THE ILLUSTRATED HISTORY OF WORLD WAR II

THE ILLUSTRATED HISTORY OF WORLD WAR II

Consultant Editor: Barrie Pitt

TEMPLE PRESS AEROSPACE

Published by Temple Press/Aerospace
an imprint of The Hamlyn Publishing Group Limited
Michelin House, 81 Fulham Road,
London SW3 6RB

Produced by Stan Morse
Aerospace Publishing Limited
179 Dalling Road, Hammersmith,
London W6 0ES

First published 1986 as *The Military History of World War II.*

This edition first published in 1989.

ISBN 0 600 567 63X

Printed in Italy by Poligrafici Calderara S.p.A. Bologna

Contents

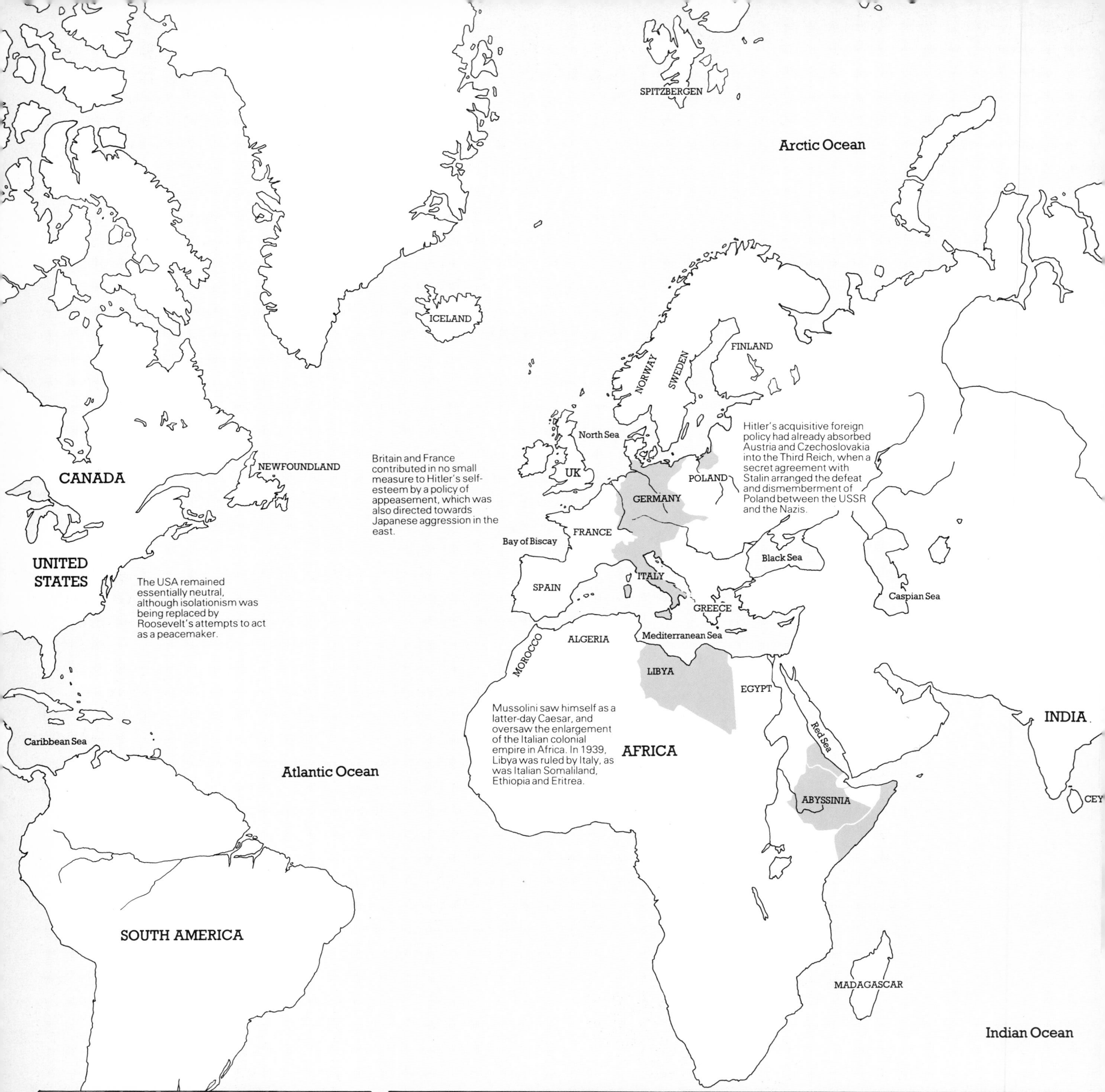
SPITZBERGEN
Arctic Ocean
ICELAND
FINLAND
NORWAY
SWEDEN
North Sea
Hitler's acquisitive foreign policy had already absorbed Austria and Czechoslovakia into the Third Reich, when a secret agreement with Stalin arranged the defeat and dismemberment of Poland between the USSR and the Nazis.
NEWFOUNDLAND
Britain and France contributed in no small measure to Hitler's self-esteem by a policy of appeasement, which was also directed towards Japanese aggression in the east.
CANADA
UK
POLAND
GERMANY
FRANCE
Bay of Biscay
UNITED STATES
The USA remained essentially neutral, although isolationism was being replaced by Roosevelt's attempts to act as a peacemaker.
Black Sea
ITALY
SPAIN
Caspian Sea
GREECE
ALGERIA
Mediterranean Sea
MOROCCO
LIBYA
EGYPT
Mussolini saw himself as a latter-day Caesar, and oversaw the enlargement of the Italian colonial empire in Africa. In 1939, Libya was ruled by Italy, as was Italian Somaliland, Ethiopia and Eritrea.
INDIA
Red Sea
Caribbean Sea
AFRICA
Atlantic Ocean
ABYSSINIA
CEY
SOUTH AMERICA
MADAGASCAR
Indian Ocean

British Prime Minister Neville Chamberlain naïvely accepts Hitler's assurances that he has no more territorial demands in Europe. After so many concessions, Hitler did not believe Britain and France would go to war over Poland.

Japanese troops are transported through Manchuria, where they have been fighting since 1932. Even after going to war with the Western Powers, the Japanese army deployed much of its strength on the Asian mainland.

Clouds of Conflict

August 1939

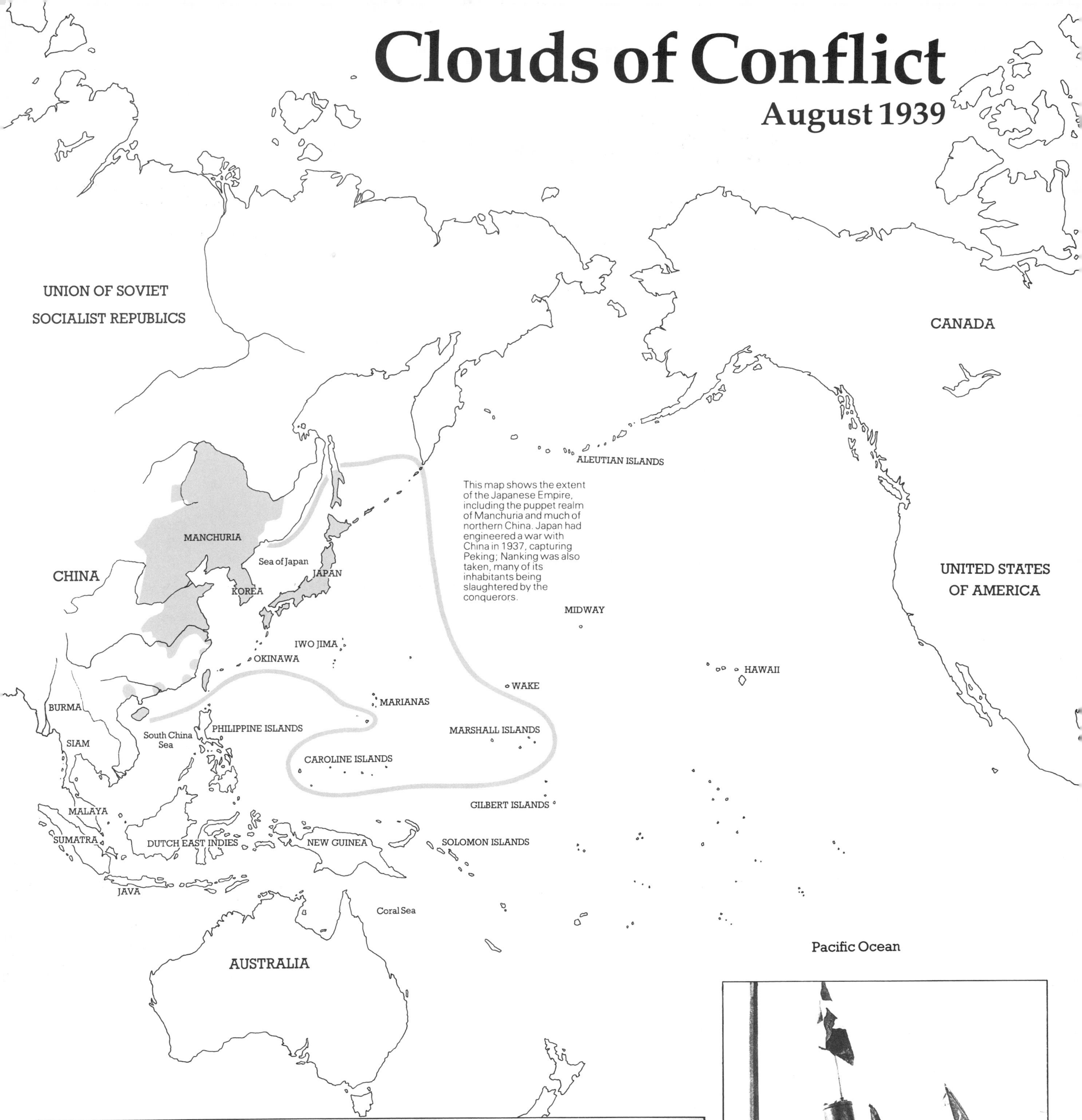

This map shows the extent of the Japanese Empire, including the puppet realm of Manchuria and much of northern China. Japan had engineered a war with China in 1937, capturing Peking; Nanking was also taken, many of its inhabitants being slaughtered by the conquerors.

Russian troops follow a BT-5 tank into action against Japanese positions on the Khalkhin-Gol river, Manchuria. This summer victory was followed by the inglorious episode in Finland during the winter.

Italian troops leave Naples, bound for Abyssinia. With the aid of aircraft and poison gas, the battle of Adowa was avenged and Emperor Haile Selassie driven from Addis Ababa.

Chapter 1

Prelude to Conflict

The Treaty of Versailles which ended World War I sowed the seeds of another conflict by handing large parts of eastern Germany to Poland. The demands for vengeance were given added stimulus by the depression and, to many Germans, Adolf Hitler and the Nazi party offered the only real leadership.

The outbreak of World War I was greeted throughout Europe by waves of enthusiasm and patriotic fervour. The people of Europe reacted in this way, historians have suggested, because in their innocence they positively wanted a war. The start of World War II, however, was received everywhere with grim resignation. This time the majority of the world's population knew only too well what hardships would now fall upon them. That they had had no say in its instigation made their resignation grimmer still. The outbreak of war had been decreed by one man, Adolf Hitler, the Chancellor of Nazi Germany, and the leaders and peoples of other countries could influence only its timing. By the summer of 1939, all avenues of escape from a military solution to Europe's problems had been blocked. The final, violent stage of Hitler's triumphant march to world domination had, he believed, begun.

Hitler had never made the slightest attempt to conceal his determination to achieve first mastery of Europe and then world hegemony – and to do so by arms. In February 1933, three days after taking office as Chancellor of the German Reich, he addressed a huge gathering of Nazi Party officials and senior officers of the German armed services upon the necessity of 'unqualified Germanization' in the east as

Left: A parade of Panzers at the Brandenburg gate in the late 1930s manifests the extent of German re-armament. In spite of the fact that the Panzer Is which took part in this parade were light tanks of minimal fighting power, they were to form the bulk of the armoured forces of the Blitzkrieg.

Adolf Hitler addresses the SA at Dortmund in 1933, only a year before he was to sacrifice that huge organization in the 'Night of the Long Knives'. The Evil Genius of the 20th Century, Hitler combined an enormous ambition for power, crackpot social theories and immense magnetism.

Chronology of War: 1933-1936

1933

January 30
Adolf Hitler becomes Chancellor of the German Reich

February 23
Japanese occupy northern China (Manchuria)

February 27
Reichstag fire; German civil liberties suspended

March 23
Reichstag passes Enabling Acts, granting Hitler absolute power

October 14
Germany leaves League of Nations

November 12
Elections throughout Germany give Nazis 92 per cent of the vote

1934

June 30
'Night of the Long Knives': Nazi purge of the SA

July 25
Attempted Nazi coup in Austria, Chancellor Dollfuss murdered

August 2
Death of President Hindenburg; Hitler becomes 'Führer' of the German Reich and assumes Supreme Command of the German Armed Forces

October 1
Hitler orders expansion of army and navy, and creation of air force in contravention of the terms of the Treaty of Versailles

December 19
Japan denounces the Washington and London naval treaties of 1922 and 1930

1935

January 13
Saar votes to return to Reich

March 16
Conscription re-introduced to Germany; disarmament repudiated

June 7
Stanley Baldwin becomes British Prime Minister

June 18
Anglo-German naval agreement signed

September 15
Nüremberg laws against Jews signed in Germany; swastika becomes official German flag

October 3
Italy invades Abyssinia

October 19
Sanctions imposed against Italy by League of Nations

December 1
Chiang Kai-Shek elected President of Chinese Executive

December 24
US Neutrality Act passed

1936

January 20
Edward VIII succeeds to British throne

February 16
Military junta appoints Hirota Prime Minister of Japan

March 7
German troops enter Rhineland

March 23
Rome Pact signed by Italy, Austria and Hungary

March 25
London Naval Convention signed by USA, Britain and France

April 1
Conscription introduced in Austria

April 13
General Metaxas becomes Prime Minister of Greece

May 3
Italian troops occupy Addis Ababa. Abyssinia declared part of Italian Empire

far at least as the Urals. During the months which followed, it seemed to those who had heard him that day that some divine force was aiding his every ambition.

Three weeks after his speech, the Reichstag Fire (which he blamed on Communist revolutionaries) gave him the excuse to suspend all civil liberties in Germany, and by the end of March the so-called Enabling Act had given him dictatorial powers. Within a year he had rid himself of rivals within his own party by his purge of the SA storm troopers and the murder of their leader Ernst Röhm, proclaimed himself Chancellor and Führer of the German Reich upon the death of the President, Field Marshal Hindenburg, and ordered the creation of a German air force (forbidden to Germany under the terms of the 1919 Versailles Treaty) and the rapid expansion of the German army and navy – the tools with which he intended to achieve his ends.

Germany re-arms

But his fleets and divisions and squadrons would need weapons, and these must come from the industrial heartlands of the Saar and the Rhineland – the areas until recently occupied by troops of the Allied

Adolf Hitler was photographed in a crowd in Munich on the outbreak of World War I. Hitler fought on the Western Front as an NCO, was wounded several times and won the Iron Cross as a battalion runner.

powers of 1918, still 'demilitarized' and still denied by treaty to German control. The Saar region he regained in January 1935 by the simple expedient of holding a plebiscite, which naturally he won, enabling him to present the resumption of German control as a *fait accompli* to a generally uninterested and as yet unsuspicious world. Next, in March 1936, he sent his troops into the Rhineland – with some trepidation – and watched while Britain and France rationalized both his aggression and their own inaction with such casuistries as 'He is, after all, only walking into his own back yard.' If Hitler's ambition was the main cause of the world conflict which followed, the pusillanimity and shortsightedness of other European leaders were by no means blameless.

Their response was an encouragement to others as well. While German troops were exercising their new-found strength in their reclaimed territories, Italian troops were extending the empire of their Duce by large-scale depredations and ferocious tactics against native forces in both Libya and Abyssinia. The former country had been wrested from Turkey in 1911, so Italian flags and Fascist emblems already decorated buildings from Tripoli to Tobruk, and a triple wire fence marked the border between Italian-controlled Cyrenaica and British-controlled Egypt. Then in 1935 Mussolini sent his troops into East Africa and invaded Abyssinia, and two months after Hitler had retaken the Rhineland the Italian flag flew over Addis Ababa; Abyssinia was proclaimed an Italian colony.

Spanish Civil War

Two months later still, the Spanish Civil War broke out, and it was quickly evident that there were political sympathies between the rebel leader General Franco and the two dictators Mussolini and Hitler – sympathies which were quickly cemented by material help in the form of weapons, 'advice' and indeed personnel. Spain would provide an ideal theatre in which to experiment with new military techniques and to train young officers in their use. By the end of 1936 the teams were being drawn up for the forthcoming trials of strength, a scenario which Hitler confirmed at the end of the year by signing an Anti-Comintern Pact with Japan.

During 1937, France and Britain began reluctantly to stir themselves into action. An extension of France's main defences against possible German aggression – the Maginot Line – was agreed and construction actually began, while Britain passed an Air Raid Precaution Bill through Parliament – though any further or more rigorous preparation for war by the British was nullified by the succession to the office of Prime Minister of Neville Chamberlain, a man whose whole character and ambition were devoted to securing for himself in history the fame and title of the Saviour of Peace. As such, in November he despatched the Foreign Secretary, Lord Halifax, to Germany to discuss with Hitler the latter's recent claims regarding the inhabitants of the Sudetenland, the German-speaking regions of Czechoslovakia.

Having successfully extended the borders of the Reich westwards, Hitler's eyes had now turned to the east. Czechoslovakia in Hitler's opinion was an anachronism, carved by ignorant Americans and their democratic European lackeys out of the old Austro-Hungarian Empire; therefore, it must cease to exist and become instead a part of the German Reich. Any arguments that the Empire had not been governed from Berlin could be dealt with.

***Above:** Germany and Italy supplied large quantities of military equipment such as these Heinkel He 70 bombers to Nationalist forces in the Spanish Civil War. German aircrew, serving there in the Condor Legion, developed the tactics which were to prove so effective in 1939-40. Russia provided aid for the Republican forces.*

***Below:** The net result of the policy of appeasement was the enlargement of the Reich, as in succession the Saar, the Rhineland, Austria, the Sudetenland, Bohemia and Moravia were engulfed, and victory parades through Vienna and Prague ensured that Hitler now felt that he could take what he wanted.*

Chronology of War: 1936-1938

July 18
Outbreak of Spanish Civil War

August 24
Two-year military conscription declared in Germany

October 1
Russia agrees to London Naval Convention

October 25
Benito Mussolini and Hitler declare Rome-Berlin Axis

November 1
F.D. Roosevelt becomes US President for the second time

November 18
Italy and Germany recognize Franco's government in Spain

November 25
Germany and Japan sign Anti-Comintern Pact

December 11
Edward VIII abdicates; accession of George VI

1937

February 8
General Franco's Nationalist troops take Malaga

April 27
Guernica destroyed by Franco's aircraft (mostly from the Luftwaffe's Condor Legion)

May 28
Neville Chamberlain becomes British Prime Minister

June 1
Prince Konoye becomes Japanese Prime Minister

June 12
Stalin's purge of the Red Army commanders begins

July 7
Japanese and Chinese troops clash on Marco Polo Bridge, near Pekin; Sino-Japanese War begins

July 17
Naval Agreement signed between Britain and Germany

October 13
Germany guarantees Belgian inviolability

November 5
Air Raid Precautions Bill introduced in British Parliament

November 6
Italy joins Anti-Comintern Pact with Germany and Japan

November 9
Japanese take Shanghai

November 17
Lord Halifax visits Hitler regarding Sudetenland; appeasement begins

December 11
Italy leaves League of Nations

1938

February 4
Hitler declared Germany's Supreme Military Commander

March 12
German troops march into Austria

March 13
The 'Anschluss' declares Austria part of Germany

April 16
Anglo-Italian Pact signed, recognizing Italian sovereignty over Abyssinia

April 23
Full autonomy demanded by Sudeten Germans

May 3
Hitler visits Mussolini in Rome

***Above:** German rearmament was accompanied by a cavalier disregard for any international treaties. The treaty of Versailles was intended to restrict the German navy to coast defence vessels, but the 'Deutschland' class (supposedly of 10,000 tons but actually displacing up to 16,000 tons at full load) emerged as long range commerce raiders.*

The other expansionist power in the 1930s was Japan. The initial target for the militarists in Japan was China and the first step was the occupation of Manchuria in 1932. Over the next five years a number of incidents, mostly engineered by Japan, led inexorably to war. It broke out in 1937.

Initially the senior partner in the Fascist movement, Italy found room for expansion in Africa. The spear armed cavalry of Ethiopia stood no chance against a modern European army using poison gas.

On 12 March 1938, after the ground had been carefully prepared by the Nazi Propaganda Department with the help of an indigenous Austrian Nazi Party formed and nurtured during the preceding months, Hitler, who had assumed supreme military command of all Germany's forces, sent his troops across the border and into Vienna to a rapturous welcome. The following day he himself travelled to Vienna to declare 'the Anschluss' – the indissoluble reunion of Austria and Germany into the Greater German Reich.

In the face of such success, surely the Czechs would realize the ideological benefits of Nazi rule, or at least accept its inevitability, and follow Austria's example?

But both the leaders and people of Czechoslovakia were more inclined by their Bohemian blood towards independence than were the more Germanically atavistic Austrians, and to Hitler's fury and frustration they objected strongly to his proposals that the Sudetenland, which contained all their defences and a great part of their industry, be handed over to him without demur. Disregarding any vague promises he may have made to Lord Halifax the previous November, the Führer announced in a secret directive on 30 May 1938 his irrevocable decision to destroy Czechoslovakia, and mobilized what had now become 'his' Wehrmacht. As rumours of an imminent German strike sped across Europe, the tension was raised still further by the increasingly strident demands by the Sudeten German leaders for Sudetenland self-government. Throughout the summer, Hitler could watch with detachment the diplomatic scurryings to and fro between London, Paris and Prague.

Munich Agreement

Both his patience and his objectivity were rewarded. On 15 September Chamberlain flew to Germany to try personally to persuade Hitler not to carry out his threats against the only true mid-European democracy, but such was the result of those talks that by 21 September both he and the French premier, Édouard Daladier, were delicately suggesting to the Czechs that perhaps the Führer's proposals were not so unacceptable as had first appeared ('Herr Hitler is a gentleman!' Chamberlain had announced upon his return to London). By 22 September Chamberlain was back with Hitler at Bad Godesberg for a further talk upon the European predicament, and on 30 September in Munich Chamberlain, Daladier, Mussolini and Hitler agreed that the Sudetenland should after all be transferred to the Reich – as the final stage of Hitler's territorial aggrandizement. Chamberlain then returned to England, waving the signed agreement and declaring 'I believe it is peace for our time!'

By the end of 1938 German engineers were dismantling Czech defences in the Sudetenland and transferring them westwards, Hungary had annexed Southern Slovakia and Poland had grabbed Teschen – and in Britain, despite their Prime Minister's assurances, volunteers were flocking to join the Territorial Army while civilians dug trenches in Hyde Park and built air-raid shelters in their gardens.

Of course, 1939 was the year for democracy's chickens to come home to roost. It began with the defeat of the Spanish loyalist government and the almost immediate recognition of Franco as the new Spanish ruler by Chamberlain's government. But by mid-March the British Prime Minister was facing a far more bitter reality. German troops had moved forward from the Sudetenland, first to Prague and then on into the whole of Bohemia and Moravia. Before leaving Berlin to make another triumphant entry, this time into Prague, Hitler announced that 'Czechoslovakia has ceased to exist' – and Chamberlain was sadly complaining that the Führer had broken his word.

As it became obvious almost immediately that Hitler now intended Poland as his next victim, there followed further diplomatic activity as Britain and France tried to form some cohesive alliance against the forces of Fascist dictatorship (though offers from Russia to join were rejected), and conscription for men aged 20-21 was introduced in Britain.

Throughout May the diplomatic charade continued, the 'Pact of Steel' was triumphantly announced between Germany and Italy, and in August, at the prompting of Winston Churchill, a mission went to Moscow to explore the possibility of a military alliance with the only country likely to field an army large enough to oppose Hitler's. The mission was still there when to an astonished world was revealed the existence of a new non-aggression pact between Russia and Germany (it contained secret clauses which were to become obvious only too soon) – in response to which Chamberlain announced Britain's guarantee of Poland's independence.

On 31 August Hitler ordered the invasion of Poland. The following day Britain and France demanded the instant withdrawal of all German forces, and in the face of the contemptuous silence with which this was greeted in Berlin, consulted on how best to implement their promises to Poland. That they must be implemented was unanimously agreed; but how, when and where were matters for lengthy discussion, and indeed remain the subject of controversy.

An ultimatum was sent – and ignored; at 11 a.m. on Sunday, 3 September 1939, Chamberlain broadcast the news that Britain was now at war with Germany. The world would realize, he felt sure, what a bitter disappointment it was to him.

At 4.45 on the morning of 1 September 1939, bombers and fighters of the German Luftwaffe crossed the Polish frontier and began their systematic destruction of Polish airfields and aircraft, of road and rail centres, of concentrations of troop reserves, and of anything which intelligence or observation had indicated as likely to house command headquarters of any status. The first Blitzkrieg had begun.

Aircraft of the Polish Air Force

Compared to the German aggressors, the Polish air force was ill-equipped, with obsolescent types in service. Despite their brave defence, the Polish aircraft were cut down by the sleek German fighters, a harbinger of doom for air forces yet to face the professional Luftwaffe.

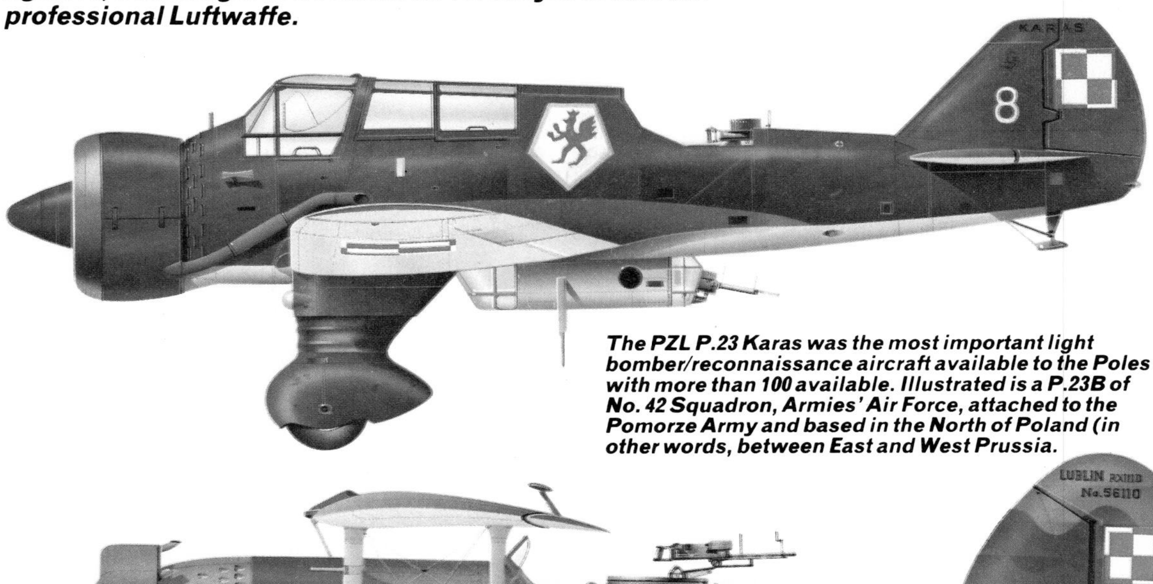

The PZL P.23 Karas was the most important light bomber/reconnaissance aircraft available to the Poles with more than 100 available. Illustrated is a P.23B of No. 42 Squadron, Armies' Air Force, attached to the Pomorze Army and based in the North of Poland (in other words, between East and West Prussia.

The standard observation type used by the Poles was the Lublin R-XIII parasol wing monoplane. Some 49 were in service on 1st September, but losses were heavy (a number being shot down by friendly fire). Only 17 got away to Romania.

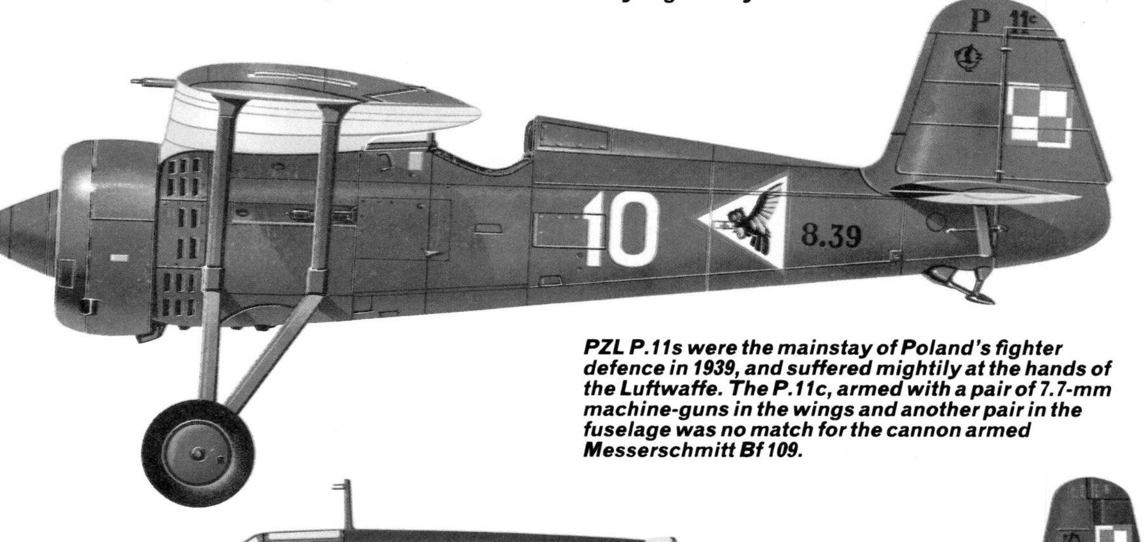

PZL P.11s were the mainstay of Poland's fighter defence in 1939, and suffered mightily at the hands of the Luftwaffe. The P.11c, armed with a pair of 7.7-mm machine-guns in the wings and another pair in the fuselage was no match for the cannon armed Messerschmitt Bf 109.

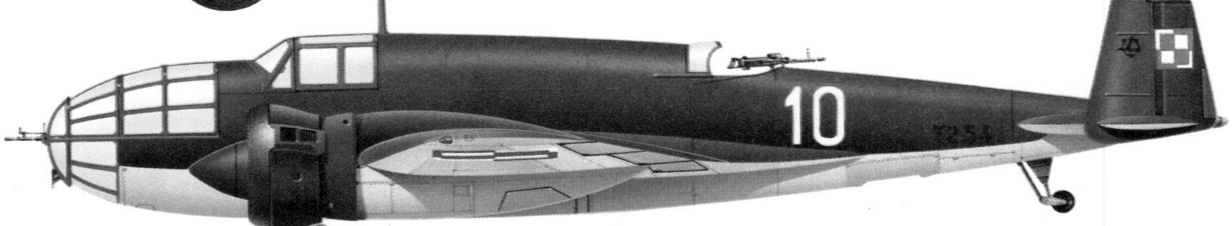

The PZL P.36 Los (Elk) was the most advanced strike aircraft available to the Poles, but only 36 were in service. Comparable in performance to the Heinkel He 111P series, the Los was never able to make a contribution to the battle for Poland.

Chronology of War: 1938-1939

May 30
Hitler announces his 'unqualified decision' to destroy Czechoslovakia

September 7
Sudeten Germans break off talks with Czech Government

September 15
Chamberlain flies to Germany to meet Hitler regarding Czechoslovakia

September 21
British and French advise Czechoslovakia to accept Hitler's terms

September 22
Chamberlain flies to Bad Godesberg to see Hitler again

September 29
Munich Conference begins

September 30
Britain, France and Italy cede Sudetenland to Germany. Chamberlain declares 'Peace in our time'

October 1
German troops enter Sudetenland

November 2
'Vienna Award' announced by Germany, ceding large areas of Czechoslovakia to both Hungary and Italy

November 9
'Crystal Night' anti-Semitic pogroms throughout Germany

November 26
Non-aggression pact renewed between Russia and Poland

December 6
France and Germany sign non-aggression pact

1939

February 27
France and Britain recognize new Spanish government

March 15
German troops cross Czech frontier

March 16
Hitler announced 'Czechoslovakia has ceased to exist' and accepts Protectorate of Slovakia. Hungary annexes Ruthenia

March 17
Chamberlain accuses Hitler of breaking his word

March 22
Germany annexes Memel. Lithuania forced to accede

March 28
End of Spanish Civil War

March 31
Chamberlain announces British and French guarantees to Poland

April 7
Italy invades Albania

April 13
British and French offer guarantees to Greece and Romania

April 26
Conscription announced for all men in Britain aged 20-21

April 28
Hitler renounces Anglo-German naval pact and Polish-German non-aggression pact. He also rejects Roosevelt's peace proposals

May 22
'Pact of Steel' signed between Germany and Italy

May 23
Hitler tells Hermann Goering, General Keitel and Admiral Raeder: '. . . we are left with the decision to attack Poland at the earliest opportunity.'

The Junkers Ju 87 came to symbolize the new form of war that the Wehrmacht unleashed upon Poland. Caught here in the act of dropping a typical load of one SC 250 and four SC 50 bombs, the Stuka added to their terrifying aspect by the fitting of 'Jericho Trumpet' sirens to the legs of the fixed landing gear.

Poland was an ideal theatre for such warfare. In addition to being fairly flat (and at this time dry and hard-surfaced), her frontiers were much too long for them to be well defended. She was, moreover, flanked by her enemy on both sides – East Prussia to the north and the newly occupied Czechoslovakia to the south – and the most valuable areas of the country lay between those flanks. Poland, in fact, protruded like a tongue into hostile territory – and her armies in September 1939 were deployed in that tongue, instead of behind the river lines of the Vistula and San where their defences would have been stronger. But the fatal weakness in Poland's defences lay in her lack of armour, for the bulk of the army consisted of 30 divisions of infantry supported by 11 brigades of horsed cavalry and two motorized brigades. Against them were to be launched six German armoured divisions and eight motorized divisions, together with 27 infantry divisions whose main role would be to engage the attentions of the Polish infantry while the German mobile forces raced around the flanks to strike at the centres of control and supply.

Spearheads into Poland

One hour after the Luftwaffe had struck, Army Group South under General von Rundstedt smashed their way forward: Eighth Army on the left wing driving for Lodz, Fourteenth Army on the right aimed for Krakow and the line of the River Vistula, and the bulk of the armour of Tenth Army under General von Reichenau in the centre piercing the gap between the Polish Lodz and Kracow armies, linking with Eighth Army mobile units and racing on for Warsaw.

By 4 September, Tenth Army spearheads were 50 miles into Poland, curving up towards the capital and isolating the Lodz Army from its supplies, while to the south Fourteenth Army panzers had reached the River San on each side of Przemysl.

Meanwhile Army Group North under General Guderian was driving down from Pomerania and East Prussia; Fourth Army down along the line of the Vistula towards Warsaw, Third Army down the line of the Bug towards Brest-Litovsk, Lwow and eventual junction with Fourteenth Army coming up from the Carpathians.

Thus two huge encirclements would take place, the outer intended to block any escapees from the inner – and at the end of the first week only the immediate confusion of battle masked the extraordinary success of the German attack. The inner pincers had certainly met successfully, but the chaos inside the trap was such that no one could be sure what was happening. Polish columns marched and counter-marched in frantic efforts to make contact either with the enemy or with their own support, and in doing so raised such clouds of dust that aerial observation could report nothing but general movement by unidentified forces of unknown strength, engaged in unrecognizable activity in pursuit of incomprehensible aims.

Wehrmacht triumphant

As a result there was some doubt at German headquarters whether or not the bulk of the Polish forces had been trapped, and as a result Tenth Army armour wheeled north to form another block along the Bzura, west of Warsaw. Here was fought the most bitter battle of the campaign, but it could only end in defeat for the Poles. Despite their desperate gallantry, they were fighting in reverse against a strong, well-entrenched enemy who had only to hold on to win, and after the first day they were harried from behind by troops of Eighth Army from the southern group and of Fourth Army from the north. It is hardly surprising that only a very small number managed to break through the German armoured screen to join the garrison at Warsaw – where they very soon found themselves again cut off from escape to the east by the outer encirclement.

From this double encirclement only a small fraction of the Polish army could hope to escape, and on 17 September even this hope was dashed. The contents of the secret clauses of the Russo-German Pact signed the previous month were cruelly revealed when the Red Army moved in from the east to collect its share of the spoils; Poland as a nation ceased to exist and a new international frontier ran from East Prussia past Bialystok, Brest-Litovsk and Lwow as far as the Carpathians.

Common frontiers had existed between Russia and Germany before, and had rarely proved anything but a source of friction and animosity. Many wondered now how long such essentially antagonistic neighbours could exist side by side.

Poland in Pincers

The invasion of Poland gave the world its first taste of the power and swiftness of Blitzkrieg. Three armies were involved in the inner pincer movement, with two spearheaded by armour making up the outer drive. It was very effective, victory taking only one month to achieve (although assisted by the Soviet invasion on 17th September). The pincers were to meet on the Vistula and the Bug rivers, encircling most of the Polish army in the field. The inner encirclement closed on Warsaw by the 10th September, and the outer, with the Panzers under General Heinz Guderian, reached Brest-Litovsk on the 14th. There was only one large scale counter attack, on the River Bzura near Warsaw, when the Poles were routed.

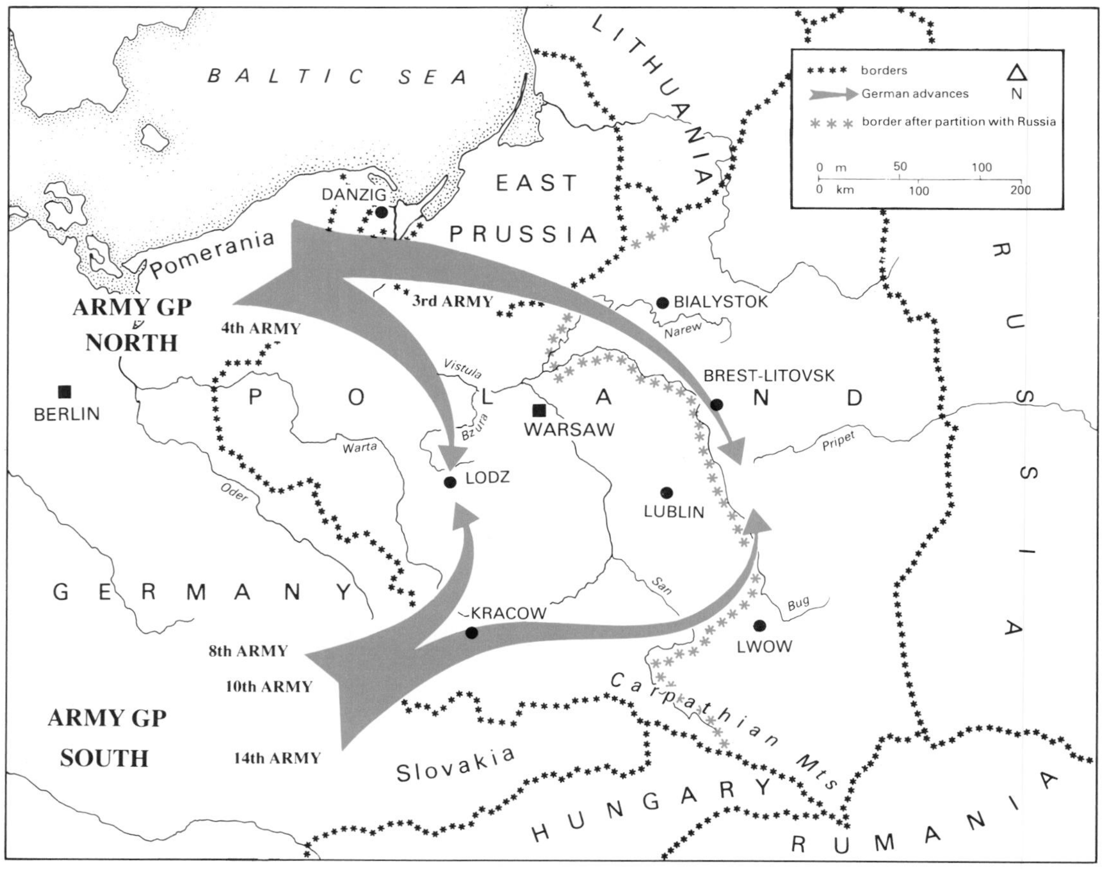

A Panzerkampfwagen II, armed with a 20-mm main gun, precedes a machine gun-armed PzKpfw. I in the winter of 1939. Designed as training tanks, these two and three man vehicles bore most of the responsibility for German success until the much more capable Panzer III and IV were produced in numbers after the fall of France in 1940.

Chronology of War: 1939

July 1
France warns Germany of her firm decision to stand by Franco-Polish guarantees

July 9
Winston Churchill urges military alliance with Russia

July 26
US denounces old trade pact with Japan

August 2
General Wavell appointed C-in-C British Land Forces Middle East

August 12
Anglo-French mission to Russia

August 23
Germany signs non-aggression pact with Russia, including secret clauses partitioning Poland. Chamberlain warns Germany that Britain will honour agreements with Poland

August 24
Emergency Powers Bill passed through British Parliament

August 25
Anglo-Polish Mutual Assistance Pact signed. Mussolini tells Hitler that Italy is unprepared for war

August 26
Hitler guarantees to respect the neutrality of Belgium, Holland, Luxembourg and Sweden

August 26-31
Last-minute attempts by Roosevelt, French Premier Daladier, and Chamberlain are made to avert German invasion of Poland

September 1
Poland invaded at 4.45 a.m.; Germany annexes Danzig. Evacuation of children from London commences

September 2
Chamberlain sends ultimatum to Hitler. Luftwaffe bombs Warsaw

September 3
Britain, France, Australia and New Zealand declare war on Germany. The passenger liner SS Athenia *is torpedoed off Ireland*

September 5
German troops cross Vistula

September 9
Panzers reach Warsaw

September 10
British Expeditionary Force (BEF) begins move to France

September 17
Soviet troops invade eastern Poland. British aircraft-carrier HMS Courageous *torpedoed*

September 22
Red Army occupies Lwow

September 27
Warsaw surrenders

September 29
Soviet-German agreement regardng partition of Poland comes into force

October 6
Polish resistance ceases. Hitler broadcasts his 'offer of peace'

October 14
British battleship HMS Royal Oak *torpedoed in Scapa Flow by U-47 commanded by Günther Prien*

October 27
US Neutrality Bill passed in Senate

November 3
'Cash and Carry' clause introduced into US Senate

November 8
Bomb attempt made on Hitler in Munich

November 30
Red Army invades Finland through Karelian Isthmus. Helsinki bombed

Early German Armoured Vehicles

German armoured vehicles used in the early stages of the war were not as large as one might think, the majority having been envisaged as training machines. It was the new tactics which were to make the difference in battle.

The German annexation of Czechoslovakia gave the Wehrmacht access to the products of the noted armaments manufacturer Skoda. The PzKpfw 38(t), originally designed for the Czech army as the LT vz 38, was roughly equivalent to the PzKpfw II but with a more powerful gun. It formed a significant part of the Wehrmacht's Panzer strength in the first years of the war, by 1940 equipping two complete Panzer divisions in the invasion of France.

The Panzerkampfwagen II was designed as a training machine intended to prepare the German armoured forces for the arrival of the PzKpfw III and IV medium tanks. Despite this, the PzKpfw II with its 20-mm gun provided the larger part of Wehrmacht Panzer strength in the operations of 1939 and 1940. More than 1000 were used in the invasion of Poland, and a similar number in the lightning campaign in the West.

The kleiner Panzerbefehlswagen (armoured command vehicle) was adapted from the PzKpfw I light tank. It had a crew of three, and the fixed superstructure contained two radios, a map table and extra electrical equipment. Their main benefit was to allow commanders to keep up with the armoured formations which were the cutting edge of the new style of battle now known as 'Blitzkrieg'.

One of the characteristics of the German infantry battalion as developed by theorists between the wars was the provision of integral artillery support, particularly in the shape of the 15-cm schwere Infantrie Geschütz 33 (sIG 33, or heavy infantry gun). The rise of mechanization saw the weapon self-propelled on a modified Panzer I chassis.

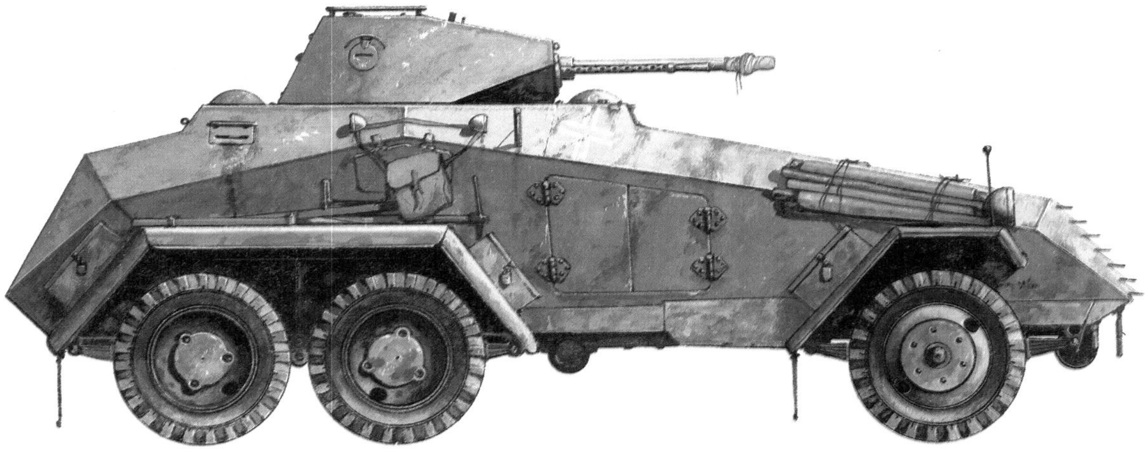

The first German armoured vehicles were armoured cars, based on truck chassis and developed abroad to avoid the constraints of the treaty of Versailles. The Panzerspähwagen SdKfz (Sonderkraftfahrzeug, or special purpose vehicle) 251 was not really suitable for prolonged cross country use, but nonetheless saw action in Poland and France. This example is armed with a 2-cm cannon (earlier models only being fitted with a 7.92-mm MG).

A column of Panzer I light tanks ford a river in Poland. The distinctive black Panzer uniform and the padded beret which served as a kind of crash helmet came into use with the founding of the Panzer arm, and immediately gave the members of the young service a sense of identity.

The first German armoured cars designed as such were the 8-Rad (8-wheeled) SdKfz 231 series, which replaced the 6-wheelers which had been adapted from truck chassis. This Waffenwagen mounted a 20-mm KwK-30 or -38 cannon, and formed part of the equipment of the armoured reconnaissance units of the Panzer Division.

Air Forces of the Winter War

The Winter War saw the small Finnish air arm outnumbered by at least four to one by the Soviets, yet for the first few weeks the well trained and highly motivated Finns put up considerable resistance. Fighting spirit can only do so much, however, and the massive weight the USSR threw into battle eventually proved decisive.

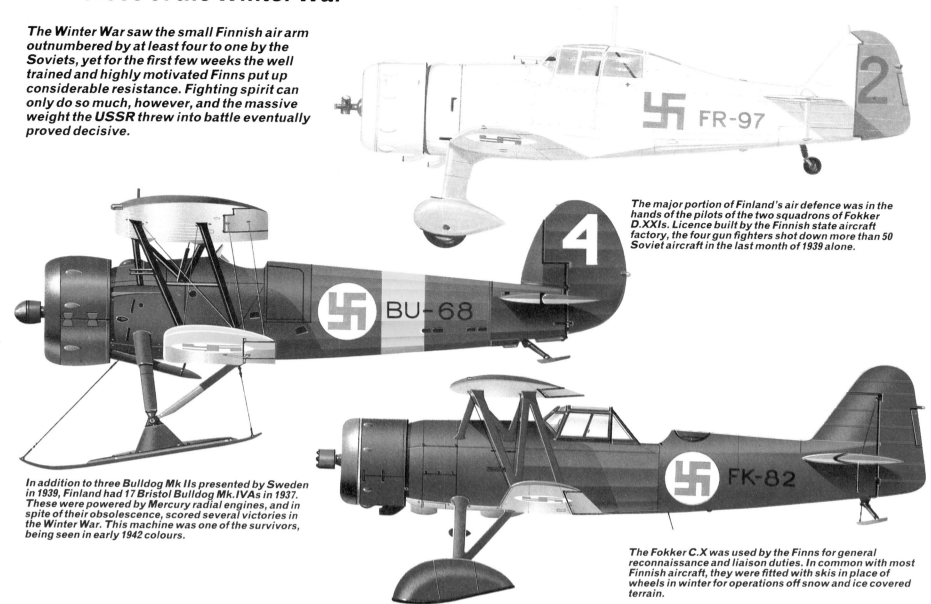

The major portion of Finland's air defence was in the hands of the pilots of the two squadrons of Fokker D.XXIs. Licence built by the Finnish state aircraft factory, the four gun fighters shot down more than 50 Soviet aircraft in the last month of 1939 alone.

In addition to three Bulldog Mk IIs presented by Sweden in 1939, Finland had 17 Bristol Bulldog Mk.IVAs in 1937. These were powered by Mercury radial engines, and in spite of their obsolescence, scored several victories in the Winter War. This machine was one of the survivors, being seen in early 1942 colours.

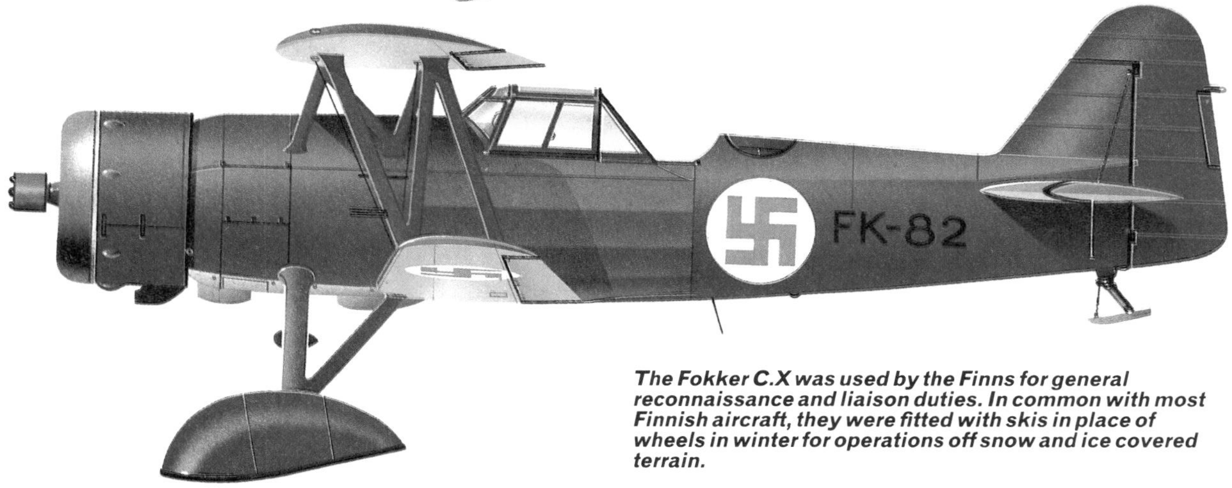

The Fokker C.X was used by the Finns for general reconnaissance and liaison duties. In common with most Finnish aircraft, they were fitted with skis in place of wheels in winter for operations off snow and ice covered terrain.

Russian armoured development was to lead to the most effective tanks of WWII, but some interwar experiments were to lead up blind alleys. The multi-turreted tank, such as the T-100 seen here, was tested in Finland and found wanting, being ponderous and overly complicated.

In the summer of 1939, before the disasters in Finland, Soviet units scored an impressive victory against the Japanese in the Far East. This was never forgotten by the Japanese, and throughout World War II they maintained nearly a million troops in Manchuria.

Poland was not the only country to figure in those secret clauses in the Russo-German Pact. They also mentioned the Baltic republics of Estonia, Latvia and Lithuania, together with Finland, placing them all 'within the sphere of interest of the USSR' – and Joseph Stalin, having watched Hitler's army conquer one small nation so spectacularly, seems to have felt that it was time for the Red Army to bring him similar gains.

Political pressure – and geographic realities – were enough to persuade the three Baltic republics to sign treaties of mutual assistance which allowed the USSR to establish garrisons and bases within their borders, but Finland felt herself protected in her most vulnerable area by the Gulf of Finland and Lake Ladoga, and by the wilderness of forest, swamp, lakes and sheer arctic distances which made up her eastern frontier, stretching from Lake Ladoga up to the Arctic Ocean. The Finns also believed that the spirit and training of her armed forces would be enough to hold the first onslaught, and that the sight of their own David fighting off the Russian Goliath would evoke first sympathy and then active aid from the rest of the world.

And when, on 28 November, after two months of verbal bullying by Molotov and defiance by the Finnish leaders Paassikivi and Tanner, the Soviet Union broke off negotiations and attacked the Finnish defences two days later, it looked at first as though the Finns had been right. Certainly, all Western Europe and the United States applauded the Finnish stand – and Finnish military successes at first exceeded all expectation. Despite the size of the Finnish army – at its peak it could never produce and support more than 16 divisions – despite their acute shortage of artillery and heavy ammunition, despite their shortage of transport, signals equipment and total lack of armour, they held the Russian attack which came up through the Karelian Isthmus, along the whole of the Mannerheim Line (the main Finnish defences) from the Gulf of Finland to the River Vuoksi, and between there and Lake Ladoga they held the Russians in their forward positions *in front* of the line. The Finnish II and III Corps, in fact, beat back the Russian Seventh and Thirteenth Armies, inflicting astonishing losses on the Red Army infantry by the accuracy of their rifle and machine-gun fire, and on the Russian tanks with petrol bombs. By 22 December, after six days of pointless battering against a seemingly impregnable line, the Russians broke off the action and withdrew, obviously to regroup – and to rethink.

Finland defiant

Matters had not gone so well for the Finns north of Lake Ladoga. The six divisions of the Russian Eighth Army crossed the frontier and advanced implacably to the line of Finnish defences between Kitela and Ilomantsi. But in doing so they had given some hostages to fortune: incredibly, the Russians had no ski troops, whereas every Finnish soldier was well trained on skis and many were expert in their military exploitations. Russian divisions thus found them-

Early German Armoured Vehicles

German armoured vehicles used in the early stages of the war were not as large as one might think, the majority having been envisaged as training machines. It was the new tactics which were to make the difference in battle.

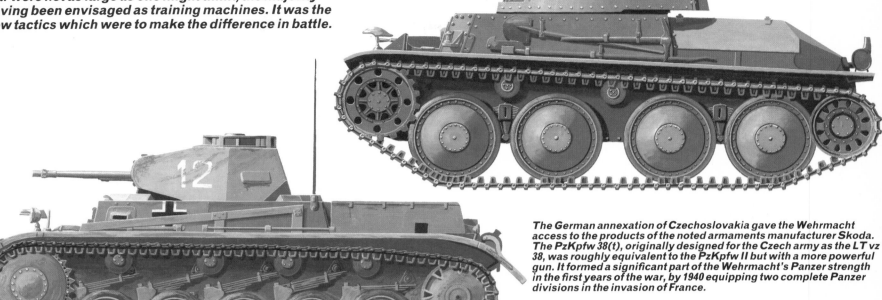

The German annexation of Czechoslovakia gave the Wehrmacht access to the products of the noted armaments manufacturer Skoda. The PzKpfw 38(t), originally designed for the Czech army as the LT vz 38, was roughly equivalent to the PzKpfw II but with a more powerful gun. It formed a significant part of the Wehrmacht's Panzer strength in the first years of the war, by 1940 equipping two complete Panzer divisions in the invasion of France.

The Panzerkampfwagen II was designed as a training machine intended to prepare the German armoured forces for the arrival of the PzKpfw III and IV medium tanks. Despite this, the PzKpfw II with its 20-mm gun provided the larger part of Wehrmacht Panzer strength in the operations of 1939 and 1940. More than 1000 were used in the invasion of Poland, and a similar number in the lightning campaign in the West.

The kleiner Panzerbefehlswagen (armoured command vehicle) was adapted from the PzKpfw I light tank. It had a crew of three, and the fixed superstructure contained two radios, a map table and extra electrical equipment. Their main benefit was to allow commanders to keep up with the armoured formations which were the cutting edge of the new style of battle now known as 'Blitzkrieg'.

One of the characteristics of the German infantry battalion as developed by theorists between the wars was the provision of integral artillery support, particularly in the shape of the 15-cm schwere Infantrie Geschütz 33 (sIG 33, or heavy infantry gun). The rise of mechanization saw the weapon self-propelled on a modified Panzer I chassis.

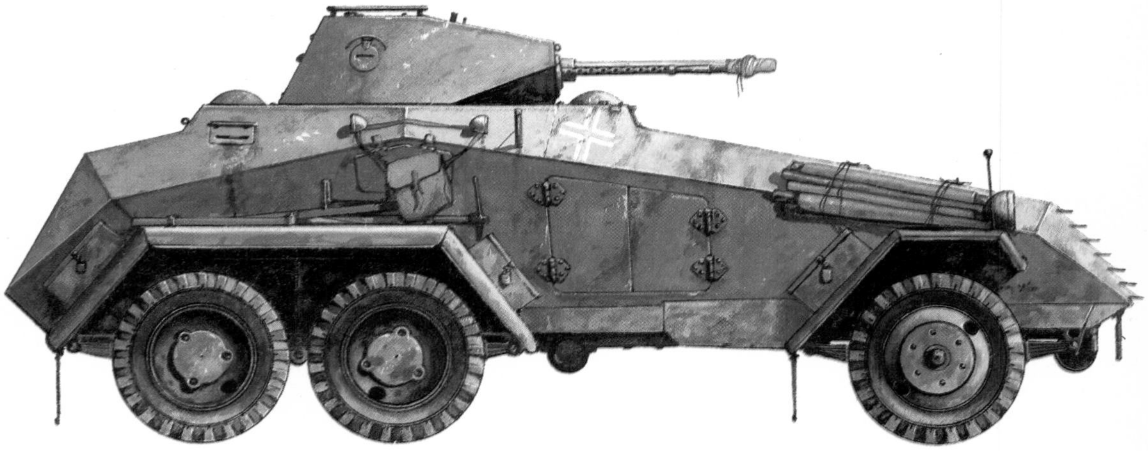

The first German armoured vehicles were armoured cars, based on truck chassis and developed abroad to avoid the constraints of the treaty of Versailles. The Panzerspähwagen SdKfz (Sonderkraftfahrzeug, or special purpose vehicle) 251 was not really suitable for prolonged cross country use, but nonetheless saw action in Poland and France. This example is armed with a 2-cm cannon (earlier models only being fitted with a 7.92-mm MG).

A column of Panzer I light tanks ford a river in Poland. The distinctive black Panzer uniform and the padded beret which served as a kind of crash helmet came into use with the founding of the Panzer arm, and immediately gave the members of the young service a sense of identity.

The first German armoured cars designed as such were the 8-Rad (8-wheeled) SdKfz 231 series, which replaced the 6-wheelers which had been adapted from truck chassis. This Waffenwagen mounted a 20-mm KwK-30 or -38 cannon, and formed part of the equipment of the armoured reconnaissance units of the Panzer Division.

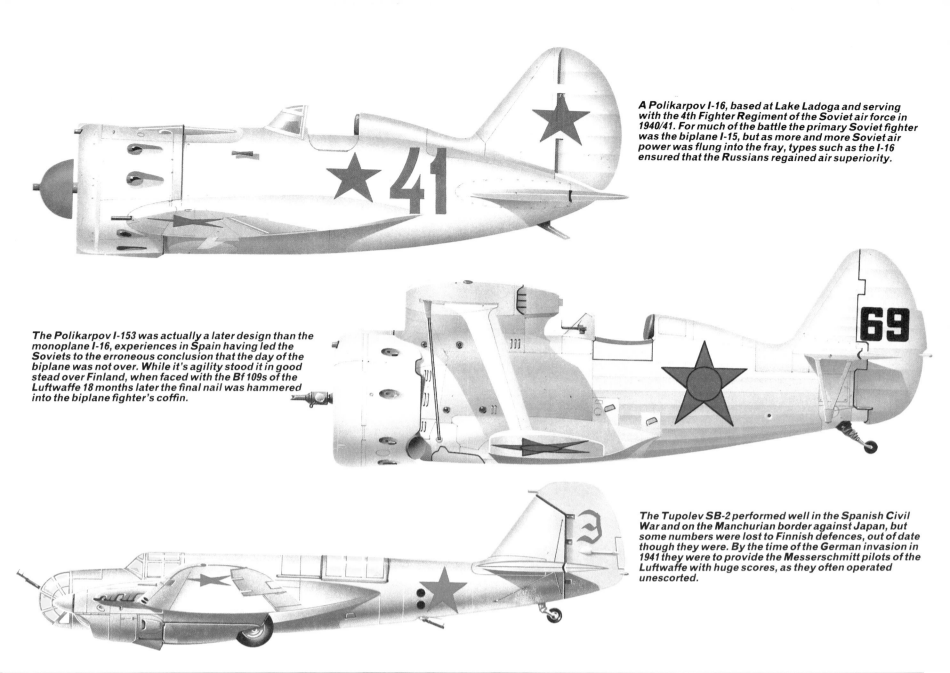

A Polikarpov I-16, based at Lake Ladoga and serving with the 4th Fighter Regiment of the Soviet air force in 1940/41. For much of the battle the primary Soviet fighter was the biplane I-15, but as more and more Soviet air power was flung into the fray, types such as the I-16 ensured that the Russians regained air superiority.

The Polikarpov I-153 was actually a later design than the monoplane I-16, experiences in Spain having led the Soviets to the erroneous conclusion that the day of the biplane was not over. While it's agility stood it in good stead over Finland, when faced with the Bf 109s of the Luftwaffe 18 months later the final nail was hammered into the biplane fighter's coffin.

The Tupolev SB-2 performed well in the Spanish Civil War and on the Manchurian border against Japan, but some numbers were lost to Finnish defences, out of date though they were. By the time of the German invasion in 1941 they were to provide the Messerschmitt pilots of the Luftwaffe with huge scores, as they often operated unescorted.

selves cut off from communication and supplies; small formations were decimated, some units annihilated.

Much further north at Suomussalmi the Russian 163rd Division was surrounded, subjected to concentrated small-arms and short-range artillery fire until 29 December, when it broke completely, the survivors fleeing across the frozen wilderness leaving 11 tanks, 25 guns and 150 lorries to the elated victors.

But of course it could not go on. First of all, although Britain, France, America and Sweden all professed a desire to help, they produced very little of it – the first two because they needed for their own use every man and every weapon they could produce, the others because of their carefully cultivated neutrality; and when plans were laid to send British and French reinforcements in, Sweden refused to allow them passage.

By early January, Stalin had decided to bring it all to an end. Command of the campaign was given to General Timoshenko, siege artillery was brought up and on 15 January 1940, the systematic destruction of the Mannerheim Line commenced. As the Finns had no long-range artillery, they could mount no counter-battery fire; Finnish troops spent the days in the trenches connecting the strong-points, their nights desperately trying to reconstruct the smashed concrete boxes, the obliterated gun-posts: and soon on every night they had also to beat off Russian tanks, supported by infantry brought up on towed sledges. Sheer exhaustion spelt the end of the Mannerheim Line – and in due course of every other defence line the Finns could man.

By the beginning of March the Russians had driven them back to Viipuri, and from there the Finnish line curved back almost to Tali and on to Vuosalmi, then to the water-line to Taipale on Lake Ladoga. On 3 March Timoshenko sent a battalion and a brigade across the ice to Vilajoki. So the Finnish positions were turned – and the road to Helskinki open.

On 13 March, bowing to the inevitable, Prime Minister Ryti signed the Treaty of Moscow, which returned the Russo-Finnish border more or less to where Peter the Great had drawn it in 1721; where, in fact, it remains today.

The Finnish Winter War

The Soviet Union learned a bitter lesson in its attack on neighbouring Finland in 1939. Attacking on a number of fronts, the Red Army was to suffer hideous losses in its attempt to break the Mannerheim Line between Lake Ladoga and the Gulf of Finland, and further north it received a stunning blow at the bloody battle around Suomussalmi. Nevertheless, and in spite of the courage and fighting ability of the Finns, superior numbers told, and the line was pierced.

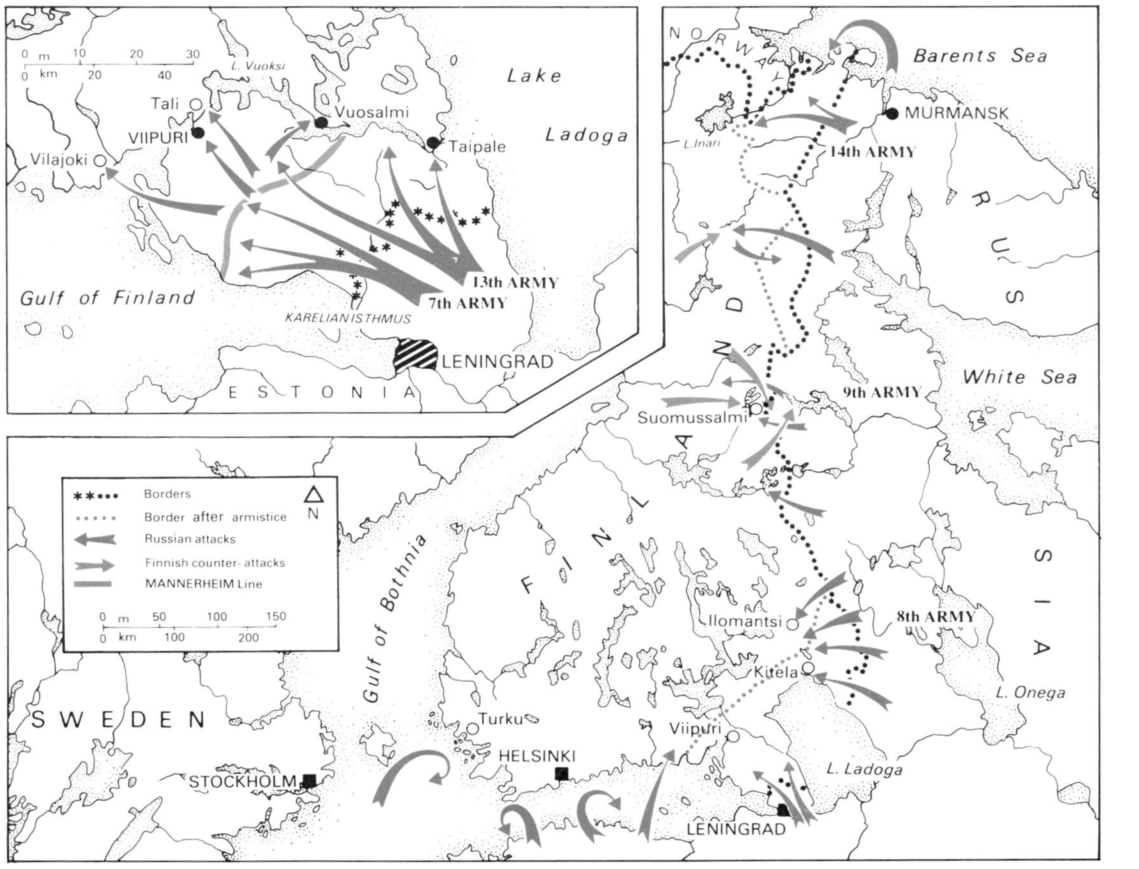

Chapter 2

Blitz in the West

The lightning German victory in Poland took place while the Allies sat supine in their positions along the German border. Then, in May, months of 'Phoney War' ended abruptly as the German army fell on Western Europe like the wolf upon the fold.

Although the Russo-Finnish War excited great sympathy among the British and French, in practice it did not affect them a great deal, for their main enemy – Germany – was not involved; thus once the subjugation of Poland was completed in early October, it almost seemed to the peoples of Western Europe that military operations had ceased. The 'fighting war' was apparently over and what United States Senator Boragh dubbed the 'Phoney War' began; Chamberlain called it the 'Twilight War', the Germans called it the 'Sitzkrieg', and one perspicacious observer called it the 'Winter of Illusion'.

This it certainly was for the British people and their leaders, for there grew in Britain (and in the United States, though to a lesser degree in France) a dangerous feeling that perhaps it would be possible to get through this war without too much unpleasantness, such as actual battle. True, there had been losses at sea – the aircraft-carrier *Courageous* had been torpedoed and sunk in September and the *Royal Oak* inside Scapa Flow in October – but the defeat of the *Graf Spee* levelled that out to some extent, and there was a growing impression that, ever since the torpedoing of the passenger liner *Athenia* a few hours after the declaration of war, there were influential circles in Britain who felt that the whole thing was a sad mistake.

Chamberlain would, of course, allow no suggestion that any sort of deal could be done with Hitler, but once the German people 'had realized that they can't possibly win this war' – a condition he visualized developing by spring 1940 – they would undoubtedly rid themselves of their Führer, and probably an agreement could then be arrived at with some other German statesman, for instance Marshal Goering. In the meantime, 18,000,000 printed leaflets informing the Germans of the wickedness of their Führer would be dropped over Germany by the RAF, who would doubtless continue to suffer their resultant losses with knightly forbearance, at the same time ensuring that no damage whatsoever occurred to German citizens' private property, in case it upset them.

As for the Western Front, the French troops occupied the Maginot Line, and the British Expeditionary Force had proceeded smoothly to their positions along the Franco-Belgian border where they built pill-boxes and dug trenches. But as Chamberlain put it to Major-General Montgomery when he visited his division in December, 'I don't think the Germans have any intention of attacking us, do you?' The general's reply is not recorded, but the Prime Minister's feelings reflected those of the British population as a whole, and was echoed in France, especially at the top of the French Command.

Certainly, there had been no attempt to take pressure off the Poles during their ordeal by military action across the Rhine – much to the relief and astonishment of some of the senior Wehrmacht officers, who revealed after the war that a powerful thrust into the Saar during the first month of the war would have been almost uncontested and could quite possibly have precipitated that popular revolt against the Nazi

The German blitz in the west began on 10 May with a speed and ferocity which stunned the Allied armies; meticulously executed combined arms attacks smashed the front wide open. Here a 105-mm light field howitzer opens fire.

France had some fine tanks, but obsession with a defensive strategy left her armoured forces unfit to face the German onslaught. Here a late model Renault R-35 lies burning as the blitzkrieg continues.

Below: A generation of French youth perished in the holocaust at Verdun in 1916. The vast casualty list and the apparent impregnability of fortresses led France to construct the Maginot Line which was expected to hold the German attack in 1940. The ammunition chamber seen here is many storeys below ground.

Chronology of War: 1939-1940

December 13
Battle of the River Plate between the British cruisers HMS Exeter, Ajax *and* Achilles *and the German 'pocket battleship'* Admiral Graf Spee

December 17
Graf Spee *scuttled in River Plate estuary*

December 31
Finnish victory at Suomussalmi announced. Russian advance north of Lake Ladoga repulsed

1940

January 2
Russians attack on Karelian Isthmus

January 8
Finns claim destruction of Russian division near Suommulsami

January 15
Belgium refuses Allied request for passage through her territory

February 11
Fierce fighting in Karelia

February 15
'Mannerheim Line' of defences across the Karelian Isthmus is breached by Russians

February 16
HMS Cossack *rescues British prisoners from* Altmark *in Norwegian waters. Plans announced for evacuation of 400,000 children from British cities in event of air raids*

February 21
Work begins on the construction of a new concentration camp in Poland near the small town of Oswiecim (Auschwitz)

February 24
German plans for invasion of Western Europe completed

March 5
Finnish delegation goes to Moscow to accept terms

March 11
Chamberlain announces plans for aid to Finland

March 13
Russo-Finnish Peace signed in Moscow

March 28
Britain and France pledge not to conclude peace separately

April 2
Hitler orders preparation for invasion of Denmark and Norway under the code name Operation Weserübung

April 5
Chamberlain announces that Hitler has 'missed the bus'

April 7
Allied expeditionary force sails for Norway

April 9
German troops invade Denmark and Norway

April 10
First Battle of Narvik

April 12
Second Battle of Narvik

April 15-18
British troops landed at (from north to south) Narvik, Bodo, Namsos, and Åndalsnes. Germans advancing from Oslo

April 21-30
Heavy fighting in Norway

May 1
Norwegians at Lillehammer surrender

May 2
Allies evacuate Norway at Namsos

The Sinking of the Graf Spee

The 'pocket battleship'* Graf Spee *sailed into the Atlantic two weeks before war broke out. Her mission: to wreak havoc among Britain's vital merchant shipping lanes while evading the Royal Navy's cruisers.

Germany well understood the vulnerability of the UK's maritime trade and had constructed ships designed expressly for the destruction of such trade. Among these was the trio of 10,000-ton *Panzerschiffe* (perhaps better known by their popular British label of 'pocket battleships'). These were well protected, featured multiple-diesel drive for great endurance, and had an armament including six 280-mm (11-in), eight 150-mm (5.9-in) and six 105-mm (4.1-in) guns. It was thought that what they could not outfight, the *Panzerschiffe* could outrun.

A fortnight before war commenced, two *Panzerschiffe* sailed unobtrusively into the Atlantic. One was the *Admiral Graf Spee*. Her orders, in the event of hostilities, were to disrupt trade but avoid action with warships that could cause her injury far from dockyard facilities.

The enemy commenced operations near the end of September, sinking the Booth liner *Clement* off the Brazilian coast. To catch the *Admiral Graf Spee* the French and British put together eight separate hunting groups of which Force G comprised the South American division reinforced by the Royal New Zealand Navy's HMNZS *Achilles*, a sister to the *Ajax*. Under the command of Commodore Henry Harwood, these four ships had an enormous area to cover but, despite the raider's widespread depredations, Harwood was convinced that she would eventually strike at the important River Plate trade. His convictions were well-founded, though when his force sighted the *Admiral Graf Spee* off the Uruguayan coast on the morning of 13 December, his concentration was of only three ships, the *Cumberland* being near the Falklands.

HMNZS* Achilles *joined Force G to hunt for the* Graf Spee. *When the German cruiser was located on 13 December, she and* Ajax *engaged her from one side and* Exeter *from the other.

Harwood, like Nelson before him, had thoroughly discussed his plans with his captains and dispositions were smoothly carried out to split the enemy's fire. The *Exeter* took one side and the two light cruisers the other. Fire was opened at over 17375 m (19,000 yards) the *Admiral Graf Spee* first taking on the two light cruisers, whose volume of fire must, initially, have appeared more of a threat. She very soon switched, however, as the larger splashes of the *Exeter*'s 203-mm (8-in) weapons began to straddle.

Turning nearly 180° from her original course of near south east, the *Admiral Graf Spee* put the *Exeter* slightly abaft her port beam, with all six 280-mm (11-in) guns bearing. Simultaneously, she engaged the two smaller ships with her 150-mm (5.9-in) secondary armament.

The enemy had the advantage of a radar set which could pass ranges to the gunlayers and the *Exeter* was soon hard hit by three 280-mm (11-in) projectiles, losing a turret and her steering. Under emergency control, she continued doggedly, launching her starboard torpedoes without effect. Hit again, she developed a starboard list and turned in that direction to fire her portside torpedoes, which were again evaded. Her injuries began to tell on both the accuracy and rate of her fire.

Still shooting well at a comfortable range, the *Admiral Graf Spee* hit her twice again, putting another turret out of action and starting a serious fire. Blinded and burning, the gallant *Exeter* was spent; pulling away, she disengaged to the south.

Comparatively untroubled to this point, the two light cruisers had to manoeuvre to deter the German from making after the *Exeter*. The enemy's resolve seemed broken, however, and from an hour after the action commenced, her course was generally westward, the *Ajax* and *Achilles* hanging on to her, eventually shepherding her into Montevideo.

Though the *Graf Spee* had lost 36 killed (in comparison, the *Exeter* alone suffered 61 dead) the damage from the 27 hits that she had suffered was superficial. Nevertheless, without hope of making it back to Germany, this still-formidable fighting machine was scuttled by her crew. This, and the suicide of her respected commander, Langsdorff, brought a sombre note to what had been to the British a sparkling little action.

Named after the gallant German Admiral of World War I,* Graf Spee *was designed to outrun any ship she could not outfight but Commodore Harwood's boldness paid off.

Party and the Führer of which Chamberlain so ardently dreamed.

But nothing had happened, and once the Poles had been beaten the now-experienced German divisions moved swiftly back across their country to the Siegfried Line. Here they settled down to do little for the moment but glower at their opposite numbers and exchange insults with them daily through loudspeakers; but neither side did anything to disturb the other's physical comfort.

As for British civilians, their lives were disturbed by the torrent of bureaucratic regulations which descended upon them from every old and several new departments of government, and their homes were either emptied of their own children if they lived in important cities or filled with other people's children if they lived in the country. A lot of them suffered disability or even death as a result of accidents in the black-out, and life, commented one observer afterwards, 'seemed to have become a continual exhortation, as posters sprouted everywhere enjoining every civic virtue from thrift to celibacy'.

As winter passed and the first signs of spring of 1940 began to show themselves, boredom with the war and all its petty nuisances was a general feeling.

Then on 8 April 1940, the First Lord of the Admiralty, Winston Churchill, announced that the Royal Navy were laying mines in Norwegian waters in order to stop the iron-ore traffic between Narvik and Germany – a flagrant violation of Norway's neutrality apparently to be justified on the curious ground that Germany's reaction was likely to be even more flagrant. As Norway was a distinctly friendly neutral, this struck many British people as odd.

But not so odd as the news next morning.

It was the Russo-Finnish War and the possibility that British and French reinforcements and supplies might cross from Narvik to Luleå in Sweden, and thus interrupt Germany's supplies of iron-ore, that first brought Hitler's attention to Norway. Before that, his attention in the west had been concentrated on the Low Countries, but once he had seen the dangers which the exploitation of Norway might hold for Germany, and the advantages which would accrue to his Kriegsmarine by possession of Norwegian ports and control of her coastline, he ordered planning for what became known as Weserübung – Exercise Weser.

On 16 February 1940, British intelligence discovered that the *Altmark*, one of the *Graf Spee*'s supply ships, with a large number of British seamen aboard taken prisoner during the *Graf Spee*'s raiding cruise, was steaming down the Norwegian coast. When threatened by the British 4th Destroyer Flotilla under Captain Vian, she took refuge in Jösenfjord. With typically Churchillian panache the orders went out from Whitehall: Vian disregarded Norwegian neutrality, entered the fjord, forced the *Altmark* aground and rescued the prisoners, his boarding party making minor popular history with the call 'The Navy's here!'

The British public were delighted, United States and other Western powers applauded discreetly – and Hitler ordered a speeding-up and consolidation of Weserübung. Two days later General von Falkenhorst and his staff were given control of the operation – and it was one of Fortune's extravaganzas that at the end of March, Hitler decreed that it would be launched at dawn on 9 April.

The result was that, to the watching world, Germany's reaction to the Royal Navy's mining of the Norwegian Leads, flagrant violation or not, appeared bewilderingly rapid. By dawn the following day German troops were swarming ashore at Oslo, Bergen, Trondheim and even – to the astonishment of a world steeped in the tradition of British supremacy at sea – at Narvik, over a thousand miles from the German homeland. German paratroops seized Sola airport near Stavanger and dropped later on to Fornebu airport near Oslo, while the Kriegsmarine ferried the army formations across the Skagerrak and Kattegat (Denmark had been totally overrun in a few hours), though not without loss. Both the *Blücher* and the *Karlsruhe* were sunk, the first by Norwegian coastal guns and the second by the submarine *Truant* – and the cruiser *Hipper* had 120 feet torn out of her starboard bow when she was rammed by the British destroyer *Glowworm* in a self-sacrificial attack, an action which won her commander, Lieutenant-Commander G.B. Roope, the first posthumous Victoria Cross of the war.

On land only the Norwegian forces, reacting with admirable determination after the first shock, could offer any resistance, but the Royal Navy could at least help up at Narvik. Destroyer strikes led by Captain Warburton-Lee created chaos among the German

German paratroops land in Norway, 9 April 1940. The invasion was a deftly-executed combined operation, although the German navy was to be seriously punished.

German aircraft played a vital role in the invasion of Norway, dropping parachutists, providing close air support and, in theory, discouraging the Royal Navy from interference.

The German destroyer Georg Thiele *lies beached in the upper part of Rombaks Fjord after the Royal Navy's aggressive sortie of 13 April.*

warships in the harbour and on 12 April the old battleship *Warspite* raced up the Ototfjord and completed the destruction; but to the south the preponderance of German artillery and trained battalions – and the complete domination of the air by the Luftwaffe – ensured the ultimate conquest.

In eight days brigades of the German 163rd and 196th Divisions had advanced 180 miles and now controlled the vital southern region; when eventually hastily landed British reinforcements arrived, they were incorporated piecemeal into the ragged defences, and beaten, as were the Norwegians, by better trained, better armed, and much better co-ordinated and commanded troops. The survivors of two British brigades landed at Andalsnes in the middle of April were re-embarked and evacuated by 1 May, and central and southern Norway virtually abandoned to the Germans.

However, in the far north at Narvik, the situation for the German General Dietl and his 2,000 mountain troops was not at first so favourable. Their naval transport and supply had been destroyed and they were chased out of Narvik itself by a combined force of British Guardsmen, French Chasseurs Alpins and Polish Chasseurs du Nord. By 28 May Narvik was at last firmly in Allied hands. Thus it was somewhat ironic that orders had already been issued for the rapid return home of all Allied forces, as they and their weapons were urgently needed elsewhere.

Perhaps the most illuminating comment upon the Allied conduct of the Norwegian Campaign was written ten years after the war by the man appointed to command the British reinforcements in central Norway. As Major-General Carton de Wiart, VC, walked along Whitehall to answer an urgent summons to the War Office in early April, 'It dawned on me that it might be Norway, as I had never been there and knew nothing about it!'

But if the Norwegian Campaign was a setback for the British arms, it was a disaster for the Prime Minister.

Leadership crisis

The House of Commons was packed, the mood of the members frustrated and angry – the anger concentrated on the figure of Neville Chamberlain sitting in his usual place on the front bench, so pale with fury and humiliation that Churchill, despite the bitter arguments of the past few years, was filled with sympathy for his harassed leader.

The First Lord of the Admiralty could hardly remember such bitter attacks being mounted in the House before. These were attacks against the policies of appeasement to which the government had clung for so many months, against the pathetic optimism exhibited by the Prime Minister both in his dealings with Hitler before the war and in his attitude to Britain's defences since its outbreak, and especially against the contents of a speech Chamberlain had made but a month before which had included the unfortunate statement that he believed 'Hitler has missed the bus!'

Nor was the attack delivered entirely by members of the Opposition, for it reached its zenith with a speech from one of Chamberlain's oldest friends and political colleagues, Leo Amery. Quoting Cromwell's scathing indictment of the leaders of Hampden's army as 'old decaying service men,' he turned directly on the Prime Minister and quoted Cromwell for the second time: 'You have sat here too long for any good you have been doing,' he proclaimed. 'Depart, I say, and let us have done with you! In the name of God, go!'

It was a devastating shock to the Prime Minister's ego, underlined by howls from the backbenchers chanting 'Go! Go! Go!' as he left the House. Later that day he admitted to Churchill that he felt that he could not continue to lead a one-party government in the prosecution of the war, that a national government embracing members of all parties should be formed – but he doubted if the Labour leaders would serve under his own direction.

So, in fact, it proved during the somewhat involved talks and negotiations of the next 48 hours; by 11 a.m. on 10 May Chamberlain had accepted that he must give way to another leader, and sent for the two men between whom he felt the choice must be made: Lord Halifax and Winston Churchill.

'I have had many important interviews in my public life,' Churchill later wrote, 'and this was certainly the most important. Usually I talk a great deal, but on this occasion I was silent.'

It must have been a remarkable scene: Chamberlain, still icily certain of the rightness of his every action since taking office but prepared to yield in the face of such uncomprehending and incomprehensible hostility, now sure that his preference for Lord Halifax was justifiable; Churchill silent, feeling no doubt

The German battlecruiser Gneisenau *fires a salvo from her 11-in main battery at the British aircraft carrier HMS* Courageous.

German heavy artillery advancing during the invasion of Norway. Better led and better organised, the Wehrmacht cut ruthlessly through the Allied defences.

French Armour 1940

In 1940 the French army and nation were still haunted by the memories of Verdun, France possessed the most powerful tank park in Europe but tactical thinking was rooted in the past and French armour offered little opposition to the Blitzkrieg.

Well protected and manoeuvrable, the ***SOMUA S-35*** *was the best tank fielded by the Allies in 1940. It was equipped with radio, and the 47-mm gun could fire both* ***HE*** *and* ***AP*** *rounds (a requirement which had been overlooked by British designers).*

Typical of the equipment used by the ***BEF****, the* ***Vickers Light Tank*** *was a classic example of the cavalry school of tank design. Barely suitable for use as recce machines, they were employed as combat tanks in France (mainly due to a lack of suitable types). Vulnerable to anything larger than rifle bullets, they suffered heavy losses to the advancing Wehrmacht and Luftwaffe.*

Another of the French two-man tanks of the 1930s, the ***Hotchkiss H-39*** *proved more effective than the Renault, having a respectable performance (by 1930s standards). Nevertheless, the major disadvantage of a one-man turret and their dismal tactical use against massed German armour meant that the Hotchkisses were no more effective than other Allied types.*

In common with many armies of the 1930s, France saw the need to re-equip ageing tank parks with more up-to-date vehicles. Some of the products of this change were extremely advanced, but others took no notice of the change in war since 1918. The ***Renault R.35*** *was a two man infantry support tank squarely in the Great War mould, and proved no match for the German Panzer forces in May and June 1940.*

With a development history dating back to the early 1920s, the ***Char B1*** *series mounted a powerful main gun in the hull as well as the turret gun. Potentially the most powerful tank in the world, and easily able to deal with any German tank then extant, abysmal handling and the usual French tactical errors meant that the 400 or so tanks available were largely ineffective.*

the weight of history already pressing about him; Halifax uncertain, his sense of duty unsustained by any driving ambition. It was, as Churchill wrote, 'a very long pause.... It certainly seemed longer than the two minutes which one observes in the commemoration of Armistice Day.'

It was broken, at last, by Halifax. It would be, he said, very difficult for him to direct the War Cabinet from outside the House of Commons where all the major decisions must be debated, and where, as a member of the House of Lords, he was barred from speaking (it should be remembered that these were the days before a peer could disclaim his title). When he had finished it was evident that Churchill's would be the name recommended to His Majesty, and after a little more desultory talk the three men parted.

The call to Churchill came late in the afternoon, and at 6 p.m. was shown into the presence of the King, whom he was to serve so devotedly through such crucial years.

'I suppose you don't know why I have sent for you?' asked the King with a smile.

'Sir, I simply couldn't imagine why,' replied Churchill, matching his mood.

'I want to ask you to form a government'.

So began the premiership of one of the most remarkable men in British history and it is hard to believe that, for most of the rest of the world, the appointment itself and the events surrounding it passed for the moment almost unnoticed.

Early that same morning, the Spring Offensive of the German Wehrmacht into the Low Countries (both of them neutral) had opened, with air bombardment of Rotterdam and German parachutists

French gunners load a World War I vintage 75-mm field gun as the German invasion begins. Dated equipment was not the most serious weakness in the French army in 1940.

Above: A German Panzer III heads for Paris after the breakthrough in the Ardennes. The French Third Republic died as it was born: to the sound of gunfire in the hills around Sedan.

Right: A machine-gun team of a German reconnaissance unit opens fire with a ZB-30 light machine-gun, one of the many weapons acquired by the Wehrmacht from the invasion of Czechoslovakia.

Below: A mortar team belonging to the Waffen SS regiment 'Germania'. Weighed down by the mortar legs, the soldier on the left carries a Luger pistol instead of a rifle.

Left: A German artillery battery crosses a pontoon bridge in the wake of the advancing tank divisions. Whereas the BEF was entirely motorized, the German army still relied heavily on horse-drawn transport.

dropping on to key points along an obviously carefully planned attack route.

The days of the 'Phoney War' were gone for ever.

Shortly after 2.30 on the morning of 10 May 1940, 64 men of the German army crossed the Dutch frontier; this was the pinpoint of invasion. Three hours later glider-borne troops dropped over the Belgian border to capture and demolish the huge fortifications at Eben-Emael; five minutes later the 30 divisions of Army Group B under General von Bock flooded forward across the frontiers from Maastricht up to the coast at the Ems estuary, while to the south General von Rundstedt's Army Group A of 44 divisions, including the main striking force of seven panzer divisions under General Kleist, struck forward into the Ardennes – the wooded country which French military commanders had been proclaiming impassable for tanks since 1919.

And with an almost suicidal alacrity which brought tears of joy to Hitler's eyes, the Allied armies in the north – five divisions of the British Expeditionary Force, eight divisions of the French First Army on their right and seven divisions of the French Seventh Army up on the coast around Dunkirk – left the defensive positions they had spent the bitterly cold winter so arduously preparing, and moved forward to join the Belgian army in accordance with the Dyle Plan, which envisaged a defensive line running along the Dyle and Meuse rivers. There were obviously some difficulties to be overcome on the way, for the Luftwaffe was busy overhead all the time, and this was the occasion for the baptism of Allied troops by dive-bombing – it took time for them to become accustomed to the nerve-shaking howl which accompanied it. Moreover, roads were soon choked by refugees fleeing ahead of Bock's advancing infantry.

Nevertheless, by the evening of 14 May, the Allied line was formed. From the mouth of the Scheldt to just north of Antwerp stood three divisions of the French Seventh Army; the 50 miles south-east to Louvain were held by 13 divisions of the Belgian army; between Louvain and Wavre the front was held by the BEF and from Wavre to Namur by six divisions of the French First Army. Some of the battalion and brigade commanders were dismayed by the fragmentary nature of the defences they now occupied – especially compared with those they had just left – while the divisional and higher commanders were alarmed by news of events further to the south. But as yet none of them were aware of the fact that Bock's slowly advancing Army Group was in fact 'the matador's cloak' tempting the mass of the Allied armies forward into the trap which would release Kleist's Panzer Group for the killing thrust.

This was not merely the plan; it soon became the reality. Crashing through the 'impassable' Ardennes as though on a peacetime exercise and brushing aside the French light cavalry unit which had been sent out to 'delay' them, the three divisions of General Guderian's Panzer Corps were across the French frontier and had reached the Meuse on each side of Sedan by the afternoon of 12 May; by evening German armour controlled the right bank of the river up as far as Dinant. They were across the river within 24 hours (French High Command estimates, once they had got over the shock of the German arrival on the Meuse, were that the crossing would take at least four days to organize and two to carry out). By the morning of 14 May Guderian had two bridgeheads consolidating, while up at Dinant the 7th Panzer Division of Colonel-General Hermann Hoth's XV Panzer Corps (commanded by Major-General Erwin Rommel) had formed yet another bridgehead in the face of desperate but sporadic French resistance.

Chronology of War: 1940

May 10
Germany invades Holland, Belgium and Luxembourg. The main armoured thrust is by Army Group A through the Ardennes. British and French troops enter Belgium. Chamberlain resigns; Winston Churchill becomes Prime Minister of Coalition Government

May 11
German paratroops complete capture of Fort Eben-Emael outside Liège and cross Albert Canal. British War Cabinet formed

May 13
Churchill makes his 'blood, sweat and tears' speech

May 14
German Luftwaffe terror raid on Rotterdam. German troops reach Meuse from Liege to Namur

May 15
Holland capitulates. General Heinz Guderian's Panzers break through at Sedan

May 16
Roosevelt asks Congress for 50,000 aircraft a year

May 18
Germans reach Antwerp, cross Sambre and take Amiens

May 19
73-year-old French General Weygand appointed C-in-C Allied Forces

May 20
Guderian's Panzers reach Channel coast at Abbeville

May 21
British and French counterattack at Arras fails

May 23
Germans take Boulogne

May 24
Hitler issues famous 'Stop' order which halts German armour south of Dunkirk

May 26
Operation 'Dynamo' – Dunkirk evacuation – begins

May 28
Belgian Army capitulates and King Leopold signs surrender. Calais falls. Capture of Narvik by British and Norwegian forces

May 31
Roosevelt announces 'million dollar' defence programme

Allied Air Forces 1940

The Allied air forces found themselves facing the might of the Luftwaffe, and despite having some up-to-date aircraft among the obsolescent Gladiators and Battles these were no match for the sleek Messerschmitts and Dorniers fielded by the Germans.

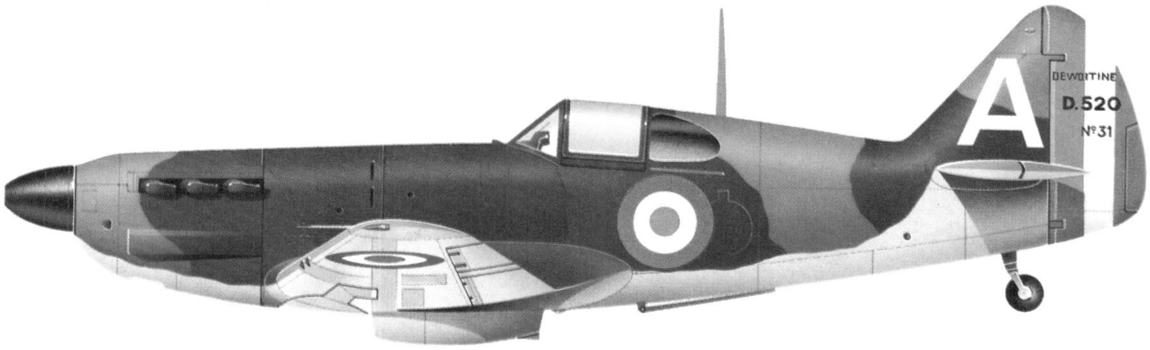

Dewoitine D.520 No. 31 was on the strength of the Escadrille de Chasse de Defense, based at the SNCASE plant at Toulouse and tasked with the local defence of that important part of the nationalized aircraft industry.

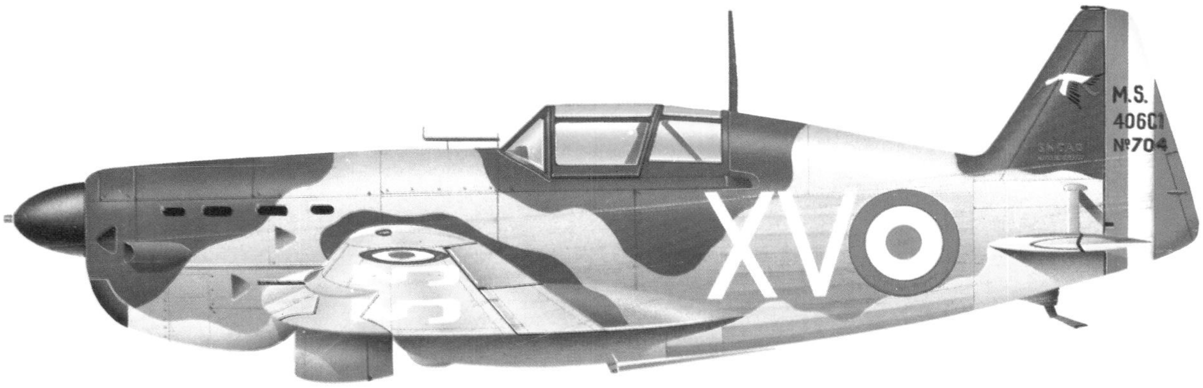

Left: Despite its lack of power and relative crudity, the Morane-Saulnier MS.406 served the Armée de l'Air with honours. Nevertheless, even in the hands of famous units such as the Cigognes (1ère GC 1/2) it was hopelessly outclassed by Bf 109s.

The Potez 63.11 army co-operation and reconnaissance aircraft was forced to operate without fighter cover in the Battle of France, and 225 out of 700 in service were lost.

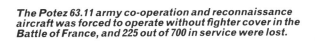

A Fairey Battle of 5e Escadrille, III Groupe, 3e Regiment based at Evère. The Belgian Battles were as woefully ill-equipped for the new kind of war as those of the RAF, and losses were high.

Gladiators of No. 615 Squadron based at Croydon went to France with the BEF, based at Vitry, Poix and Abbeville. The squadron was heavily engaged in May flying bomber escort, interceptor and ground attack missions.

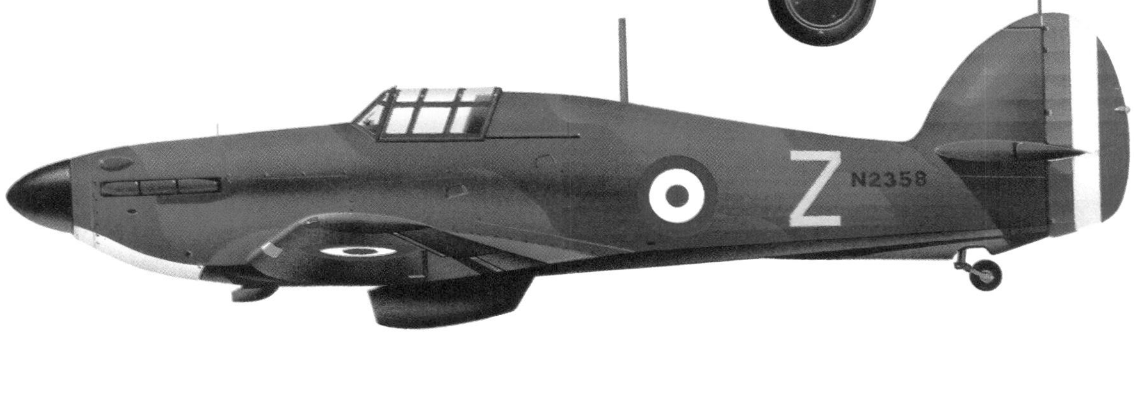

A Hawker Hurricane Mk 1 of No. 73 Squadron, one of the two component squadrons of the Advanced Air Striking Force's No. 67 (Fighter) Wing, based at Rouvres until the German attack on 10 May.

No. 218 Squadron's Fairey Battles suffered heavy losses during their brief sojourn in France. Initially used for reconnaissance and leaflet drops, the squadron was later used for bombing attacks against the rapidly advancing Germans. It returned to RAF Mildenhall in June 1940.

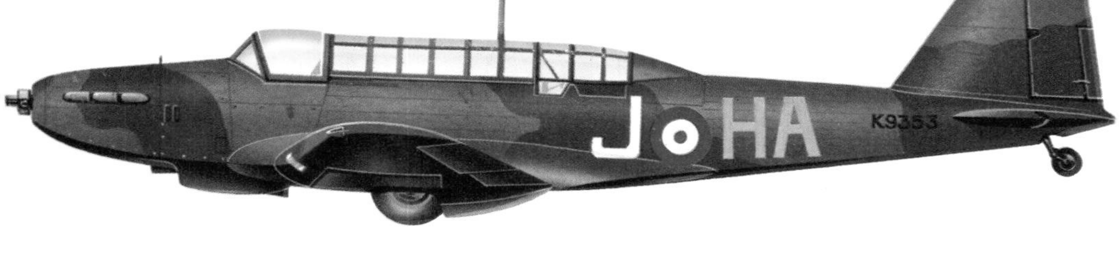

A German gunner fuzes shells for an FH18 150-mm howitzer on the Aisne. Following in the wake of the Panzers, the infantry divisions attacked the by-passed Allied units.

Above: Two Panzer 38(t) light tanks and a pair of Panzer IV medium tanks advance at a leisurely pace with hatches open and crews enjoying the sunshine.

Early on 15 May, the flood burst into France. From each of the bridgeheads the panzers roared out, preceded on every advance by a cloud of screaming Stukas, covered against attack from British or French fighters by marauding Messerschmitts. Refugees choked the roads, harried by Luftwaffe fighters, bullied by frightened and demoralized soldiers or gendarmes of their own side, or forced into the ditches by strange, ominous, foreign vehicles manned by blond young giants who waved triumphantly at them, rarely deliberately harming them but leaving in their wake an impression of total invincibility.

That evening, German panzers were reported only 12 miles from Laon, and when Daladier, now France's Minister of National Defence, ordered a counter-attack, the French commander-in-chief, General Gamelin, replied that he had no reserves because the bulk of French strength was locked up in the outflanked Maginot Line. At the same time Gamelin announced that he could no longer take responsibility for the defence of Paris, and he issued orders for a general retreat of all French forces in Belgium. A copy of these orders came, solely by good fortune, to the notice of the British commander-in-chief, Lord Gort, enabling him to ensure that the BEF divisions on the Dyle were not left there on their own.

In the face of apparently imminent disaster – and a devastating indication of French morale from the French premier, Paul Reynaud, who woke him with a telephone call announcing 'We have been defeated! We are beaten; we have lost the battle!' – Churchill flew to Paris on the evening of 16 May both to put some iron into the French political backbone and to discover for himself the true state of affairs. These became distressingly obvious when in answer to his question 'Où est la masse de manoeuvre [the strategic reserve]?' Gamelin answered 'Aucune! [None!] But even at this setback Churchill refused to abandon hope.

Allied impotence

There were still considerable French forces to the south of the German breakthrough, and even larger forces – including the British Expeditionary Force – to the north. Between them, could they not first manoeuvre to channel and then contain the German breakthrough, then counter-attack from both north and south and so cut the enemy spearheads off from

German troops storm over a river while under mortar fire. Allied air attacks on captured bridges over the Meuse failed disastrously and the Blitzkrieg continued unchecked.

One of the few officers to protest against the supine French strategy was Colonel de Gaulle, who launched one of the very few armoured counter-attacks mounted by the French army in 1940.

German Anti-aircraft Guns

While German aircraft provided devastatingly effective close air support for their advancing army, Allied ground attack aircraft which broke through the Messerschmitt Bf 109s were met with a hail of anti-aircraft fire which inflicted prohibitive losses.

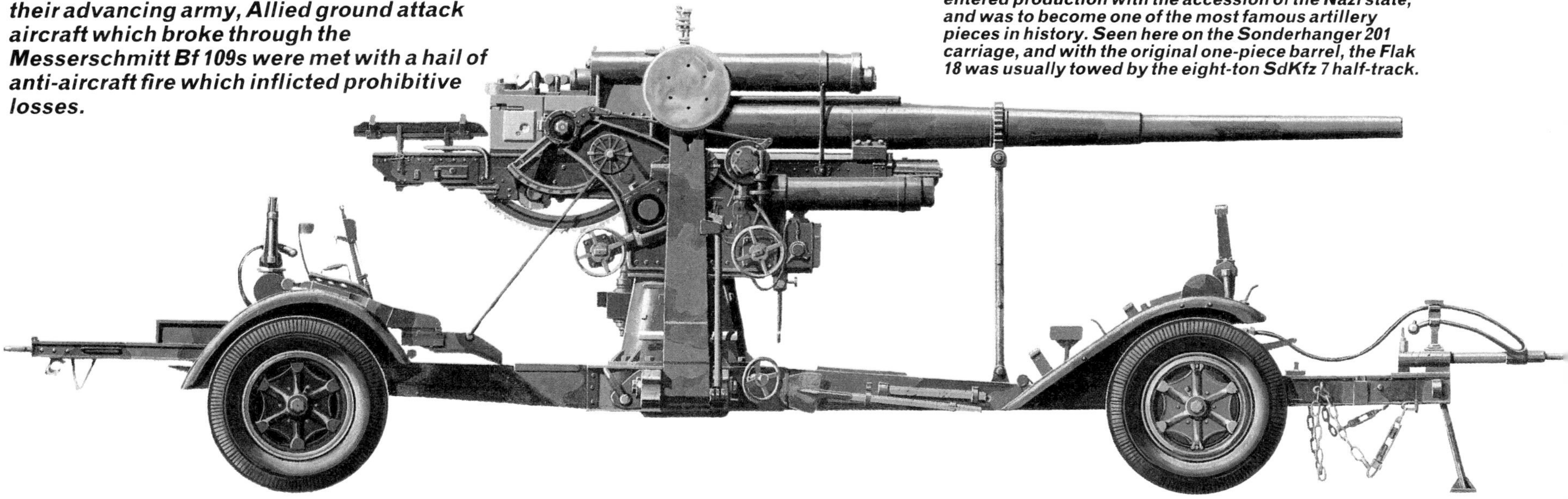

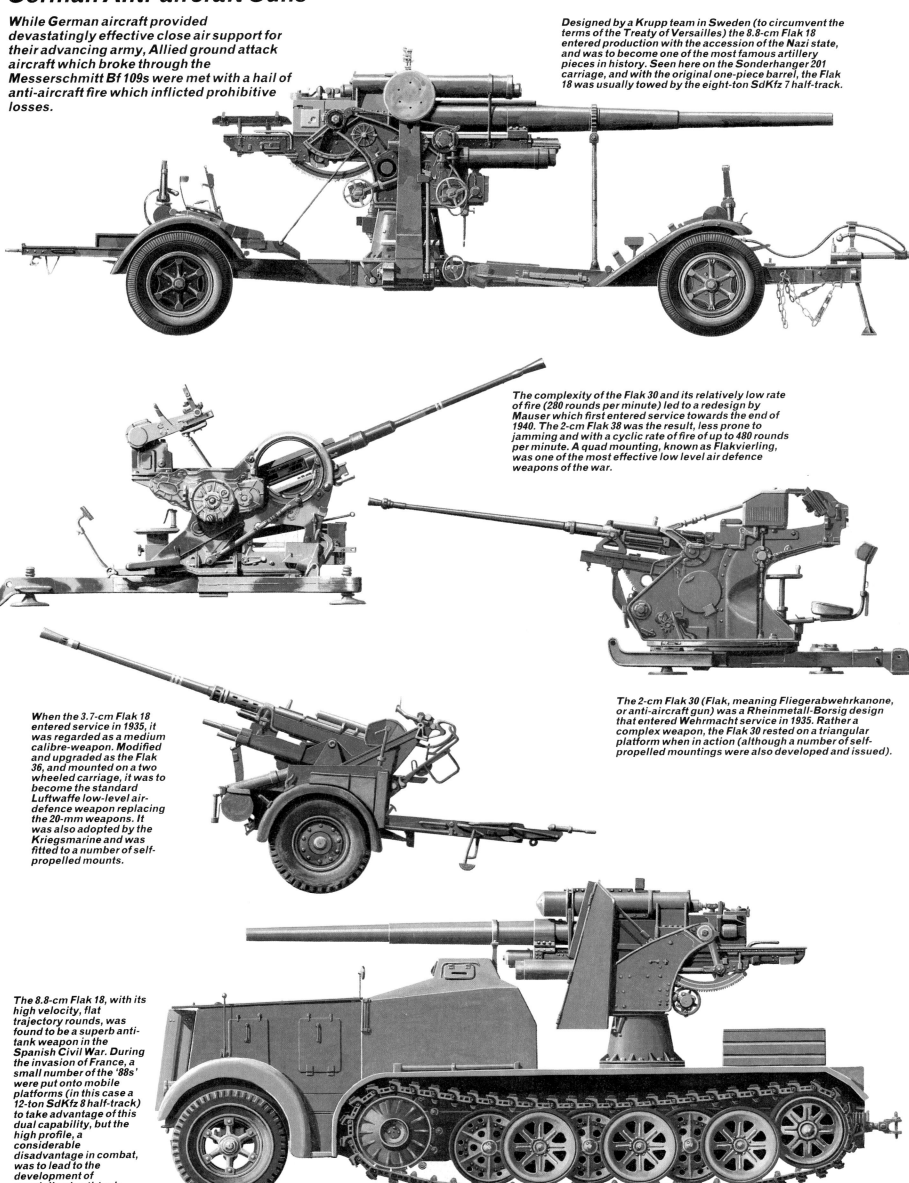

Designed by a Krupp team in Sweden (to circumvent the terms of the Treaty of Versailles) the 8.8-cm Flak 18 entered production with the accession of the Nazi state, and was to become one of the most famous artillery pieces in history. Seen here on the Sonderhanger 201 carriage, and with the original one-piece barrel, the Flak 18 was usually towed by the eight-ton SdKfz 7 half-track.

The complexity of the Flak 30 and its relatively low rate of fire (280 rounds per minute) led to a redesign by Mauser which first entered service towards the end of 1940. The 2-cm Flak 38 was the result, less prone to jamming and with a cyclic rate of fire of up to 480 rounds per minute. A quad mounting, known as Flakvierling, was one of the most effective low level air defence weapons of the war.

The 2-cm Flak 30 (Flak, meaning Fliegerabwehrkanone, or anti-aircraft gun) was a Rheinmetall-Borsig design that entered Wehrmacht service in 1935. Rather a complex weapon, the Flak 30 rested on a triangular platform when in action (although a number of self-propelled mountings were also developed and issued).

When the 3.7-cm Flak 18 entered service in 1935, it was regarded as a medium calibre-weapon. Modified and upgraded as the Flak 36, and mounted on a two wheeled carriage, it was to become the standard Luftwaffe low-level air-defence weapon replacing the 20-mm weapons. It was also adopted by the Kriegsmarine and was fitted to a number of self-propelled mounts.

The 8.8-cm Flak 18, with its high velocity, flat trajectory rounds, was found to be a superb anti-tank weapon in the Spanish Civil War. During the invasion of France, a small number of the '88s' were put onto mobile platforms (in this case a 12-ton SdKfz 8 half-track) to take advantage of this dual capability, but the high profile, a considerable disadvantage in combat, was to lead to the development of specialized anti-tank guns.

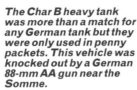

The Char B heavy tank was more than a match for any German tank but they were only used in penny packets. This vehicle was knocked out by a German 88-mm AA gun near the Somme.

Above: Endless columns of British troops wait for evacuation on the beach at Dunkirk. It was indeed a miracle that most of the BEF escaped, Hitler halted the German divisions poised to storm the port.

their main sources of supply and support?

In the depths of their despondency, the French leaders were reluctant to admit the practicability of such a scheme, pleading lack of air strength unless Churchill were to abandon all thought of retaining RAF fighter squadrons for the defence of Britain and send them all to France instead. Even then it seemed most likely that the German forces would be either on the Channel coast or in Paris – or both – in a matter of days, in which case the British and French armies to the north most probably faced early dispersion and disintegration, and, unless a general armistice saved them, possibly physical destruction.

Churchill was home by the following morning, but before he left he managed to instil something of his own dogged courage into the French leadership, so that they at least agreed to order some form of counter-attack on the German spearheads as he had suggested. But at the pace of Allied military planning it was four days before it could be attempted, and even then it was bungled.

By the evening of 20 May, Guderian's panzer spearheads had reached Abbeville at the mouth of the Somme, and at this point their line was as attenuated as it ever would be. On 21 May, four British infantry brigades and the First Army Tank Brigade were launched southwards from Arras, in theory supported by two French infantry divisions on one flank and one light mechanized division on the other, while equally strong French forces were assumed to be attacking up from the south to meet them.

In the event, only the British forces and the French light mechanized division moved at all, and they quickly found themselves blocked by Rommel's 7th Panzer Division, which after a brisk battle (it at least managed to worry Rommel seriously) drove them back to their original positions and threatened them with encirclement. By the evening of 23 May, General Gort was withdrawing the British brigades further north, and two days later it became evident to him that only a rapid retreat to the coast and evacuation to England would save even a quarter of his command.

On his own responsibility he issued the necessary orders: the British III Corps withdrew to the beaches on each side of Dunkirk, the I Corps fell back to hold the western flank with one French division on their right and the British II Corps on their left, while the Belgian army held the eastern end of the perimeter. However, on 28 May King Leopold of the Belgians signed an armistice with the Germans, the Belgian army ceased to exist and a large gap yawned on the left of the British positions – filled during that night by a manoeuvre of extraordinary difficulty carried out with admirable efficiency by the 3rd Infantry Division under command of Major-General Montgomery. It is not too much to say that this operation saved the British Expeditionary Force.

Now 'Operation Dynamo' began – the attempt to evacuate the British army and as many as possible French soldiers from the trap into which they had been lured. Over a thousand boats took part in this evacuation, varying in size from a Royal Navy anti-aircraft cruiser down to dinghys which were sailed across the Channel by their owners from a hundred tiny slips along the south coast or along the reaches of the Thames. At least 250 of these craft were sunk; many of the yacht owners were killed or wounded; but an astonishingly large number of soldiers were saved to fight again, and to form the basis of new armies.

The highest hopes before the evacuation began were that perhaps 50,000 men might escape capture or worse; in the event 338,226 reached the shores of Britain during those miraculous nine days, of which, on Churchill's insistence, over 100,000 were French. He had returned to Paris on 31 May, and there agreed that British troops would share in holding the rear-guard with French formations, and that French troops in the bridgehead would be evacuated in the same proportion as the British. As it happened, French formations were fighting furiously to the south of the bridgehead (thus holding back powerful German forces which would otherwise have been free to attack Dunkirk), and these never reached the sea. Many of those that did arrive towards the end of the operation refused the chance to escape, and the last ships to sail were thus almost empty. As quite a large number of French troops who did get away quickly decided that they did not care for life in Britain and chose to return to France (where most of them soon found themselves in German prison-camps), Churchill's well-meant gesture was to a great extent wasted.

But, to the British people, the escape of the bulk of the BEF at Dunkirk was a miracle. To such an extent did their spirit rise, indeed, that Churchill found it necessary to sound a cautionary note. 'We must be very careful not to assign to this deliverance the attributes of a victory,' he said in his report to Parliament; 'wars are not won by evacuations.' He then went on to finish his speech with what was to become one of the most famous passages of rhetoric in British history:

> Even though large tracts of Europe and many old and famous States have fallen or may fall into the grip of the Gestapo and all the odious apparatus of Nazi rule, we shall not flag or fail. We shall go on to the end. We shall fight in France, we shall fight on the sea and oceans, we shall fight with growing confidence and growing strength in the air; we shall defend our island, whatever the cost may be. We shall fight on the beaches, we shall fight on the landing-grounds, we shall fight in the fields and in the streets, we shall fight in the hills; we shall never surrender; and even if, which I do not for a moment believe, this island or a large part of it were subjugated and starving, then our Empire beyond the seas, armed and guarded by the British Fleet, would carry on the struggle, until, in God's good time, the New World, with all its power and might, steps forth to the rescue and liberation of the Old.

Below: A French soldier contemplates the utter defeat of his country. After the Armistice the revered Marshal Pétain became President of the Vichy régime.

In a lightning campaign the German army had defeated all its European enemies and now faced the Channel. Across the water, England braced itself for invasion.

Luftwaffe Aircraft

Employing the same Blitzkrieg tactics that had shattered Poland, the bombers of the Luftwaffe swept through Western Europe, their superior tactics and modern aircraft beating the determined but ultimately futile defence that rose to meet them.

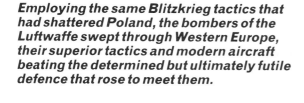

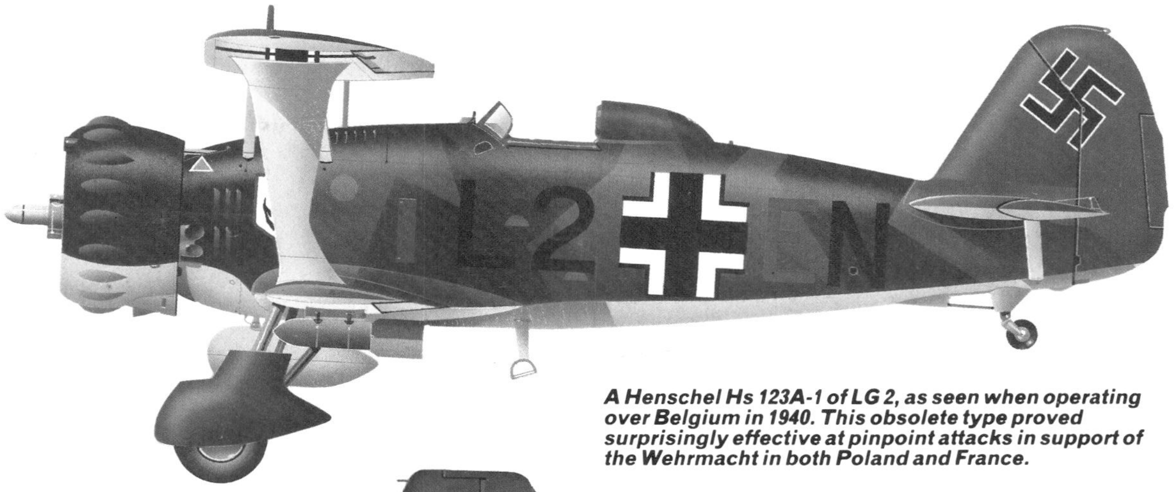

A Henschel Hs 123A-1 of LG 2, as seen when operating over Belgium in 1940. This obsolete type proved surprisingly effective at pinpoint attacks in support of the Wehrmacht in both Poland and France.

A Junkers Ju 87 B-2 of 3./StG 2 'Immelmann', as it looked in the summer of 1940. The Stuka was Blitzkrieg personified, a terrifying weapon that was only to be blunted in the early stages of the Battle of Britain. This particular aircraft was shot down near Selsey, Sussex, in August 1940.

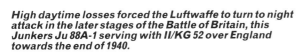

High daytime losses forced the Luftwaffe to turn to night attack in the later stages of the Battle of Britain, this Junkers Ju 88A-1 serving with II/KG 52 over England towards the end of 1940.

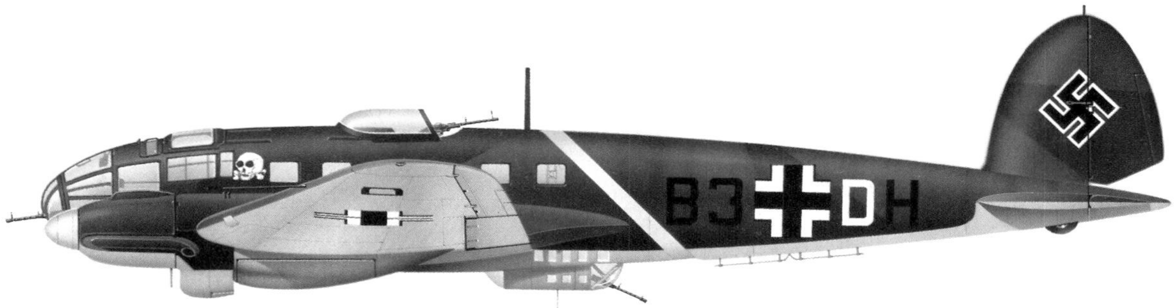

A Heinkel He 111H-3 of 1./KG 54, the appropriately named 'Totenkopf' (Deathshead) Geschwader. It was 57 aircraft from this formation which gutted the city of Rotterdam on 14 May.

This Dornier Do 17Z of 9./KG 76 based at Cormeilles-en-Vexin, south of Le Havre, was part of Sperrle's Luftflotte III. It was in position to attack Channel convoys and targets on the south coast of England.

A Messerschmitt Bf 110C of the Stabsschwarm (staff flight) of I Gruppe, Zerstörergeschwader 2 based at Amiens in July 1940. Unfortunately, the heavy Zerstörer fighter vulnerable to the Hurricanes and Spitfires of the RAF.

This Messerschmitt Bf 109E-3 was in action with III Gruppe, Jagdgeschwader 2 'Richthofen' over France in May/June 1940. The cannon-armed Bf 109 had a great advantage over most other fighters it encountered, being able to fire a greater weight of metal than even the eight-gun RAF fighters.

Chapter 3
Britain Alone

After the incredible triumph in France, the victorious German forces stood poised to finish off their one surviving enemy. The Luftwaffe fought to win air superiority preparatory to invasion, and Britain's vital merchant convoys began to take a hammering. All that stood between the British and defeat were 21 miles of sea, German fear of the Royal Navy and the fighters of the Royal Air Force.

Right: The Junkers Ju 87 Stuka dive-bomber provided close support for the rapidly advancing German tank divisions, but its success depended on air superiority. When they were launched against Britain they suffered prohibitive casualties.

Once the German army had occupied Dunkirk and the French coast as far west as Abbeville and the mouth of the Somme, there was nothing except Hitler's orders to stop them turning south and driving down into the body of France; and as early as 29 May the Führer had intimated to both Rundstedt and Bock that his next plans would be to 'settle the French army's account'. Britain could wait – or better still, come to terms.

As a result, even before the Dunkirk evacuation was over Bock had deputed his Eighteenth Army to clear up Belgium and press on westwards, and had directed the remainder of his Army Group B down to take position along the line of the Somme, on the right of Rundstedt's triumphant infantry and panzer divisions closing up to the coast. By 5 June, the ten panzer divisions of both army groups had been redeployed into five armoured corps, three under Bock, two under Rundstedt, and that morning at dawn, preceded as usual by clouds of dive-bombers, two of them burst out of bridgeheads west of Amiens and drove for the Seine.

'The second great offensive is starting today with formidable new resources!' announced Hitler, while General Weygand, who had been recalled from the Levant to take command of the French army when it became obvious that Gamelin had lost control, appealed to his troops: 'May the thought of our afflicted country inspire in you an unflinching resolve to stand firm. The fate of your country and the future of our children depend on your firmness.' This was hardly the most inspiring message for troops in a desperate situation.

Nevertheless, for a few hours French troops hurriedly assembled into 'hedgehogs' around what their commanders considered strategic nodal points and held back the flood, destroying the leading panzer formations as they came within range, and giving the German commanders pause for thought. 'The French are putting up strong opposition,' reported one of them. 'We are seeing a new French way of fighting.'

But in a very short time the 'hedgehogs' were being bypassed, and by 11 June Hoth's XV Panzer Corps controlled the Seine from Vernon to Le Havre; two of Bock's panzer corps, XXXIX and XLI, had passed the Chemins des Dames and were driving down between Rheims and the Aisne; and his Ninth Army was driving straight for Paris. The following day Rommel's 7th Panzer Division reached St Valéry and captured the western flank of the French Tenth Army, including the survivors of the British 51st Highland Division under their beloved General Fortune. Two days later, on 14 June, German troops drove into Paris, which was saved from damage by an 'Open City' declaration by the French government as it hastily left for Bordeaux.

Above: A German 8-cm mortar in action, France 1940. While the Panzer divisions continued their hectic advance, German infantry units engaged in a series of battles against the Allied forces which had been bypassed.

It must be said that the spectacular advance of the German army was aided throughout by the dilatoriness and uncertainty of the French Command. Under Gamelin this had been a major factor in precipitating disaster, and under Weygand it showed little improvement. Even the formation of 'hedgehogs' was described by one French general as 'only a last resort to enable these weak but brave troops to resist with honour before being overwhelmed'. Reynaud, the French premier, when asked on the evening of 7 June if hope was fading, replied, 'No, it can't be! And yet I know that the battle is lost!'

Some French divisions, nevertheless, defended their positions resolutely, especially on the eastern sector where the 14th Infantry Division under General de Lattre de Tassigny held XLI Panzer Corps (and in one action took 800 prisoners), while a little further

During the Battle for France, many German tank units were still equipped with light tanks like these Panzer IIs, and the Wehrmacht was actually outnumbered in tanks by the combined Allied armies.

west at Rethel the 2nd Division for a whole day fought off every attack mounted against them. Instead of continuing to assault these positions, the panzers found the space between and drove through to Rheims. Even at the lower level there seems to have been no understanding of the impracticability of static defence against strong and mobile armour.

At one point an armoured battle did take place, when a counter-attack was put in by a formation of French heavy 'B' tanks – the strongest in the world at that time – which worried Guderian when he saw his anti-tank shells ricocheting 'off the thick plate of the French tanks'. The French armour drove north towards a small village called Perthes where they rescued an infantry regiment which had been surrounded – only to find that they were surrounded themselves and out of petrol!

But everywhere else the French divisions were overwhelmed or cut off, control from headquarters at all levels was lost, and as the panzers cut deeper and deeper into the heart of France and the grey-clad columns marching so cheerfully behind them occupied more and more villages and towns, morale plummeted and the French army moved ever closer to disintegration.

As early as 9 June, Weygand had stated, 'our armies are fighting the last possible defensive battle. If this attempt fails, they are doomed to rapid destruction.' Two days later he moved his GHQ out of Paris to Briare on the Loire where that evening the last of the Anglo-French conferences was held. Churchill arrived accompanied by Eden and Generals Ismay and Spears, while General Weygand was supported by Marshal Pétain and attended – somewhat guardedly one suspects – by Brigadier de Gaulle.

Weygand opened the meeting with the declaration that 'the last line of defence has been overrun and all the reserves are used up. We are on a knife-edge, and don't know which way we will fall from one minute to the next.' When eventually the argument and discussions died away, he closed the conference with the warning: 'Once our disposition is upset, and that won't be long now, there is no hope of reforming it, because of our lack of reserves. In this case I can see no way of preventing an invasion of the whole of France.'

'These three hours of discussions achieved nothing,' wrote de Gaulle later. 'I thought how empty this chatter was, because it was not directed towards the only viable solution; recovery across the sea.'

This was indeed a solution which Weygand was to reject with venom. On the evening of the day Paris fell, Reynaud suggested that Weygand should follow the example of the Dutch chief of staff, and surrender to the Germans the army on metropolitan soil, while the government went to North Africa with the whole of the French navy, whatever formations of the French air force could fly there, and every French soldier who could escape, there to continue the struggle alongside Britain – and America and every other freedom-loving country as soon as they saw fit to join in.

'I rejected the proposal with indignation!' Weygand claimed later. 'I would never agree to inflicting such shame on our flag! . . . This would have been the ultimate crime, damning and doing irreparable harm to the military honour of our nation. . . . I cannot think of such an ignominous proposal without a shiver of disgust!'

What 'ignominy' Weygand saw in this proposal is difficult to understand, especially as only eight days later he was to order the remaining French army

Above: Mounted on BMW motorcycles, German reconnaissance companies probed ahead of the main body. Here, a sidecar combination passes a Pz.38 (t), which equipped the 7th and 8th Panzer divisions during the invasion of France.

Below: Versailles revenged! German field guns take their turn in parading through the Arc de Triomphe after the fall of Paris on 14 June 1940. The speed of the German victory stunned the world and convinced Hitler that his grasp of strategy was better than that of the General Staff.

Chronology of War: 1940

June 3
Dunkirk evacuation ends with a total of 338,226 men having been rescued. Paris bombed. British troops evacuate Narvik

June 4
Germans claim 40,000 prisoners taken at Dunkirk. Churchill makes 'We shall fight on the beaches . . .' speech

June 5
Battle of France begins. German Panzer divisions drive south and west extremely quickly, bypassing the Maginot Line and demoralizing French forces

June 8
British aircraft-carrier HMS Glorious sunk by German battlecruisers Scharnhorst and Gneisenau

June 10
Italy declares war on Britain and France

June 11
British patrols from Egypt cross 'The Wire' into Italian-controlled Cyrenaica. RAF attacks Turin

June 12
51st Highland Division trapped at St Valery. Churchill flies over to France to see Weygand and Reynaud

June 14
Germans enter Paris

June 16
British offer of Franco-British Union rejected. Marshal Pétain, formerly France's deputy prime minister, forms Cabinet

June 17
Pétain asks for Armistice terms

June 18
French forces in total retreat. Hitler and Mussolini meet in Munich. Churchill makes 'This was their finest hour' speech

June 20
France allows Japanese military missions into Indo-China, requests armistice with Italy

June 22
Franco-German Armistice signed in the same railway carriage at Compiègne where Germany had surrendered in November 1918

June 24
Franco-Italian Armistice signed in Rome

June 25
All hostilities in France end

June 27
German troops reach Spanish frontier

June 28
Britain recognizes de Gaulle as Free French leader. Channel Islands demilitarized. Marshal Balbo, Italian governor of Libya, killed by Italian anti-aircraft fire over Tobruk

June 30
Germans occupy the Channel Islands, the only part of the British Isles to be held by the enemy in the entire war

July 1
French Government moved to Vichy. Romania breaks off French accord. Marshal Rodolfo Graziani succeeds Balbo as C-in-C, Italian North Africa

July 2
Hitler orders plan for invasion of England, codenamed Operation 'Seelöwe' (Sealion). German casualties in France are 17,000 killed; 1,900,000 prisoners taken (mostly French)

July 3
Royal Navy attack French battle squadron in Oran and Mers-el-Kebir, causing heavy damage. 1,300 French seamen are killed. French warships in British ports incorporated into Royal Navy. SS Arandora Star sunk. Skirmishing between British and Italian forces takes place around Fort Capuzzo

July 4
Petain government breaks off relations with Britain

formations in and behind the Maginot Line, *amounting to 400,000 troops*, to 'ask for a cessation of fighting, with war honours'. Under the French Code of Military Justice, the 'ultimate crime' is 'to surrender without having exhausted every means of defence', so the behaviour of the French C-in-C during June 1940 presents something of an enigma.

On 16 June Reynaud resigned and Marshal Pétain took his place, with a determination to obtain an armistice from the Germans as quickly as possible and to establish a form of government of which Hitler would approve.

The fall of France

By 20 June, German troops were in Lyons and Grenoble in the south, along the Swiss border to the east and controlling the Biscay coast to the west as far south as Royan; and Mussolini, who had declared war on both France and Britain ten days earlier, was endeavouring furiously to prod his soldiers into crossing the Franco-Italian frontier and capture Nice before the Germans got there.

They were prevented by the events of the following day. At 3.30 p.m. on 21 June, a French delegation headed by General Huntziger was led into the very railway carriage at Compiègne in which the 1918 Armistice had been signed, where they were awaited by Hitler and his entourage. Little negotiation took place for Hitler was certain that he had won, and any arguments which Huntziger might have put up had to be referred back to Pétain, who tended to agree wholeheartedly with Hitler.

By 7 p.m. on 22 June, the Armistice had been signed, the limits of German occupation agreed – and the promise made that the French battle fleet in Toulon and other Mediterranean ports would remain there under French command. Hitler was very satisfied with this, for one of his main fears had been the powerful French battleships might join the Royal

To complete the humiliation of France, the Germans insisted on signing the surrender in the same railway carriage at Compiégne which was used for the signing of the Armistice in 1918. Hitler dances with glee.

Navy.

On 25 June Marshal Pétain announced over French radio, 'Honour is saved! We must now turn our efforts to the future. A new order is beginning!' Seventeen days later he indicated the form of the new order with an announcement of the 'First Bill of the Constitution' which opened: 'We, Philippe Pétain, Marshal of France, in accordance with the Constitutional Law of the 20th of July, hereby assume the functions of the Head of the French State.' The Republic was abolished; parliament was dismissed.

France had been betrayed by her military leaders, and although many attempts were later made to blame her defeat on social causes which had sapped the morale of the rank and file of her army, it should be remembered that one of the aphorisms of her most famous soldier had been: 'There are no bad soldiers; only bad officers.'

Assault on Britain

The speed and completeness of the victory of the German forces in the west astonished the whole world, not excluding Hitler and his command staff.

A Fieseler Fi 156 Storch lands a senior officer in the Place de la Concorde after the French surrender. Marshall Pétain established the new French regime at Vichy, and German thoughts turned to the invasion of Britain.

Not for one moment had they believed that within a month of opening their campaign would they be faced with the problems of mounting an invasion across the English Channel, and when they did realize that they now controlled the Channel coast from the Frisian Islands to Brest, they allowed hope to persuade them that the British would be so impressed by their victories that they would be willing to make peace.

But in order to add that small degree of extra pressure, the Luftwaffe were ordered to mount bombing raids against Britain.

This they did throughout the latter part of June and the first weeks of July, their pilots gaining valuable experience in night operations and the use of navigational aids. The Luftwaffe administration services made the necessary plans for moving the bomber squadrons to airfields in the Low Countries and northern France for use should the British prove stubborn. On 19 July Hitler made a formal peace offer, broadcast to the world; on 22 July it was rejected. Surprised and disappointed, Hitler ordered that planning for the invasion of Britain should assume a more serious aspect.

According to meteorological experts, weather conditions for a sea-borne crossing of the Channel by large numbers of troops and their impedimenta (and the German army considered that six divisions would be the minimium to be put ashore in the first wave) would remain satisfactory only until mid-September. So, disregarding the protests of both naval and army commanders that time was far too short for even the planning, let alone the basic preparations, Hitler decreed that Seelöwe (Sea Lion) would be launched on 15 September.

As the only point of unanimous agreement among all parties in Berlin was that air supremacy must be achieved before the ships and barges could even leave port – and as Goering was anxious that the Luftwaffe should quickly expunge the stain of the broken promise he had made to the Führer that they would stop the evacuation of the BEF from France – the opening stage of the invasion of Britain would be the destruction of the RAF. This Hitler ordered on 1 August: 'The German air force is to overcome the British air force with all means at its disposal, and as soon as possible.'

RAF Fighter Command

To Air Chief Marshal Sir Hugh Dowding, Air Officer C-in-C of Fighter Command, the problem he faced when the battle opened was one of stark simplicity. He had 46 squadrons of effective day-time fighters – Spitfires and Hurricanes – plus another eight squadrons of Blenheims and Defiants which against Bf 109s and 110s were unlikely to prove effective; with probable losses and mechanical troubles he could reasonably count on about 800 serviceable fighters. Against this, the Luftwaffe could deploy some 2,600 aircraft, of which 1,000 would be Messerschmitt fighters, the others Dornier, Heinkel or Junkers bombers.

To offset his numerical inferiority, however, Dowding had at his disposal the most advanced and efficient radar system in the world, which would provide warning of the direction and size of any airborne attacking force. Spitfires were moreover marginally faster and more manoeuvrable than Bf 109s and they were coming off the production line at an ever-increasing rate. On the other hand, pilots to fly them were not becoming available at the same pace, so those already on his strength would have to bear the brunt of the attack. It was therefore important that

Chronology of War: 1940

July 7
French warships in Alexandria neutralized by agreement between Admirals Godefroy and Cunningham

July 9
British and Italian fleets meet briefly off Calabria; Italians retreat. RAF begins night bombing of Germany. Romania placed under German protection

July 10
Battle of Britain begins; 70 aircraft raid Cardiff and Swansea

July 11
Marshal Petain assumes title of Chief of French State after the Vichy assembly elects to give him full authority

July 13
Italians attack British garrison at Moyale in Ethiopia. Hitler issues Directive 15 regarding invasion of Britain, which outlines the general strategy to be followed

July 14
Latvia, Lithuania and Estonia united with USSR by general elections in all three countries. Soviet ultimatum in June – 'Join USSR or be invaded' has had its effect

July 16
Prince Konoye appointed Prime Minister of Japan

July 19
Hitler makes his 'Last Appeal to Britain'

July 21
Hitler orders preliminary preparations for attack on Russia. Russia officially annexes the Baltic states

July 22
British set up SOE (Special Operations Executive) to co-ordinate undercover operations in occupied Europe

July 25
Italian air force bombs Alexandria. Luftwaffe and German torpedo boats attack shipping in the North Sea

July 29
Dover harbour heavily bombed by Ju 87 'Stukas' with heavy fighter escort. 11 German aircraft shot down

July 30
Demobilization of French North African and Syrian armies

July 31
Fifteen ships with war materials sail from America for Britain. Civilian casualties from air raids in UK are 258 killed, 321 injured

August 1
Soviet Commissar for foreign affairs Vyacheslav Molotov delivers verbal attack on Britain and USA. Japanese announce plans for 'Asian Co-prosperity Sphere'. Hitler orders Luftwaffe to destroy RAF

August 3
Italians invade British Somaliland

August 5
Italians capture Hargeisa

August 7
Gaullist Free French Forces set up

August 8
US aircraft production reaches 900 units per month. German attacks on shipping in the English Channel continue.

August 9
British troops begin to withdraw from Shanghai and North China

August 11
Italians attack Tug Argan in Somaliland

August 12
Battle of Britain intensifies; Portsmouth heavily bombed

August 13
'Eagle Day' (Adlertag) of Battle of Britain launches full scale Luftwaffe assault on RAF stations, control centres and aircraft factories

Royal Air Force fighters at the Battle of Britain

For the German invasion of Britain to have a chance of success, the Luftwaffe had to gain air superiority. In early August 1940 large formations of German aircraft opened the battle with a series of raids against RAF airfields. Although Air Chief Marshal Dowding had jealously hoarded the RAF's limited fighter strength, the RAF was still badly outnumbered and the fate of Britain hinged on the efforts of some 3,000 aircrew.

This Hawker Hurricane Mk 1 of No. 85 Squadron was commanded by Squadron Leader Peter Townsend, who shot down six enemy aircraft during the battle.

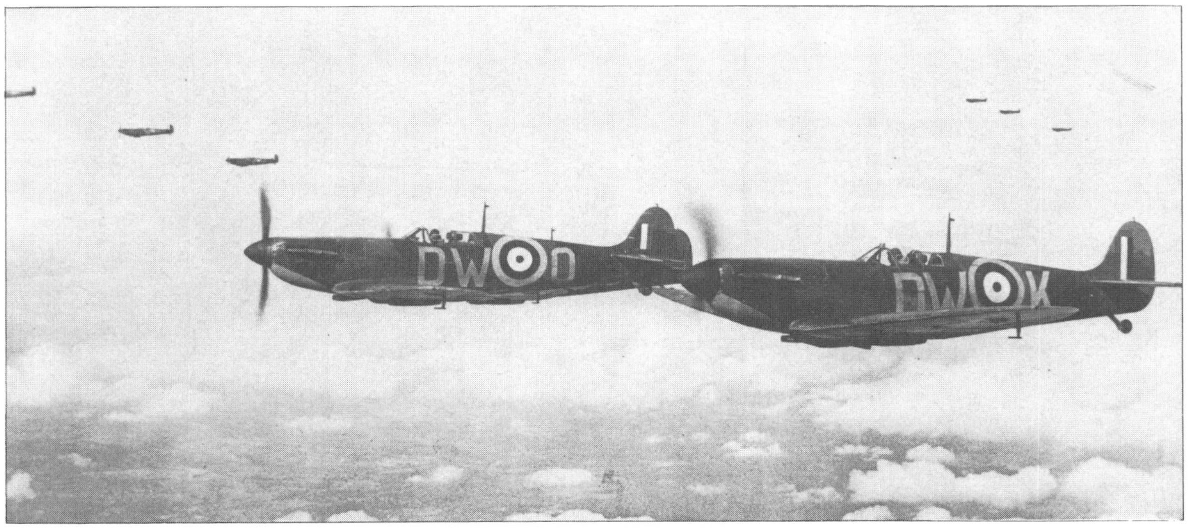

Supermarine Spitfire Mk 1As of No. 610 Squadron, Royal Auxiliary Air Force, on patrol over Kent. This squadron was heavily engaged in August 1940 before being withdrawn north for the defence of Newcastle.

A formation of Hurricanes above the clouds: when possible, RAF Fighter Controllers vectored the Hurricanes against the German bomber stream and the Spitfires to engage the swarms of Messerschmitt Bf 109s.

Above: This Spitfire Mk II was presented to the RAF by the Observer Corps and flown by Squadron Leader Finlay, commander of No. 41 Squadron.

Left: The Boulton-Paul Defiant scored a few victories when German pilots mistook it for a Hurricane, but it was hopelessly outmatched by the German fighters.

A Bristol Blenheim Mk 1F of No. 25 Squadron, Fighter Command, based at North Weald in early 1940. During the first phase of the battle the squadron was based at Martlesham Heath in the North Weald sector.

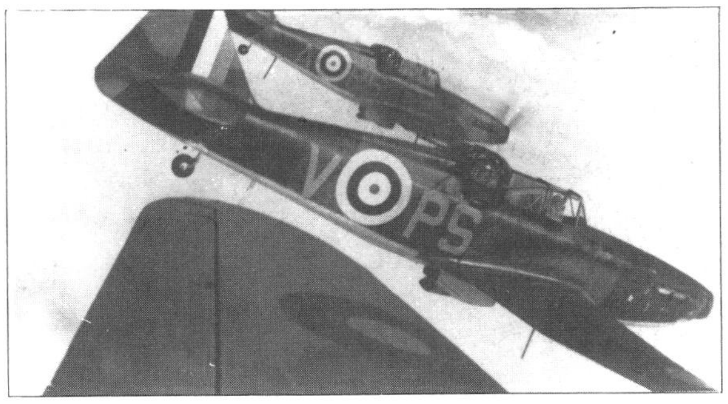

A formation of the ill-fated Defiants, which had their armament concentrated in a turret behind the pilot.

Above: Bristol Blenheim Mk 1Fs of No. 604 Squadron, Auxiliary Air Force, are seen in parade-ground array at Northolt before the battle.

No. 25 Squadron was one of the first to receive a Bristol Beaufighter, taking delivery of this aircraft on 2 September 1940. Fitted with primitive radar sets, Beaufighters soon proved themselves very effective night fighters.

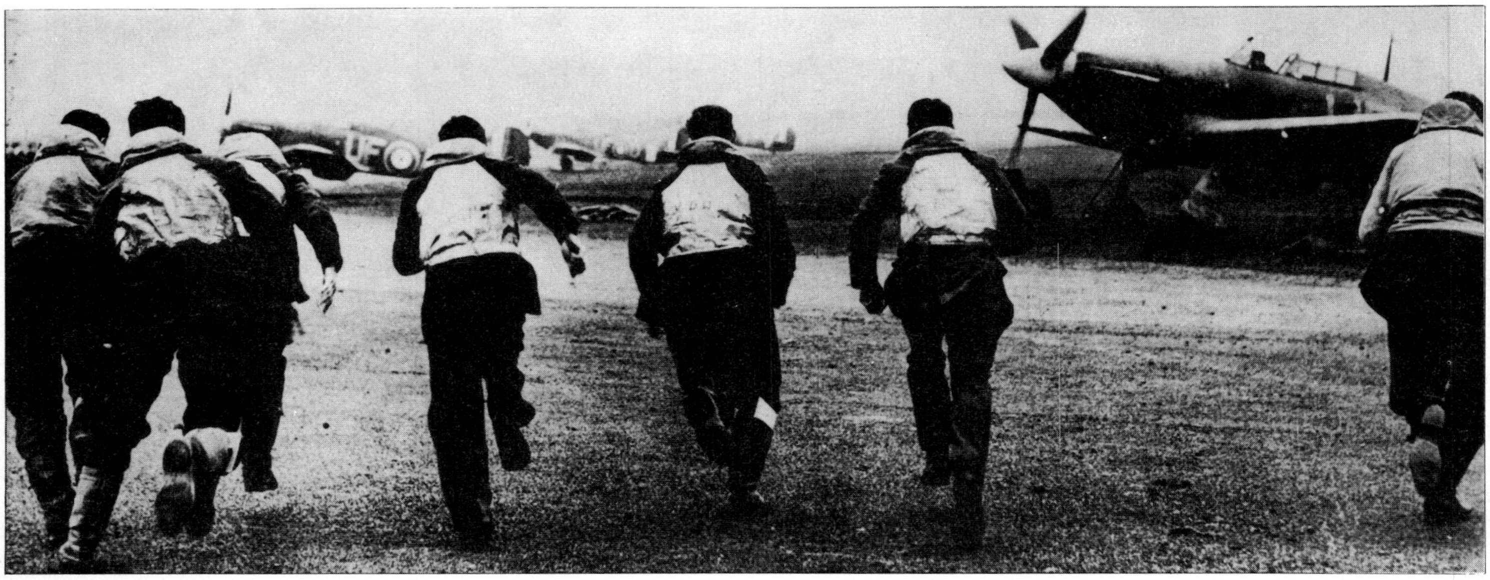

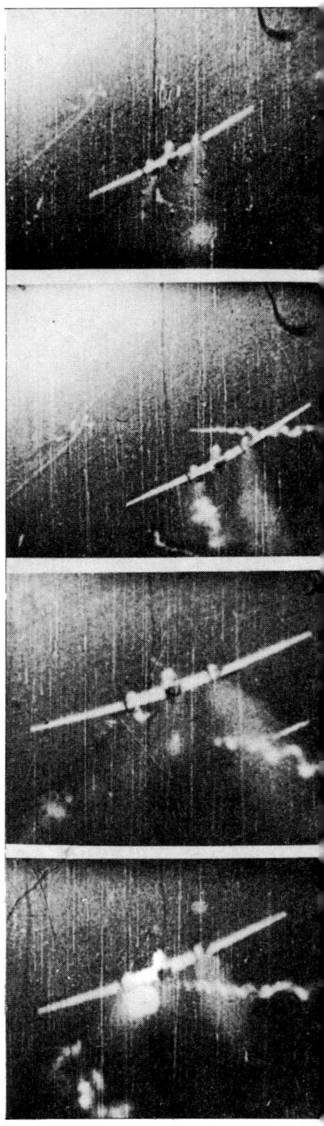

Above: Pilots of No. 601 (County of London) Squadron scramble at Northolt on their return to operational flying late in 1940. No. 601 was a squadron of the Auxiliary Air Force.

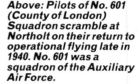

Right: A camera-gun sequence shows the fate of a Messerschmitt Bf 110 over Britain in 1940. The Zerstörer-type fighter proved extremely vulnerable to modern fighter opposition.

Above: WAAF plotters at work in the operations room of an RAF station during the Battle. It was Britain's command and control system as much as radar that proved decisive in 1940.

Above: The Heinkel He 111P, developed in accordance with the prime mission of the Luftwaffe – support of the Wehrmacht – was less suited to the strategic role demanded in the Battle of Britain.

Hurricanes of No. 257 Squadron are seen returning to their field after a sortie. The squadron was heavily involved in the battle, flying from Hendon, Northolt and Debden.

they should be conserved as far as was practicable, protected from exhaustion by being employed only to fight off genuine threats, and none of their energy wasted by inefficient direction. At least, those who managed to bail out would do so over home ground and, unless badly burned or wounded, would be quickly back on duty.

The first phase of the Battle of Britain occurred during the opening days of August and was directed by the Luftwaffe against Channel shipping. A modest tonnage of shipping was sunk, but perhaps the greatest profit to the Luftwaffe was the experience it gained at the periphery of the British defensive system, tempting the RAF fighters out from their shores. But it cost the Luftwaffe 217 aircraft against 96 lost by the RAF.

On 11 August the second phase opened and German aircraft crossed the Channel to begin the assault on the Fighter Command airfields ringed around London, together with radar stations along the south coast and shipping in the Thames estuary. For the first time the anxious watchers on the ground saw the intricate pattern of condensation trails in the sky, heard the faint chatter of machine-guns above, and watched the occasional plummeting fireball, the white canopy opening with its minuscule figure dangling beneath. By the end of the day 31 German aircraft had been destroyed, 27 British; one radar station (Ventnor) had been badly hit, five slightly damaged; and Lympne, Manston and Hawkinge airfields put out of action – though only for a few hours.

Then on 15 August came the most exhaustive attack the Luftwaffe was to launch. Nearly 1,800 sorties were flown in seven raids attacking targets from Northumberland to Hampshire, employing bombers and fighters from three Luftflotten – Nos 2 and 3 operating respectively from Belgium and northern France, No. 5 from Denmark and Norway. In the morning 40 escorted Ju 87s attacked Lympne and Hawkinge airfields in Kent; in the early afternoon 65 He 111s with Bf 110s in support arrived over Northumberland, followed soon by Ju 88s over Yorkshire. Mid-afternoon saw the attack renewed against Kent and the Thames estuary stations, while at 5.20 p.m. some 80 heavily escorted bombers attacked Portsmouth harbour and then went on to airfields at Middle Wallop and Worthy Down. The evening saw more bombers over Kent, and during the night another 60 bombers cruised over southern England, bombing every light they saw.

But every raiding force had been attacked, and 75 German aircraft had been shot down at a cost of 34 assorted Spitfires and Hurricanes. On the other hand, if the damage to airfields had not been extensive it still had to be repaired by men on the spot, and

Chronology of War: 1940

August 15
Greek cruiser Helles *mysteriously sunk, probably by Italian submarine. Massive assault by all three 'Luftflotte' facing Britain. More than 70 German aircraft are destroyed*

August 16
British evacuate Berbera in British Somaliland. RAF raid Turin and Milan. Luftwaffe bombs London docks

August 17
Germany announced 'total blockade of Britain'

August 18
RAF destroys 71 German aircraft, losing 27

August 19
British withdraw from Somaliland

August 20
Churchill makes speech on the Battle of Britain – 'Never in the field of human conflict has so much been owed by so many to so few.' Italy announces 'total blockade of British African possessions'

August 21
Romania ceded Southern Dobrudja to Bulgaria. Trotsky assassinated in Mexico City by an agent of the Soviet NKVD. Mussolini postpones planned invasion of Greece.

August 24
First German bombs fall on Central London; St Giles Cripplegate damaged

August 25
Eighty-one RAF bombers raid Berlin by night in retaliation

August 26
Luftwaffe intensifies operations against RAF airfields

August 29
French Equatorial Africa, Chad and the Cameroons declare for de Gaulle

August 30
'Vienna Award' Hitler forces settlement of territorial dispute between Hungary and Romania

August 31
RAF Intelligence reports assembly of landing-craft in French ports. Civilian casualties in UK are 1,075

September 3
Britain cedes West Indian bases to US in exchange for 50 old destroyers. Operation 'Sealion' fixed for September 21

September 4
General Antonescu assumes power in Romania with the consent of King Carol. Hitler promises air reprisal for RAF bombing of Berlin

September 5
London's longest night alert so far – seven and a half hours

September 6
King Carol of Romania abdicates following popular unrest over the outcome of the 'Vienna Settlement', largely provoked by the anti-Semitic 'Iron Guard' movement

September 7
'Invasion imminent' signal sent out to southern Britain. Goering changes main focus of Luftwaffe attacks to London, in retaliation for the Berlin raids (unwittingly giving the RAF a chance to recover)

September 9
First US destroyers supplied under the September 3 agreement are accepted by the RN, soon to sail for the UK

September 11
Buckingham Palace damaged

September 13
Italians invade Egypt and occupy Sollum

September 15
Climatic moment of the Battle of Britain – in an all-day battle 56 German aircraft are shot down, proving that the RAF remains a force to be reckoned with. Iron Guard declared only legal party in Romania

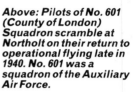

The Battle of Britain

If Operation Sea Lion, the German invasion of Britain, was to have any chance of success, the German air force needed to win air superiority over southern England. As the summer of 1940 wore on, Britain's hopes rested on a dwindling number of RAF fighter pilots.

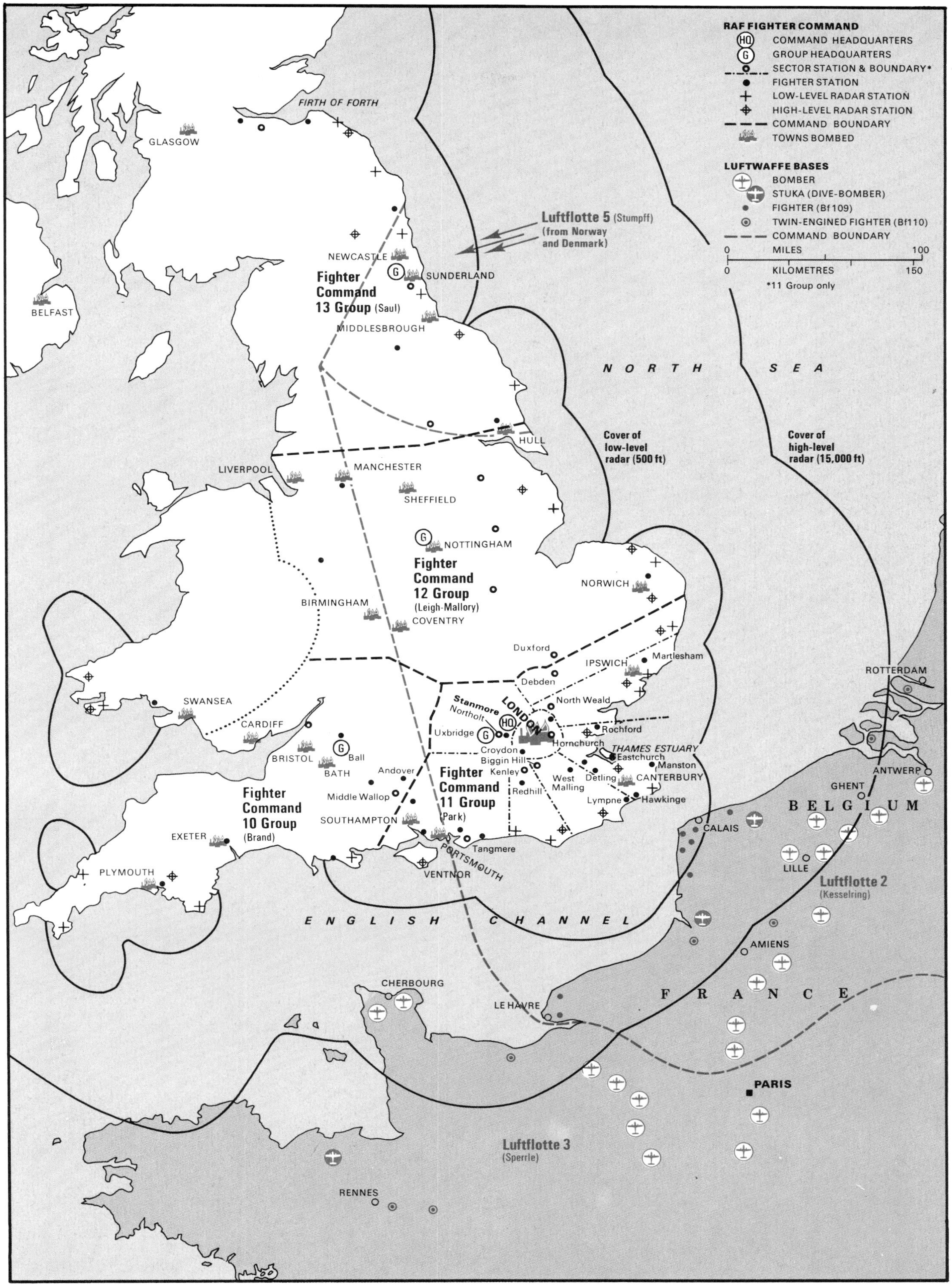

though the RAF pilots were triumphant, they were also tiring.

The pattern continued. On 16 August the Luftwaffe attack was almost as heavy – 1,700 sorties flown – and as German Intelligence was forecasting the reduction of RAF strength to an ineffective 300 after four days of such attacks, they were repeated the following day – and the day after. On 18 August the Luftwaffe lost another 71 aircraft, and their returning pilots reported no obvious diminution of RAF strength: this puzzled German Intelligence officers, though not so much as it would have done had they learned the truth. Dowding on that day had nearly 600 Spitfires and Hurricanes in the front line, plus 120 assorted Blenheims, Defiants and Gladiators – though not enough pilots for all of them.

Then on 23 August a German pilot, frustrated in his attempts to reach the Midlands, off-loaded his bombs over London. In retaliation Churchill ordered the bombing of Berlin, which took place two nights later. As Goering had declared that this would never happen, and as the RAF was thought to be at its last gasp, Hitler decided that the time had come for the morale of the British people to be shattered by the destruction of London and other major cities, in order that his invasion troops should meet the merest semblance of opposition – if not actual welcome – when they landed. He ordered the Luftwaffe attack to be switched from the RAF stations to British cities.

Thus began the Blitz. Wave after wave of bombers crossed the coast to attack London, great fires raged across dockland and the East End, guiding the bombers back night after night; streets were laid waste, ancient buildings destroyed, men, women and children killed or badly hurt. But the emotion kindled in their hearts was defiance, not fear – and out in the

Adolf Galland, commander of JG/26, was one of the finest fighter pilots in the war, and a great opponent for the RAF.

surrounding counties the airfields were resurfaced, the control-towers rebuilt and the radar stations re-equipped, while the factories produced more Spitfires and Hurricanes. And the old pilots caught up on some of their sleep while the training schools turned out fresh ones.

On 11 September Hitler postponed the date of Operation Sea Lion for nine days, prompted by the undiminished vitality of the RAF – which not only attacked his bombing fleets with increasing vigour, but over the last few nights had also successfully bombed the accumulation of shipping and invasion barges assembled in coastal harbours.

The broad, spade-shaped wings of the Heinkel He 111 were to become a familiar sight to Londoners, as the Staffels in their tight Kette (vics of three) passed overhead.

Below: Flying Officer A.V. Clowes climbs into his No. 1 Squadron Hurricane at RAF Wittering. Each victory he scored added another stripe to the wasp insignia.

The Night Blitz

By abandoning the onslaught on RAF airfields and turning the fury of the Luftwaffe on London, Hitler made a major strategic error but this was small consolation to Londoners.

If the Luftwaffe's switch to attacks on London on the evening of 7 September 1940 signalled Fighter Command's victory of survival in the daylight Battle of Britain, it also heralded a savage foretaste of a form of warfare to which the hapless civilian populations of Warsaw and Rotterdam had already been subjected – the ordeal by bomb and fire. The difference now would be that Goring's bombers would keep up their night attacks on British cities for nine long months, London itself being ruthlessly bombarded with high explosive and incendiary without let-up for 57 consecutive nights.

A disturbing fact that for obvious reasons was concealed from the public at large was that the RAF was virtually powerless to counter these night raids. The radar chain could detect and report their approach, but overland the Observer Corps was able to give no more than a superficial indication of their general strength and direction. The majority of British night fighters were the obsolete Blenheim Mk IF twin-engine aircraft whose performance scarcely even matched that of a laden German bomber. The real antidote to the night Blitz lay in the introduction of airborne interception (AI) radar. The RAF, which had been experimenting with a small number of Blenheims of the Fighter Interception Unit (FIU), for some months introduced a new two-seat, twin-engine purpose-designed night fighter with Mk IV AI, the Bristol Beaufighter, a big aeroplane with the heavy armament of four 20-mm cannon and six machine guns.

As London continued to suffer heavy raiding nightly throughout October, the daylight Battle of Britain petered out with a period of high altitude attacks by bomb-carrying fighters which also did little damage. By the end of the month the Luftwaffe had deployed the equivalent of 12 Geschwader with 1,150 bombers in Holland, Belgium and France for the systematic destruction by night of British cities. During the last 61 nights of 1940 an average nightly force of two hundred aircraft would unload a total of 13,900 tons of bombs on 36 towns and cities, killing 8,381 civilians and severely injuring 11,246 others, bringing the civilian death toll to 23,002 suffered in air raids by the end of 1940.

Major cities

During the first half of November Birmingham, Liverpool, Southampton, Brighton, Plymouth, Bristol and London were all hit. On the night of the 14th/15th however it was to be the turn of Coventry, a major centre of the British aircraft industry. This time the Luftwaffe sent almost 450 bombers, gaining the necessary concentration of raiders by employing a specially trained and equipped pathfinder force of He 111s of Kampfgruppe 100. These aircraft, flying from their bases in Western France, employed equipment known as X-Gerät; a narrow radio beam was transmitted from a ground station to pass directly over the intended target and the pathfinders would fly along this until their radio operators received signals intersecting the approach beam, at which point incendiary bombs would be released to illuminate the target. Three streams of bombers, approaching from other directions, then converged on the target and dropped their loads of high explosive. In the attack on Coventry a total of 56 tons of incendiaries and 394 tons of high explosive was dropped. 380 civilians died and 800 were injured; every main railway line out of the city and twelve aircraft factories were hit.

A series of vicious attacks on British cities in December marked the climax of the Winter Blitz, but also marked a shift in the fortunes of the RAF's night defences. The old Blenheim night fighter was replaced as production of Defiants and Beaufighters gained pace. By January Defiants equipped six squadrons, while the excellent new Beaufighter became fully operational on five others. Not only was the training of the Beaufighters' radar operators speeding up; the skill of fighter controllers at the ground radar stations – required to bring the night fighter into radar range of its target, much closer than daylight visual contact – was quickly improving.

The early months of 1941 also brought a shift in the Luftwaffe's night bombing aim as the Blitz assumed a phase of the Battle of the Atlantic with determined attempts to destroy British sea ports. Raids were stepped up on Avonmouth, Bristol, Cardiff, Clydeside, Hull, Merseyside, Portsmouth, Plymouth, Southampton and Swansea, as well as the Port of London. Increasing use was made of the so-called 'land mine' – an adaptation of the 2,000-lb (908-kg) naval mine, dropped by parachute, two of which could be carried by the He 111 over

Seen under a full moon, these Junkers Ju 88s head for England. Equipped with the most advanced bombing aids, the Ju 88s of KGr 100 served as pathfinders.

This Heinkel He 111 flew from Vannes in Brittany with 2.KGr/100, the Pathfinders. It was fitted with X-Gerät radio pathfinder gear, much used during the Night Blitz.

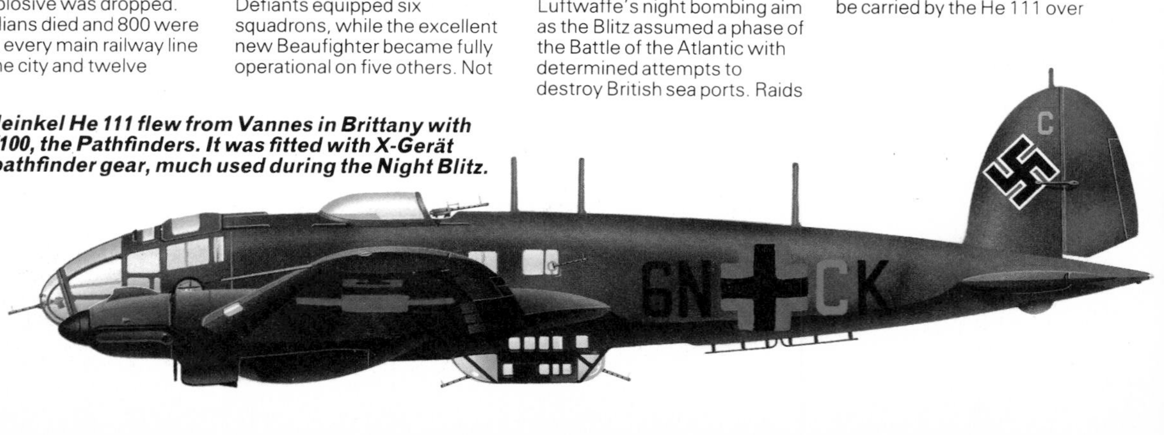

Left: Dockland ablaze: a sombre backcloth to Tower Bridge and the Tower of London as the Luftwaffe struck at London on 7 September.

The morning of 15 September dawned with mingled clouds and sunshine. By 11.30 a.m. Luftwaffe squadrons were crossing the Kentish coast while from every airfield south of London the fighters swarmed up to meet them, vectored in and accurately positioned by the renovated radar chain. Squadrons from Fighter Command No. 11 Group challenged the Luftwaffe in successive waves all the way to London, and once the bombers were over the capital they were then hit by more squadrons coming down from Fighter Command No. 12 Group. They dropped their bombs over south London, turned and fled – only to run once more into No. 11 Group's fighters, refuelled and waiting.

Two hours later the radar chain detected another mass of German aircraft building up over the Pas de Calais, and once again No. 11 Group were awaiting them over Kent and Surrey, and No. 12 Group fighters over London – east London this time – where again the bombers were forced to jettison their bombs and flee back through the gauntlet they had just run. During the afternoon, attacks by Luftflotte 3 aircraft on Portland and Southampton met such sustained and accurate fire from Ack-ack batteries that they too turned back, decimated and unable to inflict any worthwhile damage.

That evening the Luftwaffe commanders faced a daunting bill. Over 60 of their aircraft had been shot down, at a cost – though they did not yet know this – of only 26 RAF fighters, of whose pilots 13 were safe and well.

Two days later, Hitler postponed Sea Lion 'indefinitely' and ordered the invasion craft dispersed 'for the time being'. In fact, the invasion threat was over; the Battle of Britain had been won.

The bombing of London and Britain's major cities continued, of course, for many months to come. Coventry, Southampton, Cardiff, Swansea, Liverpool, Bristol, Plymouth, Portsmouth and many other cities were to feel the force of the Blitz in their turn, some 40,000 British civilians were to be killed, another 50,000 injured and over 100,000 homes destroyed.

But the invasion of Britain was never to become a serious threat again, principally because Hitler's attention had moved elsewhere. Early in 1941 he turned his back on the stubborn islanders to gaze again at the snowy reaches past the Carpathians which have haunted Teutonic imaginations for centuries. Soviet Russia had always prompted his most violent antagonism.

Right: For Londoners, the autumn of 1940 presented an unforgettable sight. White condensation trails marked out the battle for survival in the deep blue sky above their heads.

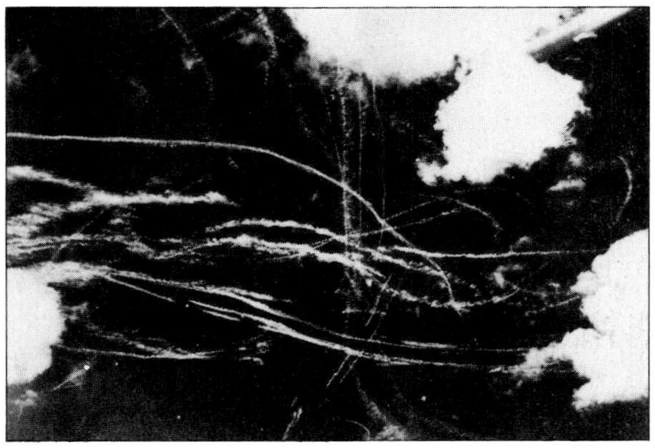

moderate distances and which proved particularly effective against dockyard installations; these weapons, exploded barostatically above ground level, caused considerable damage by blast.

On 10 January 1941 the RAF's first Ground Control Interception (GCI) radar stations became operational. Using the rotating aerial of the Type 7 metric radar, the ground controller was now presented with a plan view (on the Plan Position Indicator, or PPI) of the fighter and target. By April 11 GCI stations were operational.

The successes gained by the night fighters now began to increase sharply. Hitherto the guns had claimed the majority of raiders destroyed: in January the fighters had destroyed three, the guns 12; in February the fighters four, the guns eight. March brought the welcome change as fighters shot down 22 compared to 17 by the guns, followed by 48 and 39 respectively in April. Added to the aircraft now being shot down over Britain was the growing number of bombers being destroyed by the RAF's night intruders whose pilots patrolled in Hurricanes and Havocs in the vicinity of the bomber bases across the Channel awaiting the return of the weary German crews.

During May the night defences destroyed a total of 138 enemy aircraft, of which 96 fell to the fighters, a figure that represented the loss of an entire Geschwader in a single month. Hitler, however, having abandoned all idea of an invasion of Britain in the foreseeable future, was now ready for his great assault in the East and, to support the massive attack on the Soviet Union, Goering began shifting his bomber forces away from the West to bases in Poland. Britain's first ordeal by the night bomber came to an end.

Above: Hastily blackened, with flame damping exhausts and darkened roundels, No. 85 Squadron began night fighting in November 1940 with Hawker Hurricanes.

Right: a Heinkel He 111 is seen flying north-west over the Thames, with Surrey Docks beneath the right wingtip and the East End under the nose.

THE WAR AT SEA

'The only thing that every really frightened me during the war was the U-boat peril,' Winston Churchill was to write, and by the end of 1940 that peril was alarmingly evident.

Germany had started the war with only 48 operational U-boats, all sailing from Baltic or North Sea ports, their commanders enthusiastic but short of experience. The torpedoing of the liner *Athenia* was not regarded with favour even in Berlin, though Gunther Prien's exploits in sinking the *Royal Oak* inside Scapa Flow was, of course, greeted throughout the Kriegsmarine with acclaim, as was the sinking of the *Courageous* in the Channel.

But on the whole for the first eight months of the war U-boat activity against Britain's vital supply lines was small – indeed during the Norwegian Campaign all U-boats were withdrawn from the Atlantic for operations in the North Sea – and almost entirely directed against the few ships which sailed independently rather than in convoy.

Then in the summer of 1940 the fall of France gave them the Biscay ports, and the Battle of the Atlantic could really begin.

The early use by British destroyer escorts of their Asdic systems, whereby the range and bearing of an underwater object could be determined and then attacked, had given the U-boat commanders great respect for all Royal Naval escort vessels, but now they discovered a method of avoiding those escorts completely. For one thing, there were fewer of them, for the actions off Norway and Dunkirk had taken their toll of destroyers and the frantic building programme undertaken to replace them with sloops and corvettes had not yet reached peak production. So the ever-growing convoys of empty ships going to America could only be escorted to a line some 300 miles west of Ireland, where the escort would meet a deep-loaded convoy coming home. And the areas east of that line were now well within operational reach of the new U-boat bases at Brest and Bordeaux.

Above: U-38, one of the two original Type IXA ocean-going U-boats to serve through the war (being scuttled at Wesermunde in May 1945), is seen after returning from the first patrol of the war. These long-range boats were at sea before the war started, ready to go into action immediately hostilities commenced.

Thus began what U-boat commanders were to call the first 'Happy Time'.

In the period July to October 1940, 144 unescorted British ships were sent to the bottom, and several convoys had been so meagrely escorted that from these another 73 ships had been sunk. Morever, some of the more daring U-boat commanders soon uncovered a fatal flaw in the Asdic system itself; it could not detect a submarine approaching on the surface! The 'wolf-pack' attack developed and was soon spectacularly successful.

Convoy SC 7 of 34 ships left Nova Scotia on 5 October with a single sloop in attendance; by the 16th it was 500 miles west of Ireland, where it was met by another sloop and one of the new Flower-class corvettes. Also in attendance was one lone U-boat which promptly signalled all relevant details to headquar-

Left: Type VIIA boats of the Second Flotilla are seen at Kiel pre-war. All the boats in the picture were war losses, U-27 on the left being sunk in the first month of the war north-west of Scotland. U-33 went down in 1940 in the Firth of Clyde.

Below: U-boats were not the only threats to Britain's maritime life line, as for a time the German long-range patrol aircraft seemed an almost equal danger. One of the hasty counters to attack from the air took the form of CAM ships.

Kretschmer against the convoys

The most successful of German U-boat skippers did not operate in the manner laid down by the pre-war textbooks. In the October 1940 attack on convoy SC-7 from Canada to Britain, one of the premier U-boat aces, Otto Kretschmer in U-99, executed what was to become the classic U-boat attack. Going in on the surface, at night, Kretschmer made use of his boat's high surface speed to get in amongst the helpless ships of the convoy, where he sank nine out of the 17 ships lost that night.

The crippling loss of allied shipping in the early years of the war at sea was out of all proportion to the number of submarines causing that loss, with rarely more than a dozen at sea at any one time. To the merchant seamen, the prospect of U-boat attack was not pleasant; even if you survived your ship sinking there was the peril of being adrift in the hostile waters.

ters and then, in bright moonlight, torpedoed two of the transports and slipped away.

In their inexperience the escorts stayed behind to pick up survivors. The convoy steamed on unescorted until the following evening when another U-boat damaged a third transport, by which time other help had arrived from home. By nightfall on 18 October, two sloops and a corvette were shepherding the remaining 31 ships – and just over the horizon was waiting a patrol-line of six U-boats whose commanders knew exactly where and when their quarry would arrive. Two of these commanders were the acknowledged 'aces', Joachim Schepke of U-100 and Otto Kretschmer of U-99.

They struck just after midnight, and a night of chaos and confusion followed, filled with death and destruction for the unfortunate convoy – and high excitement and triumph for the U-boat crews. All around ships were burning, blowing up, sinking. Some settled slowly and tiredly, the frigid waters lapping higher and higher until the final lurch; others broke in half, with one section sticking upright out of the water until the imprisoned air leaked out and it went down with a rush and a gulp. The steamship *Sedgepool*, with her bow blown off, knifed down into the sea like a U-boat doing a crash dive, propeller still whirling high in the air.

The escorts could do little but pick up survivors, for their Asdic was useless and radar to replace it had not yet been fitted. By morning the convoy had disintegrated and of the original 34 ships only 12 reached port – they did so only because word had reached Kretschmer and his comrades that yet another convoy, HX 79, was close behind and ripe for their attention. Of the 49 ships of this convoy, the U-boats sank 12 and damaged two more.

Above: Built in 1919 as part of the massive US naval construction programme, the 'Clemson' class destroyer USS Bailey was one of the 54 stackers transferred to the RN in the 1940 'Bases for destroyers' deal.

Below: In the early stages of the war the bulk of convoy escort duty fell to old destroyers such as the World War I vintage 'V and W' class, even though they were not really suitable.

Below: A Type VIIC U-boat is readied for launch after undergoing maintenance at a base in France.

U-BOAT THREAT

Given how close the Germans had come to starving Britain into defeat during World War I, it is surprising that greater efforts were not made before 1939 to create a large U-boat fleet. Nevertheless, the U-boats came within an ace of winning the Battle of the Atlantic.

Type II U-boat

The Type II coastal boats were the first submarines produced by Germany after Hitler decided to break the treaty banning Germany from operating submarines. Short-range vessels displacing just over 300 tons, they carried a crew of 25 and were armed with six 533-mm torpedoes fired through three forward tubes;* U-3*, illustrated here, was an early command of the U-boat ace Schepke.

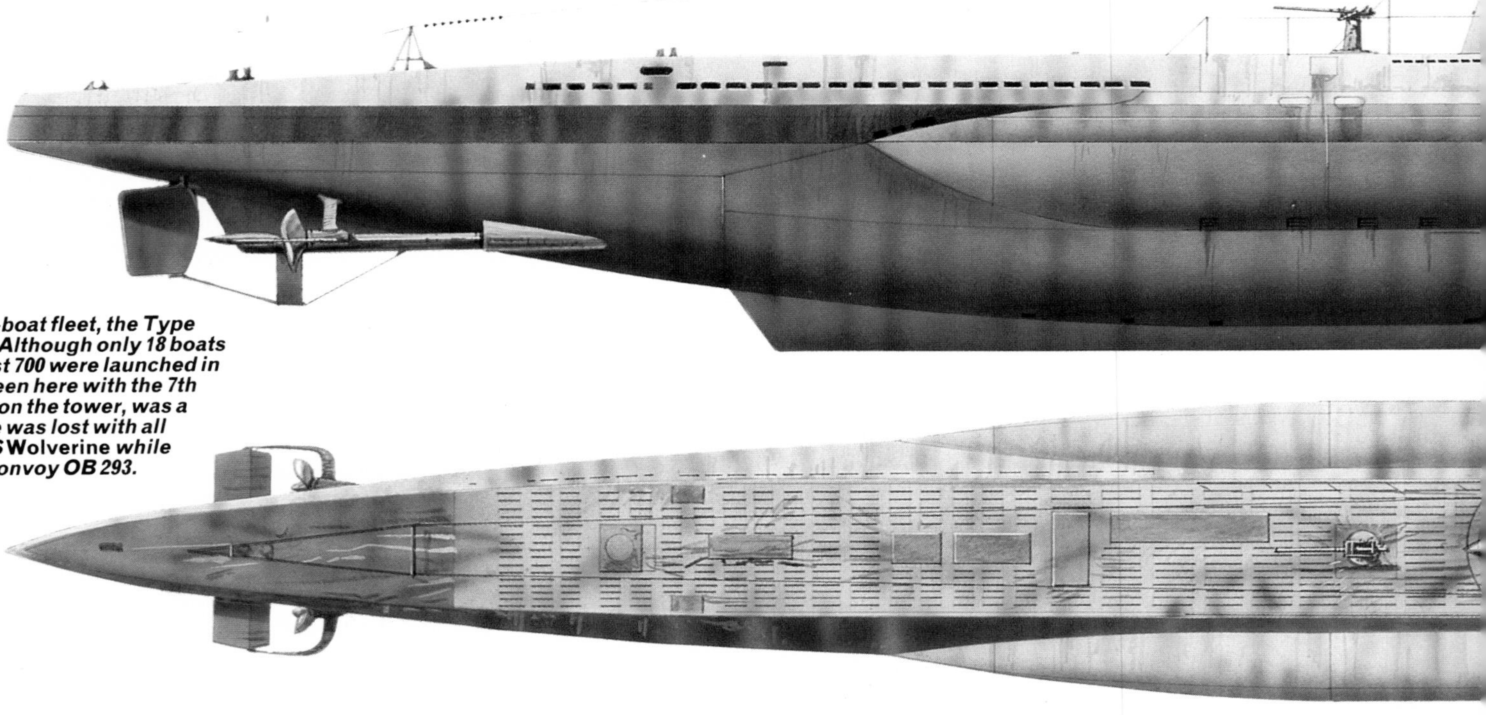

Workhorse of the Kriegsmarine U-boat fleet, the Type VII appeared in six main variants. Although only 18 boats were in commission in 1939, almost 700 were launched in the next five years. Prien's* U-47*, seen here with the 7th Flotilla's 'Laughing Bull' emblem on the tower, was a Type VIIB, completed in 1938. She was lost with all hands in March 1941, sunk by HMS* Wolverine *while stalking the westbound Atlantic convoy OB 293.

By December the convoy losses promised to reach such proportions that defeat through starvation threatened Britain. Only immediate and drastic measures could avert catastrophe, and the only measures which would work would be more escorts guarding more closely controlled convoys, with better detecting equipment. Fortunately, these measures could be taken – just in time.

A deal was struck with the United States: in return for 99-year leases of main base sites in the Bahamas, Jamaica, St Lucia, Trinidad and Antigua, the US Navy handed over 50 destroyers – true, they were old four-stackers from World War I, but they filled the gap (and were stocked by American generosity with everything the crews could want); fast escort destroyers were released from anti-invasion duties once it was seen that the danger was passed; and the corvettes were coming off the slips at an increasing rate. Most significant of all, a small 'resonant cavity magnetron' had been invented by British scientists which would soon provide the essential radar system to catch U-boats on the surface. The 'Happy Time' was soon to end.

But the U-boat menace continued, and bitter battles were fought over the Atlantic wastes during 1941. The menace would not be completely subdued until the United States Navy and the Royal Navy came to amalgamate their energies and experience, and operate together, either in close convoy escorts or in what became known as hunter/killer groups.

Not all the dangers to Britain's supply routes came from U-boats, however; Hitler's Kriegsmarine also had surface vessels to throw into the battle.

In the early months the *Graf Spee* had plundered the trade routes until she met her end in the mouth of the River Plate; and her sister ship *Deutschland* had also made an early foray into the North Atlantic which claimed two unescorted ships. But in October 1940 the pocket-battleship *Admiral Scheer* began her raiding career, and soon caught a convoy of 37 ships escorted by the lone armed merchant cruiser *Jervis Bay*, whose gallant defiance earned her captain a posthumous Victoria Cross, and herself undying fame in the annals of sea warfare.

The convoy scattered as the *Jervis Bay* fought off the attacker, but when the merchant cruiser had been sunk *Admiral Scheer* chased and sank five of the transports, then continued her cruise into the South Atlantic and Indian Ocean, where she sank another 16 ships before returning to Germany.

The episode which gained the most publicity, however, was the short but spectacular cruise of the *Bismarck* in May 1941, which is described in detail on page 40.

Gunther Prien: U-boat Ace

At 01.16 on 14 October 1939 the British battleship HMS *Royal Oak* was torpedoed whilst in the protected fleet anchorage of Scapa Flow. Within 15 minutes the veteran of Jutland had gone down in only 13 fathoms but taking with her 833 of her crew. An outstanding coup, the sinking marked the highpoint of the brief career of Gunther Prien; commander of the *U-47*.

The war was only two days old when Prien accounted for his first British merchantman, the *Bosnia*; by his recall two days later he had added two more.

It was the beginning of October when he was summoned to a conference at which was outlined an audacious plan to penetrate the British naval anchorage at Scapa Flow. Dönitz himself had worked it out and, asked his opinion, Prien thought the scheme feasible. He was promptly given the assignment, sailing on 8 October.

Scapa Flow was, indeed, a poor abandoned place

Left:* U-47 *is seen approaching the battlecruiser* Scharnhorst *before the war. The U-boat was to be the more successful vessel.

***Gunther Prien after the award of his Ritterkreuz (Knight's Cross) following the sinking of HMS* Royal Oak.**

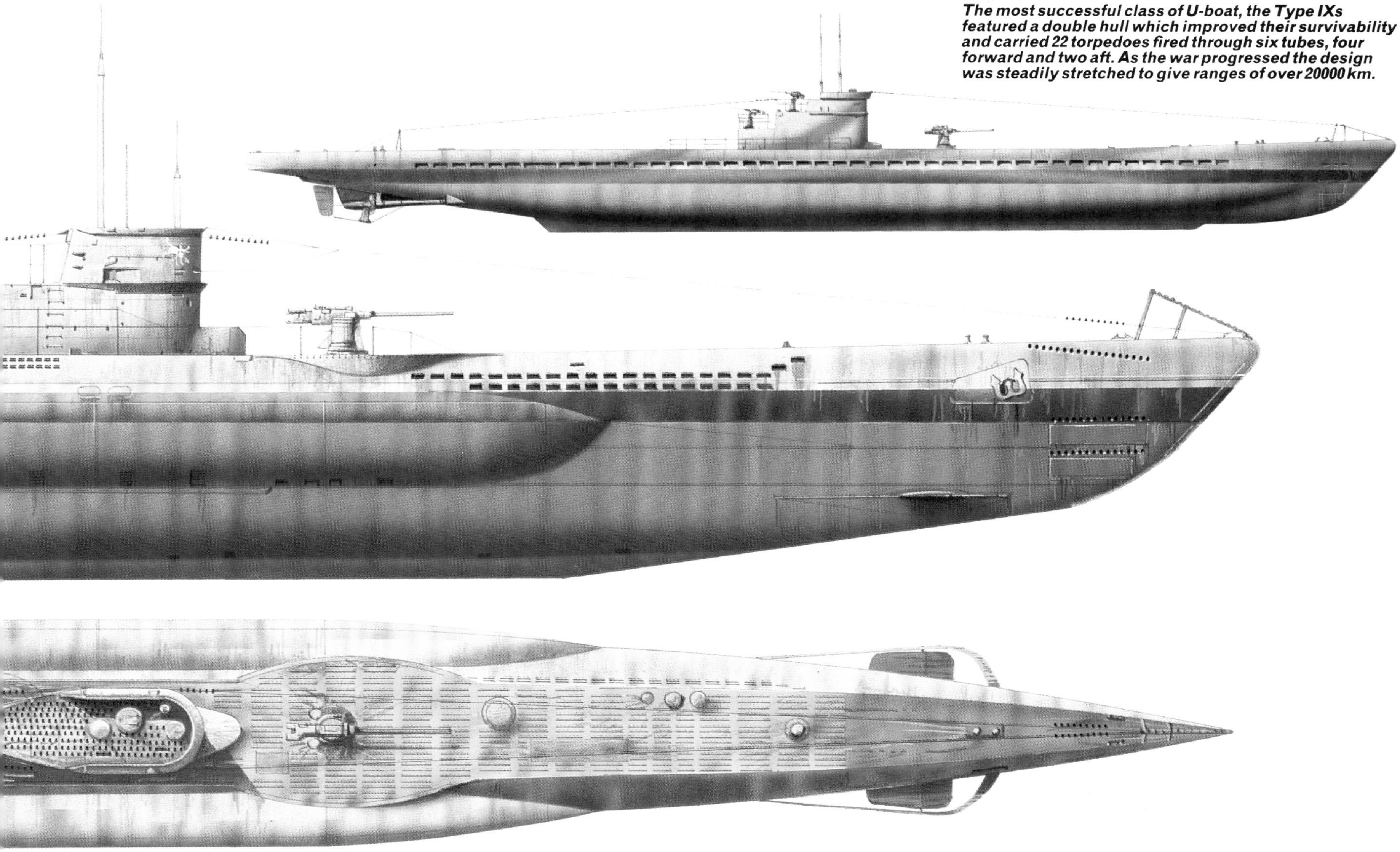

Type IXB U-boat

The most successful class of U-boat, the Type IXs featured a double hull which improved their survivability and carried 22 torpedoes fired through six tubes, four forward and two aft. As the war progressed the design was steadily stretched to give ranges of over 20000 km.

compared with its heyday 20 years before, when it had harboured most of the Grand Fleet. Its defences were run down, and pre-war plans to upgrade them were as yet unexecuted. So poor were the defences that the Home Fleet had been long billeted on Loch Ewe, and few ships were now to be seen. The Flow itself is a wild, bleak water about 6 miles across, surrounded by the treeless hills of the Orkneys. Access to it is by a dozen navigable channels, subject to fierce tidal flows and, for the most part at that time, boomed and defensively mined or obstructed by blockships. Dönitz had reasoned correctly that the moveable obstructions were more likely to be patrolled than the fixed blockages which is why, shortly before midnight on 13 October, Prien was approaching the 700-yard wide narrows between the islet of Lamb Holm and Mainland on the Flow's eastern side.

Aerial reconnaissance had suggested that this channel, though encumbered by a boom and four rotting blockships, could be negotiated at high water. The submarine shouldered her way through, scraping both beach and barrier. Boldness paid off and, running free, the *U-47* found the net barrier beyond of small consequence. With diesels murmuring from the open hatch behind them the bridge watch stared into the shifting gloom of the Flow that was opening up ahead. Initially, there was nothing to be made out then, to starboard, close under the hills of Mainland, could be seen the massive tophamper of a battleship. Beyond her was another. Prien identified them as HMS *Repulse* and an 'R' class battleship, and swung *U-47* around to close.

In fact the ships were the battleship *Royal Oak* and the seaplane carrier *Pegasus*.

Remaining on the surface, Prien fired three torpedoes. At this time, German torpedoes were prone to both depth-keeping and magnetic pistol problems, and all that rewarded Prien's efforts was a muffled detonation of no great intensity. Aboard the target herself, opinion differed as to whether it had been an air attack or an internal explosion.

Prien calmly reversed his boat and loosed his single stern tube. Again no result and, incredibly, no apparent alarm. Labouring mightily the crew reloaded and a further salvo of three was unleashed. Only two hit, but it was more than enough, the old ship flooding rapidly. In 13 minutes her remains joined those of the German High Seas Fleet just 5 miles to the west.

Prien blasted back the way that he had come, and was in open water again by 02.15. Returning the 'hero of Scapa Flow', he was received by the Führer himself and awarded the Knight's Cross of the Iron Cross.

Royal Oak was an old ship of limited value but her loss was a severe blow and led directly to others. With Scapa clearly vulnerable, the Home Fleet needed to use other anchorages, a point not lost on the Germans who used submarines to mine them. Thus *U-31*'s mines at Loch Ewe were to damage the battleship HMS *Nelson* heavily and sink two minesweepers, while *U-21*'s mines in the Firth of Forth broke the back of the cruiser HMS *Belfast* and sank two other ships.

Faulty torpedoes were to dog Prien in the Norwegian campaign from April 1940. In June the so-called 'Group Prien' was formed with U-47 and six others. The group operated successfully in the Western Approaches, accounting for 32 merchantment of about 175,000 gross registered tons.

Using the effective tactic of entering a convoy on the surface at night, possible until the general fitting of radar to escorts, Prien sank four out of the five ships lost by the Halifax-UK convoy SC 2 in August 1940. In the October, he sighted HX 79, vectored in five other U-boats and mounted a co-ordinated onslaught that accounted for 14 ships, three to Prien.

On 6 March 1941 Prien located the westbound OB 293 and brought in four other boats. The convoy was stoutly defended, losing four ships at an initial cost to the Germans of one U-boat sunk and one severely damaged. Prien hung on. Using his surface speed and the cover of rain squalls, he kept the convoy in sight but neglected to watch his flanks. The veteran destroyer HMS *Wolverine* surprised him, forced him down and sank him with all hands.

Besides the *Royal Oak*, Gunther Prien's personal score included 30 merchantships of about 165,000 gross registered tons. His loss was admitted by the German high command a fortnight later, together with the posthumous award of the Oak Leaves to his Knight's Cross.

The 'R' class battleship, HMS Royal Oak, is seen before the war. The loss of the World War I veteran was a blow to British morale.

Prien on his return to Germany as the 'Hero of Scapa Flow'. After this success, he was to sink a further 165,000 tons of shipping before his own death in the Atlantic some 18 months later.

THE CRUISE OF THE *BISMARCK*

***For the spring of 1941 the German navy planned a large raid on the Atlantic convoys by a squadron of German battleships, but in the event only the pride of the fleet,* Bismarck *made the voyage, accompanied by the heavy cruiser* Prinz Eugen.**

To Grand-Admiral Erich Raeder it seemed during the early months of 1941 that the time was ripe for his major strategic stroke. The battleship *Bismarck* and the heavy cruiser *Prinz Eugen* were completing their operational training in the Baltic; the battle-cruisers *Scharnhorst* and *Gneisenau* were at Brest; he had available five tankers, two supply ships and two reconnaissance ships to support them.

Unfortunately for Raeder *Gneisenau* was hit first by an aerial torpedo as she lay in Brest roads, then bombed repeatedly in dock; *Scharnhorst*'s machinery developed faults which required time to correct and *Prinz Eugen* was slightly damaged by a magnetic mine. Admiral Lütjens, who would have operational command of the force, recommended cancelling the whole project or at least postponing it until the ships at Brest were ready – but Raeder refused: if a complete Rheinübung was not to be, then at least a part of it would take place. *Bismarck* and *Prinz Eugen* would sail from Gdynia on 18 May.

The Commander-in-Chief, Home Fleet, Admiral Sir John Tovey, was himself at Scapa Flow as the news came in, flying his flag in the battleship *King George V*. He had immediately at his disposal the famous battle-cruiser *Hood*, the battleship *Prince of Wales*, newly-commissioned and not yet completely worked up, the aircraft carrier *Victorious*, four cruisers and nine destroyers. At sea on patrol in the Denmark Strait (watching for just such an event as was now developing) were the cruisers *Norfolk* and *Suffolk*, while two more, *Manchester* and *Birmingham* were on duty in the Iceland–Faroes gap. The battle-cruiser *Repulse* was in the Clyde, the battleship *Rodney* on convoy duty already out in the Atlantic.

Fortune at first favoured Sir John; during the evening of 23 May *Bismarck* and *Prinz Eugen* were seen by *Suffolk* as they gingerly edged their way down the narrow lane between the Greenland ice pack and the minefield which the British had laid in the Denmark Strait. Vice-Admiral L.E. Holland aboard HMS *Hood*, with the *Prince of Wales* and six destroyers in close attendance, was racing across south of Iceland towards the exit from the Denmark Strait and by midnight was only 120 miles from his quarry – they should meet about dawn. The commander-in-chief himself with *King George V* and *Victorious* were away to the south, also on a converging course but some 300 miles away.

The actor Esmond Knight was serving as a lieutenant aboard the *Prince of Wales*:

> . . . There they were, in deep sharp silhouette on the horizon – *Bismarck* and *Prinz Eugen*, steaming in smokeless line ahead, unperturbed and sinister. 'Ye gods! – what a size!' I heard someone mutter.

Almost immediately the *Hood*'s main armament thundered out, then the *Prince of Wales*'; and as infinite seconds of the wait for visible results ticked by, brilliant flashes and black smoke jetted from the *Bismarck*. Huge spouts of water rose just astern of *Hood*, then alongside *Prince of Wales*.

Then *Bismarck*'s fifth salvo crashed down through *Hood*'s thinly protected deck and detonated in a magazine. A huge explosion tore the ship in half, the whole forepart rising up out of the sea before dropping back and disappearing. A vast cloud of smoke bloomed, then rolled away to reveal an empty sea: the *Hood* was gone, leaving one midshipman and two seamen of her complement of 1,419 alive. *Prince of Wales* was soon under fire again, from which she quickly received orders to withdraw.

During the next 24 hours, Admiral Lütjens planned to throw off his shadowers, elude the enemy forces he felt sure were closing about him, and make for a port where the damage suffered in the action could be repaired. It was not much, but one shell from the *Prince of Wales* had isolated 1,000 tons of his fuel, and a torpedo launched in the evening by a Swordfish from *Victorious* hit the *Bismarck* amidships. Now not only were the *King George V* and the *Victorious* in the hunt, but *Rodney* had left her convoy to join them – and the famous Force H consisting of the aircraft-carrier *Ark Royal*, the battle-cruiser *Renown* and the cruiser *Sheffield* were coming up from Gibraltar.

HMS* King George V*, is seen at about the time of the* Bismarck *hunt, when she still carried UP (Unrotated Projectile, or unguided anti-aircraft rocket) launchers atop her turrets.

The* Bismarck *leaves Gdynia on trials. At the time, she was thought to be one of the most powerful battleships built.

***Right: The heavy cruiser* Prinz Eugen *enters Brest after detaching from the ill-fated* Bismarck.**

Above: 16-in shells from HMS* Rodney *dwarf even the mighty* Bismarck*, as dawn on 27 May saw her battered into a shambles by the Royal Navy.

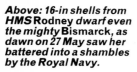

HMS* Rodney *and* Nelson *were the only British battleships to be fitted with 16-in guns. Each of the nine guns carried weighed over 100 tons, and could fire a 2000 lb shell a distance of 40,000 yards.

Warships in the hunt for the Bismarck

But in the early hours of May 25 *Bismarck* vanished from *Sheffield*'s radar, and none of the other shadowers could help. Throughout the next 30 hours, fury and frustration grew in Whitehall and among the Royal Navy in the Atlantic, and their hopes fell – for their fuel tanks were emptying fast and the weather was deteriorating.

In their dilemma, the Admiralty appealed to Coastal Command, and soon their prayers were answered. At 10.36 on the morning of 26 May a Catalina flying-boat sighted the *Bismarck* some 800 miles from Brest. Force H was between *Bismarck* and the French coast.

The first attack was delivered by 15 Swordfish from *Ark Royal* that night, launching 13 torpedoes at her: two scored hits, one amidships which did little harm – and one on her starboard quarter which sealed her fate. It damaged her starboard propeller and wrecked her steering-gear, jamming the main rudder; observers in the planes above saw *Bismarck* turn two complete circles, obviously out of control and with her speed dropping dramatically.

The night of 26/27 May was one of desperation for the crew of the battleship. A howling gale added to their toils. At 8.30 a.m. Nemesis arrived in the shape of the *King George V* and the *Rodney*, and within 20 minutes both had opened fire.

Bismarck was still capable of fighting back, of course: her first few salvos straddled *Rodney* without hitting her, and raised waterspouts alongside *King George V*. But *Rodney*'s third salvo crashed aboard the *Bismarck*, another shortly afterwards knocked out both her forward turrets, and one by one the rest of her main armament fell silent.

At 10.15, her chief engineer officer, Lieutenant-Commander Gerhard Junack, received the order to prepare the ship for sinking, and, having done so, he made his way up on deck.

Quickly realizing that he was the senior officer left, Junack organized the survivors into parties, then after a triple 'Sieg Heil!' he ordered 'Abandon Ship', and hardly were they overboard and clear of the ship when it keeled over.

The bows rose slowly into the air and, stern first, *Bismarck* slid down beneath the waves, taking over 2,000 of her complement with her. Rheinübung was over, the *Hood* had been avenged.

Contemporary with* Bismarck*, the 'King George V' class was unlike the German vessel in that it was built in accordance with the London Treaty displacement limit of 35,000 tons.

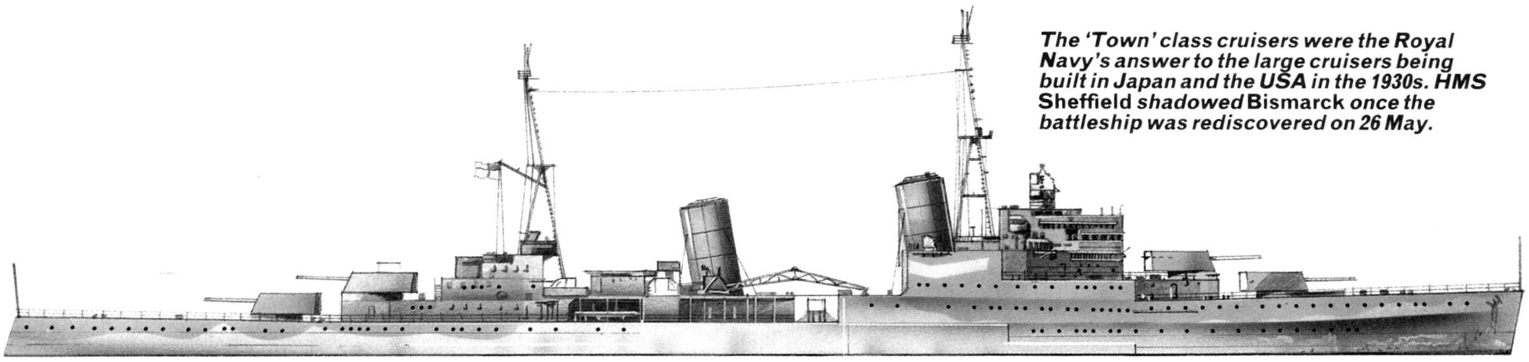

The 'Town' class cruisers were the Royal Navy's answer to the large cruisers being built in Japan and the USA in the 1930s. HMS* Sheffield *shadowed* Bismarck *once the battleship was rediscovered on 26 May.

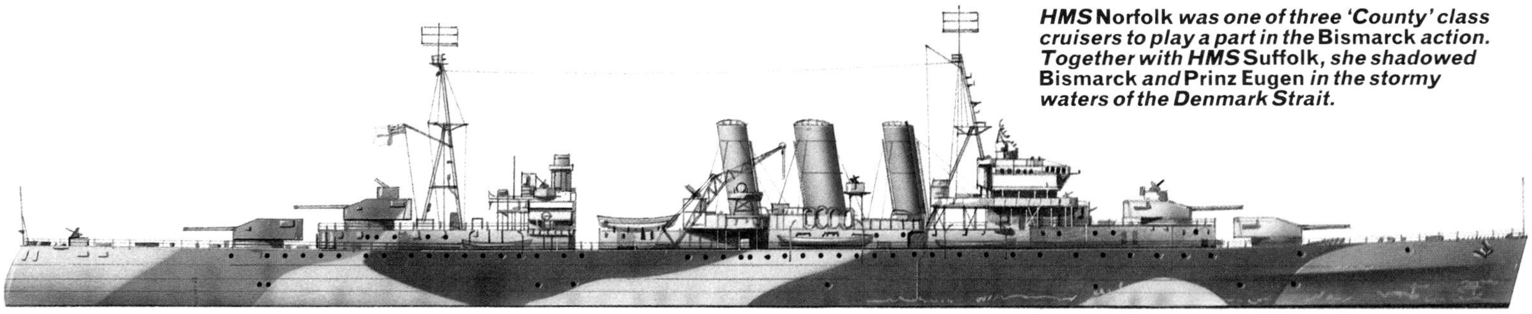

HMS* Norfolk *was one of three 'County' class cruisers to play a part in the* Bismarck *action. Together with HMS* Suffolk*, she shadowed* Bismarck *and* Prinz Eugen *in the stormy waters of the Denmark Strait.

HMS* Victorious *was in company with HMS* King George V*, and was to launch the first strike against the* Bismarck*. Given the antiquity of the Fairey Swordfish, and the terrible weather conditions, it is remarkable that even one torpedo got home (unfortunately to little effect).

Supposedly built to Washington Treaty displacement (10,000 tons), the 'Hipper' class could approach 20,000 tons when fully loaded.* Prinz Eugen*, seen here as she was painted at Bergen, was ordered to make her way to Brest independently, and parted with* Bismarck *during the night of 24 May.

KMS* Bismarck *was by far the most powerful unit in the Kriegsmarine, and was the first genuine battleship laid down in Germany since World War I. Armour arrangements followed those of the last German battleship* Baden*, though upgraded in order to cope with contemporary threats. The very broad beam made* Bismarck *a very stable gun platform for her eight 380-mm (15-in) guns, as proved in the action against HMS* Hood.

Chapter 4

Italy Falters

When Adolf Hitler began his political career he did so in conscious imitation of a leader he admired fervently: Benito Mussolini, founder of the Fascist State. But the relationship was soon reversed as Hitler's European conquests began. Mussolini entered the war scenting rich pickings, but the Italian army proved unequal to the task.

If Hitler's preoccupation during the early part of 1940 had been military, it was political consideration which came to dominate much of his time in mid-summer and autumn, his attention fixed upon the geopolitical heartlands of 'Mittel-Europe'.

In the immediately pre-war days he had incorporated Austria and Czechoslovakia into the Reich, and the larger part of Poland had been his first military acquisition – but still between his domains and his great objective, Soviet Russia, lay the states carved by League of Nations theorists from the body of the old Austro-Hungarian Empire: Hungary itself, Romania and Bulgaria. They must all, sooner or later, become part of his empire, if only to clear his eastern border for the great sweep to the Urals and beyond. In the case of Romania there was the added necessity of securing the oilfields at Ploesti in order to fuel his conquests.

His naturally Machiavellian cast of mind now combined with events to make this possible. Shortly after Mussolini had attempted to leap aboard Hitler's bandwagon and annex Nice and parts of Savoy, Stalin decided to follow suit. He demanded the return to Russia by Romania – the most pro-French of the Balkan countries – of the province of Bessarabia between the Rivers Pruth and Dniester, plus a sizeble piece of Northern Bukovina, all of which had been lost to Russia by the decisions of 1919 and after at Versailles. Bulgaria, not to be left behind in the grab for territory, moved troops and her own boundaries northeastwards 40 miles into Southern Dobruja.

Politics in Central Europe

The highly unpopular King Carol II, who with his mistress Mme Lupescu had been the sole rulers of Romania since before the outbreak of war, now decided that only an alliance with Hitler could save them, and in an effort to curry favour they encouraged the re-emergence of the Iron Guard, Romania's equivalent of the Italian Fascists.

It was at this point that Hungary decided that she too had claims to press – to some 17,000 square miles of Transylvania which included not only some of Romania's richest countryside but also the provincial capital of Cluj. In desperation, King Carol and his advisers turned to Hitler for arbitration. Romanian ministers were called to Vienna where Ribbentrop and the Italian Foreign Minister, Count Ciano, informed them of Hitler's unshakeable decision: they were to hand over the disputed territory immediately and without further argument. In so doing they reduced their already diminished political weight almost to zero.

Romania had thus been removed as a block to Hitler's ambition, and at the same time Hungary had become directly indebted to him – and Bulgaria too, though indirectly, in default of any criticism from Berlin of her actions in Dobruja. What Stalin thought was for the moment of little consequence.

Mussolini's reactions, however, were of a certain – at least temporary – importance. Il Duce had been surprised and indeed awed by his fellow dictator's successes in Poland and France, and was greatly frustrated when what his son-in-law Ciano ironically referred to as a sudden 'outbreak of peace' robbed him of greater military glory and a larger proportion of the pickings from the French Empire. Moreover, when the two dictators met in Munich in June, Hitler made it clear that Italian pretensions to more territorial gains in Corsica, Tunisia or French Somaliland would have to await final peace settlements and the announcement of the 'New Order' which would be proclaimed when Hitler was finally satisfied with global 'reallocations'.

Mussolini therefore remained frustrated, and as he watched Hitler extend his own political domain further eastwards towards the Black Sea, his chagrin grew. It grew even more in July when his suggestions –

Il Duce planned a new Roman Empire in the Mediterranean and Africa, but waging war against another major power proved a very different business from making the trains run on time.

Chronology of War: 1940

September 25
Vidkun Quisling assumes power in Norway. Dakar expedition abandoned, after damage to British battleships HMS Barham *and* Resolution. *US bans iron exports to Japan*

September 27
Germany, Italy and Japan sign the Tripartite pact

September 28
US supplied destroyers reach Britain

September 30
UK civilian casualties in September are 6,954 killed, 10,615 injured

October 1
Japanese occupy Wei Hai Wei after the withdrawal of British troops from the China station

October 3
Garrison at Malta reinforced. Neville Chamberlain resigns from British Cabinet due to ill health

October 4
Hitler and Mussolini meet at Brenner Pass on the Italian/Austrian border

October 7
German troops enter Romania, occupy the Ploesti oilfields and commence the rebuilding of Romania's armed forces

October 8
Burma Road to China to be re-opened

October 11
Finnish-Soviet Convention signed

October 12
Hitler announces 'Sea Lion' postponed until April 1941

October 15
Worried by German occupation of Romania, the Italian leaders decided to attack Greece

October 16
RAF bombs Kiel

October 22
de Gaulle visits French forces in Equatorial Africa

October 23
Hitler meets Franco on French/Spanish border but is unsuccessful in persuading Spain to enter the war

October 24
Hitler and Petain agree collaboration between France and Germany

October 28
Italians invade Greece. Hitler is irritated, but offers assistance in the shape of the Luftwaffe's parachute divisions

October 29
British troops sail from Egypt for Crete

October 31
UK civilian casualties in October 6,334 killed, 8,695 injured

November 1
Italians reach Kalmas River in Greece – but Greek resistance has completley blunted the Italian drive. RAF bomb Berlin

November 3
British troops land in Greece

November 5
Franklin D. Roosevelt re-elected for third term as President. The 'pocket battleship' Admiral Sheer *sinks the armed merchant cruiser HMS* Jervis Bay

The Italian navy

Italy entered the war with a powerful fleet headed by modern fast battleships, backed by a series of excellent cruisers and a submarine force larger than that of Germany. However, a fatal combination of politically appointed officers, restrictive operational orders and Admiral Cunningham ensured a dismal war record for all the major units.

Vittorio Veneto
Together with her sister Littorio she formed the spearhead of the Italian fleet in 1940. Escaping damage at Taranto, she led the Italian forces at the Battle of Cape Matapan where she was disabled by a torpedo dropped by one of HMS Formidable's Albacores. She was repaired only to be torpedoed by the British submarine Urge in December 1941.

Zara
The four excellent 'Zara' class cruisers had the sad distinction of losing three of their number in a single engagement. Pola was torpedoed by British aircraft during the Battle of Cape Matapan and left dead in the water. Zara and Fiume remained behind to assist her, but during the night Admiral Cunningham's battleships caught up and demolished them with point-blank salvoes of 15-in gunfire.

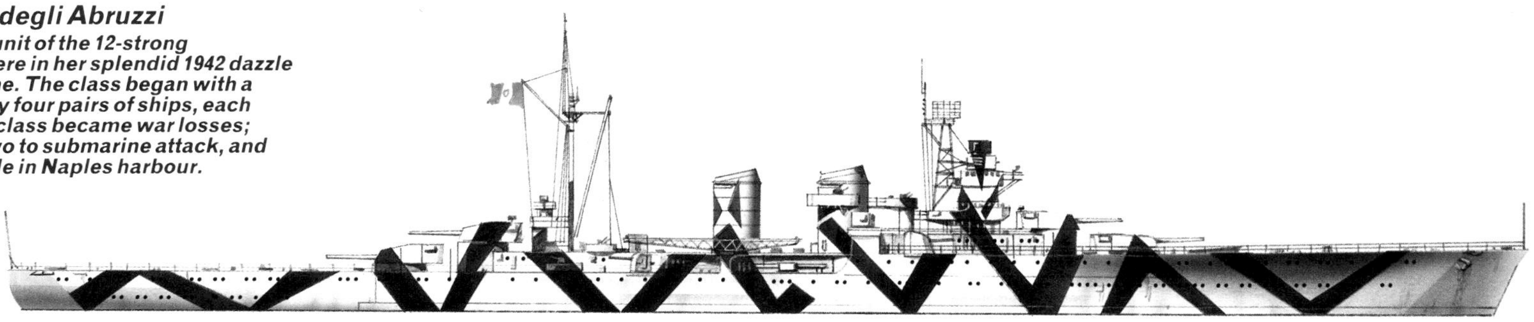

Luigi di Savoia Duca degli Abruzzi
This was the penultimate unit of the 12-strong 'Condottieri' class, seen here in her splendid 1942 dazzle pattern camouflage scheme. The class began with a four-unit series followed by four pairs of ships, each slightly different. Half the class became war losses; three in surface actions, two to submarine attack, and one bombed and sunk while in Naples harbour.

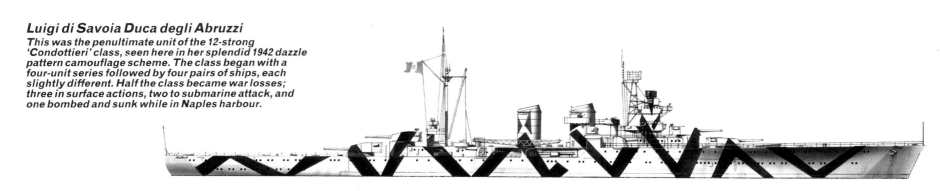

Soldato
Italian ship designers had been encouraged to produce very fast warships, and the large 'Soldato' class of destroyers were capable of up to 39 kts. The design was developed with four similar 'Maestrale' class vessels and the repeat 'Orianis'. However, two foundered in the gale after the second Battle of Sirte, not because of any damaged sustained but simply because of their light design.

Cagni
The four 'Cagni' class submarines were unusual because they were full-sized ocean-going boats, unlike the coastal vessels that made up the bulk of Italy's submarine fleet. Their construction, in 1939, perhaps anticipated a war against a major maritime power, but in the event they were flung into the battle for the Mediterranean and only the nameship survived.

made in Berlin this time, by Ciano – that it would be dangerous to leave the Greek Ionian islands perhaps to be leased by Greece to the British as naval bases, and that Yugoslavia, being 'a typical Versailles creation working against us' must be neutralized, did not receive from Hitler the response he wanted: the endorsement of his plans for an Italian invasion of both countries, plus several tons of military equipment to enable him to carry it out.

The Führer did agree that the Yugoslavian problem should eventually be settled in a manner satisfactory to Italy, but only when the moment was 'favourable'. This was not so at the moment, for Russian interest in the Balkans in general and in Yugoslavia (with its strong Communist movement) in particular must for the time being be respected. As for Greece, she would be most cheaply and effectively brought to heel by the humbling of the power upon whom she was totally dependent, Britain, the main foe whose strongholds in Egypt and the rest of the Middle East were far more worthy targets for Italian military ambition than anything nearer.

Unfortunately, attempts to eliminate the British in Egypt were proving more difficult than had been expected, which meant that the Royal Navy was still the dominant force in the Mediterranean. But surely it would be possible to strike at Britain *through Greece*? 'The Greeks represent for Italy what the Norwegians represented for Germany before the action in April,' Mussolini complained to Ribbentrop on 19 September. But without even bothering to ask Il Duce for further explanation of this dubious claim, Ribbentrop repeated Hitler's *diktat* that all conflict in the Balkans must be avoided. Britain and British bases across the Mediterranean were the only approved objectives for Blackshirt aggression.

The French navy

The French navy had to wage a long struggle against governmental indifference between the wars, but by 1939 was developing into a well-modernized fleet. After France's defeat Britain was understandably anxious that the Germans should not capture these valuable warships, and the Royal Navy was compelled to take action.

Richelieu

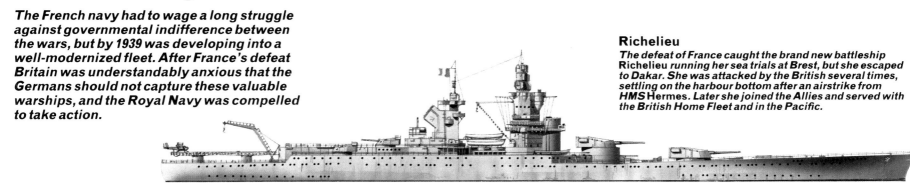

The defeat of France caught the brand new battleship **Richelieu** *running her sea trials at Brest, but she escaped to Dakar. She was attacked by the British several times, settling on the harbour bottom after an airstrike from* **HMS Hermes**. *Later she joined the Allies and served with the British Home Fleet and in the Pacific.*

Le Fantasque

These very large destroyers were a product of the intense naval rivalry between France and Italy during the inter-war years. Designed to defeat enemy destroyers, they were well armed and exceptionally fast, capable of up to 43 kts and able to sustain 37 kts even in a seaway. Their fates reflected the division of France during the war, two being sunk by the Allies and the other four fighting with them.

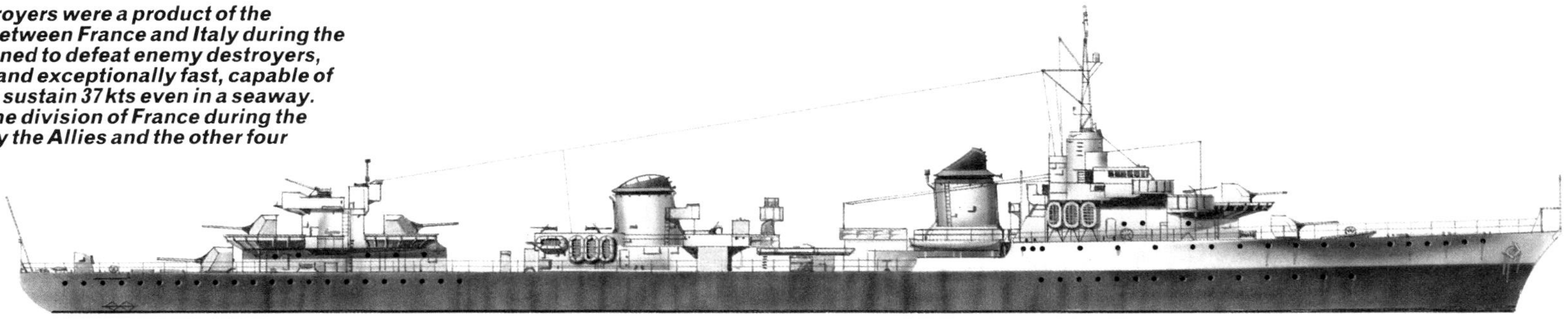

L'Adroit

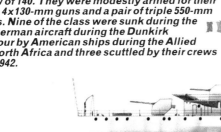

Built in the late 1920s, the 14-strong 'l'Adroit' class of fleet destroyers displaced 1,900 tons at full load and carried a crew of 140. They were modestly armed for their size, sporting 4x130-mm guns and a pair of triple 550-mm torpedo tubes. Nine of the class were sunk during the war, two by German aircraft during the Dunkirk evacuation, four by American ships during the Allied landings in North Africa and three scuttled by their crews at Toulon in 1942.

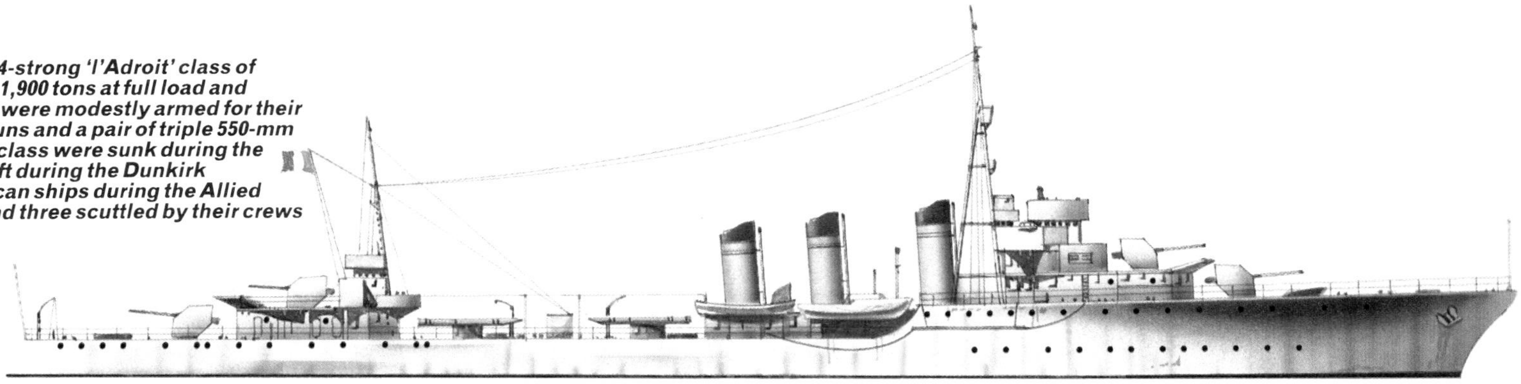

Elan

The 13-strong Elan class were 740-ton minesweeping sloops completed between 1938 and 1940. Some were used as escort vessels by the Free French Navy, fitted with British guns and depth-charge racks, while others served with the Vichy, Italian and German navies. Despite their fine lines their low power diesels could only manage 20 kts, although endurance was impressive.

Surcouf

The massive **Surcouf** *was a 'cruiser submarine' designed for long-range commerce raiding. She carried a specially designed floatplane and a pair of 203-mm guns in a pressure-tight turret as well as torpedoes. Technically, she was a successful boat but never had the opportunity to fight the sort of war for which she was designed.*

Saphir

Saphir *and her five sister-ships were short-range minelaying submarines designed for operations in the Mediterranean. Three were captured at Bizerta in 1940, two being operated by the Italian navy, and one was scuttled at Toulon.*

A pair of M13 tanks provide fire support for Italian infantry against a Greek position. The fierce resistance of the Greek army came as a disagreeable surprise to the Italian army and to Mussolini.

Mussolini might consult Hitler upon his thoughts and ambitions for the future, but Hitler did not reciprocate. The dismemberment of Romania had not been a subject upon which Mussolini's opinion was solicited, and in September came further developments. In the wake of the cessions of territory to Russia, Bulgaria and Hungary, King Carol and his government had fallen. The king and his entourage had fled the country and in his place the Iron Guard leader Marshal Antonescu had assumed control, to be bolstered by a 'military mission' from Germany, invited by Antonescu to 'help train the Romanian army'. With the Ploesti oilfields but a hundred miles from the nearest Red Army units, Hitler accepted with alacrity – and on 20 September issued his orders.

He met Mussolini at the Brenner Pass on 4 October and apparently did not think the matter of the entry of his 'military mission' into Romania worthy of mention, so Mussolini did not hear of it – or of its size – until some days later. A German motorized division strongly reinforced by panzer units had moved into Romania – and right across that country to the Bulgarian border and the lower reaches of the Pruth.

Later in the month, the Nazi officials who had followed the panzers as far as Bucharest held a celebration for Romania's 'bloodless occupation' to which a few junior Italian officers were invited, but not Mussolini. Il Duce was furious about the whole affair; and in his fury he resolved to disregard all Hitler's warnings about starting an offensive in the Balkans.

'Did they tell us about the campaign in Norway?' he shouted to Marshal Badoglio when the latter queried the wisdom of the move. 'Or the opening of the offensive on the Western Front? They behave as though we did not exist – I shall repay them in their own coin.' He gave orders for the Italian divisions in Albania, which Italy had occupied since April 1939, to advance in three drives across the border into Greece.

This they did during the morning of 28 October, their northern prong driving along the road from Korcë towards Florina, the middle prong through the mountainous Pindus region along the Vijose valley, and the third southwards along the flatter coastal belt. Even with the aggressors' advantage of surprise, however, they made only slow progress: they advanced only six miles in the the first two days along the coast and the parallel road towards Ioannina; in the centre they got as far as the small town of Konitza, which they captured in the face of no opposition at all; and in the north it would seem that the formations sent out from Korcë barely reached their own Albanian border, let alone crossed it.

By 2 November Mussolini's pride and joy, the 'crack' III 'Julia' Division of Alpini, were solidly blocked in the valley of the Vijose while (though they did not realize it) Greek units were infiltrating past them along the ridges which line the valley. Further south the coastal advance was still creeping reluctantly down towards the River Thyamis, which was reached on 8 November. This was the limit of their advance, and they began to withdraw five days later in view of developments in the north.

General Papagos, commanding the Greek army, had a more realistic view of tactical necessities than his opponent. Realizing that potentially the most dangerous advance into his country would be the move in the north against Florina, which if successful might break through to Thessalonika and cut off western Thrace and his divisions guarding the border with Bulgaria, he mobilized those divisions, gambled on Bulgarian passivity, moved them across to Florina and threw them westwards and across the border. Six days after the invasion of Greece had begun, Greek troops had captured Pissoderi, three miles inside Albania! Three days later the main road linking Korcë with the centre of Albania had been cut and the town itself came under Greek artillery fire.

By 16 November 5,000 men of the 'Julia' Alpinis had been taken prisoner; the remainder had been killed or were making their way back towards Albania at such speed that they swept away the convoys of reinforcements coming out to them, and by the 18th they were scurrying back across the border, hotly pursued by the Greeks. On the coast the withdrawal of the formations which had reached the Thyamis, which had been commenced in order to conform with developments along the Vijose, now accelerated as more of Papagos's army came across to attack them, and by the end of November they were fleeing

Left: Italian Cant Z.1007 'Alciones' (kingfishers) bomb the mountain passes of north west Greece. Just six days after the Italian invasion, the outnumbered Greeks were counter-attacking into Italian-held Albania.

Raid on Taranto

The Italian fleet's main base was the southern port of Taranto, only a few hour's dash from Malta. The British, old Mediterranean hands, had long planned an air strike on the port as a war-game. This plan was dusted-off once two carriers were available, and preparations began for a raid on Trafalgar Day, 21 October 1940. To this end the RAF, using Malta-based Martin Marylands, began a regular reconnaissance schedule, but a delay was imposed by a fire in the hangar of the *Illustrious*, which destroyed or damaged several aircraft.

Urgency was then injected by the unexpected invasion of Greece on 28 October, which presented the British with a whole new range of naval commitments. Clearly the east-west route through the Mediterranean had to be kept open, and dealing with Taranto would be a step in the right direction.

It was resolved to hit the base at the next favourable moon-phase, on 11 November, naval activity being disguised in a series of convoy movements, necessary because the enemy anticipated an attack but needed to be kept unaware of its timing. Unfortunately the venerable *Eagle*, which had been heavily shaken-up by bombing following the action off Calabria in the previous July, had to withdraw with a major failure of her aircraft fuelling system. She left *Illustrious* with a legacy of five Swordfish and night-trained crews to make up numbers.

On the morning of the attack, one of the carrier's Fulmars called at Malta for the latest reconnaissance update. It showed that delay had served the British well, for five of the enemy's six battleships were at home, the sixth joining during the day. All were lying in the Mar Grande, the spacious outer harbour.

Attack would be opposed by the warships' armaments, backed up by an estimated 21 medium-calibre AA gun emplacements and 22 searchlight installations. Fortunately for the British, only about one-third of the enemy's planned length of anti-torpedo nets could be seen in position, and his comprehensive balloon barrage had suffered damage in a recent storm. Even so, the reconnaissance pictures showed that, taking into account both nets and balloons, air attack was possible on only narrow fronts, and it was resolved to use small numbers of aircraft for the actual strike, backed by extensive diversionary attacks. Only 21 aircraft were to be involved in the night attack, a first strike of 12 and a second of nine. Of the first group, six carried torpedoes and of the remainder some carried 16 parachute-retarded flares and four small bombs, and some four 250-kg (551-lb) bombs. The flares were to silhouette the main targets for the low-flying torpedo-carriers, and the bombs were for diversionary attacks on smaller warships in the Mar Piccolo, the seaplane base and the oil fuel depot.

In dead calm conditions under a three-quarter moon, the first 12 Swordfish lumbered, heavily loaded, into the air. By 20.40 they were all away on the 275-km (170-mile) two-hour flight, their crews freezing in their open cockpits. Long before their arrival the port was marked by a multi-coloured cascade of fire, arcing aimlessly in the clean air, the jittery Italians being warned of aircraft noises by listening apparatus but, fortunately, lacking night-fighters.

At 23.02, the first British flare blossomed at 1370 m (4,500 ft) followed by others in a neat line at 805-m (880-yard) intervals. The torpedo aircraft had gone their own way, splitting further into two groups to attack from the south west and north west. Of these the first had to fly between the invisible balloon cables, and here the stately 85 mph (137 km/h) of a Stringbag was a positive advantage.

Miraculously, only one of the aircraft was lost, while a single hit put the *Cavour* on the bottom and another holed the new *Littorio*'s port quarter. The bombers, meanwhile, had raised a hearty blaze in the seaplane base, which thus served as a beacon to welcome the second strike, about 40 minutes behind the first.

Again the flare-line worked well, throwing the stationary Italian ships into sharp relief. Only five torpedo aircraft were in this group. One crashed and another was hit, but so was the *Duilio* and, again, the *Littorio*. The bombers suffered from faulty fusing and many of their weapons failed to explode, including one that penetrated well into the cruiser *Trento*.

In the early hours, close aboard the Greek Island of Cephalonia, the *Illustrious* received her brood as they arrived singly and in pairs, tattered and elated. For the loss of only two aircraft, three enemy battleships had been bottomed. In deep water they would have been lost; as it was, two were eventually salvaged and returned to service.

The value of the attack lay in its demonstration of the sheer economy of a well-planned carrier strike, the further moral ascendancy given to the outnumbered Royal Navy and the withdrawal of all Italian heavy units to points north.

***Above:** The British attack on the Italian fleet in its base at Taranto put three out of six enemy battleships on the harbour bottom.*

***Below:** The forecastle of* **Littorio** *is visible as she rests on the harbour bottom after being struck by three torpedoes. She was in dockyard hands for six months.*

A Vickers Mk 6 light tank hurtles across the desert in pursuit of the retreating Italian army. Operation Compass succeeded beyond the wildest expectations.

through Sarande, 15 miles up the Albanian coast.

But it was again in the north that disaster struck most keenly. Mussolini had fed into the area, with some desperation, the Ninth Army, the 'Army of the Po', and its best-known formations – some of them special Blackshirt units – had arrived in Korcë just before it was cut off and the shelling began. They were still there when the town fell on 22 November, together with a great deal of military equipment, much of it supplied at Il Duce's special request by Hitler; some of it had not even been unpacked.

Such were the blows which had fallen on Mussolini's military adventure in the Balkans; and to add to his discomfiture, on 11 November three of his proudest battleships – *Littorio, Duilio* and *Cavour* – had been severely damaged, the first two put out of action for many months and the last permanently, after attacks by Swordfish from HMS *Illustrious* on the Italian fleet while it lay at anchor in Taranto harbour.

But much worse for Italian arms was soon to follow.

It thus came – as General O'Connor later commented – as something of a disappointment when the Italian invasion ground to a halt at Sidi Barrani, 60 miles short of Mersa Matruh, having apparently run out of petrol, water and perhaps energy. The leading Italian formations then spent the next two months building a number of fortified camps running in a quadrant out into the desert from Maktila on the coast to Sofafi at the top of the Escarpment, and stocking them with food, wines, excellent soft furnishings for the officers' and senior NCOs' quarters, some well-sited artillery and some ammunition.

On 9 December General O'Connor launched Operation Compass, a 'five-day raid' by both divisions of Western Desert Force, intended to attack and perhaps destroy two or more of the fortified camps, menace the others on the Escarpment, shell Italian barracks and garrisons in Sidi Barrani and Maktila, and, if all went well, advance as far as the frontier wire and destroy any other enemy installations there. They were then to collect as many prisoners as possible before withdrawing either along the coast to Mersa Matruh or down into the desert.

The Royal Navy and the Royal Air Force mounted diversionary attacks that night, attracting Italian attention out to sea and up into the skies, while Western Desert Force probed cautiously into a gap beween the Escarpment and the strongpoint at Nibeiwa. By dawn they were in position, 4th Indian Infantry supported by newly arrived Matilda tanks of the 7th Royal Tank Regiment on the right and now facing the rear, unprotected sides of Nibeiwa and two other camps; the tank brigades and Support Group of the 7th Armoured on the left, facing west as a shield against interference from any Italian support from their reserves. And at 7.30 a.m. the guns roared out and the attack went in.

It caught the Italians totally by surprise, the majority of the garrisons in the course of preparing breakfast. The shock of the attack was total. Ponderous and irresistible, the line of Matildas appeared over the crest half a mile from the main entrances to the camps, brushed aside any vestige of defence put up against them, burst through the gateways and fanned out across the camp areas like avenging furies. They were impervious to any fire, even from the Italian artillery, and only minefields could have stopped them – and they were all on the far sides of the camps.

Britain strikes back

Nibeiwa was in British hands by noon, the Tummar camp to the north by evening and the camp nearest to the coast surrendered the following morning without firing a shot. Meanwhile Sidi Barrani had been occupied, the forward patrols of the 7th Armoured Divisions were probing westwards to the wire, and by the evening of 10 December one of the greatest problems facing Western Desert Force was dealing with some 20,000 prisoners. Operation Compass was succeeding beyond the wildest dreams and if exploited could go much farther than the limits of the 'five-day raid'.

It did not take long for General O'Connor to obtain permission for such exploitation. He lost the 4th Indian Division on account of plans made by General Wavell for an attack on the Duke of Aosta's fief down in Ethiopia, but the gap was filled with enthusiasm by men of the 6th Australian Division, who made up in sheer physical strength what they may have lacked in equipment or experience. By 13 December all Italian positions in Egypt had been reduced and their garrisons were marching glumly eastwards towards hastily constructed prison camps. The leading units of 7th Armoured Division were now through the wire and circling north to cut the road between Bardia and Tobruk.

Bardia was surrounded by the Australians by 17 December and assaulted by them on 3 January; by the evening of 6 January the last Italian defences had collapsed, thousands more prisoners were trudging eastwards, and one British armoured brigade – the 7th – had reached El Adem on their drive to seal off Tobruk. Their engines needed overhaul, their tank

Above: The one that got away – the mighty battleship* Vittorio Veneto *fires a salvo from her 15-inch guns in December 1940. The following March she led the Italian force at the Battle of Cape Matapan.

Chronology of War: 1940

December 6
Marshal Badoglio, Duke of Addis Ababa, resigns as Chief of the Italian General Staff. Luftwaffe to operate in Italy

December 8
Heavy incendiary air raid on London by 413 German night bombers

December 9
General Wavell, C in C Middle East, launches 'Operation Compass' against Italian positions in Egypt. Two Divisions under General Richard O'Connor attack the Italian 10th Army (10 Divisions)

December 11
British recapture Sidi Barrani

December 12
20,000 Italian prisoners taken in operations so far

December 17
British occupy Sollum and Fort Capuzzo; 38,000 Italian prisoners taken so far

December 18
Hitler issues secret memorandum on Operation 'Barbarossa' as the projected invasion of Russia is called. Invasion to be launched in May 1941

December 23
Anthony Eden appointed Foreign Secretary

December 24
British and Australian troops surround Bardia

December 29
Roosevelt declared America the 'Arsenal of the Democracies'. Heaviest incendiary raid on London; Guildhall and eight Wren churches damaged or destroyed

December 31
UK civilian casualties in December 3,793 killed, 5,244 injured

Australian troops examine an Italian L6/40 light tank. The 6th Australian Division reached Bardia on 17 December and launched their assault on 3 January. Three days later the city fell, and thousands more Italian soldiers trudged into POW camps.

Italian army equipment

The Italian army, which was to be so heavily defeated in December 1940, was by no means ill-equipped; its problems stemmed more from politically appointed commanders and poor motivation. But as the war progressed Italian equipment began to look increasingly dated compared to the new AFVs being introduced by both the British and the Germans.

Fiat L6/40

A two-man light tank armed with a 20-mm cannon and a co-axial light machine-gun, the Fiat L6/40 was the Italian equivalent of the German Panzer II. The commander acted as both gunner and loader and entered the vehicle either via a hatch in the turret roof or through a door in the right side of the hull.

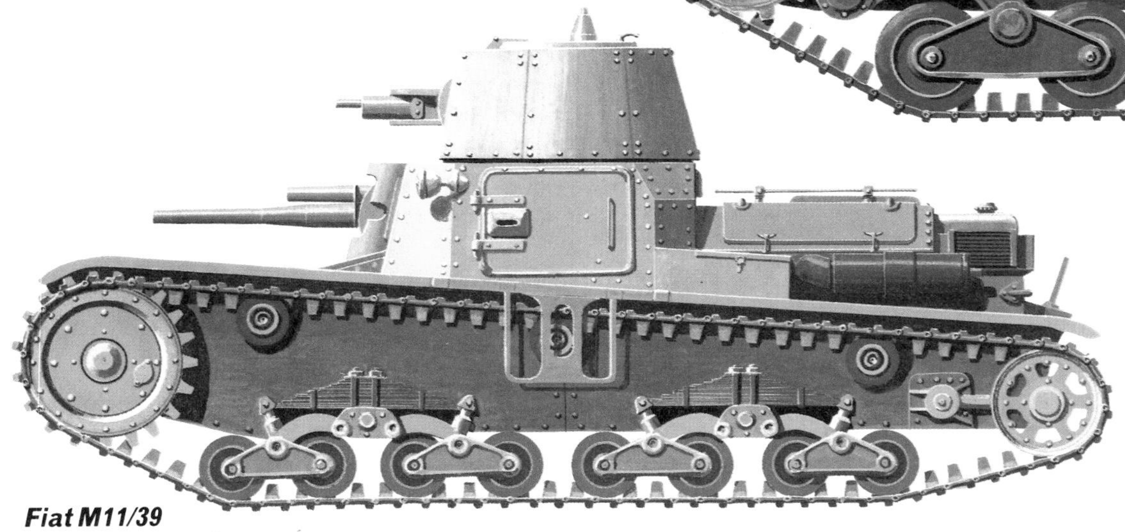

Fiat M11/39

Similar in conception to the American M3 Lee tank, the M11/39 mounted a 47-mm gun in a sponson on the right hand side of the hull front and carried a pair of 8-mm machine-guns in the turret. The chassis and suspension became the basis for the M13/40, which mounted the gun in the turret and became the most numerous Italian tank in service. The M11/39 was recognized as obsolescent by 1940 and only 100 were built; most were destroyed or captured in the British offensive launched in December.

Semovente L3 da 47/32

The Italians were among the first nations to develop tank destroyers, fitting powerful anti-tank guns to light or old tank chassis to produce essentially a self-propelled anti-tank gun. The L3 was an early effort, sporting a 47-mm gun, 32 calibres long (hence the designation) on this open mounting.

Autoblinda 41

This was one of the most numerous Italian cars encountered in the desert war, and proved a sturdy and reliable vehicle although prone to steering problems. Armed with a 20-mm cannon and a co-axial machine-gun, it weighed 7½ tons (compared to the 7 tons of the L640) and carried a four-man crew. In addition to service in the reconnaissance units, many were used on anti-partisan operations in the Balkans.

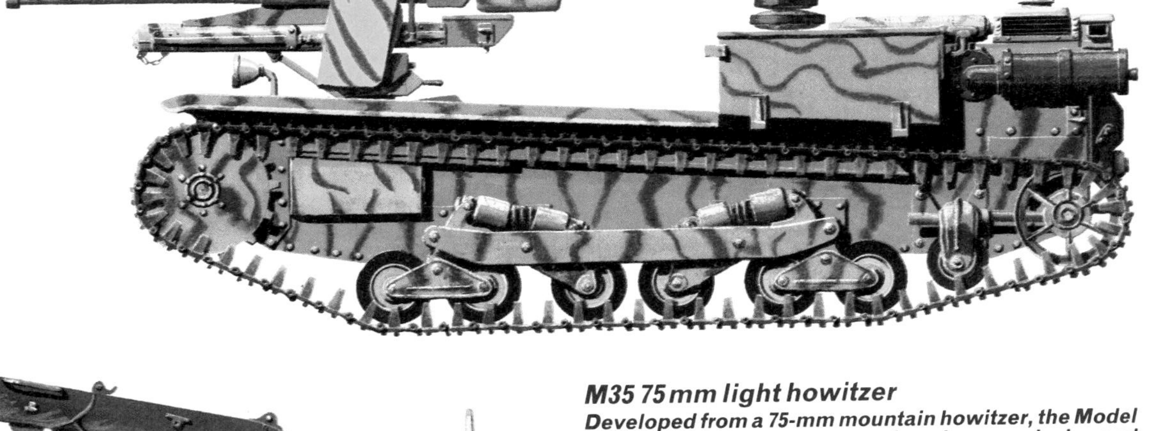

Semovente M41M da 90/53

The success of the German 88-mm anti-aircraft gun in the anti-tank role encouraged the Italians to employ their 90-mm anti-aircraft gun in the same manner. Unfortunately they lacked a large tank chassis to carry the gun, and the weapon was finally fitted to an M14/41 tank chassis, which was too small for anything but this lightly-protected mounting.

M35 75 mm light howitzer

Developed from a 75-mm mountain howitzer, the Model 1935 light howitzer was a sound modern gun design and probably the best weapon equipping the Italian artillery arm in 1940. The Fascist government had perversely sold many of these guns abroad for valuable foreign exchange, with the result that the Italian army was consistently short of them.

Westland Lysanders fly over the Suez canal – the glittering prize which formed the Axis objective in the North African campaign. The Lysander was designed for artillery spotting and liaison duties, but won real fame later in secret missions to occupied Europe.

An Australian cavalry regiment on parade: Vickers Light Tanks and Bren gun carriers fitted with Boys anti-tank rifles. Note the vital spare track sections on the side of the tank in the foreground.

tracks had already grossly exceeded their statutory mileage, the drivers' eyes were red-rimmed and everyone was hungrier and thirstier than they had believed possible – but they were winning and this made up for everything.

The Australian 19th Brigade and the riflemen of the 7th Support Group arrived on the Tobruk perimeter on 12 January, the other two Australian brigades following on the 17th, and on 21 January, covered by the guns of the Support Group and the small-calibre fire of the tanks, the Australian infantry mounted the first attack on Tobruk. It was all over in 36 hours: few of the Italian posts were held with any degree of determination, and the naval garrison around the port gave up without a shot fired, an Australian trooper hoisting his slouch hat to the top of the main flagpole in place of the Fascist flag which he had just taken down.

The following morning new orders reached the men of Western Desert Force; they were now to mount a raid on Benghazi, so their advance must continue westwards, the Australians moving on Derna, 7th Armoured Division concentrating at Mechili, on the Trig el Abd, south of the Jebel Akhdar bulge. They were there by 2 February.

At Mechili it was evident to all that, for an advance across the length of the bulge, time must be made available for the accumulation of at least 3,000 tons of stores and replacements, plus water for all, and for running repairs on all 7th Armoured Division vehicles. Time was also needed for the exhausted, underfed, thirsty and now extremely unwashed men to get themselves into better shape. The absolutely minimum necessities might be achieved in five days; six would be preferable.

They got two hours. Vehicle bonnets were open, men were washing and shaving in what minuscule driblets of water they could find, nominal rolls were being consulted for names of missing – for inevitably some had been killed and some wounded – the adjutant was catching up on his paperwork. Then a staff car drew up; the enemy were showing signs of quitting Benghazi, of giving up Cyrenaica altogether, and somehow an armoured force must be immediately assembled to drive southeastwards the rest of the way to the coast – about 150 miles – and there cut the road from Benghazi to Tripoli where it ran along the edge of the Gulf of Sirte. The Australians would drive around the Jebel coast, through Derna, Cirene, Barce and El Abiar to Benghazi and hound the Italians down into the trap.

Excitement kept them all going. They were driving vehicles in dire need of service and maintenance, over appalling country about which almost nothing was known except that it led in the right direction. They had aboard the vehicles two days' supply of food and water, just enough petrol to get them to the

British Mk IV Cruiser tanks kick up the dust as they speed across the stony desert. Their suspension made them very nimble, but they were weakly protected and armed with the ineffective 2-pdr gun.

Chronology of War: 1941

January 1
British bombard Bardia, the Italian strongpoint on the Egyptian border, from sea and air

January 3
Australians break into Bardia. Greek counteroffensive begins in Albania

January 5
Bardia captured; 30,000 prisoners taken

January 6
Churchill advises Chiefs of Staff to give priority to Greek operations

January 10
Lend-Lease Bill introduced to US Congress. Luftwaffe units in action for the first time in the Mediterranean, attack a convoy

January 16
Malta attacked by 80 German Ju 87 Stukas – the first in a long series of raids

January 19
British open campaign in Eritrea

January 20
Roosevelt's third inauguration. Attempted Iron Guard putsch in Romania

January 21
Tobruk defences broken by Australians and British

January 22
Tobruk falls; 25,000 Italian prisoners taken. Allied casualties under 500

January 24
Lord Halifax meets President Roosevelt aboard the battleship HMS King George V

January 29
Death of General Metaxas. Emmanuel Tsouderos succeeds as Greek premier

January 30
Wavell's troops capture Derna, 100 miles west of Tobruk

February 3
German battle cruisers Scharnhorst *and* Gneisenau *break out of Kiel into the North Atlantic. British occupy Cyrene with the general retreat of Graziani's troops. Battle of Keren opens in East Africa*

February 6
Rommel appointed commander of Afrika Korps. Allies enter Benghazi

February 7
Italian collapse at Beda Fomm

February 8
Lend-Lease Bill passed by US House of Representatives. El Agheila occupied by Allies

February 12
General Erwin Rommel arrives in Tripoli

February 14
German units arrive in Tripoli. Yugoslav ministers meet Hitler

February 19
Australian 8th Division lands at Singapore

February 22
Anthony Eden, Sir John Dill (Chief of the Imperial General Staff) and General Wavell arrive in Athens. Rommel attacks at El Agheila

February 24
British Cabinet agree to send force to Greece

February 26
Eden and Dill arrive in Ankara for talks with Turkish government

February 28
UK civilian casualties for two months 2,289 killed, 3,080 injured

target area – and as much ammunition as they could find room for; God only knew what would happen when it ran out.

But the leading armoured cars were chasing an astonished garrison out of the fort at Msus by the afternoon of 4 February, the first cruiser tanks arrived there the following morning, and by that afternoon guns and infantry of the Support Group had raced down to Antelat and then across the coast road at Beda Fomm. By 4 p.m. a battalion of the Rifle Brigade was established across the road with gun positions in support to their rear and armoured cars patrolling the stretch of beach on their left. Altogether, the force consisted of about 600 men.

The first onslaught was not long in coming. Within half an hour of the riflemen taking up their positions, they saw the head of what proved to be the leading column of the rump of the Italian Tenth Army on their way out of Cyrenaica, bowling unconcernedly towards them. The ensuing action was brief but bloody; from then on the mass of Italian soldiery, with their guns, their lorries and their light tanks, built up inexorably as the rest of Tenth Army came south.

The riflemen were saved by their own expertise and their own sense of survival, for they had nowhere to escape to and they knew that every shot they fired must hit its target, every shell take its toll. Having demonstrated their efficiency by decimating the leading Italian formations, they at last received paramount support when the sound of tanks – labouring, but full of menace to the listening Italians – came through the thickening dusk. Such was the effect when the first half-dozen arrived and began rampaging up and down the flanks of the ever-lengthening Italian column, that literally hundreds of soldiers of all ranks threw down their arms and rushed towards the nearest rifleman or tank to surrender – to such effect that the accumulation of prisoners became almost more of a problem than the possibility of battle with those still showing signs of hostility.

But there was little need to worry come nightfall, although the British knew that their stocks of petrol and ammunition were running dangerously low, and that every minute that passed added numbers to the enemy column building up in front of them (for word had arrived that the Australians had reached Benghazi and were driving every last Italian down towards them). But the mood prevailing opposite them was of resignation, if not actual panic.

On 9 December General Wavell's counterattack began: two divisions against seven. In four days, four Italian divisions were destroyed. For just over 600 casualties, the British captured 38,000 Italian soldiers, 240 guns and over 70 tanks. What started as a raid ended in the British capture of all Cyrenaica; 31,000 British troops inflicted 20,000 casualties and captured a staggering 130,000 Italians.

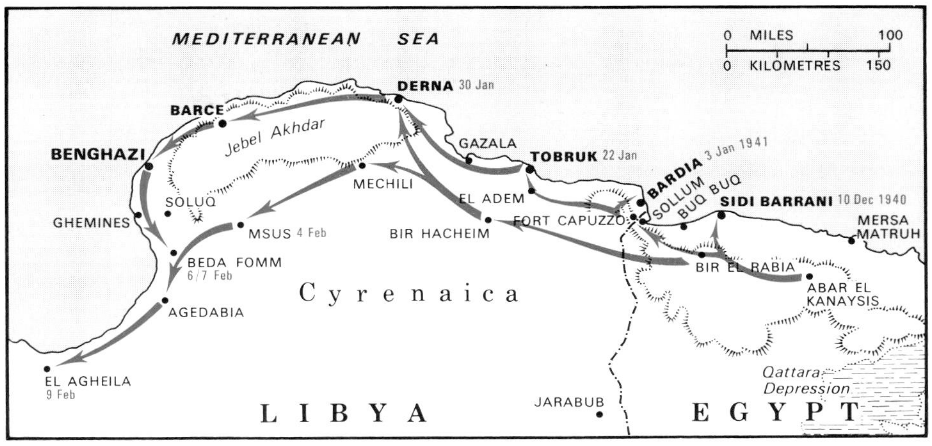

When the morning came, one small attack was launched against the British lines, by 13 M13 tanks which had been brought up to the head of the column during the night; but it was met by a storm of fire – which in fact emptied the artillery magazines and left many riflemen with the prospect of using their bayonets as a last resort. When the smoke of battle cleared, the astonished watchers saw 13 smoking and stationary Italian tanks, some with their tracks blown off, some with their crews shot by fire through turrets or hatches, one stopped only yards from the tent from which the action had all been directed.

There followed a silence over the battlefield, broken only by the crackle of burning vehicles and the occasional sharp crack of burning ammunition. Then white flags began to appear along the length of the column, then at the front, more and more until the whole road from Beda Fomm up towards Ghemines had become a forest of waving white banners. Operation Compass was at an end.

In ten weeks, General O'Connor's force had advanced 500 miles and destroyed the Italian Tenth Army, taking 130,000 prisoners including seven generals – at a cost to themselves of 550 killed or missing, 1,373 wounded. It was a remarkable feat by any standards, and now, despite the condition of the bulk of their equipment, all the men of the force from O'Connor down to the youngest private were sure they could drag themselves further, on and into Tripoli, thus driving the Italians completely out of North Africa – possibly even out of the war altogether!

With this in mind, O'Connor's chief staff officer travelled post-haste back to Cairo. He arrived early on the morning of 12 February and at 10.00 was ushered into General Wavell's office.

All the maps of the desert which had previously covered the long wall were gone; in their place was a huge map of Greece.

'You see, Eric,' said Wavell, gesturing towards it. 'I am planning my spring campaign!'

Developments in the Balkans had conspired to rob General O'Connor and his men of their greatest victory.

British 25-pdr field guns bombard Bardia on the last day of 1940. The port fell on 5 January, yielding 40,000 prisoners; British casualties were under 500.

Below right: Some of the 130,000 Italian soldiers captured during the British offensive in Cyrenaica. Only the fateful decision to intervene in Greece prevented O'Connor's division from advancing further.

Below: A Bren gun carrier brings in another batch of prisoners of war. The Boys anti-tank rifle gives the vehicle a slight measure of defence against Italian armour.

Chapter 5

Hitler Strikes South

Yugoslavia's stand against Hitler was rewarded with instant invasion but the German foray into the Balkans became more extensive as the Greeks doggedly resisted Italian conquest. Britain made a vain attempt to save Greece from the German onslaught, but the British forces proved unequal to the task and were ejected from the Greek mainland in less than a month. Worse was to follow in Crete, with German paratroops spearheading the forces which inflicted yet another crushing defeat on the British Empire.

German troops move into the Balkans to assist their Italian allies. The arrival of the Germans changed the face of the battle in this theatre, their hard, professional army making short work of the opposition.

Mussolini's invasion of Greece had infuriated Hitler, both because of the blatant disregard of his stated opinions on the subject and because of its effect upon his own long-term plans. Even the lamentable performance of the Italian troops in the face of Greek resistance can have provided only the most fleeting temptation towards *Schadenfreude*, for it soon became obvious that Hitler could not leave Mussolini's chestnuts merrily blazing in the fire. And pulling them out would necessarily be a military, not a political, matter.

In order to clear his southern flank when the time came for his onslaught on Soviet Russia, Hitler had already laid plans for a drive down through Bulgaria 'to occupy the north-east coast of the Aegean'. Although the wording of the Directive for Operation Marita then continued 'and, should this be necessary, the entire mainland of Greece', he had hoped that the bonds between his own dictatorship and that of the Greek ruler, General Metaxas, would be sufficient to avoid actual battle and bring about a peaceful occupation similar to those already in operation in Romania and Hungary, and intended for Bulgaria.

He also hoped for a peaceful solution to the problem posed by Yugoslavia. In this regard he had even before the war arranged to take Yugoslavia's entire production of copper plus substantial quantities of lead and zinc, in return for supplies of aircraft and guns. That Hitler had no particular intention of fulfilling Germany's part of the bargain need have no effect, in his opinion, upon Yugoslavia's compliance with his wishes. He summoned the Yugoslav Foreign Minister, Aleksander Cincar-Markovic, to Berchtesgaden on 27 November 1940 to suggest that his country place herself unreservedly upon the side of the Axis.

But the ruler of Yugoslavia was the Prince-Regent Paul, who was married to a sister of Princess Marina of Kent, had been educated at Oxford, and was well aware that popular feeling throughout the bulk of his country was either pro-Soviet or pro-British; it was almost unanimously anti-Nazi.

Nonetheless, realities had to be faced. Hitler, by spring 1941, was undoubtedly the most powerful figure on the continent of Europe and, in view of the apparent acquiescence in his every action by Soviet Russia at that time, probably in the world. Moreover, Yugoslavia's advances to Britain, although received with welcoming cordiality and strong encouragement to stand firm against the Axis dictatorships, evoked no more than a firm regret that because of the active theatre in Libya and commitments made to Greece, there was nothing to be spared in the way of arms or divisions. 'You big nations are hard,' remarked Paul sadly. 'You talk of our honour but you are far away.'

Invasion of Yugoslavia

The main attack on Yugoslavia came from List's Twelfth Army, which was already in position in Bulgaria and which would also be responsible for the invasion of Greece. The German advances from the north, east and south east were added to by an Italian attack down the Dalmatian coast towards Dubrovnik. The campaign was a masterpiece, lasting only 10 days.

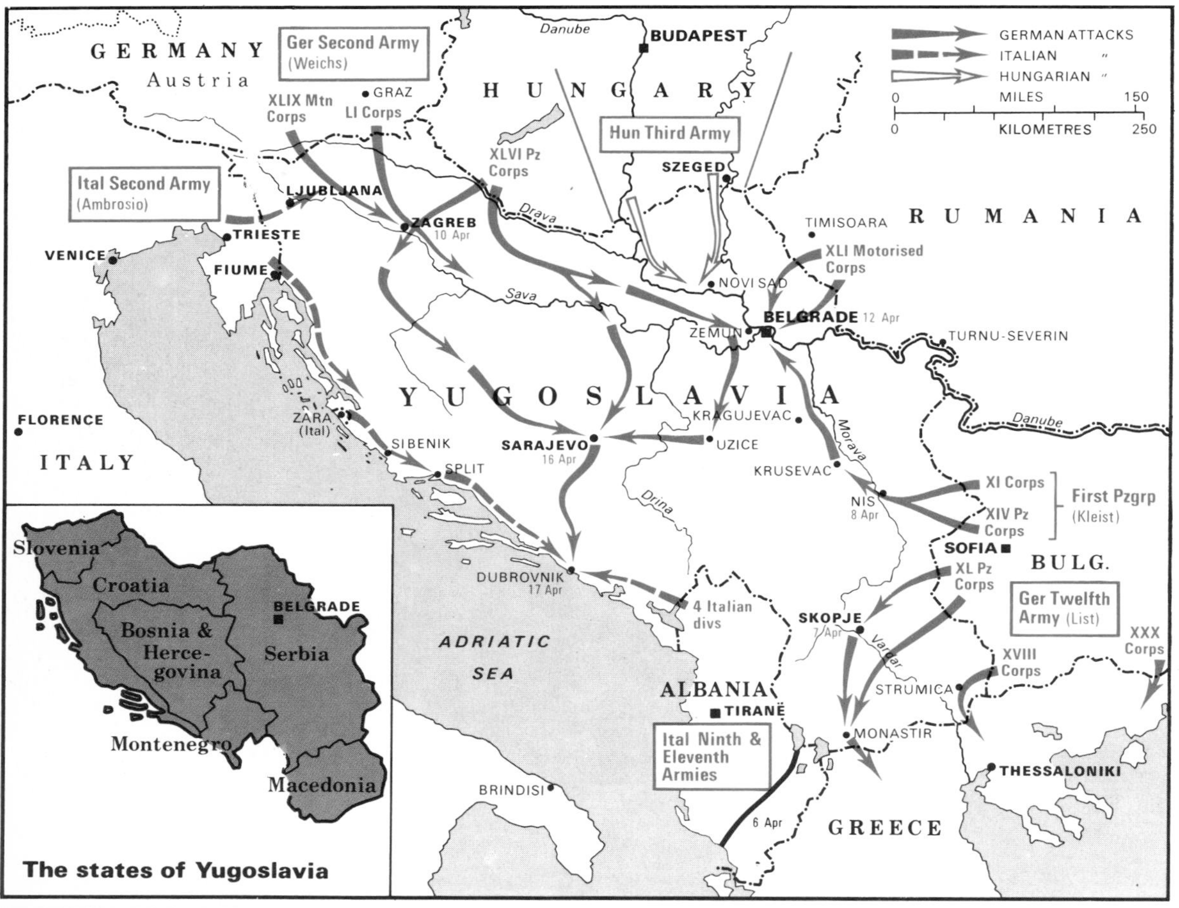

Ultimatum for Yugoslavia

On 19 March Hitler gave Yugoslavia five days in which to sign a pact which guaranteed their frontiers and gave her unrestricted use of the port of Salonika (which Hitler intended to control quite soon) in return for neutrality and the demilitarization of the Adriatic coast – and made it quite obvious that if she failed to sign, life would become increasingly difficult in the very near future. On 25 March, Cincar-Markovic signed the pact at a ceremony so lacking in the festive spirit that even Hitler likened it to a funeral.

But neither Hitler nor Prince-Regent Paul had correctly gauged the temper of the Serbian people. Early on the morning of 27 March tanks and guns moved into the centre of Belgrade, and at dawn a radio programme announced a palace coup, the immediate exile of Paul, the assumption of the throne by the 17-year-old King Peter II, and the renunciation of the pact with Germany signed 48 hours before. Any doubts as to the popular validity of the new regime were dispelled by the rejoicings throughout Belgrade, the cheering, the flags and the continuous shouting of the slogan 'Better war than pact; better grave than slave!'

When the news reached Hitler he thought at first that it was a joke; but any amusement he might have felt vanished as soon as he realized the truth of the situation, and he was possessed by a consuming fury. A meeting of the Wehrmacht commanders at Zossen presided over by General Halder, Chief of the German General Staff, was interrupted at noon and by mid-afternoon they had received new and unequivocal orders. 'The Führer is determined . . . to make all preparations for the destruction of Yugoslavia militarily and as a national unit. . . . Politically it is especially important that the blow against Yugoslavia is carried out with pitiless harshness. . . . The main task of the Luftwaffe is to start as early as possible . . . and to destroy the capital city, Belgrade, in waves of

Chronology of War: 1941

March 2
Bulgaria joins Axis. German troops enter Bulgaria in preparation for invasion of Greece

March 4
British commandos raid Lofoten Islands, west of Narvik. British troops sail for Greece from Egypt

March 7
Allied troops land at Piraeus and Volos

March 8
US Senate passes Lend-Lease Bill

March 9
Italians launch offensive in Albania

March 11
Lend-Lease Bill signed in Washington

March 12
Roosevelt asks Senate for Lend-Lease appropriation of $7,000,000,000. Churchill calls it 'A new Magna Carta'

March 19
Germany issues ultimatum to Yugoslavia

March 25
Yugoslavia signs Tripartite Pact

March 27
Revolt against Tripartite Pact in Belgrade. King Peter forms new Cabinet. Agreement signed between USA and UK for lease of Caribbean bases in exchange for 50 US destroyers

March 28
Battle of Cape Matapan off the southern tip of Greece. The British Mediterranean fleet annihilates an Italian cruiser force

March 30
Rommel launches attack in Cyrenaica. The heavy cruiser HMS York sunk at Suda Bay, Crete. Scharnhorst and Gneisenau bombed by RAF in Brest

March 31
Eden and Dill in Athens. UK civilian casualties in March 4,259 killed, 5,557 injured

April 2
Rommel's troops reach Agedabia. British retreat from Mersa Brega

April 4
Germans capture Benghazi and Msus

April 6
Germans invade Greece and Yugoslavia; large scale Luftwaffe bombing of Belgrade. British occupy Addis Ababa in Ethiopia

Axis aircraft in Greece and Crete

Air power played a considerable part in the conquest of the Balkans, and made the operation to take Crete possible. Italy had had varying fortunes in this theatre, but the Luftwaffe, honed to a fine edge by the campaigns in Poland and France, attained an almost complete superiority in the air.

The Macchi MC.200 series Saetta (lightning) entered service with the Regia Aeronautica in October 1939. Over Yugoslavia and Greece it proved adequate, but was soon outclassed in North Africa. This example is in the colours of 371ª Sq, 22° Gruppo in June 1940.

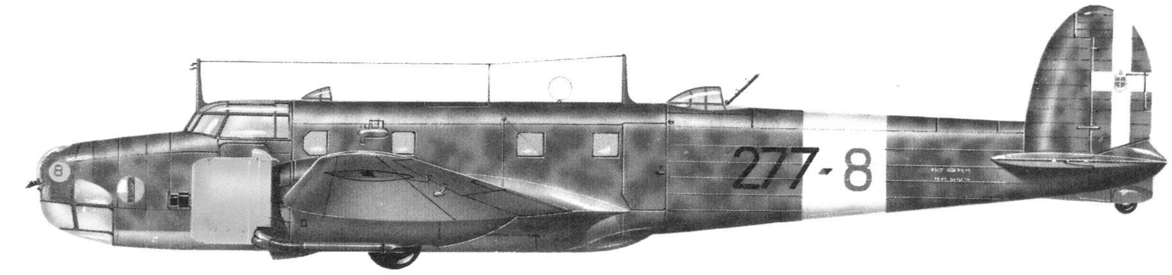

A Fiat BR.20 M of the 277ª Sq, 37° Stormo operating over the Greco-Albanian front from its base at Grottaglie in 1940/41. Popularly called the Cicogna (stork) the BR.20 was not a great success in spite of a fair bombload.

The first German forces to get involved in the Mediterranean were the aircraft of the Luftwaffe. This Junkers Ju 88A-4 of 9./KG 30 'Adler Geschwader' was used on anti-shipping strikes in early 1941.

A Messerschmitt Bf 110C of I/ZG 26 'Horst Wessel', based in the Peloponnese for Operation 'Mercury'. The unit played a major part in softening up the defences of Crete before the airborne assault.

A Junkers Ju 87R of 7./StG 77, based at Deta in Romania. Operation Marita, the German invasion of Greece saw StG 77 under control of Fliegerkorps VIII in the role for which the 'R' model was designed – long range anti-shipping missions.

A Junkers Ju 52/3m g4e of the Stabsschwarm, IV/KGzbV 1, based around Corinth in May 1941, and under the command of Oberst Buchholz. Operations over Crete were severely hampered by having to operate off sand airfields, greatly degrading aircraft performance.

attack.' There was to be no misunderstanding of the form Operation Strafgericht (punishment) was to take.

As Field Marshal List's Twelfth Army had by now moved south from Romania into Bulgaria in order to carry out Operation Marita, there was no reason why both operations should not take place together. And in view of the presence in Greece itself of British armour and aircraft and several brigades of Australian and New Zealand troops, there was obviously now no point in limiting Marita to Thrace and Macedonia. The whole country would be occupied, straight away.

Britain had signed an agreement with Greece in April 1939 guaranteeing to come to her aid if her independence were threatened and in 1941 the British Foreign Secretary, Anthony Eden, was determined that, if necessary, Britain would keep her promise. In his desire to send armed assistance to Greece he was supported by Churchill, whose romantic nature responded immediately to the idea of rescuing 'the cradle of civilization' from the barbarians, and by General Wavell, who did not regard battles in Libya against the Italians as very important, and felt that the sooner a 'Balkan Front' against the main enemy, Germany, could be formed, the better.

Under General Metaxas, the Greek government had viewed British offers of help with some scepticism. Greece's fight against the Italians was proceeding better than could have been expected, the main difficulties during the months from October to February 1941 being the weather and the lack of medical support and transport for casualties. Certainly, the Greek army was dreadfully short of air support, and some RAF fighter and light bomber squadrons had proved very useful. But so far as men on the ground were concerned, the last thing Metaxas wanted was a force large enough to attract Hitler's attention – unless it was also large enough to repel the invasion which would inevitably follow. Eleven divisions, at least two of them armoured, would be fine; otherwise Metaxas would far sooner have just their boots, for the lack of adequate footwear was causing Greek troops in the mountains unbearable suffering.

But on 29 January Metaxas died of a heart attack, and his successor, Emmanuel Tsouderos, was more open to suggestion. He met Eden, accompanied by the CIGS (Chief of the Imperial General Staff) Field Marshal Sir John Dill, General Wavell, Air Chief Marshal Longmore and Captain Dick, RN, at the Royal Palace on 2 February 1941, and after other meetings – and the eventual resolution of one or two misunderstandings – it was agreed that the 1st Armoured Brigade Group, the 6th Australian Division and the 2nd New Zealand Division would be sent to Greece as quickly as possible, to be joined later perhaps by the 7th Australian Division and the Polish Independent Brigade Group. The first convoys arrived early in March.

On paper the Greek army consisted of 21 divisions, but of these 15 were in Albania, short of ammunition, equipment or men to replace casualties; only hope and their dogged determination to hold back the Italians kept them in place. The other six divisions had already been stripped of their best men, who had volunteered for the Albanian front, but they could at least man the main forts in Thrace and much of the length of the Metaxas defence lines in Macedonia.

If the British took a central position between Salonika and Florina, with some of them in the Aliakmon Line, they would be available to support one Greek army against German invasion from Bulgaria's southern border, or the other Greek army if the Italians should manage to mount a strong push east from Albania. They would also be squarely in the path of any invasion which came down through Yugoslavia, especially if it funnelled through the Monastir Gap.

Operations Punishment and Marita both opened on 6 April (Palm Sunday) with spectacular strikes by the Luftwaffe. The citizens of Belgrade were awakened by the noise of aircraft circling above them at 5.30 a.m. (there was no declaration of war) and by 6.00 a.m. bombs were raining down on the railway station, the Royal Palace and the airfield at Zemun where much of the Yugoslav air force was caught on the ground. For the whole of that day the attack continued, until the centre of Belgrade had been reduced to rubble; by the following evening 17,000 people had been killed and fires were raging.

German Panzer IIs roll through Yugoslavia. While the Balkans is not ideal armour country, the Germans made use of their superior skills.

Waffen SS troops pass through Belgrade in April 1941. They were to prove extremely efficient soldiers.

Five hundred miles to the south were similar scenes of disaster. On that fatal Sunday evening, Piraeus harbour was congested with shipping from convoy AFN 24, which had brought more administration units in to support the Anzac Corps, now moving up towards the Kozani area. Shortly before 9.00 p.m. the menacing drone of approaching aircraft was heard and soon afterwards mines were being parachuted down into the water, effectively blocking any escape route out of the harbour for the trapped ships. The bombers followed; sticks of bombs rained down across the water, the shipping, the sheds and warehouses along the harbour edge – and particularly across the SS *Glen Fraser* anchored by the main quay. Red and orange flame lit the whole scene as wooden buildings caught fire, petrol drums burst and spread lakes of fire across the concrete and lapping waves.

Then a bomb burst aboard the *Glen Fraser*, and the 250 tons of explosive in her holds blew up with a shattering roar that devastated Piraeus harbour, blew apart the smaller ships anchored nearby and split the hulls of the larger ones, rained white-hot metal everywhere to start yet further chains of fires, and smashed doors and windows in Athens seven miles away.

The last two Balkan states were now feeling the weight of German ambition.

On the ground, two German armies were on the move. From Bulgaria, the German XX Corps of List's Twelfth Army drove south from the Arda region into Thrace, isolated the two fortresses at Nymphaea and Ekhinos and shelled them into submission, annihilated the Greek Evros Brigade, reached Xanthi and Alexandroupolis, then turned and probed towards the Metaxas Line over the River Nestos – all in one day. To their east the 2nd Panzer Division had first driven west into Yugoslavia at Strumica, then hooked south across the border, and by the morning of 9 April had reached Salonika *behind* the two spurs of the Metaxas Line, destroying the remnants of the desperately outnumbered rearguard and precipitating the collapse of the entire Greek Eastern Macedonian Army.

German command of the air meant that troops and equipment could be moved with ease around the theatre. Command of the sea was another matter, however, and in the face of determined opposition from the Royal Navy the projected invasion of Crete, Operation Merkur could only be carried out from the air. As in all German theatres of war, the primary transport aircraft was 'Tante Ju', the Ju 52.

German infantry weapons

German infantry weaponry in the early stages of the war differed little from those of other nations, with bolt-action rifles remaining the major arm of the infantryman. However, changes were to become evident after early combat experience, but mainly in terms of ease of manufacture. The real small arms revolution was not to come until later in the war.

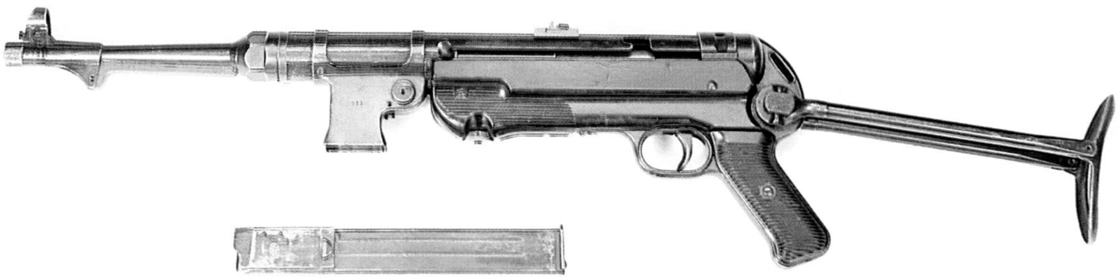

The MP38 was designed for rapid mass production, with simple metal stampings and die-cast parts making up much of the gun. Even so, the receiver and some other parts were machined and took up too much manufacturing capacity. The MP40 was outwardly very similar, and handled much the same but made use of simpler methods of manufacture.

The well known Parabellum Pistole 08, known far and wide as the Luger, was an excellent weapon but one that could not be manufactured in the numbers required by German rearmament.

Developed to replace the P.08, Walther's P.38 was (and still is) an excellent service pistol. Robust, hard-wearing and accurate, it remains in service to this day, although ironically it never completely replaced the Luger in Wehrmacht service.

Derived from the classic Mauser Gewehr 98, the Karabiner 98k was the German army's main service rifle of World War II, in production from 1934 to the very end of Nazi Germany, even though far more appropriate battle rifles had appeared in the meantime.

Members of the Waffen SS in their distinctive camouflage smocks wrestle a motor-cycle combination through an arid gorge.

The Junkers Ju 87B-2 may have been shot out of the skies over Britain, but once again proved its worth against limited air opposition.

The Sturmgeschutz III passing the foot of the Acropolis in Athens in 1941 is symbolic of the German victory in the Balkans, a victory that caused almost fatal weakening of British Empire forces in North Africa.

From Bulgaria, too, had come the first strike against Yugoslavia, by 9th Panzer Division advancing from Petrich, first to Stip and then to Skopje; then on 8 April Kleist's armoured corps drove along the valley of the Nisava to capture Nis, pressing on the next day up the Morava towards Belgrade. On the same day, LI Corps of Field Marshal von Weichs' Second Army struck south from Styria to take Maribor and drive on to Zagreb, one division veering west to Ljubljana; and on 11 April the 8th Panzer Division crossed the Drava River from Barcs and drove down towards Belgrade from the northwest.

Their advance was rapid, owing to the panic and confusion amid the Yugoslav ranks – underarmed and under-equipped, poorly supplied with transport – but also because of disaffection among them. Weichs' units were advancing into Croatia – and Croats had long rebelled aganst the Serbian majority which had for years ruled Yugoslavia with an arrogance towards minorities which rankled bitterly. The Croats were largely Roman Catholics, their leader Ante Pavelic a refugee in Rome; and now Croat Ustase formations threw down their arms and on several occasions welcomed the Germans, and even joined them in their advance.

By 10 April Zagreb was firmly in German hands, and two days later the mayor of Belgrade officially surrendered his city to an SS captain who had driven his company in ahead of the main column of the German XIV Corps. Early on 14 April the Yugoslav army capitulated, its chief of staff formally requesting an armistice, King Peter and his government flying out to Athens.

Amongst other immediate consequences was the opening of the Monastir Gap for German invasion of central Greece.

The invasion of Greece

The first German patrols had come through the gap as early as 8 April. General Maitland Wilson had brought up New Zealand machine-gunners to support the men of the 1st Armoured Brigade there, and to extend the defences of the Vevi Gap inside Yugoslavia through which the Germans evidently intended to penetrate.

General Wilson was in an unusual situation, even for a military commander working with allies who, though valorous, were unequipped for the war they were forced to fight, commanding Commonwealth troops in a foreign though friendly country. For in addition to the knowledge of his own weakness, he knew from day to day not only the enemy's order of battle, but also their local intentions; Ultra, the deciphering of the German Enigma code, was coming on stream.

As early as 7 April Wilson had known of German intentions regarding List's army in Thrace and Macedonia, and the following day he knew what formations would follow the first probes through the Monastir Gap to attack the British and Anzac forces under his command. And he knew perfectly well that they were neither strong enough on the ground nor well enough armed and equipped to withstand them; his duty therefore would not be to repel the invader, but to withdraw from an impossible situation as large a proportion of the forces under his command as was possible, in order that they might fight another day.

By 12 April he knew that the victors of Salonika were about to outflank him on the east, so he ordered the evacuation of the Vevi Gap and by the 14th those who had got away were joining New Zealanders along the line of the Aliakmon River and the passes around Mount Olympus. Here they held the flood of German armour and infantry for four days while lorries full of exhausted men, accompanied by trudg-

The invasion of Greece

The majority of Greek forces at the time of the German invasion were deployed against the Italians on the Albanian front; the balance, together with the Commonwealth troops sent from Egypt, held the Metaxas and Aliakmon defensive lines. The German advance through the Monastir Gap forced the surrender of the Greeks in the east and pushed the British back to Thermopylae and beyond to the evacuation at Kalamata.

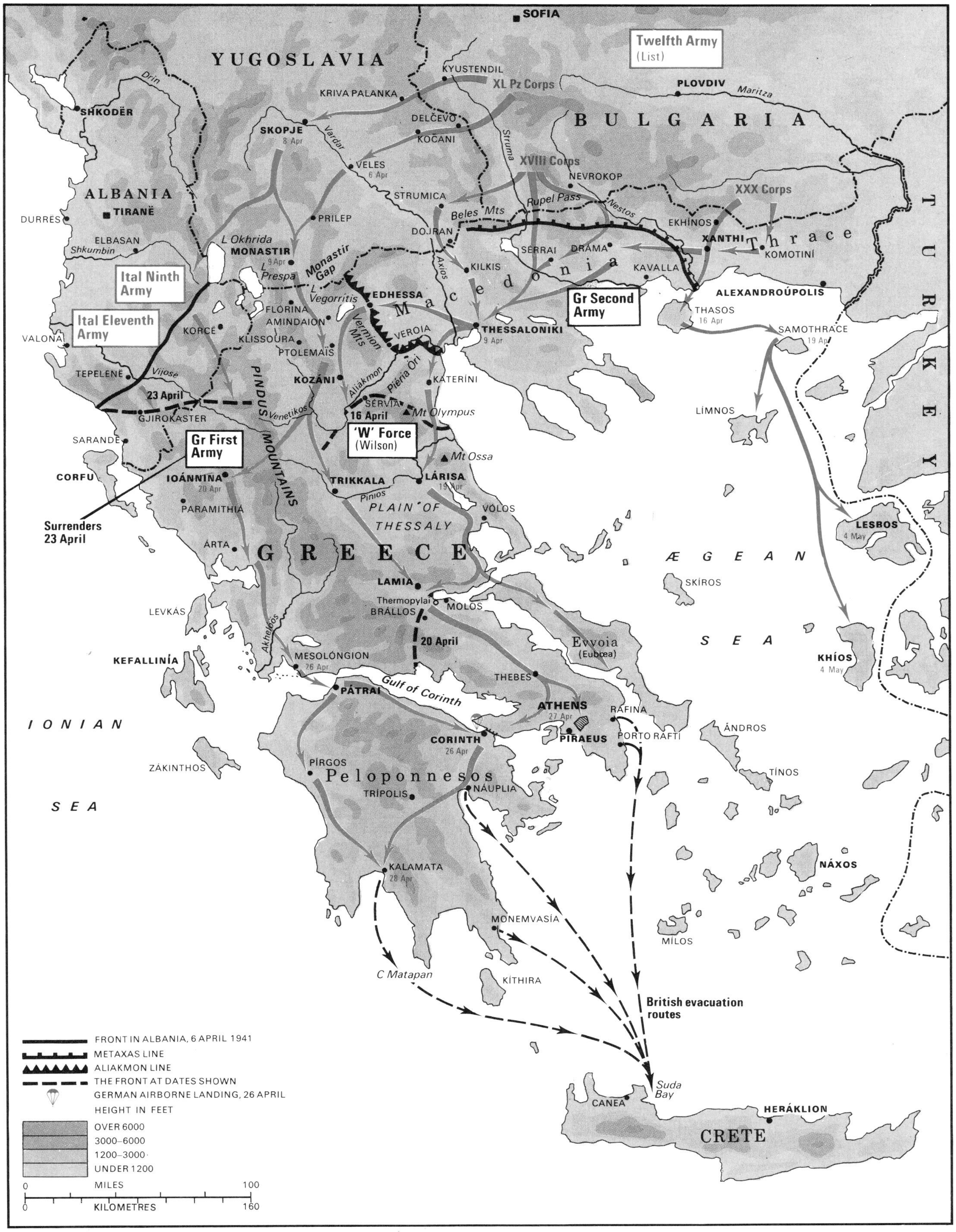

ing files of troops, farm carts full of bewildered Greek families and their belongings, broken-down trucks laden with Greek wounded, all shuffled through – harried by Stukas, machine-gunned by Bf 109s – until 18 April, when Wilson learned through Ultra that German armour was driving for Ioannina and the Thessaly region, thus outflanking him again, this time on the west.

On 19 April Australian, New Zealand and British troops were streaming back past Thermopylae, the rearguards digging their positions for yet another 'last stand'. Already Royal Navy ships were evacuating base personnel from Piraeus. But 50,000 men could not be lifted from one port, so the 4th Hussars were sent south to keep open the bridge over the Corinth Canal and also to guard the open beaches on the Peloponnesian coast at Navplion, Monemvasia and Kalamata, for a Dunkirk-style evacuation.

General Papagos advised his King on 21 April that the Greek army could fight no more; to General Wilson he said that the British promise to fight alongside the Greeks had been faithfully kept, but now the time had come for them to go. The rearguards at Thermopylae held on until 24 April, then slipped away; General Wilson left Athens on the morning of 26 April and crossed the Corinth Bridge, glad to know that he had been preceded by over 40,000 men. But just after he reached the Peloponnese, German paratroops dropped nearby to capture the bridge, and German gliders landed in support; the bridge was blown even as the Germans raced over it searching for the charges – dropping them and the bridge neatly into the canal below.

For the next two days, only the Luftwaffe could harass the evacuation, and this they did, sinking one transport and two destroyers on the night of 26 April. But the Royal Navy carried on: 21,000 men were lifted off five open beaches on the 27th, 5,000 New Zealanders the next night.

But shortly after dawn on 28 April, 5th Panzer Division and the SS 'Leibstandarte Adolf Hitler' crossed the Corinth Canal and drove south. The panzers headed for Kalamata, where after a vicious fight it became obvious that no ships would be able to get in to rescue the 7,000 Imperial troops still there, many of whom had fought in all the rearguards from the Vevi Gap southwards.

When the losses had all been counted it was reckoned that the Imperial Expeditionary Force had lost nearly 12,000 men including 900 dead and 1,200 wounded; 104 tanks, 400 guns, 1,800 machine-guns and 8,000 vehicles. The RAF had lost 72 aircraft shot down and 137 destroyed on the ground; the Royal Navy had lost two destroyers, and in addition some 25 other ships had been sunk.

Rightly or wrongly, the British had kept their promise.

Retreat to Crete

Almost all the men lifted off the Poloponnesian beaches were taken to Crete, thus releasing the ships for a quick return to pick up more of the hard-pressed British and Anzacs. One of the last to come out was

In spite of intensive German suppression of the air defences on Crete, the incoming Ju 52s, and DFS gliders, suffered a great deal. It was an extremely close run thing; with a little change of luck the battle could easily have gone the other way.

Major-General Bernard Freyberg, VC, DSO, and on 30 April, the day after he had disembarked at Suda Bay, he was told that he was to command the troops on the island and should prepare them to receive a German invasion in the near future. He protested at first, until he discovered that two of his own New Zealand brigades were on the island with him, instead of back in Egypt where he thought they had been taken.

In addition to these two brigades, Freyberg found that he had a Brigade Group of Australians plus an extra battalion of Australian infantry, one of their machine-gun battalions and a Field Regiment of Artillery; one brigade of British infantry and part of the 1st Armoured Brigade (with two light tanks) from Greece, and some 10,000 enthusiastic but almost untrained Greek recruits. There were also some 400,000 Cretans who in the event would prove valiant supporters, though unskilled. In addition there were 14,000 Italians who had been taken prisoner in Albania. They all had to be fed, and now the only source of everything the island needed to exist, let alone to fight off an invader, was Egypt, the only supply route across the Mediterranean from Alexandria.

There was no doubt in anyone's mind that Hitler would order the invasion of Crete. He must ensure first that its three airfields – at Maleme, Retimo and Heraklion – were not available to the RAF (whose bombers could attack from them the vital oilfields at Ploesti), nor its port facilities in Suda Bay to the Royal Navy (from which control of the Aegean and Ionian Seas could be exercised). In German hands, moreover, those airfields would be invaluable for attack on British positions in Egypt or Libya, and ideal for harassing British shipping in the southern Mediterranean. He could not leave Crete unattacked.

The island of Crete is about 160 miles long east to west, averaging 36 miles from north to south, and is dominated by a steep and narrow mountain range which falls sharply to the sea along the south coast, but which in the north leaves three areas of flatter, cultivable ground. The westernmost of these is around Cania and Suda Bay (and included the airfield at Maleme), the centre area is around Retimo and the most eastern area is around Heraklion, both with their own airfields.

These were the areas in which Freyberg concentrated his defence. The two brigades – 4th and 5th – of his own New Zealanders he posted around Maleme and supported them with three Greek battalions; in the Suda Bay area he left some 2,000 men of the original garrison force known as MNBDO – Mobile Naval Base Defence Organization – plus one British, one Australian and one Greek battalion; to the Retimo section he sent three Australian infantry and their machine-gun battalions, plus two Greek battalions; while to Heraklion he sent the two remaining battalions of the 14th British Brigade, one Australian battalion, a medium artillery regiment which had left its guns in Greece but still had rifles, and two more Greek battalions. By 7 May the defending force consisted of about 15,000 British, 7,750 New Zealanders, 6,500 Australians and 10,200 armed Greeks.

The German Fallschirmjäger, *or parachutists, were amongst the elite Wehrmacht (or strictly, Luftwaffe) formations. In spite of the victory on Crete, they were never again to be used en masse from the air.*

General Wavell, as conscious as Freyberg of the lack of heavy armament with which to fight off a powerful invasion, helped as much as circumstances allowed. From his depots he scraped 16 light tanks – old, battered and obsolescent – six Matildas, and nearly a hundred pieces of artillery, though these last were in such bad shape that Freyberg's artillery commander cannibalized many of them and in the end could supply only 49. One infantry battalion, the 2nd Leicesters, arrived on 16 May and was sent to Heraklion.

They trained, they dug – and they waited.

Every morning German aircraft arrived overhead, either on reconnaissance or on the 'morning hate', but at dawn on 20 May the note and emphasis was entirely different. German fighters wove along the north coastal strip between Maleme and Retimo, strafing the olive groves and shooting up anything that moved, in such numbers that to one startled observer there seemed to be a Bf 109 to every human target.

Then, as men ducked into their trenches and the wiser ones hurriedly gobbled their breakfasts and piled all the ammunition they could get hold of into convenient heaps, a new note sounded – a prolonged buzz, like that of an approaching swarm of angry bees. As it rose in a crescendo, the New Zealanders around Maleme saw a huge fleet of great transport planes come in towards them across the sea, so many of them that it seemed impossible that they should not crash into each other. As they arrived overhead, the sky blossomed with a thousand parachutes dangling men and containers, and the battle for Crete had begun.

Invasion of Crete

Operation Merkur (Mercury) called for airborne landings at four places along the north coast of Crete, but owing to shortage of transport planes was to be launched in two waves. Thirty-six gliders would land first, to destroy anti-aircraft guns, attack the camp to the south of Maleme airfield and capture Tavronitis Bridge; then three battalions of the XI Air Corps Assault Regiment would drop close by, capture the airfield and hold it until reinforced by units from the 5th Mountain Division flown in by heavy Ju 52 transports. They would then drive east and link up with men of the 3rd Paratroop Regiment who had been dropped at the same time, some 25 miles away around Galatas and Canea, the capital of the island. Together the combined force would then capture all the ground necessary to control Suda Bay.

While this was going on, the transport aircraft would have returned to Greece and taken aboard the 1st and 2nd Paratroop Regiments with all their engineer and artillery support, for the second wave. This would be delivered in the afternoon, 2nd Regt going to Retimo, 1st to Heraklion. By this time the first wave of seaborne support would be at sea – 25 shallow-draught motor cutters escorted by Italian MTBs, carrying two more battalions from the 5th Mountain Division with their vehicles, support weapons and anti-aircraft guns, plus those men of the paratroop regiments for whom there had been no room in the aircraft. They should arrive off Maleme during the evening.

A second wave of seaborne reinforcements would make the trip in 38 cutters on the following day, in

Operation Merkur: the Battle for Crete

The airborne assault on Crete consisted in its initial stage of a three-pronged parachute, glider assault and airborne landing. The bitter fighting at Malème and Canea, Retimo and Heraklion came as a surprise, and only at great cost was a foothold established at Malème. German losses of more than 4000 killed and missing appalled Hitler, and future large-scale parachute actions were looked on with some disfavour.

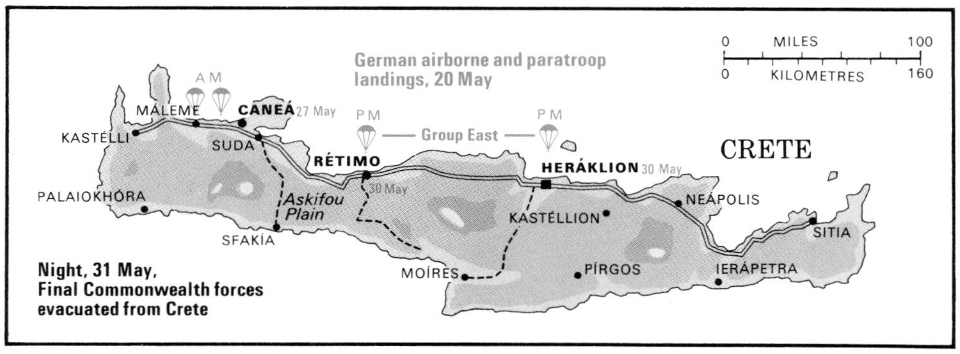

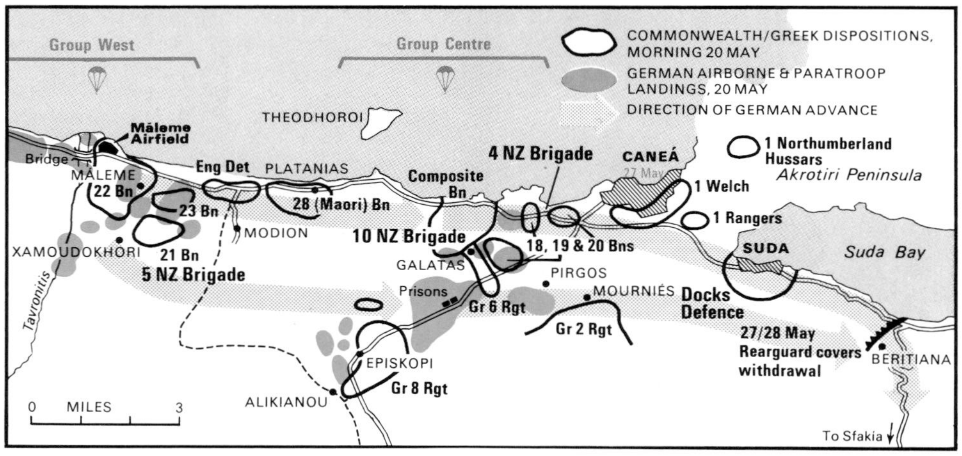

Chronology of War: 1941

April 7
General O'Connor, the commander of the British Desert Force, and General Neame captured in Jebel Akhdar. Rommel captures Derna

April 9
In North Africa Rommel takes Bardia. In Greece German armour enters Salonika

April 10
Australian 9th Division withdraws into Tobruk; decision to accept siege there. Germans reach Monastir and capture Zagreb in Yugoslavia. The 'Benson' class destroyer, USS Niblack is the first US Navy vessel to depth-charge a U-boat after a Dutch freighter is sunk off Iceland

April 11
Blitz on Coventry. Italian and Bulgarian units invade Yugoslavia

April 12
Belgrade occupied by Germans

April 13
Rommel encircles Tobruk. Malta heavily bombed

April 14
Australians beat off German attack on Tobruk. Germans through Kleisoura Pass in Greece

April 16
London's St Paul's Cathedral damaged in bombing

April 17
Yugoslav army capitulates. Largest RAF raid to date on Berlin; 118 bombers including the new Short Stirling four-engine heavy

April 20
Greek army in Epirus surrenders to SS Div Leibstandarte Adolf Hitler

April 22
Battle of Thermopylae. First evacuation of British Imperial Forces begins. Greek army in Thessaloniki capitulates

April 23
Greek King and ministers fly to Crete

April 24
German breakthrough at Thermopylae

April 25
Germans invade Lemnos and in North Africa capture Halfaya Pass. British retreat to Mersa Matruh

April 26
German paratroops capture Corinth

The British Mediterranean fleet

The British fleet in the Mediterranean was ranged against a substantially larger enemy navy, equipped with more modern warships fighting on its home territory and often with air superiority: a daunting prospect indeed.

HMS Eagle

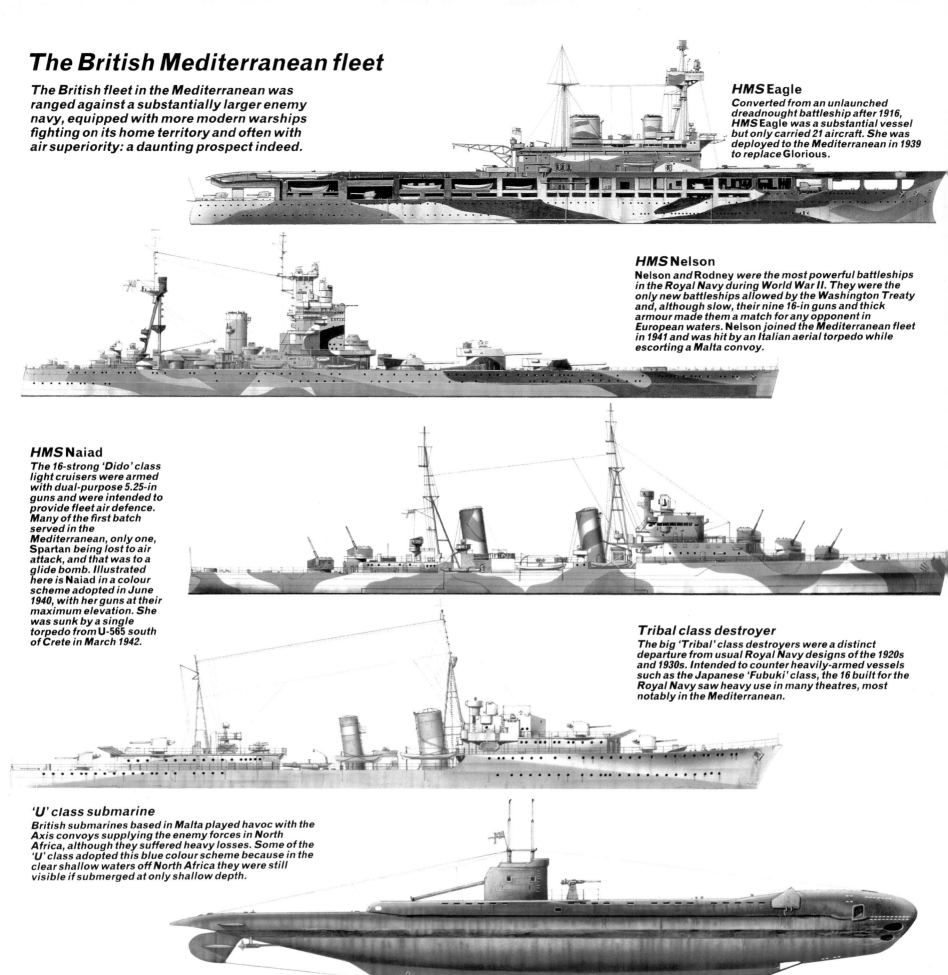

Converted from an unlaunched dreadnought battleship after 1916, HMS **Eagle** ***was a substantial vessel but only carried 21 aircraft. She was deployed to the Mediterranean in 1939 to replace*** **Glorious.**

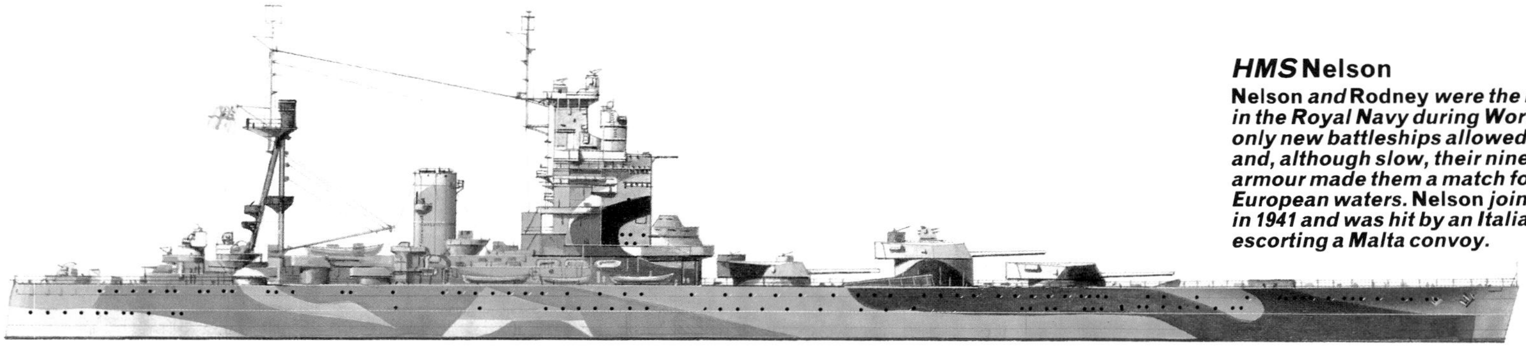

HMS Nelson

Nelson ***and*** **Rodney** ***were the most powerful battleships in the Royal Navy during World War II. They were the only new battleships allowed by the Washington Treaty and, although slow, their nine 16-in guns and thick armour made them a match for any opponent in European waters.*** **Nelson** ***joined the Mediterranean fleet in 1941 and was hit by an Italian aerial torpedo while escorting a Malta convoy.***

HMS Naiad

The 16-strong 'Dido' class light cruisers were armed with dual-purpose 5.25-in guns and were intended to provide fleet air defence. Many of the first batch served in the Mediterranean, only one, **Spartan** ***being lost to air attack, and that was to a glide bomb. Illustrated here is*** **Naiad** ***in a colour scheme adopted in June 1940, with her guns at their maximum elevation. She was sunk by a single torpedo from*** **U-565** ***south of Crete in March 1942.***

Tribal class destroyer

The big 'Tribal' class destroyers were a distinct departure from usual Royal Navy designs of the 1920s and 1930s. Intended to counter heavily-armed vessels such as the Japanese 'Fubuki' class, the 16 built for the Royal Navy saw heavy use in many theatres, most notably in the Mediterranean.

'U' class submarine

British submarines based in Malta played havoc with the Axis convoys supplying the enemy forces in North Africa, although they suffered heavy losses. Some of the 'U' class adopted this blue colour scheme because in the clear shallow waters off North Africa they were still visible if submerged at only shallow depth.

support of the 1st Paratroop Regiment at Heraklion. And on the especial insistence of Hitler, once Suda Bay was firmly in German hands, as many panzers as could be loaded into the available shipping would be hurried across.

Altogether the plan allowed for the landing of 22,750 men on Crete – 750 by glider, 10,000 by parachute, 5,000 in air transport, 7,000 by sea. They would be protected by 280 bombers, 150 dive-bombers and 180 fighters, and their progress checked by 40 reconnaissance planes; over 1,200 aircraft would be engaged.

As is inevitable on such occasions fortunes were mixed, but at no stage in the planning had anyone envisaged the fire which would come up to greet the gliders and parachutists as they came in. The glider-borne troops at Maleme and the 3rd Assault Battalion which had dropped just east of the airfield found themselves the targets of New Zealand farmers who had shot for the pot since childhood and the paratroops were almost totally wiped out before they hit the ground. Of the 3rd Paratroop Regiment, which landed amid the Australians around Galatas, only those dropped into 'Prison Valley' to the south of Galatas managed to collect together in sufficient numbers to form an effective unit, all the others being decimated in the air and pinned down on the ground.

As for the paratroops dropped at Retimo and Heraklion, the fire which came up to meet them was not only just as devastating as that around Maleme, it had not been even momentarily checked by the element of surprise; by nightfall those men of 1st and 2nd Paratroop Regiments who were still alive were counting the costs of the operation and beginning to accept that they were most likely the victims of Germany's first military defeat since 1918.

By nightfall of 20 May, then, to the commander, General Student, in his headquarters at Athens, the situation of the German airborne forces on Crete looked dangerous – if not catastrophic; but he had been a soldier for most of his adult life and learned long since that nothing is ever so good – or so bad – as it first looks. Some 8,000 of his men had been landed and although signals from most areas were not encouraging, there were some significant gains. Tavronitis Bridge had been captured by Major Braun's men, though Braun himself had been killed; Colonel Heidrich had nearly 1,000 fit men in 'Prison Valley' and despite being the centre of a positive cauldron of Australian fire would probably be able to break out in due course.

Best of all, a large number of the parachutists of the Assault Regiment had been dropped by mistake to the west of Maleme, and although this had meant that they had not been at hand to support the glider-borne troops and the unfortunate 3rd Assault Battalion, they had at least been out of range of New Zealand riflemen and had thus been able to coalesce and organize themselves. They had moreover, advanced and made contact with the men at Tavronitis Bridge,

The old battleship HMS* Barham*, veteran of the Battle of Jutland, joined the Mediterranean Fleet in 1941. Unlike* Warspite*,* Queen Elizabeth *and* Valiant *(and to a lesser extent* Malaya*) she was not given a second modernization in the 1930s, and it is perhaps significant that she was the only one of the five to be lost (in November 1941).

After its poor showing when faced with modern fighter opposition in the Battle of Britain, the Messerschmitt Bf 110 was switched to other tasks and theatres, where less capable opposition and powerful armament made it suitable for long-range missions. The type was used extensively over the Mediterranean.

fought off a New Zealand attempt to recapture it, and were now in position to mount an attack on Point 107, which if succesful would give them a dominating position above Maleme airfield.

In the meantime, Student still had at his disposal a reserve of some 600 parachutists and almost the whole of 5th Mountain Division. The latter were of course intended for Heraklion but were not yet committed; he would hold them back until he could best judge where they would be of most use. At least the radios of the Assault Regiment HQ were now working well, and by dawn he should have a clear picture of where all his men at Maleme were and what opposition they faced.

The New Zealanders' radios were not working at all well. In addition all telephone lines had been cut by bombing, and runners kept failing to get through or, having got through, failing to return. To Lieutenant-Colonel Andrew, VC, DSO, commanding 22nd New Zealand Battalion on and around Point 107, his position that night looked obscure and dangerous. He was out of touch with two of his companies, had grave doubts about another and could get only the weakest of signals from HQ. Moreover, his attempt to recapture Tavronitis Bridge had been beaten off, and he had no doubt that the German forces there were being reinforced and that shortly after dawn his decimated battalion would be attacked in considerable strength. He must withdraw to his reserve positions and cover his flanks by contact with 21st and 23rd Battalions.

He was wrong in his belief that two of his companies had been destroyed, but right in his predictions of the morning assault. It opened with attacks both from the area of the bridge and from the village of Vlakheronitissa, the paratroops overrunning the 'lost' companies of 22nd Battalion and, greatly to their astonishment, finding Point 107 virtually unprotected. Well before noon Student knew that Maleme airfield was within his grasp and, without waiting for complete victory, sent in the remaining parachutists under command of the tough old World War I veteran, Colonel Ramcke, followed by the first battalion of mountain infantry. Their orders were simple. 'Roll up Crete from the west!'

Battle for Maleme

When the first Ju 52s arrived, Maleme airfield was still the scene of bitter fighting, still under a hail of rifle and machine-gun fire and the fire of the nine heterogeneous pieces of artillery which had been allocated to the New Zealanders. But the Ju 52s landed, and during the late morning and early afternoon others came on in despite the inferno of blazing planes and exploding shells which greeted them. Transport planes were piled up everywhere, shot to pieces and blazing fiercely – one had even landed on top of the wreck of another – but still the pilots brought them in, still the mountain infantry poured from the aircraft, manhandled out their guns, mortars and heavy machine-guns and threw them into action. And as the hours passed, the New Zealander's fire slackened; the paratroops – now all under Ramcke's direction – fought their way implacably along the coast towards Galatas and their comrades still pinned down there by the Australians.

The turning point

Few people realized it at the time, but these few but furious hours at Maleme on the afternoon of 21 May sealed the fate of the resistance on Crete. Like the fall of a grain of sand which starts a landslide, the withdrawal of 22nd New Zealand Battalion from Point 107 eventually gave Crete to the Germans, for from then on General Student's forces could be regularly supplied and augmented while General Freyberg's were inexorably whittled way. A commando battalion did manage to land at Suda Bay before the whole peninsula fell under German control, but that was on 24 May, and thereafter the German pressure built up all the time in the area between Maleme and Armenoi; and still the Junkers flew into Maleme.

On 26 May General Freyberg ordered a withdrawal by all his forces over the mountains to the south coast and asked General Wavell to begin organization of an evacuation from the beaches at the village of Sfakia. On 28 May the last rearguard action in the plains was fought, the long trudge over the White Mountains in progress; Colonel Robert Laycock's commandos formed a perimeter across the ridges and ravines above Sfakia through which the exhausted remnants of Freyberg's command made their painful way.

The Royal Navy, with Narvik, Dunkirk and Greece behind them, were only too accustomed to the part in the drama which now befell them. They began taking troops off the beachhead on 27 May and by the 31st it was evident that the operation must end. Altogether, they lifted off some 16,500 men and took them back to Alexandria, at a cost to themselves of three cruisers and six destroyers sunk, and about 2,000 sailors killed or taken prisoner. Left behind on Crete were 13,500 Allied prisoners (of whom 2,250 were wounded), the bodies of 1,750 more (of whom 1,283 were Anzacs), and an unknown number of assorted Greek, British and Anzac soldiers who were to fight guerrilla campaigns in the mountains for weeks, months and in some cases for years.

The Royal Navy had gained extensive experience of fighting retreats by the time it became necessary to evacuate Crete. Such operations are costly; this is the wreck of the cruiser HMS* York *in Suda bay.

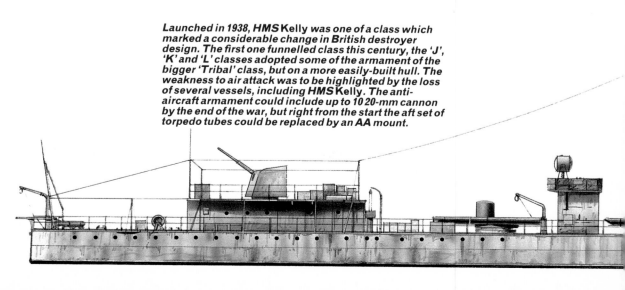

Launched in 1938, HMS* Kelly *was one of a class which marked a considerable change in British destroyer design. The first one funnelled class this century, the 'J', 'K' and 'L' classes adopted some of the armament of the bigger 'Tribal' class, but on a more easily-built hull. The weakness to air attack was to be highlighted by the loss of several vessels, including HMS* Kelly*. The anti-aircraft armament could include up to 10 20-mm cannon by the end of the war, but right from the start the aft set of torpedo tubes could be replaced by an AA mount.

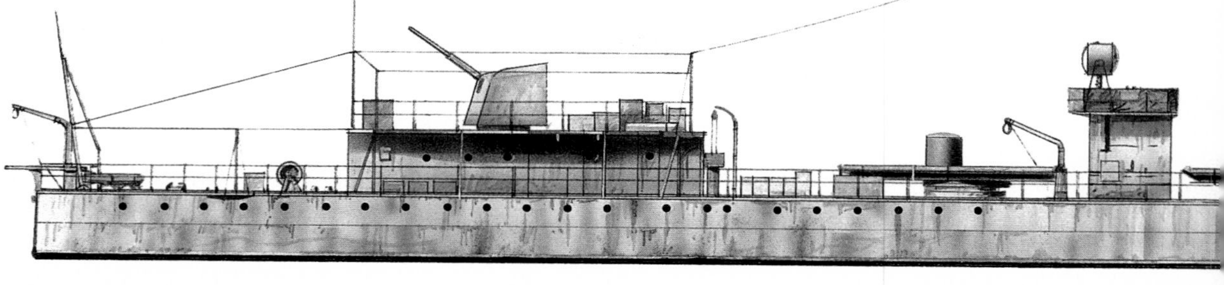

Kelly's last voyage

Spring 1941 found a newly worked-up *Kelly* and her flotilla at Plymouth. Life was eternally busy but without major event until, in April, they were ordered to Malta. Existence in the Mediterranean was, at that time, precarious: the Greek campaign had collapsed and, at considerable cost, the navy was evacuating 50,000 troops to Crete. With the Sicilian-based Luftwaffe reducing Malta slowly to dust and enemy land forces tightening their grip on the significant islands in the Aegean, the future of both Crete and Malta was looking less than bright.

Smaller naval units were still working out of Valletta, and the 5th Destroyer Flotilla formed part of the Malta striking force, Force K, that nightly contested enemy efforts at conveying supplies from Italy to their armies in North Africa. Returning from one of these sweeps on 2 May, the *Kelly* saw her sister destroyer HMS *Jersey* mined at the entrance to the Grand Harbour; she was brought in, but was in effect a total loss.

From the middle of May it was apparent that Crete's time had come. The Royal Navy patrolled in sufficient force to deter a landing by sea, but with superiority in every other department the enemy chose to come by air. Their paratroops fought fanatically with nowhere to retreat, but every available warship was at sea to prevent reinforcements arriving. On consecutive nights 5th Destroyer Flotilla ships slaughtered virtually helpless convoys of caiques, but by day the Luftwaffe was supreme. On 21 May HMS *Juno* disappeared within two minutes of taking a heavy bomb. Next day it was the turn of HMS *Greyhound*, together with the cruisers HMS *Fiji* and HMS *Gloucester*, which had fought until their AA ammunition was exhausted.

On the same grim day *Kelly* arrived from Malta, accompanied by HMS *Kashmir*, HMS *Kelvin*, HMS *Kipling* and HMS *Jackal*. Together with *Kashmir* and *Kipling*, she was directed to bombard Maleme airfield after dark. Though the last-named fell out as a result of mechanical trouble, the operation began well with the interception and destruction of a pair of heavily-loaded caiques. Unfortunately the short, late-spring night was nearly spent by the time the British ships' mission was done.

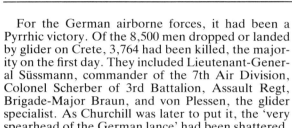

With the main strength of the fleet recalled earlier to Alexandria, they were on their own. Dawn found them barely clear of the island but an early high-level bombing was easily evaded. This attack was, however, closely followed-up by the dreaded dive-bombers: 24 Ju 87s of I Stuka-geschwader, operating from airfields only minutes away in the Peloponnese, approached from astern. Both ships manoeuvred violently, with 2-pdrs, 12.7-mm (0.5-in) machine-guns, 20-mm cannon and even the 4.7-in guns on opportunity throwing everything at an enemy who attacked from all quarters. Within minutes *Kashmir* was broken-backed, her smoke-shrouded hulk barely losing its way before it was *Kelly*'s turn. Turning at full speed, she was heeling when squarely hit aft of amidships. Such was the impact she did not recover, rolling over onto her beam ends and then capsizing completely to port, hanging thus for a long 30 minutes with many of her crew trapped inside before sliding under in 1,500 fathoms.

Fortunately, *Kipling* had overcome her mechanical problems and was close enough to pick up a total of 279 survivors. To the discredit of the enemy, she was heavily bombed and strafed throughout, several men being killed, Still under attack, she withdrew and successfully reached Alexandria the next day.

The loss of the ships emphasized the varying fortunes of the war at sea, for they had been sunk south of Gavdo Island in the same spot that had seen, less than two months earlier, the opening skirmish of the Battle of Cape Matapan. The very next day, 24 May, saw the fleet stunned by the news of the loss of HMS *Hood*, far from the warmth of the Mediterranean she knew so well.

HMS* Kelly*, passing a message by line, clearly shows the limited field of fire forward for the quad pom-pom that was the main anti-aircraft weapon of the class – a fatal flaw facing the Mediterranean air threat.

The 5th Flotilla at sea, with HMS* Kashmir *and* Kelly *in view (*Kelly*, the flotilla leader having the funnel stripe). Both were to be lost on 24 May during the evacuation of Crete.

For the German airborne forces, it had been a Pyrrhic victory. Of the 8,500 men dropped or landed by glider on Crete, 3,764 had been killed, the majority on the first day. They included Lieutenant-General Süssmann, commander of the 7th Air Division, Colonel Scherber of 3rd Battalion, Assault Regt, Brigade-Major Braun, and von Plessen, the glider specialist. As Churchill was later to put it, the 'very spearhead of the German lance' had been shattered.

As for the price in aircraft, this had been so high that Hitler came to a very similar conclusion to that of the British Prime Minister. Some days later he decorated the more outstanding of the officers who had fought in Crete, then entertained them to lunch. Over coffee, he turned to Student and said: 'Of course, you know, General, that we shall never do another airborne operation. Crete proved that the days of parachute troops are over.'

Hitler was wrong about that – as Allied forces were to prove in later months – and indeed German paratroops were to go into action in Italy, the Dodecanese and during the Ardennes Offensive of Christmas 1944; but never again in such numbers as had been employed at Crete.

They may have captured the island in May 1941. But it proved to be 'the grave of the German paratroops'.

Following the serious losses in the Mediterranean the Royal Navy was reinforced by the presence of HMS* Queen Elizabeth*. Considerably more capable than the ill-fated HMS* Barham*, especially in terms of anti-aircraft armament, HMS* Queen Elizabeth *had a career stretching from Gallipoli to the East Indies in 1945.

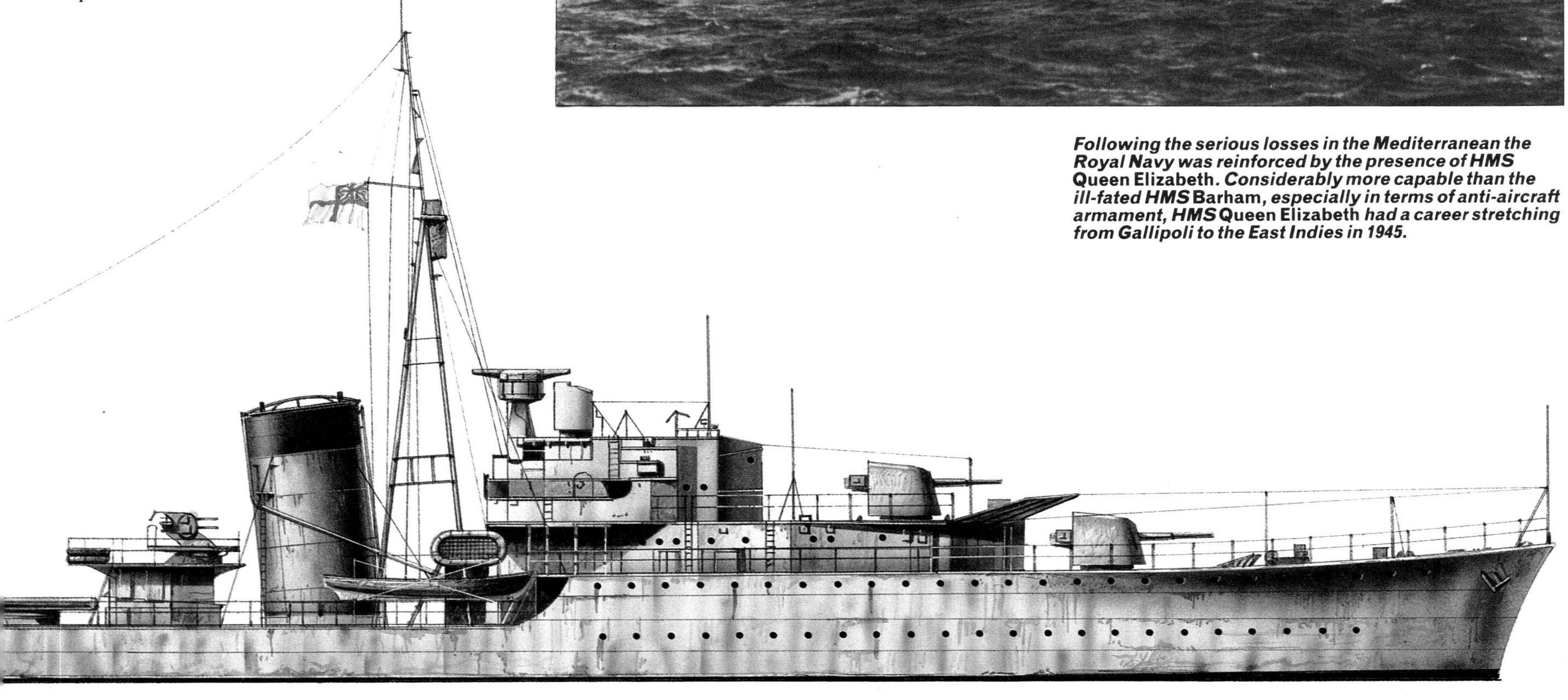

Chapter 6

Enter Rommel

Wavell's campaigns against the Italians in North and East Africa had been marvellously successful – so successful that Hitler had to step in to give aid to his Axis partner. Not the least of that help was a general called Rommel.

The first units of the Afrika Korps to reach North Africa were soon to prove more than the simple blocking force that the Führer had intended. Under the command of Major-General Erwin Rommel, they were to prove extraordinarily effective.

Greece had not been the only theatre in which Hitler had felt he must take steps to avoid too humiliating a reverse for his fellow dictator. He had watched with caustic amusement Il Duce's attempts to get the Italian armies on the move in Libya and Egypt, but was as disappointed as Mussolini himself at the paltry advance which followed such apparently gigantic labour. O'Connor's 'raid' riveted his attention from the moment the first news reached him, and from then on his alarm grew as the arrows on the maps indicated the rout which was attending the Italian Tenth Army. By the time the arrows had reached Tobruk he had decided to take action; by the time they had reached Benghazi his orders had been issued and by 12 February 1941 the first contingent of German support had reached Tripoli. It was not very large, in fact it consisted of one general and two staff officers, but it was to prove highly significant.

Arrival of the Desert Fox

Major-General Erwin Johannes Eugen Rommel flew into Castel Benito airfield in the morning and by the evening had already given those who met him an exhibition of the extraordinary mental and physical energy which was to be the hallmark of his command. He had received the details of his new command from the Führer himself on the afternoon of 6 February, and later they had been confirmed by Field Marshal von Brauchitsch, commander-in-chief of the German army; he was to co-operate with the Italian forces in Libya and use the German contingent consisting of the 5th Light Division and the 15th Panzer Division, when they arrived, to help form a *Sperrverband* – a blocking force – along a line running south from the area of Buerat. There the British were to be halted – and perhaps in due course plans might be laid and orders issued to him for their further discomfiture and possible repulse; but he was to await receipt of such orders before even contemplating more offensive action.

But it was not in General Rommel's nature to hold defensive positions or even to fight defensive battles, especially when he had reason to believe that the enemy forces ranged against him were neither aggressively intentioned nor particularly well organized for their own protection. And of these characteristics he became more and more convinced.

Personal reconnaissance persuaded him that the country beyond Buerat at least as far as Nofilia and perhaps El Agheila was unoccupied by British forces, and could be efficiently defended even by Italian troops if they were properly posted and supervised. Moreover, behind them was a level plain in which he could marshal his panzer division when it arrived. Before then he could bully his immediate Italian superior, General Italo Gariboldi (Graziani had, not unexpectedly, resigned) into releasing some Italian armour into the area so that at least he could evaluate their potential use in his future plans.

These plans were to throw the British forces in Cyrenaica back into Egypt and possibly further, an ambition which was encouraged by intelligence reports on the departure of both the 6th Australian Division and the 7th Armoured Division from the Jebel Akhdar area – the first to Greece and the second to Cairo – and their replacement by formations which were apparently uncoordinated and certainly inexperienced. They also appeared to be unsoundly disposed.

German intelligence had not been in error in its assessment of the condition and organization of the British forces now occupying the area between the Gulf of Sirte and Tobruk. One of the reasons for their sorry state was that General Wavell's attention had for the time being been directed towards other theatres. It was not only affairs in Greece and Yugoslavia which were looming large in Wavell's mind; he was also deeply concerned in developments to the south east where the reduction of the Italian Empire in Eritrea and Abyssinia was proceeding apace. This was being carried out in the northern areas by the 4th and 5th Indian Divisions, and in the south by South African troops assisted by brigades from both East Africa and the Gold Coast.

But by mid-March, matters seemed to be progressing well down there, so Wavell had gone to see how things stood in Benghazi. He was appalled by what he found. The obvious person to have left in command there had been General O'Connor, but unfortunately he had been in bad health by the end of Operation Compass and been forced to spend some time in hospital. In his place Wavell had sent Lieutenant-General Philip Neame, VC, of whom Wavell knew nothing except that he was a friend of O'Connor's – and his possession of a Victoria Cross obviously indicated at least an abundance of courage.

But Neame was not, Wavell quickly concluded, possessed of great tactical imagination – though not even O'Connor could have built an impregnable defence in the area with the forces the unfortunate Neame had at his disposal. In place of the 7th Armoured Division – and to form the core of the defence – Neame had cruiser tanks of the 2nd Armoured Division (of which there was only one brigade, since the other had been sent to Greece) and of those 52, half were already in the workshops and the rest liable to break down as both their track and engine mileages had been grossly exceeded. So far as infantry were concerned, one single brigade of Australians was all that was available for the defence of Benghazi, and Neame had placed them in the middle of the plain between Benghazi and El Agheila where they could be outflanked on both sides.

Ordering their immediate removal to better defensive positions above Benghazi, Wavell returned to Cairo to think matters over and to arrange for more troops and supplies to be moved up to Cyrenaica. By 23 March having absorbed the the latest reports supplied by his chief intelligence officer, helped again by Ultra, he had made the best rearrangement possible. The new German commander, Rommel, was undoubtedly an energetic and forceful character and he had to be carefully watched. He would probably mount an attack as soon as possible, but before he could move he must build supply dumps in the forward areas, and even for the limited forces now at his disposal (5th Light Division had now arrived) this would take at least 30 days. According to Ultra, a panzer division would follow but could not possibly be deployed for action until mid-May. Surely Rommel would wait for it. So Neame probably had until June to organize all the forces Wavell could spare for him, and perhaps by that time some of the Indian or South African formations down in Abyssinia would be free to come north.

Time, for the moment, appeared to be on the British side; however imaginative, aggressive or daring the new enemy commander might be, he could not ignore the iron laws of logistics.

But Wavell did not yet know Rommel.

The attack

Rommel had flown to Berlin on 19 March, spent two days explaining his intentions to Hitler and then to Brauchitsch and Halder, and from all of them received discouragement ranging from scepticism about his tactical capability to flat prohibition of his plans. Hitler was kind but cautious, Halder unequivocally hostile – possibly because Rommel had once called him a bloody fool and asked what he had ever done but sit on his backside on an office stool.

How Rommel occupied his thoughts on the journey back to Tripoli is unknown, but once there he proceeded to disobey his orders with a diligence which compels respect. The day after he arrived back (23 March), he launched all forward units of the 5th Light Division against the fort and landing-ground at El Agheila, and a week later, with the somewhat specious excuse that there was a better water supply there, had driven them 16 miles further on to Mersa el Brega – and down through the vital defile there.

There had been no sign of British armour (held back on the ground that they must await clear indication of the enemy intentions) and as air reconnaissance reported an apparently empty space in front reaching east for at least 25 miles, Rommel ordered 5th Light to plunge on forward towards Agedabia. He set up his headquarters there on 3 April, and then proceeded to disregard all established principles of warfare by deliberately splitting the already tenuous forces at his disposal into three.

A mixed German and Italian force under Graf von Schwerin he sent off eastwards in a swing even wider than that taken by 7th Armoured Division two months before, but in the opposite direction, through

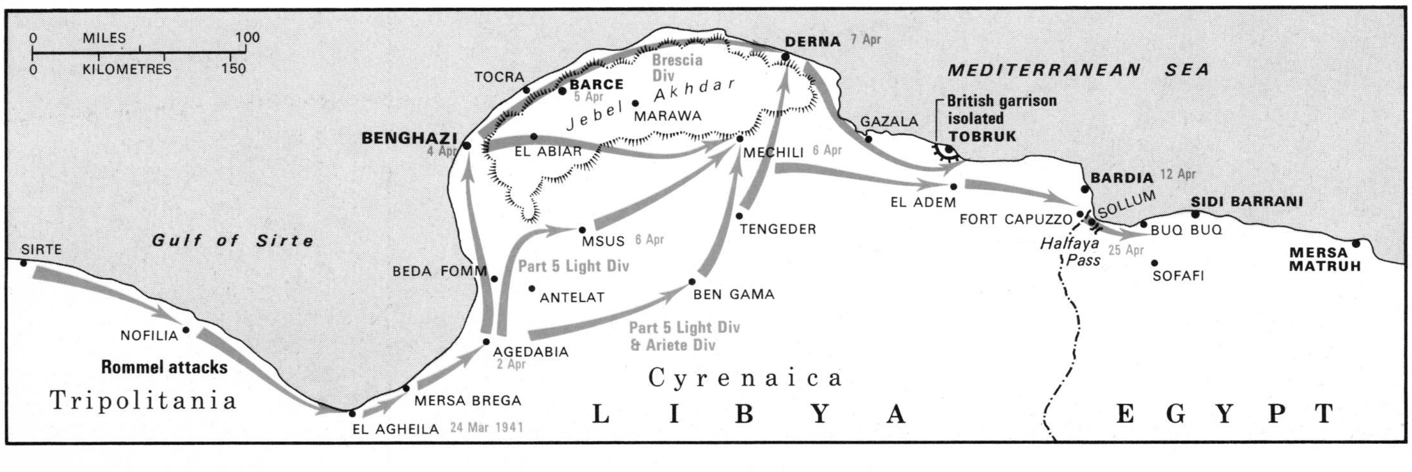

Rommel's first offensive

Commonwealth forces in North Africa were sadly depleted by February 1941, calls to the Balkans and replacement of battle-weary units leaving an inadequate force in control of Cyrenaica. Rommel had only one of his two Panzer divisions when he decided, on examining the situation on his arrival, to take advantage of Wavell's weakness and to attack. His aim was to recover Cyrenaica, and to drive into Egypt. In a lightning campaign, his forces forced the British back from the ground taken from the Italians.

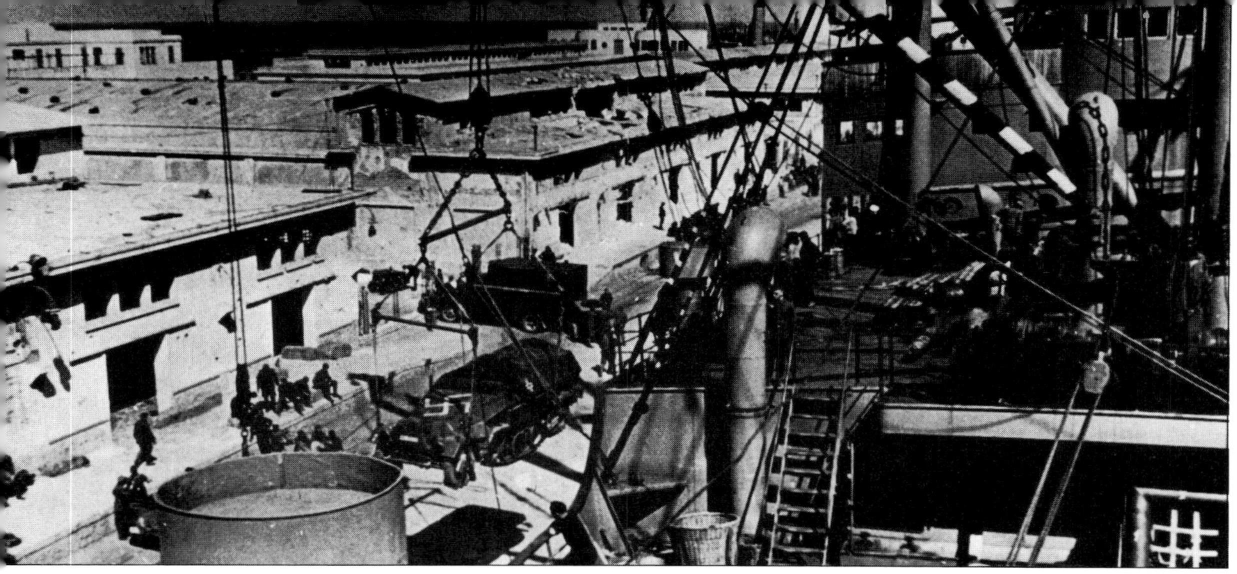

Above: German equipment is unloaded at Tripoli at the end of March. In spite of the fact that his 5th Light Division would not be fully equipped until mid-April, Rommel commenced his attack on 24 March.

Left: A patrol of the Long Range Desert Group (LRDG) deep in the desert. From the early stages of the war, such patrols were used to scout behind enemy lines.

Right: Erwin Rommel was a gifted commander, inspiring to his men and respected by his opponents.

Giof el Matar and up through Tengeder towards Mechili; the bulk of 5th Light he directed to advance through Antelat and Msus. He himself accompanied the armoured cars and light vehicles of 3rd Reconnaissance to the north, towards Suluch and Ghemines; then, having heard rumours that the British were evacuating Benghazi, he ordered them to drive straight for the port, where they were welcomed with such wild enthusiasm by the inhabitants that it reminded one American observer of the jubilation with which the Australians had been received. History has given the Libyan peoples a keen sense of survival.

By 7 April Rommel had captured Derna and isolated Mechili, and his reconnaissance units were probing eastwards south of Tobruk. An even more significant success had been granted him by an indulgent Fortune, though he was not yet fully aware of it. As his columns probed aggressively along every road, path or track which led in the right direction, they isolated more and more of the bewildered British formations (whose radios were once again proving ineffective) and in that *danse macabre* of military reverse – changes of command, role and deployment planned by commanders and staffs frantic to plug

Right: The result of one of the early meetings between the Afrika Korps and the British. The German philosophy of avoiding tank versus tank actions, and luring enemy armour into carefully prepared anti-tank positions (equipped with the fearsome 8.8-cm Flak gun) was to lead to the loss of many tanks such as this Valentine.

Below: The Royal Navy had established a dominant presence in the Mediterranean with vessels such as HMS Renown (although at one stage, Axis air power almost swayed the balance in the central region), and Rommel's supplies of armour and precious fuel often ended up on the bottom of the sea.

gaps', one of them under Lieutenant-Colonel Ponath, driving up during the night from Mechili at Derna, stopped a British staff car on one of the minor tracks. At the wheel was Lieutenant-General Philip Neame, giving his driver a rest; in the back and fast asleep was Lieutenant-General Sir Richard O'Connor, newly knighted, despatched by Wavell from hospital with orders to stem the disaster which was negating all the triumphs he had so recently won. It was probably the most valuable car-load of booty to fall to the Afrika Korps during its entire existence.

Mechili fell to Rommel's troops on the morning of 8 April. By the 9th his reconnaissance units had arrived in Bardia with the Egyptian frontier, Halfaya Pass and Sollum just a few miles on; those British motorized formations not actually surrounded or on the point of surrender, were scurrying past them towards the bases from which Operation Compass had been launched four months before.

But behind lay Tobruk – now the haven into which retreated the Australian infantry who had been at Benghazi. They were reinforced in Tobruk first by a trickle, then by a flood of platoons, sections, half-companies, isolated and random groups of British and Indian soldiers – exhausted, bewildered, parched with thirst, but still resolute and often very angry. It did not take long for the Australian commander, Major-General Leslie Morshead, to integrate them with his Australians and institute the first stages of what later became an epic siege.

Rommel's first attack on Tobruk – little more than an attempt to 'bounce' the defenders out – took place on 10 April, but it stalled in a sandstorm and ran into unexpectedly heavy and accurate artillery fire. So Rommel withdrew his forces, deployed them in greater strength and launched a joint German-Italian attack on 16 April. But by now Morshead and his mixed garrison, ably assisted by Brigadier John Harding, had manned the line of Italian defence positions along the Tobruk perimeter, cleared them out and installed every piece of artillery they could find – from their own 25-pounders to Italian 37-mm and 75-mm anti-tank and field guns. They thus constructed so strong a defence system that after 48 hours the Italian armour had been reduced from over 100 tanks to less than 10, and Rommel's panzers to less than 20, all in need of maintenance and new tracks.

In the circumstances, Rommel decided he could do nothing more about Tobruk until reinforced by both men and tanks, preferably German. In the meantime he would turn his attention to clearing up the rest of the front.

British counter-attack

By now the front line east of Tobruk consisted of an intermediate area between the line held by the Germans from Bardia down through Fort Capuzzo towards Sidi Omar, and positions held by the only force Wavell could move up in a hurry from the Delta, basically the 7th Armoured Division Support Group, commanded by Brigadier 'Strafer' Gott with Colonel Jock Campbell as second in command.

By 19 April, Gott had brought up 22nd Guards Brigade to Halfaya Pass, and in the area to the south-east and back along the escarpment he stationed four mixed columns (known as 'Jock Columns' after Campbell, who had commanded the first of them), which he used to probe forward across the Wire in order both to harry the enemy and to gather intelligence for Wavell and the Cairo staff. Their efforts were noted and appreciated, but at that moment at Cairo headquarters attention was concentrated on events on the other side of the Mediterranean (the Yugoslav army capitulated on 17 April and by the 19th the Greek retreat had reached Thermopylae). So for the rest of the month Gott was left to consolidate the frontier positions, while a new force under Lieutenant-General Beresford-Pierse was gradually built up in the rear areas.

Halfaya Pass, on the Egyptian border, was one of the key strategic points of the North African campaign. Captured by the Germans in their first drive, it was fortified and was one of the pivots of the disastrous British Operations Brevity and Battleaxe. Under the command of Major the Reverend Wilhelm Bach, the Halfaya strongpoint was to remain a thorn in the side of the British until November and Operation Crusader. Some of the defenders are seen here in the summer of 1941.

It was mid-May before any form of counter-attack against Rommel could be mounted (by which time Cairo's attention was increasingly drawn to Crete), but on 15 May Operation Brevity was launched – only to come up quickly against the fact that Rommel too had been consolidating his forces opposite. He had, moreover, brought up to the frontier some of the newly arrived formations of 15th Panzer Division which, although without their panzers, had sufficient heavy machine-guns and light anti-tank weapons to fight off all attempts by Durham Light Infantry to take and hold Fort Capuzzo. By the morning of 17 May, although the British held Halfaya Pass, they had been beaten back on every other attack front and had lost most of their admittedly worn-out armour. Communications had failed again, with the result that a suggestion from Gott to Beresford-Pierse that withdrawal would be advisable remained unanswered for so long that when the withdrawal was eventually put into effect it took place in the face of orders forbidding it, which had arrived too late.

Ten days later, Rommel sent a combined panzer and infantry force to Halfaya Pass and retook it, later placing it under command of a remarkable soldier-priest, Major the Reverend Wilhelm Bach. He also constructed a strong defensive arc in the area, the main strong-points consisting of 88-mm anti-tank guns sunk so deep into the ground that little was visible from the front except the barrels, though each commanded a wide field of fire. 'I had great hopes of the effectiveness of this arrangement,' wrote Rommel later, with all the complacency of hindsight.

Not surprisingly, the disappointment felt in Cairo about events in both the Balkans and Cyrenaica was echoed in Whitehall. But defeat always called forth Churchill's greatest qualities and his reaction to the reverses was magnificent; the nagging ceased, there were no recriminations – only sympathy, understanding and an immediate concern to help. And one of the most practical aids the Prime Minister could give to his hard-pressed commander in the field was to override the apprehensions of his advisers in England, strip the Home Defence of every tank and aeroplane that could be spared (Coventry had just been virtually destroyed by Luftwaffe bombing), and send them by the fastest means possible through the Mediterranean to Alexandria. By 28 April Wavell had been informed that he would receive nearly 300 new tanks and over 50 Hurricane fighters by mid-May.

Churchill's courage was rewarded. Of the five fast transports making up the 'Tiger' convoy, only one was lost. The others arrived at Alexandria on 12 May, so that by mid-month Wavell's armament had been theoretically increased by 135 Matildas, 82 cruiser tanks of which 50 were the new Crusaders, and 21 light tanks, while RAF strength had been increased by 43 Hurricanes. In practice, all the tanks had to go into workshops for the installation of dust filters and modifications to their cooling systems to adapt them to desert conditions; then their new features had to be studied by the crews who would take them into action.

Units of Rommel's 5th Light Division (later known as 21st Panzer Division) drive across Cyrenaica from Agedabia towards Derna and Tobruk in the first week of April. Within days Tobruk was to be encircled, and an epic siege would be under way.

Chronology of War: 1941

April 27
German troops enter Athens

April 28
Rommel captures Sollum on the Libyan/Egyptian border. Last Allied forces evacuated from Greece

April 30
Iraqi troops surround RAF base at Habbaniyah. New Zealand General Freyberg appointed C-in-C Crete. Germans occupy Greek mainland. UK civilian casualties in April 6,065 killed, 6,926 injured

May 1
Heavy Axis attack on Tobruk beaten back by Australians

May 6
US Navy to protect supplies across Atlantic for Britain

May 10
British raise siege of Habbaniyah in Iraq

May 10
Deputy Führer Rudolf Hess flies to Scotland

May 11
Germans complete occupation of Aegean islands

May 12
'Tiger' convoy with 238 tanks arrives in Alexandria

May 13
Martin Bormann succeeds Hess as Nazi Party secretary

May 15
First British offensive against Afrika Korps, Operation Brevity, launched

May 16
Last British reinforcements reach Crete. UK bans rubber exports to Japan

May 18
German battleship Bismarck *and heavy cruiser* Prinz Eugen *leave Gdynia for North Sea*

May 20
Operation Merkur; Germans invade Crete with largest airborne assault to date. 1,500 paratroops are landed

May 21
Germans capture Maleme airfield

May 22
General Freyberg orders withdrawal to short defence line. British battleships HMS Warspite *and* Valiant *damaged off Crete*

May 24
British battlecruiser HMS Hood *and battleship* Prince of Wales *engage* Bismarck *and* Prinz Eugen *at long range;* Hood *sunk*

May 25
Bismarck *escapes British pursuit*

May 26
Bismarck *located off south-west England, attacked by naval aircraft and halted. On Crete Freyberg orders withdrawal to Sfakia*

May 27
Bismarck *sunk. Germans take Canea and control Suda Bay; Freyberg receives permission to evacuate Crete. In North Africa Rommel retakes Halfaya Pass*

May 28
British evacuate Heraklion in Crete

May 29
British rearguard defends beachhead at Sfakia. Retimo surrenders

May 30
Iraqi revolt collapses

May 31
Evacuation of Crete completed. UK civilian casualties in May 5,394 killed, 5,181 injured, 75 missing

June 2
Hitler and Mussolini meet at Brenner Pass

June 5
Germans complete occupation of Crete. 15,000 Allied prisoners are taken

Afrika Korps equipment 1941/43

The stunning early victories of the Afrika Korps were not due to any preponderance of equipment but to the leadership of Erwin Rommel and the high quality of the German units he commanded. The Afrika Korps began its campaign with a high proportion of light tanks, which were gradually replaced by more capable vehicles, and as the Desert War drew to its conclusion the new PzKpfw VI Tiger tanks made their first appearance.

Above: The mighty PzKpfw VI Tiger tank made its combat debut in Tunisia in 1943. With its thick armour and powerful long-range 88-mm gun, it was a far cry from the light tanks which began the desert war. All but invulnerable to standard Allied anti-tank guns, it was an excellent defensive tank but, fortunately for the Allies, it was a complex machine which took a long time to build.

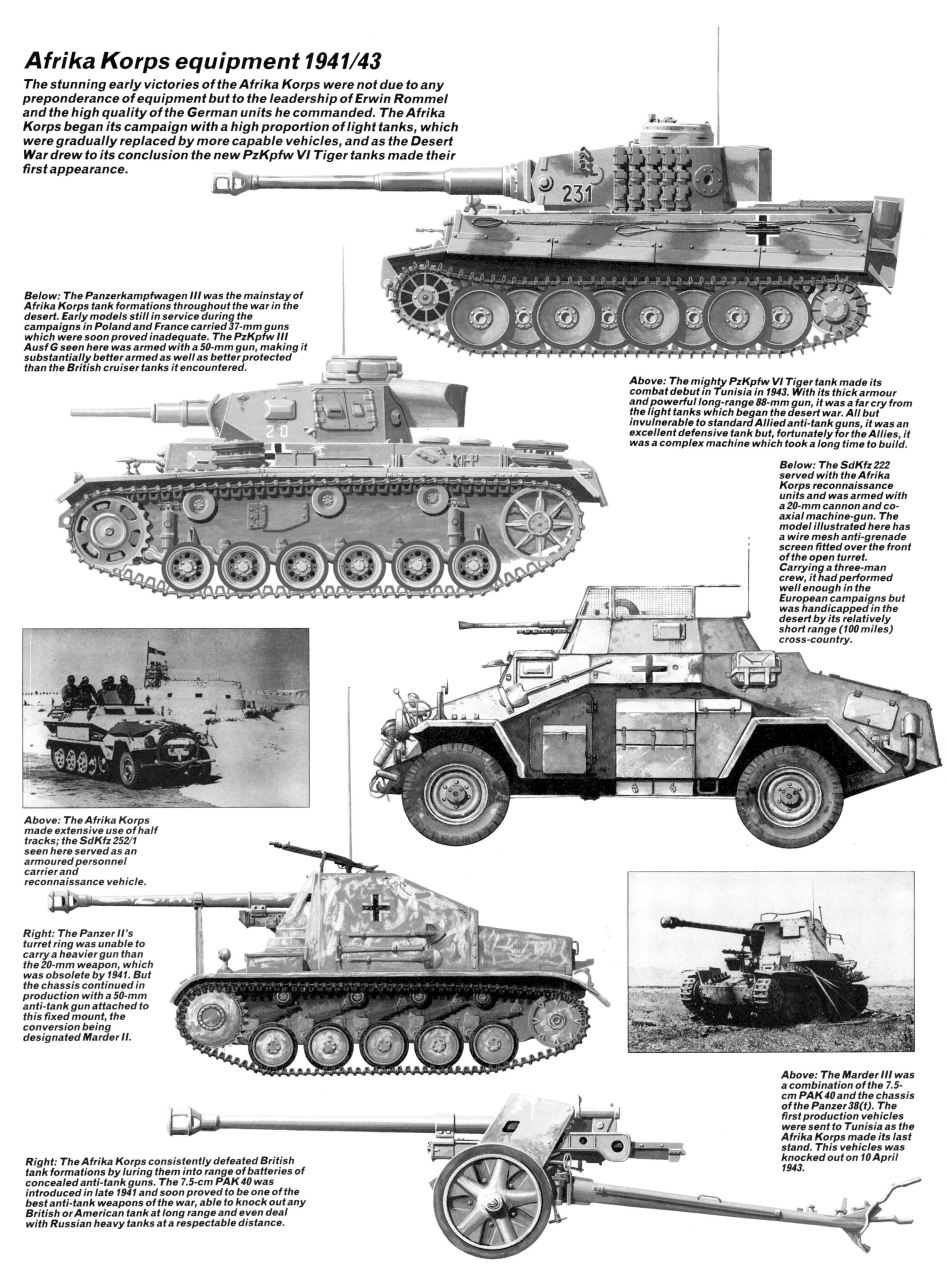

Below: The Panzerkampfwagen III was the mainstay of Afrika Korps tank formations throughout the war in the desert. Early models still in service during the campaigns in Poland and France carried 37-mm guns which were soon proved inadequate. The PzKpfw III Ausf G seen here was armed with a 50-mm gun, making it substantially better armed as well as better protected than the British cruiser tanks it encountered.

Below: The SdKfz 222 served with the Afrika Korps reconnaissance units and was armed with a 20-mm cannon and co-axial machine-gun. The model illustrated here has a wire mesh anti-grenade screen fitted over the front of the open turret. Carrying a three-man crew, it had performed well enough in the European campaigns but was handicapped in the desert by its relatively short range (100 miles) cross-country.

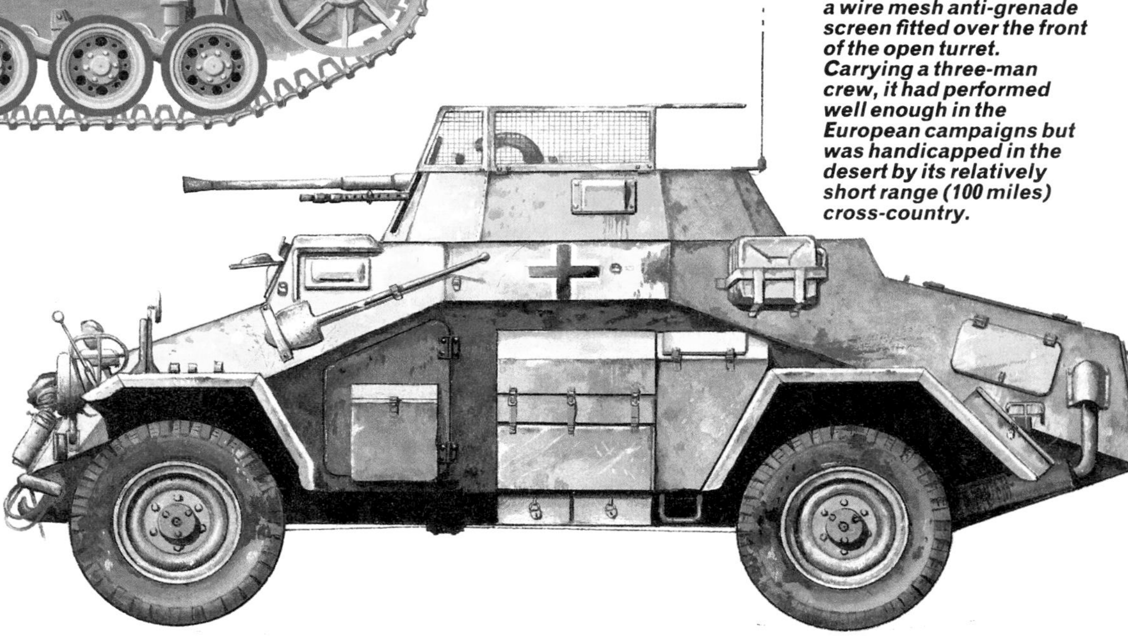

Above: The Afrika Korps made extensive use of half tracks; the SdKfz 252/1 seen here served as an armoured personnel carrier and reconnaissance vehicle.

Right: The Panzer II's turret ring was unable to carry a heavier gun than the 20-mm weapon, which was obsolete by 1941. But the chassis continued in production with a 50-mm anti-tank gun attached to this fixed mount, the conversion being designated Marder II.

Above: The Marder III was a combination of the 7.5-cm PAK 40 and the chassis of the Panzer 38(t). The first production vehicles were sent to Tunisia as the Afrika Korps made its last stand. This vehicles was knocked out on 10 April 1943.

Right: The Afrika Korps consistently defeated British tank formations by luring them into range of batteries of concealed anti-tank guns. The 7.5-cm PAK 40 was introduced in late 1941 and soon proved to be one of the best anti-tank weapons of the war, able to knock out any British or American tank at long range and even deal with Russian heavy tanks at a respectable distance.

Lieutenant-General Sir Richard O'Connor prepares to be flown to captivity in Italy. The loss of O'Connor, commander of the victorious offensive against the Italians, was a crippling blow to the British. His cool, capable leadership might well have changed the face of the North African campaign.

All this took time – and time was the one aspect of warfare that Churchill hated to see wasted and which he never completely understood. Between 14 May and 15 June, the pressure on Wavell from Whitehall increased a hundredfold, the nagging became incessant. When were the tanks going to lead XIII Corps into battle? When did Wavell intend to expel Rommel and his Afrika Korps from Egypt?

Operation Battleaxe was launched at dawn on 15 June 1941, and for the British it was a disastrous failure. Some portion of the blame can be attributed to Churchill's impatience, but the failure was mainly due to a superior German battle technique. They did not believe that it was the task of their panzers to do battle with enemy tanks; that task they left to their artillery. Panzers were for crushing infantry, especially those occupying trenches or other dug-in positions.

But the Royal Armoured Corps hungered for the armoured battle as their cavalry forefathers had hungered for battle against enemy hussars and dragoons. So on 15 June they drove out, hunted down their enemy, Panzer Regiment 5, chased them and their soft transport up and over the first crest of Hamid Ridge – and ran straight into the line of 88-mm anti-tank guns, augmented by 50-mm and 37-mm guns, all very effective at that range. Within minutes 11 of the new Crusaders had been knocked out and six more badly damaged. This was a tale to be repeated time and time again during that traumatic day. By the end of it, of the 100-odd Matildas with which 4th Armoured Brigade had gone into battle that morning, only 37 were still capable of action when darkness fell; overall, British armoured strength had been reduced by 50 per cent. After three days' unavailing conflict Wavell called off the operation, his mauled forces retiring to their original positions.

On the last day of the battle, Churchill, shaken by the accumulating evidence of the loss of what he had romantically come to look upon as his own contribution to a desert victory, left London and went down to his home at Chartwell, which he had shut up for the duration of the war, to roam disconsolately through the empty rooms and once-immaculate gardens, now shabbier, now showing the signs of less exact attention. It was not an atmosphere conducive to optimism or impartiality of judgement; and while he was there Wavell's report on the battle arrived, opening with the words 'I regret to report the failure of "Battleaxe."'

During the next few days the figures of British losses came in – XIII Corps had lost 122 officers and men killed, 588 wounded and 259 missing; the RAF had lost 36 aircraft; and the artillery had lost four of their guns. But the figures which rubbed salt into Churchill's wounds were those which revealed that 64 Matilda and 27 cruiser tanks had been totally lost – for no benefit whatsoever. He had not stripped Britain of her defences, ignored the advice of his Chiefs of Staff and braved the dangers of the Mediterranean passage for results such as these.

Wavell must go. As it happened, the solution to the problem of removing so senior and so well-regarded a commander without causing a considerable rumpus throughout both military and political circles was quite simple. Churchill wished command of the armies of the Middle East now to devolve upon the present commander-in-chief in India, General Auchinleck, who during the past months had demons-

British armour in the desert

British tanks were divided into two categories in 1939: infantry tanks, which were intended for close support of the infantry, and cruiser tanks, which would act as armoured cavalry. Unfortunately, all of them were armed with the ineffective 2-pdr gun; the infantry tanks were very slow indeed, and the cruisers ill-protected. These problems were compounded by the Afrika Korps tactic of goading British armour into ill-conceived cavalry style charges against dug-in anti-tank guns.

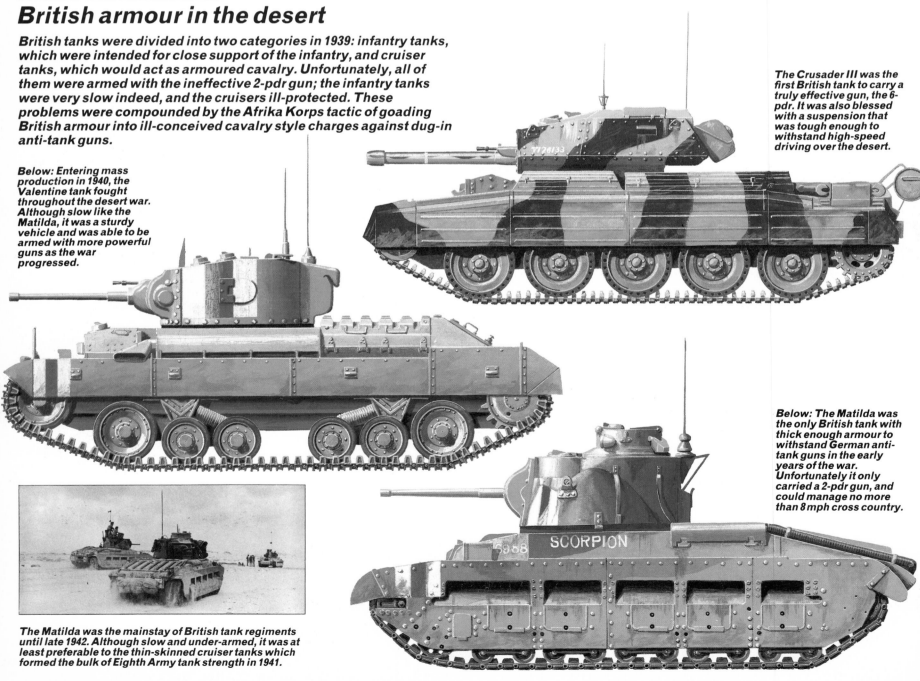

The Crusader III was the first British tank to carry a truly effective gun, the 6-pdr. It was also blessed with a suspension that was tough enough to withstand high-speed driving over the desert.

Below: Entering mass production in 1940, the Valentine tank fought throughout the desert war. Although slow like the Matilda, it was a sturdy vehicle and was able to be armed with more powerful guns as the war progressed.

The Matilda was the mainstay of British tank regiments until late 1942. Although slow and under-armed, it was at least preferable to the thin-skinned cruiser tanks which formed the bulk of Eighth Army tank strength in 1941.

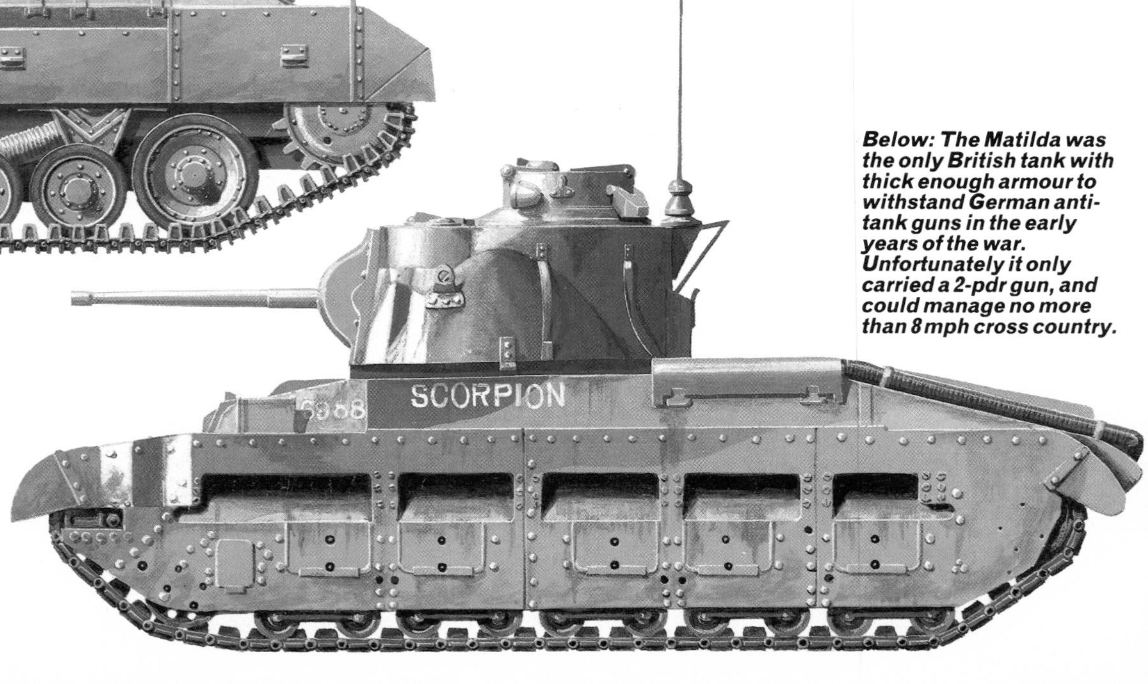

Below: The Matilda was the only British tank with thick enough armour to withstand German anti-tank guns in the early years of the war. Unfortunately it only carried a 2-pdr gun, and could manage no more than 8 mph cross country.

trated many times a generosity of spirit and a willingness to take risks which had appealed to Churchill's nature. As Wavell had great experience of military service in India, the generals could simply exchange commands. The matter should be put in hand immediately.

Auchinleck in command

General Sir Claude Auchinleck took command of the British and Commonwealth armies in the Middle East on 1 July 1941, and immediately found himself holding an opinion of the overall situation totally different from that held in Whitehall.

The most fundamental change in the situation between the one which had faced Wavell and now faced Auchinleck had been brought about by the German invasion of Russia on 21 June, which indeed introduced an entirely new dimension into the war. To Auchinleck it seemed that the invasion had given him a breathing space in which to reorganize his forces, get to know the men now under his command, ensure that they were properly equipped, and train them thoroughly for the tasks he had in mind for them in the operation to recapture Cyrenaica. To Churchill – and his Chiefs of Staff – it seemed that Auchinleck had been presented with a golden – but fleeting – opportunity to strike at Rommel and destroy him and his forces while all attention in Berlin was focused on Russia. And not one tank, one plane, one soldier or even a passing thought could be spared for events in Cyrenaica.

The cables flew, the arguments multiplied, tempers grew warmer. But at least supplies and men were still despatched to Suez, and the convoys still sailed, mostly making the long haul around the Cape, where they often picked up yet more supplies and men from South Africa.

By November, Auchinleck undeniably had a force at his disposal powerful enough to rate the term 'Army'. Eighth Army consisted in November 1941 of two corps – XIII and XXX – comprising three infantry divisions plus a guards brigade, an armoured division of three brigades and a support group, an army tank brigade of heavy infantry support tanks, all necessary headquarters and corps troops – and yet another infantry division in reserve. As one major purpose of his proposed operation was to relieve the Tobruk garrison, he could also count among his forces the fortress troops consisting of four infantry brigades, another army tank brigade, a considerable quantity of artillery and a machine-gun battalion.

So far as armour was concerned, the total British tank strength was 724, of which 201 were heavy infantry tanks (Matildas and Valentines) and 523 cruisers of various marks and ages but including at least 158 Crusaders. XXX Corps under Lieutenant-General Willoughby Norrie was regarded as the armoured corps and had 491 of the cruiser tanks; XIII Corps was the infantry corps under Lieutenant-General A. R. Godwin-Austen and had under command the Matildas of 1st Army Tank Brigade.

The whole Eighth Army was commanded by Lieutenant-General Sir Alan Cunningham, who had recently led the main and final stages of the reduction of the Duke of Aosta's fief down in Abyssinia, and had personally restored the Emperor Haile Selassie, Lion of Judah and King of Kings, to the throne from which the Italians had driven him five years before. Now Cunningham was to command the best-equip-

Outside Agedabia, a British Crusader tank burns. While very mobile, the cruiser was thinly armoured and undergunned, and was to prove extremely vulnerable to German anti-tank tactics. Nevertheless, had they been used in the German fashion, concentrated in large formations, they could well have been more successful. Unfortunately, the British were never able to match German understanding of armoured war, and victory eventually came through vastly superior numbers and total air superiority.

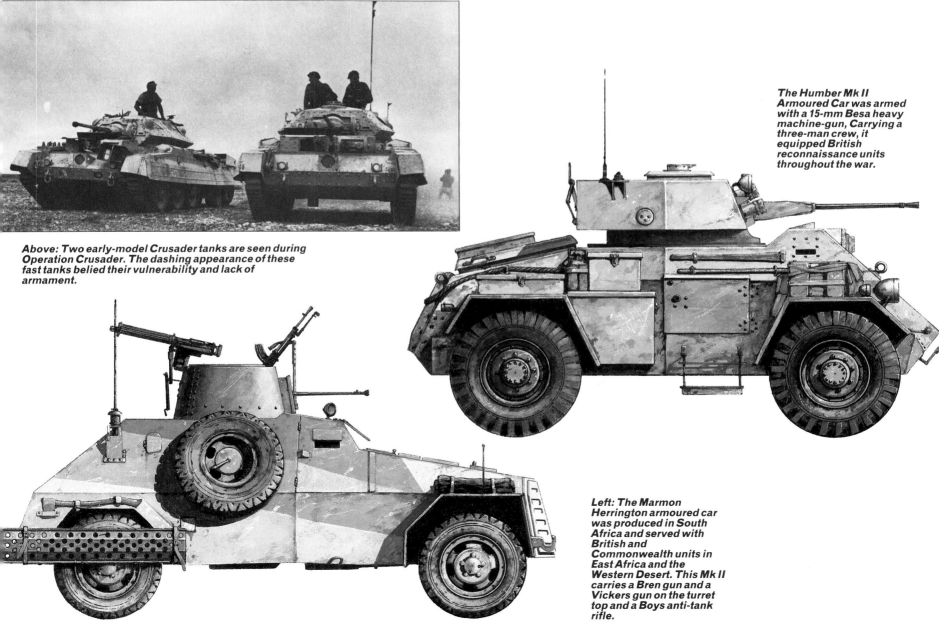

Above: Two early-model Crusader tanks are seen during Operation Crusader. The dashing appearance of these fast tanks belied their vulnerability and lack of armament.

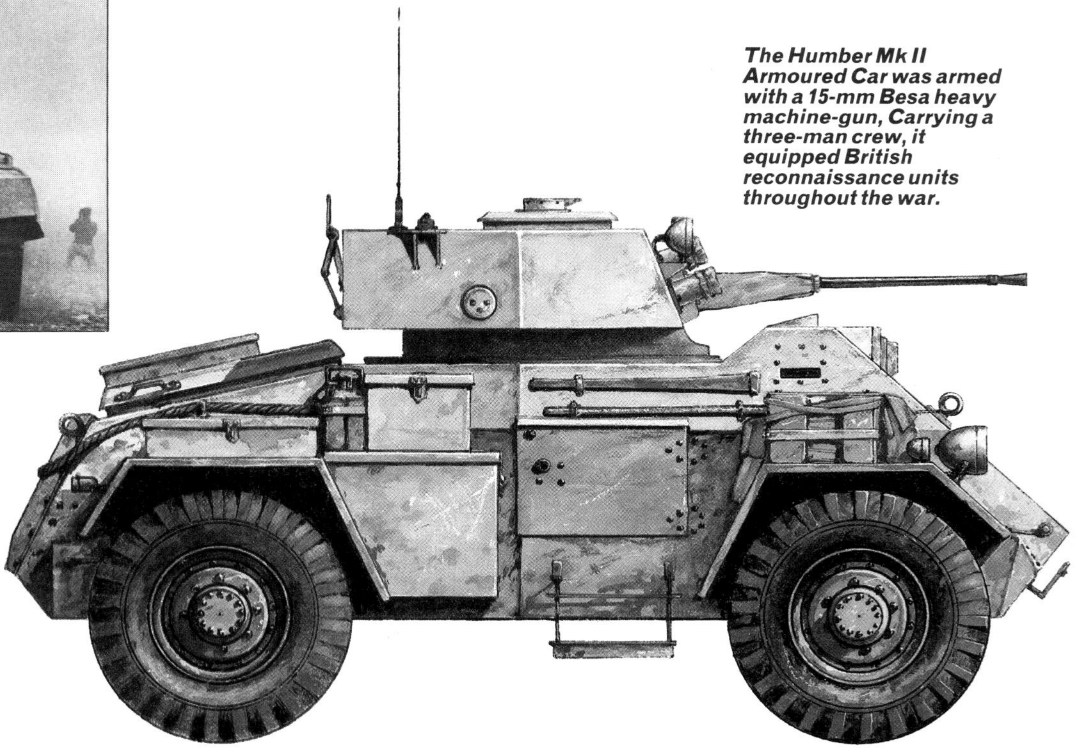

The Humber Mk II Armoured Car was armed with a 15-mm Besa heavy machine-gun, Carrying a three-man crew, it equipped British reconnaissance units throughout the war.

Left: The Marmon Herrington armoured car was produced in South Africa and served with British and Commonwealth units in East Africa and the Western Desert. This Mk II carries a Bren gun and a Vickers gun on the turret top and a Boys anti-tank rifle.

ped army Britain had put into the field so far in World War II against an opponent who, whatever his reputation, commanded an army known to be numerically inferior in men, armour and aircraft. Surely Cunningham could not fail.

At the moment of the launch of Operation Crusader, Rommel was suffering a further disadvantage. The capture of Tobruk had become an obsession with him, and all his efforts were directed to his latest attempts on the fortress – a powerful onslaught upon the south-east face of the perimeter by one panzer division and one light division, supported after the break-in by three Italian infantry divisions. Italian armour would wait to the south of Tobruk in case the British attempted to intervene from Egypt; should this happen the British would also be attacked in flank by the newly arrived 21st Panzer Division held back in and around Rommel's main stores dump at Gambut.

So intent upon this assault on Tobruk was Rommel that he dismissed as scaremongering rumours all warnings from his intelligence staff of a possible powerful attack into Cyrenaica by the British (for which there was not much evidence, as Eighth Army security was excellent). The more the warnings were repeated, the angrier he became. Any interference by the enemy with his plans, Rommel announced, would easily be dealt with by 21st Panzer Division under Major-General Ravenstein.

Crusader is launched

The Eighth Army crossed the frontier on the morning of 19 November after two days of torrential rain which had reduced large areas of the desert to bog. The infantry and heavy tanks of XIII Corps drove north to isolate the German and Italian garrisons from Sidi Omar to the coast, the brigades of 7th Armoured Division drove north west towards Bir el Gubi and Tobruk, and the semi-independent 4th Armoured Brigade Group occupied the ground between the two corps to the east of Gabr Saleh.

By evening, 7th Armoured Brigade cruisers with the 7th Support Group were 10 miles from Tobruk and had captured the landing-ground at Sidi Rezegh; the two brigades of South African infantry were in position to the south of Bir el Gubi; and both the New Zealand and Indian Divisions of XIII Corps had reached their destinations encapsulating the Axis frontier garrisons. The only slight disappointments in the advance were the blocking of 4th Armoured Division in the gap by elements of Ravenstein's 21st Panzer reacting with admirable speed to danger, and the absolute repulse by Italian artillery of 22nd Armoured Brigade (which had failed to absorb the lessons of Battleaxe) at Bir el Gubi itself.

During the following day (20 November) the opposing formations skirmished and attempted to consolidate. The New Zealanders pushed further north towards Sidi Azeiz; the Stuart tanks of 4th Armoured Brigade fought another indecisive action with elements of 21st Panzer; and 7th Armoured Brigade at Sidi Rezegh attempted to make contact with the 'break-out' force from Tobruk, but failed because their tanks were the oldest and most worn of those in Eighth Army and because the Italian divisions along the perimeter were well dug in and much better led than before.

At 9.00 that evening the BBC announced on the news that a powerful armoured force of 75,000 men was advancing victoriously into Cyrenaica. The scales fell from Rommel's eyes, he cancelled his own assault on Tobruk and turned his whole attention upon defeating the Eighth Army . . . and during the days which followed, he came close to success.

He himself drove immediately to Ed Duda, taking two of his 88-mm anti-tank guns with him, and with the Italian forces there he stemmed during the morning of 21 November all attempts by 7th Armoured Brigade and the Tobruk garrison to link up. He also sent 15th Panzer Division down to join all of 21st to the east of Gabr Saleh, where they administered a sharp and severe blow to the assembled Stuarts of 4th Armoured Brigade Group, after which the entire Afrika Korps turned north west and sped off towards Sidi Rezegh, 7th Armoured Brigade and the Support Group.

The first to feel the weight of this Armoured hammerhead were the 30 old cruiser tanks and 20 Crusaders of 7th Hussars, the only force not committed to the attempt to reach Ed Duda further down the Sidi Rezegh valley, which Brigadier Davy now flung this force into the path of the Afrika Korps in the hope of delaying them until he could bring more of his strength back up to help. During the holocaust which followed, all but 10 of the Hussars' old cruisers and all of their Crusaders were destroyed; not just knocked out but completely wrecked as the panzers rode over their positions and pumped shell after shell into their hulls until they were reduced to scrap iron. Only the reserve guns of the Support Group and the fact that they were running short of petrol halted the Afrika Korps at the head of the Sidi Rezegh valley, leaving the airfield temporarily in British hands. Davy withdrew his armour from Ed Duda, the Support Group dug in around the airfield and everyone awaited the arrival of the South African Brigade coming up to reinforce them from the south.

***Above left:** The capture of Tobruk became an obsession with Rommel. Here a 10.5-cm howitzer bombards Australian positions during the first German attempts to take the port.*

***Above:** Inside Tobruk, an Australian Bren-gunner fires at an attacking Axis aircraft. The Australians in Tobruk confirmed their reputation for toughness and fighting ability and came to be much respected by the Germans.*

Operation Crusader was the most wildly fluctuating battle of a wildly-fluctuating campaign. Here a British cruiser tank passes a burning German Panzer IV during the opening stages of the battle.

Aircraft of the Desert War

While mainland Britain was under daily air attack, the RAF squadrons in North Africa had to manage as best they could against the Regia Aeronautica but the desert air war changed radically with the arrival of the Afrika Korps. In six weeks the Germans accounted for more Allied aircraft than the Italians had in as many months. With both sides often fighting at the end of long lines of communication, air attacks on transport columns could have heavy impact on the campaign.

In this still taken from a German propaganda film of 1941, the camouflage scheme carried by this Bf 109E-4 Trop of I/JG 27 blends miraculously into the desert background. Of course, this only occurs at those brief moments during the day when the shadows are of the right length and are viewed from the correct angle.

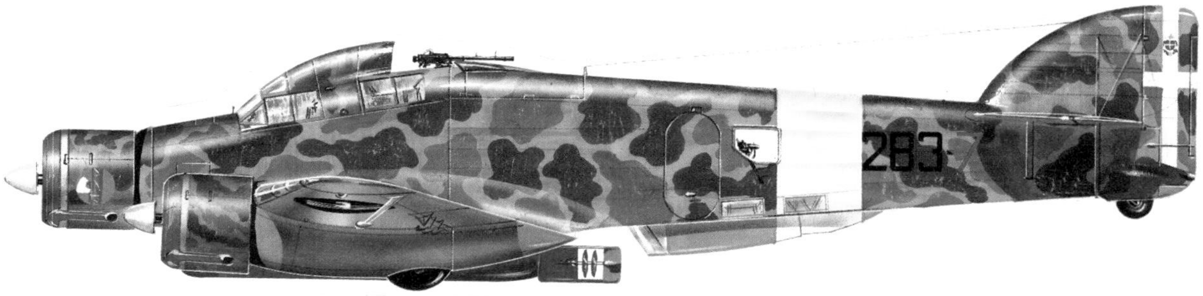

Left: The Savoia-Marchetti S.M.79 Sparviero proved an effective torpedo-bomber, scoring a string of victories against British warships. This machine of 193ª Squadriglia was based on Sicily in 1941 for strikes against the Malta convoys.

Right: A Macchi M.C.200 Saeta based in Cyrenaica in 1941. Underpowered and undergunned, it could cope with early model Hurricanes weighed down by tropical air filters, but soon suffered heavy casualties.

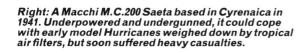

Left: The Messerschmitt Bf 109F carried a 15-mm Mauser cannon in its nose. This is a tropicalized model with dust filter, which was based at Qasaba in late 1942.

Right: Both sides introduced anti-tank aircraft into the Desert War. This Messerschmitt Bf 110E operated from Barca, North Africa, in September 1942, carrying a 30-mm cannon which could pierce the thin top armour of most Allied tanks.

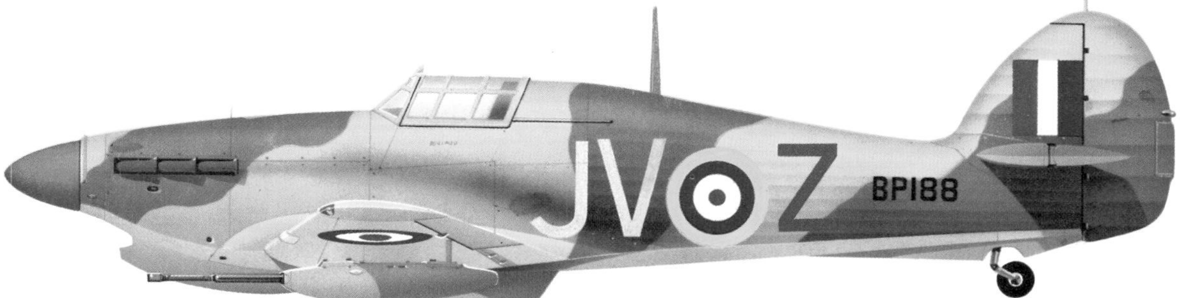

Left: The Hurricane Mk IID tank buster carried a pair of 40-mm cannon, making it a cumbersome beast to fly but a powerful threat to Axis armour.

Right: This Curtiss Kittyhawk Mk 1 was flown by Flying Officer Neville Duke of No. 112 Squadron, based in Egypt in September 1942.

But, as was to happen so often, messages failed to get through and Rommel snatched at every opportunity. He brought the 5th Panzer Regiment around in a loop from the top to the bottom of the Sidi Rezegh valley and the following day (22 November) sent them up the valley to the airfield while 15th Panzer drove in from the top. The first battle of Sidi Rezegh was fought – and by the end of it so many British tanks had been shot to pieces by the efficient German anti-tank guns that Jock Campbell was leading charges across the airfield by random units in a staff car, waving red and blue flags as directing signals. No man ever won his Victoria Cross more gallantly.

The Afrika Korps retook Sidi Rezegh on the 22nd, and on the 23rd they were to fight an even more destructive action. They had massed after the battle at the head of the valley; the following morning revealed their enemy scattered over the ground to the south – in great numbers still but apparently disorganized, except for two South African brigades laagered some 10 miles apart, 5th Brigade just south of Sidi Rezegh, 1st Brigade east of Bir el Gubi. At Bir el Gubi lay the Italian Ariete Division.

'Death Sunday'

Leading Afrika Korps under Rommel's overall command was Major-General Cruewell, and his plan for Sunday, 23 November (*Totensonntag*) was simple. At 8.00 a.m. 15th Panzer Division followed by 21st set off southwestwards for Bir el Gubi, cutting through between the South African brigades, spreading chaos and confusion among the heterogeneous British units over which they rode, and joining the Ariete soon after noon. They then turned and faced north east, marshalled the Ariete armour on their left flank, and shortly after 2.00 p.m. moved implacably forward on the 5th South African Brigade which they overran and virtually annihilated in one of the fiercest battles the Korps were ever to fight. It was over by dark; the cost to the Eighth Army was clear, that to the Afrika Korps was still to be reckoned.

To Rommel, however, it seemed obvious that the British were paying exorbitantly for the battle so far. According to reports from Cruewell and Ravenstein, the British 7th Armoured Brigade had been destroyed at Sidi Rezegh; the 4th Armoured Brigade Group near Gabr Saleh, the 22nd Armoured Brigade at Bir el Gubi and now the 5th South African Brigade no longer existed. Along the frontier there were New Zealand and Indian infantry brigades but they would be powerless against the Afrika Korps – and all that lay between them were the tatterdemalion remains of the British XXX Corps. Once these Commonwealth infantry formations were defeated the road to Cairo and the Nile would be open.

So 24 November was the day of Rommel's 'Dash to the Wire'.

It began at 10.00 a.m., 21st Panzer Division in the lead (with Rommel himself at the head), 15th Panzer following and Ariete collected en route and holding the right flank position for a part of the way. The scenes which resulted as the panzers roared through the British dumps, supply echelons and the regrouping armoured and infantry units between Sidi Rezegh and the Wire at Gasr el Abid live in legend – a legend with its hilarious side, for the Afrika Korps cut through the remains of XXX Corps like a hot knife through butter; but the butter remained when the knife had passed, and coalesced again.

By that night, Rommel and those formations which had kept up with him – for his panzers were just as dependent upon fuel and maintenance as the British tanks – were isolated in Egypt. Just to their north 4th Indian Division stood inviolate, and back in Cyrenaica the men of XXX Corps had time to sort themselves out, resupply themselves from their dumps and echelon services, and thoroughly prepare themselves for the next stage of the battle. Moreover, the New Zealanders had now turned west and were driving along the Trig Capuzzo towards Ed Duda; they arrived on 26 November and on the following day, after heavy hand-to-hand fighting with Italian Bersaglieri, the link-up with the Tobruk garrison was at last made.

Ironically enough, the link-up took place a few hours after Auchinleck had replaced Cunningham as army commander with one of his own staff, Major-General Neil Ritchie. Cunningham had been very upset by the losses of the first few days, and had been visiting Norrie at Gott's headquarters when Rommel's Dash had caused him to make an undignified rush for his plane, from which he had a bird's-eye view of the German knife-thrust and the chaos it spread on each side: but he did not see the healing process behind it. He arrived back at his own headquarters in a very depressed and even negative frame of mind and as Auchinleck was there at the time he could see that Cunningham was no longer the man to lead Eighth Army to the victory which was still within their grasp.

Ritchie took over on 26 November but for some days could have little real effect upon the battle, which had become to a great extent a contest of wills between two men – Rommel and Freyberg. The former had soon realized that his Dash to the Wire had been premature and that an unbeaten foe still waited behind him; by 28 November he was leading his panzers back towards Tobruk and from then until 1 December the New Zealanders fought off attack after attack with a resolution which inspired admiration from friend and foe alike.

By now Rommel's losses and his expenditure of fuel and ammunition were causing deep concern at his headquarters – concern exacerbated by the knowledge that many miles away the Royal Navy and the Royal Air Force were doing as much as Eighth Army to defeat Rommel; 14 ships had been sent to the bottom of the Mediterranean since the battle began, taking 60,000 tons of Rommel's supplies, especially of fuel (of which only 2,500 tons had arrived). On 4 December he was told by his staff that he could expect no replacements for the 142 panzers, 25 armoured cars, 83 guns or 60 mortars he had lost, nor, worse still, for 16 commanding officers or the 4,000-odd other ranks who were now dead, badly wounded or missing.

Rommel's staff told him that there was every indication that the new Eighth Army commander was about to launch a powerful drive toward El Adem and the area to the west of Tobruk; as Ritchie now had all the resources inside Tobruk to help him, together with another infantry division coming up from reserve, there was little that could be done to stop him. Reluctantly, Rommel agreed that if he had not beaten the British by the evening of 7 December

The siege of Malta

At the time of Italy's entry into the war on 10 June 1940 Malta served two purposes: a British naval replenishment base on the maritime route through the Mediterranean to and from the Suez Canal and the Far East, and as a limited staging-point for long-range flights from the UK to the Middle East.

Despite the completion of four bases (at Hal Far, Luqa, Takali and a flying-boat station at Kalafrana), there was no organized fighter defence and only a naval gunnery flight. When the Italians began somewhat desultory air attacks, however, four Sea Gladiators were hurriedly uncrated and used to fly patrols against the raids (three of them ultimately being dubbed *Faith, Hope* and *Charity*); before a fortnight was out, four Hurricanes on their way out to North Africa were commandeered by the island for its defence.

On 2 August 12 Hurricanes were flown off the carrier *Argus* to the island, a second instalment of 12 Hurricanes, flown off *Argus* on 17 November, was overtaken by tragedy, eight of them being lost at sea after running out of fuel.

Throughout General Wavell's brilliant offensive in Egypt and Cyrenaica during the winter of 1940-1 the Wellingtons from Malta constantly raided Tripoli and Castel Benito – operations that brought swift reaction by the Axis with the arrival in Sicily late in December of the advance units of the German Fliegerkorps X, a force that within a month had grown to some 250 modern aircraft. On 10 January 60 Ju 87s and He 111s attacked a British convoy in the Sicilian narrows, severely damaging the carrier *Illustrious* and the cruisers *Southampton* and *Gloucester*.

With losses increasing among the Hurricanes, the Wellingtons now had to be withdrawn to North Africa and, with Malta thus largely disarmed, the Germans were able to send about half of Fliegerkorps X to Cyrenaica to support Rommel's counteroffensive in the Western Desert. The relief of pressure on Malta now allowed the British to sail a large convoy almost unscathed through the Mediterranean to Alexandria in May. In June, X Fliegerkorps was moved to Greece. At once the Wellingtons returned to Malta, together with Blenheims and Marylands, and these aircraft renewed the attacks on the Italian ports and convoys. When two convoys reached Malta without loss Hitler resolved to eliminate the island once and for all, ordering Luftflotte II from the USSR to Italy before the end of the year under Albert Kesselring. There now started a four-month nightmare for Malta. Throughout January and February 1942 attacks by several dozen bombers were commonplace with never a day without raids, the targets in the main being the airfields.

The Wellingtons were withdrawn once more, and April found the island seriously short of food, fuel and fighters, three out of four supply ships having been sunk. At the height of the assault, on 20 April, 47 more Spitfires arrived, followed by 62 on 9 May (having flown off the American carrier *Wasp*). Amidst rumours that the Germans were preparing to invade the island, Malta was awarded the George Cross for its sustained resistance.

It was now that Hitler stepped in with changed priorities (the first being the recapture of Cyrenaica), and Kesselring moved a large proportion of his aircraft to North Africa to support Rommel. The following month two convoys were sailed to Malta from east and west, of which one from Alexandria was forced to turn back. Two supply ships managed to reach the beleaguered island and the German offensive ran out of steam at El Alamein.

Left: Savoia-Marchetti S.M.79s over the Mediterranean. The attack on Malta took the form of long periods of air assault, as the Axis powers (and more specifically the Luftwaffe's Luftflotte II, under Kesselring) tried to eliminate the Maltese threat to their forces in North Africa.

Below: The cost of maintaining Malta was heavy, resupply convoys being particularly hard-hit. Nevertheless, convoys got through, to enable the island to withstand the attack.

Although in general the Royal Navy had the best of the struggle in the Mediterranean, it was not achieved without terrible cost. The veteran battleships of the fleet were to see hard service, all being seriously damaged at one time or another. HMS* Barham *was torpedoed by* U-331 *off Sollum in November, exploding with the loss of over 860 of her crew.

he must withdraw – and when in the late afternoon he realized that British pressure and especially British artillery fire was increasing all the time, he accepted the inevitable and gave orders to fall back as far as Gazala.

But there was no particular defence line there and he soon announced that the retreat must go on back to the Gulf of Sirte. There, in bad weather and worse tempers, Operation Crusader, or 'The Winter Battle' as the Germans called it, fizzled out, in the desolate sands around El Agheila, from which, nine months before, Rommel had launched the first spectacular advance of the Afrika Korps.

The third stage of what the irreverent-minded were calling the 'Benghazi Handicap' had been run.

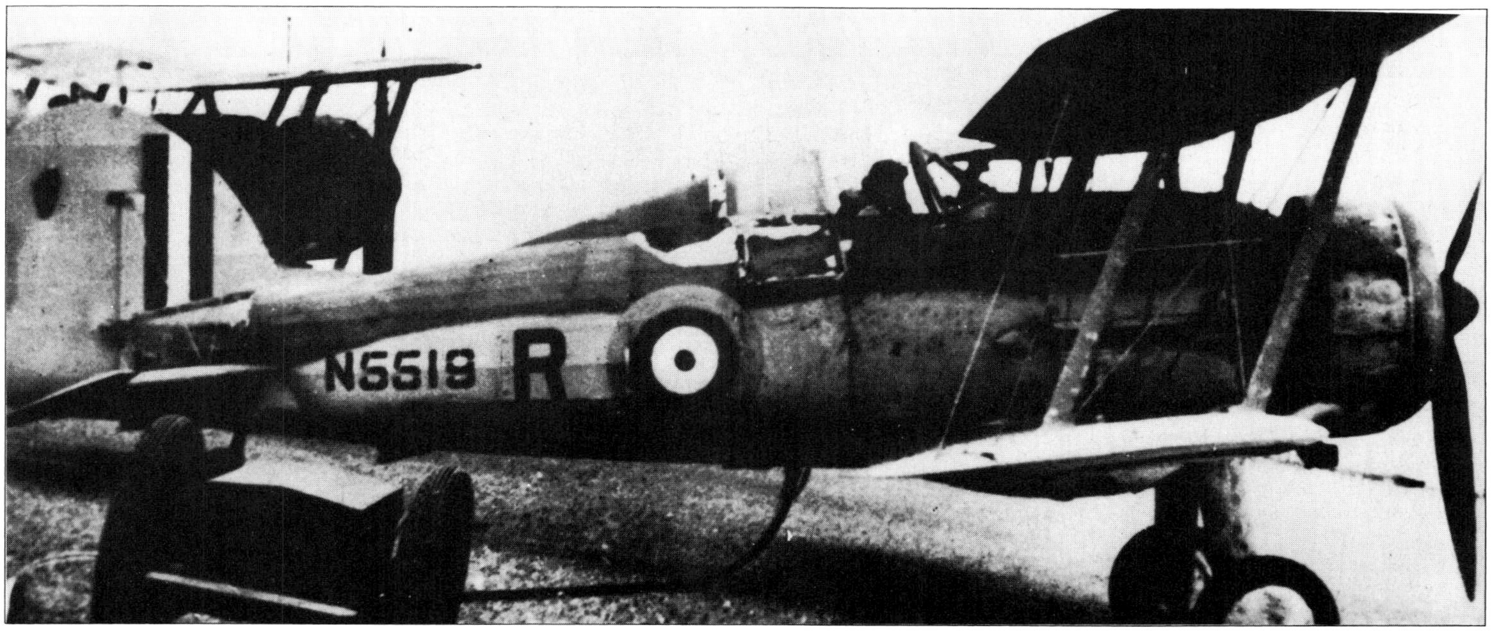

Right: One of three famous sisters which briefly shouldered the burden of the defence of Malta: 'Faith', together with 'Hope' and 'Charity', were Sea Gladiators which flew against the original Italian bombing raids.

***Below: The 'Pedestal' convoy to Malta in August 1942 saw a convoy of 14 merchantmen escorted by three carriers, two battleships, seven cruisers, 32 destroyers and six submarines. Here HMS* Indomitable *(damaged by air attack on 12 August) leads HMS* Eagle *(sunk by submarine torpedo 11 August). Three of the convoy arrived, to be followed by the heavily damaged but vital tanker* Ohio.**

Chapter 7

Barbarossa

On 22 June 1941 Hitler turned on his sometime ally, the Soviet Union, planning to achieve a lightning victory, just as he had in the west. As the summer wore on, German divisions plunged deep into the Russian heartland and by September Smolensk had fallen and the road to Moscow lay open.

'When Barbarossa is launched,' declared Hitler, 'the whole world will hold its breath!' – indeed, the forces massed along the Soviet frontier from the Arctic Circle to the Black Sea that early summer of 1941 represented the greatest concentration of military force the world had seen to that date.

Three German army groups disposed between them 80 infantry divisions, 18 panzer divisions and 12 motorized divisions, while behind them in reserve waited another 21 infantry, two panzer and one motorized divisions: some two million men, 3,200 tanks, 10,000 guns. By mid-June already in position to supply them were enough stores dumps, fuel and ammunition reserves to feed them over a 350- to 400-mile advance; and 500,000 lorries waited in massed parks from East Prussia to Romania to rush it forward on demand. To the modern mind the only questionable, indeed alarming, figure to emerge from the tables of statistics among the planning memoranda for Operation Barbarossa is that for 'stabling': 300,000 horses were to play an apparently essential part in this monumental military exercise.

The disposition of the army groups and the directions of their advances were dictated to a large extent by one inescapable geographical factor, namely the Pripet Marshes, a virtually uncrossable swamp measuring nearly 100 miles from north to south and 300 miles from east to west, dividing Belorussia from the Ukraine. Because of this, there could be little contact during the first stage of the operation between Army Group South launched from Lublin towards Kiev and the lower reaches of the River Dnieper, and the two groups to the north, Army Group Centre aimed first at Smolensk and then (at least in the minds of the military leaders) at Moscow, and Army Group North launched out of East Prussia first towards Lake Peipus and then towards Leningrad.

It was in the northern sector that the greater weight of the attack lay: the army groups comprised 50 infantry, 13 panzer and nine motorized divisions, and, of the two, Army Group Centre was the stronger. Under the command of the icily aristocratic Field Marshal Fedor von Bock were two infantry armies, the Ninth and the Fourth, and two panzer formations, III Panzergruppe under General Hermann Hoth and II Panzergruppe under General Heinz Guderian. These were the armies whose commanders intended to reduce Napoleon's feat of arms of 129 years earlier to historical obscurity, for they planned to reach Moscow in less than eight weeks and to annihilate the Soviet army in the process.

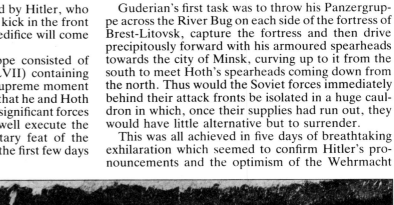

German tanks pass abandoned Soviet transport in a Russian village as they race eastwards. Note the Nazi flag on the back of the tank in the foreground, for aerial recognition.

In this hope they were encouraged by Hitler, who had assured them, 'We have only to kick in the front door and the whole rotten Russian edifice will come tumbling down!'

To Guderian, whose Panzergruppe consisted of three corps (XXIV, XLVI and XLVII) containing four panzer divisions, this was the supreme moment of his military career. It was evident that he and Hoth between them commanded the most significant forces in the entire operation, and could well execute the most exciting and spectacular military feat of the century, perhaps of all history. And the first few days seemed to confirm the prospect.

Guderian's first task was to throw his Panzergruppe across the River Bug on each side of the fortress of Brest-Litovsk, capture the fortress and then drive precipitously forward with his armoured spearheads towards the city of Minsk, curving up to it from the south to meet Hoth's spearheads coming down from the north. Thus would the Soviet forces immediately behind their attack fronts be isolated in a huge cauldron in which, once their supplies had run out, they would have little alternative but to surrender.

This was all achieved in five days of breathtaking exhilaration which seemed to confirm Hitler's pronouncements and the optimism of the Wehrmacht

Right: Soviet militiamen surrender to SS men in July 1941. Moments after this picture was taken, both prisoners were shot out of hand on the excuse that they were not in proper uniform.

Below: The Luftwaffe rapidly won air superiority, which made it easy for light aircraft to maintain contact with the armoured spearheads. Isolated Soviet units had no such facility, and proved unable to co-ordinate their actions.

Below: German infantry divisions had to maintain a ferocious pace to surround the Soviet forces left in the wake of the Panzer divisions. Many Soviet units offered stubborn resistance even when all hope of relief had vanished.

The invasion forces

In June 1941 the German army fielded 205 divisions, of which 133 were earmarked for the invasion of Russia, 38 garrisoned the west, 12 were in Norway and two fought the British in North Africa. This proportion of effort was to remain roughly the same for the rest of the war.

Above: Minsk fell in July to a German pincer movement from the north west and south east, which trapped a large force of Soviet troops to the west.

Left: Russia ablaze – the wooden houses of a Ukrainian village burn fiercely after a Soviet rearguard action. Only the stone chimneys were to remain.

Above: The war in the East was characterized by utter barbarity, the Germans soon giving notice that 'Bolshevik sub-humans' would receive savage treatment. Here, captured partisans were summarily executed.

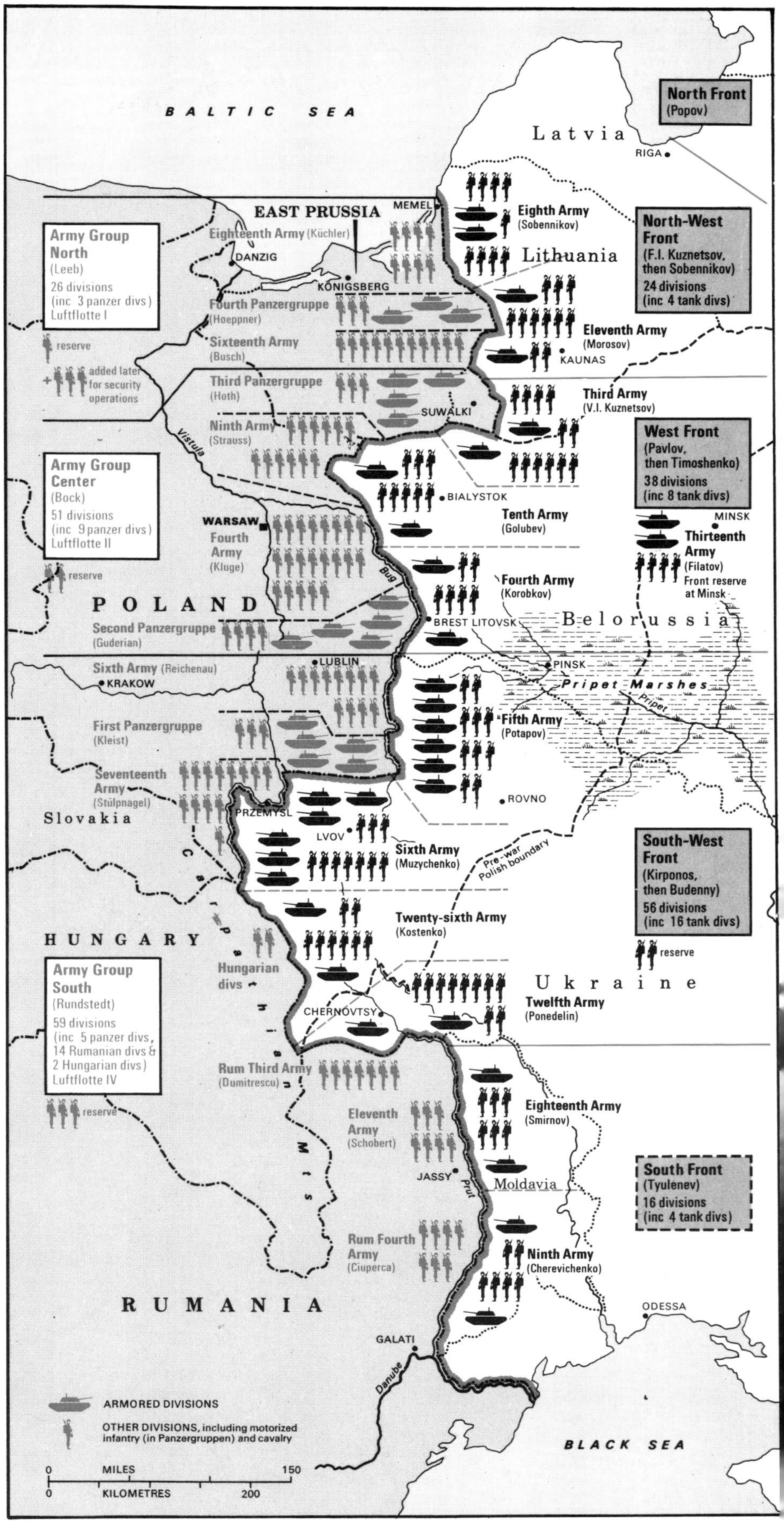

leaders. Operation Barbarossa was launched on 22 June 1941. The water-proofed tanks of the 18th Panzer Division forded the Bug before dawn, and Guderian himself crossed the river in an assault boat soon afterwards. His XXIV Corps captured intact all the bridges immediately to the south of the fortress, and although the Brest-Litovsk garrison reacted quickly and organized a resolute defence which lasted some days, Guderian's mobile units sped past and were 30 miles on at Kobrin by the evening of their first day.

By 24 June, only 60 hours after the launch of the attack, the 17th Panzer Division was driving into Slonim, over 100 miles from the frontier and half-way to the Germans' first objective. There Guderian visited the division, taking part in a skirmish with Soviet infantry just past the village of Rozana, in which he himself acted as machine-gunner. He narrowly avoided capture by more Soviet infantry on his way back to his command post, escaping this fate by rapid acceleration through the surprised enemy. It was all very exciting; and three days later, on the afternoon of 27 June, the leading tanks of the 17th Panzer Division drove into Minsk to meet the spearheads of Hoth's III Panzergruppe, which had covered 200 miles in five days and accomplished the first stage of their mission.

But behind them they had left pockets of Soviet troops who, unlike enemy forces similarly encircled the year before in France, showed little inclination to lay down their arms and surrender. There were four of these pockets: the fortress at Brest-Litovsk, six divisions around Bialystok, six more at Volkovysk, and another 15 between Novogrudok and Minsk itself. The task of first containing and then destroying and capturing them was assigned, in Hoth's and Guderian's minds, to the German infantry of the Fourth and Ninth Armies trudging stolidly behind the panzer divisions.

The trouble was that the infantry were now quite a long way behind, for the roads shown on the Barbarossa maps proved in the majority of cases to be little but mud tracks which were quickly reduced to foot-deep dust, through which it was impossible to move at more than 3 mph. Of the half million lorries which were supposed to be bringing not only troops but also the next issues of ammunition and fuel, a large proportion had been captured in France; the rest proved to be totally inadequate for carrying heavy loads across rough country, besides having no reserve of spare parts. Moreover, they had already been driven from France across half Europe and their useful mileage had been almost consumed.

Not surprisingly, arguments arose. Guderian and Hoth were convinced that they must immediately race further ahead, first to Smolensk and then to Moscow, confident that speed would prove the decisive factor in this campaign. With a burst of that insubordination which was later to mark the whole of the Russian invasion, on 1 July Guderian and Hoth released panzer units towards the next obstacle, the River Beresina, and were threatened with court martial for so doing by their immediate superior, General Günther von Kluge.

The summer campaign

The priority accorded to the advance on Moscow was changed in August, Hitler deciding that the wheatlands of the Ukraine and the oil fields of the south west were more important. Before winter he was to change his mind again, but it was too late and Moscow remained tantalizingly beyond his grasp.

On the same day, Guderian's panzers met for the first time a Soviet T-34 tank, which blocked their advance for three hours, knocked out five PzKpfw III tanks and was only removed by an attack from the rear with an 88-mm gun. Fortunately no more T-34s were encountered in the area and then, on 3 July, the order came for the next stage of the advance. So from his illicit bridgehead over the Beresina, Guderian launched the 18th Panzer Division towards the River Dnieper, which was reached on 5 July.

On the Dnieper

Here the division beat off a Soviet counter-attack and then waited until all three of the Panzergruppe's corps were lined up along the river between Orsha and Stary Bykhov – with both flanks 'in the air', an increasingly tenuous supply organization and the support infantry two weeks' hard marching behind them! No wonder Kluge remonstrated violently, and at first expressly forbade any attempt at further advance.

But every day that the Germans waited there the Soviet defences would stiffen until the task of crossing the Dnieper would become impossible for anything less than an army group. Eventually Kluge gave way: 'Your operations always hang by a thread!' he muttered, but gave permission for the next stage.

The next three weeks were occupied with the hardest fighting III Panzergruppe had yet experienced, for although advanced units of the 29th Motorized Division reached Smolensk on 16 July, fierce fighting still raged behind them and there was as yet no sign of Hoth's III Panzergruppe spearheads. For 10 days II Panzergruppe had three separate objectives to pursue: to bar the Soviet forces they had bypassed since crossing the Dnieper from escape south or east, to seek to contact III Panzergruppe fighting their way down from the north west, and to widen their hold on the land east of Smolensk (towards Roslavl and the River Desna at Elnya) into a solid bridgehead for the final thrust towards the Germans' great goal, Moscow.

But on 29 July Hitler's adjutant, Colonel Schmundt, arrived at Guderian's headquarters, bringing with him Hitler's felicitations and the Oak Leaves to the Knight's Cross (Guderian was only the fifth man in the army to receive them). He also brought with him the first hint of changes of plan and emphasis.

Moscow was perhaps not so important after all. The rolling wheatlands of the Ukraine would provide the granary from which the ever-growing Axis armies could be fed. Moreover, down in that direction lay the Baku oilfields.

Moscow could wait. Guderian for the moment must go no further east.

Above: German infantry shelter behind the bulk of a Panzer IV on the outskirts of a Russian village. Note the jerrycans of fuel and length of spare track carried on the side of the vehicle.

Left: A Soviet BA-10 armoured car blazes after a direct hit from a German tank gun. The Soviet army had over 1,000 of these large armoured cars in service in 1941 and most were lost by summer 1942.

Right: One of the first T-34s to see action, knocked out at point blank range by a German anti-tank gun battery at Rozana on 5 July 1941. Used in handfuls they achieved little, but when deployed en masse in December it was a different story.

Soviet armour in 1941

When Germany invaded the Soviet Union in June 1941, the Red Army had more tanks than the rest of the world put together. While the majority of their estimated 20,000 tanks were light vehicles, the Soviets fielded a large number of multi-turreted monster tanks and had already developed a medium tank destined to become a war winner.

The T-34 was the most important tank of World War II and its influence can still be detected in modern armour. It was superior to any German tank in 1941 and was produced in vast numbers until well after the war. Stalin held back the limited number operational in 1941 for his December counter-attack.

The KV-1 was the most powerful tank in service in 1941: its armour made it invulnerable to most German weapons, and it carried a heavier gun than any rival tank. It equipped Soviet heavy tank regiments until 1944.

The T-28 was the only one of the Soviet multi-turreted tanks to be even moderately successful; the 'land battleship' concept soon proved a blind alley in tank design.

The T-35 had five turrets carrying three main guns and two machine-guns and a crew of 11, making it an impressive centrepiece for the huge pre-war military parades. After Stalin's slaughter of his officer corps the Red Army was good for little else.

The T-37 two-man amphibious light tank performed badly in the Russo-Finnish war in 1939, but many were still operational in 1941. Its flimsy armour only offered protection against small arms fire.

Under development in 1941 was the T-70 light tank, which replaced the similar T-60 during 1942. The Soviets persevered with their two-man light tanks well into 1943, despite their indifferent performance.

A graphic illustration of the exceptional mobility of the BT-2 light tank, which spawned a whole generation of agile tanks leading eventually to the T-34.

A German machine-gun team in action in the Ukraine after Army Group South's advance received top priority. Napoleon's veterans had complained that the heat of the Russian summer was worse than Egypt, and many of Hitler's soldiers soon shared the sentiment.

Below: Gleeful Waffen SS men remove the remains of a Soviet tank crewman from a knocked out BT-7 light tank on the northern front. The Russian tank reserve in the north was thoroughly defeated in July.

More Russian prisoners are led away into captivity, July 1941. Herded westwards and eventually used as slave labour in the Reich, Soviet POWs had a poor chance of survival.

Field Marshal Leeb's drive out of East Prussia towards Leningrad, though not so powerful as Bock's in the centre, was at the beginning equally successful. Army Group North consisted of two infantry armies – the Sixteenth and the Eighteenth, containing 15 infantry divisions between them – and the IV Panzergruppe, which contained three panzer divisions, three motorized infantry divisions and two infantry divisions. Three infantry divisions were held in support.

It was a matter of some acrimony between the staffs of Leeb and Bock (not between the two principals themselves, who were far too aristocratic to squabble though they encouraged their subordinates to do so) that although Army Group Centre held the bulk of the Wehrmacht's mobile striking power, Army Group North had further to go and, on paper, a much deeper enemy defence to penetrate. Leningrad lay 500 miles from East Prussia, and the seven divisions of General Georg von Küchler's Eighteenth Army were to sweep along the Baltic coastline through Lithuania, Latvia and Estonia, all occupied by recently installed Russian garrisons, with reserves stretching back into the territory of the old Russian Empire.

To the south of this drive the main striking force of IV Panzergruppe would break through the first Soviet defences across the Neiman and, presumably, be quickly into open country behind – but according to German intelligence a large reserve of Soviet tanks was held to the east of Pskov, so Sixteenth Army on the right wing of the advance would have to do everything possible to keep up with the armour. The Sixteenth Army would thus aim for Staraya Russa just south of Lake Ilmen, the Eighteenth on the left would go for Tallinn and then Nerva, while the Panzergruppe went straight for Leningrad itself. As in the other Barbarossa plans, surprise and speed were the basic essentials, the Panzergruppe forming the apex of a wedge, the infantry armies on the flanks. The final words of Army Group Order issued on 5 May 1941 read 'Forward! Don't stop for anything. Never let the enemy consolidate, once he has been thrown back!

Drive on Leningrad

By midnight on 21/22 June, every unit was in position and at 3.05 a.m. the leaders crossed their start-lines and the drive to Leningrad began. The only resistance encountered by the vital centre drive was near Taurage but this was quickly brushed aside, and by the evening of the first day the leading panzers were 37 miles into Lithuania, the only menace a rumour of massed Soviet armour moving north from Wilno, apparently towards Kedaynyay. This town had been the objective of 8th Panzer Division, but there was no sign of Soviet tanks when they reached it – and it was only the following day that it was realized

Chronology of War: 1941

June 8
British Commonwealth and Free French forces invade Syria

June 14
US freezes Axis assets

June 15
British attack Sollum. British attempt to relieve Tobruk, Operation Battleaxe, begins

June 15
British attack Sollum

June 17
Japanese-Dutch negotiations fail. Rommel forces British back into Egypt, Battleaxe fails

June 21
Damascus occupied by Free French forces. General Auchinleck appointed to replace Wavell as C-in-C, Middle East; Wavell appointed C-in-C, India

June 22
Germany invades Russia with 120 divisions along a 2300-km front in Operation Barbarossa. Churchill promises aid to Russia

June 23
Germans cross the river Bug

June 24
Germans take Vilna and Kaunas in Lithuania

June 25
Heavy British merchant shipping losses in Battle of the Atlantic announced in Parliament

June 26
Germans reach Daugavpils, Dvina river crossings and Brest-Litovsk

June 27
Japan declares 'Greater East Asia Co-Prosperity Sphere'

June 30
Germans occupy Lwow. UK civilian casualties in June 309 killed, 461 injured

July 1
Germans occupy Riga on the Baltic. Red Navy shells Constanza in Romania. Guderian's panzers cross Berezina and Army Group North panzers advance on Pskov

July 3
Stalin calls for 'scorched earth' policy

July 8
Germany and Italy partition Yugoslavia. Hitler plans to raze Moscow and Leningrad

July 9
German forces take Minsk pocket and Vitebsk

July 10
Army Group Centre panzer cross Dnieper. Kleist's forces within 10 miles of Kiev. Finnish forces invade Russia

July 11
Ceasefire between Vichy authorities and Allies in Syria

July 12
Anglo-Soviet Mutual Assistance Agreement signed

July 15
Smolensk captured by Army Group Centre. 300,000 Russian troops encircled

July 19
BBC announces existence of Resistance Forces in Europe

July 20
Field Marshal von Bock orders Guderian to close Smolensk pocket

July 22
German Army Group North halts at Lake Ilmen, south of Leningrad

July 24
Vichy France agrees to Japanese occupation of Indo-Chinese bases

that the enemy armour had actually crossed in front of 8th Panzers, eventually reaching Rasenyay in the path of XLI Panzer Corps, who promptly surrounded and destroyed them, none of the 200 Soviet tanks escaping.

The main thrust of the Panzergruppe was thus threatened and by the afternoon of 24 June, 7th Panzer Division was racing along the main road from Kaunas to Daugavpils (Dvinsk) in the River Dvina; by the early morning of the 26th they had captured the two river bridges there. Counter-attacks were beaten off, more panzers came roaring in and by the end of the day the city was firmly in German hands. The first objective of Army Group North – bridgeheads across the wide River Dvina, 185 miles from East Prussia – had thus been achieved in five days, and during the next five days the entire XLI Panzer Corps arrived at Livani to the north, to cross the river there and link up with 7th Panzer to form a bridgehead nearly 18 miles deep. A supply base for the next stage of the advance was thus secure, so on 2 July the Panzergruppe set out on the 155-mile race to the Ostrov/Pskov area.

It seemed incredible to the German command as it did to the watching world that 1st Panzer Division had captured Ostov on 4 July, 6th Panzer Division had smashed a way through the northern extension of the 'Stalin Line' about 18 miles south of Ostrov on the same day, and three motorized divisions of the Panzergruppe had crossed the old Latvian-Russian border opposite Opochka and were also driving up towards Ostrov. As a result, when the mass of Soviet tanks held east of Pskov were thrown into the battle on 5 July in a counter-attack on Ostrov, the German armour had been thoroughly reinforced, and by the end of the second day only the wrecks of 140 Soviet tanks lay betwen the panzer divisions and Pskov itself.

Into the Baltic states

Now, of course, the immutable problem arose: the panzers streaking ahead at such a rate, how could the infantry keep up? The problem was further complicated by the terrain encountered east of the old borders with the Baltic states, which proved so marshy and generally impenetrable that the pace of even the motorized infantry was reduced to little more than that of the marching columns – and they were just clearing Daugavpils back in the Dvina.

Nonetheless, it was quite evident that chaos and confusion reigned throughout the opposing forces, and advantage must be taken of this. Panzergruppe must drive on forward, and if their own supporting infantry and that of the Sixteenth Army on their right could not keep up, perhaps that of the Eighteenth on their left could help.

As the roads in Lithuania, Latvia and Estonia were so much better than those in Russia, the progress of Eighteenth Army had in fact been almost as spectacular as that of the Panzergruppe. Yelgave and Riga had both been taken on 29 June by which time some 12 Soviet divisions had been annihilated, and by 7 July both Tallinn and Narva were under Eighteenth Army artillery fire, while four divisions were driving towards the southern end of Lake Peipus. Here indeed lay help for the Panzergruppe.

Infantry support weapons

German and Soviet infantry regiments included a large number of mortars to provide local fire support. German units began the war using light artillery as well, but the combination of firepower and ease of production represented by Soviet heavy mortars led the Wehrmacht to follow suit, even directly copying some Russian mortars.

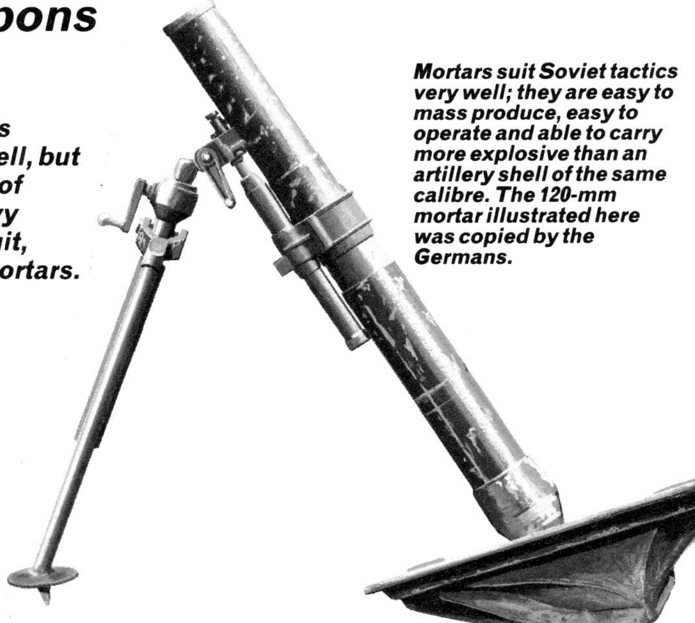

Mortars suit Soviet tactics very well; they are easy to mass produce, easy to operate and able to carry more explosive than an artillery shell of the same calibre. The 120-mm mortar illustrated here was copied by the Germans.

A Soviet 120-mm mortar is aimed against German positions on the Caucasian front, 1942. The 120-mm HM 38 was the best mortar produced during World War II, and is still in widespread service today.

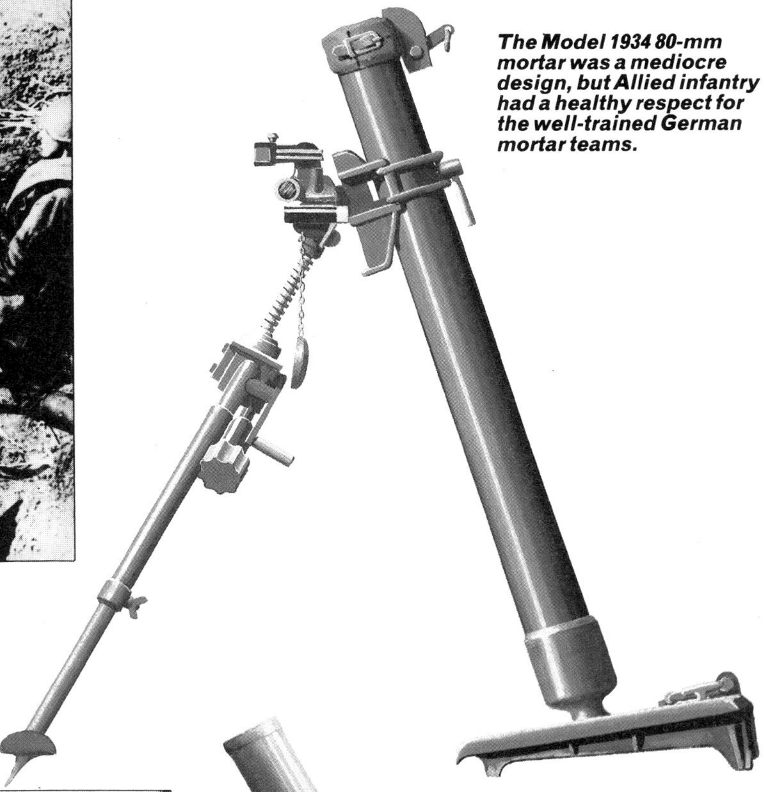

The Model 1934 80-mm mortar was a mediocre design, but Allied infantry had a healthy respect for the well-trained German mortar teams.

German infantrymen fire a Model 1936 50-mm mortar at the Russian lines. A light mortar of this size would have been useful, but this weapon was unnecessarily complicated, fragile and expensive to produce.

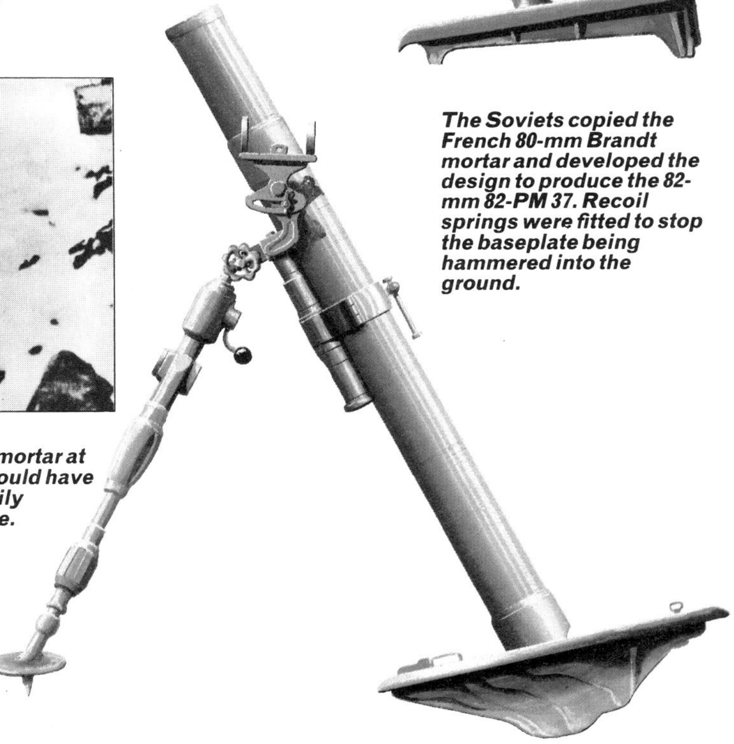

The Soviets copied the French 80-mm Brandt mortar and developed the design to produce the 82-mm 82-PM 37. Recoil springs were fitted to stop the baseplate being hammered into the ground.

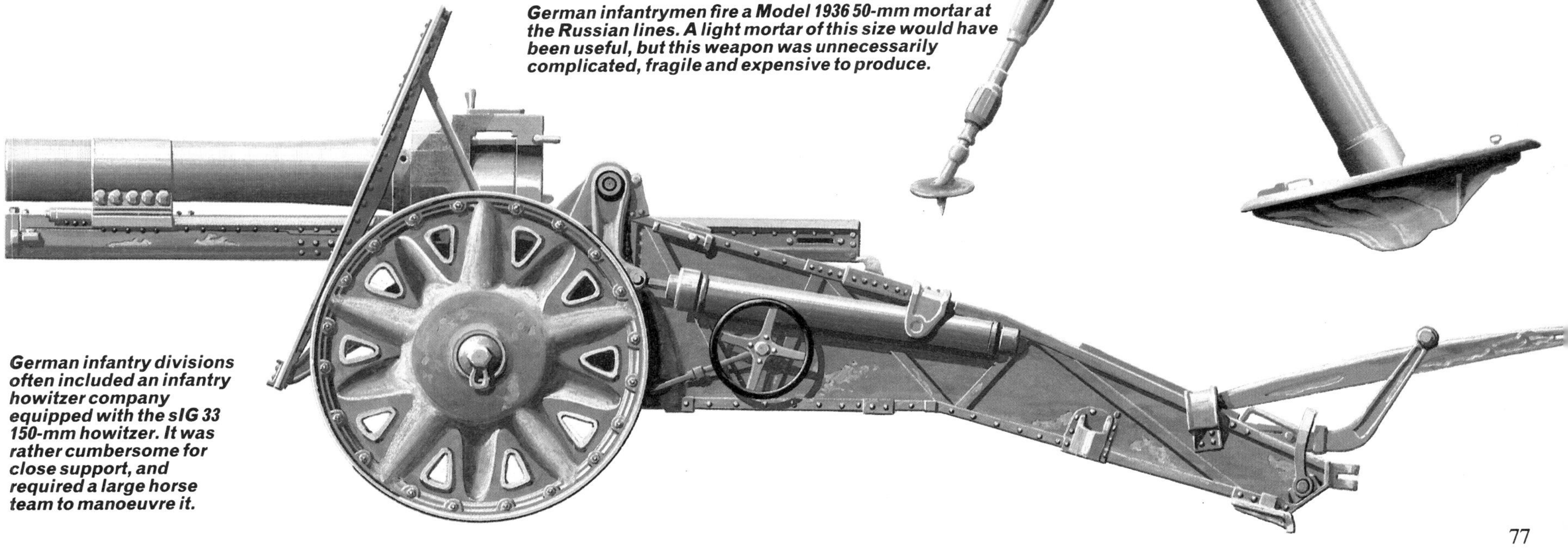

German infantry divisions often included an infantry howitzer company equipped with the sIG 33 150-mm howitzer. It was rather cumbersome for close support, and required a large horse team to manoeuvre it.

Left: German infantry march past some of the vast quantities of equipment captured in the Kiev pocket. Over 500,000 Soviet troops surrendered.

German infantry debus from SdKfz 251 half-tracks to assault a Russian village. The use of half-tracks as armoured personnel carriers was central to the combined arms tactics of the Panzer divisions.

Millions of Russians regarded the Germans as liberators, freeing them from the barbaric rule of the communists, but the Nazis' racial policies soon led to disillusionment and resistance behind the lines.

On 7 July, the decision was taken: 1st and 58th Infantry Divisions were moved from Eighteenth Army to Panzergruppe command and ordered to drive eastwards into Pskov while the panzer divisions themselves raced ahead to the River Luga between Kingisepp and Sabsk, only 60 miles from Leningrad itself. By 15 July they were across the lower Luga, and to their triumphant eyes it seemed that Peter the Great's city was theirs for the taking. But the caution which was to restrain Guderian west of the Desna now held them back. To the commanders back in Germany – and to Hitler especially – the picture across the whole Barbarossa Front was one of increasing danger. Not only were the gaps opening too far between German armour and German infantry, they were also gaping widely between the army groups themselves – and though the enemy forces in these gaps were all evidently in conditions varying only from confusion to chaos, they consisted of an apparently unlimited number of brave soldiers who seemed incapable of realizing when they were beaten.

Surrounded Russians

The number of pockets of enemy resistance bypassed by the Panzergruppen of both Northern and Central Army Groups grew every day, and none of them evinced the slightest inclination to surrender until the last bullets had been fired. So although steps could be taken to ensure that no further ammunition got into the pockets, time must elapse before the German infantry could all join the panzers and ensure a stable platform from which to launch the next stages of the invasion of Russia. Despite the anguished pleas of the panzer commanders Reinhardt and Manstein, the idea of an immediate thrust into the heart of Leningrad would have to wait.

Behind them, the infantry fought and marched, fought and marched again – and gradually the strength waned. Casualties were inevitably suffered, and formations – battalions, regiments, even divisions – had to be left behind to deal with the pockets. Then in mid-July the orders came that a drive up from the northern wing of Army Group Centre to fill that ominous gap between the two groups needed help, so one corps of Sixteenth Army must now veer further to the right towards Nevel and the Upper Dvina, well south of the army groups' planned borderline at Velikiye Luki.

Though it was not realized at the time, this development killed the idea of the capture of Leningrad by a rapid *coup de main*. Not only would the lapse of time give the Russian defenders opportunity to strengthen their positions enormously, but as the arrows on the maps showing the infantry advance crept north-eastwards, they also revealed the magnetic influence of that gap to the south. The first two infantry divisions from Eighteenth Army which had gone to Pskov were in fact moved north along the eastern side of Lake Peipus towards Narva, but two more – 11th and 21st – were ordered to Pskov, then further east to Porkhov and north to Soltsy, which they captured on 22 July. But an attempt to drive further north was checked west of Lake Ilmen, largely by another immutable factor of warfare: after more than a month of constant fighting and forced marches, often in great heat, the German infantry were suffering mounting exhaustion.

In these circumstances, a weakening of the Panzergruppe now began, for Hitler had decided that Novgorod and Chudovo were essential objectives, and, as the infantry drive towards them had stalled, panzers must come across to help. The position was stabilized, but Manstein's panzers did not return to the lower Dvina, remaining with the infantry for a projected drive on Lyuban, to be co-ordinated with one on Krasnogvardiesk by Reinhardt's corps.

This began, in pouring rain, in the early morning of 8 August, and consisted of drives from the the original bridgehead on the lower Dvina and from the newly won ground west of Lake Ilmen; but the assault on the left ran into an attack planned by the Red Army on the Panzergruppe for exactly the same moment, and the storm of fire that blanketed the area stunned even the most experienced soldiers on each side. Eventually, however, German training and efficiency prevailed, four panzer divisions broke through, and by 11 August were clear yet again for the drive on Leningrad – only to be held back by more problems caused by Russian intransigence. Five divisions holding ground just north of Luga refused to budge and now had to be 'stabbed in the back' from the north, to free the right-hand wing for the first stage of its advance on Novgorod.

Novgorod remained inviolate until 16 August, after which Chudovo fell quickly to Manstein's pan-

Chronology of War: 1941

July 25
Japanese assets in US, UK and Dominions frozen. Vital RN convoy arrives in Malta after two-day battle. Italians make unsuccessful night attack on Grand Harbour with human torpedoes and explosive motor boats

July 28
Japanese troops land in Indo-China. Japan freezes US, UK and Dutch assets

July 31
UK civilian casualties in July 501 killed, 447 injured. Göring, on Hitler's instruction orders Heydrich, head of the Nazi security service, to make 'all necessary preparations for a complete solution to the Jewish problem'

August 1
US oil embargo against 'aggressors'. Roosevelt establishes Economic Defense Board

August 3
Generals von Kleist and von Stülpnagel seal Uman pocket. Finnish forces occupy Karelian Isthmus

August 5
Odessa under siege by Romanian forces. End of all resistance in Smolensk pocket

August 12
Atlantic Charter signed by Churchill and Roosevelt. Army Group North advances on Leningrad. Hitler postpones advance on Moscow in favour of encirclement of Kiev

August 16
Novgorod taken by Army Group North

August 18
Army Group North captures Nikolayev and Kingisepp

August 19
Leningrad almost encircled

August 24
Russians counterattack at Gomel. Guderian heads south from Army Group Centre towards Kiev and Army Group South

August 25
Panzer units consolidate at Dnepropetrovsk

August 29
Russians evacuate Karelian Isthmus

August 31
UK civilian casualties in August 169 killed, 136 injured

September 1
German long-range artillery bombards Leningrad

September 4
Finland re-occupies pre-war frontier

September 5
Germans complete occupation of Estonia

September 6
Japan decides on war against the USA and the Colonial powers of SE Asia

September 8
Leningrad cut off by German Army Group North

September 12
First snow on Russian Front

September 15
Von Kleist's and Guderian's panzers meet at Lokhvitsa, trapping four Soviet armies. Siege of Leningrad begins

September 17
STAVKA (Soviet High Command) agrees Red Army withdrawal from Kiev

September 19
Germans take Kiev and Poltava

September 25
Surrender of vast Russian forces in Kiev Pocket

Air forces of Hitler's allies

A host of national contingents fought side-by-side with the Germans on the Eastern Front. They varied widely in quality and quantity, and included forces from the states Hitler created from the conquered nations of Central Europe as well as neighbours of the Soviet Union caught between the two aggressive dictatorships.

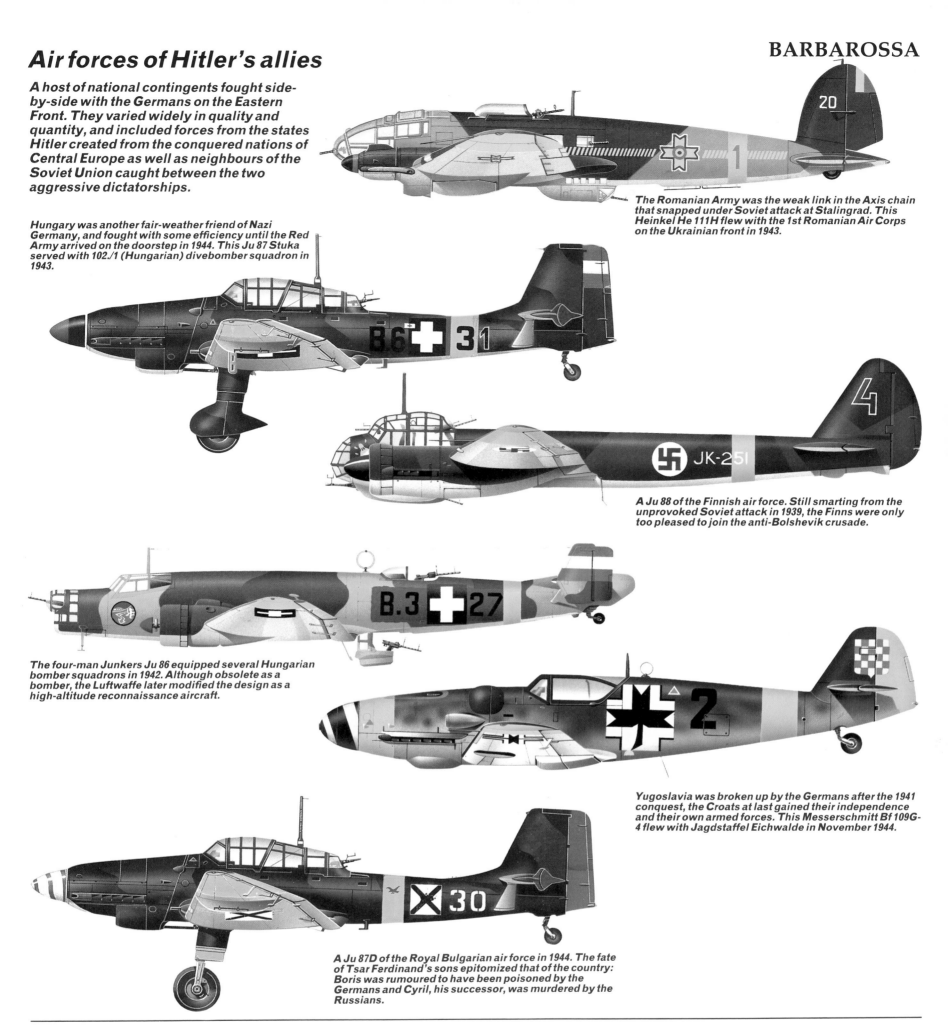

The Romanian Army was the weak link in the Axis chain that snapped under Soviet attack at Stalingrad. This Heinkel He 111H flew with the 1st Romanian Air Corps on the Ukrainian front in 1943.

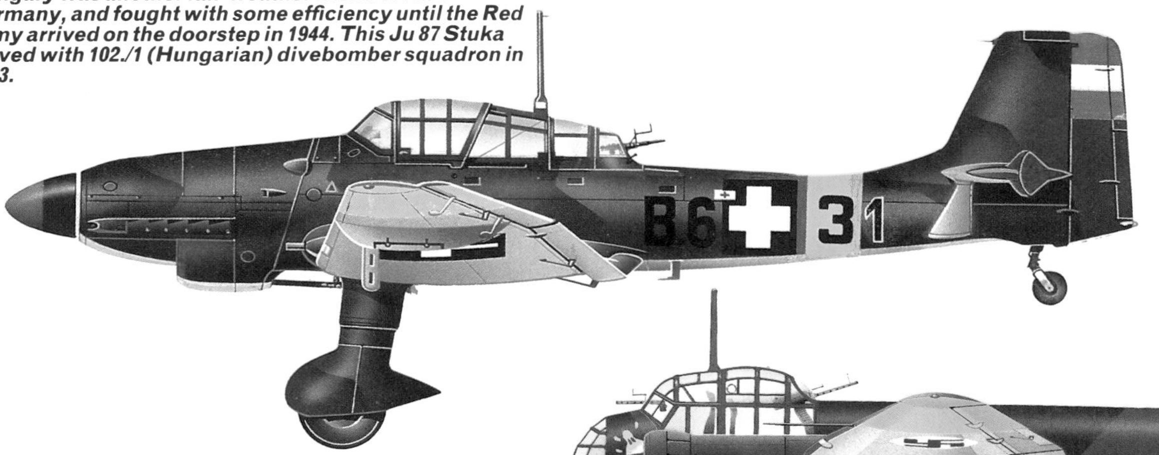

Hungary was another fair-weather friend of Nazi Germany, and fought with some efficiency until the Red Army arrived on the doorstep in 1944. This Ju 87 Stuka served with 102./1 (Hungarian) divebomber squadron in 1943.

A Ju 88 of the Finnish air force. Still smarting from the unprovoked Soviet attack in 1939, the Finns were only too pleased to join the anti-Bolshevik crusade.

The four-man Junkers Ju 86 equipped several Hungarian bomber squadrons in 1942. Although obsolete as a bomber, the Luftwaffe later modified the design as a high-altitude reconnaissance aircraft.

Yugoslavia was broken up by the Germans after the 1941 conquest, the Croats at last gained their independence and their own armed forces. This Messerschmitt Bf 109G-4 flew with Jagdstaffel Eichwalde in November 1944.

A Ju 87D of the Royal Bulgarian air force in 1944. The fate of Tsar Ferdinand's sons epitomized that of the country: Boris was rumoured to have been poisoned by the Germans and Cyril, his successor, was murdered by the Russians.

zers, which then went on to reach Lyuban on 28 August. Moreover, Hitler had now ordered Army Group Centre to release one of General Hoth's Panzer corps to help Army Group North on its right wing, and this came up on the west bank of the Volkhov. Its leading units drove into Ishora, only 11 miles from the centre of Leningrad, on the day that Lyuban was captured, while its accompanying motorized infantry swung up to the east towards the River Neva and the shores of Lake Ladoga. The old capital of Russia was now surrounded.

Assault on Leningrad

But not yet occupied – and in some disregard of directions which were now reaching him, Leeb sent Reinhardt's XVI Panzer Corps in for the final blow. It began on the morning of 9 September, and the two leading divisions were soon enmeshed in a labyrinth of anti-tank ditches and straggling earthworks thrown up by the desperate Leningraders while the Germans had waited. These were the worst conditions for attacking armour, the best for stubborn infantry defence and though by the evening of 10 September German units had reached the Dugerdorf Heights, six miles south east of the city, so many panzers had been hit or had broken down that the momentum of attack had been dissipated. German infantry crept up on their left during the following day, entered the Leningrad suburbs of Slutsk and Pushkin, and in the evening occupied the Summer Palace of the Tsars at Krasnoye Selo. But the impetus had gone.

And by now the lure of the wheatlands of the Ukraine and the Baku oilfields had taken complete control of Hitler's mind. Like Moscow, Leningrad must wait – indeed, Hitler had decided that he no longer wanted Leningrad at all, for its civilian population of some three million would be nothing but an embarrassment! It should be encircled by infantry – perhaps in time even by an electric fence – its inhabitants starved to death, its architecture eventually pounded to dust by the Luftwaffe. When it had been flattened, the area could be handed over to the Finns, despite the fact that Marshal Mannerheim had declined to involve the Finnish army more closely in the attack on Russia than to advance just past the old Russo-Finnish border of 1939, thus merely reoccupying Finnish territory.

All material strength the Werhrmacht could muster, all reserves, all military attention, must be focused on the vast reaches to the south, beyond the Dneiper, beyond the Crimea, into the Donets Bend, and even across and into the Caucasus.

Military ambition had never mounted higher.

Left: Troops of Colonel-General von Kleist's I Panzergruppe advance to the south of the Pripet Marshes after Hitler's decision to strike into the Ukraine. The Soviet Fifth Army retreated into the trackless wastes of the marshes in order to re-group.

There is some irony in the fact that by August 1941 Hitler had decided that the southern front of Barbarossa was the most important, for in order to capture it Field Marshal Gerd von Rundstedt had originally been given command of by far the weakest group. In the northern section of 600-mile-wide attack front, launching from the Lublin area of southern Poland, were his more powerful forces, but these consisted of Sixth Army under Reichenau, 1st Panzergruppe under Kleist and Seventeenth Army under Stulpnagel; in the south, driving out of Moldavia, was only one German Army – Eleventh under Schobert – accompanied by Third and Fourth Romanian Armies, a Hungarian army corps and an Italian army corps, all armed with out-of-date rifles and machine-guns and a bare minimum of artillery and vehicles.

Nonetheless, tactics were envisaged for the advance similar to those employed by the two northern army groups. Kleist's panzers accompanied by Reichenau's infantry were ordered to break through along the southern edge of the Pripet Marshes driving east to reach the Dneiper just below Kiev, while Stulpnagel's infantry drove south east along the northern edge of the Carpathians towards Vinnitsa, eventually meeting Kleist's armour even further east on the river. They would thus trap the whole Russian 'South-West Front' between two gigantic pincer arms, and so occupy the greater part of the Ukraine. To their south, Schobert's army and his conglomerate were first to ensure the safety of the Ploesti oilfields; then, once these were fully protected, they were to drive east and capture south-west Ukraine, occupying the Black Sea coast probably as far as the Crimea.

So far as the principal drive was concerned, it made excellent progress from the start, for the Russian commander, General Kirponos, in his haste to block their advance committed his forces piecemeal as they became available. Thus they were all separately shattered, though this was not the end of early resistance. In their first powerful thrust, I Panzergruppe had shouldered the Russian Fifth Army aside and into the Pripet Marshes where neither German armour nor vehicles could follow – and with that infuriating tendency towards survival that typified other bypassed Soviet troops, Fifth Army reorganized and in mid-July struck south west from Korosten towards Novograd Volynski, where it hoped to meet the Soviet Sixth Army driving up from below Berdichev.

The Germans' expertise and their skilful use of the 88-mm flak gun in an anti-tank role broke this attempt to snap off the German spearhead, but Fifth Army then retreated back into the marshes and for the next six weeks both Kleist and Reichenau were uncomfortably aware of the threat hanging over their north-western shoulder.

Battle of the Ukraine

But the main drive to the south west continued down between the Bug and the Dniester, while at the same time Soviet forces, now under command of the flamboyant but inexpert Marshal S. M. Budenny and his political commissar Nikita Khrushchev, concentrated around two important centres – Kiev and Uman. Avoiding both by cutting between them, Kleist's Panzergruppe with Sixth Army in close attendance (the ground was much harder here in the

Soviet small arms 1941-5

Soviet small arms, like most other Soviet weapons, were simple to manufacture, sturdy in the extreme and highly effective. Over 2 million German troops were killed in action on the Eastern Front, and half of them fell to bullets fired from these weapons.

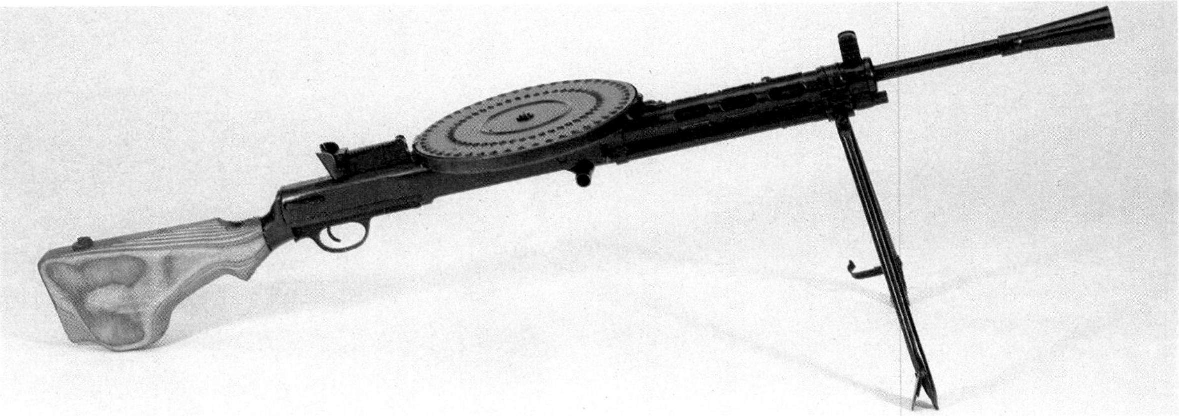

Easily distinguished by its flatpan magazine, the Degtyarev DP Model 1928 was an outstandingly successful light machine-gun and served throughout the war.

The Tokarev TT33 was a semi-automatic pistol developed from the Colt/Browning designs and chambered for 7.62-mm ammunition. It can still be encountered today in the hands of Warsaw Pact security forces.

While the mass of Soviet infantry used cheap SMGs, the Russians were among the first countries to introduce a self-loading rifle, the SVT 40 which was usually issued to NCOs or Guards units.

Ukraine than further north, so infantry could move more quickly) drove down the land-bridge between the rivers, and part of Reichenau's forces curved west towards Pervomaisk where they were joined first by Stulpnagel's division and then by Schobert's coming up from Moldavia. The Russian Sixth and Twelfth Armies and part of the Eighteenth were thus isolated between very strong forces and held there additionally by orders from Stalin, who refused to recognize the danger they were in. By 3 August they had been sealed in, by the 8th they were being subjected to pressure from every side under heavy artillery fire, and when two days later their resistance ceased, some 20 Russian divisions had been annihilated and 103,000 prisoners taken.

Romanian offensive

Moreover, while this had been happening, the two Romanian armies had marched along the coast and begun a siege of Odessa which, although it was to last 64 days and inflict an almost unbearable toll of Romanian casualties, nevertheless tied up the huge Russian garrison, which could thus play no part in the drama unfolding to the north. Here the largest concentration of Red Army troops lay at Kiev and in the area immediately to the north. On Hitler's orders, Guderian's II Panzergruppe was now driving down to meet Kleist's curving up, thus cutting off three complete Russian armies and the remnants of at least two more.

Guderian had not, in fact, immediately obeyed the orders which had reached him on 29 July, because his eyes – and wholehearted ambition – were still focused on Moscow. He thus invented a threat by Russian divisions around the small town of Roslavl, launched his Panzergruppe in an attack upon it which he hoped would so embroil them that it would be almost impossible to detach them until they had 'eaten' their way much nearer to Moscow – and was thus disappointed when complete and rapid victory attended their efforts.

On 4 August Hitler travelled forward to Novo Borosow and talked to his senior commanders (as a result, one of Hoth's panzer corps was despatched north to Leningrad) and for the moment was sufficiently impressed by the arguments of Bock and Guderian not to insist upon the abandonment of the drive on Moscow. But during the next three weeks his attitude hardened, and on 24 August in a solitary interview with Guderian he ordered him to lead his entire Panzergruppe down to assist in the occupation of the Ukraine, in the capture of the huge and vitally important industrial region stretching from Kiev to Kharkov and beyond, in the neutralization of the Crimea as a base from which the Ploesti oilfields could be bombed – and perhaps even in the penetration into the the huge Donets Bend.

During the next two days Panzergruppe Guderian (as it had been renamed as something of a sop to Guderian's feelings) swung its axis through 90 degrees and set out for Novgorod Severski, Konotop and the meeting with Kleist.

A new army group – the Bryansk Front – had been formed by the Red Army Command (STAVKA) along the east bank of the Desna with the specific aim of stoving in Guderian's flank as it moved down (for

***Right:* After a siege of nine weeks, the Black Sea port of Odessa fell to German and Romanian forces. Here Romanian troops load the spoils of victory before the offensive continues.**

Not all Soviet gun designs were crude, hastily-produced weapons; the PPD-34, which completed production in 1940, was developed from pre-war German SMGs but introduced two features which were to become common: a chrome-plated barrel and a 71-round drum magazine.

During the siege of Leningrad an engineer called Sudarev designed one of the crudest sub-machine guns ever made. It was a runaway success and was developed into the PPS-43, which became one of the standard Soviet SMGs.

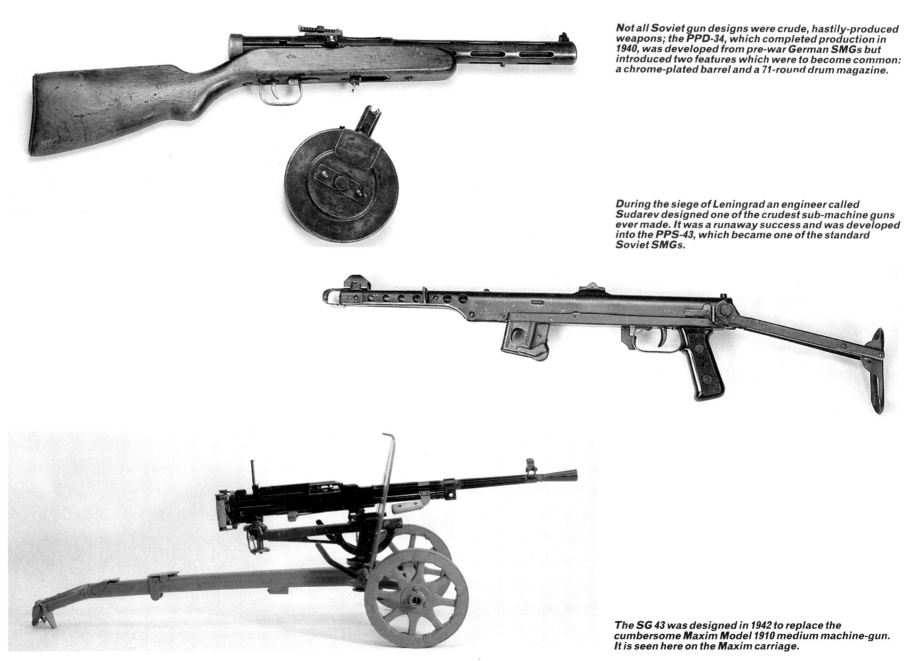

The SG 43 was designed in 1942 to replace the cumbersome Maxim Model 1910 medium machine-gun. It is seen here on the Maxim carriage.

General Zhukov was now in the area and already exhibiting that uncanny gift for divining his enemy's thought processes). Unfortunately, the Red Army Chief of General Staff, Marshal Shaposhnikov, believed that Moscow was still Guderian's objective and that the Panzergruppe would veer east just north of Bryansk and attempt to cut off Moscow from the south. He thus ordered the most powerful elements of the Bryansk Front to line this route, so they were unavailable to attack Guderian as he drove south.

Nonetheless, two armies of the Bryansk Front under General Yeremenko moved forward on 30 August to attack Guderian's left flank, but lack of co-ordination and, more importantly, of air cover (for the Red Air Force had by now been virtually emasculated) left them at the mercy not only of the Panzergruppe but also of the remainder of Kluge's Fourth Army (renumbered Second Army). By 2 September Bryansk Front was in tatters, and eight day later Stalin was receiving direct appeals from both Budenny and Khrushchev for permission for their still large but disintegrating forces to be allowed to escape through the rapidly narrowing gap between Konotop and Kremenchug where Kleist's Panzergruppe had crossed the Dnieper and were preparing to drive north.

Stalin sought the views of Kirponos in the Kiev pocket and promptly rejected the advice given, which was to allow the Kiev garrison also to escape the trap which was obviously about to be sprung; he then dismissed Budenny and appointed Marshal Timoshenko to preside over the ensuing débâcle. During the remaining days that the gap remained open, Stalin insisted through Shaposhnikov that all fronts, all armies, all divisions should stand fast where they were.

Guderian's panzers met Kleist's at Lokhvitsa on 15 September, infantry and guns from Second Army to the north and from Seventeenth to the south came up to harden the ring, and by the evening of 17 September the biggest encirclement of the entire Barbarossa campaign – probably of history – had been formed, and this time hardly anyone would escape. That night permission was at last given for the remnants of the Soviet armies to attempt to break out to the east, but the bulk had too far to go and lacked the heavy mobile equipment to smash through the waiting German ring. Budenny and Khrushchev were flown out, Major-General Bagramyan brought out about 50 men; but Kirponos and most of the staffs of the South-West Front and of the Fifth Army were killed as they tried to escape, or were rounded up and captured. And with them into graves or prison-camps of the most appalling nature went nearly 500,000 Russian soldiers, making this in terms of numbers the biggest military catastrophe in Russian history, perhaps in all history.

Above: A dramatic scene at Mariepol on the Sea of Azov, which was reached by German forces in early October, isolating several Soviet divisions against the coast.

Right: Dead SS men lie in the snow after the Soviet counterattack from Moscow in December 1941. At the beginning of the month, German units penetrated to the very suburbs of the city, just 23 miles from Red Square.

Above: A KV-1 heavy tank trundles purposefully through Moscow to join the counter attack in December 1941. Invulnerable to most German anti-tank guns, these vehicles were instrumental in saving the capital.

The Kiev pocket

Guderian and Kleist were jubilant, Rundstedt modestly gratified that the greatest single success of German arms had been won by the army group under his command. In that atmosphere of heady euphoria, few remarked that for all their triumphs and all the ground won, something had been lost: time.

But Kleist at least was aware that time was passing. With admirable speed he drew his Panzergruppe back south to the area around Dnepropetrovsk and on 30 September it erupted from a bridgehead over the Samara at Novomoskovsk and drove down to the Sea of Azov, neatly trapping Ninth, Twelfth and Eighteenth Soviet Armies between Orekhov and Osipenko, while Eleventh Army, now under command of General von Manstein, drove eastwards along the coast. Another 106,000 prisoners were taken, together with 212 tanks and nearly 700 guns – but now haste and perhaps over-confidence tempted Army Group South too far.

By October, rain, wind and the first snow flurries were bringing a hint of the white chaos which would soon engulf the whole Russian front, and by the end

Chronology of War: 1941

September 26
Operation Typhoon, offensive against Moscow, ordered

September 27
Estimated two-thirds of Red Army strength on Russian front destroyed, 500,000 prisoners being taken at Kiev

September 28
First Allied convoy to Russia leaves Iceland

September 30
UK civilian casualties in September 217 killed, 269 injured

October 2
German attack on Moscow is launched

October 7
Panzer spearheads seal Vyasma (six Soviet armies encircled) and Bryansk pockets (two Soviet armies encircled)

October 8
Guderian's panzers capture Orel

October 14
Resistance in Vyasma pocket ends

October 16
Soviet Government leave Moscow for Kuybyshev; Stalin remains. Odessa surrenders

October 17
General Hideki Tojo replaces moderate Prince Konoye as head of Japanese government

October 20
Resistance in Bryansk pocket ends; total Soviet losses in Vyassma/Bryansk battles in excess of 70 divisions, yielding 673,000 prisoners. Germans capture Stalino. Japanese navy prepares for Pearl Harbor attack

October 21
General Georgi Zhukov appointed as defender of Moscow

October 24
Von Runstedt's Army Group South takes Kharkov

October 26
Australians withdrawn from Tobruk

October 27
Russian counterattack around Moscow

October 29
German breakthrough in Crimea

October 31
UK civilian casualties in October 262 killed, 361 injured

November 1
Germans capture Simferopol

November 3
Germans capture Kursk. Approval of Yamamoto's plan to attack Pearl Harbor by Japanese Imperial Command

November 4
Germans capture Feodosia

November 5
Japanese Command issues final war orders

November 6
Russian casualties to date given as 350,000 killed, 378,000 missing, 1,020,000 injured

November 9
Important railhead at Tikhvin captured by Army Group North

November 14
British aircraft carrier HMS Ark Royal sunk off Gibraltar

November 15
20 degrees of frost halts German offensive against Moscow

November 16
German Army Group South captures Kerch

November 17
Commando raid on Rommel's North African headquarters. Lt. Col. Keyes killed

Eastern Front Air War

Like the Soviet tank arm, the Air Force had vast numbers of obsolescent machines in 1941 and the Luftwaffe made short work of them, some pilots running up prodigious tallies of victories.

The assault on the Soviet Union was launched before dawn on 22 June 1941 along a front that stretched from the Baltic to the Black Sea, the three army groups (under Leeb, Bock and Rundstedt) advancing 50 miles (80 km) in the first 24 hours. Supporting the huge offensive were four *Luftflotten* (air fleets) which between them deployed 19 *Jagdgruppen* of Bf 109Es and Bf 109Fs (600 aircraft), seven *Stukagruppen* of Ju 87 dive-bombers (more than 200 aircraft) and 24 *Kampfgruppen* of He 111s, Do 17s and Ju 88s (about 850 aircraft), as well as more than 1,000 other transports and reconnaissance aircraft.

So widely dispersed were the Soviet airfields that the Luftwaffe was only able to send three or four aircraft against each yet, by use of large numbers of 2-kg and 10-kg (4.4-lb and 22-lb) fragmentation bombs, they were able to devastate the grounded aircraft. The relatively small numbers of outdated I-16 fighters which rose to defend their bases were swatted like flies by the experienced Luftwaffe pilots in their superb Bf 109s. During that first day the Soviets admitted the loss of more than 1,200 aircraft.

The airfield strikes were quickly followed by an attack by 127 He 111s and Ju 88s on Moscow, 104 tons of HE and 46,000 incendiary bombs being dropped; this was followed within 48 hours by two further raids by 115 and 100 aircraft. The massacre of Soviet aircraft continued to occupy the Luftwaffe throughout July and August, and not unnaturally huge personal victory tallies were amassed by individual pilots; by mid-August four of the *Jagdgeschwader* (JG 3, JG 51, JG 53 and JG 54) had each passed a score of 1,000 enemy aircraft destroyed.

The autumn rains slowed the pace of the German advance but air operations continued relentlessly. On 23 September Ju 87s of Stukageschwader 2 based at Tyrkowo attacked the Soviet fleet at Kronstadt, and a single bomb dropped by Oberleutnant Hans Rudel sank the Soviet battleship *Marat*. By the end of that month the front stretched from the Crimea in an almost straight line to Leningrad.

Despite the weather the German armies managed to struggle forward and by early December reached Rostov, Voronezh and the outskirts of Moscow itself just as the first snows fell. This effectively brought air operations to a halt.

The Soviet December offensive pushed back the German spearhead and the air forces prepared for the next year's fighting; both the Luftwaffe and V-VS were hurriedly introducing improved aircraft. The Bf 109E was now finally being replaced in all units by the Bf 109F; the Do 17 had almost disappeared from front-line service, being replaced by the Do 217, while new versions of the He 111, Ju 88 and Ju 52/3m were starting to arrive at the front. Among the Soviet aircraft the I-15 and I-16 were being withdrawn at last as deliveries of modern LaGG-3s, MiG-3s and Yak-1s were frantically stepped up. Production of the Il-4 bomber (which had first raided Berlin on 8 August 1941) and Il-2 close-support aircraft was accelerating, and the first British convoys bringing Hurricane fighters had been arriving at Murmansk since September.

Above: MiG-3 fighters are seen lined up at a factory, awaiting delivery to the hard-pressed squadrons of the V-VS (Air Defence Force) in late 1941.

Above: Soviet I-16 fighters litter a field after being destroyed on the ground by German air attack, the fate of many Soviet aircraft in the summer of 1941.

Above right: Ju 87 Stukas are shown with an escorting Bf 109 over the Ukraine, autumn 1941. As usual the Stuka proved highly effective against an enemy lacking first-rate interceptors.

Left: An I-16B fighter takes off to face the might of the Luftwaffe. Few were destined to return.

Above: In September the first British convoys arrived to bring numbers of Hawker Hurricanes to bolster the Soviet fighter squadrons.

of that month Kleist's Panzergruppe were edging their way slowly into Rostov; although they did not know it, they were also edging into a Soviet trap as dangerous as any they had themselves set. STAVKA had at last learnt the effectiveness of the traditional Russian tactic of trading space for time; and many of the units threatened with encirclement by both Panzergruppe and by the armies of Reichenau and Stulpnagel in the drive for Kharkov had in fact been allowed by Stalin to escape and were now being re-formed into the Soviet Thirty-seventh Army in the angle of the Donets Bend.

On 19 November they began to move implacably forward into Rostov, The following day they were joined by shock troops of the Ninth Army, and by 28 November 1st Panzergruppe had been squeezed out of Rostov, back through Taganrog to the line of the Mius River. It was the first time in World War II that the German army had had to face an enemy attack, prepared and launched after adequate organization – and one of the immediate results was Hitler's anger, followed by Rundstedt's resignation and der Alte Herr's departure for ever from the Eastern Front.

Guderian and Bock were facing a similar phenomenon in front of Moscow.

At the gates of Moscow

On 23 July, General Halder had reported to Hitler that the Soviet forces now facing the Wehrmacht amounted to 93 divisions, of which 13 were armoured; on 1 December his estimate was of 200 infantry divisions, 35 cavalry divisions and 40 armoured brigades – with another 70 mixed divisions deep inside Soviet territory. And of these, 18 divisions of excellently trained, well-equipped and warmly clothed long-service troops, with 1,700 tanks and 1,500 aircraft, were on their way to the Moscow Front from the Far Eastern Front in outer Siberia. The brilliant Soviet agent, Richard Sorge, had been able to assure the Soviet leaders that there was no need to hold them along the frontier with Japanese-occupied China, as Japan had no intention of going to war with Russia.

These divisions were reviewed in Red Square in early December and went straight on to launch an attack from the front lines of Moscow defences. By mid-December, three Russian commanders all later to become world famous – Koniev, Zhukov and Timoshenko – were directing attacks by large armies against the German ring around Moscow, and making advances which, though small (in comparison with army movements during the preceding months), were nonetheless significant.

Early in the month, both Kluge and Guderian had come to the conclusion that they must give their troops time to form defensive positions in which to shelter, not only from the Russians but also from the fierce cold which now gripped the Eastern Front and for which no preparations had been made in the Barbarossa plans. Frostbite caused more hospitalization now than Russian guns, hypothermia would soon be killing more. And now Russian attacks were forcing them out of their hard-won positions, causing the German commanders to look over their shoulders and seek safer defences to the rear.

Hitler would have none of this! Haunted by the spectre of Napoleon's retreat from Moscow, he would allow not the slightest suggestion of the Wehrmacht turning their backs, even momentarily, on the Russian capital; and when his commanders protested, he sacked them.

The most senior to go was Brauchitsch, the commander-in-chief, whose place Hitler took himself, thereby completing the subjection of the German army to his personal control, a process upon which he had embarked almost as soon as he reached the Chancellory. Also to go were the other two army group commanders, Leeb and Bock – they were dismissed; only Rundstedt, for whom Hitler to the end had great respect, was allowed to resign – and, just before Christmas, Guderian also was dismissed. Thirty-five other corps or divisional commanders were likewise dismissed, and Hoepner, who had commanded the 4th Panzergruppe in the north, was cashiered, then called back into the army as a private.

So far had the reputation of the German army fallen in two months of the Russian winter, from those triumphant heights of summer when it had seemed that they were conquering the world! Vaulting ambition had betrayed them all.

November 19
Operation 'Crusader' launched by General Alan Cunningham's Eighth Army in Cyrenaica. Sir Alan Brooke appointed CIGS in London

November 20
Japanese negotiators present Washington with an ultimatum

November 21
Germans complete occupation of Rostov-on-Don

November 22
Heavy fighting btween South African 5th Division and 21st Panzer Division at Sidi Rezegh

November 23
'Totensonntag'; 5th South African Brigade destroyed by Afrika Korps

November 25
British battleship HMS Barham *sunk by* U-331 *off Sollum. 862 killed in magazine explosion*

November 26
Japanese carrier fleet sails from Japan for Hawaii. Major-General Neil Ritchie takes command of 8th Army in the desert

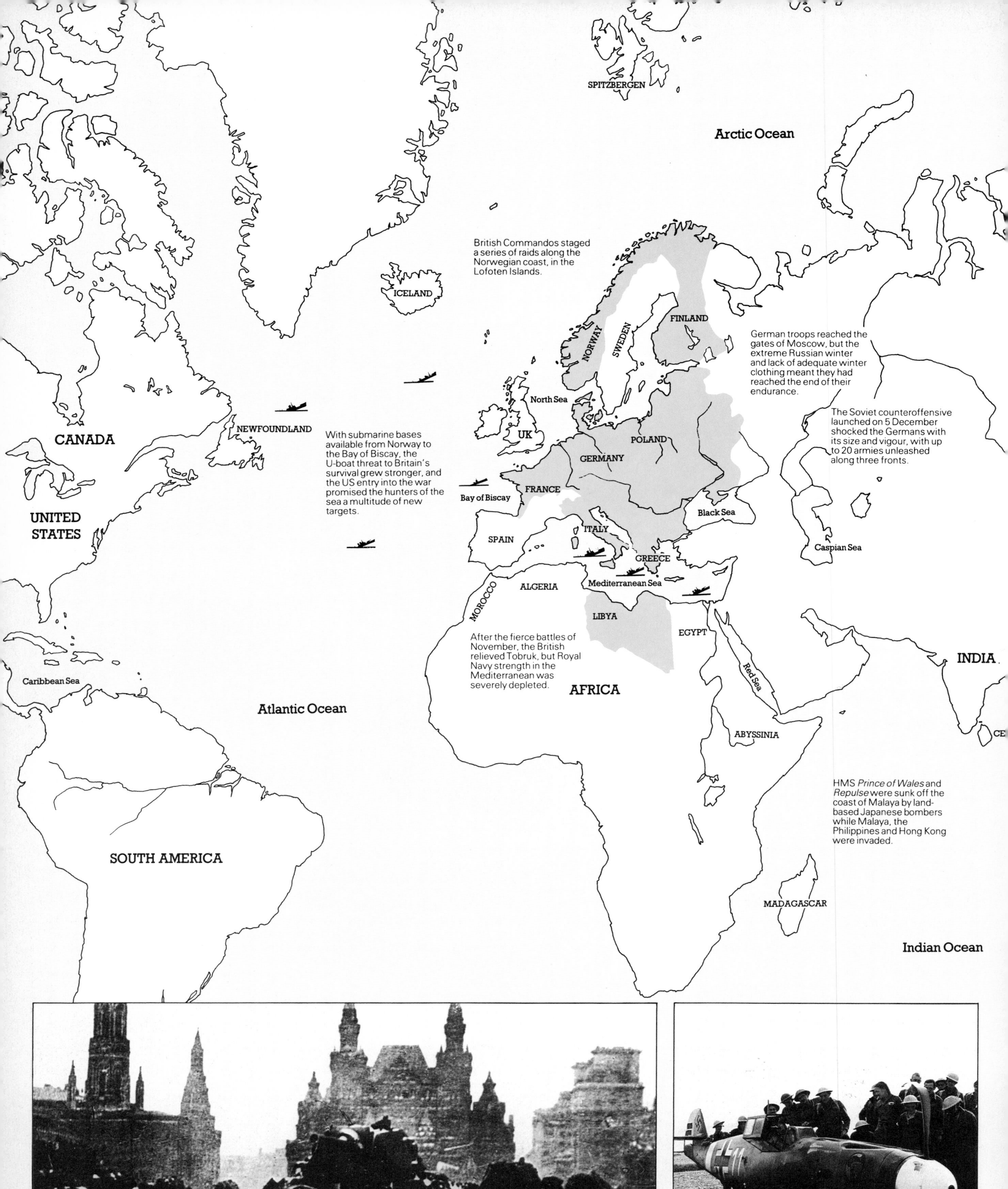
SPITZBERGEN
Arctic Ocean
British Commandos staged a series of raids along the Norwegian coast, in the Lofoten Islands.
ICELAND
FINLAND
NORWAY
SWEDEN
German troops reached the gates of Moscow, but the extreme Russian winter and lack of adequate winter clothing meant they had reached the end of their endurance.
The Soviet counteroffensive launched on 5 December shocked the Germans with its size and vigour, with up to 20 armies unleashed along three fronts.
North Sea
CANADA
NEWFOUNDLAND
With submarine bases available from Norway to the Bay of Biscay, the U-boat threat to Britain's survival grew stronger, and the US entry into the war promised the hunters of the sea a multitude of new targets.
UK
POLAND
GERMANY
FRANCE
Bay of Biscay
UNITED STATES
Black Sea
ITALY
SPAIN
Caspian Sea
GREECE
Mediterranean Sea
ALGERIA
MOROCCO
LIBYA
EGYPT
After the fierce battles of November, the British relieved Tobruk, but Royal Navy strength in the Mediterranean was severely depleted.
INDIA
Red Sea
Caribbean Sea
AFRICA
Atlantic Ocean
ABYSSINIA
HMS Prince of Wales and Repulse were sunk off the coast of Malaya by land-based Japanese bombers while Malaya, the Philippines and Hong Kong were invaded.
SOUTH AMERICA
MADAGASCAR
Indian Ocean

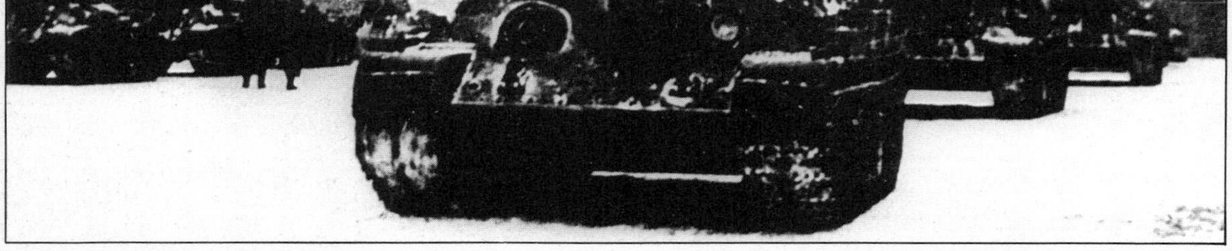

T-34s clank through Red Square in Moscow, forming up for the Soviet counter-offensive which drove the Germans away from the capital. Many of these superb fighting machines drove straight from the factory, unpainted, direct to the front line west of the city.

British troops regrouping after Operation Crusader come across a crashed Messerschmitt Bf 109 in Cyrenaica.

Axis High Point
December 1941

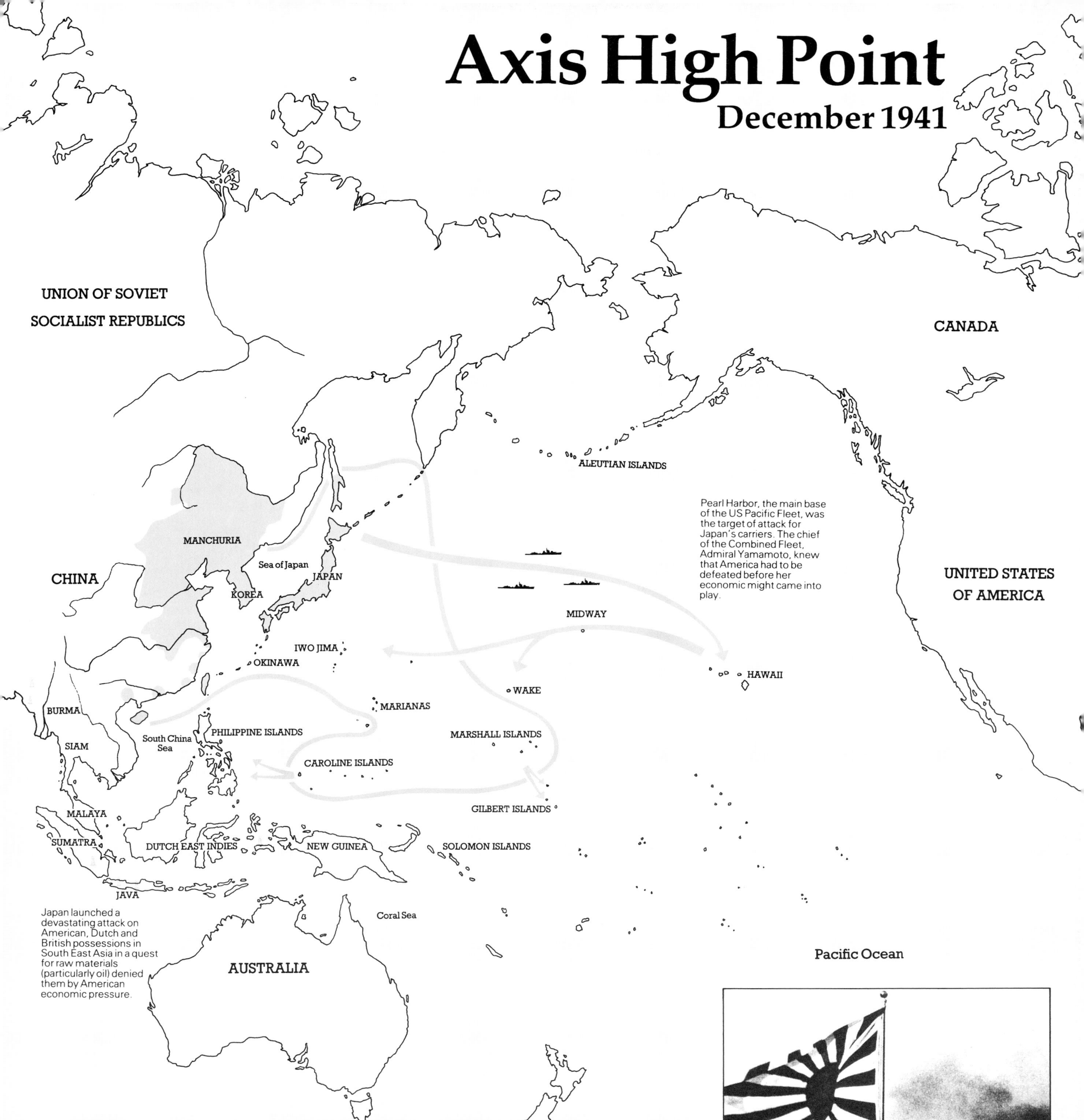

Pearl Harbor, the main base of the US Pacific Fleet, was the target of attack for Japan's carriers. The chief of the Combined Fleet, Admiral Yamamoto, knew that America had to be defeated before her economic might came into play.

Japan launched a devastating attack on American, Dutch and British possessions in South East Asia in a quest for raw materials (particularly oil) denied them by American economic pressure.

A Mitsubishi A6M 'Zero' launches from the flight deck of the Japanese flagship* Akagi *during the infamous attack on Pearl Harbor. Six carriers launched 183 aircraft in the first wave of the attack, comprising dive bombers, torpedo bombers and escorting fighters.

Marines of the Imperial Japanese Navy hoist the naval ensign outside Manila during the invasion of the Philippines.

Chapter 8

The War Against Japan

The might of Imperial Japan was unleashed early in the morning of 7 December 1941. As the message flashed from Ford Island 'Air Raid Pearl Harbor – this is not a drill', the conflict truly became a world war.

Japan's adventures on the Asian mainland during the 1930s had stirred great antagonisms in the Western world. One effect was a build-up of the American fleet; though this was matched by the Japanese, the latter lacked the oil resources to use it in a prolonged war. Japan, indeed, lacked most natural resources and felt in addition the need for what Hitler called *Lebensraum* (living room). Finally, when the European war had brought about the capitulation of France, Japan saw her opportunity and invaded French Indo-China. Well understanding the Japanese weakness, the West embargoed her oil supplies in retaliation.

To the Japanese there could now be no going back without unacceptable loss of prestige. Europe was virtually a German vassalage; of the major Far Eastern colonial powers, the Netherlands had fallen like France and the defeat of Britain appeared to be only a matter of time. A short but intense war could gain Japan what she needed, namely Malaya, the Philippines, the East Indies and a defensive perimeter of outlying islands. Only the American fleet was really to be feared and a massive riposte from this source could be prevented by an effective pre-emptive strike on Pearl Harbor, its Hawaiian base. It was argued that the Americans, though incensed, would be faced with both a *fait accompli* and a two-ocean war, and would be driven by its strong isolationist lobbies to accept the situation.

Once decided, the Japanese planned thoroughly. That part of the US Pacific Fleet forward-based at Pearl Harbor was in a slack peacetime routine despite world tensions. Even so, it presented a formidable target. A conventional gunned fleet could never have undertaken the job – only the power of a modern carrier group made it possible, and then only if concentrated on a previously undreamt-of scale.

The possibilities of carrier-based air assault on a defended naval base had been demonstrated in the British raid on Taranto in November 1940, and the precedent for a Japanese pre-emptive naval attack was that of February 1905 at Port Arthur.

Pearl Harbor's geography was well known, and for months beforehand the Japanese exercised in order to perfect their tactics. Only aircraft were to be used, which meant bomb and torpedo attack. Suitable armour-piercing bombs were not available, so fins were added to 356-mm naval shells to produce 800-kg projectiles that proved highly effective. The standard 400-mm aerial torpedo was of low lethality against major targets, so large numbers would be used to guarantee a sufficient percentage of hits. As the harbour was shallow, frangible wooden fins were added to the torpedoes to prevent an initial dive into the muddy seabed.

Although the Imperial Japanese Navy, with the numerous simultaneous undertakings that were planned, was deeply committed, the importance of the Pearl Harbor operation was emphasized by the allocation to it of the fleet's six best carriers. Under the command of Vice Admiral Nagumo, the force was termed the 1st Air Fleet; the *Akagi* was its flagship and was accompanied by *Kaga*, *Soryu*, *Hiryu*, *Shokaku* and *Zuikaku*, their normal aircraft outfits swollen to over 430 for the occasion. These were mainly Aichi D3A 'Val' dive-bombers, Nakajima B5N 'Kate' torpedo and level bombers, and Mitsubishi A6M 'Zeke' fighters. No surface action was planned or expected and, in any case, gunned warships were in short supply, so supporting forces included only two battleships, three cruisers (two of which were adapted to carry five reconnaissance seaplanes apiece) and nine destroyers.

The force concentrated in great secrecy at an isolated and desolate anchorage in the Kuriles. As Hawaii was half an ocean distant and a circuitous route would need to be taken, the fleet was accompa-

Attack on Pearl Harbor

The first wave of more than 180 Japanese aircraft, led by Commander Fuchida, closed on Oahu from the North, with dive bombers and fighters peeling off to deal with the various air bases, and the torpedo bombers splitting to take Pearl Harbor from two sides. Overhead, more dive bombers waited to complete the destruction.

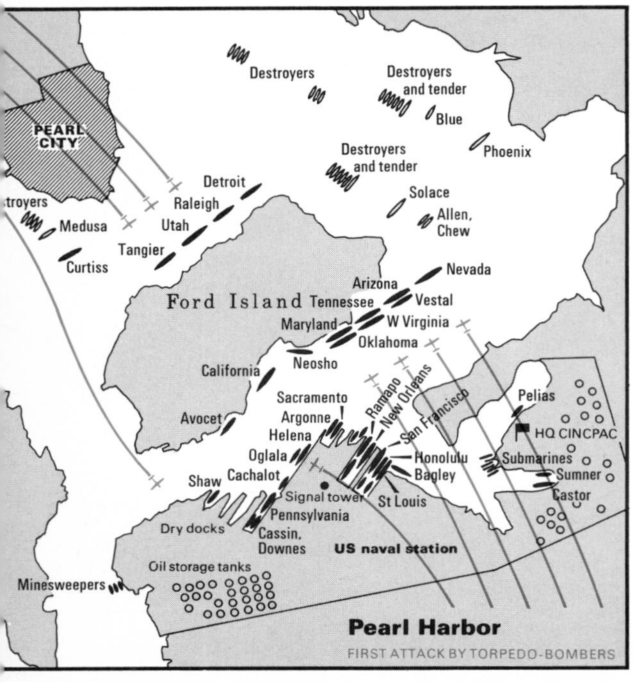

Pearl Harbor, as seen from a Japanese aircraft in the first wave of the attack. The torpedo burst alongside 'Battleship Row', which has hit either USS West Virginia or USS Oklahoma, places the time the photo was taken at about 08.00.

War in the Pacific

Japanese expansionism, fuelled by the ambitions of the Imperial Army, led to war with China in 1937. Any southward actions would make the neutralization of US forces on the Philippines and perhaps of the US Pacific Fleet itself necessary.

Pearl Harbor ablaze after the devastating Japanese strike. Only 29 Japanese planes were lost, and the US Pacific Fleet seemed crippled. Appearances can be deceptive, however, because the Japanese aircraft had missed the most vital target of all. By sheer chance, the three Pacific Fleet carriers were at sea during the attack, and remained unscathed.

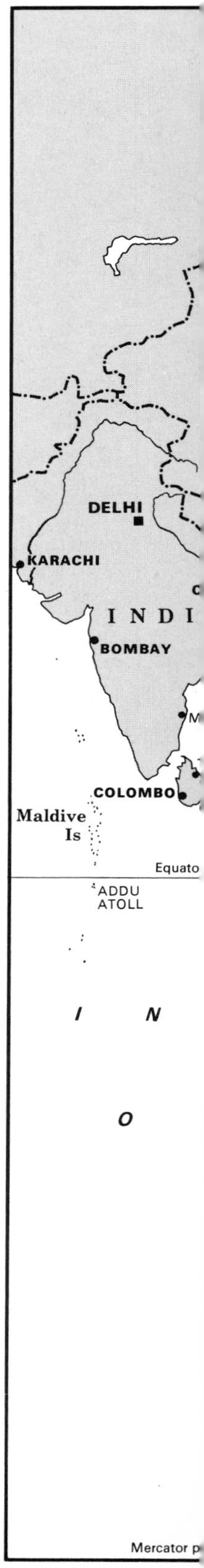

***Oklahoma** and **Maryland** after the attack. **Maryland** was least damaged of the battleships at Pearl, but 400 men were trapped in the capsized hull of the **Oklahoma**.*

*USS **Nevada** actually got under way, and was slowly steaming down Battleship Row when the second attack came in. The Japanese concentrated on the moving vessel, and she was hit repeatedly.*

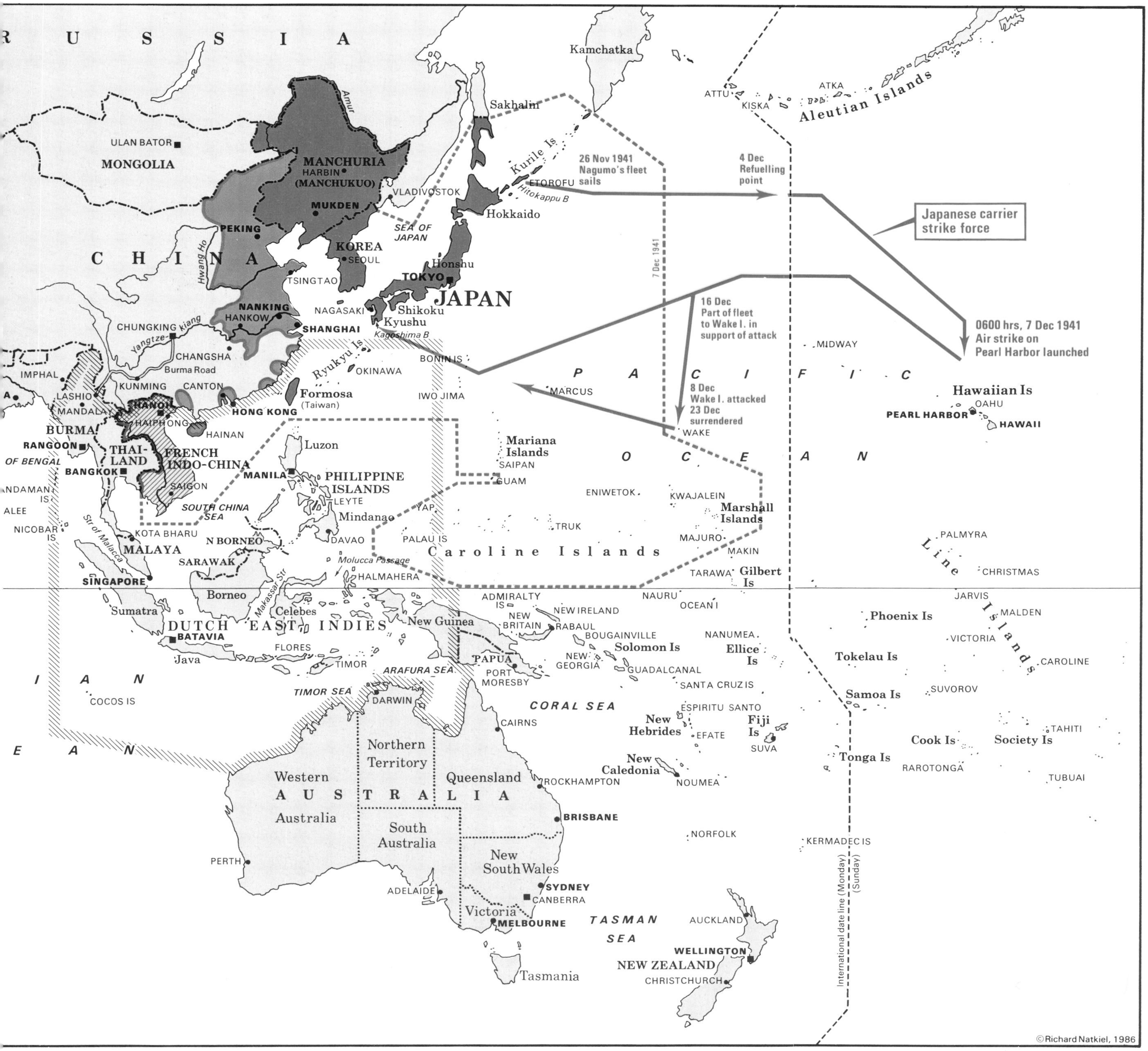

nied by tankers and supply ships. Although these would limit the speed of the group, this was not important before the event.

Sailing on 26 November 1941, the Japanese kept to a northern route, beset by concealing fog and poor weather. The track was well clear of trade routes and beyond the radius of Consolidated PBY aircraft working out of Midway Island. Submarines had been sent ahead to reconnoitre.

The attack is launched

The attack order was received by Nagumo on 1 December and, two days later, far to the north west of Hawaii, his force refuelled from the support ships. Replete, unreported and unsuspected, the force worked up to 25 kts and began the run-in from the unlikely direction of north. For maximum effect, the strike was scheduled for breakfast time on Sunday 7 December. The evening before, Nagumo was given a final update on the American fleet in port and was disappointed to learn that no carriers were present. Japanese intelligence did not appear too good where these were concerned, for of the five they believed to be in the Pacific two were in fact in the Atlantic. Of the remainder, the *Saratoga* was on the west coast and, as luck would have it, the two actually based on Pearl Harbor (*Enterprise* and *Lexington*) were away delivering aircraft to Wake and Midway.

Dawn, 7 December 1941, north east of Hawaii: aboard the carrier* Shokaku, *Mitsubishi A6M2 'Zero' fighters prepare to launch.

The destroyer USS* Helms *(the only vessel actually under way when the attack started) forced one of the two-man submarines taking part in the attack to beach and surrender.

As the Japanese approached their launch point, 275 miles north of Hawaii, however, they knew that targets still abounded in the form of eight battleships, eight cruisers, 29 destroyers and 40 other assorted warships and auxiliaries.

First aloft, in the pre-dawn gloom, were four Aichi E13A 'Jake' floatplanes from the cruisers, tasked with reconnoitring the track. Because of deteriorating weather conditions, the first strike began to get airborne before 6.00 a.m. In 15 minutes 183 aircraft were flown off, marshalled and away, a considerable achievement for its day.

With its Saturday night still heavy upon it, the American fleet slumbered in the brilliant light of an early sun as the waves of aircraft bore in: 40 torpedo bombers, 51 dive-bombers, 49 bombers with large AP projectiles and 43 fighters for escort and ground support. A veritable armada by the standards of the day, the Japanese formations were detected by surveillance radar and reported. That the reports were not acted upon is a subject of debate to this day; probably, as at Savo Island, yet to come, the reason was no more sinister than sheer disbelief born of acute unlikeliness.

Slightly early, at about 7.55 a.m., all hell broke loose about the heads of the Americans. At low states of readiness, with large numbers of crew ashore, the fleet found itself in a war in its own backyard. The Japanese formations split, with groups making for the various airfields on the island that, between them, could field over 400 aircraft. Suppression of these was vital to avoid instant retribution, and the tactic was savagely effective: on six airfields, nearly 200 aircraft were destroyed and 160 damaged in various degrees. Only a handful were able to take to the air.

The main drama, meanwhile, unfolded in the harbour. In the centre of this spacious inlet lay Ford Island, off which was 'Battleship Row'. Seven battleships, together with auxiliaries, were moored singly and in pairs in a gleaming line. Though this represented an apparently unmissable target some 1,300 yards in length, only about 800 yards separated the line from the opposite, or dockyard, shore. This meant that split-second timing was required but the target was neither moving nor shooting, and the aviators were well practised. The water became alive with torpedo tracks and the muddy discoloured rings from bomb bursts.

The end of the USS *Arizona*

Barely 10 minutes after the attack had begun came a heart-stopping moment as the *Arizona* erupted; hit by only one torpedo, her forward magazine had detonated on being drilled by one of the improvised AP bombs. Nearly 1,200 perished.

Just astern, the *West Virginia* absorbed six torpedoes and settled on the bottom, shielding in the process the *Tennessee* that lay on the inshore berth. The *California*, at the end of the trot, took two torpedoes and began to flood. Fuel oil from ruptured tanks blazed on the water and a pall of grey-black smoke formed the sombre backdrop to the activities of a growing number of small craft feverishly engaged in the task of rescue.

At the head of the line the *Nevada*, though hit, succeeded in getting under way; but even as the momentum of the first strike began to slacken, the second wave of 167 Japanese aircraft arrived.

The stricken *California*, hit twice more, settled to the level of her upper turrets while the gallant *Nevada* had to be beached. All, including the docked *Pennsylvania*, had also been hit by bombs and damaged in

The spectacular explosion of the destroyer USS* Shaw, *hit in the attack on the dry-docked fleet flagship USS* Pennsylvania. *Burning oil reached two other destroyers, which were lost.

Chronology of War: 1941

November 27
German offensive halted in Moscow outskirts. Tobruk garrison links up with 8th Army

November 28
Germans forced out of Rostov

November 29
Rommel counterattacks in Cyrenaica

November 30
UK civilian casualties in November 89 killed, 155 injured

December 1
Russian counterattack at Tula

December 5
Hitler agrees abandonment of Moscow offensive

December 6
Soviet counteroffensive around Moscow begins

December 7
Pearl Harbor attacked by Japanese aircraft. Singapore bombed; Japanese land in Thailand and Malaya

December 8
Japanese attack Hong Kong, Guam, Midway, Wake Island and Philippines

December 10
British battlecruiser HMS Repulse *and battleship* Prince of Wales *sunk off Malaya. Japanese land on Luzon, Philippine Islands*

December 11
Italy and Germany declare war on the USA. In return, US declares war on Italy and Germany

December 12
British begin withdrawal from mainland Hong Kong positions

December 13
Fierce battles in Cyrenaica

December 15
British withdrawals in Malaya, Burma and Kowloon begin. Rommel decides on withdrawal in Cyrenaica

December 17
British advance in North Africa to Gazala line. Japanese land in North Borneo. British withdraw to Perak river in Malaya

December 18
Japanese land on Hong Kong

December 19
Italian frogmen damage battleships HMS Queen Elizabeth *and* Valiant *in Alexandria harbour. British retake Derna and Mechili*

December 22
Japanese land in Gulf of Lingayen in the Philippines

December 24
Japanese capture Wake Island. British retake Benghazi

December 25
Hong Kong surrenders. Some 3,700 Leningraders die of starvation

December 26
Japanese break through Perak River in Malaya and advance to Ipoh. Russians land on Kerch peninsula in the Crimea in attempt to relieve Sevastopol

December 27
Allied commandos raid Vaagsö and Lofoten Islands

December 29
Russians retake Feodosia

December 31
South Africans attack Bardia. Japanese advance towards Manila. UK civilian casualties in December 34 killed, 55 injured. Convoy war losses in 1941 are (Allied and neutral) 1,299 ships, totalling 4,398,031 tons; (Axis) 35 U-boats, 18 Italian submarines and three Japanese submarines

The US Pacific Fleet, 1941 and 1942

The US warplan 'Orange' assumed a war against Japan with the Philippines as the primary objective. Air power was expected to play a major role in preparing the way, but the issue would be decided by a massive battleship engagement, probably in Japanese home waters. Curiously, the US Navy began the war with only a meagre force of cruisers, but soon embarked on a colossal building programme.

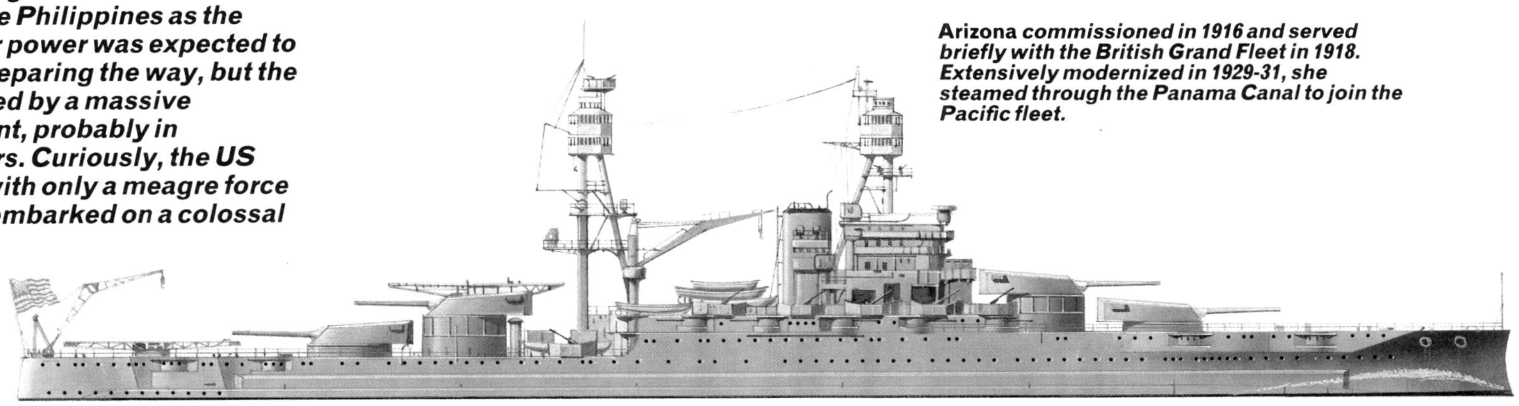

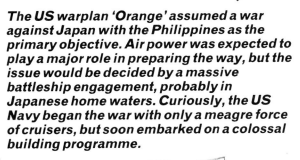

Arizona *commissioned in 1916 and served briefly with the British Grand Fleet in 1918. Extensively modernized in 1929-31, she steamed through the Panama Canal to join the Pacific fleet.*

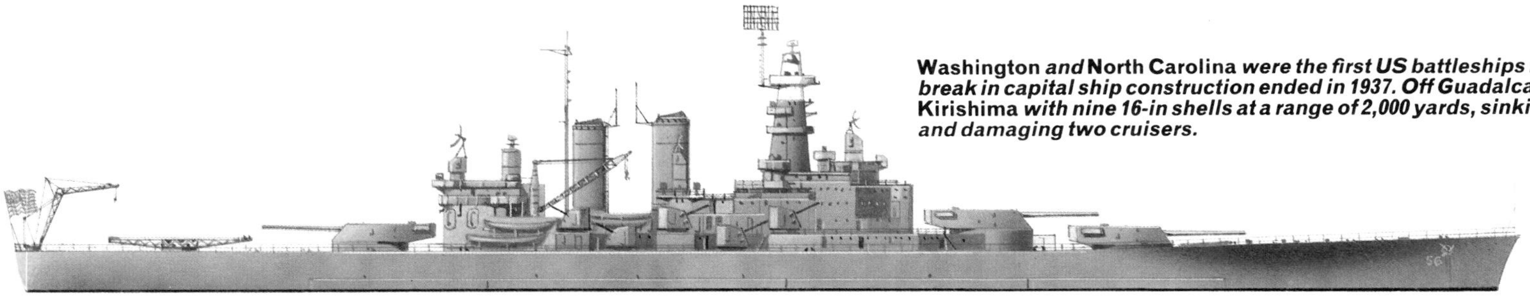

Washington *and* **North Carolina** *were the first US battleships built after the 15-year break in capital ship construction ended in 1937. Off Guadalcanal* **Washington** *hit* **Kirishima** *with nine 16-in shells at a range of 2,000 yards, sinking the enemy battleship and damaging two cruisers.*

South Dakota *was the name ship of a four-strong class of battleships which all commissioned in 1942. She suffered electrical failure while in action against the Japanese battleship* **Kirishima**, *and was only saved by the timely intervention of USS* **Washington**.

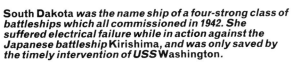

Arizona *cruises gracefully off Hawaii before the war. In the inner line of Battleship Row at Pearl Harbor, her magazine was detonated by a Japanese bomb and she sank at her moorings with over 1,000 of her crew.*

West Virginia *was one of the 'Big 5': the backbone of the pre-war Pacific fleet. She needed major reconstruction after Pearl Harbor and she rejoined the fleet with massively enhanced anti-aircraft batteries.*

The strong emphasis on battleship construction during World War I meant that by the early 1930s the US Navy's destroyer flotillas were obsolescent. The 18 'Mahan' class destroyers launched in 1935-6 introduced new boilers, designed for long range operations in the Pacific.

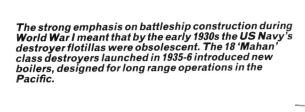

Invasion of Malaya

The main force of the Japanese 25th Army landed near Singora in Siam, while a smaller force made an assault on Kota Bharu in Malaya. Opposed by elements of the 9th Indian Army Division, the Takumi force established the first beachhead of Japan's new empire. Meanwhile, the main thrust down the west coast was being led by the 5th Division.

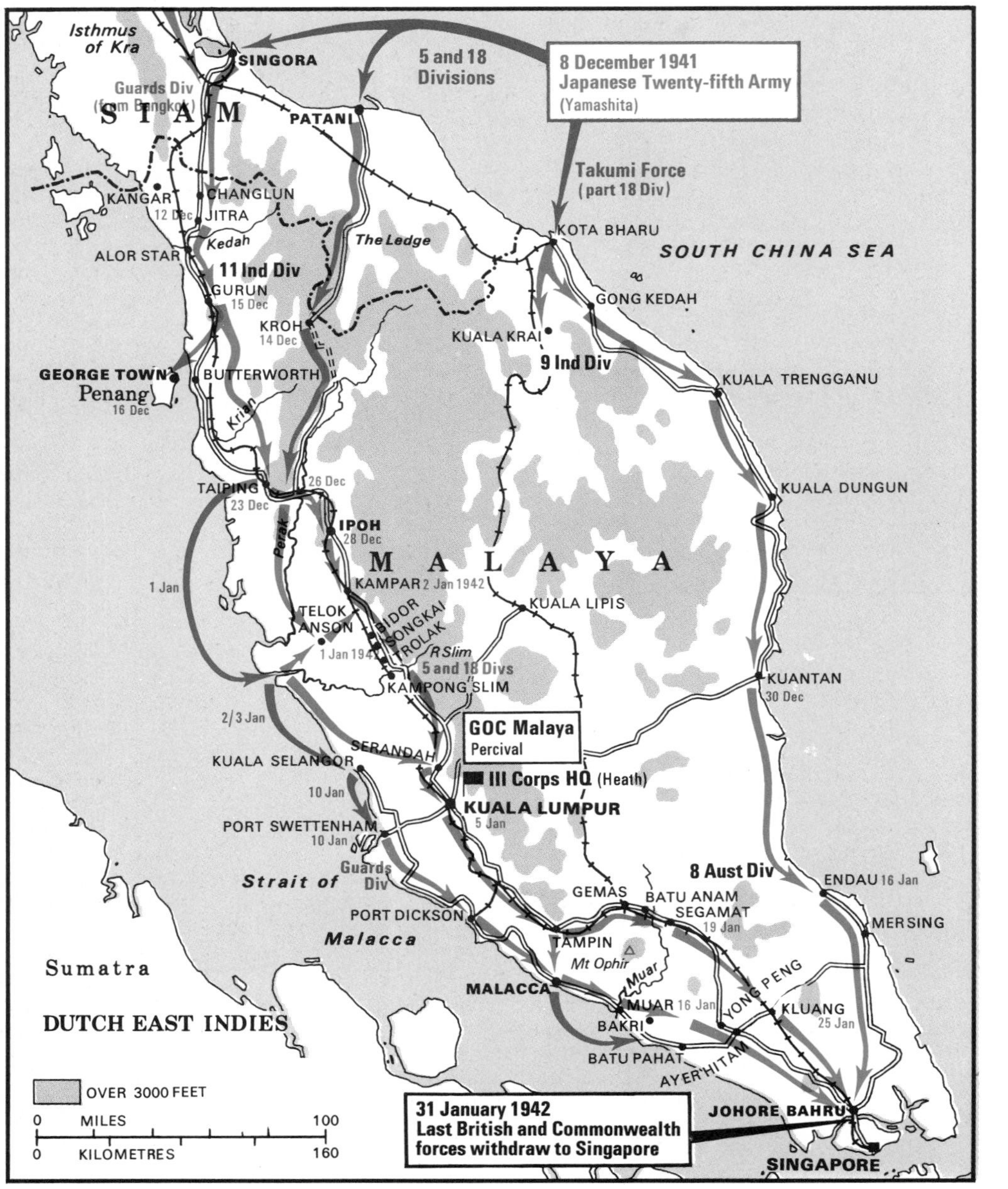

varying degrees. The defences were now better organized, preventing the second wave from causing damage on a similar scale.

By mid-day Nagumo had recovered his aircraft and had begun a high-speed withdrawal. For the loss of 29 aircraft he had both made history and set in train the process that was to devour his country. The old battleships, which only time would show to have been obsolescent, had absorbed the ordnance that would, more profitably, have laid waste the fleet base facilities. Worse, the American carrier and submarine forces remained intact and were to spearhead the great naval effort that, eventually, was to bring about the Japanese downfall.

The Japanese gamble had failed. America did not flinch from war, and this war would not be the short affair anticipated by the Japanese. In a contest of attrition with the world's greatest industrial power there could only ever have been one result.

Malaya and Singapore

But Pearl Harbor was not, of course, the sole target of Japanese military expertise on the morning of Sunday, 7 December 1941. Even while Nagumo's Vals, Kates and Zekes were still airborne, Japanese bombers and fighters were taking off from airfields on Formosa to attack selected targets on Luzon in the first phase of a plan drawn up by the Japanese Imperial Staff to give them control of Luzon Island in 50 days and of the entire Philippines in three months. To their north-west, nine infantry battalions supported by ample artillery and six squadrons of aircraft – 20,000 men altogether – moved south towards the lightly held British colony of Hong Kong; and west of Luzon in the Gulf of Siam a convoy of 22 ships was closing up to the coasts of Thailand and Malaya to put ashore an army which in five months would sweep away all British power, from Singapore to the borders of India.

Pearl Harbor Strike Force

The 1st Air Fleet, which made the attack on Pearl Harbor, consisted of six aircraft carriers under the command of the stalwart Vice Admiral Nagumo, flying his flag in the* Akagi*. Two carriers,* Shokaku *and her sister* Zuikaku*, were brand new in December 1941, and the inexperience of their aircrew limited them to a supporting role. The main strike of 183 aircraft flew from the decks of* Kaga*,* Soryu*,* Hiryu *and the flagship herself.

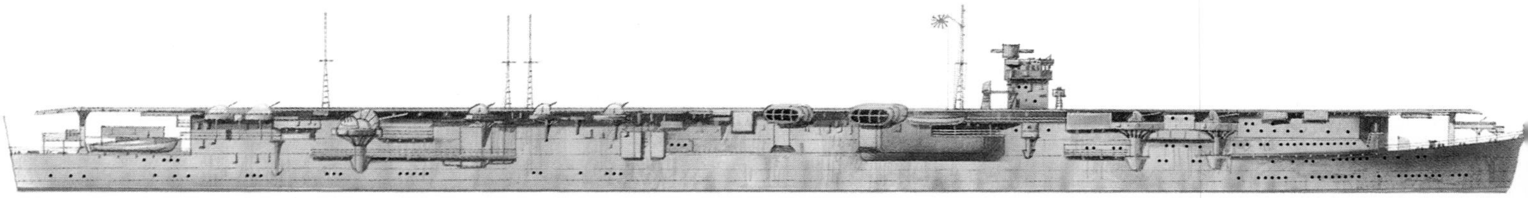

Right: Although displacing under 20,000 tons,* Soryu *carried 63 aircraft in her cramped hangars. With her half-sister* Hiryu *she formed Carrier Division 2, and after Pearl Harbor joined the other fast carriers for their six-month rampage over the Pacific before meeting her end at Midway.

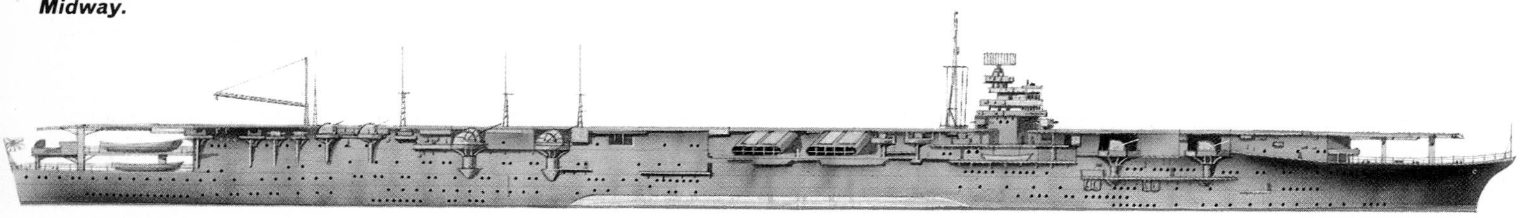

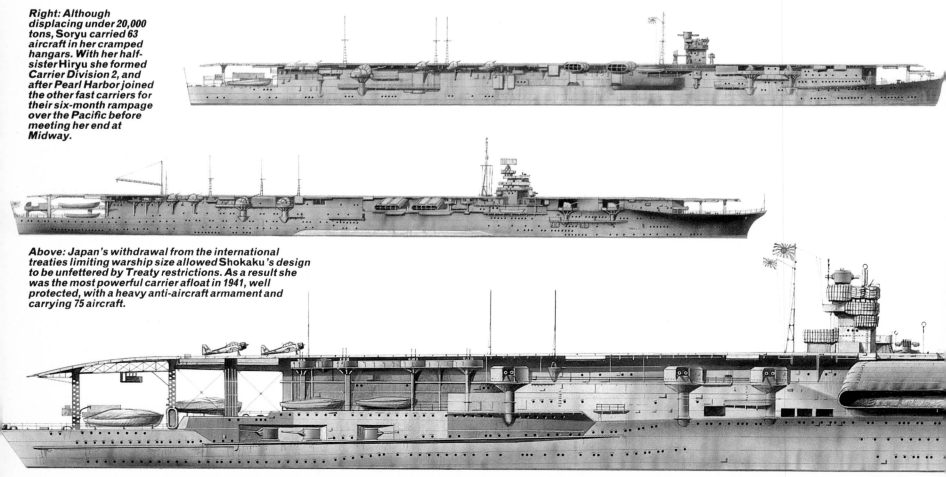

Above: Japan's withdrawal from the international treaties limiting warship size allowed* Shokaku*'s design to be unfettered by Treaty restrictions. As a result she was the most powerful carrier afloat in 1941, well protected, with a heavy anti-aircraft armament and carrying 75 aircraft.

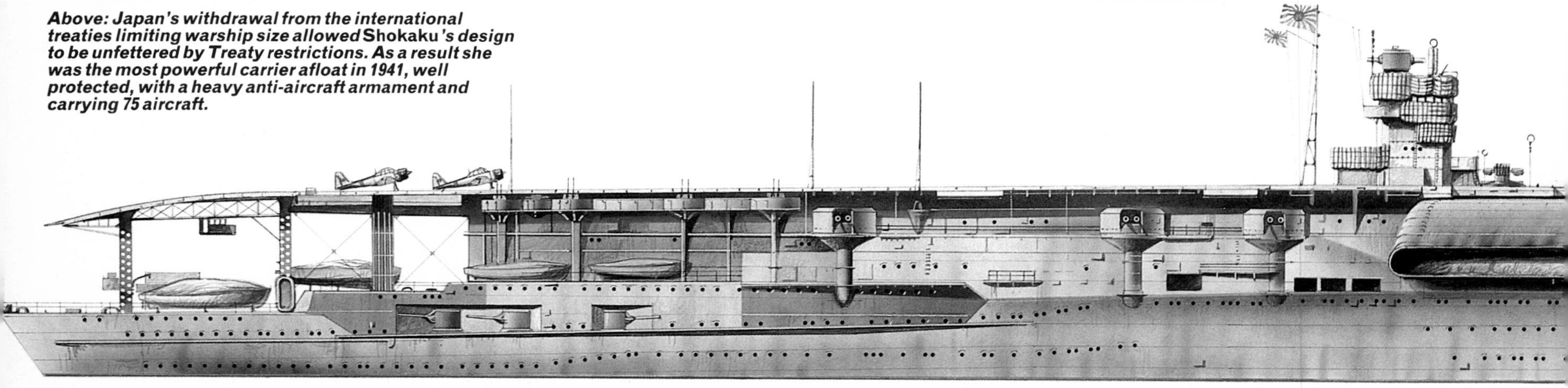

Malaya and then Burma were the main Japanese objectives of the gigantic military and naval planning and movements of the closing months of 1941: those lands plus the islands of the Dutch East Indies, would provide spoils to allow Japan to continue, and perhaps complete, her conquest of China, begun in 1937, and also to realize her long-term strategic aspirations of driving Europeans from the Far East and establishing Japanese hegemony in their place. Malaya produced 38 per cent of the world's rubber and 58 per cent of its tin; from Burma and the Dutch East Indies would come all the essential oil to fuel Japan's ships, aircraft and army transport; with American naval and military bases in the Pacific either destroyed or in Japanese hands, their movements throughout the vast area would be unhindered. Only Hitler's ambition matched that of the Japanese Imperial Staff.

The convoy carrying the armies for those first vital conquests was seen soon after midday on 6 December by a Hudson reconnaissance plane operating from Kota Bharu, high up on the eastern border of Malaya; but soon afterwards deteriorating weather covered all movements at sea, so the fleet moved safely northwards until the dispersion point was reached. Then, shortly after 9.00 a.m. on 7 December, the individual sections left for their own selected landing areas; three sections went north east to land along the Kra Isthmus to await orders for the move up into Burma, four large transports escorted by three warships moved south east, the first party to land troops unopposed at Singapore, the larger party in three transports to go ashore at Kota Bharu. Here, under cover of a naval bombardment, they would attack the known positions of the 8th Indian Brigade at Baluch, Dogras and Frontier Force Rifles, the northernmost outposts of what was in effect the defences of Singapore.

Landings at Kota Bharu

The shelling of the British positions began just before midnight, the first Japanese troops swarmed ashore soon after 1.00 a.m. on 8 December, and such was their reception that one naval commander suggested that the landings be abandoned. The sea had become unexpectedly rough, and many soldiers had been drowned either in transfer to the landing craft or as they scrambled through the surf. Those who did reach the beach came under such severe and accurate rifle and machine-gun fire that the first officer to arrive quickly realized that they must advance or die; they thus gave the first example of that incredible courage in the face of Allied opposition which was to astonish the Western world. By 3.45 a.m. the two central positions of the Dogras had been overwhelmed (at a cost to the Japanese of over 500 men killed on a hundred-yard front) while two miles inland the Frontier Force Rifles were under strong attack around the airfield, which had already been bombed and shelled from the sea.

By mid-morning, the second and third waves of Japanese troops were ashore, and so was their commander, Major-General Takumi, whose headquarters ship had been bombed and set afire by the one attack mounted by the Royal Air Force. He quickly organized outflanking attacks on the Indian positions still opposing his own men, and when more transports arrived off Kota Bharu bringing the rest of his force, he sent them off on a rapid march south towards the Baluch positions about 15 miles away on the coast. By 7.00 p.m., Brigadier Key, commanding the Indian brigade, was urgently requesting permission to withdraw his troops down the coast towards Kuala Trengganu, or even as far as Kuantan, for there were no sound defensive positions in between.

To the British GOC, Malaya, Lieutenant-General A. E. Percival, and his staff, the second week of December 1941 was to bring a seemingly unending catalogue of disaster. The Japanese landings at Singapore and Kota Bharu had not, in fact, been totally unforseen; it was their almost instantaneous success which caused at first surprise, and then shock. Next came realization of the reversal of naval balance in the Pacific caused by the attack on Pearl Harbor, followed by news of the virtual elimination of their own air cover in northern Malaya. The Japanese III Air Group had established themselves at Singapore after it had been occupied by 5th Division, and dealt devastatingly with every RAF base within striking range. Meeting only ineffective fighter defences (Hurricanes were no match for Zeros) and light anti-aircraft fire, Japanese pilots in 24 hours reduced the operational strength of the RAF in northern Malaya from 110 to 50, and in the days following were to whittle even this remaining strength down almost to nothing. From then on in this campaign the Japanese were to enjoy total air superiority.

The Japanese drive south

Under this sheltering cover, the Japanese 5th Division under command of Lieutenant-General Matsui now commenced their spectacular drive from Singapore across to and down the west coast of the Malayan peninsula. By 11 December they had crossed into Malaya's northern province, Kedah, and in the early morning were grouped to storm reported positions at Changlun with a strong reconnaissance unit supported by 10 tanks. By noon they had outflanked the Punjabi troops occupying the forward posts, who promptly began withdrawing in pouring rain to their reserve positions at Nangka, two miles north of the main base at Jitra. Here disaster overcame them. According to one of the Japanese officers, 'Ten guns with their muzzles turned towards us were lined up on the road, but beside them we could not find one man of their crews. The enemy appeared to be sheltering from the heavy rain under the rubber trees ... and through this slight negligence they suffered a crushing defeat,'

A column of Type 95 Ha-Go light tanks en route for Singapore. Adequate for the early campaigns, Japanese armour was to be sadly outmatched later in the war.

The main Japanese infantry came up fast behind the reconnaissance unit and were soon close up to the main Jitra positions held by brigades of the 11th Indian Division. All that night they tried to break through between the Leicesters and the 22nd Gurkhas, but despite casualties on a scale which would have been unacceptable to Western troops, the morning revealed Jitra still covered by the defending force – in front of it. Then General Kawamura, commanding 5th Division infantry arrived, a flanking attack was launched and Major-General D. M. Murray-Lyon saw that he must try to get his division back behind a viable tank obstacle.

Permission to withdraw was received at 10.00 p.m., and at midnight and in pouring rain the 11th Indians began a retreat back to Alor Star on the south bank of the River Sungei Kedah. Retreat, always a difficult manoeuvre, along a single road by poorly trained troops at night, pressed from the rear by an exultant enemy whose troops have learned how

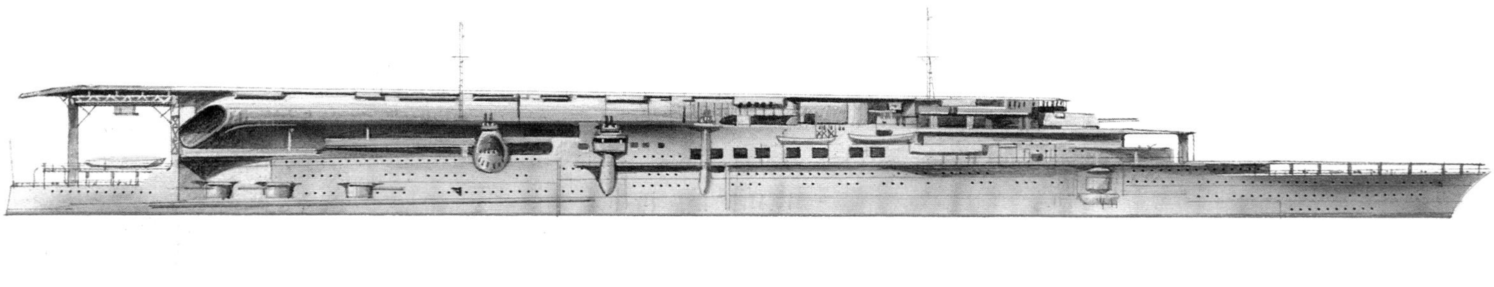

Right: As constructed, Kaga ***trunked her smoke ducts down the starboard side, had two short flying-off decks forward of the hangars, and had no island. The design was not a success and she was returned to dockyard hands for 4½ years before emerging as a powerful fleet carrier.***

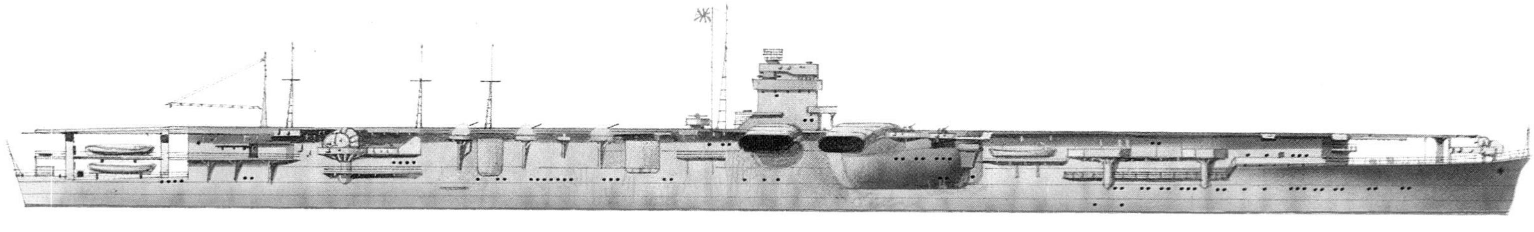

Left: Hiryu ***had a port side island to form a clockwise landing circuit when operating with a conventional carrier, but it did not prove successful. She launched the one successful Japanese air strike at Midway, which scored three devastating hits on USS*** Yorktown.

Below: Akagi ***as she appeared in December 1941. She led the Pearl Harbor strike and the brilliantly executed follow-up raids through the East Indies and into the Indian Ocean, sinking the British carrier*** Hermes ***and bombing Australia.***

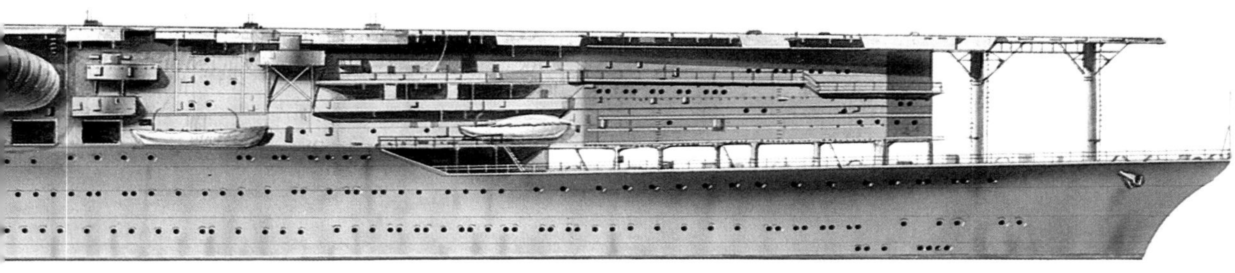

Kaga ***as she appeared after her extensive modernization programme. She could embark up to 90 aircraft; 73 of her complement were launched against Pearl Harbor.***

The surrender of Singapore, the most humiliating capitulation in British military history, was accepted on 15 February 1942 by Lieutenant-General Tomoyuki Yamashita, commander of the Japanese army in Malaya, in the Ford factory on Bukit Timah hill.

to move swiftly through jungle, spells disaster – and so it proved in this case. By daylight, two brigades of the 11th Indian Division had lost over 1,500 men – and guns, vehicles and ammunition on an alarming scale. Gone, too, was most of the division's morale.

It has been said that the action around Jitra was a major disaster for the British and a disgrace to British arms. Certainly it proved to be a key action in the Malayan campaign, for from now there was always insufficient time to deploy reinforcements sent up from Singapore, to organize firm defences anywhere back down that long coastal road or to allow British divisions which were being landed in Singapore time to acclimatize themselves. The British and Indian forces now in Malaya were never to regain their balance, and the more they retreated, the lower sank their morale. They were doomed probably because of lack of training and firm leadership, certainly because they began to believe they were doomed.

Japanese confidence

The Japanese, on the other hand, felt that they were winning and no thought of hunger, thirst, exhaustion or wounds would divert any of them, from general to private, from their course. They hurled themselves at every sign of resistance, swung around the flanks if it persisted, mended every blown bridge within hours of reaching it, treated with harsh contempt every enemy soldier who surrendered to them and, as a general rule, bayoneted every wounded enemy soldier they came across. Such behaviour was well within the rules of warfare as they understood them, and their treatment of their own wounded was little better; had any Japanese soldier surrendered to the British, his fate once his own countrymen had recovered him would have been no different.

A Japanese bomber's view of the doomed British capital ships HMS Prince of Wales *and* Repulse. *Leaving Singapore on 8 December, they were to be lost only two days later. Winston Churchill later recorded that the news of the sinkings was his most direct shock of the war.*

By 15 December the Japanese were at Gurun, by the 16th Penang Island had been evacuated and what was left of Murray-Lyon's force was behind the Krian, while Percival was attempting to form another defence line behind the Perak. In this he was singularly ineffective, though he was allowed rather more time for his dispositions than could have been foreseen: the Japanese Imperial Guards Division had crossed into Kedah Province from Patani and driven down through Kroh and along the line of the northern Perak to join 5th Division, and the army commander, Lieutenant-General Yamashita, waited until they arrived. He sent them in against the Perak defences on 26 December and ordered them to drive forward and take Ipoh.

Kampar was outflanked on 2 January 1942, hurriedly thrown-together British forces were scattered on 7 January along the line of the Slim River – and now the whole of central Malaya lay open to the attackers, while Johore and the last defences before Singapore were seriously prejudiced. Then on 8 January forward elements of the Japanese 18th Division under their choleric commander Lieutenant-General Mutaguchi landed at Endau, barely 100 miles from Singapore; and three days later the Japanese 5th Division marched into that epitome of English colonial power, Kuala Lumpur, with its enormous stocks of food, arms, clothing, vehicles and ammunition. Petrol and oil dumps had been set alight, but not all had burned, and Yamashita was so satisfied with 5th Division's progress that he decided to rest them, sending the Guards Division on down to Malacca. He also issued orders that the bulk of Mutaguchi's division could now come down through eastern Malaya by road instead of to Endau by sea, as there was evidently no military resistance worthy of the name to oppose him. As the only powerful force of the Royal Navy in the area – Force Z, consisting of the modern battleship *Prince of Wales* and the elderly battlecruiser *Repulse* – had been sunk by Japanese aircraft on 10 December off Kuantan in an action as successful as the Royal Navy's own attack on the Italian fleet at Taranto, there was little enough naval opposition.

General Wavell, whose first six months as Commander-in-Chief, India, had so far been as testing as any time he had spent in the Middle East, had flown into Malaya for his first emergency conference on 8 January. He promptly suggested the move of the 8th Australian Division from Johore, where they had been doing little but wait, into the path of the invaders along the river-line between Muar and Batu. There they administered a sharp rebuff to the Imperial Guards. Wavell then flew to Java, where he found himself in command of the ABDA theatre (American, British, Dutch, Australian). 'I'm getting used to holding babies,' he commented, 'but this looks like being the worst behaved of all!'

This prognosis received sharp confirmation on the morning of 19 January, when he discovered that no detailed scheme for withdrawal of forces on to Singapore Island, or for its defence, had as yet been drawn up. He cabled warnings to Whitehall, and sped back to Singapore, where his worst fears were realized; practically nothing had been done to strengthen the island's northern defences anywhere. His difficulties were increased by Percival's differing views on what needed to be done, and further complicated by the arrival of a cable from Churchill reading, 'I want to make it absolutely clear that I expect every inch of ground to be defended, every scrap of material for defences to be blown to pieces to prevent capture by the enemy, and no question of surrender to be entertained until after protracted fighting among the ruins of Singapore City.'

Debacle at Singapore

Both Wavell and Churchill were talking to a man who had made up his mind along other lines. Disregarding Wavell's tactical advice, General Percival divided Singapore Island into three sectors, Western to be held by the Australians, who were to be brought back from the Muar River, Northern by the 18th Division which had just arrived, and Southern by whatever Indian formations had survived and would form a reserve. As it happened, 1,900 more Australians arrived during the next few days, together with 7,000 men of the 44th Indian Infantry Brigade – and these buttressed the allotted sectors. By 31 January, all British and Commonwealth formations still existent in Malaya had been withdrawn into the Singapore defences, and the Japanese forces under General Yamashita were closed up for the final attack.

This, after adequate reconnaissance, was launched across the Johore Strait on the night of 7/8 February, Imperial Guards making a feint on the east, 5th and 18th Divisions crossing to the western end of the island – all under artillery cover. As can be seen on any sportsfield, fortune favours the winners; Japanese gunfire wrecked the British communications, their strongest probes went in through the defenders' weakest points and although they lost men to rifle and machine-gun fire, the bulk of both 5th and 18th Divisions was ashore by dawn on 9 February. By mid-morning they had reached Tengah airfield, where they found British planes in working order and neatly parked, fresh bread and soup on the messroom tables, clothes and suitcases in the quarters; and although British artillery fire was accurate and at times effective, when the Japanese stormed through it they found little but confusion and disorganization beyond.

By 13 February, they had fought their way forward implacably until the British troops – who now numbered some 80,000 – were penned inside a 28-mile perimeter around the city, with no plans for a counter-attack, no morale and no confidence in their leaders. In this lack of confidence they were undoubtedly justified; on 15 February – to be known in British history from then on as 'Black Sunday' – General Percival, ignoring Churchill's strategic directions as he had ignored Wavell's tactical directive, ordered a white flag to be hoisted. In due course he met General Yamashita in the Ford factory at Bukit Timah and within minutes of the opening conference, Percival had agreed to surrender unconditionally – presumably to avoid a 'bloodbath' among the Allied troops under his command.

Had he, or they, foreseen their sufferings as prisoners of the Japanese during the next four years, they would probably have chosen the 'bloodbath' with its possibility, however remote, of victory; and its certainty of avoiding the humiliation they now suffered.

Once the Japanese Imperial Staff could feel confident that their control of the Malayan peninsula was assured, they turned their attention to Burma, with its oil, and with its jungle-clad mountainous countryside which would barricade their 'Greater East Asia Co-Prosperity Sphere' against interference from India. Its conquest – or at least the conquest of the British and Indian air and land forces stationed in

Japanese carrierborne aircraft

The Japanese aircraft-carriers had a mixed complement of dive bombers, torpedo bombers and fighters, which rapidly proved themselves to be the best of their kind in the world. However, wartime experience demonstrated graphically that it was the quality of the aircrew that was critical, and once the veteran fliers of the 1st Air Fleet had been lost the Japanese carriers were doomed to defeat.

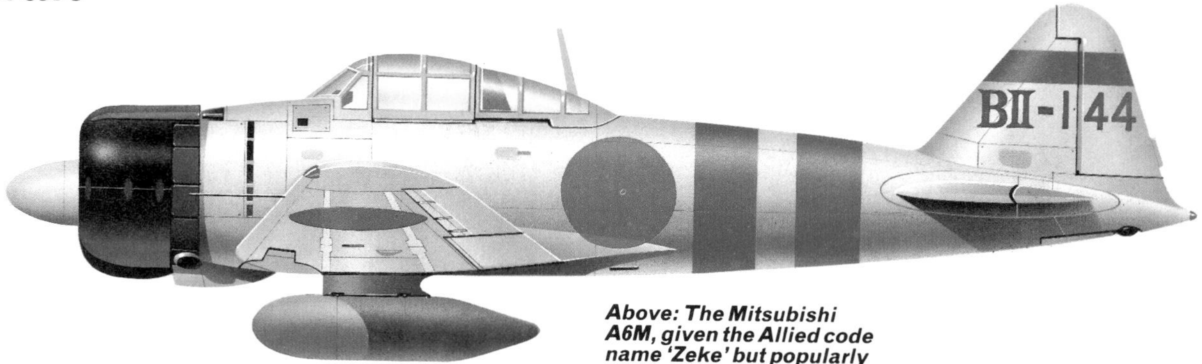

Above: The Mitsubishi A6M, given the Allied code name 'Zeke' but popularly known as the 'Zero', was a superlative fighter which was to dominate the early air battles of the Pacific War. The aircraft illustrated is an A6M2, which was operated from **Hiryu** ***during the Pearl Harbor attack.***

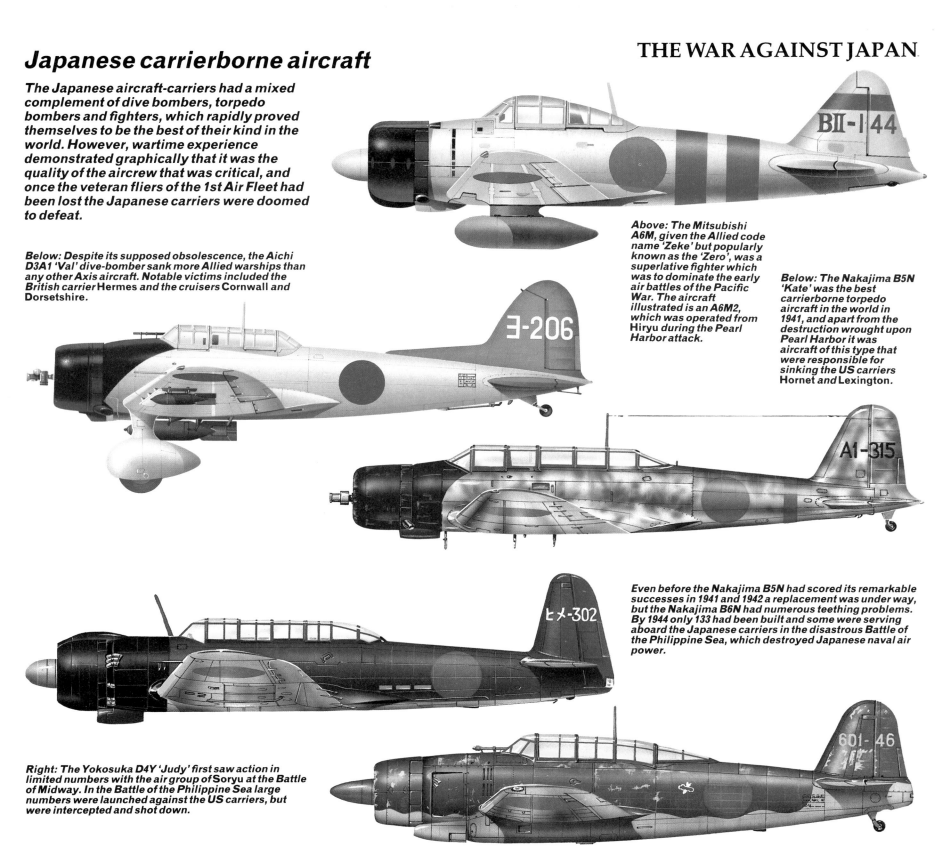

Below: Despite its supposed obsolescence, the Aichi D3A1 'Val' dive-bomber sank more Allied warships than any other Axis aircraft. Notable victims included the British carrier **Hermes** ***and the cruisers*** **Cornwall** ***and*** **Dorsetshire**.

Below: The Nakajima B5N 'Kate' was the best carrierborne torpedo aircraft in the world in 1941, and apart from the destruction wrought upon Pearl Harbor it was aircraft of this type that were responsible for sinking the US carriers **Hornet** ***and*** **Lexington**.

Even before the Nakajima B5N had scored its remarkable successes in 1941 and 1942 a replacement was under way, but the Nakajima B6N had numerous teething problems. By 1944 only 133 had been built and some were serving aboard the Japanese carriers in the disastrous Battle of the Philippine Sea, which destroyed Japanese naval air power.

Right: The Yokosuka D4Y 'Judy' first saw action in limited numbers with the air group of **Soryu** ***at the Battle of Midway. In the Battle of the Philippine Sea large numbers were launched against the US carriers, but were intercepted and shot down.***

Burma – did not pose any insuperable or indeed major military problems, and the first step was taken against no opposition at all.

The Japanese Fifteenth Army under Lieutenant-General Iida, which had landed along the northern section of the Kra Isthmus shoreline, reached Bangkok on 8 December and immediately became master of Thailand, controlling all airfields and railways. On 23 and 25 December, Japanese aircraft bombed Rangoon, and on 16 January – the day after the Imperial Guards had received a sharp setback from the Australians on the Muar river-line – Iida sent a single battalion across the narrow strip at Burma's southernmost extent to occupy Victoria Point and its airfield, the British garrison there having been evacuated a month before.

Three days later another Japanese battalion captured Tavoy, 250 miles to the north, overwhelming a company of Burma Rifles and an artillery battery there and cutting off the garrison at Mergui, between Victoria Point and Tavoy. That garrison was evacuated by sea two days later, so in less than a week and at no cost to themselves the Japanese had gained three vital airfields from which to provide fighter cover for land operations, from all of which Rangoon could be bombed.

But the main Japanese drive was further north, where Fifteenth Army was massed for a swift attack from their base at Raheng, across the Burmese border through Kawkareik, first toward Moulmein and yet another airfield, then around the Gulf of Martaban, across the Sittan River and into Rangoon itself. It was given eight weeks to complete the operation.

There was not a great deal of military power to oppose it. The British Commander-in-Chief, Burma, Lieutenant-General T. J. Hutton, had only just been appointed by Wavell and had spent almost all his previous military life in staff appointments. As commander in the field he had Brigadier (acting Major-General) 'Jackie' Smyth, who had won the Victoria Cross during World War I but was not, in early 1942, in the best of health, and whom Hutton had met for the first time on 9 January. And the troops at Smyth's disposal to hold back an entire army of well-trained and experienced Japanese troops, eager to emulate the deeds of their triumphant brothers in Malaya, were the 46th Brigade of the 17th (Black Cat) Division (the other two brigades were in Malaya), the 16th Indian Brigade under Brigadier J. K. Jones, who was already at Kawkareik (one company of the 1st/7th Gurkhas down at Three Pagoda Pass) and the 2nd Burma Brigade under Brigadier Bourke, who were spread over 300 miles of jungle and had been expected to provide the garrisons of Tavoy, Mergui and Victoria Point.

None of Smyth's formations had been seriously trained in jungle fighting, every battalion had long since lost their best British and Indian officers and NCOs to the 4th and 5th Indian Divisions in North Africa, and they had no air cover at all. To General Smyth it was quite obvious that the only area in which they could be expected to block an otherwise irresistible Japanese advance was in the open ground immediately west of the Sittang River, 100 miles short of Rangoon. His requests to General Hutton to be allowed to concentrate there behind the the quite formidable river barrier was categorically refused.

Smyth therefore concentrated his forces as best he could, though he was to be immediately disappointed when the remnants of 16th Brigade arrived back at Moulmein on 23 and 24 January – shattered and having lost all their transport and most of their support weapons. By 26 January, Moulmein was under close attack by the Japanese 55th Division, and two

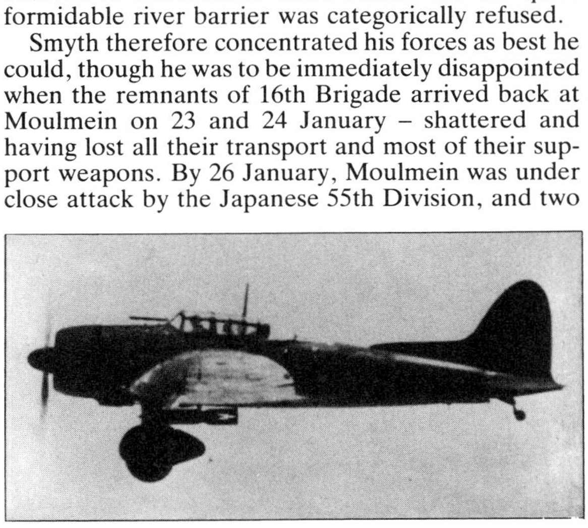

The Aichi D3A1 took part in every major carrier battle during the first 10 months of the Pacific War. From late 1942 it was to be replaced by the improved D3A2, recognizable by the streamlined cockpit canopy.

The Japanese occupation of Thailand gave them a ready base from which to launch their drive through the unprepared British forces in Burma, and from the start they dominated the battle.

days later Smyth's surviving formations were evacuated by sea (and by a minor miracle!) leaving behind 600 dead or wounded and most of their equipment. Now only 100 miles separated the Japanese from the vital bridge over the Sittang, and the only natural defence line for Smyth's men was the River Bilin – at that time of the year little more than a muddy ditch.

But soon afterwards, much to his relief, Smyth received reinforcements in the shape of the 48th Gurkha Brigade and a number of independent units, some of battalion strength, until by the end of January he had the manpower of a complete division, though they were split into four brigades who had never worked together, and they lacked line-of-communication troops. Moreover, Smyth was also informed that the 7th Armoured Brigade would arrive in Rangoon (from the Western Desert, where it had fought at Sidi Rezegh) and would come under his command – an addition to his strength which reinforced the suggestion that the Japanese could best be blocked in the open country west of the Sittang.

But permission to withdraw across the river was still refused, so during the first weeks of February 1942, the four brigades sweated out the battle in thick jungle and appalling, dusty heat, devoid of air cover, and conscious all the time of open flanks around which the enemy was more than capable of creeping. Martaban fell, the Japanese pushed up the railway line towards Bilin itself and then came reports that their 33rd Division were driving down from the area of Papun towards the Sittang Bridge and the only escape route eastwards.

Japanese troops enter Moulmein after outflanking the British by an amphibious operation.

On 19 February General Hutton at last visited Smyth in the forward area and gave permission for the withdrawal; now all that remained was to carry it out. Remarkably, the brigades managed to detach themselves from the Japanese – sometimes only a few yards away when the operation commenced – and all through the night of the 19th and through the following 24 hours they leapfrogged back towards the bridge – the railway lines partially planked over to take road transport.

Then at dawn on 21 February Smyth's headquarters were attacked by a Japanese raiding party. It was driven off, but it marked the beginning of a most unpleasant and disastrous day. The weather was very dry and hot, thirst grew intense and was made worse by the clouds of thick red dust – which revealed to marauding Japanese pilots the trails the retreating brigades were trying to follow, allowing them to bomb and machine-gun them, not only from their own Zeros but also from the Hurricanes – still bearing RAF markings – which they captured at Tavoy. Ambulances full of wounded men, staff cars and pick-ups were ditched; mules bearing weapons, ammunition and wireless sets broke loose and bolted, casualties mounted and many had to be abandoned. That evening, Smyth, inspecting the Sittang Bridge and ensuring that it could be efficiently blown when his men were across it, was approached by a staff officer from Hutton's HQ with the news not only that 7th Armoured Brigade was now deployed to the west, but also that Japanese parachute troops were expected in the same area the following morning. The sooner he got back the better.

Sittang Bridge

Smyth and some of the 1st/4th Gurkhas had crossed the bridge to survey possible dropping zones for enemy paratroops when a burst of firing from the side they had just left indicated another Japanese raiding party trying to capture the bridge itself. A strong counter-attack had to be mounted, which was successful in pushing the raiders away into the jungle, but soon it became obvious that the Japanese were arriving in strength and a pitched battle commenced with the Japanese coming down through the jungle to the north, the 48th Gurkha Brigade holding the bridge and its approaches, and the remnants of 16th and 46th Brigade trying to fight their way through increasingly tough resistance, from the south and east.

All next day the battle raged. It showed signs of slackening in the evening, so Smyth and one of his brigadiers moved back off the bridge to plan for the morrow, eat and snatch some sleep, which they had now been without for nearly three days. At 4.30 a.m. they were awoken by the brigadier commanding the 48th Gurkhas; pressure on the bridge was increasing rapidly and he doubted if his men could hold it for more than an hour more. He requested permission to blow it, despite the fact that the bulk of the other two brigades had not yet crossed.

There was only one answer. If the bridge could not be held, it must certainly not be allowed to fall intact into enemy hands – and at 5.30 a.m. on 23 February the charges were blown. In one of the few really efficient operations carried out so far by Allied troops in Burma the bridge was totally destroyed.

As it turned out, the cost in human terms was not as high as might have been expected. With sound sense of military reality, the Japanese immediately moved north to find another river-crossing, ignoring for the moment the survivors of the two Allied brigades. Of these most of those fit enough managed to swim or float themselves across the river during the next few days. But they left behind them all the badly wounded, and almost all their arms and equipment, so the force left to defend Rangoon was even further weakened.

Rangoon is taken

In fact the fate of Rangoon was now inevitable. The thousands of Indian dockworkers had panicked under the air raids, the police had deserted, Burmese and Indians fought out old antagonisms, looting was rife, and now a wave of incendiaries swept the city. Plans for evacuation of non-native inhabitants were put in hand and hundreds of thousands found their way by sea to India – including 'Jackie' Smythe himself, who was now in urgent need of hospitalization, and General Hutton, who was replaced on 5 March by Lieutenant-General the Hon. Harold Alexander. Within a matter of hours of arriving in Rangoon, Alexander escaped capture by the narrowest margin as the result of the premature removal from a crossroads on the Prome highway of a Japanese roadblock, whose members might otherwise have brought about the curtailment of a promising career.

He was at the time on his way north to form a defence line between Prome and Toungoo, where the Chinese 200th Division, sent down the Burma road by Generalissimo Chiang Kai-Shek, was already under pressure from the Japanese, who had arrived there almost as soon as the Chinese. Alexander brought back 'Burcorps' – assembled from Hutton's formation in the south plus the 1st Burma Division, and under command of Lieutenant-General Bill Slim – to hold the line on the Chinese right, but, even as the line formed, the Japanese swung east and the line was outflanked.

On 16 April Slim knew that he would have to drop further back, so he ordered the destruction of the oilfields at Yenangyaung and Chauk, and then for ten days Burcorps and the Chinese 38th Division were embroiled in desperate defensive battles south of Mandalay while the Japanese 56th Division outflanked them yet again in a drive on Lashio – and the Burma road. To General Alexander and the American General Stillwell, who was in charge of the Chinese armies in the field, it was becoming increasingly obvious that the defence of India was becoming hourly of more strategic importance than tactical battles in Burma – which was already evidently lost to Japanese aggression and military efficiency.

By 29 April the Japanese had completely cut the Burma Road at Lashio, and the following day, with breathtaking thrust and speed, they reached Monywa and then drove on towards Shwegyin. The Chinese armies had no choice but to begin withdrawal back to China, while Burcorps began theirs into India. During mid-May they arrived in batches in Assam – 'gaunt and ragged as scarecrows', as Slim was later to write, 'Yet as they trudged behind their surviving officers in groups pitifully small they still carried their arms and kept their ranks.'

With Slim watching them one day was General Stillwell, who had himself marched out from Shwebo. 'Well, General,' said 'Vinegar' Joe, 'I don't go very far with all this stuff about the British and the Americans having a common outlook, a common language, and common heritage and all that stuff. But they sure as Hell share one common ancestor. Ethelred the Unready!'

Chronology of War: 1942

January 1
United Nations Declaration signed by 26 nations in Washington

January 2
Japanese occupy Manila and Cavite. British and South African troops recapture Bardia

January 5
Further Japanese landings on west coast of Malaya. Russians hold most of Kerch peninsula. British attack Halfaya. Stalin orders massive Russian offensive

January 6
Auckinleck's advance started by Operation Crusader ends at El Agheila

January 7
General Wavell, C-in-C India, arrives in Singapore

January 8
Rommel retreats from Agedabia

January 9
Russian counterattack reaches area of Smolensk

January 10
ABDA (Australian, British, Dutch, American) Command set up under Wavell

January 11
Japanese enter Kuala Lumpur. Tarakan captured. In North Africa British recapture Sollum

January 16
Japanese troops cross Burma border from nominally-neutral Thailand

January 21
Rommel attacks again in Cyrenaica

January 22
US troops retreat into Bataan Peninsula on Luzon in the Philippines. Rommel reaches Agedabia

January 23
Japanese land at Rabaul, Kavieng and Balikpapan on New Britain, New Ireland and Borneo. Rangoon bombed. Russians break through towards Smolensk

January 24
Battle of Makassar Straits; US destroyers hold up a Japanese convoy. Australians evacuate Lae and Salamaua on New Guinea

January 25
Rommel captures Msus

January 28
Rommel recaptures Benghazi

January 29
Rommel advances on Barce

January 30
British withdraw from Malaya across the Jehore causeway into Singapore

February 3
Japanese bomb Port Moresby, New Guinea

February 4
Rommel captures Derna

February 5
Rommel's advance slows short of Gazala

February 7
Japanese land on Singapore Island

February 10
Japanese take Martaban and land at Makassar on Celebes

February 11
The Channel Dash: Scharnhorst, Gneisenau *and* Prinz Eugen *escape up Channel from Brest*

February 15
Singapore surrenders

February 16
Japanese airborne attack on South Sumatra. Palembang oil refinery captured

February 18/19
Battle of Lombok Strait, east of Bali

February 19
Japanese invade Bali, cross River Bilin in Burma and bomb Darwin

Japanese army weapons

The stunning victories achieved by the Imperial Japanese Army were not due to any superiority in equipment. Japanese tanks were generally inferior to those of the Allies, and their artillery was hardly overwhelming. Japanese use of armour was influenced by their experience in China against hordes of ill-armed troops with little tank or anti-tank capability.

***Above:** The Type 95 light tank carried a four-man crew and was armed with a 37-mm gun and a pair of machine-guns. Like French tanks of the 1930s, the commander had to operate the main armament as well as command the vehicle.*

***Left:** The Type 4 HO-RO was one of the few self-propelled guns produced by Japan. Built and deployed in only small numbers it used the chassis of the Type 97 medium tank to carry a 150-mm howitzer.*

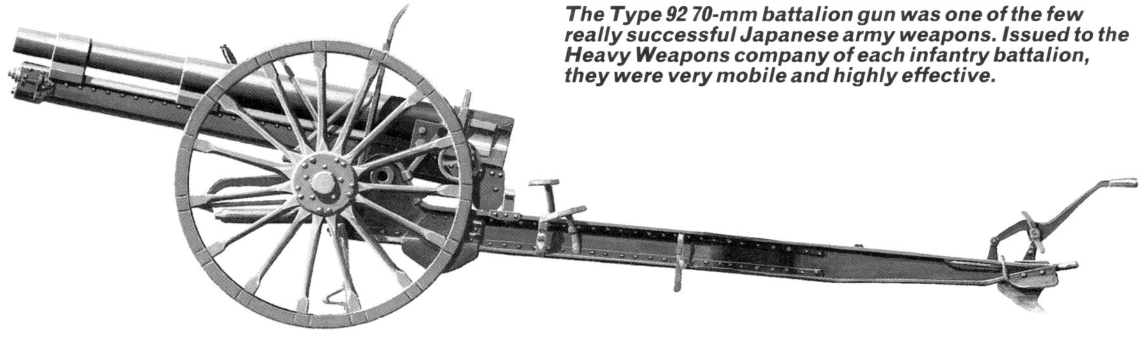

The Type 92 70-mm battalion gun was one of the few really successful Japanese army weapons. Issued to the Heavy Weapons company of each infantry battalion, they were very mobile and highly effective.

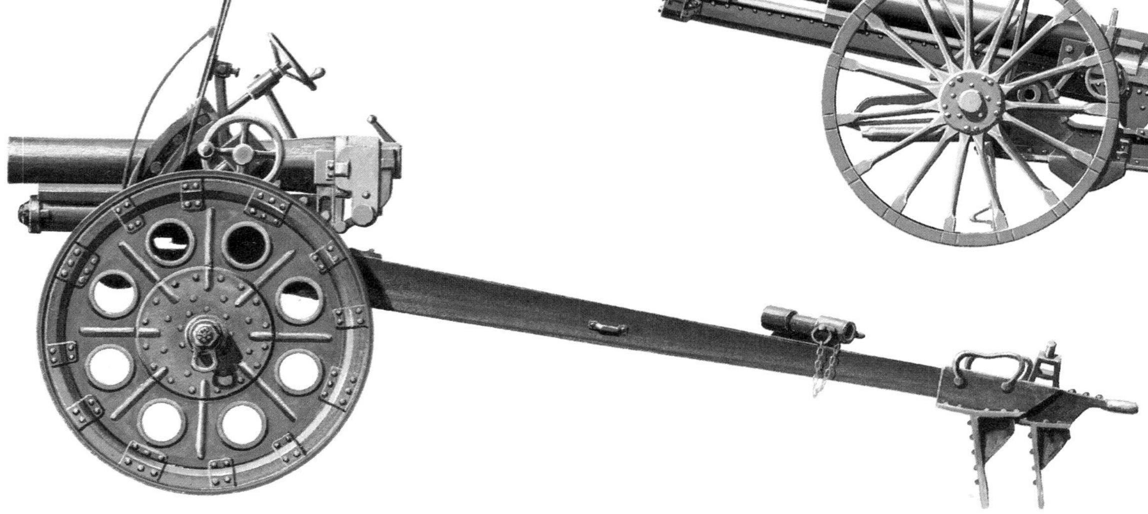

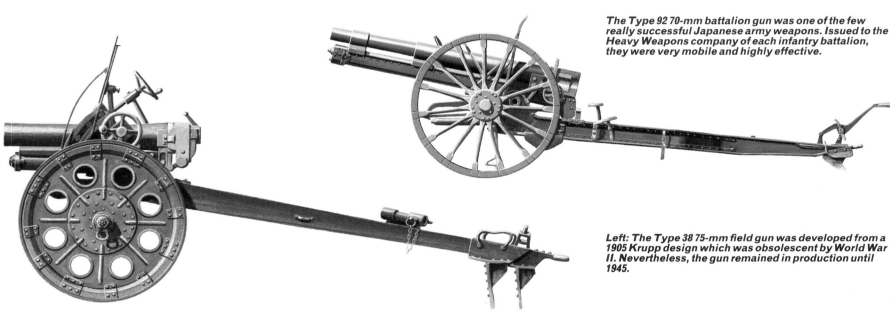

***Left:** The Type 38 75-mm field gun was developed from a 1905 Krupp design which was obsolescent by World War II. Nevertheless, the gun remained in production until 1945.*

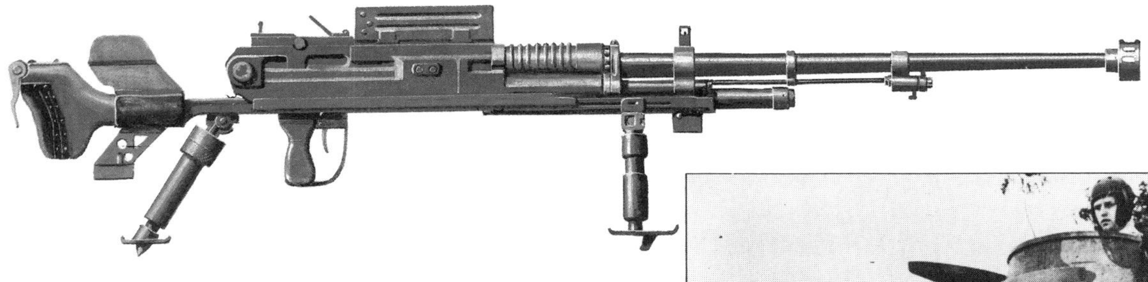

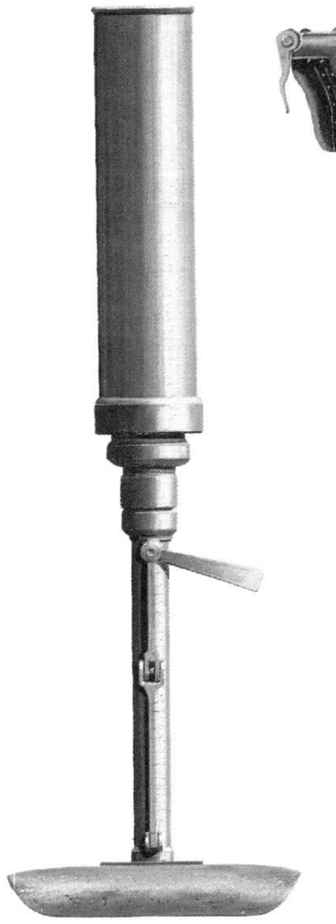

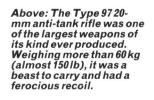

***Above:** The Type 97 20-mm anti-tank rifle was one of the largest weapons of its kind ever produced. Weighing more than 60 kg (almost 150 lb), it was a beast to carry and had a ferocious recoil.*

***Right:** This Type 95 light tank was captured intact by the US Marines on Makin Island. In an early effort to reduce the heat inside a tank operating in a tropical climate, asbestos lining was fitted to the walls of the crew compartment.*

***Left:** The Type 10 50-mm mortar was a light and handy weapon suited to jungle fighting. It was incorrectly dubbed the 'knee mortar', which led to many US troops injuring themselves by firing captured weapons with the baseplate resting on the thigh.*

Chapter 9

The Onslaught Continues

From the moment that the aircraft of the Imperial Japanese Navy struck an unprepared Pearl Harbor and Japanese army troops landed on the coast of the Malayan peninsula, a seemingly endless cataract of disaster befell the Allies. Over a six-month period, Japan was to gain vast territories and the raw materials that went with them. Guam, Wake, the Phillippines, French Indo-China, Burma, Thailand, Malaya, the Dutch East Indies, most of new Guinea and Papua, the Bismarcks, the Solomons and the Gilberts were taken in a lightning campaign to match that of the Germans in the West.

A week after the Japanese forces had gone ashore on the Kra Isthmus in their attack on the British, one of their supporting convoys had veered south of Saigon and landed on the Sarawak coast; by Christmas the entire province was under Japanese control. On the day after the main Japanese attacks on Luzon had been launched, a fleet sailed from Palau and quickly occupied Mindanao, concentrating large naval forces in the anchorage at Davao.

There could be little doubt as to the purpose of these moves, and on 10 January, when General Wavell attended the first conference of ABDA in Java, the declared intention of all present had been to set up a defence of the Malay barrier along the line Malaya/Sumatra/Java/Sunda Islands/Australia; 14 days later the suggestion was made by Wavell that the eastern end of the defence line should specifically include Port Darwin and its surroundings.

Whether or not the British, American, Dutch and Australian military and naval commanders attending the conferences admitted it – even to themselves – there was little they could do to stem the flood of Japanese aggression about to swamp the area, except manoeuvre vaguely in an attempt to confuse, and evacuate as many people as could be collected together before they were captured. That, and watch events with some of the fascination of a rabbit trapped by a stoat.

From the Davo anchorage on 7 January sailed two Japanese convoys with their escorting naval forces – Eastern Force bound through the Molucca Passage to occupy the islands of Ceram, Ambon and Timor on one flank, the Celebes, Makassar and Bali on the other; Central Force to sail down the Straits of Makassar, coastal-hopping at the important places along the south-east Borneo coast as far as Bandjermasin, then crossing to Java. Once the Japanese Imperial Staff were assured that those operations were proceeding satisfactorily, Western Force would sail from Camranh Bay on the Indo-China coast and take Sumatra,

Were if not for the success which was attending Japanese forces elsewhere during this astonishing explosion of military energy, it would be difficult to believe the speed with which this programme was carried out, and the almost derisory price the aggressors paid for their triumph.

A Type 95 Ha-Go light tank crashes through the jungle on the Bataan peninsula of Luzon. The Japanese victory in the Philippines was a result of superior air power crushing American air strength and supporting numerically inferior, but better trained, troops.

By 11 January Japanese troops of the Central Force had landed around Tarakan, and troops of Eastern Force at five points along the north-eastern Celebes coast; the following day they had captured respectively Tarakan and Manado, the first with an adjacent oilfield, the second with an airfield. Nine days later Central Force was off Balikpapan, though here they did suffer some losses: one steamer had been sunk by US Martin bombers, one had been torpedoed, and while the Japanese fleet had been silhouetted against burning oil installations it had been attacked by four US four-stacker destroyers, which sank another three steamers. Not that this interrupted Japanese plans to any great extent; the fleet landed its soldiers, and three days later Balikpapan was firmly in their hands, the fleet auxiliaries assembling for their next step.

Eastern Force had kept pace and, on the day Balikpapan fell, so did Kendari, with the best airfield the Dutch government had built outside Holland itself. In the meantime the Japanese air fleets had been bombing Ambon continuously since 16 January, so that on the 25th the Allies withdrew their own remaining aircraft. As a result, when the Japanese fleet arrived offshore on 31 January the defenders had no air cover, the town of Ambon was taken immediately, and three days later the main Australian force on the island was forced to surrender. So far Eastern Force had lost one minesweeper sunk and two damaged in a minefield on this flank, and one destroyer torpedoed on the other flank when the fleet was en route for Makassar. Makassar fell on 9 February.

Meanwhile Central Force had 'pacified' Balikpapan and its surroundings. It then left on 27 January to carry out what was perhaps its most vital task – the capture of Bandjermasin and the main airfield 16

Japan's requirement for raw materials made the oil fields of the Dutch East Indies a prime target for conquest. Palembang, on Sumatra, was the target for attack by naval parachutists.

Chronology of War: 1942

February 19
Japanese invade Bali, cross River Bilin in Burma and bomb Darwin

February 22
General MacArthur ordered to leave Philippines; appointed C-in-C Allied Forces, Australia

February 27
Crushing defeat inflicted on Allied fleet in Battle of Java Sea. British paratroops attack Bruneval on north west coast of France

February 28
Japanese invade Java. UK civilian casualties in February 22 killed and 21 injured

March 2
Japanese land on Mindanao in the Philippines

March 5
General Harold Alexander appointed GoC Burma

March 8
Japanese land at Lae and Salamaua on the north coast of New Guinea and enter Rangoon. General Yamashita appointed C-in-C Philippines. Dutch East Indies capitulate

March 12
MacArthur embarks at Corregidor

March 19
General William Slim arrives in Burma to command Imperial troops

March 24
Japanese drive down into Bataan Peninsula

March 28
Raid on St Nazaire; HMS Campbelltown *rams dock gates*

March 31
UK civilian casualties for last four months 189 killed, 149 injured

April 1
Japanese land on Dutch New Guinea

April 3
Japanese launch final drive in Bataan

April 6
Japanese land on Bougainville and Admiralty Islands

April 9
General King surrenders Bataan; Wainwright escapes to Corregidor

April 18
Doolittle raid on Tokyo

April 29
Japanese reach Lashio, terminus of the 'Burma Road'

April 30
Japanese complete conquest of Central Burma. UK civilian casualties in April 938 killed, 998 injured

May 2
All British troops in Burma withdrawn across Irrawaddy

May 4
Japanese transports leave Rabaul for Port Moresby

May 5
Japanese landings on Corregidor. British commandos land on Madagascar

May 6
Corregidor garrison surrenders. All US forces in Philippines surrender

May 7
Battle of Coral Sea opens. Japanese light carrier Shoho *sunk*

May 8
In continuing battle fleet carrier USS Lexington *sunk. Japanese forces occupy Akyab and Myitkyina in Northern Burma. German offensive in Crimea*

May 9
Russian offensive towards Kharkov

miles south east at Ulin, from which air cover could be provided to dominate the Java Sea and the Banka Strait. Both were firmly in their hands by 10 February.

With the success which was attending every Japanese move, it is hardly surprising that Western Force from Indo-China was now despatched to Sumatra. It left Camranh Bay on 11 February, arrived off Muntok on the 14th and landed troops on Banka Island the same day, occupied Muntok airfield against no opposition, then sailed troops up the Musi River to join 700 paratroops who had been dropped at night near Palembang. The town with its oilfields intact was taken on 16 February, though there had been attempts to interrupt the operation at sea. ABDA had sent a 'Combined Striking Force' from Oosthaven aound the eastern end of the island to attack Western Force, but one Dutch destroyer hit a reef and had to be scuttled by its crew, and the rest of the force was sighted by a Japanese spotter plane and then subjected to such concentrated carrier-borne air attack for four hours that Admiral Doorman turned back. (The day before, Singapore had capitulated.)

Eastern Force's next target was the island of Timor, which from 12 to 18 February was subjected to heavy and continual bombing raids. On 19 February these were suddenly switched to the Australian mainland at Port Darwin, and every aircraft available from their new base at Kendari, plus those from four aircraft-carriers now cruising north west of the port, was sent over in a succession of waves which killed 240 people and wounded 150 more. The next day the Japanese landed troops at two places on the Timor coast, dropped paratroops around the airfield at Penfui that day and the next, and by 22 February controlled the island's main centres and communications. On Timor, however, the defenders managed to withdraw into the interior, where they carried on a gallant guerrilla warfare for nearly a year before they were rounded up and killed.

Bali was the next island to fall – its airfield at Den Passar was in Japanese hands by 19 February, but here again an attempt at interference was made. Two naval forces mustering between them three cruisers, seven destroyers and a number of motor torpedo-boats attacked the Japanese fleet during the night of 19/20 February – after the Japanese troops had been landed – but the Battle of the Lombok Strait, despite the element of surprise achieved, was hardly an Allied victory. For one Dutch destroyer lost and a light cruiser hit 11 times, they had damaged two Japanese destroyers and a transport – and had not impeded the Japanese operations by a single day.

Java Sea

With the capture of Bali the air link between Australia and the command structure throughout the Dutch East Indies was cut; the way was now open for the invasion of Java.

The Battle of the Java Sea was fought out between 27 February and 1 March, repeating the pattern of every previous engagement between the Japanese and Allied navies so far, and hardly delaying the invasion of Java itself by more than a few hours. The Japanese Eastern Force destined for Kragan consisted of 41 transports escorted by two heavy cruisers, two light cruisers and 14 destroyers, covered by air squadrons from Kendar and the airfields recently captured on Borneo.

The heavy cruiser HMS Exeter *fights off a Japanese air attack while escorting an Allied convoy through the Bangka Strait off Sumatra just before the fall of Singapore. Within a month she was to be destroyed by vastly superior Japanese surface forces.*

The Allied fleet to oppose them consisted of four cruisers – one from each of the ABDA countries – and a dozen mixed destroyers; their air cover was to have been provided by 32 Curtiss P-40 fighters (Kittyhawks), but as a portent of the battle to come, the light aircraft-carrier *Langley* was sunk by Japanese aircraft on 27 February and took the P-40s with her. Not only was Admiral Doorman to fight bereft of air cover, he was also to fight blind – against an enemy, moreover, armed with a weapon of which the Allies had as yet no equivalent; the Japanese had cracked the problem of liquid oxygen propellant for torpedoes and were using these for the first time. With them, the Japanese sank four Allied destroyers and two cruisers – including the *De Ruyter*, Doorman's flagship.

The only significant successes scored by the Allies occurred during the night of 28/29 February when two cruisers, *Perth* and *Houston*, which had just refuelled at Tandjong Priok were endeavouring to slip away through Sunda Strait, came across the Japanese Western Force disembarking troops at Merak and went straight into the attack. A fierce battle followed which resulted in both allied cruisers being sunk – but they took with them a Japanese minesweeper and a transport, and damaged three destroyers and three more transports to such an effect that they had to be beached. But all the troops and most of their equipment had already been landed.

Late on 28 February, HMS *Exeter*, which had been badly hit in the first encounter and sent back to Surabaya for repair, left the port escorted by two destroyers, heading for Fremantle. But they were seen early on 1 March and all three were sunk by air attack. Of the entire Allied fleet which had operated during those dreadful days throughout the Dutch East Indies, only four American destroyers – *Edwards, Alden, Ford* and *Paul Jones* – managed to escape to Australia.

The situation throughout that island barrier was now lost to the Allies. On 7 March the Japanese C-in-C demanded talks with the Dutch C-in-C and the Governor-General, and during the afternoon of 8 March under threat of a devastating bombardment of Bandung, an unconditional surrender was agreed. The Japanese conquest of the East Indies had been completed in three months; they could be well content, for they had expected it to take six.

The Philippines

Pearl Harbor and the US fleet there had been removed from the Pacific military chessboard on 7 December 1941. By the beginning of March 1942 Japan had taken possession of the Dutch East Indies with all the oil, tin, bauxite, rice and coffee the region could produce, and two months later she completely controlled Malaya and Burma, together producing enough rubber, tin and oil to satisfy the gargantuan appetite of the most ambitious war programme. By 1 May all that remained was to remove the last vestige of resistance to Japanese aggression still in the area – the 15,000 half-starved American soldiers isolated on Corregidor, an island off Luzon, itself the largest of the Philippine islands.

Japanese troops on Luzon use a flamethrower on a pillbox. Only limited pockets of stiff resistance had to be dealt with, and before long Manila was taken and the American and Philippine forces were under siege.

The major Japanese assault on the Philippines was launched by forces under the command of General Homma. Landed in the area of Lingayan Gulf, their advance south soon forced the forces of General MacArthur.

Attack on Luzon

The Japanese took a calculated risk in their attack on Luzon, the most important of the Philippine Islands. The first landings were by small forces in the north and south, with the main thrust from Lingayen Gulf in the West some two weeks later. The destruction of American air power was to prove the deciding factor, allowing Japan command of the skies over the battlefield.

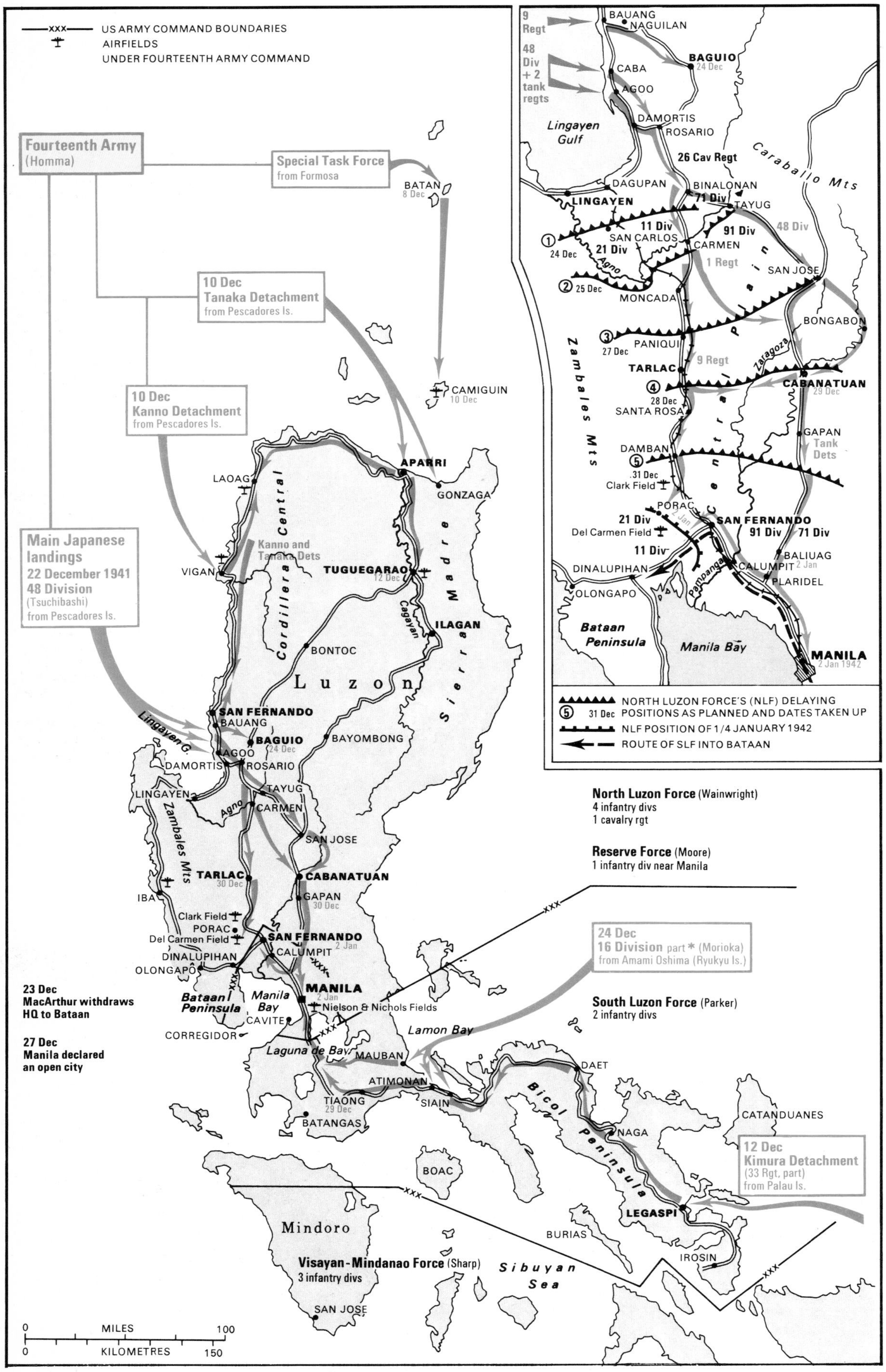

Although General Homma was given only two divisions from the Japanese Fourteenth Army to deal with the 11 divisions under the command of MacArthur, the troops he had were well equipped, well trained and imbued with the warrior spirit peculiar to Japan.

Five time zones and 5,000 miles separate Pearl Harbor from Luzon, so it had been 2.30 a.m. in Manila on 9 December when the unbelievable news of the attack on Pearl Harbor came through and 3.30 a.m. before General MacArthur learned of it from a commercial broadcast. By 5.00 a.m. General Brereton, commanding the US air force in the Philippines, was seeking from MacArthur permission to bomb the Japanese in Formosa. Warned from Washington not to allow his bombers to be caught on the ground by a sudden attack, Brereton sent his B-17s (Flying Fortresses) out on patrol at 8.00 a.m. – for the moment without bombs. At 10.45 a.m. all permissions had been obtained and loading crews were ready, so the patrolling bombers were brought back to Clark Field to bomb-up and refuel, while fighters of the 20th Pursuit Squadron were being prepared, alongside. By 12.15 p.m. all were lined up and ready to take off.

On Formosa, crews of the Japanese 'Betty' bombers and Zero fighters, and the commanders of V Air Group, had had a frustrating 12 hours. Thick fog had closed in on their airfields at midnight and was still dense at daybreak. All hope of surprise was thus lost, for they knew that Manila would have been informed of the Pearl Harbor attack within minutes of its taking place; as the light grew they fully expected American B-17s to arrive overhead, but as time passed their spirits rose and the fog thinned. All would apparently be well; they had 25 bombers in the air making for north Luzon by 8.00 a.m., and by 10.15 a.m. – their commanders still apprehensively searching the skies for signs of retribution – naval aircraft of the Japanese XI Air Fleet were taking off, their target the USAAF base at Clark Field.

Escorted by 84 fighters, 108 Japanese bombers arrived over Clark Field at 12.15 p.m. to see, beautifully lined up as though for inspection, all the bombers of the US 19th Bombardment Group and the fighters of the Pursuit Squadron, all with full fuel tanks, loaded bomb bays and ammunition racks. Even the battleships at Pearl Harbor had not been so conveniently laid out for destruction.

The next two hours reduced Clark Field to a flaming mass of destruction wherein flights of enemy bombers accurately pinpointed B-17s and P-40s and reduced to rubble the hangars, warehouses and barracks alongside the runways, while the Zeros sprayed everything that moved. At a nearby fighter base at Iba another Japanese force hit the control tower and the radar station, then caught P-40s of the 3rd Pursuit Squadron circling to land because they were almost out of fuel, and shot all but two of them out of the sky. The total Japanese score between noon and 2.00 on the afternoon of 8 December 1941 was 17 B-17s, 56 P-40s and some 30 miscellaneous aircraft, together with vitally important ground installations and 230 men killed or wounded – all for the loss of seven Zeros.

The following day the Japanese attacked installations at Nicholas Field, and on 10 December they hit three air bases around Manila and left the naval dockyard at Cavite ablaze – repair shops, warehouses, barracks, radio station all wrecked and 500 men killed or wounded, a submarine hit, and a store of some 200 torpedoes destroyed.

Such was the speed of the Japanese attack, and so accurately had they assessed MacArthur's weaknesses that large coastal guns designed to repel attacks from the sea were overrun from the rear.

Japanese battleships and cruisers

By 1941 Japan possessed a mighty battleship fleet which was intended to crush the US Pacific Fleet in a classic sea battle. Ironically, the original American war plan involved sending the fleet to the support of the Philippines.

In 1942 the Japanese fleet was joined by **Yamato** *and* **Musashi**, *the largest and most powerful battleships the world has ever seen. Tight secrecy had surrounded their construction and only after the war did the full details of these magnificent warships emerge.*

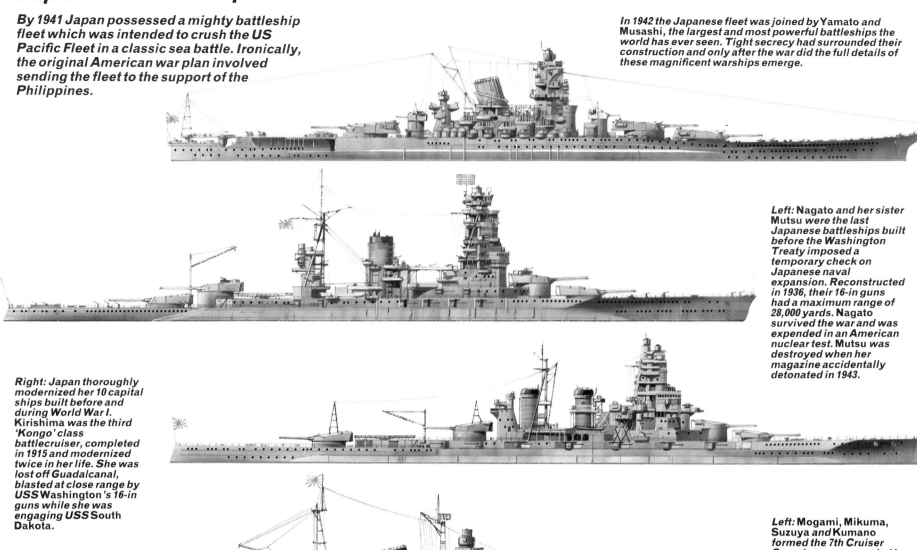

Left: **Nagato** *and her sister* **Mutsu** *were the last Japanese battleships built before the Washington Treaty imposed a temporary check on Japanese naval expansion. Reconstructed in 1936, their 16-in guns had a maximum range of 28,000 yards.* **Nagato** *survived the war and was expended in an American nuclear test.* **Mutsu** *was destroyed when her magazine accidentally detonated in 1943.*

Right: *Japan thoroughly modernized her 10 capital ships built before and during World War I.* **Kirishima** *was the third 'Kongo' class battlecruiser, completed in 1915 and modernized twice in her life. She was lost off Guadalcanal, blasted at close range by USS* **Washington***'s 16-in guns while she was engaging USS* **South Dakota**.

Left: **Mogami, Mikuma, Suzuya** *and* **Kumano** *formed the 7th Cruiser Squadron, commanded by the redoubtable Admiral Kurita. Armed with 10x8-in guns and 12x24-in torpedoes, they were fine ships,* **Mogami** *proving a very tough vessel indeed.*

Right: *The four units of the 'Myoko' class were* **Myoko, Nachi, Haguro** *and* **Ashigara**. *These aggressive-looking warships were responsible for many Allied losses in the Java Sea in 1942.*

Mogami *working up to full speed on her trials in 1935. After Japan abrogated the Treaty of London, the triple 6-in turrets were replaced by double 8-in mountings.*

Her tripod mast now enclosed in the characteristic 'Pagoda' structure, **Fuso** *cruises majestically off the Bungo Straits before the war. Thirty years after her launch she perished in the Battle of the Surigao Strait, torpedoed by US destroyers.*

Within a week, therefore, the United States Far East air force had been as thoroughly incapacitated as had been the US battleship fleet at Pearl Harbor, and from then on the US Army in the Philippines would have to fight without air cover and learn the bitter lesson expounded later by Rommel: 'Anyone who has to fight, even with the most modern weapons, against an enemy in complete command of the air, fights like a savage against modern European troops, under the same handicaps and with the same chances of success.'

The first landings of Japanese troops in the Philippines took place on 8 December, when a small force landed unopposed on the island of Batan; two days later they moved on to take the seaplane base at Camiguan from which they could cover more important landings the same day at Aparri, and Gonzaga and Vigan. By 12 December the Vigan force had pushed north and taken the airfield at Laoag, the Aparri force had taken one at Tuguegarao, and during this operation they had been attacked only once by a few US bombers, and had to beach two of their transports. But the troops had been landed quite successfully, and with air cover guaranteed, both forces moved south to concentrate around Lengayen Gulf, where the main bulk of the Japanese Fourteenth Army under General Homma was to land.

Homma arrived on 22 December, and despite choppy weather, an attack by B-17s from Darwin and some shelling by two 155-mm guns along the coast, by the following day the 48th Division with an extra infantry regiment, four well-equipped artillery regiments and nearly 100 tanks were ashore, and probing inland for opposition – of which they found very little. Then on 24 December, 7,000 men of General Morioka's 16th Division went ashore on the narrow strip of land between Siain and Mauban on the isthmus south of Manila, virtually isolating south Luzon and its garrisons from Manila and the north.

In Manila itself, General MacArthur was facing up to the unpleasant reality that the Philippine army was no match for the Japanese, and that higher authority

Japanese marines move towards Corregidor as the last American foothold in the Philippines is bombed and shelled.

Captain Marc Mitscher talks with the crews about to launch their B-25 bombers from USS* Hornet *on the Doolittle raid.

felt they could do little to help him. He had hoped for reinforcements to arrive on a convoy of seven ships escorted by the cruiser *Pensacola*, but the convoy never even braved the Japanese fleet, and a request that US Navy planes should be flown in from aircraft-carriers was turned down because they were needed elsewhere – and in any case could prove too vulnerable at that time to be of much use.

MacArthur, in fact, was on his own, and as a result by 23 December he had decided to remove himself and his headquarters to Corregidor Island, to concentrate his forces solely for the defence of the Bataan Peninsula, and to declare Manila an 'Open City'. By 2 January, therefore, Morioka's troops were in Manila (which they treated exactly as though they had fought for it), all of southern Luzon was under Japanese control, and the American and Philippines troops in northern Luzon were being penned into an increasingly narrow neck of land between Manila Bay on the east and the South China Sea on the west. By 9 January, the defence line ran from the west coast north of Moron across the foothills of Mt Santa Rosa, and on behind the line of the Calaguiman River to Manila Bay near Abucay. Three infantry divisions, a cavalry regiment and an artillery regiment made up I Corps under Major-General Jonathan M. Wainwright on the left flank, four infantry divisions plus a regiment of Filipinos making up II Corps under Brigadier-General George M. Parker and holding the ground between Santa Rosa and Manila Bay. To their rear were packed over 30,000 administration troops and some 26,000 civilian refugees, and sufficient fuel and food, it was reckoned, to last for about two months; but there was a shortage of quinine, and malaria cases were already filtering into the hospitals.

Assault on Bataan

At 3.00 p.m. on 9 January a concentrated artillery barrage opened up on Parker's men, and soon Japanese infantry were seen crossing the Calaguiman River. American artillery caught many of them, but by midnight the Japanese were in a sugar plantation only 150 yards from American positions, and soon afterwards, under cover of another artillery and mortar barrage, the infantry rushed forward again in a suicidal *banzai* charge. Over 200 Japanese dead were counted on the field there the following day – but the defence line had been bent back and when Colonel Takechi's 9th Regiment attacked Parker's left flank the whole US position began to crumble. Savage fighting continued all the way back to the rear defence line along the Pilar-Bagac Road, but it was only the US artillery which really held the Japanese flood, the US infantry lacking the aggression and experience of their opponents.

On the western flank, Wainwright's corps was under the same pressure, one of its divisions routed to such an extent that they fled in disorder down the coast, abandoning even their rifles. By 25 January, the line ran from Bagac to Orion – only 12 miles from Mariveles at the point of the Bataan Peninsula.

But now General Homma found himself facing unexpected difficulties. The American artillery held high ground from which it could pour heavy – and increasingly accurate – fire down on every Japanese position and movement, and Fourteenth Army was weakening as every day went by. By the end of February (by which time they were all closed up on the Bagac-Orion line) the Japanese had suffered some 7,000 casualties of whom 2,700 had been killed, and those who remained were no more proof against malaria and other tropical diseases than their enemies. Nearly 12,000 of Homma's men were down with a variety of illnesses from dysentery to beri-beri, and he had hardly enough fit men to muster three effective battalions: if his situation had been appreciated by MacArthur the whole story of the war in the Pacific might have been different.

But if Homma's formations lacked numbers, they made up for it in aggression and ingenuity. Every night the patrols were out, and every night they kept the men in the long defence line awake, itchy, irritated and nervous. Rifle and pistol shots rang out all the time, every one from a different – and, to one or other defender, more threatening – point. Loudspeakers would suddenly blast out terrifying booms as though of barrage or bombardment, then a voice would announce some distant, or occasionally nearby, disaster to American arms followed soon by soft voices crooning 'Home, Sweet Home', 'Home on the Range', or some other nostalgic lullaby. The Japanese seemed also to have an unlimited supply of fire-crackers and a device for hurling long strings of them up into trees behind the defence lines; suddenly it would seem to the exhausted American and Philippine soldiers that they were being attacked from the rear.

And all the time fresh troops were arriving to reinforce Fourteenth Army. During March, the 4th Division arrived from Shanghai with detachments of extra infantry, artillery and engineers; more significantly, another 60 twin-engined bombers arrived at the repaired and re-equipped air base at Clark Field, and plans were laid for the final liquidation of American strength on Luzon by the beginning of April.

Those forces would no longer be commanded by General MacArthur. At the time of his decision to withdraw to Bataan and Corregidor he had assured General Marshall, Chief of Staff in Washington, that he intended to 'fight to destruction' on Corregidor, and on 8 February his report ended 'there is no denying the fact that we are near done.' But shortly afterwards America and her Pacific allies agreed that a new joint South-West Pacific Command should be formed with MacArthur at its head, and, on orders from President Roosevelt, on 8 March MacArthur handed over command to the unfortunate General Wainwright. MacArthur arrived in Darwin on 12 March and there delivered his valedictory 'I shall return' message to the men he had left behind.

On Good Friday, 5 April 1942, the Japanese bom-

A Japanese field artillery battery in action in China. It should be remembered that the main strength of the Japanese army remained in China, not only for the the first months of 1942 but for the whole war.

The Indian Ocean Raid

After the attack on Pearl Harbor, the 1st Air Fleet of the Imperial Japanese Navy went on to demonstrate its strike power and the superb skills of its fliers against new targets-most notably against the Royal Navy.

The shock effect of Japan's Pearl Harbor strike remains so great that it is widely overlooked that Nagumo's 1st Air Fleet went on within a few months to essay a similar exercise on the British. Four of his six fast carriers engaged in a preliminary warm-up on 19 February 1942 against Darwin and Broome in north-western Australia. For the loss of two aircraft the Japanese sank 12 assorted ships and spent a leisurely, and largely uncontested, hour reducing the base facilities and much of the towns.

By late February 1942, the Japanese had gained most of their objectives in the East Indies, Malaya and the Philippines, and the 1st Air Fleet carriers had a months' well-earned rest before sailing for the Indian Ocean on 26 March.

An Allied agreement about this time defined the Indian Ocean west of the Malayan peninsula as a British zone of responsibility, but the Royal Navy could muster only a scratch force for its protection. Admiral Sir James Somerville had on paper a powerful force built around five battleships and three carriers. Only two of the carriers were modern, however, and four of the battleships were 'R' class units, too much outclassed by the enemy to be of more than sacrificial value. Sensibly, Somerville formed two separate forces, the older ships based in East Africa and the remainder in Ceylon and the secret facility at Addu Atoll, 600 miles away in the southern Maldives.

Intelligence reports indicating strongly a Japanese strike against Ceylon on or about 1 April 1942, Somerville kept his still-complete force well to the west by day, when he considered himself at greatest disadvantage, steaming eastward by night onto the expected Japanese approach.

Although correct in essence, Somerville's intelligence was badly wrong with respect to time. By the evening of 2 April, the British force needed to fuel and provision and had to return to Addu, except for the heavy cruisers HMS *Cornwall* and HMS *Dorsetshire*, the old carrier HMS *Hermes*, and the destroyer HMS *Vampire* which, because of other commitments, were sent to Ceylon.

Barely had Somerville reached Addu, on the evening of 4 April, than an air search spotted Nagumo less than 400 miles south-east of the island. Caught flat-footed, the British sailed immediately, although with no hope of forestalling the attack. Ceylon, uncovered, sailed the two cruisers to meet Somerville and braced itself for the onslaught.

As at Pearl Harbor the Japanese picked a Sunday before breakfast for the raid, and shore-based radar tracked in the force of 126 aircraft as they made for Colombo. Being protected by organized AA defences and the RAF, the harbour was not cleared of shipping. As it happened, the 40 or more fighters that met the Japanese lost half their number without managing to break up the attack. But after the 30-minute attack, which lost the enemy seven aircraft, the port still functioned.

Unfortunately, just before midday, an Aichi E13A 'Jake' floatplane from the cruiser *Tone* sighted the two hurrying cruisers. For over three hours the aircraft dogged their heels until it vectored in a 90-aircraft strike. Lacking any air cover, the two British ships were swamped and sunk within 20 minutes, with the loss of over 400 lives.

Seeking to redress the balance, Somerville steered to intercept Nagumo at dawn on 6 April. The victorious Japanese did not oblige, probably fortunately for the British, who would almost certainly have been worsted.

To exploit the likely panic resulting from the Colombo attack, Nagumo had formed a separate raiding force, centred on the smaller carrier *Ryujo* which was, in any case, too slow to operate as part of the main group.

This force had sailed on 1 April from newly-occupied Burma, and had divided into three divisions to mop up mercantile traffic on the Orissa coast. In the space of 10 days the surface warships, backed by submarines and the *Ryujo*'s 48 aircraft, accounted for 28 merchantmen totalling 145,000 tons and had bombed a couple of ports for good measure.

The *Ryujo* group disengaged on 7 April, but the British were allowed no respite for, on the afternoon of the following day, Nagumo was spotted by a Ceylon-based PBY, some 450 miles to the eastward. Again, Somerville was at Addu, having just detached his older ships for the less hazardous waters of East Africa. The Japanese course suggested either Trincomalee or Madras and, with no hope of naval interception, the ports were cleared. Some 15 hours after the PBY's sighting report, 85 enemy aircraft hit Trincomalee. They found no shipping and few targets ashore, but again roughly handled the RAF.

A 'Jake' from the *Haruna* found the veteran carrier *Hermes* close inshore. She sailed when the harbour was cleared, carried no fighters of her own, and was prevented by communications problems from calling up shore-based air cover. No fewer than 85 escorted dive-bombers saturated her with bombs. Within minutes, having absorbed an estimated 40 250-kg projectiles, she capsized and sank.

Nagumo recovered his aircraft and turned for home. He had defeated the British as soundly as he had the Americans and, for the moment, the seas beyond the western Japanese defence perimeter were secure. Although the enemy never again penetrated the Indian Ocean in such strength, the scale of his activities had guaranteed that a counter-offensive would be a long time coming.

Admiral Chuichi Nagumo was to lead the First Koku Kantai (First Air Fleet) of the Imperial Japanese Combined Fleet through six months of the most stunning naval action the world has seen, from the attack on Pearl Harbor to the Battle of Midway.

Following Pearl Harbor, the First Air Fleet struck at northern Australia, causing serious damage in Darwin. The conquest of the East Indies now freed the fleet to enter the Indian Ocean to attack the British possessions there.

Darwin was the main supply base for the hastily cobbled together ABDA naval force, and one of the 12 vessels sunk or destroyed was the* Neptune*, an ammunition ship.

Once in the Indian ocean, the battle-tested pilots found such new targets as the cruiser HMS* Dorsetshire *brave but helpless in the face of attacks by up to 90 bombers.

HMS* Hermes*, the first carrier to be designed as such, was sunk by more than 40 bomb hits by planes from the Pearl Harbor veterans* Akagi*,* Soryu *and* Hiryu*.

bardment opened on the positions of the Bagac-Orion defence line, augmented by 60 tons of bombs dropped by the newly arrived aircraft from Clark Field; by evening Japanese infantry were through the line in most places and 1,000 yards on, and on the following day, having spent the night moving up his guns and rearming his bombers, General Homma repeated the pattern. The Japanese 65th Brigade smashed through the central positions, by dawn on 7 April they were commanding the northern slopes of Marivales range, where they beat off an attempted counter-attack with tanks, and the US II Corps began to disintegrate.

Wainwright now suggested to the commander of the Luzon defences that I Corps should be thrown into a flank attack, but the US forces in Bataan had been reduced to a condition not far from rout – defeated, it must be said, as much by their own fatalism as by the enemy forces. They knew they could not be reinforced or evacuated; they had watched the implacable advance of the enemy with the same resignation as had overcome the Dutch in Java and Sumatra, and the British in Singapore; and, as they had no conception of the treatment they would receive at Japanese hands, they lacked the ferocity of cornered rats which might, even at this stage, have thrown the Japanese back.

On 9 April, the surrender of Bataan was agreed. Some 2,000 people including nurses and some sailors escaped to Corregidor – for what that was worth – and 78,000 men of a demoralized army went into dreadful captivity from which a comparatively small number ever returned.

At their peak, General Homma's forces had never exceeded 30,000.

The siege of Corregidor

The bombing of Corregidor had begun on 29 December 1941, and the first stage lasted a week. During the following days a great deal of clearing up and repair work was carried out, but while they were doing it the garrison could also watch the arrows on the Luzon map, pointing towards them from all sides and creeping inexorably closer. On 6 February shelling from a medium battery in the Cavite Province began, and then in mid-March 10 240-mm howitzers arrived in the hills to the south and began regular shelling of Corregidor and the nearby island of Fort Frank, Fort Drum and Fort Hughes. On 24 March day-long bombing began by 60 military and 24 naval aircraft operating from Clark Field.

Corregidor garrison went on half rations on 1 January, their stocks of food and quinine as low as those in Bataan; and when Bataan fell, they knew that it would be their turn next.

General Homma took his time. He brought up every sizeable piece of artillery he had and sighted it carefully with Corregidor as the bullseye – 46 155-mm guns, 28 105-mm guns, 32 75s in addition to the huge 240s; and to guide the efforts he appointed a strong

intelligence team, with a squadron of observation planes and a balloon company to assist them.

Monday, 29 April was Emperor Hirohito's birthday, and the gunners had stockpiled ammunition with which to salute it. At 7.25 a.m. the barrage opened and during the hours which followed bombers from Clark Field added to the chaos, though no one on Corregidor noticed. The din was indescribable. Jagged steel and concrete flew through the air only too often accompanied by pieces of bleeding flesh, trees were uprooted and flung about like rushes, and by noon fires had started all over the Rock, while exploding ammunition dumps added to the danger and to the uproar.

For two days this continued, and on 2 May, incredibly, it seemed to increase, until finally a time-fused armour-piercing 240-mm shell crashed through the weakened concrete of a main battery into the magazine, and to the watchers in one of the balloons it looked as though Corregidor itself blew up. To the men on the island it seemed as thought the guts of their fortress had been spewed up on to the surface – one 13-ton mortar was found on the golf course 150 yards from its emplacement – and to General Homma it was obvious that now was the time to put his troops in.

For a few days, however, the garrison was spared invasion while more landing-craft were brought down from Lingayen, but on 5 May yet another bombardment began, concentrating on communication centres, searchlights and mined beaches. Then in the evening the beaches of the north shore at the tail of the island were blasted; at 9.00 p.m. the shelling rose to an even greater pitch, and sound locators on the main fort picked up the noise of marine engines. The Japanese were on their way.

Incredibly, there would seem to have been little but a heterogeneous group of marines, soldiers, sailors and Filipino Scouts massed to meet the invasion, and most of these were basically administration personnel armed with whatever they could scavenge from the chaos. When the landing craft came within range, they opened up with every rifle, pistol and machine-gun they had, but uncoordinated and without direction. Meanwhile Colonel Gembachi Sato and his men of 61st Infantry Regiment slipped ashore unseen, gathered the survivors of other units which had reached land through the American fire, and set off for the Malinta Tunnel, where the US command structure – what was left of it – still attempted to function: but from 15,000 men on the island, they were apparently unable to organize even 1,000 into a useful reserve.

On 6 May 1942 the last defenders of the Philippines surrendered on Corregidor. The Japanese were to treat those who surrendered with a brutal hand, the infamous 'Death March' leading to the deaths of thousands.

While the Japanese army equipment was not of as high a quality as that in the west, it was sufficient to handle the war in China (seen here) and the first stages of the Pacific War and the war in South East Asia.

By 10.00 a.m. on 6 May, Japanese tanks had been brought across, light artillery was ashore and firing into the main headquarters area. In the confusion and dismay which reigned by then throughout the American forces at all levels General Wainwright felt that the end had come so he broadcast a surrender message to General Homma. Corregidor was finished and the Japanese conquest of Luzon – and the Philippines – was complete.

Long before the final fall of Corregidor, the only practical way into and out of Manila Bay was by submarine. What few supplies could be run in helped a little, and a few wounded people could be evacuated. One cargo was somewhat different – USS* Trout *removed a vast quantity of gold bullion from the doomed fortress.

The carrier war

The atmosphere of euphoria brought about by a run of spectacular military success does not necessarily lead to contented agreement among the victors; in 1942, in fact, it led almost immediately to acrimonious argument.

By the beginning of April 1942, the Japanese army leaders were already proclaiming that their successes along the line of the Malay Barrier should be followed there by nothing but consolidation, and that Japan's main aim now should be to strengthen the forces in Manchuria in order to combine with the German Wehrmacht in a double-pronged onslaught on Russia which would see, once and for all, the end of Communism. The Japanese navy, on the other hand, believed that it was essential for Japan's final victory – and indeed for her continued existence as a powerful nation – to expand even further their hold on the southern Pacific, to allow the fullest possible exploitation of the areas newly under their control – an objective which required as its first task the elimination of the remaining American naval strength there.

The arguments raged quite fiercely until 18 April. Then 16 B-25 Mitchell bombers led by Lieutenant-Colonel James Doolittle took off from the US air-

Chronology of War: 1942

May 14
Russians withdraw in Kerch Peninsula

May 15
Last of British forces retreats across Burma-India frontier

May 16
Germans capture Kerch

May 17
Russian offensive towards Kharkov halted

May 20
Germans control Kerch Peninsula

May 24
General Stillwell, C-in-C US Forces SE Asia and Chief of Staff to Chiang Kai-Shek, arrives in Delhi after 20-day trek through jungle

May 26
Operation 'Venezia'; Rommel attacks British and Commonwealth troops in Gazala Line

May 27
'Hangman' Heydrich is assassinated near Prague

May 28
Russian forces in Kharkov area destroyed. Fierce battle around Bir Hakeim

May 30
US Task Force leaves for Midway. First RAF Thousand-Bomber raid on Cologne; thousands made homeless, nearly 500 killed, 39 bombers lost

May 31
UK civilian casualties in May 399 killed, 425 injured

June 4-7
Battle of Midway – the decisive battle of the Pacific War

Allied aircraft over the Pacific

Much of Japan's success in the early stages of the war was due to the ease with which their aircraft gained superiority over Allied types. Most of them lacked the outstanding agility and range of the Japanese, and poor tactical use was to lead to high losses.

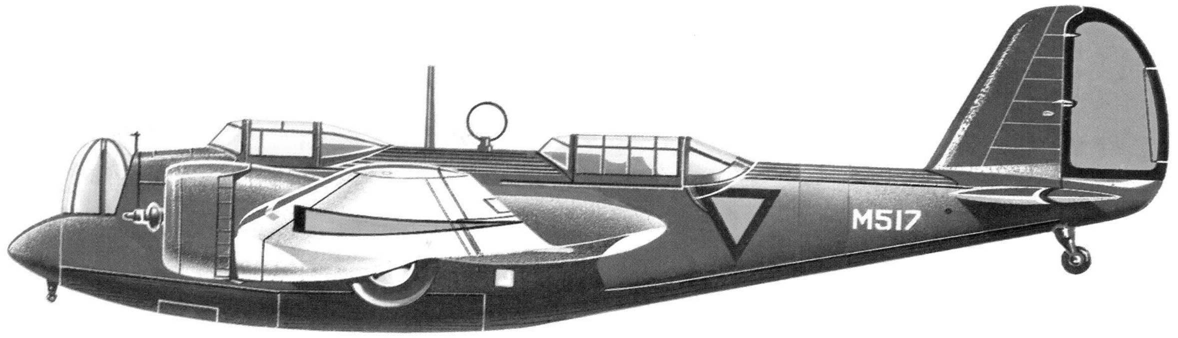

***Left:** Part of the American strategy designed to hold the Japanese in check, the B-17 bombers based at Clark Field in the Philippines in December 1941 were singularly unsuccessful.*

***Above:** One of the most important aircraft designs in history, the Martin B-10 was sadly out of date by the time this example served with the Royal Dutch East Indies Army Air Corps.*

***Right:** A Curtiss Hawk 75 of the KNIL (Royal Dutch East Indies Air Force), flown by Colonel Boxman from Madioen in what is now Indonesia.*

***Left:** This Hawk 81A-2 (basically the same as the USAAF P-40B) was flown by Charles Older of the 3rd Squadron (Hell's Angels) American Volunteer Group (the Flying Tigers) in China early in 1942.*

***Right:** The Bell P-39 was ordered by the RAF, but found to be unsatisfactory at altitude. With US entry into the war, the USAAF took over the RAF planes (still armed with a 20-mm cannon) and used them in the Pacific in 1942.*

***Left:** One of the first Commonwealth Boomerangs to enter service, with a training unit in October 1942. Although outpaced by Japanese types, the Boomerang proved extremely tough and manoeuvrable.*

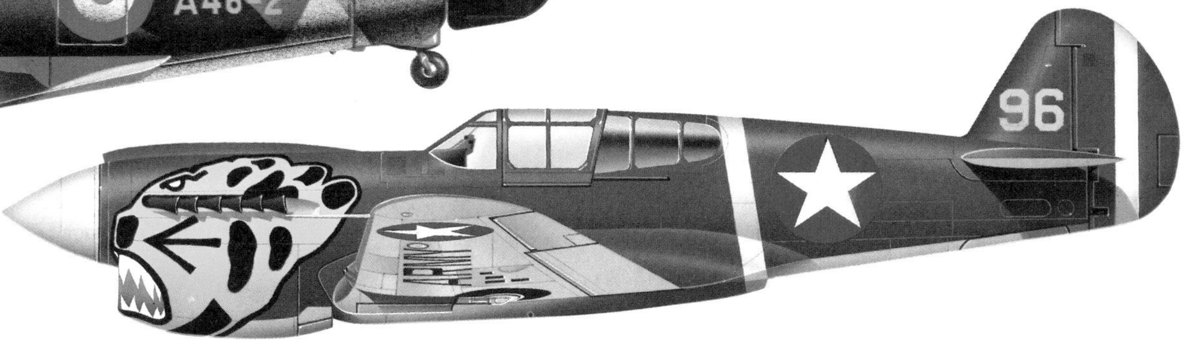

***Right:** This P-40E Warhawk served with the 11th Fighter Squadron, 343rd Fighter Group based at Fort Glenn in Alaska in 1942.*

craft-carrier *Hornet* and bombed Tokyo, Kobe and Yokohama, executing very little material damage, but so alarming Japan's military leaders that they at once abandoned their plans for action in the north, and agreed that plans should go immediately ahead for the capture and occupation of Port Moresby in Papua, followed in June by the occupation of Midway Island (near the Hawaiian Islands) and the Aleutians (in the Bering Sea) and then of New Caledonia, Fiji and Samoa. Admiral Isoroku Yamamoto, commander-in-chief of the Japanese Combined Fleet, was to have his way.

The first moves in this ambitious scheme were those against Port Moresby – vital to the Allies not only for the security of Australasia but also as a springboard for future American and Australian offensives in the south-west Pacific. The moves of the Japanese fleets thereby prompted swift covering action by General MacArthur and the commander-in-chief of the US Pacific Fleet, Admiral Chester Nimitz. This resulted in the Battle of the Coral Sea, noteworthy not only as being the first naval action between aircraft-carriers – and thus between two fleets which never came within sight of each other – but also because this was the first occasion upon which the American commanders could draw benefit from the cracking of the Japanese naval codes by their cryptographers, an even more notable achievement than that of the Bletchley codebreakers vis-à-vis the German Enigma machines.

THE BATTLE OF THE CORAL SEA

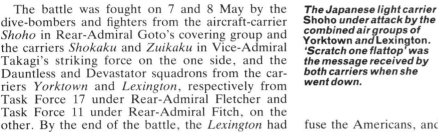

The Japanese light carrier* Shoho *under attack by the combined air groups of* Yorktown *and* Lexington. *'Scratch one flattop' was the message received by both carriers when she went down.

The sinking of* Shoho *was more than matched by the Japanese sinking of USS* Lexington *a day later. She was hit by two torpedoes in an attack just before noon, 8 May, and was wracked by internal explosion at 12.45.

The battle was fought on 7 and 8 May by the dive-bombers and fighters from the aircraft-carrier *Shoho* in Rear-Admiral Goto's covering group and the carriers *Shokaku* and *Zuikaku* in Vice-Admiral Takagi's striking force on the one side, and the Dauntless and Devastator squadrons from the carriers *Yorktown* and *Lexington*, respectively from Task Force 17 under Rear-Admiral Fletcher and Task Force 11 under Rear-Admiral Fitch, on the other. By the end of the battle, the *Lexington* had been sunk, the *Yorktown* had been damaged and sent back for repair to Pearl Harbor – and the *Shokaku* too, had been damaged and sent back to Truk. Admiral Goto's carrier *Shoho* had also been sunk, but this was a light carrier – only 30 aircraft as against *Lexington*'s 70 – so it seemed as though this had been yet another victory for Japanese arms; but there were other factors to be taken into consideration. The Japanese had lost 43 aircraft and their highly experienced pilots, of whom there were now comparatively few left; the Americans had lost 33 of each, but those pilots who survived were learning fast, and indeed the whole US naval force in the Pacific were to gain advantage from lessons learned in the Coral Sea.

Moreover, the Japanese believed that they had sunk the *Yorktown* when in fact the damage they had wrought was repaired in a few days and she was again ready for battle by 29 May, whereas not only was the *Shokaku* to be out of action during the critical days ahead, but the battered aircrews of the *Zuikaku* too were to be absent from the vital areas.

Finally, the Japanese invasion fleet for Port Moresby had been turned back and thus the main object of the Japanese incursion into the Coral Sea had been thwarted. And the scene had been set for the Battle of Midway.

The failure of the invasion of Port Moresby did not greatly concern Admiral Yamamoto. With the destruction of the *Lexington* and, apparently, of the *Yorktown*, the US Pacific Fleet was now so weakened that any confrontation with his own Combined Fleet would, he felt sure, result in another overwhelming Japanese victory. In order to bring this confrontation about, he amassed together the bulk of the naval strength under his command, sent a small force off to the Aleutians as a tantalizing bait with which to confuse the Americans, and sailed for Midway.

His plan called for the arrival of Vice-Admiral Nagumo's 1st Carrier Striking Force consisting of the four aircraft-carriers *Akagi, Kaga, Soryu* and *Hiryu* plus two battleships and three cruisers, to arrive off the Midway atoll at dawn on 4 June and deliver a heavy bombardment of the American base there in order to soften it up for the arrival of the assault troops in a transport group two days later.

This move, Yamamoto was sure, would bring to the rescue the strongest force which Admiral Nimitz could marshal out from Pearl Harbor, and on the way to Midway the American ships would have to pass over two, if not three, cordons of submarines. Those that survived would then face not only the Zeros, Kates and Vals of Nagumo's striking force, but also the huge guns and expert gunnery of five battleships (including his own flagship the *Yamato*, the biggest battleship in the world), four heavy cruisers and over 30 destroyers of the main body and the main support force. The battle should spell the end of American naval power in the Pacific.

Action off Midway

But by the beginning of June Admiral Nimitz was in possession of most of the details of Yamamoto's plan, and his main force was thus no longer at Pearl Harbor. Task Force 16 under command of Rear-Admiral Spruance, consisting of the carriers *Enterprise* and *Hornet* plus six cruisers and nine destroyers, and Task Force 17 under Rear-Admiral Fletcher were waiting some 200 miles to the north of Midway, secure in the knowledge that the commanders of the oncoming enemy fleet had not the slightest inkling of their presence.

Despite this enormous advantage, at the outset the battle went badly for the Americans. The Kates and Vals flown off the Japanese carriers to attack Midway were guarded by Zeros, which with almost contemptuous ease shot the Brewster Buffaloes defending Midway out of the sky; and although there were some losses among the bombers, the bulk got through and dropped their loads on the specified targets. Moreover, as the Buffaloes took off, so had six Grumman Avengers and four Marauders, to attack Nagumo's carrier striking force, which they found at 7.10 a.m.; but with no fighter support, these too were shot out of the sky, only three escaping to crash-land back on Midway, and no damage at all was done to any of Nagumo's ships.

Moreover, just before 8.00 a.m., another American force arrived above the 1st Carrier Striking Force, this time consisting of 16 dive-bombers, 15 Flying Fortresses and 11 Vindicator scout bombers – but the Zeros again clawed their way off the carrier-decks and up into the sky to chase them off. Although the American bombs were released, not one of them scored a hit.

Nevertheless, Nagumo faced severe organizational problems. There had been losses among the first flight to attack Midway and it seemed advantageous

***The internal damage to the Lexington was so great that she had to be abandoned as a blazing hulk. She was eventually put down by torpedoes from the destroyer USS* Phelps.**

Left: Douglas TBD Devastators were the main torpedo-bombers aboard the US carriers for the first year of the war. Slow and vulnerable, they were torn out of the skies at Midway.

Above: The Grumman F4F was to serve throughout the war, and at Coral Sea and Midway was the standard US Navy fighter. These examples are seen on* Lexington *after the torpedo strikes at Coral Sea, while the carrier could still handle her air group.

US aircraft carriers 1941-42

The US Navy displayed keen interest in aircraft carriers after observing the growing naval air power of the Royal Navy in 1917-18. By the time of Pearl Harbor the US Navy possessed six fleet carriers. Luckily, none were in port when the Japanese struck, and these half-dozen carriers bore the brunt of the fighting which followed. A year later, four had been sunk.

Above: Hornet *launched the famous B-25 raid on Tokyo on 18 April 1942 and fought at Midway. While her aircraft were en route for Japanese carriers at the Battle of Santa Cruz she was attacked and crippled by a wave of enemy strike aircraft.*

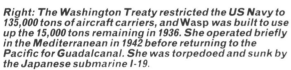

Right: Lexington *in pre-war days. She carried 8x8-in guns to defend herself against enemy cruisers, although these were landed by the time of her loss. When the Japanese attacked Pearl she was away delivering aircraft to Midway Island.*

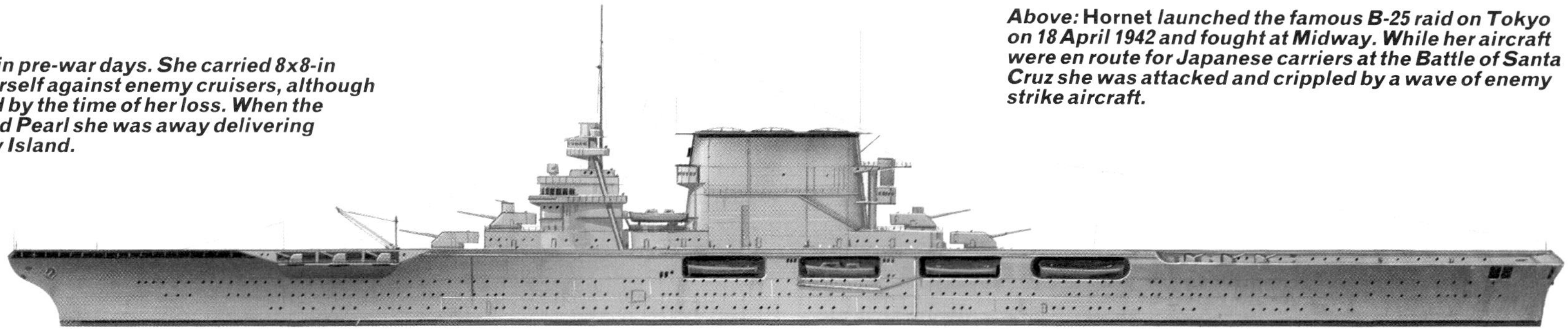

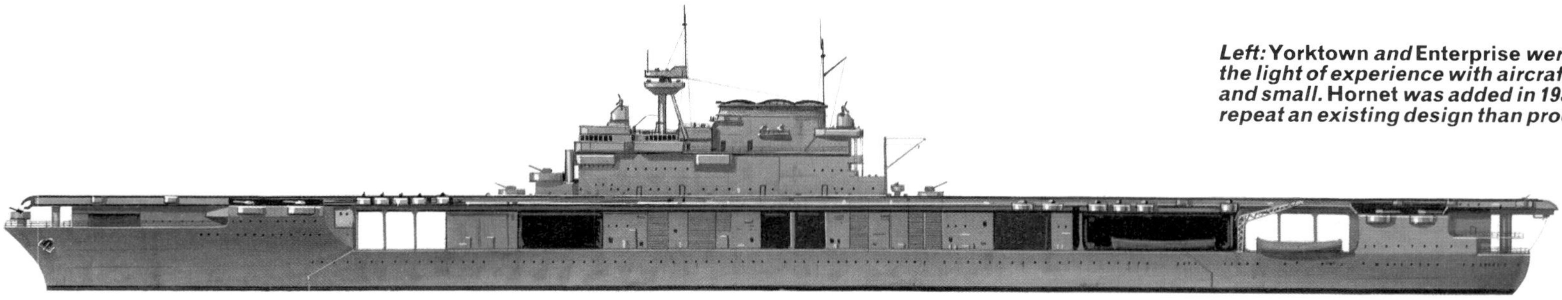

Left: Yorktown *and* Enterprise *were laid down in 1934 in the light of experience with aircraft carriers both large and small.* Hornet *was added in 1939 as it was easier to repeat an existing design than produce a new one.*

Right: The Washington Treaty restricted the US Navy to 135,000 tons of aircraft carriers, and Wasp *was built to use up the 15,000 tons remaining in 1936. She operated briefly in the Mediterranean in 1942 before returning to the Pacific for Guadalcanal. She was torpedoed and sunk by the Japanese submarine I-19.*

Enterprise *fought in most of the great carrier battles of the Pacific War, from Midway to the Battle of the Philippine Sea. Holding 19 battle stars, the 'Big E' should have been preserved as a memorial.*

Right: Saratoga, *seen here in 1932, was* Lexington*'s sistership and the two carriers fought each other in annual manoeuvres. She was a tough ship, taking a series of heavy blows.*

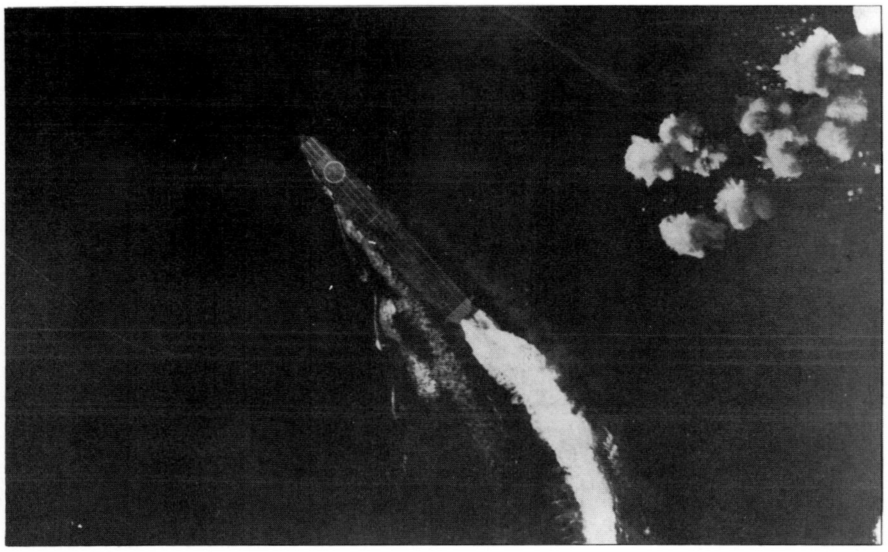

A Japanese carrier (probably **Akagi**) under attack by Midway-based B-17 bombers early in the battle that was to mark the high water mark of the Japanese tide that had swept the Pacific.

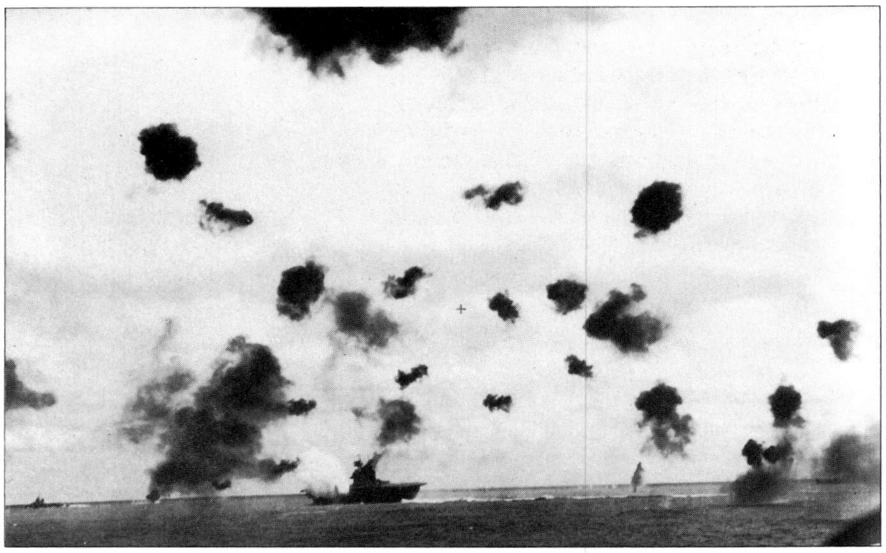

Yorktown, heeling as she turns hard to starboard in an attempt to avoid a torpedo attack by the aircraft of **Hiryu**, is struck by one of the two that got through.

to send in a second wave; Kate bombers already loaded with torpedoes aboard *Akagi* and *Kaga* were therefore struck down into their hangars to have their torpedoes replaced by bombs. But at 7.45 a.m., one of his scouting planes suddenly reported the presence of 10 enemy ships heading in his direction – information which caused him to reverse his last orders and have the Kates' torpedoes replaced. Then came the second American onslaught, which sent the last of his Zeros up into the air. When they had chased away the Flying Fortresses and accompanying aircraft, they had to be landed and refuelled – especially as they would be needed to escort the Kates whenever they took off, on whatever mission. Half an hour later, at 8.30 a.m., the survivors of the first Midway attack were arriving back, some damaged, all short of fuel, so the decks of all four aircraft carriers now had to be cleared to allow the returning heroes safe landings. It was 9.18 a.m. before they were all safely aboard and the next stage of the operation could proceed.

Meanwhile, 67 Dauntless dive-bombers, 29 Devastator torpedo-bombers and 20 Wildcat fighters of Task Force 16 had been assembling above *Enterprise* and *Hornet*, but the job had taken an hour and resulted eventually in the aircraft departing to find their enemy in four separate groups – and when they all arrived over the estimated position of Nagumo's carriers, they found only empty sea, as Nagumo had altered course. *Hornet*'s dive-bombers went south east, found nothing and had to return with their loads to Midway or the *Hornet*, while their escorting fighters all had to ditch when they ran out of fuel. Another group consisting of two torpedo-squadrons, however, found the Japanese striking force at 9.30 a.m. and, with great courage but no protection, streaked in low over the water to the attack; a few even launched their torpedoes, but all were shot down, only one pilot escaping alive. No damage at all was sustained by their targets.

Five minutes later two more torpedo-squadrons arrived, one from *Enterprise*, and one at last from Task Force 17's *Yorktown* – but none of them were a match, either for the Zero fighters which streamed off Nagumo's decks to get at them, or of even for the anti-aircraft fire levelled at them. Of the 26 torpedo-bombers in that attack, only three survived, and the few torpedoes launched were easily avoided by Japanese carriers.

And now the Zeros could return to their ships, and Nagumo's Vals and Kates, all refuelled, re-bombed and re-armed, were ready to take off from the crowded decks of *Akagi, Kaga, Soryu* and *Hiryu* to complete the destruction of the Americans. It was just before 10.00 a.m., all Japanese eyes and attentions were focussed on the decks of these huge ships and the furious but expert activities on them – when suddenly they heard the high-pitched rising scream of dive-bombers; as they turned to look upwards, the thousand-pound bombs swung away under the bellies of 35 Dauntlesses from *Enterprise* and *Yorktown* which had arrived overhead a few moments before. It was Clark Field again, but in reverse, and much more dangerous for those aboard the carriers than it had been for those on land.

Akagi was hit first, squarely amidships by a bomb which exploded in the hangar below near a torpedo store, and was hit again in the midst of assembled Kates whose petrol-tanks exploded in vast sheets of flame. Within minutes Nagumo's flagship was doomed. Four bombs hit *Kaga* with similar results, though she was to remain afloat for some hours, wracked by internal explosions and eventually torpedoed by a US submarine. *Yorktowns*'s dive-bombers concentrated on *Soryu*; three hits spelled her end, and her crew abandoned her 20 minutes later. Thus in five violent minutes half of Japan's most modern carrier force had been destroyed together with her most experienced fighter force – and the myth of Japanese invincibility.

Only *Hiryu* was left – she had been detached some miles to the north east – and she was to be found and sunk by American pilots before the day was out, though not before she had wreaked some revenge for her sister-ships' fates. Her aircraft found *Yorktown* just before noon and hit her with three bombs which started internal fires and brought her to a halt; but her crew fought for her and in the early afternoon she was under way again, the fires dying. But then *Hiryu*'s Kates arrived and their torpedoes put an end to her, at last.

When darkness came on 4 June in mid-Pacific, the smoking hulls of four Japanese aircraft-carriers signified the turning of the fortunes of war. The US Pacific Fleet had not been destroyed; in fact it, would grow and grow from now on until it far overshadowed its opponents in both size and experience. Though few realized it at the time – or for some time afterwards – the Battle of Midway was one of the most decisive battle in history.

The Battle of Midway

The Battle of Midway was one of move and counter-move, the main participants never being within 100 miles of each other. Together with Coral Sea, it highlighted the new prominence of the aircraft-carrier in the war at sea. Thanks to superior intelligence, the US Navy dive-bombers were able to rip the heart out of the Imperial Japanese Navy.

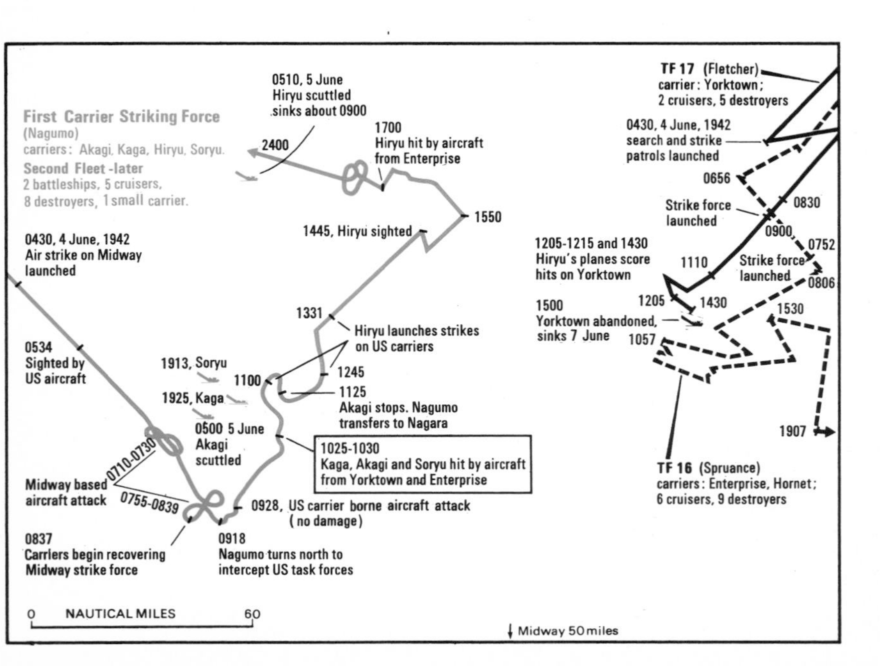

The shattered Japanese carrier force retreated westward, leaving the crippled 'Mogami' class cruisers **Mogami** and **Mikuma** to make for the safety of Wake Island.

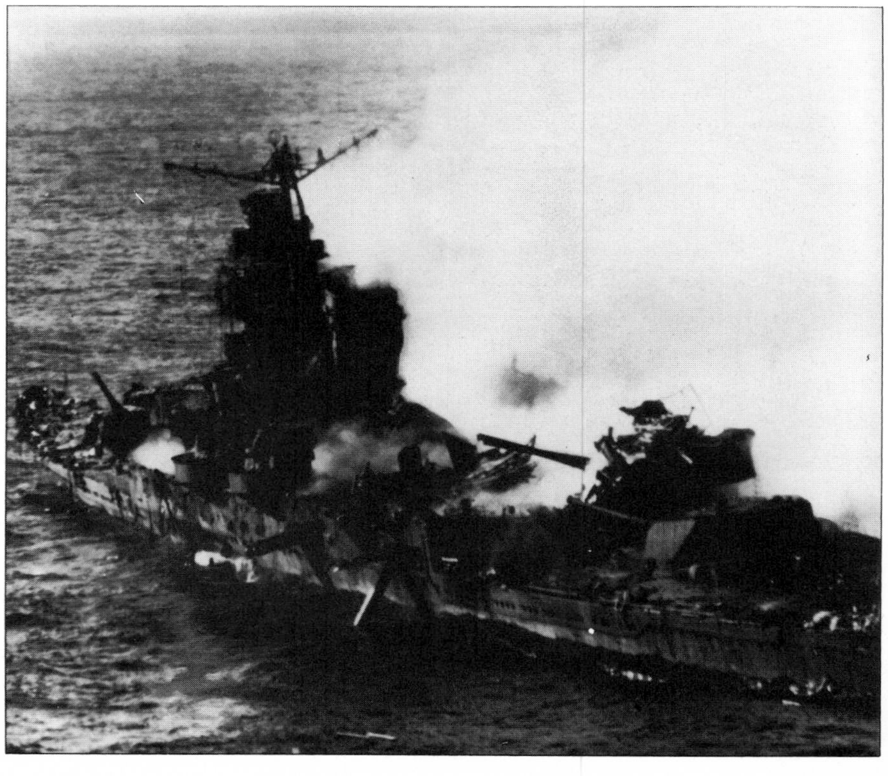

American carrier aircraft 1941-2

In many respects, the US Navy had been one of the great innovators in the use of aircraft at sea, having introduced the original 'Helldiver' dive-bomber. At the outbreak of war the machines were rugged, but much less manoeuvrable and of shorter range than their Japanese opponents.

Above: Heavy, unstable and ponderous, the Brewster Buffalo was no match for the Japanese Zero. This example was flown by VMF-221, US Marine Corps, out of Hawaii in early 1942.

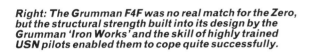

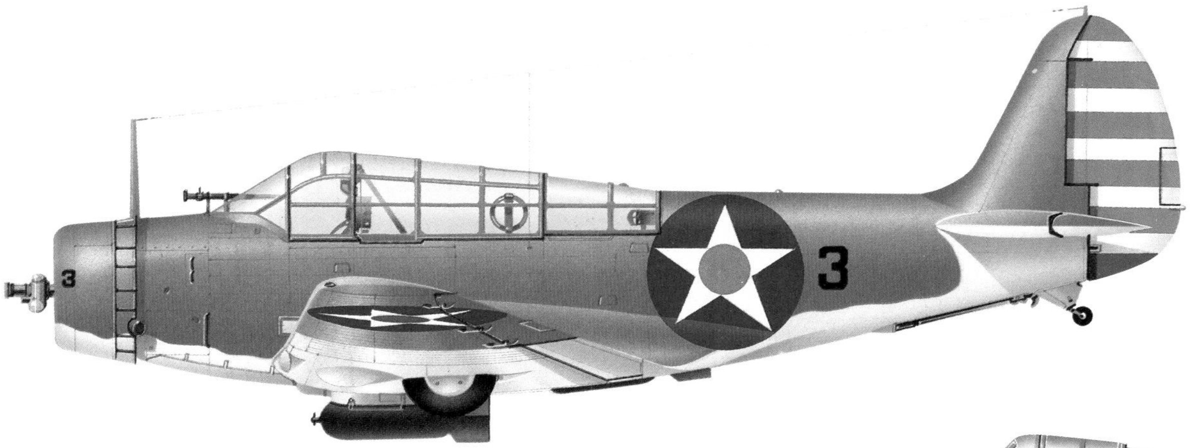

Left: A Douglas TBD-1 of VT-6, aboard USS Enterprise *in April 1942. Only a month later, 'Torpedo Six' was to be shot to pieces in the attack on the Japanese fleet at Midway.*

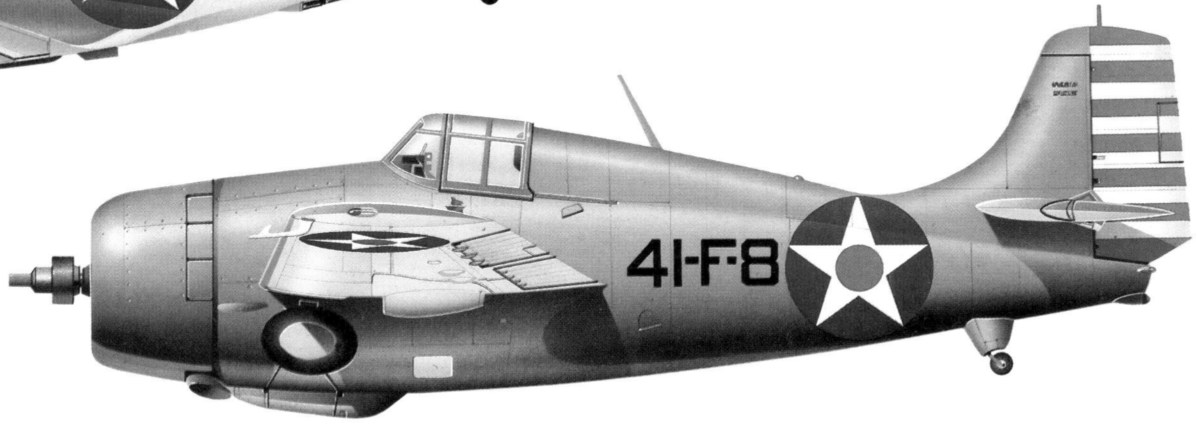

Right: The Grumman F4F was no real match for the Zero, but the structural strength built into its design by the Grumman 'Iron Works' and the skill of highly trained USN pilots enabled them to cope quite successfully.

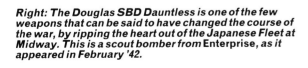

Left: US Marine Corps aircraft, being acquired through the navy, were carrier-capable, although more often than not they served ashore. This SBD served with Marine Corps Air Group 21, based at Oahu in 1941.

Right: The Douglas SBD Dauntless is one of the few weapons that can be said to have changed the course of the war, by ripping the heart out of the Japanese Fleet at Midway. This is a scout bomber from Enterprise*, as it appeared in February '42.*

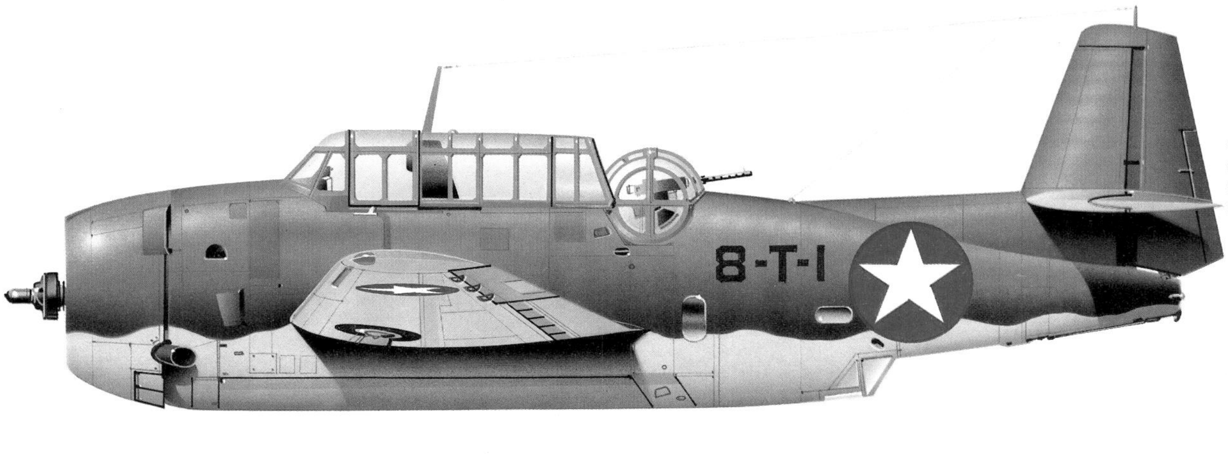

Left: This TBF-1 Avenger was to have joined USS Hornet *as one of the first of the type to go to sea. Missing the boat, it was one of six Avengers to attack the Japanese fleet from Midway Island – disastrously.*

Chapter 10

From Moscow to Crimea

By December 1941 the German army stood poised before Moscow, and panic reigned in the Soviet capital. But the Germans were desperately short of supplies, and had pitifully little protection against the bitter Russian winter. Stalin ordered a counter-attack led by his toughest troops, the Siberian divisions, and in a desperate battle in the snow the Germans were driven westwards.

At the end of 1941 an objective observer would not have rated the chances of an Allied victory over the combined forces of Germany and Japan very highly. In the east, catastrophe attended every sphere of Anglo-American interest, while after some 150 days of war the Soviet Union was apparently bleeding to death.

Huge slices of territory had been lost during the previous four months, including vital agricultural and industrial resources and major transport and communication facilities. Those industries that had not fallen into enemy hands were now out of action, because they they were being hurriedly transported beyond the Urals in a pell-mell evacuation which, although in the end recognized as a magnificent achievement, at the time was a major distraction from direct military action, evidence of gross miscalculation and unpreparedness on the part of the Soviet leaders.

As for manpower, it was reckoned that some 35,000,000 Soviet citizens had by now been engulfed in the German invasion, Soviet industrial manpower was down to 20,000,000 from the 31,000,000 at which it had stood in 1939, and at the end of November the Red Army's strength was down to 2,250,000 – the lowest figure since the middle 1930s, and indeed the lowest figure during the war. According to German figures, the Wehrmacht had taken 3,335,000 prisoners.

But by mid-December some of the effects of the gigantic Soviet mobilization system were being seen. The Red Army now had 4,196,000 men under arms, though there were not always arms for them and a large proportion of the soldiers were totally untrained; no matter – they could be fed into battle, pick up arms where they found them and, to use one of Churchill's expressions, 'always take one with them'. And they had one advantage over the German enemy: they were warmly clad, for every Russian knows about the Russian winter which was coming as such a shock to the invaders.

On 5 December, on Stalin's instructions, the Red Army went over to the offensive on both the Kalinin and West Fronts in order to push the German Army Group Centre back from Moscow. On the following day they were joined on their left flank by the armies of South-West Front – 15 armies altogether, plus one cavalry corps, and if the Soviet army of those days barely exceeded a German corps in manpower, this first counter-offensive was nonetheless conceived on a grand scale. And because it was attacking forces at the end of lengthy communications and supply lines who were also tired from their recent efforts – and suddenly ragged and freezing – the counter-attacks succeeded despite the lack of heavy weapons or armour to support them.

Gradually German armies were levered away from the outskirts of Moscow, the pincers on each side bent back; and if the distances the Red Army advanced during those days were miniscule compared with those of the Wehrmacht in the summer, this did not affect the fact that the Red Army were going forwards, the Wehrmacht backwards – with inevitable effects upon their morale, and upon Stalin's. On 17 December he issued orders to armies of the Leningrad Front and the Volkhov and North-West Fronts beside them, to drive south west against German Army Group North, both to check the encirclement of Peter the Great's city and to prevent a link-up between German and Finnish forces. Stalin also planned to drive a wedge between Army Groups North and Centre with a drive by the 4th Shock Army aimed – with rather extravagant optimism – at Smolensk.

Far to the south Stalin's directives also launched 20,000 men in 14 transports and a Force 8 gale across nearly a hundred miles of the Black Sea, from Novorossiisk to the Kerch Peninsula, where they landed to pose what General Manstein admitted was a serious threat to his Eleventh Army besieging Sevastapol. Then on 5 January, at a suddenly convened meeting of STAVKA, Stalin announced an all-out offensive along the entire front, from the Baltic to the Black Sea.

The Soviets strike back

It was certainly a grandiose plan. The main blow was to be delivered in front of Moscow by the armies of Western, Kalinin and Bryansk Fronts with the left wing of North-Western Front, all against Army Group Centre. Army Group North were to be defeated by Leningrad Front, the right wing of North-Western Front and the Baltic Fleet; Army Group South were to be flung out of the Donbass by South-Western and Southern Fronts, while the Crimea was to be liberated by the Caucasus Front and the Black Sea Fleet. All offensives were to start immediately; were there any questions?

Zhukov had few questions to ask, but a number of statements to make. At both the northern and southern ends of the proposed offensive line, he claimed, German forces had had time to build and occupy strong defences; in the centre, however, the present pressure on Army Group Centre had not only pushed the Germans back, it had also thrown them into considerable organizational chaos. Here, undoubtedly, lay chances for great Red Army gains should it be possible to supply them with sufficient reinforcement and re-equipment – but it was certainly not possible to reinforce and resupply the entire length of the front; therefore the proposed actions on the wings should be abandoned, and everything concentrated in the centre.

His words fell on deaf ears; Stalin held to his plans. As the meeting broke up Shaposhnikov said to Zhukov, 'You were wasting your time arguing; the Supremo had already decided. The directives have already been sent to the Fronts.'

'Then why did he ask our opinion?' asked Zhukov.

'I don't know, my dear chap, I don't know,' replied Shaposhnikov, sighing heavily.

Zhukov was, of course, right. Stalin by dictatorial decree might be able to produce another three or four armies from the apparently limitless population of the Soviet Union, but that decree would not produce weapons of quality or weight with which to arm them, nor within days the training those armies needed to use the weapons with expertise – certainly not the expertise of the Wehrmacht soldiers against whom they would be pitted. Nevertheless, attacking across 1,000 miles of front, they did push the Germans back between 50 to 200 miles, partially cleared the Kalinin, Moscow, Orel and Kursk regions, and below Kharkov drove in a deep salient (known later as the Izyum

The Eastern Front was the scene of many of the greatest manoeuvre battles in history, yet both sides were well aware of the importance of artillery. Large-calibre weapons such as the German 21-cm M18 could be used en masse to smash front-line defences prior to an armoured breakthrough.

The Germans had originally expected Moscow to be taken before winter, and had not laid in sufficient supplies of cold weather equipment. This is an SS dressing station outside Moscow.

In spite of the mechanized nature of 'Blitzkrieg', much of the Wehrmacht remained dependent on horse power. This was not always a handicap – in nearly 40° of frost, vehicles and fuel are frozen solid but a horse (as long as it is fed) can survive.

Bulge) between Balakeya and Slavyansk which penetrated nearly 80 miles to reach the banks of the Orel River in the north and Lozovaya in the south.

German defence hardens

But these gains were made almost as much by the willingness of the German forces to go back – despite the draconian penalties for doing so threatened by Hitler – as by Russian pressure, and as soon as conditions favoured a stubborn German defence, then Russian lack of experience and supply shortages compelled a halt to the advance. At times, according to Zhukhov, their main purpose in attending STAVKA meetings was literally to wheedle out of Stalin 10 or 16 more anti-tank rifles, a hundred light machine-guns or, even more vital, mortar and artillery shells. At times guns were limited to one or two shells a day – and that when the Red Army were supposed to be conducting a vigorous counter-offensive along a 1,000 mile front!

A few more small but terribly expensive gains were made during the last week of February, but by March even Stalin had to admit that the Winter Offensive was over, and that until Soviet industry could produce the necessary armaments in vast quantities the best that could be expected of the Red Army was that they might hang grimly on to their recent gains – and, in doing so, gather experience at all levels.

It is not in the nature of dictatorships, however, especially in wartime, to allow a condition of *status quo* to last for long; by the beginning of May, STAVKA had produced plans for another Soviet offensive, albeit a local one and thus on a small scale – small, that is, in comparison with the January all-out offensive. It was to take place on the South-West Front under command of Marshal Timoshenko and consist of a main drive by Sixth Army north west out of the Izyum Bulge (now referred to as the Barvenkovo Salient) and a secondary drive south west from Volchansk mainly by Twenty-eighth Army, the armies to meet west of Kharkov. Thus would this important rail and communication centre be liberated and the stage set for a summer offensive to the south, which would cut off the German armies around Taganrog and the entrance to the Caucasus, and then liberate the Crimea. Optimism reigned in Moscow.

On 12 May the opening phase was launched, and by the 14th advances of nearly 15 miles had been made from the salient and 16 from Volchansk. But here the advances stalled, partly because the army staffs had not yet learned the logistic techniques necessary for rapid support in such circumstances, and partly because the Red Army were still too short of essential supplies. But even more they were stalled because the great Summer Campaign of the Wehrmacht was due to begin on 17 May, and the preliminary task assigned to Army Group Kleist was the removal of the Barvenko Salient and the establishment of German arms on the east bank of the Donetz as far north as Kupyansk. It was nearly yet another case of 'the bear blew first'; the German bear certainly blew hardest.

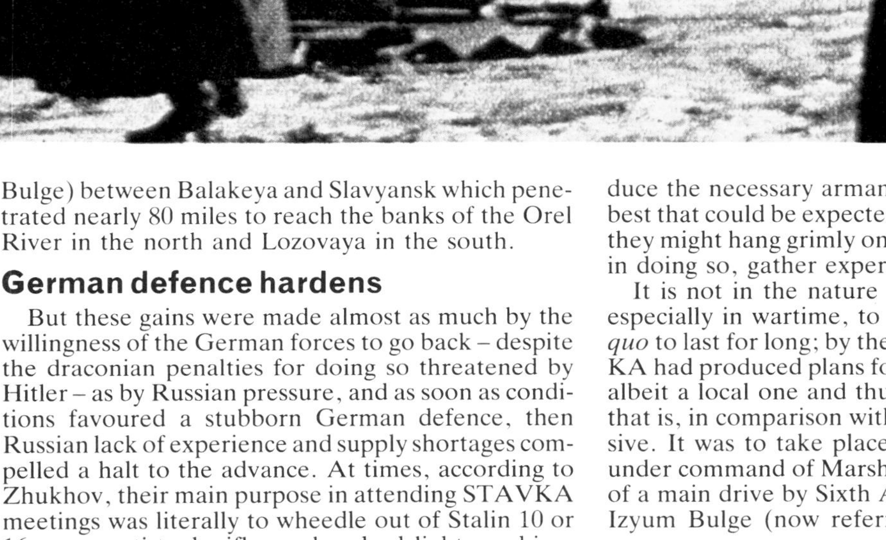

So cold is the Russian winter that soldiers would risk carbon monoxide poisoning to be warm over the engine vents of a tank. The tanks themselves had to be kept intermittently running all night, otherwise they and the petrol in the tanks would freeze solid.

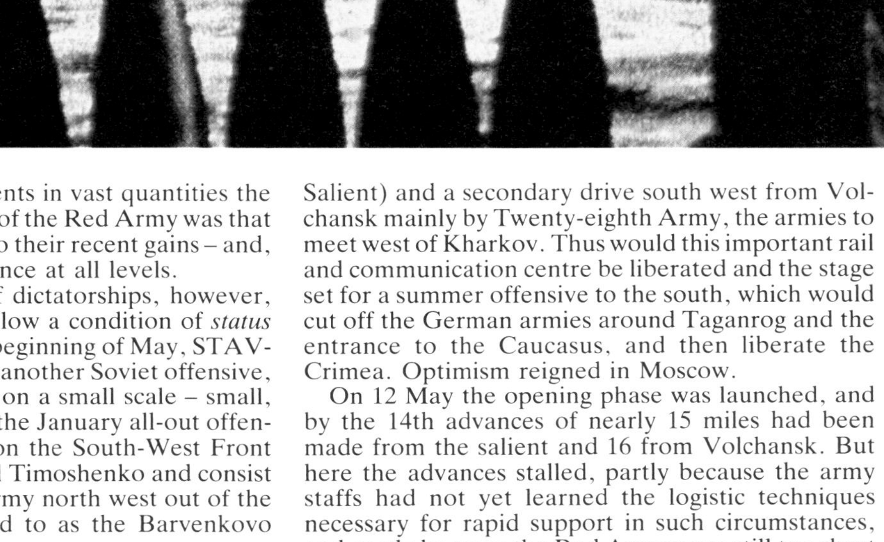

The Germans came up against a number of problems when fighting 'General Winter'. The oil normally used to lubricate the moving parts of weapons had exactly the opposite effect, freezing in the low temperatures and completely jamming the action.

HITLER'S 1942 PLAN

It had been on 15 February that Grand Admiral Erich Raeder in his capacity as commander-in-chief of the Kriegsmarine had had an audience with an unusually receptive Führer, during which he had pointed out that Britain's purpose in defending the Middle East from General Rommel's Panzergruppe was to safeguard her main oil supplies at the head of the Persian Gulf. If these could be captured then not only might Britain be knocked out of the war, but German and Japanese hands might be linked on the shores of the Indian Ocean.

This was by no means the first time that Hitler's mind had dwelt upon that strategic interpretation of affairs, but now it made a deeper impression than before and he ordered Raeder to examine the possibilities of what later became known as 'The Great Plan' – a reinforced drive by Rommel's forces across the Nile swinging up into and through Palestine to meet an even more powerful drive coming down through the Caucasus, Persia and into Iraq. This would not only sweep away Britain's oil supplies, it would augment his own to such an extent that he would never have to worry about fuel again. Moreover, it would almost certainly bring Turkey at last into the Axis camp.

Thus it was that on 5 April 1942 Führer Directive No. 41 for the Summer Campaign was issued, laying down the following instructions for Army Group South, now under command of Field Marshal Bock, replacing Reichenau, who had died of a sudden heart attack:

(a) Eleventh Army and Fourth Panzer Army were to break out north of Kharkov and with Sixth Army destroy all enemy forces west of the Don, then drive south from Voronezh as far as Boguchar, affter which they would swing east and cross the Volga north of Stalingrad. This force would constitute Army Group B.
(b) First Panzer Army and Seventeenth Army would drive east from the Donbass to cross the Volga south of Stalingrad, curve north to meet the armies coming down from the north (Army Group A).
(c) With Stalingrad and the Lower Volga under control, elements of both army groups would reorganize and drive into the Caucasus towards Maikop, Grozny and Baku.

Further developments would depend upon the speed and efficacy with which those plans were carried out, but in the meantime the first steps should be taken in mid-May.

Army Group A, consisting of First Panzer Army and Seventeenth Army, drove north from the Kramatorsk area on 17 May and hit the flank of the Soviet Ninth Army the same afternoon, slicing across its communications and capturing a large proportion of the Soviet artillery. The rear echelons of Ninth Army promptly withdrew from the salient and fled back across the Donetz. And as First Panzer Army drove north along the west bank of the rivei, South-west Front anxiously contacted Moscow and asked for permission to call off the Kharkov offensive. This request Stalin refused, so the Soviet Sixth Army on the Ninth Army's right flank plunged deeper into the country behind Kharkov and the chaos in the pocket increased: on 23 May Kleist Group joined up with detached elements of General Paulus' Sixth Army, which had driven down to the west of Balakleya, thus sealing the mouth of the Sixth salient. To the north of Kharkov itself, one half of Sixth Army drove solidly forward towards Valuyki and the River Oskel, while in the gap between Kharkov and Balakleya the other half drove east to Kuplansk, the lower Oskel and the meeting with Kleist's right flank.

By this time, of course, STAVKA had realized the trap into which the south-west armies had been led and, too late, gave orders for them to turn and fight their way back. But the problem with such a manoeuvre is that when a column turns in its tracks, its front-line units are furthest away from the point of action and by the time they arrive their support and supply echelons have usually been the victims of wholesale slaughter.

Cut into small groups, short of fuel and ammunition, out of contact with headquarters and with each other, the survivors of the Soviet Sixth and Ninth Armies found themselves committed to battle as isolated units against a solidly based and waiting enemy whose air force completely dominated the skies. Few of them reached the Donetz or the Oskel, even fewer crossed either into safety.

***Above:** Waffen SS troops occupy a foxhole during the fighting before Moscow in the first days of 1942. Even digging a trench became a major engineering problem with the temperature dipping below –35°C.*

***Left:** A German MG post on the front line. Between the vast movement of armies, the war in Russia often settled down to a static trench action, with those at the front every bit as uncomfortable as their fathers were in the Great War.*

***Below:** Soviet snipers run through a snow flurry wearing proper winter clothing. Their German targets had to make do with thin summer uniforms stuffed with newspaper and straw plus any warm clothing they could obtain.*

'Stalin's Organ'

Two weeks after the German invasion began, the Red Army tested a new weapon against enemy positions on the river Berezina. It was brutally simple: a welded launcher frame fitted to a truck which fired mass salvoes of rockets; sheer volume of fire more than compensated for individual lack of accuracy.

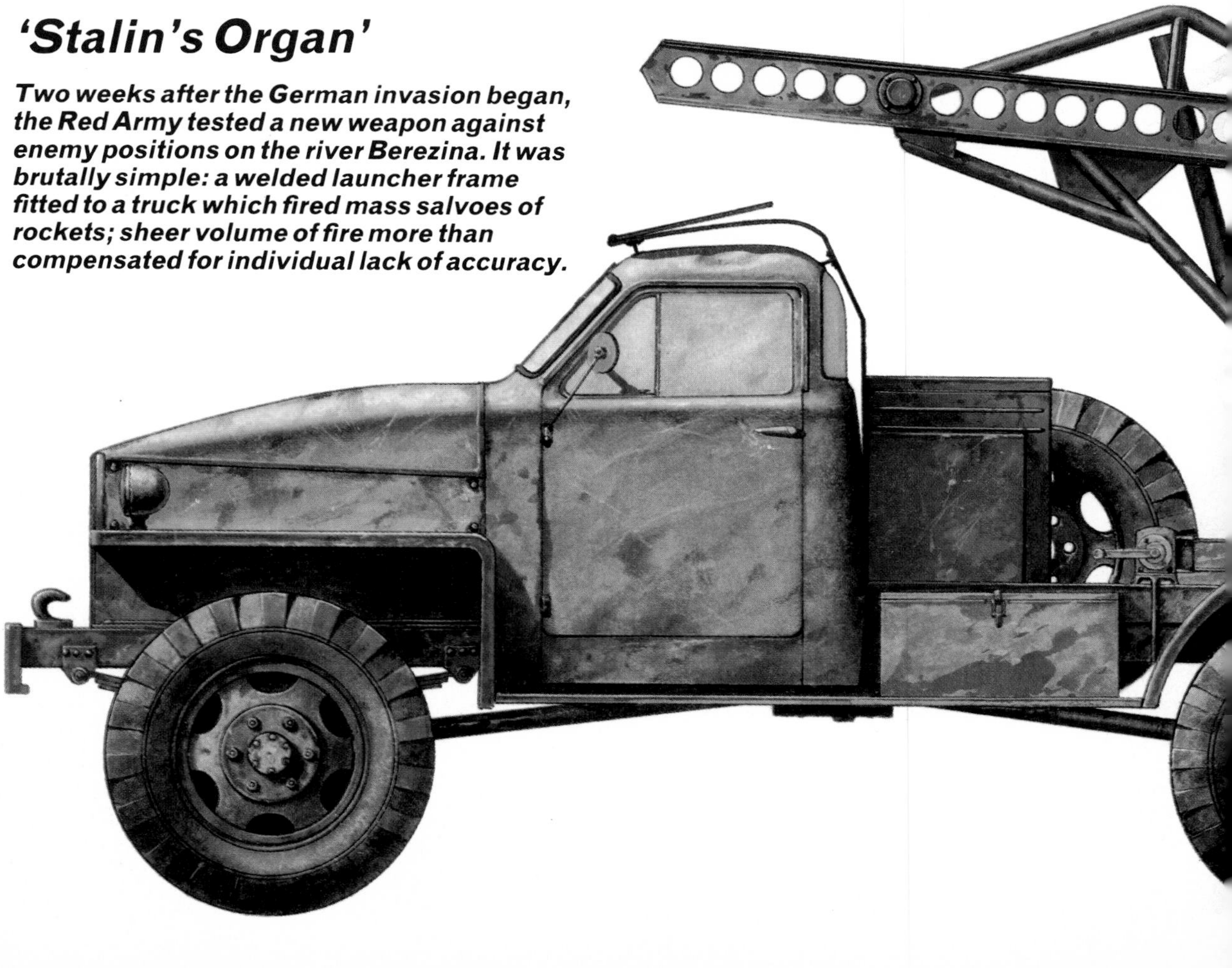

Above: One of the major differences the Germans found on the Eastern Front as compared with France was the incredible endurance of the average Russian soldier.

M-13 132-mm rocket launcher

The M-13 was the most widely used of the various Red Army rockets, and the launchers were manufactured in staggering numbers.

M-31 300-mm rocket launcher

The monstrous M-31 300-mm rocket had a range of only 2 miles, and it was not until 1944 that it was fitted to a mobile launcher. It proved very useful in reducing the fortified cities of Poland and Germany.

Below: Waffen SS troops fire their 15-cm sIG 33 heavy infantry gun on the instructions of an artillery spotter plane. Two of these relatively heavy weapons were issued to each infantry battalion.

Right: A 'Katyusha' battery opens fire, heralding a new counter-offensive by the Red Army. As the war progressed the Soviets were able to supplement their already powerful artillery arm with massed batteries of rocket launchers

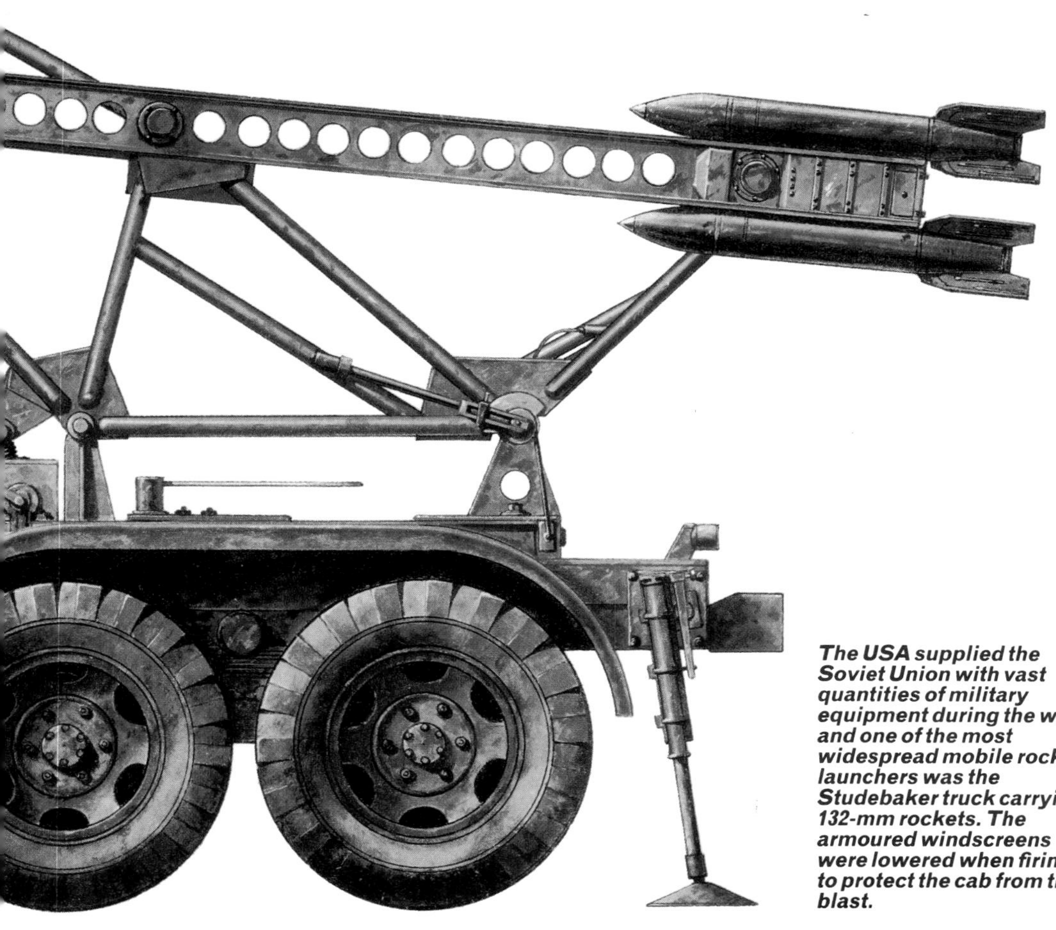

The USA supplied the Soviet Union with vast quantities of military equipment during the war and one of the most widespread mobile rocket launchers was the Studebaker truck carrying 132-mm rockets. The armoured windscreens were lowered when firing to protect the cab from the blast.

The 3.7-cm Pak 35/36 was the standard anti-tank weapon of the Wehrmacht in the early stages of the war, but ineffective against British and French heavy tanks in 1940, not to mention being almost useless against the Russian T-34 (on one occasion in 1941, a T-34 was hit 21 times without effect from a range of less than 200 metres!).

Armoured Trains

In central Europe railways remained the logistic arteries of the German war economy and the Wehrmacht's logistic effort. On the Eastern Front both sides used armoured trains, but the Germans employed them to a greater extent; their main functions was to protect the rail networks from partisan attack and to escort particularly valuable equipment being transported.

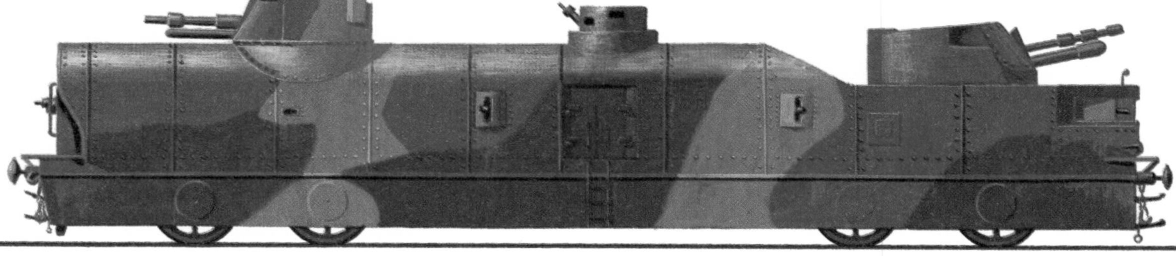

Above: Crew members of a German 105-mm howitzer carriage connect a battery for charging. Note how even the connection between two carriages is protected by armour.

Above: A complete Soviet armoured train, captured intact by the Wehrmacht. The main armament comprises turreted 76.2-mm guns atop each armoured wagon, with a quadruple anti-aircraft Maxim mount atop the armoured tender.

Below: A Soviet armoured train put out of action by the advancing Germans in July 1941. Note the ball-mounted Maxim MGs on the side. The sloped armour was designed to give protection all the way down to the rails (obviously to little effect in this case!).

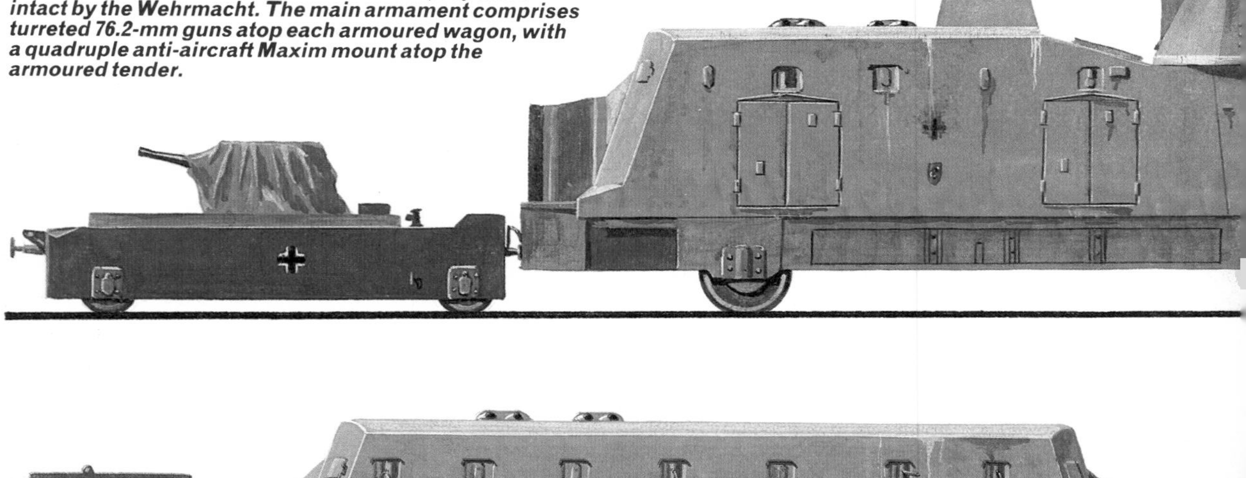

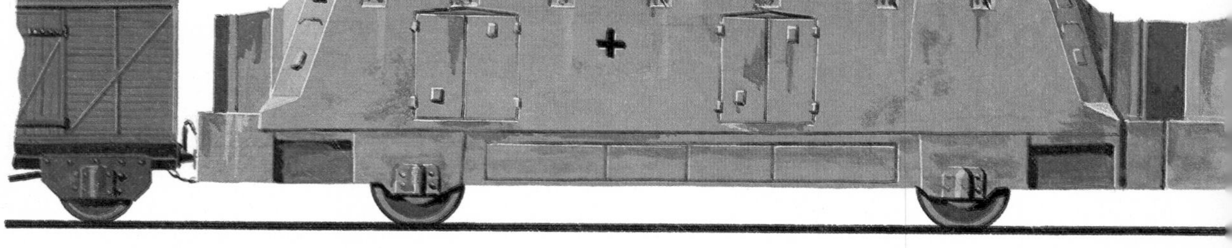

The attempt to relieve Sevastopol by landing a force of 20,000 men on the Kerch Peninsula the previous December had resulted in the formation of bridgeheads around the town of Kerch and the port Feodosia. There had followed a build-up of strength until by April five Red Army brigades had been formed, consisting of nearly a quarter of a million men, together with some supporting artillery and 200 tanks. This was a considerable force, but it had been fed in piecemeal – like so much Soviet strength in those early days – and committed to battle in the same unskilful way.

In the Crimea

Manstein had mounted a counter-attack on the Feodosia bridgehead in January which failed to eliminate the bridgehead but took a heavy toll of its defenders. When in February and March the Soviet forces in their turn launched attacks both to expand their hold in the Crimea and perhaps to relieve Sevastopol, they were bloodily repulsed by Manstein's Eleventh Army, which by April had itself been reinforced by the 22nd Panzer Division and the 28th Light. Moreover, the VIII Fliegerkorps of Ju 88s and Stukas had also arrived in the Crimea, with sufficient fighter cover to ensure air supremacy, so on 8 May Manstein launched an attack on the bridgeheads which opened with a massive drive along the south-eastern coast.

The sheer weight of German men and metal forced the Soviet rifle divisions in Feodosia backwards, then drove through the peninsula waist towards Kerch itself, protected above by Bf 109s and their way prepared by screaming dive-bombers. Manstein's task was also apparently made easier by the inefficiency of the Soviet command, and the constant nagging and wrangling of the STAVKA representative, L. Z. Mekhlis (he was also Deputy People's Commissar for Defence and Head of the Main Political Directorate of the Red Army). Between them, they scattered the available Red Army formations so wide that they had no chance of co-ordination, completely failed to arrange co-operation between ground and what little air support was available, had little contact with the fighting units and spent much of their time in fruitless conferences.

Needless to say, they were among the 86,000 men, including 23,000 wounded, who were evacuated between 15 and 20 May across the Kerch Strait to Taman and Cape Chushka – leaving behind nearly

A fairly typical scene on the Russian front, as an SS Reiter (Cavalry Trooper) passes through a burning farmyard. German brutality towards the conquered population united them in an opposition which the equally brutal Stalin could never have hoped for.

Left: Danuta was one of a number of armoured trains operated by Poland in 1939, although their deployment was restricted by the country's several different railway gauges. Those armoured carriages which survived the German invasion were soon pressed into service with the Wehrmacht.

Right: One of the last purpose-built German armoured trains is seen at the Gare St Lazare in Paris after the Liberation. Most of the equipment used by the Germans was captured or commandeered in Central Europe or Russia. Note the number of anti-aircraft mounts ahead of the 10.5-cm turret; necessary in France at that time because of Allied air power.

Below: By 1943 the Germans had 80 armoured trains operating in East and Central Europe. This example includes (left to right) a small truck with 75-mm gun, a carriage with an FH-18 105-mm howitzer, and an armoured locomotive and tender. The rear section (bottom) sports a Flak 38 quadruple 20-mm anti-aircraft mounting and a 7.5-cm PAK 40 anti-tank gun. Other armed, but not usually armoured, trains served in Germany as mobile anti-aircraft batteries, sent to areas under repeated attack from Allied bombers.

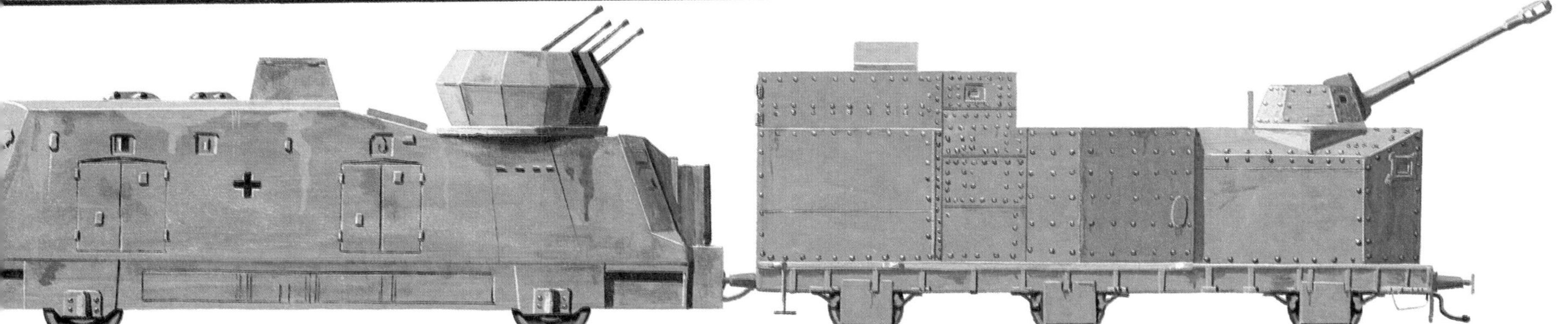

100,000 men and all the remaining tanks – but at least there was no doubt in Moscow where responsibility for much of the disaster lay. Both Mekhlis and the Front Commissar were dismissed and General Kozlov was reduced in rank.

General Manstein could now turn his attention and the enormous weight of artillery and air power at his command to the reduction of the port of Sevastopol. To defend Sevastopol the Soviet Coastal Army had some 106,000 soldiers, sailors and marines, 600 guns including those in the heavy coastal batteries, about 100 mortars, 38 tanks and, in the airfields within their perimeter, 55 aircraft. Manstein now marshalled against them 204,000 men of Eleventh Army, 670 guns including those of enormous calibre in a siege train which he had assembled, 450 mortars, 720 tanks (at something of a disadvantage in such limited space) and 600 aircraft. Most of those who survived the battle were deafened for some time afterwards and, indeed, suffered from hearing problems for the rest of their lives.

The opening barrage

The siege opened with a five-day barrage from every piece of artillery Manstein's experts could bring into action and reminded some of the older members of Eleventh Army staff of Verdun and St Quentin 25 years before. The shaking of the earth caused by the 615-mm mortars, not only when their bombs landed but also when they were fired, would have registered quite high on the Richter Scale – and the shelling was augmented by the bombs dropped by the Luftwaffe, flying in to support Eleventh Army from bases as far away as Perekop and even Odessa.

The main blow fell on the Kmaytsjly-Belbek sector and heralded a drive by LIV Corps towards the eastern end of North Bay. All through the first half of June there was the most bitter fighting, the Russians defending their trenches and holes in the ground with an astonishing tenacity, disappearing back into them whenever close action paused, and demonstrating that indestructibility which was to impress – and indeed frighten – the men of the German Sixth Army later at Stalingrad.

'Don't believe Ivan is dead just because his legs have been blown off, his scalp is half torn away by shrapnel and somebody has stuck a bayonet through his guts,' warned one of Manstein's NCOs. 'If he has an arm left and a rifle within reach, he'll roll over and shoot you in the back as soon as you're past him.' Many German soldiers were to die when they forgot this.

By the third week of June, Manstein was sufficiently worried by the apparent lack of progress that he fed the 46th Division into the ring around Sevastopol, bringing it in from Kerch, and then begged more formations from Seventeenth Army upon the Donbass.

The Black Sea Fleet contributed large numbers of sailors and marines to the desperate defence of Sevastopol, serving heroically in the face of one of the heaviest bombardments of the war. These sailors are armed with PPSh sub-machine guns and a Moisin-Nagant rifle.

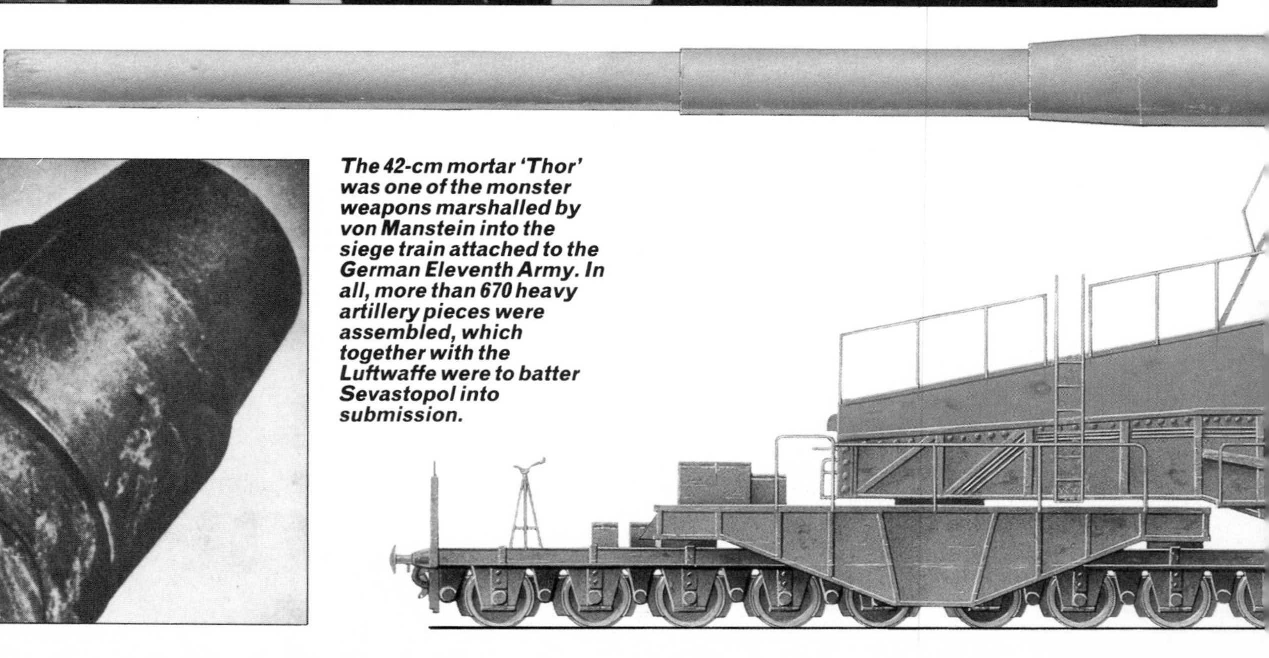

The 42-cm mortar 'Thor' was one of the monster weapons marshalled by von Manstein into the siege train attached to the German Eleventh Army. In all, more than 670 heavy artillery pieces were assembled, which together with the Luftwaffe were to batter Sevastopol into submission.

'Gustav' at Sevastopol

To prepare their attack on the Soviet fortress of Sevastopol the Germans assembled a massive gun park, including the largest artillery piece in the world – 'schwere Gustav' (heavy Gustav), an 80-cm calibre monster gun mounted on a railway train which trundled to the Crimea on specially re-laid track. Well ahead of its progress a small army of labourers started to prepare the gun's chosen firing position at Bakhchisaray, a small village outside Sevastopol. Well over 1,500 men under the control of a German army engineer unit dug through a small knoll to form a wide railway cutting on an arc of double track, and the sides of the cutting were raised to provide cover and protection for the gun. On the approaches railway troops laboured to re-lay track and strengthen possible trouble points against the passing of the 'schwere Gustav'. Work on the eventual firing site reached the point where the area behind the curve of firing tracks resembled a small marshalling yard.

Two guard companies constantly patrolled the perimeter of the gun position, and at all times there was a small group of civilian technicians from Krupp who dealt with the technical aspects of their monster charge and advised the soldiers.

Firing commenced on 5 June 1942. 'Schwere Gustav' was but one voice in a huge choir that heralded one of the largest and heaviest artillery bombardments of all time. By the time Sevastapol fell early in July 1942 it was calculated that no fewer than 562,944 artillery projectiles had fallen on the port.

'Schwere Gustav's' first targets were some coastal batteries that were engaged at a range of about 27,340 yards, and all shots were observed by a special Luftwaffe flight of Fieseler Fi-156 Storchs assigned to the gun. Eight shots were all that were required to demolish these targets, and later the same day a further six shots were fired at the concrete work known as Fort Stalin. By the end of the day that too was a ruin and preparations were made for the following day.

At best the firing rate was one round every 15 minutes. The preparation of each shell and charge was considerable and involved taking the temperature of each charge, accurately computing the air temperature and wind currents at altitude, and getting the shell and the charge to the breech. Projectile and charge then had to be rammed accurately, and the whole barrel had to be elevated to the correct angle. It all took time.

'Schwere Gustav' was in action again on 6 June, initially against Fort Molotov. Seven shells demolished that structure and then it was the turn of a target known as the 'White Cliff'. This was the aiming point for an underground ammunition magazine under Severnaya Bay, and so placed by the Soviets as to be invulnerable to conventional weapons. It was not invulnerable to the 80-cm K (E), for nine projectiles bored their way down through the sea, through over 100 ft of sea bottom and then exploded inside the magazine. By the time 'schwere Gustav' had finished its ninth shot the magazine was a wreck, and to cap it all a small sailing ship had been sunk in the process.

The next day was 7 June, and it was the turn of a target known to the Germans as the Südwestspitze, an outlying fortification that was to be the subject of an infantry attack. After seven shots the target was ready for the attentions of the infantry, and the gun crews were then able to turn their attentions to some gun maintenance and a short period of relative rest until 11 June. On that day Fort Siberia was the recipient of a further five shells, and then came another lull for the gun crews until 17 June, when they fired their last operational shells against Fort Maxim Gorki and its attendant coastal battery. Then it was all over for 'schwere Gustav'.

Once Sevatopol had fallen on 1 July the German siege train was dispersed all over Europe once more, and 'schwere Gustav' was taken back to Germany, where its barrel was changed. Including the 48 operational shells fired against the Crimean targets, 'schwere Gustav' had fired about 300 rounds in all, including proofing, training and demonstration rounds. The whole 80-cm K (E) project had absorbed immense manpower and facilities of all kinds, all to fire 48 rounds at antiquated Crimean fortifications.

By May 1945 'schwere Gustav' was scattered all over central Europe. The carefully-planned trains had been attacked constantly by Allied aircraft and what parts were still in one piece were wrecked by their crews and left for the Allies' wonderment. Today all that is left of 'schwere Gustav' are a few inert projectiles in museums.

***Above:* The largest piece of artillery ever built fires on its first day of action. The 80-cm 'Schwere Gustav' bombarded Soviet coastal batteries at Sevastopol, only eight shots being required to demolish the target completely.**

7 June 1942 'Gustav' has been turned on an outlying Soviet fortification; only seven shots were required to allow a successful infantry attack. The massive shell and charge are seen here being moved towards the breech.

Part of the crew of 'Gustav' see to the ramming-home of one of the special 7100-kg concrete-piercing shells which were to destroy the supposedly invulnerable underground magazines beneath the waters of Severnaya bay.

80-cm Kanone (Eisenbahn)

Quite simply the largest gun ever built, it is unlikely that such an enormous piece will ever be seen again. Although of fairly conventional design, 'Gustav', as it was known, weighed over 1350 tonnes, with a barrel length of nearly 29 m. It had a range of over 47 km, and required a crew of up to 2000 men to set up and fire it.

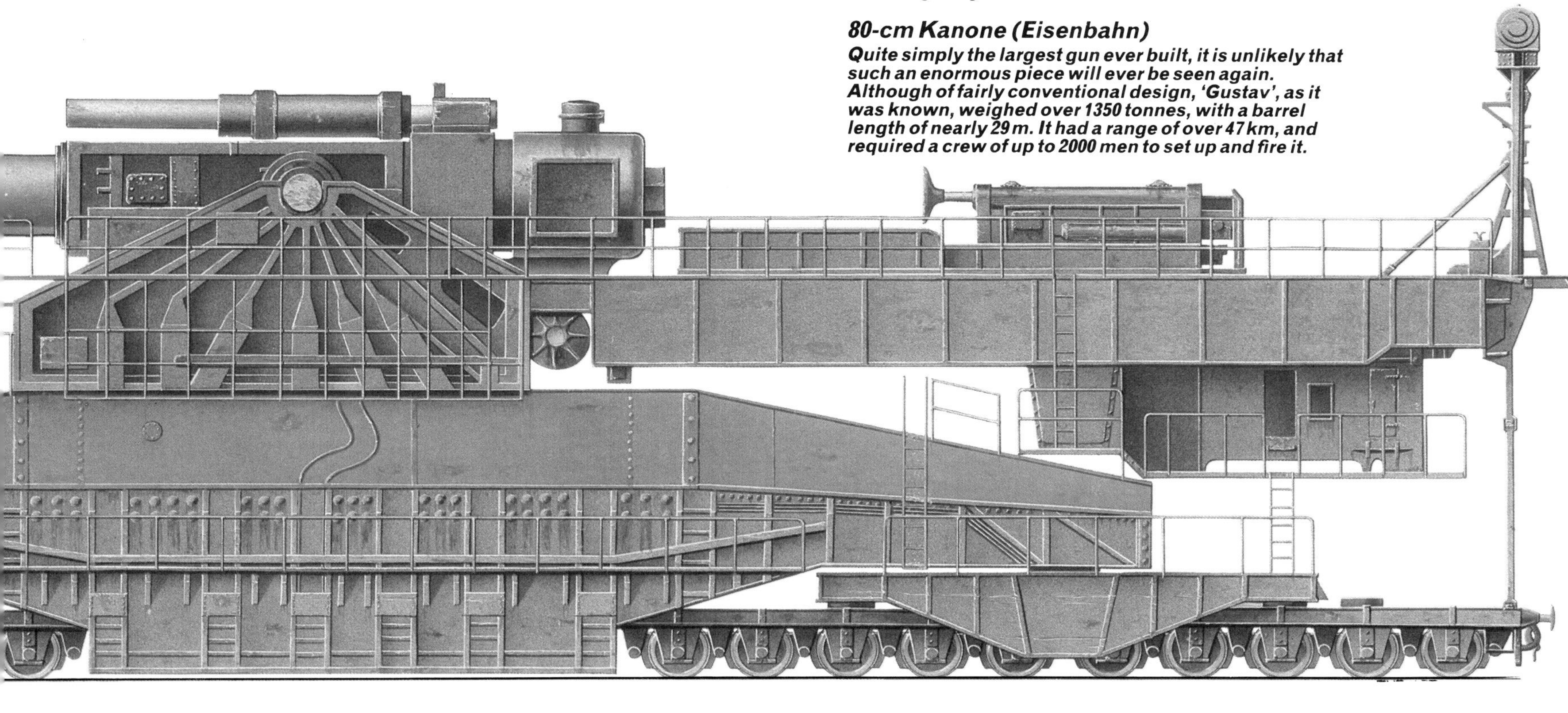

THE FALL OF SEVASTOPOL

But eventually, of course, experience plus guns, mortars and their ammunition won the battle, though the Red Army and the Red Navy performed miracles in reinforcing Sevastopol. Destroyers, minelayers, minesweepers, torpedo-boats, even submarines were used to ferry men, weapons and ammunition into the besieged port, on occasion the ship's officers being told that there was no chance of them all reaching the shore; they should try to get as near as possible before they were sunk so that at least some of their cargo might be able to swim or wade in, with luck carrying in also some weapons or stores.

All the time, the huge mortars and guns of Manstein's siege train hurled their massive shells and bombs into the fortress. The huge 80-cm gun 'schwere Gustav' began firing its 7-ton shells into the fortress from nearly 20 miles away on 5 June, and systematically destroyed the main forts and the huge 'Maxim Gorky' Battery during the next three weeks. Gradually, ammunition shortages, smashed artillery, complete lack of air cover or support after 28 June – not to speak of such human problems as hunger, thirst and lack of sleep – began to take effect, and the German attacking infantry fought their way into the port.

The end of the siege

On the night of 28/29 June the Germans managed at last to cross North Bay under cover of a smoke screen, and the following morning other formations drove in from the Fedyukhin Heights towards Sapun Gora; by the morning of 30 June German troops were fighting inside the town of Sevastopol, taking cover in the ruins of the buildings they had themselves demolished.

During the next three days a Dunkirk-style evacuation was organized, with every craft that could sail coming in from Novorossiisk and the neighbouring Black Sea ports, some even braving the perils of the Kerch Straits and coming down from the Azov ports. It is not known how many Russian servicemen and women, how many civilians, died in the siege of Sevastopol; but it had lasted 250 days since it had first been surrounded by German troops who had driven down into the Crimea. And the last 24 days had been of close hand-to-hand combat and devastating bombardment.

The battle had been by no means without cost to Eleventh Army, and General Manstein – awarded his field marshal's baton with the occupation of Sevastopol and the whole of the Crimea – found in July that he was commanding an army, if not desanguinated, at least decimated. It was not immediately available for the next stage of the Führer's plans, which had to be left to Sixth Army to the north under its ambitious commander, General Friedrich Paulus.

He knew exactly where his fame and, he hoped, his fortune were to be made, and his eyes were firmly fixed upon it: Stalingrad.

Above: Maintenance is carried out on a Panzer IV in Russia. The autumn rains turned roads into rivers of mud, which then turned to ice as hard as steel at 40° below zero.

Below: An armoured half-track passes through one of the outlying fortresses of Sevastopol after it had been blasted into rubble by massed German artillery.

Above: While the battle for the Kerch Peninsula continued, massed Axis armour was driving from Kharkov and Rostov towards the Volga and the Caucasus, in the process stopping a Soviet counter-offensive and taking another huge number of prisoners.

The Soviet offensive around Kharkov at the beginning of the year and the German drive for the Caucasus left numerous pockets of Soviet troops behind the German lines, many of whom joined partisan groups to harry the two German Army Groups' supply lines.

Right: The result of 'schwere Gustav' shelling the coastal batteries of the Crimea. Massive concrete gun emplacements were pulverized by enormous high explosive and even larger concrete-piercing shells.

Chronology of War: 1942

June 5
Germans besiege Sevastopol

June 7
Japanese invade Aleutians. Afrika Korps attacks Bir Hakeim for second time

June 10
Free French forces withdrawn from Bir Hakeim. Germans obliterate Czechoslovakian town of Lidice in reprisal for Heydrich killing

June 13
Convoys set out for Malta from Gibraltar (Operation Harpoon) and Alexandria (Operation Vigorous)

June 16
Two out of six merchantmen in the Gibraltar convoy arrive; Alexandria convoy turns back

June 17
British withdraw towards Egypt, leaving garrison in Tobruk

June 18
Churchill arrives in US for consultations with Roosevelt. Rommel despatches column towards Egypt

June 19
Churchill and Roosevelt discuss atomic bomb

June 21
Tobruk falls to Afrika Korps. Rommel promoted to Field Marshal

June 24
Afrika Korps drives forward to Sidi Barrani

June 25
General Auchinleck takes personal command in desert. Eighth Army retreats to Mersa Matruh

June 27
Germans reach Mersa Matruh. Convoy PQ 17 sails from Iceland

June 28
Eighth Army withdraws towards El Alamein

June 30
Afrika Korps reaches Alamein. UK civilian casualties in June 300 killed, 337 injured

July 1
PQ 17 spotted by Luftwaffe in Barents Sea

July 3
British force Afrika Korps back from Alamein. Sevastopol falls to Germans

July 4
Germans reach River Don. PQ 17 attacked by Luftwaffe; convoy scatters. Over the next six days 24 out of 37 ships are sunk

July 7
Germans capture Voronezh

June 12
Australian troops from Port Moresby reach Kokoda over the Owen Stanley range in New Guinea

July 14
Battle at Tel el Eisa and Ruweisat Ridge

July 19
Japanese invasion force leaves Rabaul for Buna, on the north coast of New Guinea

July 22
Germans attack Rostov

July 24
US and UK reach agreement on invasion of North Africa

July 31
Germans cross Don on wide front. UK civilian casualties in July 411 killed, 871 injured

August 3
Churchill and CIGS Brooke fly to Cairo

German field artillery

The German army began World War II with a well-balanced artillery park which served it well until 1945. During the war many captured weapons were employed, particularly Soviet guns taken in the great encirclement battles of 1941-2. Many German artillery batteries remained horsedrawn, although the armoured divisions started the war with towed guns and eventually acquired self-propelled weapons.

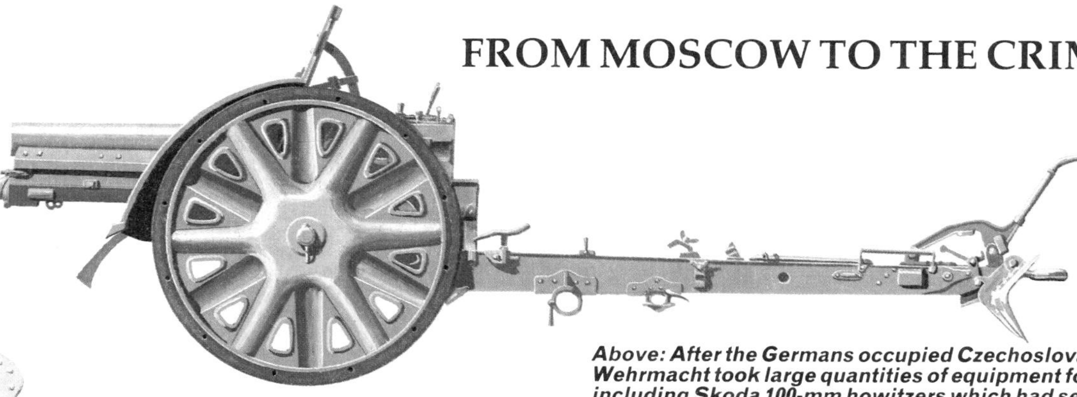

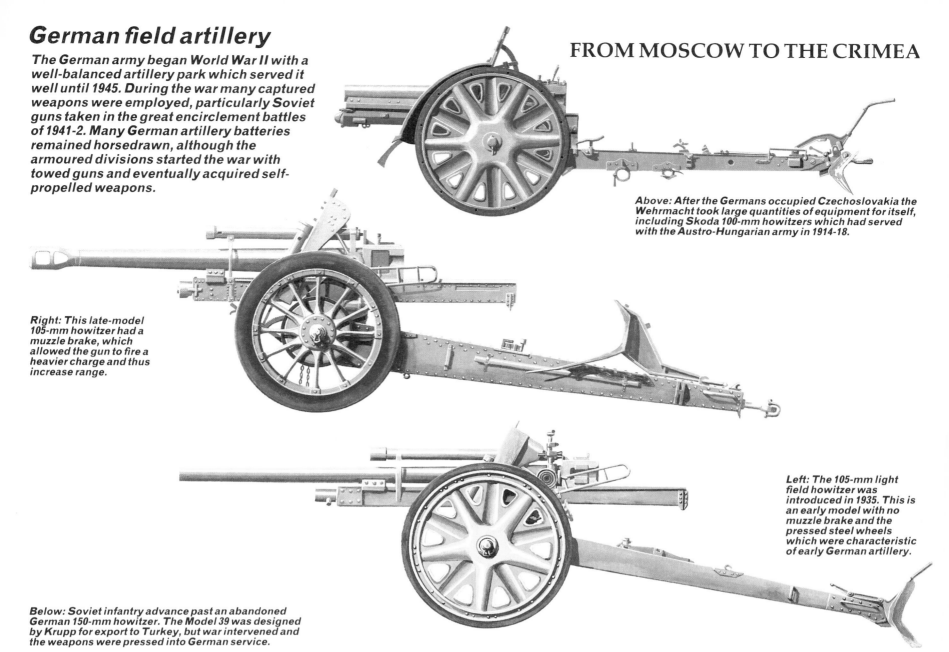

Above: After the Germans occupied Czechoslovakia the Wehrmacht took large quantities of equipment for itself, including Skoda 100-mm howitzers which had served with the Austro-Hungarian army in 1914-18.

Right: This late-model 105-mm howitzer had a muzzle brake, which allowed the gun to fire a heavier charge and thus increase range.

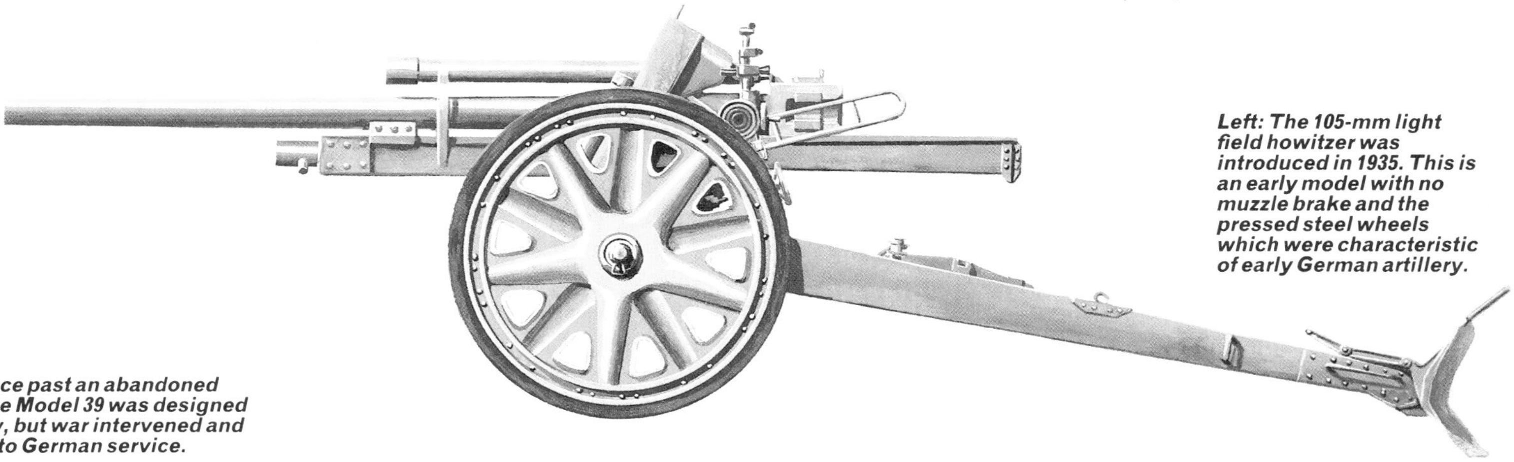

Left: The 105-mm light field howitzer was introduced in 1935. This is an early model with no muzzle brake and the pressed steel wheels which were characteristic of early German artillery.

Below: Soviet infantry advance past an abandoned German 150-mm howitzer. The Model 39 was designed by Krupp for export to Turkey, but war intervened and the weapons were pressed into German service.

Above: Preparing for a sustained bombardment, the shells are removed from their wicker boxes and their fuses set with a spanner before being stockpiled near the guns.

Below: Tanks had to be protected by artillery, and the only way to allow the artillery to keep up was to mount it on tracks, as seen here with the 15-cm SP howitzer 'Hummel'.

August 7
Churchill visits Auckinleck's desert headquarters. US Marines land in Guadalcanal and Tulagi in the Solomon Islands

August 8
Lt Gen 'Strafer' Gott killed. Battle of Savo Island; Admiral Mikawa annihilates Australo-American cruiser force

August 9
Germans capture Krasnodar and Maikop

August 13
General Bernard L. Montgomery takes command of Eighth Army

August 15
General Alexander takes command in Middle East from General Auchinleck. Australians contact Japanese in Owen Stanley Range

August 17
Germans reach Kuban. US Marines landed from submarine raid Makin Island. Operation Jubilee; Dieppe Raid by British and Canadians. First mission flown by 8th US Air Force bombers over Europe

August 19
General Paulus orders VI Army to take Stalingrad

Chapter 11
Turning Point in the Desert

By the beginning of 1942 Rommel was ready to resume the offensive in the desert and, in a lightning counterattack, the Afrika Korps smashed forward. Bewildered and fast losing confidence in its leadership, the British Eighth Army retreated eastwards to make a final stand at the gates of Egypt.

Right: Both sides laid extensive minefields in the desert to channel and disrupt enemy movement. Efforts were soon underway to develop an effective mineclearing device; this British Matilda tank pushes a 'Fowler Roller' to detonate mines ahead of the tank.

Rommel's fortunes improved remarkably during the four weeks following the dire predictions given him by his staff on 4 December 1941. For one thing, the morale of the men under his command – somewhat battered by the repeated chaos of the Crusader battles and dampened further by the final retreat to behind El Agheila – recovered quickly once they turned to face their enemy and found that he was no longer directly menacing them.

Moreover, that iron logistic rule of warfare was now favouring them instead of the British: now all British supplies had to cross hundreds of miles of desert, while German supply and communication lines were far shorter than they had been two months before. Indeed, just before Christmas convoys had brought more men and panzers into both Tripoli and Benghazi, and on 5 January an even larger consignment arrived at Tripoli with a further 55 panzers, 20 armoured cars and a large supply of fuel. This was, as Rommel's chief of staff, Fritz Bayerlein, remarked, 'as good as a victory in battle'. Rommel was not the man to allow either men or material stay idle if he could see a worthwhile purpose for their employment.

He struck early in the morning of 21 January – just 16 days after his rearguards had retired to El Agheila, cautiously pursued by probing British patrols – and found as he had expected that the opposing formations were still in a state of disorganization, due partly to the euphoria of a successful advance, partly to lack of experience of the headquarters staff in the problems of supplying what had been an exceptionally rapid advance across barren terrain. Everything which Eighth Army needed, from ammunition to biscuits, had had to be carried with or directly behind them, from the Delta at least as far as Derna.

By the end of the second day, one panzer division had reached Agedabia while a detached column had reached Saunnu and cut off a British armoured brigade. Six days later the 90th Light drove into Benghazi; Barce, Marawa and Derna were occupied by 2 February, Tmimi and Mechili by 6 February. From all positions they had chased bewildered and very annoyed British troops, taken a lot of prisoners, ransacked their stores which had been surprisingly well restocked, and thoroughly recreated the legend of Afrika Korps invincibility which had recently been dented.

By 10 February, weary, weatherworn, thirsty but triumphant, Panzerarmee Afrika under their remarkable leader were well back into Marmarica, with Tobruk – for so long their apparently unobtainable objective – again only 35 miles beyond their grasp.

Here, for the moment, they were forced to pause. The Italian C-in-C, General Bastico, had been appalled by Rommel's initiative from the moment he first heard of it, and regarded the advance past Benghazi as the height of recklessness. Even Rommel's superior, Field Marshal Kesselring, advised against further precipitate action – at least until more men, more panzers, more ammunition and especially more fuel were to hand.

Even Rommel saw the wisdom of this, so for the moment only his reconnaissance units pressed much further forward than Tmimi, quickly to find that the British and Commonwealth troops had reassembled on a line running south from the Gazala inlet as far as the Beau Geste fort at Bir Hakeim. They were in the process of building themselves into defence positions of considerable strength in the north and centre, with deep minefields bridging the gap down to Bir Hakeim, and it was soon abvious that Panzerarmee Afrika would need all its expertise to break through or to bypass these defences, plus great mobility and time to marshal it.

Left: The crew of a British Daimler 'Dingo' scout car approach a burning truck in the spring of 1942.

Right: Afrika Korps motorcycle teams probe ahead of the advancing German tank formations en route for Tobruk.

Forward to Tripoli

So far as the British were concerned, they needed time, too, for their C-in-C, Middle East, General Auchinleck, disappointed at the abrupt retreat from El Agheila, was determined that the next Eighth Army move would be forward – and as far past El Agheila as possible, perhaps even as far as Tripoli. For such an advance the army needed not only a strong shield against further attacks by Rommel's men, but a reserve behind the line, an armoured striking force available to smash the Afrika Korps, and a vast stockpile of every conceivable military necessity from which to feed that advance.

He fed forward the men and materials and instructed Lieutenant-General Ritchie, now confirmed as Eighth Army commander, both to plan for the battle and to ensure against a sudden strike by Rommel, who, in Auchinleck's opinion, would most probably strike at the centre of the defence line and try to smash a way through.

Ritchie, however, thought it more likely that Rommel would try a hook around the southern extremity of the line at Bir Hakeim, and, while trying to obey

Chronology of War: 1942

August 20
Germans drive across Don towards Stalingrad. First American aircraft fly in to Henderson Field on Guadalcanal

August 24
Sea battle off Eastern Solomons. Russians drive across south of Lake Ladoga in an attempt to raise the Siege of Leningrad. Henderson Field attacked by Japanese aircraft

August 26
Japanese land at Milne Bay, south east of Port Moresby

August 28
Fierce fighting around Stalingrad

August 31
Battle of Alam Halfa begins. UK civilian casualties in August 403 killed, 509 injured

September 5
Australians drive Japanese from Milne Bay. Germans capture Novorossiysk

September 6
Australians fall back to Efogi Spur in Owen Stanley Range

September 11
Japanese halted at Ioribaiwa on Kokoda Trail

September 13
Operation Daffodil; combined operation British commando raids on Benghazi, Barce and Tobruk

September 16
German VI Army moves into Stalingrad suburbs. Australians hold Japanese 32 miles from Port Moresby

September 23
Australians attack along Kokoda Trail

September 30
UK civilian casualties in September 307 killed, 238 injured

October 11
Battle of Cape Esperance off Guadalcanal

October 14
Air, land and sea bombardment of Henderson Field, Guadalcanal. Australians in fierce battle at Templeton's Crossing, high in the Owen Stanleys

October 17
More bitter fighting on Kokoda Trail at Eora Creek. Convoys assemble for Operation Torch, the invasion of North Africa.

October 23
Battle of El Alamein opens

October 26
Battle of Santa Cruz; American carrier USS Hornet sunk by Japanese carrier aircraft. Heavy attacks on US positions on Guadalcanal. Fierce fighting in Stalingrad

October 27
Montgomery regroups Eighth Army formations for second thrust at Alamein

October 30
Australians drive north towards sea at Alamein, trapping Afrika Korps formations in salient

October 31
UK civilian casualties 229 killed, 370 injured

November 2
Operation Supercharge; second thrust at Alamein launched

November 4
Start of retreat by Afrika Korps

November 5
Eighth Army breaks through past Fuka

November 6
Heavy rain slows Eighth Army near Mersa Matruh

Right: The dreaded 88-mm gun accounted for so many British tanks in the desert. The Afrika Korps frequently lured impetuous British tank units into prepared '88' killing grounds, where they were shot to pieces by dug-in anti-tank guns.

Auchinleck's orders to concentrate his armoured strength behind the centre of the line, felt it essential to have powerful forces in reserve in the south as well. The result was an uneasy compromise, with what were called 'boxes' of self-contained units of about brigade strength scattered around the area behind the main defence line, with armoured brigades 'within supporting distance'. Unfortunately, Ritchie's junior commanders at both corps and divisional level thought Auchinleck more likely to be right than Ritchie, and tended to drag their feet in response to Ritchie's orders.

When, therefore, on the night of 26/27 May, Rommel led his two panzer divisions, 21st and 15th, with Ariete on his left flank and 90th Light on the right, in a huge sweep around the southern end of the carefully prepared defence line, they first of all refused to believe the reports that were coming in from their own reconnaissance units, and then responded slowly and almost sulkily to Ritchie's orders to concentrate and meet Rommel's challenge in strength.

As a result, the Retma Box was quickly annihilated, the French at Bir Hakeim were isolated, the headquarters of the 7th Armoured Division was overrun and the division thus without direction until General Messervy managed to escape and reassume command, two British motor brigade groups were scattered and two armoured brigade groups, 4th and 22nd, virtually destroyed for the time as fighting units – all by noon on 27 May, at a cost to Rommel of about one-seventh of his armoured strength.

The battle of the Cauldron

But shortage of fuel and ammunition now imposed a pause in the remarkable achievement of the Afrika Korps, exacerbated by the actions of groups of British and South African soldiers, cut off from headquarters control, who attacked Rommel's supply columns as they tried to get through and caused the Afrika Korps more trouble than any of the organized British defences so far. Both panzer divisions and the 90th Light were then sandwiched for some time between the British 150th Infantry Brigade in the defence line and the men of the 201st Guards Brigade Group in the Knightsbridge Box, with the 32nd Army Tank Brigade on their right, and it looked as though the Afrika Korps had been caught in what became known as The Cauldron. But in the fierce fighting which followed, the British never seemed able to co-ordinate their attacks, so in the end the panzers broke out, rolled over two more 'boxes', and reached the Via Balba.

If the panzer crews had not been so exhausted by days and nights of unending combat, the South African and British divisions still in the northern half of the defence lines would all have been cut off and captured. As it was, during the night of 14/15 June, the South Africans filtered down to the coast and along the Via Balba, sometimes practically tiptoeing between rows of sleeping *Soldaten*, to make their way first into Tobruk and then on and back into Egypt while two brigades of the British 50th Division drove *westwards* out of the line and circled south to make their own escape.

Eighth Army were now in considerable disarray. Only the scattered remains of the British armour, some infantry reserves and odd units from the 'boxes' stood between Rommel's forces and the Egyptian frontier – except for the garrison of troops in Tobruk strengthened by the 2nd South African Division, held in reserve under their newly promoted commander, Major-General H. B. Klopper.

To General Auchinleck, the situation on 15 June looked disappointing but not yet disastrous, for the reports coming into Cairo had been both incomplete and inaccurate. He issued instructions to Ritchie that night ordering him to stand on the line running from Tobruk through El Adem to El Gubi, to ensure that there would not arise the danger of any Eighth Army troops being invested in Tobruk, and again to concentrate his forces – plus others being sent up to him – so that the Panzerarmee could be attacked and destroyed. He stressed that Tobruk must be neither invested nor captured by Rommel.

Above: Italian M13 medium tanks head for the Egyptian frontier with their weak armour bolstered by piles of sandbags on the hull front. The Italian commander, General Bastico, displayed extreme reluctance to join Rommel on his renewed offensive.

Attack on Tobruk

Not surprisingly, this was in direct contradiction to Rommel's plans, Tobruk had withstood his every assault in 1941 and he was determined that it would be his in 1942, but first of all he desperately needed more ammunition, more guns, more food for his triumphant but hungry men; above all more petrol for his panzers. Where better to find it than in the huge supply dump built up by the British at Belhammed, a few miles to the east of Tobruk and near to the RAF airfield at Gambut, from which a few Hurricanes were still harrying his forces?

During 16 and 17 June, 21st Panzer, 90th Light and

Below: French Foreign Legion units fighting for the Free French defended Bir Hakeim with their customary stubbornness. Rommel was obliged to reinforce his units besieging the position.

Below: A German transport column carries forward vital supplies for the Afrika Korps. The headlong advance placed enormous strain on Rommel's transport resources

the Ariete formations drove between the scattered British formations still holding out at El Adem and Sidi Rezegh, curved north east, and hit the 20th Indian Brigade at Belhammed during the morning of the 17th. By noon the immense stores dump was in German hands, while to the south the amalgamated panzer divisions (for 15th had come up and joined 21st) fought off with but little difficulty an attempt by the remaining British armour, now reconstituted into the 4th Armoured Brigade, to break through to the relief of the Indians and the now obviously surrounded troops in Tobruk. By early morning on 18 June, Rommel's troops had reached the coast across the Via Balba, Gambut airfield was in their hands – with 15 serviceable aircraft and considerable quantities of petrol and oil – and whatever of Ritchie's forces not pinned inside the Tobruk perimeter in retreat back into Egypt.

Rommel launched his attack on Tobruk at 5.20 a.m. on the morning of 20 June, on the south-eastern quadrant of the defence perimeter. In this choice of attack sector he was doubly fortunate, for both Klopper and Ritchie had considered that if ever Tobruk was attacked it would be in the south-western quadrant, so most of the artillery and the entire 2nd South African Division were stationed in the western half of the fortress; and most of the mines which had been sown in the southern section of the Gazala Line had been lifted from the minefields laid out by the Australians the previous year – opposite Rommel's chosen point.

By noon the leading Mark IIIs of 21st Panzer had driven over the positions held by the unfortunate 2nd/5th Mahrattas, whose centre company, despite a gallant fight, were wiped out. Rommel himself arrived at King's Cross, the centre of Tobruk, shortly after 2.00 p.m. and stood in his command truck to look down at the port and harbour which had been for so long denied to him. Along each side of his vehicle trudged dejected, bewildered files of prisoners, few of them – if any – realizing who he was. They had certainly never seen any of their own senior commanders as close to the battle as this.

The unfortunate General Klopper was now completely out of his depth. He had held only senior staff appointments since he had commanded a battalion back in South Africa, his administration and communication staffs were as inexperienced as himself, and most of his brigade and battalion commanders were of the opinion that it was more important for the lives of 'the flower of South African manhood' to be spared, than for Rommel to be beaten.

Throughout the night of 20/21 June, Klopper faced the utter solitude of a commander, with little but depressing advice from his colleagues, while, ironically, the bulk of the enemy soldiers lay once again prostrate with exhaustion and his own rank and file waited with eager anticipation for the orders – which they were sure would come – to drive forward into the darkness and slaughter the strangely quiescent foe.

They waited in vain, for the orders never came and to their astonishment and fury, shortly after daybreak a huge white flag was hoisted above brigade headquarters. As it flapped open in the first morning breeze, a great moan of disappointment, anguish and misery welled up from all over the western half of the garrison area.

Defeat is bitter in any circumstances, but now, in the minds of thousands who were experiencing it, it was compounded by disgrace.

First Battle of Alamein

The capture of Tobruk brought exultation to the Panzerarmee and a field marshal's baton to Rommel, but it brought no rest for either of them. Rommel dismissed the news of his promotion with the comment that he would far rather have had another panzer division, and to congratulations from his staff he responded with the brusque order, 'All units will assemble and prepare for further advance.' For his eyes were now on the Egyptian frontier and the vast prize of the Nile Delta, the Suez Canal and all the horizons beyond.

Italian armoured cars come under British shell fire as they pursue the retreating British into Egypt. The Eighth Army had entirely lost confidence in its leadership by the time Auchinleck assumed personal command.

Remonstrances from Kesselring and the Italian commanders were answered with statements that the enemy were in such disarray that they would be able to offer little or no resistance to the swift and powerful drive Rommel was about to launch – and that, with the stores dumps of both Tobruk and Belhammed now at his disposal, no critical shortage would impede his progress. As for previous plans and agreements, such overwhelming victory swept away the need for caution, a conclusion in which he was later supported by both Mussolini and Hitler. By the evening of 22 June, 90th Light were in Bardia and 21st Panzer were on their way to join them; by the following day 15th Panzer and Ariete were closing up to the Egyptian frontier to the south, shepherding the remains of Eighth Army in front of the them – and Rommel was examining another huge supply dump which 90th Light had seized at Fort Capuzzo, which contained 'particularly large quantities of fuel'. Fortune was favouring the successful.

General Ritchie sacked

Fortune had hardly spared Ritchie a sympathetic glance since Eighth Army had arrived at El Agheila at the end of the previous year. Nothing he could do went right, even now that he was back in Eygpt and men and supplies were more easily available. The *danse macabre* of military disaster continued: orders failed to get through, reports were late and inaccurate, battalions had lost confidence in their brigade command and support battalions, the infantry distrusted the armour, the artillery and engineers withdrew into a world of their own; and men who would willingly risk – indeed give – their lives in what they believed a worthwhile exploit, withdrew their loyalty and obedience from leaders who in their eyes were unworthy of their trust, and who would probably waste their efforts through incompetence.

A plan for holding Panzerarmee along a line south of Mersa Matruh failed for a combination of many of those reasons, but by the time it had been demonstrably shattered Auchinleck had taken a step which many people, including Churchill, thought he should have taken much earlier: he took command of the battle himself and sent General Ritchie home. In doing so he effectively saddled Ritchie with the blame for all the disasters which had happened: and he thus gave some hope to the men under his command, most of whom had always greatly respected him. Of course, he would now fight a battle with the iron laws on his side; his base and main sources of reinforcement and supply was now but a hundred miles behind him, while Rommel's supplies, once those he had captured were expended, had to come from Tripoli – or from Tobruk, when all the damage done to the port by the Royal Navy elements before they left had been repaired.

By the morning of 29 June, 90th Light accompanied by the Italian Littorio Division, with the Italian XXI Corps in close attendance, was past Mersa Matruh and driving along the coast road past Fuka towards El Daba. The two panzer divisions and Ariete were driving south west towards El Quseir. Across the front of them all ran a desert track connecting the twin peaks of Himeimat in the south on the edge of the Qattara Depression, to the newly created, wire-bound defence post around the little railway station of El Alamein, of which few people at that time had ever heard.

Rommel's orders were short and clear. There was no reason to believe that these new British defences would be any more difficult to smash than those which the veterans of the Afrika Korps had burst through before, and although their commander did realize that after the tremendous efforts of the past four weeks they were tired (and hungry; and thirsty; and very dirty!), he called for just one more extra effort which would take them through the last barriers to their well-earned rest and relaxation amid the delights of Cairo, Alexandria and the fabled Nile!

As always, they did their best, but by the time they moved off for this last great effort, they had already experienced a succession of heavy bombing raids by Wellingtons from the Delta, against which the Luftwaffe could only send an occasional lone Bf 109. In the late afternoon of the first day – 1 July – the men of 90th Light suddenly found themselves under a storm of fire the like of which none of them had ever experienced. Nothing was missing from it – heavy guns, howitzers, light and medium field guns, mortars, anti-tank guns, all contributing to a *Trommelfeuer* which shook even Rommel, who came hurrying up in an armoured car immediately the extent of the opposition to 90th Light's advance became evident.

That night, for the first time in any account of the battle of the Afrika Korps, the word 'panic' appears – in the War Diary of the 90th Light itself. Auchinleck had found a method of stopping Rommel at last.

The opening phase of the First Battle of Alamein lasted three days and ended on the afternoon of 3 July, with the Alamein Box still firmly in British – or rather South African – hands, Ruweisat Ridge and Alam Baoshaza just to the west in the hands of 21st Panzer Division, and both sides withdrawing a short distance and regrouping for the next phase.

This opened with a number of small manoeuvres and skirmishes which effectively drew the German armour to the south around Bab el Quattara, and climaxed with another tremendous bombardment by the massed British artillery on the unfortunate Italians in the north. This was followed by a sweeping advance from the Alamein Box by a brigade from the 9th Australian Division which reached Tel el Eisa, destroying two battalions of the Sabratha Division en route, and bringing a dismayed Rommel hurrying

A pall of smoke hangs over Tobruk after General Klopper surrendered the port and 30,000 British and Commonwealth troops, winning Rommel a Field Marshal's baton and compelling General Ritchie to retreat on Mersa Matruh in Egypt.

British small arms

British and Commonwealth infantry were equipped with a wide variety of small arms ranging from cheaply-produced mass production weapons to classic firearms like the Bren gun and the SMLE.

Above: The Enfield No. 2 Mk 1 revolver was the most widely used handgun in British and Empire forces. The hammer spur of earlier revolvers had tended to snag in clothing; the No. 2 Mk 1 had it removed, which meant it could only be fired double action.

Left: The Webley Mk 4 was used as the basis for the Enfield No. 2 Mk 1, but was passed over in favour of the government-sponsored weapon. However, demand for revolvers exceeded Enfield's production capacity and the Webley was issued in large numbers.

Right: The Sten gun was designed after Dunkirk as a cheap and easily produced sub-machine-gun. This is the Mk 2; introduced in 1941, it was a crude and ugly weapon but easy to clean and maintain.

Right: The Sten Mk 5 appeared in late 1943 and introduced several refinements to the original design. It carried the foresight of the No. 4 rifle and first saw extensive action in the hands of the paratroops in 1944. It became the standard British SMG after the war.

Right: The original production version of the world's finest light machine-gun: the Bren. The name comes from Brno, the Czech armaments works which produced the original gun and Enfield, where British designers modified it. The Bren Mk 1 entered service with the British army in 1937 and its direct descendants are still in service.

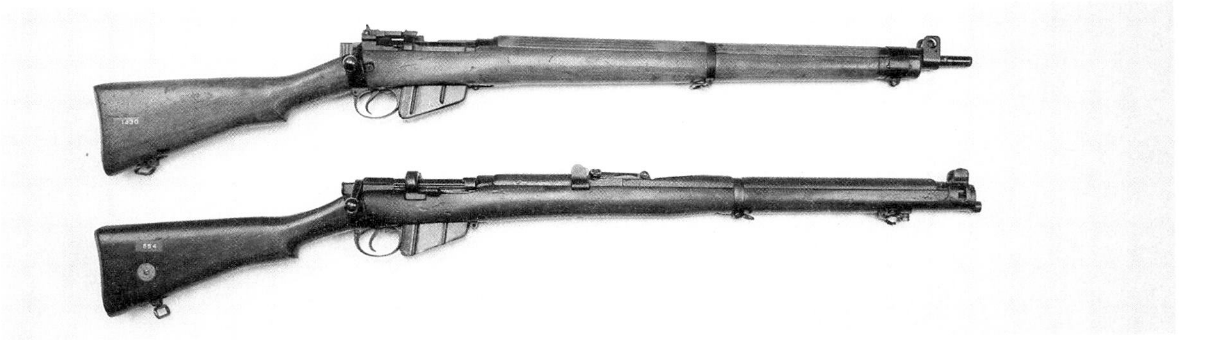

Right: A No. 4 rifle dating from 1941 (above) compared to an SMLE of 1914-18 vintage. The British SMLE (Short, Magazine, Lee-Enfield) rifle had given sterling service during World War I, but most of the parts had to be produced by hand and for World War II a mass-production version was introduced. The No. 4 was not as accurate a rifle as its predecessor, but it was still a sound weapon.

Italian M13 tanks halted in the desert just behind a crest. The terrain in North Africa could be very deceptive with apparently open ground containing hidden wadis and false crest lines. It was all to easy to blunder into an enemy killing zone.

north. For the first time he gained the impression that he was being out-thought.

On 22 July the third phase of the First Battle of Alamein began. It lasted three days, pushed Rommel's formations a mile or so backwards, cost both sides a great deal of ammunition (which Rommel could not afford but Auchinleck could), each size losing about 1,000 men, and the British about 100 tanks. It also revealed with blinding clarity the lack of sound administration and co-operation throughout the Eighth Army, its general amateurism compared with the professionalism of the Afrika Korps divisions and, as Auchinleck's chief of staff was to write, the necessity for complete reorganization and thorough training.

First Alamein produced one success and one failure for each side. Auchinleck had halted Rommel's drive for the Nile – but the Panzerarmee was still in existence and no one could foretell when it would strike again, and whether or not it would succeed.

Churchill intervenes

It had seemed at the time an especially cruel stroke of fate that Churchill had been with President Roosevelt when the news came through that Tobruk had fallen. They had been discussing a programme of mutual assistance when the American Chief of Staff, General Marshall, entered and handed Roosevelt a telegram. After glancing at it, the President handed it without a word to Churchill.

'Tobruk has surrendered,' it read, 'with twenty-five thousand men taken prisoner.'

It was, Churchill wrote, one of the heaviest blows he was about to receive during the war.

The kindness now extended to him by Roosevelt stands as a landmark in human generosity and compassion. 'What can we do to help?' was the first question the President asked, and with its answer put in train movements which were to send 300 Sherman tanks and a hundred self-propelled guns – all of which the US forces badly needed themselves – in six fast American ships to the Suez Canal.

The news also sent Churchill home in short order. Having first defeated, practically on his own, a vote of 'no confidence in the central direction of the war' (by 475 votes to 25), he immediately made arrangements to visit the Middle East himself in order to find out what had gone wrong and take steps to put the situation right.

He arrived in Cairo shortly after dawn on 3 August, held several meetings at the British Embassy with such trusted advisers as the British Chief of Staff Sir Alan Brooke, the South African Prime Minister Jan Smuts, Air Chief Marshal Sir Arthur Tedder, and General Wavell, who had been flown back from Delhi. Present also, of course, was General Auchinleck, for whom Churchill still had great respect. On 7 August both Churchill and Brooke flew up to Burg el Arab, and then drove across to visit Auchinleck in his desert headquarters just behind Ruweisat Ridge.

Churchill was not impressed, either by the plans and arguments put up by Auchinleck and his Chief of Staff, Major-General Eric Dorman-Smith, or by the conditions he found there. But on his way back he lunched at RAF Headquarters at Burg el Arab, where he found not only a much more youthful and aggressive atmosphere, but also some outspoken and obviously competent young officers who were not afraid to give tongue to their own criticisms – with which Churchill found that he agreed. By the time he returned to Cairo his mind was made up; however great his admiration for General Auchinleck, too much failure had occurred under his command for him to remain as Commander-in-Chief, Middle East. He must go, and a reorganization of the Middle East must take place.

There followed many hours of discussion and argument, and in the end it was decided that General the Hon. Sir Harold Alexander should be appointed C-in-C, Middle East, in Auchinleck's place, and that Lieutenant-General 'Strafer' Gott, who had served in the desert since the beginning of hostilities against the Italians in 1940, first commanding the Support Group, then the 7th Armoured Division and recently commanding XIII Corps, should now command Eighth Army, taking Ritchie's place.

Fortune, however, decided otherwise. On the afternoon of 7 August, as General Gott was flying back to Cairo to take up his new appointment, the plane in which he was travelling was shot down, and, as he tried to help rescue other passengers, Gott was killed by the returning fighters. He was greatly mourned throughout Eighth Army for he had been very popular and was, in many eyes, the last of the great desert fighters.

That evening a cable was sent to Whitehall and five days later a special flight brought out his replacement from England. He was Lieutenant-General Sir Bernard Law Montgomery and, as one of his opponents in the Afrika Korps was later to write, 'Nothing was ever the same in North Africa after he arrived. The war in the desert ceased to be a game.'

Montgomery arrives

One of the reasons for this was that no greater contrast could be drawn than that between the characters and personalities of Auchinleck and Montgomery. Auchinleck was a big man, handsome in a soldierly manner, generous of spirit, slow in speech and very slow to anger; one cutting but perceptive description of Montgomery of those days was 'Quick as a ferret; and about as likeable.'

He quickly demonstrated the truth of both parts of that apothegm. He was everywhere. Within days of his arrival he had visited every part of the front, every headquarters of every army brigade or RAF group, every formation to which his staff car or jeep could travel. Bewildered soldiers who had never in their military careers ever seen anyone higher in rank than their colonel, suddenly found themselves being questioned by this small, wiry, almost electric figure with piercing grey-blue eyes which gave an instant impression of total authority and an almost Messianic certainty.

As for the second part of the description, nobody had ever said he was a 'nice chap' and he would have been furious if they had, and his general unpopularity was increased within a few weeks as a stream of officers found themselves sent back to England under the cloud of Montgomery's stinging disfavour. He had always been a great believer in physical fitness for every soldier whatever their rank or duties, and at one time had decreed that even headquarters administrative staff were to do a seven-mile run every week. One pear-shaped colonel remonstrated that such an effort would surely kill him. 'Good!' replied Montgomery crisply. 'Die now and we can get a fit replacement before the battle starts!'

Not surprisingly, however, he was at first regarded with some scepticism by the bulk of the men of the Eighth Army, for they were suspicious by then of all commanders beyond those of their own battery, battalion or squadron, and especially if they had just come out from England and had still 'to get their knees brown'. But he did impress them in one respect.

Rommel would next attack, he told them, towards or at the end of that month, August. He would attack in the south, and he would be stopped as though he had run into a brick wall; after which Rommel and his famed Panzerarmee would have to withdraw to the positions from which they had started their attack – and there await what Montgomery and the Eighth Army intended for them. This was the defeat and eventual expulsion from North Africa of all Axis forces.

Soldiers quickly grow tired of long-term promises by their commanders, so the second part of the prophecy was treated with a certain ribald scepticism; but the first part was different. It was close in time and specific, and would therefore soon be exposed to reality. No recent commander of British troops in the desert had ever before so publicly and clearly committed himself, and this they found reassuring. But of course they would wait and see.

Battle of Alam Halfa

By mid-August, Rommel knew that he had no choice but to make a last, desperate bid to break through the Allied line in front of him and reach the Delta. Otherwise, sickness throughout all ranks (he was ill himself with blood-pressure problems and nasal diphtheria) and shortage of every sort of supply would so impoverish his army that the enemy would have no problem in just moving forward and steamrolling over his positions. So he made his plans and, of course, did not abandon all hope.

'We placed particular reliance in this plan on the slow reaction of the British command and troops,' he was to write. 'Things were to move fast. . . . the decisive battle was to be fought out behind the British front in a form in which the great aptitude of our troops for mobile warfare and the high tactical skill of our commanders would compensate for our lack of material strength.'

Two hundred panzers including 26 of the new Mark IV Specials with the long 75-mm gun and 243 Italian medium tanks moved off as darkness fell on 30 August, and by midnight were attempting to cross the minefield which the British had sown between Himeimat and Deir el Munassib. There seemed to be more of them than they had been told to expect, and their problems were being exacerbated by the continual bombing from flights of Wellingtons above, and from anti-tank shelling from just in front. Despite what Rommel had said, it seemed that surprise was not on the side of the Panzerarmee.

By 8.00 a.m. the next morning, General Bismarck

Left: The backbone of the Eighth Army tank force until the end of 1942, a Matilda Infantry tank. Its thick armour conferred far better protection than any other British tank, but the lack of an effective main gun was keenly appreciated.

Desert air war

Before the arrival of the Afrika Korps, honours had been roughly even in the air war over the North African desert but the appearance of German aircraft in Libya radically changed the picture.

The air war over North Africa occupied a total of almost exactly three years, between the summer of 1940 and that of 1943. At the outset an impoverished RAF, equipped in the main with a fighter force of a few Gloster Gladiator biplanes, faced Italy's equally obsolescent Fiat CR.42s. On the relatively infrequent occasions these protagonists met, honours were roughly even; by and large the Regia Aeronautica pilots were skilled fliers, the tactical balance between the two sides being maintained by the more aggressive attitude to combat among the RAF pilots.

Certainly, faced with aircraft like the Hurricane and Curtiss Tomahawk equipping six squadrons of the RAF and SAAF, the Italians had failed to gain the initiative over the Western Desert. The Italians had moreover adopted a dangerously debilitating practice of rotating combat-weary fighter units away from the war theatre and replacing them with inexperienced units, rather than simply resting individual pilots in turn for short periods. There was therefore little or no tactical continuity in the front line, with the result that few really accomplished Italian fighter pilots remained at the front long enough to pass on their experience to newcomers.

By contrast the German Bf 109E pilots of I/JG 27, led by Eduard Neumann, were exuding self-confidence when they arrived in the Mediterranean early in 1941. Within six weeks the 37 pilots of I/JG 27 had destroyed 63 Allied aircraft in air combat, almost as many as had the entire Italian fighter force in North Africa in eight months; their own losses amounted to six killed and two wounded.

Among the pilots on JG 27's 3.Staffel was a 22-year-old Berlin-born Oberfähnrich Marseille, who had already claimed seven Supermarine Spitfires shot down while flying 'Emils' with LG 2 and JG 52 over the English Channel. By the beginning of 1942 his score was around 50 and beginning to increase rapidly. On 3 June, Marseille destroyed six Kittyhawks in 11 minutes, using only 10 20-mm rounds and 180 from his MG17 machine-guns. A fortnight later, he despatched six more RAF aircraft, this time in an even six minutes. The following day, his score standing at 101, he was awarded the Swords to his Knight's Cross.

The first day of September 1942 was to see JG 27 at its zenith of achievement. On that day, aircraft of Tedder's Middle East Command flew a total of 674 sorties to protect the British Eighth Army. Marseille himself flew three times in the course of the day. On his first patrol he ran into a large group of Kittyhawks and Spitfires, shooting down three of the former and a Spitfire between 08.26 and 08.39, all south-east of Imayid. Two hours later his *Gruppe* engaged a wing of Kittyhawks, Marseille alone shooting down eight between 10.55 and 11.05 near Alam el Halfa. In the late evening the same day, Marseille accompanied his *Gruppe* against a wing of Hurricanes and Kittyhawks, this time claiming five of the American fighters between 17.47 and 17.53. That day JG 27 destroyed 20 Kittyhawks, four Hurricanes and two Spitfires for the loss of one pilot killed, one taken prisoner and one posted missing.

Marseille's feat of shooting down 17 Allied fighters in a single day (all of which are identifiable in Allied records) brought the award of the Diamonds on the next day. On 15 September he reached a score of 150 victories when he shot down seven Allied aircraft in 11 minutes.

On the morning of 30 September, now flying a Bf 109G-2 near Imayid, Marseille was heard on his radio to report that his engine had caught fire and his cockpit was filled with smoke. A few minutes later he called to report that he was baling out in the vicinity of Alamein. His wingman, Pöttgen, reported seeing Marseille leave his cockpit but saw his parachute snag the tailplane, adding as the 'Gustav' dived into the ground and blew up, simply *'Er ist tot'* (he is dead). The loss of Marseille had a profound effect upon the other young pilots of the *Geschwader*, the more so as it had been suffered accidentally and unnecessarily.

As the two great Allied advances from east and west followed the final battle at El Alamein and the 'Torch' landings, JG 27 and all the other Axis forces scrambled back to the final toehold in Tunisia, never again to reap such prolific harvest in air combat. Marseille's own I Gruppe was withdrawn from Africa to western Europe in November, although the II and III Gruppen stayed in Africa to the end. No matter how much the Luftwaffe could scrape together by way of reinforcements, the final outcome was inevitable in the face of enormous Allied air superiority.

Above: Messerschmitt Bf 109Es of I/JG 27 over the desert. They provided the vital top cover for German bombers attacking Eighth Army positions in North Africa and cut a swathe through the RAF fighter squadrons operating in Egypt.

Below: Messerschmitt Bf 109s take off from a desert airstrip, kicking up great clouds of dust. Tropicalized models of the Bf 109 were soon introduced and were superior to the RAF fighters operating over the desert.

Left: A Messerschmitt Bf 110 under maintenance in the desert. The Luftwaffe was as dependent as other German units on the long supply lines stretching back to Libyan ports.

Right: A Messerschmitt Bf 110 soars above the palm trees. After suffering catastrophic losses in the Battle of Britain it proved more successful in the desert, where it did not have to face the same concentration of single-engined fighters.

Left: A British officer leads off into the smoke during the Battle of Alamein. Montgomery's masterly handling of this set piece battle decisively defeated the Afrika Korps.

Right: Oberstleutnant (Colonel) Fritz Bayerlein took temporary command of the Afrika Korps after General Nehring was wounded during a British air strike on 1 September.

commanding the 21st Panzer Division had been killed and General Nehring commanding the Korps badly wounded, but at least the bulk of the panzers were through the minefields; unfortunately, as they were now well behind schedule, they must turn north along the line which led to the centre of the Alam Halfa Ridge, instead of further on towards Hamman. The panzers needed more fuel by 1.00 p.m. as they drew near the ridge – there was much softer sand on the way than was shown on the British map they had captured a week before, and both tracked and wheeled vehicles had run into trouble. But a welcome sandstorm cloaked them while the tanks were refilled; there was still no sign of the British armour, which should have offered itself for its usual destruction by now at the hands of the 88-mm guns.

It never did. It stayed out of range for the whole of this engagement, moving occasionally into place to act as mobile artillery, to add to the gradually increasing barrage of 25-pounder shells which crashed among the assembled panzers until the crews were blinded and deafened and longing for darkness. After this barrage, precedent demanded that a decent silence should fall upon the battlefield, the British withdrawing into remote laagers, the Afrika Korps refilling their fuel tanks yet again and replenishing their ammunition racks.

Bombing and shelling

But someone was making new rules. All that night the British artillery poured their shells into the area in which the panzers were now penned, while the RAF carried out a long session of pattern bombing which caught the supply and petrol echelons as they tried to come up, banished all hope of sleep for the Panzerarmee, wrecked too many of their vehicles and killed and wounded many of their most experienced men.

When the morning of 1 September came, lack of fuel limited Rommel's forces to only one more attack, on the western end of Alam Halfa Ridge, and this was beaten back by the same implacable gunfire as before. That night the pattern of the previous night was repeated, and the following day Rommel noticed yet another portent of the times ahead: amid the formations of aircraft which harassed and bombed his unfortunate formations were now appearing Mitchells and Liberators bearing the white star of the USAAF.

This incessant bombardment of Axis armour trapped below the Alam Halfa Ridge continued for another two days and nights during which neither the panzers nor the guns gave each other much rest, and during the night of 3/4 September, the Axis infantry lining the gap through which the panzers had passed had also to fight off New Zealand and British infantry attempts to close it. The gap remained open, however, and in the course of 5 September the remains of 15th and 21st Panzer and of the Ariete, Trieste and Littorio Divisions withdrew through it, leaving behind wreckage of a large number of Axis tanks and, as killed or prisoner, 1,859 Germans and 1,051 Italians. A number of British soldiers were now wondering hopefully if, after all this time, they at last had a general who knew his job and would again do as he promised.

As for the Panzerarmee, it had now to wait for the next move, which must come from the enemy. And wait, for the moment, without their commander, whose illness made it essential that he return home, his place taken by General der Kavallerie Georg Stumme, straight from the rigours of the Russian Front.

Panzerarmee Afrika waited until 8.40 on the evening of 23 October, when suddenly their eastern horizon turned pink, and an astonished silence gripped the world.

The Battle of Alamein

The opening barrage at Alamein remained or will remain in the memories of those who heard it for the rest of their lives. For 15 minutes Wellington bombers had plastered the rear Panzerarmee lines with 125 tons of bombs; then, with a gigantic roar, 882 field and medium guns opened fire at once, pounding the known German and Italian artillery positions, then shortening range until they were dropping a creeping curtain of fire in front of the advancing infantry of the British XXX Corps.

On the right, from a standing point about two miles in from the coast near Tel el Eisa Station, the 9th Australian Division drove due westward with, on their left flank, the 'Jocks' of the 51st Highland Division, fanning out as they attacked from a start-line just over a mile long towards an objective nearly three miles long, its south-eastern end touching the point of Miteiriya Ridge. On the Scots' left, two brigades of New Zealand infantry with the 9th Armoured Brigade, all under direct command of the famous Major-General Bernard Freyberg, VC, would take the length of the ridge itself and drive down to the foot of its forward slope; on their left the South African Division would aim for a continuation of the line, leading down to where the 4th Indian Division were holding static positions.

Behind the infantry would come first of all the sappers and specialist infantry to clear the minefields – 'devil's gardens' as the Germans called them – in places nearly two miles wide, thickly sown but apparently randomly placed; no wonder General Montgomery had chosen to call this phase of the battle Operation Lightfoot. And through the two wide swathes cleared by the minefield task-forces would pour the armour of General Lumsden's X Corps, 1st Armoured Division in the north between the Australians and the Highlanders, 10th Armoured Division in the south, through the New Zealanders and then up and over the Mitieriya Ridge. Such was the plan.

By the end of the first night (dawn, 24 October) the infantry had attained a large part of their objectives. The Australian 26th Brigade had reached and consolidated their position at the top corner of the objective (the Oxalic Line); on their left, their own 20th Brigade had dug in about a mile short, linking on their own left, with the Jocks of 153rd Brigade (also short of Oxalic), whose brothers of 154th Brigade had pushed on further and held their objective on the end of Mitieriya Ridge. Almost the whole of the ridge itself had been taken by the New Zealanders, and as dawn broke their 5th Brigade were dug in at the foot of the forward slope, 6th Brigade were on the crest to their left, and the South Africans were almost level to continue the line.

Moreover, units of the 9th Armoured Brigade, acting closely with the New Zealand infantry, had crossed the ridge, though at the loss of many tanks in uncleared minefields, and had broken out to attack advanced German gun positions before daylight had revealed them to the waiting anti-tank guns. Then, however, they had been forced back behind the ridge – a foretaste of what was to come.

But behind the infantry, in the salient they had punched into the Axis line, something like chaos reigned, and the armour of X Corps was well behind schedule. Not only had armoured progress depended upon the clearance of the gaps through the minefields (and an accident or breakdown at the head of a column caused an endless tail-back), but their paths lay across the logistic support routes of the infantry preceding them – ammunition trucks, support weapons, ambulances. Moreover, previous battles plus the tramp of thousands of men and enemy return fire had broken the surface of the desert into a foot-thick carpet of dust. As their own tracks churned it into a fog, it thickened an already dark night, to blind and choke everyone who moved in it.

Thus by morning 1st Armoured Division were still behind the Australian and Highland positions through which they should have advanced (and these too were a mile short of Oxalic), while 10th Armoured Division, although they had closed up well with the New Zealanders, were now held back by their commander, Major-General Alec Gatehouse, who had seen what had happened to the tanks of 9th Armoured Brigade in daylight beyond Mitieriya, and was unwilling to subject his own units to the same fate.

Above: A Messerschmitt Bf 109 escorts a Ju 87B Stuka back to base. Provided enemy fighters could be kept at bay by the Luftwaffe the Stuka was a formidable ground attack aircraft.

Left: An SdKfz 231 8-wheeled armoured car leads a German reconnaissance unit. Carrying a four-man crew, it was armed with a 20-mm cannon and a machine-gun.

Afrika Korps transport

The tactical brilliance of Field Marshall Erwin Rommel won the Afrika Korps a string of remarkable victories, but Rommel stretched his supply lines to breaking point in his efforts to reach Egypt. German transport had to provide all his supplies over thousands of miles of desert road.

The Kübel was the German equivalent of the Willys Jeep, and some 55,000 of them were produced during the war. This is the original model which equipped the first German formations to arrive in the desert.

Tanks suffer serious wear and tear making long journeys on their tracks although the increasing size of tanks made early tank transporters rapidly obsolete. This Bussing-Nag 454 6½ ton truck carries a Panzer I Command Tank.

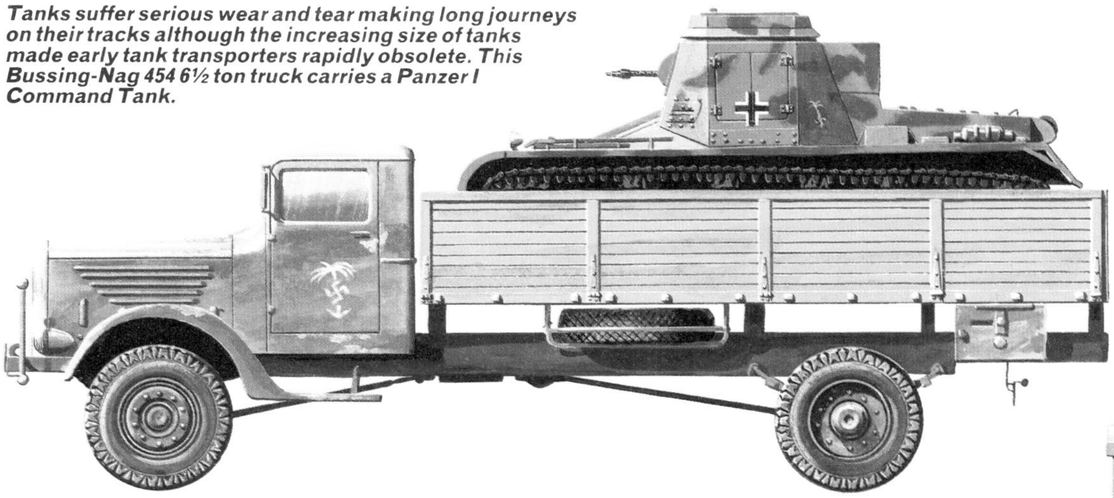

The Opel Blitz was the most widely used German truck and served in many different roles. This is the Kfz 31 ambulance model which worked in conjunction with mobile operating theatres on the same chassis.

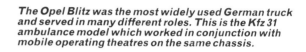

The workhorse of the German logistic effort, the Opel Blitz did not perform as well in the desert as comparable British trucks because its double rear wheels tended to clog up with sand. Just over 100,000 of these lorries were produced from 1938-45, compared to the 500,000 2½-ton trucks delivered to the Allies by GMC.

Left: A German Panzer III enters the battle with spare track mounted on the hull front for added protection. By late October 1942 Rommel's tanks were severely short of fuel.

Right: A British 25-pdr field gun joins in the formidable bombardment which preceded Montgomery's counter-attack. 882 British guns subjected the German positions to a concentrated barrage on the night of 23/24 October.

If General Montgomery was disappointed by the lack of progress by the armour, he was still determined that they should break out across the Oxalic Line to their own objective some three miles beyond – the Pierson Line – where they would stand and await the inevitable attack by Afrika Korps armour, and there destroy it. If not on the first night, then the second; there would be no change in the plan.

But during the second day, and especially in the late afternoon and evening, it became evident, to General Freyberg at least, that the armour was not being 'set up' properly for the battle. By midnight such confusion reigned behind the Mitieriya Ridge and up in the 1st Armoured Division sector (where the leading tank units were convinced they were already over a mile further forward than they really were, and were arguing with the infantry about it) that Montgomery's chief of staff decided that one of his superior's strictest edicts – that he was never to be disturbed at night – must be broken. A conference with XXX Corps and X Corps commanders was held at 3.00 a.m. that morning.

At this meeting, Montgomery 'spoke very firmly' to the armoured commander, General Lumsden, and he later had a telephone conversation with Major-General Gatehouse, which left both parties with bruised sensibilities. Montgomery still insisted that the armour must break out, if necessary under another heavy bombardment such as that of the opening night, and this would be quickly organized.

However, the following day 25 October was spent by the general in deep thought, his conclusions influenced by two pieces of news which had come in. The southern section of the Alamein line was held by XIII Corps, and their main duty had been to mount against the Axis forces down there such attacks as would keep them in place, tying them up so that they could not go to the help of their hard-pressed comrades up in the XXX Corps sector. In order to initiate and hold this pressure, XIII Corps units had launched attacks in the Himeimat sector, and had then tried to penetrate two Axis minefields covered by Italian and German paratroop formations. Both attacks had been repelled, and on the second night the famous 7th Armoured Division, like its brothers to the north, had been held up by well-sited German anti-tank guns.

The other piece of news was that arguments between Highlanders and 1st Armoured Division had been resolved, and the armour was by no means as far forward as Montgomery had been led to believe. It seemed that – for whatever reasons – the British armour either would not, or could not, break out. It was time for a new plan.

Rommel returns to the front

Rommel had by now been recalled from his sick leave in Germany, for his replacement, General Georg Stumme, had suffered a massive heart attack within hours of the opening bombardment. Rommel arrived back on the evening of 25 October to fight a battle which he knew he 'could not win' and to find himself forced to dance to the enemy's tune. With that vast salient now jutting into his northern positions, he had no choice but to order 21st Panzer Division to move north, knowing that he would not have the petrol available to move them back again, whatever the developments down in the south. He also found himself faced with the problem of finding troops and tanks to fight in a battle of appalling ferocity about to take place up near the coast.

Montgomery had abruptly shifted the axis of his attack. He had decided that he needed time to reorganize his armour, and in order to gain it he must pin down the enemy in one sector, forcing them to 'crumble' away their strength in a battle of attrition in which he possessed the greater strength.

For this he used what he later described as 'that magnificent Australian Division'. On the night of 25 October, their 26th Brigade began a drive north from their top corner of Oxalic, first towards the high Point 29, then on across the road and railway toward the coast. It thus threatened the Bersaglieri and the Germans of 164th Infantry Division, who had been holding – relatively undisturbed in the battle so far – the salient along the northern flank of the Australian advance, pointing them down towards Tel el Eisa. It was a battle which was to rage for the best part of a week, and it drew German and Italian infantry tanks into a maelstrom of fire in which they were devoured as though with the appetite of Moloch. In the battles around Thompson's Post two Australian battalions were practically annihilated and one of the finest VCs in history won – posthumously, alas.

Right: A South African engineer digs out an enemy mine while a colleague continues to probe forward with his mine detector. The engineers also had to clear paths through the British defensive minefields as the Eighth Army counterattacked.

Below: British Crusader tanks head off towards the German positions. Montgomery made great efforts to inject some ginger into his armoured commanders, but combined arms tactics still seemed to elude them.

And in the meantime, equally ferocious battles were being fought in front of the northern sector of the Oxalic Line. In order to assure himself of time and space for reorganization, Montgomery sent out screens of infantry with supporting tank units, behind which he withdrew the bulk of his armour and one of the New Zealand Brigades, while he also brought 7th Armoured Division and some of the XIII Corps infantry up north. And upon those protecting screens fell much of the force of Rommel's attempt to reduce the British salient.

The 2nd Battalion, The Rifle Brigade, had advanced from Highland Division's positions on the Oxalic Line during the night of 26/27 October to a location on the map known as 'Snipe'. By morning Lieutenant-Colonel Victor Turner had established defensive positions for his riflemen and 19 attached 6-pounder anti-tank guns inside an oval perimeter – positions he was instructed he must hold on his own until supporting armour reached him in a couple of hours. As it happened, Shermans from 24th Armoured Brigade did arrive by 8.30 a.m. Such was the enemy shellfire they attracted, however, that they were forced to withdraw – much to the relief of the embattled riflemen, who were left on their own for the rest of the day, though not by the enemy.

Since early morning Rommel had been aware of this impudent encroachment into his defences by a small unit, and as the day wore on it attracted more and more of his attention, for it seemed to epitomize all the lessons of desert fighting to date, and also those qualities of the British soldier which he most admired – stubbornness and resilience.

The great lesson which the action at 'Snipe' underlined was that well-dug-in effective anti-tank guns could wreak havoc in the ranks of attacking armour when served and protected by men of high morale. By the end of the day, 34 Axis tanks or self-propelled guns lay smoking around the edges of the battlefield and at least as many had been towed away; but a third of 2nd Rifle Brigade lay where they had fallen when, on the following night, the survivors marched back to Oxalic. But their sacrifice had even greater effect than just on numbers, for, after 'Snipe', Rommel and his staff began to look over their shoulders.

They had good cause. By now their infantry strength and morale were being slowly but surely eroded, to such an extent that reports were reaching Rommel that after allied bombardment even some of his staunch Panzergrenadiers were surrendering to the first enemy troops who arrived; and his panzer strength was falling so rapidly that, ironically, he now had sufficient petrol to move what was left about the northern sector with some freedom.

As there was now no doubt whatsoever in his mind how the battle would end, and with the lives of his splendid Afrika Korps men at stake, he began drawing up plans for a general retreat, at least as far as what the Italians called the Fuka Line some 50 miles to the west. First, however, he would make one last stand in the hope that it would weaken the resolve of his opponent, who might not have the stomach for an ever-lengthening casualty list. In the course of 31 October, therefore, he set up a command headquarters near Sidi Abd el Rahman and put together an assault group from both 21st Panzer and 90th Light Divisions, augmented by batteries of mobile artillery; these he sent off down the line of the road and railway to attack the Australians who had formed a block there, and thus to relieve the beleagured Italians and Germans still holding out in the Tel el Eisa salient.

They suffered first from a frightening and almost devastating attack by bombers of the Desert Air Force, but, when heat haze and a sandstorm gave them a respite, they moved cautiously down under Rommel's personal goading towards the Australian positions between the road and the railway, where they then found themselves opposed not only by the Australian infantry but also by Rhodesian anti-tank guns and over 20 Valentine tanks of the 40th Royal Tank Regiment. The latter reared their 7½ feet of thin armour up out of the desert, their only built-in armament the old, out-ranged 2-pounder gun, and it is incredible that against the Panzer IIIs and IVs which now attacked them, the Valentines lasted as long as they did. They were sustained as much by the pride of the crews as by the encouragement shouted at them by the surrounding Australians, who stood themselves in the trenches cheering them at every move, and by the support given them by the valiant Rhodesians.

As the panzers closed in inexorably from the west and north, the anti-tank guns were wrecked one by one, and the Valentines sacrificed themselves in open manoeuvre to tempt the panzers to expose their thin sides either to other Valentines or to the remaining guns. By early evening the whole saucer of the battlefield was cloaked in smoke from burning vehicles, blown sand and gun-smoke, at which moment, perhaps because they had run out of ammunition, to the onlookers' astonishment and delight the panzers began a slow and cautious withdrawal.

Nevertheless, 21 Valentines had been wrecked and 44 crew-members killed, and later the Australian historian wrote, 'The courage of these men made the action one of the most magnificent of the war.'

But it had not been enough to keep shut the block which had been thrown across the neck of the Tel el Eisa salient, and Rommel was now in a position to withdraw the troops who had been bottled up in it. Yet despite urgings from two of his staff officers he hesitated to give the necessary orders, partly because he was loath to abandon heavy weapons in the salient, partly because of a traditional reluctance to vacate positions which, while occupied, would constitute a threat to enemy movements and thus a possible check to their plans. And shortly afterwards, these doubts were vindicated by his intelligence staff, who told him that General Montgomery seemed to be massing forces for another gigantic onslaught, this time in the area immediately south of the Australian positions, to the north of the 'Snipe' battlefield and towards the derisory Aqqaqir Ridge running diagonally across the line of attack and defence.

In this Rommel's staff were correct. At 1.05 on the morning of 2 November, another formidable barrage was opened, and under its cover the New Zealand, Scottish and British infantry were again grouping for attack. Operation Supercharge had opened.

The operation's birth and conception had not been entirely without anguish for, as has been mentioned, it had entailed the withdrawal of formations from the battle line for regrouping into a new striking force; and when the news of the withdrawal reached Whitehall, Churchill's anxiety reached bursting-point. The storm broke that same morning over the head of the Chief of the Imperial General Staff, General Sir Alan Brooke – why was Brooke's protégé

Above: German 105-mm howitzers return fire from temporary positions as the British breakthrough imperils the Afrika Korps' position. The British enjoyed a great superiority in artillery.

Right: This Ju 87 Stuka was brought down by ground fire from British infantry and crashed just in front of them. No attempt was made to destroy the machine, and it was overrun.

Right: Bren gun carriers of the Rifle Brigade pursue the retreating Axis army. The sand thrown up by each vehicle can be seen over a considerable distance.

Montgomery taking troops out of the battle? Why was he allowing the battle to peter out? Why did he say he would break out in seven days if he only intended to fight in a half-hearted manner?

'Haven't we a single general who can win even one battle?' Churchill had cried, and for a moment Sir Alan thought he was going to hit him.

The storm calmed somewhat under Sir Alan's defence of Montgomery, but flared up again later, this time to be soothed away by the South African Field Marshal Smuts, but later Alan Brooke confided to his diary, 'I told them what I thought Monty must be doing . . . but there was just that possibility that I was wrong and Monty was beat.'

The CIGS would have been much comforted could he have attended a meeting held at Eighth Army headquarters the following day when the C-in-C, Middle East, General Alexander, accompanied by his own chief of staff and the Minister of State, Middle East, Richard Casey, questioned Montgomery on the situation and his immediate plans. The Eighth Army commander 'radiated confidence', explained his tactics, and was fully backed up by his subordinates when Casey questioned them, somewhat unorthodoxly, behind his back. The party returned to Cairo and their report to London reassured the authorities there, who awaited the next stage with rather more optimism.

Armoured breakthrough

The next stage was, in effect, a concentrated repeat of the opening onslaught by XXX Corps, on a smaller scale and aimed along a more northerly axis. Once again, a shattering bombardment opened along the length of the advance, once again the infantry marched forward with minefield-clearance teams immediately behind to clear the way, firstly for the infantry support armour – including again the 9th Armoured Brigade – then for the mass of armour from the 1st Armoured Division. The infantry were to reach and hold an objective line just short of the Rahman Track, their immediate armoured support was to thrust on *in the darkness* up and over the Aqqaqir Ridge, and the 1st Armoured Division were to crash out through the gap thereby opened, and destroy the bulk of the Axis forces beyond. Speed and exact timing were essential.

So far as the infantry attack was concerned, it went as near like clockwork as any movement in battle can be expected to go. Both the Durham Brigade on the right and the Seaforths and Camerons of 152nd Brigade on their left reached their objectives well on time, the Scots suffering less than 80 casualties of which very few had been killed. Opposition they encountered had been slight, for both German and Italian soldiers in the area had been exhausted by their battles of the last eight days, and shattered into near panic first by the bombing attacks by the Desert Air Force, and then by the artillery bombardment which had just passed over them.

But as the Valentines and assorted cruiser tanks of 9th Armoured Brigade attempted to follow, they found themselves in conditions worse than any they had previously experienced. Traffic, exploding shells and the tramp of thousands of marching feet over the last few days had reduced the desert floor to a sea of powder, feet deep, in which vehicles moved in a brown fog comparable only with a London 'pea-souper' in the days before smokeless fuel.

Fortunately, trust and co-operation between the units in the brigade and the infantry with whom they had worked closely proved strong, and with men on foot guiding the leading tanks in each column and the rest following more by sound and hope than by sight, two regiments – the 3rd Hussars on the right and the Wiltshire Yeomanry to their left – reached the infantry objective in time, though by no means in full strength. Twelve of the Hussars' tanks and all their anti-tank guns were missing for the moment, and 11 of the Wiltshires' tanks had been lost – but, more important, the third regiment, the Warwickshire, were missing *in toto*, and despite the urgings of the regimental commanders, the brigade commander refused to press forward without them.

Half an hour passed before the Warwickshires arrived, and only then did the covering barrage crash out and the brigade move forwards across the Rahman Track, and on towards the foot of the Aqqaqir Ridge – at first with astonishing success. In the darkness they overran both German and Italian gun positions; at one point Wiltshire tanks broke through a gun-line, turned and wrecked all the guns by driving over their trails, chasing the crews off into the night. But all the time the sun was rising behind them and, as they drove up the slope of the ridge, they moved dramatically from shadow at the foot into full daylight on the crest. 'At this,' as one of them was to say later, 'the whole world blew up!' – for they met the massed fire of almost all of Rommel's remaining anti-tank guns. In less than 30 minutes, 75 of the 94 tanks which had set out across the Rahman Track had been wrecked, and of the 400-odd crew members, 230 had been killed, wounded or were missing. And the formations of 1st Armoured Divisions intended to exploit their efforts were still a long way behind.

They too, had been delayed by the appalling conditions in the narrow salient, and by dawn, when 9th Armoured Brigade were enduring their Calvary, they were just arriving at the advanced infantry positions. There they stayed – to fight the last main action of the Battle of Alamein.

Rommel's intention to rescue his men from the fate which must overtake them if they stayed where they were had been foiled by Hitler, just as Rommel had begun to put it into effect. Plans and orders for withdrawal had already been issued when the infamous

Left: German prisoners are brought into the British lines on 6 November 1942, two days after British units had finally broken through the main German defences at Alamein. In defiance of Hitler's orders, Rommel ordered his men to retreat, leaving the battlefield to the Eighth Army.

Above: A German Junkers Ju 88 bomber lies wrecked after being forced down by an Allied fighter. The retreating Afrika Korps was vigorously harried from the air as it fell back westwards.

Below: An 88-mm gun begins the trek to the west, but only after German anti-tank guns once again inflicted heavy losses.

Below: Italian M13s on the move at the height of the Alamein battle. The Ariete Division fought until the bitter end in October.

The Long Range Desert Group

Operating in small units the LRDG preyed on the German supply lines which stretched back across the vast expanse of the North African desert. Airfields and supply dumps would be raided at night: a handful of men swooping out of the desert to wreak havoc and then vanish as suddenly as they had appeared.

The Long Range Desert Group (LRDG) acted very much on its own. It had no particular operational base other than Kabrit in the Suez Canal Zone, and once away from the rest of the military in the desert it acted primarily as a reconnaissance unit. It operated by stealth and guile, only rarely daring to assume a directly hostile posture, choosing rather to melt away into the desert wastes whenever trouble threatened. But if it was ever caught by enemy forces the LRDG was well equipped with numbers of automatic weapons of all kinds, and the men of the LRDG were experts in their use.

A typical LRDG mission was normally formed around a small number of vehicles. The central unit of the small forces was a 4×4 Chevrolet or another type of truck converted by the addition of extra fuel and water tanks, racks for equipment and radios, and space for the crew's kit and weapons. This truck would also carry the main support weapons of the force, usually a captured Italian 20-mm cannon or a heavy machine-gun. The rest of the force would use Jeeps liberally festooned with air-cooled machine-guns (Vickers 'K' guns or Brownings) and yet more fuel and water-tanks. These small forces would make their way behind enemy lines by driving far to the south beyond the open enemy flanks and then driving north to the area of choice. The final approaches were usually made by night, and the units holed up by day.

During the day the reconnaissance function came to the fore. All manner of military information was gathered, such as the number of tanks visible, unit markings, types of trucks and loads visible, the numbers of aircraft on airfields, and so forth. At times prisoners were taken for later interrogation, and the results of all this intelligence-gathering was sent back to Cairo by radio.

Not all the LRDG activities were confined to this passive role. From 1941 onwards the LRDG acted as the carriers for the newly-formed Special Air Service, or SAS, which had a primarily offensive raiding role to disrupt activities in the enemy's rear areas. Not all these missions were effective but some were quite spectacularly successful. On one occasion the SAS approached an enemy airstrip and under covering fire from the LRDG proceeded to break up an officers' mess party with Thompson sub-machine guns while another party rushed up around the strip blowing aircraft with grenades; when the SAS party ran out of grenades one aircraft remained intact, but this was disabled when one SAS man tore out the instrument panel by hand! Then the SAS and LRDG men joined up and made off into the desert once more.

Raids as spectacular as that were not common, but the SAS and LRDG often combined on similar nuisance raids well behind the enemy rear. Airfields were a particularly favoured target, for a few Jeeps could sweep in, create havoc, and then vanish leaving precious aircraft as wrecks. But the prime role of the LRDG was reconnaissance, and time and time again their reports enabled the British and Commonwealth commanders to make important decisions that enabled the rest of the army to attack when and where it counted most.

The LRDG operated well in advance of the Allied advance right up to the approaches to Tunisia, where the terrain was not so well suited to its tactics. But the LRDG units remained in being, albeit on a more formal basis than the free and easy days of the desert campaigns, and they were later used to good effect during parts of the Sicily and Italy campaigns. Gradually the LRDG was absorbed into the expanding SAS, and to this day the SAS maintains some of the old LRDG spirit and traditions. Even the modern SAS Land Rovers with their arrays of machine-guns evoke memories of the adventurous

Above: A Long Range Desert Group patrol prepares to leave its oasis base for a reconnaissance mission into the desert in May 1942 as the German advance on Egypt continues. Small reconnaissance units such as this provided much useful intelligence.

Above: LRDG members pose for the camera to show off their hardware: this Chevrolet truck carries a typical mixture of a Lewis gun behind the driver and a Browning 0.30-in machine-gun next to him. The metal sheeting on the side of the vehicle is for extracting it from soft sand.

Above: The LRDG on patrol in the Western desert; one of the vehicles of the New Zealand patrol undergoes engine repair in the heat of the sun. From the lack of lookouts they are unlikely to be under enemy air threat. From 1941, LRDG teams operated with the newly formed SAS in clandestine operations behind the German lines.

Above: Two LRDG patrols meet in the desert, both groups drawn from Commonwealth units – in the foreground Rhodesians, and in the background New Zealanders. Reconnaissance remained the prime role of the LRDG despite the spectacular success of some of its raids on German bases.

'Halt!' order arrived, instructing Rommel not to yield a metre of ground and ending with the stony valediction 'As to your troops, you can show them no other road than that to victory or to death!' – and this, in a few words, entailed a total change in Rommel's attitude to the battle.

No longer could he afford to fight a defensive battle, for if his troops were not to yield ground, then that dangerous salient must be eliminated before it could erupt and wreck Axis communications. This meant attack – possibly even frontal attack. So instead of sheltering in hull-down positions or behind their superb anti-tank screens while the British tried to attack them – as in the battle so far – Rommel's panzers must now themselves attack, across open ground towards whatever defences awaited them. It was a situation not dissimilar to the one in which they had already suffered severely at 'Snipe'.

Thus during the late morning and all the afternoon of 2 November the remains of 15th and 21st Panzer Divisions hurled themselves at the 'Durham Corner' where, in broken ground and with the support of strong artillery and anti-tank guns of 1st Armoured Division, the Afrika Korps at the end of the day had only 35 of their panzers left, and only 20 of the Italian M13s. British tank losses were by no means inconsiderable, but they had greater reserves upon which to draw and many of the less badly damaged tanks could be repaired. The enemy, however, had been forced off the field of battle, leaving their wrecks, their dead and many of their wounded behind: this was the action in which the strength of the famous Deutsches Afrikakorps was finally broken.

It was also the day when the Panzerarmee defence at Alamein were first punctured, albeit by a small force. During the previous night, armoured cars of the Royal Dragoons had found their way out of the south-west corner of the salient, and had threaded their way through and into the rear areas of the enemy defences – much to the astonishment, when full daylight came, of the formations whom they had shot up on the way.

But their signals that they were out into the desert convinced Montgomery that the way was opening for the great break-out. So during the 48 hours which followed, the main armoured weight of Eighth Army was regrouped to smash out through the south-western corner of the salient. There were still some clearing battles to be fought by the infantry – and in one of them, the Highland Division were again to suffer grievous and unnecessary casualties as a result of armoured inability to read a map properly – but by dawn on 4 November, Argyll and Sutherland Highlanders were out south of Tel Aqqaqir, to find that the Afrika Korps – indeed the whole of the Panzerarmee – had withdrawn.

Rommel had disobeyed his Führer and had pulled his forces back, leaving behind them a few stragglers, some wrecked artillery, random areas of uncleared mines, and a large number of ingenious booby traps.

The Battle of Alamein was over, and all that remained was for Eighth Army to organize an effective pursuit.

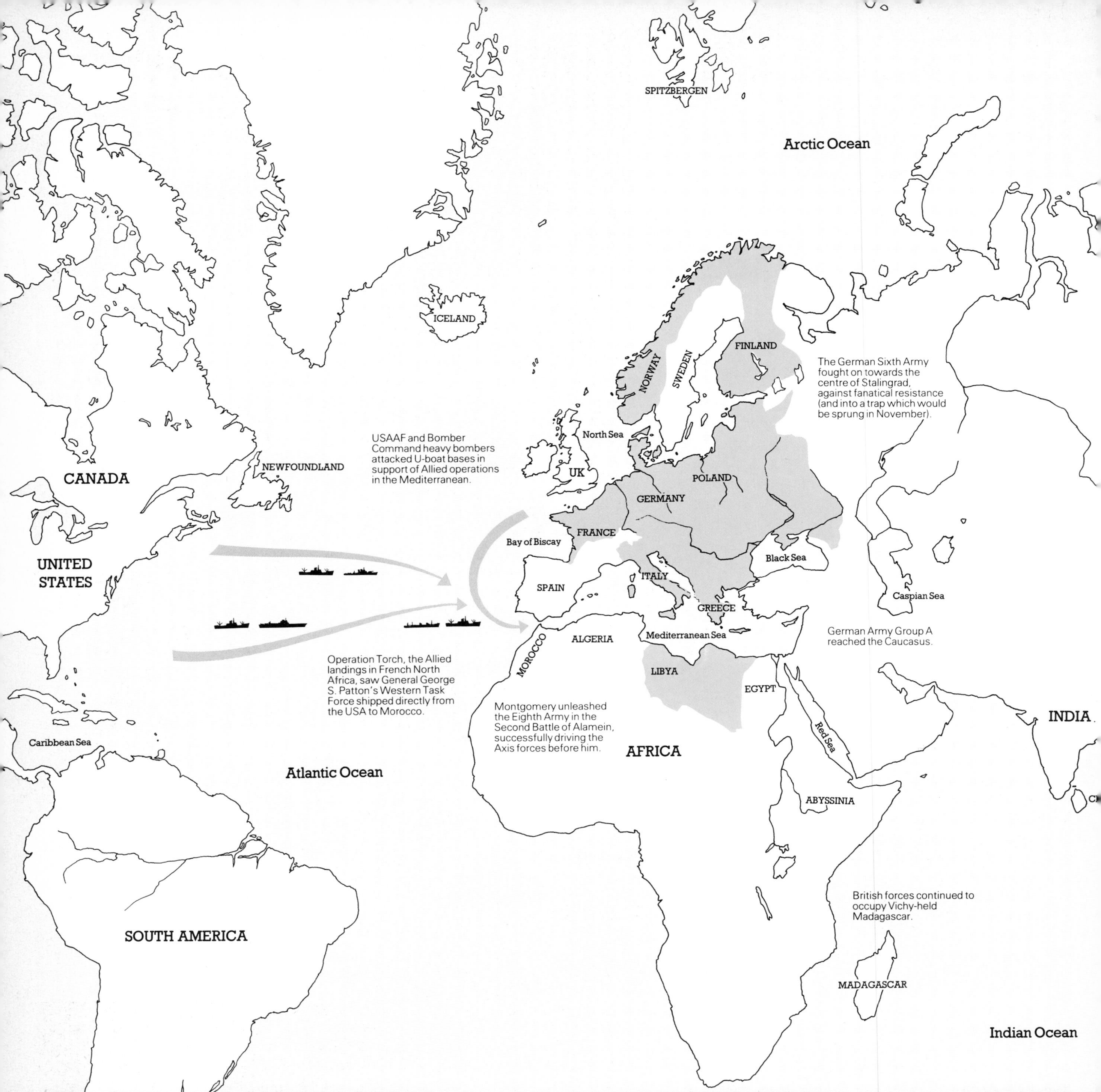
SPITZBERGEN
Arctic Ocean
ICELAND
FINLAND
NORWAY
SWEDEN
The German Sixth Army fought on towards the centre of Stalingrad, against fanatical resistance (and into a trap which would be sprung in November).
USAAF and Bomber Command heavy bombers attacked U-boat bases in support of Allied operations in the Mediterranean.
North Sea
NEWFOUNDLAND
CANADA
UK
POLAND
GERMANY
FRANCE
Bay of Biscay
UNITED STATES
Black Sea
ITALY
SPAIN
Caspian Sea
GREECE
ALGERIA
Mediterranean Sea
German Army Group A reached the Caucasus.
MOROCCO
Operation Torch, the Allied landings in French North Africa, saw General George S. Patton's Western Task Force shipped directly from the USA to Morocco.
LIBYA
EGYPT
Montgomery unleashed the Eighth Army in the Second Battle of Alamein, successfully driving the Axis forces before him.
INDIA
Red Sea
Caribbean Sea
AFRICA
Atlantic Ocean
ABYSSINIA
British forces continued to occupy Vichy-held Madagascar.
SOUTH AMERICA
MADAGASCAR
Indian Ocean

In his familiar crumpled beret festooned with badges, General Montgomery scans the horizon of the Western Desert after leading the Eighth Army to its decisive victory at El Alamein.

Some men of von Paulus' ill-fated Sixth Army joke about the autumn mud on the outskirts of Stalingrad. In just six weeks they will be surrounded and the temperature will drop to as low as −35° C.

The Turn of the Tide

October 1942

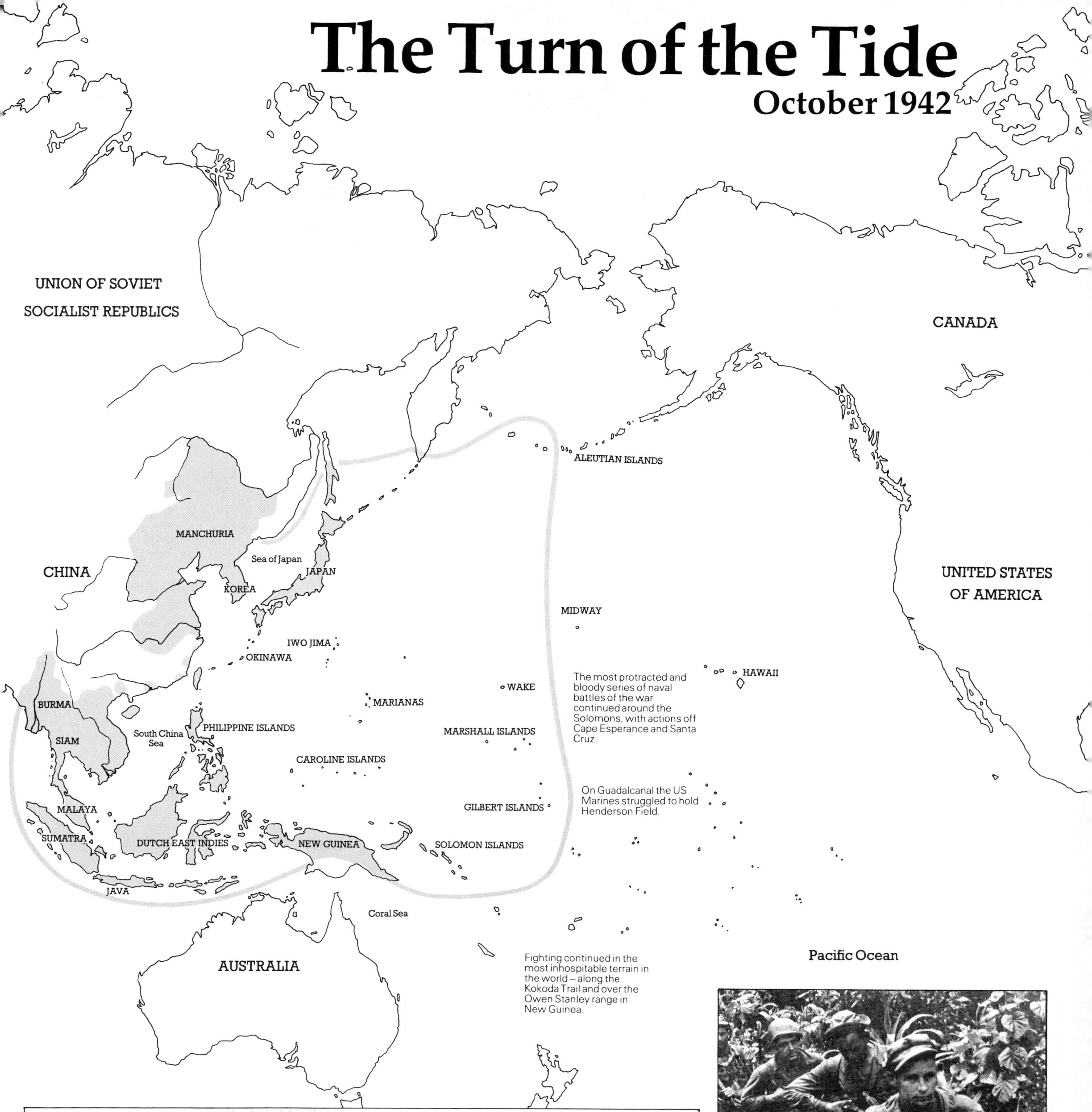

A column of von Kleist's armoured forces clatters across the steppe in early November 1942, just days before the massive Soviet offensive on the Volga which left them dangerously isolated.

US troops advance warily through the dense jungle foliage on the Solomons, where the Japanese ferociously resisted the American offensive.

Chapter 12

Stalingrad to Kursk

1942 saw the Wehrmacht at its most forceful. Unsuccessful in its attempt to take Moscow, the main axis of German attack was directed southwards, towards the Caucasus and the oilfields of the Middle East. Few could envisage that within a year the initiative would be snatched away and the summer of 1942 would mark the high point of German conquest. It takes two sides to make a battle, however, and the rebirth of the Soviet army was to change the nature of the war in the East beyond all imagining.

On 28 June 1942 the great Summer Offensive of the Wehrmacht opened with Hoth's Fourth Panzer Army sweeping forward to the north of Kursk, while Paulus' Sixth Army, which included 11 infantry divisions and a panzer corps of its own, drove parallel with them to the south of the city. Their first objective was the Don bend, but a hundred miles beyond lay the prize of Stalingrad and control of the Lower Volga and its oil traffic to the industrial centres of Russia.

Two days later, Army Group A under Field Marshal Siegmund List burst over the Donetz bend and drove southeast towards Proletarskaya, the Caucasus and the oil centres themselves, Maikop, Grozny and Baku.

It seemed at first that the days of easy victory had returned, for whatever Russian forces were encountered were swept away with almost contemptuous ease. For the first time in many months the ground favoured the large-scale, sweeping advances, hundred of miles of open rolling corn and stepped grass offering perfect country for the massed armour of both Hoth's and Paulus' legions; indeed to those who watched the huge motorized squares with panzers forming the frames and soft transport and artillery crashing along inside, it seemed that the day of the modern Roman legions had dawned. Their advance was visible from miles away – smoke from burning villages, dust-clouds as the heavy vehicles crunched their way over the fields signalling the implacable progress of a perfectly functioning war machine.

Hoth's panzers were at Voronezh by 5 July, throwing both the local Red Army Command and STAVKA into turmoil as they tried to foresee which way – north towards Moscow again or south towards the oil – this huge offensive would turn. General Vatutin was hurriedly ordered to form a new 'Voronezh Front' and was so successful in herding together the remnants of the Red Army divisions swept away to the north by the Panzer army in those first few days that Field Marshal Bock, commanding the whole Army Group South, proposed to swing both Hoth's panzers and part of Paulus' infantry left to deal with Vatutin before driving on towards the main objectives.

The drive for the Caucasus took German troops through some of the most fertile lands of the Soviet Union. Here a machine-gun team armed with an MG 34 make their way through fields of waving maize. Note the hills in the background, so different from the Ukraine.

But excitement had gripped the German High Command (Oberkommando der Wehrmacht, or OKW). Bock was summarily dismissed, Paulus was entrusted wholly with the advance and capture of Stalingrad while Hoth's panzers, instead of leading Paulus' divisions, were to swing southeast, drive down between the Donetz and the Don to 'assist in the early passage of the lower Don'. At this time the oil was still the major objective, Stalingrad merely another Russian city to be despoiled in due course and one not likely to give the Wehrmacht a great deal of trouble.

Hitler was in a happier frame of mind than he had been for months. 'The Russian is finished!' he announced on 20 July, and even the generally overcautious Halder agreed. 'I must admit, it looks like it.'

It continued to do so for a few weeks yet. The only problems posed in the south were those of traffic control, for both Kleist's and Hoth's panzers arrived at the Donetz crossing at the same time, and a certain amount of acrimony resulted, especially as Kleist saw

To the Caucasus

The German summer offensive of 1942 began well, but almost inevitably lost momentum later on. It was enormously ambitious, and was not helped by Hitler changing his aims several times. Hoth's Fourth Panzer Army was detached from Paulus's Sixth Army (just when he needed armoured support) to von Kleist's First Panzer Army (who did not need more Panzers at that moment). By the time Hoth's tanks had been switched north again to help the stalled offensive at Stalingrad, von Kleist's Army had gone far enough to be thinly stretched and in need of support.

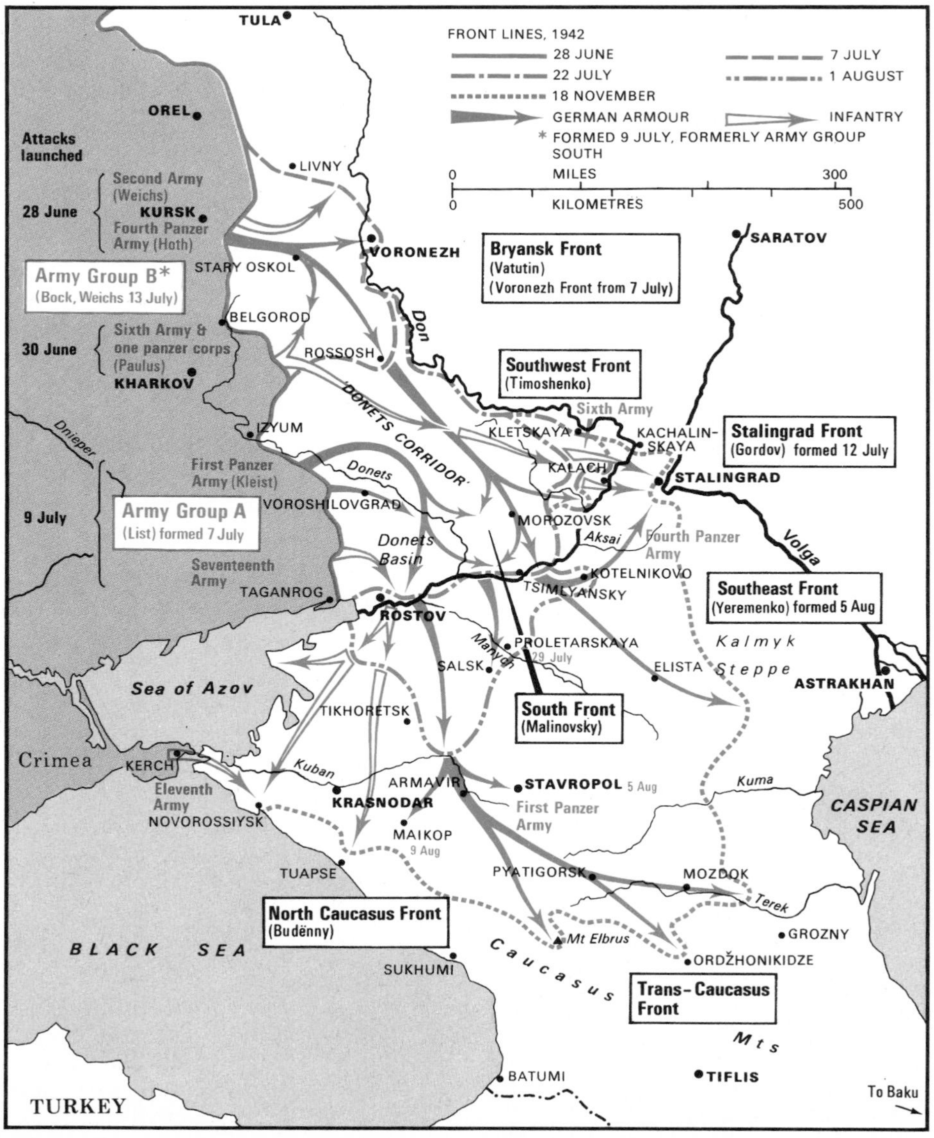

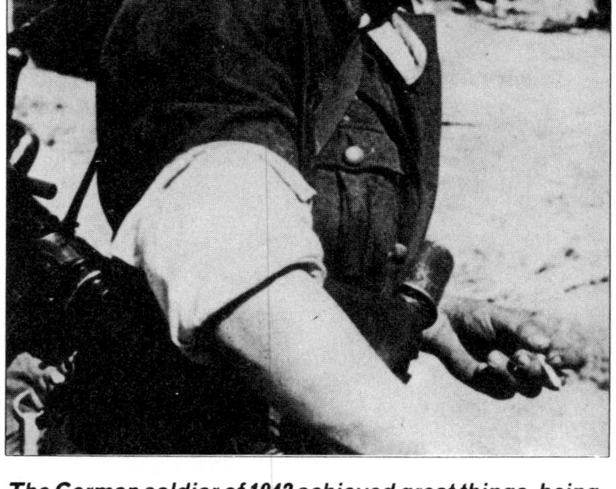

The German soldier of 1942 achieved great things, being tough, well trained and possessed of more individual initiative than that of any other country. Given equal terms, German soldiers could beat any other army.

Demyansk

The successful supply of German troops trapped in a pocket at Demyansk outside Moscow made the Luftwaffe overestimate its airlift capacity, which was to cost dearly at Stalingrad a year later.

On 9 January 1942 the Red Army launched a two-pronged offensive north-west of Moscow from Bologoye and Kuvshinovo, with four armies penetrating the German front between the Army Group North and Army Group Centre. Within a month six German divisions, totalling more than 110,000 troops of General Graf Brockdorff-Ahlefeldt's X Armee Korps, had been isolated in a pocket some 40 miles by 20 around the small town of Demyansk to the north-west of Lake Seliger.

As fresh Soviet forces poured into the region it seemed inevitable that these German forces faced annihilation. A hurried meeting was called at Chernyakhovsk, Luftflotte 1's HQ, on 18 February, at which Keller asked Oberst Fritz Morzik, then commanding the Transportflieger in the East, if sufficient aircraft could be assembled to sustain the trapped army from the air.

Within 24 hours seven transport Gruppen had been assembled on airfields at Ostrov, Pskov and Riga and others in Estonia and Latvia, amounting to about 100 Ju 52/3ms, many from training schools, as well as such aircraft as Fw 200C-3/U2s from the Instrument Flying School B36 at Gardelegen in Germany.

On 20 February the first 30 Ju 52/3ms landed on a makeshift strip at Demyansk, bringing in ammunition, while others air-dropped large bundles of blankets and clothing; the aircraft that landed were used to evacuate more than 200 wounded. By the end of the month the number of aircraft on the airlift had grown to almost 300 as three more Gruppen arrived at the base airfields.

Early in March the Germans completed a second airstrip at Pyesky a few miles north of Demyansk, allowing more aircraft to land, although by now the V-VS had started fighter patrols to spot and intercept incoming supply flights. As losses among the transport aircraft started to increase rapidly, the Luftwaffe in turn was forced to use Bf 109Fs as escorts, and there were a number of fierce air battles as the Soviet fighters tried to attack the lumbering transports. Soon Pyesky became extremely hazardous as a landing-ground so that often only air drops could be made, landings being confined to the Demyansk strip.

Nevertheless, although heavy fighting around the pocket continued throughout April and its defence was conducted almost entirely without the benefit of tanks and heavy guns, with the gradual improvement of the weather a relief offensive was mounted from the south-west, and early in May a narrow corridor was opened to the main positions of the Wehrmacht.

Bearing in mind that the normal cargo load of the Ju 52/3m was no more than about two tons, the achievement of the transport units at Demyansk was remarkable, and unprecedented. In 90 days they had supplied 24,300 tons of food, clothing, fuel and ammunition, airlifted 15,446 troops into the pocket, and evacuated 20,093 wounded personnel. A total of 238 Ju 52/3ms had been lost (out of a total of 413 employed), together with 24 other transport aircraft and 49 fighters. Three hundred and eighty-five aircrew and other personnel had been killed.

The saga of Demyansk illustrates not only an outstanding achievement by the German air transport arm, but explains why it came to represent a fallacious precedent when, nine months later, the German Sixth Army was encircled at Stalingrad. Despite a belief that what had been accomplished at Demyansk could be repeated at Stalingrad, the disaster that befell the Wehrmacht was also to a considerable extent that outcome of events at Demyansk. The Luftwaffe had been unable to make good the earlier heavy losses in transport aircraft – and the V-VS had also become immeasurably stronger in the meantime. Survival at Demyansk had indeed been for the Germans a victory of Pyrrhus.

Originally designed as an airliner, the Fw 200C was pressed into service in the operation to supply the pocket at Demyansk. Although successful the air supply technique was to be put to a much sterner test at Stalingrad.

Although the year started with a Soviet offensive, pockets such as Demyansk were to hold out, giving the Wehrmacht time in which to prepare counterattacks and to plan the spring and summer offensives.

not the slightest reason for the change in plans and the introduction of a rival panzer commander into his theatre. To demonstrate his own virtuosity, he accelerated the pace of his advance once across the river, captured Proletarskaya on 29 July, and by 9 August was at Maikop, with another column guarding his left flank at Stavropol. The great prizes of Grozny, Batumi and Baku seemed within grasp.

But for General Paulus, matters were not going quite so well. In Sixth Army's progress down the Donetz/Don corridor, there was little problem for his panzer corps (under General Weitersheim) driving alongside Hoth's panzers; but of course the 11 infantry divisions, many of whose formations were on foot, found it difficult to keep up and even to remain in touch. By the time they had reached Chernyevskaya on the River Chir in the Don bend they were all well strung out, and only the lack of a well-organized Red

A Panzer III together with infantry from General von Kleist's First Panzer Army head towards the Don. Once across, von Kleist's army moved at a tremendous pace towards the Caucasus.

The 1942 offensive was spearheaded by Panzer IVEs with a long 75-mm gun (foreground), which gradually supplanted the Panzer IIIs (rear). It was to be the last year during which the Wehrmacht were superior on the Eastern Front.

These Soviet prisoners were taken at the start of the summer offensive. Hitler was certain that the USSR had nothing left to fight with, so the stiffening resistance and increasing professionalism of the Red Army came as an unpleasant surprise.

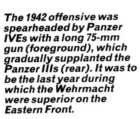

Army block allowed them to close up to the huge river itself.

Nevertheless, there was some fighting in the bend, and Paulus became more and more convinced that without Hoth's support he would not be able to get Sixth Army across the Don in sufficient strength to take Stalingrad 'on the march' – which had been his original ambition. As Hoth's panzers were doing little but annoying Kleist, OKW agreed that Fourth Panzer Army should now hook around to the north-east and drive along the south bank of the Don. But unexpected resistance along the River Aksay delayed them, so that from 10 to 19 August Paulus' army waited in the bend, its artillery massed and ready for the great attack.

The plan was straightforward and conventional. Weitersheim's XIV Panzer Corps would form the northern flank, three of Hoth's panzer divisions and two motorized divisions would form the southern flank, while nine infantry divisions would fill the centre. They were all across the Don within 24 hours and, to the delight of every German headquarters organization between Stalingrad and Berlin, Weitersheim's panzers reported that they had reached the banks of the Volga across the northern suburbs of Stalingrad by the evening of 23 August. It was only a narrow penetration, but support was driving through to bolster the advance, Hoth's panzers were slowly forcing their way through from the south (though they still had some way to go) and it seemed that only one more heavy blow would secure triumph.

On the night of 23/24 August, Stalingrad was subjected to an air raid reminiscent of the heaviest London blitz. The bulk of the bombs dropped were incendiary, and the wooden section of the city – most of the workers' shopping and housing blocks – burned in a holocaust as spectacular as the destruction of the London docks. By morning the pyre rose a thousand feet into the air, acres of Stalingrad suburbs had been reduced to charred ashes and it was evident to the thoroughly satisfied German observers that only the main factories and stone-built offices remained for the attention of the German artillery.

But during the next few days something else became evident: the Russian determination to fight, not only every step of the way to the city, but every step through it to the banks of the Volga.

The Battle of Stalingrad

There had been changes in command on the Russian side. During July Marshal Timoshenko had been moved up to the North-West Front and by August the same team which had conducted the successful defence of Moscow had come south and established headquarters on the east bank of the Volga: Voronov, the artillery specialist, Novikov of the Red Air Force, and General Georgi K. Zhukov, the general who had never lost a battle and had no intention of doing so now.

Commanding the troops of the Sixty-second Army, defending Stalingrad, was General V. I. Chuikov, who took command in early September just after Hoth's panzers had at last hammered a way through to the Volga in the southernmost suburb of the city, at

The Germans recruited some units from conquered areas, but few gave such unstinting service as the Don Cossacks, who were eventually to form a division under von Pannwitz in the Balkans. They were among the main victims of the Yalta agreement.

Chronology of War: 1942

November 8
Operation Torch begins with landings at Algiers, Oran and Casablanca

November 10
Afrika Korps retreat from Sidi Barrani to Buq Buq. US troops take Oran

November 11
Operation Anton: German troops occupy Vichy France. Allies occupy Casablanca and Bougie. Eighth Army reaches Bardia

November 12
First naval battle at Guadalcanal; a chaotic night action. British paratroops capture Bône airfield, Algeria

November 13
Eighth Army reaches Tobruk

November 14
Eighth Army reaches Tmimi, Allied reinforcements reach Bône; Australians capture Wairopi in Papua. In second battle of Guadalcanal, US Navy wins battleship vs. battleship action

November 15
Entire Japanese convoy transports destroyed by US forces off Guadalcanal, four out of 11 transports beaching before being destroyed by marine aircraft and artillery

November 16
Australian and US forces meet on Buna-Gona beachhead

November 18
British Eighth Army reached Cyrene

November 19
Red Army winter offensive opens with massive attacks on each side of Stalingrad, smashing the Romanian and Italian armies to each side of the German 6th Army

November 20
Eighth Army reaches Benghazi. Rommel at El Agheila

November 23
Red Army closes ring around German forces in Stalingrad

November 24
Montgomery plans attack on El Agheila

November 27
Germans enter Toulon, French Fleet scuttled

November 28
Large-scale Russian offensive on Central Front

November 30
In naval Battle of Tassafaronga US Navy less than successful in stopping 'Tokyo Express'. UK civilian casualties in November 24 killed, 38 injured

December 1
Australians capture Gona, New Guinea

December 4
British driven out of Tebourba, Tunisia, by von Arnim's Vth Army

November 7-11
RM Commandos penetrate Gironde River in 'Cockshell Heroes' raid

December 13
Rommel withdraws from El Agheila

December 18
Australian and US troops in fierce battles with Japanese in Papua

Soviet anti-tank weapons

The enormous quantity of German armour faced by the Soviet army on the battlefield was matched by an extremely wide variety of anti-armour weaponry, ranging from grenades to artillery equipment.

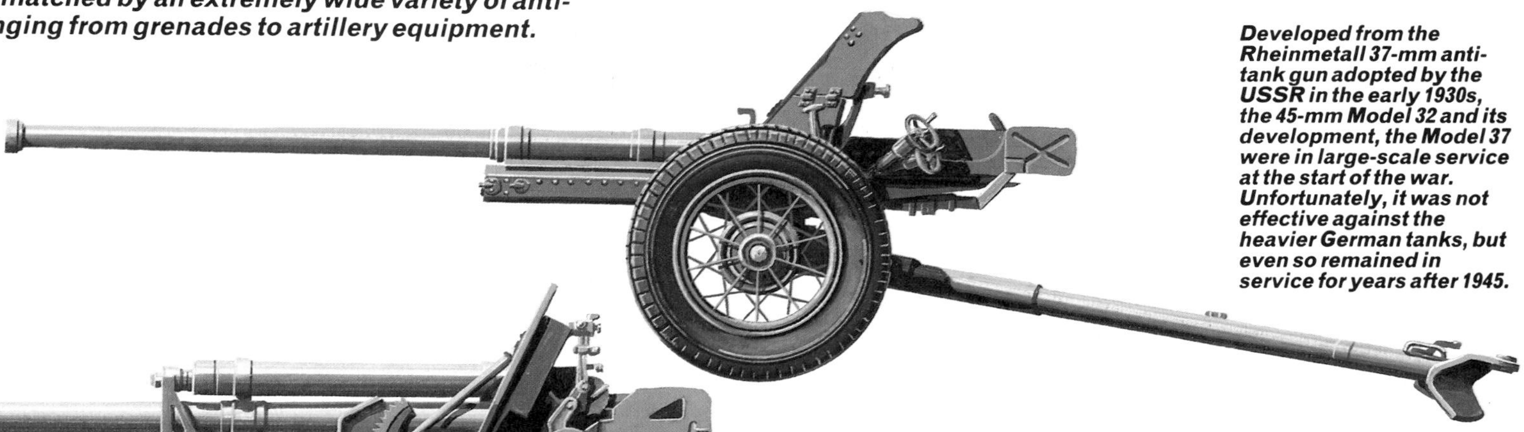

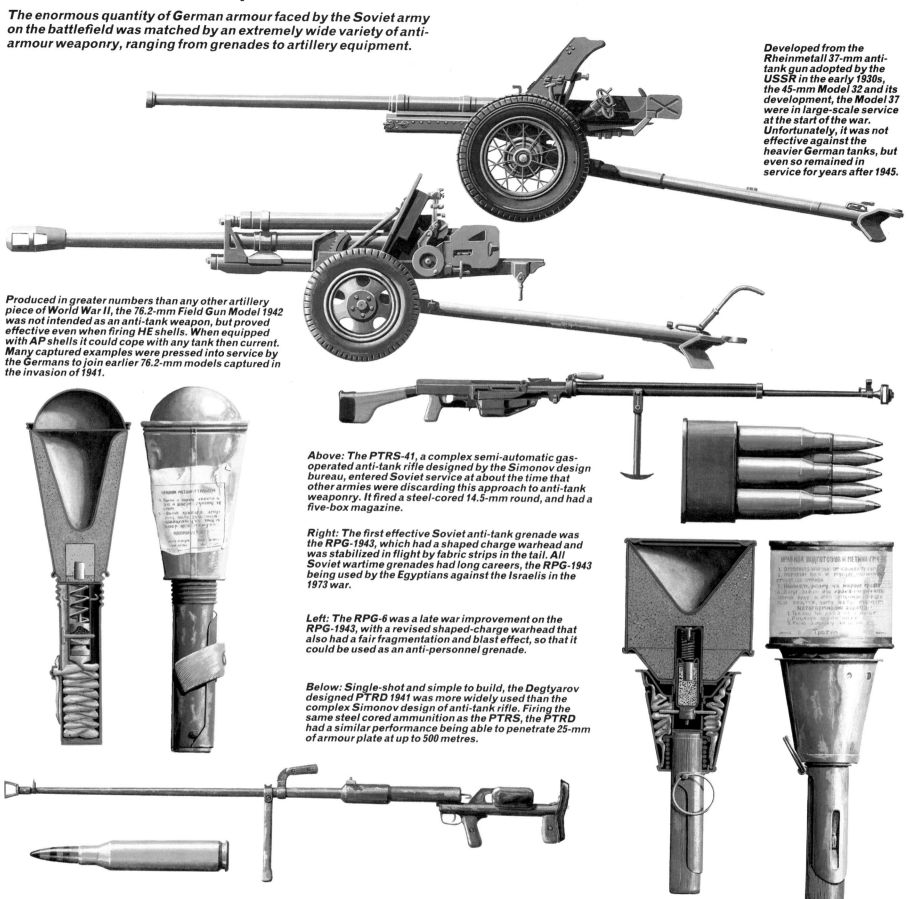

Developed from the Rheinmetall 37-mm anti-tank gun adopted by the USSR in the early 1930s, the 45-mm Model 32 and its development, the Model 37 were in large-scale service at the start of the war. Unfortunately, it was not effective against the heavier German tanks, but even so remained in service for years after 1945.

Produced in greater numbers than any other artillery piece of World War II, the 76.2-mm Field Gun Model 1942 was not intended as an anti-tank weapon, but proved effective even when firing HE shells. When equipped with AP shells it could cope with any tank then current. Many captured examples were pressed into service by the Germans to join earlier 76.2-mm models captured in the invasion of 1941.

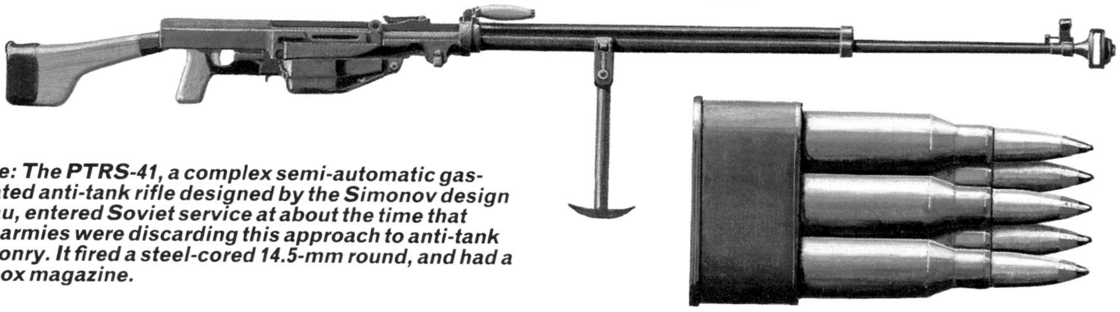

Above: The PTRS-41, a complex semi-automatic gas-operated anti-tank rifle designed by the Simonov design bureau, entered Soviet service at about the time that other armies were discarding this approach to anti-tank weaponry. It fired a steel-cored 14.5-mm round, and had a five-box magazine.

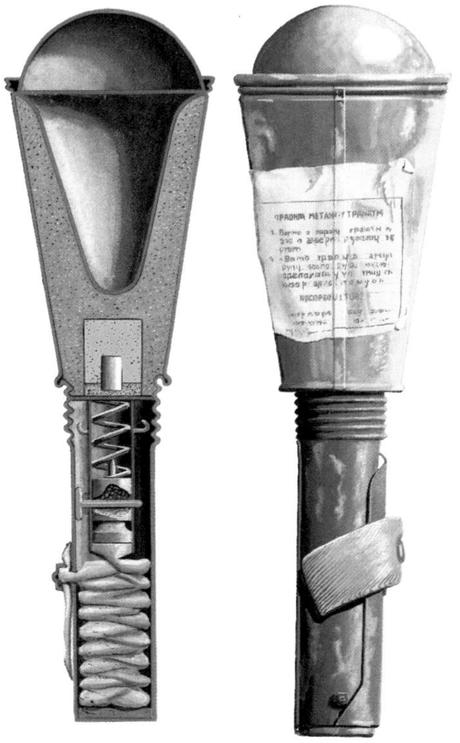

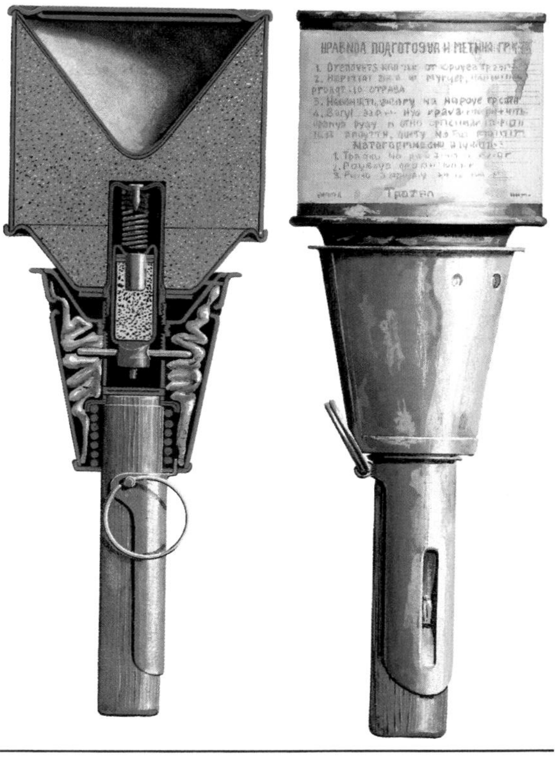

Right: The first effective Soviet anti-tank grenade was the RPG-1943, which had a shaped charge warhead and was stabilized in flight by fabric strips in the tail. All Soviet wartime grenades had long careers, the RPG-1943 being used by the Egyptians against the Israelis in the 1973 war.

Left: The RPG-6 was a late war improvement on the RPG-1943, with a revised shaped-charge warhead that also had a fair fragmentation and blast effect, so that it could be used as an anti-personnel grenade.

Below: Single-shot and simple to build, the Degtyarov designed PTRD 1941 was more widely used than the complex Simonov design of anti-tank rifle. Firing the same steel cored ammunition as the PTRS, the PTRD had a similar performance being able to penetrate 25-mm of armour plate at up to 500 metres.

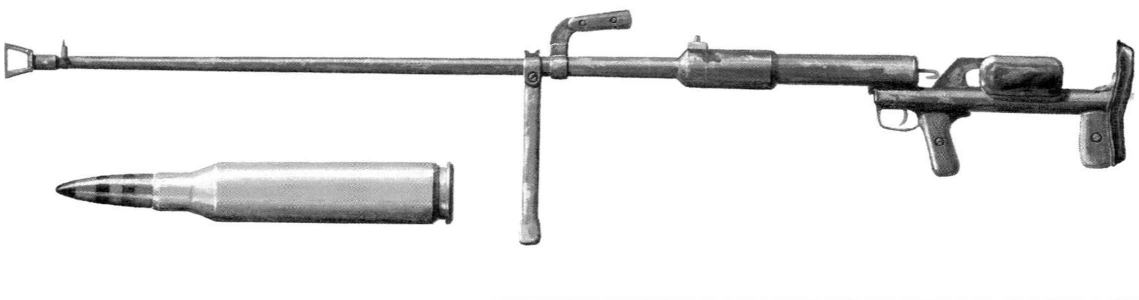

Kuporosnoye. He was to conduct a street-by-street defence of Stalingrad from a deep cave cut into the west bank of the Volga.

By this time the Germans had all reached the outskirts of the city, Weitersheim's armour pressing down towards the vital bridge at Rynok, Hoth's armour at Kuporosnoye pressing up into the mining suburb of Yelshanka, while four of Paulus' infantry divisions were in the gap between, all units intent on driving through the narrow band of massive concrete blocks and the shells of buildings, which separated them from the Volga. Once there, they believed, all would be over – locally at any rate, perhaps everywhere, for had they not been promised victory in 1942?

But the Russian soldiers were now fighting for their own famous city (spurred on by propaganda calling for national patriotism, to which they could respond) and in circumstances in which their own natural talents were at advantage and their lack of armour and mobility did not matter. They fought from holes burrowed in rubble, from the blackened caverns of burned-out offices, from behind parapets of gaunt, towering blocks; they fought for every yard of every street and every alleyway within that area of bitter contest. Here all the panzers could do was to creep into range until they could be blasted by liquid fire, or their tracks blown off by grenade, the crews left to burn or to be shot as they bailed out. As for the German infantry, at first they were mowed down by machine-gun fire as they tried to shelter behind the panzers, for the Russians knew every yard of every route towards the river and could set ambush after ambush; the battles moved down a metre or so, and men crawled all the time like moles through ditches and culverts, then even farther down into and through the sewers. Then the miners were brought in

A captured armoured train on the Don front near Stalingrad in the autumn of 1942. Within weeks, the besiegers were to become the besieged when a huge Soviet attack put the Romanians on each side of the Germans to flight.

German troops enter the outskirts of Stalingrad following large-scale incendiary and dive-bomber attacks at the end of August. The 'final' assault on the city began on 13 September.

Panzergrenadiers take cover in a shell hole during one of more than one hundred separate attacks against the Krasny Oktyabr (Red October) steel works (in the centre of the city).

and began their deep, subterranean tunnelling.

The first heavy and concentrated attack by the Germans, after careful preparation, took place between 14 and 22 September, with the attackers in control of the air above and with a three-to-one majority in manpower. During these nine days of bitter action, Paulus' infantry cleared the bed of the River Tsaritsa and reached the Volga, captured Stalingrad's Number 1 Railway Station, forced Chuikov to change his headquarters position and brought German artillery close enough to the main landing stage severely to jeopardize the nightly passage of ammunition and stores from the main dumps on the east of the river.

But both sides were then so prostrated by exhaustion that for a few days a sullen silence fell upon the area, punctuated only by sporadic machine-gun fire and mortar bursts; but quite soon the battle amid the ruins began again, and what seemed to some observers a battle of attrition recommenced in which the side with the larger numbers would inevitably win.

But those observers were wrong. German losses were far in excess of Russian losses, and indeed there was a different purpose and mentality controlling each side. Berlin was already proclaiming the capture of Stalingrad, and to Hitler's eyes no loss of life could compensate for his own loss of face if it were not quickly confirmed; Paulus must have as many men as could be shipped to him and he must feed them into the cauldron without scruple. But Zhukov had a different view; he had plans for the employment of the armies being formed on the east side of the Volga, and they did not include immolation in the devastated city, no matter what the men of the desperate Sixty-second Army might be suffering. He would bleed in just enough men to keep the defence of Stalingrad alive – and dangerous to the besiegers – but the mass of men and arms accumulating under his command had a more strategic purpose.

This was revealed on 19 November – after six different offensives by Sixth Army against Stalingrad defenders, who by then were confined to the area around the Krasny Oktyabr and the Barrikady factories along some five miles of the river bank, and after such a Calvary of fighting one tortured soul wrote in his diary, 'when night arrives, one of those scorching howling bleeding nights, the dogs plunge into the Volga and swim desperately to gain the other bank. Animals flee this hell; the hardest stones cannot bear it for long; only men endure.'

At dawn on 19 November, a thunderous barrage opened to the north from 2,000 of Voronov's guns and Katyusha batteries, and all who heard it sensed

Stalingrad

Marshal Georgi Zhukov opposed the German 6th Army with the minimum force necessary to hold them – Chuikov's 62nd Army, which had borne the brunt of the fighting so far. Meanwhile he prepared crushing blows against the Romanian armies north and south of the city. Having up to 11 armies available, he first loosed the 1st Guards, 5th Tank and 21st Armies on 18 November, and 51st, 57th and 64th Armies in the South. The Romanians were crushed, and the remorseless jaws of the trap closed around von Paulus and his army.

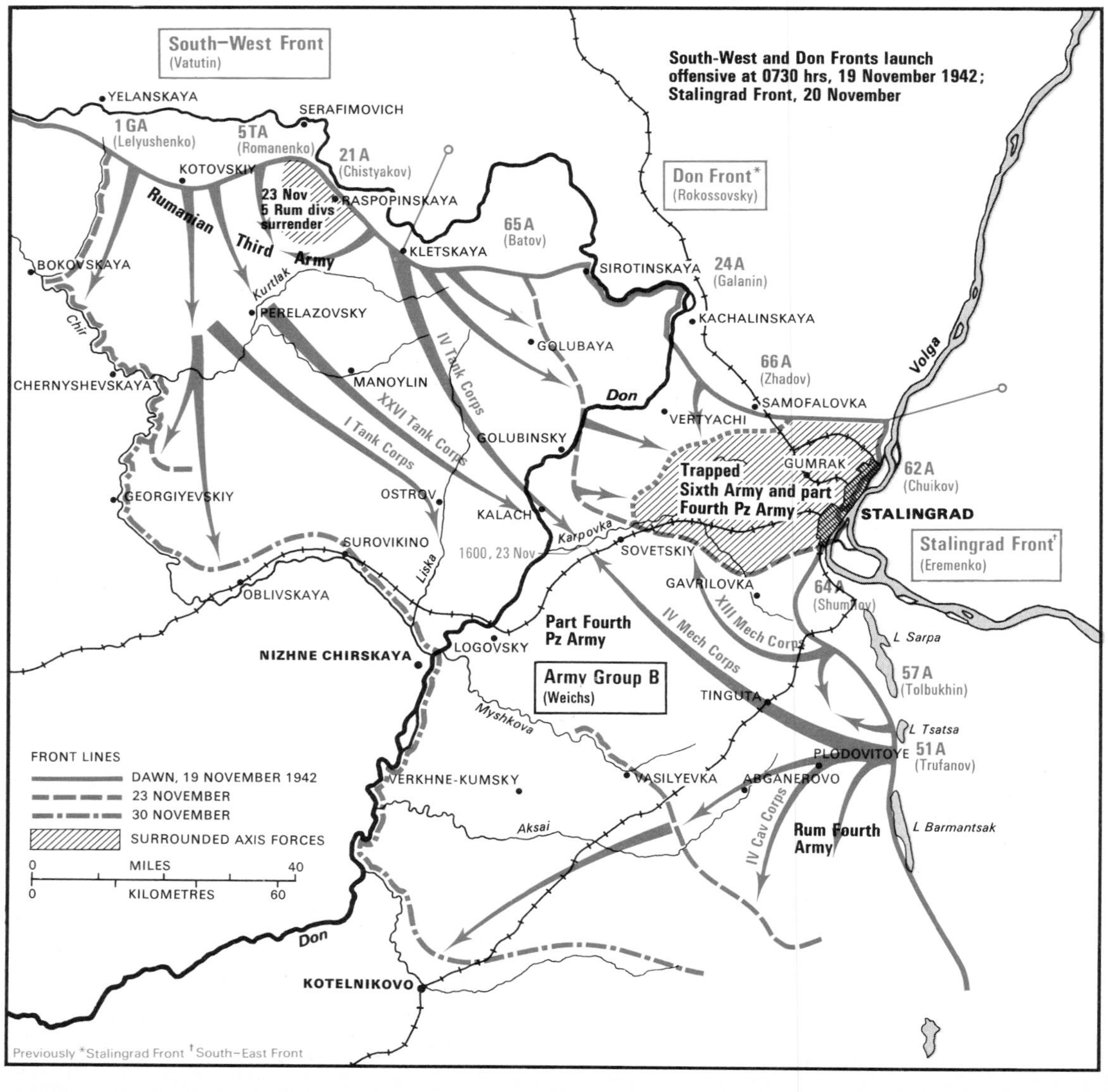

A veteran of a year fighting against the Russians waits for support in the lee of a building. Note that he has acquired a Soviet PPSh 41 sub-machine gun. These were simple weapons, but extremely reliable.

Stalingrad airlift

The trapped Sixth Army at Stalingrad, numbering about 300,000 men, needed supplies. Goering's Luftwaffe, having already successfully helped the troops in the Demyansk Pocket to survive, thought to try again – but with greater numbers to feed, and opposition considerably stronger, the result was very different.

Above: The major strength of the Luftwaffe transport Staffeln was provided by 'Tante Ju', the reliable old Ju 52/3m. More than 300 would be required to supply Stalingrad from the air, when at the best of times there were usually less than 100 available.

Right: The gigantic Messerschmitt Me 323 brought supplies as far as Rostov, but could not be risked over Stalingrad. They could carry considerable loads, an Opel Maultier and a light field howitzer being unloaded here.

Initially, no great concern was evinced for the safety of the quarter-million Wehrmacht troops surrounded at Stalingrad: German troops had frequently been isolated in the past, and had fought their way out. Remembering the successful air support provided at Demyansk, on 24 November the OKL gave orders for the trapped army to be supplied from the air, Goering informing Hitler that at least 300 tons of supplies could be flown in daily. Assuming a 50 per cent serviceability among the aircraft, this would have demanded the availability of around 300 Ju 52/3ms alone; in fact, there were immediately available no more than 70 such aircraft, of which only 25 were serviceable. In an attempt to make up the shortfall General von Richthofen appointed Oberst Dr Ernst Kühl (CO of the He 111 unit KG 55) to become Lufttransportführer 1, to take charge of all He 111s available for use as transports; some 250 aircraft, including obsolete He 111Ds and He 111Fs as well as the bomber He IIIHs and He-IIIPs, were thus employed.

During the first two days of the airlift no more than 65 tons of supplies were landed at Pitomnik and Tazinskaya, but with the arrival of the first He 111s, as well as another Gruppe of Ju 52/3ms, the daily total reached 100 tons by the end of the month. Early in December about 60 old Ju 86 transport and instrument trainers arrived, and between 19 and 21 December the transport aircraft succeeded in delivering to Pitomnik a total of 700 tons – the highest total achieved during the Battle of Stalingrad. The next day freezing fog blanketed the whole of the city and its airfields, preventing any flying, and on the 23rd Soviet shells began to erupt all over Tazinskaya; in desperation and utter confusion 108 Ju 52/3ms and Ju 86s scrambled into the air and hurried back to Novocherkassk and Rostov. The same day Russian tanks began to threaten the He 111 base at Morosovsk, and Kühl ordered his aircraft back to Novocherkassk.

Losses among the transport aircraft, as much from enemy action as from flying accidents in the atricous weather, so reduced the airlift that by the New Year the average daily tonnage of supplies delivered fell to little more than 140 tons.

On 2 January 1943 the Viermotorige Transportstaffel (four-engine transport squadron) was formed, with seven Ju 90s, two Ju 290s, a Ju 252 and an Fw 200B; 18 Fw 200Cs of KGrzbV 200 (previously part of I/KG 40) under Major Hans-Jürgen Williers joined the airlift, some aircraft landing at Pitomnik early on, but forced later to parachute supply containers to the trapped army. About 20 He 177A-3s of Fernkampfgruppe 2 also flew supply missions, but lost at least seven of their number due to engine failure. Other transport aircraft included such giants as the Me 321 glider and Me 323, though these huge aircraft were only used to deliver supplies as far as Rostov for onward transport by the Ju 52/3ms, Ju 86s and He 111s.

Between 25 November and 11 January the transport fleet flew 3,196 sorties, delivering a total of 8,500 tons of supplies, including 1,700 tons of fuel, 2,500 tons of food and 3,100 tons of ammunition – a paltry effort when compared with the achievement at Demyansk. During the final three weeks the total crept up to nearly 10,000 tons. On 16 January the airfield at Pitomnik fell to the Russians, and the last airfield, Gumrak, was captured on the 23rd.

On 31 January von Paulus surrendered, and two days later the last German gun fell silent to the north of the city. Losses had been prodigious, with nearly 120,000 Wehrmacht troops, as well as some 20,000 Italians and Romanians, killed; about 110,000 were taken into captivity by the Russians, fewer than 10,000 surviving to return home long after the war.

Disaster had befallen the Luftwaffe. Total aircraft losses amounted to around 700 aircraft out of 1,180 engaged around Stalingrad. These include 168 Heinkel He 111s, 276 Ju 52/3ms, and 41 Ju 86s. Neither the bomber nor transport arms of the Luftwaffe were ever again able to make good the heavy losses suffered in crews and aircraft.

---

that a new phase of the battle was about to begin. Later in the morning another bombardment crashed out, this time in the south – and the Sixth Army staff officers suddenly became acutely conscious of the weakness of their flanks, for these were held by Romanian armies, whose soldiers and commanders were not so dedicated to the destruction of Soviet Russia as themselves – nor so well armed, for the bulk of their weapons and vehicles had been captured in France two years before.

There was a leavening of German formations among them, of course, but even here there was some incipient weakness, for all their best officers, NCOs and men had long since been drawn into one or other of the recent offensives.

Three days later, the staff officers knew that their fears had been well founded. Along 50 miles in the north and 30 in the south, Zhukov's Shock Armies had broken the Romanian front into shards, driven all before them back over the Chir, captured intact the vital supply bridge at Kalach – and encircled Paulus and the remaining quarter of a million soldiers of Sixth Army. Now the besiegers were themselves besieged.

At first, of course, in both Berlin and Stalingrad the view was taken that an army of such size constituted a positive tactical advantage when behind enemy lines. Its reinforcement and supply was just a problem to be solved, and in the meantime the Red Army were faced with the difficulties of maintaining their encirclement and in doing so employing hundreds of thousands of men and guns which could not be put to use elsewhere.

Field Marshal Manstein, his Eleventh Army now incorporated into a new Army Group Don between B in the Don/Volga theatre and A down in the Caucasus, was given the task of correcting the predicament which had arisen as a result of Zhukov's counter-offensive. At first he felt that his best course

Above: Italian troops in action near Stalingrad before the great Soviet counter-attack. The Soviets soon recognized the fragility of the Romanian and Italian units.

Right: In spite of the best attempts of von Paulus and his army, the Soviet 62nd Army maintained several footholds on the west bank of the Volga, supported by artillery and Katyusha fire.

Left: The newly-promoted Field Marshal von Paulus and his staff after the surrender of the surviving remnants of the 6th Army. Hitler had promoted him after being told that no German Field Marshal had ever surrendered.

Right: This is what remained of the interior of the Krasny Oktyabr factory, after months of fighting. The complex changed hands several times during the battle, these Soviet troops are clearing the last pockets of German resistance.

would be to tempt the Russian armies westward away from Stalingrad, thus taking some of the pressure off Sixth Army and allowing Paulus room and time to organize a break-out to meet a drive up from the south by some of Hoth's panzer divisions; but Operation Winter Storm, launched on 21 December from the Don on each side of Kotelnikov, was solidly blocked on the Myshkova by Second Guards Army – and there seemed little inclination by Sixth Army commanders to order a break-out.

Then on 25 December Zhukov launched yet another attack, drove Hoth's army back beyond their starting point around Kotelnikov and the German forces to the north well back beyond both the Chir and the Aksay – and suddenly the distances separating the two German fronts were too great for supplies to get through to Paulus by land, while Richthofen was becoming more and more gloomy about the prospects of air support as the weather closed in. Paulus and his army were evidently in some danger. Could it be that Stalingrad was not quite so firmly in German hands as the Berlin propaganda machine had said?

As 1943 dawned, the German Sixth Army began desperately to protect itself with dense fortifications around an area some 30 miles from east to west and 20 from north to south. They were surrounded by 10 Soviet armies, and although some Red Army formations were guarding the distant borders against possible German relief columns, the main energies and attentions were directed against the pocket. On 8 January Lieutenant-General Rokossovsky, who had been given the task of destroying Sixth Army, sent in a proposal for its surrender, and when this was rejected began the last phase of the Battle of Stalingrad with a bombardment from thousands of guns and mortars, augmented by attacks by the bombers and ground-attack aircraft of Sixteenth Air Army.

By 17 January the area in German hands had been halved, by the 21st the last German airfield at Gumrak had been captured and the battle was being fought out again in the concrete tombs of Stalingrad – but with the roles reversed. By this time Sixth Army had been depleted by over 160,000 casualties of one category or another.

The last act was played out as January ended and February began. On 31 January the shell of the Central Department Store was captured and Paulus and his staff surrendered – unconsoled by the fact that Hitler had promoted Paulus to field marshal two days before; and on 2 February the remainder of the army laid down its arms. More than half the 300,000 men trapped in Stalingrad had been killed by the time of the surrender. A fortunate few, some 35,000, had been evacuated by air, but the surviving 90,000 men were herded to Siberia on foot. Many died on the march from cold and starvation, and the rest were condemned to a slow death in the mines and work camps. Many of those still alive in 1945 were never released, and only about 5,000 of the doomed army ever returned.

Left: Fresh Soviet infantrymen close in on the battered remnants of the German army. Note the number of PPSh sub-machine-guns, ideal for house-to-house fighting.

Above: Months of fighting left Stalingrad an almost surreal picture, with buildings destroyed, cellars opened up, holes through walls, any of which could conceal a hidden sniper, or from which a grenade could drop. It was a cruel, bitter struggle.

Chronology of War: 1942-1943

December 21
Eighth Army units reach Sirte. British and Indian troops advance towards Akyab in First Arakan campaign (Burma)

December 22
Red Army drives Germans back in Stalingrad, threatening Army Group B

December 23
Field Marshal von Manstein's Don Army Group is in danger from the Russian offensive while trying to relieve von Paulus and the 6th Army in Stalingrad

December 25
British Eighth Army moves into Sirte. Germans resist strongly on Longstop Hill in Tunisia

December 28
Hitler agrees to withdrawal of forces in Caucasus. Japanese withdraw from Buna

December 31
Russians advance past Kotelnikovo to reach Zimovniki. UK civilian casualties in December 109 killed, 201 injured. In Battle of the Barents Sea British destroyers foil attempt by German heavy units to get amongst convoy JW 51B

1943

January 1
Russian southern and south west fronts open offensive towards Rostov

January 3
Von Kleist's Army Group A withdraws from Caucasus

January 4
Japanese evacuation of Guadalcanal begins

January 5
Lt Gen Mark Clark appointed Commander 5th US Army

January 8
Surrender of German VI Army in Stalingrad demanded by Rokossovsky, commander of the Soviet Don Front

January 11
President Roosevelt requests war budget of $100,000,000,000

January 14
Casablanca Conference opens attended by Churchill, Roosevelt, and respective chiefs of staff

January 15
Eighth Army offensive against Buerat in Tripolitania

Luftwaffe aircraft in the East

The Luftwaffe's prime role had always been to provide close support for the German army and, as the titanic struggle on the Eastern front began to turn in favour of the Red Army, more dedicated ground attack aircraft were developed to try and stem the tide.

***Left:** The Messerschmitt Bf 110 was still operating in its original role as a heavy fighter and fighter-bomber in the second summer of the war in the East. This machine operated over the Caucasus in October 1942.*

***Above:** A Messerschmitt Bf 109G of 4./JG 54 'Grunherz' operating out of Siverskaya on the northern sector of the Eastern Front in the summer of 1942 where German endeavours to take Leningrad continued while the lunge at the Caucasus was under way.*

***Right:** a Focke-Wulf Fw 189 Uhu (owl) army co-operation and tactical reconnaissance aircraft seen in the winter colours worn while operating from the Rostov area in support of von Paulus and his doomed 6th Army at Stalingrad.*

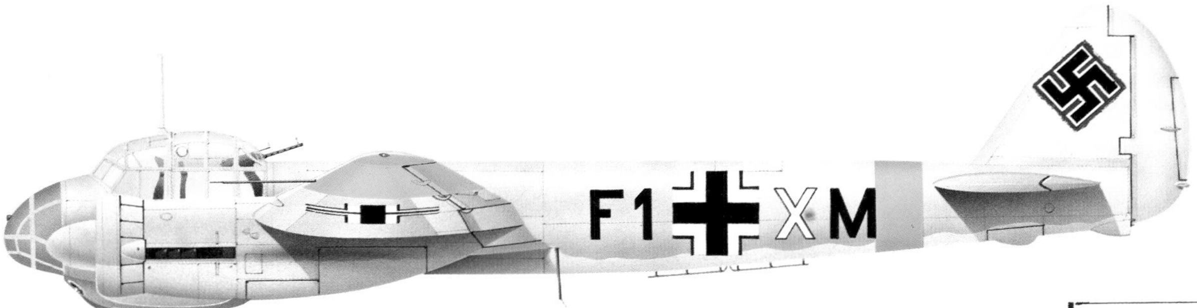

***Left:** The Junkers Ju 88 was a very adaptable design, being produced in a number of variants. The first fighters were converted from bomber airframes on the production line, but were soon being built from the start as heavily-armed Zerstörers. This is a Ju 88C-6, which operated in the Ukraine in late 1942 with a dummy glazed nose to fool attacking fighters.*

***Right:** In early 1943 the Germans introduced the most powerful tank-busting aircraft yet seen to deal with the ever-growing Soviet tank formations. Heavily armoured, and carrying a 75-mm anti-tank gun, the Henschel Hs 129B-2 made its combat debut in the massive armoured battles in the Kursk salient that summer.*

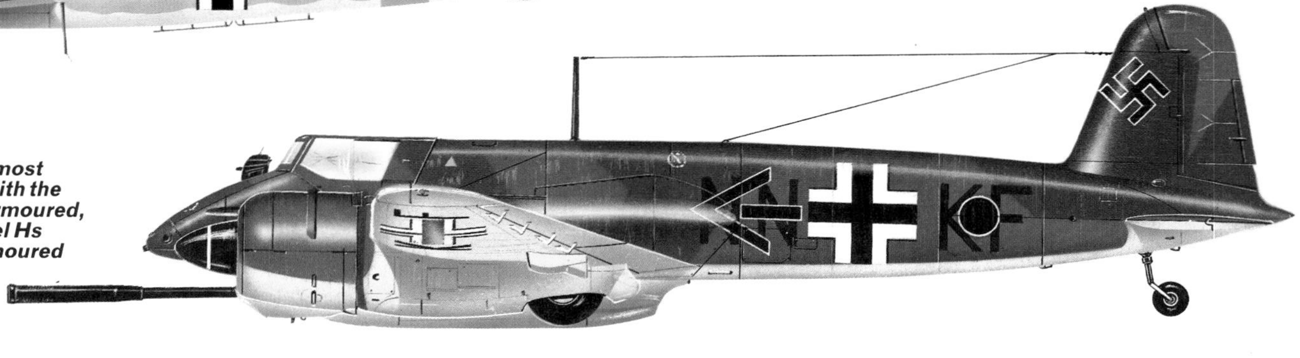

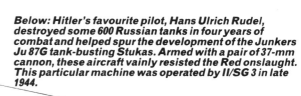

***Below:** Hitler's favourite pilot, Hans Ulrich Rudel, destroyed some 600 Russian tanks in four years of combat and helped spur the development of the Junkers Ju 87G tank-busting Stukas. Armed with a pair of 37-mm cannon, these aircraft vainly resisted the Red onslaught. This particular machine was operated by II/SG 3 in late 1944.*

Left: KV (Klimenti Voriloshov) heavy tanks pound their way forward at Kursk. Although T-34s formed the bulk of Soviet tank strength in 1943, KV-1s were to play an important part.

Above: An SS officer is seen during Manstein's brilliantly executed counter-attack at Kharkov, which was destined to be the last major German victory on the Eastern Front.

Left: The Soviet T-34 was so much better than contemporary German machines that captured examples were pressed into front line service by the Wehrmacht.

Below: Panzer VI Tiger tanks make their ponderous way through the spring rain to join the tank units assembling near Kursk.

If Stalingrad was the coffin of Germans hopes of victory, Kursk was the hammer which nailed the lid down.

The Russian winter still gripped the land when Paulus and his army surrendered, so this fact and Red Army elation at their victory tempted them into widespread attacks wherever the German line could be penetrated, followed by intoxicating advances of spectacular speed and depth.

On 26 January they recovered Voronezh; by 8 February they were through Kursk and driving for the railway at Suzemka; a week later they had liberated Kharkov and two weeks after that they were at Pavlograd, only 25 miles from the Dnieper – and quite close to Hitler, who was paying a flying visit to Zaporozhye.

Manstein strikes back

Then the iron laws of logistics forced themselves upon Russian attentions, and the leading formations found that they were separated by miles of devastated country from their bases, that the Red Army staffs lacked experience of feeding huge, rapidly advancing armies – and that their enemies were now reorganized and well supplied, poised to cut them to pieces.

Manstein sprang his first trap on 20 February, and on the day that the forward Russian patrols reached Pavlograd, panzers were driving up the west bank of the Donetz behind them to smash into the flank of the Third Soviet Tank Army and destroy it. By 3 March the Russians had been forced to abandon nearly 6,000 square miles of their recent gains; by the middle of the month, Kharkov and Belgorod were back in German hands; and by the end of the month, the line had stabilized – running from just west of Rostov in the south, up to Velikiye-Luki west of Moscow, then

German armoured fighting vehicles at Kursk

Hitler's determination to launch an offensive against the Kursk salient overrode all the arguments against the operation, and to bolster the attack new vehicles just entering production were hastily rushed to the front before their teething problems had been overcome.

*Left: Mounting the new PAK 43 8.8-cm gun, some 90 **Elefant** tank destroyers were employed for the first time at Kursk where their unreliable engines proved a source of constant anxiety to their crews. Worse, the vehicle had no machine-guns and could not defend itself against Soviet infantrymen armed with anti-tank weapons.*

*Above: The **Sturmgeschutz III** assault gun was cheaper and quicker to manufacture than a tank and by 1943 the assault gun battalions were being employed as substitute armour. The limited gun traverse was a serious disadvantage when on the offensive.*

An SKfz 251/6 ammunition carrier halftrack supplies 88-mm shells to a Tiger tank. The corrugated surface of the tank is a coating of Zimmeritt anti-magnetic paste to prevent enemy infantry fixing magnetic mines to the hull.

*Built in response to the indescribably bad road conditions in Russia, the **Maultier** (mule) was an Opel truck with the rear axle replaced by a new assembly using tracks and wheels of the obsolete Panzer II light tank.*

*Left: The **Panzerkampfwagen V Panther** is often described as the best tank of World War II, and its balance of mobility, firepower and protection has been the inspiration behind two generations of post-war Western tanks. However, its combat debut at Kursk was disastrous, the very first production vehicles being rushed into action where they proved (not surprisingly) mechanically unreliable and disagreeably inflammable.*

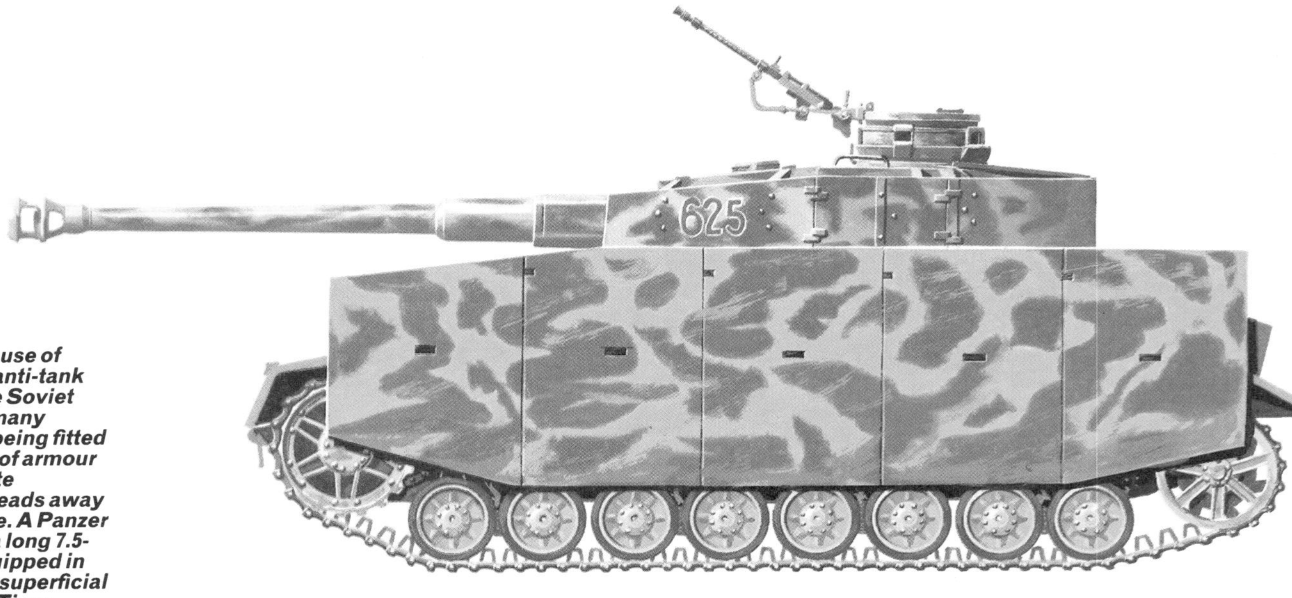

Panzer IV

The increasing use of hollow charge anti-tank weapons by the Soviet infantry led to many German tanks being fitted with thin skirts of armour plate to detonate incoming warheads away from the vehicle. A Panzer IV armed with a long 7.5-cm gun and equipped in this way bore a superficial likeness to the Tiger heavy tanks.

Troops and tanks of SS Division 'Totenkopf' head into the cauldron of the Kursk salient in July 1943. The greatest tank battle in history, it was also one of the greatest air battles.

Above: A T-34 lies blazing at Kursk, where German tank losses soon began to spiral upwards in the face of concentrated anti-tank gun batteries.

Right: Knocked-out T-34s in their green summer paint scheme are examined by curious German soldiers.

up to Leningrad – but with a huge salient jutting 50 miles westwards in front of Kursk, from just north of Belgorod up to the line of Ponyri.

This was the bulge on the map which drew all German eyes during the weeks which followed. It stuck out far more awkwardly than any sore thumb, and positively invited attack; not only would its removal flatten the line of the front, but it would provide a sound strategic base for a drive deep into Russia which would show the world that the German army was still the most powerful factor in the world.

The plan for Operation Zitadelle was quite simple. From the district around Orel, Ninth Army Group Centre would drive down through Ponyri towards Kursk, to meet Fourth Panzer Army (still commanded by Hoth) and Group Kempff from Army Group South driving up from just south of Belgorod. Fifty divisions, 16 of them panzer or motorized, containing 900,000 men would make up the original strike force, with 20 more divisions waiting to support or exploit their efforts. Ten thousand guns and 2,700 tanks and assault guns – including all the Tigers and Ferdinands available – would support the ground battle, while in the air 2,000 aircraft from the most famous bomber and fighter squadrons in the Luftwaffe would keep the skies clear of the enemy.

Everyone was as well-trained and properly briefed as was possible, the best and most experienced soldiers from the entire Wehrmacht had been concentrated into the attack area; as General Mellenthin was to write, 'No offensive was ever prepared as carefully as this one.' Hitler's order for the operation ended, 'Victory at Kursk will be a beacon for the whole world.'

There was thus considerable disquiet throughout the Wehrmacht when at 2 a.m. on 5 July – an hour before their own opening barrage was due to launch the great offensive – hundreds of Soviet guns opened up and blanketed the German assembly area, killing

Left: The distinctive silhouette of a Soviet PPsh sub-machine-gun in German hands. These brutally simple Russian SMGs became very popular with the Wehrmacht.

Right: The majority of the 2,700 tanks assembled for Operation Zitadelle were Panzer IIIs and IVs, which suffered heavy losses from the massed Russian anti-tank guns.

Below: A Russian anti-tank gun in action opens fire. At Kursk they were grouped into batteries which fired volleys at individual German tanks.

Chronology of War: 1943

January 16
British outflank Buerat. Australian offensive in Sananander sector of New Guinea

January 18
Siege of Leningrad broken by Red Army. Germans use Pzkpfw VI 'Tiger' tanks for the first time in Tunisia

January 19
Eighth Army reaches Homs and Tarhuna to the east of Tripoli. Russians advance in central and south areas. Japanese retreat from Sananander on New Guinea

January 23
Eighth Army moves into Tripoli. Casablanca Conference ends; Roosevelt states Allies aim as 'Unconditional Surrender' of Axis

January 26
Russians capture Voronezh on the Don due east of Kursk, taking 52,000 prisoners

January 27
US 8th Air Force makes first bombing attack on Germany, attacking Wilhelmshaven

January 31
Field Marshal von Paulus surrenders at Stalingrad. UK civilian casualties in January 328 killed, 507 injured

February 1
Japanese evacuation of Guadalcanal completed

February 2
With the surrender of XI Corps, all German forces in Stalingrad have capitulated. German casualties since August 1942: 110,000 dead, 50,000 wounded and 107,000 prisoners. Soviet casualties (including civilians) exceed 1 million

hundreds of waiting troops, wrecked important communication networks, destroyed quite a few guns and panzers and made it abundantly evident that the Red Army knew of all their preparations, and were waiting for them.

It had been, to a great extent, the work of one man and his immediate confederates. Rudolf Rössler and his colleagues of what became known as the Lucy Ring in Switzerland had been supplying Moscow with German military intelligence of a high order for so many months that now their information was implicitly believed – and rightly so. By the end of June the commanders of Central Front (Rokossovsky), Voronezh Front (Vatutin) and Steppe Front (Koniev) knew almost exactly the forces which would be ranged against them, what their immediate objectives were and when they would strike.

Moreover, all this information had been coming in over quite a long time, and every opportunity had been given the Russian commanders to prepare their defences. In the north, Model's Ninth Army would run headlong into the Soviet Thirteenth Army with the Forty-eighth and Seventieth Armies on each side, while in the south Hoth's panzers and Kempf's motorized infantry faced the Sixth Guards Army with the Seventh Guards Army on their left – all ready and waiting, all dug in behind belt after belt of murderous anti-tank defences which first channelled the panzer formations into killing grounds, and then demolished them.

The Battle of Kursk was undoubtedly the greatest tank battle in history. At one time it would seem that over 3,000 tanks were manoeuvring on the battlefield, and German losses on that first day were reminiscent of those on the Western Front in 1916. By nightfall 25,000 men were killed in the northern battle alone, 200 panzers were knocked out and 220 German aircraft shot down – and the days which followed increased the cost proportionately. Whole regiments were wiped out, batteries destroyed, squadrons crushed, before the leading formations broke clear of the defence belts, only to run into the waiting Russian infantry and armoured formations.

By 12 July Model's army had penetrated a mere 10 miles towards Ponyri, while Hoth's panzer army had reached the Prokhorovka area, only 20 miles from their start line; then the huge Soviet counter-offensive began. By 23 July the Germans were all back out of the salient, by 5 August Orel and Belgorod were again in Soviet hands and on 23 August Kharkov was at last permanently relieved.

Operation Zitadelle had been a disastrous failure of German arms, and never again were they to appear to the watching world as anything but a dogged and courageous army, retreating before an ever more powerful antagonist towards inevitable defeat.

***Below:** T-34s of Vatutin's Voronezh front advance to drive the Fourth Panzer Army back and eventually to retake Kharkov, signifying the utter failure of the German plan.*

***Right:** SS troops try to relax after action. Such was the strength of the prepared Russian positions at Kursk that the German attack was doomed to fail.*

Chapter 13

Victory in the Desert

As Rommel retreated from the Alamein battlefield he received news that Allied troops had landed at the opposite end of North Africa, in Morocco and Algeria. The Vichy French garrisons fought against the Allied invasion force, but once Hitler sent troops into the unoccupied zone of metropolitan France the Vichy units ended their opposition and the way was clear for a pincer movement against the Axis army in North Africa.

On 8 November 1942, Anglo-American armies were landed on the north coast of Africa between Casablanca and Algiers in an operation which still commands incredulity when its details are examined, even though such enterprises as the Sicily and D-Day landings, the war in Korea, the Six-Day war and the Falklands conflict have taken place since.

A fleet of 102 ships, including 29 transports carrying 35,000 American soldiers with all their impedimenta, had crossed the 4,000 miles of the Atlantic to Casablanca; another task-force carrying 39,000 American soldiers and escorted by Royal Naval escorts had left the Clyde on 26 October, passed through the Straits of Gibraltar and landed at Oran while a third which had left the Clyde at the same time went on to land at Algiers. This third force carried 23,000 British and 10,000 American, and some 160 Royal Navy ships had acted as cover down the Atlantic and into the Mediterranean to the 250 merchantmen carrying the forces from the Clyde; only one transport of the entire joint fleet had been lost to enemy action, the men aboard quickly being transferred to landing-ships which took them ashore.

By the end of the first day at Algiers the men were all ashore despite a brisk resistance from French marines and native troops during the first attempt to storm the port. At Oran the plan to encircle the city had gone well, the troops had all disembarked but by evening it was becoming evident that the French troops were organizing for strong defence to follow. At Casablanca, although the landings had all been virtually unopposed – to the surprise of their charismatic commander, Major-General George Patton – some confusions had delayed their deployment and by the end of the second day a combination of maladministration and growing French opposition seemed likely to block expansion of the bridgehead.

One of the great imponderables of the entire operation had been, from the beginning, the extent of opposition which might be expected from the French. After centuries of Anglo-French antagonisms, exacerbated by the destruction of the French fleet by the Royal Navy at Oran and Mers El Kebir after the Fall of France in 1940 – plus the attacks on French positions at Dakar and Syria – it was considered unlikely that even the grim realities of German occupation would persuade the French to lay down their arms and welcome British soldiers as liberators. But the relationships between France and the USA had been close since the days of Lafayette, and many American troops and their commanders expected something more in the manner of brass bands and flag-waving to greet their appearance, than the doubtful approaches and occasional shots which occurred during the first hours.

Attempts had been made to clarify the situation before the landings – Major-General Mark Clark had been smuggled ashore by British Commandos and had talked to the French General Mast, commander of the troops in the Algiers sector, while the chief American diplomatic representative in North Africa, Robert Murphy, had tried sounding out French military opinion throughout the whole theatre. But such investigations must by their very nature be tentative, and security demanded that the Americans gave very little specific information to men who might have been attempting to entrap them, and who would in any case remain under German control and even in their hands when the questioning was over.

As a result, the landings came as almost as much as a surprise to General Mast and his associates (who genuinely wanted to help as much as they could) as to the remainder of the French forces. These all certain-

After the Battle of Alamein and Operation Torch, victory in North Africa was all but assured. Here a mechanic confidently guides a taxiing Kittyhawk during a sandstorm in the desert.

US troops come ashore at Arzan near the port of Oran. It was hoped that French units would be more reluctant to engage American troops, but each Allied landing was opposed.

Chronology of War: 1943

February 4
Eighth Army forward units enter Tunisia

February 6
Red Army reaches Sea of Azov, cutting off part of von Kleist's German Army Group A

February 8
Russians liberate Kursk, trapping the German 2nd Army in a pocket

February 14
German counterattack in Tunisia against Allied First Army. Chindits cross river Chindwin in Burma. Russian south front takes Rostov at the mouth of the Don

February 16
Red Army liberates Kharkov and Voroshilovgrad on the Voronezh and south west fronts. Eighth Army reaches Mareth Line in Tunisia

February 19
Germans break through Kasserine Pass, mauling the American II Corps of the Allied 1st Army

February 20
Eighth Army takes Medenine

February 25
Allied troops recover Kasserine Pass

February 27
German attack at Hunt's Gap, Tunisia

February 28
Norwegian commandos destroy heavy water installation at Norsk Hydro, depriving Germans of raw material for A-bomb research. UK civilian casualties in February 252 killed, 347 injured

March 2-5
In Battle of the Bismarck Sea Allied aircraft and torpedo boats shatter Japanese re-inforcement convoy off Lae (New Guinea)

March 6
Afrika Korps attack on Medenine repulsed with heavy losses. Rommel leaves Africa

March 17
Japanese attack in Arakan, Burma

March 20
Eighth Army attacks Mareth Line in Tunisia

March 28
Eighth Army breaks through at Mareth and take Toujane and Matmata

March 29
Eighth Army occupies Gabes and El Hamma

March 30
British retreat in Arakan peninsula, Burma

March 31
UK civilian casualties in March 293 killed, 439 injured

April 6
Eighth Army attacks at Wadi Akarit

April 8
British and American patrols meet in Tunisia

April 12
Eighth Army reaches Sousse

April 14
Eighth Army reaches Enfidaville line

April 18
Admiral Yamamoto killed over Bougainville when aircraft shot down by American P-38s of the 339th Squadron operating from Henderson Field, Guadalcanal

April 21
Eighth Army takes Enfidaville

April 26
Longstop Hill, Tunisia, captured by First Army

Operation Torch

The landings in North Africa were a remarkable success; no amphibious landing on such a scale had been attempted before, and yet the invasion force came ashore with the loss of only a single ship to enemy action. The Germans responded with customary efficiency; reinforcements poured into Tunisia from Sicily but the scales of the North African campaign had been tipped irrevocably in favour of the Allies.

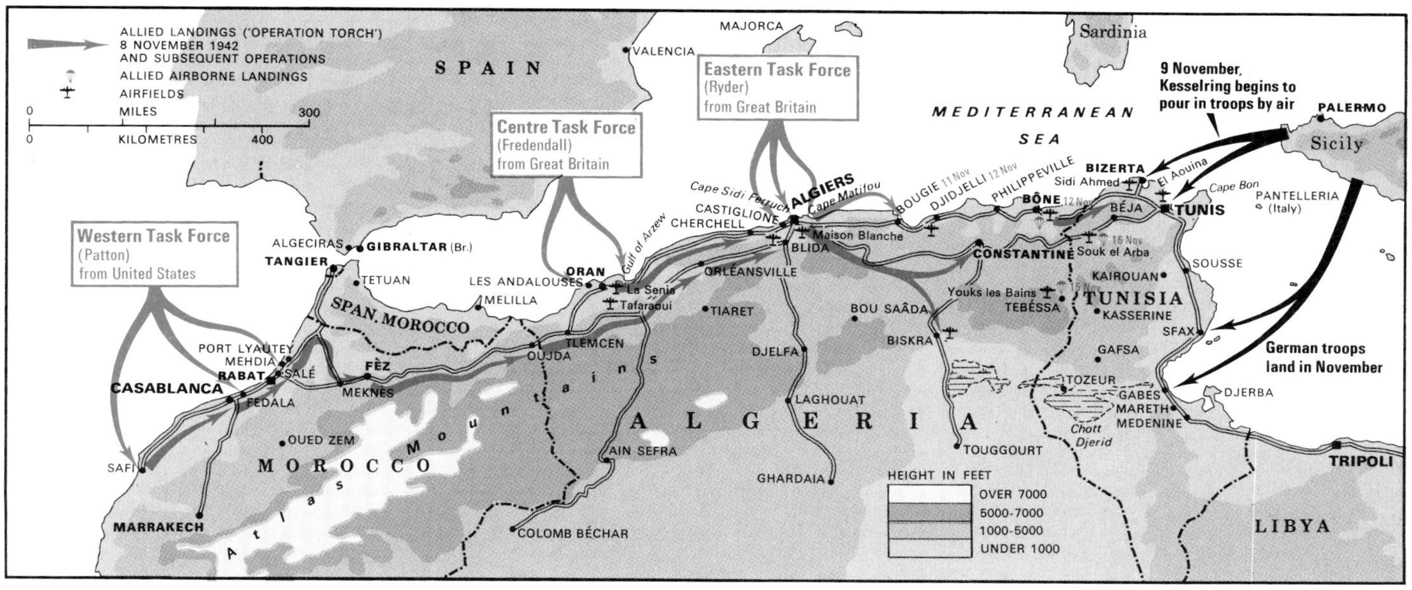

ly disliked the German occupation, but they were unsure of where their real responsibilities lay and as a result their resistance during the first few days was patchy – sometimes fierce, sometimes hesitant, but never prolonged – owing to their commanders' doubts while they awaited orders from some properly constituted authority.

That authority was vested in Marshal Pétain, but by a piece of astonishing good fortune for the Allies his deputy, Admiral Darlan, was in Algiers visiting his son who had recently contracted poliomyelitis. The Admiral's immediate reaction was not promising ('I have known for a long time that the British were stupid, but I always believed the Americans were more intelligent') and his reputation as collaborator with the Nazis would have made him a most unwelcome ally had he not been so important – but by a combination of diplomacy and straightforward bullying, Mark Clark persuaded him that his best course of action would be co-operation, and at 11.20 on the morning of 10 November he ordered an end to all French resistance in North Africa.

French loyalties

Generally he was obeyed in Morocco and Algeria, though the extraordinary rapidity of the German reaction in Tunisia held up matters there – but the whole picture clarified when the news came in that Hitler's infuriated reaction to the Anglo-American landings had been to order German troops to move into the Unoccupied Zone of southern France, which they did on 11 November. This, in the opinion of the French Command in North Africa, relieved them of their pledge of obedience to Marshal Pétain who they judged, quite rightly, would now be acting under duress: from then on the Allied moves went smoothly. By 12 November British airborne forces had been dropped at Bône and had captured the airfield there, five days later they had advanced to Souk el Arba, 300 miles east of Algiers, while the 503rd US Parachute Regiment had dropped at Youks les Bains nearly 100 miles to the south and within two days had taken Gafsa airfield inside Tunisia.

Behind them, American troops had shaken out and were moving up, Lieutenant-General Kenneth Anderson had landed and taken command of the British First Army, who were commandeering every piece of transport they could find in order to lift supporting units forward to help the airborne formations – and everyone was now facing up to the unusual, indeed extraordinary, geographical realities with which they were faced. The distance from Casablanca to Tunis is 1,274 miles, and the road system throughout the entire theatre to which the invasion force was committed – over a million square miles! – was rudimentary, and neither sufficiently well constructed nor diverse enough to carry heavy military traffic; only one narrow-gauge and somewhat dilapidated railway line wound its uncertain way between the various town and ports.

It was evident that a taxing and monumental effort lay ahead of everyone – and within a week it also became obvious that some very tough fighting awaited them as well. Already the Luftwaffe was making things very difficult in the country east of Algiers, and then news came that German and Italian troops were pouring into Tunisia; there would be no easy victory there. Nevertheless, optimism reigned: the landings had been accomplished at trifling loss of either men or material, the locals were certainly not hostile, by the end of the first week the French were co-operating fully and claiming that they were more than will-

A Grumman F4F Wildcat is flagged off the deck of USS Ranger to attack French military installations in North Africa. Ranger was the first purpose-built US aircraft-carrier, completed in 1934.

The garrison of French North Africa was mostly equipped with obsolete equipment like this World War I Renault FT light tank.

April 30
New convoy protection command formed in Atlantic. UK civilian casualties in April 173 killed, 204 injured

May 8
British and US forces reach Tunis and Bizerta

May 10
First Allied Army cuts off Cape Bon Peninsula

May 12
General von Arnim surrenders with bulk of Axis forces in North Africa. Second Washington Conference starts

May 17
RAF Lancasters of 617 Squadron breach Möhne and Eder dams in 'Dambuster's' raid

May 30
Churchill and de Gaulle arrive in Algiers. UK civilian casualties in May 584 killed, 733 injured

June 9
Allies announce 291,000 Axis prisoners taken in North Africa

June 14
RAF 2nd Tactical Air Force formed in UK

June 16
Japanese lose 100 aircraft over Guadalcanal

June 18
Field Marshal Wavell appointed Viceroy of India; General Auchinleck made C-in-C

June 20
Japanese launch attack in New Guinea

June 25
Allies bombing targets in Sicily

June 30
Operation Cartwheel; amphibious operations against Japanese positions in Solomons. UK civilian casualties in June 201 killed, 285 injured

***Left:** The natural alternative to barbed wire – cacti! Italian gunners pose by their anti-tank gun amid spiky Tunisian cover. Their line of retreat must have been interesting.*

A Daimler armoured car fires on enemy positions outside Tripoli which fell to the British on 23 January 1943. The next day Rommel was replaced by General Giovanni Messe as Axis commander in North Africa.

ing to fight the Germans once they were given modern arms – and from the other end of the North African coast came news that the Eighth Army was now in hot pursuit of Rommel's Panzerarmee and the famous Afrika Korps.

Perhaps First and Eighth Armies would meet somewhere in Libya by Christmas?

The hounding of Rommel

The German defences at Alamein had been punctured on the morning of 4 November, and by the following day there was no disguising the fact, even from Hitler, that the Afrika Korps was in full flight. A flimsy defence line at Fuka was brushed contemptuously aside by Eighth Army early that day, and a long line of fleeing Axis transport, packed with depressed Germans and thoroughly disheartened Italians, snaked back westward – easy targets for the RAF.

Then on 6 November Fate seemed momentarily to relent. Heavy rain fell, relieving Rommel's hard-pressed men of attentions from the air, slowing the pursuit and thus giving the German officers time to effect a little re-organization. By 8 November some sort of defence existed south of Mersa Matruh and morale, among the Germans at least, rose sharply when the paratroops of General Ramcke's Brigade, who everybody thought had been wiped out in the fighting south of Ruweisat Ridge, arrived after an epic march across the desert. They reported, moreover, that the British did not appear to be attempting a flank march in the south to cut the Axis escape route.

But this relief did not last long. Later that day came new of the Allied landings in Morocco and Algiers, and Rommel knew that if anything were to be saved of his army he must get it back as quickly as possible towards an escape port at Tripoli. Gone, therefore, were German plans to make a stand at Halfaya or Gazala – gone in fact were all ideas but to get back to El Agheila, twice already the backstop to which Axis forces had fallen.

Rommel moved fast and efficiently. By 20 November his army was there – minefields in position, stores brought down from a gutted Benghazi before final evacuation, left flank on the sea, right flank on the deep gorge of Wadi Faregh; and on 12 December, after what seemed an over-cautious follow-up, the British attacked the outposts after a heavy bombardment, drove them in and followed with an apparently even greater hesitancy. Hopes and speculations arose in German breasts – had the British outrun their supplies? Then one of the German reconnaissance planes spotted a column of almost 300 vehicles sneaking past down south of the Wadi Faregh, and Rommel had the feeling that not only was his army outfought, but that he himself was being out-manoeuvred.

When Eighth Army realized that Rommel was now pulling out of El Agheila, their last remaining doubts vanished. This time they were not to be sent reeling back, this time they were going forward to the end – and in steady, methodical advance which brooked no resistance, 7th Armoured Division drove forward through mixed German and Italian rearguards, 2nd New Zealand Division curved up from their flanking march, driving in Rommel's screens to reach the coast, while all the time the main Axis force retired, just as methodically, to the next defensive line at Buerat. On Christmas Day, though they were quite a long way from a link-up with First Army, Eighth Army patrols pushed forward into Sirte.

Here General Montgomery spent some time reorganizing his supply lines, and it was not until 15 January 1943 that he sent his divisions forward again – 7th Armoured and 2nd New Zealand swinging around the southern flank of the Buerat position, 51st Highland pressing in front. It was a repeat of the El Agheila tactic, and again Rommel held the flank attack until his main force was clear of the trap. But this time there was to be no let-up after the retreat, for Montgomery recognized quite clearly that behind Rommel now was an excellent defensive position in the hills of the Djebel Nefusa along the Homs-Tarhuna line – indeed Rommel had wanted to retreat to these positions from El Agheila, but Hitler had forbidden so distant a withdrawal.

Montgomery was determined not to be held up here and he switched his tactics. As Rommel sent a screen southwards to guard against the flanking attack which had so far manoeuvred him out of two positions, the weight of the British attack switched abruptly to the north. The 51st Highland Division with the 22nd Armoured Brigade in close attendance smashed straight forward into Homs on 19 January, and then on into Tripoli by the 23rd. Rommel had been 'bounced' out of a good position.

Mediterranean strategy

In the meantime, matters had been taking unexpected turns elsewhere in the Mediterranean theatre.

The startling rapidity with which the German command reacted to Operation Torch has already been mentioned; within two days German troops were occupying commanding positions along the perimeter of a bridgehead effectively guarding Bizerta

***Left:** A US B-25 bomber lands at El Aouina airport, Tunisia, which is littered with the remains of German Junkers Ju 52 transport aircraft.*

German halftracks

The German army used a wide variety of half-tracked vehicles during World War II and they served in every theatre of operations, although some of them became synonymous with the Afrika Korps. Initially introduced as artillery prime movers and recovery vehicles, half-tracks were soon used for an incredible variety of tasks.

SdKfz 7

This 8-ton half-track became famous as the usual prime mover for the 88-mm gun. Over 3,000 of these vehicles were in service by 1942, and the British were so impressed that Bedford Motors was ordered to make a direct copy for evaluation.

The combination which destroyed so many British tanks in the desert war: a Flak 18 88-mm gun and its SdKfz 7 half-track. The vehicle could carry 12 men and their kit plus ammunition.

The diminutive Kettenrad was originally developed as an air-portable vehicle to tow the 37-mm anti-tank guns of the parachute units. It was often used to bring supplies up to front-line troops.

SdKfz 251

The SdKfz 251 series was developed as an offshoot of the German half-tracked artillery tractor series to provide an armoured personnel carrier for infantry accompanying the newly-formed panzer divisions. This is one of the more numerous variants, the SdKfz 251/1, which could carry up to 12 soldiers and was armed with two MG 34 machine-guns. By the end of the war 22 discrete models of the SdKfz 251 were serving with the German army.

SdKfz 9

The 18 ton SdKfz 9 was the largest half-track produced by the Germans. It entered service before the war as a tank recovery vehicle and a prime mover for heavy artillery pieces like the Krupp K 38 210-mm gun.

SdKfz 11

The SdKfz 11 was a light vehicle weighing only 3 tons, and served to tow medium field artillery such as the 105-mm howitzer or 50- and 75-mm anti-tank guns. Like most German half-tracks it also formed the basis for self-propelled anti-aircraft guns.

A US M-10 tank destroyer enters Bir Marbatt pass, Tunisia. The American conception of a lightly-protected tank destroyer proved a failure, but nearly 5,000 of these vehicles had been built by the end of 1942 and they served until 1945.

and Tunis, and other forces were flooding ashore in the south to protect Sfax and Gabés. By the time the main Allied forces had arrived forward to support the gallant but frail airborne thrusts, German battalions were solidly in position, soon to be immeasurably helped by torrential winter rains which effectively swept away all chances of an early Allied advance eastwards, either to the Tunisian coastline or even around the corner into Tripolitania.

Another disappointment for the Allies was the fact that the powerful French fleet, for so long inactive in their main base at Toulon, had not sailed out to join the Allied navies in their fight against Hitler. Admiral de Labord was far too loyal to Marshal Pétain to move without his direct order, and in the absence of such an order he ignored a suggestion cabled to him from Darlan that he should sail his fleet to Oran. On the other hand, he had no intention of allowing his command to fall into Hitler's hands. When German forces moved into the Unoccupied Zone he gave orders for scuttling charges to be brought to readiness in every ship under his command, and when on 27 November elements of three panzer divisions swept down on Toulon naval establishment, the order 'Scuttle! Scuttle! Scuttle!' was flashed from the masthead of practically every ship in the dockyard.

Seventy-three ships, including one battleship, two battle-cruisers, seven cruisers, twenty-nine destroyers and sixteen submarines, went to the bottom of the harbour where they remained until the war was practically over – and they did not fight on the Allied side.

One positive development for the Allies, however, was the holding of the Casablanca Conference. Winston Churchill and his advisers left England in a Liberator on 12 January and arrived the following day, President Roosevelt flew in on 14 January with his staff, and within two more days both General Eisenhower, appointed Supreme Commander Operation Torch, and General Alexander, soon to take operational command of all troops in the theatre, had arrived.

The Conference lasted until 23 January and the outcome was remarkable – far better than anyone had thought likely, or even possible, at the beginning. Agreement was quickly reached that the immediate strategic priority was the defeat of the U-boats, especially those operating against the Atlantic convoys bearing the build-up of American troops for the Second Front, whenever that should prove possible. Sicily should be the next objective as soon as North Africa was finally liberated of all Axis forces, the air war against Occupied Europe was to be stepped up by both the RAF and USAAF – and the eventual defeat of Nazi Germany was confirmed as the first main objective.

Nevertheless, an autumn campaign was to be opened by the British against the Japanese in Burma, and the US Navy Commander-in-Chief, Admiral Ernest J. King, who believed deeply that Japan was the main enemy and should be the prior target, was given permission to undertake operations against the Marshall and Caroline Islands.

But for the moment, the immediate task was to clear the Axis out of Africa.

Caught in the pincer

Logistics were still posing enormous problems. By the end of January Eighth Army was 200 miles past Tripoli but its main supply base was still the Delta, and the distance from Tripoli to Cairo was nearly as far as that from Whitehall to the Kremlin. Benghazi was now in full use as a port, but until Tripoli was in like shape supplies for the forward divisions had to travel along a single road stretching for 705 miles – the distance from London to Vienna. Already, Montgomery had been forced to strip all transport from the reserve corps in order to keep the forward corps sufficiently mobile to rebuff Rommel should the latter suddenly attack, and it came as some relief to Eighth Army when they heard that instead he had turned his attention to the US 1st Armoured Division at Kasserine Pass in Tunisia.

It proved a bitter introduction to battle for the GIs, who were as unprepared for it as the British had been in Cyrenaica on two previous occasions. Between 14 and 22 February, the Axis forces in Tunisia, now under the overall command of General Sixt von Arnim, came close to success in an attempt to break the separate jaws of the Allied vice which were closing in on them by a lightning attack on the US 2nd Corps, spread between the passes at Gafsa, Faid and Fondouk.

Faid was taken by 21st Panzer Division, who then enticed the US armour forward and destroyed over 100 of their tanks with the same tactics which had wrecked so many British onslaughts – tempting them

Above: A Jagdpanzer 38(t) Hetzer is knocked out by an American armed with a 2.75-in anti-tank rocket launcher. The simplicity and effectiveness of the 'Bazooka' impressed the Germans and they soon produced similar weapons themselves.

Right: No. 60 Squadron's Hawker Hurricane Mk IIDs armed with two 40-mm anti-tank cannon taxi out for take-off. These weapons could easily penetrate the thin top armour of most German tanks in North Africa.

Tank killing-ground at Medenine

The way the desert war had changed in the 12 months since the German victories of early 1942 was graphically illustrated by the fate of Rommel's counterattack at Medenine. The familiar tank tactics of the Afrika Korps met with bloody defeat at the hands of a well co-ordinated British defence.

After the long advance across the desert the British Eighth Army had been halted at Medenine. The original Allied objective had been to link up the Eighth Army advancing from the east with the First Army that was advancing from the west following the successful Allied landings in North West Africa during Operation Torch. When the halt at Medenine was made the two Allied armies were still some 250 miles apart, but if the two could join they would form a ring that would contain the Axis forces in Tunisia. Thus the halt at Medenine provided the Germans with an opportunity to attack the Eighth Army, put it off balance and so provide time for the Axis forces either to attack the First Army or simply to prolong the campaign and build up their own defences.

Unfortunately for the Germans their plans were detected at an early stage. Thus the British forces had plenty of time to formulate their defensive measures. It was known that the Germans had to make a frontal attack supported by what was left of the once-active Luftwaffe and by as many tanks as the Afrika Korps could muster.

The XXX Corps preparations were thorough. Main defences rested on two elements: the use of a carefully drawn-up fire plan by the artillery of the entire corps and the use of anti-tank guns located well forward.

The anti-tank guns involved were almost all 6-pdr weapons, though scattered among them were numbers of the novel 17/25-pdr guns. These were conversions of 25-pdr field gun carriages to accommodate the long 17-pdr barrel.

When the attack came on 6 March all was ready. The Germans appear to have had no idea of what they were advancing into, and following the expected artillery preparation the tanks and infantry of the 10th, 15th and 21st Panzer divisions plus supporting formations were allowed to advance to within 100 yards of the anti-tank gun screen. This screen was not laid out on any linear basis but was carefully emplaced and concealed in positions that made the best use of any local cover. Most were emplaced and organized as batteries, nearly all of them manned by the Royal Artillery. Where possible these guns were controlled as batteries, but on many occasions the individual gun crews were able to select their own targets.

The Germans advanced directly against the centre of the three divisions of XXX Corps. Once they were within the prepared range the guns opened up. The close range had been selected for two reasons: firstly, at such close ranges the 6-pdr guns could be used to best effect, and secondly, to entice as much of the enemy's armour into the killing ground as possible. Once within the area their chances of getting out were much reduced. The result was a virtual slaughter of the German tanks (35, 60 and 46 respectively by division). Individual tank-guns produced some remarkable scores: one gun of the 75th Anti-Tank Regiment was able to hit six tanks with the first six rounds fired. In another position the battery watched as a line of German tanks moved side-on right across their front. When they opened fire few of their targets survived. The anti-tank gun fire was not all that the Germans had to face, for as they advanced they also moved directly into the pre-planned barrage of fire produced by 172 field and medium guns that constituted the entire Corps artillery strength. This fire seriously affected the hapless German infantry, who attacked with their usual determined fervour but were able to dislodge the defenders at only one location, where a spirited counterattack threw them out.

But it was the anti-tank screen that caused the most damage. Without the support of the German tanks the infantry could do little unaided. In the first two hours 50 of the main force of 141 Afrika Korps tanks that moved into the killing ground had been knocked out. Some of these were the much-vaunted Tigers. Their armour, as expected, was proof against the projectiles fired from the 6-pdr guns, but it was not proof against the fire from the 17/25-pdr weapons. The 6-pdr guns also attempted to use a tactic that was later to become a standard practice – the manhandling of the guns round the flank of a Tiger.

The German attack was decimated. The killing ground in front of the XXX Corps positions was a graveyard of German tanks – tanks that the Germans would be hard put to replace and which would be sorely missed during the forthcoming campaign in Tunisia itself.

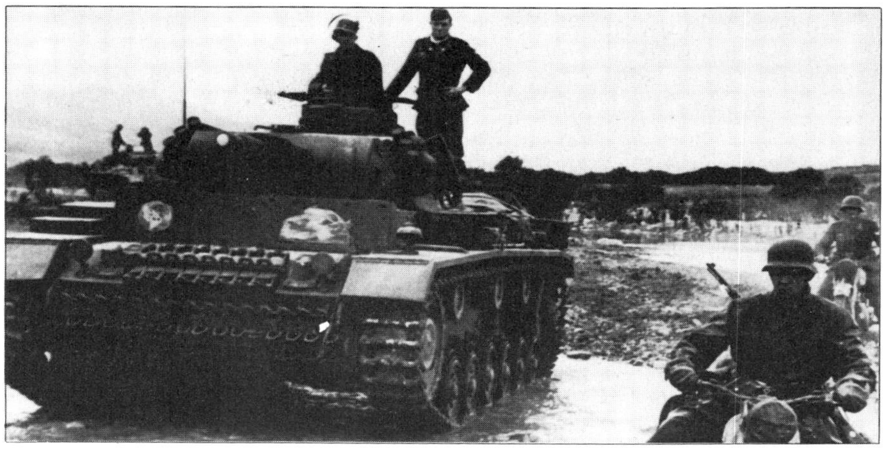

Above: A Panzer II moves up for the counter-attack which came to grief at Medenine. Extra armour has been bolted to the hull front and a length of track fixed to the glacis.

The most common anti-tank gun at Medenine was the 6-pdr, which was able to deal with Panzer IIIs and IVs but could destroy a Tiger only by a close-range shot into the side. The 17-pdr gun which was to replace it had not been completed in early 1943, but some 17-pdrs were fitted to field gun carriages and rushed to Tunisia in time for Medenine.

on to the lines of concealed 88s. A second Panzer division, the 10th, now joined in and chased the American armour back towards Thala, while another Afrika Korps detachment came up from the south to combine at Kasserine, through which narrow gap was flooding the chaos of an Allied retreat, with American, French and British units all intermingled. By 10 February the position looked desperate, but then a halt was caused by disagreement between Rommel and his superiors, and during it the Americans sorted themselves out and rallied in new positions which they held stubbornly when the attack was renewed.

Within days the lost ground was recovered by joint British and American action, and from then on, but with ever-growing certainty, the ring around the Axis forces in Tunisia was to tighten. By early March, after a resounding defeat of one of Rommel's counter-attacks at Medenine, the Eighth Army was closed up to the powerfully built defences of the Mareth Line, and on the 20th the attack opened; eight days later the First Army reopened the offensive which had been closed down by the winter weather three months before, and on 8 April patrols from the US 2nd Corps, probing south from Gafsa, met troops of the 12th Lancers from Eighth Army's 1st Armoured Division, and the link-up had at last taken place.

Rommel, a sick and exhausted man, had now left Africa for good, his place as the figurehead of Axis forces there now taken by Arnim. His removal from the scene of his greatest triumphs might be taken as a token for the future, for from that time on the entire war situation improved for the Allies. The drives by First and Eighth Armies towards their ultimate

Below: The German army had a number of massive, long range guns, this 170-mm K18 fired a 150-lb shell to a maximum range of 32,000 yards. This one was captured by the Eighth Army and its stockpiled ammunition fired into the German lines.

Right: American prisoners taken during the German counter-attack at Kasserine in February. Although outnumbered, the tough veterans of the Afrika Korps administered a sharp defeat on the inexperienced US troops.

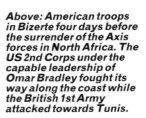

Above: American troops in Bizerte four days before the surrender of the Axis forces in North Africa. The US 2nd Corps under the capable leadership of Omar Bradley fought its way along the coast while the British 1st Army attacked towards Tunis.

Above: A Messerschmitt Me 323 evacuates German troops from North Africa. These lumbering giants proved horribly vulnerable, and after RAF fighters shot down 14 out of a 16-strong flight they were withdrawn to the Russian front.

Left: Members of the 'Earthquakers' bomber group, one of the longest-serving medium bombardment groups in the Mediterranean theatre, stand by one of their veteran B-25s. The 'Desert Warrior' flew 73 missions, dropping over 70 tons of bombs in 193 combat hours from El Alamein to Sicily.

objective gathered in strength and speed, and by the end of April the thousands of German troops that Hitler had thrown into the battle in North Africa were penned into a narrowing bridgehead around Bizerta, Tunis and the Cape Bon peninsula. The battles for Enfidaville and Longstop Hill had been fought, and behind the besieged Panzerarmee the Royal Navy were gathering for Operation Retribution, a Dunkirk in reverse for which Admiral Sir Andrew Cunningham had already issued strategic instructions: 'Sink, burn, destroy! Let nothing pass!'

On the left the US 2nd Corps, now commanded by Lieutenant-General Omar Bradley (Patton had been relieved to plan for the invasion of Sicily), were poised to drive along the coast and up through Mateur towards Bizerta. First Army held the centre of the line and the onus of the prime attack through the Medjerda Gap towards Tunis, while Eighth Army held the southern sector reaching the coast at Enfidaville, its task to hold the attention of Arnim away from the more vital areas to which, indeed, had been sent the most famous of the Eighth Army formations – 7th Armoured Divisions, 4th Indian Division and 201st Guards Brigade – on loan to First Army in a generous gesture by Montgomery, anxious as always to help his friend and commander, Alexander, in this last battle on African soil.

The onslaught began at three o'clock on the morning of 6 May with a concentrated artillery bombardment in the centre under which two brigades of the 4th Indian Division crept forward towards the known positions of a regiment of panzer grenadiers. They were on them within an hour, the leading company of Gurkhas with their kukris cutting their way through the outposts and into the main enemy positions, Bren-carriers bringing up the support companies and then fanning out to find the limits of the position. As they did so, they made contact with the British divisions on their right flank moving forward parallel with them; the two divisions then advanced, one on each side of the central valley, until by half past nine they were through the main enemy defences and the tanks of the 7th Armoured Division could pass through and drive for Tunis.

For Arnim and his troops it was soon obvious that the end had come. Their 13 sadly depleted divisions were being attacked by 19 divisions at full strength; they had only 130 panzers left and were being attacked by over 1,200 Allied tanks; 500 guns defended them against 1,500; and only 500 planes were available to hold back air assaults mounted by over 3,000. Yet they fought at first with all the efficiency and valour which had distinguished the Afrika Korps from the first, the only evidence of their decline being the ever weakening counter-attacks when they had been pushed off a hill or driven out of a valley.

Within two days both Bizerta and Tunis had been captured. Tunis was first entered by reconnaissance patrols of the 11th Hussars, the squadrons which had opened the Desert War against the Italians almost exactly three years before. Their final drive had taken place so quickly that they surprised German soldiers walking through the streets arm in arm with their girlfriends.

To the north, the Americans were mopping up in Bizerta itself and clearing out the last Axis posts in the hills and lakes close to Mateur, while to the south the 6th Armoured Division and the Guards Brigade were racing for the Cape Bon peninsula where, for a few days, the last remnants or Panzerarmee Afrika held out. Then, on 12 May, Arnim was captured by a unit from the 4th Indian Division, and the commander of the famous 90th Light Division, Major-General Graf von Sponek, was taken by his old enemies the New Zealanders; the following day the titular head of the Axis Forces in North Africa, the Italian Field Marshal Giovanni Messe, also surrendered to the famous New Zealander, Lieutenant-General Bernard Freyberg, VC.

It was claimed at the time that 250,000 German and Italian soldiers gave themselves up to the Anglo-American armies in North Africa, only a few attempting to escape to Sicily and, of those, seventy-seven were scooped out of the sea by the Royal Navy and over a hundred were later found marooned on one of the offshore islands. Those who surrendered in the north to the Americans or the First Army were subjected to a certain amount of ridicule and mockery by the comparative newcomers to the war, but those in the south – especially the Germans of the 90th Light or the 15th or 21st Panzer Divisions, who had been among the first of Rommel's troops – were watched in sympathetic silence by the men of the Eighth Army who had fought them across nearly 2,000 miles of hills and deserts, and shared too many experiences with them to feel hatred or indeed much triumph.

That evening General Alexander sent a cable to Churchill which read:

> *Sir:*
> *It is my duty to report that the Tunisian campaign is over. All enemy resistance has ceased. We are masters of the North African shores.*

The Desert War was over.

Some of the 250,000 German and Italian soldiers taken prisoner when the Axis forces in North Africa surrendered on 13 March 1943. The Afrika Korps fought with stubborn efficiency to the bitter end.

A Valentine tank of the Eighth Army carrying triumphant British soldiers. Montgomery lent Alexander some of his best units to help the 1st Army break the German defences before Tunis.

Allied light bombers in the Mediterranean, 1943

Allied air superiority over the North African desert and the southern part of the Mediterranean hastened the defeat of the Afrika Korps. Cargo vessels bearing vital supplies to Tunisia were bombed and sunk and Axis positions were subjected to regular bombing attacks.

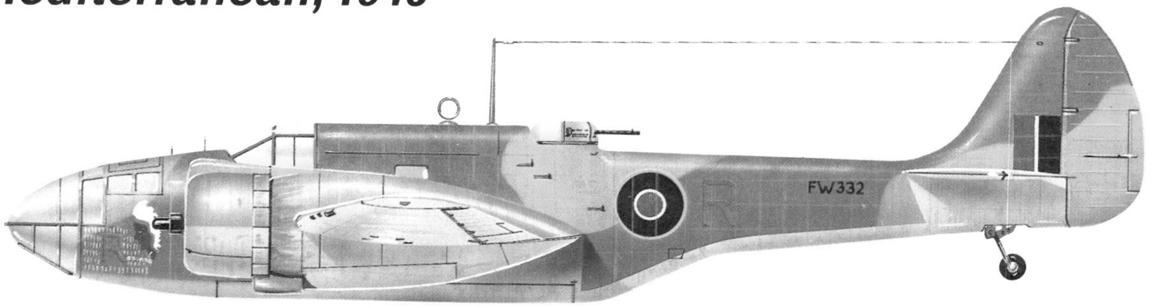

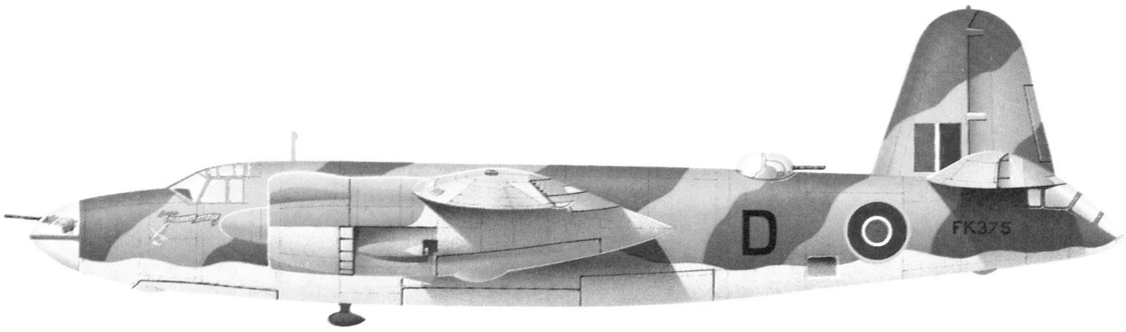

Left: *A Martin Marauder Mk 1A of No. 14 Squadron, RAF, based in Egypt and serving as a torpedo bomber. Air strikes and British submarines inflicted severe losses on Axis convoys between Italy and North Africa.*

Above: *The Martin Baltimore was an American light bomber designed to RAF specifications. It was agreeably fast and mounted up to 14 0.303-in machine-guns as well as a 2,000-lb bombload. This is a Mk V, which was the most prolific model.*

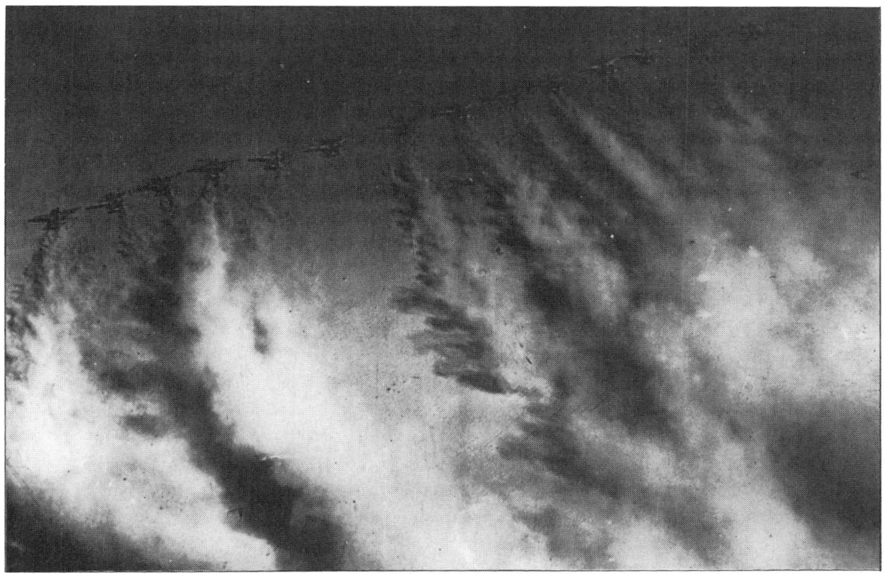

A squadron of RAF Bostons takes off from a desert airfield and throws up a veritable dust storm. The Boston was introduced to the desert air force in early 1942 to replace the ageing Bristol Blenheims.

A formation of American B-25 Mitchell bombers casts an ominous shadow over the North African desert as it flies towards its target. From their new bases in Algeria US aircraft maintained a high sortie rate against the Axis positions in Tunisia.

Right: *The Bristol Blenheim Mk V was envisaged as a low-altitude close-support aircraft, but was built as a high-altitude bomber. They operated for the last six months of the desert war without distinction, but suffered heavy losses when used over Italy and had to be withdrawn from service.*

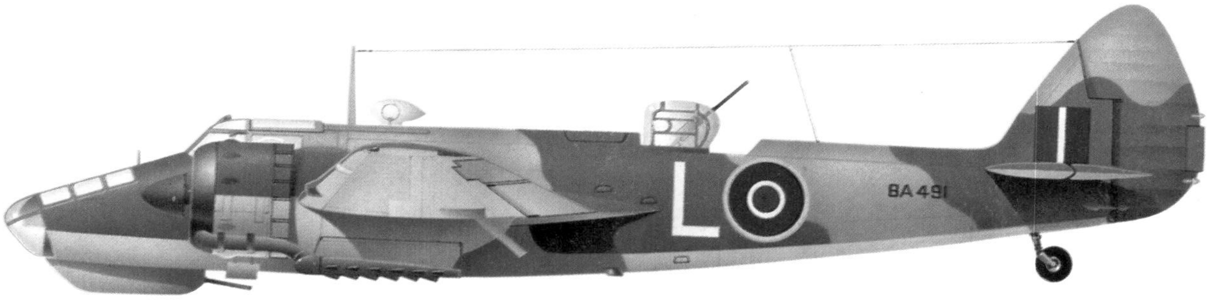

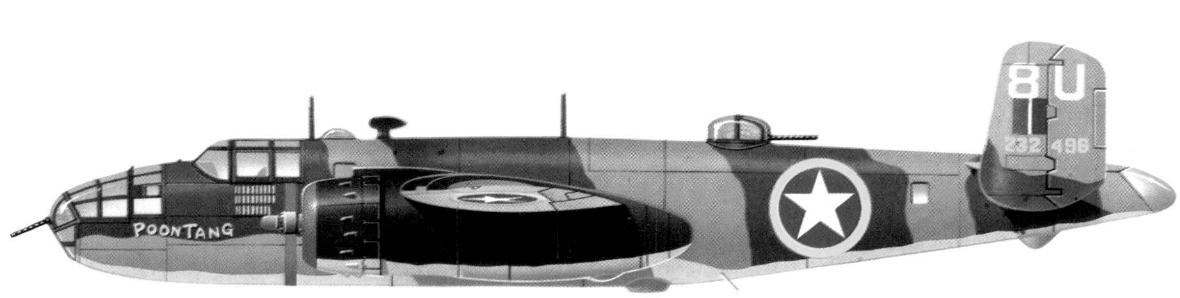

Left: *A North American B-25C Mitchell of the 488th Bomb Squadron, 340th Bomb Group, USAAF, based at Sfax, Tunisia in April 1943. The group of three Mitchell squadrons became operational with the US 12th Air Force that month.*

Right: *A Douglas Boston Mk IIIA of No. 24 Squadron, South African Air Force, based at Souk-el-Khemis, Tunisia, in April 1943. The demand for this ubiquitous aircraft exceeded Douglas's production capacity, and some 140 of the machines supplied to Britain under Lend-Lease were manufactured by Boeing.*

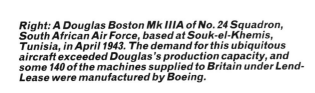

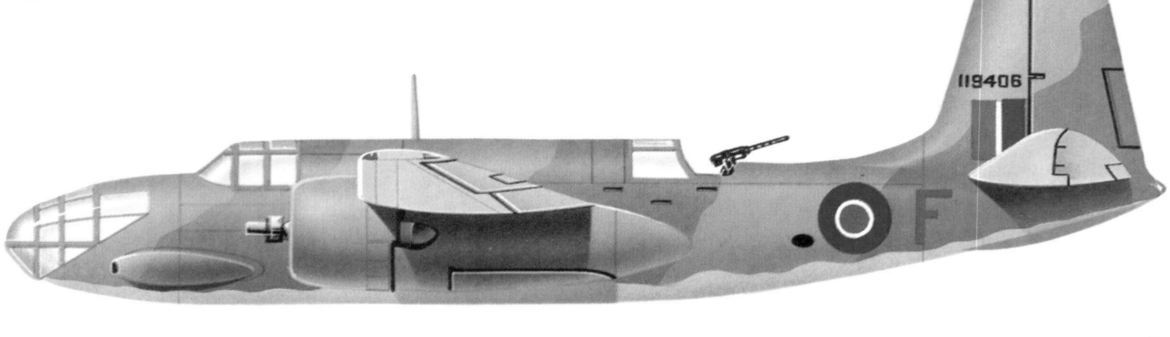

Chapter 14

The Convoy Battles

The American entry into the war led to a 'Second Happy Time' for the U-boats, with US merchant ships being sent to the bottom within sight of the American coast. However, the growth of Allied maritime air power combined with an increasing technological lead tilted the balance against the submarines.

***Right:** Depth charges are prepared for launch on the pitching after deck of USS Greer in mid-Atlantic. Conditions aboard the escort vessels could be almost as cramped and uncomfortable as on the U-boats.*

One of the reasons for the swift unanimity of agreement between the British and Americans during the Casablanca Conference in January 1943, at any rate as far as the first priority of beating the U-boats was concerned, had been the series of events referred to by the U-boat commanders as the 'Second Happy Time'.

It had been the period immediately following America's entry into the war, when Washington not only refused to profit from Britain's experience, but also decreed that in order to maintain civilian morale the Florida coastline should not be subjected to any black-out restrictions which might dampen spirits or even affect profits. As a result, for nearly six months merchant and cargo ships, tankers and coasters, continued sailing independently up from the Gulf of Mexico and the Caribbean, brilliantly silhouetted against the hundreds of miles of strip lighting which inestimably aided in their tasks the 21 U-boats which Admiral Karl Dönitz hurriedly sent to the area. By June 1942 they had sunk no less than 505 of the ships, many of them within sight of the Florida beaches.

The sinking of valuable cargoes was to continue even after the US Navy took corrective action, because of course both their own and the British and Canadian navies were still facing shortages of practically everything necessary to defeat the U-boats – shortage of escort vessels, shortage of training time for the crews, shortage of adequate weapons even when these had been put into production, shortage at that time of the technological advances required to deal with the up-to-date U-boat and her tactics; above all, shortage of long-range and long-endurance aircraft to cover the convoys throughout their entire voyage.

It was the Germans who had first demonstrated the value of air supremacy in this particular battle. In late 1940 they established Focke-Wulfe Condor squadrons along the Biscay coast which could operate 800 miles out into the Atlantic, not only spotting convoys for the U-boats but also bombing independently sailing merchantmen, and in the first two months of 1941 alone they had sunk 46 ships totalling 167,822 tons – and the U-boats had themselves only sunk 60. Only the continued acerbity between the Kriegsmarine and the Luftwaffe prevented a development which could have been catastrophic for the British, too hard-pressed for many a month to spare aircraft to beat off the Condors.

During 1941 the massacre of Allied merchant shipping had been frightening. U-boats alone sank 432 ships of 2,171,754 tons, aircraft claimed another 371 totalling 1,017, 422 tons, German surface raiders added another 84 ships of 428,350 tons, while 111 ships grossing 230,842 tons were sunk by mines laid around the British coastline; misadventure took another 301. A total of 1,299 ships was well beyond British, or even Allied, building capacity to replace in a year.

But 1942 was worse. The overall loss was 1,664 ships grossing 7,790,697 tons, of which the U-boats had sunk 6,226,215 tons – and U-boat operational strength rose throughout the year from 91 in January to 212 in December. As Churchill was to write, 'The U-boat attack of 1942 was our worst evil.'

But, imperceptibly, the tide was turning. If more U-boats were sailing into operational areas, so were more anti-submarine frigates, more corvettes, and by the end of 1942 more air cover, for at last some small escort carriers (virtually Liberty ship hulls with flying decks and hangar space) were coming off the slips. In addition Liberators could occasionally be spared, or Sunderlands operating from Iceland could help a convoy on the northern route.

More importantly, lessons were being learned, training techniques improved, and new weapons appearing. The Hedgehog, a multi-barrelled mortar which threw a pattern of 24 charges ahead of the

***Above:** An American merchantman ablaze off Cape Henry during the 'Second Happy Time'. Because the US coastline was not blacked out, merchant shipping off the coast was silhouetted perfectly for the submarines lurking off the Eastern ports.*

***Below:** A graphic illustration of what the convoy battles entailed: a storm-tossed US destroyer off the coast of Iceland. By this unsinkable aircraft-carrier the convoys formed up for the second leg of the journey to England.*

Left: A U-boat returns to the shelter of the submarine pens of the French west coast. The Allies mounted innumerable bombing attacks on these bases, but their extremely tough construction defeated all but the heaviest bomb.

Right: A lookout peers through his binoculars on the conning tower of a U-boat. Maximum visibility from a submarine was about 10 miles, so to increase the chances of spotting a convoy the U-boats were often deployed in long lines across the estimated path of the Allied shipping.

Below: A convoy forms up off Halifax for the long and dangerous voyage across the Atlantic. During 1942 1,664 Allied merchant vessels were sunk, the vast majority to U-boat attack. If the U-boats continued to sink cargo vessels faster than the Allies could build them, the British war effort would grind to a halt.

attacking ship, and the Squid, which did the same with three large depth-charges, removed the old problem of attacking a U-boat with depth-charges over the stern – losing her from the asdic (sonar) contact during the last crucial moments. Moreover, by the end of 1942 British scientists had invented the centimetric radar which when fitted to escorts could pick up U-boats on the surface (even, with experienced operators, their periscopes) without betraying that they had done so to the U-boat commander; they were also small enough to be fitted, in time, to Coastal Command aircraft.

But the most significant factor in all this development and production was the formation of Support or Hunter/Killer Groups. One of the great problems of convoy escort had been the dual duty facing each escort ship commander. Was his task to protect the convoy by remaining with it all the time as a permanent shield, or would it be better instead to concentrate on killing U-boats – a task which would inevitably lead to his abandoning the convoy for some time while he did so? Quite early in the Battle of the Atlantic the Admiralty decided that escorts must remain with their charges, and many U-boats which had been located on asdic or radar escaped destruction because their antagonists could not be spared to hunt them down.

Now the necessary numbers and types of ships were arriving at British and American ports for different groups to be formed to undertake the different tasks. By September 1942 the first support group, under Commander F. J. Walker, was trained and at sea, ready to race straight to any convoy judged to be sailing into danger – first to strengthen the normal escort then when their assailants had shown their presence, to drive them off, leaving the convoy still with its own close defence, and hunt the U-boat menace to its death.

The decision taken at the Casablanca Conference in November, therefore, was not only wise but appeared capable of comparatively rapid and smooth fulfilment, and it is ironic that other decisions taken at the same time should have imposed a delay of several months. The convoying to North Africa of 84,000 American and 23,000 British soldiers from the United States and Britain had only been successfully accomplished by the deployment of an immense range of Anglo-American naval strength, and every vessel from trawler to huge battleship that could be found had been employed upon that task. No sooner had Commander Walker assembled his group for action in the North Atlantic than they had been sent south to waters around Gibraltar, and owing to the continuation of the North African campaign through and into the first months of 1943, it was April before much shipping could be released from the Mediterranean area back to the Atlantic.

A Sunderland of RAF Coastal Command keeps a watchful eye on a convoy. Bristling with machine-guns and carrying a goodly store of depth charges, these massive flying-boats were highly effective, especially once fitted with airborne radar sets which enabled them to surprise U-boats at night or in inclement weather.

Above: British knowledge of U-boats was dramatically improved when this vessel, U-570, surrendered after being depth-charged by an RAF Hudson. Towed to Britain, it was thoroughly examined.

Left: British sailors observe the thunderous explosion of a depth charge from the stern of a destroyer. Depth charges generally served to pin down a U-boat and keep it submerged while the convoy passed by.

Above: Admiral Dönitz (right), commander of the U-boat fleet, watches the launch of a U-boat with Albert Speer, Minister of Armaments, in 1944. By then the submarines were fighting a losing battle: less than one in five of the U-boat crews were destined to survive the war.

During the intervening period the losses from the Atlantic convoys rose to appalling heights. In January 1943 they reached 203,000 tons and would have been higher had not wild winter gales effectively kept the U-boats either in port or under the waves; in February they rose to 359,000 tons. And in March 1943 occurred one of the biggest and most disastrous convoy battles (from the British point of view) of the war.

The fast convoy HX 229 had left Halifax at the end of the first week of March, and on the 13th it was accidentally found by U-653, struggling back to base after a breakdown. The commander dropped back and sent off a report to U-boat HQ and Dönitz quickly directed on to the convoy the 12 U-boats of the Raubgraf Group, which concentrated an attack through the thin escort group on the starboard side and was soon wreaking havoc amid the convoy's 11 columns. Eight ships were sunk on the first attack and most of the escorts dropped back to pick up survivors; but then rallied and during the next 24 hours kept close enough escort to keep the group away; but on the following night another two ships were sunk. However, in the meantime the U-boats of Sturmer Group, which were hurrying in to add weight to the attack, came across an even larger convoy – SC 122 – but this had a much stronger escort than the first, so the Sturmer U-boats were driven off during the first hours of the encounter.

SC 122 was a slow convoy, HX 229 was fast, but by the night of 18/19 March the two convoys had virtually amalgamated; so had their attackers, and between Raubgraf and Sturmer there were 25 U-boats, sufficient effectively to swamp the defence. By the morning of 19 March 21 ships of the two convoys had been sunk, and only the fact that early on 20 March the survivors arrived within range of protective air cover – and one U-boat was sunk by an RAF Liberator – saved a far worse massacre. As it was, the 140,842 tons lost in that encounter brought the total for March up to 627,000 tons, making it one of the worst months of the war.

Not surprisingly, Admiral Dönitz was delighted, morale among his crews rose and thoughts of yet a 'Third Happy Time' occurred to many. But during April the Hunter/Killer groups were released from their Mediterranean duties and, moreover, President Roosevelt took a hand in the battle, ordering the USAAF to release more Liberators for use over the Atlantic. There were 41 by mid-April and by the beginning of May they were operational and experienced.

In the middle of that month a large westbound convoy was scattered by a violent storm south of Greenland, and 12 U-boats gathered to take advantage; soon they had sunk nine of the convoy ships. But two support groups arrived from Nova Scotia, the gale dropped and when the U-boats recommenced their onslaught they were first driven away, then chased and some were sunk. Four were destroyed by depth charges the first night, two were sunk by bombers the following day – and two collided in darkness and both went to the bottom.

The next fast convoy lost three ships, but three U-boats paid the price; the next slow convoy lost two ships but the escorts sank two U-boats and severely damaged two more — and the next pair of convoys arrived in port unscathed, leaving in their wakes the sunken hulls of six U-boats. The April 1943 Allied shipping losses had been 245,000 tons for 15 U-boats, May's had been 165,000 tons for 40 U-boats – and June's 18,000 tons for 17 U-boats. Dönitz was keeping his craft in port while he thought out new tactics.

In fact, the Allies had won the Battle of the Atlantic. Although German ingenuity and courage was to continue to develop the U-boat threat almost to the last days of the war, so also developed Allied techniques – especially the use of the centimetric radar – and experience. They never lost the lead they had won so painfully.

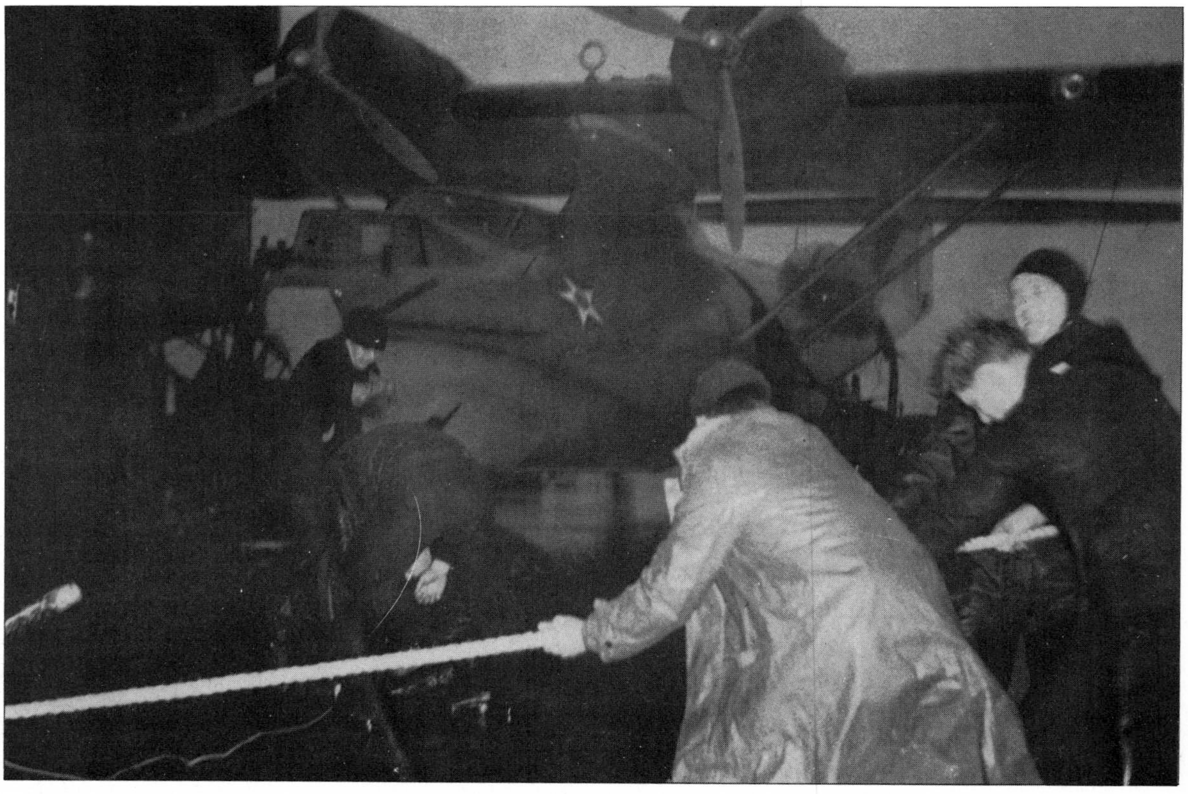

Walker: U-boat hunter

Captain F. J. Walker had specialized in anti-submarine warfare before the war, but this was not the way to win promotion and the outbreak of war found his career at an apparent dead end. But when he at last went to sea in 1941 he revealed an uncanny talent for U-boat hunting. More important, he evolved many of the techniques which were to prove vital in the defeat of the U-boat menace.

Some thrive in the peacetime navy; others need a war to develop their true potential. Captain Frederick Walker was one of the latter. He first went to sea as a cadet in 1913 and, between the wars, specialized in anti-submarine warfare. This field was then less than glamorous, and war found him in 1939 a commander with few prospects of further promotion.

For the first two years of World War II Walker fretted ashore while enemy U-boats sank well over 4 million GRT of merchant shipping. Finally, he was appointed in the autumn of 1941 to command the sloop HMS *Stork* as Senior Officer, 36th Escort Group.

Groups such as these existed to give close cover to convoys, the ships being kept together as a team as far as was possible. Newly formed, the 36th was Liverpool-based, having seven 'Flower' class corvettes led by two faster sloops.

The group's first task was to escort an OG convoy to Gibraltar, a passage in which the only enemy was the weather. The return run was with HG76 and was a very different affair. It sailed on 14 December 1941, accompanied for the first time by an escort carrier, the pioneer HMS *Audacity*, and three locally-based destroyers.

First sighting was by an aircraft, 20 miles distant and illustrating the value of the presence of a carrier. Walker's impulsive nature was then evident by his taking five ships of the 'close' escort to deal with it, a prolonged absence that was eventually justified only by the successful outcome.

A second U-boat was sunk by two of the Gibraltar destroyers on the next day but, in the darkness before the following dawn, one of these was in turn sunk by torpedo. Walker himself was quickly on the scene in the *Stork* and demonstrated his unique 'nose' for a U-boat by running down its anticipated line of retreat, detecting it and blowing it to the surface with just two passes. Too close to depress his guns sufficiently, Walker engaged in a sort of nautical dogfight, finally sinking the submarine by ramming.

As the carrier could not operate her aircraft at night, her safest night station was in the centre of the convoy; but late on 21 December she was out to one side, just where Walker ordered a 'Buttercup' (a barrage of starshell) following the torpedoing of a merchantman. *Audacity* was then herself torpedoed and sunk, Walker blaming himself for the loss.

Walker was shortly afterward promoted Captain, taking over the 2nd Support Group of six 'Black Swan' class sloops, headed by HMS *Starling*, which was crewed largely by 'old Storks'. Five of these groups were operating by the spring of 1943, their function being to join any threatened convoy and allow more U-boats to be hunted to the death without denuding the convoy of its escort.

This freedom suited Walker's style admirably. On 1 June 1943 a 'Huff-Duff' radio intercept warned of a U-boat and gave its bearing; the six sloops headed in this direction in line abreast at 6.4-km (4-mile) spacing. This deliberate sweep was rewarded, with *Starling* gaining first sonar contact and thus the privilege of the first attack.

When this produced no apparent result, Walker sent three of his ships to patrol the 'outfield' escape routes while he and the remaining two delivered a 'special', steaming abeam in close order while laying a dense carpet of depth charges. The target, *U-202*, survived 76 charges by virtue of going exceptionally deep. Up top, the group sat back to wait. Inevitably coming up for air during the night, the enemy was duly gunned down. Her destruction would never have been possible with the group responsible also for a convoy.

It was in mid-1943 too that the Admiralty embarked on a combined air and surface blitz on U-boats traversing the Bay of Biscay, to and from their French bases. On 24 June the 2nd Support Group opened the season with two U-boats before tea. With five sloops trolling along in search formation, *Starling* unexpectedly had a contact close aboard and immediately laid a pattern on it. To everybody's surprise a U-boat suddenly staggered to the surface in her wake. Between them the ships could muster 30 4-in guns and most of these opened up at the hapless submarine. However, Walker reversed course and took his ship through an enthusiastic friendly barrage, ramming the enemy which rolled under the keel, and dropping a valedictory shallow depth-charge pattern for good measure.

In January 1944, with seven 'kills' so far to their credit, six sloops of the group left for the central Atlantic, accompanied by two CVEs. Two days out, *Wild Goose* (the group's best sonar ship) flushed a U-boat tracking HMS *Nairana*. A 60-charge 'plaster' from her and *Starling* accounted for the submarine.

On 9 February three U-boats were sunk in 15 hours. The group had left the carriers and covered a point where up to 22 submarines were threatening a series of passing convoys. Two were located in sequence on the surface in the early hours, and each dived and then succumbed easily to immediate attack. The third required prolonged tracking and patience. A day later, several hours' pursuit in poor sonar conditions accounted for another. The last was the result of a Walker 'hunch' that the logical place for U-boats at daybreak would be just astern of a convoy. One was. It was sunk and gave the group a tally of six boats in 19 days.

By July 1944, the group's total 'bag' had risen to 16 but Walker was feeling the strain. He was proud of his ability to stay on watch far longer than his younger officers but endless wet nights on open bridges had taken their toll. On 7 July he went ashore from *Starling* at Liverpool for some much-needed leave and two days later he was dead. A stroke, occasioned by overwork, struck him with a finality that no enemy had matched. He was not quite 48 years old.

Above: Walker's 2nd Support Group consisted of six 'Black Swan' class sloops headed by Walker's ship HMS* Starling. *Many of her crew had served aboard his previous command, HMS* Stork, *and were used to Walker's aggressive anti-submarine tactics, which included the occasional ramming attack. By July 1944 the group had sent 16 U-boats to the bottom.

Below: In his characteristic leather jerkin Walker exhorts HMS* Woodpecker *to press home her depth-charge attack in February 1944. On this patrol Walker's group netted six U-boats, three during a 16-hour period, which established a record,* Woodpecker *was later hit by an acoustic homing torpedo and foundered while on tow.

Right: Victory in the Atlantic: a dawn panorama taken from the escort carrier USS* Bogue. *Better technology, better tactics and the massive shipbuilding capacity of the United States ensured that by 1944 the U-boat campaign had been defeated. Although submarines continued to put to sea they now faced a formidable combination of maritime and aerial power, and many boats were last seen heading out into the Atlantic, never to return.

Left: US sailors struggle to secure equipment on the deck of the seaplane carrier USS* Albemarle *in an Atlantic gale. The addition of aircraft like this PBY flying-boat to a convoy greatly enhanced security, forcing U-boats near the convoy to stay submerged and probably lose contact.

In sharp contrast to the U-boat offensive, the fortunes of the German surface fleet had gone from bad to worse after the loss of the *Bismarck*. The British Admiralty was acutely concerned at the prospect of a surface attack on the Arctic Convoys but the Battle of the Barents Sea, the botched attack on convoy JW 51B which appeared to Hitler such a failure of both communications and ordinary seamanship – a lore of which he remained all his life in total ignorance – that he issued his famous 'Scrap the Battlefleet' order which virtually gave the Allies a resounding victory at no price to them whatsoever. Admiral Erich Raeder's arguments were dismissed with contempt, and Raeder himself was replaced by Admiral Dönitz, though he, despite the fact that he was the Reich's leading exponent of U-boat warfare, persuaded Hitler to keep at least the battleship *Tirpitz* and the battle-cruiser *Scharnhorst* in commission, as some form of 'fleet in being' to constrict British naval activities.

This the two ships did by simply sitting in Altenfjord at North Cape, posing a potential but continuous threat to any ship which attempted the Murmansk run, and during the whole of the summer of 1943 this threat was enough to halt the convoys. Russia fought the huge Eastern Front battles of that summer without weapons or stores from the Allies via the northern route, and *Tirpitz* and *Scharnhorst* spent the months idly swinging around their anchors.

But the convoys did start again in November, and on 22 December German reconnaissance aircraft found convoy JW 55B coming up from the west. After some delay owing to the absence of Dönitz in Paris and the unwillingness of the German C-in-C North to take the responsibility of sending *Scharnhorst* and the accompanying destroyers out, the flotilla eventually left Altenfjord on the evening of 24 December under command of Rear-Admiral Bey, who proceeded to demonstrate with startling clarity the deleterious effects of prolonged inaction; he made almost every mistake possible.

Catalogue of errors

During Christmas Day the weather was vile, but with a following sea his ships made good time on a northward course towards his calculated interception point; and at midnight he broke radio silence to discuss the whole situation with HQ North. By the time he had finished his report and his questions had been answered, he was about 100 miles short of the convoy. Admiral Sir Bruce Fraser aboard the battleship *Duke of York*, with the cruiser *Jamaica* and four destroyers was 150 miles to his west and coming up fast, while the three cruisers *Sheffield, Belfast* and *Norfolk* under command of Admiral Sir R. L. Burnett were coming in from the east and about the same distance away. They knew where Bey was but he had no idea of their presence.

Bey made his second gross error the following morning when he turned southwest in the belief that he had crossed the convoy's route, and then ordered his destroyers to fan out ahead in search. Shortly afterwards he found himself under fire from Burnett's cruisers, which should have been easy prey for *Scharnhorst*'s guns – but perhaps distrusting his crew's competence, Bey turned away without for the moment informing his destroyers. Burnett's cruisers raced around to head Bey off from the convoy – successfully, for Bey swung around with them until his ship was facing in the direction from which Fraser aboard the *Duke of York* was coming; and at this point he would seem to have remembered his destroyers for, in view of the appalling weather and their failure to find the convoy, he ordered them back to Altenfjord.

At 4.17 p.m. on 26 December *Scharnhorst* appeared on the *Duke of York*'s radar; at 4.50 both of Fraser's big ships opened fire while Burnett's cruisers closed in from the other side; at 6.20 *Scharnhorst* abruptly lost speed as at least one of the *Duke of York*'s heavy shells went home, and her fate was then similar to that of the *Bismarck*'s. Dead in the water by 7.30 but with her secondary armament still firing bravely, she took several torpedoes from the circling destroyers, rolled over and sank at 7.45 – only 36 of her complement of about 1,800 being saved.

So ended the last battle of Hitler's High Seas Fleet.

Above:* Scharnhorst *made a brief foray into the Atlantic in 1941 with her sistership* Gneisenau*, but they returned to Germany after a dramatic dash along the English Channel.* Scharnhorst *joined* Tirpitz *in Norway.

Below: Survivors of* Scharnhorst *are led ashore. Only 36 of her 1,800 crew were rescued from the bitter Arctic waters; the sudden call to general quarters on the afternoon of 26 December had come as a shock to most of the company.

Above: The mighty battleship* Tirpitz *photographed from the heavy cruiser* Hipper *in a Norwegian fjord. Although the German heavy surface units represented a considerable problem for the Royal Navy, their sorties against the Arctic Convoys were characterized by muddle and hesitancy which compared badly with the aggressive confidence of the British warships.

HMS* Duke of York *blows a smoke ring from her aft quadruple 14-in gun turret. Flying the flag of Admiral Sir Bruce Fraser,* Duke of York *pounded the* Scharnhorst *into a blazing wreck with assistance from the heavy cruiser* Jamaica *after a destroyer attack brought the German battleship to bay.

Above: HMS* Belfast*, foredeck encrusted with frozen spray, steams to North Cape to take part in the sinking of the* Scharnhorst*. She was no stranger to Arctic waters, having escorted several of the Russian convoys.

The science of U-boat hunting

The Battle of the Atlantic was determined as much by scientific progress as by the seamanship of the protagonists, the campaign swinging to and fro as new equipment was introduced. Although the Allies established a healthy lead during 1943, by the end of the war the Germans had produced a formidable new generation of submarines which could have sharply reversed the Battle.

It could be simply demonstrated that a single group of ships was far less likely to be detected than a number of independents. Independents suffered losses at two to three times the rate of ships in convoy, but the Admiralty's belief that the latter should not exceed 40 ships came under scrutiny. Escorts were allocated (ideally, at least) at three to a very small convoy, plus one for each additional 10 ships. This principle was shown to be anomalous for, applying it, say, to two separate convoys, of 20 ships, each would need to be accompanied by five escorts, yet by combining the two convoys into one of 40 ships, only seven escorts would be required.

With escorts in desperately short supply, the reasoning was attractive. It was also correct, for though twice as many ships occupied twice the area, their perimeter (assumed circle) increased by less than 50 per cent. To extrapolate further, 60 ships had less than twice the perimeter of 20 and 100 less than 2½ times. Thus to keep the same spacing, all else being equal, only 12 or 13 escorts were required for a 100-ship convoy, where 25 would have been needed for five 20-ship convoys, together with a higher risk of detection. Larger convoys were instituted in early 1943 and halved the loss rate.

A surfaced submarine could extend its limited visual horizon (about 10 miles) by listening for a convoy's hydrophone effect or by sighting its smoke, but a group of submarines could increase its chance by forming a line of bearing across a suspected track. Should a submarine make a contact it would report to its shore-based control on HF, the latter rebroadcasting on MF to all boats to close in – the well known 'wolfpack' tactic (known to the Germans as *Rudel Taktik*). The weaknesses of the system were the amount of wireless traffic generated and the need for U-boats to run on the surface, failings both exploited by the British. The breakthrough was the development of a ship-borne high-frequency direction-finder (H/F D/F or 'Huff Duff'). Two or three ships so fitted could accompany a convoy and take bearings on any transmissions, which if close enough or on a bearing that posed a threat, would be aggressively run down by the best-positioned escort.

Asdic (now termed 'sonar') was widely fitted in Royal Naval escorts, but its effectiveness had been rather overrated before the war, and this factor was compounded by the common practice by surfaced U-boats of attacking a convoy at night, capitalizing on their small silhouettes. The answer was radar, the escorts being fitted with modified metric-wavelength ASV sets from aircraft, these being gradually replaced by centimetric sets that could detect a surfaced submarine out to about 4 miles.

It was the aircraft that proved the greatest nuisance to the surfaced U-boat. Even with radar, aircraft took a while to develop the art of submarine hunting, partly because Germans had a radio receiver that very effectively detected radar transmissions, enabling rapid avoiding action to be taken. By early 1943 shorter wavelengths confounded the German equipment and, for a space of three months, U-boat losses ran at an average of one per day.

Night-running on the surface, even to charge batteries, became prohibitively dangerous when aircraft received the 80-million candlepower Leigh Light, extra guns and improved depth charges with which to mount sudden and unannounced onslaughts from out of the darkness.

The enemy survived by developing the *Schnorkel* (snort), but slow, submerged transits now occupied most of a boat's endurance and even on station high surface speeds could not be used. Efficiency fell off rapidly. Desperately, some U-boats carried enhanced AA armament, electing to fight it out on the surface. This suited the aircraft very well, and spiralling U-boat losses soon discouraged the practice.

With the U-boat now attacking submerged, Asdic came back into its own. In 1943, if she kept her speed down to about 15 kts, an escort could obtain a contact at up to about 1.5 miles but, because of the geometry of the pencil beam, contact was lost on the run-in, some 300 yards short of target. As charges were still dropped or fired over the target's position, this gave an alert submarine commander a precious half minute to take the evasive action. Ahead-firing weapons were therefore developed: Mousetrap and Hedgehog and, later, Squid.

Any U-boat seeking to attack a convoy was then forced to tackle the escorts first, particularly as aircraft were usually present. A favoured weapon was the Zaunkönig acoustic torpedo, tuned to home on the escort's fast-running propellers. After some losses, the tactic adopted was to locate the torpedo's approach on hydrophones and stop engines. The enemy responded with more delicate tuning to detect the noise of auxiliary machinery, defeated in turn by the escort towing an acoustic decoy known as 'Foxer'.

Ultimately the Germans introduced the high-speed submarine in the Types XXI and XXIII. The former had a 16-kt submerged speed, underwater fire control and advanced torpedoes but, fortunately for the Allies, was brought into service too late to have much impact.

Through all causes, the Germans lost nearly 800 U-boats during the war. These had accounted for over 14 million gross registered tons of mercantile losses, over two-thirds the total from all causes. Science assisted the Allied victory immeasurably in both anticipating and responding to enemy developments.

Above: A Consolidated PBY Catalina delivers a depth-charge attack on a crash diving U-boat. After airborne radar cut through the cloak of darkness, U-boats found it risky to re-charge their batteries on the surface, and a snorkel device was introduced.

Right: The weatherworn hull of this 'Flower' class corvette bears eloquent testimony to the harsh conditions of the North Atlantic. Beginning life as HMS Aconite she was transferred to the Free French Navy in 1941 and fought throughout the Convoy Battles.

Below: The Type XXI was one of the most influential designs in the history of the submarine. By packing a streamlined hull with the best battery cells available the Germans produced the first submarine which travelled faster underwater than surfaced. A combination of active and passive sonar enabled them to attack without raising a tell-tale periscope. Fortunately for the Allies the war ended before the type became fully operational.

Above: The Type XVII U-boats were the first attempt at solving the problem posed by Allied radar. Now that surface operation was highly dangerous, it was essential to develop a submarine propulsion system not dependent on surface air. One solution was the Walter closed-cycle engine that used concentrated hydrogen peroxide, a system fraught with danger and which was ultimately abandoned.

Below: The small and agile Type XXIII coastal submarine was another example of a high-technology design which, fortunately, was developed too late to do serious damage. It fell to one of these, U-2336, to make the last U-boat attack in European waters, on 7 May 1945, when it sank two merchant ships inside the Firth of Forth – each with a single torpedo fired on a sonar bearing.

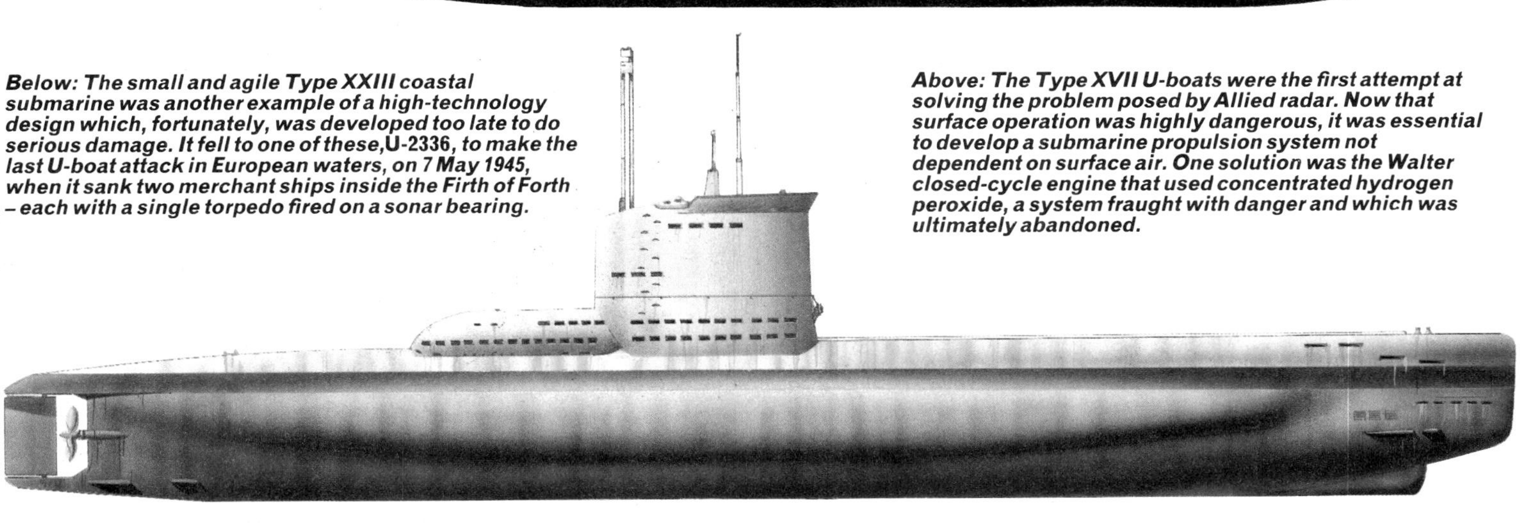

THE CONDOR THREAT

Once in possession of the Atlantic and Norwegian coasts, the Germans were able to supplement the efforts of their U-boats with air attacks on Britain's vital convoys. Lacking suitable aircraft, work was hurriedly undertaken to adapt the one proven long-range aircraft possessed by Germany, the commercial Focke-Wulf Fw 200 Condor, six development aircraft being delivered to I/KG 40 in Denmark in April 1940. Two months later, equipped with Fw 200Cs, this unit moved to Bordeaux-Merignac to start operations against British shipping, flying patrols from France over the Western Approaches and landing at Trondheim or Stavanger in Norway.

Under the command of Oberstleutnant Geisse, I/KG 40's Fw 200Cs sank 90,000 tons of Allied shipping in August and September and, on 26 October, an aircraft flown by Hauptmann Bernhard Jope attacked and crippled the 44,343-ton liner *Empress of Britain* off the Irish coast, the ship being sunk by a U-boat while under tow two days later.

By the end of 1940 a total of 26 Fw 200s had been completed, and drastic steps were being taken by the British to protect their ships. The first of these involved the erection of catapults on merchant ships from which Sea Hurricane fighters could be launched on the appearance of a Condor. The Hurricane pilots, once launched against a raider, had either to ditch in the path of the convoy in the hope of being rescued or try to reach land. The next expedient was to provide merchantmen with flight decks (MAC-ships, or merchant aircraft carriers) and a substantial conversion programme started to prepare large numbers of Sea Hurricanes to enable them to operate from catapults and flight decks.

With the appearance of fighters over the Atlantic convoys the tactics of the Condors changed, the raiders preferring to retire, only returning once the Hurricane had ditched; occasionally the big aircraft stayed to fight it out, their defensive armament undergoing progressive increase until by the end of 1941 they carried three heavy machine-guns, two light machine-guns and a 20-mm cannon. Early in 1942 the employment of Fw 200s changed again, the aircraft being used to shadow and report the position of convoys to allow U-boats to close in and attack.

The sailing of the first North Cape convoys to the USSR resulted in about half the in-service Condors being moved to Norway early in 1942, others later being transferred to southern Italy to operate against the Malta convoys. This dilution of the German raiders in the West was further exacerbated by the removal of 18 aircraft to assist in transport operations at Stalingrad at the beginning of 1943, and it was not until the middle of that year that KG 40 was able to reassemble about 40 Fw 200Cs in western France.

By then a new weapon had appeared in the German anti-shipping arsenal, the radio-controlled, rocket-powered Hs 293A missile, two of which could be carried under the outboard engine nacelles of the Fw 200C-6 and Fw 200C-8 versions.

Any account of German maritime air operations should include mention of the Heinkel He 177 four-engine bomber which also engaged in anti-shipping work, both as a carrier of the Hs 293A missiles, LT 50 torpedoes and FX 1400 Fritz X guided bomb, and as a maritime reconnaissance aircraft with KG 40.

In 1944, however, relentless pressure by the Allies and the loss of their French airbases led to the withdrawal of maritime aircraft to Germany, where they were pressed into service for defence. Aerial support for the U-boats ended.

Above: The Focke-Wulf Fw 200 Condor began life as an airliner and established several records for long-distance flights. Its military potential was obvious, and the Fw 200C was a dedicated maritime aircraft; although less than 300 were built they proved a serious menace.

Above: Before the arrival of escort carriers the only counter to the Condor threat was the CAM ship (Catapult Armed Merchantship). It was a desperate expedient, launching a Hurricane fighter which had to ditch near the convoy unless within reach of land.

Left: The Condor could range far out into the Atlantic and if it located a target it could make a bombing attack of its own and broadcast the position of the convoy to the U-boat HQ at Lorient.

Below left: A U-boat photographed from the rear of the Fw 200's gondola. In 1942 the Germans mounted a shipping search radar aboard some Condors.

Escort vessels in the Battle of the Atlantic

Victory in the convoy battles was won by a combination of maritime air power, surface vessels and technological developments, but the main burden of convoy protection fell on the escort vessels of the Royal Navy, which had to overcome not only the U-boat wolf-packs and German long-range aircraft but to endure the ceaseless battering of the North Atlantic and Arctic seas.

Above: *The 'River' class frigates were introduced to rectify the problems encountered by the 'Flower' class corvettes, and they were the first escort vessels to carry Hedgehog forward-firing anti-submarine mortars as standard. More than half the 'Rivers' were built in Canada whose shipyards played a vital role in the victory in the Atlantic.*

Below: *Many of the small shipyards building 'Flower' class corvettes were unable to accommodate anything much larger, and the 'Castle' class was introduced to keep them occupied after the 'Flower' class ceased production. The 'Castles' were mainly used to form homogeneous escort groups and carried Squid launchers, which could bracket a U-boat with three heavy bombs 500 yards ahead of the ship while retaining sonar contact.*

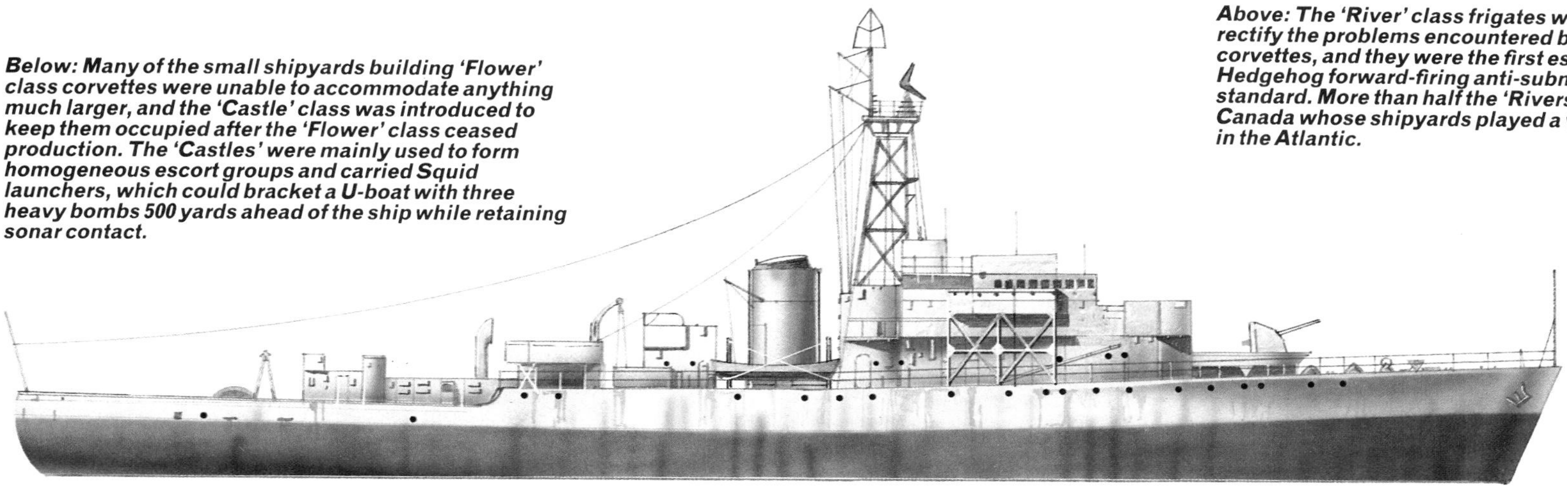

Right: *Developed before the war as Fast Escort Vessels, the 'Hunt' class lacked the endurance for Atlantic convoy operations and served around the British coast as well as in the Mediterranean. Over 80 were built and their anti-aircraft armament stood them in good stead; only three of the 19 lost during the war fell to aerial attack.*

Right: *HMS Mermaid was a modified 'Black Swan' class frigate. Twenty-four of these very successful anti-submarine vessels were constructed, later units carrying over 100 depth charges and a Hedgehog launcher. Best-known ships of the class were Walker's Starling and HMS Amethyst of the 1948 'Yangtse Incident'.*

Below: *Workhorse of the battle of the Atlantic was the 'Flower' class corvette. This is HMS Loosestrife as she appeared in 1944, with her armament including six 20-mm anti-aircraft guns as well as the standard 4-in main gun and the depth charges. Adapted from a Smith's Dock design for a southern ocean whalecatcher, the 'Flower' class were superb sea boats but their shortness made them disagreeably lively and wet in the deep ocean and they quickly exhausted the fittest crew.*

THE PQ 17 DISASTER

The Arctic Convoys

Hitler's ill-advised assault on the USSR in June 1941 gave the beleagured British an unlikely and problematical ally. Supplies were needed urgently and had to come by sea, adding to the responsibilities of the already sorely-stretched Royal Navy, and only the Soviet Arctic ports could be considered for shipments. Dependent upon the season this would demand a 10- to 15-day passage for convoys, the route flanked to the eastward by a German-occupied Norway. Winter pack ice forced their track closer towards this hostile coast, with near four months of unbroken darkness and deep gloom affording some cover but at the expense of weather conditions of unrelenting vileness. With the ice sheet retreating in summer, the route could be more distant, but was in permanent daylight and open to virtual round-the-clock attack.

Where the North Atlantic convoys were threatened predominantly by submarines and those in the Mediterranean by surface forces and aircraft, the Arctic run was menaced by all these forms and the escort system organized accordingly. This soon developed the form of an immediate escort, usually of corvettes and anti-submarine trawlers/whalers in the early days; a close cover of free-manoeuvring cruisers with destroyer escort which could rapidly reinforce the convoy on demand; and a distant cover of Home Fleet heavy units to guard against forays by the substantial naval forces built up by the enemy in northern Norway.

On 21 August 1941 the first, unnumbered seven-ship convoy sailed from Iceland for Archangel, arriving without incident 10 days later. This was shortly after the invasion of the USSR and was a political gesture as much as experiment. The PQ/QP convoy cycle commenced soon after, the inability of the enemy to interfere allowing escort strength to drop to as little as a cruiser and a pair of destroyers.

With the coming of the dark period the cycle was accelerated, so that by early February 1942 12 northbound PQs totalling 93 ships had been passed, with the loss of only one ship to a U-boat. With lengthening daylight in March 1942 things livened up with the passing PQ12 and QP8 narrowly avoiding interception by the newly-arrived battleship *Tirpitz* and her destroyers.

Only three weeks later the enemy achieved something like co-ordination, and PQ13 lost five ships: two to the very effective Junkers Ju 88 torpedo bomber, two to U-boats and one to a marauding destroyer force. In tackling the latter, the now usual close cover was unfortunate to lose the cruiser HMS *Trinidad* to one of her own rogue torpedoes. Two U-boats were sunk, one rammed by one of the ocean minesweepers that gave such yeoman service on the route.

Unpredictable weather reduced to mere chance planned interceptions by both sides. Sixteen of PQ14's 24 ships were obliged to return because of ice conditions but Ju 88s out of Kirkenes sank two of the empty QP10.

Over 260 Luftwaffe aircraft and over 30 U-boats were by now available, and both remaining 'pocket battleships' had been moved north. Despite the daylight lengthening ominously, politics demanded the running of PQ 16 in May. It suffered seven losses, six of them to aircraft.

By the end of June, when PQ17 sailed, German surface forces in the north had been reinforced by the battleship *Tirpitz*, a heavy cruiser and all remaining serviceable destroyers. By 1 July eight U-boats were concentrating on the convoy, which was also under continuous aerial surveillance. Only on 4 July, however, did the attack develop and the Admiralty ordered the convoy to scatter, firmly believing that

Above: A British convoy bound for Russia. Admiral Cunningham described the Arctic convoys as 'the most thankless task of the war at sea': at a terrible cost, equipment was delivered to Russia in exchange for abuse and non-cooperation.

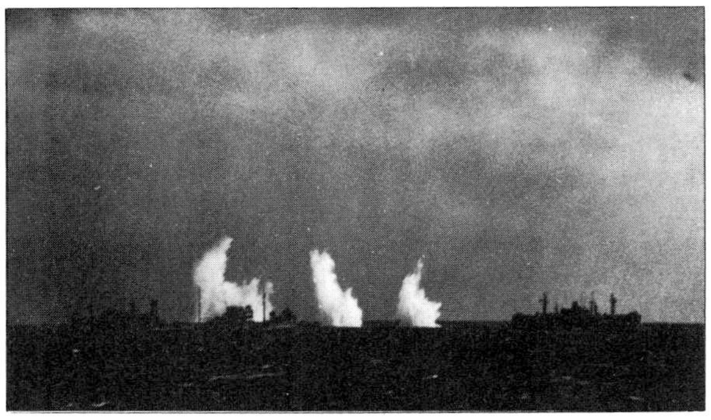

Above: A stick of bombs from a German Junkers Ju 88 lands amongst a convoy. The Luftwaffe concentrated over 260 aircraft in Norway to attack the Arctic convoys in the summer of 1942, and the air threat was enough to halt the convoys during the perpetual daylight of the Arctic summer.

Below: The Royal Navy's nightmare – major units of the German navy leave a Norwegian anchorage for a sortie against a convoy. Seen from the fantail of Tirpitz ***are the cruiser*** Hipper ***ahead of a 'pocket battleship' and four destroyers.***

Escort vessels in the Battle of the Atlantic

Victory in the convoy battles was won by a combination of maritime air power, surface vessels and technological developments, but the main burden of convoy protection fell on the escort vessels of the Royal Navy, which had to overcome not only the U-boat wolf-packs and German long-range aircraft but to endure the ceaseless battering of the North Atlantic and Arctic seas.

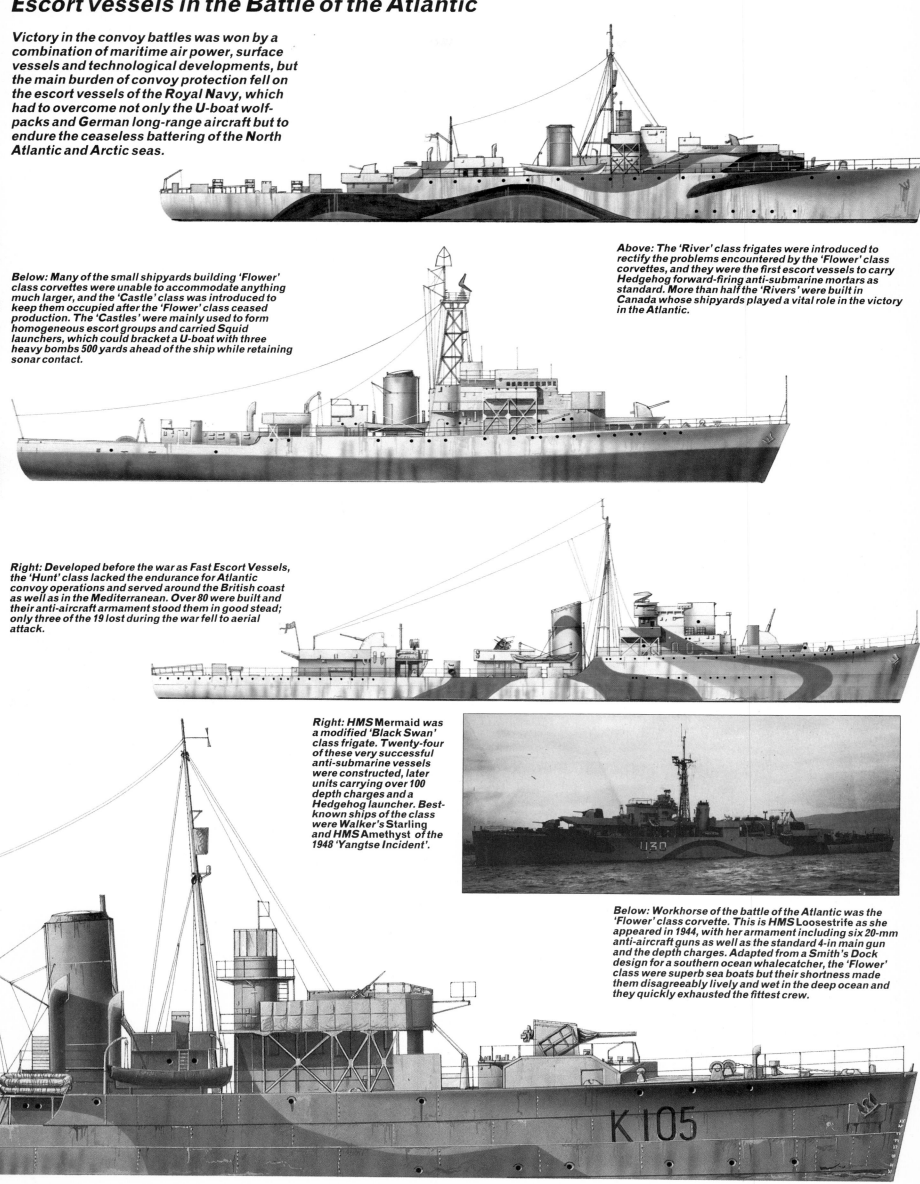

Above: The 'River' class frigates were introduced to rectify the problems encountered by the 'Flower' class corvettes, and they were the first escort vessels to carry Hedgehog forward-firing anti-submarine mortars as standard. More than half the 'Rivers' were built in Canada whose shipyards played a vital role in the victory in the Atlantic.

Below: Many of the small shipyards building 'Flower' class corvettes were unable to accommodate anything much larger, and the 'Castle' class was introduced to keep them occupied after the 'Flower' class ceased production. The 'Castles' were mainly used to form homogeneous escort groups and carried Squid launchers, which could bracket a U-boat with three heavy bombs 500 yards ahead of the ship while retaining sonar contact.

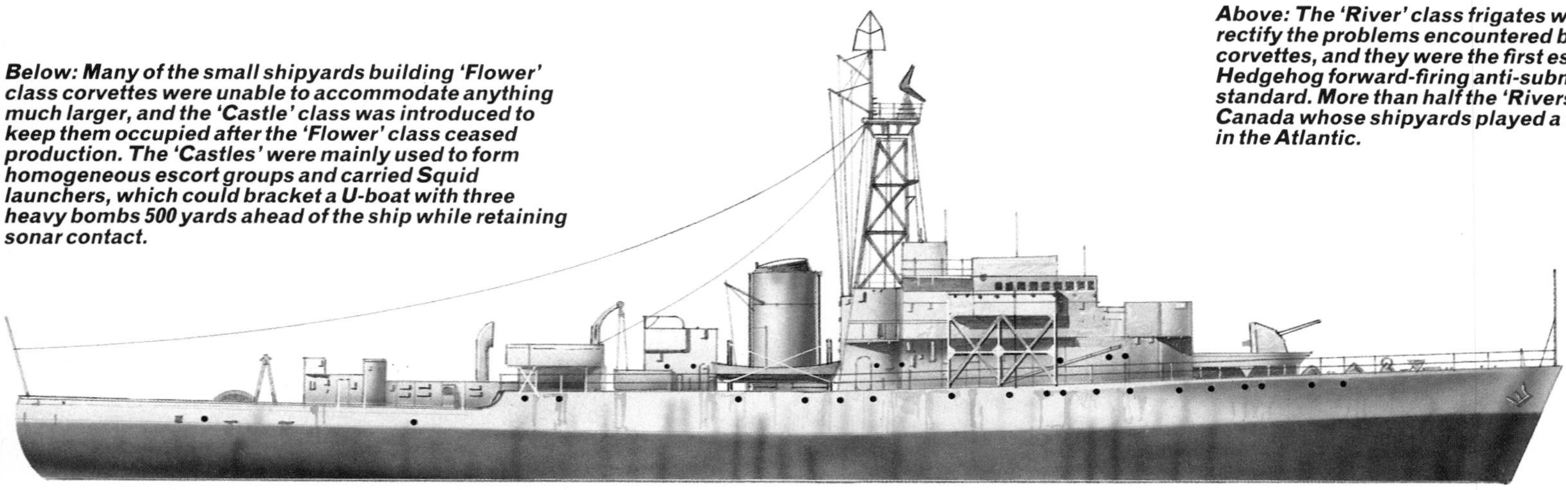

Right: Developed before the war as Fast Escort Vessels, the 'Hunt' class lacked the endurance for Atlantic convoy operations and served around the British coast as well as in the Mediterranean. Over 80 were built and their anti-aircraft armament stood them in good stead; only three of the 19 lost during the war fell to aerial attack.

Right: HMS Mermaid was a modified 'Black Swan' class frigate. Twenty-four of these very successful anti-submarine vessels were constructed, later units carrying over 100 depth charges and a Hedgehog launcher. Best-known ships of the class were Walker's Starling and HMS Amethyst of the 1948 'Yangtse Incident'.

Below: Workhorse of the battle of the Atlantic was the 'Flower' class corvette. This is HMS Loosestrife as she appeared in 1944, with her armament including six 20-mm anti-aircraft guns as well as the standard 4-in main gun and the depth charges. Adapted from a Smith's Dock design for a southern ocean whalecatcher, the 'Flower' class were superb sea boats but their shortness made them disagreeably lively and wet in the deep ocean and they quickly exhausted the fittest crew.

***Above:** A U-boat noses through the wreckage of a ship from the ill-fated convoy PQ-17, which scattered in the belief that* Tirpitz *was closing in. The isolated ships were easy targets.*

***Right:** The triple 6-in gun turrets of HMS* Belfast *encased in ice. Providing escorts to the Arctic convoys severely stretched the Royal Navy.*

the *Tirpitz* was out. As it happened she did not sail until the next day and then returned almost immediately. This, however, did not help the convoy which lost 23 out of its 34 ships to aircraft and submarine as, singly or in small groups, they struggled the last 800 miles virtually unescorted.

Not until September 1942 did the next convoy run, PQ18. Its 40 ships enjoyed a formidable escort that, at last, included an escort carrier. The enemy mounted a major effort but, though mass air attack sank 10 ships and U-boats a further three, the price was the loss of three U-boats and 27 aircraft.

Subsequently northbound convoys were recoded JW, starting at JW51. This much-delayed operation ran in two parts. Neither suffered loss but the cruiser and the destroyer close cover of JW51B fought a spirited defensive action against superior enemy surface forces on the last day of 1942.

Between February and November 1943 no convoys ran as all escorts were diverted to the Atlantic route, where the U-boat offensive had reached its peak. Then, within the space of nine weeks, a total of 106 ships passed north in six operations for the loss of only three ships.

From spring 1944 the convoys doubled in size and were accompanied by one, or even two, escort carriers. The aircraft from these made short work of shadowers while ever less-experienced U-boat commanders found themselves pitted against 20 destroyers and a battle-hardened support group before being able to penetrate as far as the corvettes of the close escort itself. Not surprisingly, the convoys ran to the close of hostilities with small inconvenience other than from the eternal, remorseless weather.

In all, 1,526 ship movements were involved in 77 convoys to and from North Russia, 98 ships being lost. Overall success was due to the dedication and perseverence of both merchantmen and escorts alike.

A convoy arrives in Russia bringing supplies Britain could ill afford. The contribution the convoys made to the Soviet war effort is difficult to assess, as current Soviet history completely ignores them.

Bombing the *Tirpitz*

Following the sinking in May 1941 of her sister ship *Bismarck*, the *Tirpitz* became the primary headache of the British Admiralty, who feared that she too might break out to raid Atlantic and Arctic convoys. That this fear was well founded was amply demonstrated in March 1942 when she left her refuge in Trondheim whilst convoy PQ 12 was bound from Iceland to the USSR. During the morning of 9 March a spotting aircraft from HMS *Victorious* sighted the enemy ship, and a strike was mounted by Fairey Albacores of Nos 817 and 832 Squadrons. All succeeded in dropping their torpedoes, but none found the target, and two of the attacking aircraft failed to return. This was destined to be the Fleet Air Arm's first and only chance of finding the *Tirpitz* on the open sea. She made one further foray in July 1942 for an intended attack on the ill-fated convoy PQ.17, but hastily returned to Norway after learning that HMS *Victorious* was once again with the Home Fleet.

The next attack on *Tirpitz* was to have been made at her moorings in Altenfjord early in 1943 by Swordfish from HMS *Dasher*, but that escort carrier blew up near the Isle of Arran on 27 March, many lives being lost. It was not until a year later that a fresh strike could be mounted, but by this time more modern equipment was available in the shape of the Fairey Barracudas of the 9th and 52nd Naval Torpedo Bomber Reconnaissance Wings.

Midget submarines

The *Tirpitz* had been damaged six months earlier in an attack by midget submarines as she lay at anchor in Kaafjord, but was ready for sea running trials in Altenfjord at the beginning of April 1944. However, by the early morning of 3 April the two fleet carriers were with the Home Fleet Battle Squadron, only 120 miles to the north west of the fjord. Accompanying the fleet carriers were the escort carriers HMS *Emperor, Fencer, Pursuer* and *Searcher*, the first three with two fighter squadrons each, and the last named with a mixed squadron of Fairey Swordfish and Grumman Wildcats for anti-submarine and fighter defence. At 4.24 a.m. Operation Tungsten began with the launch of the Barracudas of the 8th TBR Wing, accompanied by an escort of 40 fighters. They arrived at the fjord just as the enemy ship was ready for departure. With the element of surprise, all the Barracudas were able to make an attack, and they succeeded in making six direct hits on the stationary target. A further attack an hour later by the other TBR wing was less fortunate, a smokescreen having been laid in the meantime, but nevertheless they claimed a further eight hits as well as some probables.

The next effective attack was carried out on 17 July from HMS *Formidable* and *Indefatigable*. On this occasion a single strike was carried out, by 44 Barracudas, accompanied by 48 fighters, but the element of surprise was lost when the strike force was spotted from a new-built mountaintop observation post. This enabled the enemy to lay a dense smokescreen, and as a consequence only one near-miss was recorded.

Barracudas were again the main striking force in Operation Goodwood in late August. The first strike (Goodwood I) on 22 August proved fruitless as a result of further bad weather, and an evening strike by Hellcats (Goodwood II) was also abortive.

More successful was Goodwood III on 24 April. In this attack each of the 33 participating Barracudas carried a 1,600-lb armour-piercing bomb, whilst some of the Corsairs and Hellcats had 500-lb bombs. Once again the enemy had sufficient warning to put up a smokescreen, but undaunted by this the attackers dived in from various directions to confuse the AA gunners. Despite all the difficulties, one large and one small bomb found their target, but although the former penetrated the armoured decking, it failed to explode. The Fleet Air Arm's best opportunity of disabling or even sinking the ship was thus lost. A final raid on 29 August (Goodwood IV) was once more frustrated by a smokescreen, and no hits were recorded in the resulting blind attack.

The fate of the *Tirpitz* was finally sealed on 12 November 1944, when RAF Lancasters dropped 28 'Tallboy' bombs, each weighing 12,000 lb. At least two of these scored direct hits, and the ship capsized.

Above: A photograph of Tirpitz at her moorings in Kaafjord, Norway, taken by an RAF reconnaissance aircraft. If this mighty battleship intercepted an Arctic convoy it would have made short work of escorts and merchant ships alike, but aggressive air and sea attacks paralysed the German battleship for most of her career.

Left: HMS Emperor launches a Grumman Wildcat during Operation Tungsten, a mass airstrike from two fleet – and four escort-carriers which caught the Tirpitz preparing to leave her anchorage.

Below: The upturned hull of Tirpitz lies forlornly in Tromsöfjord after RAF Lancasters dropped 28 'Tallboy' 12,000-lb bombs, scoring at least two hits, on 12 November 1944. The battleship capsized rapidly, entombing 1,000 of her crew.

Above: Lancaster bombers of No. 617 Squadron RAF bomb Tirpitz through a dense smokescreen generated by smoke pots mounted atop the cliffs (the battleship is in the right hand corner indicated by an arrow).

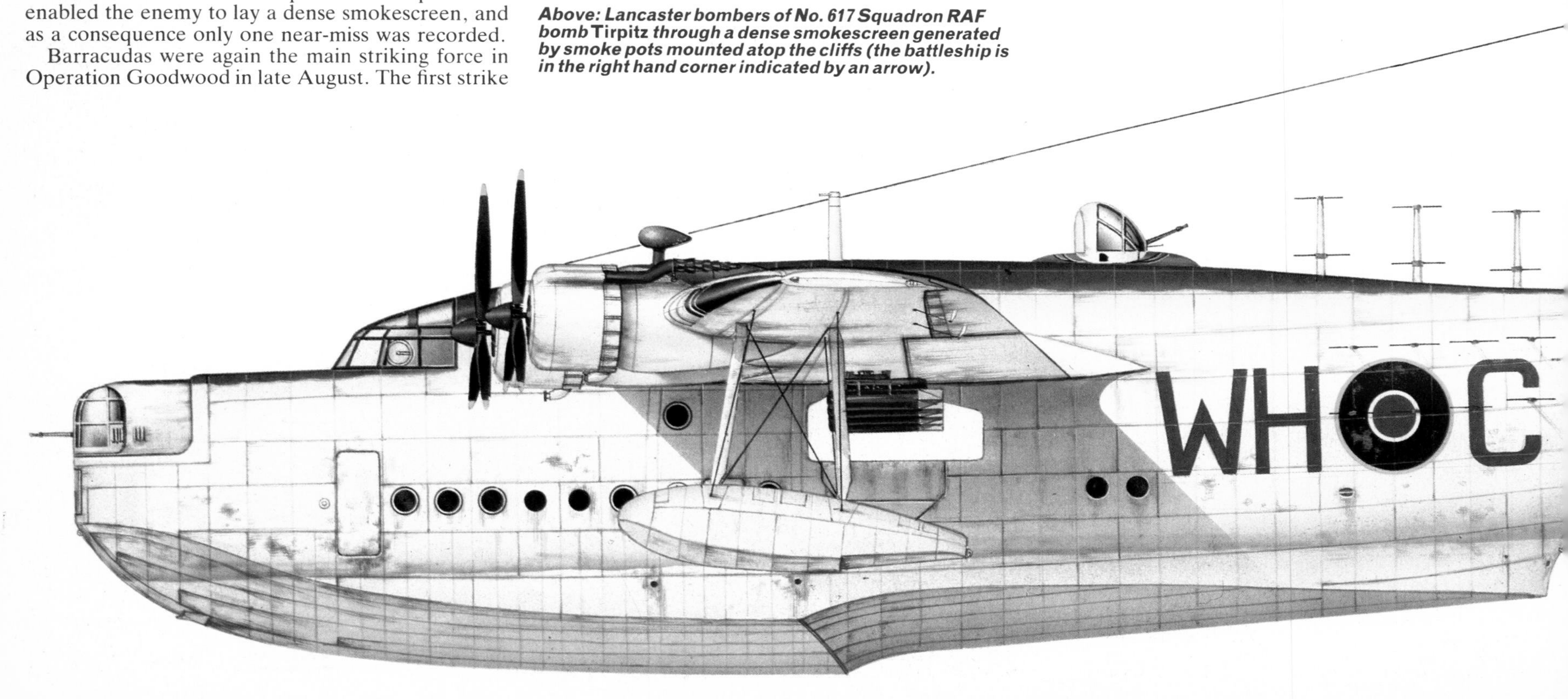

Allied anti-submarine aircraft

With the exception of the Type XXI boats, the German submarines had very limited underwater endurance and cruised on the surface whenever possible. Long-range aircraft equipped with depth charges had an immediate impact on the convoy battles, and the advent of airborne radar cut through the cover of darkness and placed the U-boats on the defensive.

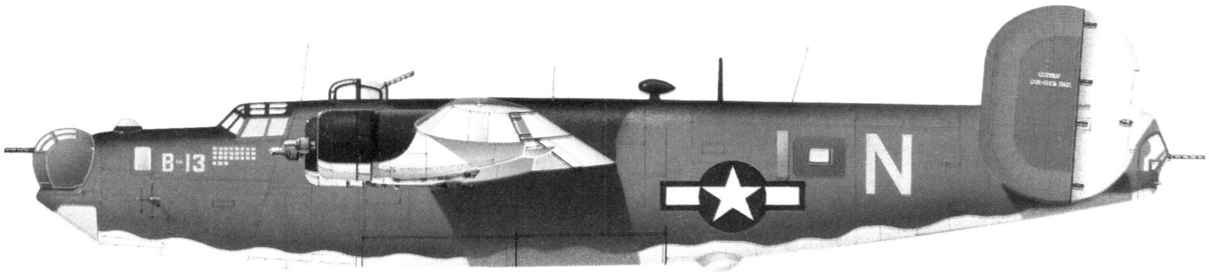

Left: After the USA entered the war the convoys received aerial protection over the western Atlantic, but American ASW aircraft also operated from Britain. This Consolidated PB4Y-1 Liberator of patrol Bomber Squadron VPB-110 was based in Devon during the winter of 1944.

Above: A Vickers Wellington Mk XIV in the markings of No. 304 (Polish) Squadron, RAF Coastal Command. This aircraft is fitted with a Leigh Light (an airborne searchlight) which was widely used by anti-submarine aircraft from 1943, with an average of two U-boats attacks per month.

Right: A Whitley Mk VII of No. 502 Squadron, RAF Coastal Command, is shown in the colour scheme adopted in late 1942. Fitted with ASV radar, this elderly bomber gave valuable service on anti-submarine patrols over the Bay of Biscay, and it fell to a Whitley to score the first kill with ASV by sinking U-206 in November 1941.

Left: 19 Boeing B-17F bombers were loaned to RAF Coastal Command and operated as maritime patrol aircraft in 1942-3 as Fortress GR Mk IIs. Illustrated here is one of 45 GR Mk IIAs issued, in this case operated by No. 220 Squadron at Ballykelly.

Right: The RAF began purchasing Consolidated PBY Catalinas in early 1941 and eventually acquired some 700 of them, equipping 11 squadrona of Coastal Command and another 12 squadrons operating overseas. Catalinas located and shadowed *Bismarck* enabling Royal Navy surface units to regain contact, and it was a Catalina which scored the last kill by Coastal Command, sinking a U-boat on 7 May 1945.

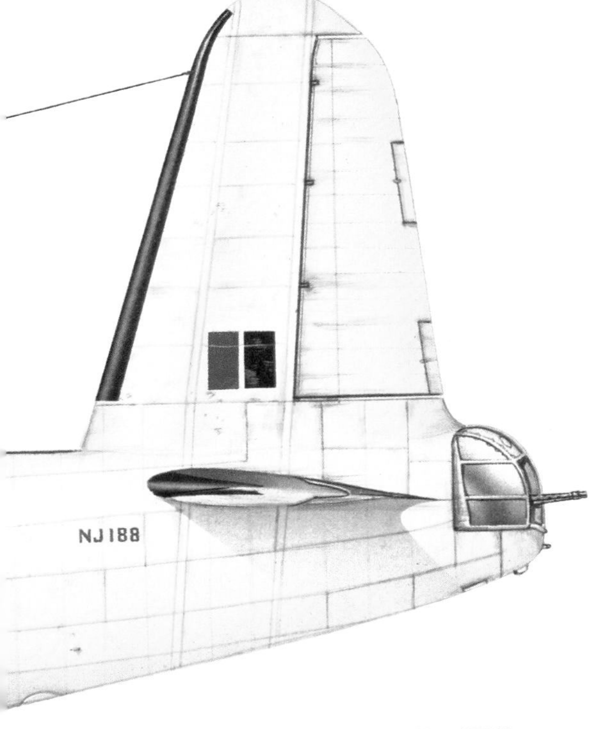

The Short Sunderland flying boat was dubbed the 'Flying Porcupine' by the Germans because of its numerous machine-guns and tough construction, which made it a formidable opponent.

Right: The US Navy valued the endurance of airships, which made them excellent anti-submarine patrol aircraft. This blimp is wafting over a 'Type IXD' long range U-boat which has surrendered in 1945.

Chapter 15

Hitting Back at the Japanese

Two months after the Imperial Japanese Navy was decisively beaten at Midway, the hitherto invincible Japanese army was checked by staunch Australian resistance in New Guinea. Over 600 miles eastwards the Americans launched their first full-scale counter-offensive against Guadalcanal in the Solomon Islands and began what was to become a protracted struggle on land, sea and air. Although the Marines around Henderson Field started the campaign with inadequate resources, within months the full industrial might of the USA was coming into play.

New Guinea presented one of the most hostile environments in which to fight a battle, with trackless mountains towering to over 13,000 ft adding to the problems of jungle war. It was here that the Japanese were first checked.

While the main drive of the great Japanese offensive during the months following Pearl Harbor had been to the southwest of the home islands on each side of a central axis aimed at Singapore, the Japanese commanders also appreciated that in the end they would have to defend themselves from American forces from the east. They had therefore consolidated control of the island chains to the south – the Marianas, the Carolines and especially the island and harbour of Truk – and as early as 23 January 1942 they had put a small force ashore at Kavieng in New Ireland, then one at Rabaul where their force of 5,000 quickly overcame the 1,400 Australian troops garrisoned there.

In early March Japanese troops landed unopposed at Lae and Salamaua in Huon Bay on the north coast of New Guinea, and busied themselves for several weeks building up stores and workshops for a possible further advance to the south. Because they were subjected to so little interference – even while they built a fair-sized airfield of obvious tactical importance – and as they soon heard that a large fleet under Admiral Hara was sailing from the Carolines to capture Port Moresby, they remained fairly confident that their progress to the south would be comparatively easy, their greatest problems being presented by the admittedly difficult terrain.

The defeat of the invasion force at the Battle of the Coral Sea put an end to such comfortable assumptions, however, though not to headquarters plans for the capture of Port Moresby; as the Japanese navy had failed to reach the place, then the Japanese army would do so. But the necessary reorganization took time, and meanwhile the Australian presence in the area increased.

Already Australian Commandos – Independent companies – had been harassing the Japanese perimeters, and in April they were joined by another company. Shortly afterwards two Australian brigades arrived at Port Moresby, another was sent to Milne Bay on the eastern tip of the peninsula and two battalions were ordered to push up and over the Owen Stanley Range along the Kokoda Trail to try to reach Buna on the north coast. There they were to construct an airfield from which the Japanese positions along the coast could be attacked.

Not surprisingly, the Japanese reacted swiftly and in some strength. On 21 July 2,000 men went ashore at Buna (the Australian battalions were still on their way); by the end of the month 13,500 men of Lieutenant-General Harukichi Hyakutake's Seventeenth Army had followed them, driven south along the trail sweeping up the Independent companies as they went, almost effortlessly driving back the two battalions as well, and by 27 July had arrived at Kokoda. By mid-August they were driving even farther south, though by now General Rowell, commanding the Australians, had pushed more men up to meet them, while Australian and American fighter aircraft were very effectively shooting up the narrow and overflowing Japanese communications. And yet again, that iron law was coming into operation: the Japanese were nearly a hundred miles of appalling going from their bases, the Australians were only 30 from theirs.

Moreover, the Australian homeland with many more divisions, many more aircraft of every category and, compared with the Japanese, a positively inexhaustible storehouse, was just behind them.

The Japanese advance was stopped by 25 August, but on the following day the second prong of the Japanese attack formed with a landing of nearly 2,000 men at Milne Bay. But their Intelligence was at fault for they had expected to find only two or three companies of Australian infantry there, as guard to the small airfield. Instead they found nearly two brigades (the first had been reinforced), two fighter squadrons and batteries of well sited artillery, and although after five days of fierce fighting the Japanese – who had landed a few tanks – did reach the edge of the airfield they were gradually driven back, their casualties mounting implacably and on 6 September the survivors were evacuated. Japanese soldiers had at last been forced to retreat!

It was beginning to happen, too, on the Kokoda Trail.

Both the 6th and 7th Australian Divisions were now concentrated in Papua, and on 23 September General Sir Thomas Blamey arrived to take command, under General MacArthur as Allied Commander-in-Chief, South-West Pacific. Slowly but relentlessly, the Australians began to force the Japanese back up the 'golden stairs' from Uberi, the 'stairs' formed by steps some 10 to 18 inches in height, the front edge of the step consisting of a small log held by stakes, with behind it little but mud and water; and they rose 1,200 feet in the first three miles!

For the Australians, the physical exhaustion of just climbing the 'stairs' was almost unsupportable, and were it not for the 'fuzzy-wuzzy angels' – Melanesian

Australian troops were recalled from the sands of North Africa to a very different terrain in the defence of their home. Stopping the Japanese, until then masters of jungle war, they saved Port Moresby and forced their way back across the Owen Stanley range.

Island-hopping

The landings on Guadalcanal were to be the first step in a long series of actions aimed at isolating Japan's key bastion in the south west Pacific, Rabaul, on New Britain. Operating in conjunction with General MacArthur's forces clearing New Guinea, the 'island hopping' drive up the chain of the Solomons would be bitterly contested, but the union between the two Allied campaigns (with the ultimate aim of launching an assault on the Philippines or the East Indies) could not be prevented.

8 August 1942, and at last American forces have come to grips with the Japanese on Guadalcanal in the Solomons. Just inshore from Lunga, the 1st Marine Division is battling for control of the airstrip that was to become famous as Henderson Field.

porters who carried everything (and almost everyone) with a loyalty and enthusiasm which astounded all who saw it – the job would have taken ten times longer. As it was, by early October the leading Australian brigade had reached Templeton's Crossing at the ridge of the Owen Stanley Range, and by the 17th had forced the Japanese away from three positions they had formed there – though hunger must have played its part in the Japanese defeat, for evidence of cannibalism was found, and most of the bodies of the dead Japanese soldiers were thin and discoloured with starvation and disease. Allied control of the air was beating them just as much as the assault on the ground.

The Australians retook Kokoda on 2 November and reopened the airfield there from which they could be well supported all the way to Buna. An attempt by the Japanese to stand on the Kumusi river was thwarted by flank attacks by fresh Australian and American troops, and their final stand at Buna came to an end on 21 January 1943, when more Australian and American troops were brought up along the trail and even more were landed along the north coast, isolating the Japanese garrisons at Lae and Salamaua.

The New Guinea campaign cost the Japanese over 12,000 men, the Australian battle casualties amounted to 5,700 and the American figure was 2,800 – but at least three times as many had succumbed to tropical hazards from malaria to sheer heat exhaustion.

But they had proved that they could fight and beat the Japanese, even in such appalling conditions – so long as they had air supremacy.

The Solomon Islands

In 1942 the Solomon Islands suddenly became a key strategic position in the developing war in the South Pacific. In Japanese hands they would threaten the supply routes between America and Australia, in Allied hands they would form first a shield for the build-up of Allied strength in Australia, second an essential springboard for an Allied offensive to drive the Japanese back to their own islands.

By May the Japanese had already installed a sizeable garrison at the magnificent anchorage of Tulagi on the small Florida Island at the eastern end of the Solomons, and at the end of that month they began ferrying troops across the Nggela Channel to the larger island of Guadalcanal. Soon reports were reaching MacArthur from the team of Australian 'coastwatchers' that the Japanese were constructing an airfield near Lunga Point and the village of Kukum, and the danger of Japanese bombers being able to operate from there against Allied shipping, and even against the Australian mainland, became obvious.

On 7 August somewhat to the surprise of all concerned, a force of 19,000 US Marines under Major-General Alexander Vandegrift was landed successfully at both Lunga Point and Tulagi, and by the evening the Marines had chased the 2,200 Japanese construction workers off into the jungle, while 36 hours later the 1,500 Japanese soldiers at Tulagi had also been eliminated. By 8 August the airfield was being completed by US engineers and had been rechristened Henderson Field, and by 20 August the first Wildcat fighters and Dauntless divebombers had landed.

But before that, of course, the Japanese had reacted. The Battle of Savo Island had severely weakened Allied naval strength, and the withdrawal of Admiral Turner's force had left the Marines very short of materials with which to build strong defences; fortunately, there was quite a lot of Japanese material around, and in the next two weeks it was put to good use.

This was proved on 18 August when a Japanese force of some 6,000 troops commanded by Colonel Ichiki, who was under the impression that only 2,000 US Marines had been landed, attacked Henderson Field and ran into a deadly storm of fire which quickly wiped his command from the face of the island. Thereafter, Japanese attacks were a trifle less reckless, but the Imperial Command never seemed able accurately to foresee the US Marines' strength on the island.

Every battle of the Slot, from each phase of the Battle of the Eastern Solomons, through the Battles of Cape Esperance and the Santa Cruz Islands to the last engagements which the Japanese called the Naval Battle of Guadalcanal, were fought to take more Japanese troops to the island in order to regain con-

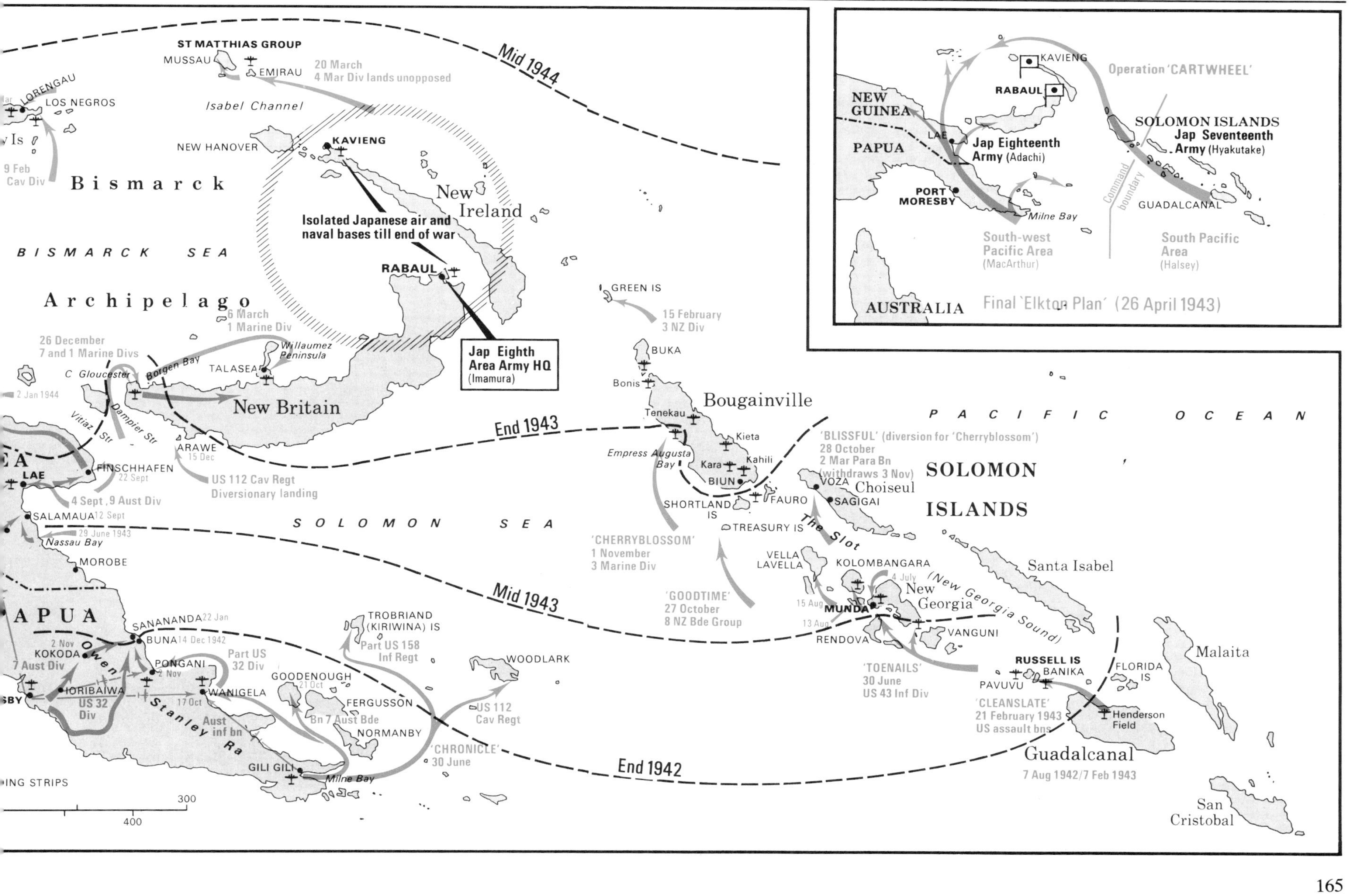

The bitter sea battles around Guadalcanal were to cost so many ships that the passage between Guadalcanal and Florida Island became known as 'Iron Bottom Sound'.

An entrenched Japanese army signaller. Once the tide of military success had turned, Japan had to maintain a far-flung empire with limited natural and manpower resources, against the awesome capacity of America.

trol of Henderson Field. The Tokyo Express had brought in another 8,000 men by 13 September – and over 1,200 of them were killed that night on Bloody Ridge.

A month later, after Cape Esperance, the Japanese strength had risen to 22,000 troops on the island – but there were now 23,000 marines with another 4,500 on Tulagi, for it was far easier for the Allies to reinforce from Australia than for the Japanese from their own homeland, or even from Luzon. Bombardment of Henderson Field by the heavy guns of two Japanese battle-cruisers set fire to fuel stocks, destroyed over half the aircraft there and so thoroughly ploughed up the field that the bombers had to return to Australia for a time – but the land attack on the field was beaten off yet again at the end of October with Japanese losses running into thousands, while the Marines, fighting from well-sited and well-dug defensive positions and gaining experience with every hour, lost only a few hundred. American medical teams were now saving a large proportion of the wounded and most of the sick.

On the night of 14/15 November, when seven of the transports Admiral Tanaka was trying to bring down the Slot were sunk, only 4,000 of the 11,000 Japanese troops sent to Guadalcanal arrived, and as they went into action the Americans abandoned the defensive which they had held so successfully for nearly four months, and went over to the offensive. During the last days of the month, the marines enlarged their perimeter so that in the early days of December there was space for the 25th Infantry Division, the 2nd Marine Division and the 'Americal' Division – XIV Corps under General Patch – to come in and relieve Vandegrift's gallant but now tired 1st Marines. Quickly Patch organized for a drive out, to clear the Japanese from the island.

Left: Once Guadalcanal was under control, Henderson Field-based bombers could harass enemy forces and shipping all along the Solomon chain. This Boeing B-17 has just bombed an island in the New Georgia group.

Left: A PT boat rests up for the day in one of the innumerable inlets along the Slot. The main function of these small craft was to interrupt the regular night runs of the 'Tokyo Express'.

Above: The Marines quickly learned the rules of fighting a determined enemy in the jungles. Much of the combat was at close range, in thick vegetation.

Savo Island

The aircraft-carriers which covered the landings on Guadalcanal soon withdrew, leaving the invasion fleet protected by cruisers and destroyers. But on the night of 8/9 August a Japanese cruiser squadron attacked with devastating success; better armament and above all, better night-fighting led to a decisive victory over an Allied force.

Above: A 'Takao' class cruiser displays the heavy armament which, together with superior night-fighting capability, was to prove decisive in the battle of 9 August.

Following the heavy Japanese defeat at Midway in June 1942, the Americans began to go onto the offensive in the Pacific. This resulted, among other operations, in the seizure of Guadalcanal and neighbouring Tulagi as a first stage in the reconquest of the Solomons. This early example of an amphibious assault entailed the presence offshore of a considerable number of transports, which would need an estimated four days to discharge. In addition to local naval cover, there was distant support from Admiral Fletcher's carrier group. These three carriers were virtually all the flightdecks remaining to the Americans in the Pacific and, anxious not to hazard them a moment longer than necessary, Fletcher made the controversial decision to withdraw after only 36 hours.

The Japanese reacted swiftly, Vice Admiral Mikawa sailing immediately from Rabaul with his heavy cruiser flagship *Chokai*, accompanied by two light cruisers and a destroyer. By 14.00 on the day of the landing, he was 200 miles on his way, making rendezvous near Bougainville with a powerful reinforcement of four more heavy cruisers. Driving on south-eastward, Mikawa used the passage between the double chain of the Solomons, a channel that was to become all too familiar as the Slot.

Americans had early established aerial reconnaissance patrols, and Mikawa was spotted twice during the forenoon of 8 August. The war was still young, however, and the air reports were poorly worded, filed without urgency, and spent hours filtering through the official machine. As a result, Rear Admiral Turner, commander of the amphibious force, learned (between 18.00 and 19.00 local time) both that a Japanese force was approaching and that Fletcher's carriers were leaving. Though the latter news was alarming, the former indicated wrongly that the enemy consisted largely of seaplane tenders. Imminent attack was not anticipated, therefore, and no special precautions taken. Indeed, there was available the not-inconsiderable force of six heavy cruisers, two light cruisers and four destroyers.

The evening of 8 August came in very dark, with low cloud and intermittent heavy rain, overlaid with the all-pervading heat and humidity so characteristic of the area. Turner, disturbed by the implications of Fletcher's withdrawal, summoned Crutchley to a conference to discuss the situation; the latter, reasonably enough in the conditions, travelled the 20 miles or so in the *Australia* herself, leaving the southern force to his deputy in the *Chicago*. Crutchley arrived at 22.30.

At 00.43 on 9 August the Japanese, in line ahead and led by the *Chokai*, made a visual sighting on an American destroyer at over 5 miles despite the velvet darkness. She was the USS *Blue* which, with the USS *Ralph Talbot*, was slowly crisscrossing the strait as radar picket. Despite the length of the Japanese line and its approach from the very direction expected, it was not detected and passed between the two ships at about 26 kts.

Mikawa, anxious to attack and withdraw before the inevitable morning air strike from Fletcher's carriers, which he believed still to be present, risked losing surprise by launching reconnaissance aircraft. These were seen by the Americans but the significance of their being floatplanes (and, therefore, cruiser-based) was not grasped.

Still unsuspected, the Japanese had Savo abeam at 01.25 and sighted the two remaining southern force cruisers shortly after that.

At 01.38 they opened their attack characteristically with a salvo of torpedoes and, minutes later, the peace of the night was split by air-dropped flares blooming simultaneously with two torpedoes slamming into the somnolent *Canberra*. Her senior ship, the *Chicago*, was equally surprised, her captain in his bunk. Even as general quarters sounded, the *Chicago*'s bows were shattered by a torpedo.

Desperately, the two injured cruisers struggled to respond but Mikawa swept by, scything in an arc around the back of Savo. The manoeuvre disrupted his line, so that it advanced in two parallel columns; as luck would have it these neatly bracketed the northern force cruisers. Incredibly, the *Chicago* had not alerted them to the situation and neither did they respond to the brief racket of battle only 5 miles away.

Proceeding in line ahead at a stately 10 kts, unprepared, with guns unmanned and pointing fore-and-aft, they found themselves suddenly illuminated at close range by searchlights. It was worse than Matapan. At barely 400-yard range the Japanese used everything, including 25-mm automatic weapons. The action lasted a bare 10 minutes, leaving the three American cruisers blazing.

Nothing significant now stood between Mikawa and his primary target – the transports. As though unnerved by his own success, however, he left them and ordered a retirement. It was shortly after 02.00. The predictible shooting-up of the picket destroyers was the last act and, after the final salvo from the *Yubari* at 02.23, peace returned. From the Japanese ships, Savo's serrated outline was etched clear against the glow of four burning ships, all of which sank within the next 12 hours, their bones being the first to grace what was to become known as 'Ironbottom Sound'.

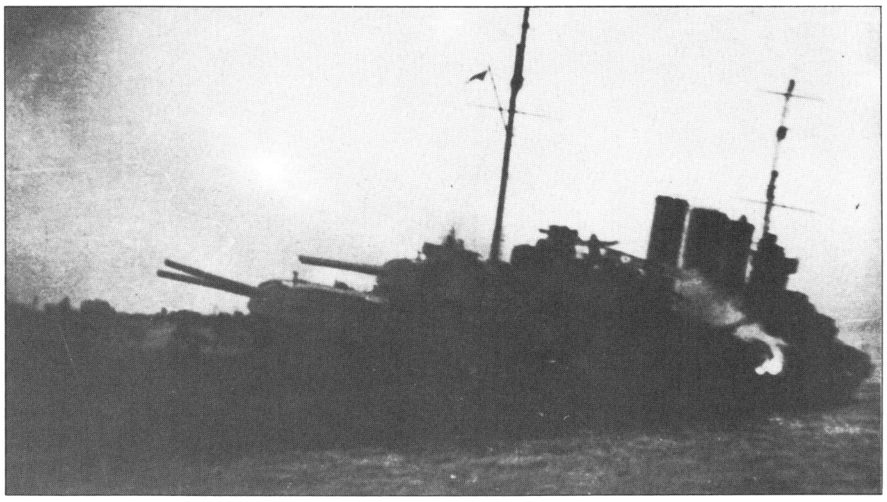

HMAS* Canberra *settles in the water early on the morning of 9 August 1942. Savo Island was a bitter lesson to the Allied navies in the Pacific, costing the lives of over 1,000 sailors.

Of the Japanese, only two van ships, the *Chokai* and *Aoba*, suffered damage of any consequence, losing 38 dead. Over 1,000 Allied seamen perished, but their deaths were not in vain, for Guadalcanal was held, becoming a symbolic prize in a six-month war of attrition in which, finally, the Americans were undisputed victors.

The 'New Orleans' class had the unhappy distinction of losing three ships in one action, USS* Vincennes, Quincy *and* Astoria *were all sunk at Savo.

But by now Imperial Japanese Headquarters was beginning to count the cost. Since 7 August losses totalled 65 naval craft and more than 800 aircraft; as for men, the calculations were difficult to make but it was apparent that while there were over 50,000 American troops on Guadalcanal, well supplied and well fed, whatever number of survivors of Hyakutake's army remained they were on one-third of normal rations and so weakened by hunger and disease that a new offensive was beyond them.

On 4 January 1943 the reality was accepted in Tokyo and the orders went out. Between 1 and 9 February destroyers of the Tokyo Express came back to Guadalcanal for the last time, and successfully evacuated 11,000 men – whose rearguard had tenaciously kept back the American advance for the required time, and who left only their dead on the beaches.

Offensive in Burma

As befitted a traditional and conservative Commander-in-Chief, General Wavell began planning for a return into Burma almost as soon as the last of General Slim's troops passed back into Assam. Such a move was necessary first to improve the morale of all troops in the India Command, then to show the world that the Japanese were not invincible, and thirdly to reassure the Burmese peoples and other races in the area that the protection of the British Empire, under which they had lived for so long, was not so fragile as had recently appeared.

Wavell's first operational plans, issued to the commanders of the Eastern Army in September 1942, envisaged an amphibious landing of the British 29th Independent Brigade on the island of Akyab and the capture of its landing fields, followed by the establishment of RAF air supremacy from those airfields, to cover larger-scale land operations back into Burma as soon as the next monsoon season was over.

As a diversionary movement to draw off the attention of the weak Japanese garrison at Akyab, the 14th Indian Division under Major-General Lloyd was to drive down the length of the Mayu Peninsula from Chittagong, through Cox's Bazaar and the important port of Maungdaw and, once it had reached Foul Point at the end of the peninsula the 6th Brigade Group, which had been amphibiously trained in India, would cross the Mayu estuary to join the 29th.

By the end of September 14th Division had indeed begun its march south from Chittagong, only slightly bemused to find that for over forty miles north of Cox's Bazaar the only road was a four-foot-wide cart track, and that all their heavy equipment would have to go by sea to that first objective. But they slogged

Sikhs wade through the monsoon mud in Burma. General Wavell's offensive into Arakan was not well omened, inexperienced troops being sent into some of the worst terrain and weather in the world.

Japanese troops on the attack in Burma. They are manpacking disassembled mortars and mountain guns through the jungle to counter a Commonwealth offensive out of India.

their way onwards, then to be told that their next objective would be to form, by 1 December, a line from Maungdaw across to Buthidaung, with one battalion across the Mayu and even further south at Rathedaung.

Thirteen inches of rain fell on one day in November, washing away much of the new roadwork just built by the slaving engineers; typhoon conditions reigned in the Bay of Bengal. The comment by an old Arakan hand that the area in the dry season can often 'be very wet', plus the news that neither 29th Independent Brigade nor its landing-craft were going to be available after all, made it clear to General Lloyd that his task was to be rather more difficult than he had imagined. Even discounting the benefits of hindsight, it is difficult to see why at that moment General Wavell did not cancel the entire operation. He should have learned by now that if Churchill admired swift reaction to setback, he nevertheless, wanted the reaction to be successful; and already the odds were mounting against the inexperienced and unfortunate troops he was sending into some of the worst country in the world.

But they stayed and they went on down, forcing their way through mangrove swamps and across numerous tidal creeks until at last on 23 October an advance patrol reached the Maungdaw-Buthidaung line – to find the Japanese already there. It took some days for the rest of the leading brigade to come up, and then General Irwin, commanding Eastern Army, overrode Lloyd and ordered that he await the arrival of 123rd and 47th Indian Brigades before he attacked the Japanese; and as heavy rain again washed out the roads, it was 17 December before all was ready.

It was then discovered that the Japanese had not waited for the attack and had fallen back to Kondan, on the west bank of the Mayu opposite Rathedaung. With understandable but perhaps over-confident optimism, 14th Division now pressed on along the narrow, tortuous route leading to Donbaik and Foul Point, only the over-imaginative sensing the ominous sounds of the local nomenclature. On 1 January 1943 patrols of 47th Brigade actually reached Foul Point and chased some Japanese troops, with suspicious ease, off into the foothills; but a week later when first a company and then a battalion of the 1st Inniskillings came up to secure the point, they ran into a maze of well-sited fox-holes hidden in scrub and small hillocks from which they were sniped from the rear, while heavy cross-fire poured in from the jungle and from a high, bamboo-covered escarpment in which the Japanese had built several strongpoints. The Inniskillings and all 14th Indian Division had plodded determinedly into a well-laid trap.

Japanese attack

They continued to do so for a while yet. Lloyd had split both his brigades to some extent, units from 47th both fighting in the tip of the peninsula and attempting to storm Donbaik, units from 123rd Brigade split between both sides of the Mayu River, one battalion of Lancashires vainly attacking Rathedaung while the rest of the brigade were on the Mayu Range around Kondon. And it was in this extended position that they found themselves at the beginning of March being attacked by three complete regiments of Lieutenant-General Takishi Koga's 55th Division, brought down from the Toungoo/Prome area.

Yet still the reality of the situation was not accepted in Delhi, and the attempt to snatch victory from a hopeless defeat went on while more troops and even some tanks were fed into the attack on Donbaik. All through March fierce fighting occurred

Japanese troops and Type 89B medium tanks cross a temporary bridge during a Japanese attack. The Japanese army was notably deficient in heavier armour, although in Burma that was no handicap as the lightest of armoured vehicles was operated with great difficulty.

The Tokyo Express

Once the Americans won air superiority over Guadalcanal, Japanese ships bringing supplies and reinforcements to the island had to do so under cover of darkness. They did so with startling efficiency, confident of their superior night-fighting techniques.

Above: A 'Fubuki' class destroyer making 34 kts would have been typical of the Tokyo Express.

Below: USS Wasp, providing cover to American reinforcements, was torpedoed and crippled by the Japanese submarine I-19. She was abandoned and sunk by a US Navy destroyer.

Below: Admiral Raizo Tanaka, whose ships wreaked such havoc off Guadalcanal.

May 1942 saw the Japanese consolidating their hold on the Solomons, from which they could threaten Australia itself. Encouraged by their great success of Midway, the Americans resolved that the Solomons would be the point at which the seemingly inexorable enemy tide would be stemmed. The landing, virtually unopposed, took place on 7 August and by 9 August apparently only mopping-up operations remained for the Americans.

Any complacency was rudely shattered on the night of 9 August when Vice-Admiral Gunichi Mikawa's cruisers bore in to inflict a bloody defeat off Savo Island on the naval forces covering the landing.

The US transports withdrew, leaving 16,000 US Marines unsupported ashore. Working feverishly in the damp, enervating heat, their engineers had the incomplete Japanese airstrip open for business by 15 August, and named it Henderson Field; it was to play a crucial role in the campaign.

On the night of 17/18 August nearly 1,000 Japanese troops were landed by high-speed transports escorted by seven fleet destroyers. Their speed was just sufficient to be in and out again within the hours of darkness, and their nocturnal activities were to become so regular as to be named the Tokyo Express.

For a week the enemy ran in small parcels of troops to build up the strength to take the island, but on 24 August the enemy tried direct assault. While the inconclusive Battle of the Eastern Solomons was being fought between the main fleets to engage the American presence, a bombardment force of four destroyers under the redoubtable Rear-Admiral Raizo Tanaka ran a group of transports down the Slot, the long channel dividing the double chain of the Solomons.

Supplemented by pottering Daihatsu barges, the destroyers built up the Japanese strength for an offensive. Meanwhile, the Americans landed 4,000 more marines, but at the cost of the carrier USS *Wasp* and a destroyer from the covering force. During October Tanaka's destroyers worked miracles, the nightly runs of the Tokyo Express delivering 20,000 men with equipment. Henderson-based aircraft were a continuing aggravation and heavy cruisers came down on the night of 11/12 October to bombard the airfield. They ran straight into a superior American force, had their 'T' crossed and lost a cruiser and a destroyer.

Determined to reduce Henderson, the Japanese bombed it heavily twice in daylight on 13 October, interfered with repairs to cratered airstrips by artillery fire and then, after dark, brought down two battle-cruisers. In a 90-minute bombardment the airfield was plastered with over 900 rounds of 356-mm ammunition.

Simultaneously, the Express brought in heavy reinforcements in transports, gambling on the parlous state of Henderson's defenders to lie offshore during the day. Fielding everything that remained, the Americans destroyed three transports and forced Tanaka to withdraw. He returned with heavy cruisers on the night of 15/16 October, laying 900 rounds of 203-mm and 300 of 127-mm fire within the shattered perimeter.

Impatient for a decision, the Japanese brought their main fleet south and engaged the new American commander, Vice-Admiral William F. Halsey, off Santa Cruz on 26 October, adding the carrier USS *Hornet* to the cost of Guadalcanal.

On 12 November the Japanese brought down 11,000 men in transports, covered by a force that included two battleships. American intelligence was good and they were ready but the battle, early on 13 November, degenerated into a confused melée, the Americans losing four destroyers and two cruisers for one Japanese battleship and two destroyers. Undeterred, the Japanese returned during the following night, the airfield again being swept by 1,400 assorted cruiser and destroyer rounds in the space of 37 minutes. With daylight Henderson-based aircraft caught the culprits, sinking a heavy cruiser, but the night action had diverted attention from the 'Express', which had run in no less than 10 transports. Six were lost to frantic air attack and the remainder beached to guarantee their deliveries. The enemy certainly did not lack resolve. A heavy covering force also came down the Slot and was met by a similar American force near Savo Island.

The battle-cruiser *Kirishima* was overwhelmed by gunfire from the battleship USS *Washington*, and together with two American and one Japanese destroyer laid her bones alongside the remainder already littering what was now known as Ironbottom Sound.

The cost had resulted in only 2,000 of 7,000 Japanese troops actually being landed. The Americans now outnumbered their foe by 40,000 to 25,000, and only Tanaka could prevent disaster.

During the night of 30 November eight of his destroyers, cluttered with supplies and personnel, were surprised by an American force of five cruisers and six destroyers of Tassafaronga. The seasoned Japanese reacted instinctively and freely with torpedoes, while the less experienced Americans betrayed their positions by reliance on radar-laid gunfire. Four cruisers were torpedoed, one was lost. Tanaka lost one destroyer but had turned a potential defeat into victory and still delivered the goods.

Early December saw a spate of runs by up to 10 destroyers at a time, that on 12 December losing the destroyer *Teruzuki* to a PT boat's torpedoes. Mechanically unsound and bereft of air cover, the Japanese called a halt until the next moonless phase in early January 1943. By now the Japanese high command had resolved on Guadalcanal being evacuated as untakeable and, on 14 January 1943 Tanaka ran in 600 crack troops to act as rearguard. The evacuation itself was, unbelievably, not opposed. In three operations between 2 and 7 February, Tanaka used a cruiser and 20 destroyers to remove every last soldier: the Americans either did not appreciate the position or were just relieved to see the back of the Japanese, the only loss being a mined destroyer.

The island had cost the Americans about 1,600 troops, and many more sailors; the enemy had lost over 23,000. Both sides had lost 24 ships apiece of destroyer size and above in numerous skirmishes and seven major actions. The Japanese fleet, experienced but outnumbered, acquitted itself admirably; while the Americans, starting as 'rookies', stuck to their task, eventually emerging not only victorious but much the wiser.

This is one of the merchant vessels that the Tokyo Express beached on Guadalcanal on the night of November 13/14, although only four out of 10 transports made it, and only 2,000 out of 7,000 troops got ashore.

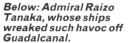

A patrol of an Indian Army division tries to smoke out a Japanese bunker. The Japanese fell back, luring Wavell's forces into a carefully-prepared counterattack

within the Kondan, Rathedaung, Donbaik triangle, and it was not until the end of the month that the danger of the entire force being cut off by Koga's division was recognized. It was too late for most of 47th and 6th Brigades, including its commander Brigadier Cavendish, who is reputed to have suffered a particularly barbaric death at the hands of his captors, but during April the remainder of the force fought its desperate way back up north again, first to the Maungdaw-Buthidaung line and eventually, after General Slim had taken command of the entire area, back to their original start lines.

By May 1943, the First Arakan Campaign was over. Lessons were undoubtedly learned from it, but it cannot really be regarded as much other than an unrelieved failure.

First Chindit

At the northern end of the Burma front there was taking placed at the same time as the last phase of the Arakan disaster an operation which, however similar the results may first have appeared to be, was in fact a promise for the future.

Orde Charles Wingate was at this time a brigadier and 40 years old, a direct spiritual descendant of those puritan, deeply religious soldiers who have played such an important but uncomfortable part in Britain's imperial history. Havelock and Gordon would both have regarded Wingate with stern admiration, agreeing with him immediately, of course, that all praise was due to God and not to man.

He had first made a strong impression on several influential people in 1938, when as a young captain he had formed the Special Night Squads from young Jews in Palestine, to combat the Arab bands which were already attacking the Jewish Kibbutzim (he had no Jewish blood himself). Then in 1940 he had been sent into Ethiopia to organize a guerrilla campaign against the Italians, but after this comparatively minor success his star seemed somewhat to wane, and in a fit of depression brought on by malaria he even attempted suicide. But Wavell had been impressed by Wingate's ideas and his almost fanatical zeal, and when in 1942 he realized the certainty of Japanese occupation of Burma, he sent for Wingate to repeat his Ethiopian adventures beyond the Chindwin.

By mid-1942 Wingate had formulated his plans and put them forward. He would raise and train Long Range Penetration Groups to strike at Japanese communications as well as at Japanese outposts, and those groups must be of a specified size – large enough to strike with effect, small enough to evade the enemy. A brigade from which the inevitable weak links had been eliminated would be right, every man trained in jungle fighting to a standard higher even than the Japanese, every man with a specialization such as demolitions, signals, medical or navigation. Every column, moreover, must contain a strong air-to-ground co-operation team, for once across the line and into enemy territory it would depend solely upon air support for supply and evacuation of wounded. Pack animals would provide transport with the columns.

On the night of 14 February 1943 the first 'Chindit' Brigade crossed the river Chindwin in two groups – Northern Group comprising five columns, totalling 2,200 men with 850 mules, Southern Group of two columns, 1,000 men with 250 mules.

By 1 March Wingate with the Northern Group had reached Pinbon, and he then sent off two columns to attack and destroy railway lines, the other three to ambush roads in the locality and to attack Japanese posts. One of the latter ran into a far bigger force than they had reckoned with and was scattered, many of the men making their own individual and precarious ways back to the Chindwin; Bernard Fergusson's Column 5 reached the railway, drove off the Japanese

Brigadier Wingate, seen talking to some of his men at a transit camp on the Burma/Assam border, was a charismatic, prickly character, fired with an almost evangelical zeal.

A Japanese soldier stands watch over a ruined bridge in Burma. While Wingate's raids could be thought mere pinpricks, they did prove to the British and Indian soldier that the Japanese were not invincible in the jungle.

patrols in a brief but bloody encounter, and then dynamited the bridge near Bongyaung in a spectacular and satisfying explosion. To the south and on the same day, Michael Calvert with Column 3 blew up two more railway bridges, one with a span of 300 feet.

Meanwhile Southern group had blown up stretches of the railway near Kyaikthin, though a day later the group headquarters and Column 2 were both themselves ambushed and scattered. But by 10 March three of Wingate's columns had moved so far into enemy territory that they had reached the Irrawaddy and were asking permission to cross it. Air drops were working satisfactorily, so Wingate gave permission, and indeed ordered a concentration of his entire force on the far side – well beyond the planned limits of the operation.

By 19 March the Northern Group columns were across, though Calvert had lost all his mules, and Wingate ordered his column and Fergusson's off to find the huge Gokteik Gorge viaduct which carries the Lashio road down to Mandalay. But now a significant setback occurred; Wingate found to his horror that the triangle of country in which he had thought to base his brigade across the Irrawaddy for as long as two or three months, although ideal for air drops, was in fact a belt of hot, trackless and – most inhibiting of all – waterless scrub. It was totally impracticable as base country. Moreover, HQ control was becoming nervous of the distances the supply aircraft had to traverse, and on 24 March issued orders to Wingate to withdraw.

Japanese troops in Mandalay, central Burma. Wingate's first operation beyond the Chindwin was centered to the north of Mandalay, where Japanese lines-of-communication to Myitkina and the Chinese border were raided and the Mandalay/Myitkina railway blown up at several points.

This, Wingate admitted somewhat reluctantly, was the sensible course; but he found that boats to cross the Irrawaddy had become scarce and the crossing-points often guarded by Japanese, for General Mutaguchi had by now become conscious of the Chindit presence. Moreover, Wingate's men were nearing exhaustion, many of the mules had escaped, died or been eaten; malaria, dysentery and the stifling heat were all taking their toll. The journey back was a dreadful experience for them all.

Nevertheless, of the 3,000 officers and men who crossed the Chindwin with Wingate, 2,182 returned to Imphal, though many of them were never to soldier in any front line again. Many observers – especially those of conservative outlook – claimed that the experience had proved that Wingate's ideas would not work, but Wavell disagreed and so did Wingate's column commanders.

So did General Mutaguchi. So impressed was he by the achievement of the first Chindit operation that he was convinced the British would soon mount another and larger operation of the same type. In order to forestall it he made what some might call the gravest strategic error of the Imperial Japanese Army; he determined to march into Assam and capture Imphal and Kohima.

Vella Lavella

As the land battle for Guadalcanal wore on, the Japanese and American fleets fought a long series of savage night actions, during which the Americans had the advantage of primitive radar sets, but the Japanese lookouts were incredibly efficient. So many ships went down that the area was christened 'Ironbottom Sound'.

Vella Lavella typifies the vicious night encounters of the Solomons campaign. Some 200 miles from Guadalcanal, the island of Vella Lavella was invaded by the Americans in August 1943 and, by the following month, the comparatively quiescent Japanese garrison was penned into the north-western corner. The Japanese planned to evacuate them on the night of 6-7 October in three destroyers and some auxiliaries covered by six seasoned destroyers of the Tokyo Express under Rear Admiral Matsuji Ijuin in the destroyer *Akigumo*.

The force was sighted by air reconnaissance and its position and likely destination signalled to Captain Frank R. Walker, commanding the destroyers USS *Selfridge*, USS *Chevalier* and USS *O'Bannon*, who was directed to rendezvous with three more destroyers off the likely Japanese evacuation point. Walker knew that he, in turn, had been sighted by an enemy aircraft but when, at 22.30, radar contacts were reported to the west he immediately advanced toward what he knew to be a greatly superior force even though his reinforcement had not yet arrived.

With the evacuation force keeping clear, Ijuin's destroyers moved into two roughly parallel columns. They almost crossed Walker's 'T' at 22.45 but, still sizing up the strength of the Americans, took no action. His mind apparently made up, the Japanese commander made two abrupt changes of course but put his force into some confusion. At the second change of course, the range had dropped to about 7,000 yards and Walker opened the bowling with the Japanese tactic of a torpedo salvo: 14 torpedoes were launched, the Japanese at the time largely masking each other's fire. It was a dark night, lit by a quarter moon but punctuated by rain squalls and both sides were moving at high speed. With the American torpedoes running the nearest Japanese destroyer, the *Yagumo*, broke formation and now at only 3,000 yards range three parts of a circle, launching eight torpedoes as she turned. Walker's ships smothered her with gunfire while Ijuin, his manoeuvre frustrated, pulled his remaining three ships into line ahead and turned 16 points under the cover of smoke.

At 23.05 the impetuous *Yagumo* was hit by an American torpedo but, almost simultaneously, the *Chevalier*, second in the US line, was struck by one from the *Yagumo*. Her bows gone, she slewed around at almost full power and was promptly rammed by the tail-ender, *O'Bannon*, which was thus immobilized.

Walker, now alone in the *Selfridge*, bore on after the pair of Japanese yet unengaged. About six minutes before, however, these had launched their full complement of 16 torpedoes and the *Selfridge* ran into them. One exploded beneath 'B' gun, removing the complete bow section and leaving the heavy twin mounting hanging by a hair over the mangled forward plating.

Warned of the approach of American reinforcements, Ijuin chose to quit while he was winning and, having launched his remaining torpedoes at 8-mile range toward his now-stationary adversaries, he withdrew at high speed. It was 23.17 and the whole affair had taken only 22 minutes.

Only 15 minutes later Walker's reinforcements arrived, finished off the stricken *Chevalier* and covered the withdrawal of the other two. Materially honours were even, with one ship lost to each side, but the Japanese gained the victory in that, keeping the Americans occupied, they permitted their evacuation force to perform its mission without disturbance.

Arashi, *a 'Kagero' class destroyer, is seen at speed. Typical of the inter-war Japanese fleet destroyer, she was fast, well armed and, in the early stage of the war, manned by a crew highly skilled in the kind of night fighting common to the Solomons campaign.*

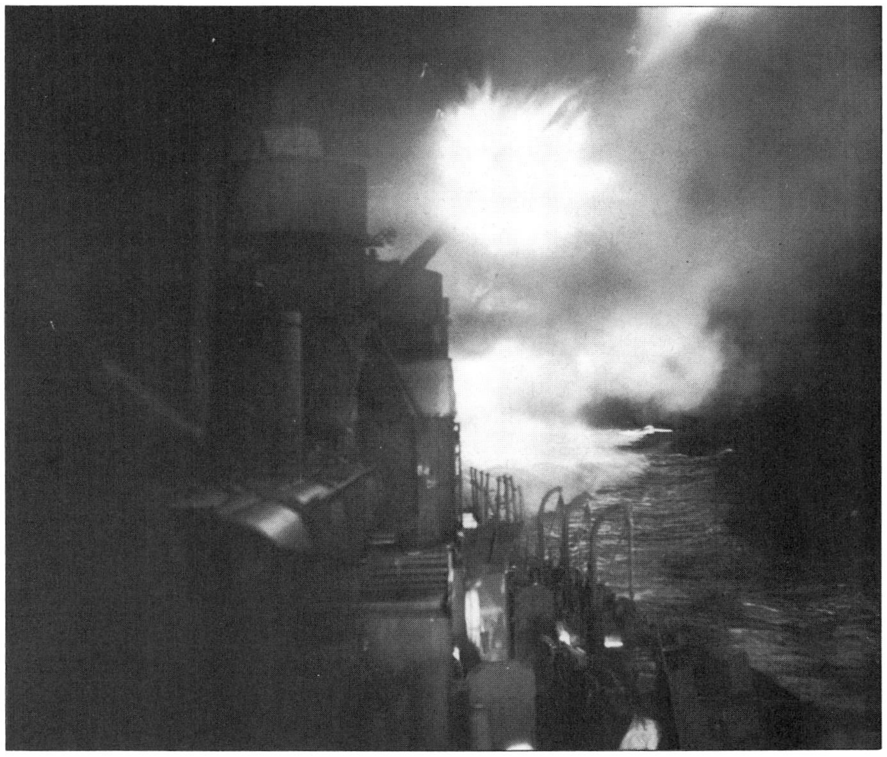

One of the two 'Fletcher' class destroyers (USS* Chevalier*, sunk, and* O'Bannon*) fires her midships 5-in gun during the battle of Vella Lavella. While each side lost a destroyer, the Japanese succeeded in withdrawing the last of their garrison on the island while the American force was engaged.

America started the war with a destroyer construction programme just gearing up to meet the demands of possible hostilities. By the time the first of the 'Fletcher' class was launched, that programme was in full swing. Indeed, in an astonishing display of sheer industrial muscle, 175 of these large destroyers were launched between February 1942 and September 1944.

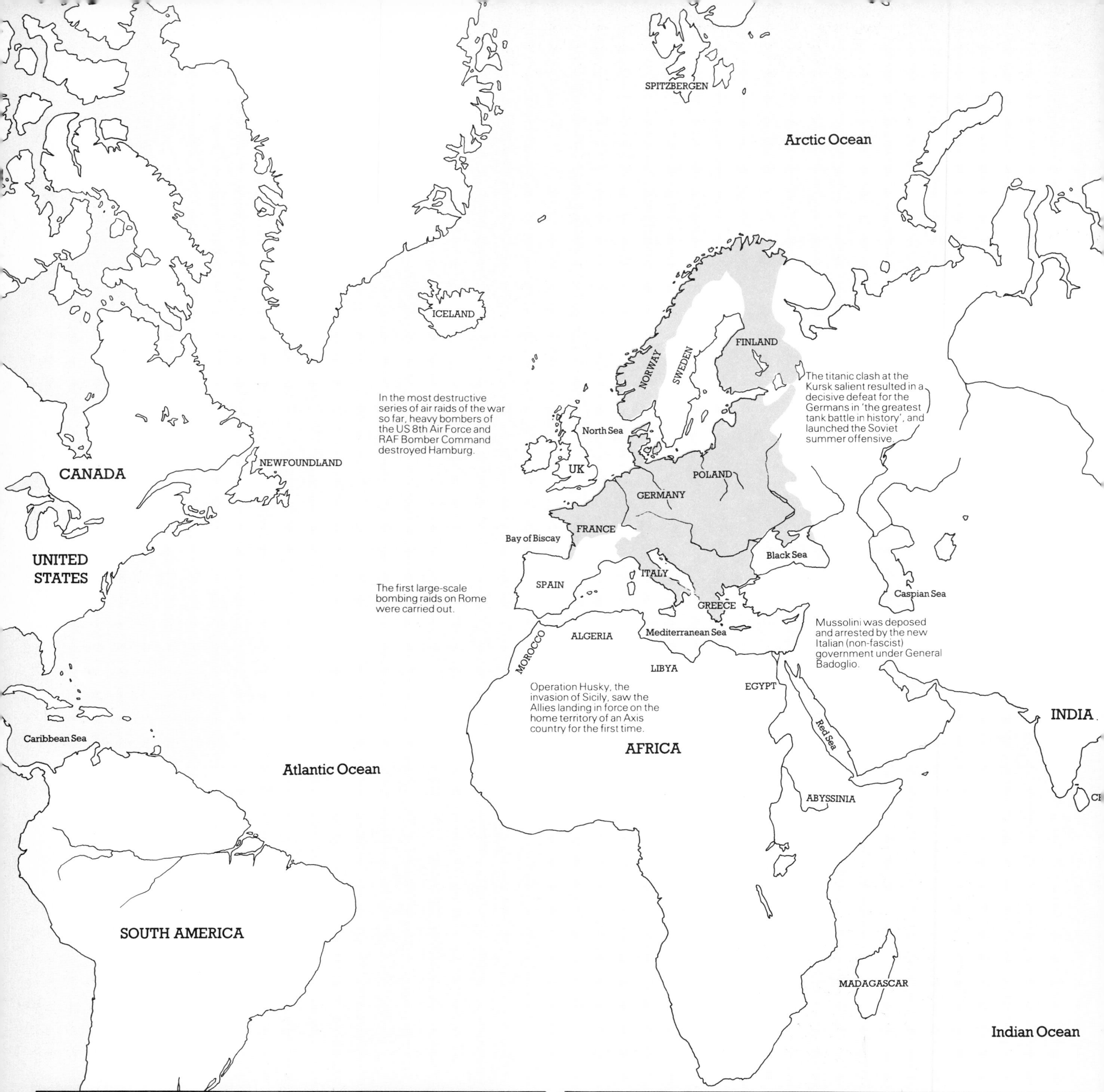
SPITZBERGEN
Arctic Ocean
ICELAND
FINLAND
NORWAY
SWEDEN
The titanic clash at the Kursk salient resulted in a decisive defeat for the Germans in 'the greatest tank battle in history', and launched the Soviet summer offensive.
In the most destructive series of air raids of the war so far, heavy bombers of the US 8th Air Force and RAF Bomber Command destroyed Hamburg.
North Sea
NEWFOUNDLAND
CANADA
UK
POLAND
GERMANY
FRANCE
Bay of Biscay
UNITED STATES
Black Sea
ITALY
SPAIN
The first large-scale bombing raids on Rome were carried out.
Caspian Sea
GREECE
Mussolini was deposed and arrested by the new Italian (non-fascist) government under General Badoglio.
ALGERIA
Mediterranean Sea
MOROCCO
LIBYA
EGYPT
Operation Husky, the invasion of Sicily, saw the Allies landing in force on the home territory of an Axis country for the first time.
INDIA
Caribbean Sea
Red Sea
AFRICA
Atlantic Ocean
ABYSSINIA
SOUTH AMERICA
MADAGASCAR
Indian Ocean

In spite of Allied air supremacy, Axis aircraft were a threat over the Mediterranean. This is the result of bombing a ship full of ammunition off the coast of Tunisia.

The Wehrmacht threw massive forces against the Kursk salient, including large numbers of the massive new Panzer VI 'Tiger' as an armoured spearhead.

The Cauldron at Kursk
July 1943

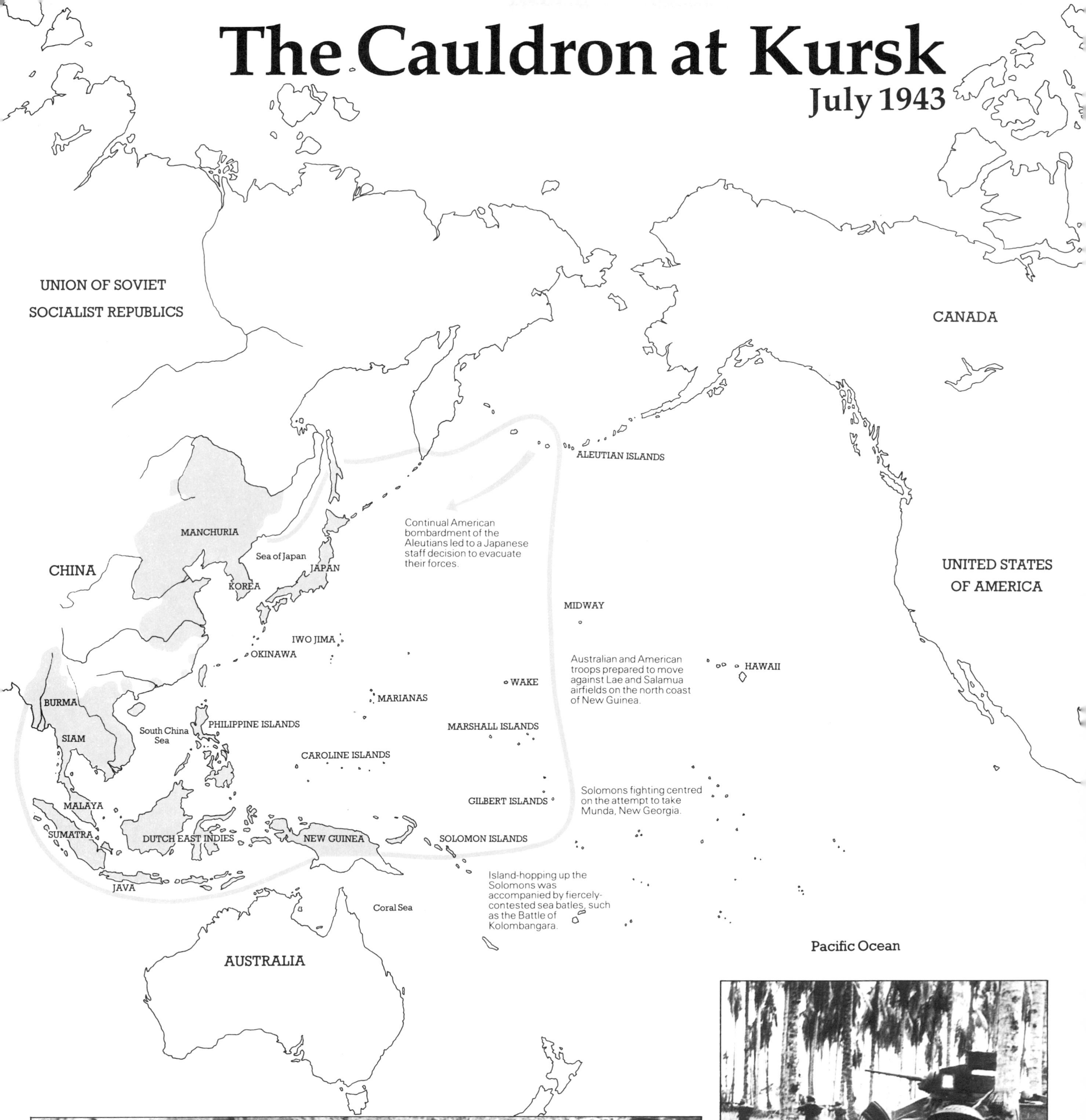
UNION OF SOVIET SOCIALIST REPUBLICS
CANADA
ALEUTIAN ISLANDS
Continual American bombardment of the Aleutians led to a Japanese staff decision to evacuate their forces.
MANCHURIA
Sea of Japan
JAPAN
CHINA
KOREA
UNITED STATES OF AMERICA
MIDWAY
IWO JIMA
OKINAWA
Australian and American troops prepared to move against Lae and Salamua airfields on the north coast of New Guinea.
HAWAII
WAKE
BURMA
MARIANAS
PHILIPPINE ISLANDS
South China Sea
SIAM
MARSHALL ISLANDS
CAROLINE ISLANDS
Solomons fighting centred on the attempt to take Munda, New Georgia.
MALAYA
GILBERT ISLANDS
SUMATRA
DUTCH EAST INDIES
NEW GUINEA
SOLOMON ISLANDS
Island-hopping up the Solomons was accompanied by fiercely-contested sea batles, such as the Battle of Kolombangara.
JAVA
Coral Sea
AUSTRALIA
Pacific Ocean

SS panzergrenadiers rest before an assault at Kursk. The delay in launching the attack gave the Red Army time to prepare an extremely warm welcome, and in spite of their fighting ability the Germans were unable to achieve success.

An Australian Bren gunner is seen with an M3 Stuart light tank on the north coast of New Guinea as MacArthur's forces drive the Japanese westwards.

Chapter 16

The Italian Armistice

The conclusion of the successful campaign in North Africa brought the necessity of further Allied operations against the Axis. The Soviet Union, having borne the brunt of German strength, was now demanding the opening of a second front in Europe, as promised by the other Allies. The Americans were all for a cross-Channel invasion as soon as possible, but were persuaded to the British view that operations in the Mediterranean were more appropriate for 1943.

Throughout the morning of 9 July 1943, the invasion fleets steamed past Malta, those carrying the US Seventh Army under the command of Lieutenant-General George Patton on the west of the island, those carrying the British Eighth Army under General Bernard Montgomery on the east. Two thousand, five hundred ships and landing-craft escorted or were carrying 160,000 men, 14,000 vehicles, 600 tanks and 1,800 guns in what was to that date the largest amphibious operation in history, due within hours to enter waters heavily mined and possibly guarded by U-boats, threatened by the existence of large enemy battlefleets well within striking distance as well as both German and Italian air squadrons operating from shore bases.

Upon reaching the shores of Sicily the armies would storm open beaches, and in order to occupy the entire island they must defeat an enemy force of nearly 300,000, of whom 40,000 were German veterans of the 15th Panzer Grenadier Division and the Hermann Goering Division.

During that day, as the huge concourse of ships moved slowly past the badly battered island of Malta, the wind rose steadily in a typical Mediterranean summer storm and by evening had reached gale force; aboard the crowded transports sea-sickness claimed victims at every rank, the heaving decks were slimy with vomit, and an overpowering stench filled the holds as the sailors fought their way between the sweating, groaning soldiers, to help when they could and to work the ship all the time. Back at his headquarters in Malta, General Eisenhower watched the maps, listened to the weather reports and to the advice from the naval staff, and at the crucial moment took his own counsel. Then he nodded; despite the weather, the operation would go on.

On crowded airfields in Tunisia, the engines of 109 American C-47s and 35 British Albemarles were warming up, their crews climbing aboard, while behind each plane was linked a Waco or Horsa glider packed with the 1,500 officers and men of the British 1st Airlanding Brigade. Just before 7 p.m. they began to take off, flying at first into clear evening air, but by the time they were approaching Malta for their assembly and turning point the sky had darkened, they were into the gale centre and the winds were driving the planes off course and buffeting the gliders.

Two hours after the British airborne forces had taken off, another 222 C-47s filled with 3,400 American paratroops had lifted off from Tunisian airfields, soon to find themselves in the same chaos and disorder as that which was engulfing the British brigade. Nearly 40 of the tows of the combined force wisely turned back, but only 54 of the British gliders landed in Sicily, the rest going down into the sea with their cargoes drowned. Of the American paratroops, though they were dropped into Sicily, only some 200

Right: The light cruiser USS Boise shells enemy positions at Gela on the southern coast of Sicily, while a crowded LST heads for the coast.

Below: Task Force 85, carrying troops and equipment for General George S. Patton's US 7th Army is shown on its way to Sicily.

The invasion of Sicily

Operation Husky, the Allied invasion of Sicily, was the largest amphibious operation mounted to that date. Two and a half thousand ships carrying over 160,000 men of the British Eigth and US Seventh Armies were landed after heavy naval bombardment, and commenced operations against a defending force some 300,000 strong.

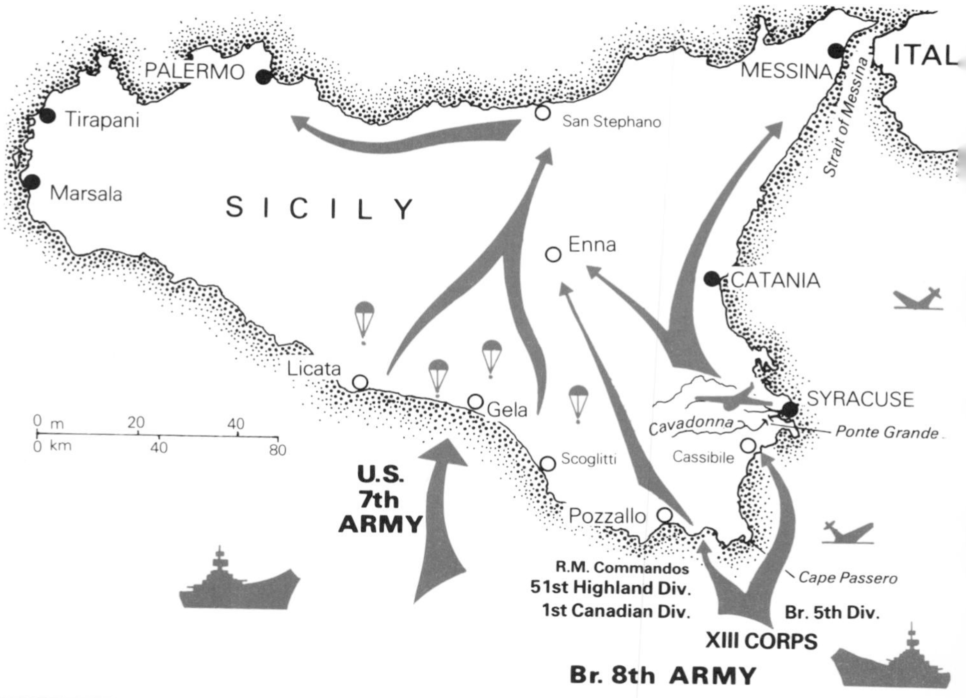

Chronology of War: 1943

July 1
US forces capture Viru Harbour and hold positions in New Guinea

July 5
Operation Zitadelle, the final German summer offensive on the Eastern Front; huge tank and air battle in Kursk Salient. Battle of Kula Gulf, New Georgia

July 9
Allies drop airborne forces on Sicily as prelude to invasion

July 10
Operation Husky: Allied invasion of Sicily

July 12
Fierce fighting in Kursk Salient, with massive Soviet counter offensives in the north sector around Kirov and Novosil

July 13
US hunter-killer groups in action against submarines in Atlantic – 12 U-boats are sunk in the next month

July 14
Germans counterattack in Sicily, but are repulsed

July 15
Russian offensives around Orel

July 16
Canadians capture Caltagirone, Sicily

July 17
Allies drive towards Salamaua on New Guinea. Hitler and Mussolini meet at Feltre. USAAF bombs marshalling yards at Rome

July 22
US Seventh Army under General George S. Patton captures Palermo

July 24
Meeting of Fascist Grand Council decides all military power to revert to the Italian Crown. RAF raid on Hamburg kills 20,000

July 25
Mussolini resigns and is arrested. Marshal Badoglio forms new Government. Hamburg bombed by USAAF by day and by RAF at night for the next week

July 26
Fascist Party in Italy dissolved

July 27
RAF incendiary raid on Hamburg generates fire storm

July 31
UK civilian casualties in July 167 killed, 210 injured

August 1
USAF bombs Ploesti

August 2
RAF raid Hamburg. Total German losses in bombing of Hamburg exceed 40,000 dead and 37,000 seriously injured

August 5
Red Army captures Orel and Belgorod

August 6
Battle of Vella Gulf in the Solomons

August 11
Russian south west front cuts Poltava-Kharkov railway

August 13
British and US forces enter Randazzo, north of Etna

August 14
Rome declared an 'Open City'

August 15
Badoglio sends peace emissary to Spain

August 17
US forces reach Messina. All German resistance in Sicily ends

August 23
Russians under Malinovsky and Konev capture Kharkov

August 24
Eight-day Quadrant Conference in Quebec between Churchill and Roosevelt ends

Italian infantry weapons

The quality of Italian infantry weapons varied sharply. Some small arms were well designed and superbly made (Beretta SMGs being much prized as war booty), yet other pieces were either over-complex in design or unsatisfactory in use.

Right: Theoretically, the Breda modello 30 LMG should have worked well, but field use exposed a number of glaring deficiencies. The cartridge oiling system was prone to clogging, and any damage to the lip of the forward-hinged, permanently-fixed magazine put the weapon out of action.

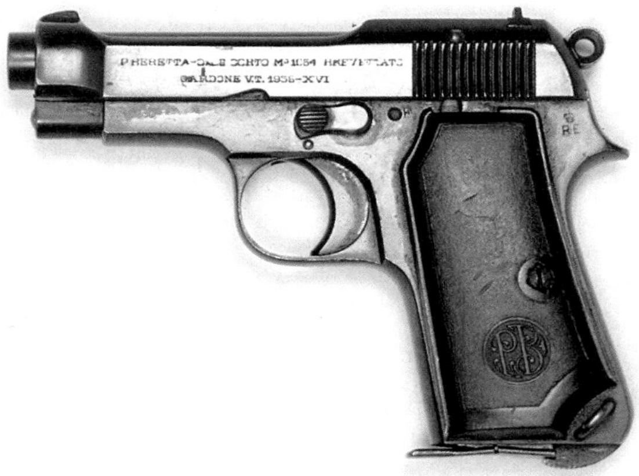

Left: Beretta automatic pistols such as the modello 1934 were of excellent design and superior manufacture, although the 9-mm short round made it underpowered for military use.

Developed at the end of the last century, the Fucile modello 91 was the basic Italian rifle through two world wars. Numerous short versions were produced.

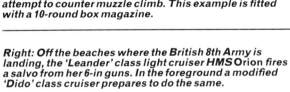

The Beretta modello 1938 was a sound, well balanced sub-machine gun that was a joy to handle. As it derived from designs dating back to 1918, it was somewhat large and heavy by contemporary standards, and was expensively made from machined steel. A bayonet could be fitted and the muzzle had four compensator slots in an attempt to counter muzzle climb. This example is fitted with a 10-round box magazine.

Right: Off the beaches where the British 8th Army is landing, the 'Leander' class light cruiser HMS Orion fires a salvo from her 6-in guns. In the foreground a modified 'Dido' class cruiser prepares to do the same.

were anywhere near their objectives and for some hours their commander, General James Gavin, was under the impression that he had been dropped into mainland Italy.

All the C-47s had turned back towards North Africa by 10 p.m. and those that had not been shot down or ditched because of mechanical failure were back at their bases well before midnight; and about an hour before midnight the wind died away even more quickly than it had arisen, and calmness reigned. The ships carrying the Eighth Army were now approaching their landing beaches more or less on time, while those bearing the Seventh Army – with farther to go and still having to cope with the remnants of the gale blowing on the south-western shores – were about an hour late.

The Italian units along the stretch between Cape Passero and Syracuse had decided that no one in their senses would attempt a sea-borne landing in such weather and had relaxed their attention once the Allied aircraft had flown off. So the first waves of the British assault landed without opposition and swept over the coastal defences almost before their presence was noticed. Belatedly, a few inland artillery units opened fire on the invasion beaches, to be immediately blanketed with shells from one or more of the six battleships – HMS *Nelson, Rodney, Warspite, Valiant, Howe* and *King George V* – which had accompanied the force for just this purpose.

Shortly after dawn on 10 July advanced units of the British 5th Division were approaching Cassibile and by 8 a.m. the town was in their hands; the whole of the British XIII Corps were coming ashore to the south of them, while the 51st Highland Division and the 1st Canadian Division of XXX Corps, with Royal Marine Commandos on their western flank, were

11 July 1943, and half-tracks of the US 2nd Armoured Division disembark at Licata on the second day of the operation. The division had taken the town the day before, immediately upon landing.

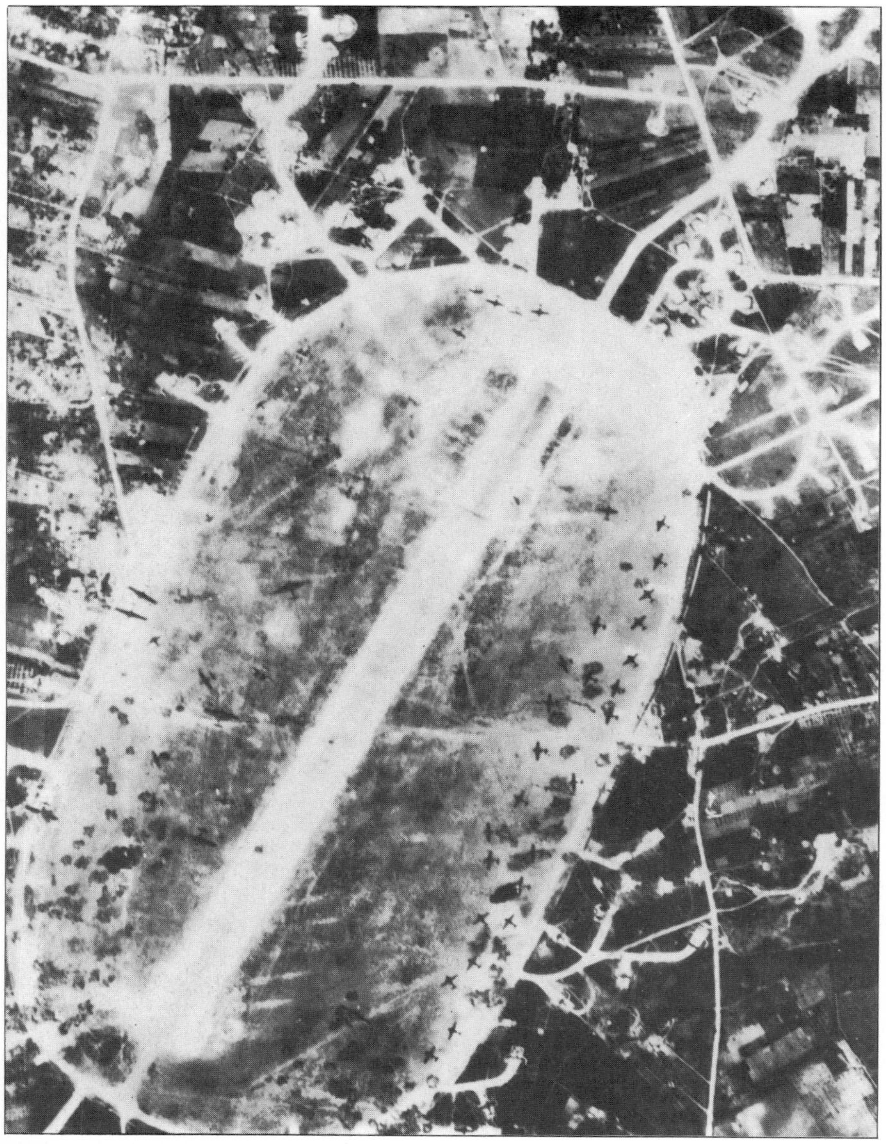

Allied air power and the hard-won lessons of the desert were used to good effect during the Sicilian and Italian campaigns. This is Castel Vetrano airfield on Sicily, during an attack by USAAF B-17 bombers.

Above: Characteristically preceded by a film cameraman, Lieutenant General George S. Patton wades ashore, pearl-handled revolver on his hip. The charismatic Patton was probably America's finest field commander of the war.

ashore around the corner of Cape Passero, between the point and Pozzallo.

Farther to the west, the US Seventh Army had not been quite so fortunate. The coastal defenders had not been asleep along their stretch and the ships and landing craft came under fire from almost the moment of their arrival. Again, fire from the heavy naval guns soon obliterated most of the opposition (much to General Patton's astonishment – and delight – as he had placed little reliance upon naval assurances), but the pier at Gela which would have been very useful for a quick build-up was blown to pieces by demolition charges as two Ranger battalions were actually sailing for it, and by 4.30 a.m. Italian and German aircraft were over the crowded beaches to sink two transports in awkward positions.

But by mid-morning all the forward strike formations of both Eighth and Seventh Armies were ashore and probing inland; the latter were suddenly to receive an unexpected bonus. If their airborne colleagues were not in exactly the right positions, they had coagulated during darkness into 20 or 30 independent groups and were creating chaos in the country just behind the landing beaches, cutting communications, ambushing lone cars, lorries or even small convoys, attacking crossroad guard posts and on one occasion holding up an entire Italian mobile regiment which had been sent to find out what was happening at Gela.

At the other end of the invasion beaches, however, the tiny part of the British airborne force which had been landed in the correct place – just a hundred of them – had assumed the task of the entire 1,500 strong brigade, rushed and taken the Ponte Grande over the River Cavadonna just south of Syracuse, and by mid-afternoon were in desperate straits. Attempts to annihilate the eight officers and 65 men on the bridge itself had begun shortly after dawn and had hardly slackened since then. Italian soldiers, marines and sailors had been sent out from Syracuse in ever stronger waves, and by 3 p.m. all but 15 of the defenders had been killed or wounded, and ammunition was running low. At 3.30 a massed assault overran the survivors, but eight managed to escape and, as the British had removed all the demolition charges while in possession of the bridge, the Italian marines had now to try to emplace some more. Two of the escaping eight therefore took position half way up an overlooking hill and from there sniped at every movement on the bridge, while the remaining six, stumbling with exhaustion, made their way south towards Cassibile. Three miles along the road they met a mobile column from the 5th Division which they led back to the bridge, which fell immediately into British hands again, and by 5 p.m. the column was driving into Syracuse itself.

By the end of the first day, the British therefore held the coastal strip from Pozzallo around to Syracuse and this vital port was in their hands, sufficiently undamaged for immediate use, while the American Seventh Army held nearly 40 miles of beach between Scoglitti and Licata. Inland, scattered bands of British and American airborne troops were loose over the southern half of the island, successfully spreading alarm and confusion.

It was not to be expected that matters would continue quite so smoothly for the Allies, especially with two highly efficient German divisions deployed against them, but the next few days saw the satisfactory development of the overall plan. The Eighth Army consolidated and began their advance up the eastern coast towards Messina, while the seventh drove north alongside, aiming for the northern coast near San Stephano and at the same time guarding the

Left: A motley collection of Italian prisoners of war is shepherded along one of the British-held beaches.

Above: There were more than 300,000 Axis troops defending Sicily, including 40,000 Germans in the veteran 15th Panzer Grenadier Division and the elite 'Hermann Goering' Division, seen here relaxing before going into battle.

German anti-ship missiles

German military science and technology produced a number of highly advanced weapons during the last years of World War II. Amongst them, the guided air-to-surface missile in its anti-ship form was one of the first to show success, particularly during the early stages of the Italian campaign.

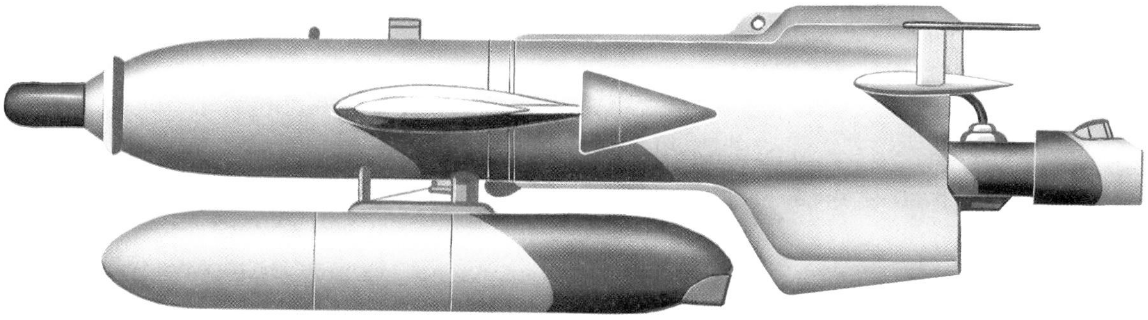

Above: The Henschel Hs 293A guided bomb was dropped from a carrier aircraft on a parallel course to the target, radio command guided by the aircraft crew (who were aided in their task by flares affixed to the rear of the missile).

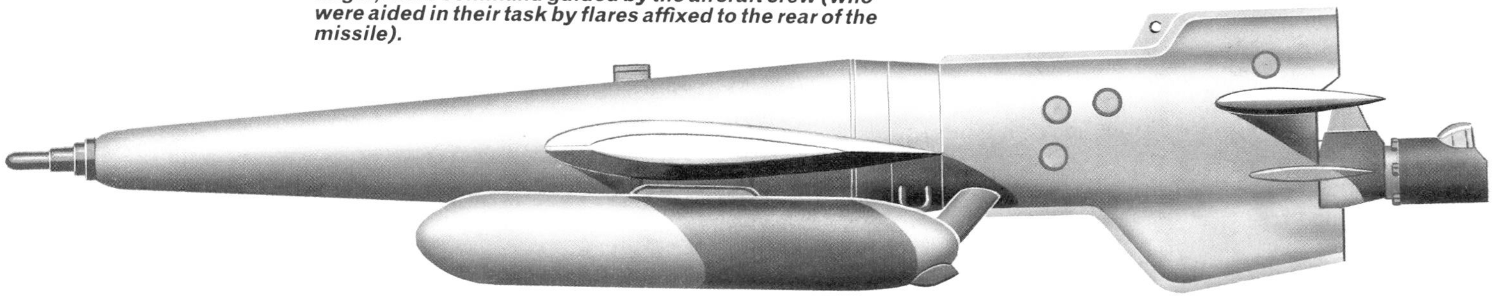

A developed version of the Hs 293, the Hs 294 was designed to dive into the water to attack heavily-armoured vessels below the waterline (a capacity even modern missiles do not have). The wings and rear fuselage broke away on entering the water, the warhead being fitted with a torpedo proximity fuse.

Above: The autumn of 1943 saw the agreed-upon surrender of the Italian fleet to the Allies, a threat the Germans could not ignore. This is all that remained of the 45,000-ton battleship Roma.

Below: The first successful attack by German anti-ship missiles was when a Dornier Do 217E-5 of II/KG 100, based at Cognac, made an attack on British forces in the Bay of Biscay.

Two 'Littorio' class battleships are seen at speed two months before the Italian surrender. Roma *was destroyed and* Italia *severely damaged.*

inner flank of the British advance.

Within 10 days Canadian units had reached Enna in the centre of the island, and two days later Patton's troops had not only reached the north coast but had turned west and occupied Palermo, taking prisoner thousands of Italian soldiers who were more than happy to stop fighting, and welcomed everywhere by delighted Sicilians to whom quite a number of the American soldiers were related. Very soon it became evident that the bulk of the inhabitants of the Italian mainland felt the same way.

The fall of Mussolini

The Italian people had never been enthusiastic about the war, finding themselves from the start fighting with inadequate weapons against an enemy they did not hate, yoked to an ally for whom they felt no particular affection. Before El Alamein the majority had hoped that their country might emerge from the conflict at least as influential and well off as it had been when Mussolini took them into it, but after Alamein and the unbroken succession of defeats since they knew that the best they could hope for was defeat at the hands of a kindly enemy, at worst total devastation of their country. And if they were to avoid this last fate, then the regime that had ruled their country for 21 years had to go.

The various landings on the coast of mainland Italy, and the obvious desire of the Italians to conclude an armistice led the Germans to send troops such as this SS Tiger unit on the Brenner Pass.

By the time of the Armistice, some Italian fighters like these Fiat G.55s were at last capable of fighting the allies on equal terms.

Dissatisfaction with the military control of the war – which Mussolini had assumed the moment he decided that Italy must earn her place at the Peace table when England and France had been beaten – had grown during the long retreat across Africa, and with the Allied landings on Sicily it appeared openly in every circle, including even the Fascist hierarchy itself. As for the army, the new Chief of Staff, General Vittorio Ambrosio who had been appointed early in the year, made no secret of his belief that it lacked every military necessity from artillery to boots for the infantry and, most of all, any vestige of sound morale.

Mussolini and Hitler had made a habit of meeting at fairly regular intervals; faced with the hard reality of the successful Allied landings in Sicily, Hitler called for an immediate conference, which took place on 17 July in a villa near Feltre, some 50 miles north of Venice. On his way there Mussolini agreed with Ambrosio that he must tell Hitler of Italy's desperate need for an armistice and their wish for withdrawal from the Pact of Steel.

He was given little chance. Hitler announced that he could spare only one day from the Russian front, and as usual his interpretation of the term 'conference' was of a gathering which listened sycophantly to everything he had to say, without interruption, and certainly without any hint of disagreement. He occupied the whole of the three-hour session with his explanation of the course of the war to date, with his immediate plans to stem the reverses which had recently plagued them all, and with a diatribe against the Italian army which, he complained, was inadequate at every level from Commander-in-Chief down to private soldier. His suggested remedy for this was the immediate appointment of a German general to reform and command the Italian army, under Mussolini. Sicily, he announced, must be turned into another Stalingrad!

There was a brief break for lunch, which the two delegates took separately. Ambrosio and Bastianini of the Foreign Office pressed Mussolini to keep to their agreement and use the only time left – the journey by car back to the airfield where Hitler's plane waited, and which the two dictators would share alone – to make it clear to Hitler that Italy must get out of the war. This Il Duce promised to do, but one look at the faces of both when the dictators emerged from the car revealed that nothing of the sort had occurred; Mussolini had, in fact, merely accepted Hitler's suggestion of a German commander-in-chief to buttress his own position.

They arrived back in Rome to discover that during their absence some 700 Allied planes had bombed the capital. Marshalling yards had been very badly hit and millions of leaflets dropped explaining the dire state of their country and the available remedies for that condition to a thoroughly demoralized populace, most of whom were eagerly collecting and reading them.

That evening Mussolini actually drafted a letter to Hitler setting out the true position, but it was not sent, and when it became obvious that he would never break with Hitler himself, the members of the Fascist Grand Council – which had not met for three and a half years – decided it was time to take action themselves. A meeting was convened for the evening of 24 July and one of the members, Dino Grandi, who had in the past been one of Mussolini's closest friends and supporters, proposed that military power should immediately revert to the Crown, and that all established governing bodies should be allowed to function as had been intended and not be controlled solely by the whim of one man. In a scene not unlike the one which had taken place three years before in the House of Commons, he turned to Il Duce and said:

> It is not enough that you assume responsibility. We are also in it, and so is the country. Among the many absurd and empty phrases you caused to be written on walls all over Italy is one you pronounced in 1924 from the balcony of the Palazzo Chigi – May all factions perish! May even our own perish – provided the nation lives! Well, now is come the time for your faction to perish!

The vote was finally taken at about two o'clock in the morning, and to Mussolini's discomfiture 19 members supported Grandi's motion and only nine were against.

'Then there is no more to be said,' he announced as he got to his feet. 'The session is over. Gentlemen, you have provoked the crisis of the regime.'

But after a few hours' sleep he had sufficiently recovered his spirits to believe that when he took the

A powerless Mussolini is seen with Hitler after his dramatic rescue from confinement by Skorzeny's commandos. The Führer treated him well, possibly with the aim of using him should the situation in Italy ever favour a restoration of Fascism.

September 1943, and the Italian Armistice and Allied landings in southern Italy and at Salerno have brought the Germans south in force. This half-track mounted flak gun and its Luftwaffe crew guard a bridge on the German line of communication.

Allied self-propelled artillery

The mobile war that was ushered in by the mechanized spearhead of the Wehrmacht's Panzers also required artillery to be much more mobile. British and American self-propelled artillery differed greatly, however, from the heavily armed and armoured assault guns used by both sides on the Russian front.

Above: The first production models of the M7 105-mm SP howitzer (based on an M3 medium tank chassis) were for the US Army, but many were supplied to Britain under Lend-Lease. Legend has it that the name 'Priest' was suggested by the pulpit-like machine-gun mount.

Below: The 25-pdr gun howitzer was used in anti-tank actions in the desert, but the lack of mobility of towed batteries made them vulnerable. The Bishop (continuing the ecclesiastical theme established by the Priest) was an attempt to provide mobility, placing the gun on a Valentine tank chassis. It was not a great success.

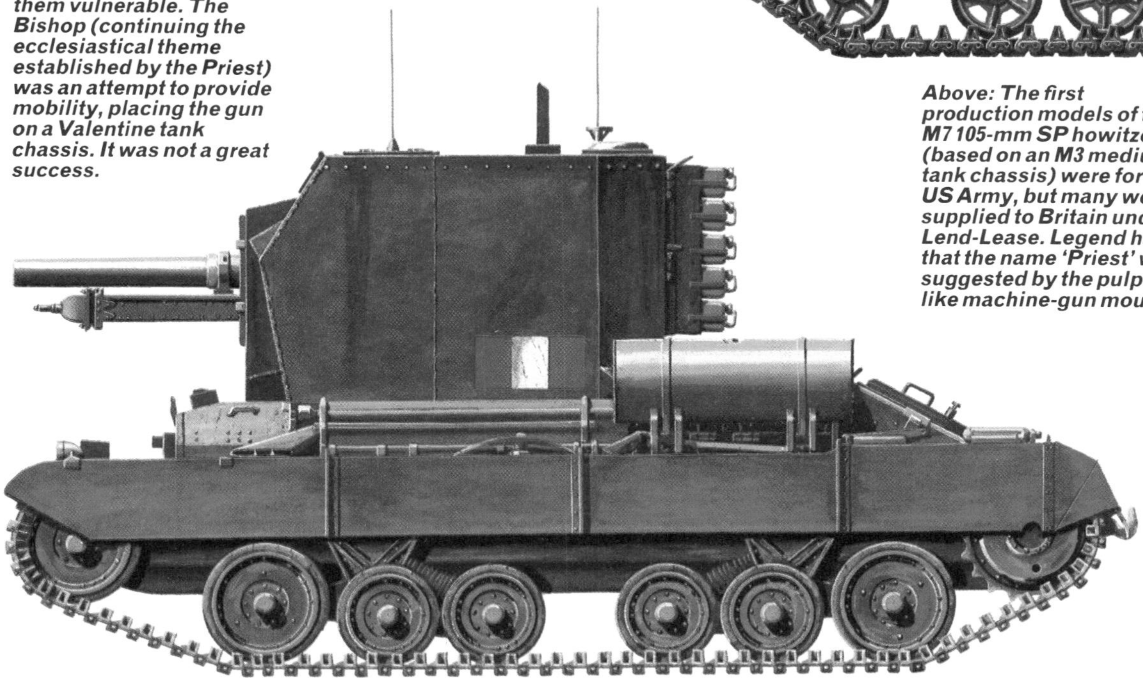

Above: This M7 is being used by a Free French unit in training in Morocco. The similarity to the M3 medium tank hull is evident, as is the prominent 'pulpit' for the Browning .50-in heavy machine-gun.

Below: Britain wanted a self-propelled 25-pdr, and after requesting a version of the M7 from the Americans settled on a version of Canada's Ram tank called the Sexton. Similar to the M7, it was a reliable vehicle that served on for many years after the end of the war.

A head-on view of the 'Sexton' self-propelled 25-pdr gun shows the semi-circular gun shield, which indicates the 25° left and 40° right traverse, and was designed with anti-tank use in mind.

Below: One of the best of wartime self-propelled artillery pieces, the M40 motor gun carriage used the chassis of the M4 Sherman tank to mount the long-range M1A1 155-mm 'Long Tom' gun, which had a range in excess of 14 miles. It arrived in Europe during the last months of the war.

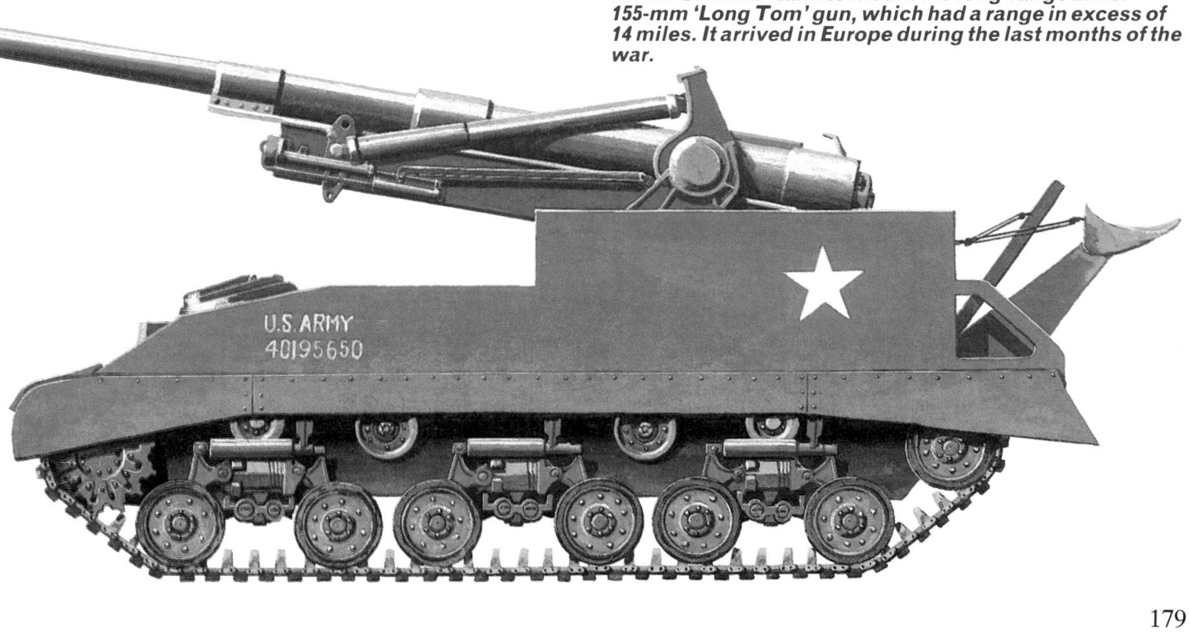

The M12 was originally acquired by an army uncertain of how to use a World War I vintage 155-mm piece mounted on a obsolescent M3 tank chassis. With the invasion of France, however, the M12 came into its own.

The rapid clearing of Sicily gave the Allies a secure base from which to deploy a massive superiority in air power until airfields could be captured or built in southern Italy. These Spitfire Mk IXs are seen near Naples, probably operating out of an airfield on the mainland.

A Bishop self-propelled gun of General Mark Clark's 5th Army is seen in action on the Naples front two weeks after the landings. A troublesome enemy machine-gun position is just being dealt with by the 25-pdr gun.

results of the Grand Council vote to the King that evening, Victor Emmanuel would just refuse to accept it and order him to 'deal with the matter as he thought best'.

But it was not like that at all. The King received him quite warmly, but when he reported the Grand Council vote His Majesty nodded, announced that he supported it too and was quite sure that both the army and the Italian people would be delighted when they heard the news. A shocked and astonished Duce was then let out into the courtyard where he was promptly arrested and driven away in an ambulance; the next day a new government was formed, headed by the venerable and lifelong anti-Fascist Marshal Badoglio. His Cabinet did not include a single member of the Fascist Party, and 21 years of dictatorship were at an end.

Armistice

The Badoglio Government lasted for 45 days, and it is impossible not to feel some sympathy for the Marshal and his colleagues in the predicament in which they found themselves.

They and the whole Italian population wanted to get out of the war, but they were realistic enough to know that there was a price to be paid. The Allied armies were in Sicily and complete control of the island by them, was obviously only a matter of days away – but German divisions were on the Italian mainland itself, better equipped and far more strongly motivated than the Italian formations alongside them. Obviously some part of the Italian mainland would shortly become a battlefield, but what could the new government do to ensure that the area devastated by war was kept to a minimum?

Clearly, they must play for time and they must also manoeuvre with consummate diplomacy, and indeed delicacy. Put more bluntly, the Marshal's position was perhaps best summed up by Churchill's comment: 'Badoglio knows that he is going to doublecross someone – let us ensure that it is the Germans, not us!'

The process began on the evening Badoglio took power (25 July) when he announced that he and his country would continue the fight alongside their German comrades until the Allies were beaten, at the same time instructing the Italian counsellor at the Lisbon Embassy to make contact with the British Ambassador to suggest that the Allied government should not take this announcement too seriously.

This piece of Machiavellianism set the tone for the rest of the month. During the days which followed there took place a sequence of devious moves by all parties concerned (including the Germans, who had little doubt of the new Italian Government's real intentions), and as a result of these – coupled with several Allied bombing raids on targets in southern Italy – a 'short armistice' was signed in an olive grove near Syracuse on 3 September 1943. Under its terms all Italian air and ground forces would lay down their arms when approached by Allied soldiers, the Italian fleet would sail for Malta, Allied prisoners of war in Italian hands would be released and in no circumstances allowed to fall into German hands, and all Italian territory including the Mediterranean islands would be made available to the Allies as operational bases from which to continue the war against the remaining European enemy.

In return for this, the Allies were willing to guarantee 'kindly and sympathetic' treatment to the Italians; they also gave the Badoglio Government the impression that they were contemplating an early landing on the Italian coast north of Rome – with a genuine plan for the dropping of an airborne division on to the Rome airfields – and would react very favourably if Italian troops in the area attacked nearby German units at the same time.

Landings in Italy

Italy's surrender was announced on 8 September; the following day to Badoglio's surprise, Lieutenant-General Mark Clark's Fifth Army stormed ashore in Salerno Bay, south of Naples and nearly 150 miles short of Rome – where German troops, acting with their customary efficiency, were already disarming the Italian units in the neighbourhood and moving in some force to every commanding position.

Eighth Army formations had already crossed the Straits of Messina on to the toe of Italy on the morning the armistice had been signed, while other British formations had sailed for the port of Taranto, which they captured against only the slightest opposition on 9 September. Although it took until 20 September for all three groups to join up, by the end of the month the Allies were in possession of Naples on the west coast, Termoli on the east and thus, with the countryside between and to the south also in their hands, they held most of the 'foot of Italy'. The long drive up the peninsula had begun and no part of the Italian mainland was to escape the horrors of war.

King Victor Emmanuel and his family, together with Marshal Bodoglio and the other members of his government, had managed to escape (on the evening of 9 September) from Rome to Pescara, where they were picked up by an Allied corvette and taken safely to the south. On the same day the Italian battlefleet had duly sailed from its northern ports for Malta, where it arrived the following day, having lost the battleship *Roma* to Luftwaffe bombing en route. On the morning of 11 September a cable from Admiral Cunningham arrived at Whitehall informing their Lordships of the Admiralty that 'the Italian battle fleet now lies at anchor under the guns of the fortress of Malta.'

An M15 Multiple Gun Motor Carriage, based on an M3 half-track and armed with a 37-mm cannon and two Browning 'fifties' on a rotating mount, is seen on the beach at Salerno following the landings in early September 1943.

A British AEC Matador medium artillery tractor tows its charge ashore at Salerno, south of Naples. The landing came as a surprise to many Italians, who had expected (indeed, hoped for) a landing nearer Rome.

The Ploesti raids

For all its armed might, Germany was desperately short of oil and the need for a secure fuel supply exerted a powerful influence on German strategy, particularly when the Soviet oilfields seemed within reach. Existing German resources were well protected; the important Romanian wells at Ploesti were defended by a heavy concentration of anti-aircraft guns plus German, Romanian and Bulgarian interceptors. In January 1942 the Allies recognized Ploesti as a strategic target and began a bombing campaign that was to last for two years.

During one of the early raids by North Africa-based B-24s a Liberator flies low enough to feel the heat of a burning oil tank.

In many ways, Ploesti was a typical strategic target. Its eight refineries processed about ten million tons of fuel annually, including the high-octane aviation gasoline that helped keep the Luftwaffe airborne.

Ploesti had been specified as a strategic target in January 1942. It was a well-defended target and by the time of the later strikes was the third-best defended enemy area, ringed with anti-aircraft sites, concealed by smokescreens, and protected by German, Romanian and Bulgarian fighter units.

Five heavy bombardment groups, all equipped with Consolidated B-24s, were chosen for the mission. For this strike, the planners decided to attack at low level, hoping to catch the defenders by surprise. The planes were modified: bombsights were replaced by a simple mechanical sight; top turrets were altered to fire straight ahead; extra .50-in machine-guns were installed in the noses. Bomb bays held two auxiliary fuel tanks to raise the normal 2,480-US gal fuel supply to 11735 litres.

They trained across desert wastes, roaring wingtip to wingtip a few feet above the sands, dropping dummy bombs on an outline of the refineries they had been briefed to attack. Instead of working with conventional vertical reconnaissance photos, the pilots memorized detailed, accurate sketches of their targets as they would look on the run-in from treetrop level.

And at 7.00 a.m. local time on Sunday morning, 1 August, the lead Liberator lurched under the full power of its four engines, rumbled and rolled down the runway and struggled into the air, followed by 176 more. One remained – a burning wreck following an engine failure on takeoff, a turnback, and a crash.

The force headed north for the island of Corfu, where they would turn in toward the north-east and Ploesti. The Germans were waiting. One of their signal interception units near Athens, having cracked the code, had been reading 9th Air Force message traffic. The Athens station broadcast the news to all defence units, and the hunt was on.

The bombers encountered haze; in spite of the experienced crews in the formations, the mass of planes began to separate into its five groups. They came out of the clouds and over the mountains, letting down over the Danube for their runs to the three initial points northwest of Ploesti. But the leading 376th made a wrong turn, mistaking another town for its initial point; the 93rd, followed. They flew directly toward Bucharest, and were nearly there before discovering the error. They swung back toward the northeast, now far off course, with the attack plan destroyed and with the defenders both alerted and informed of the target.

Only six B-24s from the 376th hit their assigned targets; the rest and the 93rd dropped on targets of opportunity, most of which had been assigned to other groups. The 44th and 98th made their bomb runs, one on each side of a railroad, and were hit hard by heavy and accurate fire from a German flak train that was steaming at full throttle along the rails. Kane and Johnson led their groups into an exploding target array, identified and bombed their own target amidst the flames and blasts of erupting tanks of fuel. The 389th reached its target with all of its force intact, and destroyed the refinery at Campina with accurate bombing.

It was hell. The refinery tanks, bursting in spectacular gouts of flame, scorched the paint on the low-flying B-24s. Heavy smoke hid key reference points, concealed factory chimneys, power lines and other obstacles. Fighters harassed them. When they came off target and headed for home, they were a badly mauled force.

Forty-one bombers had been lost in the action over the targets, and another 13 on the way in or out. About 42 per cent of the refinery capacity was destroyed. It was far from enough; Ploesti had been running at about 60 per cent of capacity for lack of crude oil. It took the Germans a few days to repair some pipes, open some valves, and get the fuel flowing again.

Ploesti continued to operate, untouched, for more than eight months following the 1 August strike. During that time, the USAAF and the RAF argued long and often bitterly about the best way to stop the Germans. The Americans wanted to bomb the oil production and storage system; the British wanted to hit transportation. When Eisenhower finally bought the transportation concept, the USAAF obediently went after railway marshalling yards, and some were in the Ploesti area. By strange coincidence, bombs often fell short or long of the yards, and hit refineries.

The Ploesti 'yards' were hit 5, 15 and 24 April 1944; 5, 6, 18 and 31 May; and 6 June. But the deception was no longer necessary, if it ever was. The legitimate targets included oil, and Ploesti was being bombed for what it was.

On 23 June, 761 heavy bombers, the largest of the forces sent against the Romanian target, hit the refineries. On 24 June 377 went back again. On 9 and 15 July, both raids were led by pathfinder planes, directing the bomb drop with the relatively new H2X system. More strikes followed: 22, 28 and 31 July; 10, 17, 18 and 19 August. On 24 August, Ploesti shut down. The Russians captured the city on 30 August.

The striking forces dispatched almost 7,500 bombers against Ploesti over 26 months of attacks. The considerably lesser number that reached the target dropped 13,469 tons of explosives and incendiaries. Perhaps as many as 12 per cent of the bombs never detonated – a chronic problem that plagued both USAAF and RAF. Ploesti's death throes cost 350 heavy bombers.

Left: A year later, the same target is bombed by Italian-based bombers of the 451st Bomb Group, 15th Air Force.

Above: A late-war shot shows a 15th Air Force Liberator just after making a high-level bomb run over Ploesti. Note the vapour trails and open bomb bay.

B-24 Liberators of the 9th Air Force depart from their field on the first mass raid, on 1 August 1943.

Chapter 17

To the Gustav Line

The Allied plans for a three-pronged attack on the Italian mainland, culminating in two drives up the Italian coasts by the US Fifth and British Eigth Armies could well have succeeded rapidly had the Germans followed Rommel's plan of concentrating forces in the north of Italy. Unfortunately, Rommel's successor, Kesselring, had very different ideas, and in a brilliant, flexible defence blunted both Allied advances. Instead of a rapid push up the boot of Italy, threatening the Reich via Austria, the campaign was to be fought to the bitter end, being resolved only during the last days of the war in Europe.

It could not be expected that the Allied drive towards the north would be unopposed. Nor was it. There were eight German divisions in Italy under the overall command of Field Marshal Kesselring. Two of them were near Rome and the others were in the south, commanded by Generals Hube and Vietinghoff. These were rapidly reassembled and the counter-attacks began on 11 September 1943. Hube had been in command in Sicily and did not intend to be defeated again. He had to contend with General Montgomery's Eighth Army and the Fifth Army of two British and two American divisions under Patton's successor, General Mark Clark; but his own resources included the formidable Hermann Göring Panzer Division. Their tanks drove the British from the Molina Pass on the 12th and added considerably to the harassment of the Allies in the Salerno beachhead.

Within two days the situation had become critical. Withdrawal in the southern sector was considered by the Americans, and Generals Eisenhower, Alexander and Admiral Cunningham went into conclave, the admiral being particularly explosive in his protests against any such re-embarkation. Alexander had the assurance from Churchill that '*Nothing* should be denied which will nourish the decisive battle for Naples. Ask for anything you want, and I will make allocation of necessary supplies, with highest priority irrespective of every other consideration.' With this backing from the Prime Minister the idea of withdrawal was abandoned.

In the event, however, it was the Royal Navy that played the biggest part in saving the day. Two of Cunningham's battleships, *Warspite* and *Valiant*, which had been engaged in the formalities attending the surrender of the Italian fleet at Malta, were ordered to return to Salerno and take up positions close inshore. Their continuous bombardment caused such havoc that any significant progress in driving a wedge between the British and American forces was impossible, though the Germans got to within a mile of the beaches and drove the Americans from their hard-won positions at Persano.

Alexander made a rapid tour of the Fifth Army's front and promised the weary troops reinforcements, rest and air support. He was as good as his word. Almost in his wake as he sped from formation to formation, 1,600 men of the 82nd Airborne Division landed on the Salerno beaches and throughout the three days and nights from 13 to 16 September pitched battles ensued. Three landing strips were laid down in record time and by the 16th Spitfires had engaged with the Luftwaffe opposition and a further 1,500 infantry were on their way in fast cruisers from Philippesville in Algeria. Alexander was able to boost his reassurances as messages reached him that Eighth Army had ousted the enemy from Cosenza, Bari and Belvedere and was fast driving north to link up with the Fifth and the British 1st Airborne Division that had captured Taranto and, reinforced, was fanning out across the peninsula. Though the actual link-up was not achieved until the 20th, Alexander had the gift of inspiring confidence in men of all arms and nationalities and despite heavy losses their spirits were unvanquished. He was able to report to Whitehall, 'I can say with full confidence that the whole situation has changed in our favour and that the initiative has passed to us.'

The invasion of Italy by the Allies was met by considerably more resistance than was expected, largely because of the swift German response to the Armistice and the rapid movement southwards of crack troops such as this 88-mm gun team.

Germany and Italy

In another sense the initiative had passed to the Germans. The Badoglio government had imprisoned Mussolini in the stronghold of Gran Sasso in the Abruzzi mountains; but like much else touching Italian organization, too little attention was given to the essential detail of keeping him there. A German paratroop detachment daringly stormed the citadel, captured the deposed dictator, and whisked him away to Munich. There he virtually grovelled before the Führer and was rewarded by restitution of dictatorial rights – for what they were worth. The new Fascist Social Republic was proclaimed with much drum-beating and waving of banners; but the shadow of the swastika was behind the flags. New or not, the 'republic' had no independent power at all; it was a puppet of Hitler's, a bedraggled phoenix rising from a doused fire and prodded into half-hearted squawkings by the German High Command, which control-

Left: SS troops begin one of the many German counterattacks against the Allied beachhead at Salerno. In early September there was serious talk of conceding defeat and evacuating the landing force, but rapid reinforcement and naval gun support kept the Germans at bay.

Left: Men of the 2/6 Queens Regiment rush past a knocked out Panzer IV Ausf H tank. Vastly more capable than the Panzer IV of 1939, the late models had a long barrelled 75-mm gun and additional armour.

Below: It must have seemed strange to troops used to fighting in the relatively open expanses of North Africa to find themselves in cities fighting a very different kind of battle. These Fifth Army men are in the streets of Cava, north of Salerno.

A Sturmgeschütz III rumbles southward to bolster the German defences in Italy. the outnumbered German armour made excellent use of the constricted Italian terrain and proved very costly to dislodge.

Members of the RAF Regiment examine bombs that had been on a train destroyed outside Taranto during the initial stages of the Eighth Army's drive up the Adriatic coast.

led its destiny, its headquarters (on Lake Garda), its piecemeal army, and its courts of justice, such as they were. Into these courts were pushed the nineteen members of the Grand Council who at the insistence of Count Grandi had voted for the transfer of power from the Duce to the King. They were ceremoniously tried for treason, found guilty and shot.

Among them was Galleazo Ciano, who had married Mussolini's daughter Edda and after the Abyssinian war had been appointed Italy's Foreign Minister. A playboy and social climber, Ciano had nonetheless had the percipience to see that his father-in-law was being forced by Hitler into the position of being '*Gauleiter* for Italy'; so he had defected his loyalties to an extent that even the megalomaniac Duce could hardly fail to notice. With unconscious humour Mussolini withdrew his son-in-law from the Ministry and posted him to Rome as Ambassador to the Holy See. 'He thinks I can do no harm there,' confided Ciano to his diary. 'He will see.' As soon as the Allied invasion of Italy was launched he joined the rebels of the Grand Council that brought about the Duce's downfall. 'And now his own punishment is wrought,' Mussolini exclaimed hysterically in his *palazzo* at Salo, where he had surrounded himself with the illusory trappings of a power he no longer held.

Obstacles

By that time – January 1944 – there had been considerable changes in the fortunes of the Allies in Italy. Although Alexander had rightly said back in September that they had seized the initiative, the

Stalemate on the Gustav Line

Forcing the Allied advance to a crawl in the mud of a rainy Italian winter, the Luftwaffe Field Marshal Albert Kesselring fortified a line to the north of Naples, as well as preparing fall-back positions for his forces still further north. Such was the nature of the terrain that the only alternative to a bloody frontal assault would be a flanking amphibious operation. In the event both had to be attempted, and the battle for Cassino was one of the most ferocious of the European war.

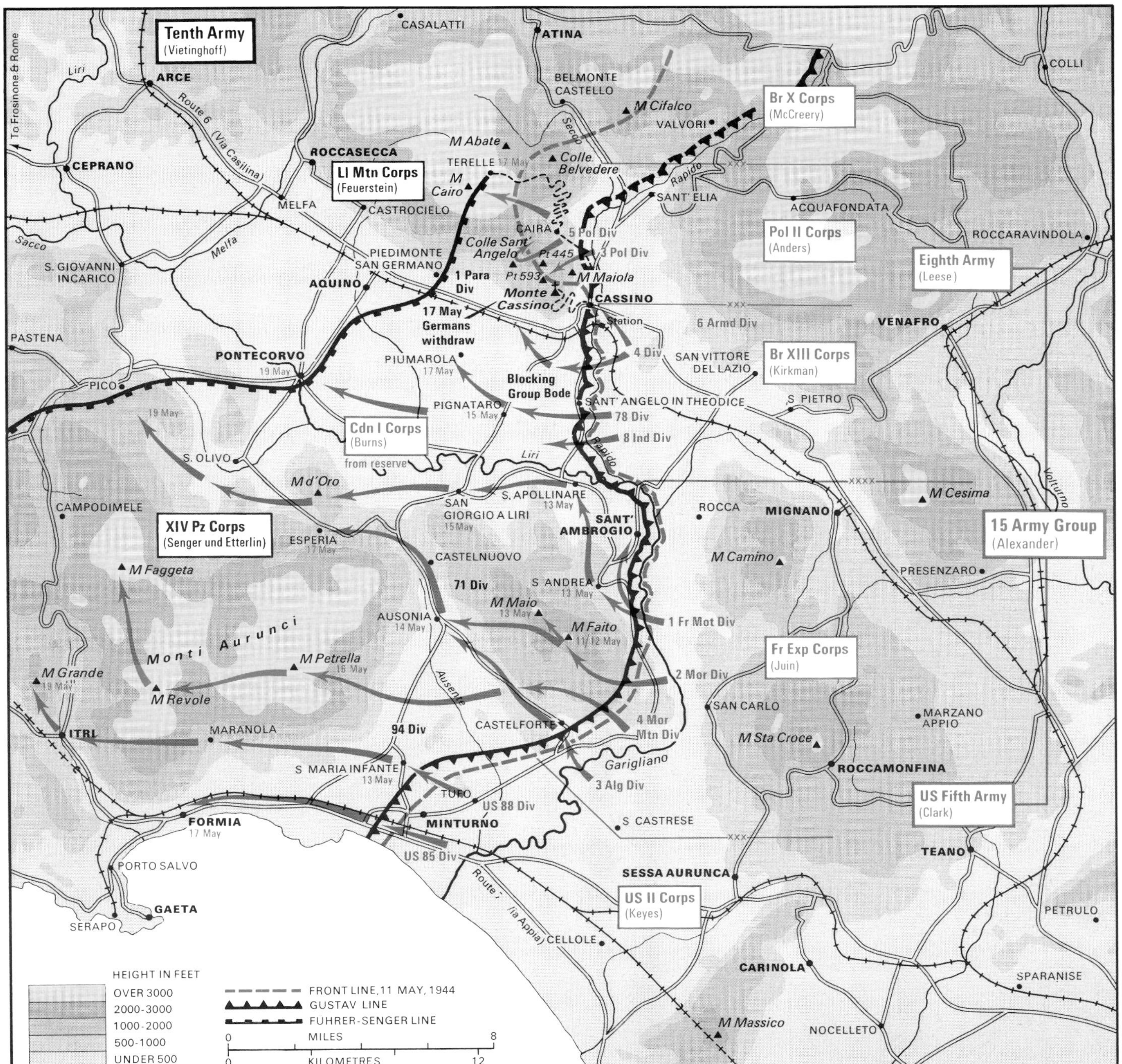

One of the most fearsome sounds heard on the battlefields of World War II was the 'tearing linoleum' snarl of the German MG 42 machine-gun. The distinctive sound was due to an exceptionally high rate of fire.

succeeding months were to throw up many obstacles on the road to complete victory.

The small-scale invasion of Taranto by 1st Airborne Division, which had fought its way – reinforced but largely unopposed – north west to join hands with the Fifth and Eighth Armies for the drive on Naples, had been codenamed Slapstick, and there was much of an element of farce about it. It had been a rushed affair, with the troops transported from Tunisia in a small armada of five cruisers and a minelayer. They were lacking the tanks that would have enabled them to consolidated their unopposed capture of the important port, and had only six jeeps in the way of motor transport – a situation that prevailed for nearly a week. When reinforcements and transport arrived their exploiting movement was hampered by command caution on the grounds that a large-scale advance up the east coast needed methodical planning. No such caution was exercised by the Germans, who quickly realized that the capture of Taranto, Brindisi and Bari on the heel of the peninsula would avail the British nothing for the maintenance of an east coast advance when the occupation of Salerno was still in dispute.

Politics and war

The choice of Salerno for the main invasion of Italy had not been altogether a wise one. The port was hemmed in by mountainous country that was very easy to defend against an advance north towards Naples and Rome. General Clark had himselve suggested that Gaeta, nestling in the gulf north of Naples, would be a more appropriate place for an unopposed landing; and indeed it would have been. But it was outside the range of successful air support and the idea was abandoned.

There were other factors, both military and political, that led to the Allies' inability to effect a quick and complete takeover in Italy. One was American caution over expending too much strength in Italy when Overlord, the main invasion of Europe, was planned for mid-1944; there was also still much to do against the Japanese in the Pacific. The American commanders agreed to the Italian venture only when Sicily had so easily crumbled against the assault of the US Seventh Army and Montgomery's Eighth. By which time Kesselring had had time to reassemble his forces, prepare his defences, and plan the counterattacks that disrupted the landings on 11 September and drove the British from the Molina Pass on the 12th.

Another factor was the Allies' political indecisiveness. They deliberately misunderstood the Soviet request to be involved in the Italian campaign, a request derived from Stalin's designs on the Balkans. Their snubbing of the Soviet Union cost them a great deal later on when it came to the liberation of Romania, Hungary and Bulgaria; but the vagueness was of more immediate importance in that it wasted political time and spread into military matters. Montgomery was ordered to land on the toe of Italy and 'secure a bridgehead . . . to enable our naval forces to operate through the Straits of Messina'. This order was given without any regard for the nature of the terrain, which was ideal for the defenders and necessitated the massing of vast forces of artillery to ensure the success of the assault, thus causing further delay that could give the enemy nothing but an advantage. There also seemed to be a lack of clarity in communication and definity of purpose between the war directorate in Whitehall and the commanders in the field. Churchill was telling Eisenhower what he thought should be the proportion of troops required for spin-offs such as the occupation of Corsica and Sardinia and the capture of the islands of the Dodecanese, and the Supremo was replying in terms that politely ignored the suggestion and answered a question that had not been asked – explaining that the reason for the delay in the linking up of the Fifth and Eighth Armies was caused by tactical and administrative forces being stretched to their limits. The Prime Minister recorded that 'Eisenhower's answer did not refer as specifically as I had hoped to what I deemed the all-important part of the message, namely, the small proportion of troops required for subsidiary enterprises.' But his protests were ignored as the battle flowed on. And in the event no troops at all were required to overcome Sardinia, which was evacuted by the Germans without a shot being fired; and Corsica fell to French liberationist troops and American Rangers, who cleared it of 50,000 Germans and Italians in five days.

Less success attended British efforts in the Aegean, which were aimed at clearance of German and Italian troops from the Dodecanese islands and the capture of airfields on the Turkish mainland. It was thought that the Italian surrender would bring the Italian garrisons to the side of the British, but that did not happen. Nor did Turkey assist. An all-too-easy capture of the islands of Samos, Leros and Cos turned out to be an ambush, for there was no adequate air support to back the invasion, and after allowing a period of lull in which the British could settle into a routine of over-confidence, the Germans returned in overwhelming force to overrun Cos and in two days took 4,500 prisoners. The same design was followed for Leros and Samos, though in the case of the latter the occupying troops were evacuated before nemesis overtook them. Slapstick was not the only operation that had a touch of farce about it.

All these side issues of minor campaigns, abortive arguments and political manoeuvring took time and had their delaying effect on the course of the main battle. Supplies were tied up, air support diverted, and the Soviet leaders, who were disgruntled about the indeterminate talk of a Second Front that seemed to them to be illusory, had to be mollified by assurances that the Second Front was in Britain and that the Italian campaign was the 'Third Front' – which may have made sense to them if to nobody else.

Naples taken

At the heart of the conflict events had gone swimmingly – or so some of the more ebullient of the home press would have had its readers believe. 'Naples Today – Rome Tomorrow!' screamed one headline.

To be sure, the German defence of Naples had been thrust back some 20 miles and on 1 October Allied forces entered the city unopposed. With the Eighth Army on the left and the Fifth on the right of a broad front Alexander brooked no delay in following up the enemy with tanks. Four days after the Allied occupation of Naples the 7th Armoured Division had reached the river Volturno and established itself on a 12-mile front from Capua to Cancello, while the Americans were deployed some 15 miles to the east, where they faced three German divisions. All of which could be interpreted (and indeed was, by the optimists) as irresistible force. The general jubilation seems to have muted any talk of the 'immovable mass' part of the equation.

The achievement of the capture of Naples and the advance to the river line had been costly in terms of

Left: Bishop self-propelled guns of 506/142 Field Regiment RA give fire support to the troops of the 56th Division. They were among the first artillery units ashore at Salerno.

German reaction to the Italian armistice was swift. Within days, most Italian units were disarmed, and tanks such as the mighty PzKpfw VI Tiger were to become familiar sights in Rome.

casualties – 7,000 British and 5,000 American. The element of surprise had been lost by the choice of Salerno for the initial invasion, even though it had been forced by the limitation of the range of air cover. Serious damage had been inflicted on *Warspite* during the inshore bombardment that had turned the Salerno landings from a threatened failure and humiliating withdrawal into an initial success: the battleship had been hit by two glide bombs. (The US cruiser *Savannah* had been hit by another.) But on the credit side the combined RAF and USAAF had gained valuable experience in covering the landing forces and collaborating with them as they advanced. This experience was to stand them in good stead later in the campaign and in Overlord.

The capriciousness of the weather took another delaying hand; but even before the machinations of that hand were seen the demonstrable ease with which narrow mountain passes could be defended slowed down the Fifth Army as it forced its way tardily up the west coast. On one occasion three divisions (the 46th, 56th and 7th Armoured) plus an armoured brigade were pitched against a bottleneck that was held by a mere three battalions of the enemy – which in any case were never overcome but simply withdrew in good order when they had gained the time necessary for the regrouping of other German formations on their flank. Demolition of roads and bridges was painstakingly carried out as Kesselring's forces withdrew to the Volturno, and there was no

The performance of the German soldier in Italy, outnumbered and in the face of overwhelming air power, was usually better than his Allied counterpart, as was the case on every front and at almost every stage of the war.

A PzKpfw V Panther heads for southern Italy in the autumn of 1943. The Allies had nothing to match this vehicle, which has some claim to being the finest all-round battle tank of the war.

***Most of the major units of the Italian fleet were sailed to Malta under the supervision of the Royal Navy, but a number of smaller units remained in service to fight with the Allies. This is the Co-Belligerent corvette* Driade.**

Nearly 10,000 North American B-25 Mitchells were built, making it the most numerous of the Allies' medium bombers. This machine was with the 414th BS at Pontedera, late in the Italian campaign.

While the Lockheed P-38 was not a great success as an escort over north west Europe, in the Pacific, Africa and Italy it proved its worth. This formation is returning to its Italian field after escorting heavy bombers over Austria.

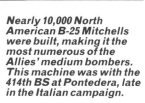

lack of air cover for them; but this was when the combined Allied air forces showed their mettle, and the Luftwaffe fared badly.

The usual weather in this part of Italy was for the winter rains to begin early in November. This year they came a month early and the plain of Nocera, which had to be crossed before entering Naples, was a sodden mass and the approaches to it treacherous with rubble and mud washed down from the hills. Tanks and heavy vehicles got bogged down, troop movements were hampered, and supplies delayed. Churchill either had his tongue in his cheek or was speaking figuratively when he sent a message to Montgomery on 2 October: 'I am delighted to see the Eighth Army striding on so splendidly.' He added congratulations and reminded Monty that they had pledged to meet in Rome.

Replying with thanks the General emphasized that the Eighth had advanced a long way (which they had) and done so very quickly (which they had not – though that was hardly his fault). He explained that because his administration had had to be switched from the toe to the heel of Italy its resources had been stretched to the limit and he would shortly have to halt and reorganize it. During that period of reorganization, he said, he would have to rest his main forces and harass the enemy with lighter ones – though these, he added, could be very effective if 'directed in sensitive areas'. He seemed in no doubt that he would keep the initiative and gain ground and would then 'advance with my whole strength on Pescara and Ancona. I shall look forward to meeting you in Rome.'

Kesselring too had to suffer the effects of the weather, but he succeeded in holding the line of the Volturno until 16 October, when he ordered a fighting withdrawal to a line some 15 miles to the north. Here he planned to pause while fortifying and extending his main defensive positions – the 'Winter' or 'Gustav' Line.

Above: After a somewhat shaky start due to its reputation as a 'Hot Ship' (being more advanced and harder to handle than contemporaries), the Martin B-26 Marauder settled down to produce a lower loss rate per mission than any other bomber in the European theatre.

Above right: Armourers load 500-lb GP bombs onto a P-38L of the 94th FS, 1st FG in Italy. Because of its size the big Lockheed fighter proved a capable attack aircraft, and though outclassed by German single-engined fighters could still give a good account of itself.

A Martin B-26C of the US 12th AAF bombs a port in the north of Italy. Medium bombers in the Italian campaign were operated with the hard-won lessons of the Desert War ever in mind.

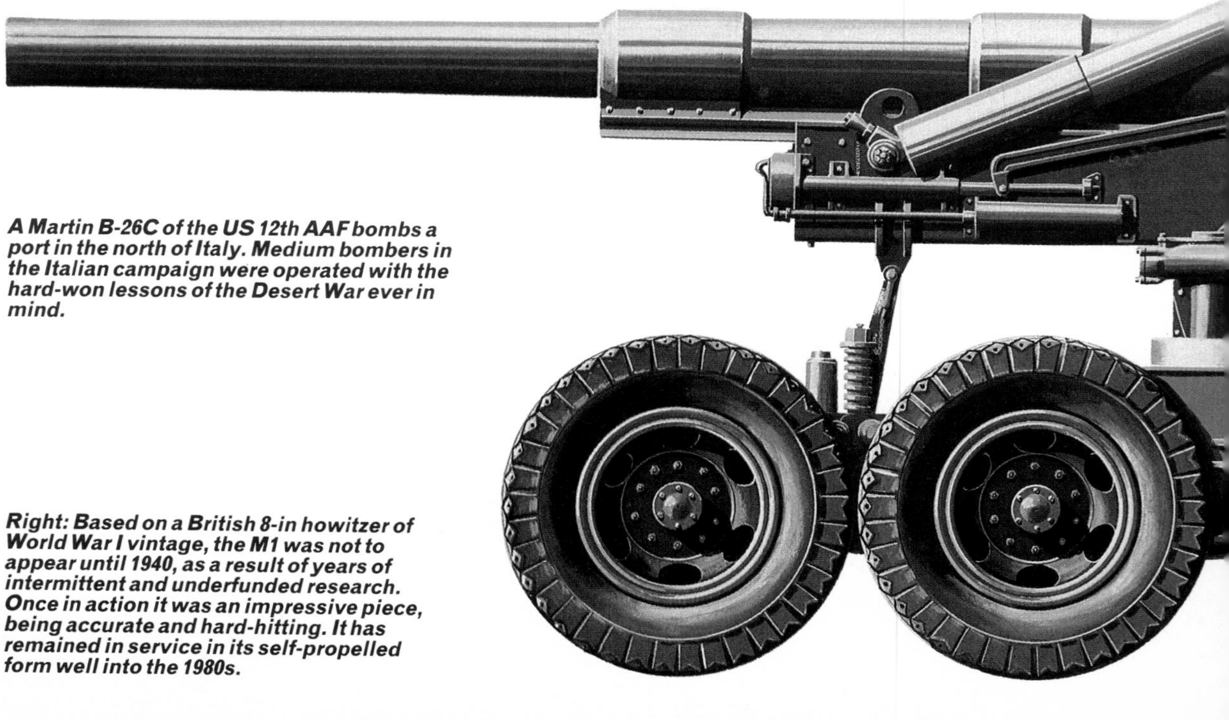

Right: Based on a British 8-in howitzer of World War I vintage, the M1 was not to appear until 1940, as a result of years of intermittent and underfunded research. Once in action it was an impressive piece, being accurate and hard-hitting. It has remained in service in its self-propelled form well into the 1980s.

US and British heavy artillery

Heavy artillery played as important a part in World War II as it had in other wars almost since the invention of gunpowder. The Western Allies used a variety of equipment, ranging from obsolescent (but still very effective) pieces dating from the Great War to sophisticated weapons that were to form the basis of artillery parks for decades after 1945.

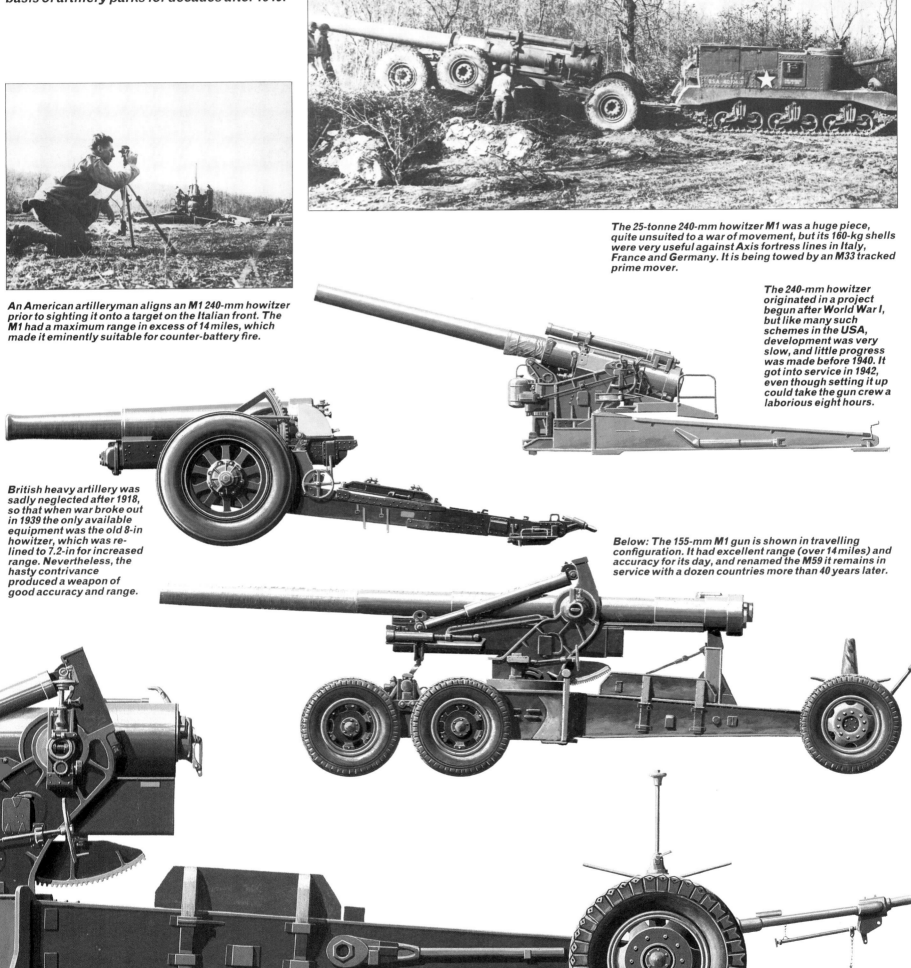

The 25-tonne 240-mm howitzer M1 was a huge piece, quite unsuited to a war of movement, but its 160-kg shells were very useful against Axis fortress lines in Italy, France and Germany. It is being towed by an M33 tracked prime mover.

An American artilleryman aligns an M1 240-mm howitzer prior to sighting it onto a target on the Italian front. The M1 had a maximum range in excess of 14 miles, which made it eminently suitable for counter-battery fire.

The 240-mm howitzer originated in a project begun after World War I, but like many such schemes in the USA, development was very slow, and little progress was made before 1940. It got into service in 1942, even though setting it up could take the gun crew a laborious eight hours.

British heavy artillery was sadly neglected after 1918, so that when war broke out in 1939 the only available equipment was the old 8-in howitzer, which was re-lined to 7.2-in for increased range. Nevertheless, the hasty contrivance produced a weapon of good accuracy and range.

Below: The 155-mm M1 gun is shown in travelling configuration. It had excellent range (over 14 miles) and accuracy for its day, and renamed the M59 it remains in service with a dozen countries more than 40 years later.

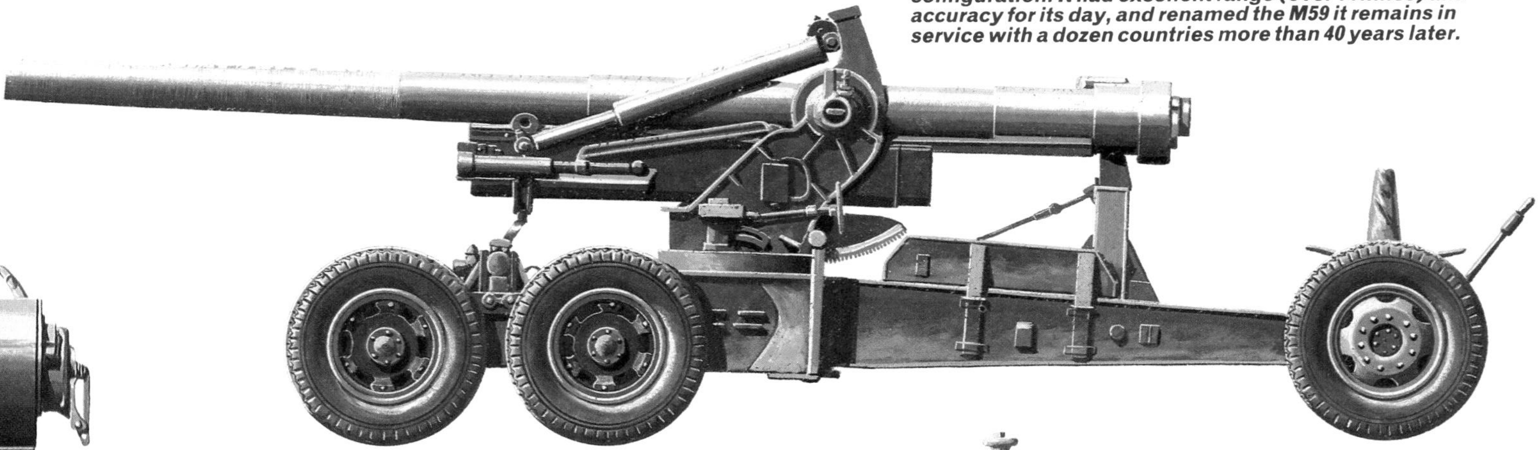

THE ROAD TO ROME IS BLOCKED

Left: A Cant Z.506B Airone, the largest floatplane of the war, forced down at Mondello beach, Sicily.

Above: This is one of the modified Panther turrets, which proved so troublesome to the troops.

The Gustav Line extended along the course of the Garigliano and Rapido Rivers from the coast road at Minturno inland for more than 30 miles and its hinge was the Cassino defile overlooked by the monastery at the summit of the rugged and precipitous hill. For almost its entire length the terrain was difficult and in many places, including Monte Cassino, virtually impregnable; yet it had to be breached before the road to Rome could be reached. Its one weakness lay in the supply links with Rome; but so long as supplies could be maintained attackers could be repelled again and again. It was to enable him to build up his supplies that Kesselring made a stand along the delaying line to which he withdrew from the Volturno.

This intermediate line of defence was carefully sited to give the Allies – particularly the Eighth Army – maximum difficulty in their progress. The area was inundated with rivers and streams irrigating the Lombardy plains, and these had to be crossed without the aid of landing craft, of which there was a great shortage because of the build-up to Overlord. Bailey bridges had to be built for all but the smallest streams.

One river, the Trigno, was reached by 78th Division of Eighth Army on 18 October; but bitter fighting held them for four days until, on the night of the 22nd, they managed to establish a small bridgehead near the coast. The attack was repelled, however, and the bridgehead force had to withdraw back across the river and reorganize – a task that, impeded by driving rain and poor visibility, took 10 days. A second attempt was made on 2 November, now supported by a naval bombardment in the coastal sector; and this time success attended the advance of 78th Division and 7th Armoured Division – which, as part of Fifth Army, actually reached the Garigliano, skirting the German intermediate defence line, which had withdrawn to the River Sangro.

Italian slogging match

But there was no easy way to Rome. As Alexander noted in a memo to Churchill, everything was being done to paralyse the German lines of communications between Rome and the Gustav Line, but bad weather had limited the activities of the air forces, and 'An examination of the enemy position has shown that his lines of communication enable him to build up in Italy, mainly in the north, to the order of sixty divisions, should they be available, and maintain them there in the winter months, despite our air superiority. . . . It would therefore appear that we are committed to a long and costly advance to Rome, a "slogging match", with our present slight superiority on the battlefield offset by the enemy opportunity for relief.'

Slogging match indeed. Clark's Fifth Army had advanced to a few miles south of the Garigliano by the first week in November. There they were blocked by another precipitous hill crowned by a monastery, Monte Camino. Their attacks were well timed but the stubborn defence by a relatively small number of German troops held them in check and they were forced to retire and re-form on lower ground that had been turned into a morass by the rain. They could not launch their attack again until 2 December, by which time they had assembled massive artillery support. Even with this the contest for the monastic crown was of epic proportions and the Germans were not flung from the slopes of Monte Camino until the 9th. Not until Christmas week was a firm hold attained on the banks of the Garigliano.

Meanwhile, on the coastal sector of the front Eighth Army had been engaged in heavy fighting on the approach roads to Ortona. The town was fiercely defended by the German 1st Parachute Division, but its capture was essential to complete the breakthrough on a 14-mile front that stretched from Ortona to Orsogna. The main attackers were the 2nd Canadian Brigade and the battle for the town was prolonged by bitter and bloody fighting from street to street and from house to house. Backed up by its parent division, the Canadians finally seized control on 23 December, on the same day that, farther inland, other Eighth Army units captured Arielli.

During this period a significant attack had been made by bombers of the Luftwaffe on ammunition and supply ships waiting to unload in Bari harbour. They had succeeded in blowing up one ammunition ship and sinking 18 transports that between them had contained 38,000 tons of supplies. It was not a good omen.

Left: A Canadian gun crew are seen manning their 5.5-in howitzer in the first stages of the assault on the Gothic Line. Artillery played an important part in these frontal battles.

Below left: A Churchill tank of the 48th Highlanders of Canada makes its way along the valley of the River Foglio, on the 8th Army sector of the assault on the Gothic Line.

Below: Italian troops fight alongside the Allies in late 1943. Most Italians had supported Mussolini until the armistice, when the majority changed sides, although a rump Fascist army continued to fight with the Germans.

German battlefield rockets

The Germany army had conducted an extensive evaluation of rocket artillery before the war, and by 1940 the first multiple rocket launchers were delivered to the Wehrmacht. Carrying a heavy payload, they were very short-ranged and were soon supplemented by smaller-calibre 'Nebelwerfers' (smoke throwers), which were able to create a dense smokescreen with impressive speed. As the war progressed, the Germans introduced an extensive family of rocket launchers.

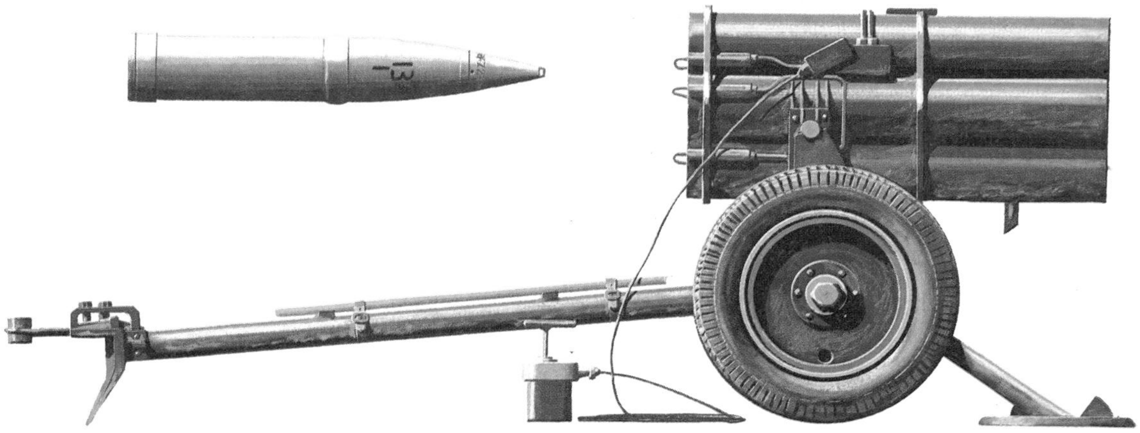

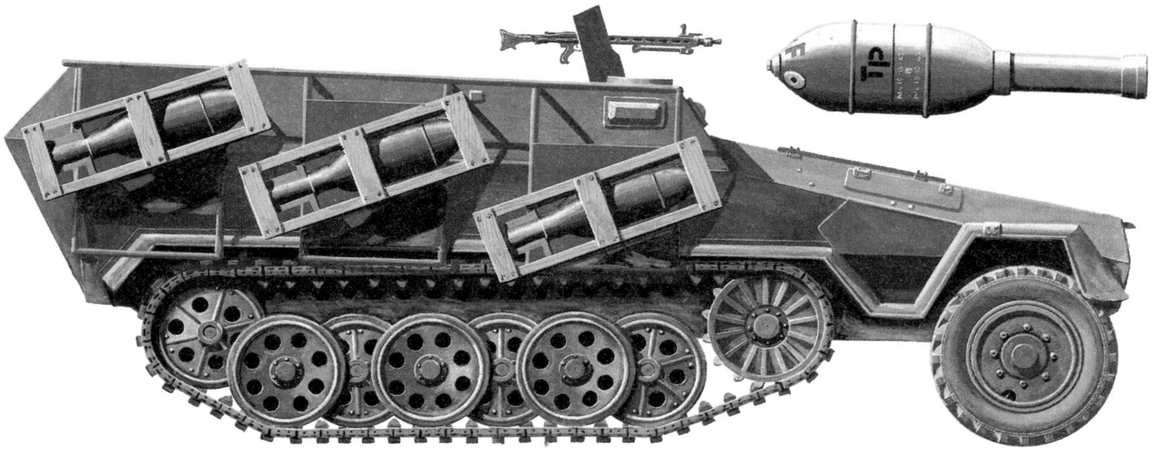

Left: The 28-cm and 32-cm Wurfkorper were among the first rockets supplied to the Wehrmacht in 1940, and though short ranged were extremely powerful. They were also among the first to be fitted to vehicles (in this case an SdKfz 251), the combination was known as the 'Foot Stuka' or the 'Howling Cow'.

Above: The 21-cm Wurfgranate 42 had a typical launcher, but the rocket itself looked at least superficially like an artillery shell. In fact, the base of the hollow-nosed projectile had 22 small venturi nozzles to impart spin stabilization.

Right: 15-cm rockets were in most widespread use with the Wehrmacht, originally fired from a towed six-barrel mount. The 10-tube launcher mounted on an armoured half-track was known as the 15-cm Panzerwerfer 42, and was much more mobile.

Below: The 15-cm Wurfgranate was almost a metre long, with an unusual layout. The spin-stabilizing and propulsive venturi nozzles were about two thirds of the way along the rocket, with the payload behind them.

Below right: The main launcher for the 15-cm rockets was the six-barrelled Nebelwerfer (smoke thrower), in which the tubes were arranged in a circle and the rockets were fired electrically in sequence.

Left: The first attack by the Fifth Army across the Rapido at Cassino literally bogged down, leaving tanks as sitting targets.

Above: February 1944, and the Benedictine monastery is shelled by American artillery from a neighbouring hill.

As the year drifted to its end through the ceaseless rain both Fifth and Eighth Armies fought on wearily against well-nigh insuperable odds posed by the German intermediate defensive positions and the determination of the defending troops to keep the Allies from reaching objectives that would aid them in their final assault on the Gustav Line. This would begin, as Alexander planned it, with an attack by the British 46th Division on a 10-mile front at the south end of the line near Minturno. But much depended on the retention of landing craft that Washington had decided must be withdrawn from the Mediterranean theatre to meet the demands of the Overlord buildup of vehicles in the United Kingdom. Even a personal appeal by Churchill to Roosevelt gained no more than an extension of the time for their withdrawal to 15 December. But it was better than nothing, the attack duly got under way on 4 January and by next day had a tenuous grip on a slight rise that gave an advantage over the enemy. Away to the right Clark's Army, which now included Italian, French and Moroccan troops (who were to acquit themselves remarkably well) began its preliminary attacks on some of the well-dug-in defences that had to be overcome before the assault on the toughest spot of all, Monte Cassino, could begin.

It was 17 January before the beginnings of a bridgehead were established by British troops at the mouth of the Garigliano, and another 10 days of desperate fighting went by before Minturno and Monte Juga were included in it. The river was also crossed, south of Saccino, by the American 36th Division; but this was a disaster, for the division was decimated. Other American attacks across the Rapido were also made and a few gains achieved; but in general the defenders had it all their own way. The look-out, like

The topography at Cassino, with the town in the valley overlooked by the castle, which in turn is dominated by the ancient monastery of St Benedict.

British and American bombs and rockets

Almost from their first introduction to the battlefield, aircraft have been used to drop weapons on an enemy. During World War II the bomber developed to the extent that a single aircraft could deliver more explosive than a full broadside from a battleship. However, sheer explosive power was not all as, bombs were developed for a wide variety of purposes, and the rocket launched from a low-flying fighter-bomber was to become the scourge of enemy transport systems, whether ships, trains or convoys of lorries.

The British 500-lb MC bomb Mk III was much more effective than earlier GP weapons, due to a higher filling-to-weight ratio.

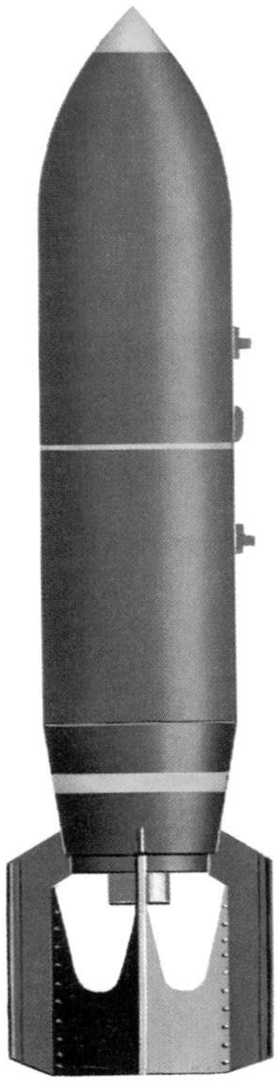

The 1,000-lb AP (Armour Piercing) bomb used by the USAAF was a thick cased weapon, which necessitated a low explosive-to-weight ratio.

The US 4,000-lb light case bomb was used for large-scale targets such as factories, with as much as 80 per cent of the bomb being explosive.

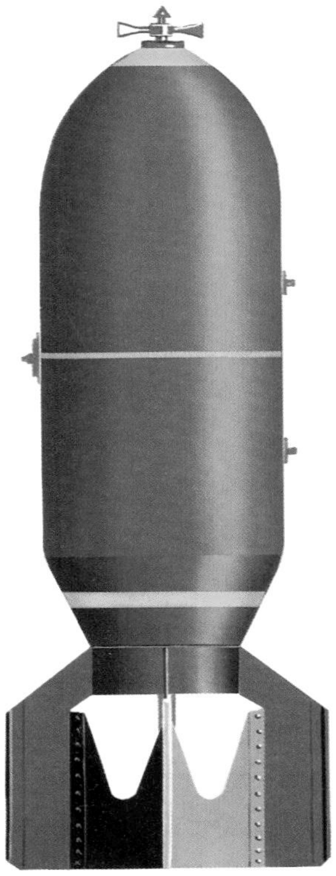

General-purpose bombs, about 50 per cent explosive, made up the vast majority of the tonnage dropped in World War II.

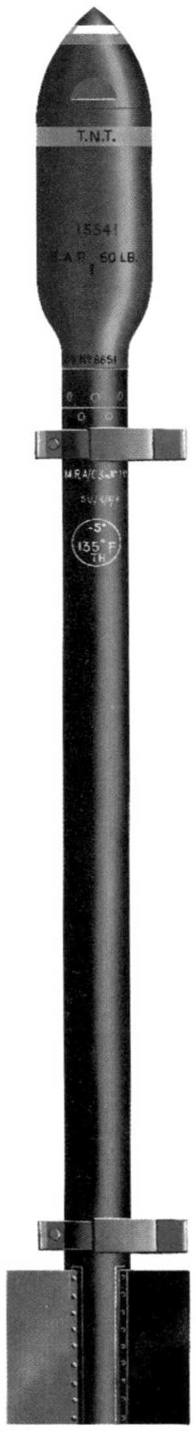

The 3-in rocket was used by the RAF for attacking a variety of targets, including ships, tanks, troop concentrations, strongpoints and submarines.

British heavy bombs, especially those designed for mass demolition, were often simply cylinders of steel packed with explosives. They were often known as 'Blockbusters'.

***Above:** A classic example of the use to which airborne rockets are put is demonstrated by Bristol Beaufighters of the South African Air Force over Yugoslavia during the course of the Italian campaign.*

***Right:** Trains and lines of communication were prime targets for the fighter-bombers of the Allied air forces. This is the result of a single 60-lb rocket hitting one of the trains seen in the previous picture.*

the weather, was bleak.

The one bright spot was that on 22 January 1944 Allied landings at Anzio on the coast due south of Rome were made with the object of cutting, or at least threatening, the German lines of communication that stretched along the highway from Rome to Cassino. The landings were completely successful and virtually unopposed – most of the forces that had defended the town having been withdrawn and added to the defence of the Gustav Line. The 36,000 men of the US 3rd Division, the British 1st Division, plus British Commandos and American Rangers were supported by forces of both navies; and at the end of the day all had been landed to find the port intact.

The Battles for Cassino

Although it is now customary to refer to the Battle of Cassino, there were in fact four Battles for Cassino, all of them infantry battles. They were hard-slogging matches reminiscent of World War I, and the casualty bill was as high as any between 1914 and 1918.

The Battles for Cassino had to be fought, for without them the Allies' northward advance up the leg of Italy would have ceased. Following the landing on the toe of Italy in September 1943 the Allies made relatively swift progress northwards, capturing Naples in the process. But as the Allies headed for Rome the Germans, although heavily outnumbered, carried out their usual skilful delaying tactics to buy time to

In a massive bombardment, the town of Cassino was reduced to rubble in an attempt to force the Germans from their positions. Unfortunately, the rubble provided ideal shelter for a defending force.

The Gustav Line, May 1944, and a heavy German artillery piece shells the troops assaulting Monte Cassino. The Germans also dominated the positions above the Anzio beachhead.

build what was then the most powerfully defended line in Europe.

The Gustav Line

From the east to west coasts of Italy the Germans built the Gustav Line. Using some of the strongest protective features that nature could supply, the Germans constructed a long line of defensive positions, both man-made and enhanced-natural, that created a major obstacle to the Allies. At no point along the Gustav Line was there any place where the Allies had even a remote chance of making any headway without a major attack in force against a strong defence. There was no way in which armoured forces could be used in the mountainous terrain which favoured geographical basis for the line, so the Allies just had to depend on a series of set-piece battles in order to break through.

In only one place was there even a remote chance of breaking the line, and that was at Cassino in the Liri valley. Even here the town was protected by an artificially swollen river and numerous fortified positions, and overlooked by what became known as Monastery Hill with its Benedictine monastery forming a natural observation post to cover the country for many miles around. Such was the strength of the Gustav Line that this fortress offered the best chance of Allied success, so it was Cassino or nothing.

If the strength of the Gustav Line was not enough, the Allies had to attack in the middle of the Italian winter. Winter in that part of Italy is a season of rains, cold and poor visibility, so the Allies had to contend with the elements. Additionally, they were hampered by a long supply line that extended back across a large number of river crossings over which supplies had to be moved on Bailey or improvised bridging. The Italian campaign was both an engineer's and an infantry campaign.

The first battle took place over a month during January and February 1944. It was very much a frontal attack and it soon stalled. The Allies found themselves attempting to advance directly into a well-organized and stubborn defence. A direct frontal attack across the Liri by an American force in brigade strength turned into a major military disaster, and even when they managed to cross elsewhere the Allies found themselves faced with an almost sheer climb to the crest of Monte Cassino.

The infanty fighting during this first battle was typical of what was to follow. It would be pointless to go through every stage of the battles for they followed one from another in a disheartening sequence and with disheartening similarity. Each battle or action started with a bombardment of the German positions, bomber aircraft sometimes taking the place of artillery. Then, following what appeared to be saturation coverage of the target, the infantry advanced, sometimes across water obstacles or up almost sheer mountain slopes, only to be cut down by defenders who struggled through the rubble to set up their machine-guns and were prepared to fight every step of the way. During the first battle it seemed that the American divisions were almost on the crest of the Cassino ridge above the town, but it was there that they were held and the position changed hands several times in the fighting that followed.

The Gustav Line was held by a variety of formations including two panzer divisions. The panzers could do little to influence the fighting directly, for the terrain was just as hostile to them as it was to the Allies, so the tanks were frequently used as pillboxes,

Above: The parachutists of the Luftwaffe were one of the elite fighting formations of the German armed forces, and the resistance they put up at Cassino more than justified their reputation.

Left: New Zealand infantrymen clear a ruined house in the town of Cassino. This was a battle to which many nations contributed troops, including France, Poland, Canada, the UK, the USA, Nepal and New Zealand.

Above: The abbot of the Benedictine monastery of Monte Cassino is escorted to Rome by German officers, when the Allies followed the bombing of Cassino town by the bombing of the monastery itself.

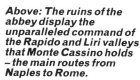

Above: The ruins of the abbey display the unparalleled command of the Rapido and Liri valleys that Monte Cassino holds – the main routes from Naples to Rome.

Right: After the battle, Humber armoured cars of the British Army rumble through the ruins of Cassino towards the new front line. The castle can be seen in the background.

often dug into strong buildings to provide added protection. The Germans also used a new ploy in the form of simplified Panther tank turrets set into steel boxes dug into specially chosen defensive positions. Most of these were inland from Cassino, up in the mountains, but where they were situated the Allies soon learned that there was no way in which they could make any headway. At no point where there was one of these dug-in turrets could the Allies break through at any stage of the battle. Prominent in the German defence of Cassino was the Luftwaffe's 1st Parachute Division, devoid of their parachutes since the invasion of Crete and fighting as infantry.

It was these paratroops who were in the thick of the fighting during the second battle, which opened in mid-February. This started with a bombing attack on the monastery itself, which was utterly destroyed by precision bombing. Unfortunately for the Allies this proved to be a major mistake, for all it achieved was to turn the monastery from a strong position into an impregnable fortress. The German paratroops promptly moved into the debris, which they found to be an ideal defensive position, and there they remained. The rest of the battle evolved into the usual round of infantry attacks met with strong defensive fire, and even hand-to-hand fighting in some areas. What advances were made were later lost in the usual German counter-attacks.

Final stages

There followed a lull, mainly imposed by the weather, which changed from bad to worse, preventing any operations. The third battle started on 15 March with a major aerial attack on the town of Cassino itself. In this bombing attack every structure in the town was either demolished or damaged in some way, and the waiting attackers believed that no one could be left alive in the inferno. But in the usual way, enough defenders did survive, and these managed to live through the artillery bombardment that followed the bombers. They managed to put up their usual spirited defence and delayed the bulk of the Allied attacks apart from one small operation in which a feature known as Castle Hill was taken. This hill was directly under Monastery Hill, and throughout that night the Germans made several attempts to retake the hill together with the old castle on the summit. In some of the most ferocious combat of all the Cassino actions the Germans were held off, but only at a fearful cost.

This third battle was noteworthy as it was the first major battle for Cassino in which the Allies attempted to use tanks. The Shermans and Stuarts of the 2nd New Zealand Division managed to find a way through the rubble of the town itself and started to climb towards the summit. They could not get far without infantry support and had to turn back, but at last a foothold on Monte Cassino ridge had been made. Farther inland the Goumiers of General Alphonse Juin's French Corps were making steady but unspectacular progress through the mountains using the time-honoured tactics and mule-carried supplies.

The third battle eventually came to a halt after only a week. Once again the defence had held, mainly because by that time it had been strengthened to the point where 23 German divisions faced 28 Allied divisions, a ratio very much in favour of the defence. The only way the Allies could really force their way through was to mass an attacking force at one point to obtain local superiority and ram their way through. Thus the pattern for the fourth battle was set and when the attack started in early May it was made by several divisions in place of the brigade-sized grouping that had been used earlier.

By the time the attacks started the winter weather was long past, and the infantry moved forward into the dust of an Italian summer. As usual the attack got under way with fire from massed artillery, over 1,600 guns in all, and as usual the Germans fought back as stubbornly as ever. But this time the Allies were attacking in overwhelming strength. In the mountains the French broke through the defences, and at Cassino itself the Polish II Corps surged forward to take the monastery. With the monastery taken the whole of the Gustav Line fell, for the old military adage that a mountain line was turned once penetrated at any point, held just as true for the Gustav Line as for any other. With the Cassino ridge in Allied hands the way through to Rome was cleared. From 19 May onwards the Allies could once more resume their advance north and Rome was duly taken in early June.

The Battles of Cassino had lasted for five months. When it was over the town of Cassino resembled one of the villages on the Western Front of World War I. Whole areas around the town were shattered and the monastery itself was a heap of ruins. Between them the Allies and the Germans had suffered over 50,000 casualties, many of whom were never found; the British alone lost over 4,000 men 'missing'.

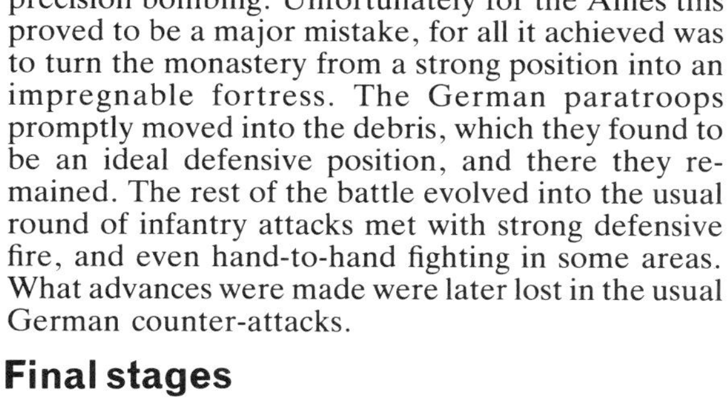

Above: Troops from the Polish 3rd Carpathian Division, part of Polish II Corps, are seen in the final assault which was to take the monastery at the same time as the French under Juin were finally making their breakthrough.

Right: A 40-mm Bofors anti-aircraft position manned by British troops in the ruins of Cassino. One of the strongest points of the German defences in Italy, it had been fought over for four months.

Chapter 18

Approach to the Philippines

The first attempts by the United States to strike back at the empire of Japan were largely pinpricks, while resources were being marshalled for the major offensives to come. The campaigns in the Solomons were the start of an island-hopping chain which was to lead to the Philippines, while at the same time a strategic drive through the Central Pacific was being planned. This too was aimed at the Philippines, from where the combined forces would launch the invasion of Japan.

During the closing months of 1942, along the Kokoda Trail and at Guadalcanal the Japanese tide of invasion had been halted and, indeed, imperceptibly turned back. This was a significant achievement – but not enough in itself to turn defeat into victory, for wars are won in men's minds and it is essential that these are clear and purposeful. It is also of great importance that there should be no large differences of opinion in top-level leadership – and this happy state cannot be said to have existed among the Allied commanders in the Pacific as 1942 drew to a close.

General Douglas MacArthur possessed one of the strongest wills and personalities in the public life of the United States of this century, and had made a clear and much-publicised statement to the effect that he intended to return to the Philippines as soon as could be arranged; and, being a firm believer in the dictum that the shortest distance between two points is a straight line, he intended to do so via New Guinea.

But even MacArthur's personality could not concentrate all American endeavour under his own, sole direction. In Admiral Ernest J. King, Chief of Naval Operations, MacArthur faced a rival with a mind and will just as powerful as his own – and in pursuit of the honour of the US Navy, King would not allow all authority to a soldier; the proud record of his own service had to be nourished, and in the wide reaches of the Central Pacific there was both room and opportunity. Thus the Allied offensive against Japan was to be delivered in two main prongs – from the Southwest Pacific Area along the New Guinea-Mindanao line under MacArthur, mainly by military formations (many of them Australian), and from the Central Pacific Area through the Gilbert, Marshal and Caroline Islands with one massive detour up into the Marianas, under King's senior deputy, Admiral Chester W. Nimitz, by naval forces including US Marine battalions with some US Army battalions in support.

One early operation was mounted by Nimitz up in the north to clear the Aleutians: on 11 May 1943 an American division was landed on Attu under a cloak of fog and supported by a bombardment from three battleships. They forced the Japanese garrison of 2,500 back into the foothills, and then wiped them out when they attempted a last suicidal assault – a phenomenon that was to become familiar as the campaign progressed; and then in July the Americans moved to Kiska where the Japanese were in greater numbers, bombarded it for nearly three weeks and then discovered that the Japanese, accepting that they were faced with overwhelming force, had evacuated the island one night under cover of yet more of the locality's customary fog.

It had been an operation employing enormous American power against a weak garrison, but it gave the Americans experience and cleared their northern flank; it also indicated to every observer that, if

The Assault on Japan

Only the immense industrial capacity of the United States of America could have sustained the immense effort required to conduct a war on the scale of the Pacific campaign, with forces committed to two immense strategic drives through the Pacific (not to mention the power involved in the European war). The two main axes in the Pacific were from Australia and along the Solomon Islands, and a fleetborne push from atoll to atoll through the central Pacific.

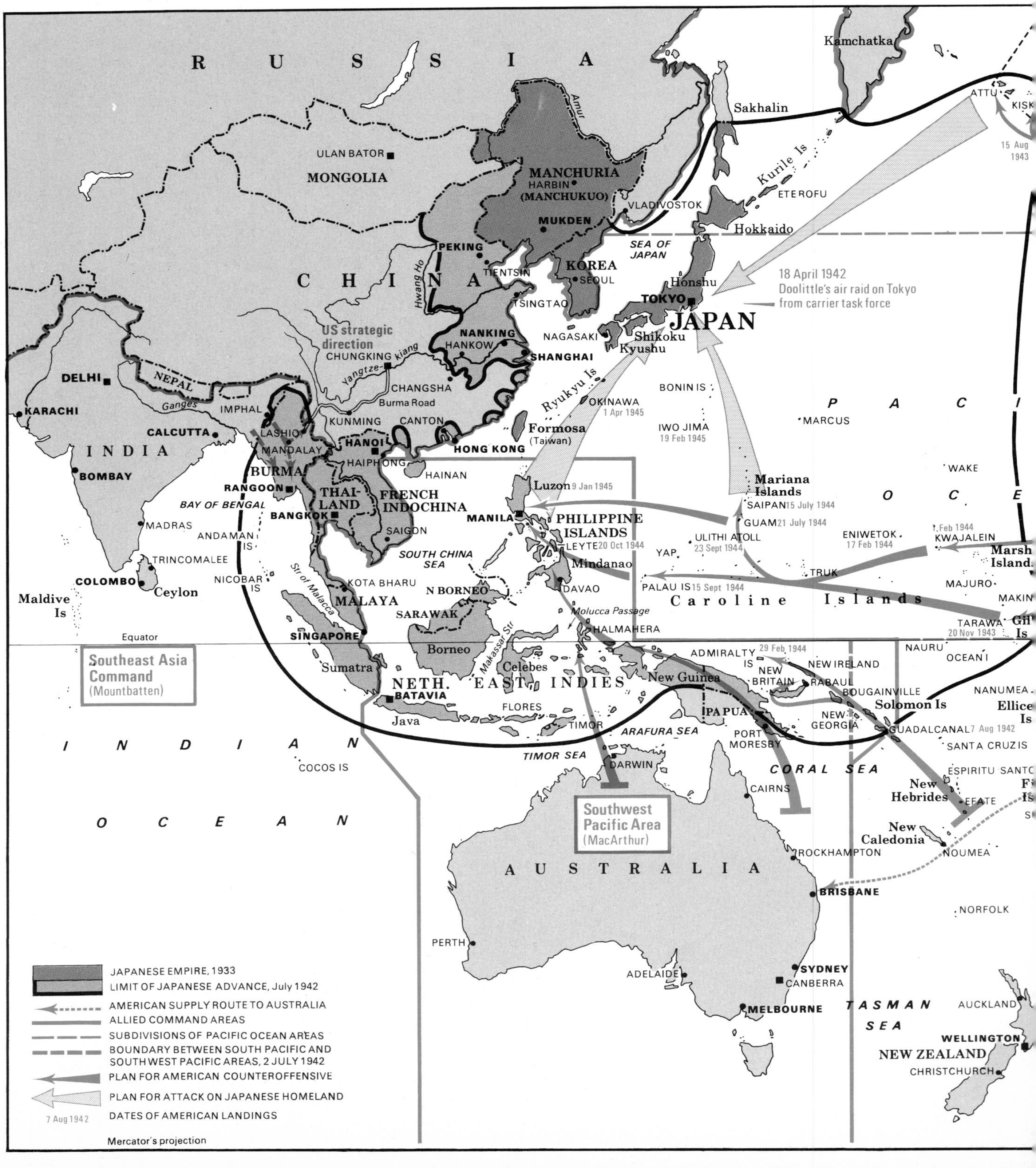

necessary, America could indeed marshal enormous power – a power that was growing all the time.

With the Aleutians cleared of Japanese troops, attention could now be concentrated on the central thrust, and the first phase – assault on the enemy garrisons in the Gilbert Islands – could be launched.

Admiral Nimitz gave Rear-Admiral Raymond A. Spruance the overall responsibility for Operation Galvanic, and his decision was that the two most westerly islands, Makin and Tarawa, were the main objectives, for with those two in American hands the remainder of the chain would inevitably be starved into surrender. The two atolls were nearly 100 miles apart (distances were to lend a distinctive flavour to this campaign) so two different fleets and expeditionary forces were necessary; they would not be able to support each other in any way.

To capture Makin Atoll, 7,000 troops of a heavily reinforced regimental combat team of the 27th Infantry Division, sailing in six transports under command of Major-General Ralph Smith, would land on the western end of Butaritari Island to form a bridgehead, out of which in due course they would drive at the main Japanese positions – pill-boxes, anti-tank ditches and a trio of 80-mm guns – all held, it was reckoned, by about 800 men under command of a junior lieutenant.

The force and its escort were off Makin by the morning of 20 November 1943, carrier aircraft and a tornado of supporting fire from two battleships, two cruisers and three destroyers covered the landing craft as they went in; it was fortunate that they kept the Japanese heads down as many of the LVTs (Landing Vehicle Tracked) hit coral long before the beaches, so the men had to wade on across a pot-holed and boulder-strewn reef. One battalion landed from the lagoon side and quickly found themselves amid the Japanese defences, so closely enmeshed that neither air cover nor naval guns could help them and it became a bitter hand-to-hand battle with rifle, gun-butt and boot or bayonet.

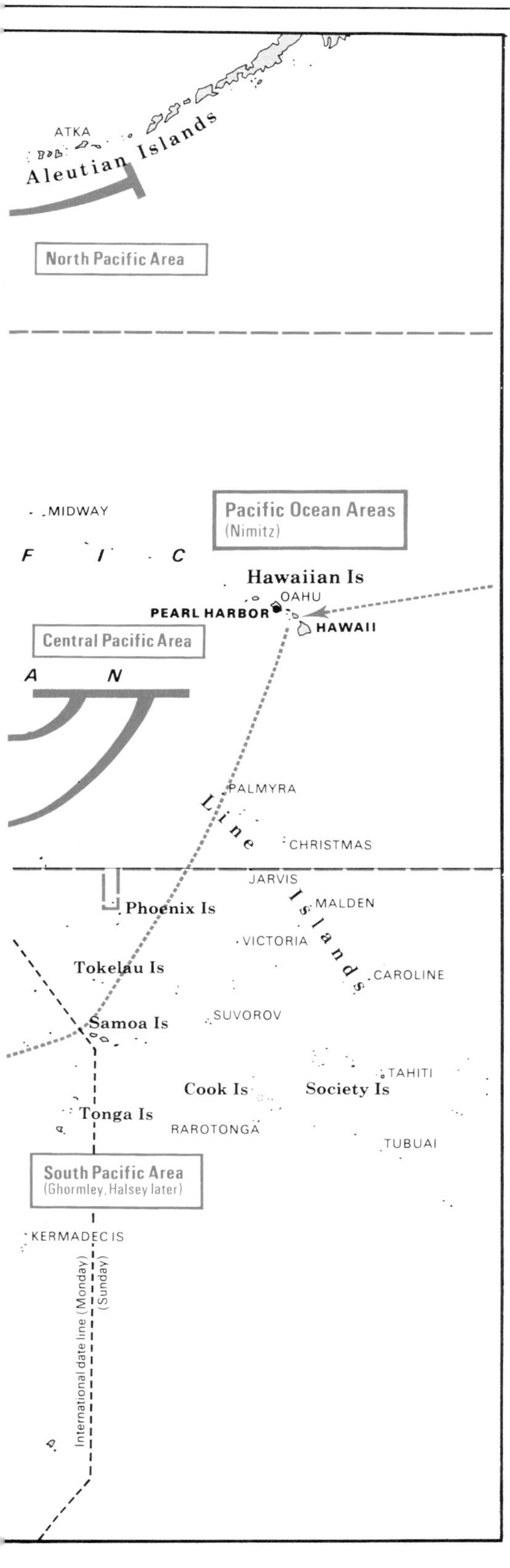

But by the evening two beachheads were secure, the Japanese positions had been identified, engineers with flamethrowers were coming ashore and heavy machine-guns and demolition teams getting ready for the next day. All through 21 November the Americans systematically brought increasing weight to bear on every enemy position until it was destroyed, and the following day they could move to the eastern end of the island to break through the last barrier of trenches and bunkers, hidden in thick vegetation. They beat off fierce counter-attacks during the night, but at 11.30 a.m. on 23 November General Smith could send off the terse message 'Makin taken.'

There were 66 Americans killed and 152 wounded, but of the 800 Japanese defenders only one wounded sailor surrendered, plus 104 Korean labourers.

To the south, the Battle of Tarawa had been fought and the fame of the 2nd US Marine Division established for all time.

The Tarawa landings

Tarawa lies some 2,500 miles south west of Pearl Harbor, and its strategic importance in 1943 rested upon its geographical position along the route from the Allied-held New Hebrides to the main Japanese south-east Pacific bastion at Truk, plus also the fact that on Tarawa the Japanese had built an airstrip capable of taking fighters and light bombers. By the same token, the Japanese had built heavily concreted defence positions in a network of underground casemates around the strip and manned them with some 2,600 well-trained troops, augmented by another 2,000 Korean construction workers who could be trusted to assist in the island's defence.

Tarawa consists of a submerged coral reef in the rough shape of an archer's bow, with several stretches of the reef rising above the waves to form islets upon which palm and scrub vegetation has taken root over the centuries. The bow encloses a lagoon into which there is only one channel, near the apex of the bow, and the nearest islet to the channel is Betio, barely 3 miles long and less than half a mile wide, upon which the airstrip and the bulk of the Japanese defences lay.

Once the Americans had recaptured the Aleutians, this provided an excellent base for maritime patrol aircraft operating over the northern sector of the war zone.

Betio, obviously, was the prime target for Allied assault.

From the point of view of the commanders of the assault force, Rear-Admiral Harry Hill and Major-General Julian Smith commanding the 2nd Marine Division, the greatest initial problem would be to get the men ashore and then supply them across a coral reef which gave at most 3.5-ft draught, and ran across an attack front varying between 600 and 1,000 yards from the target beaches. The LCVPs which would normally be used (and in any case would still have to carry the bulk of the supplies) might just scrape across the reef if they were not too heavily laden, but the LCMs carrying vehicles and (as soon as possible after the assault) light tanks would have no chance at all of going all the way in.

The only vessels available in the Pacific at the end of 1943 which might be able to save the US Marines a long and exposed walk through waist-deep water towards a defended beach were LVTs, used so far only to take supplies into an established beach-head, and either totally unarmoured or in the case of some 50 LVT 2s, very lightly armoured and fitted with only two machine-guns (one 0.3-in and one 0.5-in). Some rehearsals were carried out with those vehicles available, boiler-plate was fitted to the sides and cab-fronts of some LVT 1s, and it was piously hoped that covering fire would compensate for the lack of armoured protection.

As the Japanese commander, Rear-Admiral Shibasaki, had not surprisingly placed his heavy armament and main defences to face out to sea, the American commanders decided to put the US Marines ashore inside the lagoon. Even here, though, aerial reconnaissance reported that the defences were strong: underwater booby-trapped obstacles littered the lagoon bed, and a 4-ft high sea-wall of coconut logs at the top of the beaches which might have offered some shelter was obviously enfiladed by well-sited machine-gun posts. Admiral Shibasaki's boast that the Americans could not take Betio with one million men in 100 years did not at first glance seem totally unfounded.

On 13 November 1943 Task Force 52 left Efate in the New Hebrides, overtook on 17 November the slower-moving LST group carrying the LVT 2s and arrived some 6 miles off the outer beaches of Betio in the early hours of 20 November. The guns of the flagship, the USS *Maryland*, two other battleships

Chronology of War: 1943

August 25
Admiral Mountbatten appointed Supreme Commander, South East Asia

August 26
Russian offensive into Ukraine begins on five fronts (Central, Voronezh, Steppe, South West and South)

August 28
Japanese evacuate New Georgia and other Solomon Islands to consolidate on Bougainville and New Britain

August 31
UK civilian casualties in August 108 killed, 164 injured

September 1
German garrison at Taganrog, west of Rostov, liquidated

September 3
Allies cross Straits of Messina. Armistice arranged between Allies and Italy, but not announced

September 5
Australians and US forces land east of Lae, New Guinea. Allied bridgeheads in Italy link up

September 8
Eisenhower announces surrender of Italian forces. Russians complete liberation of Donetz Basin

September 9
Allies land at Salerno in Operation Avalanche. British 1st airborne Division lands at Taranto

September 10
Germans occupy Rome. Eighth Army captures Taranto

September 11
Allies take Salamaua, New Guinea

September 12
Skorzeny rescues Mussolini from imprisonment on the Gran Sasso

September 13
Germans counterattack at Salerno

September 15
Allies capture Lae

September 18
Allies break out of Salerno bridgehead

September 20
British and US forces link at Eboli

September 22
Allies land at Bari. Red Army captures Poltava and crosses Dnieper

September 24
US Fifth Army begins general advance up Italy

September 25
Red Army liberates Smolensk

Operation Galvanic, the attack on Tarawa, was the first major action of the Central Pacific drive, with over 18,000 Marines committed against a defending force of less than 5,000. Fanatical Japanese resistance caused some 3,500 casualties, more than 1,000 of which were killed.

On Betio Island, part of the Tarawa Atoll, the most ferocious of the fighting took place. It was on this tiny island that the Americans discovered that Japanese troops were prepared literally to fight to the last man.

and six cruisers were soon engaged in a duel with the Japanese coastal armament, while the marines of the assault combat teams from 2nd and 8th Marine Regiments clambered down the heavy debarkation nets; the first wave went straight into the LVTs, the second and third waves into LCVPs, and the fourth wave into sea boats already loading with heavy weapons and equipment. Led by minesweepers and escorted by two destroyers, the lines of landing craft made for the narrow channel through the reef, and as dawn lightened the sky they threaded their way into the lagoon and began the turn for the run-in.

As they did so the carrier-borne aircraft streaked in from the west and for nearly half an hour strafed the length of the island, especially the runways and any sign of habitation or strong-point the pilots could see. As the aircraft screamed away into the growing light, the heavy naval guns at sea opened up in a concentrated bombardment which shrouded Betio in smoke and huge billowing clouds of coral dust, effectively blinding both the defenders and, more critically, the drivers of the manoeuvring LVTs, all keenly aware of the necessity of putting their passengers down on the right beaches.

There were three of these (Red 1, 2 and 3), each the goal of a reinforced battalion, but the first marines to go ashore were a scouting sniper team under Lieutenant Hawkins, whose task it was to storm the end of a long pier which separated Red 2 and 3, neutralize its defences and hold the pier for use by the supply vessels as they came in. The team's LCVP hit the reef at the end of the pier on time and Hawkins led his men up the ramp conveniently built there by the defenders, to find himself immediately engaged in a swift and violent action among stacked fuel drums, two of which exploded during the fight. Two wooden huts were attacked with a flamethrower (and the resulting conflagration burned through an area of the pier floor, thus adding later to the problems of the supply teams), a dozen Japanese soldiers were killed and then the pier was in American hands. By this time the first LVTs had clambered across the reef and were swimming in towards the beaches. Some were hit during that last approach, machine-gun fire lacing the air across the width of all the beach-heads, but by 9.10 a.m. the first wave of marines was rolling over the sides of the craft and racing up towards the dubious shelter of the coconut palisade. Fortunately, fire from the escorting destroyers had already obliterated two of the enfilading machine-gun posts, and soon the others were also silenced. The marines dug in deeper, sniped at anything that moved inland and waited for their supporting waves to arrive.

All along the reef edge the LCVPs and LCMs grounded; the water was even lower than expected and nothing untracked could cross. Grimly, the marines slid down into the water and began the awful walk to the beaches: there was nothing to hide behind, and the Americans were held down to a slow trudge through waist high water, frothed by machine-gun crossfire and an inferno of explosions, only too often stained deep pink from the writhing bodies of their friends. But nothing stopped the survivors; as more and more craft arrived at the reef, so more and more lines of men filled the lagoon and waded implacably forward; soon the lines were reaching the beaches and running up towards the palisade.

Slow progress

Here slow progress was made. The Japanese were largely unseen, except for flickering tongues of red and orange flame stabbing from gun-ports in low-lying and concealed bunkers. Every move put the attackers in a different firelane, and casualties mounted at a worrying rate. Colonel David Shoup, the combat commander, went ashore on Red 2 just before noon and his first signal back to Admiral Hill read 'Issue in doubt'. But first impressions in battle

To reach the dubious shelter of the coconut trunk palisade that ringed the island, the Marines had to clamber from their landing craft on the reef and wade several hundred metres through the lagoon, under fire.

Chronology of War: 1943

September 29
Badoglio signs Italian Armistice

September 30
UK civilian casualties in September 5 killed 11 injured

October 1
Fifth Army enters Naples; Allies reach Foggia

October 2
Fifth Army takes Benevento, British commandos land at Termoli. Australians capture Finschafen at the end of the Huon peninsula, New Guinea

October 5
US Navy opens heavy bombardment of Wake Island in the central Pacific

October 6
US Marines land on Kolombangara by New Georgia, in the Solomons

October 7
US Fifth Army reaches the Volturno river, north of Naples

October 9
Russians occupy Kuban peninsula, east of Crimea

October 13
Italy declares war on Germany. Allies cross Volturno

October 14
Red Army captures Zaporozhye on the Dnieper

October 20
Wavell installed as Viceroy of India. Soviet Voronezh, Steppe, South-West and Southern Fronts re-named 1st to 4th Ukrainian Fronts; the Central Front becomes the Belorussian Front

October 25
Red Army liberate Dnepropetrovsk and Dneprodzerzhinsk

October 31
UK civilian casualties in October 118 killed, 282 injured

November 1
Russians cut off Crimea. US Marines land on Bougainville

November 3
Soviet Belorussian and 1st Ukrainian Fronts converge on Kiev

November 6
Red Army enters Kiev and drives the Germans beyond the Dnieper

November 8
Eighth Army reaches River Sangro just short of the Gustav line in Italy

November 12
German forces invade Leros in the Dodecanese. British-Italian garrison surrenders after four days of fierce fighting

November 18
RAF drops 350 4,000-lb bombs on Berlin

November 20
US troops land on Makin and Tarawa atolls in the Gilbert Islands. Fierce fighting on Tarawa. Eighth Army crosses Sangro on the east coast of Italy

November 23
US Marines complete capture of Tarawa. Only 17 Japanese soldiers are captured alive, together with about 130 Koreans, out of a total force of 4,836

November 28
Teheran Conference begins; Roosevelt and Churchill meet Stalin

November 30
UK civilian casualties in November 119 killed, 238 injured

December 3
Russians advance on wide front. 2nd Cairo Conference opens

are apt to be uncertain, and shortly afterwards the first of the light tanks threaded their way through the swamp of floating bodies and moved quickly to the aid of the pinned-down infantry.

More waves came into the beach, the heavy supplies trundled along what remained of the pier and reached the men who needed them, and as the long afternoon dragged by and dusk fell, the initiative passed inevitably into the marines' hands and the Japanese lost any chance they had of driving their attackers off Betio. They made no attempt to counter-attack during that night (the bombardment had smashed their communication system) and the next morning (21 November) another battalion of the 8th Marines came ashore after a wretched night spent bobbing about in LCVPs.

Pack howitzers were now ashore, the destroyers became ever more accurate in pinpointing their targets, two companies of marines broke clean through across the airstrip and reached the ocean shore where they dug in, and the whole of the western end of Betio came under American control, allowing yet more marine battalions to land. The situation closely resembled that on Crete in 1941 once Maleme airfield had fallen to the German paratroops: the attackers could be strengthened, and the defenders were being inexorably ground away.

On the last day of the battle the Japanese did mount a counter-attack, some 500 men boiling up out of the underground casemates to throw themselves through devastating destroyer and artillery fire at a marine company, and in 20 minutes of chaos and confusion at bayonet and grenade range, both sides were almost annihilated. But there were more Americans than Japanese, so the result was preordained. The following morning the 2nd Marine Division completed mopping up, destroying the last defenders in co-ordinated infantry/tank operations, and at 1.12 p.m. on 23 November General Smith declared Betio secured.

The Japanese and Korean defenders on the other islets of Tarawa atoll were quickly overcome, though in the case of the Japanese soldiers each one had to be cornered and killed; only 17 wounded Japanese were taken alive, most of the 146 PoWs being Korean. The remainder of the 4,750-strong garrison fought to the death. On the other side, over 1,000 US marines had been killed and more than 2,000 wounded.

Four Medals of Honor were won on Tarawa. And lessons were learned in the science of amphibious warfare which would save countless lives in future months.

Marines with fixed bayonets take cover behind an embankment. Only 17 wounded Japanese were taken alive, nearly 4,700 fighting to the death. These proportions were to be repeated many times.

Pacific flying-boats

Long-range patrol and air-sea rescue missions were handled mainly by flying-boats, the lack of suitable airstrips and the huge distances involved making it difficult for land-based aircraft to operate. Both sides had excellent aircraft, typified by the H6K for the Japanese and the Catalina for the Allies.

Above: Showing extremely good sea-going qualities, the Kawanishi H6K was one of the best flying-boats of the war. However, as the war progressed the H6K had to revert to mainly transport duties, as it suffered greatly at the hands of Allied fighters. This is an H6K5, codenamed 'Mavis' by the Allies.

Left: This Consolidated PBY-5 Catalina served with No. 6 Sqn, Royal New Zealand Air Force. It was based in Fiji during 1944-45, flying air-sea rescue missions and general maritime patrol.

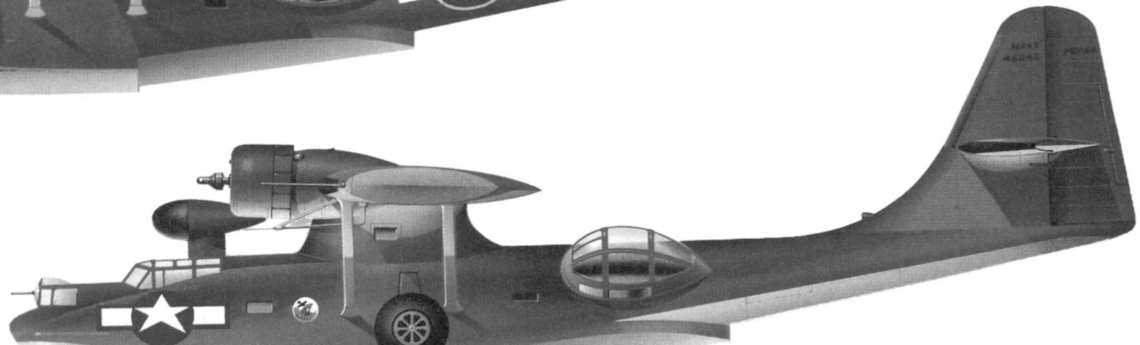

Right: Featuring many design advances, such as taller fin and aerodynamically improved hull, the final Catalina version was the NAF PBN-1 (PBY-6A). This US Navy aircraft has a search radar mounted above the cockpit.

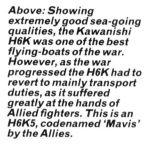

Below: Operating from Burmese bases during the latter months of the war, the Short Sunderland performed excellent work alongside the Catalinas. The type had all the attributes needed for a maritime patrol aircraft: endurance, load-carrying ability and good water characteristics.

Below: The Martin PBM Mariner was a successful flying-boat which was mainly employed for anti-submarine duties. These served from late 1943 onwards, being able to operate from seaplane tenders.

Below right: Consolidated's follow-on to the Catalina was the mighty PB2Y Coronado. A small number were built in two variants. The PB2Y-3 shown was an ASW platform, complete with radar mounted above the cockpit. The other was the PB2Y-3R transport, without such radar.

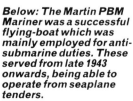

KWAJALEIN

Douglas SBD Dauntlesses were the spearhead of the Navy's attack forces, being used for all types of operations. These aircraft are seen during the attack on Param Island, in the Truk atoll.

The attack on Kwajalein was made in the light of the experience of Tarawa. An M4 Sherman follows the infantry into a battle which cost the Japanese 8,368 dead. There were no prisoners.

After the Gilberts, the Marshall Islands were the obvious objective. There was at the beginning a plan for the gradual subjection of the Marshall chain from east to west, but with the success of the by-pass plan in the Gilbert's Admiral Nimitz instructed his subordinates – Spruance, Rear-Admiral Kelly Turner who had been in overall command at Makin and Rear-Admiral Harry Hill, and the explosive Major-General Holland 'Howlin' Mad' Smith — to concentrate only on the Kwajalein and Eniwetok Atolls, though in the end Nimitz did also allow the occupation of Majuro in order to provide Spruance with a logistic base (having first made sure that it was unoccupied by the Japanese and would therefore cost neither men nor time).

The Japanese air bases at other islands in the chain – at Mili, Maleolap and Wotj – would be ignored, isolated and in due course eliminated as US air and naval power together shut off all their supplies; carrier-borne fighters would also ensure that they formed no base for interference with the main operations.

Operation Flintlock

Majuro was duly occupied on 30 January 1944, and on 1 February the 4th Marine Division forming the Northern Force of Operation Flintlock and the 7th Infantry Division forming the Southern Force were inside Kwajalein Lagoon – the largest lagoon in the world – marines storming ashore at Roi-Namur, and soldiers at Kwajalein itself, 42 miles to the south. They were supported not only by carrier-borne aircraft and gunfire from the escorting battleships, but also by medium and light artillery which had been rapidly and efficiently mounted on two or three of the myriad neighbouring islets by reconnaissance teams and engineers during the preceding 12 hours. Daring, skill and their manufacturing industry were already giving the Americans a supreme advantage.

The main problems connected with the landings had come not from the enemy, but from high surf, a rugged reef and a certain inexperience among the crews of the LVTs and LSTs. Many of the craft were gashed by coral, some had their propellers torn away and drifted helplessly for a time – to their passengers' intense fury. Nevertheless, two battalions of marines were ashore with heavy weapons at Roi by noon, the defenders, dazed by the shelling and bombing which had deluged them since dawn, giving little trouble at first; but as the marines pushed north towards the ocean, isolated groups of Japanese fought their customary bitter battles against them until they were wiped out. But by the evening Roi was securely in American hands.

The attack by the battalion on Namur differed for a variety of reasons. The island was much more thickly wooded than Roi, and the preceding bombardment had smashed the trees down into a confused mess which effectively concealed the multitude of bunkers, pill-boxes and casemates the Japanese were soon stubbornly defending. The assault LVTs could not get through the ditches and piled debris so the marines were deprived of their cannon and heavy machine-guns, but eventually some tanks came ashore and smashed their way across until slowly but surely, the attack line crept foward.

Then one of the demolition teams threw a satchel bomb charge into a blockhouse which proved to be full of torpedo warheads, and the resultant explosion blew palm trees and blocks of concrete the size of packing cases a hundred feet into the air, killed 20 marines and wounded a hundred more. Reserves were rushed in, but the momentum of the attack had been checked and by dusk a sizeable proportion of the island was still in Japanese hands. Counter-attacks during the night caused more marine casualties, but in the morning more tanks came ashore, support also came across the causeway linking Namur and Roi and at 2.18 p.m. on 2 February Namur was declared clear of the enemy.

Kwajalein

The 7th Infantry Division battles for Kwajalein itself followed a similar but more intense pattern. Four battalions of 105-mm and 155-mm howitzers were put ashore on Kwajalein and the neighbouring islets and their effect, coupled with that of the aircraft and naval broadsides, was awesome. According to one observer the 'entire island looked as though it had been picked up to 20,000 feet and dropped' – which may have been one reason why it was later used for atomic bomb tests.

Two infantry battalions went ashore on 1 February, and by nightfall they had struggled through undergrowth like that on Namur to reach the edge of an embryo airstrip the Japanese had been building. They were subjected all through that night to sniping from the rear and counter-attacks came in at them all through the following day; they had to use massed flamethrowers against some desperately defended blockhouses, and even then it took until 4 February for 32nd Infantry Regiment eventually to drive over the last Japanese strongholds and reach the far end of the two-mile-long island.

By 8 February the entire Kwajalein Atoll was in Admiral Turner's hands at a cost of 486 dead and 1,259 wounded; the Japanese killed amounted to 8,368. There were no Japanese wounded taken, and no prisoners.

Eniwetok was the next objective; as the capture of Kwajalein had been so swift (it had been expected to take at least a month) Nimitz arrived to discuss the immediate future and agreed that D-Day for the island would now be 17 February instead of 1 May. Ships were now plentiful and Admiral Hill, who was given the task, was also given use of a reserve of 8,000 men who had been earmarked for Kwajalein but had not been called upon.

However, another operation was mounted at the same time as Hill's onslaught on Eniwetok, which was not only to help him considerably, but was to have a significant effect upon the whole campaign.

Seven hundred miles to the south west of Eniwetok was the crucially important Japanese base of Truk – the 'Gibraltar of the East'. It had a superb harbour and had been almost from the outset of the Japanese offensive the headquarters of the Japanese Combined Fleet. On 12 February, Task Force 58 under command of Rear-Admiral Marc Mitscher left Majuro to eliminate it from the Pacific war chessboard. Warned of the approach of the massive American carrier fleet, quite a number of the Japanese warships fled to the comparative safety of the Palau island's harbours; nevertheless, when eventually Task Force 58 drew off on 18 February, it left behind over 270 demolished Japanese aircraft and the sunken or beached wrecks of two light cruisers, three auxiliary cruisers, four destroyers, two submarine tenders, an armed trawler, a plane ferry and 24 merchantmen – altogether comprising nearly 400,000 tons of shipping.

The raid on Truk could well be judged the most

Chronology of War: 1943-1944

December 5
Eighth Army crosses Moro river in Italy

December 7
2nd Cairo Conference ends

December 12
Rommel appointed C-in-C, Fortress Europe

December 17
US Fifth Army takes San Pietro

December 21
Russians liquidate German bridgehead over Dnieper at Kherson

December 25
1st and 7th US Marine Division units land on New Britain

December 26
Red Army attacks Kiev Salient. US Marines land on Cape Gloucester. In Battle of North Cape German battlecruiser Scharnhorst *is sunk by Home Fleet, headed by Admiral Fraser in the battleship HMS* Duke of York

December 28
Russians on the Central Front cut Polotsk-Vitebsk railway

December 29
US Marines capture Cape Gloucester airfield

December 31
Russians liberate Zhitomir. UK civilian casualties in December 10 killed, 41 injured

1944

January 1
Rommel assumes command of German Army Group B covering the north of France, Belgium and the Netherlands. General Mark Clark to command both 5th and 7th US Armies in Italy

January 2
Russians drive to within 20 miles of pre-war Polish Frontier

January 3
Russians cut railway line Kiev-Warsaw

January 5
US Fifth Army assaults Gustav Line, east of Cassino. General Sir Oliver Leese to command Eighth Army on Adriatic coast

January 6
Russians advance into Poland

January 8
Russians take Kirovograd

January 9
British capture Maungdaw on the Arakan peninsula in Burma

January 12
US Fifth Army captures Cervaro. Russians take Sarny. Germans counterattack near Kiev

January 13
Red Army offensive in north to relieve Leningrad and Novgorod

January 15
Germans withdraw across Rapido to positions around Monte Cassino

January 16
Eisenhower appointed Supreme Commander, Allied Expeditionary Forces. British 10 Corps cross river Garigliano, south of Cassino

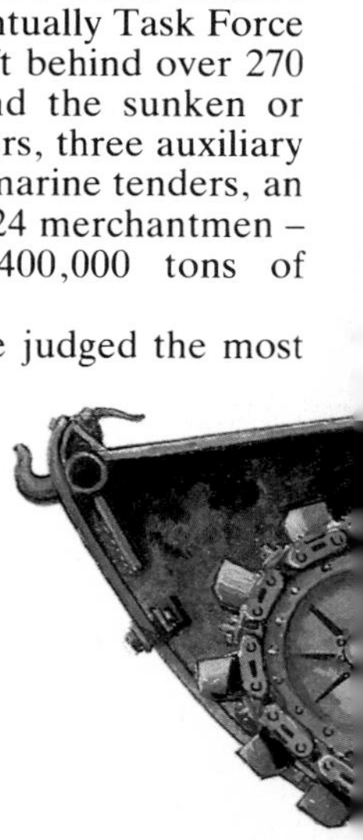

successful operation of World War II, for it was carried out at a cost of only 25 American aircraft, and 29 aircrew. And it made Hill's task at Eniwetok that much easier.

Techniques were now being perfected, intelligence gathering brought to a fine art. Before Hill's force left Kwajalein it was known how many Japanese troops garrisoned Eniwetok Atoll, which of the islands must be taken and which of the neighbouring islets could be used as artillery bases from which the bombardments could be augmented. By nightfall on 17 February artillery and men were all in position and at dawn on the 18th the guns roared out, the aircraft dropped their bombs, two battalions of the 22nd Marines went

While the atolls of the central Pacific were being fought over, the rapidly growing US carrier force was striking at the major Japanese fleet and logistics base at Truk in the Carolines, seen here from a US plane in February 1944.

Amphibious vehicles of the Pacific War

The nature of the war in the Pacific with the necessity of fighting from island to island, and each new island presenting yet another defensive line, meant that amphibious operations grew to a size that would have been unimaginable in the 1930s. A new war requires new equipment, and many amphibious vehicles were developed, both for fighting and for supply.

Left: The DUKW was developed from the ubiquitous GMC 6x6 2.5 ton truck, and was used as a logistical stores carrier ferrying supplies from ships offshore to supply dumps inland. It was used in amphibious operations worldwide.

Above: From the start, Japan realized that an amphibious capability would be essential in its far-flung island empire. The Type 2 Ka-Mi amphibious tank was one of the more commonly used light tanks, largely by the Imperial Navy.

Right: Originally a civil design for use in the Florida swamps, the LVT1 was the precursor of a large number of vehicles for the Marine Corps. The assault version had an M3 tank turret to provide fire support in the initial stage of a landing.

Below: The LVT4 differed from previous tracked landing vehicles in having a loading ramp at the rear, which allowed the carriage of larger loads such as jeeps or light artillery. It had four pintle-mounted machine-guns, as well as a bow-mounted weapon.

No aircraft turned the tide against the Japanese more than did the Grumman F6F Hellcat, represented here by an F6F-3 from USS Yorktown.

A Japanese-eye view of the invasion of Saipan, from one of the bunkers battered to oblivion by the preparatory air and sea bombardment.

ashore, and by 2.50 p.m. the first island, Engebi, was overrun; snipers were winkled out during the afternoon and evening, the last strongpoints burned out with flamethrowers and the counter-attacks during the night all beaten off under a night sky turned to daylight by star shells, a favourite tactic of Admiral Hill's. By morning another Japanese garrison had been eliminated and, moreover, documents had been captured giving accurate information regarding the other two islands requiring attention in the atoll.

By the morning of 21 February Eniwetok was in the hands of 106th Infantry Regiment, its task made if anything easier by a sacrificial Banzai charge during the night by the mass of the Japanese survivors of the day's fighting. Then, on the morning of 22 February, three marine battalions supported by army howitzers firing from Eniwetok attacked the island of Parry and by the afternoon of 23 February the atoll and thus the whole Marshalls group were under American control. Three thousand four hundred Japanese had died but only 348 Americans, and 866 Americans had been wounded.

The scene was now set for the Battle of the Philippine Sea and what became known as The Great Marianas Turkey Shoot.

The Marianas

The islands of the Marianas stand roughly halfway between the Gilberts and Japan, Tokyo being some 1,500 miles away to the north. Guam is the southernmost island, the others curving northwards for about 400 miles, the most important – Saipan, Tinian and Rota – in the southern half of the arc.

The operation now mounted to capture these islands remains one of the most ambitious in the history of amphibious warfare. It was carried out by a fleet consisting of 7 battleships, 21 cruisers, 69 destroyers, 15 aircraft carriers in four groups together carrying 956 aircraft, all shepherding transports carrying nearly 130,000 troops; many of the ships sailed direct from Pearl Harbor 3,500 miles away and the shortest voyage for anyone was the 1,000 miles from Eniwetok. It was a superbly executed operation, and on the morning of 15 June 1944 two marine divisions stormed ashore on the relatively small island of Saipan under yet another massive artillery and air bombardment, against stubborn opposition from a Japanese garrison of nearly 30,000 who had been on the island long enough to construct deep bunkers and well-sited blockhouses.

By nightfall, 20,000 marines were ashore but to a great extent pinned on the beaches by a stubborn Japanese defence pouring fire down upon them from the strong, commanding heights. That night was the first of many long, anguished sessions of bitter fighting, but the marines gradually edged their way forward, aided all the time by air strikes and powerful naval gunnery. It was fortunate that by 17 June General Smith had brought ashore the 27th Infantry Division as reinforcement and that both marines and soldiers were by then well consolidated, for on the following day a large proportion of both air and naval support had to be withdrawn to the west, to meet the threat brought about by the Japanese A-Go Operation and the approach of Admiral Ozawa's Combined Fleet.

This threat was fought off by Admiral Mitscher's superb aircrews of Task Force 58 guarded by the Battle Line under Vice-Admiral W.A. Lee, and the menace of Japanese naval air supremacy was removed by them for ever from the Pacific scene (see below); by the time this had occurred, American divisions were eating their way implacably across Saipan. It was, nevertheless, a difficult and bloody task, and it was not until 7 July that the end came when the biggest recorded Banzai attack was launched by the desperate Japanese survivors, to be repulsed in the same way as its predecessors, and at the same cost.

To the horrified Americans, what followed then was far worse than the battle itself. Convinced by Japanese propaganda that the Americans would now torture and mutilate them, thousands of Saipan civilians killed themselves and their families, some by throwing their children and themselves off the high northern cliffs on to the jagged rocks below. To the US combat soldiers – real veterans by now – this was the worst of the operation, made more awful by the fact that every move made by them to prevent it only provoked more urgent and often more painful mass suicide.

Tinian and Guam

The operations against Tinian and Guam took until 12 August to complete, the one on Tinian comparatively easy, that on Guam tough, though not so tough as that on Saipan. At the end of it, the Marianas had cost the US forces 5,367 dead and 16,843 wounded; it cost the Japanese something like 46,000, though some of that number were Korean labourers who were taken prisoner.

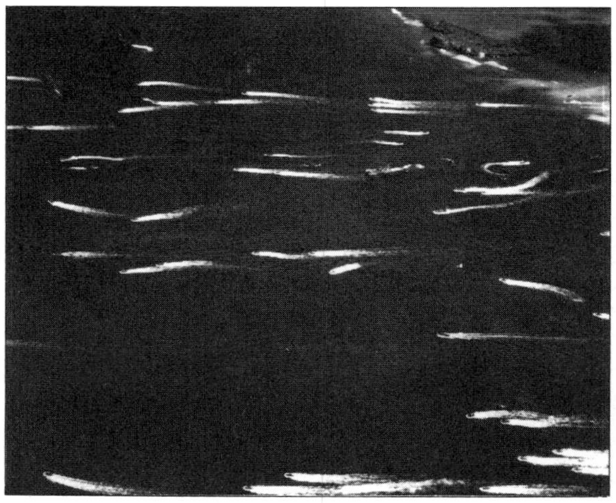

The first wave of Marines land on Saipan. The Marianas were substantial islands which would take much longer to subdue.

Landing craft head from ship to shore at Guam, the last of the major islands in the group to be landed upon.

Aircraft-carriers in the Pacific, 1944-45

Aircraft-carriers played the dominant role in the Pacific war, and the massive US Navy carrier Task Forces were to play the decisive role. Japan continued to construct carriers, many incorporating the lessons of the early days of the war, but the Empire's small industrial base was never remotely capable of matching that of the USA.

By far the largest carrier of the war, Shinano *was to have been the third 'Yamato' class battleship. Converted while building, she would have been used as a repair and resupply ship to front-line carriers. She was torpedoed and sunk by the US submarine* Archerfish *on her first sea voyage, on her way to be fitted out at Kure.*

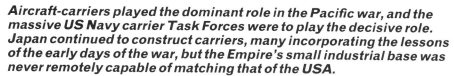

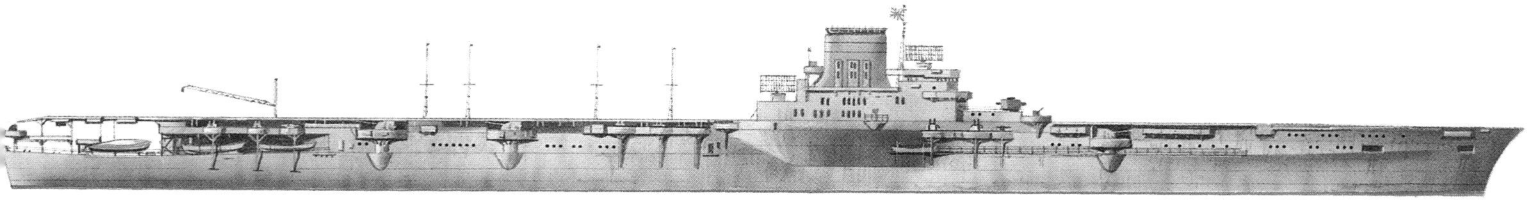

Left: Probably the most advanced of Japanese carrier designs, Taiho *had an armoured flight deck, an enclosed bow and could carry up to 85 aircraft. She was torpedoed by the US submarine* Albacore *during the Battle of the Philippine Sea, and sank five hours later by internal explosion (due to poor damage control).*

Right: In the single year from July 1943, no less than 50 'Casablanca' class escort carriers were commissioned into the United States Navy. While of limited capability, they made a significant contribution to the war in the Pacific and it was vessels of this class which stood off the Japanese at Samar during the Battle of Leyte Gulf.

Left: 'Princeton' class light carriers were converted on the stocks from cruiser hulls in the grim days after Pearl Harbor. Although cramped, the CVLs had the advantage of being able to operate with Fast Carrier Groups. Towards the end of the war, they carried night fighters for the protection of the fleet.

Right: As a result of the success of the British armoured flight deck, the Americans designed a carrier incorporating that feature with the standard side protection of US Navy carriers. The outcome was a very large carrier, commissioned days before the end of the war. That size has stood her in good stead, and the much modified USS Midway *is still in service and likely to complete half a century with the US Navy.*

Below: One of the most successful classes of warship in history, the 'Essex' class formed the backbone of the fast carrier task forces which hounded the Imperial Japanese Navy from the seas in the Pacific War. This is USS Intrepid *(CV-11) as she appeared in June 1944, on her return to combat in the Pacific. In spite of severe torpedo and kamikaze damage she survived to serve in a very different kind of war off the coast of Vietnam.*

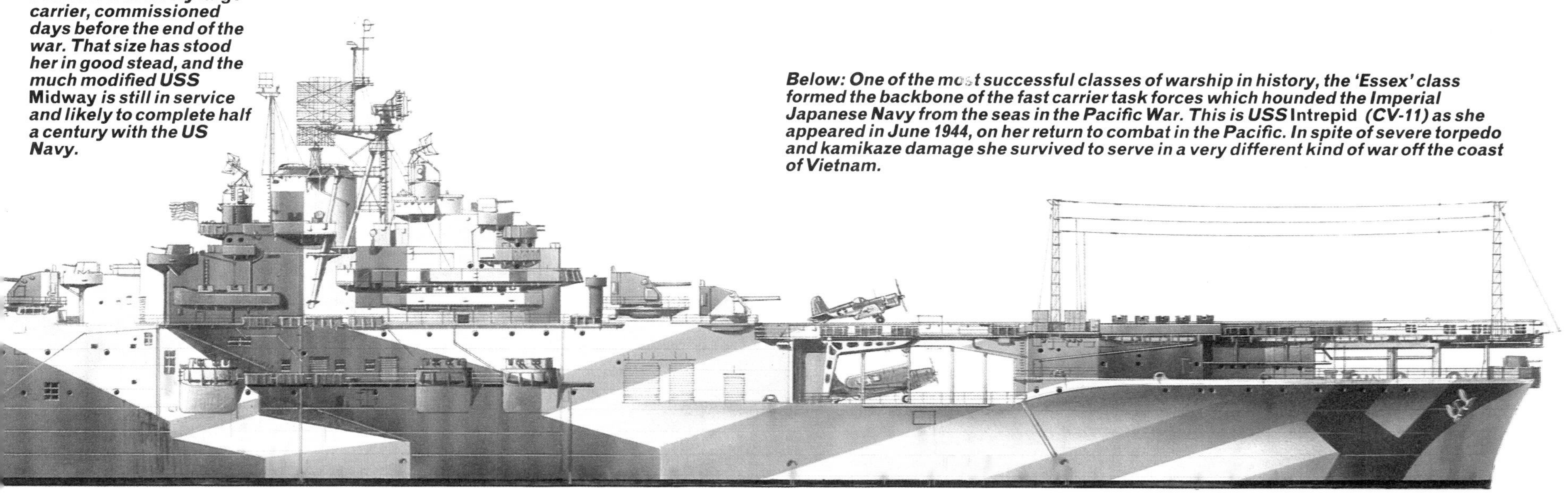

A Nakajima B5N torpedo bomber receives a direct hit from one of the 5-in guns of an American carrier, the deadly torpedo falling away harmlessly from the blazing wreckage. Very few Japanese aircraft got through the 5th Fleet's defences off Saipan.

A Japanese bomber goes down in flames while attacking the escort carrier USS Kitkun Bay off the coast of Saipan. The pre-invasion bombardment of the islands by sea and air forces left very few such aircraft to attack the amphibious force.

But the fall of the Marianas and the shattering naval defeat suffered at the hands of Mitscher's task forces revealed to the world the ever weakening situation in which Japan found herself by mid-1944.

The Battle of the Philippine Sea

The invasion of Saipan by American forces in mid-June 1944 forced the Japanese to react in strength. The reason was quite simple: from bases in the Marianas Islands American bombers would be able to bomb targets in Japan itself. To avoid this, the Imperial Japanese Navy decided to throw in its remaining carriers and trained aircrews.

Admiral Jisaburo Ozawa, commanding the newly established First Mobile Fleet, planned to put large numbers of land-based aircraft into the islands of Guam, Yap and Rota. These would attack the US carriers west of Saipan, greatly outnumbering their aircraft. As Ozawa's lightly constructed carrier aircraft had just over 200 miles more range than those of the US Navy he would be able to launch a strike outside the range of the American aircraft, attack the fast carriers, refuel and rearm on Guam, and attack a second time on the way back. In theory strikes should have been very destructive, for the American carriers would already have suffered severe damage from the land strikes.

In practice it went very wrong. Right at the beginning the commander of the land-based air forces, Vice-Admiral Kakuta, failed to inflict significant damage on the carrier aircraft. Instead the American Admiral Spruance had launched heavy attacks on the Japanese airfields, wiping out the aircraft on Guam and Rota. What remains unexplained to this day is the fact that Kakuta failed to warn Ozawa of this failure in the plan, and continued to reassure him that the Americans were suffering a heavy rate of attrition. Nor were the Americans short of intelligence about Ozawa's movements, for their submarines had spotted the carriers moving through the Philippines.

The Japanese carrier force was out in strength: the light carriers *Zuiho, Chitose, Chiyoda, Hiyo, Junyo* and *Ryuho* and the fleet carriers *Taiho, Shokaku* and *Zuikaku*, as well as 5 battleships, 12 cruisers, 27 destroyers and 24 submarines. But this force was dwarfed by Task Force 58: the light carriers *Langley, Cowpens, San Jacinto, Princeton, Monterey, Cabot, Belleau Wood* and *Bataan*, the fleet carriers *Hornet, Yorktown, Bunker Hill, Wasp, Enterprise, Lexington* and *Essex*, as well as 7 battleships, 21 cruisers, 62 destroyers and 25 submarines. Even these heavy odds were lengthened by the superb training of the American aircrews, for the Japanese pilot-training programme had totally failed to keep up with wartime attrition, and many of Ozawa's pilots were barely capable of landing on board their carriers.

Spruance divided his force into four task groups (TGs 58.1, 58.2, 58.3 and 58.4) and a Battle Line (TG 58.7) under Admiral Willis A. Lee. To attack the carriers the Japanese aircraft would first have to fly through a barrage of anti-aircraft fire from the Battle Line, and then fight off each carrier task group's combat air patrol and face the fire from their escorts. The land attacks had done nothing to weaken this defence in depth, but Ozawa had no idea of what sort of opposition his pilots would be facing.

On 18 June the main Japanese force moved into position to the west of the Marianas, and detached the van force of three light carriers under Vice-Admiral Takeo Kurita, with the intention of launching the first strikes next morning. When the van force launched its strike of 16 fighters and 53 bombers it was detected by the Battle Line on radar, giving time for the US carriers to launch every available fighter. They inflicted grievous losses on the Japanese (42 aircraft) and the only damage achieved was a bomb hit on the battleship *South Dakota*.

A second strike was launched from the six carriers of the main body: 48 fighters and 62 bombers, but 10 minutes after the launch sequence had begun the US submarine *Albacore* torpedoed the carrier *Taiho*. Once again the massed anti-aircraft fire of the Battle Line slaughtered the air strike, shooting down 79 out of the 110 aircraft, and all that was achieved was a near-miss. A third strike of 47 aircraft managed to avoid the Battle Line but found very few targets, and lost only seven planes. A fourth strike launched from 11.30 a.m. also lost its way; only 33 out of 82 aircraft found TG 58.2, and suffered heavy losses.

The Japanese carriers had made the strongest possible effort and had failed to inflict more than trifling damage on TF 58. At 12.22 p.m. Ozawa suffered a further setback when the submarine USS *Cavalla* put four torpedoes into the *Shokaku*. She blew up and sank at 3.10 p.m., followed shortly afterwards by the *Taiho*. But Ozawa had no intention of

After making mincemeat of the Japanese carrierborne aircraft sent to attack it, Task Force 58 struck back at the Japanese fleet, making contact late in the day and at the limits of aircraft range. Many planes did not make it back to their carriers that night, but a good proportion of the crews were picked up by SAR flying boats the next day.

Chronology of War: 1944

January 20
Russians liberate Novgorod. US troops reach Rapido

January 22
Anzio Landings – an Allied attempt to outflank the Gustav Line

January 24
US Fifth Army occupies Anzio and Nettuno

January 27
Leningrad relieved after a siege of 872 days. 1,500,000 Soviet lives lost, 80 per cent of which were civilian. Large German forces trapped near Kanyew. US Naval Task Force moves into Marshall Islands area

January 30
US Fifth Army unsuccessfully breaks into Gustav Line

January 31
US troops land on Kwajalein and other Marshall atolls. Russians reach Kingisepp. UK civilian casualties in January 107 killed, 260 injured

February 4
Japanese offensive in Arakan (Burma). Coast of Gulf of Finland now totally in Russian hands

February 5
US troops mop up on Kwajalein. 16,300 Japanese dead in Marshalls campaign – only 264 prisoners

February 6
British forced back in Arakan

February 7
Field Marshal Albert Kesselring launches German counterattack at Anzio. 'Admin Box' in Arakan cut off

February 8
Operation Overlord plan (the invasion of north west Europe) agreed in Whitehall

February 11
Airborne supplies dropped to 'Admin Box' in Burma

February 13
Russians clear shores of Lake Peipus

February 15
Massive air and artillery bombardment destroys Abbey at Cassino but fails to dislodge German defenders

February 16
Heavy German counterattack at Anzio. US Task Force opens assault on Truk

February 18
Truk airfield and harbour wrecked by US naval attack; 400,000 tons of shipping destroyed, and over 270 aircraft. Luftwaffe begins 'Little Blitz' on London. US troops land on Eniwetok atoll

February 21
Tojo appointed Chief of Japanese Army Staff

February 22
US Task Force attacking Marianas shoot down many Japanese aircraft. Red Army 3rd Ukrainian Front under Malinovsky captures Krivoi Rog

February 23
US Task Force 58 launches assault on targets in Marianas

February 25
British break through Ngakyedyauk Pass in Burma and relieve 'Admin Box'

February 29
US troops land in Admiralty Islands

February 29
UK civilian casualties in February 961 killed, 1,712 injured

US infantry weapons

US infantry weapons were by no means the most advanced to be built before 1945, but the sheer numbers manufactured made them of vital importance both during the war and afterwards, when they came into the hands of armies and guerrilla movements worldwide.

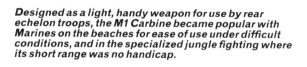

*The **Colt .45 Automatic** was designed as a result of **US** experience in the **Philippines** in the first years of this century, and became a standard pistol before **World War I**. It remained in service for the next 70 years, and was the standard **US Forces** sidearm through **World War II**.*

*Designed as a light, handy weapon for use by rear echelon troops, the **M1 Carbine** became popular with **Marines** on the beaches for ease of use under difficult conditions, and in the specialized jungle fighting where its short range was no handicap.*

*Right: The .30 **Caliber, M1 Rifle** (known as the **Garand**) was the first self-loading rifle to be accepted as a standard military weapon. Strong and sturdy, the gas-operated **Garand** was slightly heavier than the bolt-action **M1903** it replaced.*

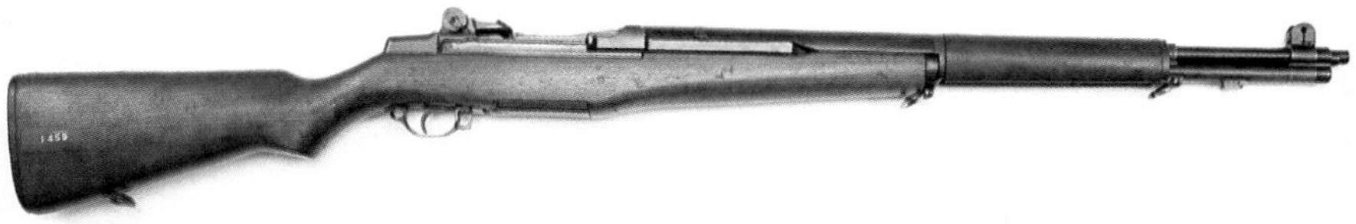

*Left: The **M3 'Grease Gun'** was an equivalent to the **British Sten** and the **German MP 40**, being designed for mass production. It was a sound enough weapon, but the troops never really took to it although it found a measure of acceptance in the **Pacific** where there was no alternative sub-machine gun.*

*Right: The **M1A1** was the last production version of the famous **Thompson** sub-machine gun, much simpler than the original design but still made almost solely from machined components. As such it was still far more expensive to make than the **M3**, and was considerably heavier.*

*Left: The last production variant of the **Browning Automatic Rifle** (usually known by its initials as the **BAR**) remained in use into the 1950s as a light machine-gun/automatic assault rifle, but by then it was an anachronism, having only a 20-round magazine and no quick-change barrel facility.*

giving up, for he still believed that Kakuta's land-based forces had inflicted heavy casualties, and he therefore felt that his 102 remaining aircraft could turn the tables on Spruance. In addition Kakuta had told him that many of the survivors of the carrier strikes had landed safely on Guam.

The US Navy hits back

Next day the two opposing fleets were moving to the north west on roughly parallel courses. When Spruance learned of Ozawa's position it was late in the afternoon, and he was faced with a difficult choice. A strike against the Japanese carriers would be at maximum distance, and the return flight to the carriers would have to be made in darkness. Nevertheless at 4.20 p.m. he ordered an all-out strike by 85 fighters, 77 dive-bombers and 54 torpedo-bombers

The Japanese could only launch 80 aircraft before TF 58's tempest overwhelmed them. The light carrier *Hiyo* was sunk by two torpedoes; the *Zuikaku, Junyo* and *Chiyoda* were badly damaged, and other ships were damaged. Ozawa managed to extricate the remnants of his forces without further loss, but he had lost what he knew to be the last chance of a decisive victory. His inexperienced pilots had been shot down in such numbers that the American pilots had called the air battle on 19 June the 'Great Marianas Turkey Shoot'. Even when stretched to the limit, the US Navy's pilots were more skilled; after the strike on 20 June the aircraft returned to their carriers at 10.45 p.m., many of them virtually out of fuel. In a classic signal Vice-Admiral Mitscher ordered the carriers to turn on their landing lights, to make sure that the pilots could find a friendly deck in the darkness. Losses were heavy, but 116 aircraft landed safely. The remaining 80 crash-landed or 'ditched' nearby, allowing destroyers to pick up the majority of the aircrew.

Left: Vice-Admiral Marc Mitscher, one of the first US Navy flyers and captain of the* Hornet *during the Doolittle raid, was unfairly criticized for allowing the Japanese fleet to escape.

An M1 flamethrower is shown in action on Guam. This was often the only way to neutralize a bunker manned by fanatical defenders. To the horror of the American troops even Japanese civilians on the islands preferred death to the dishonour of captivity.

In retrospect it is difficult to criticize Ozawa's handling of the battle. The major tactical error, attacking the Battle Line, was the result of the naval pilots' lack of experience. The extraordinary lies told by Kakuta led Ozawa to believe that his four strikes would have much more effect than they did, and he was even misled into believing that his aircraft were safe in Guam, whereas in fact they had been destroyed. Given these circumstances, and the fact that he was vastly outnumbered, it would have been difficult to do better.

Even if Ozawa had been blessed with better luck and a more capable subordinate he would have needed a miracle to give him victory against TF 58. The best that could have happened would have been a few US carriers badly damaged or even sunk. That would have resulted in a short respite, but the Japanese were now being overwhelmed by sheer numbers. Not only were trained pilots in short supply; even the raw materials and oil for which Japan had gone to war were difficult to transport to Japan, because of the lack of shipping. It was now impossible for Japanese shipyards to maintain shipping at pre-war levels. The fleet could not get sufficient refined oil, and was forced to use volatile oil from Borneo – a major cause of the explosions which destroyed the *Taiho* and *Shokaku*.

Aftermath

On the American side there were bitter recriminations against Spruance, particularly by Admiral William Halsey and his supporters. They felt that the caution of Spruance had lost TF 58 the opportunity to sink all Ozawa's carriers, and thus eliminate the Imperial Japanese Navy. What the critics could not accept was that Spruance's dispositions at all times took account of the overriding need to prevent Ozawa from evading his task groups and getting at the vulnerable amphibious forces off Saipan. No mercy would have been shown to Spruance if his carriers had lost Ozawa, and massive losses thus inflicted on the invasion force. The critics tend to overlook the fact that only three months later at Leyte Halsey swallowed the bait offered by Ozawa. Although the Japanese carriers were severely punished the main force under Admiral Kurita got through to the invasion areas, and only the desperate bravery of the defending light carriers and escorts saved the Americans from disaster. Historians have been kinder to Spruance than his fellow admiral in 1944.

Towards the Philippines

All the time that Admiral Nimitz's vast fleet were driving through the Central Pacific, General MacArthur's forces of the South-west Pacific Area, aided by Admiral Halsey's fleets of the South Pacific, had also been fighting their way towards the Philippines, and during the month following the vast and successful operation against the Marianas, MacArthur's US Army XI Corps took up positions on Morotai Island to the north of Halmahera, well on the way to Mindanao. But it had been a difficult road there, and the 20 months since the liberation of Buna by the Australians, and Guadalcanal by the Americans, had been long and bloody.

By mid-February 1943, with Guadalcanal free of Japanese the next phase of Operation Elkton was a planned drive up through the rest of the Solomons to Bougainville, from whose airfields it was considered

Marine infantry move fast to take up new positions in Garapan, principal town of Saipan. Street fighting was something new to the Marines of the Pacific theatre, used as they were to fighting for small atolls.

On Saipan, 1 July 1944, a reconnaissance patrol sets out into the jungle. By this time, the Japanese were penned up in the northern peninsula of the island, ready to launch a last suicidal counterattack. It failed.

Carrier aircraft, 1944-1945

The carrier aircraft bore the brunt of the fighting in the Pacific theatre, carrying first the Japanese and then the Americans across the war zone. By the latter months, the US aircraft were well on top, led by the redoubtable Hellcat.

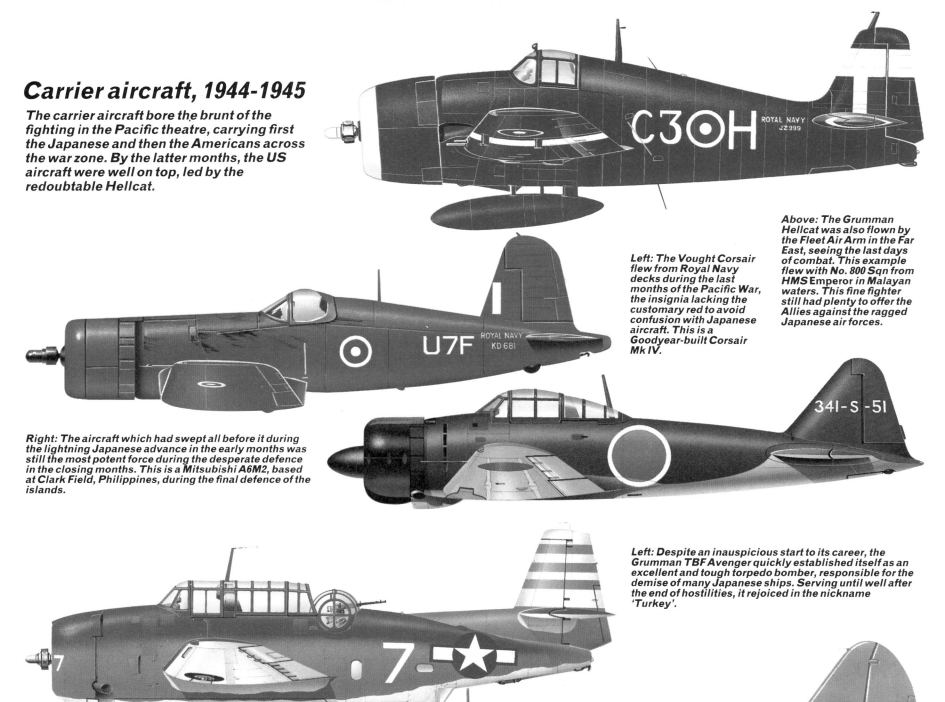

***Above:* The Grumman Hellcat was also flown by the Fleet Air Arm in the Far East, seeing the last days of combat. This example flew with No. 800 Sqn from HMS Emperor in Malayan waters. This fine fighter still had plenty to offer the Allies against the ragged Japanese air forces.**

***Left:* The Vought Corsair flew from Royal Navy decks during the last months of the Pacific War, the insignia lacking the customary red to avoid confusion with Japanese aircraft. This is a Goodyear-built Corsair Mk IV.**

***Right:* The aircraft which had swept all before it during the lightning Japanese advance in the early months was still the most potent force during the desperate defence in the closing months. This is a Mitsubishi A6M2, based at Clark Field, Philippines, during the final defence of the islands.**

***Left:* Despite an inauspicious start to its career, the Grumman TBF Avenger quickly established itself as an excellent and tough torpedo bomber, responsible for the demise of many Japanese ships. Serving until well after the end of hostilities, it rejoiced in the nickname 'Turkey'.**

***Right:* Although never fully replacing the much-loved Dauntless, the Curtiss SB2C Helldiver was introduced on to the larger carriers from November 1943. A tricky aircraft to fly and maintain, the 'Beast' never received much more than insults, but went on to compile a useful war record.**

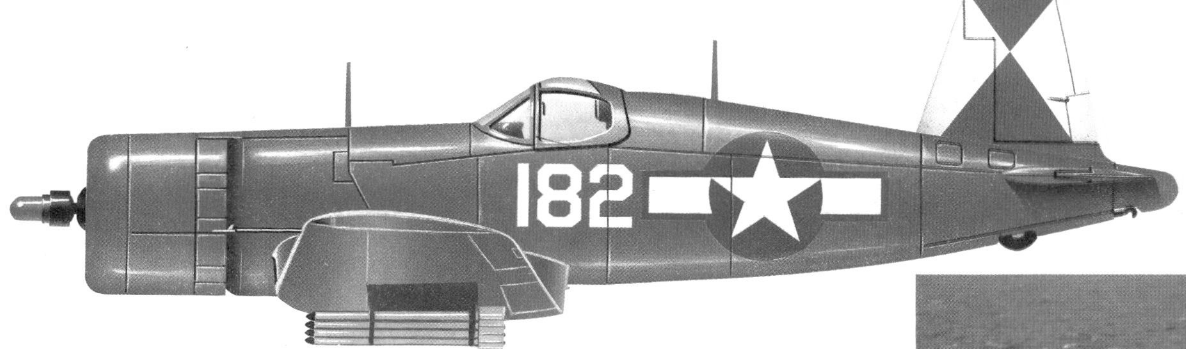

***Left:* The excellent Vought F4U Corsair took some time to see carrier service due to visibility and landing gear problems. However, once aboard the ships, it went from strength to strength, proving itself outstanding in both fighter and ground attack roles.**

***Below:* During the last few months of the war, Allied aircraft adopted a midnight blue colour scheme, complete with unit marks on the fin. The Curtiss SB2C (unkindly nicknamed 'Son of a Bitch, 2nd Class') flew continuously throughout the final assaults on Japan.**

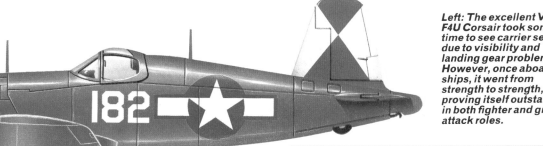

By 1944 the Mitsubishi A6M Zero-sen had been largely mastered by the Allied fighters, but its splendid manoeuvrability was still a factor when flown by an experienced pilot. The type fought bravely throughout the last months of the war and many were used in kamikaze raids.

Desron (DEStroyer squadRON) 5 pass Savo Island, as if in review over the graves of so many of their fellows in Ironbottom Sound. They are returning from a successful raid on the Japanese stronghold of Rabaul.

Marines land an M3 half-track gun motor carriage, armed with a 75-mm field gun and bristling with machine-guns, at Cape Gloucester on New Britain. This operation cut off Rabaul until the end of the war.

that the vital Japanese base at Rabaul in New Britain could be eliminated, or at least neutralized. From the five airfields there and the spacious Simpson Harbor, the Japanese Celestial Eagles strike aircraft and cruiser/destroyer squadrons were at that time a dangerous threat, not only to the Australian forces intended to drive along the northern coast of New Guinea, but also to any Allied ships using the Solomon, Coral and Bismarck Seas. They could also endanger the new Allied bases on Guadalcanal, and bomb Northern Australia.

The Allies need to drive both alaong the New Guinea coast and parallel through the Solomons was, of course, as obvious to Admiral Isoroku Yamamoto as it was to MacArthur and Halsey – and when on 21 February army and marine battalions landed on the Russell Islands as the first step 'up the ladder', he decided the time had come to act. He ordered General Imamura, commanding Japanese troops at Rabaul, to send at least one division down through the Dampier Straits to reinforce the division at Lae and Salamaua, escorted by ships from the South-east Area Fleet.

On 1 March, a convoy of eight transports carrying 7,000 troops of the 51st Division and escorted by eight destroyers, left Simpson Harbor and sailed down the north coast of New Britain – and was sighted by a B-25 of MacArthur's 5th Air Force. The following day the convoy was attacked by a squadron of B-17 Flying Fortresses which sank the large transport carrying the divisional headquarters staff, and the following day – by which time the convoy was near the Dampier Straits – the 5th Air Force struck again. Four destroyers and all of the transports were sunk, and only some thousand of the men of 51st Division ever arrived at Lae.

The following month, an even worse disaster befell the Japanese. Two Japanese Betty transport aircraft escorted by six Zeroes were attacked by 18 Lightnings and the transports shot down; aboard them were Admiral Yamamoto and his staff, and the Imperial Japanese Navy had lost its most imaginative and irreplaceable officer.

But even with the removal of their most formidable antagonist and the decimation of the Rabaul garrison and fleet, it was still to take a very long time for the Americans and the Australians to fight their way westwards. It was May before the Australians were closing in on Lae down the Markham Valley, and August before the Japanese bridgehead around Salamaua was yielding to any pressure – for in addition to Japanese courage and stubbornness, the appalling nature of the whole countryside with its thick jungles and swamps, its near vertical ravines and cliffs, made any progress overland slow and arduous.

Moreover, by mid-1943, the evident successes of Central Pacific Force gave them a degree of priority of naval shipping, and Halsey was thus always short; it was June before the first major step 'up the Solomons ladder' was mounted against New Georgia, and July before the main attack towards Munda airfield at the western end was launched. Then followed a regrouping and planning session for the next stage on towards Choiseul, Treasury Island and Bougainville itself, and it was November before the first landings on the final objective of Elkton were made, and another week before the Japanese counter-attacks were beaten off and the Battle of Augusta Bay confirmed American possession.

In the meantime, the Huon Peninsula on New Guinea had been the scene of an ambitious and well-executed three-pronged attack. On 5 September an amphibious force landed the bulk of the 9th Australian Division just east of Lae; the next day the 503rd US Parachute Regiment was dropped to the north west (the first use of airborne troops by the Allies in the Pacific) to capture an airfield there, and as soon as it was safely in their hands the 7th Australian Division was flown in. Yet it was still October before Finschafen on the point of the peninsula was taken, and almost the end of December before all Japanese opposition in the area ended.

But by that time naval and air supremacy had been achieved by MacArthur's air force and Halsey's fleets, and on Christmas Day 1943 a huge fleet sailed up the Vitiaz Strait to land the US 1st Marine Division at Cape Gloucester on the western tip of New Britain. A smaller force had landed on the south-west coast near Arawe and then on 2 January 1944 another large American force was landed at Saidot on the northern New Guinea coast, 100 miles west of the Australians at Huon. Thus control of the eastern half of New Guinea, the entire length of the Solomons,

As soon as an island had been captured, the USAAF moved its fighters in to protect the newly-gained territory from counter-attack. Here an airfield engineer plays traffic cop as two Thunderbolts live up to their name from a Marianas airfield.

As with all large scale Japanese operations, that known as 'A-Go', which resulted in the Battle of the Philippine Sea in June 1944, was meticulously planned. It was hoped to lure substantial US naval forces into waters north of the Admiralties, across a well-prepared submarine trap. Japanese tactical doctrine saw the primary roles of the submarine as a scout attacking warships, and 25 were deployed for the purpose, many in the waters mentioned and over a month beforehand.

In mid-May the three 'Buckley' class DEs USS *England*, *George* and *Raby* were on a mission to harass the enemy supply line to Bougainville when, in the early afternoon of 19 May, the first-named gained sonar contact on a submerged submarine. Only a few of the Pacific escorts were armed with Hedgehog; the recently commissioned *England* was, and attacked without hesitation. The second salvo produced the sound of two direct hits but, lacking immediate evidence of a 'kill', she followed up with three more salvoes, the last of which produced three small explosions, followed by a massive detonation which lifted the after end of the ship bodily in the water. It marked the end of the *I-16*, a submarine larger than the DE.

The little group was proceeding north-westward outside the Bismarcks when, at 3.50 a.m. on 22 May, it caught the *RO-106* charging batteries on the surface. The *George* caught her in her searchlight as she dived, and offloaded a pattern of depth charges over the spot. Again there was no instant result and the *England* waded in with a Hedgehog salvo. A first-time bulls-eye left

The most important feature of the capture of the Marianas was the ability of American bombers to strike at the Japanese mainland. This Consolidated B-24 Liberator exercises this newly-found advantage.

Hedgehog bombs are loaded on to an American escort in the Pacific. A British invention, the most astonishing use of the Hedgehog came from the **USS England*****, which sank six submarines in 12 days.***

and all the seas around were now in MacArthur and Halsey's hands – and Rabaul was isolated. The decision was then taken to leave the Japanese forces there to 'wither on the vine'.

Early in the New Year there was some argument between the 'Central' and 'Southern' schools of thought, but MacArthur was not to be outdone; in February he sent formations from US 1st and 7th Cavalry Divisions to take the Admiralty Islands, and by April had formed a sound naval base at Manus while at the same time 'coast-hopping' further west along the New Guinea coast to Hollandia, Sarmi and Wakde, then taking Biak Island in early August.

Thus by September 1944 both the Central Forces of Admiral King and the Southern Forces under General MacArthur were poised for the last phase before the assault on the Japanese homelands.

But where was it to be? For if MacArthur's eyes were still firmly fixed on the Philippines, King had looked past the Marianas and seen Formosa – that much nearer the final objective.

USS England *in the Philippine Sea*

only oil and wreckage rising to mark the spot.

This submarine had been the northernmost of a line and her neighbour, the *RO-104*, was detected before breakfast on the next morning. Both the *George*, the senior ship, and *Raby* attacked without success. It remained again for the *England* to zero in. Again there was ample evidence for a claim.

As there was now adequate evidence of a submarine line the group moved further south-westward and, sure enough, the *George* secured a radar contact on a rapidly submerging target in the early hours of 24 May. Sonar conditions were good, so the *England* carefully gauged bearing and depth before firing a deliberate salvo of her few remaining bombs. Though the target was running deep there came a muffled explosion. This fourth victim was the *RO-116*.

Returning to Manus on 26 May to refuel and rearm, the group found yet another submarine. A sonar contact was gained by the *Raby*, lost, regained by the *England* and presented with the usual precision Hedgehog pattern. Again a hole-in-one, it disintegrated the *RO-108* in a series of rumbling explosions clearly audible from the surface.

Rapidly topped up, the ships immediately sailed again to join an ASW group based on a CVE. One of the latter's destroyers flushed a submarine but could not leave to attack it. The DEs stayed in contact all night and, after a series of unsuccessful attacks by the other ships, the *England* was finally allowed a go. The almost inevitable result was the *RO-105* sunk with a single salvo at 7.35 a.m. on 31 May. The *England* had set a record which still stands: six enemy submarines sunk in 12 days. Of the 25 Japanese submarines deployed, 17 were sunk. Their tactics were poor, they were badly placed, they achieved nothing, and they were wasted.

Chapter 19

War over the Reich

The Allied bombing of Germany was the most protracted campaign of the war. As it gained momentum it inflicted untold damage on the German war machine, while diverting valuable air assets away from other fronts. Indeed, the major success of the bombers can be measured in the fighters, artillery and manpower which had to be kept from the fighting fronts for the defence of the homeland.

Air Chief Marshal Sir Arthur 'Bomber' Harris took control of Bomber Command on 22 February 1942 and brought a new dynamism to the service. Within the year, the four-engined heavies were the mainstay of the RAF.

Events in northern Europe during the first year of the war compounded the problems faced by RAF Bomber Command, lacking any continental bases after the fall of France. The pioneer trio of bombers, the Wellington, Whitley and Hampden, performed bravely against targets in Germany itself but lacked the range and bomb loads necessary to sustain a truly destructive offensive, added to which training and equipment was shown to be quite inadequate to achieve the required navigation and bombing accuracy.

In the last three years of peace three new heavy bombers had been ordered, the four-engine Stirling reaching the first squadron (No. 7) in August 1940, followed before the end of that year by the Manchester and Halifax. But these big aircraft were slow to gain production tempo and in 1941 only two further Stirling squadrons were re-equipped, while Manchester and Halifax squadrons also increased to three of each type. In addition, one squadron (No. 90) had received American B-17 Fortress daylight bombers, but these proved unsuitable and were dispersed to the Middle East. Compared with this strength of 9 'new' bomber squadrons, there still remained with the heavy bomber force some 20 Wellington squadrons, 5 of Whitleys and 7 of Hampdens at the end of 1941.

If the introduction of new aircraft into Bomber Command was painfully slow at least its weapons were increasing in destructive power. The 2,000-lb semi-armour-piercing bomb had come into use during the summer of 1940, and 4,000-pounders were first dropped by Wellingtons on the night of 31 March/1 April 1941 on Emden. February and March that year also saw the first operational sorties by Stirlings, Halifaxes and Manchesters. In June the first British 'radio' navigation aid was established with the completion of the first Gee chain of stations at Daventry, Stenigot and Ventnor, but it was not to become fully operational until the following March.

Dependence upon the older bombers in 1941 meant that Bomber Command was still obliged to concentrate its efforts on 'fringe' targets, the German and German-occupied ports of Emden, Kiel, Hamburg, Bremen, Le Havre and Brest (the latter sheltering the German warships *Scharnhorst, Gneisenau* and *Prinz Eugen*) attracting the heaviest tonnage of bombs.

Meanwhile one of the RAF bombers, the Manchester, had proved to be a failure owing to fundamental problems with the new Rolls-Royce Vulture engine – a situation that was to have a profound influence on the British bombing campaign. Difficulties with the Vulture had surfaced almost as soon as the Manchester entered service in 1940 with the result that an example of this aircraft was re-engined with four Merlins and first flown on 9 January 1941. Plans to put this version into production went ahead at top speed and the first Lancaster I was flown on 31 October the same year. First deliveries were being made to No. 44 Squadron at Waddington in December.

Use of the well-tried Merlin engine and the 30 per cent power increase transformed the Manchester into a superb bomber, and introduction of the Lancaster to Bomber Command was well underway when on 22 February 1942 Air Marshal Arthur Harris was appointed Air Officer Commanding-in-Chief, taking over from the Acting AOC-in-C, Air Vice-Marshal J.E.A. Baldwin. By then the German warships had made their escape from Brest and decisions were now quickly taken to switch the British bomber force against more distant targets, against specific industrial key points and in greater concentration. The first such raid was flown against the Renault factory near Paris on 3/4 March when an average of two aircraft bombed the target every minute for two hours. Later that month the Lancaster took part in its first raid, attacking Essen on the 10th/11th. Exactly one month later a Halifax of No. 76 Squadron dropped the RAF's first 8,000-lb bomb, also on Essen.

It was at this time that Bomber Command launched two attacks of a widely differing nature that were to represent landmarks in the bombing offensive. On 17 April, led by Squadron Leader J.D. Nettleton, 20 Lancasters of Nos 44 and 97 Squadrons attacked the MAN factory at Augsburg in daylight at low level. Enemy flak and fighter opposition was fierce and seven aircraft were lost, while damage to the target was relatively insignificant. Nettleton was awarded the Victoria Cross for his leadership, but it was immediately realized that such attacks were of little value and that the high losses suffered would seriously delay the build-up of Lancaster strength in Bomber Command. Indeed, despite the Lancaster's heavy defensive armament of eight machine-guns, it was evident that little had changed since the disastrous daylight Wellington raids of 1939.

Infinitely different in scope was the Bomber Command raid on the night of 30/31 May when 1,046 aircraft were sent to attack Cologne – Operation Millennium, the first 'thousand-bomber' raid. Launched by Harris as much for propaganda purposes as to demonstrate his theory that 'area bombing' was more devastating to enemy industry than attempts to obliterate specific targets, the Cologne raid cost the raiding force (which included bombers from other Commands) a total of 40 aircraft – just 3.8 per cent of the number sent out. As the last bombers were returning from Germany a new aircraft was making its first operational sortie as Mosquitos of No. 104 Squadron carried out an armed reconnaissance over the burning city. Dependent on its high speed to evade enemy fighters, the Mosquito light bomber henceforth spearheaded the bombing attacks on Europe both by day and night, eventually being capable of carrying a 4,000-lb bomb all the way to Berlin.

Two further 'thousand-bomber' raids were mounted in June 1942 (against Essen and Bremen), from which a total of 75 aircraft failed to return, and the second of the attacks was the last occasion on which the Manchester was flown operationally. Owing however to the inclusion of aircraft and crews from Operational Training Units, and the disruption caused to the training of new crews for Bomber Command, these very large raids were discontinued and it was to be almost three years before anything like comparable numbers of heavy bombers would be despatched against Germany on single nights.

While the build-up of Lancaster squadrons continued (by August 1942 there were nine), Harris turned his attention to the problem of improving the bombing accuracy, adopting the practice pioneered so efficiently by the Luftwaffe with the employment of a pathfinder force. On 15 August Bomber Command's Pathfinder Force (later to become No. 8 Group) came into being under the leadership of Group Captain D.C.T. Bennett, a former airline pilot, this being first flown operationally four nights later against Flensburg. As the development of target-marking bombs went ahead for use by the Pathfinders a new navigation and bombing aid, Oboe, came into operational use, this being used to enable high-flying Mosquitos to strike pinpoint targets in north-west Germany (as its range was effectively limited by the radar horizon as 'seen' by the transmitting stations in Britain); the first such attack using Oboe was carried out by Mosquitos of No. 109 Squadron against the Lutterade power station on 20/21 December 1942.

By the beginning of 1943 only the Wellington of all the old 'twins' survived in operational use by Bomber Command. Moreover raids on Berlin were by no means uncommon, the first daylight raid by Mos-

The Short Stirling was nightly on the offensive during 1941-42. This bomb trolley load is for this one aircraft, to be winched up into the cavernous wing root and fuselage bomb bays. The aircraft is from 1651(H) Conversion Unit.

Left: Bombs fall away from an RAF aircraft, the photograph entirely lit by the tracer shells from flak guns. The RAF had to fly nightly through intense defences and attrition was high.

Right: During mid-1942, the USAAF's 8th Air Force arrived in England and embarked on a massive daylight campaign which lasted until war's end. Most famous of the aircraft used was the Boeing B-17, but these were ably assisted by the Consolidated B-24 Liberator, seen here bombing over France.

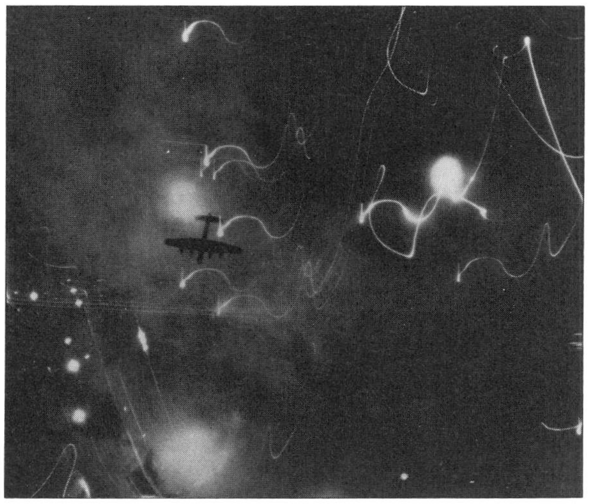

Left: Flak, flares and fires trace abstract patterns in this photograph of a Lancaster over Hamburg. This four-engined bomber greatly increased the effectiveness of Bomber Command's night operations, their huge bombload being only bettered during the conflict by that of the Boeing B-29.

quitos on the German capital being carried out on 30 January. Already 8,000-lb bombs had been dropped on Italian targets by UK-based Lancasters. In March Harris mounted the first of his set-piece 'battles' with an all-out attack on the industrial Ruhr. By then No. 8 (Pathfinder) Group comprised five squadrons, including two of Lancasters and one each of Mosquitos, Stirlings and Halifaxes. The Stirlings and Halifaxes (of Nos 7 and 35 Squadrons respectively) were now equipped with a new bombing radar, H_2S, an airborne radar on whose screen was displayed a rudimentary picture 'map' of the ground being overflown. As yet this was inadequate to provide sufficient accuracy for blind bombing but, giving a track over prominent coastlines or rivers, was excellent for navigational purposes.

The Ruhr

The Battle of the Ruhr opened with an attack on Essen by 442 aircraft on 5/6 March led by Oboe-equipped aircraft. Similar heavy raids continued for about six weeks with attacks on most of the other industrial towns and cities previously scarcely damaged owing to Bomber Command's difficulty in identifying the targets through the thick industrial haze. To fight this battle Harris had at his disposal a force of 357 medium bombers (of which 265 were Wellingtons) and 669 heavy bombers (308 Lancasters, 220 Halifaxes and 141 Stirlings).

It was during the course of the Battle of the Ruhr that Bomber Command carried out one of its most famous attacks of the war when, on the night of 16/17 May, 19 Lancasters of No. 617 Squadron, led by Wing Commander Guy Gibson (who dropped Bomber Command's first 2,000-lb bomb in 1940 and the first 8,000-lb bomb over Italy in November 1942), attacked and breached the Möhne and Eder dams whose hydro-electric stations supplied power to the Ruhr. With crews specially trained for the attack (Operation Chastise) No. 617 Squadron's Lancasters were modified to carry large cylindrical mines which were bounced along the surface of the huge reservoirs to explode against the dams. Eight Lancasters were lost in the attack but Gibson survived to be awarded the Victoria Cross; he was, however, to be killed in action over Germany a year later.

Harris' next great attack was to become known as the Battle of Hamburg when, between 24/25 July and 3/4 August, Bomber Command raided the German port four times in great strength (Operation Gomorrah). Once more a new device was introduced for the occasion by the attacking bombers; this comprised huge quantities of metal foil strips, cut to match the wavelength of enemy radar and dropped in their millions to confuse the German fighter and ground defences. This countermeasure ('Window') proved so successful that the Luftwaffe found itself powerless to locate and attack the raiders, and tremendous damage was wrought in Hamburg – as American heavy bombers joined in during the daylight hours.

There now followed a period of heavy attacks against widely dispersed targets, during which Bomber Command introduced a host of new techniques, equipment and weapons. In a raid by 595 heavy bombers on the German research station at Peenemünde on the Baltic coast on 17/18 August a master bomber was employed for the first time during a heavy raid; this technique involved a bombing leader who remained in the target area to broadcast instructions to the main force pilots, advising them of any inaccuracies in the position of the target markers. The latter on this occasion were 'red spot flares', 250-lb canisters which ignited before reaching the ground and burned with a vivid crimson fire for about ten minutes. On 15/16 September No. 617 Squadron, again re-equipped with special Lancasters, dropped the RAF's first 12,000-lb high-capacity bombs. The raid, mounted by eight aircraft at low level against the Dortmund-Ems canal, proved unsuccessful; only two bombs were dropped in the target area and five Lancasters, all with highly experienced crews were lost.

A new blind-bombing radar, G-H, was introduced into service during October, enabling Mosquitos and heavy bombers alike to strike targets shrouded by cloud, and this device remained in constant use long after the end of the war. It was first successfully used by Mosquitos of No. 139 Squadron in an attack on Aachen on 7/8 October. Also used for the first time in October was a device known as Airborne Cigar (ABC), which jammed enemy radio communications between the ground controllers and the Luftwaffe night fighter pilots: high-powered jamming was also introduced using transmitters in the UK, as well as noise transmitters using microphones placed in the bombers' engine nacelles; 'controllers' in Britain started broadcasting spurious instructions to German night fighter pilots under the codename 'Corona'.

Last of the early twin-engined RAF bombers to survive in the front line was the Vickers Wellington, which had possessed greater bombload and flexibility than the Whitley or Hampden. These were largely confined to operations close to home.

With this extensive array of equipment and tactics Harris now embarked on his third great battle, the Battle of Berlin. This distant target always posed the greatest hazards for the attacking crews, for much of the flight was visible to enemy flak, fighters and radar, while any inaccurate weather forecasting could face the bomber crews with headwinds that might force aircraft to ditch in the North Sea with inadequate fuel to reach their home bases. The new battle was fought in the depths of winter, starting on 19/20 November 1943 and lasting until 24/25 March 1944. To enable bombers to land safely in the event that fog covered their bases, the RAF introduced emergency bases equipped with FIDO (Fog Intensive, Dispersal Operation), the installation of fuel burning along the edges of runways to disperse the fog.

Although numerous attacks were mounted on other targets during the Battle of Berlin, the German capital was heavily attacked 16 times by an average of 568 four-engine bombers. These 16 raids cost Bomber Command a total of 587 aircraft destroyed and 3,640 aircrews killed or missing. This heavy loss was just sustainable although, when added to casualties suffered elsewhere, it placed a considerable strain on the bomber training units. But when it became clear from reconnaissance that neither Bomber Command nor the USAAF (whose daylight raids on the capital started on 4 March 1944) were achieving any worthwhile concentration of damage, Harris was forced to terminate his assault on Berlin.

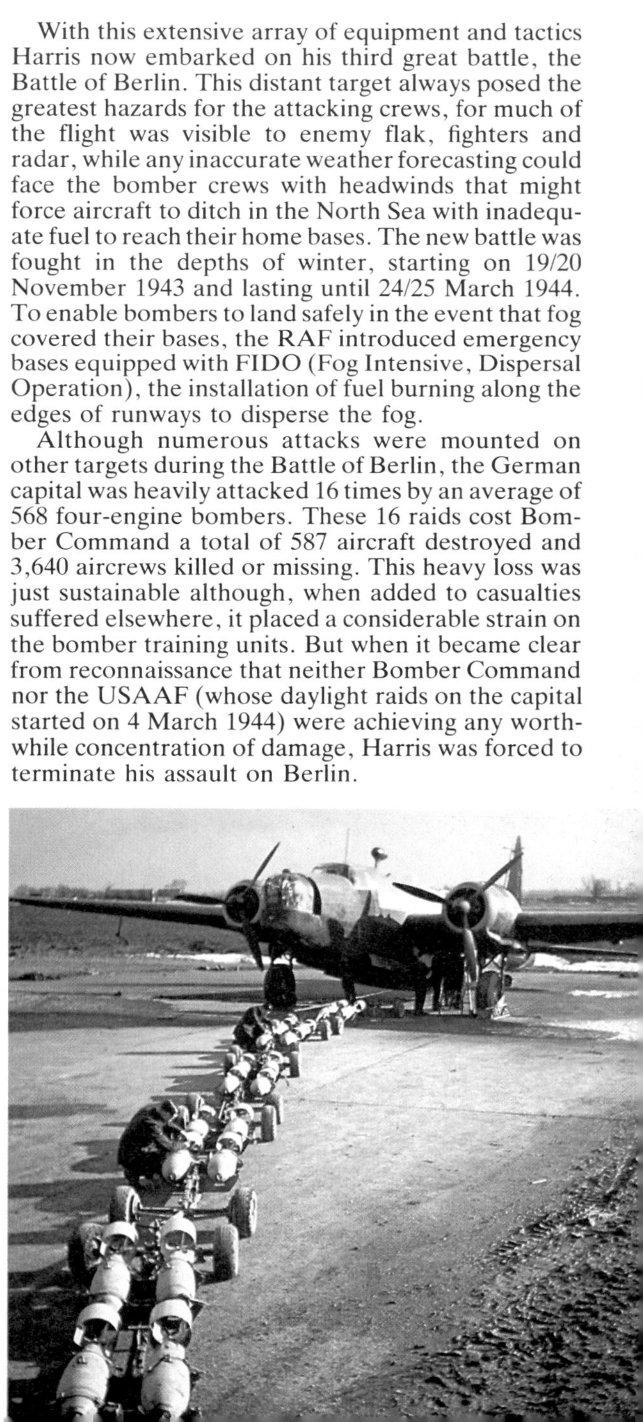

Operation Gomorrah

The RAF raids on Hamburg in July/August 1943 produced a horrific firestorm that laid waste much of the city. Amazingly, Hamburg recovered quickly from the blow, producing war matériel again in a matter of weeks.

In the most devastating series of raids up to that time launched by bombers, Air Chief Marshal Sir Arthur Harris, Commander-in-Chief of RAF Bomber Command, set out on the night of 24/25 July 1943 to give a demonstration of just what could be achieved by the systematic application of what were, by the standards of the time, sophisticated weapons, equipment and tactics.

The strategic choice of Hamburg as the target was made on account of its concentration of war industries, not least of which was the huge Blohm und Voss shipyard which contributed 45 per cent of Germany's total U-boat construction programme.

The bombers carried a new weapon in the war of the ether: millions of tinfoil strips in bundles cut to half the wavelength of enemy radar and codenamed 'Window'; one moment the Germans had been following the approach of the raid on their coastal radar, the next, their displays were covered by blossoming clouds of new signals which effectively obliterated the scopes.

Dead on schedule at 01.57 the first yellow illuminators were released by the leading parthfinders, followed by lines of red 250-lb target indicators for the 746 bombers following behind.

For three weeks Hamburg had been enjoying hot, dry weather, many of the large static water tanks were half empty, and everywhere was tinder dry. Added to this, a large area of the city consisted of ancient buildings constructed of timber. As the leading Lancasters and Stirlings unloaded huge numbers of incendiaries and fires sprang up over a wide area, the city's numerous firefighting teams started out to tackle the minor blazes. Then came the Wellingtons, each carrying a single 2,000-lb parachute mine fuzed to explode about 50 ft above the ground and designed for maximum blast effect which knocked down large buildings and blocked the streets with rubble. Finally the Halifaxes and more Lancasters unloaded a mix of 8,000-lb, 4,000-lb 'blockbusters' and delayed-action 1,000-lb bombs plus incendiary bombs, deliberately intended to collapse large buildings, destroy water and gas mains and trap the fire service in blocked streets.

Devastation was incredible, and more than 4,000 key personnel in the city's emergency services were killed or seriously injured. To add to the confusion, long-delay fuzes had been fitted to a high proportion of the bombs, which thus continued to detonate some hours after the last bombers had departed, frequently erupting to bring buildings crashing down on the rescue workers.

On the night of 27/28 July Bomber Command returned once more, as 722 out of 739 bombers despatched unloaded 2,417 tons of bombs, well over half this weight composed of incendiaries.

Within 30 minutes the congested dock area, comprising 8 square miles of narrow streets and warehouses, was transformed into a lake of fire which superheated the air to a temperature of 1,832°F; this monster conflagration, demanding oxygen, created a terrifying suction from its perimeter 'so that the air stormed through the streets with immense force, bearing upon it sparks, timber and roof beams, and thus spreading the fire still further and further till it became a typhoon such as had never before been witnessed, and against which all human resistance was powerless'.

Thus ran the subsequent report to Hitler by Hamburg's Air Protection Leader, General-Major H. Kehrl. The man-made winds of 150 mph tossed human beings like so much chaff into the flames; large trees were uprooted and reduced to charcoal in seconds; citizens strove to avoid oxygen starvation in their shelters by emerging into the holocaust, only to be driven back by the rain of high explosive. Hundreds on hundreds leapt into the canals where they remained relatively safe from incineration. This fire-storm phenomenon, for which Hamburg was to gain a terrifying immortality, laid to ashes an area of 6,000 acres.

Two nights later the bombers returned; 726 Lancasters, Halifaxes and Stirlings dropped 2,382 tons of bombs, scarcely requiring the services of pathfinders so bright were the fires still raging below. Once more a fire-typhoon erupted. By now, with more than 70 percent of the city's firefighting personnel dead or injured, the city was powerless to prevent further destruction.

One final attack was launched on the night of 2/3 August when 762 heavy bombers set out for Hamburg. Severe storms persisted all the way across the North Sea and 'only' 442 aircraft attacked. To the terror of fire and explosives were added the crash of natural thunder and the flash of lightning; not even the deluge of rain could quench the inferno, nor prevent yet a third fire-storm.

Out of 3,095 bombers despatched by the RAF, 2,630 had attacked, dropping 4,309 tons of incendiaries and 4,312 tons of high explosive. Damage in Hamburg was prodigious, with 40,385 residential houses and 275,000 flats (61 per cent of the city's residential accommodation) destroyed or made uninhabitable; 580 industrial and armament plants were destroyed. Yet despite the initial casualty figures of 41,800 killed and 37,439 severely injured (of whom many were to succumb from the injuries suffered), Hamburg recovered with astonishing speed. Overall manufacturing output recovered to some 70 percent of the pre-raid effort within six weeks.

In less quantifiable terms Operation Gomorrah provided the UK with satisfying retribution. British civilian casualties from German raids suffered thus far in World War II stood at some 49,810 killed. The German dead in the Ruhr and Hamburg already far exceeded this figure.

One final heavy night attack was carried out against Germany before the Halifaxes and Lancasters were directed elsewhere. On the night of 30/31 March 1944 795 heavy bombers set out to attack the city of Nuremburg. The raid was a disastrous failure with wrongly forecast winds causing the bomber stream to stray from its 'safe' track and to overfly enemy night fighter assembly beacons. None of the diversionary attacks succeeded in confusing the defences and the opposing Ju 88 and Bf 110 night fighters claimed many victims. Nor were the experienced Pathfinder crews any less confused and their inaccurate navigation so dispersed the main force that no more than an insignificant number of bombers crews identified Nuremberg, the majority striking hapazardly at neighbouring towns and villages. No fewer than 95 Halifaxes and Lancasters failed to return and a dozen others crashed in England.

8th Air Force aircrew are intent on the briefing at a USAAF base. Such mass briefings occurred every morning at many bases in the UK. The crews paid close attention: observing everything that was said paid dividends in this highly dangerous game.

The assaults on Berlin and Nuremburg have frequently been quoted as representative of Bomber Command's failure to hasten the war's end, as had been constantly foreshadowed by 'Bomber' Harris himself. Certainly the prowess of the German night fighter crews seemed to be capable of defending the Reich against the night bomber for, with losses such as those over Nuremburg, Bomber Command could not have sustained a worthwhile offensive for much longer. Such a verdict would be to gainsay the devastation wrought in German cities and industry, the effects of which were already being sorely felt. Harris' bombers were now switched to the task of softening up German preparations to meet the Allies' imminent invasion of Europe. Once that invasion was established the Lancasters and Halifaxes would return to Germany with even more devastating effect.

Throughout the campaign waged by Bomber Command the German defences had proved adaptable and had progressively increased in strength and efficiency. How they came to achieve the scale of victory in the skies over Nuremberg is told later in this chapter, but now we turn to the other leg of the Allied bomber offensive: the daylight raids of the United States Army Air Force.

America's daylight offensive

When the United States of America were drawn into the war in December 1941 the Army Air Force was ill equipped to mount anything but isolated bombing attacks by small numbers of aircraft whose bomb loads were – at least by RAF standards – somewhat meagre. The USAAF moreover clung doggedly to the belief that its daylight bombers, such as its B-17 Flying Fortress, were perfectly capable of defending themselves against intercepting fighters – a philosophy already discarded by the RAF after its drubbing over the Heligoland Bight during 1939. Nor, after the Battle of Britain, did the Luftwaffe consider the use of unescorted bombers particularly profitable. The Americans pointed to their Norden bombsight, popularly referred to as being able to deliver a bomb 'into a pickle barrel from 20,000 feet', and claimed much greater bombing accuracy by day than by night – a claim fairly easily substantiated having regard to the RAF's abysmal bombing accuracy during 1941.

The first elements of the US VIII Bomber Command (later to become the 8th Air Force) arrived in Britain in February 1942, and its first bombing operation, using Boston aircraft of No. 226 Squadron of the RAF, was flown on 29 June. This first tentative step was followed on 17 August by a raid by B-17Es of the 97th Bombardment Group against the rail yards at Rouen. Given an escort of RAF Spitfires, this very short-range raid did not attract air opposition by the Luftwaffe, so the daylight theories were not put to the test. Similar attacks against 'soft' targets in France by the B-17s continued for the remainder of 1942, raids

Above: The third and fourth raids on Hamburg did not require the services of the Pathfinders as the city was still a raging inferno when the bombers returned. Their bombs further fuelled the fires, ensuring the eventual destruction of 60 per cent of the city's residential areas.

Only charred, roofless shells remained of many Hamburg buildings following the devastating fire raids. The firestorm was one of the worst seen, winds reaching 150 mph as the conflagration sucked in air to feed itself, tossing bodies and debris about like leaves.

Vast amounts of 'Window' were used during the Hamburg raids. This was chaff consisting of strips of metallic foil half the wavelength of enemy radars. The radar screens showed a huge cloud in which the bombers flew unseen. Ironically, the Germans had developed a similar technique known as 'Duppel'.

that provided useful training for the 10-man American crews. In October they were joined by the 93rd Bomb Group, the first in Britain to be equipped with the B-24 Liberator.

These early raids, mounted usually by fewer than 50 aircraft, began to attract the Bf 109Gs and Fw 190As of fighter groups JG 2 and JG 26 into the air, the German pilots initially experiencing considerable difficulty in getting to grips with the bomber 'boxes' which were well defended by a veritable deluge of crossfire from the bombers' massed 12.7-mm machine-guns. It was not long, however, before the Luftwaffe pilots discovered the B-17s' and B-24s' weak spot – the forward arc of fire – and began to employ that most unnerving of all attacks, the head-on pass. At once, despite efforts by escorting Spitfire pilots to protect their charges, losses among the American bombers began to increase perceptibly – losses that not only slowed the build-up of B-17 and B-24 groups in England but prompted caution among the Americans when planning raids against the Reich itself.

During the closing weeks of 1942 VIII Bomber Command Groups attacked such targets as the submarine bases at St Nazaire, Lorient and La Pallice, but on 27 January 1943 B-17s and B-24s launched their first attack on Germany, bombs being dropped on the northern port of Wilhelmshaven.

Smoke markers snake up through the formation as Boeing B-17s unload over their target. The B-17 bore the brunt of the American offensive and carved a niche for itself in the hearts of many of its crews for its ability to miraculously struggle back to base.

B-17s of the 381st Bomb Group display immaculate formation-keeping. Such flying was extremely important to the USAAF day raids as the bombers covered each other with defensive fire. This group suffered the highest loss during the disastrous first Schweinfurt raid.

At this time the American fighters (almost exclusively P-47s) were under the control of RAF Fighter Command, their principal tasks being confined to relatively short-range sorties over northern France. Thus the raid on 27 January was flown without the benefit of fighter cover, the P-47s not possessing adequate range – and their pilots lacking experience in efficient fuel management. Fortunately for the bomber crews the Luftwaffe deployed only small forces of fighters to defend the Reich at this time, and losses among the raiders were light.

Raids by the VIII Bomber Command Groups at the beginning of 1943 seldom involved more than about 50 aircraft, the build-up in Britain having been delayed by the diversion of units to North Africa to assist the creation of the 15th Air Force in the Mediterranean theatre. After the attack of 27 January poor weather forced the British-based bombers to return to their French targets for the time being. On 15 February Major-General Ira C. Eaker (who had led the first raid on Rouen the previous August) was appointed to command the US 8th Air Force and, following decisions taken at the Casablanca Conference in January , the B-17s and B-24s were once more sent against Germany: on 22 March they again raided Wilhelmshaven, and on 17 April they attacked the Focke-Wulf factory at Bremen.

Daylight raids increase

May brought an intensification of the daylight attacks as P-47s (now equipped with drop tanks) escorted 79 B-17s throughout a raid on Antwerp. Despite being attacked by German fighters the American escort pilots managed to hold their own and protected the bombers from serious loss. Already early wartime lessons with the B-17E had resulted in a new version being introduced, the B-17F, and this version predominated among the UK-based groups throughout 1943; it featured strengthened landing gear and increased fuel and bomb loads, as well as improved armament and armour.

If the raids by American heavy bombers had thus far escaped lightly, those by the medium bombers were much less fortunate. The newly formed 322nd Medium Bomb Group, with twin-engine B-26C Marauders at Great Saling, had flown an initial sortie on 12 May, and on the 17th sent 11 aircraft on a low-level raid against Ijmuiden and Haarlem; one aircraft returned early with technical trouble while every one of the remaining 10 B-26s, with 60 crewmen, succumbed to flak and Bf 109Gs. The B-26 was promptly reassigned to medium-altitude operations, and retraining of new crews was not completed for more than two months.

Misfortune was by no means limited to the RAF and USAAF. Increasingly widespread fighter and light-bomber activity over France and the Low Countries was beginning to subject the Luftwaffe fighter units in the west to considerable strain. Losses, already fairly heavy – though supportable – in 1942 increased sharply during the spring of 1943. During May eight *Jagdgruppen* (fighter groups) lost 61 fighters shot down, with more than 50 others damaged; among the pilots killed were seven experienced squadron leaders. For the first time since 1940 German fighter losses consistently exceeded those of the Allies.

The reason lay not so much in inferior aircraft, but more in the increasing pressure on a relatively small force of defending fighters. Prominent among the German aircraft were the Fw 190A-5 and Bf 109G-6, fighters more than able to match the Spitfire VB and P-47C, and fairly evenly matched with the Spitfire IX and P-47D (the latter starting to appear during the spring of 1943). Only now were the German aircraft carrying increased gun armament in an effort to combat the American bombers, but the pressure was on to introduce new forms of armament of which the 21-cm Waffengerat 21 mortar proved fairly effective; mounting two of these weapons under the Bf 109G's wings reduced its performance significantly, however, so that it became particularly vulnerable if caught by Allied fighters.

By June 1943, with the slowly growing number of American raids over Germany, the decision was taken to reduce the Luftwaffe's fighter strength in France and two Fw 190A-5 groups were moved east to help bolster the Reich's defences. This reduction of fighter strength in the west encouraged the British and Americans to mount a series of co-ordinated sweeps and raids (Operation Starkey) by fighters, fighter-bombers, light and medium bombers and B-17s and B-24s over France and the Low Countries, the object being to draw the remaining Luftwaffe fighters into the skies where they could be overwhelmed by sheer weight of numbers. Between 25 August and 9 September 'ramrods' and heavy-bomber raids were mounted, principally against enemy airfields around Paris. JG 2 and JG 26 duly reacted against them, losing 51 aircraft shot down, 30 damaged and 43 pilots killed (about 20 per cent of the forces still based in France). Allied losses however amounted to 49 fighters and fighter-bombers, 8 British medium bombers, 7 B-26 Marauders and no fewer than 65 B-17s and B-24s. Clearly the RAF and USAAF were still far too weak to claim or dispute air supremacy in the west.

These heavy losses followed hard on the heels of the Americans' first major long-distance raids flown on 17 August against targets deep inside Germany. The objectives selected were the Messerschmitt factory at Regensburg near the Austrian border and the ball-bearing plants at Schweinfurt in south Germany, a raid on the first being intended to draw defending fighters away from the second, its aircraft flying on to land on Allied airfields in the Mediterranean theatre. Close fighter escort was not possible owing to the distances involved, it being planned to give cover up to the point at which the bombers penetrated German airspace. The two raids were intended to set out about 10 minutes apart but unfortunately the Schweinfurt bombers were delayed by more than three hours by fog on their airfields. To ensure that they would be able to land at their airfields in the south, the Regensburg bombers set out on time, leaving the Schweinfurt raiders to face the enemy fighters which were waiting for them, having landed to refuel and rearm. The second raid accordingly suffered enemy fighter attacks almost

Arriving later in the theatre than the B-17, the Consolidated B-24 Liberator went on to compile a useful record against the Germans. Possessing greater range but smaller bomb load, the B-24 was built in greater numbers. These are B-24Ds.

British night bombers

Throughout the war, the RAF stuck to night bombing, preferring to use the expertise of the Pathfinders and their radar navigation sets to pinpoint targets in the dark.

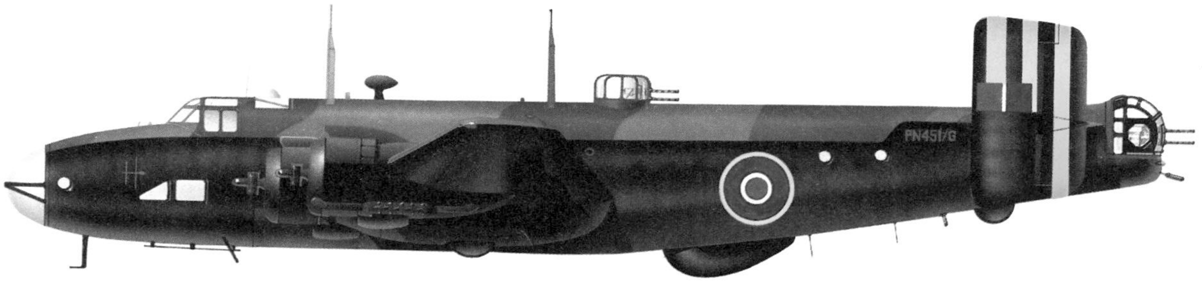

***Above:** This Handley Page Halifax B. Mk III was flown by **No.** 462 (RAAF) Sqn, and was used on electronic countermeasures duties by No. 100 Group. Following service as a chaff carrier, the aircraft received 'Airborne Cigar' and 'Carpet' jamming gear. These operated during the last months of the war in Europe. The 'G' in the serial meant the aircraft had to be guarded on the ground.*

***Above:** This Vickers Wellington Mk IC served with No. 310 (Polish) Sqn from 1940 to 1943, when the squadron was disbanded. These capable bombers were sometimes used for special operations such as clandestine supply drops to resistance groups. No. 310 was also involved with minelaying, a lesser task for Bomber Command.*

***Above:** No. 571 Sqn was formed late in the war as part of No. 8 Group's Fast Night Striking Force, and used Mosquito B.Mk XVIs on raids against German industrial centres. Favourite weapon of these raiders was the 4,000-lb 'Cookie' bomb, which necessitated a bulged bomb bay to accommodate it.*

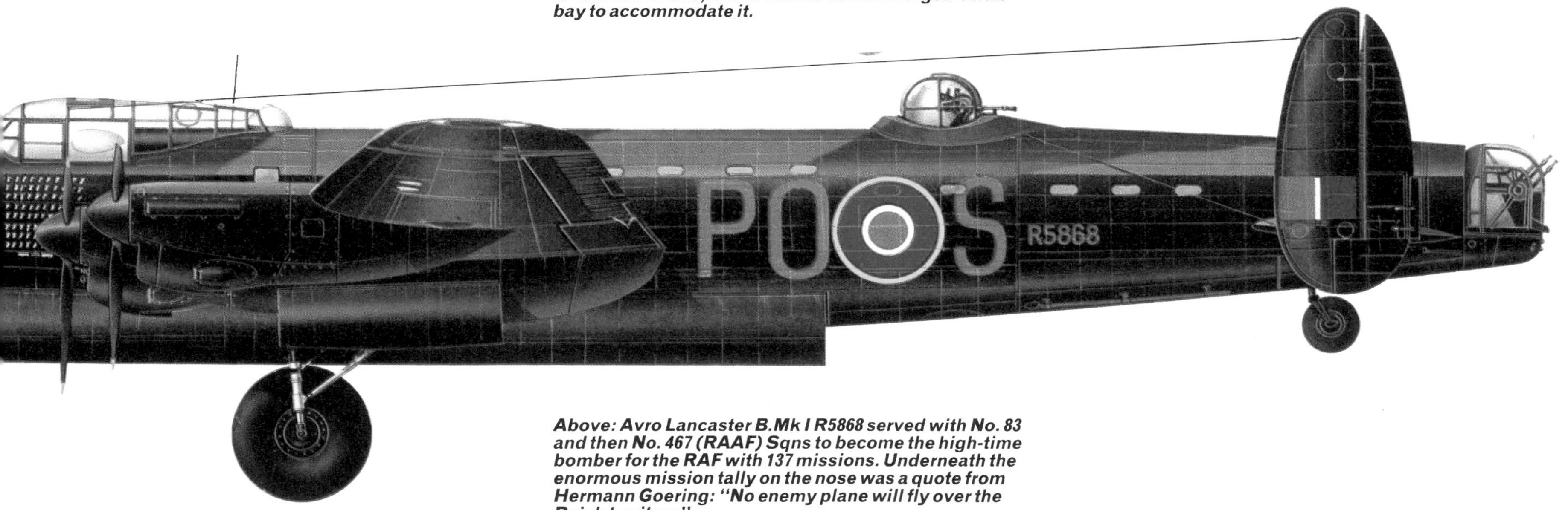

***Above:** Avro Lancaster B.Mk I R5868 served with No. 83 and then No. 467 (RAAF) Sqns to become the high-time bomber for the RAF with 137 missions. Underneath the enormous mission tally on the nose was a quote from Hermann Goering: "No enemy plane will fly over the Reich territory".*

***Above:** The Armstrong Whitworth Whitley was widely used by the RAF during the first years of the war, before most front-line squadrons converted to the Halifax or Lancaster. No. 78 Sqn flew this Whitley Mk V from Dishforth in 1940.*

***Below:** No. 149 (East India) Sqn flew the Short Stirling throughout the mid-war period. As well as performing well in the general campaign against German industry (taking part in the first 1,000 bomber raid), the squadron attacked the rocket site at Peenemünde and was also used for supply drops to the Maquis.*

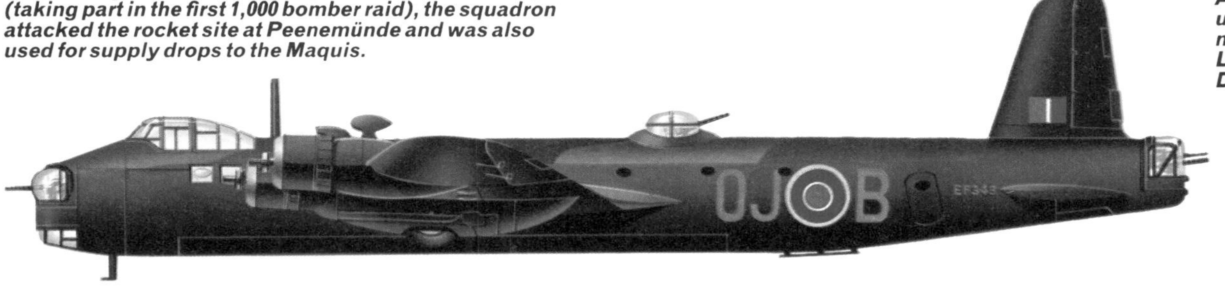

This photograph shows the town of Schweinfurt during a USAAF bombing raid. Note the explosions in several parts of the town, as well as bomb craters from previous attacks.

Flames and debris spew backwards from an 8th Air Force B-17 hit moments before bomb release. The USAAF suffered far greater losses than the RAF during the bombing raids, mainly due to their insistence on carrying out attacks during daylight, when the fighters and gunners found it easier to defend.

from the moment it crossed the Belgian coast; head-on attacks against the leading bomber elements destroyed 21 of the 36 bombers so that, without the most experienced bombardiers, accuracy over the target suffered badly and little lasting damage was inflicted. Of the 200 B-17s sent out, 59 were lost to enemy action and 7 others crashed on return.

Despite the loss of more than 120 bombers (and over 1,000 crew members) in less than a month, VIII Bomber Command had grown to 16 bomb groups (91st, 92nd, 94th, 95th, 96th, 100th, 303rd, 305th, 306th, 351st, 379th, 381st, 384th, 385th, 388th, and 390th) with B-17Fs, and four groups (44th, 93rd, 389th and 392nd) with B-24D-Js, between them fielding some 480 bombers. Disappointing results in the 17 August raid prompted a second attack on 14 October when it was intended to send 420 bombers (of the 1st and 3rd Air Divisions) back to Schweinfurt. Recent losses, however, reduced the number of bombers sent to 291 but, with recently improved drop tanks being carried by the P-47s, at least close fighter escort could be provided for much of the outward journey. As the 3rd Division's aircraft flew a zig-zag course to confuse the enemy's fighter defences, and thereby escaped with relatively light losses, the 1st Division flew an almost direct route and was accordingly heavily attacked. Sixty B-17s were shot down and five others crashed in Britain, while the Luftwaffe lost 62 fighters and 29 pilots. Bombing results on this occasion were shown to be much improved, resulting in an almost 50 per cent drop in bearing production for several months.

Escort fighters

Schweinfurt was to be raided several more times by the USAAF, the next occasion being on 24 February 1944 when 238 B-17s of the 1st Division were despatched. This time, given the benefit of long-range fighter protection, the Americans' losses were held to only 11 bombers, and the appearance of these all-important escorts must now be described for they were to engender the survival of the American daylight bomber offensive over Germany.

Although the Americans had not originally planned to deploy fighters in Europe for bomber escort duties, necessity had caused the Spitfires of the 4th Fighter Group and the P-47s of the 56th Group to be employed for such duties where range permitted. The P-38 Lightning had been intended for escort work but was found to be generally outgunned and outfought by the Bf 109G and Fw 190A, and most were reassigned to fighter-bombing and long-range sweeps; others equipped photo-reconnaissance groups. As experience was gained by P-47 pilots in combat, and 150-gallon drop tanks were introduced, the P-47D was found to be adequate for escort missions of up to about 650 miles, but bearing in mind that the Schweinfurt raid involved the bombers in a 900-mile flight the problem was acute.

On 1 December 1943 the 8th Air Force in Britain took delivery of its first P-51B and C Mustangs, powered by Packard-built Rolls-Royce Merlin engines. Soon these superb aircraft were to carry 269 gallons of fuel internally as well as 110-gallon drop tanks, increasing their range to just over 2,000 miles. They flew their first bomber escort mission when aircraft of the 354th Fighter Group accompanied bombers to Amiens on 5 December, and on the 13th tank-carrying P-51Bs of the 354th, together with P-38s of the 55th Group, accompanied B-17s to Kiel – the longest raid (almost 1,000 miles) thus far accomplished with fighter escort all the way. In due course the 8th and 9th Air Forces were between them to deploy 11 P-51 groups, and in 1944 the P-51D, with cut-down rear fuselage, sliding canopy, more powerful Merlin and six-gun armament was introduced, this being the most widely used American fighter in Europe during the war; almost 8,000 were produced.

Returning to the American bomber offensive, the raids of 13 December 1943, apart from the Kiel attack, included raids on Bremen, Hamburg and Schiphol airport, and involved a total of 1,462 aircraft – the largest number of Allied aircraft flown thus far in a single day's operations. On 6 January 1944 Lieutenant-General James H. Doolittle (leader of the famous Tokyo raid of 1942) took command of the 8th Air Force in Britain. On the 11th the Americans sent almost 800 aircraft to attack Halberstadt, Brunswick and Oschersleben, escorted by P-51s; 55 bombers were lost as well as 5 fighters. On the 29th they attacked Frankfurt, and the following day it was the turn of Hanover and Brunswick once more. On 3 March it was planned to mount the USAAF's first raid on Berlin (Harris' Battle of Berlin was nearing its climax), but poor weather prevented the B-17s and B-24s from reaching their target – and the only American aircraft to arrive over the capital were P-51s!

The first Schweinfurt raid

The map below follows the first raid on Schweinfurt, when 66 out of 200 bombers were lost. Later attacks on the town were more successful, due to the presence of an effective fighter escort.

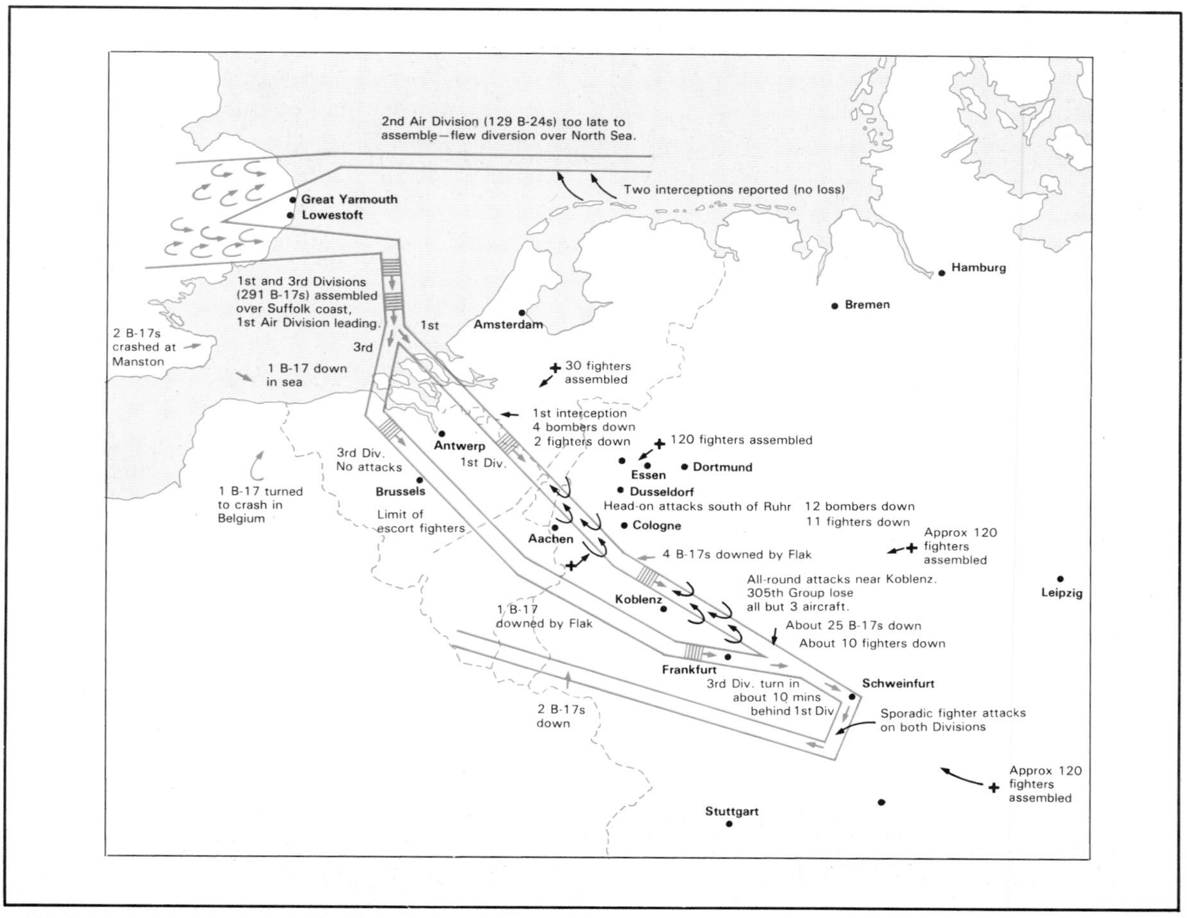

Hitler addresses munitions factory workers at the end of 1940. At that high point in the success of the Wehrmacht, few could have foreseen that the most pressing need for the heavy 10.5-cm Flak 38 would be for the defence of the Reich itself against almost overwhelming attack from the skies.

The first successful American raid on Berlin was launched on 6 March when 609 B-17s and B-24s set out with a fighter escort of some 90 P-51s. This fighter strength proved inadequate and, with air battles raging for more than three hours over northern Germany, 68 bombers were lost as well as 11 fighters; 37 German aircraft were shot down.

This first raid on Berlin represented a landmark in the American daylight bombing offensive, and the appearance of single-seat American fighters over the capital came as a rude shock to the Luftwaffe which had hitherto seemed capable of inflicting prohibitive losses on unescorted bomber formations. Henceforth fast-increasing numbers of P-51s were to be encountered deep inside German airspace and desperate tactics were to be adopted by the German fighter pilots to penetrate the swarms of escorting P-51s to get to the bombers. More heavy raids were made by American bombers on Berlin on 8, 9 and 22 March by forces of 540, 330 and 610 aircraft respectively, of which a total of 57 failed to return. During the next two months the target list grew steadily with the addition of Augsburg, Coblenz, Cuxhaven, Frankfurt, Friedrichshafen, Hamm, Karlsruhe, Kassel, Lippstadt, Mannheim, Metz, Münster, Oranienburg, Osnabrück, Saarbrücken, Stettin, Strasbourg and

With its heavy cannon armament the Focke-Wulf Fw 190 gave the Luftwaffe much-enhanced bomber destroyer capability.

German heavy anti-aircraft guns

In spite of the best efforts of the British and American bomber forces, German war production went up by leaps and bounds even at the height of the bombing. However, the bombing campaign tied up scarce German resources in the production of air defence equipment, forcing the Luftwaffe to deploy much of its strength in Germany, and the million men assigned to air defence were not available on the battlefront.

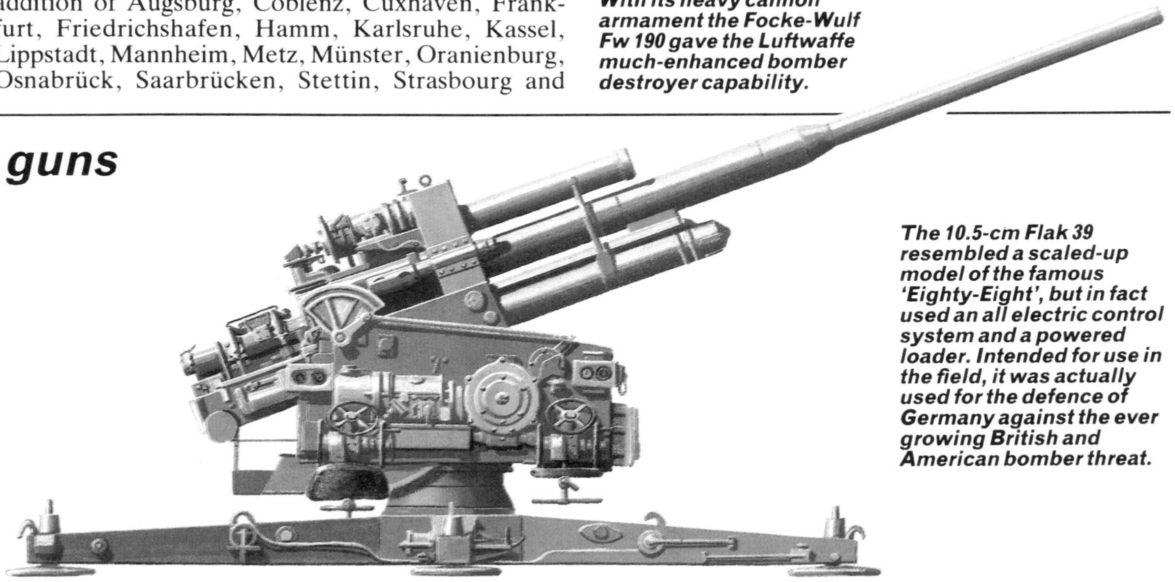

The 10.5-cm Flak 39 resembled a scaled-up model of the famous 'Eighty-Eight', but in fact used an all electric control system and a powered loader. Intended for use in the field, it was actually used for the defence of Germany against the ever growing British and American bomber threat.

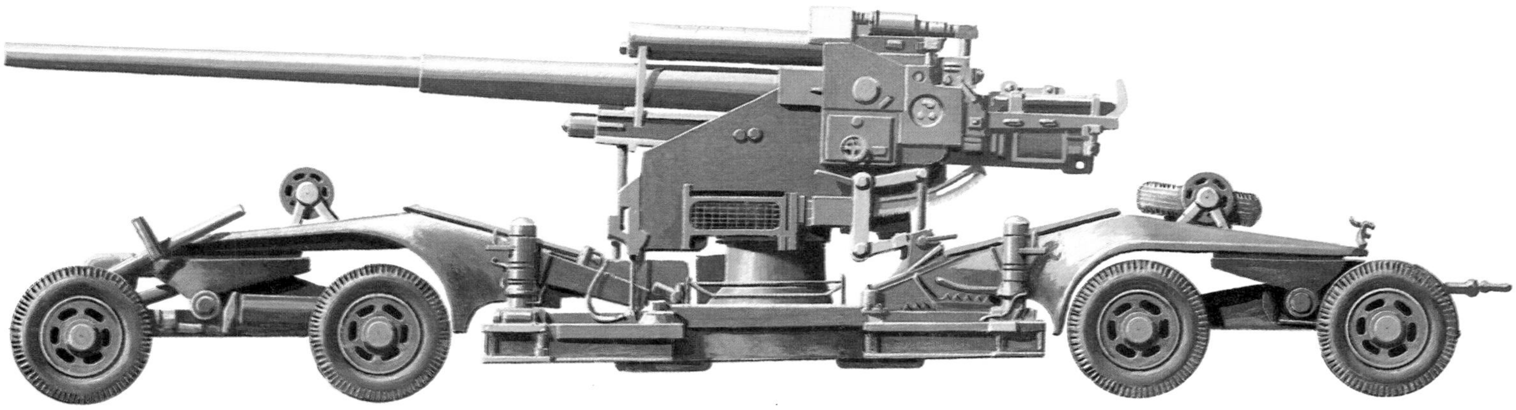

The 12.8-cm Flak 40 was also intended for use with the army, but so massive was the system that only six guns (one of which is illustrated) were ever completed in mobile form. A static version was produced from 1942, as well as a twin mounting (called Flakzwilling 40). Maximum effective ceiling was over 48,000 feet

One of the most famous of all weapons used in World War II was the 'Eighty-Eight', primarily because the Germans were the first to realize that the high-velocity, flat-trajectory shell of an AA gun would also be good at knocking out tanks. Designed by a Krupp team in Sweden (in order to circumvent the Treaty of Versailles), the 8.8-cm Flak 18 entered production in 1933, and was the progenitor of a series of Flak, tank and anti-tank guns that were to make no small contribution to the German war effort.

The Republic P-47 Thunderbolt was at the time the fastest and heaviest fighter in the USAAF, and in combat consistently proved its immense strength. Dive characteristics were particularly good, and it was well-armed.

This North American P-51B was the famous mount of Don Gentile, who ended the war with 23 victories to his name. He had originally enlisted in the RAF and flew with No. 133 (Eagle) Sqn. He transferred to the 4th Fighter Group in 1942.

The P-47 introduced speed and hard-hitting weaponry to the 8th Air Force and was soon piling up victories. These are from the 56th Fighter Group, the first USAAF P-47 unit. The Group went on to become the highest-scoring 8th Air Force unit.

many other objectives. By the end of April, however, much of the 8th Air Force's muscle was being diverted (as was that of RAF Bomber Command) to preparation for the invasion of France and against the enemy flying-bomb sites in the Pas de Calais. Later in the year the Americans would return in even greater strength to the Reich.

The mounting of the American daylight air offensive in Europe between 1942 and the spring of 1944 represented a monumental achievement of logistics and administration. The campaign was fought by a veritable army of young men, fighting in foreign skies far from home against an enemy frantically defending its homeland. Those were the days never to be forgotten by the survivors; the blue skies high over Europe with vast condensation trails from hundreds of bombers whose crews were battling their way to some distant target as the fighters weaved their own fleeting webs of tracer fire. History has never recorded a grimmer battlefield.

Shuttle bombing

If the Allied air forces possessed one theoretical strategic advantage against the Axis enemy it lay in the peripheral location of their bases for attack on an enemy fighting from the geographical centre. While Hitler's recurring nightmare was the spectre of simultaneous warfare on more than one front, his long run of conquests in the early years of the war, and the enlargement of the Axis bloc continued with the alignment of Italy, Romania, Hungary and Bulgaria, forced the boundaries of the 'central powers' far outwards.

Such were the relatively poor range capabilities of Britain's early heavy bombers that it proved impossible to mount raids involving one-way flights across enemy-occupied Europe and, although home-based RAF Whitley and Wellington crews performed some outstanding feats of endurance by raiding targets in northern Italy in the latter half of 1940, the very long and hazardous flights, involving a return to the United Kingdom, resulted in poor target location and relatively puny bomb load.

It was not until 1943, with the defeat of German and Italian forces in North Africa already accomplished and the establishment of bases by the RAF and USAAF in Algeria and Tunisia, that the scene was set to embark on what were to become known as 'shuttle-bombing' raids. On 20/21 June that year Bomber Command sent a force of four-engine bombers (in Operation Bellicose) to attack Friedrichshafen on the German shores of Lake Constance, the crews flying on to land at Algiers, a raid involving an eight-hour flight of over 1,250 miles. Three nights later the British bombers dropped 4,000-lb bombs on the north Italian port of Spezia on their return journey to Britain.

The demonstration of the practicality of such raids allowed plans to go ahead with further attacks on targets in north Italy, particularly such industrial and rail centres as Turin, Milan and Genoa. Milan was attacked four times in the first 15 nights of August, the raids being accompanied by Pathfinders with H_2S. This phase of shuttle bombing was launched as much to support the Allied landings in Sicily, which

Dramatic shot of a Boeing B-17 as it loses a wing over Germany. This scene was repeated many times during the daylight raids, yet the Fortress often struggled home with tailplanes, wing sections or engines shot completely away.

US aircraft over Germany

The 8th Air Force conducted a bombing campaign over Germany from 1942 until 1945, utilizing the Boeing B-17 and Consolidated B-24 bombers. Fighter Groups provided escort, while also getting in some fighter-bomber duties, particularly against enemy communications.

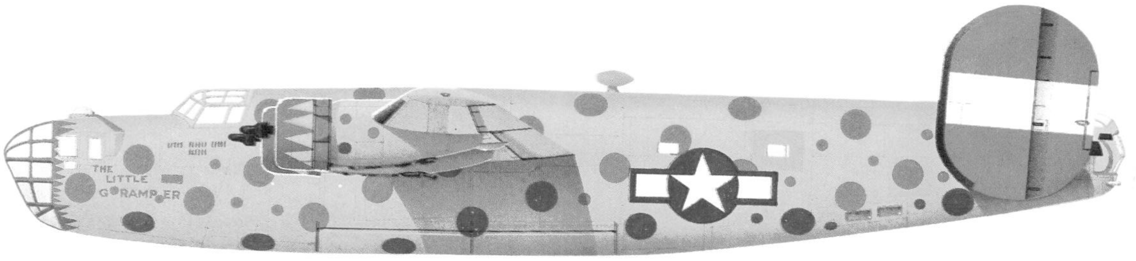

Above: The Little Gramper was a Consolidated B-24D flown by the 491st Bomb Group as a lead-ship. These aircraft were used to assemble the huge formations over England, ensure everyone was in position and then send them on their way. The colours were deliberately bright for high visibility.

Above: A Consolidated B-24 Liberator of the 93rd Bomb Group, 2nd Bomb Division of the US VIII Bomber Command, based at Hardwick in the autumn of 1942. The 93rd were later to deploy to Egypt for the Ploesti raids.

Above: Republic P-47D of the 352nd FS, 353rd FG. This unit pioneered the use of dive-bombing methods against German communications targets which were favoured until VE-day by both 8th and 9th Air Force aircraft.

Above: The 357th Fighter Group flew North American P-51 Mustangs throughout the war, including this P-51B of the 364th FS. It was the first 8th Air Force unit to receive the Mustang, and its greatest day occurred on 14th January 1945 when it scored 56 enemy aircraft destroyed, an 8th Air Force record for a single mission.

Above: The 447th Bomb Group flew from Rattlesden from November 1943 onwards, flying the B-17G variant throughout. This aircraft is one of the high-time B-17s: another from the 447th reached 129 sorties.

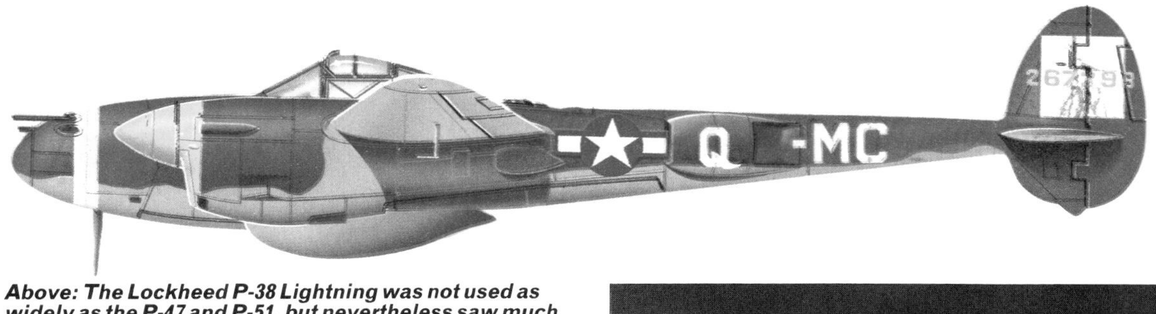

Above: The Lockheed P-38 Lightning was not used as widely as the P-47 and P-51, but nevertheless saw much action over Germany, where its long range enabled it to escort the bombers deep inside enemy territory. This example served at Kingscliffe with the 20th Fighter Group.

A feature of the daylight raids were the vapour trails pulled by the USAAF aircraft. Here the escorting fighters are seen patrolling above the bomber stream, weaving back and forth across the main path, ever vigilant for German attacks.

had taken place the previous month, as to encourage the Italian nation to defect from the Axis. In the second attack, the most destructive of the series, one of No. 218 Squadron's Stirlings was badly damaged by machine-gun fire which also sorely wounded the pilot Flight Sergeant Louis Aaron; the young pilot handed over control of the big bomber to his bomb aimer but refused morphia in order to remain conscious to land the aircraft, a task successfully accomplished at Bône in Algeria, 500 miles to the south. Aaron succumbed to his wounds, but his posthumous award of the Victoria Cross was never more gallantly earned.

The gradual Allied advance northwards through Italy in 1943-4 rendered shuttle bombing by UK-based RAF and USAAF bombers unnecessary as bases for the American 5th and 2686th Bomb Wings and the RAF's No. 205 Group became available within range of targets in southern Europe.

The next phase of long-range shuttle bombing was undertaken by the US 15th Air Force in support of the Russian summer offensive of 1944, following the liberation of the Ukraine. By June that year Soviet engineers had made ready two airfields near Poltava, 200 miles east of Kiev, and on the 2nd a force of B-17s of the 301st Group with P-51 escort took off from their bases in Italy, carried out a surprise raid on the Luftwaffe air base at Debrecen in eastern Hungary and flew on to Poltava; four days later, on their return flight to Italy, the B-17s raided the German airfield at Galati in eastern Romania.

The relative success of these shuttle flights to Poltava resulted in similar plans by the 8th Air Force in Britain being made, and on 21 June 114 B-17Gs of the 388th Bomb Group, based at Knettishall in England, took off with a P-51D escort to attack German oil installations at Ruhland, 30 miles north of Dresden. When the bombers failed to turn back after the raid the Luftwaffe realized that this was also a shuttle flight to the Soviet Union and ordered off a Heinkel He 177 to shadow the formation, pinpointing its destination at Poltava. That night Ju 88s and He 111s of KG 4, KG 27, KG 53 and KG 55 carried out a virtually unopposed attack on the base, destroying 43 B-17s and 15 P-51s. Without adequate promises of night defence of the Poltava base the Americans discontinued their shuttle raids to the Soviet Union.

The final recourse to shuttle bombing in September 1944 involved an attack on the battleship *Tirpitz*, then anchored in Altenfjord in the northernmost Norwegian province of Finnmark. This target was too far distant from any base in the United Kingdom to enable Lancasters to make a return flight, attacking with 12,000-lb bombs, so Nos 9 and 617 Squadrons flew out to Yagodnik, near Archangel to await favourable weather conditions. On the 15th their attack took place but, owing to the use by the Germans of an efficient smokescreen, only one bomb struck the *Tirpitz*, which was moved south to Tromsö for repairs. The Lancasters flew on to Britain and awaited another chance. Now the *Tirpitz* was within range of Britain and, in an out-back raid on 12 November, the great battleship was hit or narrowly missed by three of the huge bombs and capsized.

***Above:** Attacks into Europe were not only mounted from England; here USAAF Fortresses head towards France from bases in Italy. Shuttle bombing was carried out between England and Russia, and England and Italy.*

***Right:** Liberators seen unloading over Frankfurt during a 800-bomber effort against the important industrial centre. Towards the end of the war, the Luftwaffe challenge usually resulted in far greater losses for the defenders than for the bombers, largely due to effective fighter cover.*

Defence of the Reich

The early American daylight raids against German ports which started in January 1943, though anticipated by the Luftwaffe for some months, gave no immediate cause for concern in the Reich and were considered to warrant no special redeployment of fighters to counter them. Gradually, however, as the USAAF became bolder and stronger, and began to provide fighter escorts of P-47s, so the Supreme Command, Central or Home Front, began to press urgently for reinforcements.

By 17 August 1943, the date of the first deep penetration raids on Augsburg and Schweinfurt, the daylight home defences had grown considerably and included some 120 Fw 190A-4s and A-5s distributed among four *Jagdgruppen*, I and II/JG 1, I/JG 11 and II/JG 300, backed up by 60 others of I and II/JG 26 in France. Mainstay of the home defence units were however the 180 Bf 109Gs flown by JG 3, II/JG 27, II/JG 51 and III/JG 54, commanded by such star pilots as Major Wolf-Dietrich Wilcke, Captain Werner Schroer, Major Karl Rommelt and Major Reinhard Seiler. Specially boosted Bf 109Gs were also flown by JGr 25 (Major Herbert Ihlefeld), while bomber-destroyer Bf 110s equipped ZG 26 and ZG 76. Thus with more than 350 fighters available to intercept the unescorted bombers on that day it was little wonder that the Luftwaffe scored a resounding victory.

Already the Luftwaffe was experimenting with new weapons and tactics to overcome the large numbers of heavy-calibre machine-guns mounted by the B-17s and B-24s, whose range and crossfire made

A German 12.8-cm Flak 40 is demonstrated in its mobile form (only six of this model were built). The Flak 40 was one of the types to equip the flak towers which protected cities and major targets in the Reich.

A battery of 10.5-cm Flak 38s is seen early in the war, firing together in an attempt to 'bracket' the target. Later in the war such combinations were radar-directed, and as many as 16 heavy guns would be targetted on a single helpless bomber.

German fighters, 1944-1945

The Luftwaffe carried out a brave and skilful defence against the incessant tide of bombers hitting Germany both day and night. Some of the most experienced were night fighters, who wrought considerable havoc amongst the RAF bombers.

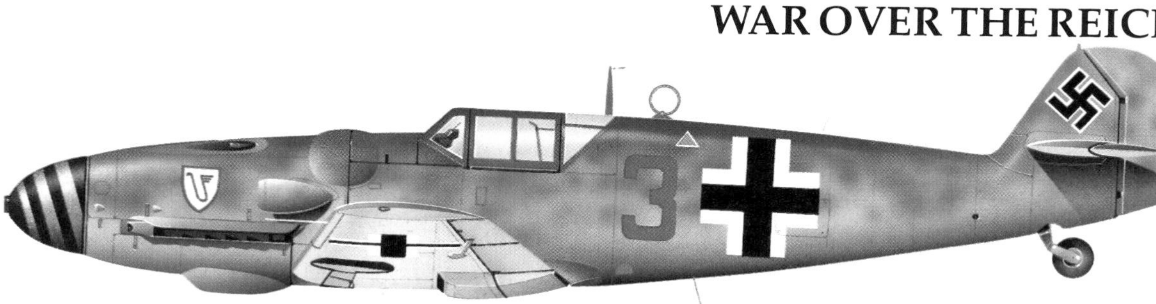

***Above:** The Messerschmitt Bf 109 was still the mainstay of the Luftwaffe fighter forces as the bombing campaign reached its peak. This is a Bf 109G-10, as flown by I/JG 3 during the German Bodenplatte offensive against Allied airfields in Belgium in January 1945.*

***Above:** This Messerschmitt Bf 109G-14/R2 served with III/JG 27 during 1945. It wears the Defence of the Reich rear fuselage band denoting its unit.*

***Above:** Bearing a disruptive wave pattern, this Junkers Ju 88G-6b of I/NJG 101 has the Lichtenstein SN-2 radar set installed and schräge Musik cannon installation, which fire obliquely upwards, allowing the night fighter to attack the unprotected underside of bombers.*

***Above:** The Ju 88 proved itself to be one of the most versatile aircraft of the war, and it excelled as a night fighter. This Ju 88G-7a of IV/NJG 6 features a fin painted to represent that of the earlier and far less effective Ju 88C variant, hoping to lull RAF aircraft into some kind of false security.*

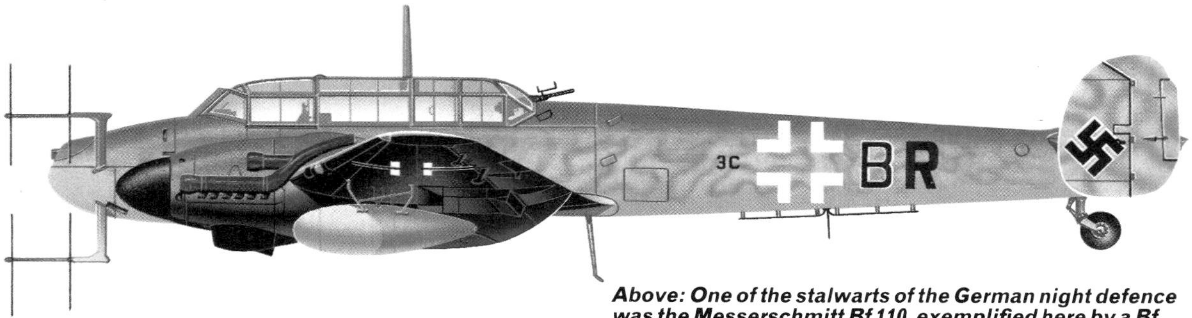

***Above:** One of the stalwarts of the German night defence was the Messerschmitt Bf 110, exemplified here by a Bf 110G-4b/R3 of 7./NJG 4. The type carried heavy armament and in certain variants the Lichtenstein radar set.*

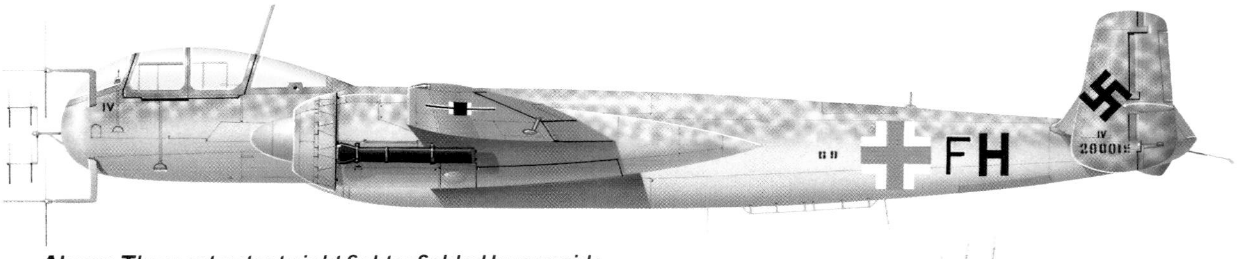

***Above:** The most potent night fighter fielded by any side during the war was the Heinkel He 219 Uhu. Luckily for the RAF it saw service in only modest numbers, but its worth was proved on its first operational sortie, when it downed five Lancasters. Notable operational firsts for the type were ejector seats and tricycle landing gear. It was the only Luftwaffe aircraft with any chance of catching RAF Mosquitoes.*

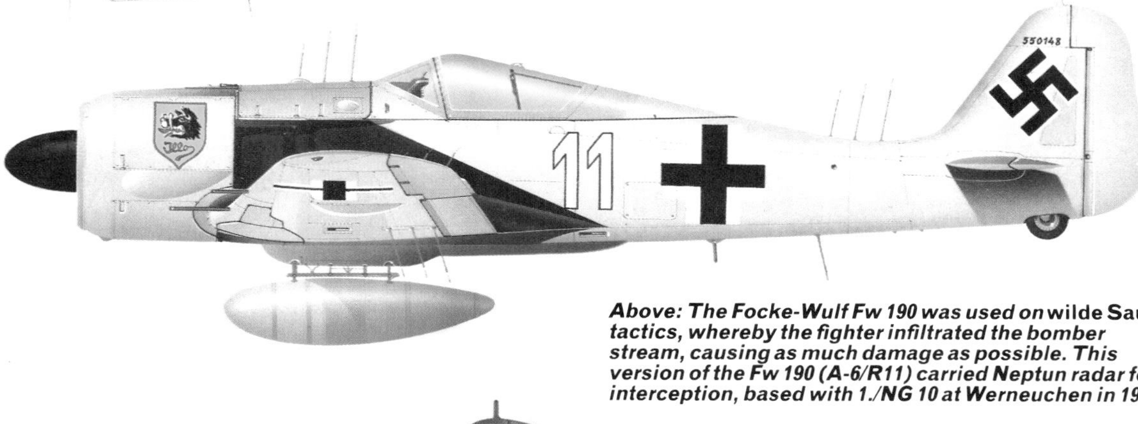

***Above:** The Focke-Wulf Fw 190 was used on wilde Sau tactics, whereby the fighter infiltrated the bomber stream, causing as much damage as possible. This version of the Fw 190 (A-6/R11) carried Neptun radar for interception, based with 1./NG 10 at Werneuchen in 1944.*

***Below:** The long-nose Fw 190D-9 was dubbed 'Dora', and was a highly capable fighter or ground attack aircraft. Many flew during Bodenplatte, while this example is seen wearing the Defence of the Reich bands of JG 4.*

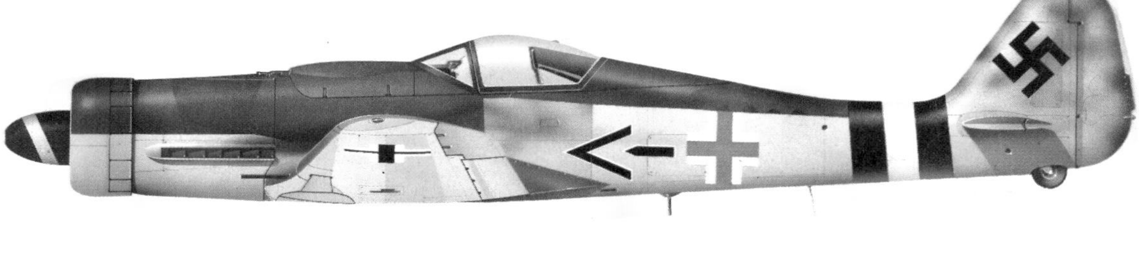

The night fighters

As well as having to contend with dense flak, the RAF bombers were up against the most experienced and capable night fighter force in the world, equipped with heavily-armed aircraft carrying sophisticated radar and radar-homing sets.

Easily the most capable of the night fighters was the Heinkel He 219, depicted here on its first sortie, when it downed five Lancasters. Heinkel designs had often suffered from political decisions, and the He 219 was no exception. Thankfully for the RAF, only small numbers reached service, yet their impact on proceedings far outweighed their proportions.

For six years, following its creation in 1934, the Luftwaffe paid scant attention to the development of night-fighters. When, on 15 May 1940, RAF bombers started attacking targets inside Germany, an immediate expedient was sought by reclassifying a single *Zerstörergruppe* (heavy fighter group), I/ZG 1, as a night fighting unit, I/NJG 1. Little success attended the efforts of this unit, and on 20 July Goering ordered Oberst Josef Kammhüber to create a night-fighter defence organization to counter the RAF's attacks. Kammhüber established a ground radar chain which extended from the Swiss border north to Denmark, each radar station comprising a pair of 'Giant Wurzburg' sets, one to track the enemy raider and one the night-fighter, to whose pilot were passed radio instructions guiding him to a visual contact.

German progress in the development of airborne radar was extremely slow in 1941, being two years behind the British, but by August that year the first set, the Lichtenstein BC, was undergoing flight trials; and entered service in 1942.

1942 was the great formative year for RAF Bomber Command under Sir Arthur Harris, with the mounting of the first '1,000-bomber' raids the introduction of the Avro Lancaster and de Havilland Mosquito bombers, the first use of the 8,000-lb bomb, and the formation of the Pathfinder Force; in the year the tonnage of bombs dropped on German industrial towns trebled. Faced with a ghastly spectre of destruction by night, the Luftwaffe redoubled its efforts to improve its night-fighters, and by the beginning of 1943 all were equipped with Lichtenstein BC or the simplified FuG 212 C-1 radar. Improvements were being introduced into the Kammhüber reporting and control system, with the result that losses among the British bombers increased rapidly during the winter of 1942-3. The introduction of the 'bomber stream', led by experienced Pathfinder crews, undoubtedly improved the effectiveness of RAF bombing, but certainly contributed to this increase as it now only required German night-fighters to intrude into the streams to achieve multiple victories among the massed raiders.

Hitherto the RAF's Mosquito bombers had operated almost unscathed over the continent, no Luftwaffe night-fighter possessing a performance approaching that of the superb British light bomber. But on 15 November 1942 there had flown the prototype of a new German custom-designed night-fighter, the Heinkel He 219, an aircraft that arrived in limited service with the Luftwaffe at Venlo in April 1943. On its first combat sortie, flown by Major Werner Streib against an RAF bomber stream heading for Düsseldorf on the night of 11/12 June, the He 219 destroyed five four-engine bombers in 30 minutes with its devastating six-cannon armament.

During the first 10 nights of operations by the small number of Venlo-based He 219s, their pilots destroyed 20 British bombers, including six Mosquitoes. It was at this point that, faced with catastrophic losses, RAF Bomber Command introduced 'Window', metal foil strips which, discharged in huge quantities by the bombers, rendered the close control of night-fighters impossible.

The Germans now quickly improvized, dividing their night fighting tactics between close control and freelance interception, code-named respectively *zahme Sau* (Tame Sow) and *wilde Sau* (Wild Sow). The former tactic, advocated by Oberst von Lossberg, consisted simply of a running commentary on the location and course of the bomber stream broadcast to patrolling night-fighter pilots, who then navigated themselves into the stream and attacked the bombers as best they could between the clouds of 'Window'. The latter, capable of being employed only on moonlit nights, involved the use of single-seat day fighters at night, a new *Jagdgeschwader*, JG 300, being created, which was later expanded into Jagddivision 30. Despite the tactic's success, the strain on pilots was too great and losses, as a result of excessive wear and tear, were prohibitive, for the same aircraft were also combating the American daylight bombers; with the onset of winter, bad weather frequently caused accidents, and operations by these aircraft gradually declined, except under the most favourable conditions.

Meanwhile the Luftwaffe had introduced new tactics and equipment to offset the RAF's jamming. The first of these, conceived by an armourer serving with II/NJG 5, Paul Mahle, consisted of a pair of 20-mm (or later 30-mm) cannon mounted amidships in the Bf 110, Ju 88 and He 219, so as to fire obliquely forwards and upwards at an angle of between 70° and 80°. This installation, codenamed *schräge Musik* (Jazz), enabled the night-fighter, whose approach to the bomber had consisted of a stern chase, to position itself below the target and open fire at the raider's engines and fuel tanks. Being thus attacked from a blind arc, the RAF crews for many months remained blissfully unaware of the lethal German tactics, and the British bombers continued over Germany without ventral armament.

Also unsuspected by the RAF was the German's ability to home on to the signals transmitted by the British H2S blind-bombing radar. Indeed, as many RAF crews switched on this equipment at the beginning of their outward journey as an aid to navigation, German night-fighters were often already well-established inside the bomber stream before the 'Window' dropping began.

Without detracting from the achievements of German pilots, those of the Allied night-fighter arm should be seen in perspective. The highest scoring RAF night-fighter pilots were Wing Commander B. A Burbridge (21 victories) and Wing Commander J. R. D. Braham (19 victories), the majority of whose successes were gained as intruder and night escort pilots over enemy territory where opportunities to shoot 'sitting ducks' were rarely gained. For that is largely what the RAF Lancasters and Halifaxes were, tied into a bomber stream, their pilots ordered to maintain a specific course and altitude in a hostile environment, their gunners cramped into freezing turrets as they searched the dark skies for darker silhouettes.

Shown in formation with two other aircraft from the same group, this polka-dotted B-24 is the lead-ship from the 458th Bomb Group. Once the brightly-painted aircraft had assembled the formation and sent it on its way to Germany, they returned to base, taking no further part in the raid.

penetration of the bomber boxes extremely hazardous. The head-on attacks, favoured by the more experienced fighter pilots, were effective only in causing the bombers to break formation but, by and large, the gun armament of the German fighters was not yet adequate to rip apart major structural components of the big American aircraft. A few of the fighters of JG 1 and JG 26 were the Fw 190A-5/R6 variant which carried a 21-cm WGr-21 rocket under each wing, a missile that was perfectly capable of blasting apart a Fortress if exploded within about 10 feet; the WGr-21 was also to be used by JG 3 and JG 27. Another novel tactic was the use of air-dropped 250-kg bombs which, released by Bf 109Gs to explode inside the bomber boxes, caused the formation to scatter – if indeed it did not actually strike an aircraft – and thus enabled stragglers to be picked off. Brainchild of Lieutenant Heinz Knocke of V/JG 1, the air-dropped bomb gained only limited success and was not widely used, particularly after the appearance of American escort fighters.

The formation of the two 'fast' fighter units, JGr 25 and JGr 50, originally conceived to combat high-flying photo-reconnissance Mosquitos, enabled the Luftwaffe to engage the B-17s' top cover – the P-47s, P-38s and, later, the P-51s – which usually flew some 8,000 feet above the bombers. Ihlefeld, himself a veteran of Spain, was one of the Luftwaffe's most experienced fighter pilots; during the war he also commanded JG 1, JG 11, JG 52 and JG 77, and he finished the war with 130 air victories, including 18 American fighters downed while leading JGr 25; he was to be awarded the Oakleaves and Swords to the Knight's Cross. Most successful of all German pilots, however, in the daylight defence of Germany was unquestionably Sergeant Herbert Rollwage, a 27-

***Left:** This photograph of a Messerschmitt Bf 110G-4d/R3 shows the diagonally-mounted aerials for the Lichtenstein SN-2 radar.*

***Right:** The Hirschgeweih (stag's antlers) aerials for the Lichtenstein SN-2 radar set were canted on later night fighters to avoid interference. This Ju 88G-7a also carries the Naxos Z set above the cockpit, which scanned the skies for RAF H2S emissions. Thus equipped, the late models of the Ju 88 were among the most capable night fighters in the world, and provided much data for post-war development by the Allies.*

year-old NCO pilot who returned home from the Mediterranean with II/JG 53 in November 1943 and who shot down 44 American heavy bombers (out of a total victory tally of 102).

The disaster that accompanied the first British use of Window in the night Battle of Hamburg had led to the creation of Hajo Herrmann's JG 300 for *wilde Sau* night defence using day fighters. In due course this force grew to three groups (JG 300, JG 301 and JG 302), but it was always emphasized that it would be too wasteful to set aside so many Bf 109s and Fw 190s solely for use on fine, moonlit nights, with the result that all had to be available for conventional day combat. This placed such a strain on pilots and aircraft alike that their availability dropped rapidly – albeit after gaining considerable success early on.

Second Schweinfurt

The second raid on Schweinfurt, on 14 October, in which a high proportion of the 60 American bombers brought down were destroyed by WGr-21 rockets, prompted desperate measures by the Luftwaffe. One of the more macabre steps taken was the formation of *Stürmstaffel* 1 at the behest of Hermann Goering himself. Staffed partly by volunteers and partly by pilots who had somehow earned the displeasure of their superiors, each man on the unit had to sign a declaration before each combat sortie that he would destroy at least one enemy aircraft – if necessary by ramming – as a means of atonement. The threat of 'cowardice in action' proved fairly effective. Equipped with specially armoured Fw 190A-6s, *Stürmstaffel* 1 gained early success and, commanded by Captain Wilhelm Moritz, formed the nucleus of IV (*Sturm*)/JG 3 in April 1944. The unit's greatest victory was gained on 7 July 1944 when, during an American raid on Leipzig, 32 bombers were brought down for the loss of only two fighters. A second unit, originally termed the *Ramm-Staffel*, was formed at Quedlinburg in March 1944 under Major Hans Günther von Kornatski; it later became II(*Sturm*)/JG 4 and flew Fw 190A-8/R7s and R8s with increased cockpit armour and 30-mm gun armament. Such was the tremendous strain on these 'assault interceptor' pilots that few lasted long in combat, and Moritz himself was obliged to give up his command owing to utter exhaustion.

One weapon employed against the bombers was the use of air-launched mortars, a WfrGr 21 unit installed under the wing of a Messerschmitt Bf 109G-6/R2. Known as Pulk-Zerstörer (formation destroyer), these aircraft launched bombs into the bomber stream, hoping to kill aircraft with the explosion. The weapon achieved most success during the second Schweinfurt raid, but thereafter the drag caused by the launcher made the 109s easy prey for escorting American fighters.

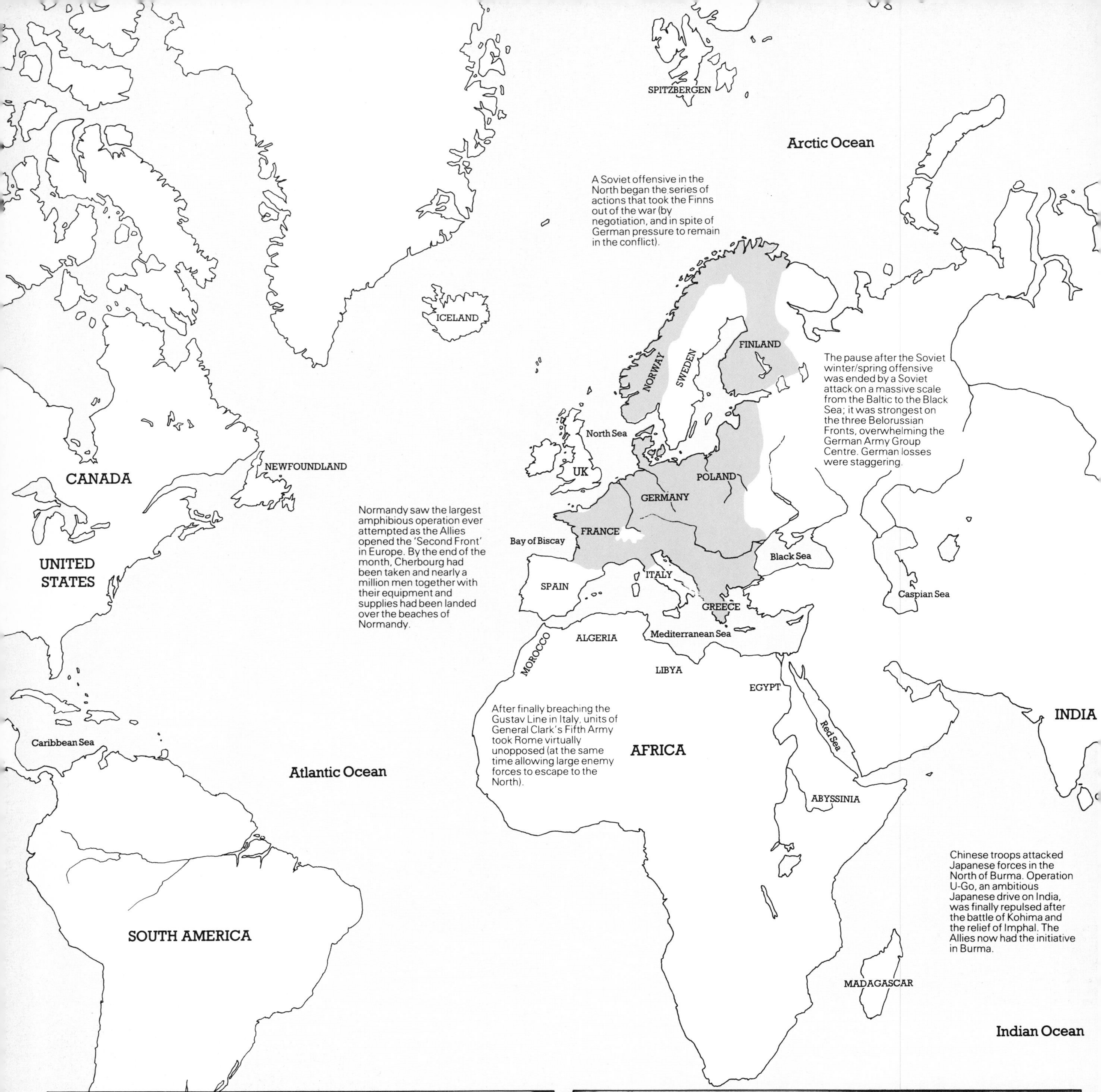
SPITZBERGEN
Arctic Ocean
A Soviet offensive in the North began the series of actions that took the Finns out of the war (by negotiation, and in spite of German pressure to remain in the conflict).
ICELAND
FINLAND
NORWAY
SWEDEN
The pause after the Soviet winter/spring offensive was ended by a Soviet attack on a massive scale from the Baltic to the Black Sea; it was strongest on the three Belorussian Fronts, overwhelming the German Army Group Centre. German losses were staggering.
North Sea
NEWFOUNDLAND
CANADA
UK
POLAND
GERMANY
Normandy saw the largest amphibious operation ever attempted as the Allies opened the 'Second Front' in Europe. By the end of the month, Cherbourg had been taken and nearly a million men together with their equipment and supplies had been landed over the beaches of Normandy.
FRANCE
Bay of Biscay
Black Sea
UNITED STATES
ITALY
SPAIN
Caspian Sea
GREECE
ALGERIA
Mediterranean Sea
MOROCCO
LIBYA
EGYPT
After finally breaching the Gustav Line in Italy, units of General Clark's Fifth Army took Rome virtually unopposed (at the same time allowing large enemy forces to escape to the North).
INDIA
Caribbean Sea
Red Sea
AFRICA
Atlantic Ocean
ABYSSINIA
Chinese troops attacked Japanese forces in the North of Burma. Operation U-Go, an ambitious Japanese drive on India, was finally repulsed after the battle of Kohima and the relief of Imphal. The Allies now had the initiative in Burma.
SOUTH AMERICA
MADAGASCAR
Indian Ocean

General Dwight D. Eisenhower pays a call on American airborne troops on the eve of their departure for Normandy. They were to spearhead the largest invasion in history.

Troops of the 1st Ukrainian Front overlook the Dniester during the Soviet Summer Offensive – a phenomenal operation which took in a front line from Leningrad to the Black Sea.

Axis Catastrophe

June 1944

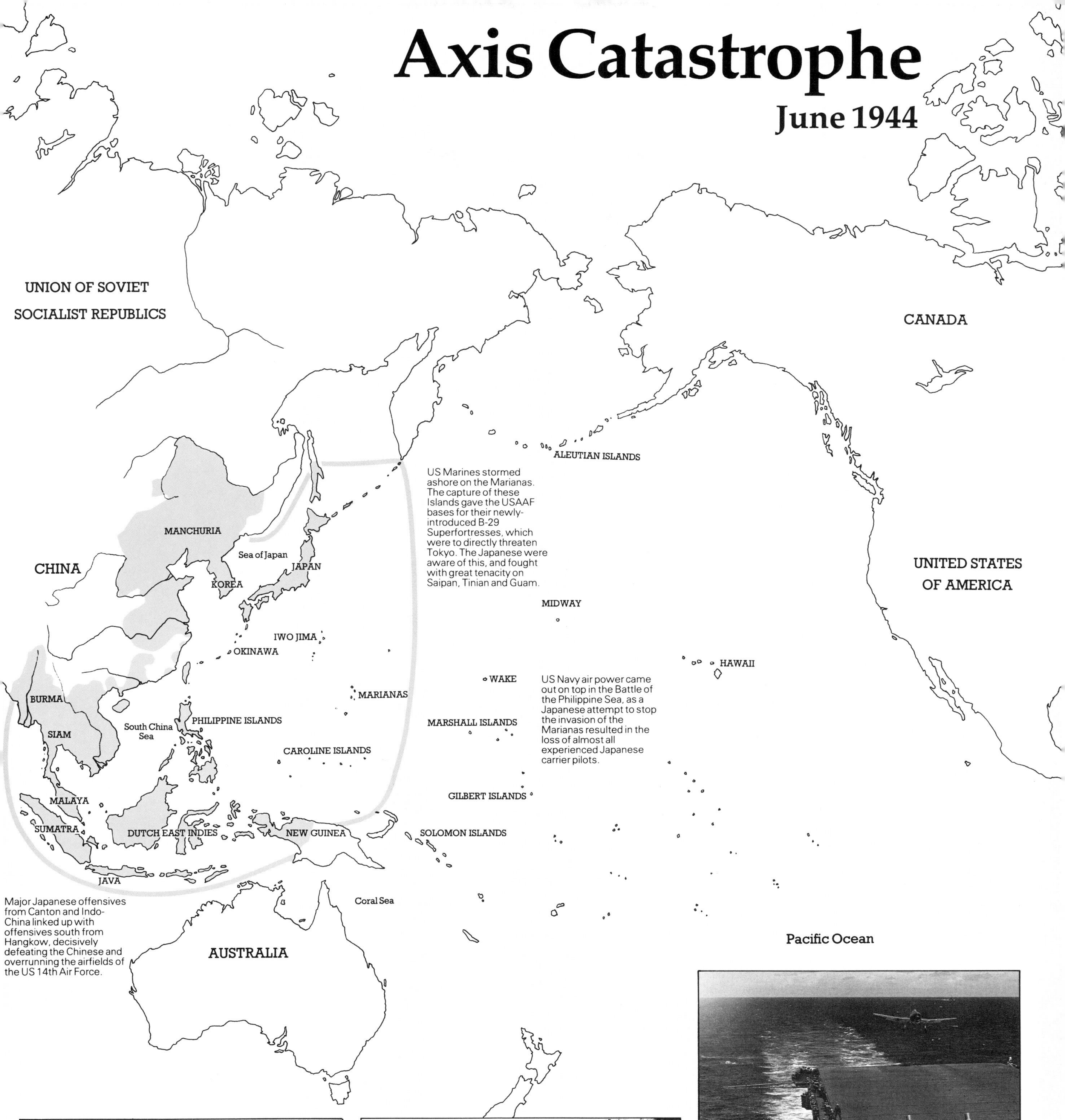
UNION OF SOVIET SOCIALIST REPUBLICS
CANADA
ALEUTIAN ISLANDS
US Marines stormed ashore on the Marianas. The capture of these Islands gave the USAAF bases for their newly-introduced B-29 Superfortresses, which were to directly threaten Tokyo. The Japanese were aware of this, and fought with great tenacity on Saipan, Tinian and Guam.
MANCHURIA
CHINA
Sea of Japan
JAPAN
KOREA
UNITED STATES OF AMERICA
MIDWAY
IWO JIMA
OKINAWA
HAWAII
WAKE
US Navy air power came out on top in the Battle of the Philippine Sea, as a Japanese attempt to stop the invasion of the Marianas resulted in the loss of almost all experienced Japanese carrier pilots.
BURMA
MARIANAS
SIAM
South China Sea
PHILIPPINE ISLANDS
MARSHALL ISLANDS
CAROLINE ISLANDS
MALAYA
GILBERT ISLANDS
SUMATRA
DUTCH EAST INDIES
NEW GUINEA
SOLOMON ISLANDS
JAVA
Coral Sea
Major Japanese offensives from Canton and Indo-China linked up with offensives south from Hangkow, decisively defeating the Chinese and overrunning the airfields of the US 14th Air Force.
AUSTRALIA
Pacific Ocean

Vehicles of the Fifth Army pass in review beneath the statue of Victor Emmanuel in Rome, the first Axis capital to fall.

The battles around Imphal and Kohima stopped the Japanese in Burma, and opened the way for an offensive by Slim's Fourteenth Army.

A Grumman F6F Hellcat comes in to land on the 'Essex' class carrier USS Lexington during a lull in the 'Marianas Turkey Shoot'.

Chapter 20

The Invasion of France

The invasion of France was one of the biggest military operations of all time. It had been contemplated for 1943, but at British insistence was postponed until 1944. The month was June, the invasion target Normandy, and in Britain millions of men and women prepared for action. Three airborne divisions, five infantry divisions and supporting armour, were to form the initial landings between the Cotentin peninsula and the Orne river, under the largest ever protective umbrella of air and sea power.

During the night of 5/6 June 1944, over a quarter of a million Allied soldiers, sailors and airmen were taking part in one of the most complex and intricate operations in the history of warfare – the D-Day landings on the beaches of Normandy, between the foot of the Cotentin Peninsula on the west, and the line of the Orne River on the east.

Nearly 5,000 ships of a hundred different types and sizes were afloat somewhere in the Channel, the majority approaching the Normandy coastline – every one in a carefully plotted position and with a specifically detailed purpose to perform – while above, squadrons of fighters ensured that the skies were clear of enemy aircraft which might interfere with the flights of 1,200 transport planes carrying 20,000 paratroops, or the gliders bearing more men, more guns, more of the special vehicles used by airborne forces. This was the culmination of years of planning, months of training, weeks of anxiety for the commanders, days of pre-action nerves for the men who would put it all to the test.

The airborne forces were the first into action.

Two US airborne divisions, the 82nd and the 101st, were to be dropped at the foot of the Cotentin Peninsula in the area astride the Merderet River and around the small town of St Mère-Eglise, in order both to spread confusion among the German troops there and to block any swift movement of German formations towards the coast on each side of the small resort of La Madeleine, designated Utah Beach, where the men of the US VII Corps would come ashore. In the event, errors in navigation by inexperienced pilots, accident, uncertain marking by Pathfinder units which had dropped beforehand, resulted in such a wide-spread dispersion of men on the ground that at dawn only 1,100 men of 101st had been concentrated out of 6,600, while 82nd were at least 4,000 men short. In addition, the whole area in the valleys of the Merderet and the Douve were subject to floods and this had been a wet spring and early summer; many of the men spent hours floundering about in the dark up to their waists in mud and water, some were drowned under the weight of kit they carried, many of the gliders carrying the airborne artillery went straight under and were not seen again until long after the battle.

Yet the total effect of the landings was a success, for the confusion among the Americans was reflected among the German formations in the area, who had not been expecting the deluge of enemy soldiers – certainly not that night, with the weather so unfavourable for parachuting – and were for a long time swamped by reports of paratroops from over a wide and apparently uncoordinated scene.

And at one place, accuracy and determination had won. One regiment of the 82nd Airborne had landed in a tightly knit group on the outskirts of St Mère-Eglise; by dawn the town was in their hands – despite a fire caused by a crashed plane, put out by French citizens at first supervised by German soldiers – and by afternoon the strongpoints had been secured, the perimeter held, more American paratroops of both divisions reporting in – and Utah Beach behind them was safely in VII Corps hands.

Field Marshal Erwin Rommel, commander of Army Group B, (the German forces on the channel coast) makes a tour of inspection of the defences along the Atlantic Wall.

At the eastern end of the landing area, the British 6th Airborne Division was charged with the task of establishing a bridgehead between the Orne River and the Caen Canal, halfway between Caen and the coast, expanding the bridgehead eastwards to form a shoulder to protect the eastern flank of the entire operation, and if possible probing further east as far as the villages of Troarn, Bures, Robehomme and Varaville, where they would blow the bridges over the River Dives.

The first down after the Pathfinders were six gliders carrying Royal Engineers and men of the 2nd Battalion, the Oxford and Bucks Light Infantry, whose task was to secure two vital bridges over the Orne and the Caen Canal. Three of them landed exactly on time and on target, and within minutes had chased away the Germans defending the eastern end of the Canal Bridge, though they had a brisk battle with those at the western end; the three gliders landing the party to attack the river bridge were not quite so close and thus ran into opposition ready and waiting for them. But the result was the same, and well before dawn a perimeter had been formed around and enclosing both bridges, the men manning it confident that they could hold on until the main forces came up from the beach-head.

To their north, paratroops had stormed the battery of 150-mm guns on the coast at Merville and, after a

Light and medium bombers were well to the fore in support of the landings, hitting German defences with pinpoint precision. A B-26 Marauder of the US 9th Air Force is seen over the beach early on the morning of 6 June.

Chronology of War: 1944

March 1
Chindit 16th Brigade marches into Burma

March 5
Chindit Brigades dropped north-east of Indaw. 'Broadway' and 'Piccadilly' strips formed

March 6
Red Army drives forward on wide front in Ukraine

March 7
Chindit strongpoint at 'Broadway' under attack

March 8
Japanese commence drive to Imphal in Operation U-Go

March 9
Japanese launch offensive on Bougainville

March 11
Indian troops take Buthidaung in Arakan. Russians take Berislav on Dnieper

March 13
British landings on Arakan coast

March 14
British forces retire from Tiddim towards Imphal in face of Japanese assault

March 15
Heavy Allied attack on Cassino preceded by bombardment

March 16
Japanese cross Chindwin and drive towards Kohima-Imphal road

March 17
British forces destroy bridge on Kohima-Dimapur road. New Zealanders reach Cassino railway station

March 18
Heavy raid on Hamburg. Over 3,000 tons of bombs dropped. Indian division flown from Arakan to Imphal

March 22
Red Army reaches Pervomaisk

March 24
Colonel Orde Wingate, commander of the Chindits, killed in plane crash

March 27
Lentaigne takes command of Chindit Forces

March 29
Siege of Imphal. US Task Force opens attack in Carolines

March 30
RAF raid Nuremberg, 95 aircraft lost.

March 31
UK civilian casualties in March 279 killed, 633 injured

April 2
Russians enter Romania

April 5
British forces in Kohima surrounded

April 10
Red Army liberates Odessa

April 11
Red Army seize Kerch and advance on Simferopol. Germans retreat into Sevastopol

April 13
Red Army captures Simferopol and Feodosia

April 16
Red Army liberates Yalta and Tarnopol, and cuts Axis front in half

April 18
British reinforcements link up with forces inside Kohima

April 22
US troops land in Hollandia, New Guinea

April 24
US War Department announces that Japanese homeland must be invaded

The invasion of Normandy was the greatest seaborne military operation in history, which required unprecedented numbers of vessels to land more than five divisions the first day alone.

desperate hand-to-hand fight amid a tangle of machine-gun posts, tunnels and earthworks, had destroyed the guns – one by firing two shells through it simultaneously, the other three by gammon bombs – and routed the 130-man garrison at a cost of 66 dead and 30 wounded. None of the paratroopers was over 21 years old.

To their south as far as La Bas de Ranville, the 3rd and 5th Parachute Brigades were in close action with men of the German 716th Division and of the 21st Panzer Division, but like the American airborne troops 63 miles away at the other end of the Normandy beach-head, they were remembering with some comfort the words of one of their commanders – 'Do not be daunted if chaos reigns. It undoubtedly will!' and it was affecting their enemy more than themselves.

The British ashore

Not long after dawn the commander of the panzer division, General Feuchtinger, whose men and armour could undoubtedly have rolled over the two parachute brigades had he been allowed to continue his arrangements to do so, received an urgent message from the Paris headquarters of his Commander-in-Chief, Field Marshal Rommel. He was ordered to break off the action and remove himself and his formations 30 miles west to attack American units pouring ashore between Vierville and St Honorine, on what the Allies had christened Omaha Beach.

By this time, the British 3rd Infantry Division and the 22nd Armoured Brigade were coming ashore between Ouistreham and Lion-sur-Mer on Sword Beach behind the paratroops, and the commandos of the 1st Special Service Brigade who had landed on the extreme left flank of the invasion force were racing through to aid the men holding those bridges and the embattled areas beyond. They reached the Oxford and Bucks Light Infantry and the men of the 7th Parachute Battalion who had been helping them at the Canal and Orne bridges by 2.00 p.m. – by which time they had by-passed several enemy strongpoints, destroyed a battery and marched nine miles – and by evening they were through to the positions around and past Ranville. The eastern shoulder of Operation Overlord was firmly held.

Further west between Arromanches and St Aubin were the Gold and Juno Beaches, Gold the objective of British XXX Corps consisting of the 8th and 50th Infantry Divisions with the 47th Royal Marine Commando on the right flank, and Juno the target for the 3rd Canadian Infantry Division and the 2nd Canadian Armoured Brigade. The DD tanks of General Hobart's 79th Armoured Division preceded the bulk of both forces. On the right, on Gold Beach, they were followed by the Flail tanks, lashing the sand amidst eruptions of mines, most of them losing their tracks but one at least beating a lane right across the beach to reach the coast road, while on each side the Bobbin tanks laid mattresses over patches of soft blue clay, and bridging tanks flung their Arks over the craters and ditches to make way for the main armour coming in behind.

For all, the actual landings had been traumatic. High winds and seas had added their own dimensions to the turmoil and thunder of the naval bombardment, the continual roar of aircraft, the crash of bombs and the whine of bullets. On both beaches some of the lighter landing craft, driven like surfboats by the wind and sea, fouled underwater obstacles and overturned, spilling their cargoes into the waves, or rode on in, half-sinking but still afloat, to skid at any angle through the surf and on to the sand. And all through the chaos of broken ships and wading men, the LCTs (Landing Craft, Tank) crashed through to the beaches, lowered their ramps and disgorged their vital cargoes, first Hobart's 'Funnies' – which on these beaches fully justified all hopes for them – then the Shermans for the main armoured thrusts.

By 11.00 a.m. 7 lanes had been cleared on Gold Beach, and 12 on Juno, and both tanks and infantry were through them, blasting the strongpoints, hurling grenades into pill-boxes, the infantry by-passing defence posts obviously too strong for them and leaving them for the armour, everyone pressing on to deepen the bridgehead to make room for the divisions and brigades coming behind. By nightfall, the two beaches had linked into a single bridgehead 12 miles wide along the coast, and between 3 and 5 miles deep. The main road betwen Douvres and Bayeux was well behind the forward thrusts.

At the western edge of the invasion beaches, American fortunes had been mixed. The first waves had gone ashore at Utah by 6.30 a.m. under the blasting roar of the main naval bombardment, the

Above: Following the establishment of a beach-head, the Allied fighter-bombers could move into makeshift strips to continue operations against defenders. Shown is a Hawker Typhoon bombing up prior to a mission.

dark sky above wild with the roar of aircraft, the scream of shells and whine of bullets, the beach ahead screened by an opaque curtain of dust and sand shot with fire. And 300 men of 2nd Battalion of the 8th Regiment waded the last 200 yards waist-deep in tumbled seas, to walk up the beach with the comforting shapes of tanks alongside them – and not a shot fired in opposition. By midday, three battalions of 22nd Regiment were ashore behind them, and soon afterwards the battalions of 12th Regiment were ashore and moving inland.

Six men had been killed by mines on the beaches, and in all that day the 8th and 22nd Regiments lost only 12 men between them; but by nightfall they were all extremely uncomfortable, having spent most of their time ashore wading, often up to their armpits, through the flooded areas in which their airborne comrades had splashed and cursed the previous night. During the night of 6/7 June they consolidated on the pockets of dry – or at least above-water – ground upon which the paratroops had positioned themselves. But further east at Omaha Beach, matters were very different. Omaha Beach was a shallow arc of sand between outcropping rocks, the sands sloping up, in places to a sea-wall, but for most of its

Above: The complicated Allied disinformation campaign to convince the Germans that the invasion would come across the Pas-de-Calais did not mean that Normandy was unprotected. Indeed, since Rommel's arrival millions of mines had been laid.

General Dwight D. Eisenhower speaks to men of the 101st Airborne Division as they prepare for their assault in the early hours of D-Day.

US Troops storm ashore from a landing craft manned by the United States Coast Guard. The Americans suffered mixed fortunes on their beaches.

Above: High and dry at low tide, a variety of shipping overlooks a Royal Navy Beachmaster's position which newly landed troops move past. The Beachmaster had the important task of organizing the inevitable chaos produced on the beach by landing the maximum of men and equipment in the shortest time.

Left: An RAF Mustang flies over a village in Normandy after attacking a German transport column. Note the prominent 'invasion stripes' carried on the wing to clearly identify the aircraft as Allied.

length to a natural barrier of heavy shingle rising in places to some 10 feet in height. It was, in fact, an ideal defensive position and the highly efficient German infantry division there – the 352nd – had turned it into a near death-trap.

At each end, gun positions in the shoulders of the bluffs could pour enfilade fire on to the sea approaches; behind the shingle bank and sea-wall they had built a system of linking pill-boxes, machine-

The Allied landings in Normandy Operation Overlord

Under the overall command of General Sir Bernard L. Montgomery, American, British and Canadian troops were landed from more than 4,000 landing ships onto five main beaches on 6 June 1944.

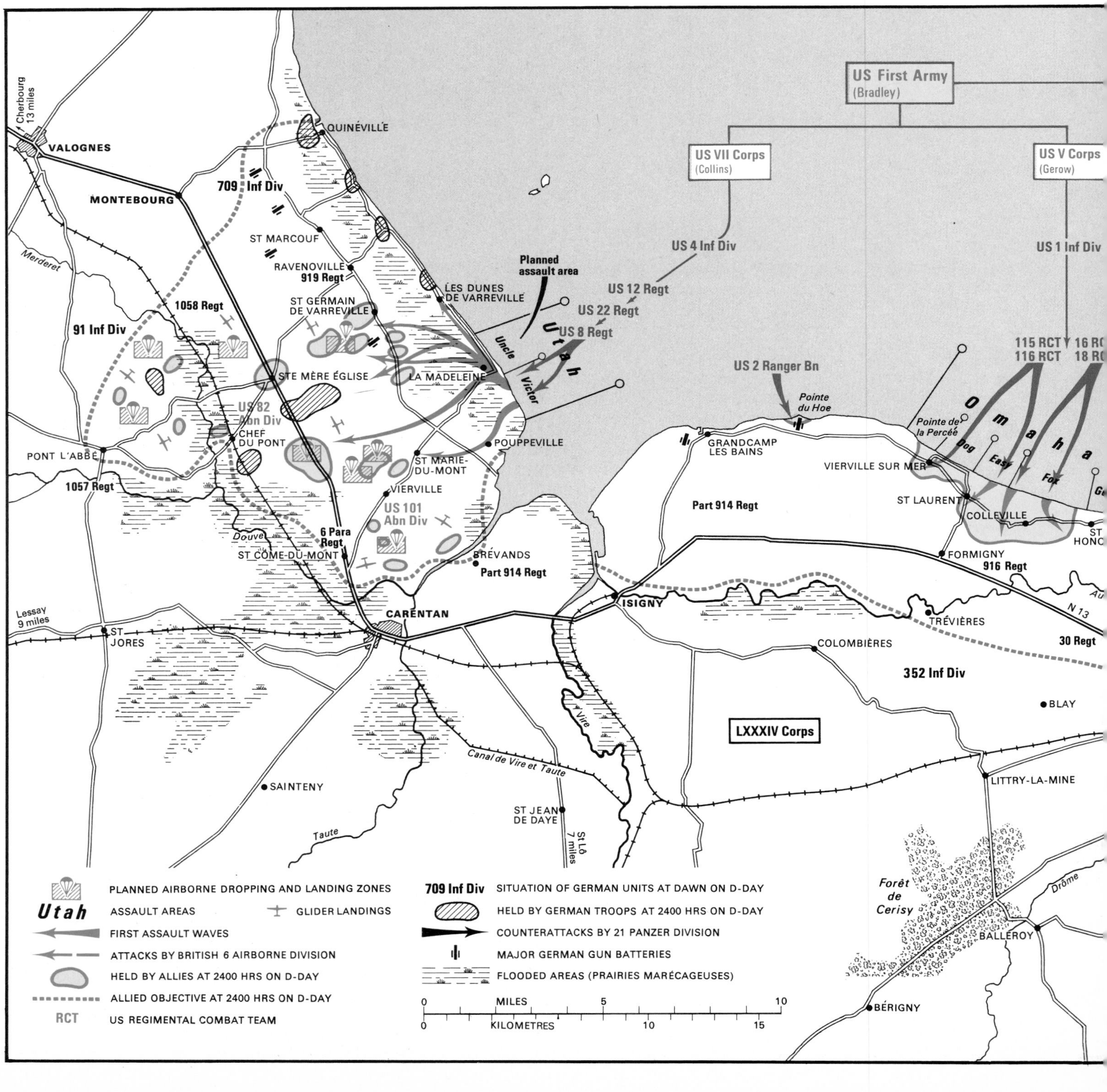

gun posts and 88-mm gun emplacements, while the sandy beach was itself a labyrinth of stakes and racked obstacles, some of them booby-trapped and all with mines sown between them. Behind the defences along the wall and shingle lay a further system of trenches, strongpoints and minefields; it was a copybook example of a shore position, plotted and equipped to repel a seaborne assault.

That assault was now to be mounted by the US V Corps under General Gerow – 34,000 men with 3,300 vehicles carried in nearly 200 assorted landing craft, approaching across a wind-tossed sea which here was producing 6-foot waves which swamped the small craft and blew the larger ones off course. Even worse for them all, General Omar Bradley, commanding the US First Army, had refused Montgomery's offer of all except the DD swimming tanks of Hobart's specialized armour, so there would be no Flails, no Crocodiles, no Bobbin tanks or Arcs to help the US infantry across that dreadful expanse and out into the relatively clear areas inland.

They very nearly had no DD tanks either, for by a piece of almost unbelievable misjudgement, the commander of the LCT carrying some of the massive vehicles began decanting them into those unruly seas 6,000 yards – nearly three-and-a-half miles! – offshore. Twenty-seven sank – with their crews – almost immediately, two by excellent seamanship and better luck reached the shore but with badly

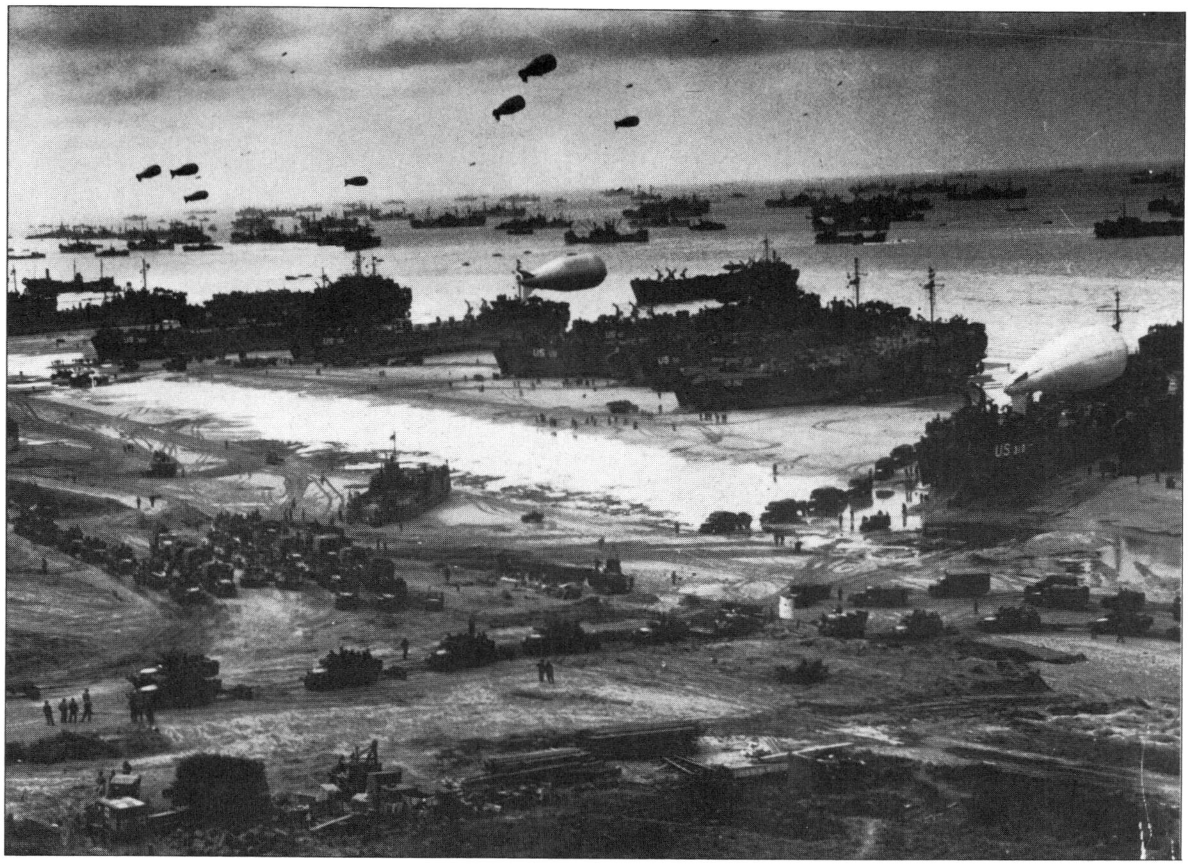

More than two million tons of matériel were stockpiled all along the south coast of England. Here, the mammoth task of unloading begins under a protective line of barrage balloons.

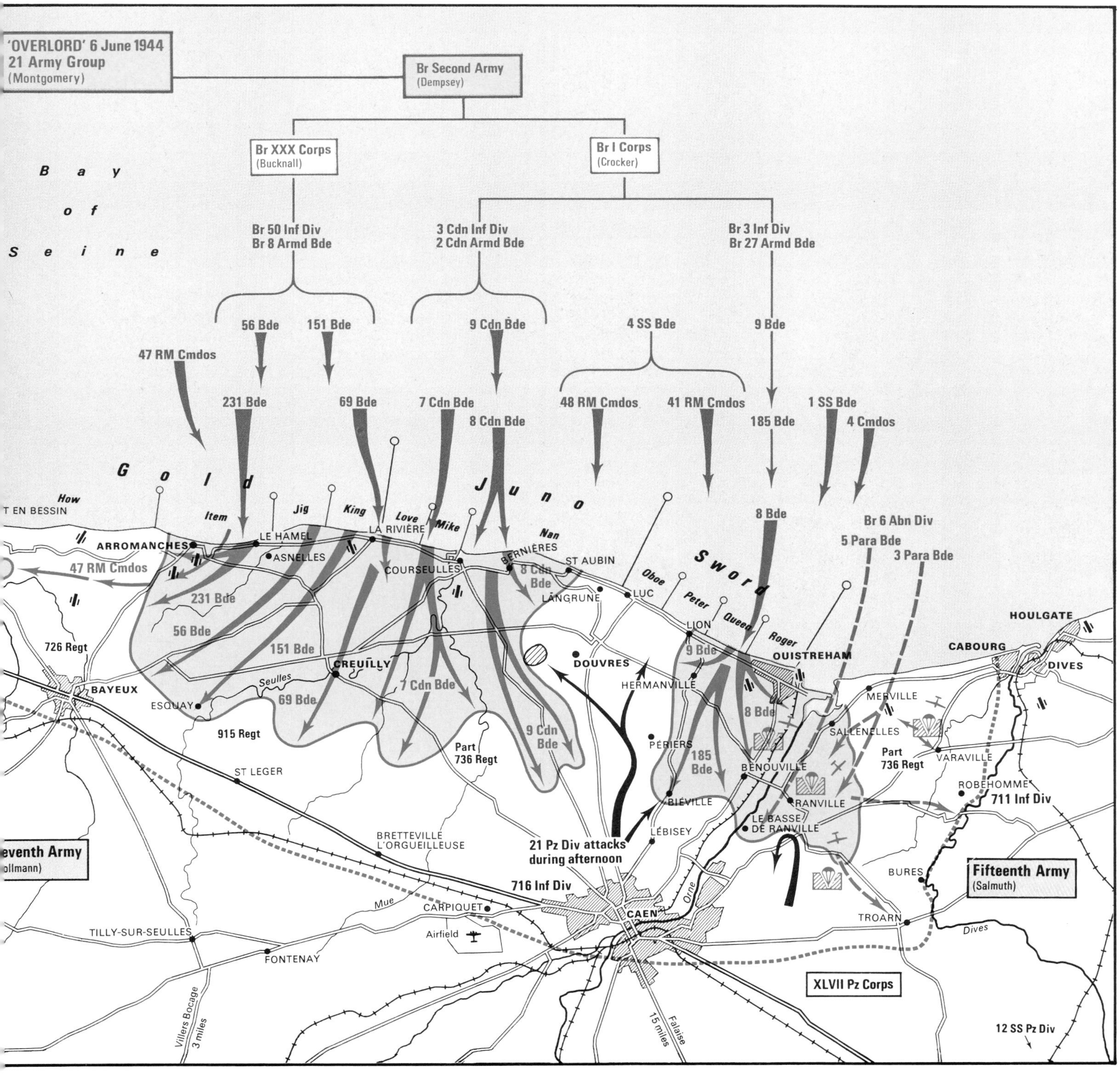

Above: Normandy fields were littered with gliders after the Allied airborne assault. Gliders enabled large numbers of troops to be landed together, but the landings were fraught with danger.

Above: British troops in a Bren gun carrier pass a crash-landed glider between Ranville and Amfreville after the seaborne troops had linked up with the airborne forces.

shaken crews and depleted fuel tanks, and three were saved by the jamming of the ramp as they had been about to follow their companions, and were thus safely landed when the LCT went ashore.

A fate similar to that of the DD tanks – but through weather conditions and enemy action – overcame many of the DUKWs taking in the supporting artillery. All the 105-mm howitzers went to the bottom save one, a whole battalion of infantry support cannon was lost with most of the guns of 7th Field Artillery, while the engineers' tractors and bulldozers were spilled off their wallowing carriers like refuse tipped into a dump.

All these tragedies at sea were taking place under a positive sheet of steel and sound as, with 40 minutes still to go to touch-down, the main armament of suporting battleships roared out, augmented by shells of smaller calibres from cruisers and destroyers, while 1,000 tons of bombs were dropped by 300 Liberators on the known strongpoints along the sea-wall and shingle bank and on the areas behind – for Intelligence had provided so many details of the defences here that it is still difficult to understand why the help of the 'Funnies' had been refused. They would have saved so many lives.

When the barrage lifted, there was only a brief pause until the guns of the defenders opened up; shells hit the leading craft as they slewed in across the waves to hit the beaches, machine-gun and rifle bullets poured into the landing craft immediately the ramps went down, and men fell into the surf, dead before they hit it. On the right flank, an LCT received a direct hit which killed all but one of the company officers of the leading tank battalion.

Nevertheless, pressure and sheer numbers were putting men ashore – exhausted, bewildered, half-drowned, their equipment and themselves soaked, leaderless if they were GIs, bereft of their men if they were officers. And if they were in the centre of the beach area they were for the first half hour without any protection in the form of tanks, or guns heavier than they ones they carried. They were in more danger when they crawled ashore than when they had been in the water.

But, slowly and surely, the engineers who had landed began to organize and tackle the tasks they had been trained for – hardly ever the ones in which they specialized, and never with the men with whom they had trained. Behind them, as the tide rose so did

Below: US Army glider pilots are ferried from the beach on their way back to England. British glider pilots were not so lucky and had to remain in action with the airborne forces.

Left: DD (Duplex Drive) amphibious Sherman tanks pass through Ouistreham. Note the twin propellers under the folded-down flotation screens.

Chronology of War: 1944

April 28
US and Chinese armies drive up Mogaung valley towards Myitkyina

April 30
UK civilian casualties in April 146 killed, 226 injured

May 3
British and Indians take control of Buthidaung road, Arakan

May 7
Red Army attack on Sevastopol opens

May 9
Sevastopol re-taken. USAF and RAF open offensive on French airfields in preparation for D-Day

May 11
US Fifth and British Eighth Armies prepare for joint onslaught on Gustav Line

May 12
Last German forces evacuated from Crimea

May 13
Allies take St Angelo, Castelforte and open road to Rome

May 15
Kesselring orders controlled withdrawal of Germans from Gustav to Adolf Hitler Line

May 16
Fifth and Eighth Armies at last through Gustav positions. Last Japanese units driven from Kohima Ridge

May 17
US troops land on Wadke island off the north coast of New Guinea. Kesselring orders evacuation of Germans from Cassino. Allies capture Myitkyina airfield, north Burma

May 18
Polish troops capture Cassino Monastery. Allied attack on Myitkyina town repulsed. Field Marshal von Rundstedt appointed to command anti-invasion forces in western Europe, Field Marshal Rommel and General Blaskowitz to command Army Groups

May 19
Merrill's Marauders and Chinese troops surround Myitkyina

May 22
Canadian troops break through Adolf Hitler Line in Italy

May 23
Operation Buffalo; under strong air support US and British troops launch breakout from Anzio

May 25
Anzio troops link up with Fifth Army troops at Terracina. In Burma Chindits withdraw from 'Blackpool' under heavy attack

May 27
US Marines land on Biak, New Guinea

May 31
UK civilian casualties in May: nil

June 3
End of Battle of Kohima

June 4
General Mark Clark and the US Fifth Army enter Rome

June 5
Allied airborne forces dropped in Normandy

June 6
D-Day: Allies land forces on French coast between Cotentin Peninsula and River Dives

June 7
Allies reach Bayeaux. US forces assemble on Eniwetok and Kwajalein for attack on Marianas Islands

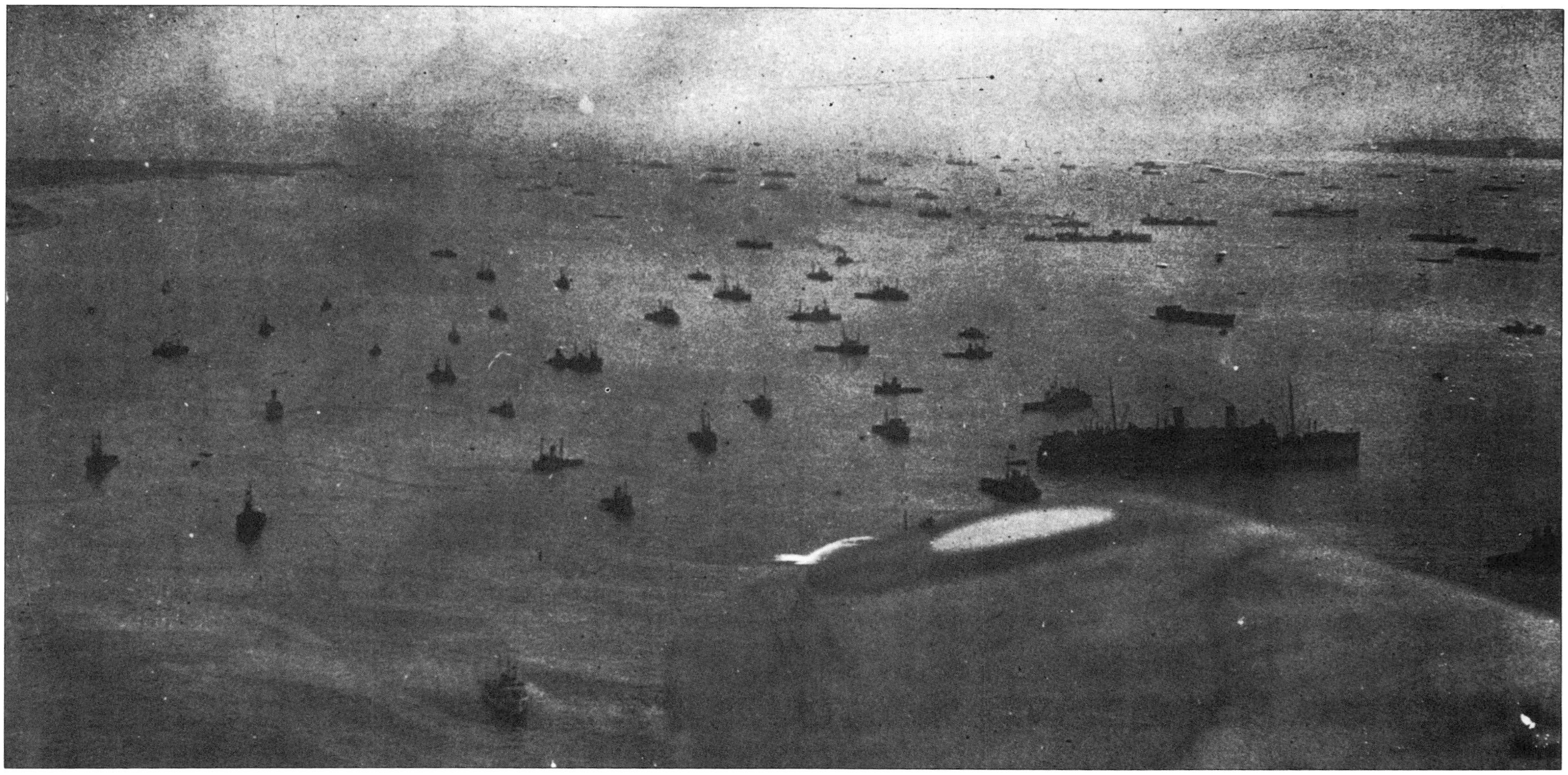

Part of the Normandy invasion fleet, seen from the air. Over 1,200 warships, 4,126 landing vessels, 1,500 merchantmen and auxiliaries were in action on D-Day alone, along with nearly 14,000 aircraft.

the pressure of men dumped on to the beach, as more and more craft forced their way through the debris offshore and as the German defenders began to run out of ammunition or became casualties themselves. Destroyer captains, realizing the extent of the catastrophe they were witnessing, took their ships close inshore and blasted the enemy strongpoints at close range.

After three hours, with the foreshore a wilderness of burning vehicles, wrecked craft and shattered men, no exits from the beach yet opened and none of the main enemy positions yet attacked, it would have seemed to an objective observer that the battle for Omaha Beach had been lost by the invaders; but in fact, the tide of men into the beach-head was now unstoppable as they were in small ships at the mercy of a following sea, which would deposit them at their destination whatever the circumstances. By the early afternoon, first platoons, then companies, then whole battalions collected themselves, and with obvious destruction staring at them if they stayed where they were, climbed over the nearest obstructions and began fighting their way through the trenches and minefields behind. Their numbers and their training gradually turned a dreadful defeat into a grudging victory, the line of their advance crept southwards across the road linking the villages of Vierville, St Laurent and Colleville, and by nightfall the Omaha beach-head was nearly two miles deep in the centre and five miles wide along the coast.

Above: A purpose-built night fighter, the Northrop P-61A Black Widow first saw action in Europe in July 1944.

Suppression of German coastal defences was a prime requisite for the invading Allies, one of the most effective methods being the LCT(R).

Below: An RAF Hawker Typhoon flies over a British transport column in Normandy. The overwhelming Allied air superiority allowed Allied vehicles to mass unhindered behind the Front, while German vehicles could only move safely by night.

NIGHTFALL ON D-DAY

Once the fighting had moved inland, the Allied logistical organization managed to deliver reinforcements and hundreds of thousands of tons of supplies through to the front lines.

German reaction on D-Day had been slow and confused for a number of reasons. Their intelligence had given them only general warning that an Allied invasion was certain, but practically everyone agreed that the weather ruled it out for the moment. Although Field Marshal Rundstedt in Paris felt that the reports arriving on his desk that morning merited instant and weighty counteraction, he half-believed that it all might be a feint and that the main Allied landings would eventually be made in the Pas de Calais. So did Keitel in Berlin when Rundstedt phoned him, and he steadfastly refused to wake the Führer who, he knew, was also of the opinion that the real thrust would be made by the Allies across the narrowest part of the Channel.

As for Rommel, whose responsibility the defences of the Atlantic Wall had been for the last six months, he was in Germany on a trip on which he hoped both to see his wife and to talk to Hitler about the need for more panzer divisions west of the Seine, when he received the news of the invasion; immediately he turned back to his headquarters. He had already voiced his opinion that any landings must be thrown back in the first 24 hours – feint or not – but even he had not the authority to move significantly powerful formations, such as panzer or even infantry divisions, without permission from Berlin. Had he possessed even the authority of a corps commander in the Allied armies, two panzer divisions – 12th SS Panzer and the Panzer Lehr Division – would have been waiting on the St Lô-Carentan line and the story of 6 June might have been far different.

Left: Some of the first German prisoners taken on D-Day rest while awaiting evacuation after treatment for their wounds.

Below left: A patrol of the 82nd Airborne Division moves warily through a churchyard in St Marcouf, aiming to link up with troops breaking out of Utah Beach.

As it was, by nightfall the beach-heads were formed and held, and during the days which followed a combination of continual air attacks under total Allied air supremacy and the valiant efforts of the French Resistance severely hampered every effort made by Rommel's armies to move into position and throw the invaders back into the sea – or even to confine them tightly inside the borders they had seized. By the evening of 10 June all beach-heads had linked up, and the area the Allied armies held ran continuously from the Dives on the east to the Douve on the west, at least 5 miles deep and in places nearly 10.

Moreover, those truly astonishing engineering phenomena, the Mulberry Harbours, were in the process of assembly off St Laurent in the American sector and off Arromanches in the British, thus bringing closer to fulfilment the Allied plans for introducing into northern France a force of 26 to 30 divisions – 2,000,000 men, 500,000 vehicles and some 3,000,000 tons of supplies – during the next two months. Hopes were high for an early breakout, and General Montgomery professed himself satisfied with results so far, for the centre of the beachhead was now firm and unthreatened, the flanks firm and strong enough to hold off the three German infantry divisions facing the Americans on the west, and the six divisions – three of them panzer divisions – around Caen at the eastern end.

The LST(2) was a compromise between the seagoing quality of the first experimental Tank Landing Ships and the ease of construction of landing craft. It succeeded admirably, but such was the demand for the diesel-powered US-built design (more than could be supplied) that a modified steam powered variant was built in Britain as the LST(3), distinguishable by its funnel. The mixed cargo on deck includes an LCT.

The amphibious armada at Normandy

The greatest amphibious operation in history had participants both great and small, from the lonely paratrooper in the night to the commander of a bombarding battleship. Yet without one group of unglamourous vessels, there would have been no invasion. Largely unsung, the amphibious warfare vessels and their crews made the invasion possible.

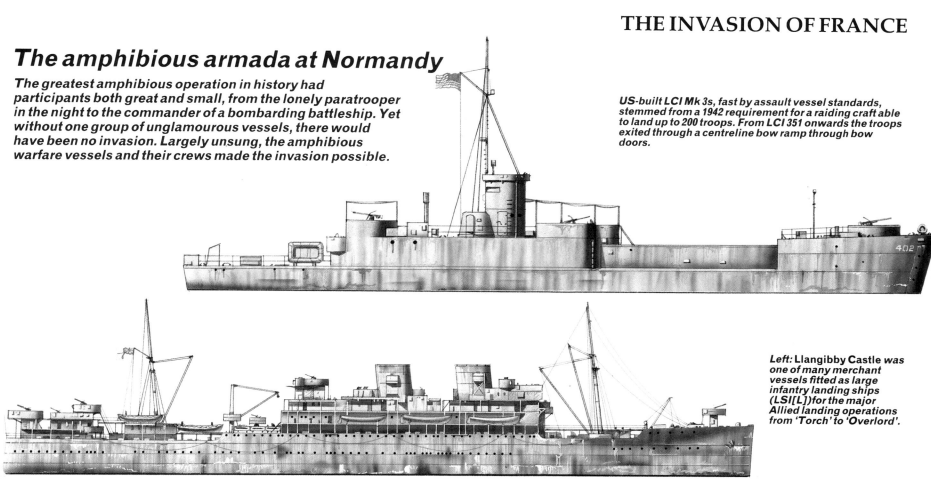

*US-built **LCI Mk 3s**, fast by assault vessel standards, stemmed from a 1942 requirement for a raiding craft able to land up to 200 troops. From LCI 351 onwards the troops exited through a centreline bow ramp through bow doors.*

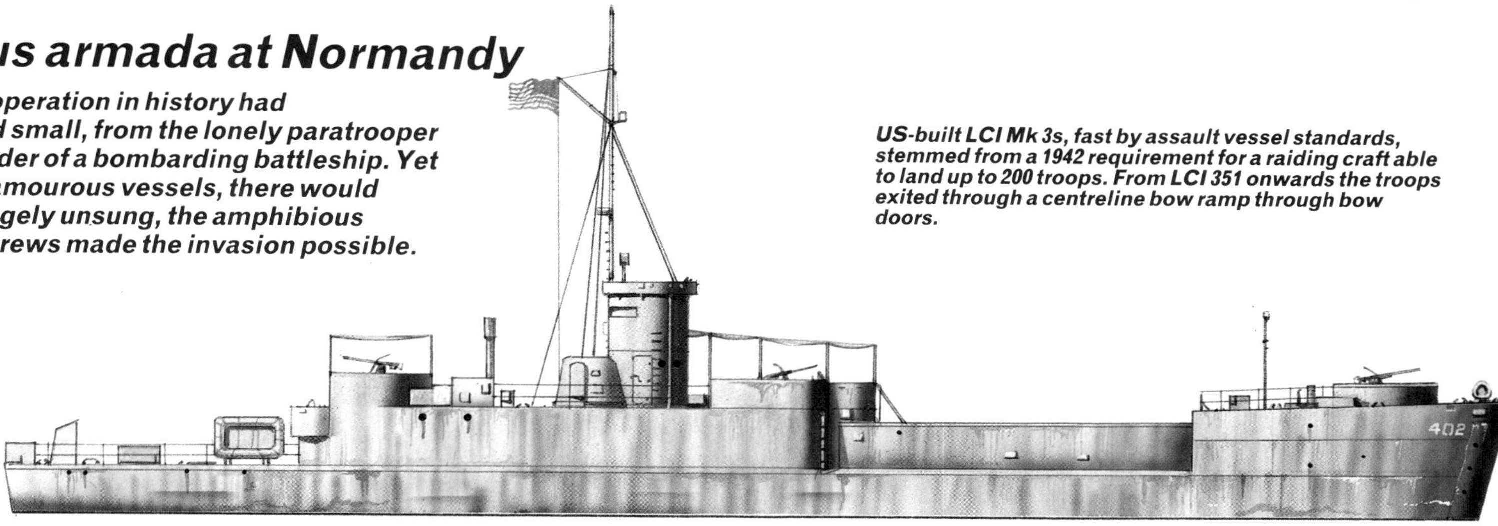

Left: **Llangibby Castle** *was one of many merchant vessels fitted as large infantry landing ships (LSI[L]) for the major Allied landing operations from 'Torch' to 'Overlord'.*

Right: *Formerly a liner, the* **USS Ancon** *was taken over in 1942 as a transport, but soon became an amphibious force flagship with the US Navy. She was used as an LSH (Landing Ship Headquarters) at Sicily, Salerno, Normandy and Okinawa, and was present at the Japanese surrender.*

Left: *A short, beamy, drive-through craft, the* **LCT(6)** *was designed to be portable on the deck of an LST, to be able to ferry vehicles ashore or to act as a bridge if the draught of the mother ship was too great.*

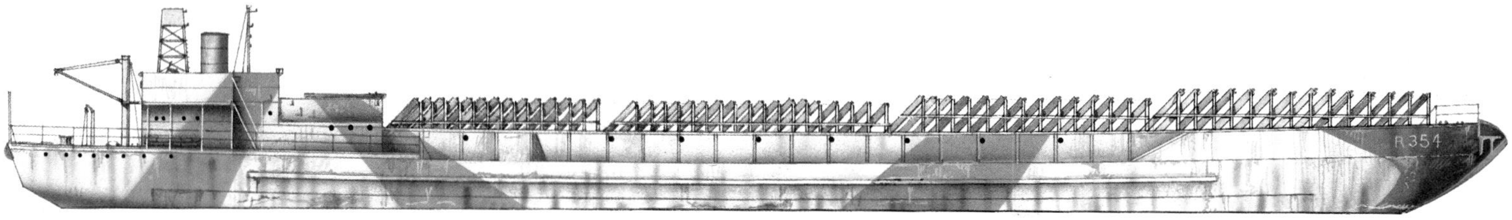

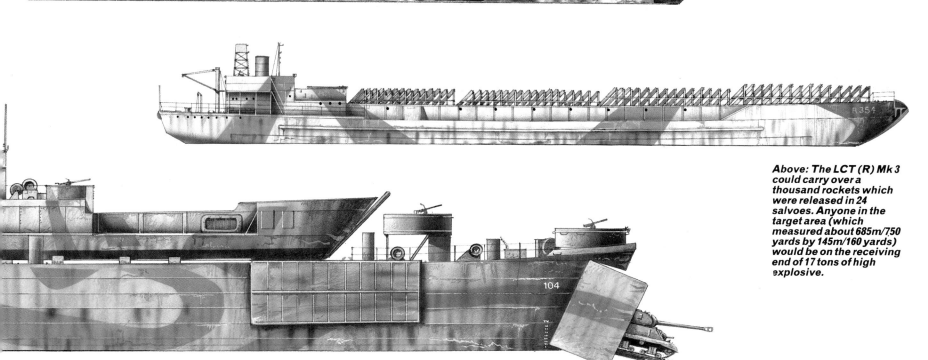

Above: *The* **LCT (R) Mk 3** *could carry over a thousand rockets which were released in 24 salvoes. Anyone in the target area (which measured about 685m/750 yards by 145m/160 yards) would be on the receiving end of 17 tons of high explosive.*

Troopers belonging to the 13/18 Hussars operating south of Caen take up a defensive position at the side of the road after losing their tank to a German mine.

US troops under fire at St Lô duck across a typical hedgerow-lined, sunken lane typical of the bocage country. Note the knocked out German Panther tank in the foreground.

The only disappointment had been that Caen had not fallen to the British by the end of the first day, and now was occupied by a strong German force which was obviously determined to hold this vital road and communications centre – not only as an anchor point for attacks on the beach-head, but also for the level ground immediately south, from which Luftwaffe planes could have operated if only the Expeditionary Air Force had allowed them off the ground. Even in this situation, however, Montgomery found some cause for satisfaction. Caen was as essential to the defence against his forces as it was to him for the next stage of his campaign; therefore the Germans would have to feed more and more strength into its defence as his own pressure against it grew, and in doing so they would leave the American armies at the western end free, first to build up their strength, then to fight their way through the tangle of the *bocage* country – small fields bordered by high banks and hedgerows, liberally sown with hidden German machine-guns, mortars and anti-tank weapons – and burst out towards Avranches and Brittany beyond.

The battle at the eastern end of the bridgehead therefore grew in ferocity as the days passed, more German panzer divisions made their way around the blown bridges, collapsed tunnels and ripped-up roads towards Caen, and the British strength was concentrated more and more in the area. On 10 June, after careful preparation, 7th Armoured Division was launched out of the end of the beach-head with 51st Highland Division crossing the Orne into the tiny airborne bridgehead still there, and in two days of fierce fighting swung around to cross the Caen-Villers bocage road – only to run into the redoubtable SS tank commander Michael Wittmann in his Tiger tank, who abruptly halted the advance, destroyed 25 mixed Shermans, Comets and Cromwells, and provoked an abrupt change of tactical plan for the British.

Obviously, an even more carefully planned and more powerful offensive was needed before Caen would be wrested from the Germans; so Montgomery massed the divisions of the newly arrived VIII Corps just south of the original junction between Gold and Juno Beaches for a proposed onslaught on 23 June. But on 19 June a summer gale of quite extraordinary ferocity sprang up, wrecked the Mulberry in the American sector, severely damaged the one at Arromanches and effectively halted all reinforcement of the invasion force for three days, thus causing a crucial imbalance of the opposing forces. So far, the Allied build-up had managed to keep significantly ahead of the Germans, but by the end of the storm the 10 American and 10 British divisions inside the bridgehead – including two armoured – were opposed by 18 German divisions outside, of which five were armoured.

It was 26 June before Operation Epsom could now be launched, when the 'furious Scotsmen' – as the Germans later described them – of the 15th Scottish, and the Wessex men of the 43rd Division and the Hussars and Yeomen of the 11th Armoured, drove south from Bretteville l'Orgueilleuse to Cheux and then to Tormeauville, aiming for the major prize of Hill 112. German reaction was as efficient and as rapid as the conditions allowed, and the battle raged on until 1 July with the panzer divisions holding the onslaught but paying a dreadful price – as Montgomery intended them to – under the constant bombing of Allied aircraft and the heavy and remarkably accurate and effective shelling by 15- and 16-inch naval guns of the battleships, still on patrol off the beach-head. The Shermans of 11th Armoured eventually drew back from Hill 112, but they left behind the wrecks of over 100 panzers among those of their own tanks – and the Shermans could be quickly replaced, while the Tigers and Panthers could not.

Above: A PzKpfw V Panther is seen on the way to the invasion front in 1944. This tank was superior to any of the Western allies' tanks; only the Sherman Firefly had a gun that could knock it out at a respectable range.

British Cromwell tanks are seen east of the river Orne, 8 July 1944. The Cromwell, which first saw action in Normandy, was the last and best of a long series of British cruiser tank designs.

Chronology of War: 1944

June 9
In Normandy St Mère Eglise and Trevières liberated. Allied aircraft operate from French airfields. German counterattack west of Caen beaten off. Russian offensive on Karelian Isthmus opens

June 10
Allied bridgeheads in Normandy linked up. Montgomery establishes headquarters in bridgehead. Carentan taken by US troops

June 13
First V1 flying-bombs land in England

June 15
US Marines land on Saipan. Further US reinforcements reach Eniwetok and Kwajalein. Japanese fleet sails for Saipan area. US Navy aircraft attack Bonin and Iwo Jima

June 16
V1s fall on southern England day and night. Japanese launch unsuccessful counterattack on Saipan. Eighth Army drives for Perugia

June 18
Russians break through Mannerheim Line into Finland. Eighth Army reaches Assisi

June 19
Battle of Philippine Sea; Marianas 'Turkey Shoot' (250 Japanese aircraft destroyed). Severe storm in Channel damages Mulberry Harbours

June 20
US Fleet destroys or damages 14 Japanese warships, including three aircraft-carriers, during Battle of Philippine Sea. US troops drive on Cherbourg

June 21
One thousand US bombers attack Berlin. Viipuri (Finland) falls to Red Army

June 22
British Fourteenth Army under General Slim drives through and relieves Imphal. Chindits begin attack on Mogaung. Thousand-bomber raid on Cherbourg takes place as US forces drive into suburbs. Red Army southern offensive launched

June 23
Red Army offensive involves 1st Baltic and the three Byelorussian fronts with massive air and artillery support attacking on a front of 350 miles (560 km)

June 24
Russians reach Dvina on Baltic Front

June 26
Mogaung in Burma taken by British and Chinese armies. Operation Epsom; British drive for Caen

June 27
German pocket near Vitebsk destroyed. Severe fighting on Saipan

June 29
US forces liberate Cherbourg. Russians capture Bobruisk. US troops mop up Cotentin Peninsula

June 30
UK civilian casualties in June 1,935 killed, 5,906 injured

Storming the Atlantic Wall

German intentions of creating a formidable defensive barrier on the Channel coast – the West Wall – were soon to be put to the test by a strange array of unusual armoured vehicles. Wary of the difficulties of making an opposed amphibious assault, the British created the 79th Armoured Division specifically to deal with the German beach defences.

When the first waves of special vehicles of the 79th Armoured Division swept ashore on the Normandy beaches on 6 June 1944, it was the highpoint of a long process of training and preparation that had in some cases been going on for years. In the event it was in most cases a practical demonstration of the old military maximum 'train hard, fight easy', for the men and machines of the 79th Armoured Division had been working up to the invasion through a long series of excercises, tactical analysis and individual training sessions.

79th Armoured Division had to start completely from scratch, but it had a major advantage in that it was commanded by Major General Sir Percy Hobart, one of the most remarkable officers in a remarkable generation of army officers. His drive, organization and overall direction enabled the untrained and unprepared 79th Armoured Division to become one of the most successful armoured formations of World War II.

Equipment had to be developed from scratch. It was appreciated that tanks would have to move ashore in the early assault waves, and as it might not be possible to land them directly on a beach they would have to swim ashore somehow. From this came the Duplex Drive (DD) tanks, usually Shermans, with their high collars that enabled them to float in relatively calm waters, moved by twin propellers at the rear. Then there was the need for an armoured vehicle type to provide combat engineers with some form of protection and in time the Armoured Vehicle Royal Engineers (AVRE) was born. Minefields would be an obvious obstacle, and mine-clearing tanks with their various forms of attachment or flail systems had to be developed. All manner of special equipment had to be devised, from assault bridging to obstacle demolition charges.

The flamethrowers were an important component of the 79th Armoured Division. Most of the equipments involved were known as Crocodiles – based on the Churchill tank.

By the summer of 1943 the 79th Armoured Division carried out its first large-scale training exercises at Linney Head in Wales, and for the first time the division worked together as a cohesive whole. The Royal Air Force provided a constant stream of low-level photographs, and daring raids by commando teams produced actual dimensions of the types of beach and other obstacles that the division would have to face. Replicas of these obstacles were built on a training range at Orford in Suffolk and were used to determine exactly how they could be tackled. In this way the division began to lay out exactly what equipment such as bridging would be required, and even got down to the task of determining which vehicles would be in any particular landing craft at each stage of the landings.

During early June 1944 the 79th Armoured Division took its turn in the long lines of traffic that moved to the invasion ports along the south coast of England. The 79th Armoured Division had to disperse itself quite widely, for by the very nature of its operational task it had to land on every beach which British and Allied troops would be using. The 79th Armoured Division was thus divided among three divisions. On the west the British 50th Division would be landing on 'Jig' and 'King' beaches, in the centre the 3rd Canadian Division would be landing on 'Mike' and 'Nan' beaches, while in the east the British 3rd Division would be landing on a brigade front on 'Queen' beach. The odd thing was that the highly specialized 79th Armoured Division was the only formation of its kind to be landing on the invasion day. The US Army had decided not to employ specialized vehicles other than DD tanks, and relied entirely upon their ordinary divisional resources. In part this was due to the fact that many of the beaches they were to use were backed by cliffs or other terrain where armour of any sort would be difficult to use; but in places specialized armour would have proved invaluable.

On the morning of 6 June all the training came to fruition. On almost every beach the carefully rehearsed drills were used and proved entirely successful. Of course things did go wrong in places, especially on the western beach where the sea was so rough that it proved impossible to launch the DD tanks and the assault teams had to provide their own fire support. Not surprisingly, the carefully-laid plans were set aside and improvization and common sense had to be used. It was here that all the training was shown to be fully justified. Tactics were rapidly evolved to overcome the defences at the same time as the obstacles were cleared, and the Crab Shermans proved invaluable with their 75-mm guns. In the centre, some of the minefields proved to be particularly difficult to clear and the mine-clearing teams suffered heavy casualties in men and equipment before they won through with the close support provided by accompanying Canadian infantry.

By nightfall some Allied troops were nearly 6 miles inland and much of this advance was due to the success of the 79th Armoured Division in clearing paths across and from the beaches. In contrast the Americans to the west were at best only 3 miles inland and they had suffered proportionally far greater casualties. This alone provides a yardstick of the success of the 79th Armoured Division, but it should not be forgotten that much of their success was due to the fact that their preparations had been so thorough that the invasion 'came easy'.

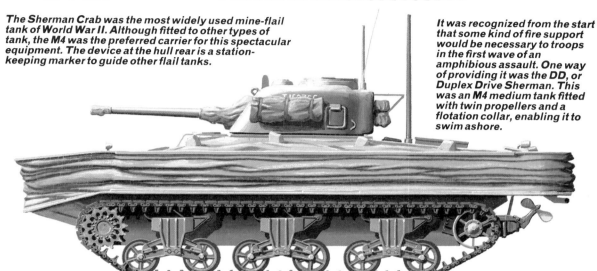

The Sherman Crab was the most widely used mine-flail tank of World War II. Although fitted to other types of tank, the M4 was the preferred carrier for this spectacular equipment. The device at the hull rear is a station-keeping marker to guide other flail tanks.

It was recognized from the start that some kind of fire support would be necessary to troops in the first wave of an amphibious assault. One way of providing it was the DD, or Duplex Drive Sherman. This was an M4 medium tank fitted with twin propellers and a flotation collar, enabling it to swim ashore.

The Sherman BARV (Beach Armoured Recovery Vehicle) featured a high box-type superstructure that allowed it to be driven into deep water to recover stranded vehicles. It was fitted with a nudging nose to push them out of trouble.

The Jones Onion was a tank transportable demolition device carried on a steel frame that could be placed against an obstacle such as a sea wall.

Once the carrying tank was safely away, the charge was exploded electrically. The tanks could then come through the gap in the obstruction.

Left: American-equipped troops of the Free French 2nd Armoured Division prepare to move out on 1 August 1944 at the first stage of the operation that would liberate Paris less than a month later.

Above: The US Army's 331st Regiment fights house-to-house through St Mâlo, some soldiers covering possible or suspected sniper positions while their comrades dash for the next piece of cover.

Montgomery by now had been confirmed – in his own mind – by his tactics, and he was determined to continue them. On 18 July, Operation Goodwood opened, its declared objective 'to engage the German armour in battle and to "write it down" to such an extent that it is of no further value as a basis of the battle'. It was the most massive armoured onslaught carried out by the British up to that time, three divisions debouching from the original Orne bridgehead, supported by the artillery of three separate corps and preceded by an immense carpet of bombs which had been dropped from 2,000 heavy and medium bombers, augmented by naval shelling. Such was the effect that prisoners taken during the first advance had been so deafened that they could not be interrogated for 24 hours.

Goodwood lasted until 20 July and by that time, although the front had been advanced at the eastern end of the bridgehead only a matter of a few miles, the ruins of Caen were in British hands, German strength had been sucked as though by a gigantic vacuum pump to the eastern end of the bridgehead – and Operation Cobra had been launched from the western end.

An M10 tank destroyer of the US Army is seen in Normandy in 1944. This was a successful vehicle, although still no real match for the powerful German tanks.

Operation Cobra

At the end of June 1944 there were many seriously worried men in Whitehall and Washington, men whose whole attention had been concentrated for months (in some cases years) upon the successful liberation of Europe from Hitler's domination, and who now suspected that their plans were going awry. On 6 June the Allied armies had stormed ashore in Normandy as part of the greatest amphibious operation in the history of warfare, and during those first, heady days had secured such apparent success as to raise the hopes and banish all doubts. Now the hopes were lower, the doubts back and growing.

At the eastern end of the beach-head the British Second Army under Lieutenant-General Sir Miles Dempsey was still edging its way forward towards Caen, one of its earliest objectives, while at the western end the US First Army, under General Bradley, had captured the vital port of Cherbourg on 29 June, but was still caught in a nightmare of frustration by the *bocage* country.

The invasion programme was thus well behind schedule, for by this time the planners had hoped that the Allied armies would be in possession of the whole of Normandy, and that 62 squadrons of fighters and bombers on 27 airfields would have been established. All they had taken, in fact, were 17 airfields supporting only 31 squadrons, contained in less than a quarter of the area that it had been hoped the Allies would hold by this time.

But there was an exception among these downcast Allied leaders, the man in command of the formations actually engaged in the fighting, General Montgomery, whose rocklike confidence provided balm to those who believed in him and was a source of deep annoyance to the many who did not. The believers were right. As early as 11 June Montgomery had stated that his objective was to draw the greatest possible weight of enemy forces on the eastern end of the bridgehead, towards Dempsey's forces aimed at Caen, thus weakening the opposition in front of Bradley's forces until the time came when they could break out, first to occupy the whole of the Cotentin Peninsula, then to cross the Selune River just south of Avranches and release the US Third Army under the flamboyant Lieutenant-General George Patton, to flood out to the west and take the whole of Brittany and the vital ports of Brest, Lorient and St Nazaire.

And to the delight of Montgomery's friends, the grudging approbation of his enemies, and the relief of all, by the end of July all this seemed possible. On 24 July Bradley had launched Operation Cobra, and four days later the American tank crews were out of the *bocage*, their infantry holding a line from the Cotentin coast eastwards through Coutances, Roncey and St Lô; and on 30/31 July they swept into Avranches to cross the Selune River with Brittany (and as it happened the whole of north west France) open to them. It was enough to cause Major-General Leland Hobbs, commanding the US 30th Division, to deliver himself of the excited comment 'This thing has busted wide open. We may be the spearhead that broke the camel's back!'

Left: An escaped Russian prisoner-of-war talks with American soldiers he and his resistance colleagues have met. The original newspaper caption to this photo quipped 'What the well-armed man in Brittany is wearing'.

Above: One of the few areas where it could have been said that the Allies had a qualitative superiority over the Germans was in the field of artillery. This US howitzer crew is firing at retreating Germans near Carentan.

Churchill engineer vehicles

For centuries, the military engineer has been an important part of any army, as has the bridging train. In mechanized war, it is not surprising that the engineer should also become mechanized, and one of the most versatile of all engineer vehicles was the Churchill AVRE – Armoured Vehicle Royal Engineers.

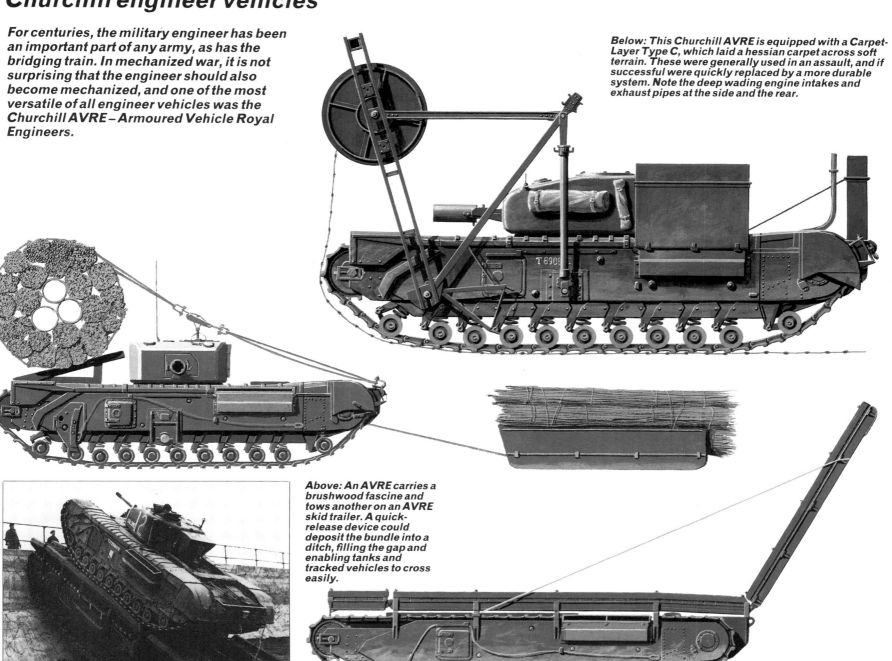

*Below: This Churchill **AVRE** is equipped with a Carpet-Layer Type C, which laid a hessian carpet across soft terrain. These were generally used in an assault, and if successful were quickly replaced by a more durable system. Note the deep wading engine intakes and exhaust pipes at the side and the rear.*

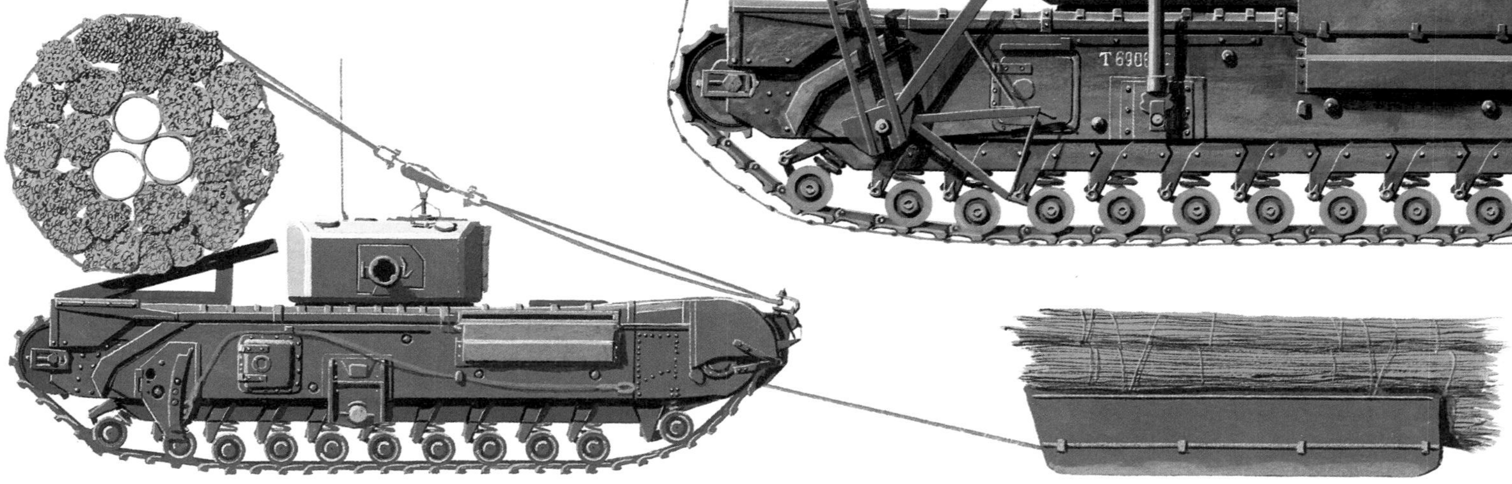

*Above: An **AVRE** carries a brushwood fascine and tows another on an **AVRE** skid trailer. A quick-release device could deposit the bundle into a ditch, filling the gap and enabling tanks and tracked vehicles to cross easily.*

*Above: A Churchill **ARK** demonstrates the use for which it was designed, as a mobile ramp that other tanks could use to get past or over seawalls or anti-tank defences.*

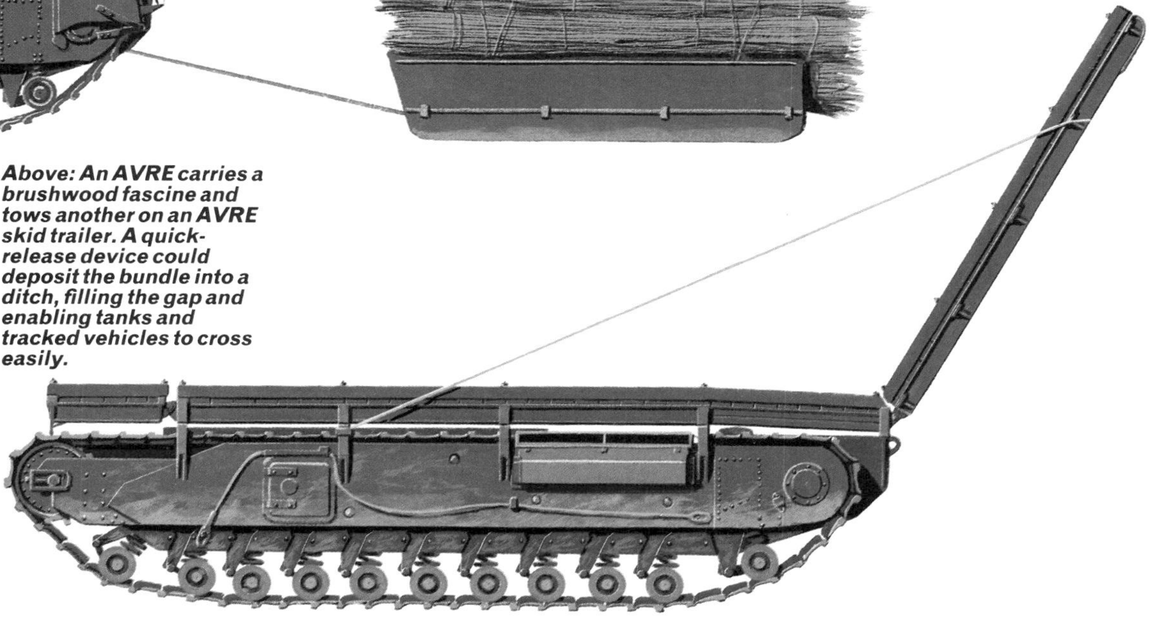

*Above: A Churchill **ARK** is depicted unfolding its ramp. The **ARK Mk II** differed in having two such ramps, increased in length, which gave it the capacity to bridge larger gaps.*

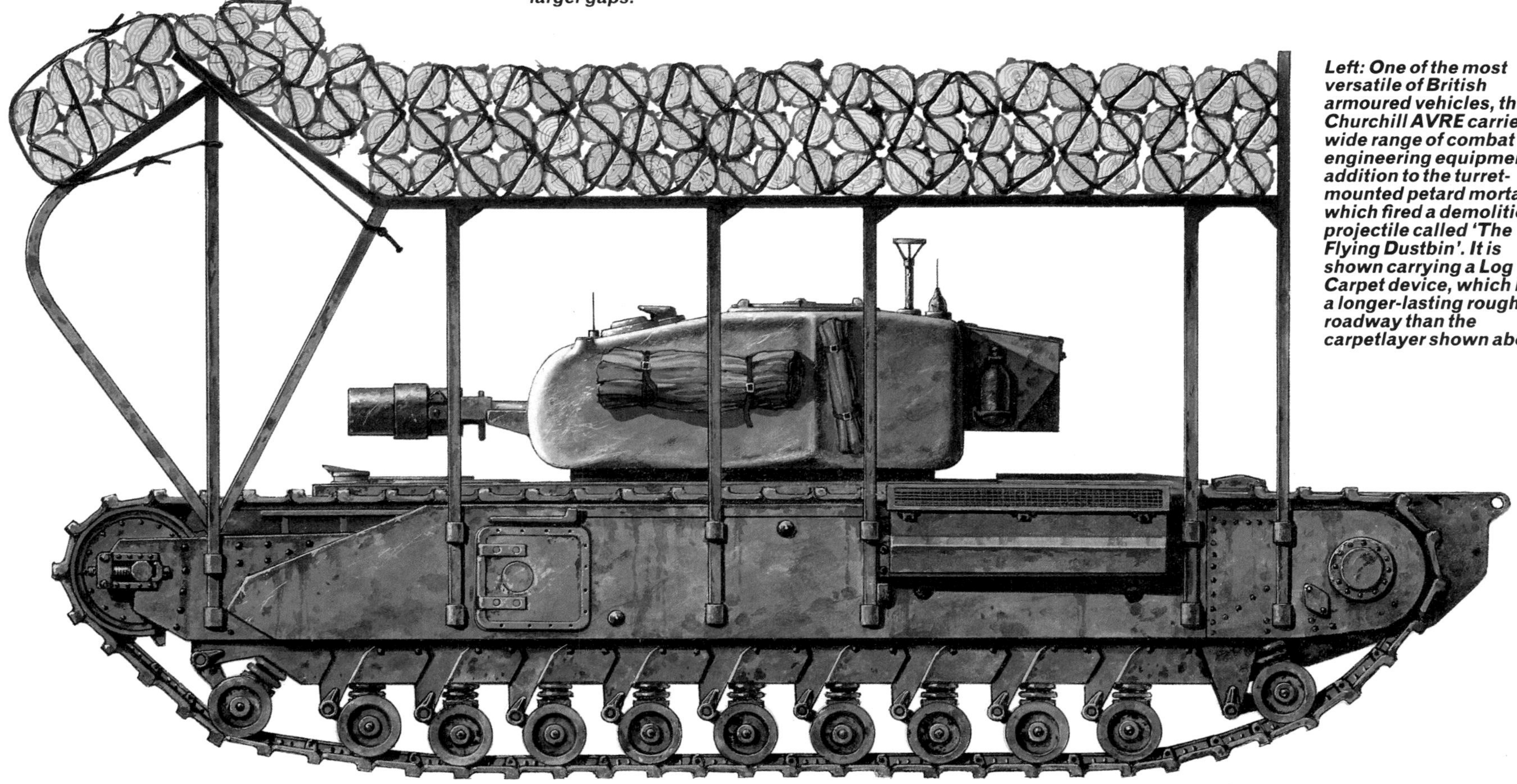

*Left: One of the most versatile of British armoured vehicles, the Churchill **AVRE** carried a wide range of combat engineering equipment in addition to the turret-mounted petard mortar which fired a demolition projectile called 'The Flying Dustbin'. It is shown carrying a Log Carpet device, which laid a longer-lasting rough roadway than the carpetlayer shown above.*

***Left:* When the Allies took Cherbourg in the first month of the invasion, it was soon realized why it had taken so much effort to knock out the U-boat pens by air attack.**

***Above:* Train-busting was a favourite occupation of Allied fighters as they edged their way towards the Rhine. Here is a Lockheed P-38 scoring a direct hit on a locomotive.**

Patton was equally excited, especially as on the morning of 1 August his Third Army became officially operational, though his own presence in Europe, for reasons which now seem curiously unreal, was not yet officially acknowledged except by the Germans, who had known about it for days.

Patton's position before 1 August had been somewhat equivocal, for the US VIII Corps under Major-General Troy Middleton was really a part of Patton's Third Army but had been loaned to Bradley's First Army for the invasion. This was the corps on the western flank of Cobra which had swept down the Cotentin coast to take Avranches and cross the Selune, and on 28 July, Bradley had asked Patton to assume responsibility for VIII Corps area as Deputy Army Commander, despite the fact that Patton was not supposed to be in Europe, and was officially commander of the Third Army.

But at noon on 1 August, all this changed. Patton was now in undisputed command of four corps (VIII, XII, XV and XX) containing eight infantry and four armoured divisions, under operation orders issued before D-Day and confirmed by Montgomery on 27 July and by Bradley that morning; his first and prime task would be to liberate Brittany and its vital ports as quickly as possible. It was typical of Patton that hardly had he swallowed the drink celebrating his assumption of command than he had seen chances of far wider objectives for his divisions and requested permission to exploit them, but began putting them into operation without awaiting reply.

Instructing the armoured divisions of Middleton's VIII Corps to race straight for Brest, Vannes and Lorient without worrying about their flanks or anything except their speed, he turned away from the Atlantic and directed his attention eastward to the gap between Chartres and Orléans, over 100 miles away, beyond which lay the Seine; on the Seine lay Paris, and Patton, an ardent Francophile, purposed to be the first Allied commander to reach the French capital.

Race to the Seine

By now XV Corps under Major-General Haislip was forming just south of the Avranches gap in order to hold enemy pressure off the hinge of Middleton's corps and in theory to protect its left flank, but as the divisions came up, either by accident or design they faced east, away from Brittany and towards the heart of France. The gap between Mayenne and Laval on the Mayenne River beckoned, and by 4 August both Bradley and Montgomery had reached the same decision as Patton. 'The main business', proclaimed Montgomery, 'lies to the east.' And as Haislip's XV Corps prepared to crash through the Mayenne-Laval gap, Patton threw his XX Corps under Major-General Walker even farther south, aimed at Angers and the passage east along the north bank of the Loire.

Haislip's XV Corps moved first, on 5 August, and by 8 August was not only across the Mayenne but had reached Le Mans 40 miles on; Walker moved on 7 August, took Angers on 11 August and raced forward to cover Haislip's flank towards the Chartres-Orléans gap, moving at 16-20 miles per day. It was all very exciting, but it must be remembered that compared to the battles farther north, the Third Army was advancing into a partial vacuum; what little opposition the Americans found they by-passed.

Patton split his command into comparatively small combat units; reconnaissance teams in their jeeps and fast halftracks probing continually ahead, tanks close behind, lorries and infantry carriers in support. It soon became more a matter of logistics than of battle, for the rate at which the Third Army was advancing needed about 250,000 US gallons of petrol per day, all rushed forward in anything which could move, particularly anything fast and capable of moving across country without choking the already packed roads. M3 half-tracks were in constant demand for the task.

But there now occurred a slight check on the onward rush. Other eyes than Montgomery's and Patton's were watching strategic developments, and whatever the Wehrmacht generals might prescribe, Hitler was still in command. Field Marshal Günther von Kluge might recommend a rapid withdrawal of all German forces to behind the Seine and the water-barriers of the Somme and the Meuse, but Hitler's eyes were on that narrow gap between Mortain and Avranches through which all Patton's supplies must be fed. On 4 August four panzer divisions of General Paul Hausser's Seventh Army struck westwards through Mortain and were 7 miles on towards Avranches before being stopped as Bradley, now commanding the Twelfth Army Group, sensed the danger and threw in two corps from the US First Army.

Driving out of Normandy, US forces demonstrated a natural flair for a war of movement, which when allied to solid British professionalism soon forced the Germans back to the French border. This M4 Sherman is close to the Marne, in late August 1944.

Once the invasion of France was well and truly under way, there was a general rising of the Resistance who made it extremely difficult for Germans to move around the country by means of sabotage and attacks on German troops.

Normandy air war

Thousands of sorties were launched from British soil on 6 June, and within a few days of intense action aircraft were flying from French strips. Most of the effort was aimed at disrupting German supplies to the new front line, in particular the slowing of German armoured reinforcements from other parts of France. In this regard they were highly successful.

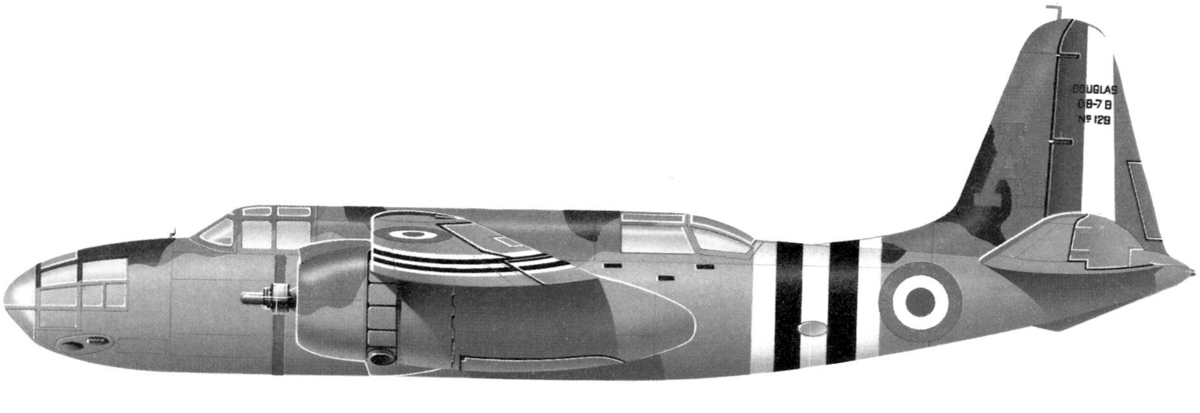

The Douglas A-20/Boston/Havoc series proved a handy light bomber with Allied air forces. Many examples were flown in support of the Normandy raids. This aircraft is from the French air force, several of whose Havocs were the first French aircraft to land back in the country.

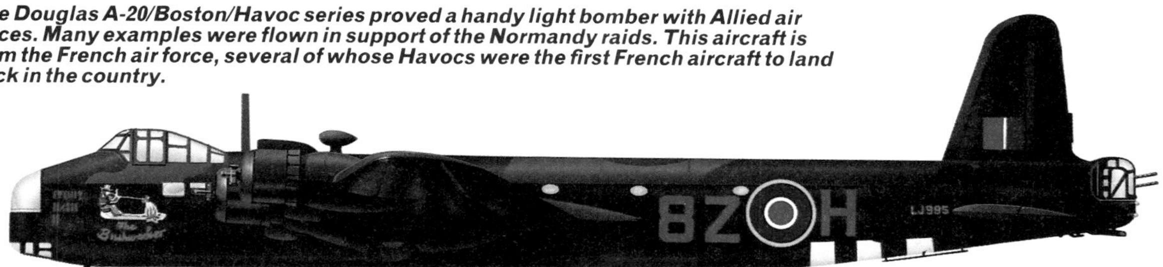

After its days as a long-range heavy bomber were over, the Short Stirling was employed for various transport duties, the most important of which was glider-towing. Note the towing hook mounted underneath the rear turret.

For some months past the RAF and USAAF had been preparing the way for the invasion, British and American heavy bombers striking at key points in the French road and rail system to prevent the movement of reinforcements once the invading forces had landed. To this task was added the offensive against the flying bomb sites in the Pas de Calais, while the fighter-bombers and light bombers of the 2nd Tactical Air Force struck at coastal targets (the E-Boat bases, radar stations, airfields and coastal gun batteries) along the French coast. On the eve of the landings themselves the Allied Expeditionary Air Force comprised 173 squadrons of fighters and fighter bombers, 59 squadrons of light and medium bombers, and 70 squadrons of transport aircraft; in addition to some 50 other support squadrons, there was also the might of RAF Bomber Command and the US 8th Air Force. In all, the Allies could count on close to 12,000 aircraft with which to support the invasion.

The assault on the French coast was indeed a highly co-ordinated effort by the land, sea and air forces. As 145,000 men went ashore from the sea on the first day, considerable use was made of airborne forces, the US IX Troop Carrier Command's C-47s dropping large numbers of paratroops behind the American beach-head area, their task being to consolidate an area from which an advance could be made up Cotentin peninsula to capture the port of Cherbourg. In the event the American airborne operations were not wholly successful, the 82nd and 101st Airborne Divisions being scattered over too wide an area to be fully effective. In the eastern sector, behind the British and Canadian beaches, the Stirlings, Albemarles, Halifaxes and Dakotas of the RAF's Nos 38 and 46 Groups dropped 4,310 paratroops and towed about 100 gliders to secure vital objectives such as coastal batteries, river bridges and road junctions.

As part of the elaborate deception plans undertaken to conceal the true location of the assault area, during the night of 5/6 June a squadron of Lancasters (No. 617) had flooded the skies over the Channel far to the north east with 'Window' in a slow-moving cloud designed to suggest on enemy radar an approaching invasion fleet; a similar operation was carried out by Halifaxes and Stirlings off Boulogne. And these feints certainly played their part in discouraging the Germans from committing their reinforcements until the real landings had gained a powerful foothold in Normandy.

Throughout that first day, as more and more men and vehicles stormed ashore, the Allied air forces put up an enormous umbrella of protective fighters to keep watch for the Luftwaffe. Indeed the German air force reacted slowly and sluggishly with the relatively small number of aircraft available (a total of around 500 serviceable aircraft in the whole of Luftflotte III's assigned area). Only a small number of enemy air attacks developed and the damage caused by them was negligible. The Allies, on the other hand, recorded a total of 14,674 operational sorties on that first day, for the loss (mainly to flak) of 113 aircraft.

The initial assault phase ended with the delivery of 256 gliders to the inland dropping zones, carrying reinforcements to the men of the British 6th Airborne Division. Heavy tank-carrying Hamilcar gliders were now used for the first time to bring the Tetrarch tank into action.

For four days after D-Day the Allies were content to consolidate their beach-head as the tactical support Typhoons, Spitfires, Mustangs, Lightnings and Thunderbolts ranged over northern France, attacking road convoys and trains struggling to deliver German reinforcements to the battle area. Within 10 days more than half a million men had been landed on the Normandy beaches, scarcely troubled on their voyage from the UK by the Luftwaffe, thanks to the continuing efforts of the 2nd Tactical Air Force to pin the German aircraft to their bases. By 10 June (after only three days' work by the airfield engineers) the first landing strip on French soil had been completed and thereafter RAF Spitfires and Typhoons were able to operate close up behind the land battle.

Rocket stores at forward bases in France did hectic business during the initial days of the Normandy campaign, supplying the Hawker Typhoons.

Newly introduced into the fray, the Hawker Tempest was a Typhoon derivative with a laminar wing. It was one of the fastest fighters of the war, later employed against the flying bombs.

Above: Railways were an inviting target for Allied fighters, proving fairly easy to knock out with rockets, as illustrated by this Hawker Typhoon. The effect on the German counter-attacks were marked.

Right: A stalwart of the D-Day and Normandy campaigns was the Martin B-26 Marauder. A tricky aircraft to fly on account of its high wing loading, the B-26 packed a heavy punch and was manoeuvrable.

Left: British troops gaze curiously at a knocked-out German Panther tank as they push out of Normandy. In spite of such superior armour, Allied control of the sky proved decisive.

Above: An SS sniper lies dead in Falaise, killed by Canadians in closing the Falaise pocket. Although most of the German armour escaped the trap, 50,000 Germans were taken prisoner.

Only a minority of the armour that the Germans used in Normandy were the massively powerful Tigers and Panthers; Mk IV Panzers made up the bulk of strength. However, these were not the same vehicles which had reached the Channel only four years before: they had extra armour and a long 7.5-cm gun.

There was bitter fighting, but Avranches remained inviolate. Now two German armies and a Panzergruppe (nearly 100,000 men) were concentrated west of a line running south from Falaise to Alençon, while Dempsey's British and Canadians were a few miles north of Falaise and Haislip's tanks were at Le Mans. It needed no great imagination to see what would happen if they were to meet, and Montgomery was playing it cool when he said 'If we can close the gap completely, we shall have put the enemy in the most awkward predicament.'

The Falaise Gap was not closed with total effectiveness, though the destruction of German equipment and their loss of some 60,000 men was a severe blow; but Haislip's XV Corps did reach Argentan on 13 August and could probably have gone on to Falaise had not demarcation lines and poor liaison prevented it. XV Corps was ordered instead to form the southern shoulder of the gap. But Patton was not pleased to hear that one of his corps had been allotted a purely static role. Moroever, he did not feel that the whole corps was needed at Argentan, so on the following day he sent two XV Corps divisions off to join the race eastwards again, aimed first for Dreux which they reached on 16 August.

200 miles in 21 days

To the south of them, Walker's XX Corps had the same day reached Chartres while by another feat of organization Patton had fed in his fourth corps (XII Corps under Major-General Manton S. Eddy) even farther out on the right flank to take Orléans. Some 300 miles now separated the farthest-flung divisions of Patton's Third Army (Middleton's men at Brest and Eddy's at Orléans) and the gap was to widen even farther. Haislip's men left Dreux on 16 August and reached Mantes-Gassicourt on 19 August, Walker's XX Corps left Chartres on 16 August to reach Melun and Fontainbleau on 20 August (thus XV and XX Corps cut the Seine both above and below Paris almost simultaneously) and Eddy's XII Corps drove into Sens from Orléans on the afternoon of 21 August.

In 21 days, therefore, Patton's Third Army had advanced eastward from Avranches 200 miles to the Seine, and westward 150 miles to Brest. The Americans had liberated some 45,000 sq miles of France, and played a significant part in the destruction of the immense German forces trapped in the Falaise pocket.

This was a considerable military achievement by any standards and, in terms of logistics, a classic.

Left: An M4 Sherman fires point-blank at German positions while on each side of the street GIs peer out, very much aware of one of the constant perils of streetfighting – the threat of snipers.

Below: American soldiers sample some of the local produce as they head into the interior of France, before pushing on to the battle line and the eventual liberation of the whole country.

Allied light vehicles

World War II saw much in the way of innovation, and one of the major changes was the vastly increased mobility conferred upon troops by the motor vehicle. Smaller models were used for a multitude of services, and the Willy's Jeep was undoubtedly the most famous; but there were many other light vehicles making a contribution to the war, of which these are but a very small sample.

***Left:** While the M3A1 White scout car was not a great success in its designed role, it was widely used as a lightly armoured utility vehicle. It also provided the base for the even more widely used M2/M3 series half-tracks.*

***Above:** The Dodge T214 range of ¾ ton trucks were introduced in 1942. They were used to transport personnel, weapons, tools and equipment, and were sometimes known as 'Beeps' (Big Jeeps).*

***Below:** The Dodge T214-WC53 command and reconnaissance version of the 'Beep' was often used as the nickname suggests – as a much more roomy Jeep. The sturdy design has contributed to the fact that T214s can still be found in use in many parts of the world.*

***Right:** British military vehicles were built very much to standard designs laid down by the War Office. This Bedford MWD with GS body is typical of a type of vehicle which saw numbers in service increase from about 15,000 in 1939 to 230,000 in 1945.*

***Above:** While France may be a land of sunshine, there were times in the summer of 1944 when the weather was atrocious. It was at times like those that the 'go anywhere' ability of vehicles like the Jeep were most appreciated.*

***Left:** A four-wheel drive estate car, the Humber Heavy Utility was the basic staff and command car in British service, and remained so for some years after 1945. It was the only British built 4x4 vehicle of this type.*

Chapter 21

Destruction of Army Group Centre

While the Allies were landing in France, the Soviet summer offensive swept all before it from the Balkans to the shores of the Baltic, and as the Russian spearheads advanced inexorably westward, Hitler's allies began to desert him.

At Stalingrad, the Red Army had learned how to stop the German Army; after Kursk it was to show that it could drive them backwards. Techniques had improved considerably; reconnaissance before an offensive was now thorough and efficient, huge formations moved into position at night in complete silence, staff control during the approach marches was excellent, camouflage when daylight came was effective. And when the battle started, co-operation among infantry, tanks and cavalry was good.

The Germans reflected the other side of the coin. Before Stalingrad they went to the Russian Front with their spirits buoyed up in the crusading ideal and the stout belief that German efficiency and courage would inevitably bring victory; after Kursk new recruits went up, and experienced men returned, hag-ridden by legends of Mongol hordes descending on the German homelands. Even before Kursk, the lines on the maps revealed enormous withdrawals and the loss of huge tracts of territory won in the days of triumph. In addition to the great losses between the Don and the Donetz following the fall of Stalingrad, almost the whole of Army Group A under General Kleist – which had in August looked likely to capture the vital Caucasian oilfields and perhaps even break down into Persia and the Middle East – had been hastily withdrawn in the face of the drive south by armies of the Stalingrad Front and had only got out through Rostov in February by the narrowest of margins.

After Kursk, which had stripped them of so many trained men and so many precious tanks and aircraft, the Germans faced a new and terrifying factor; although the Soviet forces had suffered the same losses in both men and weapons, they had apparently no difficulty at all in replacing them immediately with new ones. This had been demonstrated by their capture of Orel only a few days after Operation Zitadelle had been called off, and their permanent relief of Kharkov at the end of the month.

Continuous offensives

The offensives continued, one beginning as its predecessor slowed in a manner which reminded an observer of the winning tactics of Marshal Foch on the Western Front in 1918. Kharkov fell in the south, and in the north General Popov launched an attack out of the newly won ground around Orel towards Bryansk, while even further north, Kalinin Front under Eremenko drove down towards Smolensk. Two drives were launched in the direction of Kiev – from Central Front under Rokossovsky and Voronezh Front under Vatutin – while at the far south of the line, Tolbukhin's armies of South Front crossed the River Mius, outflanked Taganrog (from which the last of Kleist's men hastily withdrew) and drove along the Azov coast to Mariupol.

A posed propaganda picture well illustrates the confidence of the Soviet army after the great strides made in 1943. 1944 was to be the decisive year, when the Soviet army advanced 400 miles in only two months. The bulk of German strength was deployed on the Eastern Front, but it was defeated nevertheless.

By mid-September, the whole Soviet front from Smolensk down to the Black Sea was on the move towards the Dnieper. Within a few days, Central Front had swept through Sevsk as far as Konotop, Voronezh Front was through Piryatin, Steppe Front at Poltava, South-west and South Fronts between them had cleared all enemy forces from the Donetz Basin and were within striking distance of the Dnieper at Zaporozhe – and by the end of the month not only were Red Army troops on the river from just north of Kiev down almost to Nikopol, but at Kanev Vatutin's men were actually across and forming a bridgehead.

Kiev to the north, Dnepropetrovsk in the centre and the Perekop Isthmus with the Dnieper Estuary were the next immediate targets, and no logistical

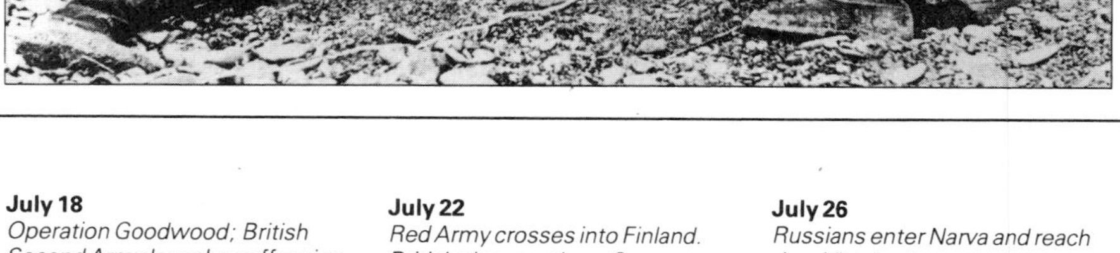

One of the German army's biggest problems lay in keeping their long lines of communication open in the face of relentless partisan pressure. It was a vicious struggle, with very little quarter given by either side, and these saboteurs knew that their life expectancy would be short if they were caught by the Germans.

Chronology of War: 1944

July 3
Russians recapture Minsk

July 4
US Marines push ahead on Saipan

July 7
Admirals Nagumo and Yano killed on Saipan. British Second Army attacks Caen under heavy RAF bombardment

July 9
Caen and Bretteville-sur-Odon taken by British

July 12
US Fifth Army reaches Laiatico and Castiglioncello in Tuscany

July 13
Red Army launches offensive in North Ukraine. Vilna, in Lithuania, is taken by the forces of the 1st Baltic Front

July 16
Eighth Army takes Arezzo, reaches river Arno in the Italian campaign

July 17
Red Army cross Bug into Poland. Eighth Army crosses Arno and advances towards Florence. US troops enter St Lô in Normandy

July 18
Operation Goodwood; British Second Army launches offensive around Caen, drawing German forces into battle in preparation for Operation Cobra six days later. Japanese XV Army retreat back towards Chindwin from positions around Imphal in Burma

July 19
Fifth Army takes Leghorn. Russians enter Latvia

July 20
July Bomb Plot: attempt to assassinate Hitler

July 21
After two weeks' continuous bombardment US marines land on Guam

July 22
Red Army crosses into Finland. British clear southern Caen

July 23
Red Army breaks through north of Carpathians and 1st Belorussian Front captures Lublin. Allies reach Pisa

July 24
US Marines land on Tinian in the Marianas. Heavy fighting on Guam. Operation Cobra; US forces break out of Normandy stalemate across Periers-St Lô road under strong air support

July 25
Canadians drive across south of Caen

July 26
Russians enter Narva and reach river Vistula. Japanese counterattack on Guam

July 27
US forces break through west of St Lô. Russians capture Lwow, Stanislavov, Daugavpils and Rezekne. US Marines drive across Guam and Tinian

July 28
Red Army takes Brest-Litovsk, Yaraslov and Przemysl. US troops reach Countances. Last resistance ends on Biak, north west of New Guinea

July 30
First US Army reach Avranches. Russians form bridgehead across Vistula

July 31
UK civilian casualties in July 2,441 killed, 7,107 injured

August 1
Warsaw Rising. Tinian held by US Marines. US Twelfth Army Group operational in France under General Bradley. General George S. Patton takes command of US Third Army, General Courtney Hodges takes command of US First Army

considerations were allowed to check an immediate onslaught. To the astonishment – and terror – of the German armies standing in their way, the Soviet forces stormed relentlessly on. With the help of Ukrainian partisans a bridgehead to the north of Kiev was formed, and the one to the south held despite the fierce counter-attacks it attracted and the comparative lightness of the artillery the holders had been able to bring up. From both of these, aided by units of the Thirty-eighth Army rushed up to the east bank, the liberation of Kiev was launched on 1 November. By 4 November more and more T-34s were arriving and grinding their way across the hastily but efficiently built wooden bridges, 2,000 guns and heavy mortars were pounding the German defences – and Soviet infantry, many of whom had learned their trade at Stalingrad – were into the city streets, fighting their way through. On 6 November Kiev was once more in Soviet hands.

Now the ground was frozen, the Russian winter again chilling the hearts of the German forces even more terrifyingly than in the previous two winters – and the Red Army was content for the moment just to clear the rest of the Dnieper in the south, and recapture a few significant places to the north. Steppe and South-west Fronts drove across the river and formed a wide and deep penetration pointing past Dnepropetrovsk at Krivoi Rog, and past Kremenchug at Kirovograd. South Front drove on down to the Dnieper mouth and effectively shut off all German forces left in the Crimea; to the north Vatutin and Rokossovsky had driven their fronts as far as Korosten and the eastern edge of the Pripet Marshes respectively, and Sokolovski had taken – by the use of seven armies and at great cost – the massive defensive bastion that the Germans had made of Smolensk.

Consolidation

Time was now briefly taken to consolidate that immense line, but winter was the time for Russian victories and the pace must be kept up. In particular, it was time to bring to an end the ordeal of the people of Leningrad – now in its twenty-eighth month of siege.

The passage out to the rest of Russia which had been forced through in January 1943, though enough to save the city inhabitants from starvation, was still under German fire and thus constant threat; but it had allowed the evacuation of the sick, the elderly and the too young, and even more important had allowed during the last months of the year the build-up of forces in the Oranienbaum bridgehead to the west of the city and in the main Leningrad Front, and the provision to them of massive artillery and strong tank forces.

They struck at the German lines on the night of 13 January 1944, under a massive bombardment not only from the main artillery but also from the guns of the Baltic Fleet in which some 100,000 shells were fired, and by morning the infantry had driven two miles in towards Ropsha. Two days later, a second onslaught under a similar barrage was launched on the left from the Pulkovo Heights, and the following day yet another from even further left, aimed at Pushkin.

Those first days of the breakout saw some of the fiercest fighting of the entire war, for the German defences were sound, had been well constructed over many months, and the men in them knew that, once forced out of them, there was little they could look forward to but death in the freezing wastes behind. It was five days before the men of the Second Shock Army from Oranienbaum and the Forty-second and Sixty-seventh Armies on the left had advanced as much as five miles, to sense the first creakings in the German defence lines. But by 19 January Krasnoye Selo and the important heights of Voronya Gora had been taken, and the clearance of Ropsha was complete. Behind the attackers lay the 85 heavy guns of the batteries which had bombarded Leningrad so unmercifully during so many months.

By now also armies of the Volkhov Front on the eastern flank had moved forward. On 20 January they took Novgorod after flank attacks to the south across the frozen waters of Lake Ilmen, while further north Fifty-fourth Army drove down on Lyuban and Chudovo, then swung west to reach the Luga River above Luga itself, while Leningrad Front also curved west to reach it from Kingisepp to the Baltic.

Leningrad relieved

By the end of the month the Siege of Leningrad was at last over, massive salutes were fired there and in Moscow, and for the first time for 900 days the people of the city could walk their streets without fear of Wehrmacht shells or Luftwaffe bombs. But the northern offensive was not yet over. Luga fell on 12 February, 2nd Baltic Front under General Popov drove west below Lake Ilmen, and when on 1 March *Stavka* called a halt, Soviet troops had reached the shores of Lakes Piepus and Pskov, and so held that wilderness of forests and lakes which runs along the Estonian Border.

Meanwhile, just south of Kiev a battle of truly gigantic proportions was developing. At the turn of the year, the Germans had still held one small stretch of the Dnieper around Kanev where they had thrown back the Soviet bridgehead, and behind them to the west they occupied a salient nearly 20 miles deep, and, at its base between Belaya-Tserkov and east of Shpola, over a hundred miles wide. But such distances were beginning to mean nothing on the scale of Red Army movements, and on 24 January opened the battle of the 'Korsun-Shevchenkosky.'

On 24 January, the right-wing armies of General Koniev's renamed 2nd Ukrainian Front smashed through the eastern end of the salient and drove eight miles in on the first day, after which Koniev sent up the Fifth Guards Tank Army; on 26 January, Vatutin's 1st Ukrainian Front attacked from the north and on the 28th the two forces met, trapping 10 German divisions in the pocket, from which all attempts to escape were doomed to fail. The equipment of four panzer and six infantry divisions plus 18,000 men were abruptly wiped from the strength of Field Marshal Manstein's Army Group South; and this was just the beginning of a far greater strategic move.

No more of it, however, was to take place under command of General Vatutin. On 1 March as he was

A typical German frontline soldier after three years in the hell of the Eastern Front. The spit and polish so beloved of the Prussian army is gone, but the fighting ability of the individual German soldier remains high.

Above: Troops of the Second Ukrainian Front move forward towards the attack line, in the southern sector of the overall front which stretched from Estonia to the Crimea.

Left: Late-model StuG III assault guns are seen on the streets of a city in Russia. The superiority of Soviet armour was a considerable shock to the Germans, and forced the upgrading of their AFVs as far as the chassis could stand it. These have had side skirts added as a protection against shaped-charge warheads.

August 3
Chinese armies capture Myitkyina in north Burma. Japanese transports sunk off Bonin, north of Iwo Jima

August 4
Eighth Army reaches Florence. US Third Army takes Rennes

August 6
US Third Army reaches outskirts of Brest

August 7
Thousand-aircraft support for Canadian attack south of Caen

touring the front his car was ambushed by anti-Soviet Ukrainian partisans, and he died later in Kiev General Hospital; his place was taken by the deputy supreme Commander-in-Chief, Marshal Zhukov, who thus once more assumed a dominant role on the battlefield.

There was, briefly, a pause in the centre, but further south Malinovsky's 3rd Ukrainian Front had opened an attack on the Krivoi Rog area and the River Ingulets beyond, while Tolbukhin's 4th Ukrainian Front attacked over the lower reaches of the Dnieper. General Chuikov's Eighth Guards Army took Krivoi Rog on 22 February, and in some desperation Manstein transferred divisions down from the central sector which had seemed for the moment unthreatened.

Zhukov struck almost immediately. On 4 March his armies were driving out through Korosten in a huge arc which was to cut down through Rovno, Shepetovka and Volochisk to threaten Tarnopol, and by 10 March they had reached the valley of the Dniester, with the Carpathian Mountains looming over the western horizon – and with Army Group South still in a pocket to the south-east.

Here they were attacked by armies of the 2nd Ukrainian Front under the newly promoted Marshal Koniev, driving clear of the Korsun-Shevchenkovsky base-line, through and past Uman, over the Yuzhny Bug to reach the Dniester between Mogilev Podolsky and Rybnitsa. Manstein had thrown everything he could find into a defence of the rail link between Odessa and Lwow, for this provided the best chance of escape for his armies from what was by now obviously a near-fatal trap – though few of them had a chance to use it. Most were thrown back over the River Pruth, while First Panzer Army, consisting of 10 infantry divisions, 9 panzer divisions and an artillery division, were cut off around Kamenets Podolsky between Zhukov's forces and Koniev's.

Advances continue

Perhaps there was a misunderstanding between Zhukov and Koniev about whose responsibility this pocket was, but at the end of March the trapped divisions formed themselves into a vast striking force akin to the Roman Legion in movement, and burst out to the west, reaching the safety of the German lines at Buchach on 7 April. But in the spring of 1944 this was the only achievement the Wehrmacht could look upon with any satisfaction.

By the end of March the whole length of the Bug had gone, Malinovsky's armies had driven from Krivoi Rog to take Nikolayev and reach the lower Dniester, while Chuikov had swung his army further south to attack Odessa from the north. He captured it on 10 April – and by this time Koniev's troops were across the Pruth and into Bessarabia, and the whole of the Ukraine except the area around Lwow was back under Soviet rule.

The traditional spring campaigning season was now almost at an end, but one task remained in the south – the reduction of the German forces in the Crimea. This was entrusted to Tolbukhin's 4th Ukrainian Front, helped by a newly-created independent Coastal Army under General Eremenko and by the Black Sea Fleet.

It did not take long. On 11 April, two armies broke through the narrow neck at Perekop, while Eremenko's divisions drove westwards from the Kerch Peninsula, both soon finding themselves in a labyrinth of trenches, strongpoints and mined areas. But between them they comprised 470,000 men with nearly 6,000 guns and mortars and 560 tanks, supported by 1,250 combat aircraft; the German and Romanian forces there, despite their defence lines, were overrun in a matter of hours and fled back into Sevastopol – and by the beginning of May, the Soviet assault upon the port was ready for launch.

It took four days of massive artillery and air bombardments poured down on to specified sectors, followed immediately by assaults through streets, tunnels and trench lines by the never-ending streams of Soviet infantry – almost all of them now armed with sub-machine-guns. By 10 May, the fighting was over, Sevastopol was once more a base for the Russian Black Sea Fleet; a small part of the German and Romanian garrison had escaped by sea but the greater part were dead or on their way to prison camps.

Now a lull fell along the length of the Eastern Front from the Baltic to the Black Sea. The Germans could do little but count their losses and fear for the future; the Red Army, however, could lay their plans, strengthen further their lines of communication, amass storehouses through the areas now again under Soviet control – and take considerable satisfaction from their recent achievements and their present condition.

A Soviet 45-mm anti-tank gun is seen in action under fire. Copied and enlarged from a German design, the weapon was really too small for use against the heavier German armour, but the Soviet practice of retaining obsolete weapons even when their replacements were in large-scale service saw it in action against second-line targets.

Left: Luftwaffe paratroopers prepare for action in March 1944. The first of the major Russian offensives was to the south of the Pripet Marshes, and in spite of leavening with such elite troops the German Army Group South was pushed back almost to the Polish border (leaving Army Group Centre exposed in the middle of the Front).

Below: An officer of the Waffen SS in the southern Army Group. By this late in the war, the SS were no longer the all-German elite that they had been, taking volunteers from all over Europe. Nonetheless, they were still formidable (and on occasion ruthless) opponents.

Chronology of War: 1944

August 8
Canadians driving south towards Falaise

August 9
General Eisenhower sets up his HQ in France. US Third Army turns north towards Falaise, approaches St Malo and mops up Le Mans

August 10
Japanese garrison on Guam annihilated (although last Japanese soldier does not surrender until 1972)

August 11
US forces take Angers. Falaise Gap closed to less than 20 miles. Red Army attacks near Pskov

August 12
PLUTO pipeline from Isle of Wight to Cherbourg in operation, ensuring Allied fuel supplies in France

August 13
Germans begin withdrawal through Falaise Gap

August 14
Red Army launch offensive from Vistula bridgehead

August 15
Operation Anvil; Allies invade southern France

August 16
Canadians take Falaise

August 17
Russians reach East Prussia

August 19
Field Marshal von Kluge, Commander of Army Group B (but implicated in July 20 plot), commits suicide. Two German armies surrounded in Falaise-Argentan pocket. Patton's forces reach the Seine on each side of Paris. Malinovsky's 2nd Ukrainian Front launches powerful offensive south towards Jassy and the oilfields of Ploesti

August 20
US Third Army forms bridgehead across Seine at Mantes-Gassingcourt. Falaise Gap closed. French troops liberate Toulon. Russians cross into Romania and drive down to the Danube

August 22
Fleet Air Arm attack German battleship Tirpitz *in Altenfiord*

August 23
Coup d'etat in Bucharest. The dictator, Marshal Antonescu, arrested; Romania accepts Russian terms. Russians encircle German divisions near Kischinev in Moldavia

August 25
Allied forces headed by General Leclerc's French 2nd Armoured Division liberate Paris. US troops assault Brest. British Second 2nd Army crosses Seine at Vernon

August 26
UK and US divisions drive eastwards from Seine. Bulgarian government announces withdrawal of Bulgaria from war

August 27
Last Chindits evacuated to India

August 28
Marseilles liberated

August 29
Soissons liberated. French troops cross the Rhône. Russians take Constanza and Buzan. Allies capture Pinbaw, Burma

August 30
Russians take Ploesti

August 31
British Second Army reaches Amiens and captures Somme bridges intact. Eighth Army attacks Gothic Line. Montgomery promoted to Field Marshal, commanding 21st Army Group. UK civilian casualties in August 1,103 killed, 2,921 injured

Soviet air force, 1944-1945

After a few weeks of the German advance in 1941, the Red air force lay in tatters. Soviet industry set to work, transforming the force into a large and effective fighting machine, able to sweep the Luftwaffe away with relative ease during the last year of the war.

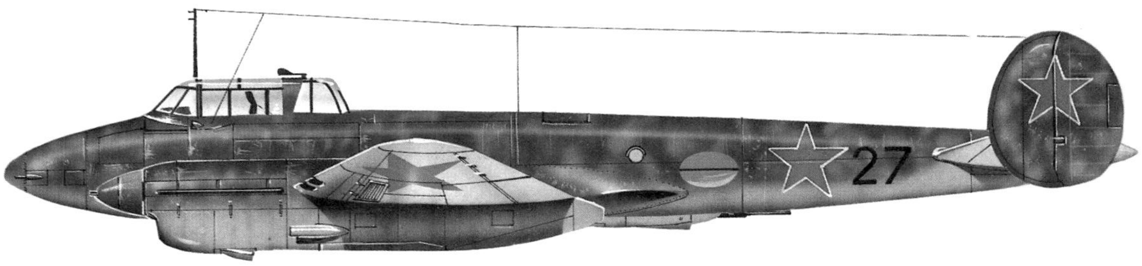

Above: The Petlyakov Pe-2 was dubbed the 'Russian Mosquito', and it certainly lived up to the versatility of its RAF ally. Mainly used as a fast light bomber, the Pe-2 first rose to fame during the battle of Kursk.

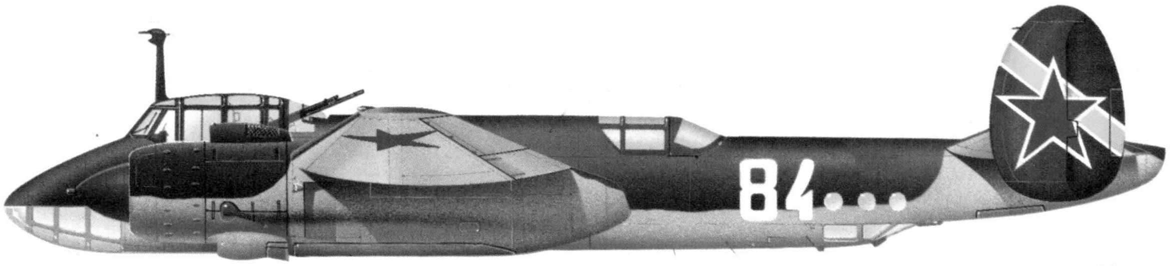

Left: Heavier than the Pe-2, and in the class of the B-25 Mitchell, the Tupolev Tu-2 was another excellent product. When freed from the shackles of bomb carriage, the Tu-2 surprised many Luftwaffe pilots with its ability to turn and fight.

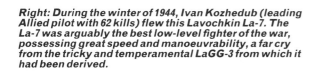

Right: During the winter of 1944, Ivan Kozhedub (leading Allied pilot with 62 kills) flew this Lavochkin La-7. The La-7 was arguably the best low-level fighter of the war, possessing great speed and manoeuvrability, a far cry from the tricky and temperamental LaGG-3 from which it had been derived.

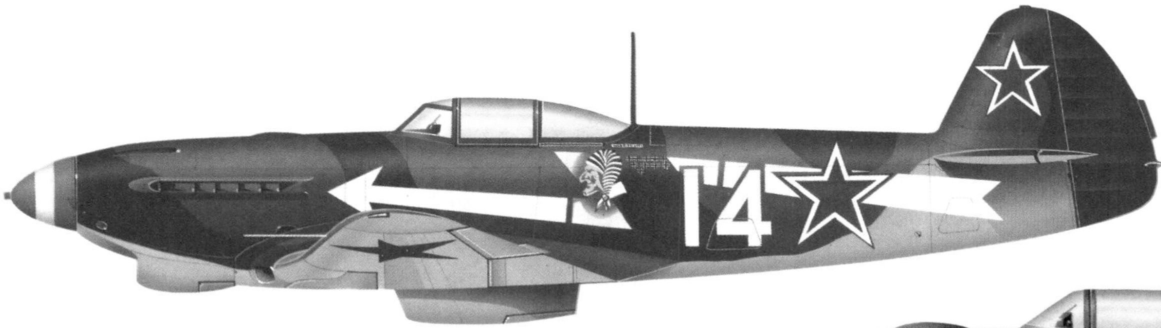

Left: The Yakovlev single-seat fighters were built to the tune of some 37,000 units – the highest figure for any fighter, and they did more than any other aircraft to defeat the Luftwaffe. This is a Yak-9 of the Normandie-Niemen regiment, crewed by expatriate French pilots.

Right: The most manoeuvrable fighter of the war at low level was the Yakovlev Yak-3, which entered service in late 1944. The Luftwaffe soon learned not to tangle with this machine, issuing orders to their pilots to 'beware of the Yak fighter without an oil cooler under the nose.'

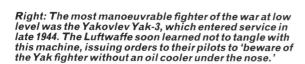

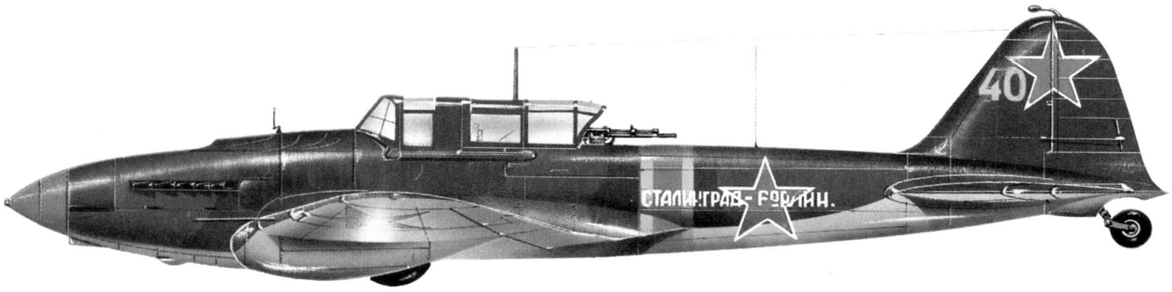

Left: The Ilyushin Il-2 'Shturmovik' led the aerial charge against the German armour, artillery and ground positions. Although losing many to German fighters, the factories were producing more and more. Stalin proclaimed: "The Red Army needs the Il-2 as it needs bread and water: I demand more! This is my final warning!", and so 36,000 aircraft were constructed.

Right: While other air forces found the Bell Airacobra unsuitable for their requirements, the Soviets used it widely as a fighter and ground attack platform. One pilot who enjoyed the type was Major Aleksandr Pokryshin, who downed most of his 59 kills in this Bell P-39Q.

Left: The purposeful lines of the La-7 are readily apparent in this photograph. Most of the Eastern Front air battles were fought at low level, needing no supercharged engines, and such Soviet aircraft proved very manoeuvrable near the ground.

Where the Soviets had a great advantage was in the ability to function normally in the cruel winter. Even a highly capable fighting machine such as this Yak-3 could start in any weather, and be serviced by the roughest of mechanics.

THE SOVIET ARMY IN 1944

By the early summer of 1944, the Red Army was the biggest land force ever put into the field of battle in recorded history. It seems possible that by that time close to 20 million Russian men and women were wearing service uniform, and although both the Red Air Force and the Red Navy were enormous by any standards, the bulk of the fighting forces were in the Red Army. And in the army itself, a very high proportion of those serving were at what the Western Allies called 'the sharp end' – a far higher proportion than in those Western armies. The Sharp End for the Russians was more akin to a Sledgehammer Head.

The Red Army was basically an infantry force with a primitive supply and administration service, manned by soldiers of immense toughness and physical strength which enabled them to carry heavier loads for longer distances than most; and their birthright had accustomed them to far colder temperatures, withstood on far smaller rations, than many in the West would have believed possible. No welfare services absorbed Red Army personnel strength for there were no such things as leave, regular pay or even contact with the family; all of that was of the past. The Soviet soldier was trained to expect discipline of a type not seen in the British army since the days of the Crimean War, a high rate of casualties, little medical attention if he was wounded, and none if he was ill. And very little food. One of the best of the divisional German commanders, Hasso von Manteuffel, later wrote:

> The advance of a Russian Army is something that Westerners can't imagine. Behind the tank spearheads rolls on a vast horde, largely mounted on horses. The soldier carries a sack on his back, with dry crusts of bread and raw vegetables collected on the march from the fields and villages. The horses eat the straw from the house roofs – they get very little else. The Russians are accustomed to carry on for as long as three weeks in this primitive way, when advancing.

By 1944 the factories which had been evacuated beyond the Urals were at full stretch and were turning out some 2,000 tanks and self-propelled guns every month, and nearly 9,000 aircraft. Moreover, those tanks and guns were largely of the same original designs, sound and reliable, and, if not as sophisticated as the German Tiger tank or the 88-mm gun, there were hundreds – and soon thousands – of them. When the new Royal Tiger appeared it might well be able to knock out 10 T-34/85s within minutes; but it would be attacked by 50 of them and broken by sheer weight.

It cannot be said that many of the tanks and weapons sent to the Soviet armies by their allies were of much direct use to them. The British Valentines saw some service down in the Caucasus, but elsewhere Western-made tanks were too narrowly tracked for the conditions in Russia, and too thinly armoured – as the British had themselves found out – to brave the German anti-tank guns. But American supplies of basic material – sheet steel, leather, blankets, canvas tents, first-aid packs and shiploads of iron rations – were appreciated by the Soviet soldiers though they rarely knew who supplied them. However, there was one significant contribution that Western industry made towards the Soviet advance – some 500,000 motor vehicles (including 100,000 of the Studebaker version of GMC's famous 2½-ton 6×6 truck), which were putting the Red Army on wheels for the first time in its history. Now the 'Deuce and a halfs' were lifting forward to that immensely long line – which would itself soon start moving forward – everything the vast Red Army would require to smash the force which had so brutally invaded their country, and whose more extreme elements had carried out such appallingly bestial crimes upon their people. In June 1944 the men of the Red Army were motivated by patriotism and the normal military companionship of arms; by the time they reached Berlin, fury at what they had discovered on the way had wiped away any vestiges of compassion.

Great summer offensive

Three years to the day after Barbarossa had been launched, the great Soviet Summer Offensive opened – 22 June 1944. From Velikie Luki in the north around a huge arc to Kovel below the Pripet Marshes, the artillery of four Red Army fronts – 15 armies – crashed out, while the aircraft of four air armies flew overhead, and the infantry and tanks – increased over normal establishment by more than 60 per cent – moved out of their concentration areas into the attack. Their objective – to obliterate the German Army Group Centre which consisted of three infantry armies and one panzer army under General Busch (altogether over a million men with 1,000 panzers and 1,400 aircraft) smash through them and all their defences and drag out of the Soviet Union the Finnish

Soviet T-34/85s are seen before an offensive. This superlative weapon has a claim to being the finest fighting vehicle of the century, being a generation ahead of any contemporaries, produced in enormous numbers throughout the USSR (11,000 of this more heavily-gunned model being produced in 1944 alone).

Designed by the Germans in response to the T-34, the PzKpfw V Panther was perhaps an even better tank but, lacking the brute simplicity of the Soviet design, was much harder to produce and appeared in far smaller quantities.

Both sides on the Russian Front saw the value of heavy artillery pushed well forward in the assault gun role. The SU-152 mounted a heavy 152-mm howitzer on the chassis of the KV (later IS) heavy tank.

Air combat on the Russian Front

German fighter pilots found themselves up against ever-increasing swarms of Russian warplanes, led by the massed ranks of Yakovlev fighters and Ilyushin attack aircraft. The Soviets began to increase their personal tallies, while only the luckiest German aces survived. Those that did survive flew constantly, until at the top of a Luftwaffe of decreasing quality was a band of the most experienced combat pilots in history, with literally thousands of hours of fighting experience showing in phenomenal personal scores.

With the recapture of Sevastopol by the Soviet armies early in May 1944 the scene was set for a great surge forward, both westwards towards Germany itself and south-west through the Balkans. The air forces on both sides were being heavily reinforced, but much of the German strength in the air was the strength of the reinforcements dissipated throughout the Balkans, reflecting Hitler's fear for the safety of his oilfields in Romania (now being heavily attacked by American bombers from the Mediterranean). The remainder amounted to around 800 aircraft, and supported Generalfeldmarschall Ernst Busch's Army Group Centre along the line of the Pripet marshes and northwards to the Baltic coast.

It was at this time that the V-VS committed to widespread operation its new Tu-2 fast attack bomber and the Yak-3 and La-7 fighters; these excellent machines – more than a match for the latest Bf 109G-10 when flown by a German pilot of average ability – were being turned out in staggering numbers. By June 1944 Soviet aircraft on the central front outnumbered German aircraft by five to one.

On 22 June the Soviet 1st Baltic and 3rd Belorussian Fronts opened their offensive with powerful attacks against Vitebsk. In support of the attack were ranged some 2,300 aircraft, and from the beginning of the great offensive the Tu-2s and Pe-2s kept up constant raids on the Luftwaffe's airfields behind the immediate front as the inevitable swarms of Il-2m3s – with heavy fighter cover – attacked battlefield targets.

The attack appears to have caught the Luftwaffe wholly unawares, no more than 40 Bf 109Gs and Fw 190s of JG 51 at Bobruisk, Orscha and Mogilev being available for combat. These airfields were quickly rendered unusable by the Russian attacks; even the hurried arrival from Germany of 30 further Bf 109Gs of III/JG II at Dokudevo was scarcely noticed. The German armies in the centre of the Eastern Front disintegrated and when, on 9 July, Soviet forces entered Vilna it seemed that the northern plains of Poland would be swiftly overrun.

The air operations by the V-VS in support of this enormous advance had been prodigious, with some 98,000 sorties flown in 55 days. The Luftwaffe had claimed to have destroyed around 2,800 Russian aircraft, while the Soviets themselves claimed about 1,500 German aircraft; although both figures were almost certainly exaggerated, the relative proportion of losses was probably fairly accurate. The great Soviet fighter pilot, Ivan Kozhedub, took his personal victory tally to 57 by the end of the year, and with an ultimate score of 62 became the highest-scoring Allied pilot.

While Soviet fighter pilots now began to increase their own individual victory scores, Luftwaffe losses included some of its most experienced pilots. On 17 June Oberleutnant Anton Hafner (204 victories) was killed in combat at low level with a Soviet fighter when his 'Gustav' struck a tree; two days later Leutnant Helmut Grollmus (75 victories) was killed over Finland; and on 10 August Fritz Luddecke was shot down by Soviet flak over East Prussia. Others, such as Erich Hartmann of JG 52 who added the Diamonds to his Knight's Cross on 25 August when his score reached 301 victories, continued to lead charmed lives.

Above: Ivan Kozhedub finished the war with 62 victories, and was thrice Hero of the Soviet Union. Here he is seen (left) being congratulated by colleagues.

Right: The Pe-2 (illustrated) and Tu-2 bombers were available in large numbers and the Luftwaffe had great difficulty putting up enough fighters to counter their attacks. Once in the air, they had to contend with escorts and the bombers were no slouches either.

Below: The Focke-Wulf Fw 190F-8 was introduced late in the war as a fast ground attack aircraft, able to outrun fighters yet able to deal effectively with the massed Soviet ground onslaught. Four bomb racks were mounted under the wings, with one under the fuselage.

Below: Second highest-scoring pilot for the Allies was Aleksandr Pokryshin, seen here in 1943 in front of his Bell P-39. Thrice a Hero of the Soviet Union, Pokryshin ended his wartime career flying Lavochkin La-7s.

Left: A tank crewman of SS Division 'Viking' in the Kowel sector, April 1944. 'Viking' was recruited from occupied Norway and Denmark and had a well-earned reputation as one of the toughest SS Panzer divisions.

Right: The commander of an Su-122 self-propelled gun poses for the camera as the Soviet army heads westward. Note the crude construction of the gun mantlet: ugly, but quick to produce and no less effective than more polished German equivalents.

and German armies to the north, and the Hungarian, Romanian and German armies to the south.

This was the onslaught which would clear the invader from the soil of Mother Russia.

Within a week, the three main bastions of the German defences had been first cut off, then captured – Vitebsk in the north by converging attacks from one army of Bagramyan's 1st Baltic Front above and one of Chernyakovsky's 3rd Belorussian Front below; Mogilev by two armies of Zakharov's 2nd Belorussian Front, and Bobruisk by the armies of Rokossovsky's 1st Belorussian Front, which moved massively but secretly over countless small rivers and lakes at night, then attacked out of marshy ground that their opponents had considered impassable. Parts of two panzer corps were cut off and bombed into disintegration, and then Rokossovsky's armies took Bobruisk with 24,000 prisoners.

By 4 July, both Zakharov's men and Chernyakovsky's had driven forward nearly 150 miles leaving only one pocket of German resistance behind (it surrendered on 11 July), Rokossovsky's Twenty-eighth Army was approaching Pinsk – and except in the north around Daugavpils (Dvinsk) the Germans were back over the old pre-war Soviet-Polish border.

The momentum never flagged. Everywhere the Germans were in full retreat, though they turned and struck back ferociously at times. Nevertheless, armies of the 1st Baltic Front forced the Dvina and took Polotsk within days; Chernyakovsky's and Zakharov's armies – having already cut off 105,000 Germans as they crossed the Beresina – drove for Vilnyus and Bialystok, taking the latter at the end of the month and causing General Guderian to note caustically in his diary, 'Army Group Centre has now ceased to exist.'

Immediately north, Chernakovsky's right flank drove on from Vilnius to Kaunas in Lithuania and by the end of August had reached the borders of East Prussia, while further north Bagramyan's Baltic Front armies crossed into both Latvia and Lithuania, and sent an armoured raid up to the Gulf of Riga. Brest-Litovsk fell to Rokossovsky on 28 July and soon afterwards his forces had reached the Bug north of Warsaw, while on his left Chuikov's Eighth Guards Army had stormed out of Kovel in mid-July, captured Lublin and reached the Vistula, which they crossed on 2 August.

Soviet artillery

By 1944 the Soviet army had brought its use of artillery to a fine art, massed heavy guns in 'breakthrough' artillery divisions in combination with massed armour being able to penetrate German defences with ease. Unfortunately, lack of flexibility was a weakness in such huge organizations, and exploitation was often less effective than the initial attack.

Above: The SU-122 was a conversion of the T-34 to accommodate a front mounted 122-mm howitzer in a well-armoured hull of good ballistic shape.

Above: The 152-mm gun-howitzer M 1937 was a tough and reliable weapon (typical Soviet characteristics) that was produced in vast numbers. A good indication of the worth of the weapon is the fact that it is still in service worldwide in the 1980s.

Above: The SU-152 was first of the Soviet heavy self-propelled artillery carriages, built onto a KV-2 heavy tank chassis and first appearing at Kursk.

Right: The ISU-152 was a straightforward conversion of an IS-2 tank to carry a 152-mm howitzer as a close support artillery weapon. The thick superstructure and enormously dense frontal armour made it a particularly difficult weapon to knock out.

Marshal Koniev's armies on the Ukrainian Front had not been embroiled at the start of the offensive, but on 13 July they drove forwards against very strong resistance from Army Group North Ukraine (for this was where the Wehrmacht had expected the Soviet onslaught) and it was not until two more tank armies had been brought up from reserve on 16 July, and this tremendous weight of men and fire-power began to tell, that the defences cracked. Forty thousand Germans were surrounded near Brody, Rokossovsky's right-hand army drove straight to the Vistula, crossed it and formed a bridgehead at Sandomir, one tank army flanked Lwow to the north and another was thrown into a direct assault which captured the city on 27 July; Przemysl fell, then Mielec at one end of the front and Nadvornaya at the southern end.

By the end of August, the Carpathians had been reached along their main length, the Polish border was behind the Red Army positions which had now closed up to the old borders with Czechoslovakia and with Hungary. In two months the Soviet troops had advanced 450 miles – at great cost but also inflicting enormous losses on their enemies – and now the time had come again to reorganize the supply lines for the next advance on this front.

Southern offensive

But to their south, another campaign was about to open, with perhaps more political motivation than military; the Balkans were as great an attraction to Stalin as they had been for centuries to the Romanovs.

On 20 August, the Fifty-second Army of Malinovsky's 2nd Ukrainian Front broke through the defences of Army Group Ukraine in the Pruth valley opposite Jassy, the Sixth Tank Army immediately followed and by the 24th were near Leovo, where they met two of Tolbukhin's mechanized corps which had forced the lower Dniester into Bessarabia.

They had isolated the German Sixth Army and intended to grip and destroy it, when political events intervened. A *coup d'état* took place in Bucharest,

Fighting through a village, a soldier of the Red Army takes a prisoner, while dead German defenders lie scattered around. Life as a prisoner on either side was not sweet, with the notorious SD and Gestapo on one side and the equally unsavoury NKVD on the other.

Soviet T-34 tanks (carrying a full load of infantry in default of any personnel carriers) push forward against crumbling German positions. The sheer scale of Soviet operations in the summer of 1944, with 124 divisions committed to the Central Front alone, was overwhelming, and in spite of staunch resistance the Soviets were able to push forward in the Balkans, on the Central Front and in the Baltic states.

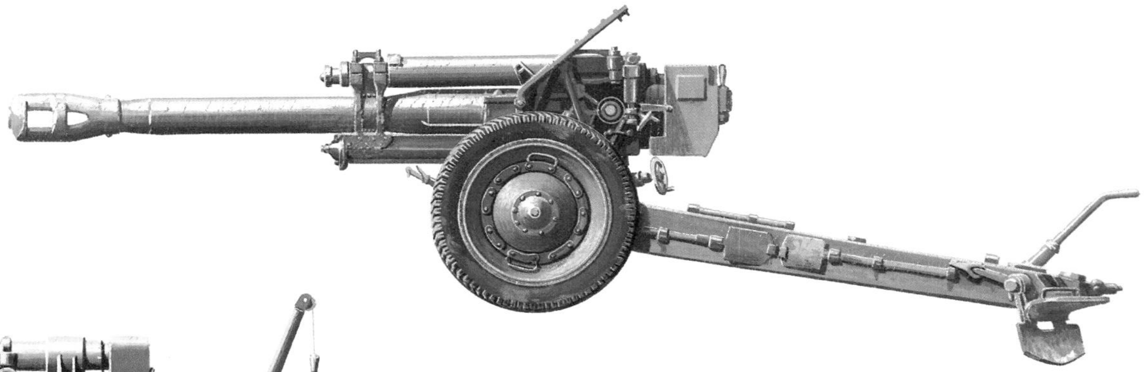

Above: Designed by the Petrov design bureau in Sverdlovsk, the 152-mm Howitzer M1943 was produced in prodigious quantities, and served for many years after the war in Soviet motor-rifle divisions until replaced in the last decade. Today it remains in service with many Soviet client states.

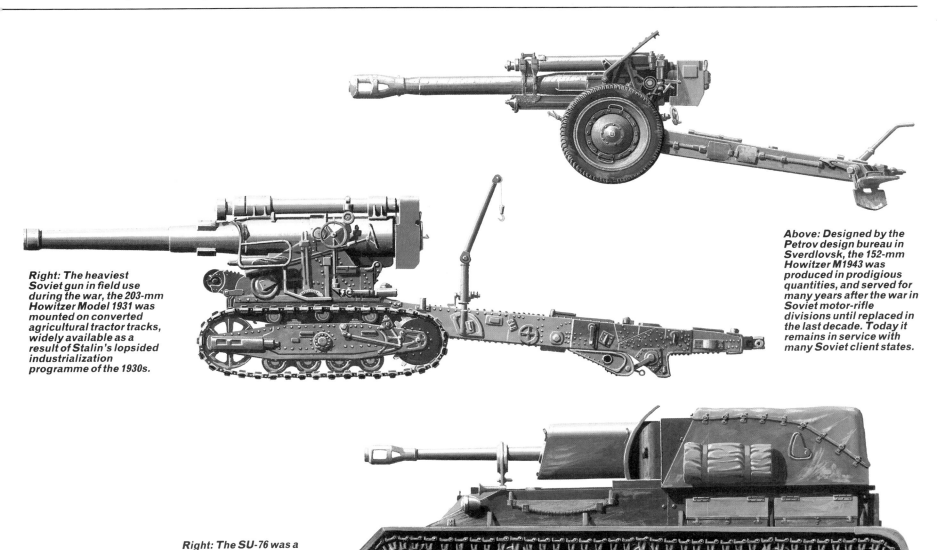

Right: The heaviest Soviet gun in field use during the war, the 203-mm Howitzer Model 1931 was mounted on converted agricultural tractor tracks, widely available as a result of Stalin's lopsided industrialization programme of the 1930s.

Right: The SU-76 was a rather rushed wartime conversion of the T-70 light tank to carry a 76-mm field gun. Although it was produced in huge numbers, it was unpopular with its crews, who generally called it 'the bitch'.

Marshal Antonescu was overthrown, King Michael took his place, the government promptly sued for peace with the Allies, and immediately two Romanian armies laid down their arms, and southern Bessarabia, the Danube delta and the Carpathian passes to the north lay open to the Soviet armies. By the end of the month, Romania was in the process of being occupied by the Red Army, and Bulgaria to the south was about to be invaded by one of Tolbukhin's armies, driving down the Black Sea coast through Constanta. Perhaps infected from the north, a pro-Allied group of officers now seized control in Sofia and welcomed the Red Army – so the invasion became 'a visit by friendly forces', who raced through the capital on 15 September, collected two Bulgarian armies and pressed on to the Yugoslav border opposite Bor in the north and Skopje in the south.

By 8 September, Malinovsky's armies had joined Tolbukhin's, on 28 September they moved forward together to link up with Marshal Tito's Partisans while 46th Army of 2nd Ukrainian Front, drove in over the Romanian border north of the Danube. But the German Army Group F under General Weichs was holding open an escape route for both themselves and Army Group E under General Löhr, rapidly retreating up through Greece, and put up such a stout resistance that it was 20 October before Belgrade was in Allied hands – and then only after the bulk of both German army groups had raced north through the gap to join a hastily forming defence line in Hungary, where yet another attempt to desert the Axis had been foiled.

Admiral Horthy had never been an enthusiastic

Left: Waffen SS soldiers briefly hold up the overpowering tide of the Soviet advance, but not for long. The tank they are passing is the massive IS-2, with a 122-mm main gun; this was to evolve into the forerunner to modern Soviet tank design, the IS-3 heavy tank.

Above: German Tiger tanks crunch through the frost on the borders of East Prussia. The Tiger was a fine defensive tank, being well armoured and carrying the tank version of the famous 'Eighty Eight', but its heavy weight and relative lack of engine power counted against it.

Night harassment

Night intruders were used widely on the Eastern front by both sides, used to harass the enemy by dropping small bombs and grenades. The tactic became so successful that it spread to other theatres.

The resort to widespread night harassment by German aircraft during the great campaign in the East proved to be extremely effort-effective and a number of Axis pilots became highly proficient in these unorthodox tactics.

Indeed, the German-sponsored expedient itself developed from Soviet tactics in 1942 when, having never achieved an initiative in the air since the launch of Operation Barbarossa, Soviet pilots started flying Polikarpov Po-2 light biplanes (*Nämaschinen*, or 'sewing machines', as they were dubbed by German soldiers) over the advancing German forces. These

follower of Nazi or even Fascist doctrine, and had only agreed to Hungarian co-operation in the war against the Soviet Union the previous March, when Hitler threatened full-scale occupation of the country. On 16 October Horthy declared a withdrawal from the Pact and announced he wished for an armistice with the Allies, but before he could implement it in any way, he had been virtually kidnapped by the German commando Otto Skorzeny (who had rescued Mussolini from the Gran Sasso where he had been imprisoned), and German armies from Austria poured in, later to be reinforced by the formations from Greece and Yugoslavia.

By the time Malinovksy's and Tolbukhin's armies had assembled for a drive up from the Lake Balaton area, not only were the Germans in some force throughout Hungary, but Budapest in particular was strongly held and fortified. In November, the Soviet armies were fighting their way north on each side of the Hungarian capital, slowly, implacably, but at great cost and with little of the energy and momentum of the previous months; and on 25 December 1944, when divisions of the two Ukrainian fronts which had fought all the way from the Dniester met to the west of Budapest, it was decided that with 180,000 Germans and Hungarians encircled there was no chance of taking the city by storm.

They therefore organized for a full-scale siege, calling up super-heavy artillery from hundreds of miles back in the Soviet Union, extra divisions from reserves, supplies and food from wherever they could be found.

The final assault must wait until 1945.

Above: The exhaustion shows on the faces of these men of Grossdeutchsland Division, regrouping for a counter-attack. Although German units fought with their customary efficiency they were simply too outnumbered to halt the Soviet advance.

Right: A Soviet tank formation presses on into the forests of East Prussia. As ever, the tanks' supporting infantry ride atop their vehicles, accepting the worst of the weather. By carrying their infantry this way the Soviets cut down upon the need for extra transport, which could then be assigned important tasks such as ammunition, fuel and food (in that order of priority).

operations, while scarcely ever achieving the slightest damage by their haphazard nature and with the tiny bombs carried, did nevertheless act as abrasive on the nerves of the Germans, so that even before the front began to stabilize towards the end of 1942 the Luftwaffe had itself created a number of *Behelfskampfstaffeln* (provisional bombing squadrons). These were regularized in November as *Störkampfstaffeln* (literally disturbing bomber squadrons), with units assigned to specific sectors of the front, such as Behelfsnachtkampfstaffeln Don and Volga; of these the task of the former was, for instance, to harass the Soviet night workers in the Stalingrad munitions factories. Flying such obsolete aircraft as the Gotha Go 145 and Arado Ar 66 biplanes, many of the pilots were past the normal age accepted for combat or, at the other end of the scale, young pilots awaiting posting to regular combat units.

The operations by these units were carried out with the utmost bravery, not to mention the difficulties involved. In many instances the pilots flew their old aircraft from dirt roads, often (through lack of radio and dependence on mapreading as their only means of navigation) being unable to find their 'base' and, having landed, to contact their scattered support personnel. Bearing in mind that almost all their missions were flown in darkness, the successes achieved by the 'night assaulters' provide ample testimony of their devotion to duty.

Until 1944 the *Nachtschlachtgruppen* were able to deliver only very small weapons against the enemy, these being confined to an occasional 50-kg bomb, or perhaps three or four 20-kg bombs. The favourite weapon, was, however, the 2-kg SD 2 fragmentation bomb, most of the old biplanes being racked to carry up to 20 such weapons for attacks against Soviet truck parks and tented encampments. Many pilots also carried panniers of hand grenades in their cockpit which they would toss out as they flew low over enemy troop concentrations. There were also recorded instances of fairly large fuel and ammunition dumps being destroyed simply by the use of Molotov cocktails thrown from the cockpits! Attacks were almost invariably carried out by relays of single aircraft throughout a single night, seldom returning to the same target on successive nights so as to avoid unnecessary losses from strengthened and alerted flak defences.

A new chapter in the affairs of the night assaulters began in 1944, when most of the Ju 87D-equipped *Schlachtfliegersgeschwäder* (SG) began converting to the ground-attack versions of the Focke-Wulf Fw 190. Apart from the dedicated anti-tank Ju 87G, which had to remain in service as being highly effective against the mass of Soviet armour despite enormous losses among the 'old hands', almost all the redundant Ju 87s (Bs and Ds) were distributed among the *Nachtschlachtgruppen*, particularly NSGr 9 which achieved a measure of success against the British and American forces in Italy.

It was at that time that a new name rose to prominence among the night assaulters. Kurt Dahlmann had been an experienced bomber pilot almost since the beginning of the war before commanding the fast bomber *Gruppe*, SKG 10. Under his command this fighter-bomber unit flew the Fw 190G-1 in night/bad-weather attacks against southern England, being renamed III/KG 51 and then NSGr 20 in November 1944 when based at Twenthe in the Netherlands. Led by Dahlmann (who had received the Knight's Cross earlier in 1944), small sections of Fw 190s, each carrying a 1800-kg bomb, carried out sneak raids, often in appalling weather, against key targets behind the Allied lines, including headquarters buildings, tank parks, road and rail junctions, bridges and lock gates. The attacks were skilfully planned and executed, and considerable damage was done in dozens of instances, the Allied authorities not always aware that an air attack had been responsible simply because only a single bomb might have been dropped. On at least one occasion the destruction of a fuel dump in Belgium was ascribed to the work of saboteurs, but it is now clear that it was caused by one of Dahlmann's pilots. That, surely, was the very essence of night harassment. Major Dahlmann himself survived to receive the Oakleaves on 24 January 1945.

One other *Gruppe* remains to be mentioned. Following attempts by NSGr 20 to destroy the vital bridge over the Rhine at Remagen in March 1945, some Junkers Ju 88P-3s were assembled from NSGr 4 and 9 (with pilots from IV/NJG 2 and KG 3) and formed into NSGr 30 for operations against the American and British forces in the West. Flying low level by night in pairs (one of the aircraft illuminating the target with flares) the Ju 88 crews carried out a score of attacks in the closing weeks of the war, particularly against crossing points on the Rhine and on Allied airfields in the Low Countries but, after suffering heavy casualties, were eventually grounded through fuel shortage. Alas, on account of the hastily improvised nature of so many *Nachtschlachtverbände* operations, the vast proportion of their work went unrecorded and remains only in the memory of a dwindling number of survivors.

Many types of aircraft were employed on night harassment sorties, one of the most common being the Henschel Hs 123 shown here. These usually operated singly and randomly so that they would not suffer too much from flak.

Equipped with many types of obsolete aircraft and trainers (such as the Polikarpov U-2 at right), the women pilots of the 46th Guards Air Regiment flew night harassment missions. This group contains six Heroes of the Soviet Union.

Chapter 22

The Seine to Arnhem

Even before the conclusion of the battle for Normandy, Allied forces were racing to bridge the Seine and push their way to the Rhine. The advance was extremely rapid – almost too fast for logistical lines stretching back to Cherbourg to cope with. Not surprisingly with such extended lines, they pushed once too far.

The arrival of the Allied armies on the Seine only 80 days after D-Day was undoubtedly a cause for celebration and congratulation for the troops and their commanders; it was a matter of some concern for those charged with the mundane business of keeping the men supplied with food and ammunition, and even more crucial – and difficult – the vehicles with fuel.

Cherbourg, though in Allied hands, was still not fully operational because of the damage and sabotage it had suffered before capture, one Mulberry harbour was wrecked and the other half-operational, and the fact that the Germans had fought so hard during the early weeks had constricted the size of the bridgehead in which the original stores dumps had been formed. The British had now wrenched themselves away from Caen and the Falaise area and the Americans were 200 miles away or more down past Fontainebleau – but they all had to be fed from those dumps, and although there were nearly half a million trucks and lorries ashore, only 15,000 of them were long-distance load carriers.

On 26 August thirty Allied divisions – Canadian First Army with six, British Second with nine, US First with nine, US Third with six – lay in an arc from the mouth of the Seine up the river past Paris to Troyes, and if the vast proportion of the men viewed their situation with relaxed confidence, their leaders were worried and argumentative. Quite obviously, with the Seine reached, the next main objective was the Rhine, 250 miles eastwards, behind which lay the hearts of German industry, the Saar and Ruhr; equally obviously, with the supply difficulties the Allied armies now faced, not all the divisions could immediately race forward to take full advantage of the dishevelment to which the German forces had been reduced – a state which all agreed was unlikely to last long.

In General Montgomery's opinion, both Army Groups – his own Twenty-first and General Bradley's Twelfth – should together drive north eastwards into Belgium as a solid mass, so strong that it need fear nothing, then divide shortly before they both crossed the Rhine with the British and Canadians sweeping along the northern edge of the Ruhr, to meet the Americans who would have taken the southern route on the far side.

General Eisenhower, who by previous agreement was due very soon to take over command of the land forces in Europe from Montgomery, accepted the attractions of the plan, but felt that it was his duty to be more conservative. Moreover, General Patton's Third Army was undoubtedly the one 'with the ball' at the moment, it was eager to press onwards, was aimed at the moment through such stirringly memorable places to the Americans as Chateau Thierry, Belleau Wood and St Mihiel towards Metz, and Patton was triumphantly declaring that given the supplies, his army would be through Metz and over the German border within ten days.

Moreover, there were now more American divisions coming up from the south, thus weighting that flank. On 15 August, 12 battalions of the US VI Corps had landed on the 35-mile stretch of beach to the east of Toulon, between Cavalaire and Agay, and, aided by French commandos and the enthusiastic population of the area, had occupied Toulon and Marseilles within a few days. They were now poised to drive northwards up the Rhône valley and the Route Napoléon, and like the divisions under Patton these too were eager, excited and likely to gain and maintain a vital and perhaps even decisive momentum.

There was thus great pressure on Eisenhower to stick to the original pre-D-Day concept of a 'broad front' advance across France to the German border, which would in fact enable the fullest use of the excellent road system in western Europe (a boon not to be found in other theatres) and also make available that tactical 'ace' in almost any situation – an alternative strategy should one be blocked. Although the British and Canadian Armies should indeed drive north east through Belgium – and be supported too, by Lieutenant-General Courtney Hodges' US First Army on its right flank – the bulk of Bradley's Twelfth Army Group would drive east from the Seine

The invasion of Normandy and the subsequent movement of German forces against the Allies was the signal for the French resistance to come out into the open. This group is in the South, just before Operations Anvil and Dragoon.

American troops are ferried into the old port of Marseilles, August 1944. The successful landings gave the Allied commanders another option when choosing the best route to defeat Hitler, making the German defensive problem that bit more complicated.

On the beachhead near Toulon one of the Free French colonial units assigned to the US VI Corps is landed. Note the interesting variety of personal equipment sported by these soldiers; most of it is American, but headgear includes British and French helmets.

Chronology of War: 1944

September 1
British troops reach Arras; US forces cross the Meuse and reach Verdun

September 2
Canadian troops enter Dieppe and Rouen. US Fifth Army enters Pisa, British Eighth Army drives for Rimini. Russians reach Bulgaria

September 3
British Second Army liberates Brussels. French troops enter Lyons. US Navy shells targets in the Palau Island and the Carolines, sinking 13 Japanese ships

September 4
British Second Army reaches Antwerp

September 5
US forces cross Meuse. Ghent captured

September 6
Canadian forces surround Calais. US forces cross Meuse at Dinant and Namur. Russians reach Yugoslav border

September 7
US troops cross Moselle

September 8
First V2 rocket attack on London. Red Army drives unopposed into Bulgaria. Fifth Army launches big offensive against Gothic Line in Italy

September 10
Russians capture Prague. Russo-Finnish armistice signed in Moscow. US troops enter Luxembourg. Canadians enter Zeebrugge

September 11
US First Army patrols cross into Germany near Stalzenburg. British cross Meuse-Escaut canal

September 12
US First Army crosses German border near Aachen. Germans in Le Havre surrender

September 15
US First Army break through Siegfried Line. US landings on Morotai (west of New Guinea) and Pelelieu in the Palau Islands

September 17
Operation Market Garden; Allied 1st Airborne Army drop at Eindhoven, Nijmegen and Arnhem

September 18
Germans mount heavy counterattacks against all Allied airborne positions. Brest garrison surrenders

September 19
British paratroops at Arnhem Bridge cut off. US and British troops meet at Nijmegen

September 20
Bridges at Nijmegen secured by Allies. Polish troops reach Scheldte Estuary

September 21
Russians clear ground between Lake Peipus and coast in Estonia. Polish Parachute Brigade dropped in support of British at Arnhem. British force at bridge destroyed. Eighth Army takes Rimini

September 22
Russians enter Tallinn in Estonia, Arad in Romania. Boulogne garrison surrenders

September 23
Russians reach Gulf of Riga

September 24
British Second Army closes up to Rhine

Above: General LeClerc, 25 August 1944. Paris is in the process of Liberation, and appropriately it is the Free French 2nd Armoured Division, part of General Hodges' First US Army, which is in the van of the forces entering the city.

Right: An M8 Armoured car of the US 4th Infantry Division looks down the Champs Elysées from the Arc de Triomphe. Militarily, Paris was a minor target, but as a political symbol it was of great value.

and pass the German border to the south of the Ardennes.

Once the supply situation was satisfactory, the first divisions could move.

Liberation of Paris

But first there was the problem of Paris.

Given the choice, General Eisenhower would have by-passed Paris and left it severely alone until the Germans there decided to surrender. It had been calculated that the city would need 4,000 tons of supplies each day once it was liberated, and certainly for the first week or more it would not be able to find any of that 4,000 tons for itself. That meant 4,000 tons less of petrol, ammunition and other essential supplies for Montgomery's and Bradley's armies, and General Eisenhower grudged every ton brought over the Normandy beaches that was not used in the front line.

But politically there was no choice. The whole world was watching to see what would happen to the French capital, and if Hitler did not in fact ever enquire if Paris was 'burning', on 23 August he quite specifically ordered that it 'should not fall into the hands of the enemy except as a field of ruins'. Fortunately, neither General Dietrich von Choltitz, the German Commandant in Paris, nor General Hans Speidel, commanding the German Army Group in whose area Paris lay, wished their names to go down in history as the despoilers of such a centre of civilization and art; Choltitz had already arranged a somewhat precarious truce with the leaders of the French Resistance in Paris, in order to suppress to some extent the possibility of wide-scale insurrection and consequent damage.

General de Gaulle, of course, had every intention of being among the first of the liberators into the city, and he also intended that French troops should lead the way in – and who better than the men of the French 2nd Armoured Division under their brilliant and gallant commander, General Jacques LeClerc – a choice the British who had fought with him in North Africa would fully endorse? But the French 2nd Armoured were a part of US V Corps under General Gerow, whose reaction to the suggestion that he should release one of his divisions for a special, privileged duty was unfavourable – and to the further suggestion that LeClerc was really under de Gaulle's command and not his own, explosive.

But LeClerc was not so easily to be diverted, and on 21 August – in flagrant disobedience of his orders – he detached a column of 150 men, ten tanks and ten armoured cars, under a colonel, and sent it forward with instructions to get itself mixed up with any American formations who seemed likely to be intent upon entering Paris. He also flew to General Hodges' headquarters and could possibly have faced court martial had not, at that moment, a message arrived from Eisenhower indicating that he had at last given way to political pressure; the liberation of Paris by Allied troops should take place as soon as possible and the French 2nd Armoured should be in the van. The US 4th Infantry Division should accompany LeClerc's armour, the whole group would be commanded by General Gerow and would include a British contingent, and all groups would go in flying their national flags.

As it happened, General Montgomery felt that, despite the Supreme Commander's wishes, French sensibilities regarding such matters as Dunkirk, the destruction of the French Fleet at Oran and Mers el Kebir, Syria – and perhaps even Waterloo – would make it unnecessary or even inadvisable for a British presence on this occasion, so there were no Union Jacks flying on the morning of 25 August when French tanks drove into Paris from the west, and men of the US 12th Infantry Regiment arrived from the south.

There had been opposition from German units to both formations on the way in, 2nd Armoured having already lost 71 killed, 225 wounded, 35 tanks, 6 guns

Paris rose 10 days before the arrival of the Allies, and the Resistance fought running battles with the Germans. Here an isolated German sniper fires on the crowd in Place de la Concorde.

A German soldier is seen after being taken during the capture of the Opéra. Some Germans were less fortunate, and were killed by the Paris mob. The worst fury of the mob was reserved for collaborators, who were treated brutally.

September 25
Chiang Kai-Shek requests replacement of General 'Vinegar' Joe Stillwell

September 26
British Second Army widens Nijmegen salient. Last survivors of Arnhem Battle withdrawn. Eighth Army crosses the Rubicon

September 27
German counterattack at Nijmegen

September 30
Canadians take Calais. UK civilian casualties in September 190 killed, 360 injured

German reaction to the invasion of Normandy was seriously hampered by a co-ordinated series of sabotage and guerrilla raids carried out by the Maquis. Railways were a prime target for underground groups, usually armed by the Allies as seen here.

A light tank from a US Army reconnaissance regiment brushes through a barricade outside the village of Harze, Belgium. This unit was part of General Hodges' US First Army, for the moment (September 1944) operating with Montgomery's 21st Army Group.

Once the slogging match around Caen was over, and the Allied troops made their various drives for the German border, the speed and mobility of the Cromwell, last of the British Cruiser tanks, was much appreciated, especially during the lightning push towards Antwerp.

and over a hundred vehicles of one sort or another – an illuminating example of the high cost of enthusiasm over that of caution; but the troops' enthusiasm was nothing compared to that which greeted them as they penetrated deeper into the suburbs of Paris. Flowers, drinks, girls' kisses – all held up progress as effectively as would have an 88-mm gun had one been present along the Champs Élysées; as it happened, only a Panther was stationed there – in the Place de la Concorde – and this was destroyed by a single round from a French Sherman.

It was 3.00 p.m. before General Choltitz was captured, and even after he had signed a formal instrument of surrender, fighting was to continue for some hours – in the Bois de Boulogne until the next day – not least because German soldiers were well aware of the treatment they were likely to receive at the hands of French civilians once they put down their arms. Altogether, some 1,600 French soldiers and civilians died in Paris that day, and nearly 3,000 Germans, and it was fortunate that American medical supplies were near at hand to deal with the 8,500 wounded of both sides.

While Paris was in the process of liberation, the bulk of the Allied armies was shipping itself across the Seine with one major objective – to move ahead fast enough to prevent the German armies regaining their cohesion and building new positions along any of the river lines which had served them so well in the previous war – the Somme, the Marne, the Aisne and the Meuse. The day after the US 4th Division arrived in the French capital, the other divisions of Hodges' First Army crossed the Seine and, after a number of small but brisk battles, began a drive which for speed and excitement outmatched even the race of Patton's divisions from the Mayenne to Fontainebleau.

The left hand corps (on Montgomery's right) reached St Quentin by the end of August and by 2 September was approaching Mons and Tournai (thus causing the abrupt cancellation of an air drop for the following day, intended to hold the position until Hodges' men arrived!) and Hodges then detached divisions of the V Corps and sent them along the valleys of the Sambre and Meuse towards Aachen. On the right flank, VII Corps had driven through the remnants of German Army Group B (now commanded by the 'Führer's Fireman' Field Marshal Model) as far as the point of the Ardennes near Laon, where it veered east to drive along the southern border – thus forming and then widening a gap between itself and the northern half of Hodges' command, somewhat to the general's concern.

But to the south of First Army, Patton's Third Army was cutting a triumphant swathe through the

British AFVs in north-west Europe

While British armour at the end of the war might not have matched that of the Germans for sheer fighting power, it was very mobile, and in the kind of fast-moving campaign fought by Montgomery to take the port of Antwerp, that was vital.

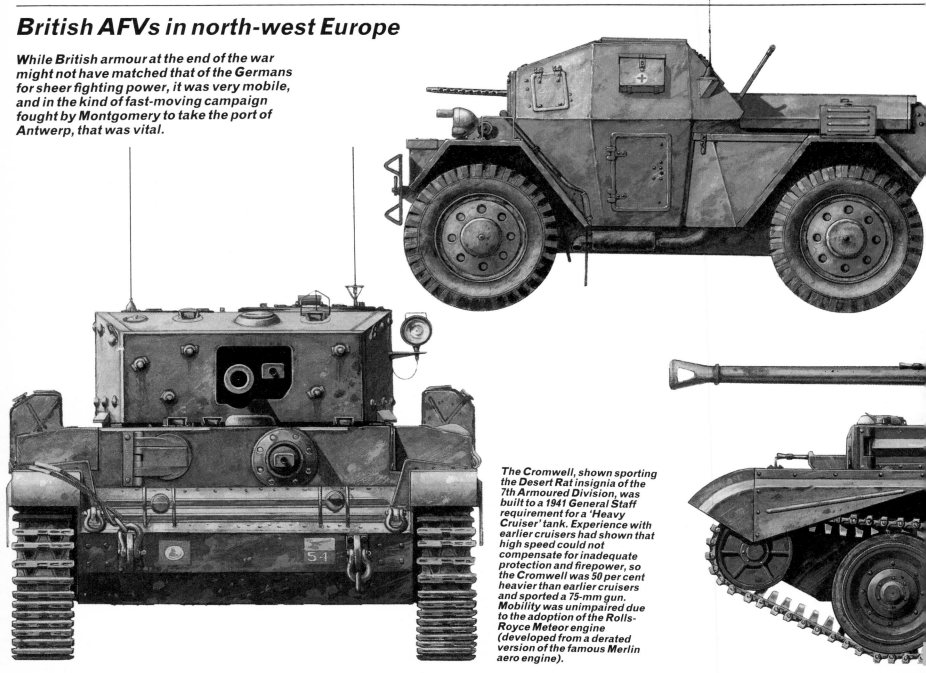

The Cromwell, shown sporting the Desert Rat insignia of the 7th Armoured Division, was built to a 1941 General Staff requirement for a 'Heavy Cruiser' tank. Experience with earlier cruisers had shown that high speed could not compensate for inadequate protection and firepower, so the Cromwell was 50 per cent heavier than earlier cruisers and sported a 75-mm gun. Mobility was unimpaired due to the adoption of the Rolls-Royce Meteor engine (developed from a derated version of the famous Merlin aero engine).

countryside and everyone and everything in it. The Red Ball Express, a fleet of fast convoys on a one-way system carrying nothing but petrol for the US armies, gave them enough fuel at the start for XX Corps on the left to reach Reims and then swing across towards Verdun, while to its south XII Corps sped towards Commercy in an exhilarating chase punctuated by short – but usually vicious – bursts of fighting. At one period XX Corps was running on petrol from a captured German supply train, and at another there was a brief and hilarious halt when XII Corps captured a German train which upon examination proved to be full of cases of wine and cognac; but mostly it was a pell-mell pursuit with everyone hanging on grimly inside jolting jeeps or lorries, outside rumbling tanks or tank destroyers, or even on prime movers whose normal tows were the heavy artillery or anti-aircraft guns which had been left behind.

Patton's fuel problem

Over all flew the fighter bombers of the Tactical Air Commands, shooting up everything not displaying the identifying white star, and the roads were lined with the wrecks of German transport and bodies of their horses – and of soldiers. Evidently, German Army Group B was in a condition of total disarray and, if the pressure could be maintained, could never hope to turn and offer a solid resistance – perhaps not even when the German frontiers were reached.

Then on 31 August the leading formations reached the Meuse – with empty fuel tanks and no sign of the Red Ball Express convoys behind them. 'My men can eat their belts,' raved Patton, 'but we got to have gas!'

But for the moment, none was available – and this time Patton could not employ the means he had used when faced with a similar situation on a training exercise in Louisiana. He had just filled all the division's vehicle-tanks with petrol from the pumps along the road, paying for it all from his own immense wealth.

Above: The final section of treadway is laid into place on a newly constructed pontoon bridge across the Seine on 24 August. By this time, there were a number of Allied bridgeheads across the river, and forward units were pushing on towards Belgium.

Right: Multiple rocket-launchers of Hodges' First Army were into German territory by November, ready to bombard positions in the Hurtgenwald, part of the Rhineland.

Left: Daimler scout cars were designed in the 1930s as a general utility 4x4 scout vehicle for use in the all-mechanized army then being envisaged. Although lightly armed, it was quiet and manoeuvrable, and proved very effective. It remained in production throughout the war.

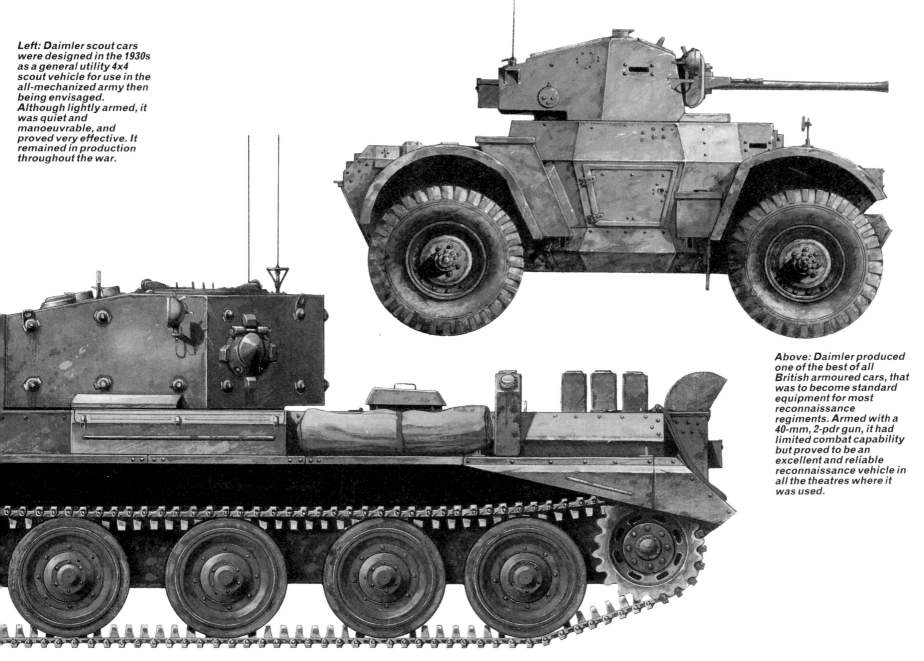

Above: Daimler produced one of the best of all British armoured cars, that was to become standard equipment for most reconnaissance regiments. Armed with a 40-mm, 2-pdr gun, it had limited combat capability but proved to be an excellent and reliable reconnaissance vehicle in all the theatres where it was used.

The main lines of General Montgomery's plan for the advance of Twenty-first Army Group were for the Canadian forces on the left to invest and capture the ports of Le Havre, Dieppe, Boulogne and Calais and then press onwards to Zeebrugge and the Scheldte Estuary, while the divisions of the British Second Army drove through Amiens and Lille towards Brussels, with one corps peeling off to the left once they were across the Belgian border to seize Antwerp. It was believed that, as in the south, the German forces available to block the advance were in such a state of disorganization that it was unlikely that they would be able to offer much other than sporadic resistance.

German opposition

Nevertheless, the crossing of the Seine by both Second Army corps was firmly resisted at first and the Bailey bridges at both Louviers and Vernon were thrown across under fire – but by 29 August the armoured spearheads were streaming across, XII Corps on the left and XXX Corps on the right. The country they faced was ideal for the type of operations for which they had been trained and for which the crews hungered – flat, open, clear of forest and with good roads – though at first it would seem to have taken the crews some hours to shake off the caution that fighting through the *bocage* had induced. On the right, XXX Corps took until midday 30 August to reach Beauvais, and that night as the Guards Armoured Division came up to take over the lead, orders came that they were to drive straight on and seize crossings over the Somme on each side of Amiens, 35 miles distant.

'A night march through enemy territory is at the best of times a tense affair,' wrote one tank officer later, but by morning it became crystal clear that these were indeed 'the best of times'. Though there were occasional spots of resistance, these were fleeting, and what became known as 'the Great Swan' gathered splendid momentum as hour followed hour.

At dawn the leading tanks of 11th Armoured Division were in the Amiens suburbs and the city bridges were in their hands before the guards realized their presence. Meanwhile 2nd Household Cavalry cars had raced along on the right flank, through sleeping villages occasionally sparked with light as some more awake inhabitant realized the difference in the engine sounds to those he had been hearing for the last four years, and flung open his window to shout greetings. They swung around the eastern skirts of Amiens and raced for three bridges – Faith, Hope and Charity – over the river there, dropping off engineers as they reached the first two and all three were in their hands before the German posts could stop the defusing of demolition charges.

Arras and Aubigny on the Scarpe were the easily reached objectives for 1 September, with only a 15-mile jaunt the next day to Lens and Douai, occasionally slowed by minor actions – in which men were nevertheless killed – cheered all the way by the enthusiastic populace who garlanded the tanks and crews, pressed wine and food upon them and sent out their prettiest girls to kiss them. The day also gave time for supplies to catch up, for some much needed servicing to the vehicles, and for the Guards to polish their boots and buckles, blanco their webbing and press the creases back into their trousers.

Prominent among the Allied forces taking part in the Allied campaign in north west Europe were the exiles, fighting for their own countries. These Netherlands Cromwells are part of the 'Princess Irene' Brigade seen here in a Belgian village near the Dutch border.

A Belgian Vickers Machine-Gun team is seen in action while serving with Montgomery's 21st Army Group as they push along the Belgian coast.

The reason for the break, they were all told, was that an airborne drop was planned the next day into the country just ahead around Tournai, so being soldiers, the vast majority just shrugged their shoulders, accepted the possibility of rest and the reality of relaxation all around them, content that the Airborne now should have as easy a time as they were having themselves.

Brussels freed

Then in the early evening the new orders arrived. The drop had been cancelled as the Americans had arrived at Tournai first and now the Guards Armoured were to get to Brussels as quickly as possible and the 11th Armoured were to drive for Antwerp. Brussels was just within a day's range for armour, Antwerp just beyond it – but in both cases only if every unit regarded it as a race.

General Sir Alan Adair organized it for the Guards Armoured Division. He plotted two separate but parallel routes for the two brigades, sent them off together and gave them a winning post inside the Belgian capital. One brigade was delayed by an action at Leuze and again at Enghien, but their momentum and luck carried them through both blocks with little loss of time, or men; but as the other brigade was as a result slightly ahead, the brigadier instructed the Welsh Guards in their faster Cromwell tanks to rush forward on their own.

They reached the winning post just ahead of the Grenadiers in their slower Shermans, but both contingents suffered their greatest delays as soon as the inhabitants of the Brussels suburbs realized who they were. The scenes that day and the next in Brussels outdid those of any other liberated city in Europe. The Guards drove through the streets 'as if floating on a sea of upturned faces', wrote one of them later. 'It seemed as if a million inhabitants had of one accord gone mad.... Spontaneously they lined the streets and pavements twenty deep, and cheered and cheered and cheered. Last war veterans saluted, wives cried and laughed alternately, young women leapt on to the vehicles embracing the dusty soldiers and youths fired rifles into the air.'

It was the most memorable day of their lives, both for the Guardsmen and for the Bruxellois.

Until a port had been freed, Allied supplies had to come the long, weary way from Normandy. Once Antwerp had been liberated, it became essential to take the German-held islands at the mouth of the Scheldte, Westkapelle, on Walcheren was the first landing, and Royal Marine Commandos are seen here coming ashore.

Alongside the Typhoon, the Republic P-47 was the classic fighter-bomber of the race to the Reich. Armed with powerful guns and able to haul bombs and rockets, the P-47 was a formidable attack craft, pulverizing German installations. It was a tricky opponent to fight against, despite its size.

Allied fighter-bombers

One of the most significant assets available to Eisenhower's forces was the tactical air power which gave the Allies such dominance over the battlefield. That air power was seen most dramatically in the direct support of the ground forces, in which the fighter-bomber performed to great effect.

A 9th Air Force Republic P-47D Thunderbolt, with a suitably impressive array of victories, gets a guiding hand from a ground crewman. The long nose of the P-47 made it difficult to see forward, and with the narrow makeshift taxiways laid down at the airstrips weaving was not possible.

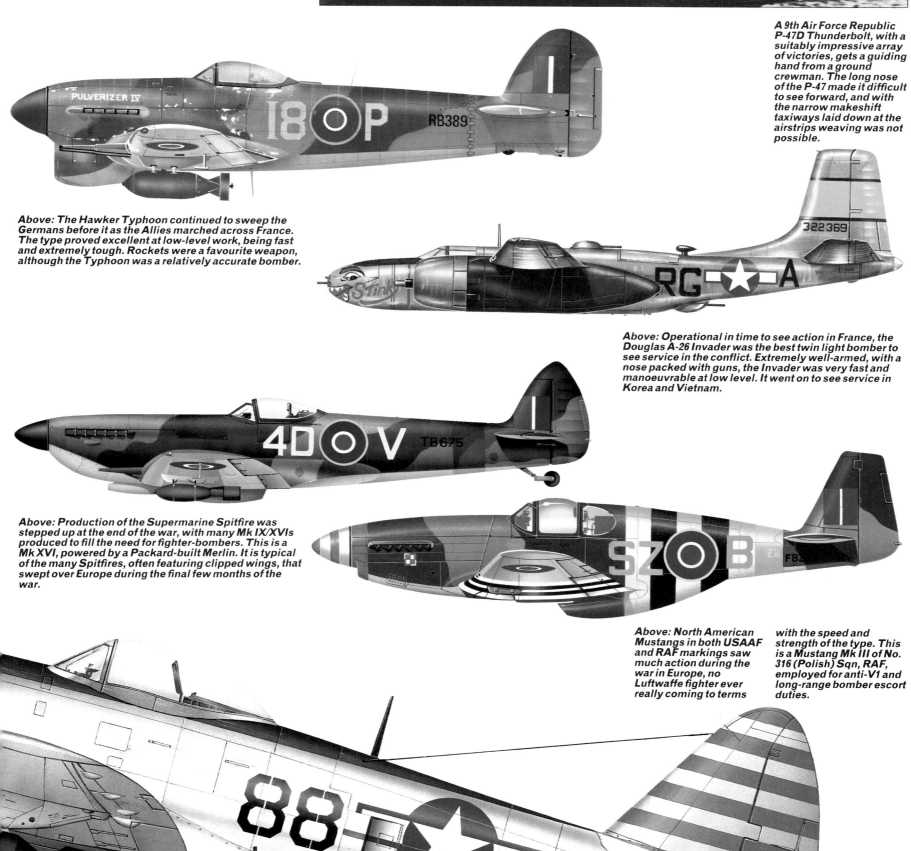

Above: The Hawker Typhoon continued to sweep the Germans before it as the Allies marched across France. The type proved excellent at low-level work, being fast and extremely tough. Rockets were a favourite weapon, although the Typhoon was a relatively accurate bomber.

Above: Operational in time to see action in France, the Douglas A-26 Invader was the best twin light bomber to see service in the conflict. Extremely well-armed, with a nose packed with guns, the Invader was very fast and manoeuvrable at low level. It went on to see service in Korea and Vietnam.

Above: Production of the Supermarine Spitfire was stepped up at the end of the war, with many Mk IX/XVIs produced to fill the need for fighter-bombers. This is a Mk XVI, powered by a Packard-built Merlin. It is typical of the many Spitfires, often featuring clipped wings, that swept over Europe during the final few months of the war.

Above: North American Mustangs in both USAAF and RAF markings saw much action during the war in Europe, no Luftwaffe fighter ever really coming to terms with the speed and strength of the type. This is a Mustang Mk III of No. 316 (Polish) Sqn, RAF, employed for anti-V1 and long-range bomber escort duties.

British troops halt at the outskirts of a German-occupied village. In the face of overwhelming odds the Wehrmacht continued to put up tenacious resistance, conscious that in the east the Russians were approaching Germany.

Above: A German machine-gunner aims through a curtain of smoke and fire in a French port behind Allied lines. Isolated German garrisons held the naval bases of Lorient and St Nazaire until the end of the war.

Needless to say, matters had not gone so triumphantly on other parts of the British and Canadian front, and during the next few days it became evident that the armour of XXX Corps had found a lucky gap between two reorganizing German forces.

It had been recognized from the start that the Germans were likely to defend the Channel ports as stoutly as they could, not only for the strategic purpose of complicating the Allied supply problems, but also because in the Pas de Calais area lay most of the sites of the V-bombs which were deluging southern England and upon which the Führer pinned his hopes of breaking the British will to fight on. Le Havre in particular was known to be strongly held, and as it was the first objective on the left flank and the Canadians were anxious to get on – especially to Dieppe where so many of their comrades had fallen in the 1942 raid – it was agreed that it should be the target of the British I Corps. As this formation included the 51st Highland Division who wished to be the first into St Valèry, for reasons similar to those of the Canadians who wanted to liberate Dieppe, there was no controversy over the decisions and a great deal of mutual pride and sympathy.

Both the formations crossed the lower Seine during the last days of August, both reached their prime objectives on 2 September, the Canadians to find Dieppe unoccupied, the Highlanders fighting a short but satisfying action before reaching the scenes of their 1940 tragedy. On 3 September the skirls of Scottish and Canadian pipes covered all sounds of battle along that stretch of coast – and did little for the confidence of the enemy soldiers who heard it.

Battle for Le Havre

In the meantime, Lieutenant-General Crocker, commanding the British I Corps, was facing an acute and unpleasant problem – as was his opponent, Colonel Wilderwuth, an officer of no great military ambition and mindful of the lives, not only of his own soldiers, but also of the 50,000 civilians within the defence lines with which Le Havre was now surrounded. He was also mindful of Hitler's 'No Surrender' order and of the fate of the families of those who disobeyed, and both he and General Crocker were aware of the 'unconditional surrender' terms which were now the official and invariable Allied proposals.

Neither man had the slightest room for manoeuvre, and thus officialdom and unthinking political decree enforced a solution of brute force. For 10 days Bomber Command sent heavy aircraft over the port to rain destruction down upon it; the guns of the monitor HMS *Erebus* and later of the *Warspite* hammered the defence batteries and all their surroundings, while along every approach the infantrymen of 49th and 51st Divisions patrolled and probed, and the crews of the specialized tanks of 79th Division, brought up from the beach-heads, serviced their engines and the equipment for their individual tasks, and awaited the hour of the attack.

It came at dusk on 10 September after a bombardment the like of which no one had seen before in which 5,000 tons of bombs were dropped into a limited area, marked out by a ring of flares dropped by the Pathfinders. As the last wave of bombers flew off, the guns of both sides opened fire, searchlights lit the scene with 'artificial moonlight' and the Flail tanks crashed forward amid the bursts of exploding mines, the Crocodiles added awful light to the fires with their 50-foot-long flares, and the Kangaroos probed through the gaps, decanting their loads of infantrymen to clear away the few anti-tank guns still operating.

Behind them, the foot soldiers marched doggedly forward, then crouched and ran as German rifle and machine-gun fire contested their advance. Such weight of fire and explosives had crashed into the city that it was a wonder that anyone had survived – but nevertheless it took all that night and most of the next day before the ring of defences was entirely in British hands, and even after another night of battle the columns fighting their way into the centre, where Wildermuth, badly wounded, was still conducting the defence, could not claim victory until the afternoon.

Only then, with Le Havre a rubble of demolished wharves and warehouses, wrecked streets and houses peopled by distraught and bewildered townsmen and women – the unhappy victims of Roosevelt's word-spinning – did Wildermuth surrender. Weeks would elapse before the port facilities would be repaired sufficiently for Le Havre to help much with the Allied supply problems.

Above: One of the most successful of all the 'Funnies' developed for the initial landings on the Normandy coast, the Churchill Crocodile flamethrowing tank was much in demand as a close infantry support weapon.

Below: The 15-in guns of the veteran HMS Warspite saw their last action off Walcheren. Even with one turret out of action due to glide-bomb damage sustained off Salerno, the veteran of Jutland lent weighty support.

German flying-bombs

German weapons development at the end of World War II was remarkable, providing the basis for many post-war technologies. But no programme had more effect than Hitler's 'vengeance' weapons, the V1 and V2, which were the first strategic cruise and ballistic missiles to go into action.

Constituting the most sinister of all strategic threats by Germany, the Vergeltungs-waffe (retaliation weapon) programme foreshadowed an entirely new concept of warfare and one that has come to dominate world politics ever since. The fact that it only achieved military reality during the final year of the war in Europe prevented the weapons from seriously influencing the final outcome of the war, but they were no last-ditch expedient. Development of long-range rockets dated as far back as 1933, with such men as Werner von Braun completing the first successful experimental rockets before the war.

First of the retaliation weapons to achieve service status was the pulse jet-powered Fieseler Fi 103 flying bomb (V1), much of whose development work was undertaken at Peenemünde in the Baltic during 1942; but after a devastating Bomber Command raid in August 1943, all launching trials were subsequently carried out in East Prussia. Soon afterwards numerous launching sites were identified in Northern France, suggesting to the Allies that a major campaign for the bombardment of southern England was being planned. Accordingly, both the RAF and USAAF embarked on a sustained series of attacks of these 'No Ball' sites, forcing the Germans to introduce much simplified 'ski sites' which proliferated rapidly and proved difficult to locate.

Constant production difficulties, as well as Allied bombing, delayed the start of the flying bomb offensive until 13 June 1944, when the first bomb fell near Gravesend. Within a fortnight more than 2,000 had been launched, of which the majority reached English shores. Although London was regarded as the major target, bombs were also deliberately aimed at various other major towns and cities throughout southern England.

To counter them, fighters patrolled the Channel while gun defences were given freedom to fire over the coastline itself; further inland the fighters were free to attack the bombs until the survivors neared the outer suburbs of London, where they were left to the gun defences and balloon barrage. The bombs proved unexpectedly fast, and the first wing of Tempest Mk V fighters, commanded by Wing Commander R. P. Beamont, was the most successful, shooting down 638 out of the RAF's total tally of 1,771 destroyed between 13 June and 5 September. Also ranged against the V1s were Mustangs, Mosquitoes, Spitfires and the first of the RAF's new twin-jet Meteor fighters of No. 616 Squadron at Manston.

As the Allied armies threatened and eventually overran the launch sites in the Pas de Calais, the Luftwaffe began discharging the flying bombs from Heinkel He 111s of KG 3 and KG 53, although Mosquito night fighters took a growing toll of the raiders. Of more than 30,000 bombs produced, only about 20 per cent reached their intended target areas in Britain, France and Belgium. For all their inaccuracy, they constituted however a useful propaganda weapon, killing 6,139 and injuring 17,239 civilians in Britain alone. The Luftwaffe launched a total of about 1,200 flying bombs from He 111s, of which only some 250 reached British soil, while nearly 80 of the bombers were lost.

Posing a much greater potential threat, on account of its immunity from interception and destruction before impact, the long-range V2 rocket was first launched against Paris by the German army in Belgium on 5 September 1944, followed by the first against London (falling on Chiswick) on the 9th, fired in Holland. Of about 6,000 rockets produced, 1,054 fell on Britain and 1,675 on the Continent, Antwerp being hit by 1,265 compared with London's 517. All the operationally-fired rockets were launched by mobile units of the Wehrmacht from rudimentary sites, some of which were pinpointed and attacked by Allied aircraft. Infinitely more menacing were huge underground concrete structures at Siracourt, Watten and Wizernes, designed to launch sustained salvoes from fixed batteries against London; fortunately they were spotted before completion by the Todt organization, and eventually demolished in attacks with remotely controlled B-17s packed with explosives.

The last V2 fell on Orpington, Kent, on 27 March 1945 – fired from a site 345 miles distant. The savage assault by rocket – whose approach and arrival was signalled by a shattering explosion – cost the lives of 2,855 British civilians, with 6,268 seriously injured.

One of the most important duties undertaken by RAF aircraft in 1944-45 was the interception of the many V1 weapons droning towards London. Cannon fire or wingtip deflections were used to bring them down. The Hawker Tempest Mk V (illustrated), was one of the fighters fast enough to catch the bombs.

An incomplete 'Ski-Jump' launch site is over-run by the Americans near Cherbourg. These camouflaged constructions were the subject of heavy RAF and USAAF attack, which forced the Germans into launching their missiles from improvised ramps (which were much harder to locate and were easier to build).

The Fieseler Fi-103 pilotless aircraft first flew on Christmas Eve 1942, and on 13 June 1944 became the first guided strategic missile to be fired in anger. More than 29,000 were produced, mostly from the vast slave-worked Mittelwerke.

Above: Ostensibly the German Atlantic Wall stretched from the Bay of Biscay to the coasts of Denmark, and in some locations the fortifications were exceptionally strong.

Right: Unfortunately for the Germans, such positions could be simply bypassed by the Allies, and along the Belgian coast the Wehrmacht had to depend upon mines, barbed wire and skills.

The same grim story had to be repeated at both Boulogne and Calais, though by the grace of the German commanders, Lieutenant-General Heim at the first and Lieutenant-Colonel Schröder at Calais, the toll among civilians was not so great, because evacuation had been agreed between the two sides. But the fighting in both cases was as fierce, and the eventual surrenders were brought about by heavy bombing and shelling, and the efficient use of Hobart's 'Funnies' which again proved their value and the genius of their inventors. By the end of September, the ruins of both ports were occupied by the Canadians, 30,000 German soldiers had become casualties (mostly prisoners) at a cost of about 1,500 Allied soldiers – but it would be a long time before the ports would be of much use to the armies which had liberated them.

The war had moved on. The day after the Guards Armoured had swept into Brussels, a squadron of the 3rd Royal Tank Regiment of the 11th Armoured Division had raced through a welcome in Antwerp, potentially as much of a hindrance as the one in Brussels, and reached the main dock installations. It was a *coup de main* which should have had the most significant of benefits, but unfortunately the euphoria of the moment was matched by the rapidity of reaction of the Germans, and before the bulk of 11th Armoured could get through to take control of the vast complex of quays and wharves and other port installations which made up the great inland harbour, all bridges across the Albert Canal had been blown, and all positions controlling the Scheldte Estuary – on both banks – had been strongly occupied. Again, the Allies might hold the port, but they could not use it.

Not that this unduly perturbed their Army Group commander, for Field Marshal Montgomery still had his eyes on the heart of Germany and his mind on a rapid thrust to it – narrow perhaps, but fatal.

On 10 September, he had met General Eisenhower at Brussels and addressed him at first with such force and acerbity that Ike had been driven, but with his normal kindness and understanding, to point out that he was Monty's boss! This done, he listened to Montgomery's arguments which were for a northern thrust through Holland, over the Rhine and into the Ruhr by the British Second Army under General Dempsey and the US First Army under General Hodges. Patton's army on the right and the Canadians on the left should receive only the supplies necessary for them to hold their positions, all else should feed this new central offensive – and for its opening thrust Mont-

The V2: Hitler's terror weapon

On 8 September 1944, Chiswick in West London was rocked by a mysterious explosion. Over the next few weeks it became clear that a new dimension had been added to warfare: the long-range ballistic missile had arrived.

In its initial form the A4 rocket system comprised 28 or 30 vehicles divided into 'soft' – which could clear the site before launch – and 'hard' – which were needed near the rocket throughout the launch. The latter were all armoured, several (including the vital launch control centre) being based on armoured cars of the SdKfz 231 or 238 types, with six or eight wheels or, increasingly, on halftrack suspension for greater towing power. There was a need for plenty of pulling power, for the rockets on their *Meillerwagen* vehicles, for the protected van with warheads, for the guidance station vehicles, for nine types of workshop, and above all for the propellant tanks.

Experimental troops even carried their own liquid-oxygen production plant. A mobile crane was needed to offer up the warhead section, weighing about 975 kg, of which a remarkable 93 per cent explosive. The fairly weak 60/40 Amatol filling was the lesser of two evils. More powerful explosive such as Trialen invariably detonated during re-entry back into the atmosphere, when the nosecone was heated to a bright cherry red by friction with the air. Despite thick glass wool insulation, which was also needed around the alcohol and liquid oxygen tanks, many rockets still exploded prematurely high above the earth, though the launch troops knew nothing of this.

From the start it was accepted that the rocket was too big to hide or to camouflage, and there was little attempt to prevent detection from the air. Early production A4s were painted mainly dark green, though from August 1944 Mittelwerke rockets were camouflaged in pale green/grey patterns. By October 1944 it was common for a single firing unit to travel by night with as many as five rockets, all supported by the same service vehicles though, of course, needing five loads of alcohol and rapidly evaporating liquid oxygen.

The transporter incorporated a giant hydraulic ram, usually powered from an external source, which slowly raised the complete cradle and missile vertically onto the launcher. The latter had to be towed to the selected spot, the wheels removed, and the platform levelled with spirit levels. Soon after elevation the loading of 4173 kg of ethyl alcohol was started. It was necessary to rotate the upper table of the launch platform to get the missile exactly aligned with the azimuth (direction) of the target, because there was no provision for changing direction after launch. All that the guidance system did was control the missile as it gently tipped over towards the target and finally cut off main-engine propulsion at exactly the right velocity (this was done in a way similar to modern inertial systems, by measuring the varying acceleration of the missile and measuring the time).

The launch troop had to work their way through two substantial manuals of procedures, which in all took a minimum of six hours. In the final two hours 5,533 kg of intensely cold liquid oxygen was carefully pumped aboard. Last of all, and with the strictest adherence to procedures, the fluids needed to drive the turbopump were loaded: Z-Stoff (calcium permanganate solution) and 172 kg of T-Stoff (concentrated hydrogen peroxide). Once these were aboard the A4 was regarded with the greatest respect. Nobody liked it if the day was windy, because a toppled-over missile invariably went up in a fireball even if the simple electric-contact fuze on the tip of the nose failed to hit the ground.

In the last minutes the radio telemetry (often carried to log the achieved trajectory) was activated with four slim aft-facing rod aerials at the trailing edges of the giant fins. By this time everyone would be far from the rocket, except for the launch control vehicle which remained linked by two heavy cables. Launch was by manual procedures, with verification between steps. Three sets of

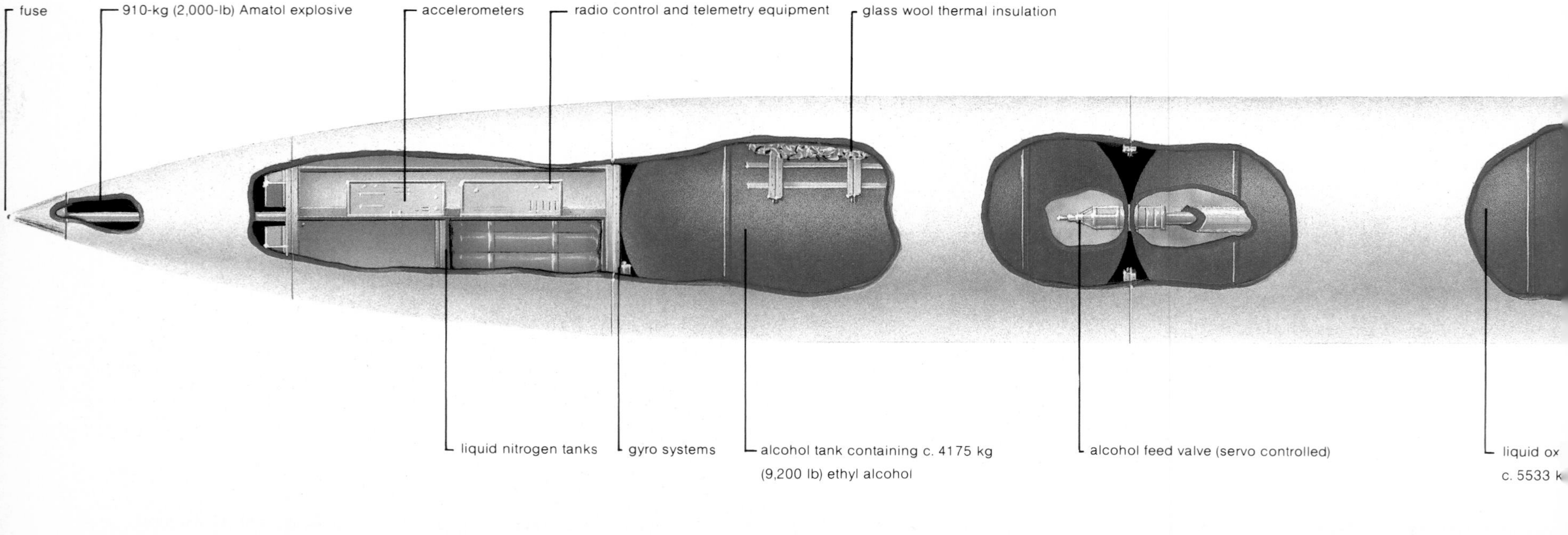

gomery proposed to use the main reserve which Eisenhower had always promised would be his to command – the three divisions of the Allied 1st Airborne Army.

They should form 'an airborne carpet' along a corridor 65 miles long from the border to cross the Rhine, taking and holding the bridges at Eindhoven, Nijmegen and Arnhem, over which Dempsey's and Hodges' armies would then stream to 'bounce the Rhine', reach the Zuider Zee on one flank and the north German plain on the other, and then, together and supported by the armies which had been temporarily left behind, drive straight for Berlin.

Thus the war in Europe might end in 1944.

Arnhem

During the morning of Sunday, 17 September 1944, the inhabitants of south east England witnessed the assembly in the skies above them of the greatest airborne armada of all time. From 22 airfields stretching from Dorset to Lincolnshire over 1,500 aircraft climbed into the air, and as the fighter and bomber units sped away on their protection or distraction tasks Douglas C-47 Dakota transports and Short Stirling bombers converted for troop-carrying, some of them towing a total of 478 gliders packed with men or vehicles, formed up for their journeys over the North Sea to the Netherlands.

One stream made for the North Foreland, then due east across the sea to Geel, then north towards their dropping zone at Eindhoven; these held the men and equipment of the US 101st Airborne Division (commanded by Major-General James Gavin). The second, larger stream, flew on a line farther north,

Left: M4 Sherman tanks provided the bulk of Allied armour. On its own it was no match for German vehicles, but it was available in sufficient quantities to overcome that disadvantage. Nevertheless, it was not pleasant to be an M4 crewman knowing that there were Panthers about.

While Eisenhower's forces were pressing on towards the Rhine, the 50,000 German prisoners taken in the Falaise pocket had to be dealt with, along with a similar number taken previously. For many Allied soldiers, this was their first look at Germans, who turned out to be men like any other men.

Below: In a small village on the Franco-Belgian border, members of the resistance take the opportunity to pay off old scores as they round up fellow countrymen who collaborated with the occupying Germans.

safety links and valves had to be activated before the actual firing, which began by opening the nitrogen feed valve and then the master valves for peroxide and permanganate. These mixed in a reaction chamber to generate high-pressure superheated steam to drive the 730-hp turbopump. As soon as this started turning it began feeding the main propellants, the liquid oxygen passing through a distributor leading to the ring of injectors in the head of the combustion chamber, and the alcohol reaching the same injectors via the double wall of the nozzle in order to provide essential cooling. Ignition of the main propellants was electrical, by an exploding bridgewire. Acceleration of the turbopump to full speed took less than two seconds, by which time the main engine should (in theory) be putting out full thrust. This would raise the missile off the launcher, its stability being assured by the graphite vanes in the rocket jet.

Within two or three seconds the great rocket would rise above the surrounding trees, which were always present to provide some protection against the wind and air reconnaissance. At this point the rocket would be seen by people in surrounding villages and probably by Allied pilots, but though several Allied fighters tried to chase rising A4 rockets not one was ever shot down. One, in fact, climbed vertically just as a Spitfire Mk XIV passed overhead in a tight turn, and disappeared into cloud before the fighter could get near it. As it climbed away, it was slowly tilted over by its guidance to an angle of 45° or even 40°, depending on the target distance. Then, about 60-70 seconds from lift-off, the propulsion was cut off, the trajectory having been established. Only a system malfunction could stop it.

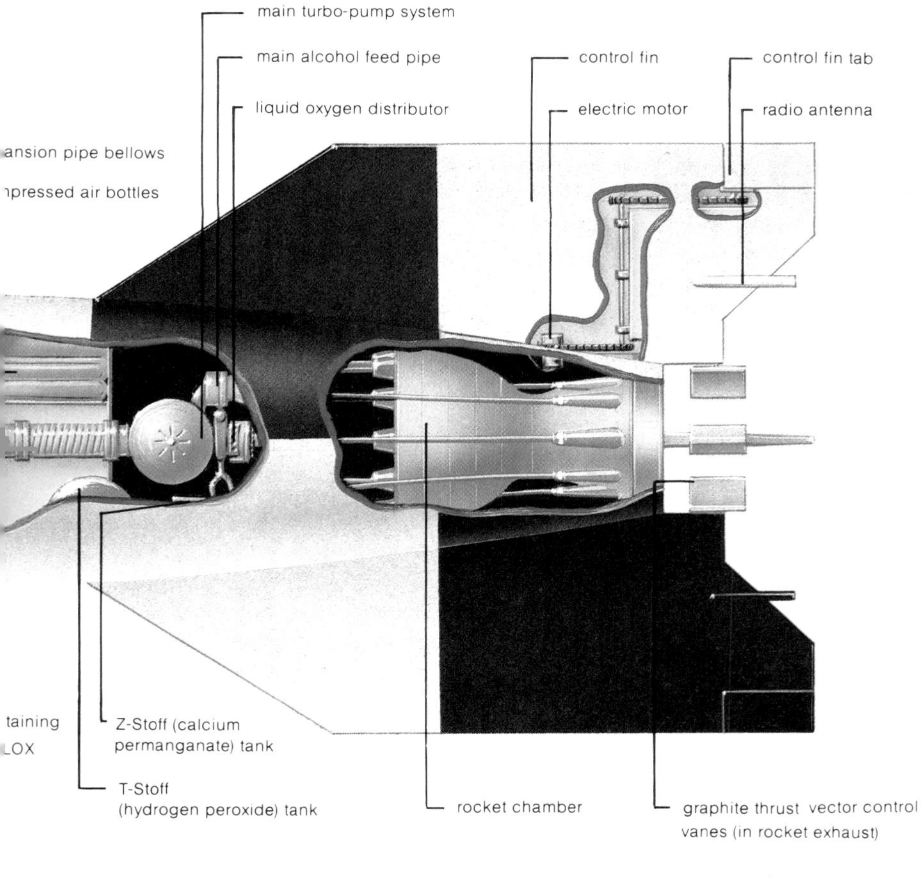

Certainly one of the most significant advances in weapons technology ever achieved, and the foundation of both Soviet and American missile development, the A4 ballistic missile was the subject of considerable investigation after the war. A captured A4 rocket is test-launched by the Americans at White Sands, New Mexico in 1946.

Above: Dutch fields lay scattered with RAF gliders, towed in by Stirlings and Halifaxes. Many of the gliders were damaged during the landing, some hitting obstacles on the ground. Miraculously, most managed to avoid each other, no mean feat in the packed landing grounds.

Above: After the gliders had landed, the paratroops dropped down from Dakotas, forming a large ground force, ready to move and fight. Note the dismembered tails of the Airspeed Horsa gliders.

over Aldeburgh, above the specially positioned vessels in the North Sea flashing their beacon lights and then Shouen Island, over the Dutch coast as far as the oddly named small town of s'Hertogenbosch where the stream split into two. The larger part carried the US 82nd Airborne Division and flew almost due east towards the area between Grave and Nijmegen, while the smaller part carried the Air Landing Brigade and one Parachute Brigade of the British 1st Airborne Division (commanded by Major-General Robert Urquhart) and flew north east to the division's landing grounds 10 miles to the west of the town of Arnhem and its vital bridge of the Neder Rijn.

That bridge and four other bridges to the south at Nijmegen, Grave, Veghel and Eindhoven, were the objectives for these airborne forces, for farther to the south (along the line of the Meuse-Escaut Canal) waited the forward troops of the British Second Army, poised to hurl themselves forward along the Eindhoven-Arnhem road and across all the canals and rivers between, outflanking the main German defences of the Siegfried Line and thus forming, in the words of their commander-in-chief, Field Marshal Montgomery, 'a springboard for a powerful full-blooded thrust to the heart of Germany'.

The bridge at Arnhem was the tip of that springboard, the *Ultima Thule* of Operation Market Garden.

Operation Market Garden failed, largely because two crack SS Panzer Divisions, of II SS Panzerkorps, had been withdrawn to the Arnhem area for recuperation; against such veterans the lightly-armed paratroopers were seriously outmatched.

Right: The airdrops over Holland took their toll on the transport fleet. Here a Douglas Dakota burns during the Nijmegen operation. The crew had managed to get out before the crash.

Twelve converted British bombers and six American Dakotas carried the Pathfinder company that dropped first, and within its time schedule the company's work was completed; as the 149 Dakotas carrying the men of 1st Parachute Brigade arrived over Dropping Zone X the flares were all burning and the marking tapes laid out, as they were for Landing Zones S and Z where the 254 Airspeed Horsa and 38 giant General Aircraft Hamilcar gliders of the Air Landing Brigade and Urquhart's headquarters were released from their tows, first to drop with stomach-wrenching acceleration then to level off and skim silently to their destinations. From the entire force only five gliders had been hit or the tows cut during the journeys, and only 35 aircraft lost – many of these after they had dropped their parachutists or slipped their tows. As a loss rate of 30 per cent had been predicted, the omens looked good at first for Market Garden.

Nevertheless, the first troop movements were slow to begin. It was 3.30 p.m. on that fine Sunday afternoon before Lieutenant-Colonel John Frost had assembled the men of his 2nd Parachute Battalion and led them off on their 8-mile march to the Arnhem Bridge. But their planned predecessors, the brigade reconnaissance squadron which should have raced off long before in their armed jeeps to take the bridge by *coup de main*, had not even started; by an unfortunate coincidence three of the gliders which had been lost had been carrying their vehicles.

A bridge is blown

Frost's battalion reached Oosterbeek, a small town half way to Arnhem, and Frost was about to detach one company to capture and cross the railway bridge over the Neder Rijn (to storm the southern end of the main bridge while the rest of the battalion took the northern end) when a loud explosion revealed that they were too late and the rail bridge had been blown.

This was the second serious setback, but the British paratroops pressed on after first brushing aside resistance by German armoured cars and snipers inside Oosterbeek town; but it was dark by the time Frost and his men reached Arnhem Bridge, and began the epic battle by which the legend of '2nd Para' was born.

Meanwhile, Urquhart was facing another severe difficulty: his signal sets were not working. This was not so uncommon in those pre-transistor days, and in fact it is fair to say that in 1944 no satisfactory small portable set had yet been manufactured; they were either too heavy for easy transport or too fragile and short in range for effectiveness in a spreading battle. So in order to find out what was happening, Urquhart set out after his paratroops by jeep.

He found Frost's HQ close to the Rhine bank, then turned back and towards the sound of battle near Oosterbeek. There Urquhart found Lieutenant-Colonel Fitch's 3rd Battalion (heavily engaged with young German troops who had been rushed down to block them and who fought with fanatical zeal) and also found the commander of 1st Parachute Brigade, Brigadier Lathbury. By now it was dark, it was evident that German panzer units were coming into position between 3rd Battalion and Arnhem, as they were also between Lieutenant-Colonel Dobie's 1st Parachute Battalion working its way along the railway line running into Arnhem from the west.

The night was spent by 1st and 3rd Battalions probing down towards Arnhem against ever-thickening resistance, and by Frost's men first attempting to cross the bridge to the southern end against withering fire from armoured vehicles and a pill-box, then repelling the first efforts by German vehicles to cross from the south. Four German lorries were set on fire, and in their light Frost's engineers cut all the leads they could find, though heat and machine-gun fire prevented them from reaching German demolition charges set among the girders.

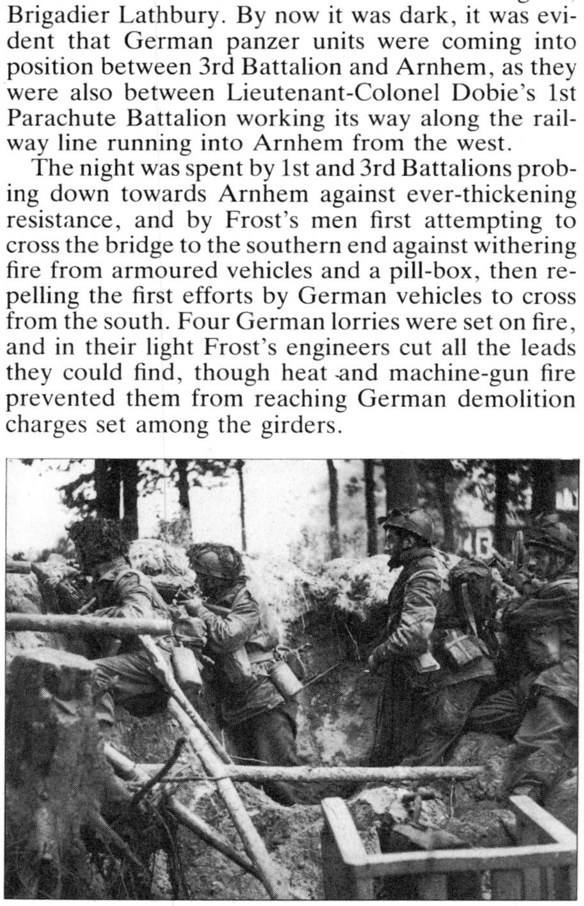

The early stages of the landing did not receive as much hard treatment as had been expected, fewer aircraft and troops being lost in the initial landings than had been allowed for. As an omen for the troops, however, it was tragically inaccurate.

A camouflaged StuG III assault gun in the streets of Arnhem illustrates the problem faced by the lightly-armed British paratroopers. If they were to survive against armour, they needed relief from the south.

A paratrooper wounded and captured at Arnhem. The lightly equipped units of the 1st British Airborne division were confronted by German armour tempered by years on the Eastern Front.

But by now the pattern of the battle had been formed; powerful and efficient German units were being fed into the gap between Frost's men at the bridge and all possible reinforcements – and even when the 4th Parachute Brigade under Brigadier John Hackett arrived on the Monday afternoon, it could only fight its way forward to join the remnants of 1st and 3rd Battalions, blocked around Oosterbeek and the small farms and houses to the west. Throughout the next two days the separate battles raged with ever-increasing ferocity, the advantage moving to the Germans as a result of dwindling numbers on the British side (and dwindling ammunition too, for to the near-despair of the men fighting in constricting areas, the RAF's supply aircraft were dropping the vital canisters in zones already occupied by the enemy).

By Wednesday night it was all over at the bridge. Frost had been wounded during the late afternoon, the Germans had shelled into chaos every building the paratroops had occupied, and now their panzers moved inexorably across the bridge; German infantry closed in and took the few fit survivors prisoner, carrying away and treating the wounded with care and courtesy.

During Thursday, the survivors of the division, now some 3,000 men, began coalescing around the village of Westerbouwing on the outskirts of Oosterbeek, their focal point St Elisabeth's Hospital, their outposts stretching down to the river bank, all their hopes resting in the promised arrival of the infantry and tanks of the Second Army. But alas, these were baulked at Nijmegen by fierce German defences, now further reinforced as more panzer formations drove down across the Arnhem bridge.

Spirits were raised briefly on the afternoon of Friday, 22 September, when the Polish Airborne Brigade under its gallant General Sosabowski was dropped just south of the river, but the ferries had been destroyed and every attempt by the Poles to go to the rescue of the British came under withering fire from both banks; in the end only about 50 Poles got across. And the ordeal of the 1st Airborne Division had still another three days to run.

The men had been told that they would be relieved certainly within four days, perhaps in two; in the event they were on their own for nine days. Three battalions of the 43rd Division at last reached the southern bank of the river on Sunday afternoon, and some men of the 5th Dorsets crossed to bring help and reassurance to the exhausted, famished, desperate paratroops still holding on, and during the following afternoon their evacuation was organized.

That night XXX Corps artillery put down a devastating curtain of fire all around the perimeter, the glider pilots of the Air Landing Brigade taped out an escape route, and when darkness had fallen, guided their dazed and staggering comrades down to the bank, where British and Canadian engineers waited in assault boats which had somehow been rushed up from Nijmegen.

And as one semi-conscious paratrooper stumbled out of his boat, into the welcoming arms of more XXX Corps infantry, he was heard repeating endlessly to himself, 'That's bloody that! That's bloody that! That's bloody that!'

Operation Market Garden had been a good idea. It was defeated by lack of information of enemy dispositions around Arnhem, by bad luck with weather which had contributed to XXX Corps' delay, and mistaken planning which had dropped 1st Airborne Division too far from its objective.

But the battle for Arnhem Bridge will live in history as long as the red beret is worn.

Paratroopers prowl through the ruins of the hamlet of Oosterbeek near Arnhem. Casualties were extremely high during the nine days of the battle, only 2,163 of the 10,000 troops committed to Arnhem escaping.

The bridge that was too far – over the Neder Rhine at Arnhem, intended to allow Montgomery's 21st Army Group to force the flanks of Germany's defences and drive into the heart of the Reich.

Chapter 23

The Empire's Last Throw

The war in Burma was slowly but surely swinging the Allies' way, as supplies and equipment finally began to reach this neglected theatre. The Japanese supply lines had to come overland, exposed to Allied air power, or by sea through the deadly ring of steel that was the US Navy's submarine blockade. Meanwhile the stage was being set for the reconquest of the Philippines, and the opening scene was to become the greatest sea battle in history.

General Renya Mutaguchi, Commander in Chief of the Japanese Fifteenth Army in Burma, was the commander of the regiment involved in the Marco Polo Bridge incident in 1937 that started Japan's war with China, which was to lead inexorably to World War II.

Weather dictates to a very great extent the activities which can take place in the regions covered by Assam, North Burma and the Yunnan Province of China, so after the débacle for the British in Arakan which ended in May 1943, several months elapsed during which all Allied energies were devoted to building up stores and training formations for the next phase of the war.

At the end of August a new and unified South East Asia Command was set up with Admiral Lord Louis Mountbatten as Supremo and the American General 'Vinegar' Joe Stillwell as his deputy; and the main British striking force was established – the Fourteenth Army, of which General 'Bill' Slim was given command.

Just as important as the manpower and its leadership were the weapons, stores and communications which would supply them in battle. In a locality such as that in which they were to be expected to operate – rugged, rough and with a minimum of sound road and rail services – this meant that immense engineering projects were necessary, together with the formation of at least one vast stores and administration centre. It also necessitated the accumulation of a large fleet of transport aircraft together with a network of airfields between which it could operate, the necessary service and maintenance systems and, most important of all, sufficient fighter cover to guarantee air supremacy over the whole area.

By the summer of 1943 quite a large proportion of such a project was possible to the Allies, as the factories of the United States were growing in number and output and the mobilization schemes of both Britain and the Commonwealth, and America, had produced the men who were now completing at least their basic training.

The Japanese, on the other hand, were facing a decline in every particular. Their best soldiers and airmen had already been killed and their factories were quite unable to produce the necessary weapons in either the quality or the quantities reached by their enemies. All they had was the unbelievable staunchness and courage of their servicemen; as General Slim was to say, 'We all talk about fighting to the last man and the last bullet. The Japanese soldier was the only one who did it.'

The decision taken by the Allies was that the campaign of 1944 would be aimed at reoccupying Northern Burma and re-establishing communications with China along the 'Burma Road', thus making it possible to resume supplies to her large but ill equipped armies. In pursuance of this road and rail communications were considerably improved throughout Assam, and the necessary vast stores centre was set up in the plain around Imphal together with all necessary airstrips, signal networks, security and protection systems, plus the headquarters of the British IV Corps under command of Lieutenant-General Sir Geoffrey Scoones. As it was obvious that such a valuable military prize as Imphal was becoming would soon attract the attention of the enemy, General Scoones deployed his three infantry divisions and his tank brigade between the Imphal Plain and the Chindwin – which still constituted the demarcation line between the antagonists – and took full advantage of the network of forward patrols and native observers who had been feeding back information of Japanese activities since the arrival of the invaders in 1942.

Arakan Prelude

Before the main battles began, however, there was a short 'trial engagement' by both sides over the same ground which had seen the spring 1943 defeat for the British – the Arakan. In the early days of January 1944, two divisions of the British XV Corps — the 5th Indian on the right and the 7th Indian on the left – drove down into the Arakan on each side of the Mayu Range, to reach, respectively, Maungdaw and Buthidaung, between which ran the Japanese defensive systems set up since the previous battle.

There they attempted to break through down to Donbaik, but were at first repulsed. They then found themselves in some danger when the Japanese 55th Division under General Hanaya hooked around their left flank, captured Taung Bazar and drove westwards to cut 5th Indian Division's supply routes, both in the north and at Ngatyedauk ('Okeydoke') Pass. The two Indian divisions then concentrated into an 'Admin Box' near Sinzweya and the whole engagement became an exercise in techniques.

First attempts to supply the box by air failed in the face of the Japanese fighter squadrons, the first attempt to relieve the box was halted by Japanese blocking forces above Ngatyedauk Pass – as was the second from the eastern approaches to the box. But all the time the men of the two divisions in the box were perfecting their defences all round, and were becoming acclimatized to the idea that they were surrounded – but not on their own. Every day more Allied aircraft appeared overhead, first to beat off the Japanese fighters, then on 11 February successfully to drop ammunition and supplies to them.

On 25 February, 123rd Brigade broke through Okeydoke Pass and reached the box, supplies were

Left: Anti-tank gunners of the 5th Indian Division engage a Japanese bunker in Burma, when the tide of battle had turned the way of the Allies. The Indian and British troops of Slim's 14th Army, at last receiving adequate support, proved that they had learned their lessons well, and the Japanese were no longer the masters in jungle warfare.

Below: Infantrymen of General Sato's 31st Division haul themselves across the Chindwin on a raft ferry (at the start of the U-Go offensive). Their aim was to take Kohima, the commanding position controlling the supply route from India to Imphal.

Chronology of War: 1944

October 1
Red Army enters Yugoslavia

October 2
Germans evacuate Athens. Polish Home Army surrenders in Warsaw after savage German attacks

October 4
Red Army and Yugoslav partisans link up. Operation Manna; British special forces land in Peloponnese

October 5
German Army Group North threatened by Red Army drive to Baltic coast

October 6
Canadians assault Breskens pocket in the Low Countries

October 9
Canadians break into pocket towards Scheldte

October 10
Russians cross Carpathians in south, reach Baltic coast in north. British occupy Corinth

October 11
US aircraft attack Luzon in the Philippines. Aachen heavily shelled

October 12
British special forces capture Athens airfield

October 13
US 1st Army enters Aachen

October 14
British liberate Athens. Rommel (implicated in July 20 plot) commits suicide

October 16
Hungary asks for Armistice, but SS Commando Otto Skorzeny kidnaps Admiral Horthy, the head of state, and forces him to withdraw request

October 19
British drive to Mohnyin, Burma, and take Japanese supply depot. Germans leave Belgrade

The Japanese drive on Kohima

Japan's Operation U-Go, ambitiously sub-titled 'The March on Delhi,' opened with an attempt to seize the major supply base at Imphal (to forestall a coming Allied offensive) and the strategically placed village of Kohima astride the route from Assam.

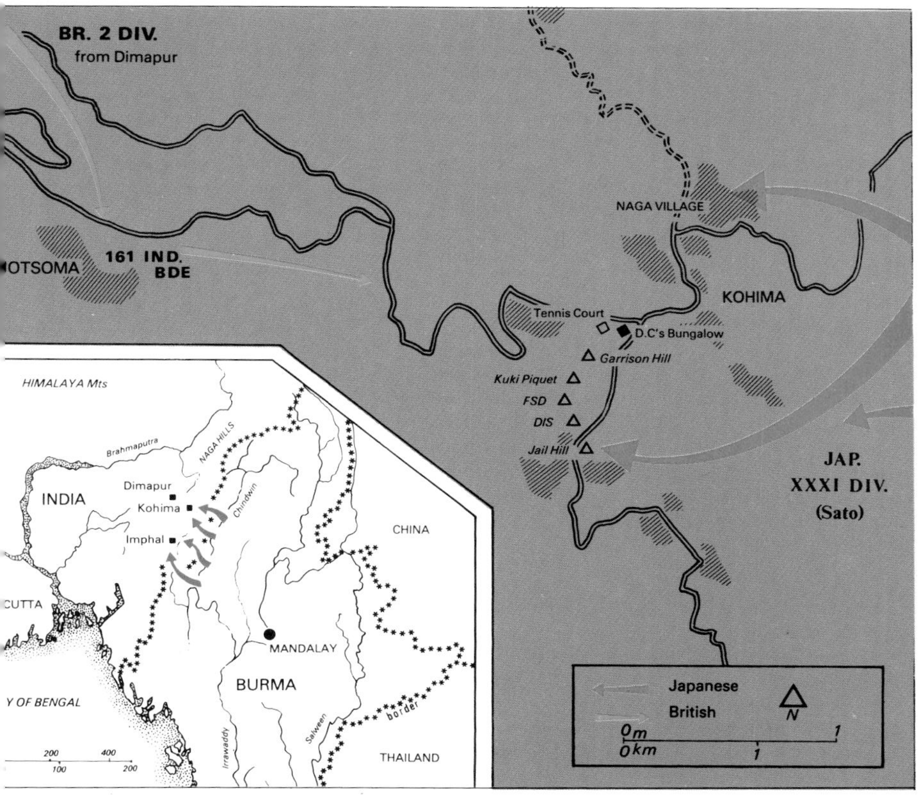

Japanese infantry push their way along jungle trails in an attempt to capture the rich supply base at Imphal. They exhibited all their familiar tenacity.

dropped again (and once more the following day), the Japanese command called off their siege and retreated, and on 11 March 7th Indian took Buthidaung. The next day 5th Indian advanced at their end of the line and took the main Japanese fortress of Razabil.

The advance down the peninsula was then abandoned, first because it was considered unnecessary, secondly because both divisions were now needed elsewhere. Imphal was under threat, as – 60 miles to the north – was the small colonial administration settlement of Kohima.

The Battle of Kohima

'I fought at Kohima!'

There can be few men alive today who can make this claim, for the bones of many rest there still and the health of the majority who lived to reach home must have been affected by their ordeal; but whoever they are and whether their skin be white, brown or yellow they should be accorded respect, for they lived through a conflict comparable only with Stalingrad or Cassino in World War II or with Mort Homme at Verdun in World War I. It was a fight to the death.

The events which led to the battle began on the night of 7 March 1944 when Lieutenant-General R. Mutaguchi, commanding the Japanese Fifteenth Army, launched Operation U-Go, throwing his divisions across the Chindwin river in an attack somewhat grandiloquently dubbed The March on Delhi. The first stage of this was to be the isolation and then capture of the vast stores and administration centre which the British had built up at Imphal.

Diversionary attacks were launched to the south of Imphal, but apart from the main assault on the depot the most important step was the move by the 31st Division under Lieutenant-General K. Sato, which crossed the Chindwin on 15 March and drove towards the small settlement of Kohima with its Naga village, its *maidan* on which the detachment of Assam Rifles drilled, its reinforcement camp in which soldiers returning from leave or hospital awaited their next move forward, its District Commissioner's bungalow with its terraced garden and tennis court, and its vital tactical position commanding the only road along which British reinforcements and supplies could reach Imphal from the railheads in Manipur.

Sato's orders, to be carried out with the utmost haste, were to drive his infantry battalions and their accompanying guns of the 31st Mountain Artillery Regiment in three columns across the countryside between the river and the settlement. Some idea of the size of his task is revealed by the fact that although the distance on the map was only 75 miles, his men had actually to march nearly 200 miles, their weapons, ammunition and supplies being carried on mules, elephants and oxen, of which the first and last categories were regarded as meat on the hoof. It is a tribute to the Japanese soldiers and their commander that their forward units reached the northern outskirts of Kohima at 4.00 a.m. on 5 April.

They found facing them a hastily organized defence perimeter manned at that moment by some 1,500 men, mostly of the 4th Royal West Kents augmented by men of the Assam Rifles (streaming back from forward positions where they had been both observing and attempting to delay Sato's advance) and the faithful, tenacious and extraordinarily courageous Naga villagers. One vital British formation of which the first Japanese arrivals remained for some time in ignorance, however, was a battery of 94-mm howitzers sited on the reverse slope of a hill at Jotsoma two miles to the west of Kohima, manned by Indian gunners of the 161st Indian Brigade, of which the 4th Royal West Kents were one battalion and 1/1st Punjabis and the 4/7th Rajputs the other two. These battalions were moving down from Dimapur to join the defence.

Within hours of arrival the men of the Japanese 58th Regiment were giving proof of their ferocity, and the Royal West Kents of their stubborness. The Japanese swept around Kohima from the Naga village to Jail Hill and on the night of 6 April, strengthened as more of their compatriots arrived, succeeded in taking two more of the features inside the defence perimeter, known as DIS and FSD. But their attacking units were annihilated on the next morning by the counter-attack of the Royal West Kents.

However, by now more and more of Sato's 12,000 infantry and their gunners were coming up, and he himself was confident of success within 48 hours,

Japanese infantrymen make an attack in Burma. Hand in hand with the increasing capacity of their enemies, Mutaguchi's troops had to contend with an ever-worsening logistics position.

Troops from the 7th Indian Division seen during the fighting at Ngatyedauk pass on the Arakan Peninsula. The Japanese defeat here could have been seen as a dress rehearsal for the larger battles to come on the Indian border.

Although outclassed in Europe, the M3 Grant medium tank was considerably more powerful than anything the Japanese had.

On the plain before Imphal, artillerymen from the Japanese 33rd Division shell IV Corps positions with a light field howitzer.

though seven days later this confidence was waning. On the night of 13 April massed attacks by wave after wave of cheering assault troops foundered on the rock of the stubborn infantry defence, aided by astonishingly accurate fire from the howitzers at Jotsoma, which broke up their formations as soon as they assembled, accompanied the waves all the way forward to the defences, and harried the survivors as soon as they were ordered back.

And on the following day reinforcements for the hard-pressed British got through to Jotsoma and began planning to blast their way through the last two miles. This was to prove appallingly difficult and a necessary delay of 24 hours almost fatal, for during that night the Japanese blasted FSD with every shell and mortar bomb their weapons could fire; the perimeter began to disintegrate, the FSD position and neighbouring Kukri Picquet was lost.

But at 8.00 a.m. on 18 April, the British at Jotsoma and the surrounding area replied with a devastating bombardment of the same kind and under its protection the relief of the original garrison was carried out. The Royal West Kents, the survivors of the Assam Rifles and those of the composite companies formed from the reinforcement depot dragged themselves out through the grisly evidence of their ordeals and the men of the Royal Berkshire Regiment and the Durham Light Infantry took their places.

Kohima relieved

But the battle was by no means over. On the British side, brigades of the 2nd Division were pouring down the road from Dimapur, while on the Japanese side more and more of Sato's 31st Division were being deployed, and as there was physically not enough room in the Kohima area for two whole divisions to operate, the encircling moves were attempted by both sides through the appallingly difficult country around Kohima. This was such that a rate of movement of one mile per day against no enemy opposition came to be accepted as the norm, and when on 27 April rain began falling with a weight and ferocity which none of the troops on either side had ever experienced before, movement became almost impossible and diarrhoea and dysentery took an even greater toll than bullets and shrapnel.

And all the time, on the central Kohima Ridge, the kernel of the battle was being fought. The Durhams fought off an attack on Garrison Hill which cost Sato such high casualties that he ordered a cessation of night attacks, and he sent a caustic signal to Mutaguchi complaining of the time the latter was taking to capture Imphal, and also of the total lack of support or supplies coming through to him at Kohima.

Now it was becoming a battle of logistics, and the British were winning it. Not only were supplies flowing down from Dimapur, but also more mountain artillery, and even mobile artillery in the form of tanks. And by the end of April the 2nd Dorsetshires had begun fighting their way into Kohima towards the District Commissioner's bungalow, and reached the edge of the the tennis court. This now became the scene of an almost Pyrrhic conflict.

The opposing forces were separated by less than 25 yards, but the Japanese had got there earlier and, great diggers always, had burrowed deep into the terrace which rose at the far end, and also under a big water-tank which dominated the area. No one could move across the open area in daylight, and Dimapur stores were astonished by the continual demands for gym shoes for night patrolling! But though these proved effective, the battle dragged on with ever increasing ferocity, and it was not until the middle of May, when a single tank managed the tortuous route up the District Commissioner's drive and began blasting the Japanese bunkers, that the British could claim even 'the first set'.

But more tanks arrived (of 149th RAC) and more infantry; and during May the men of the Manchesters, the Royal Scots, the Royal Norfolks, the Worcesters, the Queen's Own Cameron Highlanders and the Royal Welch Fusiliers came up to help the men already in Kohima, amid their ordeal of shell and bomb-burst and the incessant chatter of rifle and machine-gun, facing the almost unbelievable bravery and ferocity of the Japanese soldiers.

Nothing was coming up for them: Mutaguchi's attack on Imphal was blocked by the garrison there, and far from sending help up to Sato he had demanded the release to him of one of Sato's battalions. All Sato received during the entire campaign were words of empty encouragement, orders which he was unable to obey and promises of victory at Imphal which were never kept; all the time his men were sacrificing their lives, for as usual none of them allowed themselves to be taken prisoner and there was nothing for the wounded to do but die; and Sato's strength was falling.

By the end of May Sato knew that he could not take Kohima, and further sacrifice was pointless. After an angry exchange of signals with Mutaguchi, in one of which he pointed out that since crossing the Chindwin his force had received not a single bullet or grain of rice, let alone any reinforcements, he sent off his last angry jibe ('The tactical ability of Fifteenth Army Staff lies below that of cadets'), closed down his radio and ordered his men to retire.

This the Japanese soldiers reluctantly did, desperately fighting off the clutches of the now all-encircling British and firing off the last of their mortar bombs and shells. And the story of their agonizing walk back to the Chindwin, living on grass and roots, their clothing and boots in tatters, using canes or their broken rifles as crutches, is an epic of endurance and courage which no soldier will ever decry, certainly not the equally valorous men who fought them.

With the Japanese less than 800 yards away, Gurkhas cut bamboo stakes to front their positions at Imphal. Cut off in the first week in April, IV Corps held out against the Japanese until relieved from Kohima late in June.

Chronology of War: 1944

October 20
US forces land on Leyte Island to start the Philippines campaign

October 21
Aachen garrison surrenders. Japanese counterattack on Leyte

October 23-26
Battle of Leyte Gulf. Red Army drives into East Prussia

October 26
Japanese losses in Battle of Leyte Gulf: four carriers, three battleships, 10 cruisers, 11 destroyers. US losses: one light carrier, two escort carriers, three destroyers, two submarines

October 27
Kamikaze attacks on US naval forces in Philippines. Canadians land on South Beveland in the Scheldte estuary

October 31
UK civilian casualties in October 172 killed, 416 injured

November 1
Canadians cross Scheldte and land on east Walcheren, while British commandos seize Westkapelle

November 2
Germans leave Greece. Fifth Army takes Casetta. Fourteenth Army takes Mawlaik in Burma

November 3
Canadians and British occupy Flushing. General McCreery appointed Eighth Army commander

November 7
Roosevelt elected President for fourth term. Eighth Army drives towards Forli. Victor Sorge, the most effective Soviet spy of the war, executed in Japan

November 8
German resistance on Walcheren collapses

November 11
US Navy shells Iwo Jima

November 12
RAF Lancasters sink Tirpitz in Tromso Fiord

November 14
French 1st Army drives for Belfort Gap

November 16
Fourteenth Army cuts Japanese XV Army communications to the south and Japanese Burma area command

November 18
US 3rd Army crosses German frontier

November 19
US forces reach Geilenkirchen

November 22
US 3rd Army reaches Metz

November 24
Allies cross the Saar. French troops take Strasbourg. B-29s bomb Tokyo from Marianas

November 24
General Alexander promoted to Field Marshal. Kamikaze attacks increase in Leyte Gulf and Luzon

November 26
Port of Antwerp open for merchant shipping

November 27
B-29s bomb Tokyo heavily

November 29
Russians cross Danube

November 30
UK civilian casualties in November 716 killed, 1,511 injured

Aircraft over South East Asia

Towards the end of the war the Japanese had been decimated in the air over China and Burma. The Allies continued to harass Japanese ground positions, while swatting away what little Japanese defence was put up to fight them.

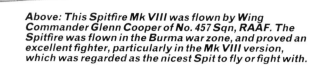

Above: This Spitfire Mk VIII was flown by Wing Commander Glenn Cooper of No. 457 Sqn, RAAF. The Spitfire was flown in the Burma war zone, and proved an excellent fighter, particularly in the Mk VIII version, which was regarded as the nicest Spit to fly or fight with.

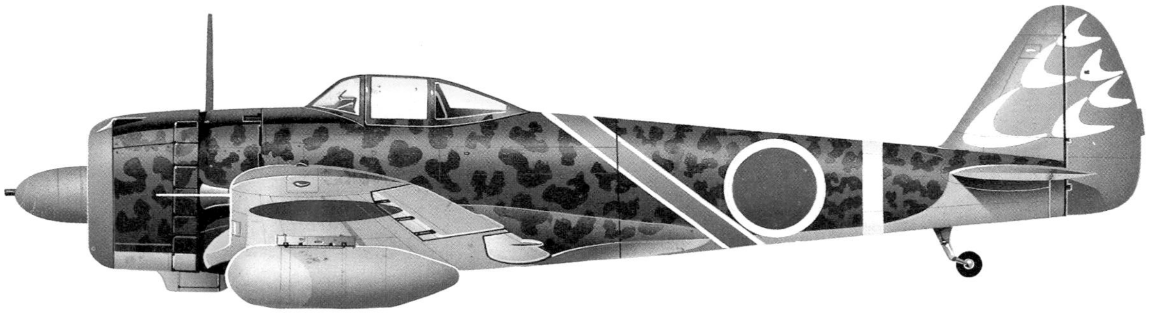

Above: The major Japanese fighter type throughout the war in Burma and China was the Nakajima Ki-43, known to the Allies as 'Oscar'. Possessing astounding manoeuvrability, the Ki-43 was slow and woefully undergunned, proving no match for the modern Allied fighters operating in the region.

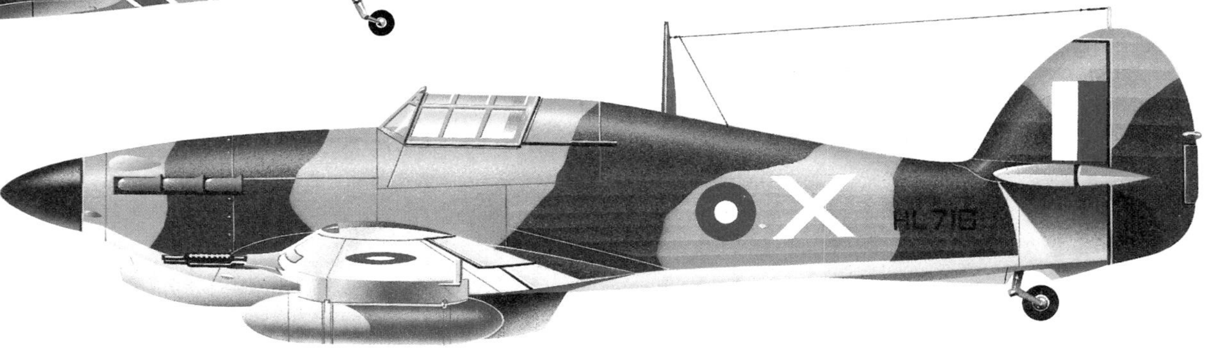

Above: The ubiquitous RAF operational aircraft throughout the last three years of the war was the Hawker Hurricane, mostly in the Mk IIC version with four 20-mm cannon. Long-range tanks helped the Hurricane fight far from base over the inhospitable jungle of this theatre.

Above: The North American P-51 Mustang replaced the famed Curtiss P-40s of the 1st Air Commando Group. This P-51A was flown by Colonel Philip Cochrane, the group's CO, over Burma in 1944.

Above: Some potent fighters were available to the Japanese in China in the latter period of the war, such as this Nakajima Ki-44-IIb 'Tojo' of the 85th Sentai. Flying from Canton, these aircraft lacked the agility of other Japanese types but made up by being fast, well-armed and bestowed with excellent climb and dive characteristics.

Below: The Bristol Beaufighter was employed on a large scale throughout Burma and India. Several were built in Australia and one of these aircraft is shown here in RAAF colours. The soft whistle of the Hercules engines earned the aircraft the name 'Whispering Death' from the Japanese.

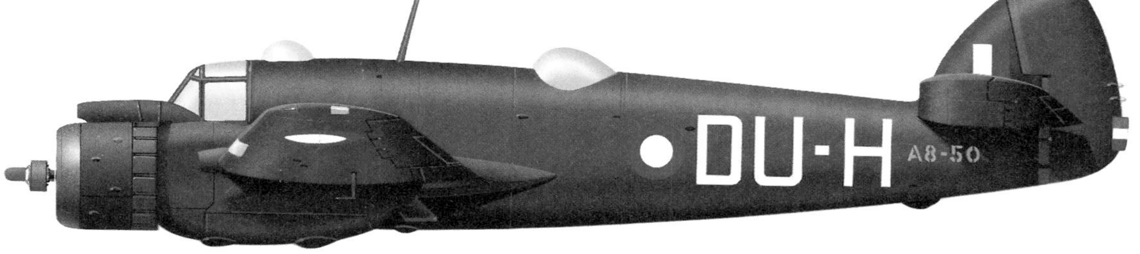

Left: The monsoons brought special problems to RAF squadrons, both in the air and in the shape of abysmal conditions at the primitive bases. Standard fighter in the closing months was the Spitfire Mk VIII, seen here with No. 607 Sqn.

Right: Seen with the aircraft it replaced, the Hawker Hurricane, these No. 5 Sqn, RAF Republic Thunderbolts taxi for takeoff in Burma. Eight 0.5-in machine-guns and long-range tanks enabled them to provide fighter support for bombing raids deep into Japanese territory.

General Mutaguchi's problems during the first half of 1944 were by no means limited to the Central Front, for his apprehensions of the previous April were realized. Wingate's Chindits had returned, and in much greater force.

Instead of nine columns, Wingate's force by the end of 1943 had become three brigades and he himself a major-general. Moreover, his ideas for the employment of his command had developed from those for a series of 'hit and run' raids to a plan for the establishment of a string of boxes or 'strongholds' in the area around Indaw – between that held by Scoones' IV Corps and the Hukawng Valley controlled by Stilwell and his Chinese armies. There, supplied by his own No. 1 Air Commando, Wingate's men would attract Japanese attack and fight it out until main advances by formations of the Fourteenth Army reached them. In essence, these Chindit brigades would therefore be the spearheads of the British reoccupation of Burma.

One brigade – 16th under Bernard Fergusson – walked into position from Ledo to Manhton between 5 February and 10 March 1944, and then set up the stronghold of 'Aberdeen'. Two other brigades – 77th under Michael Calvert and 111th under Joe Lentaigne – were flown in, and owing to last minute intelligence reports they were both eventually landed at 'Broadway' between Taungni and Bhamo. Despite some chaos during the first few hours when many of the 62 gliders used in the first lift crashed or miscarried, by 12 March some 9,000 men had been deposited by air across the Chindwin, Calvert's men had marched 30 miles south west to establish 'White City' near Mawlo with Fergusson's men 20 miles further west.

Death of a leader

Despite the fact that Mutaguchi's attention was by then firmly directed towards Imphal and that the Chindit incursion had taken Japanese headquarters by surprise, within a week an improvised Japanese division under General Hayashi was concentrating at Indaw and, moreover, Japanese fighter attacks on Broadway had destroyed half a dozen Spitfires which had been allotted to 77th Brigade and were due to operate from a landing-strip prepared inside the stronghold. From then on air cover for both Calvert's and Lentaigne's forces had to come from Imphal, by then in need of all the air support it could get for its own purposes.

But then tragedy struck. Wingate had flown in to inspect matters for himself and issue encouragement to all (he informed Calvert that he had been granted a bar to the DSO he had been awarded after the previous expedition: 'Let it go to your heart, Michael, not your head'), and on the way back on the evening of 24 March his plane crashed and all aboard were killed. His place was taken by Joe Lentaigne, but Wingate's driving spirit and creed were gone and not replaced.

Two days later 16th Brigade, instead of awaiting attack in prepared defences, themselves attacked the Japanese positions at Indaw and were repulsed; the day after that the Japanese tried to liquidate Lentaigne's positions at Broadway and were themselves repulsed; and there then followed another battle at Indaw where Fergusson's men were thrown back with losses they could ill afford.

On 6/7 April a really heavy Japanese attack was launched against White City but Calvert and his men beat it off – and then the abandonment of Wingate's ideas and principles was first signalled by the receipt of orders that all three brigades were to amalgamate, and assault Indaw in divisional strength.

On 27 March, after some argument, Lentaigne had officially taken Wingate's place as Chindit commander and had flown out of Broadway to Sylhet for a conference with Slim and Mountbatten (leaving in command of his brigade Major John Masters, later to become a famous novelist). Whatever Lentaigne's abilities as a commander, he was certainly not dedicated to Wingate's ideas of irregular guerrilla fighting; the capture of Indaw was followed first by withdrawal well north by the whole force to a new stronghold at 'Blackpool' near Taungni, the flying out of Fergusson's 16th Brigade (it was, not surprisingly, exhausted), and the virtual subjection of the remaining Chindit forces to Stilwell's command in an attempt to take Mogaung from both north and south.

Nevertheless, the Chindits had by then been in operation behind Japanese lines for over two months, and Japanese HQ regarded them as an infuriating and costly nuisance. They were also the cause of a first-class row between Mutaguchi and the commander of the Japanese 111th Air Division, who could no longer provide the Fifteenth Army around Imphal and Kohima with all the cover and support they needed, because of the necessity to search for and attack the Chindits; so in some ways the Chindit principle was being justified, even though the aim had not been maintained.

At the end of May the survivors of 111th Brigade, still under Masters, were at Blackpool under heavy pressure from continuous Japanese attacks, but sustained not only by the steadfast courage of the men but also by extraordinarily accurate bombing raids on Japanese positions by the RAF. But then the monsoon broke, a Japanese attack smashed through the perimeter and the brigade lost a lot of men before it was halted, food stocks dropped alarmingly and Masters decided they must pull out. On 25 May he led the

Right: Major General Orde Wingate briefs pilots of the 1st Air Commando Force on problems encountered during the first Chindit operation, with the intention of improving techniques for future large-scale raids. This visionary soldier was killed in a plane crash in March 1944.

Below: Protected by tanks, British infantry press north from Imphal through Kanglatongbi towards General Stopford's XXXIII corps, driving south from Kohima. The siege was lifted when the two forces met on 22 June.

Elsewhere in Burma Japanese plans had gone awry. Their Ha-Go operation was designed to counter Slim's 2nd Arakan offensive. Even with troops drawn off for the Imphal/Kohima battles, the British XV Corps was able to hold the Japanese.

The Japanese 55th Infantry Group under the command of Major General Sakurai advances to attack the Ngakyeduak Pass, with the aim of outflanking the 5th and 7th Infantry Divisions.

Over the Hump

Communications between India and China were difficult at the best of times, but in the chaos of war the only reliable method of supply proved to be by air – over the 'hump' of the Himalayas.

As well as the more famous Curtiss P-40 Warhawk, the North American P-51 Mustang also served with Chennault's 'Flying Tigers' in China, this suitably war-weary example displaying an RAF-style two-tone dark earth-dark green colour scheme.

For almost three years of the war, every single item that reached either the American forces in China, or the armies of Generalissimo Chiang Kai-Shek, got there by air. Bulldozers and typewriters, toilet paper and gasoline, shoes, rifles and medicines were airlifted to China in one of the most hazardous and difficult flying missions ever attempted.

The airlift portion was only part of a 1,300-mile tortuous supply trail. Cargo was unloaded at the Indian port of Calcutta, moved to Assam by slow train, loaded on air transports and flown to Myitkyina, in Burma. There it was transferred to barges on the Irrawaddy river and floated downstream to Bhamo, where it was offloaded and trucked to Kunming over the winding Burma Road. In May 1942, the Japanese seized the airfield at Myitkyina, and cut that route.

Only a direct air link between Assam and Kunming remained as a possibility. It was a 500-mile run above some of the worst terrain and in some of the worst weather in the world. Between the two terminals lies the Santsung Range, an extension of the Himalayas known to pilots as 'The Hump' or 'The Rockpile'. Its peaks topped 16,000 ft and its passes were above 14,000 ft. Thunderstorms, 100-mph winds, frightening turbulence, and icing at every level above 15,000 ft combined to make the route a pilot's nightmare.

It was begun with Douglas C-47s of 10th AF, valiant but out of their depth in the fierce conditions of the Hump route. Airfields were totally inadequate, from any viewpoint. The Hump region was uncharted, and any other navigational aids were non-existent. The Japanese bombed the airfields; there were only about 40 10th AF fighters for defending the bases and escorting the transports on the Hump run.

The accident rate was appalling. Veteran pilots referred to the run as 'The Aluminum Trail'; there was a wreck for almost every mile of its length, more than 450 planes downed. Maintenance had to be done at night, when the aircraft were cooler. To touch their metal skins during the day produced second-degree burns. Spare parts were in great demand and short supply.

Air Transport Command took over the Hump operation in December 1942. The tonnage began to rise steadily, only interrupted for causes like monsoon rains that turned the bases into mud sloughs. And each time that things seemed to be going well, another customer had an urgent need for air cargo.

In March 1944, British units defending against an enemy drive into Assam urgently needed air resupply. In May Lieutenant-General Joseph Stillwell began his Burma offensive and became another airlift customer. The 20th AF moved its B-29s into China and staged raids from forward bases near Chengtu, China; they also drew on ATC air supply.

And always, Generalissimo Chiang and his representatives in Washington pressed for increased tonnages of supplies, reminding US leadership of the precarious position of loyal Chinese troops.

Late in the war, the single air lane across the Hump had broadened to a 100-mile wide air corridor through which about 650 planes moved every day. The Burma Road never carried more than 6,000 tons of supplies in any month, a figure exceeded routinely by planes from several of the Assam bases. The record performance was set on 1 August 1945; Hump pilots flew 1,118 round trips, carrying 5,327 tons of supplies without a single accident or incident.

It was a prodigious accomplishment, ferrying 650,000 tons of freight by air across a treacherous stretch of mountains. It consumed men and planes, ruined health and careers, wasted money and materiel. Yet the offensive war in that theatre could not have been waged without it; it was the only way to go.

Above: The RAF and USAAF combined in India to provide a massive airlift support to all the forces in the area. Both Douglas C-47s and Curtiss C-46s were used. Here an RAF Dakota lands in China as a USAAF C-46 taxis out.

Below: The most important aircraft on the 'Hump' route was the Curtiss C-46 Commando, able to carry far greater loads than the C-47. This example is seen above the typically tough terrain these transports were required to fly over.

columns out during the night and by a series of forced marches they arrived at Mokso on the 27th, where they were safe for the moment.

Calvert had brought 77th Brigade up and was ordered to attack Mogaung from the south and east in conjunction with the 38th Chinese Division from the north and west, but it was 26 June before they entered the town and by then Calvert's force consisted of less than 400 totally exhausted men. When later they were examined by medical officers it was found that every officer and man had suffered at least three bouts of malaria and some had had six or seven, the loss of weight averaged three stones per man and at the end the death rate from cerebral malaria and typhus was rising alarmingly.

Yet a few of the men stayed in the area until August, by which time Stilwell's command had at last captured Myitkyina. Not many of Wingate's Force were still there, but some were – and although both British and American historians of their exploits have been niggardly in their tributes to the Chindit achievements, the Japanese have not. One of them was to write afterwards:

> In coming to any conclusion we must not forget Major-General Orde Wingate.... He planted himself centre stage, and conducted all fronts with his baton which he called the Chindits. He reduced the Japanese power to wage war on the four Burma fronts and so fatally affected the balance.

In particular, the Japanese praise the timing of the Second Chindit operation. A week earlier and Mutaguchi would have delayed his thrust on Imphal while he dealt with it; a week later and transport vitally needed for the Imphal front but necessarily diverted and blocked by the Chindits, would have gone forwards and might, they say, have tipped the balance in Mutaguchi's favour. 'If Wingate decided on the timing,' wrote one Japanese general, 'he was a genius of war.'

The siege of Imphal

The main assault on Imphal had begun on the same night as that on Kohima – 7/8 March – but IV Corps had been expecting it for some time and three divisions were deployed to meet it. All were Indian divisions – 17th to the south of Imphal down towards Tiddim, 20th south east of Imphal around Tamu, and 23rd held close to Imphal in reserve; all were waiting the order to put in hand appropriate moves immediately Mutaguchi's divisions crossed the Chindwin.

Needless to say, matters after the first clash did not go exactly according to plan. In the south it soon became evident that although a large Japanese formation was about to drive up the Tiddim-Imphal road to push the 17th Indian up north, other Japanese formations were moving with admirable stealth and rapidity to cut that road at Tongzang, the Manipur Bridge and around Milestone 100. Immediately, Scoones ordered 17th Indian back and sent a brigade from the reserve 23rd Division down to help – but then more Japanese formations were reported even further north along the Tiddim-Imphal road so another brigade from reserve was sent. By 15 March, the situation there resembled a Neapolitan ice cream cake; furthest south were the bulk of the Japanese 33rd Division, then the 16,000 marching men, 3,500 mules and 2,500 vehicles of 17th Indian on their way

Above: General 'Vinegar' Joe Stillwell was the acerbic American commander in Burma, and simultaneously Chief of Staff to Chiang Kai-Shek in China. He is here seen in the front seat of a Jeep fording a jungle stream during one of his frequent visits to the troops in the North of Burma.

Gurkhas advance down the Ukrul road supported by Grant tanks with their distinctive low turret and sponson mounted main armament. It was essential for infantry to probe ahead of the tanks to kill Japanese suicide anti-tank men who waited by the road with an armed bomb and a brick to set off the detonator.

Right: The road to Imphal is open: British staff officers meet Indian troops from the Imphal garrison at Milestone 109.

Below: Gurkhas from XXIII Corps take Myinmu during the drive from the Irrawaddy bridgehead, 30 miles west of Mandalay. General Slim's attack over the Irrawaddy was one of the most professionally executed and successful operations mounted by the British Army.

The Noose of Steel

It is interesting to note that the first warships allowed to Japan after World War II were dedicated anti-submarine vessels, for the Japanese had learned from bitter experience how deadly the submarine can be to a nation.

So great an impression did the nuclear bombing of Japan make in August 1945 that it is widely assumed that this weapon won the war. It did not. The rambling Japanese empire had already been defeated because it had no answers to the assaults of the fast carrier groups, to the outflanking amphibious operations and to the iron ring of the submarine blockade.

One reason for Japanese creation, of the so called 'Greater East Asia Co-Prosperity Sphere' was to gain access to raw materials, coal, iron ore, oil, tin, rubber, etc, with which the home islands were poorly provided. This wider empire was created rapidly and efficiently by the campaigns of early 1942, but thereafter, the key to sustaining it lay in the free movement of mercantile traffic.

The Japanese operated a superb surface fleet but, like the British Grand Fleet of World War I, this was drilled to think offensively against the day of the Armageddon of a sea battle that would decide mastery of the Pacific. Its considerable submarine arm existed to scout for the fleet and to ambush that of the enemy. Submarine assault on merchant shipping, despite its critically important implications, was not in line with offensive strategy. Conversely, it seems not to have been considered that an opponent would adopt just these tactics and Japan thus started hostilities with no plans for convoy, few escorts and little preparation for the rapid replacement of lost tonnage.

Paradoxically, the American submarine arm had been built on the twin precepts of home defence and 'go for the warships'. It took the assault on Pearl Harbor to force the decision to adopt unrestricted submarine warfare.

Fifty boats of various vintages were available for deployment. Though at first spread thinly, they soon began to concentrate at points where they could exploit the Japanese practice of sailing unescorted and singly, often still lit. The first enemy warship kill by SubPac boats was on 27 January 1942, when the USS *Gudgeon* sank the surfaced submarine *I-173*. On 8 February the old 'pig-boat' USS *S-37* used the German trick of exploiting her small silhouette in a surfaced night attack, sinking the destroyer *Natsushio* in the Macassar Strait. Some skippers were to develop particular affinities in sinking Japanese destroyers, eventually causing a crisis for the enemy.

It was possible by mid-1942 to commence a regular close blockade of the ocean coasts of the Japanese home islands. Though convoys were now to be encountered, these were poorly escorted and the introduction of SJ surface-search radar allowed submarines to detect and track potential targets. In the first half year to June 1942, submarines accounted for 56 merchantmen of 235,000 GRT. Over the following six months the toll rose to 84 ships of 358,000 GRT. Elsewhere things were warming up.

Extensive minelaying was also undertaken by submarines, causing further losses and disruption. For the steep rise in activity there was a premium to be paid. Only three boats were lost to Japanese countermeasures in 1942, but this rose to 15 during the following year. On the other hand, 1943 saw a further 308 enemy casualties, grossing some 1,367,000 tons. Even offset by replacement tonnage, this represented a 16 per cent decrease in Japan's available shipping.

By 1944 both sides were getting more experienced. The American boats were not only more numerous but stayed longer on station by virtue of using forward staging posts, and judiciously-sited depot ships or tenders. The Japanese convoy system was getting into its stride but the submarines regrouped into 'wolf-packs' for co-ordinated attacks.

The year 1944 saw the loss of no less than 548 merchantmen of 2,452,000 GRT. Though tanker construction kept pace with losses, the Japanese saw their dry cargo fleet halved. By making tankers priority targets, the Americans halved Japan's vital oil imports by the middle of 1944. Enemy shipping was now being constricted into a tighter area by American advances, and submarines competed increasingly with each other and both carrier- and land-based aircraft for the now diminishing number of targets. Early 1945 saw 160 submarines available, and the South China Sea was called Convoy College. The USS *Hoe* and USS *Flounder* even contrived to collide underwater. Japanese imports from the Indies dried up.

There were still losses. A particularly bitter one was that of Dick O'Kane's USS *Tang*. Having disposed of 24 enemy ships in eight months, the boat was sunk by one of her own rogue torpedoes in the course of attacking a convoy in the Formosa Strait.

A subsidiary function of the submarines was 'lifeguarding' stationed along the routes of the Boeing B-29s that were laying waste the Japanese home islands from the bases in the Marianas. Over 500 ditched aircrew were rescued in total.

The last 'Maru' of the campaign was sunk by the USS *Torsk* the day before the surrender. She was the last of 1,113, totalling 4.8 million GRT. The cost had been 52 submarines.

Above: The remains of a Japanese transport, beached on one of the Pacific islands, is mute testament to the efficiency of the submarine stranglehold on Japan. The offensively-minded Imperial Navy had never considered a defensive war, and failed to protect Japanese seaborne communications.

Left: The end of a Japanese destroyer, modified to act as a fast transport for the island-hopping war. Hit forward, the old vessel quickly succumbed, going down by the bow rapidly and sinking within seconds.

***Below: A photo taken through the periscope of USS* Archerfish *on her third patrol, in the waters off Iwo Jima in July 1944. Some five months later,* Archerfish *was to claim the biggest prize of the war in sinking the 70,000 ton carrier* Shinano.**

Right: The 'Kagero' class destroyer* Shiranui *in a Japanese dry dock with her bows removed following a US submarine torpedo hit off the Aleutians.

Below: USS* Archerfish *running on the surface, showing to advantage the lines of the US fleet submarine of World War II. Long range and a good habitability made them well suited to the long patrols required of boats in the Pacific.

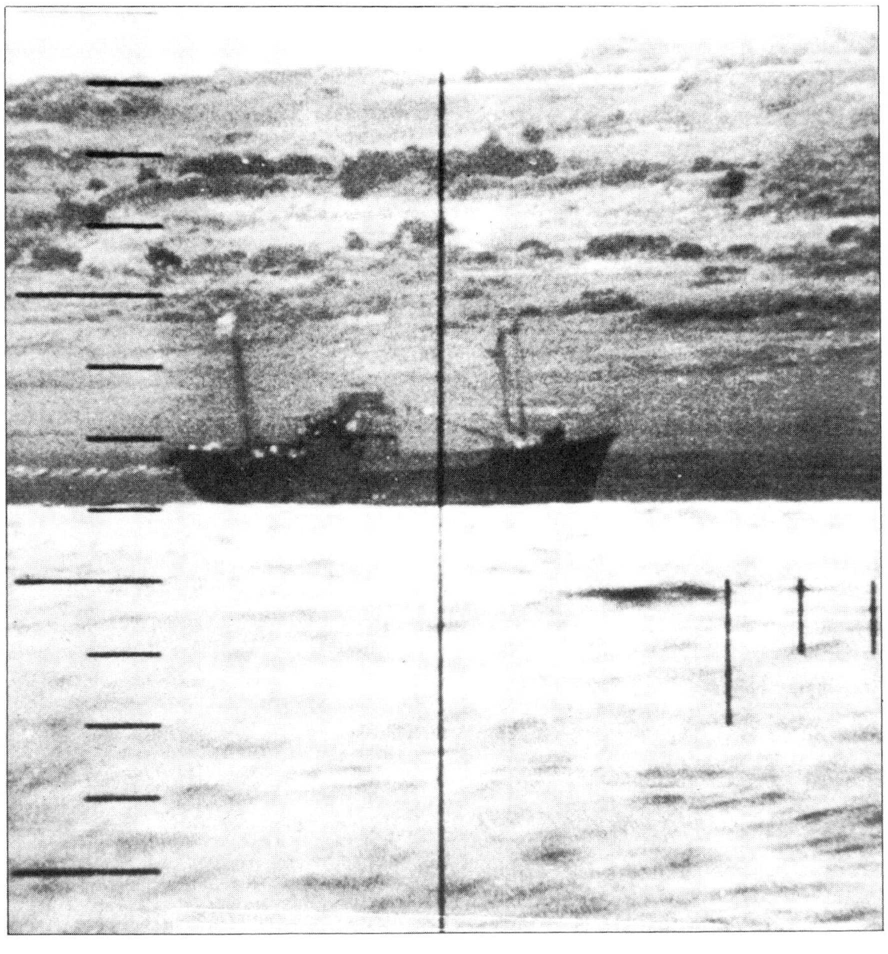

north. Above them were now the Japanese blocking forces at Tongzang, followed by a British garrison at a minor stores dump at Milestone 109, then another Japanese roadblock which by then extended nearly 10 miles to Milestone 100, then two brigades of 23rd Indian hurrying south to help.

There was considerable fighting around Tongzang and the Manipur Bridge, the stores dump at Milestone 109 was partly lost and partly destroyed, but the Japanese roadblocks were eliminated or chased away, and by the first week in April the bulk of 17th Indian were back to within 10 miles of Imphal, still on that Tiddim-Imphal road. But it had been an anxious time.

The withdrawal of 20th Indian had not been quite so traumatic. Dumps of petrol, ammunition and stores in their area had been successfully pack-loaded or destroyed, and the civilian labour force which had been building a road in the area was sent back to Imphal before danger threatened. The division moved back, first to the Shenam Saddle to form a block on the road to Imphal, then further back to form a solid defence. But to the north, the moves by Sato's division on Kohima broke through unexpectedly and reached Ukhrul, then swung south to strike at a small detachment on a hill at Sangshak which contained a hospital. So the third reserve brigade of 23rd Indian Division was sent up in support.

On paper this despatch of his last reserves seemed to leaves Scoones in a bad, if not desperate, situation and 5th Indian Division was hurriedly detached from the Arakan front and flown into Imphal – so by 4 April Scoones' command at Imphal consisted of four divisions totalling about 60,000 men, another 40,000 administration personnel in Imphal itself – and sufficient food, ammunition and equipment to keep them all well supplied for weeks, if not months. Moreover, the divisions were now well deployed – 5th Indian quickly to the north and north west, 20th Indian at Shenan covering the approach from Tamu and the east, 23rd now south on the Tiddim road while 17th recuperated in Imphal itself.

Imphal conclusions

The scene was thus set, and during the next two-and-a-half months the gallant soldiers of Mutaguchi's Fifteenth Army threw themselves at the virtually unbreakable ring with a courage and determination which compels reluctant admiration – reluctant because it was so pointless. Fanatical attacks were driven forward – sometimes at defences only yards away from the starting points – Japanese soldiers climbed over the bodies of their dead comrades still hanging on barbed wire to get at the defence posts, or came suddenly to life after lying in the open for hours on end, presumed dead. Small copses vanished in the shellfire, vegetation was stripped from hillsides and all signs of cultivation obliterated – and once the monsoon started in May, the conditions became indescribable.

Mutaguchi's troops, here as well as around Kohima, were getting little or no supplies, while the RAF were continually flying into Imphal. At the end of the siege it was reckoned that they had flown in 14,000,000 pounds of rations, 1,000,000 gallons of petrol, 1,200 bags of mail, 43,000,000 cigarettes and 12,000 reinforcements, besides evacuating 13,000 casualties and 43,000 non-combatants.

The Japanese got nothing; and their wounded died.

By early June, the Kohima Battle was over and the British XXXIII Corps were intent on driving down from Dimapur through Kohima to Imphal, and there was only the rearguard of the Japanese 31st Division to stop them. The rest of the Japanese Fifteenth Army, if not in retreat to the Chindwin, was preparing itself for death or withdrawal; and Mutaguchi sent their morale even lower by abruptly dismissing his three divisional commanders.

They and their men had striven valiantly for him, and their treatment was grossly unjust. The fault lay with Mutaguchi, in allowing the first Chindit expedition to prompt him into an attack across the Chindwin for which his army was ill equipped, especially against the growing might of the Allies. After mid-1943, there was in fact no hope of a Japanese victory in the face of American industrial regeneration and British recovery from the early disasters – but Mutaguchi's attempted onslaught across the Chindwin cost the Japanese forces in Burma so much that their eventual defeat there was easier – and far quicker – than it might have been.

British troops from the English home counties push along the alien vegetation and soil of the Arakan Peninsula as Fourteenth Army troops drive down the slopes of the Mayu Ridge near Maungdaw.

The fanatic willingness to die for the Emperor was one of the most familiar features of Japanese fighting men in all theatres. This soldier was shot while waiting to detonate a 250-lb bomb under a tank . . . by hand!

A Gurkha patrol prepares to move out against the Japanese in the South East Asian theatre. They were part of General Messervy's 7th Indian Division in the Arakan peninsula.

Indian artillerymen at Fort Dufferin, Mandalay. February and March 1945 saw the battles for Mandalay and Meiktila, with Slim making his attacks in a masterly fashion, and after two months hard fighting forcing the Japanese eastwards. At the same time, Stillwell's Chinese were pushing the Japanese on the Burma Road to the north.

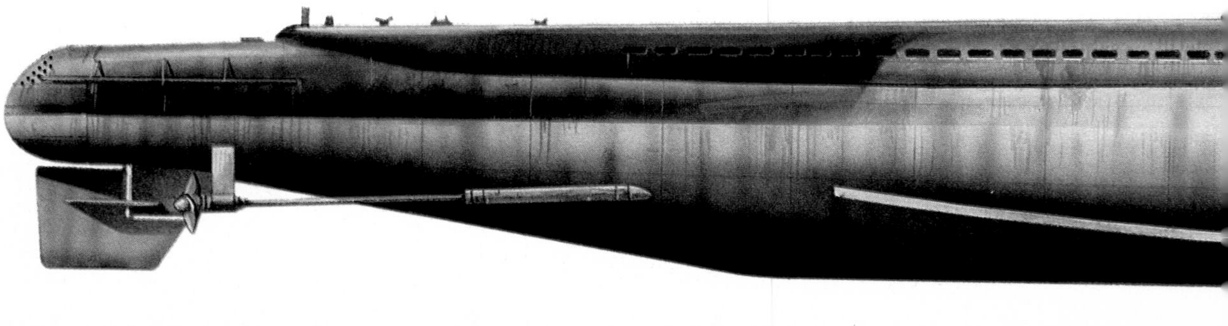

US submarines in the Pacific

To the gunnery-minded US Navy of the inter-war years, the submarine was little more than a coast defence weapon, so that when war was thrust upon them they had a submarine force woefully inadequate for the task in hand. The transformation in four short years was dramatic, with over 200 large fleet submarines in service by 1945.

The launch of USS **Swordfish** *on 1 April 1939. Few present could have foreseen that within a week of Pearl Harbor,* **Swordfish** *would sink the* **Atsutusan Maru**, *and thus open an account that would eventually close with 1,113 Japanese merchant vessels (totalling 4.8 million gross tons) falling to the US Navy's submarine force.*

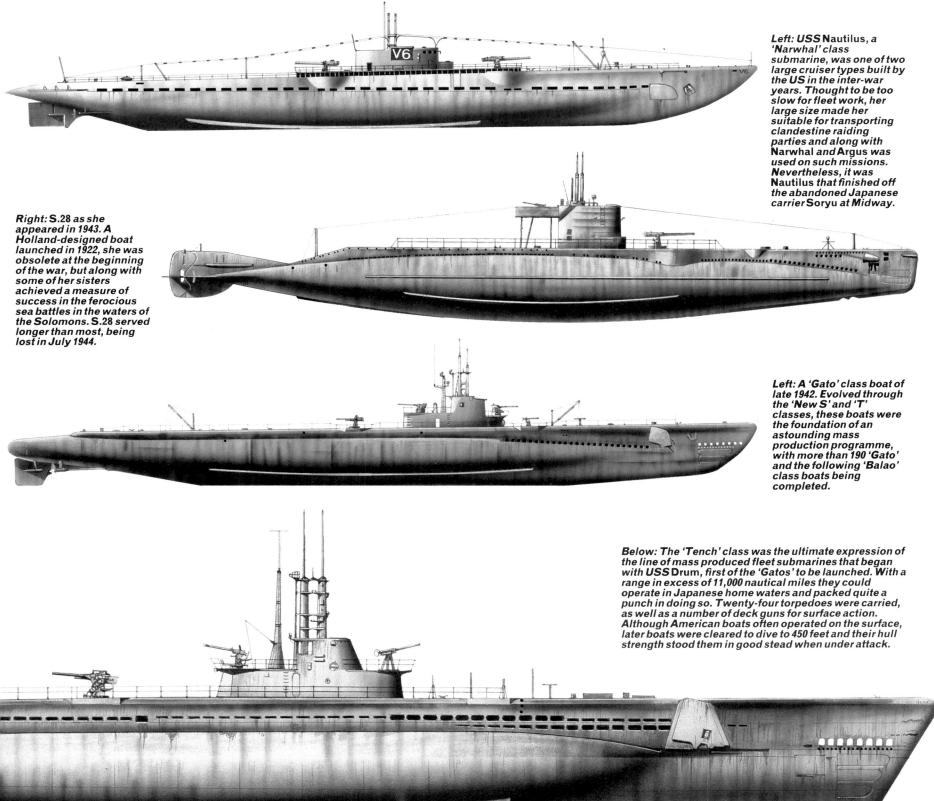

Left: USS **Nautilus**, ***a 'Narwhal' class submarine, was one of two large cruiser types built by the US in the inter-war years. Thought to be too slow for fleet work, her large size made her suitable for transporting clandestine raiding parties and along with*** **Narwhal** ***and*** **Argus** ***was used on such missions. Nevertheless, it was*** **Nautilus** ***that finished off the abandoned Japanese carrier*** **Soryu** ***at Midway.***

Right: **S.28** ***as she appeared in 1943. A Holland-designed boat launched in 1922, she was obsolete at the beginning of the war, but along with some of her sisters achieved a measure of success in the ferocious sea battles in the waters of the Solomons.*** **S.28** ***served longer than most, being lost in July 1944.***

Left: A 'Gato' class boat of late 1942. Evolved through the 'New S' and 'T' classes, these boats were the foundation of an astounding mass production programme, with more than 190 'Gato' and the following 'Balao' class boats being completed.

Below: The 'Tench' class was the ultimate expression of the line of mass produced fleet submarines that began with USS **Drum**, ***first of the 'Gatos' to be launched. With a range in excess of 11,000 nautical miles they could operate in Japanese home waters and packed quite a punch in doing so. Twenty-four torpedoes were carried, as well as a number of deck guns for surface action. Although American boats often operated on the surface, later boats were cleared to dive to 450 feet and their hull strength stood them in good stead when under attack.***

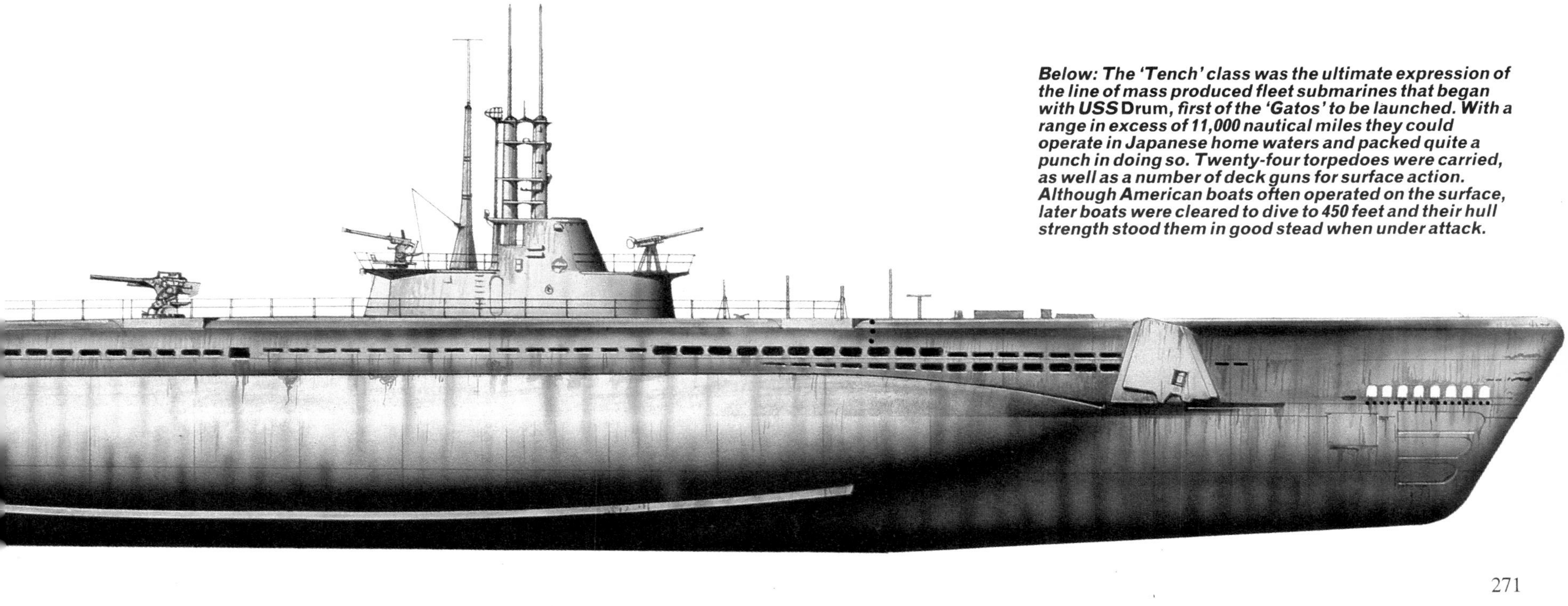

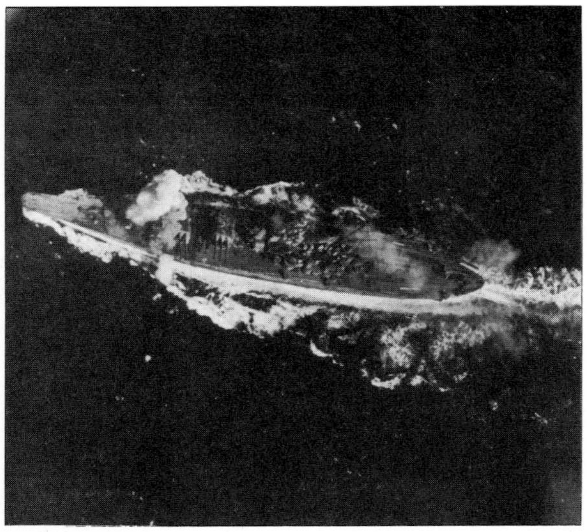

Above: IJNS Yamato *receives a bomb forward at about midday on 24 October during the first major action of the enormous sea battle of Leyte Gulf. Admiral Kurita attempted to force the San Bernardino strait, but massive US carrier air strikes in the Sibuyan Sea forced him back.*

Right: USS Pennsylvania *leads a task group into Lingayen gulf after the occupation of Leyte. The veteran of Pearl Harbor was one of the vessels in the last battleship-versus-battleship action to have been fought, when the old battleships of the Seventh Fleet met Nishimura's force at the mouth of the Surigao Strait.*

Further east the Japanese commanders were not making such gross misjudgements, but their basic weaknesses in industrial power and trained pilots were still evident.

MacArthur won the argument as to the target for the next American thrust, to some extent because his were the land forces without which final victory could not be won. Admiral King controlled the means of transport of those forces, certainly, but tanks and soldiers are necessary to occupy ground and take possession of an enemy's territory; you cannot capture a general staff in a battleship.

Thus the decision for the Philippines was taken, and on the morning of 20 October the waters in and around Leyte Gulf contained the largest and most powerful fleet of amphibious assault vessels and warships in the Pacific ever assembled. Over 700 transports and warships were concentrated east of Leyte and around the entrance to the Gulf, while scores of aircraft patrolled overhead and hundreds were massed on the carriers' decks to cover the landing on the Leyte beaches of four divisions of General Krueger's Sixth Army – 200,000 men in all.

But before they could be landed, the Battle of Leyte Gulf had to be fought. The so-called Battle of Leyte Gulf was in fact a series of air-sea battles spread over a vast area. It was not only the climax of the war in the Pacific but also the greatest naval battle of history. All the classic warship types were engaged, from battleships and carriers down to destroyer escorts, all fulfilling their designed roles.

Once the Marianas had fallen in August 1944 the Japanese high command knew that defeat stared the country in the face. All that could be hoped for was a gambler's throw, an all-out offensive by the remaining capital ships and carriers against the next big amphibious landing. As soon, therefore, as Allied forces were reported moving into Leyte Gulf in the Philippines, Plan 'Sho-1' was put into action. It called for the Japanese forces in North Borneo and elsewhere to divide into three forces. From Borneo, Force A, a portion of the First Strike Force under Vice-Admiral Takeo Kurita, was to pass through the San Bernardino Strait to attack the US landing forces from the north off Samar; a Second Strike Force, commanded by Vice-Admiral Kiyohide Shima, was to join with Force C (also from Borneo and part of the First Strike Force under Vice-Admiral Shaji Nishimura) to pass through Surigao Strait to attack the landings from the south; finally the main carrier force, the First Mobile Fleet from Japan under Vice-Admiral Jisaburo Ozawa (whose carriers had hardly any aircraft), was to lure the American carriers away from the Philippines while the First and Second Strike Forces dealt with the landings and their warship support, afterwards attacking with the returning US carriers with the 460-mm guns of the super-battleships *Yamato* and *Musashi* of Force A.

Like other complex Japanese battle plans, it went

The Battle of Leyte Gulf

The Japanese Plan Sho-1 operation was designed to disrupt and if possible destroy the American landings at Leyte. Accurately gauging that Admiral Halsey could be decoyed north by the Japanese carrier force (for which there were no planes or pilots), the plan was to filter heavy surface units under Kurita and Nishimura through the Philippines to wreak havoc amongst the amphibious force. It almost worked.

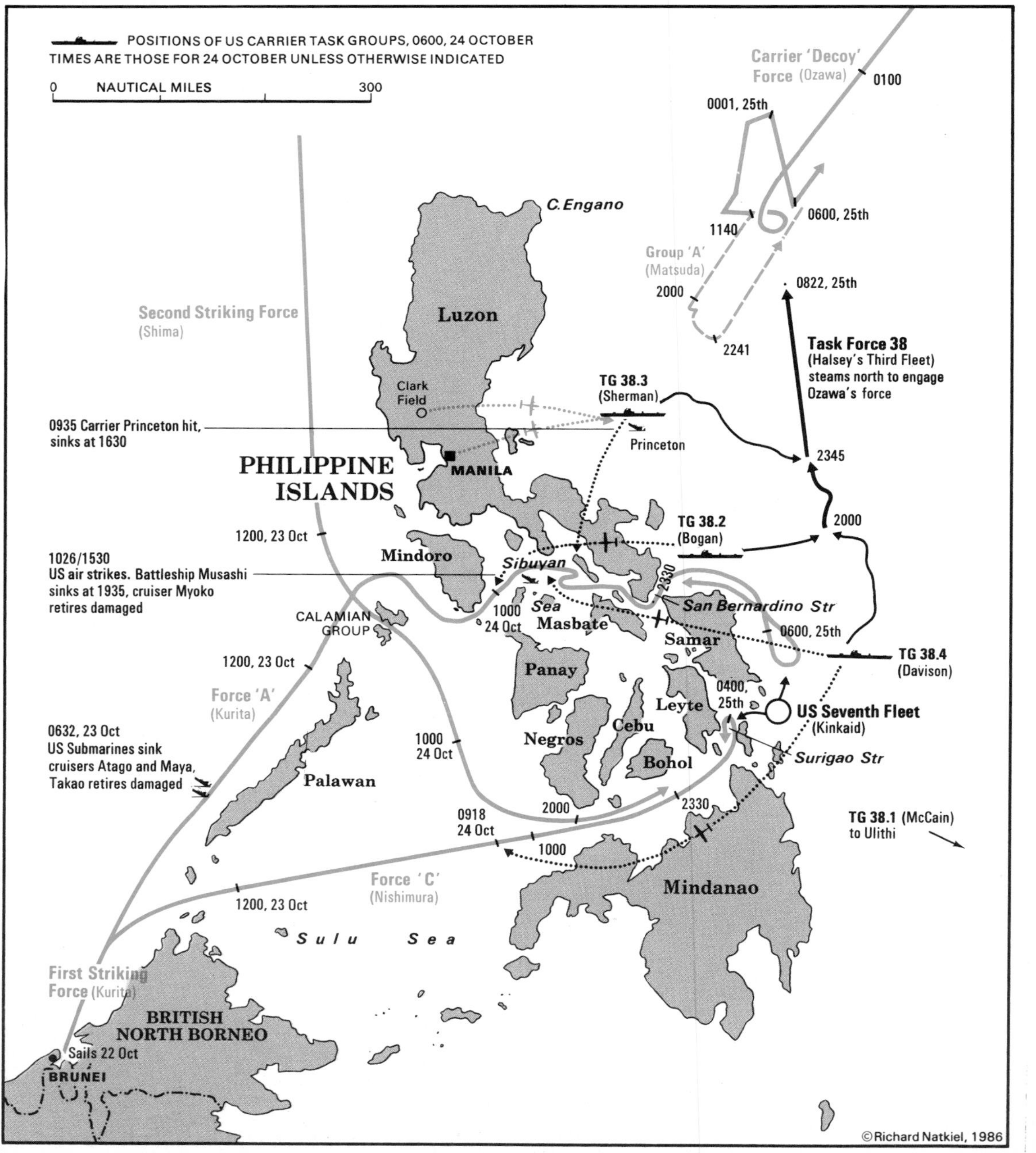

Submarines of the Imperial Japanese Navy

Japan had a unique attitude to submarine warfare, deploying squadrons of large submarines with the battle fleet and using midget submarines to attack the advancing US battle fleet.

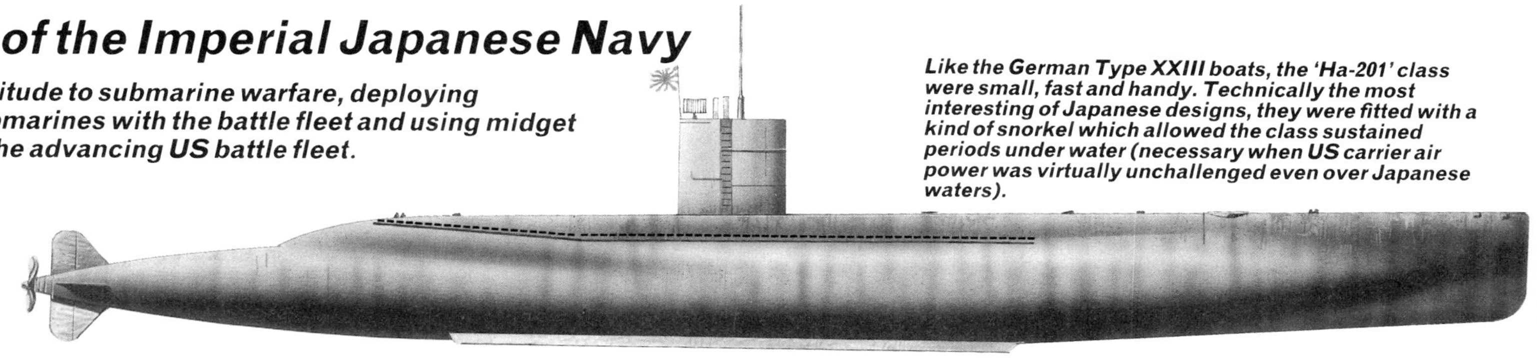

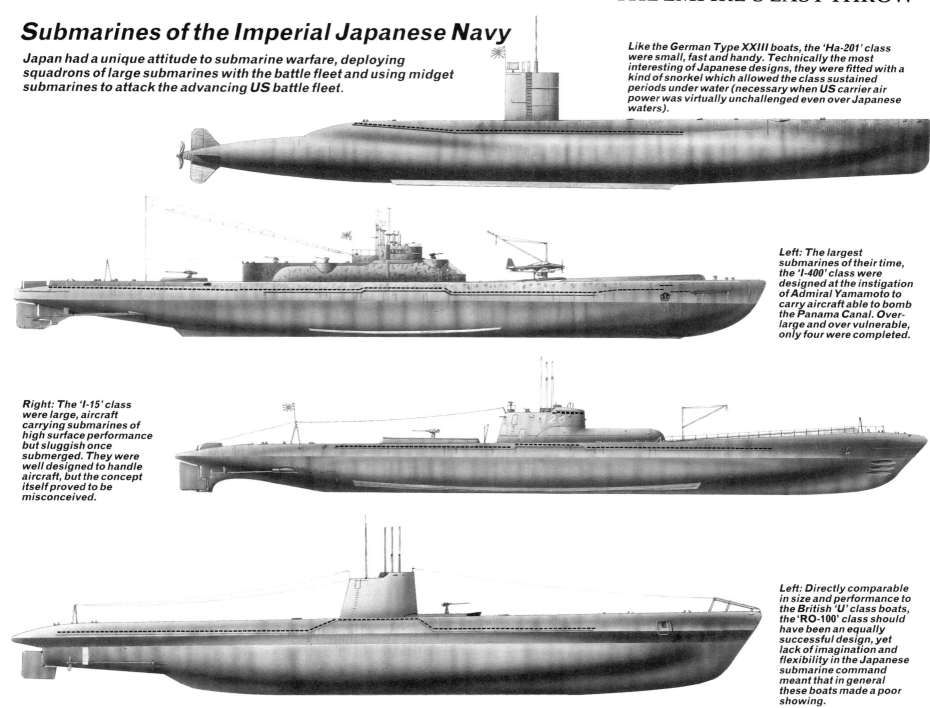

Like the German Type XXIII boats, the 'Ha-201' class were small, fast and handy. Technically the most interesting of Japanese designs, they were fitted with a kind of snorkel which allowed the class sustained periods under water (necessary when US carrier air power was virtually unchallenged even over Japanese waters).

Left: The largest submarines of their time, the 'I-400' class were designed at the instigation of Admiral Yamamoto to carry aircraft able to bomb the Panama Canal. Over-large and over vulnerable, only four were completed.

Right: The 'I-15' class were large, aircraft carrying submarines of high surface performance but sluggish once submerged. They were well designed to handle aircraft, but the concept itself proved to be misconceived.

Left: Directly comparable in size and performance to the British 'U' class boats, the 'RO-100' class should have been an equally successful design, yet lack of imagination and flexibility in the Japanese submarine command meant that in general these boats made a poor showing.

wrong almost from the beginning. Off Palawan Force A was ambushed by two US submarines, which radioed the news and also torpedoed three heavy cruisers. Admiral Kurita's ships came under heavy air attack as they passed through the Sibuyan Sea, and eventually the mighty *Musashi* succumbed to an estimated total of 19 torpedo hits. However, her sister *Yamato* and the smaller battleships *Nagato, Kongo* and *Haruna* survived and continued to plough towards San Bernardino Strait.

Thanks to a mix-up in communications, the US fast carriers left the small escort carriers off Samar to face a ferocious bombardment from Kurita's ships while they chased after Ozawa's empty carriers. Fortunately for the Americans their 'jeep carriers', destroyers and destroyer-escorts put up such a stout resistance that Kurita eventually withdrew and missed the chance to destroy the vulnerable invasion force.

The Americans now took a terrible revenge on the Japanese. Ozawa's carriers were hunted down off Cape Engano: the *Chitose, Chiyoda, Zuikaku* and *Zuiho* were all sunk. While trying to force their way through Surigao Strait Nishimura's and Shima's forces came under a withering night attack from Admiral Oldendorf's old battleships, some of them salvaged veterans of Pearl Harbor, and were all but wiped out.

Leyte was the end of the Imperial Japanese Navy as an effective force. With no fuel for operations and no aircrew to man new aircraft, the remaining carriers were reduced to swinging idly at their moorings, waiting for the inevitable air attacks which would sink them.

Land action on Leyte

The divisions of General Krueger's Sixth Army were all ashore on Leyte by the end of October, once the sea and air battle had been won, and by then they were safely in control of the whole of the Leyte Valley and the vital airfields in the east and central part of the island. Unfortunately, they now came up against an even more intractable antagonist than the Japanese Thirty-fifth Army – the weather; 35 inches of rain fell during the first 40 days of their campaign, high winds soaked men and supplies, blew over shel-

Left: Aircrewmen relax in the ready room of USS Ticonderoga (CV-14), one of the 'Essex' class fast carriers that so changed the nature of the Pacific war. After destroying the fighting power of the Japanese fleet at Leyte, they were assigned to support the operations on land in the Philippines.

Right: Leyte Gulf might have been a success for the Japanese, had they been able to get amongst the amphibious forces landing on Leyte Island. All that stood against them were the 'jeep' carriers and destroyers of TF38.3. One of the escort carriers can be seen being shelled by a Japanese heavy cruiser (just visible on the horizon).

This Japanese destroyer has been attacked by a gunship version of the B-25 Mitchell medium bomber, which has 'skip-bombed' a pair of 1000-pounders into its hull.

Vice-Admiral Takeo Kurita commanded a heavy cruiser division at Midway, and rose to command the 1st Air Fleet at the battle of the Philippine Sea. He was in command of the main battleship force at Leyte.

ters and reduced the ground to a morass of mud and sheets of water.

Only one airfield remained operational – at Tacloban – and without air cover the American divisions were unwilling to move; but the Japanese Navy found itself able to sail freely for the first time for weeks, and did so, bringing some 45,000 reinforcements to General Suzuki's embattled Thirty-fifth Army before the battle was over.

November was a dreadful month for everyone on Leyte. Although the Americans in the lower coastal regions could move on foot, the roads were few and poor and once vehicles – even tanks at first – moved off them they were mired to the axles in minutes, while the Japanese holding the central ridges and the rough, rocky hills of the mountain barrier of central Leyte could do little but glower at their enemies below and hope that food and stores might eventually be dropped to them. But when the weather was clear enough for Japanese transports to fly, it was also clear enough for American carrier-borne fighters to shoot them down.

An attempt by the Japanese to seize at least one of the airfields with airborne forces failed when the first attempt crash-landed four transports on the field and killed most of the passengers, while a larger airdrop planned in brigade strength managed in the end to put down only 350 men, who controlled Buri airstrip for a few days until they were wiped out by encircling US infantry and tanks.

Eventually, of course, overwhelming American

PT boats in the Surigao Strait

Surigao Strait has been remembered as the last battleship-against-battleship action to be fought. What has been forgotten, however, is that it was also one of the few battles in which torpedo boats were used as originally conceived: to harry the enemy battle fleet.

The 'Sho-1' plan initiated on 10 October was to use Vice Admiral Jisaburo Ozawa's carrier group to seduce Vice Admiral William F. Halsey's 3rd Fleet from its offshore station and then to attack the gulf simultaneously from both north and south. The Southern Force was an oddly divided command in two separate groups. Vice Admiral Shoji Nishimura led with the elderly battleships *Yamashiro* and *Fuso*, the heavy cruiser *Mogami* and four destroyers.

Trailing it by about two hours was Vice Admiral Kiyohide Shima's force of two heavy cruisers, one light cruiser and seven destroyers. They were to be harried throughout their approach by PT boats, then by destroyers, each using the night torpedo attacks practised so well by the Japanese themselves. Any enemy that penetrated this gauntlet-run would find itself met by the armoured wall of Rear Admiral Jesse Oldendorf's six veteran battleships, backed by three heavy and five light cruisers, plus 29 destroyers.

With nightfall, Nishimura prudently pushed the *Mogami* and three destroyers ahead to reconnoitre while his heavy units kept closer under Bohol, which lay to port. Sure enough, at 22.36 the first PT section picked up the Japanese admiral's big ships on radar. They then closed at moderate speed to avoid excessive noise and giveaway bow-waves but, even so, the cat-eyed Japanese sighted them promptly. Nishimura acted vigorously, turning toward the midget vessels and using searchlights and rapid-fire medium-calibre guns in textbook fashion. The Americans were young and inexperienced, and their attack wilted under this riposte. None of the section gained an attacking position; neither, more importantly, did they make a contact report. Worse, the *Mogami* group had passed the second section without either side being aware of the other. Not until two hours after first contact did Oldendorf hear of the enemy's approach, the message having passed by several relays. Fortunately it confirmed his dispositions.

The third PT section, meanwhile, took on the *Mogami* group near Limasawa Island just before midnight. Again they were obliged to hightail it, pursued in their snaking paths by a hail of fire laced by arcs or tracer and blue white beams of searchlights. Again no contact reports got through.

Nishimura now re-concentrated his group and sent a confident progress report to Kurita who was heading for the San Bernardino Strait to the north. Shortly before 02.00 he was passing the narrows between Pananon and the northern tip of Mindanao, beyond which he would turn northward up the strait. In this 10-mile wide chokepoint no less than five sections of PTs were concentrated. These succeeded in closing piecemeal to the point where about a dozen torpedoes were expended, again without result.

Triumphantly, Nishimura held course. Only two sections of PT boats were now left ahead of him, and both these were ordered to stand clear for the planned destroyer attacks. The time was 02.15 on 25 October; Shima was closing astern and Kurita had passed the unguarded San Bernardino Strait almost two hours before. At this point Leyte Gulf was in dire danger.

Though the little ships had enjoyed scant reward for their effort so far, they had marked the Japanese onward progress to the yard and, paradoxically, engendered a measure of overconfidence in their enemy. At 03.30, however, from the dark cover of land on each side, Nishimura was attacked by destroyers. There was no warning before 27 torpedoes were away and, seemingly paralysed by indecision, the Japanese took little evasive action. Both battleships and three destroyers were hit, one blowing up. A second wave of six destroyers followed immediately. The *Yamashiro* was hit again but pressed on; the already stricken *Fuso* blew into two separate halves which remained afloat for a while. A further destroyer disintegrated. Nishimura's force was already shattered, only the flagship, the heavy cruiser *Mogami* and one destroyer proceeding but wavering. They were already coming under fire from Oldendorf's main body at the head of the strait when the third and last destroyer attack was made.

This, somewhat discomforted by 'friendly' fire, succeeded in putting two more torpedoes into the doomed *Yamashiro*, at the cost of one destroyer heavily damaged. The Japanese flagship was dismembered within nine minutes by the American heavies, but the *Mogami* and the destroyer *Shigure* turned about and ran back down the strait, only to run (literally) into Shima: the *Mogami* collided with the cruiser *Nachi* but proceeded. At this point *PT-137*, which had hung around after fruitlessly expending two torpedoes after an advancing Nishimura, saw the enemy returning and loosed a further torpedo at the destroyer. It missed but went on to disable the light cruiser *Abukuma* beyond.

The dogged *Mogami* was tracked by *PT-491* for 20 minutes, the boat eventually missing with two torpedoes while under 203-mm (8-in) salvo fire at close range. *PT-323*, came across a burning wreck at first light. Standing by was the damaged destroyer *Asagumo*, which took the PT under hot fire, frustrating three attempts to attack. The PT's final cause for frustration was the arrival of an American cruiser/destroyer force which promptly finished off both Japanese! *PT-150* and *PT-194* unsuccessfully took on the heavy cruiser *Nachi*, the latter boat taking a 203-mm (8-in) shell hit.

The surface action was now finished, it being left to American aircraft to pick off the enemy stragglers, only two cruisers and five destroyers surviving out of the combined Southern Force. The PTs had come through their greatest test with much credit but few scalps. Interestingly, they had been repulsed mainly by that very combination of searchlights and quick-firing guns adopted by the Victorian navy to defeat its own torpedo-boat bogey.

Elco PT boats were expanded versions of a British design, able to carry four torpedoes. Seen here in its original form, with torpedoes in tube launchers and relatively light gun armament, the PT boats had a legend built around them from the early days of the war in the Philippines.

The hybrid battleship/carrier* Ise *is seen off Cape Engano during Halsey's chase after the Japanese carrier force at Leyte. The six ships in the Japanese force had only 13 aircraft available, but their main task was to draw the American fleet carriers away from the landing force, which they succeeded in doing.

USS* St Lô *explodes off Samar after being struck by one of the earliest of kamikaze strikes. The escort carrier had faced up to Kurita's battleships (including the mighty* Yamato*) earlier in the day, but an attacking Zero plunged straight through the deck of the beleaguered vessel and touched off a series of devastating blasts.

power and technological command won the day. Tractors came ashore, wide-bodied tanks and personnel-carriers which could splash their way through the square miles of water-logged ground, and gradually the Japanese forces were squeezed out of their positions in the Ormoc Valley area, and shelled unmercifully everywhere else. On 19 December the Thirty-fifth Army commander, General Suzuki, was informed by General Yamashita in Luzon that no further supplies or reinforcement could be sent to him; on 25 December a message arrived telling Suzuki that he might evacuate any troops he could to other islands, and bidding him a sad farewell.

On the same day, General MacArthur announced the end of organized resistance on Leyte, but it was not a message that reached the still obstinate though starving survivors of Suzuki's formations, and the grim and dangerous business of mopping them up occupied Sixth Army for many more months.

Leyte cost the US forces – air, land and sea – nearly 5,000 dead and 14,000 wounded, and the combination of appalling weather and the spongy ground which absorbed the water and took weeks to dry out made a mockery of the American strategy, which had hoped to make of the island a major base from which to mount the final blow against Luzon, and a solid staging-post for the thrust to the Japanese mainland.

But the destruction of the last powerful Japanese naval formations illustrated to the world the decline in Japanese fortunes. 'Our defeat at Leyte', wrote the Japanese Navy Minister, Admiral Yonai, 'was tantamount to the loss of the Philippines. And when you took the Philippines, that was the end of our resources.'

Above: PT boats were useful at Surigao Strait, not only in spotting, tracking and attacking Japanese naval units, but after the battle in picking up survivors. Here PT 321, an Elco 80-foot boat, hauls an oil-soaked Japanese survivor from the sea. Note the armed sailor standing by; in the Solomons a PT boat crewman was killed by a Japanese survivor to whom he was offering a cup of coffee.

Above: The battleships* Fuso *and* Yamashiro *had the most pronounced of all the 'Pagoda' masts so characteristic of Imperial Japanese Navy battleships during World War II. Both were lost in the Battle of Surigao Strait.

Left: Higgins boats were the other main type of torpedo craft to see active service with the US Navy. This one is seen later in the war, when the adoption of torpedoes designed for aircraft launch did away with the need for the cumbersome tubes, and the weapons were simply rolled off the brackets mounted on the deck.

Chapter 24

Victory in Italy

While the end of 1944 saw the Allies pushing forwards rapidly on most fronts, the Italian campaign was a notable exception. Kesselring's forces here conducted one of the most stubborn defences of the war.

An M4 Sherman medium tank comes ashore from a 'Large Slow Target', as the crews of the LSTs called their charges. The aim of the Anzio landings was to cut off the German troops manning the fortifications of the Gustav line, in particular those at Cassino, which was proving a singularly hard nut to crack.

During the fierce and disastrous battle for Cassino a very different situation prevailed at Anzio - a situation that was to resolve itself into stagnation.

The object of the landings there on 22 January 1944 had been to isolate General Vietinghoff's Tenth Army and sever the lines of communication that supplied Cassino; and the beach-head had been established very easily, with no more than a battalion of the 29th Panzergrenadier Division, which had been resting, to oppose it.

VI Corps, the Anzio invasion forces, were commanded by Major General John P. Lucas. Securing the beach-head were his two infantry divisions (1st British and 3rd US) reinforced with Commandos and Rangers, two tank battalions and a parachute regiment. As soon as the first landings were established another two American divisions (1st Armored and 45th Infantry) followed up. All these forces were there to exploit the landings, and they should of course have thrust out immediately to the north. But Lucas, a cautious man who had anyway never had any great enthusiasm for the enterprise, decided on consolidation before advancing and thereby lost his chance, for Field Marshal Kesselring acted with remarkable speed. He gathered together everything he could move into the area, leaving only the Tenth Army in the Gustav Line, which could safely be left to look after itself with the virtually impregnable hazard of Monte Cassino to be stormed again and again before success was finally achieved at enormous cost.

A week went by before Lucas was satisfied that he had built up his supplies and ensured follow-through for his breakout. He has been much criticized for his lack of vigour - possibly more than is warranted - but whether or not he was justified the delay was fateful. Enemy artillery (including the famous 'Anzio Annie' gun on its railway mounting) had been brought up and the Luftwaffe made concentrated strafes on the shipping gathered in the bay. There could be no easy thrust forward now to link up with General Mark Clark's forces attacking the Gustav Line. Though the Allies had nearly 70,000 men, 500 guns and 237 tanks they were effectively sealed in by the eight divisions Kesselring had manoeuvred into position while Lucas was consolidating. Kesselring's design was not simply to hold the Allied forces and prevent the link-up: he aimed to destroy them. On 19 February the Americans desperately and successfully counter-attacked an enemy thrust into the beach-head and managed to hold firm despite dreadful weather conditions. But stalemate had been reached. Further attacks were similarly resisted until the Germans seemed to realize their efforts were fruitless; but, equally, there was no further chance of a breakout. The stalemate was to persist until 23 May, when a general Allied offensive under General Lucian Truscott, who had replaced Lucas, was successfully launched.

There were other changes in command. Montgomery had been recalled to England in January to take part in the planning of Overlord and Eighth Army was now in the charge of General Sir Oliver Leese, who had led the Allied invasion of Sicily. Eisenhower too had been summoned to the planning sessions and Alexander was now Kesselring's opposite number as supremo in Italy; while in the Anzio beach-head Major-General Gerald Templer had replaced the commander of the British 1st Division, Major-General Penney, who had become a casualty.

Breakout from Anzio

The weather, that influential factor in all battles, had changed considerably for the better by the time Alexander, grasping the nettle of Kesselring's withdrawal of reserves and timing the occasion to a nicety, ordered the launching of the Allied breakout from the beach-head under Truscott. He saw it as a renewed opportunity to hem in Vietinghoff's Tenth Army along the Gustav Line and destroy their communications. Now that Cassino had at last fallen (in every sense of the word) the road to Rome was – anyway in theory – open. But the theory demanded the practice of cutting the main inland highway, Route 6, and holding the enemy against the Apennines. This is turn required Truscott's forces to hold fast such escape routes through the mountains as the Germans might resort to; and that, in the event, they failed to do.

Nevertheless, the breakout was to a large degree successful.

Within two days – that is, by 25 May – two American divisions (1st Armored and 3rd Infantry) had captured the town of Cori on the other main highway, Route 7, and had made contact with the US II Corps, which after fruitlessly hammering away at Cassino had reassembled and was actually on Route 7 and pushing northward towards Rome, Mark Clark hav-

Chronology of War: 1944-1945

December 1
Germans leave Suda Bay, Canae and Maléme on Crete. Fourteenth Army reaches Pinwe. US forces drive into Germany on 30-mile front

December 6
Eighth Army crosses the Lamone

December 7
Russians on south shore of Lake Balaton, Hungary

December 9
Red Army drives on both sides of Budapest

December 10
Fourteenth Army reaches Indaw

December 14
US aircraft attack Japanese airfields on Luzon

December 15
US forces land on Mindoro to build airfields

December 16
Battle of the Bulge; V and VI Panzer Armies drive through Ardennes in attempt to reach Antwerp. Eighth Army clear Faenza

December 19
Montgomery to command Allied armies north of the Ardennes, Bradley to command those to the south

December 21
US 101st Airborne Division in Bastogne besieged

December 22
Germans blocked on drive to Meuse

December 25
German panzers driven back from Meuse. Japanese resistance on Leyte collapses

December 26
US Third Army tanks drive up to relieve Bastogne

December 27
Red Army completes encirclement of Budapest

December 28
Mindoro airfield in use

December 31
UK civilian casualties in December 367 killed, 847 injured

1945

January 1
Operation Bodenplatte (Baseplate); last major Luftwaffe operation, against Allied airfields in France, Belgium and Holland. US Ninth Army begins four-month mopping-up on Leyte

January 2
Germans mount relief operation towards Budapest

January 4
British Eighth Army attacks at Senio. Kamikaze attacks on Task Force approaching Lingayen Gulf. Akyab, Burma, occupied by British and Indian troops

January 6
US Task Force reaches Lingayen Gulf; kamikaze attacks continue

January 7
Fourteenth Army reaches Shwebo

January 10
US Sixth Army lands on Luzon at Lingayen Gulf

January 11
Luzon beachhead expanded against fierce opposition

January 12
Russians launch Winter Offensive in south

January 15
American First and Third armies link up at Houffalize in the Ardennes

January 17
Warsaw liberated by Polish troops attached to Red Army

January 18
Germans drive through Russian lines to reach Danube

January 19
Russians capture Crakow and Tilsit

***Above:* A composite photograph of part of the Anzio landing taken at about 10.30 in the morning of 22 January. For the first six hours of the operation, the infantry divisions met little opposition.**

***Right:* Heavy and medium bombers, such as this Martin B-26 Marauder, continued to harass German line of communications as well as key points.**

ing determined that the capital should be the prize of Fifth Army. To that end he detached only one division to assist in the drive to Volmontone, the capture of which was the key to the severance of Route 6. But one division was not enough to strengthen the breakout forces sufficiently for them to triumph over the German opposition of three divisions which protected the main artery. Clark's obstinacy in securing for the Americans the glory of the seizure of the Holy City, despite Alexander's orders that the strongest effort should be made to gain Valmontone, had little effect on the ultimate victory in the Italian campaign; but it was not a move that gained him much popularity among the British, Polish, French, New Zealand, Moroccan and Indian troops who had four times stormed the heights of Monte Cassino and justifiably looked forward to a co-operative strike toward Rome rather than a star role for the Americans.

***Above right:* Field Marshal Kesselring managed to redeploy his forces to counter the landings extremely rapidly, and by the time the Allies were ready to move out from the beach-head the Germans had ringed it with eight divisions.**

***Right:* A British 4.5-in gun fires on a German command post from the Fifth Army beach-head.**

***Left:* DUKW amphibious trucks running a shuttle service between the shore and the supply ships come under fire from the guns of the German Fourteenth Army.**

THE CAPTURE OF ROME

But the star role must not be denied its triumph. Victorious US troops entered the city on 4 June to the plaudits of multitudes of Italians who lined the streets and welcomed them like long-lost relations – which indeed many of them were, a fact that had contributed from the very beginning to the lack of enthusiasm on many Italians' part to go to war with a country to which many of their compatriots had emigrated and where they had established themselves with great success.

Rome, however, as well as not being built in a day is by no means the whole of Italy. The Allies had fought their way up from the toe and heel of the peninsula and despite having made many mistakes had to a great extent overcome the ingenious generalship of the enemy and superior mobility of his forces. But there was still a long way to go. In any case the approaches to the capital were still the scene of considerable fighting. During the days prior to the entry of units of the US 88th Division into Rome, the Liri Valley towns of Monte Cairo, Piedimonte and Aquino had more or less fallen to the Allies, but Arce and Ceprano were fiercely held; and on 26 May the US 3rd Division had been halted by stiffening enemy resistance at Valmontone. It was clear to the Germans that they were being forced to withdraw on the whole front, but this intensified rather than weakened their resistance and their skilful manoeuvring and sudden counter-attacks caused much dismay among the Allies, as well as substantial losses. But morale, considerably recovered since the seasonal changes from the unmitigated awfulness of the winter to the burgeoning of spring and summer, was additionally boosted by the triumphal entry of representative forces of all Allies into Rome on 5 June; and it was sustained, though the world's interest was switched from Italy to Normandy on 6 June, when Overlord was launched and the liberation of northern Europe began.

Though it had vanished from the headlines and been upstaged by the invasion of Normandy, the Italian campaign was drawn out almost to the end of the war in Europe. To those involved in it there was no respite: there was still a long way to go.

The Lockheed P-38 Lightning performed excellently in the Italian theatre, used as fighter-bombers. The twin boom layout produced little form drag, enabling the Lightning to be one of the fastest twins of the war. This example carries long range tanks.

The Gothic Line

Alexander was to lose several of his divisions to the more urgent needs of the Normandy invasion, even though he needed them when the time came for his planned attack on the Germans' final line of defence south of the Lombardy plains, which, overrun, would give access to Austria and the Balkans.

This, the Gothic Line, ran from slightly south of La Spezia in the Gulf of Genoa right across Italy from west to east, crossing the Apennines near Florence and continuing to Pesaro on the Adriatic coast. On that line, Kesselring figured, he could hold the Allied forces during the winter after harrying their sporadic

M7 self-propelled 105-mm howitzers of the 191st Tank Battalion fire on the enemy during the German counteroffensive in early February. They formed part of the US 45th Division, which had come ashore after the initial landings.

Chronology of War: 1945

January 20
French troops drive into Colmar pocket

January 21
Russians take Tannenberg

January 22
Burma Road re-opened

January 23
US First Army takes St Vith. Fourteenth Army in Burma takes Tizaung and Myinmu. US Sixth Army approaches Clark Field on Luzon

January 25
Roermond triangle, north of Aachen, eliminated. US troops fight on Clark Field on Luzon. Beginning of the greatest seaborne evacuation in history, as up to 2 million Germans are taken from Courland, Pomerania and Prussia across the Baltic and away from the Russians

January 27
Russians take Memel and cross Vistula

January 28
Last vestige of Ardennes Salient flattened. Germans lose 120,000 dead, wounded and POW in Battle of the Bulge – US losses include 8,607 dead, 47,139 wounded and 21,144 missing

January 29
Russians enter Poznan

January 31
US Sixth Army controls Clark Field. Russians reach Oder from opposite Berlin down to Carpathians, a front of over 500 km

February 1
US Seventh Army reaches Siegfried Line. US Sixth Army drives towards Manila

February 3
US raid Berlin with 1,000 B-17 bombers escorted by 900 fighters

February 4
Yalta Conference opens. US troops capture first Roer Dam

February 5
British and Canadian offensive drive to the Rhine begins

February 6
Russians cross Upper Oder. Fifth Army reaches river Serchio in north Italy

February 7
German engineers wreck Schwammanuel Dam floodgates

February 8
British and Canadians begin clearing area between Maas and Rhine

February 10
US First Army captures Schwammanuel Dam

February 11
Russians approach Breslau and Dresden. German garrison in Budapest destroyed

February 12
Yalta Conference ends. Canadians take Cleve

February 13
Fourteenth Army cross Irrawaddy south of Mandalay. RAF 'Fire Raid' on Dresden – estimates of dead vary between 135,000 and 250,000

February 14
USAF continues raid on Dresden. US Sixth Army drives south on Bataan Peninsusla

February 15
Red Army encircle Breslau and drive towards Danzig

February 16
US Navy bombards Iwo Jima. US TF.58 raids Tokyo and Yokohama with over 1,000 carrier planes (repeated 17 Feb.)

February 19
US Marines land on Iwo Jima

advances north from Rome during the few remaining months of summer. His withdrawals would be aided by additional strongly defended positions on the Albert Line, stretching from a point halfway between Grosseto and Orvieto north east to the Tiber and Lake Trasimeno and beyond to Gubbio. Between the Albert and Gothic Lines rearguard stands would be made at the easily defensible gaps in the Tuscan mountains south of Arezzo, and along the Arno from Ribbiena to Pisa.

All this was of course in the future when Rome (which had been declared an 'open city' by Kesselring) came under Allied occupation on 4 June. The jubilation in the city continued, but a feeling of anticlimax gradually spread through the Allied lines – certainly not to the extent of affecting morale, but bringing with it a sense of lethargy which overcame the natural wish to push on while the going was good and lay hands on the whole of Italy.

Decisions at Cabinet and Chiefs of Staff levels were the main cause of the delay. The invasion of southern France as a preliminary to Overlord had occupied the consideration of these top people since the summer of 1943; and because its implementation would have meant the withdrawal of Allied forces from the Italian campaign it was naturally strongly opposed by the British. But rejigged and renamed Dragoon it was now scheduled to take place on 15 August, and Alexander had to suffer the withdrawal of three divisions of the US VI Corps and the four divisions of the French Corps, reducing his total forces to five divisions. The enemy, on the other hand, were being reinforced by four divisions and a regiment of heavy tanks to cover their losses in the fight for southern Italy. The arguments in favour of or opposing Dragoon had veered to and fro, until the beginning of July. By that time Kesselring had accepted the urgency with which he had to stem the Allies' further

Tanks of the 1st US Armored Division during the break-out from Anzio. German improvisation had kept the Allied force bottled up until the fall of Cassino and the breaking of the Gustav Line.

'Anzio Annie'

The landing at Anzio, designed to bypass the defences of the Gustav line, was soon stalled in a small beach-head. Not least of the problems besetting the troops was the regular shelling by huge railway guns.

As the Allied troops of the VI Corps stormed up the beaches at Anzio and Nettuno, south of Rome, in January 1944 their commanders supposed that between them and the city of Rome there were few German troops to oppose them. The bulk of the German forces were farther to the south manning the strong Gustav Line of defensive positions that included the mountain fortress of Cassino.

The whole landing operations were conducted on so tight a manpower and logistic shoestring that US Major General John Lucas, commanding the subsequent beachhead, deemed it prudent to build up his supplies and strength (especially in armour and heavy artillery) before he ventured forwards into the Alban Hills, despite the fact that ground and air reconnaissance found virtually no opposition.

By the time Lucas considered it possible to advance, his adversary Generalfeldmarschall Albert Kesselring had raked together existing forces and formed new units composing the 14th Army to obliterate the beachhead. When the Allies advanced they were countered by strong German forces that included some Panzer units and fresh troops from the north of Italy. They also encountered the German railway guns.

The railway guns involved were two 28-cm K 5 (E)s that had originally been sent to Italy for shipment to Tunisia, that campaign ending before they could be shipped. The guns had since spent their time near Milan and were sent south to the Anzio area via Rome at the end of January 1944. Once in position only one gun could be kept in action at any one time for, although a near-perfect firing point for a railway gun was found, it could accommodate only one gun at a time. This position was not far from Albano on the main Rome to Nettuno railway line at a point where the track entered a tunnel. The K 5 (E) could be kept under cover in the tunnel, being pushed out to fire and immediately pulled back in again once the round had been released. Although the track in and out of the tunnel was double at the site, it was deemed safer to operate only one gun at a time with the other gun kept in another tunnel farther to the north.

For four months the two guns between them made the lives of the Allied soldiers in the Anzio beachhead as difficult as possible. A constant drizzle of 28-cm shells was scattered all over the confines of the beach areas and the country inland, in conjunction with a constant bombardment from light artillery units and the continuous threat of Luftwaffe attacks. The Allied air force did what they could to find and destroy the K 5 (E) firing site but the area was well camouflaged and the gun was always kept inside the tunnel when Allied aircraft approached. In time the fire from the K 5 (E) became so regular that the Allied troops named the guns 'Anzio Annie' and the name has stuck to this day, despite the fact that two guns were involved. They wrought considerable damage between them, and remained in action until the Allies broke through the Gustav Line to the south.

With the fall of Cassino to Polish forces, the Gustav Line was broken and the Allies stormed north to relieve the Anzio beachhead. This they did by moving rapidly north, not along the coastal route but inland to the extent that they cut off the railway lines that provided the two K 5 (E)s with their escape route. The guns were thus captured almost intact and ready to move out. One gun was damaged by its crew before capture but the other was found almost complete and this example was subsequently shipped to the United States for examination and test firing. The major components of the other gun were also shipped to the USA, and when the examination programme was completed bits of both guns were put together to form the exhibit that is now on public show at Aberdeen Proving Grounds in Maryland. Now named 'Leopold' for some reason, this K 5 (E) is the only example of its kind that can be seen in the West.

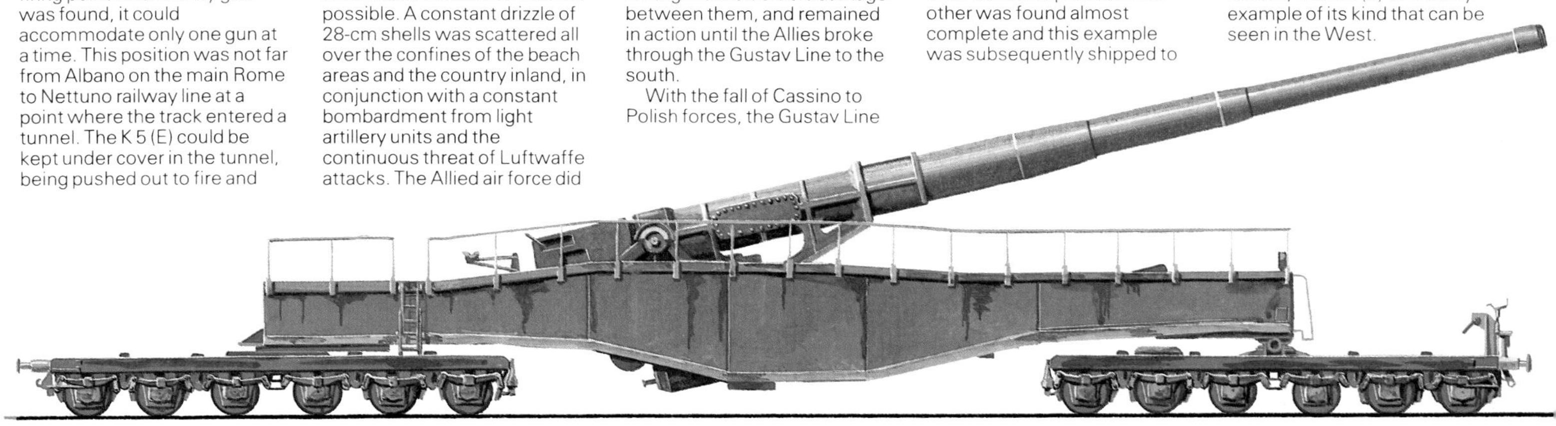

Above: The 28-cm Kanone 5 (Eisenbahn) or K5(E) was one of the finest artillery pieces made. Unlike most railway guns, the K 5(E) was used extensively from the Atlantic Wall to the siege of Sevastopol. The complete equipment weighed 218 tonnes and the gun could fire a 255-kg shell to a range of 62 km.

The awesome blast of a K 5(E) in action. The two guns which together became known as 'Anzio Annie' were positioned safely in the Alban hills, more than 32 km from the landing zones and well protected from air attack by the railway tunnels of the main Rome-Nettuno line.

February 21
21st Army Group: British and Canadian troops reach Goch, which is captured by 51st Highland Division. US Third Army advances on wide front

February 22
Operation Clarion; Allied air forces attack German road and communication system. Fifth Army overlooks Reno valley

February 23
Russians take Poznan. US Marines take Mount Suribachi on Iwo Jima

February 24
American forces control almost all of Manila

February 26
Operation Blockbuster; Canadian units drive into Holland

February 27
US Marines take airfield on Iwo Jima

February 28
Corregidor in US hands after airborne assault. UK civilian casualties in February 483 killed, 1,152 injured

Above: A PzKpfw V Panther on the Italian Front in July 1944. Note the Zimmeritt paste finish; a layer of concrete like anti-magnetic material designed to foil anti-tank weapons.

Below: Lieutenant General Mark Clark examines enemy held terrain in the company of Major General Joao Batista de Mascarenhas, of the Brazilian Expeditionary Force.

Right: An abandoned machine-gun post in a classic position designed to fire along an Italian resupply route. The Mauser designed MG 42 was one of the finest weapons of its type.

advance northward from Rome and had called for additional help besides the four divisions and the heavy tanks he had already been promised. The answer had been to conjure up yet another four divisions (switched from the Eastern Front) and to send them with all speed down through the thigh of Italy to the railhead at Bologna, from which they were siphoned off to concentrations in Pontremoli, Parma, Reggio, Modena and Ferrara to await their principal use in the climax of Kesselring's catch-as-catch-can harrying plan.

The elements of the plan were simple enough: he would lure the Allied forces forward first to the Albert Line, parry their thrust there and wait for them to reform for a major attack; then, before the attack was launched, skip back to the Arezzo line. The same tactics would be repeated there, this time the withdrawal being to the Arno line; and finally the full forces massed behind the Gothic Line would be used to repel the Allied attack and, with any luck, annihilate its formations – or, at the very least, reduce them to such numerical inferiority that any attack on Austria by way of the Lombardy plains would be out of the question. Now that he had ample forces at his command he set about implementing the plan.

Needless to say, Alexander too had a plan which he had formulated with Montgomery's successor at the head of Eighth Army, Oliver Leese. It was a plan based largely on bluff. If Kesselring could be tricked into thinking that Allied activities were to be switched to the Adriatic coast and a breakthrough to Rimini, thus causing him to drain forces away from the centre to deal with it, another feint could be aimed at Bologna with the likely consequence that the forces sent to repel the Adriatic advance would have to be hastily returned to the centre; whereupon the sham attack in the east could be turned into a real one and a speedy advance made by way of the Valli de Comacchio into the Lombardy plains. This plan took into consideration the reduction in available forces – particularly the lack of the French divisions, which incorporated highly skilled mountain troops who would have been essential in any big-scale action in the Tuscan mountains. Like all plans it had its pluses and

US fighting vehicles, 1944-1945

When the US entered the war, US armoured vehicle thinking was in the process of assimilating the first lessons of the war in Europe. It was not innovative design or powerful vehicles which were to prove decisive in 1944/45, as both German and Soviet designs had considerably more fighting power than those of the USA. Once again, it was the sheer industrial muscle which could turn out 50,000 M4 Shermans in under four years that won the victory.

Equipped with the same gun as the later models of the M4 tank, the M18 Hellcat was a fast, lightly armoured tank destroyer. The American concept of the tank destroyer was that it should survive by its mobility. The M18, with its lightweight, air-cooled radial engine and Christie suspension, was certainly mobile, having a top speed of 55 mph.

The M4A3E8 variant of the Sherman, commonly known as the 'Easy Eight', was equipped with the late-war standard 76-mm gun, which was a great improvement on the original 75-mm (although still no match for the German 88-mm or the long 75-mm). It had a new, horizontally-mounted suspension system rather than the vertical suspension unit fitted to the bogeys of earlier models.

minuses. One of the minuses was its reliance on continuing dry weather to enable negotiation by armoured vehicles of the terrain north of Rimini, which was inclined to marshiness in periods of prolonged rain. Another was the network of waterways that would inevitably impede progress. It was a toss-up whether the mountain passes or the meandering rivers offered the greater obstacles.

In the event both commanders had to cope with the vagaries of fortune as well as those of weather and terrain.

The Alexander/Leese plan was given the code-name Olive and scheduled to be launched on 15 August – the same day that the airborne and seaborne forces of Dragoon invaded the French coast between Toulon and Cannes, with initial success.

Eighth Army offensive

Olive too got off to a good start, though not until 10 days later, on the 25th. Eighth Army's three corps had been successfully deployed in the Adriatic sector without arousing the enemy's suspicions: they were the British V, the Canadian I and the Polish. In the centre sector X Corps remained poised for the second feint attack, and over to the west XIII Corps were on hand to support it if Kesselring fell for the trickery of the east-coast activities. Which in a sense he did. The movement of the Allied troops into that Adriatic sector did not attract his attention until the end of August, by which time the stop-gap transfer of a couple of divisions from the centre sector was too late to stem Eighth Army's advance north on a broad front – an advance that had easily overcome the tenacious but inadequate opposition of the sparsely held German positions. But the drive could not be maintained. Supply lines to the Eighth were being shortened – an eventuality that had been foreseen but had not taken into account the inadequate facilities provided by the Adriatic ports – and early rains settled in to give Kesselring an additional advantage.

September was a month of indecisions and revisions, of the bouncing to and fro of attacks and counter-attacks on and off the Gothic Line – though the Canadian 1st Division had successfully pushed through it at Pesaro on the 1st and had fanned out on a front of 20 miles with relatively small losses. And Kesselring had, as anticipated, been taken by sur-

Above: The war in Italy was not all vino and sun: the weather was particularly awful during the winter. The Allied air forces continued to operate in adversity, exemplified by this B-24D wading through rainwater on its way to the runway.

Left: The Germans put up a brave defence against the Allied bombers. This 15th Air Force Liberator takes a round in the wing while providing bombing support for the Allied drive.

The M10 was evolved from the chassis of the M4A2 Sherman but was fitted with the 3-in M7 gun (originally an AA weapon). The turret was open topped as it was in its successor the M18, but the lack of protection for the crew was accepted in view of the weight saved (which gave extra speed), and the superior all-round visibility, which was essential when spotting the enemy first meant survival.

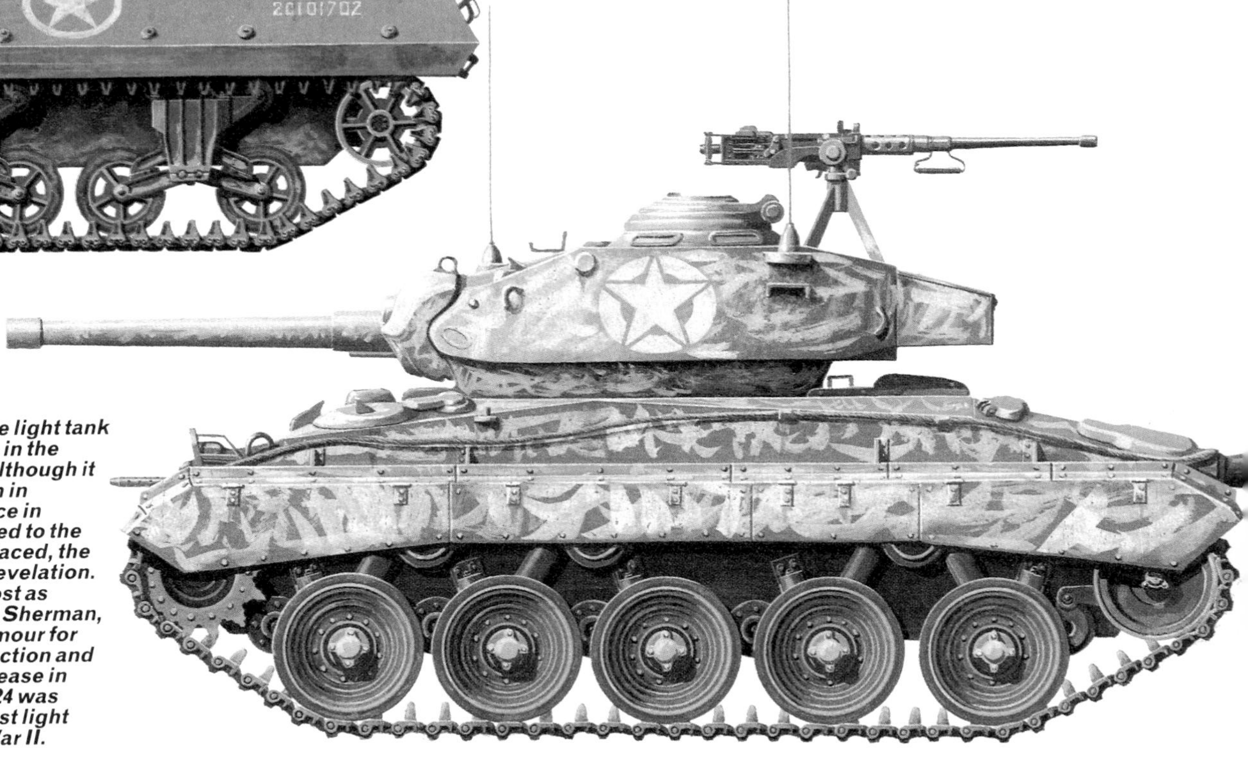

The M24 Chaffee light tank reached Europe in the winter of 1944, although it saw most action in American service in Korea. Compared to the M5 which it replaced, the Chaffee was a revelation. With a gun almost as powerful as in a Sherman, well-shaped armour for increased protection and little if any decrease in mobility, the M24 was probably the best light tank of World War II.

Left: North of Isola del Piano, in the Gran Sasso hills, tanks of 51 Royal Tank Regiment go forward support to 139 Infantry Brigade on the Eighth Army's push towards the Gothic Line.

Above: Rome was the first of the Axis capitals to fall to the Allies, being taken by American troops in June. These M10s of the Fifth Army are among the first to pass the Colosseum on 4 June 1944.

prise by the designated second feint of the Fifth Army in the western sector. Here, on the 5th, troops of the US IV Corps had captured Lucca, well north of the Arno line and Kesselring had let nearly two weeks pass before he recognized it as a major offensive and shuttled back two of his divisions from the eastern sector to deal with it.

This was the time when the big-scale Eighth Army drive into the Lombardy plains should have gone ahead and succeeded. But despite the Canadians' success at Pesaro the Eighth's momentum had slackened. Inadequacy of supplies, heavy losses in the infantry, the incapability of heavy armoured vehicles to overcome the hazards of marshy terrain and perpetual rain, were all contributory causes of the slowdown.

Stalemate

So, alert now to the threat of Fifth Army's activities on the western sector, Kesselring was able to withdraw many of the forces he had been misled into sending to the east and use them to stiffen his resistance to Mark Clark's drive toward Bologna; for it was clear to him (as it rapidly became to all ranks of the Eighth) that the drive on the eastern flank was easing to a halt and that the defence of the coastal area could safely be left to the weather and the geological features.

By the end of October, though there had been some skirmishing round Casseta just south of Bologna and V Corps had got across the River Ronco, the overall picture was as gloomy as the weather. The Eighth had lost some 500 tanks, considerable morale and their commander, Leese, who had departed to take up a new appointment in command of the Allied Land Forces in south east Asia. General Richard McCreery took over (his promotion and appointment were not confirmed until November) to direct the fluctuating fortunes of the bogged-down army, which was still being held up by waterways and weather and had to all intents and purposes come to a standstill.

Over on the left the Fifth Army too had been slowed in its drive toward Bologna – not so much by the weather (and even less by the terrain) as by the tough resistance of the enemy, who gave no ground at all and turned every defensive point along the inland highway Route 65 into an obstacle which even Clark's II Corps of four divisions could overcome only with such great difficulty that their advances were negligible. This led to the virtual abandonment of operation Olive by the beginning of November. Once again stalemate had been reached. And as the Combined Chiefs of Staff recognized the uselessness of resuscitating the Italian campaign before the spring, they depleted its forces still further by hauling out the Canadian Corps for service on the Western Front, while a substantial part of Eighth Army was transferred to Greece, where civil war had broken out.

Italian Fascists still fought for the Axis in the north of the country, but Allied air and sea power was almost overwhelming. This Italian patrol boat was bombed in Leghorn (Livorno) harbour.

The Luftwaffe continued its campaign against Allied shipping. The lack of ventral gondola and the FuG 200 Hohentwiel *radar array identify this aircraft as a Ju 88A-6/U long-range maritime aircraft.*

The last offensive

During the three months of inactivity on the Italian battlefront that ensued after the abandonment of Olive the Allies took advantage of the lull to rest and reverse the depressing effect on morale of heavy losses, failure to achieve their main objectives, and the disappearance of some of their strongest elements to other theatres of war.

Morale was considerably, if gradually, restored by the Allied air forces' complete superiority over the Luftwaffe, the buildup of manpower to a total strength of over 600,000 military personnel, and 60,000 Italian Partisans who infiltrated behind the German lines and confused enemy intelligence, and the welcome arrival of immense quantities of ammunition, bridging equipment and armoured vehicles – including tracked landing vehicles called Fantails which were designed to cope with exactly the sort of marshy areas that had proved so frustrating to the advances of Eighth Army.

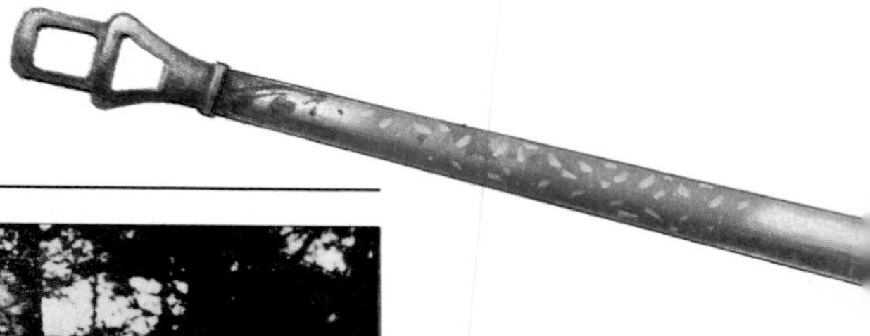

Massively powerful, the Jagdtiger mounted the 12.8-cm Pak 44 L/55 gun on the chassis of the Tiger II, or Royal Tiger. It could destroy any other vehicle it met but great weight meant low mobility and excessive tendency to mechanical failure. Only 77 production models were completed.

German tank destroyers

The Germans put their early war experience into the development of assault guns, heavily armed and armoured vehicles designed to accompany infantry to deal with strongpoints or obstacles. These often developed into tank destroyers, mounting more powerful guns than similar tanks, and cheaper to build. Although formidable weapons, they had a basic drawback; virtually defenceless outside the narrow traverse of the gun, they proved vulnerable to tank hunting infantry.

Above: Jagdpanzer IV was a Panzerjager version of the Pz IV tank and housed its main 7.5-cm gun in a well armoured mount with good ballistic shape. An early model is depicted, as later production omitted the muzzle brake.

Right: It was inevitable that the Pak 43 8.8-cm gun should be fitted onto surplus Panzer III and IV chassis. This is a Pak 43/1 auf GW IV, which went under the official title Nashorn (Rhinoceros) but was commonly called Hornisse (Hornet). It was an interim design, closer to American practice than was usual, being lightly armoured and with an open crew compartment.

Above: The light Panzer II was soon found to be unsuitable for the kind of fighting that took place on the Eastern Front. In order not to waste production capacity, a Panzerjäger was designed on the chassis, mounting the trusted 7.5-cm Pak 40. Although the result had a high profile, it was one of the most numerous German tank-hunters of the later war years.

Below: When the Czech designed Panzer 38(t) became outmoded, its chassis was found to be suitable for a number of purposes. Fitted with the 7.5-cm Pak 39, the Hetzer (baiter, as in bull-bait) proved to be one of the best gun/chassis combinations being low, well protected for its size and able to knock out all but the most powerful of Soviet armour.

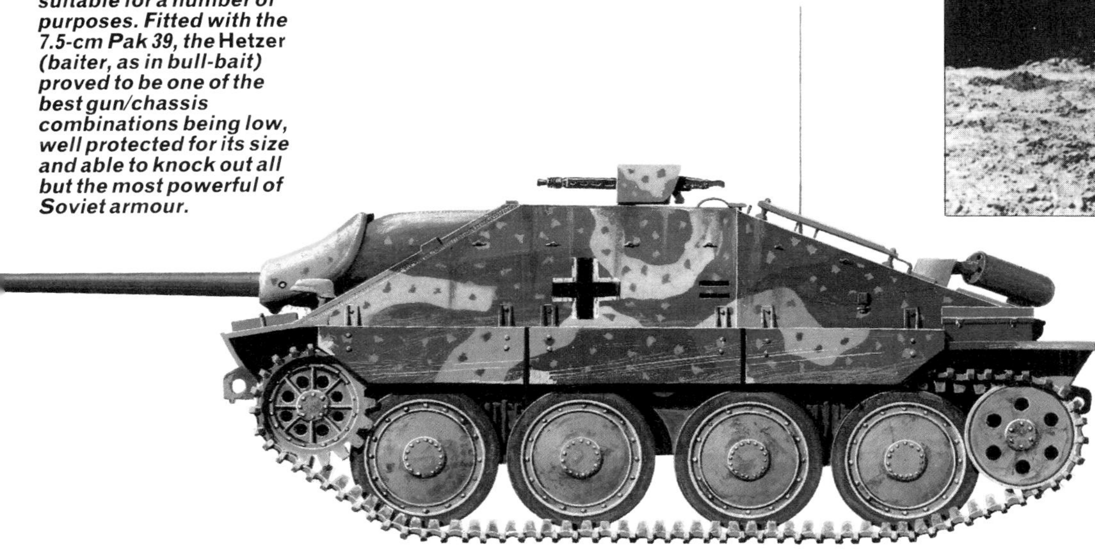

Below: The tank-killer conversion of the PzKpfw V Panther was one of the finest combat machines of World War II. Superbly armoured and shaped, the Jagdpanther was capable of destroying any Allied tank with its 8.8-cm Pak 43/3 gun. Fortunately, production was limited to a total of 382, largely as a result of Allied bombing of manufacturing facilities.

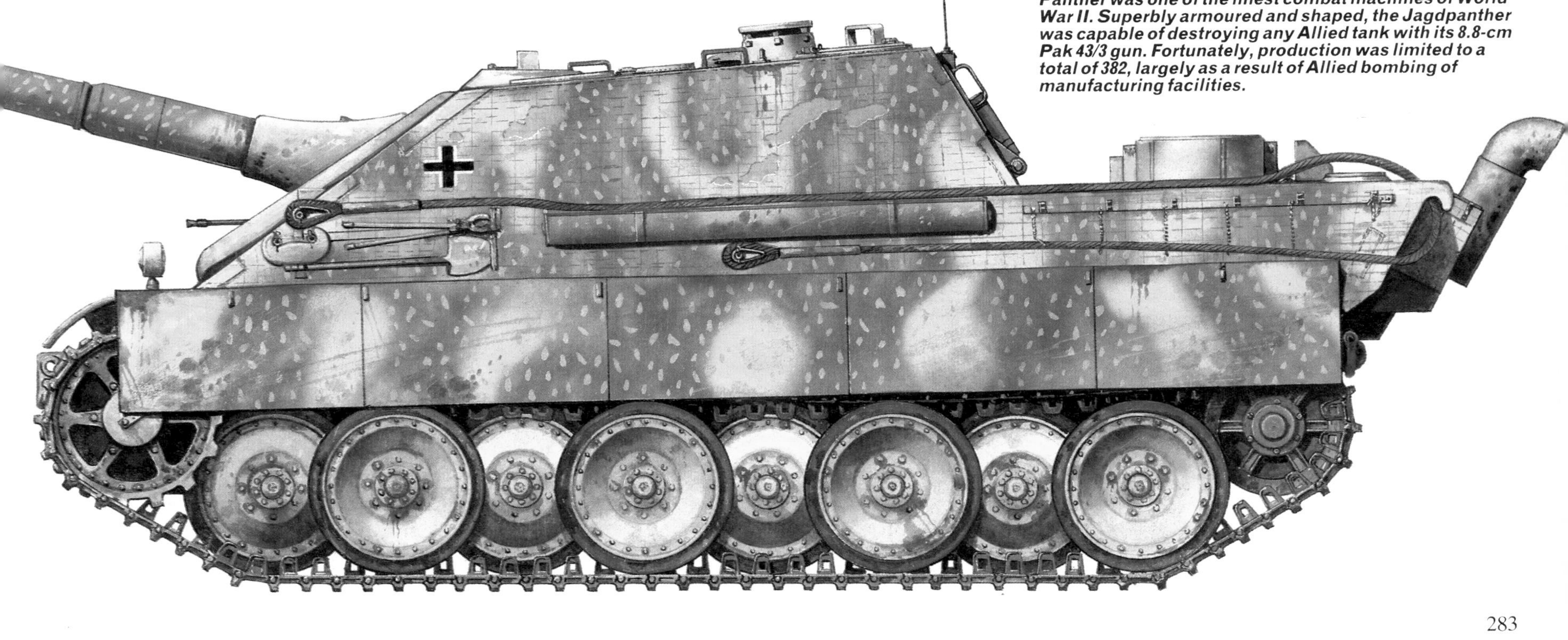

GERMAN SURRENDER

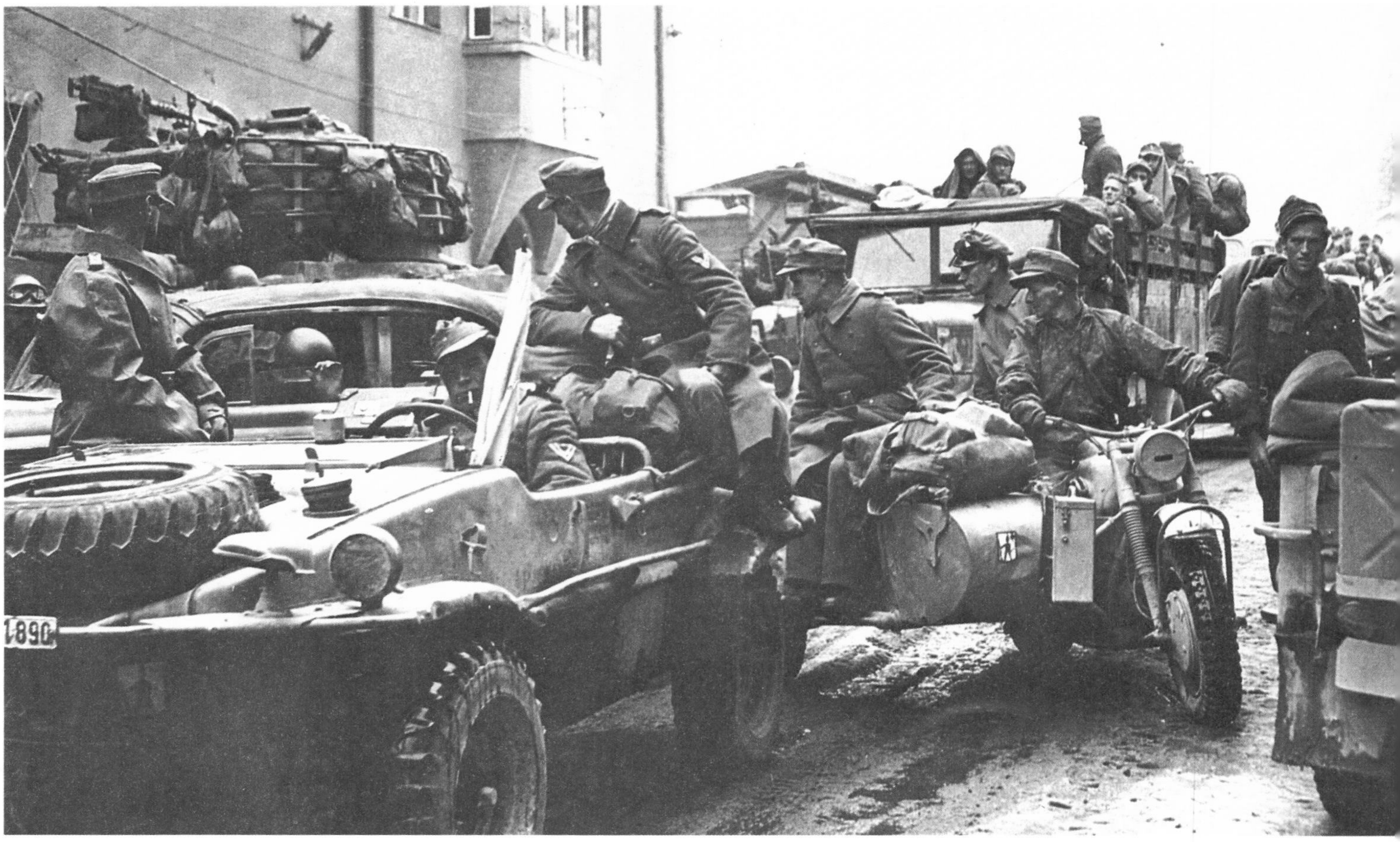

The end of the war, and units of the US Fifth Army make contact with the US Seventh Army pushing south through the Brenner Pass. Caught in the middle, the German army tries to find its way home after the surrender of 2 May 1945.

The Spring Offensive began effectively on 9 April with both Fifth and Eighth Armies heading for Bologna – the latter on a broad front that would wheel round to the north and engulf Ferrara. Once again subterfuge was used, this time by way of a preliminary attack launched by the Eighth north of Ravenna, intended to attract what few German reserves there were away from the concentration area round Bologna and thereby weaken the resistance that might be offered to the Fifth when it began its drive to the city a few days later. The plan was largely successful; all the same, the enemy, now in desperate straits, resisted fiercely and held the advances back until the 21st, when Bologna fell to units of the Polish II Corps and the US II Corps.

The Argenta Gap had already been negotiated by British troops with the highly successful Fantails, and it was obvious that with Fifth Army in possession of Bologna and its reconnaissance patrols sweeping on toward the Po, the German C-in-C, Vietinghoff (Kesselring had been withdrawn from battle after a car accident), would have to look to his laurels. His forces were concentrated in the front line, he had but a skeleton of reserves, and the general collapse of the German forces in north-west Europe after the failure of the Ardennes offensive offered little hope of a respite. In bitter frame of mind he communicated with Hitler and formally requested permission to retreat to the line of the Po. As might have been expected, permission was refused, but he ignored the rejection and ordered the withdrawal himself. It was the signal for a general retreat by all German and pro-German forces, for now that the Allies had broken through to the open ground beyond the Po the chances of stopping them amounted to nil.

Italian Partisans and British paratroops fell upon Milan and Genoa, and another happy band of Partisans fell upon Mussolini and his mistress near Lake Como and summarily despatched them. Then came the capture of Verona and Lake Garda, which split the remnants of the retreating German army as they raggedly retreated to Trieste and Turin, both of which were occupied by the Allies on 2 May, while other Allied units headed toward the Brenner Pass to link up with US Seventh Army forces from the north. Apart from the formalities of official surrender the awesomely long and difficult Italian campaign was over. As much controversy attended its conclusion as had delayed its beginning. But there can be little doubt that the retention of some 25 German divisions in Italy at a time when, following Overlord, their presence was sorely needed elsewhere, contributed to the quicker success of the Allies in the West.

The surrender had been discussed away from the battlefield as early as February. Karl Wolff, head of the SS in Italy, and Allen Dulles of the US Office of Strategic Services in Switzerland had met on neutral ground and put forth feelers. The discussions were prolonged and tricky and several times seemed on the verge of breaking down. Only when orders from Hitler were disregarded did they come to fruition. Even then they dragged on, and it was not until 25 April that orders were given to German and Italian Fascist forces to lay down their arms at 12 noon on 2 May – just as the Allies were entering Trieste. It was the only negotiated surrender of the war in Europe.

Right: Field Marshal Albert Kesselring, whose stubborn defence of the Italian Peninsula tied down the US Fifth and British Eighth Armies to the last days of the war, is seen during his imprisonment at Nuremberg after the war.

Below: American made M10 tank-destroyers of the 6th South African Division open fire on German positions flanking the Fifth Army front on Highway 64 near Bologna. The town was eventually taken by the Allies some six months later, in April 1945.

Below: The Cossack Division of the Wehrmacht lay down their arms to the British 6th Armoured Division to the east of Klagenfurt in Austria. They were handed back to the Russians, as a result of the Yalta agreement, and most were executed as traitors.

Mediterranean torpedo boats and coastal craft

While the exploits of the PT boats in the Philippines and Solomons and the nightly encounters between E-boats, MTBs and MGBs in the North Sea have often been recounted, the ferocious battles of the coastal forces in the Mediterranean have been largely overlooked.

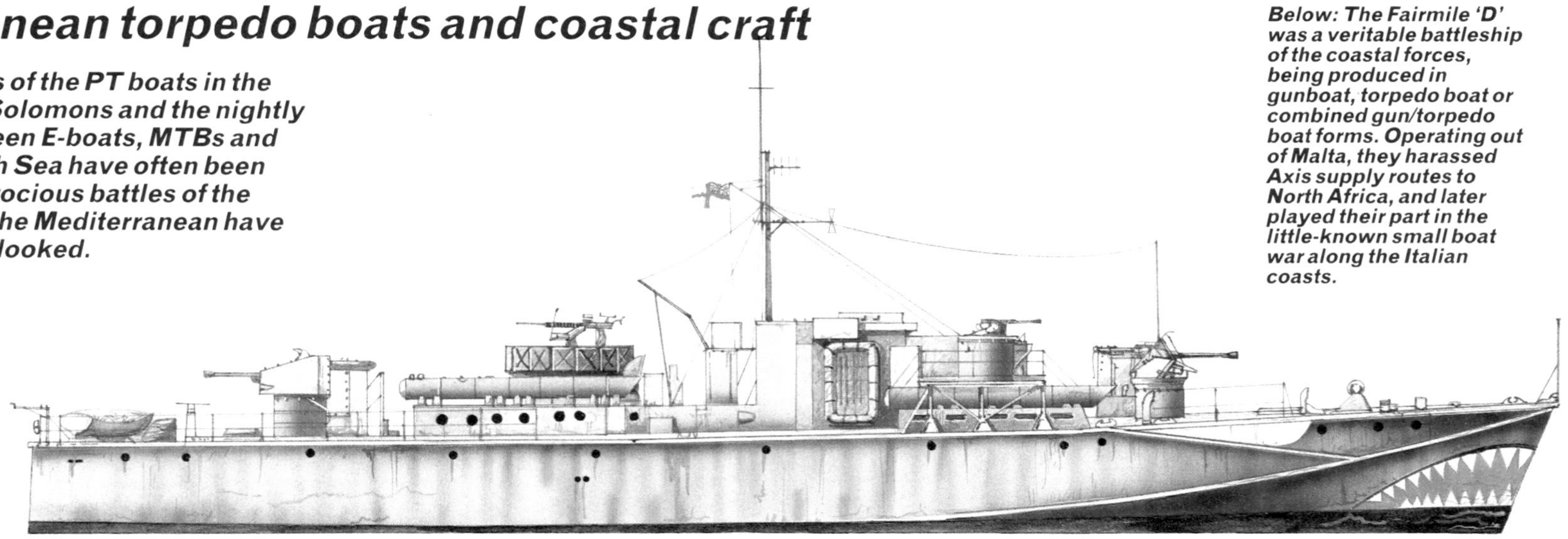

Below: *The Fairmile 'D' was a veritable battleship of the coastal forces, being produced in gunboat, torpedo boat or combined gun/torpedo boat forms. Operating out of Malta, they harassed Axis supply routes to North Africa, and later played their part in the little-known small boat war along the Italian coasts.*

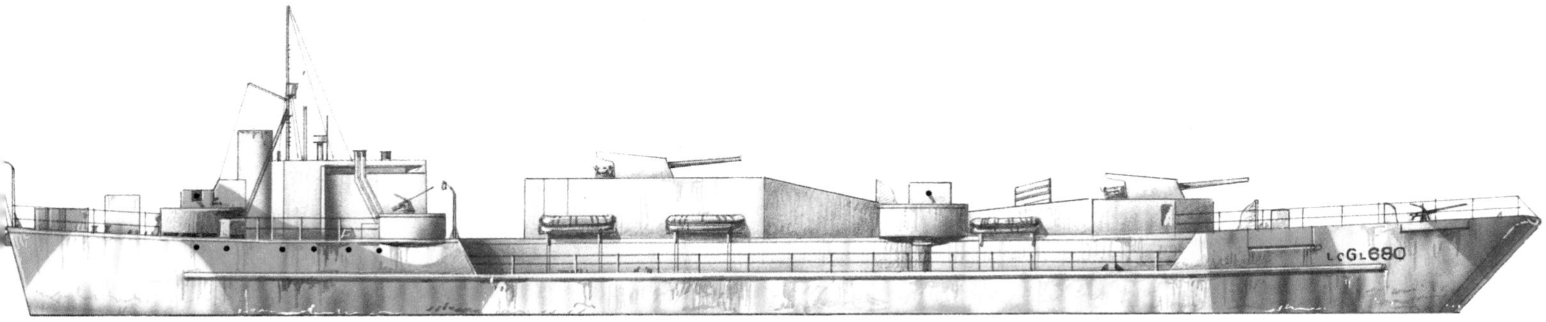

Left: *Also involved in the coastal war, the Landing Craft, Gun was fitted with destroyer armament. Operating with Royal Navy MTBs and radar-equipped US Navy PT boats, these vessels were the centre of hard-hitting groups deployed against the coastal shipping which carried much of the Wehrmacht's supplies for the Italian Campaign.*

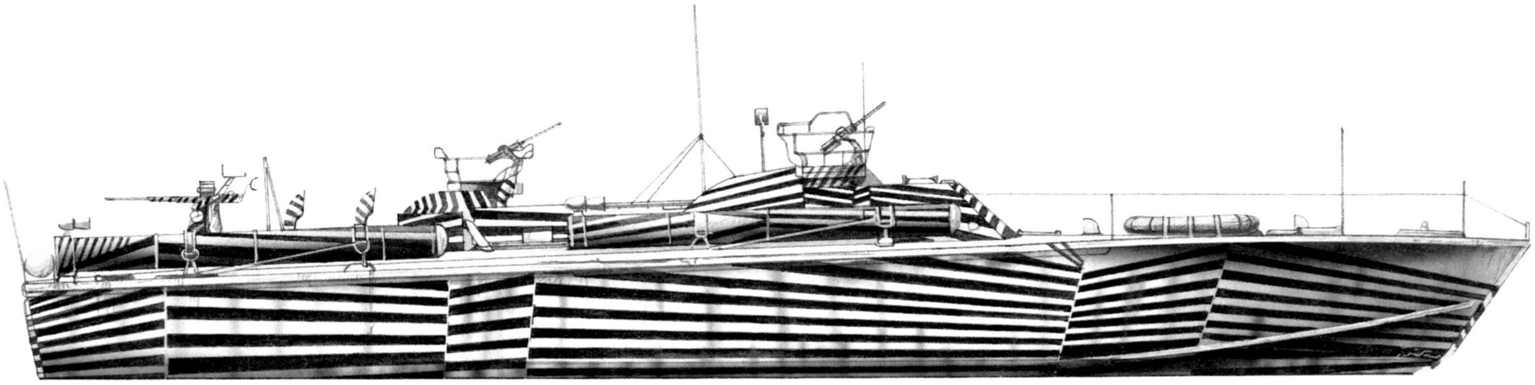

Right: *An Elco 80-foot PT boat is shown in the experimental dazzle scheme that was tried by the US Navy in the Pacific, and also on some of the boats operating out of Sardinia harassing German supply convoys.*

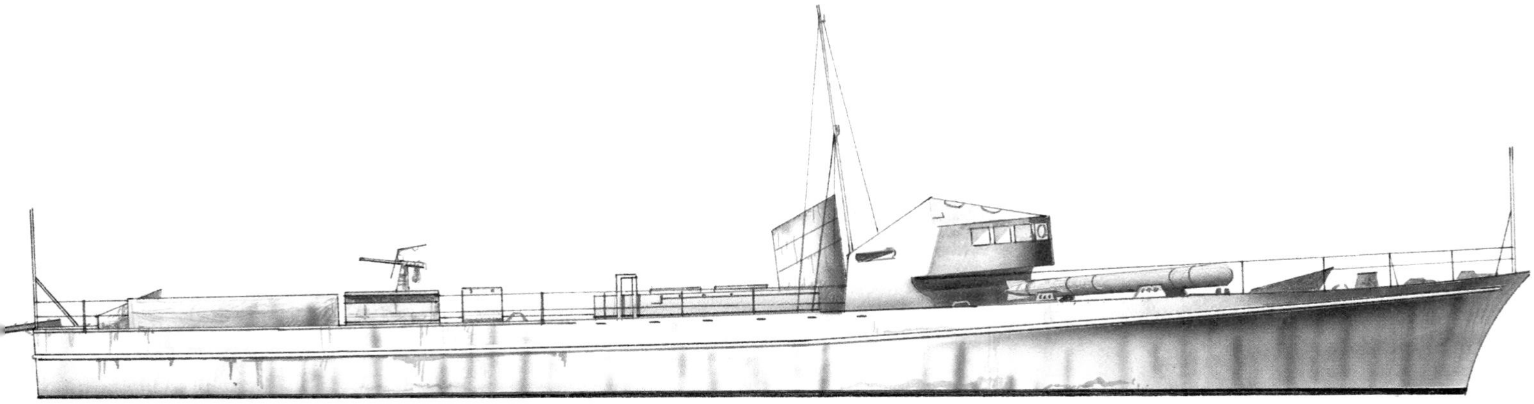

Left: *The Italian VAS (Vedette Antisommergibili) boats were designed for inshore ASW work, as their name suggests. In the event, there proved little need for such a capability, and they were used as supplementary flotilla craft.*

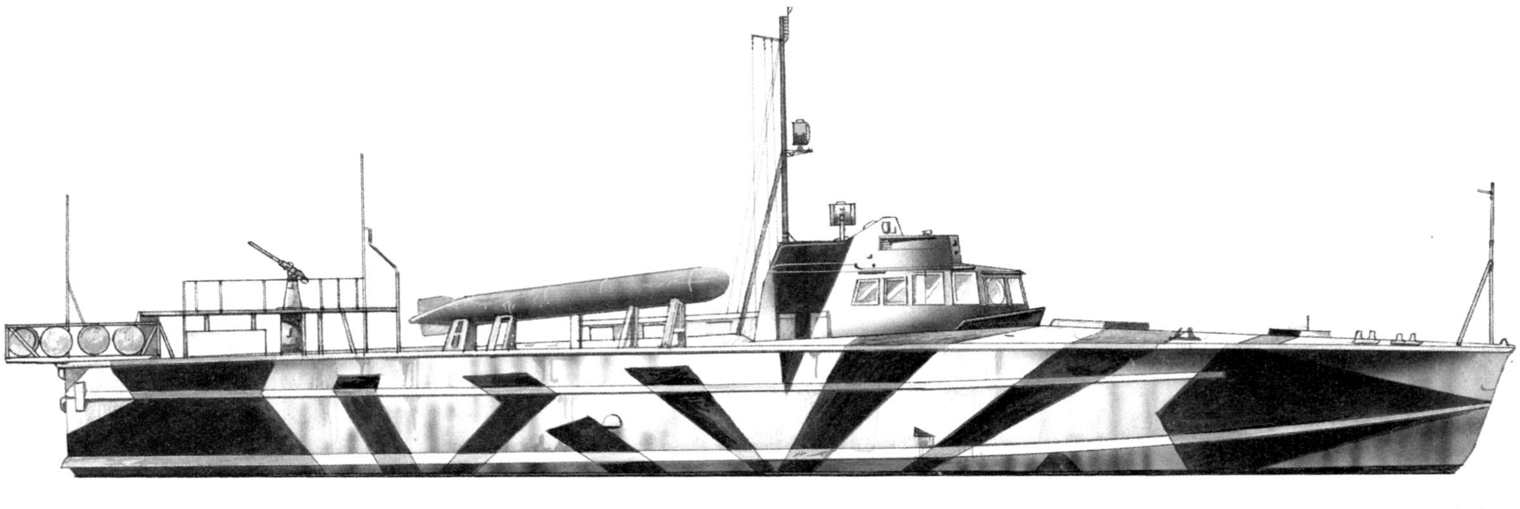

Right: *The great success achieved by Italian torpedo boats in World War I led Italy to continue work on such craft in the inter-war years. The MAS 501 series retained lightweight 450-mm torpedoes of earlier craft and carried only a single machine-gun, but were capable of 42 kts.*

Chapter 25

The End in Europe

The war that Germany had embarked on with so much success was now coming home to the German people with a vengeance, as American, British and Canadian armies drove for the western borders of the Reich. Poised in the east was the Soviet Army, honed by almost four years of bitter fighting from the Arctic tundra to the Black Sea into an overpowering war machine.

The Allied armies had reached the Seine 11 days before they had expected to, and had freed Paris 55 days ahead of schedule; by mid-September the American First Army was close to Aachen which on pre-invasion estimates had not been expected to be within striking distance until May 1945 – and on 4 September 11th Armoured Division had driven into that truly vital port, Antwerp, essential for the Allied advance into the heart of Germany.

Unfortunately, it was to take 85 days before the first heavy cargo ship could berth at one of Antwerp's quays, and another two weeks before even half of the required daily tonnage was moving through the port. Years later Montgomery wrote, 'I must admit a bad mistake on my part. . . . I reckoned that the Canadian Army could do this while we were going for the Ruhr. I was wrong.'

By the time Arnhem was over and full attention could be turned to the problem of making Antwerp operational, General Zangen, appointed by Hitler to turn Walcheren into a fortress and to deny the Allies the use of the port, had moved two infantry divisions into position – 64th on the south bank in the 'Breskens Pocket' between Zeebrugge and the Braakman inlet, and 70th in South Beveland – and had been allotted 719th Infantry Division and General Student's First Parachute Army in reserve, just to the east on the mainland. In addition, at Breskens, Cadzand and on the dunes at Walcheren were powerful defence batteries now manned by fresh crews, so far unaffected by the traumas of the retreat from Normandy.

The Canadians of the Algonquin Regiment had attempted to break into the Breskens Pocket while the Arnhem battle was in progress, and their narrow and bloody escape gave notice of what was likely to happen in the future. By the end of September, the Canadian army, now under General Simmonds, was deploying its infantry and armoured divisions for an all-out attack, with the British I Corps and the Polish 1st Armoured Division in support, and a clearer idea of what they faced. All through October, they mounted ever increasing pressure on both the pocket and the area at the neck of the Beveland Isthmus – thankful all the time for Allied air supremacy but fearful that soon the weather would rob them of it.

In the end, after massive bombing by Lancasters and Mosquitos in which vital dykes were destroyed and floods swept in across some of the defence works, it was decided that a full-scale amphibious landing on Walcheren was necessary, and on 1 November 4th Special Service Brigade with two Royal Marine Commandos and one Army Commando were landed at Westkappelle. It took them a week to quell all resistance on Walcheren, and, with the Canadians, another week before all German positions along the Scheldte were safely in their hands – and then the engineers had enormous problems of mine-clearance and repairs to essential dockyard equipment. There is little doubt that the decision to mount the Arnhem operation cost the Allies two months of vital logistic support for their armies.

As the months in question were the last of summer weather, the loss was magnified. It was not until the early weeks of December that the Canadians could establish themselves along the line of the Maas and take the bridgehead across the Waal – held by the US 82nd Airborne during the Arnhem battle – with the British Second Army moving in on their right and American armies stretching out to the south, all, by mid-December, gearing up for the crossing of the Roer and the Rhine into Germany itself.

But Christmas was only two weeks away, the weather was excessively cold, and most Allied soldiers of lesser rank than major-general wanted a break – at least until the New Year.

The fortified island of Walcheren dominated the essential port of Antwerp. Montgomery's troops eventually cleared the island by mid-November.

In a frame from a German propaganda film, SS troops pass a blazing M8 armoured car in the Ardennes. The Germans achieved initial success, with three armies pitted against a weakly held US sector.

By mid-December 1944 the main bulk of the Allied forces were concentrated (as were the attentions of the Allied high command) towards both ends of the battlefront. In the north the Anglo-Canadian armies had at last cleared Antwerp and opened the Scheldt Estuary, and the US First and Ninth Armies were set to close up to the Neder Rhine and threaten the vital Roer dams. In the south General Patton's US Third Army, after its specacular drive across France, was poised to sweep through the equally important Saar region towards the Rhine at Mannheim.

Between the two powerful groupings were strung out some 80,000 American troops along 90 miles of front, the bulk of them consisting of General Middleton's VIII Corps which had been brought across from Brittany, backed by one armoured division, the 9th, which had but lately arrived in the area and had not yet seen action. They were there because this part of the front, the Ardennes section, was a quiet part, covered in front by the sparsely settled German Schnee Eifel, and behind by the steep wooded hills and foaming trout streams which had always been, despite the events of 1940, regarded as unsuitable country for open warfare. Moreover, the first winter snows had fallen and heavy clouds overhead had lately kept the Allied and German air forces on the ground; both green and veteran troops crouched in their foxholes, listened to reports of bitter fighting to north and south with thoughts of thankfulness that they were not there, and dreamed of Christmas.

They were thus considerably shaken when at 5.30 on the morning of 16 December they were suddenly deluged by the heaviest artillery bombardment even the veterans among them had experienced, and when after periods varying from 20 to 90 minutes they peered out into the pre-dawn murk; they found themselves overrun by German shock troops surging forward through their positions, followed shortly by powerful panzer and Panzergrenadier units, many of them bearing the jagged double streak of the Waffen SS.

It had all been Hitler's idea, as usual at this period of the war, in direct contradiction to the advice tendered to him by the army's generals.

Even as the fighting in the Falaise Gap was ending, Hitler had announced that by November a force of some 25 divisions must be prepared to launch a huge counter-offensive against the Anglo-American armies; and to the astonishment of the German high command that force had come into existence, con-

Chronology of War: 1945

March 1
US Ninth Army captures Mönchen-Gladbach

March 2
US Third Army captures Trier. Last Japanese on Corregidor killed

March 3
Manila Bay finally cleared of Japanese mines and positions

March 4
First B-29s land on Iwo Jima. Meiktila in Burma taken

March 5
Allies capture Cologne. Russians approach Stettin

March 6
German panzer corps launches heavy attack at Lake Balaton

March 7
US First Army crosses Remagen bridge over Rhine. US Third Army drives towards river Ahr. Chinese units occupy Lashio

March 8
American troops enter Bonn. US troops land on Mindanao

March 9
US Third Army closes up to Rhine

March 10
'Fire Raid' by Boeing B-29 Superfortresses on Tokyo; large areas devastated. Estimates of dead range from 84,000 to as high as 200,000. US armies link up on Rhine

March 12
Russians capture Kustrin on the Oder

March 13
Fourteenth Army cuts Japanese escape route from Mandalay, at Maymo

March 14
US Third Army crosses Moselle

March 16
German drive to Budapest from Lake Balaton blocked

March 17
US Third Army captures Coblenz

March 19
Japanese driven out of Mandalay

March 22
Russians besiege Danzig and Gdynia

March 23
British and Canadians launch offensive across Rhine. US 5th Division crosses south of Mainz

March 24
British and US airborne forces 14,000 strong dropped at Wesel and link up with British and Canadians

March 25
US Third Army crosses Rhine and captures Darmstadt. US 9th Army links up with British forces east of the Ruhr

March 26
Japanese survivors on Iwo Jima launch last 'Banzai' attack. Only 216 POWs taken out of garrison of 21,000. US casualties 19,939 including 4,630 dead

March 27
US First and Third Armies link near Coblenz; Third and Seventh Armies link near Darmstadt. US forces take Wiesbaden. Bitter fighting inside Danzig and Gdynia

March 28
Red Army units reach Austrian border. British Second Army drives east towards the Elbe

March 29
US First Army drives north towards Paderborn; Third Army reaches Frankfurt. US Navy bombards Okinawa

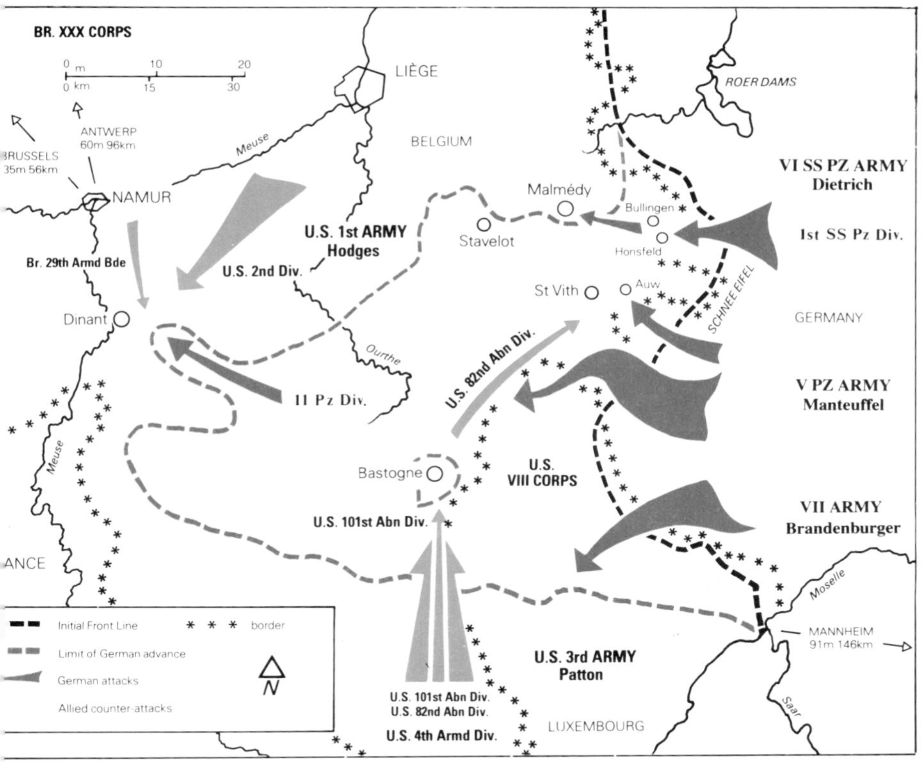

***Above:* Spearheading the German drive were eight Panzer divisions, with some of the most powerful tanks seen during the war. This SS Tiger II, of Sepp Dietrich's Sixth SS Panzer Army, is seen giving a lift to paratroops.**

***Right:* Shocked US prisoners are marched into captivity. The Ardennes had been regarded as a quiet sector, manned by the largely inexperienced US VIII Corps, so the assault came as a rude surprise to both Patton's Third and Hodges' First Armies on each side of the Bulge.**

The German Ardennes offensive

Hitler's last gamble in the West had the ambitious (and totally unrealistic) aim of driving a wedge between the Allied army groups, capturing the port of Antwerp and cutting off Montgomery's forces. All it did was to drain the remainder of Germany's fighting strength in the West, and seriously weaken the East.

jured from every corner of German life: rear-area administrative echelons, 16-year-old boys, civil servants, small shopkeepers, university students and the scourings of the prisons, all had been swept into the armed service, sometimes to join new formations themselves, and sometimes just to release experienced men to bulk them out.

Thus had been formed three German armies, and they were by mid-December marshalled under an exemplary cloak of secrecy and subterfuge opposite that thinly occupied 90 mile strip of line, so tenuously held by the US VIII Corps. In the north were poised the units of the Sixth SS Panzer Army under General Sepp Dietrich, erstwhile commander of Hitler's personal bodyguard in the street-fighting days and later of the crack 'Liebstandarte Adolf Hitler' 1st SS Panzer Division. In the middle section of the attack front waited the Fifth Panzer Army under the trusted army General Hasso von Manteuffel. And on the southern flank of the attack to form the 'hard shoulder' against any possible northward countermove by formations of the US Third Army was the Seventh Army under the dogged but unimaginative General Erich Brandenburger.

Altogether some 200,000 men would take part in Operation Wacht am Rhein, equipped with more tanks, more artillery and more ammunition than had been granted to any similarly assembled German force for many months past; and in addition to those more or less conventional fighting divisions, there waited in the rear 1,250 paratroops under Colonel von der Heydte, a veteran of Crete, to drop in front of the main assault, seize bridges and crossroads, and attack any headquarter organizations they could find. Moreover, to help them spread alarm and despondency, the famous raiding commander Otto Skorzeny commanded a special force of volunteers driving American vehicles and wearing American uniforms, a ploy which would result in their being shot if they fell into Allied hands.

The objective for this surreptitiously assembled force was Antwerp, plus the splitting of the Allied armies threatening the German frontier, the annihilation of the Anglo-Canadian armies and the US First and Ninth Armies alongside them by starvation as their main supply-port was captured, and an immense morale boost for the German public together with such a shock to the Allies that the consequent bickering between them would wreck their future strategic planning for weeks and possibly months.

It was not regarded in this light by all the German commanders. Field Marshal Gerd von Rundstedt, whom Hitler had placed in overall command of the front, was scathing: 'Antwerp?' he cried. 'If we reach the Meuse we should go down on our knees and thank God!'. Dietrich, who would seem by now to have lost his original admiration for the Führer, later remarked: 'All I had to do was cross the river, capture Brussels, and then go on to take the port of Antwerp.

***Left:* Bomb-laden Republic P-47s rev up their engines in readiness for take off from a strip in eastern France.**

***Below:* A Sherman of the 3rd Armored Division, US First Army, passes a knocked-out German Panzer V.**

March 30
Russians occupy Danzig and Gdynia and launch attacks on German garrison at Breslau

March 31
UK civilian casualties in March 792 killed, 1,426 injured

April 1
Ruhr completely encircled when US First and Ninth Armies link up at Lippstadt. US Tenth Army lands on Okinawa

April 2
British 7th Armoured Division reaches Dortmund-Ems Canal. Eighth Army formations attack between Lake Commaccio and sea

April 4
Germans leave Hungary. Fierce fighting on Okinawa

April 6
Operation Kikusai (Floating Chrysanthemums): massed kamikaze attack on US Fleet off Okinawa. Several ships sunk. First of 10 such attacks in the next two months

April 7
Russians reach Vienna. Battle of East China Sea; US Navy sinks battleship Yamato, one cruiser and four destroyers. Fifty-eight Japanese aircraft shot down

April 8
Allied armies in Germany drive east on wide front

April 9
Russians storm Konigsberg Fortress after siege of 59 days

April 10
US Ninth Army reaches Hanover. Canadians cross river Ijssel. Eighth Army crosses river Senio. Churchill announces British and Commonwealth casualties in war to date: Armed Forces 1,126,802; Merchant Navy 34,161; Civilians 144,542

Above: Two members of a cavalry reconnaissance squadron of the 75th Infantry Division are seen sniping at German snipers near Beffe.

Left: The main square at Bastogne. The town was a key to communications in the Ardennes and was held by the 101st Airborne Division against an all-out German assault.

The snow was waist deep and there wasn't room to deploy four tanks abreast, let alone six armoured divisions. It didn't get light until eight and was dark again at four, and my tanks can't fight at night. And all this at Christmas time!'

Nevertheless, aided by that essential factor of surprise, some of them did very well at the beginning. Leading elements of the 1st SS Panzer Division under their ruthless commander, Colonel Peiper, swept through a gap in American lines to Honsfeld in the north, captured a large petrol dump at Bullingen and then caught American troops on the move at Malmedy crossroads before racing on towards Stavelot. Unfortunately for all parties concerned, his men, inured to the bitter fighting on the Eastern Front, shot down 19 American prisoners at Honsfeld, 50 at Bullingen and nearly 100 at Malmedy, a piece of barbarism which defeated itself; when rumour of the massacres swept through the embattled American positions it produced feelings of both fury and desperation and caused even the greenest units, sometimes commanded by only junior NCOs, to fight with a committed ferocity which baulked the important German thrust to the south.

It also spelled the almost immediate death of any of Skorzeny's men discovered at their clandestine tasks.

One of Manteuffel's spearheads had success similar to Peiper's, but without that ruthlessness, and reached the village of Auw just in front of the vital road junction of St Vith, but here it ran into the tank destroyers and main artillery of an American infantry division which held them, forcing the main drive of Manteuffel's army southwards into the gap between St Vith and the other vital road junction, Bastogne.

And it was here that the attentions of both attackers and defenders became concentrated. It was General Bradley's Twelfth Army Group which caught the offensive in its central section, and at first Bradley wrote it off as merely a spoiling attack to disrupt the First Army's threat to the Roer in the north and the Third Army's to the Saar in the south; but he soon realized that it was more than that. On 19 December he ordered General Hodges in the north to swing some of his First Army divisions back to hold a flank and then drive down to St Vith, and Patton to do the same in the south and send his crack 4th Armoured Division up to relieve Bastogne. Being Patton, of course, he objected, but then suddenly cheered up. 'What the hell,' he said, 'we'll still be killing Krauts!', and with an efficiency which compels the greatest admiration he swung the bulk of his army through 90° in 48 hours.

In the meantime, General Eisenhower had released his reserves and they sped to the two vital points in every truck and jeep they could find: the 82nd and 101st Airborne Divisions, recently recovered from their battles at Nijmegen and Eindhoven, raced north from Patton's lines, the 101st dropping off to begin its famous stand at Bastogne and the 82nd passing on to St Vith. The battle now was becoming one of mobility, and that game the Americans knew how to play.

As Manteuffel's spearheads probed farther and farther west (they never crossed the Meuse, though the 11th Panzer Division did reach nearly to Dinant) American tank destroyers and artillery shored up the flanks of the penetration while their infantry fought doggedly forward into the gaps or held on grimly in isolated positions. For most of the time, moreover, they fought without air cover, for the weather favoured the Germans for days on end. But by Christmas Day, after some of the bitterest fighting seen in Europe, the sting had been drawn from the German onslaught; although Manteuffel mounted a last desperate attack on Bastogne, it was beaten off and on the following day Patton's tanks arrived to break the siege.

Meanwhile, Field Marshal Montgomery had taken command of the northern flank and in order to 'tidy up the battlefield' he authorized a withdrawal from the St Vith salient, and he brought the British 29th Armoured Brigade down on the Americans right flank to hold the deepest penetration; when on the following day the whole of the US 2nd Armoured Division came down to join them, Hitler's last offensive in the west was brought to a halt.

It had undoubtedly given the Allied leaders a nasty jolt, and it would be many more days before the Ardennes salient was entirely flattened, but in fact the offensive had used up a great deal of the rapidly diminishing German war matériel and it caused Hitler the loss of manpower which he could better have used on the other side of the Rhine. It had been defeated by the ability of American leadership to deploy guns and armour with supreme efficiency, and by the dogged courage of the American infantryman.

It was, indeed, a great American victory.

US troops pause to watch Douglas C-47 transports on their way to supply the beleaguered 101st Airborne Division at Bastogne. Despite besiegement, the 101st hung on until Patton's tanks broke through to relieve them.

Towards the Rhine

The Ardennes salient was almost flattened out by the New Year, and the front line ran then from the Scheldte Estuary past Nijmegen on the Waal, across a narrow land-bridge to the Maas which it followed south as far as Roermond, then the Roer itself as far as the dams (still in German hands and thus capable

Late-war armour

The tanks which were in service at the end of the war (in Europe at least) would have seemed unbelievable only six years before. Where Germany invaded Poland with the majority of its tanks weighing less than 10 tonnes armed with machine-guns or 20-mm cannon, by 1945 there were vehicles over 70 tonnes in service, able to shoot through thick armour plate at distances measured in kilometres.

Below: One of the first M26 Pershing heavy tanks to reach the ETO (European Theater of Operations, as Europe was called in American official jargon) is ferried across the Rhine at Remagen. Well armoured and with a powerful 90-mm gun, the M26 was the weapon US tankmen had wanted from the first day that their M4 Shermans had been matched against Tigers and Panthers.

Above: The massively powerful Königstiger (King's Tiger, but known to the Allies as the Royal Tiger), virtually impervious to Allied tank guns and capable of dominating the battlefield when properly handled, was armed with a new, long-barrelled 8.8-cm gun with greatly increased muzzle velocity. It could penetrate almost 200 mm of armour at 2000 m. To put that into perspective, the standard Western tanks had a maximum armour thickness between 70 and 150 mm, with Soviet tanks having similar protection.

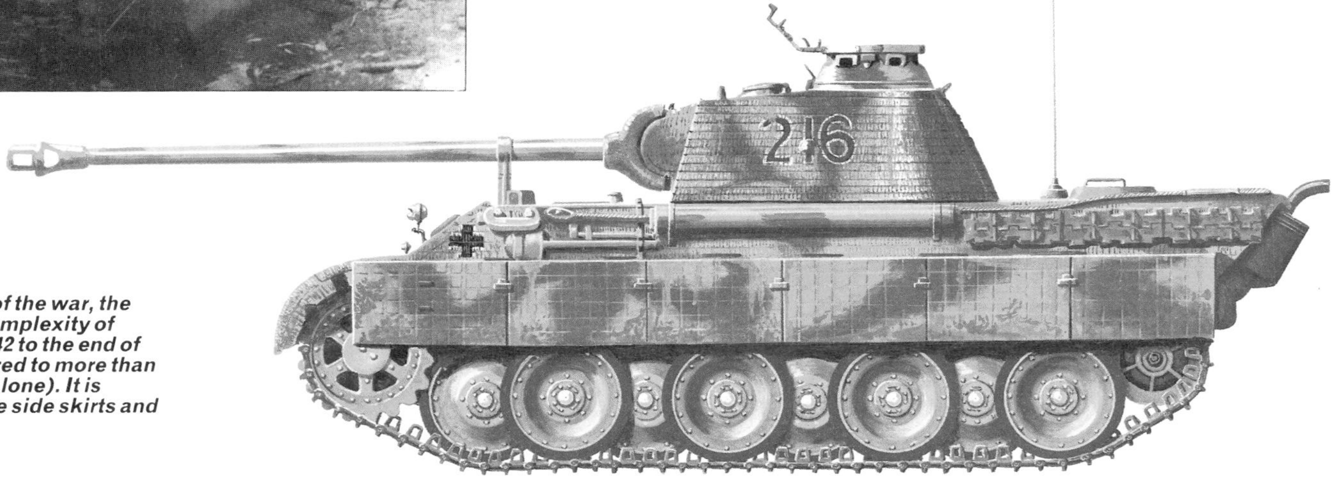

Right: Probably the finest German tank of the war, the PzKpfw V Panther suffered from over-complexity of construction. From first production in 1942 to the end of the war some 4,800 were built (as compared to more than 11,000 Soviet T-34/85s appearing in 1944 alone). It is depicted in late-war form, with protective side skirts and a covering of anti-magnetic paste.

The first 50 or so production Königstigers were completed with a turret built by Porsche, although Henschel turrets were to become standard. Incorporating the sloped armour so effective in the Panther, the Royal Tiger had a gun/armour combination that would not disgrace a modern MBT.

Developed from the KV series, and introduced into service with the Soviet Army in 1944, the IS-2 was heavily protected and had an extremely powerful 122-mm gun. In spite of their armour and gun, the IS tanks (named after Stalin) did not weigh any more than the German Panther, and had much the same mobility. This contrasted greatly with German heavy tanks, which were anything but agile.

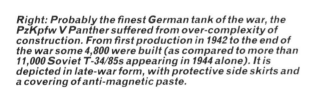

A Churchill Crocodile flamethrowing tank supports an attack by two platoons of the 1st Rifle Brigade, attacking St Joost to the north of Schilberg during the closing stages of the German offensive in the west.

The closer Germany was threatened in the west and east, the more ferocious became its defence. Boys and old men joined the Volkssturm, while regular troops such as these panzerfaust gunners used any transport to get to the Front.

of turning the Roer from a narrow river to a raging flood) then in front of the fortifications of the Siegfried Line down to the Black Forest.

The task for the Canadian army in the north, the British army next to it, the four US armies stretching down to Strasbourg, and the French army in the Vosges, was to cross the Roer and reach the Rhine; and in addition to the resistance they could expect from the German armies in the defence positions, they faced all the problems produced first by freezing weather, then by a succession of thaws which turned the ground to glutinous mud or uncertain slush. The soldiers all along that front lived until March in unadulterated misery.

It began on 15 January 1945, when British XII Corps, using two infantry and one armoured division assisted by specialized armour and massed artillery, attacked along the whole of their front into what was called the Roermond Triangle. Two German divisions waited for them behind concrete, wire and mines and the battle was never anything but a drear, dreadful slogging-match. Mines lay buried everywhere, heavy ground hampered the Flails, vast craters filled with water needed bridging, and the AVRE's floundered in mud. Strongpoints required the attention of the Crocodiles, but wooded ravines hid anti-tank guns which turned them into flaming coffins.

It took until 25 January for attrition to win, at its usual high price.

Then US First Army started for the Roer dams – seven of them, holding back 111,000,000 cubic metres of water backed by the results of the recurrent thaw, and when on 10 February they took the last one they found that the German engineers had efficiently sabotaged the valves, and any crossing of the river would have to wait until the water had all drained down into the North Sea.

At last it could all start. On 8 February Lancasters bombed Cleve and Goch, an artillery bombardment blanketed the approach area, four infantry divisions of XXX Corps rolled forward at 300 yards every 12 minutes – and the Battle of the Reichswald opened. It was one of the bitterest and most depressing battles fought on the Western Front. Canadians had to use DUKWs just to move from village to village, the most appalling traffic congestion wrecked every plan 10 minutes after it was launched; broken roads, sodden tracks, massive armoured columns jammed solid within the ranks of plodding, miserable infantry.

Incredibly, they won in the end. By 21 February, Goch, Cleve and Calcar were in British and Canadian hands, and to the south US Ninth Army could launch Operation Grenade and fling bridges across the Roer opposite Mönchen Gladbach, which they took on 1 March. Five days later Cologne was in American hands, and on 7 March, to the astonishment of the Allies and to Hitler's inexpressible fury, the Remagen Bridge over the Rhine had been taken, apparently undamaged, and was in use by US First Army. Fortunately, auxiliary bridges were thrown across, both up- and down-stream from Remagen, during the days which followed, so when on 17 March, weakened by bombing, by the attempted German demolitions, by the drumming of thousands of infantry feet and the heavy lurches of overladen vehicles, the whole bridge fell sideways into the Rhine – taking 28 US engineers to their deaths – at least the disaster did not cut off the bridgehead on the east bank from all supplies.

By then, the US and French armies to the south had all crossed the rivers, broken through the Siegfried Line (or outflanked it) and were fighting their way to the Rhine. It was often grim and desperate business for Hitler had decreed that the age-old barrier protecting the Teutons from the Latins was to be defended to the last, and any German soldier retreating across it in the face of the enemy would be subject to immediate death by firing squad. As a result, by 24 March over 150,000 German soldiers found themselves in Allied PoW camps, and a large but unknown number were killed; by the end of the month the west bank of the Rhine from the Channel to the Swiss border was in Allied hands.

They were thus now only 300 miles from Berlin.

Attack from the East

The Soviet armies, however, were only 50 miles from Berlin.

At the turn of the year, with the exception of a few pockets of resistance in the north the Soviet Union was free of German troops, and the front line ran from Memel on the Baltic Sea, around the eastern quarter of the East Prussia border, down and across the Narew towards Warsaw to reach the Vistula just south of the Polish capital, down the line of the river as far as Sandomir where it bulged westwards in a significant bridgehead, across eastern Czechoslovakia to the Danube, a bulge above Budapest, then along Lake Balaton and the river Drava into the area controlled by Marshal Tito and his Partisans.

Eleven guards armies, 5 shock armies, 6 tank armies, and 46 infantry or cavalry armies, all fully equipped and supported by 13 air armies, gave the Red Army commanders a superiority in every aspect of military strength over the 200-odd German and Hungarian divisions facing them. The only palpable advantage the Wehrmacht commanders might have had was the fear and hatred of the 'Mongol Hordes' so firmly implanted in the hearts of every Axis soldier.

The other traditional metaphor applied throughout the ages to the forces driving west across the plains of Eastern Europe, was 'Russian Steamroller' – and that was by this time a reality indeed.

The three Fronts at the northern end of the Red Army line – 1st Baltic under Bagramyan, 3rd Belorussian under Chernyakhovsky and 2nd Belorussian under Rokossovsky – were to concern themselves in the opening stages of the 1945 Offensive with Baltic matters; the Belorussian fronts exclusively with East Prussia. They both moved on 13 January.

As was fully expected, the onslaught was fiercely resisted, and within hours it was clear to Chernyakhovsky that his road to Königsberg would be won only by hard slogging. German engineers had built defence lines every few miles and after six days his five armies had only driven 15 of them; even with an extra guards army fed through, it was not until 20 January that Insterburg – a third of the way to the main objective – was reached.

As so often occurs in military affairs, it was the flank attack which redeemed the position. Rokossovsky to the south had attacked across the Narew on the same day, sent two armies through the Masurian Lakes with orders to link up with Chernyakhovsky's at Königsberg and five more armies on the left in the direction of Danzig and Bromberg. They all had two to three days of bitter fighting at first, but once the hard shell of the defences was broken, tank armies were fed in and raced ahead. By 19 January they had reached Mlawa, then broke through a gap east of Tannenberg and a week later had reached the Baltic at Elbing, cutting off the huge German garrison at Königsberg, which was now left almost to its own devices.

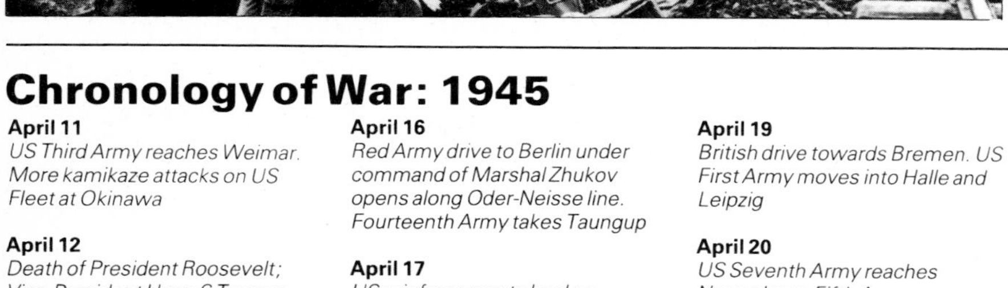

The famous Ludendorff Bridge at Remagen, whose capture relatively intact by units of the 9th Armored Division allowed General Courtney Hodges' First Army to set up the first bridgehead on the east bank of the Rhine on 7 March.

Chronology of War: 1945

April 11
US Third Army reaches Weimar. More kamikaze attacks on US Fleet at Okinawa

April 12
Death of President Roosevelt; Vice-President Harry S Truman takes office. Eighth Army cross river Santurno

April 13
Vienna occupied by Red Army. British and Americans reach Belsen and Buchenwald Concentration Camps. Fifth Army offensive into Po valley opens

April 16
Red Army drive to Berlin under command of Marshal Zhukov opens along Oder-Neisse line. Fourteenth Army takes Taungup

April 17
US reinforcements land on Mindanao

April 18
370,000 prisoners taken as Ruhr pocket collapses. British Second Army reaches Lüneberg. US Third Army reaches Czechoslovakia; Ninth Army takes Magdeberg. Allies drive through Argenta Gap in Italy

April 19
British drive towards Bremen. US First Army moves into Halle and Leipzig

April 20
US Seventh Army reaches Nuremberg. Fifth Army moves into Po valley. French 1st Army in Neckar valley

April 21
Red Army drives each side of Berlin; Chuikov's Eighth Army into south-east suburbs. French troops enter Stuttgart. US and Polish troops reach Bologna

April 22
French First Army reaches Lake Constance

April 23
US Eighth Army captures Cebu in central Philippines. US Fifth and British Eighth Armies reach river Po. Zhukov's and Koniev's forces break into Berlin. Fourteenth Army takes Toungoo

April 24
Red Army fronts join forces in central Berlin. British and Canadians enter Bremen. Dachau reached. Fifth and Eighth Armies move across Po, Spezia taken

April 25
US and Red Army units meet at Torgau on the Elbe. Fifth Army takes Verona. San Francisco Conference opens

April 26
Red Army occupy Brno and Stettin. US forces move across Danube. Fierce Japanese resistance on Okinawa

April 28
Mussolini and staff captured and killed by Italian Communist partisans near Swiss border. Fifth Army reaches Venice

April 29
German representatives of General Vietinghoff discuss armistice in Italy. Eighth Army advances towards Trieste and conacts Fifth Army at Pádua. Hitler marries Eva Braun and appoints Admiral Dönitz as successor

April 30
Hitler commits suicide. Fourteenth Army captures Pegu. In last five days kamikaze attacks sink 20 and damage 157 ships of US Fleet off Okinawa. UK civilian casualties in April: nil

May 1
Australian troops land on Tarakan. British airborne troops drop south of Rangoon

May 2
Red Army occupies Berlin. Surrender of all German forces in Italy to the forces of Field Marshal Alexander. Allies occupy Turin, Milan and Trieste. Fourteenth Army takes Prome and Pegu in Burma

Air war over Europe, 1944-1945

Allied air superiority over Europe was challenged by new German aircraft designs, but despite local setbacks the sheer number of Allied aircraft and of trained pilots proved decisive.

As the Allies advanced through France their air forces were constantly in action, and their ground echelons strove to establish and re-establish fresh bases close up behind the advancing armies. Before the crossing of the Seine, Mosquitoes, Mitchells, Mustangs, Bostons, Spitfires and Wellingtons of No. 2 Group attacked the ferries and barges at Rouen and elsewhere as German fighters attempted to interfere; these were engaged by No. 83 Group's Spitfires and the US 9th Air Force's P-47s and P-51s, which together claimed more than 100 of the enemy destroyed during the last week in August.

As RAF Bomber Command joined in attacks on German coastal garrisons from St Nazaire to Dunkirk, which had been bypassed by the advancing armies, the Dakotas, Stirlings and Halifaxes of RAF Transport Command were called on to mount the British airborne assault at Arnhem, while the C-47s of the US IX Troop Carrier Command delivered the 82nd and 101st Airborne Divisions against targets on the Maas and Waal rivers. Unfortunately there were insufficient RAF aircraft available to carry the entire British 1st Airborne Division (and the Polish Parachute Brigade) in one journey and, while the American forces duly secured their targets, the British attack at Arnhem failed despite the constant delivery by air of supplies. Unfortunately, as a result of recurring administrative problems, the 2nd Tactical Air Force was not brought fully into action to support the Arnhem action, and Nos 38 and 46 Groups lost 55 transport aircraft shot down and 320 others damaged by flak.

Elsewhere the Germans kept up attacks on the vital Nijmegen bridge over the Waal, now in British hands, sending among other aircraft the *Mistel* weapons; this comprised an unmanned Ju 88 bomber packed with explosives with a piloted fighter mounted on top, the pilot at the last minute releasing the bomber and guiding it towards its target. However, these attacks failed to hit the bridge.

Meanwhile the RAF had been engaged in supporting a major operation to clear the island of Walcheren at the entrance to the Scheldt, thereby opening up the great seaport of Antwerp. In operations which lasted from 3 October to 8 November, Bomber Command attacked gun batteries and dykes, dropping almost 9,000 tons of bombs as the 2nd Tactical Air Force flew some 10,000 sorties, dropped 1,500 tons of bombs and fired 11,600 rockets.

On 16 December the Fifth and Sixth Panzer Armies, assisted by bad weather and the element of surprise, attacked in the Ardennes between the US Ninth and Seventh Armies, and within a week had penetrated some 60 miles. The poor weather prevented large-scale air action, and it was without significant air support that the Americans were eventually able to counterattack and crush the German attack. Among the enemy aircraft that did appear were some of the new bomber versions of the Me 262 jets.

The bad weather that had dogged Allied air operations during the Ardennes attack improved gradually during the last few days of 1944, and Allied offensive action by the 2nd Tactical Air Force was resumed. However, unsuspected by British and American intelligence, the Luftwaffe had for some weeks been planning a great set-piece operation against the RAF and USAAF bases in northern Europe, the OKL believing that sufficient destruction could be caused severely to disrupt Allied operations and buy time to reorganize the defence of Germany. After assembling some 800 fighters and fighter-bombers of all types (including Me 262 and Ar 234 jets) from units all over the Reich the attack, Operation Bodenplatte (baseplate), was launched soon after first light on New Year's Day 1945. Surprise was almost universal as the attacks came in soon after 9 a.m. Considerable damage was caused and about 500 Allied aircraft were destroyed or later scrapped but, after the defences had recovered from the shock, about 300 German aircraft were shot down or crashed on the way home. Also whereas the Allies were able to replace their losses within a few days (relatively few aircrew were killed), the German losses, which included some 230 airmen, were little short of disastrous. Indeed the folly of the operation was voiced by many senior German commanders, but they were confronting Nazi leaders fanatically blind to the realities of unquenchable Allied air supremacy and, just four months away, the inevitable grounding of the Luftwaffe through lack of fuel.

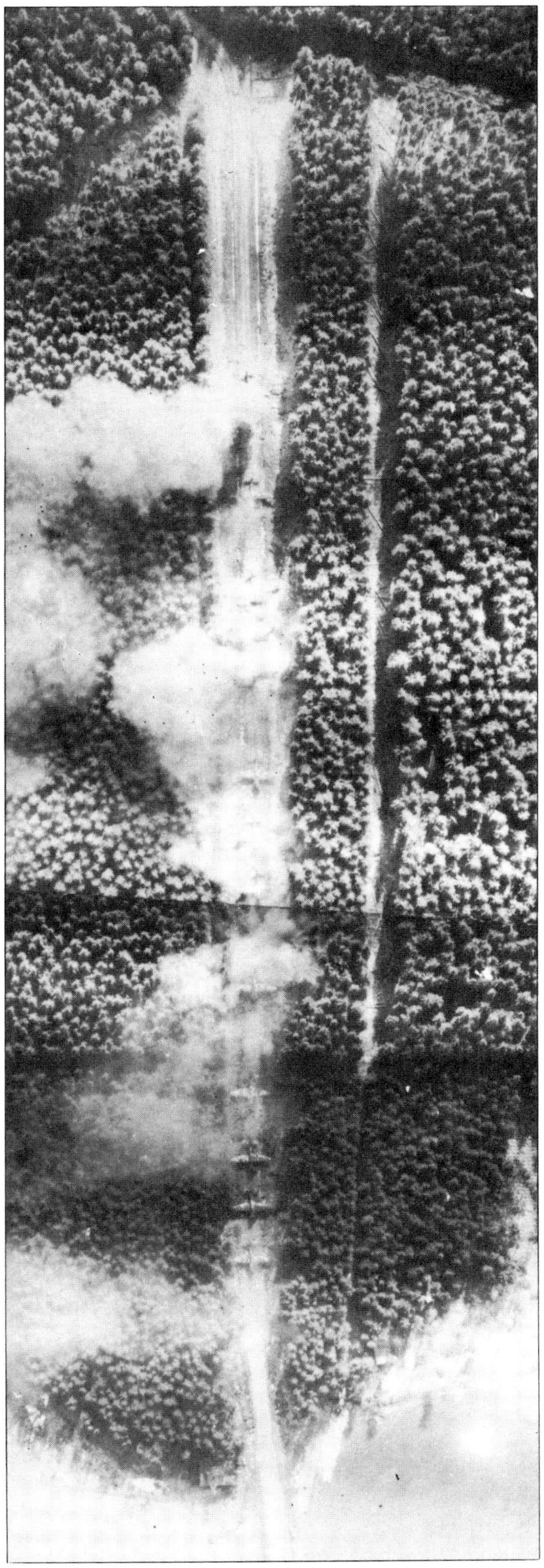

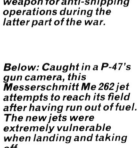

The Luftwaffe continued to fight back to the bitter end, against appalling odds. As the fighter-bombers pushed the Germans back into Germany, the Luftwaffe became increasingly vulnerable at its own airfields, illustrated here by a line of Junkers Ju 87s burning after a strike from P-47s. They had been waiting to attack the vital Remagen bridge.

Left: The war at sea continued until the end of hostilities, with RAF Mosquitoes and Beaufighters exacting a heavy toll on German coastal vessels in the North Sea. Here a Mosquito takes on a load of rockets, the favoured weapon for anti-shipping operations during the latter part of the war.

Above: Victorious P-47s operate from an ex-Luftwaffe base inside Germany. In the background are Ju 88 night fighters, left when the Germans retreated.

Below: Caught in a P-47's gun camera, this Messerschmitt Me 262 jet attempts to reach its field after having run out of fuel. The new jets were extremely vulnerable when landing and taking off.

Below: This 354th Fighter Group North American P-51D sets down on a German air base, shortly after it was hurriedly vacated by the Luftwaffe.

May 3
Montgomery receives German envoys on Lüneberg Heath. US Seventh Army advances towards Brenner Pass. Indian troops enter Rangoon

May 4
Montgomery receives surrender of German forces in Holland, Denmark and north-west Germany, effective 8 a.m.

May 5
Kamikazes sink another 17 US ships off Okinawa

May 6
Russians occupy Breslau

May 7
In General Eisenhower's headquarters at Rheims General Jodl signs instrument of surrender of all German forces

May 8
VE-Day: German surrender to Russians signed at Karlshorst, near Berlin

May 9
German surrender ratified in Berlin; Red Army occupies Prague

Winston Churchill, Franklin D. Roosevelt and Joseph Stalin are seen during the Crimean conference in February 1945. The post-war fate of Europe was decided at Yalta, although the most influential of the western leaders, the American President, was seriously ill at the time, and was to die only two months later.

But it was even further south that the greatest advances were made. Marshal Zhukov's 1st Belorussian Front attacked Army Group A along the direct Warsaw – Berlin Axis, after a hurricane bombardment from a concentration of 400 guns per mile backed up by rocket batteries, and was 10 miles into the German defences in the first 24 hours. To the south Zhukov's infantry had ripped open so wide a gap that he fed in two tank armies, and by evening of 15 January they were marauding nearly 30 miles ahead. Meanwhile, two of his armies had met west of Warsaw, and on the evening of 17 January the First Polish Army (serving with the Red Army since before Stalingrad) entered the ruined capital to succour the unfortunate survivors of the ill-fated revolt of the previous year.

By this time, the breach torn in the German defences by Zhukov's armies was 180 miles wide and there was nothing at all to stop the tank armies – and as many of the infantry as could keep up – racing ahead the rest of the way across Poland and into Germany itself. They brushed aside several German formations hastily thrown in their way, blockaded Poznan and left it behind on 25 January; on the last day of the month they reached the River Oder just north of Kustrin, where they crossed to form a bridgehead on the western bank. By the end of the first week in February, the east bank of the Oder from Zehden down to Fürstenberg was in Zhukov's hands, with another bridgehead across it at Frankfurt. The thunder of his guns could be heard in Berlin's Unter den Linden.

Marshal Koniev's armies of the 1st Ukrainian Front had done as well. This was the biggest front of all and contained 14 armies, two of them tank armies. The bulk of them broke out of the Sandomir bridgehead on 12 January under yet another massive bombardment which so stunned the defenders of the important town of Kielce that most of them were still deafened and half-blind when the town was occupied by the Russian infantry two days later. Then the armies fanned out – one driving down the west bank of the Vistula towards Kracow, another driving for Czestochowa. Within a week the 1st Ukrainian Front was advancing on a 170-mile wide sweep which penetrated at one point nearly 100 miles, smashing two German armies on the way.

It raced up past Beuthen and Oppeln towards Breslau, and then along the line of the Oder until it closed up to the demarcation line with Zhukov's 1st Belorussian Front. By the end of January the river was in Red Army hands from where its headwaters left the Carpathians up to just north west of Berlin.

Further south, in Hungary, fierce battles were fought by 2nd and 3rd Ukrainian Fronts when German and Hungarian armies tried hard to relieve the forces trapped in Budapest, and during March the Sixth SS Panzer Army put in an attack around Lake Balaton which in many ways resembled the fury and last-minute desperation of the battle in the Ardennes; but it suffered the same fate, beaten back in the end by greater numbers supplied by greater sources of weapons, ammunition and manpower. By 19 March, the SS were fleeing back over the Austrian border towards Vienna, and by that time, too, Rokossovsky's armies had fought their way across the Oder and closed up to the line of the River Neisse.

It was time to take stock of the whole situation, and prepare for the last battle.

Across the Rhine

Planning for the Rhine crossings had been started even before the previous year had ended. It was not

Advanced German aircraft designs

Tremendous advances were made by German technicians in the fields of jet and rocket propulsion, which manifested themselves in many designs powered by these engines. Some were more successful than others, and both East and West found German development more than useful in their own post-war programmes.

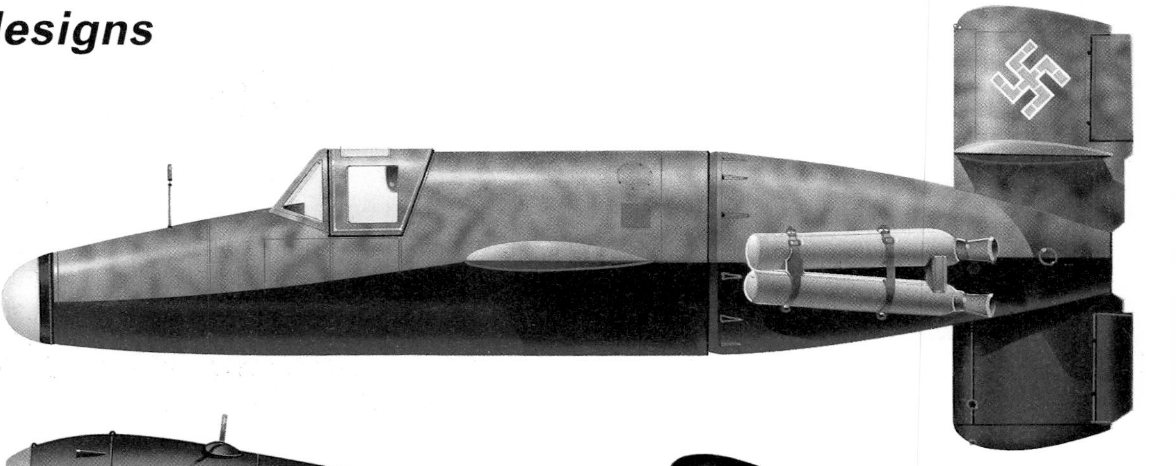

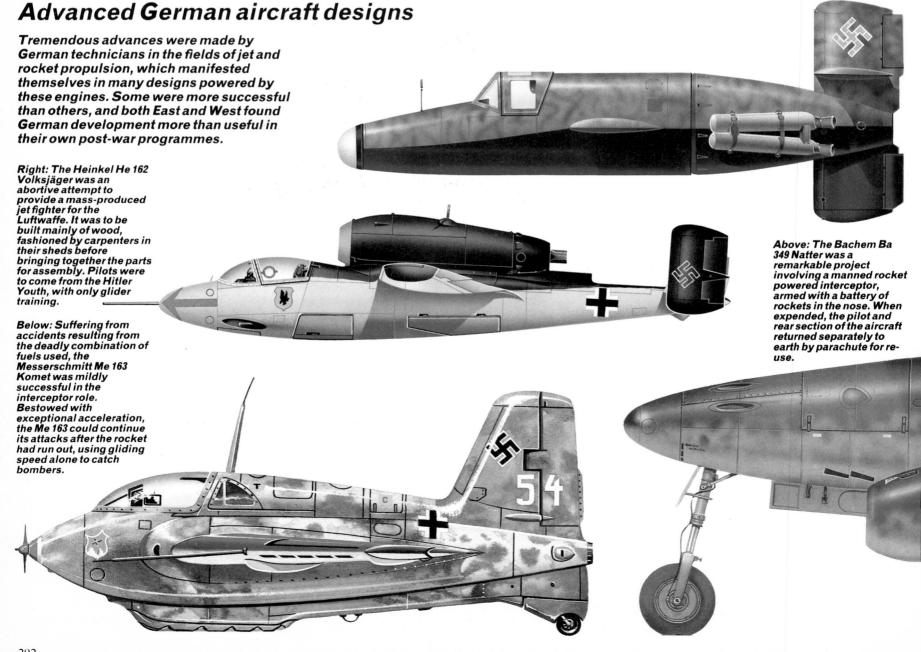

Above: The Bachem Ba 349 Natter was a remarkable project involving a manned rocket powered interceptor, armed with a battery of rockets in the nose. When expended, the pilot and rear section of the aircraft returned separately to earth by parachute for re-use.

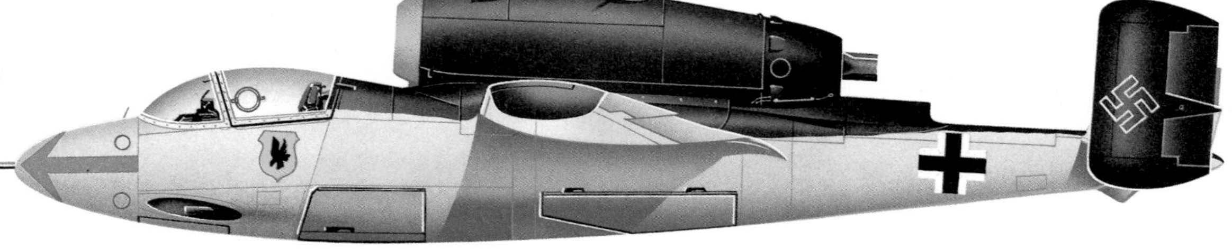

Right: The Heinkel He 162 Volksjäger was an abortive attempt to provide a mass-produced jet fighter for the Luftwaffe. It was to be built mainly of wood, fashioned by carpenters in their sheds before bringing together the parts for assembly. Pilots were to come from the Hitler Youth, with only glider training.

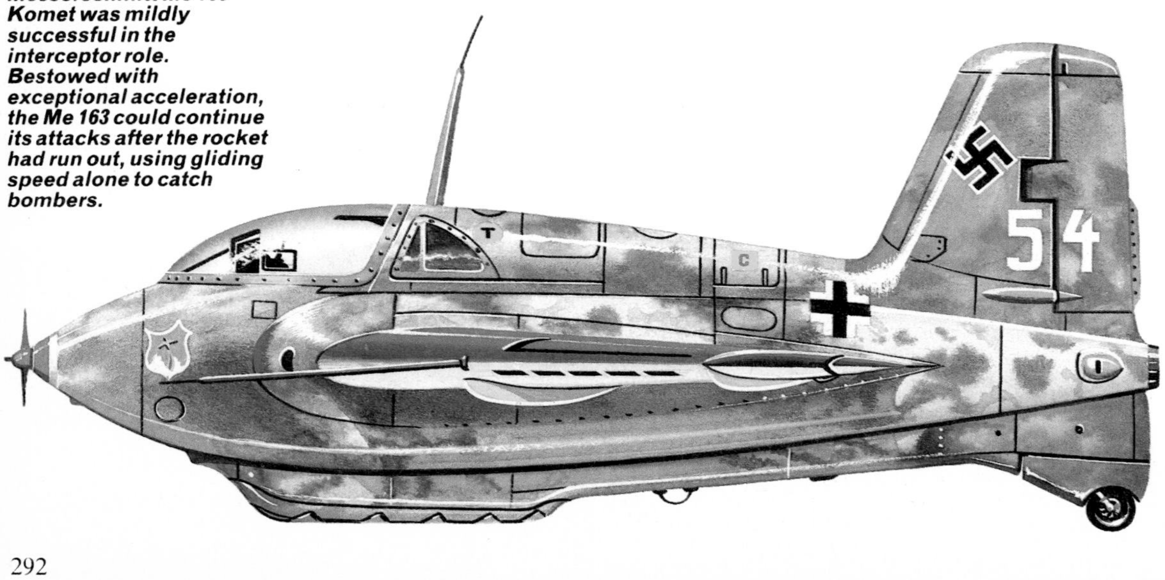

Below: Suffering from accidents resulting from the deadly combination of fuels used, the Messerschmitt Me 163 Komet was mildly successful in the interceptor role. Bestowed with exceptional acceleration, the Me 163 could continue its attacks after the rocket had run out, using gliding speed alone to catch bombers.

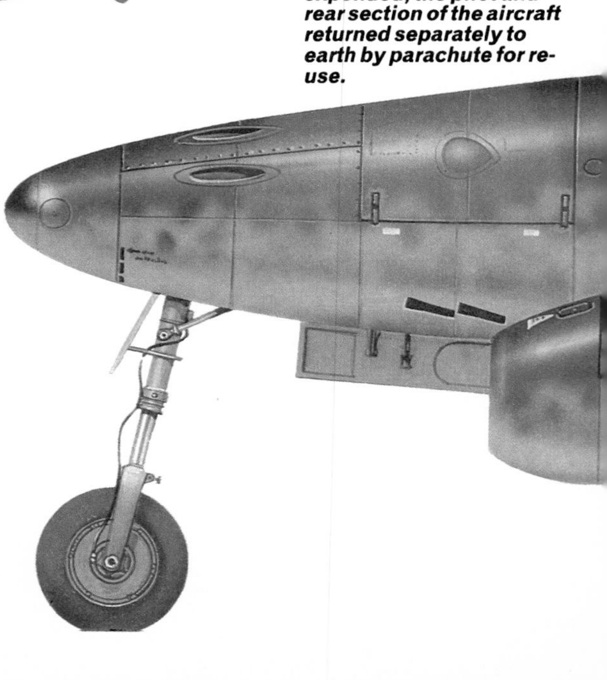

just a matter of piling up men and supplies for the crossing as a great deal of training was necessary. One of the largest programmes concerned the conversion of several tank regiments to the use of LVTs (Landing Vehicles, Tracked), or Buffaloes as they were known to the British. These were to be used to carry the first waves of men across and they were to be followed up by a second wave travelling in assault boats. The crossings were also to require a considerable engineer involvement. Not only had the bridging equipment necessary to cross the Rhine to be assembled ready for use, but approach roads and other transport facilities had to be made ready. In the end this was managed only by the allocation of several US Army engineer regiments to help out. Ultimately over a quarter of all supplies and equipment involved in the Rhine crossings was that of engineer units.

The Allies were taking no chances. The Allied air forces were provided with the task of completely neutralizing the rump of the Luftwaffe left after the Ardennes offensive of the previous winter. Standing patrols were established over all Luftwaffe airfields likely to become involved in the crossings, mainly to prevent the Luftwaffe seeing the vast build-up of men and matériel close to the crossing points. New railheads had to be established to enable 662 tanks of all kinds, 4,000 tank transporters and 32,000 vehicles of every variety to be brought up. Moreover, there were 3,500 field and medium guns to be assembled, together with a quantity of really heavy artillery that would cover the main crossings.

To add to the planners' problems the Rhine had its own say in the matter. The area where the crossings were to be made is flat and prone to flooding, and the previous winter had been so wet that by March the flood plains were still very wet: it was ideal for the Buffaloes but not so easy for the other vehicles, though it was a risk that had to be accepted.

On the night of 23 March 1945 the crossings began under a barrage from all of the artillery weapons that had been assembled. The first troops went across in Buffaloes with numbers of DD Shermans and other special vehicles in train. Air support was so intense that Wesel itself was confidently bombed by RAF Bomber Command when Allied troops were only a few hundred yards away. This not only cleared Wesel of the enemy but prevented the Germans from moving through Wesel to counter-attack.

The Allies did not have it all their own way. The mud was so bad in places that not even the Buffaloes could make much forward progress, with the result that some of the second assault waves, crossing in boats, came under intense fire and took heavy casualties.

Opposition to the landings was patchy. In places the defenders fought fiercely and in others the preliminary bombardment had been so fierce that organized defence was slight. The sheer weight of the onslaught was such that in places the Allies were soon able to wade ashore and establish sizeable bridgeheads, but the main strength of the attack was yet to come.

This arrived at about midday when the first of the Allied airborne forces came into sight. What became known as the 'armada of the air' flew over the Rhine to disgorge two divisions of parachute troops who seemed at times to make the sky dark with their numbers. They were soon followed by glider tugs that unleashed their charges to land in an area known as the Diersfordter Wald and another known as the Mehr-Hamminkeln. These glider troops did not land unscathed. Despite all efforts of the Allied air forces to neutralize flak sites near the landing points, some

An M3 half-track of the 5th Armored Division, Ninth US Army has reached Wittenmoor, 12 miles west of the Elbe and only 70 or so miles from Berlin. At this point the Russian army was about the same distance from the German capital in the other direction, and the Americans ignored a chance to take the city before their Russian allies (soon to become potential enemies).

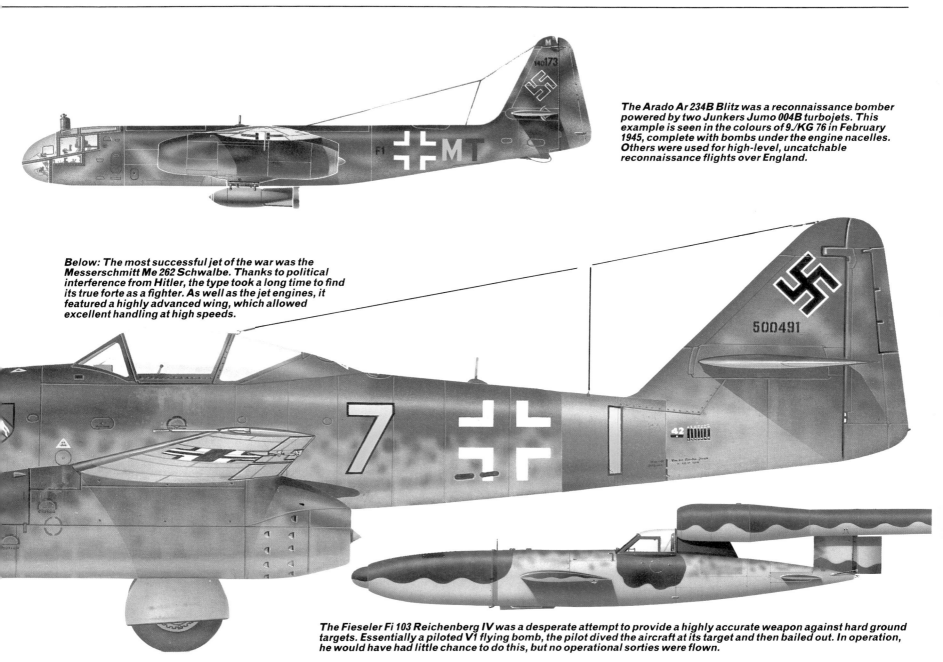

The Arado Ar 234B Blitz was a reconnaissance bomber powered by two Junkers Jumo 004B turbojets. This example is seen in the colours of 9./KG 76 in February 1945, complete with bombs under the engine nacelles. Others were used for high-level, uncatchable reconnaissance flights over England.

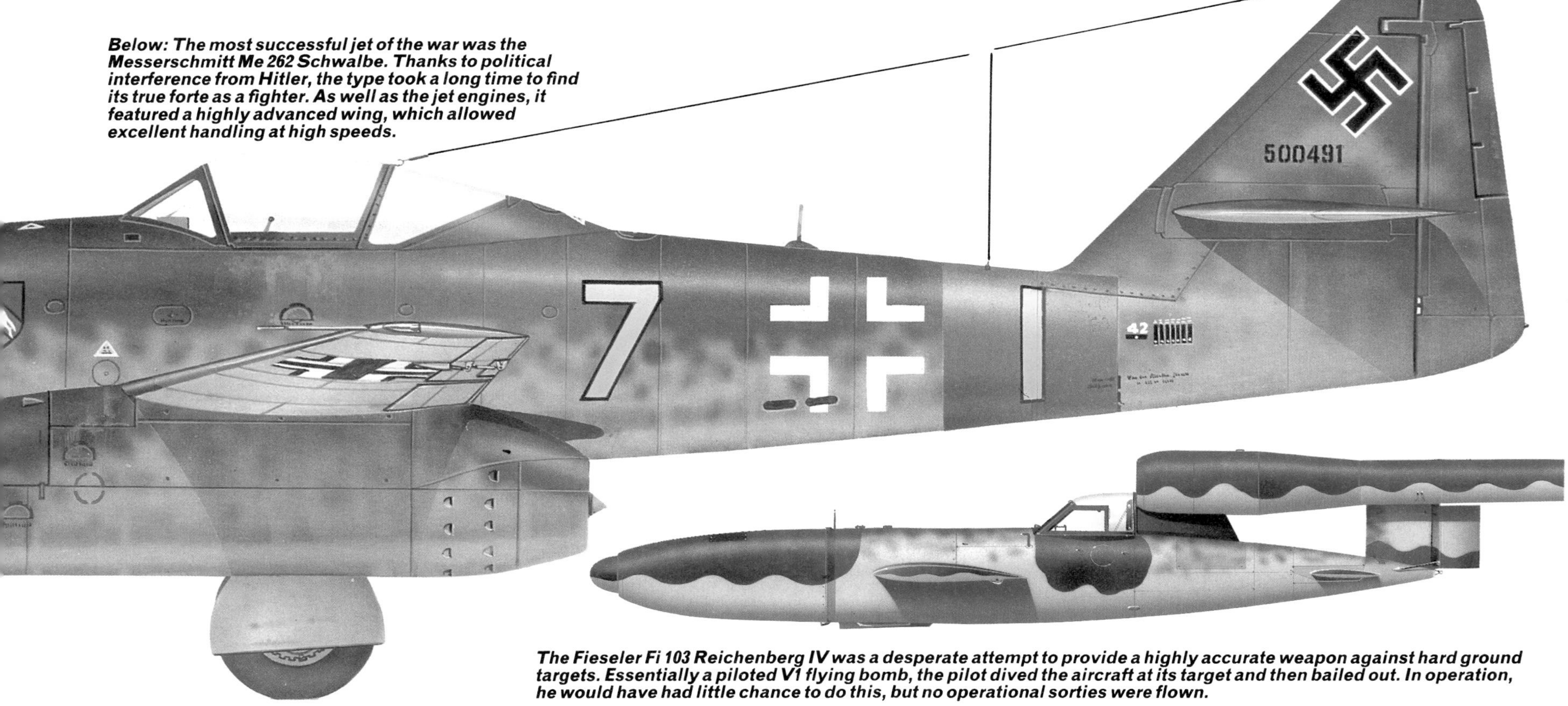

Below: The most successful jet of the war was the Messerschmitt Me 262 Schwalbe. Thanks to political interference from Hitler, the type took a long time to find its true forte as a fighter. As well as the jet engines, it featured a highly advanced wing, which allowed excellent handling at high speeds.

The Fieseler Fi 103 Reichenberg IV was a desperate attempt to provide a highly accurate weapon against hard ground targets. Essentially a piloted V1 flying bomb, the pilot dived the aircraft at its target and then bailed out. In operation, he would have had little chance to do this, but no operational sorties were flown.

The Soviet drive on Berlin

Stalin was determined to capture Berlin before the Western Allies, and summoning Zhukov and Koniev he commanded them to take the city, using the rivalry between the two Marshals as a goad. Zhukov's 1st Belorussian Front attacked on the same day as Koniev's 1st Ukrainian Front. It was Koniev's troops, however, that made the historic first contact with the Americans near Torgau on 25 April.

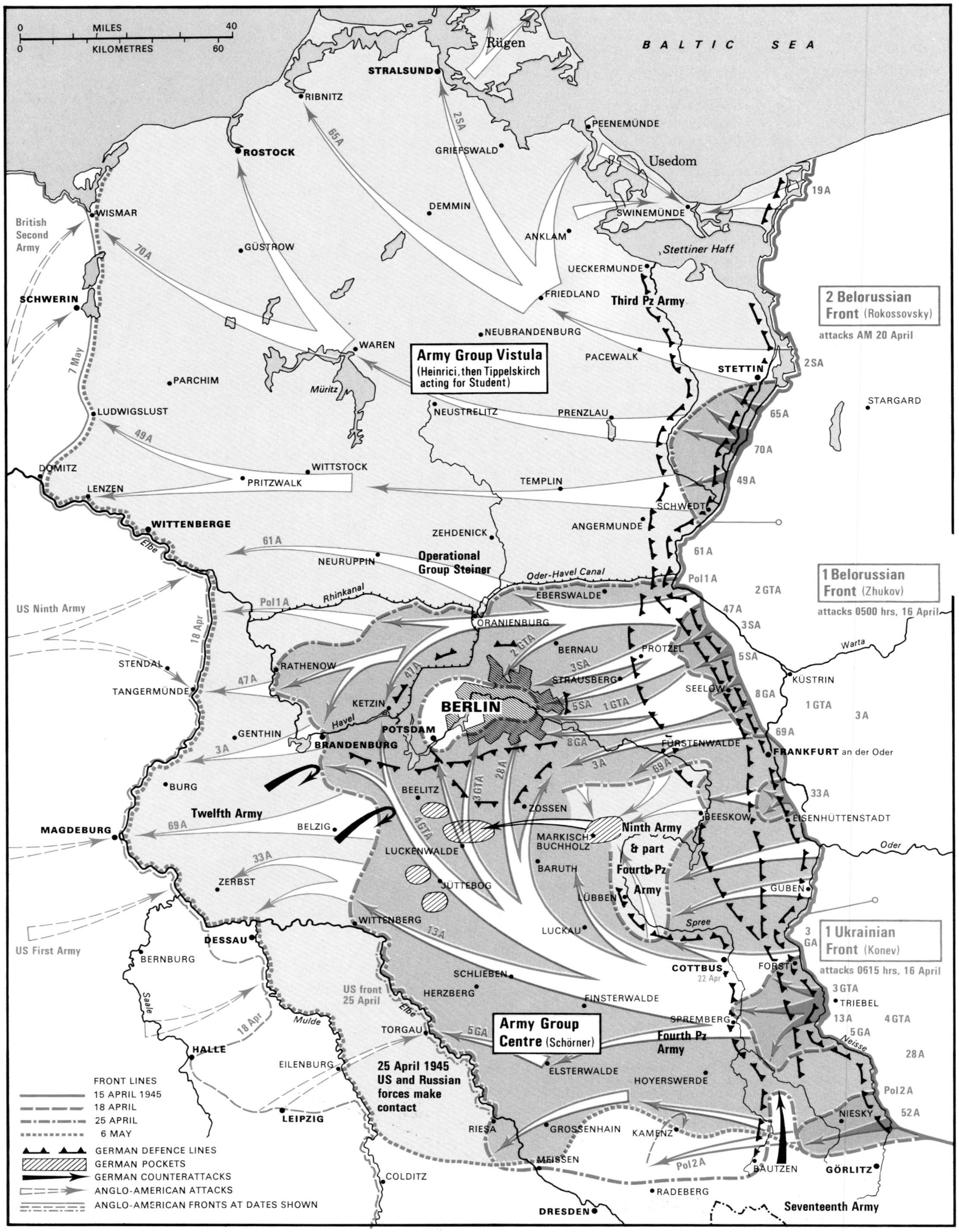

guns escaped to concentrate their fire power on the gliders, and about one quarter of all glider pilots involved became casualties in this operation. The numbers that did land safely were such that the airborne forces and the troops that had made the river crossings were able to join up, often well in advance of the anticipated times. By nightfall the Rhine bridgeheads were secure and despite some localized German counter-attacks they were across the river to stay.

It had always been realized that the crossing of the Rhine in the northern sector would be most strongly resisted, not only because of the close vicinity of the Ruhr industries but also because the gap between the Ruhr and the Dutch border led directly to the north German plain and the main route to Berlin.

As a result, attempts to cross by the American armies along the more southern stretches of the Rhine, although mounted by fewer men with smaller

An Eastern Front Flak 'Eighty Eight' crew prepare for the imminent arrival of the Russians. The offensives of January and February had seen the defences of the Reich crumble before possibly the mightiest army the world has ever seen, and now the Soviets were within 60 miles of Berlin.

The Battle for Berlin

The capture of Berlin by the Soviet army was not a gentle affair, fanatical pockets of German resistance being obliterated by a force with the memory of millions of Soviet deaths at the hands of these same Germans.

In Berlin the sound of artillery fire was an everyday adjunct to what passed for normal life in a wrecked city. Among the smoking heaps of rubble that had once been one of Europe's major cities, military and civil life somehow managed to continue. Civilians were outnumbered by the military who ranged from the last of the old regular German army to a rabble of 'foreign legions', party organizations and virtually untrained conscripts, many of whom were as young as 14 years. By day and night the Allied and Red air forces flew over the city to add to the piles of rubble below and to stoke the ever-burning fires on almost every street.

Remaining in the city, when much of the party and civil administration had already left for the southern hinterland of Germany, Hitler used his last reserves of power to condemn thousands more to death at a time when all was already lost. His party henchmen seemed to do what they could to add to the death total. All through the early days of April 1945 squads of party fanatics roamed the debris of Berlin seeking out 'deserters' and hanging them on the spot from nearby lamp posts, so that it was not long before every street in Berlin had its dangling example of the party's waning powers.

Away across the Oder the Soviets already had seen the self-same powers of the party. In their advances across Poland and East Prussia they had already uncovered many examples of concentration and extermination camps and all the other excesses of German rule in the East. Within the Soviet Union itself the brutal rule of the *Gauleiters* had already condemned millions of Soviet citizens to death by local forced labour or deportation to the labour camps of the Reich, and the Red Army was in no mood to be generous to a beaten enemy.

By 16 April 1945 the Soviets were ready for Berlin and the massed artillery of two groups of armies fell upon the German positions. There was no finesse in these massed attacks. The artillery was arranged wheel-to-wheel in rows, and thundered away for hours in a massive preliminary barrage.

When the bombardment lifted the tanks moved forward. The T-34/85s and the IS-2s lumbered from their hides, carrying with them the 'descent' infantry squads riding on their hulls with their sub-machine guns and grenades ready to fall upon any infantry positions that were left in a state to defend themselves. By 18 April the Red Army was through the Oder defences and within a few days shells were falling on the outskirts of Berlin.

Within the city Hitler continued his decline into a state of fantasy. Already unhinged by the attempt on his life in the previous July, Hitler's mind withdrew into a realm where the German army and party divisions of 1939 still existed, and he ordered nonexistent armies about his large-scale maps as though he was still in command of a mighty force. The reality was otherwise. Outside the bunkers what remained of the German army and the party machine shattered into a myriad of individuals who took the precautions for the future that they thought fit. This ranged from murdering old rivals or suspected political opponents to burying home movies and looted treasures from all over Europe. In a final frantic orgy of destruction the party anti-deserter squads carried out their last 'executions' and then ran to the west.

By 27 April Red Army tanks were in the Potsdamer Platz and through the sound of artillery fire the chatter of small arms could be heard, even in the Chancellery bunker where Hitler still held court with an entourage of the party faithful. At that point reality broke through the fantasy and in a last moment of Wagnerian grandeur Hitler shot himself along with the faithful Eva Braun and his dog. Their bodies were burned in the garden outside the bunker and the flames added their small glimmer to the holocaust about them as the Third Reich came to a fiery end.

Around the bunker the Red Army moved into a desolate wilderness of ruined buildings where isolated pockets of resistance still lingered. Many of the remaining strongpoints were manned by various of the German 'foreign legions' who knew only too well what to expect once they fell into Red Army hands, and so preferred to go down fighting. With such pockets of resistance the Red Army commanders wasted no time. They quickly called forward a number of 152-mm howitzers and sited them close to the source of the resistance. Then the howitzers simply blasted them away, as Red Army cameramen recorded the scene to show workers back in the USSR what their labours had made possible.

An SU-152 assault gun stands in the shattered streets of Berlin, jubilant Soviet soldiers atop its hull. Passing by, defeated Germans carry what belongings they have as they head towards imprisonment. Those who were sent to the camps of the USSR were unlikely to return; of the 90,000 prisoners taken at Stalingrad only 5,000 ever saw Germany again.

Right: The hammer and sickle is hoisted above the Reichstag while fierce fighting continues all around. To the Soviet army, which had fought back from the gates of Moscow, this was the crowning achievement of the war.

Below: Peace settles at last on the piles of rubble that was Berlin. This was the Foreign Ministry, once a seat of power, humming with activity as the relations of the Nazi state with the rest of the world went their course. Here it was that the ultimata were given and received, and wars were officially declared. Now, like Shelley's Ozymandias, "nothing beside remains".

resources, were just as successful. One had occurred the day before Twenty-first Army Group launched the main crossing – south of Mainz between Nierstein and Oppenheim by an assault regiment of the US 5th Division, part of XII Corps of Third Army, under command, needless to say, of General Patton.

The divisional commander, Major-General Leroy Irwin, made some small protest about the shortness of time he was given for preparation, but in the face of Patton's urgency he sent the first wave of assault boats across the 1,000-feet wide river, just before midnight, under a brilliant moon and the artillery support of a group which later complained that it could find little in the way of worthwhile targets. The first Americans to land captured seven German soldiers who promptly volunteered to paddle their assault boat back for them, and although later waves ran into sporadic machine-gun fire the regiment was across before midnight and moving towards the east-bank villages, with support regiments flooding across behind them By the evening of 23 March the entire 5th Division was across the river, a bridgehead formed and awaiting the arrival of an armoured division already on the west bank.

During the next few days crossings were made at Boppard and St Goar, Worms and Mainz, and by the end of the month Darmstadt and Wiesbaden were in US hands and armoured columns were driving for Frankfurt-am-Main and Aschaffenburg beyond; further south, the French had put an Algerian division across near Germersheim. Now a huge Allied bridgehead could be formed from Bonn down to Mannheim, from which would be launched the last Western offensive designed to meet the Russians on the Elbe and split Germany in two. The main objective for the US Twelfth Army Group would be the industrial region of Leipzig and Dresden.

To the north, Montgomery's Twenty-first Army Group were to drive north towards Hamburg, its left flank (the Canadians) clearing Holland of the enemy and then driving along the coast through Emden and Wilhelmshaven, its right flank (US Ninth Army) curving around the Ruhr to meet Hodges' First Army formations at Lippstadt, thus encircling Field Marshal Model's Army Group B in the Ruhr. After Hamburg, the British would close up to the Elbe down as far as Magdeburg, and send other forces up into Schleswig-Holstein and the Baltic.

There was some argument as to the desirability of Twenty-first Army Group racing for Berlin, but Eisenhower, solidly supported by Roosevelt, felt that the German capital was in easier reach of the Russians who – Roosevelt was sure – would prove both co-operative and amenable in regard to post-war European responsibilities.

Stalin would doubtless have been amused had he learned of the arguments.

BATTLE FOR BERLIN

On 1 April, Marshals Zhukov and Koniev had arrived in Moscow for a briefing on the subject of the Battle for Berlin. Stalin informed them that the devious and conniving Western Allies were planning a swift Berlin operation with the sole object of capturing the city before the Red Army could arrive – an announcement which, not surprisingly in view of the recent achievements of the Red Army, incensed them both.

They had expected to mount the attack on Berlin in early May, but in these special circumstances they would accelerate all preparations and be ready to move well before the Anglo-Americans could get themselves solidly inside German territory. Which of the two fronts – Zhukov's 1st Belorussian or Koniev's 1st Ukrainian – should have the task, and the honour, of driving straight for Berlin? – a question to which the wily Georgian left an ambiguous answer, by drawing on their planning map a demarcation line between their commands, which ended short of Berlin, at Lübben, 20 miles to the south east.

When the last offensive of the Red Army was launched its aims were to advance to the Elbe and to annihilate all organized German resistance before them, including the capture of Berlin and the reduction of its garrison. For this purpose, Marshals Zhukov and Koniev had some 1,640,000 men under their command, with 41,600 guns and mortars, 6,300 tanks, and the support of three air armies holding 8,400 aircraft.

To oppose them were 7 panzer and 65 infantry divisions in some sort of order, a hundred or so independent battalions, either remnants of obliterated divisions or formed from old men, children, the sick, criminals or the simple-minded, collected together by SS teams sent out from the Chancellery bunkers in which Hitler and his demented entourage were living out their last fantasies, with orders to conjure yet another army from the wreckage of the Thousand Year Reich.

Above: One of the last authentic pictures of Hitler, taken on 20 April as he inspected his last army, the boys of Berlin who were to be thrown into battle against veteran Soviet tank armies. Hitler retired to the bunker from where he dictated his political testament, married Eva Braun and at 3.30 pm on 30 April committed suicide with her.

Left: The true horror of the Nazi regime did not become clear until the concentration and extermination camps were overrun. Nothing could prepare the troops occupying Belsen for this, and it was not surprising that after the war, those responsible were charged with crimes against humanity.

Above: The comment above the gate of a Nazi camp, roughly translated as "Freedom through Work", is unlikely to have been appreciated by the victims of the National Socialist state. For millions in the camps of Eastern Europe it would be one of the last things they saw as they went naked to the gas chambers.

Unorganized and half-trained though they might be, the bulk of the German formations defending Berlin against the Red Army nevertheless fought at first with a blind ferocity and a blistering efficiency which demonstrated yet again that the epitome of high morale in combat is that of the cornered rat – which is the reason he so often escapes.

But there would be no escape for the Germans now.

At dawn on 16 April tremendous artillery and air bombardment opened all along the Oder and Neisse Rivers and out of the Soviet bridgeheads stormed the first waves of shock troops. It took Zhukov's northern thrust two days to smash through some four miles to reach the Seelow Heights, and his southern thrust to advance eight miles – and at that point they had seen no sign of a crack in the German defences despite the casualties on both sides. Koniev's shock troops, however, were not so strongly opposed and they advanced eight miles the first day; so on 18 April

***Above:* An IS-2 heavy tank leading a column of T-34/85s stamps a Soviet seal to the end of the war in Europe. The USSR had paid heavily to that end, losing 20 million people in a war that had been fought on a scale and with a ferocity unparalleled in history.**

Koniev fed in two tank armies and ordered them to fight their way to the north west, into the Berlin suburbs. His right-hand flank brushed Lübben, but only just.

Perhaps inspired by competition, Zhukov now drove his infantry and tank armies forward with ruthless vigour, and by 19 April both his thrusts had advanced 20 miles on a front almost 40 miles in width, destroying as they did so the bulk of the German Ninth Army, immobilized in the path of the attack by lack of fuel. On 21 April General Chuikov reported that his Eighth Guards Army, which he had brought all the way from Stalingrad, was into Berlin's south-eastern suburbs.

Meeting at Torgau

Koniev, having thrown his own counter into the battle for the capital, now devoted the bulk of his endeavour due westwards towards the Elbe. By 20 April two of his tank armies had reached Luckenwald – thus splitting the German Army Group Centre from Berlin and the defences in the north - and then drove two more armies given him by STAVKA up towards Potsdam where on 25 April they linked up with one of Zhukov's guard tank armies which had come around the north of Berlin – and the city, its inhabitants and its 200,000-man garrison were surrounded.

On the same day, units of Fifth Guards Army reached the Elbe at Torgau and within minutes were exchanging drinks, hats, buttons and photographs with Americans of the US First Army. The scenes of triumphant comradeship and co-operation which followed were repeated up and down the central axis of Germany, as soldiers who had fought westwards from Stalingrad met those who had fought eastwards from Normandy, and during the brief period in which they were allowed to fraternize, they learned to recognize each others' qualities. It is a tragedy that friendships made then were not allowed to continue.

***Right:* May 1945, and Marshal of the Soviet Union G. K. Zhukov stands on the steps of the Reichstag, as the principle architect of the Soviet victory in their war with Nazi Germany.**

On 1 May, General Chuikov, now well inside the Berlin city centre, was approached by General Krebs, the Chief of the German General Staff, with three other officers bearing white flags desirous of negotiating a surrender. With almost unbelievable effrontery, the German general opened the conversation with the remark:

'Today is the First of May, a great holiday for our two nations.'

Considering the outrages carried out in his country by the nationals of the man addressing him, Chuikov's reply was a model of restraint.

'*We* have a great holiday today. How things are with you over there, it is less easy to say!'

But the first moves towards an official end to hostilities in Europe had been made.

Berlin surrendered unconditionally on 2 May, on 4 May Field Marshal Montgomery took the surrender of all German forces in the north – and on 7 May the 'Unconditional surrender of Germany to the Western Allies and to Russia' was agreed, the instrument itself signed by General Jodl for the defeated, and Generals Bedell Smith and Susloparov for the victors, General Sevez also signing for France. The war in Europe was at an end.

Hitler had committed suicide on 30 April, having first married and then poisoned his mistress Eva Braun, made a will leaving the leadership of his country to Admiral Dönitz, spoken briefly to every member of his personal staff – and poisoned his dog. Afterwards, the bodies of all three were burned.

A man of enormous but demonic gifts, he had lifted his country from a position of weakness and chaos to unparalleled power, and then dropped her back into chaos again – all in the space of 12 years.

Chapter 26

Victory over Japan

With the conclusion of the war in Europe, the Allied powers were free to turn all their might against Japan. The submarine blockade that had strangled the Japanese economy made the defeat of the Empire inevitable, but not without some of the bloodiest fighting of the war. By the end, however, a new, terrifying force had been unleashed, casting a giant shadow over the future.

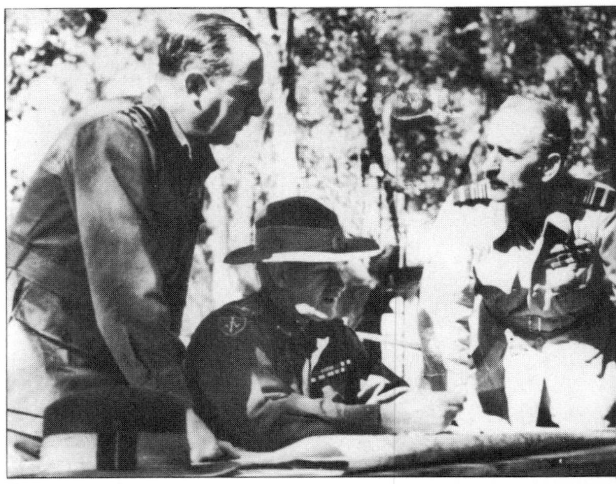

Right: General Sir William 'Bill' Slim, perhaps the finest British commander of the war, is seen at the jungle headquarters of the 14th Army. To his left is Air Marshal W.A. Coryton.

Below: Pathan troops of a Punjabi regiment attack Japanese positions near Mawchi as pockets of Japanese troops are forced to retreat towards the Thai border.

What remained of the Japanese Fifteenth Army was back across the Chindwin by August 1944, with General Honda's Thirty-Third Army up around Myitktyna facing the Chinese armies, and General Sakurai's Twenty-Eighth Army on the left flank in the Arakan. An indication of their plight can be given by the fact that in addition to the losses all three armies had suffered by battle and disease, they were informed in October that not only would they receive no more reinforcements or supplies, but that in view of the obvious menace of the buildup of American air fleets in the Pacific, they would now lose all their modern fighters and bombers. They thus faced the next Allied onslaught at the end of October with less than 50 obsolescent aircraft and no hope of more.

General Slim, on the other hand, had now three up-to-strength army corps at his disposal – XV under General Christison still in the Akyab Peninsula, XXXIII Corps under General Stopford in the centre south of Imphal, and IV Corps under General Messervy in the north. Moreover, on Messervy's left there were now several Chinese divisions with whom co-operation was likely to be far better because, at Chiang Kai-Shek's insistence, General Stilwell had been replaced by the far more amenable and competent General Wedemeyer.

Moreover, ever since Imphal and Kohima had been relieved, the great effort to improve communications in the area had been continued, and an effective plan laid for logistic support once the next campaign opened.

It did so at the end of October 1944, once the monsoon rains ended and the ground had to some extent, dried out. By mid-December Stopford had established a bridgehead across the Chindwin near Kalewa where his force was joined by one of Messervy's divisions coming down from Dimapur. Stopford's divisions then pushed eastwards towards Shwebo while another of Messervy's divisions drove parallel but well to the north to Banmauk, where they met the leading brigade of the 36th Division which had been flown in at Stilwell's request when the last of the Chindits had been evacuated. These two divisions now linked up and drove south to join Stopford for an attack on Mandalay from the north, but progress was hindered not only by the country, but by the narrowness of the roads and tracks – often between near-vertical hillocks – which made their obstruction by small Japanese rearguards comparatively easy.

As the situation developed it looked increasingly as though the bulk of the Japanese armies might escape southwards, so Slim ordered Messervy to send the half of his corps which had gone to Kalewa stealthily down the Myittha valley and across through Nyaungo to Taungtha, then on to Meiktila. This all took time – but it worked; by 3 March 1945 17th Division under Major-General Cowan was at Meiktila, and the whole of XXXIII Corps and 36th Division were closing down on Mandalay and its fortress, Fort Dufferin.

In the meantime, Christison's XV Corps had reached not only Donbaik, but also at last Akyab, which they occupied on 4 January; and then – as Sakurai's divisions had been hastily recalled to attempt to stem the threat to Mandalay and the Irrawady crossings (they arrived too late) XV Corps took ship 70 miles down the coast and occupied Ramree Island – thus providing themselves with an excellent air base, in conditions the troops quickly decided was the nearest to paradise they were likely to find this side of the grave.

The Japanese situation was now hopeless. Their Fifteenth Army on the central front had comprised only 21,000 men when the campaign opened, and by 20 March, when Stopford's men drove the last survivors out of Fort Dufferin, they had lost so many that the residue was hurriedly absorbed into General Honda's Thirty-Third Army – now back in central area having been driven away from the north and thus freeing at last the entire length of the Burma Road. By April, therefore, the Japanese had lost Mandalay, and only Rangoon still remained to them of the plums which had fallen into their hands in the days of triumph. But they were not yet ready to admit defeat, and to hold the British back from Rangoon they planned to block the way down the Irrawaddy Valley through Prome with Sakurai's Twenty-Eighth Army – now at last to hand – and the road and rail route from Meiktila through Toungoo, with the remnants of Honda's army and the disgraced Mutaguchi's.

But the planning was to little avail. By 14 April, Yamethin, 40 miles south east of Meitkila, had been taken by the British 5th Division, six days later Messervy's spearheads reached Toungoo and by 29 April were at Kadok, only 70 miles from Rangoon. Here they met quite fierce resistance at first, for Stopford's XXXIII Corps had driven down the east bank of the Irrawaddy – virtually ignoring Sakurai's army marooned on the west bank without boats – and Japanese Command, Burma, realizing that their days there were numbered, ordered the hasty evacuation of everything and everyone who could move. For this they desperately needed the gap east of Rangoon held open.

It was at this point that Operation Dracula took place. A Gurkha parachute battalion with a detachment of Special Forces was dropped on Elephant

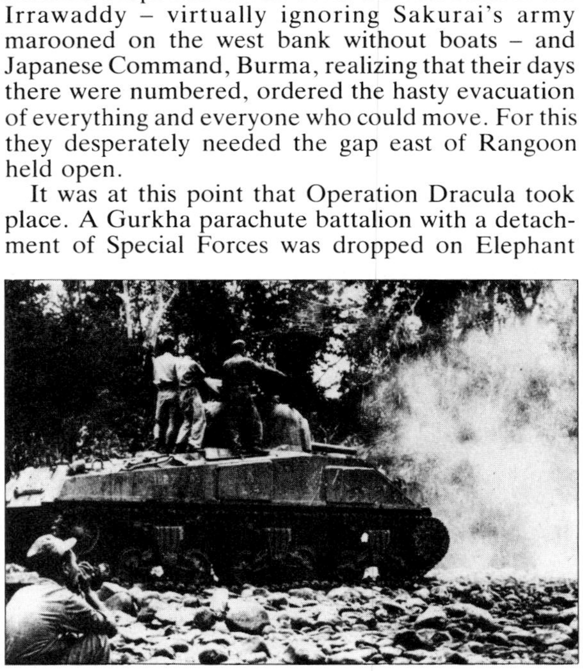

An American-supplied M4 Sherman medium tank operates with Chinese forces on the Burma Road. 'Vinegar' Joe Stillwell had been replaced, but his plan for a large-scale pincer movement between forces out of Myitkyna, Mogaung and from Yunnan in China went ahead, forcing the Japanese 33rd Army back towards Thailand.

Chronology of War: 1945

May 10
Fourteenth Army links up with forces from Arakan, cutting off all Japanese forces west of the Irrawaddy

May 11
Heavy offensive launched by US forces across Okinawa

May 12
Germans surrender on Crete

May 13
Red Army occupies Czechoslovakia

May 14
Fire raid on Nagoya starts series of B-29 raids on Japanese industry

May 19
Last Japanese resistance on Luzon ends

May 23
Wehrmacht commanders and high Nazi Party officials captured at Flensburg. Himmler commits suicide

May 25
US Chiefs of Staff complete plan for invasion of Japanese homeland

May 28
Over 100 Japanese aircraft shot down over Okinawa beaches

June 1
Japanese retreat on Okinawa

June 5
Allies agree on division of Germany into four zones of occupation; Berlin to be jointly occupied

June 10
Australian forces invade Borneo

June 15
End of series of B-29 raids on Japanese industry. 36 sq km of built-up area destroyed

June 18
US Tenth Army commander, Lt General Simon Bolivar Buckner, killed on Okinawa. New series of raids on Japanese cities commences

June 20
Japanese forces begin surrendering on Okinawa

June 22
US forces claim total control of Okinawa. Japanese casualties – 129,700 dead, 10,755 POW, c.42,000 civilian casualties; US losses – 12,520 dead, 36,631 wounded, 763 planes lost, 22 destroyers and 18 other warships sunk

June 25
San Francisco Conference draws up World Charter of Security

July 1
Australian forces land at Balikpapan

July 5
Australian reinforcements land on Borneo

July 10
TF.38 launches thousand-aircraft raid on Tokyo from its carriers

July 12
US and UK troops enter Berlin

July 16
First atomic explosion at Los Alamos

July 17
Potsdam Conference opens. One thousand five hundred Allied bombers from US 3rd Fleet (including British Pacific Fleet) attack Tokyo while surface units shell Mito-hachi on Honshu

Point on the west bank of the Pegu Estuary, and on 2 May the leading sections of the 26th Indian Division went ashore from transports which had brought them from Akyab and Ramree. The plan was for a controlled and orderly advance on each side of the River Pegu, through Kyauktan and Syiram into the outskirts of Rangoon, hoping that whatever fighting took place would neither destroy too much of the city, nor endanger the lives of the Allied prisoners known to be held in the various jails there.

In the event very little fighting took place anywhere, the appalling weather proving the greatest obstacle. Everywhere, troops and vehicles had to wade or splash through water-logged paddyfields, and the rising hopes that the Japanese had gone were confirmed when an RAF pilot flew low over one of the known jails in the city and saw the words, whitewashed on the roof, 'JAPS GONE. BRITISH HERE' – any doubts as to the veracity of the message being dispersed by the laconic instruction painted on a nearby roof, 'EXTRACT DIGIT.'

Now all that remained for the Fourteenth Army was to round up and trap the remnants of the Japanese armies who had so triumphantly swept across the country three years before. Disordered, starving, leaderless, so dejected that some of them were even prepared to surrender, these unfortunates faced the problems of crossing a countryside flooded by violent rainstorms, then attempting to cross the Irrawaddy and the Sittang, along both of which waited British, Indian and Gurkha soldiers ready and willing to kill them.

And for the 6,000 odd who made it, what was there in Thailand or Indo-China, except hostility and the prospect of a long walk back to a defeated homeland?

Seen from USS* Essex*, the might of a carrier group enters Ulithi atoll after strikes against the Philippines. Leading the group are the light carrier* Langley *and the larger carrier* Ticonderoga *(Essex class). Following behind are battleships* Washington, North Carolina, South Dakota, *and cruisers* Santa Fe, Biloxi, Mobile *and* Oakland. *The* Langley *in the foreground carries Grumman Hellcats and Avengers, some still in the old light grey scheme.

MacArthur's return

With Leyte firmly in American hands, General MacArthur's pledge to 'return' was so close to spectacular achievement that there could be no doubt as to his next objective – Luzon itself, Manila, the Bay and Corregidor.

Nevertheless, he proceeded carefully; his instructions to all his subordinate commanders were that first of all the island of Mindoro must be captured, its airfields readied to receive the bulk of 5th USAAF, and thus air supremacy guaranteed for the landings in Lingayen Gulf – where the whole Philippines campaign had started – of General Krueger's Sixth Army.

As a result, fast carrier groups from Admiral Halsey's 3rd Fleet sailed for the waters around Mindoro to arrive at dawn on 15 December 1944 when the landings were made. Their aircraft pounded the airfields around Manila only 100 miles away, then maintained an umbrella of fighters over the airfields to keep the Japanese bombers on the ground.

That night, American rangers reached the airfields on Mindoro with little trouble for there was only a 100-man Japanese garrison on the island; the engineers arrived the following day and by the end of December, B-17s and B-29s were already in operation.

On 3 January 1945, yet another armada of US warships assembled in Leyte Gulf, this time to set out for Luzon. Six battleships, 17 escort carriers and 144 other ships made up the fleets under Admirals Kincaid and Oldendorf, and when they arrived off Lingayen Gulf they found Halsey's fast carrier force awaiting them, already experiencing – and indeed suffering from – the spectacular attentions of Kamikaze attacks. During the operations which followed these attacks killed over a thousand American servicemen and sank or damaged, in varying degrees, nearly 50 ships of the combined fleets.

But on 10 January Krueger's four divisions poured ashore – against little or no opposition, for General Yamashita had decided that US naval and air power was such that his men could not live and fight within its close range – and pushed southwards towards Manila. Fearing a trap – and hearing that formations of I Corps which had fanned out to the east and north from Lingayen Gulf were being heavily opposed – General Krueger ordered caution in the southern drive, and it was 23 January before they were approaching the vital Clark Field. Here, not surprisingly, they ran into a stubborn defence.

Now began for the Americans the largest and costliest of their campaigns in the Pacific. General Krueger's forces, which in the end were to amount to six infantry and one airborne divisions, were opposed by 250,000 Japanese soldiers under Yamashita, and although the latter were poorly organised, badly deployed and desperately ill equipped, they nevertheless formed a formidable opposition, charged, as the majority were, with their usual zeal. It took eight days and two major attacks before the Americans controlled Clark Field, by which time 2,500 Japanese soldiers had died and American losses were mounting on a scale not before experienced. Meantime, MacArthur had put another corps ashore on the west coast of the Bataan Peninsula to ensure that the Japanese could not retreat down into it in the same way that the Americans had done in 1942, and it took them two weeks to consolidate all the way down from the neck of the peninsula, to Mariveles at the foot on Manila Bay.

In Burma the RAF continued to sweep the Japanese north, fighter units bolstered by the arrival of the Republic Thunderbolt. The eight-gun armament and good bomb-carrying ability enabled it to perform well in the fighter-bomber role.

Below: Dramatic shots of a Douglas A-20 catching flak and crashing during a raid on a Japanese-held island. Light bombers played a massive part in the Pacific drive, softening up targets before landings were made. Alongside the A-20 flew the North American B-25 Mitchell, which also carried out successful 'skip-bombing' raids against Japanese shipping.

MacArthur had also put the bulk of 11th Airborne Division ashore by boat to the south of Manila, and by the first week of February Manila itself was under siege from both north and south, the attackers somewhat inhibited by the knowledge that some of the larger and more important building complexes in the city housed Allied prisoners and internees – some of them women and children. However, by the evening of the second day those buildings had been captured and the prisoners released – but then it became evident that Rear-Admiral Iwabuchi, commanding the 17,000 naval troops there, had every intention of turning Manila into a second Stalingrad, despite orders from Yamashita to yield it up as an 'Open city'. Thus almost every major structure had become a minor fort, and the city would have to be pounded into a shambles.

It took until 25 February until the last bastion – the 16th century Intramuros Fort – was finally captured by the Americans, every Japanese inside having been killed and practically every wall reduced to tumbled boulders. Then came the problem of Corregidor, which was now to withstand a far heavier bombardment than it had suffered three years before. For ten days the garrison fought back against US naval shelling, USAAF bombardment, an amphibious attack by one battalion and an airborne attack by another, and in the end the survivors had to be burned out of the underground tunnels and caves with flamethrowers, or blown out by bazookas; but by 2 March, no living Japanese was still on Corregidor. The Rock was back in American hands.

On 28 February, MacArthur re-established the Philippine Commonwealth Government in Manila, ending his address to them with the comment 'My country has kept the faith!' Certainly by the end of March the centres of administration and communication in Luzon were beyond Japanese control, though large formations still existed in the north of the island and to the east and south east of Manila. They would continue fighting until the war's end.

By that time, starvation, disease and exhaustion would have killed at least as many as had died in combat, and of the 250,000 there when Krueger's armies had first landed, only 60,000 were to survive. American casualties for the Luzon operation amounted to 10,000 killed including 2,000 by Kamikaze attacks, and 30,000 wounded.

And it seemed to the survivors there was still a long way to go to Japan itself.

Above: Iwo Jima was the first part of the Japanese homeland to be invaded by the Americans, so naturally the ferocity of the defenders was greater than ever before encountered. Even with as massive a force as this, seen off Green Beach at the foot of Mount Suribachi, it took over a month of the bloodiest fighting in the history of the Marine Corps to clear the island.

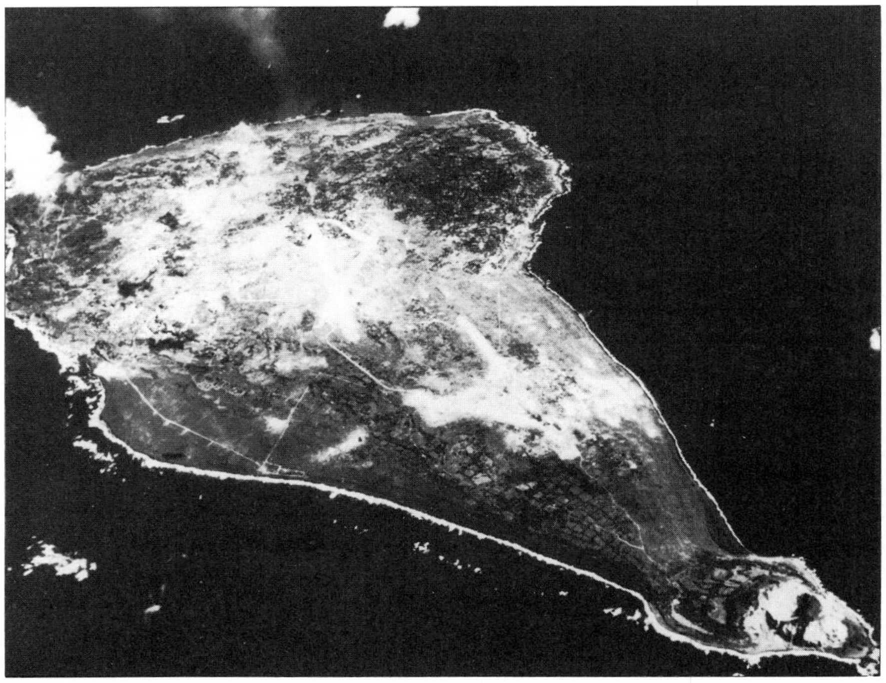

Right: The tiny island, less than eight miles square, was defended by a force of some 21,000 under the command of General Kuribayashi. The Americans took fewer than 220 prisoners, mostly wounded, and suffered 20,000 casualties in the process (a third of the troops committed) including over 7,000 dead.

Iwo Jima

By the end of 1944 it had become quite evident to the US commanders in the Pacific that in the near future they would have to mount a large-scale attack on the Japanese island of Iwo Jima.

Three factors made the decision inescapable. First, heavy B-29 bomber raids on the Japanese mainland, then being mounted from the Marianas, were proving prohibitively expensive as even North American P-51 Mustangs could not escort them on the 2,800-mile round trip, and they thus lacked essential fighter protection over the target area; Iwo Jima lies only 660 miles from Tokyo and possessed two airfields, one of which could take B-29s immediately. Second, even with no further advance towards Japan Iwo Jima was a highly desirable link in the defences of the newly captured Marianas. And thirdly, the island was traditionally a part of the Japanese homeland (it was administered by the Tokyo prefecture), and its fall would thus constitute a severe psychological blow to the Japanese people. The island must therefore be captured; isolation would not be enough.

Unfortunately for the Americans, the Japanese high command possessed just as keen an understanding of strategic realities, and had long appreciated the necessity of denying Iwo Jima to the Americans. One staff officer even went so far as to suggest that as Japanese air and naval strength had suffered an apparently irreversible erosion, serious consideration should be given to a project of sinking the island into the Pacific, or if not the whole island then at least the half which contained the main airfield. Iwo Jima is, after all, only 5 miles long, 2.5 miles wide at its broadest, and at its tallest point (the summit of Mount Suribachi) only 550 ft high.

The suggestion was turned down, but as early as June 1944 the highly regarded General Kuribayashi was sent to organize the defence of the island, and given clearly to understand that in case of failure he should not expect to see his family or homeland again; the same stricture applied to the 20,000 veteran reinforcements who followed him to Iwo Jima during the months which followed. As they were provided with heavy and medium artillery, anti-aircraft batteries, heavy and light machine-guns, mortars and tanks, together with relevant ammunition all on an ample scale, their morale was in no way cast down by their predicament.

They therefore set to work with a will, dug their artillery well into the ground, and constructed successive lines of defence across the width of the island a task in which they were considerably aided by the fact that Iwo Jima is of volcanic origin, so the soft pummice is easily quarried yet still self supporting however deep it is cut. By the following March, 3 miles of tunnelling wound its way under the northern half of the island.

A Japanese stands guard in front of a half finished steel pillbox in the heart of Manila's business district. American troops had landed on Luzon three weeks before, and the 1st Cavalry is only a week away from the city.

Two months after the Luzon landings, while the battle for Manila came to a close, the exceedingly complex task of clearing the myriad islands of the Philippines saw the 41st Infantry Division roar ashore at Zamboanga on Mindanao.

The battle for Manila was savage. The Japanese naval commander ordered his 17,000 sailors to defend the old walled city to the death, and they did so (taking over 100,000 Filipino citizens with them). US casualties exceeded 25,000 killed and wounded.

Sinking the Haguro

***It has been forgotten that the last major Japanese naval unit to be sunk in a surface battle was not put down by the US Navy, but one of the classic Royal Navy destroyer actions. The victim was the veteran heavy cruiser* Haguro.**

At 16.40 local time on 10 May 1945, the British submarine HMS *Subtle* sighted a 'Nachi' class cruiser with a destroyer and two smaller escorts in the narrows of the Malacca Strait; the cruiser was the *Haguro* which, accompanied by the destroyer *Kamikaze* and two patrol ships, had left Singapore the day before, bound for Port Blair in the Andamans. Her mission was to evacuate the garrison.

On the strength of an earlier intelligence report a powerful Allied force had already left Colombo to intercept the *Haguro*. Under the command of Vice Admiral H. T. C. Walker, it included the battleships HMS *Queen Elizabeth* and the French *Richelieu*, the Dutch destroyer *Tromp* and four escort carriers. However, this force was sighted by a Japanese reconnaissance aircraft and the alerted *Haguro* turned back.

Haguro set off again on 14 May and, with all but one of the submarines now withdrawn, entered the Andaman Sea unchallenged. Though suspecting the movement, Walker had no definite information and, in the early hours of 15 May detached the 26th Destroyer Flotilla, under Captain Manley Power, to work along the *Haguro*'s estimated track pending an air search. Power's ship was HMS *Saumarez*, and she was accompanied by four of her 'V' class sisters, HMS *Venus*, *Verulam*, *Virago* and *Vigilant*. Let off the leash, they were in sight of the northern tip of Sumatra by daybreak.

At 10.41, however, came a signal from the commander-in-chief Ceylon to Walker, repeated to Power, to abandon the operation as the *Haguro* was no longer considered a threat to wider activities in the Bay of Bengal. A true destroyer man, Power decided that Ceylon could not be in full receipt of the facts and queried the signal. This was a time-consuming process and meanwhile the 26th Destroyer Flotilla held its course.

This Nelsonian approach was vindicated when a Grumman Avenger, in locating a transport, sighted also the *Haguro* and her destroyer running north out of the strait at easy speed. Again she reversed course on being sighted but Power held on.

In the early afternoon they doubled the northerly tip of Sumatra and entered the strait at 27 kts. The weather was hot and sunny with vast banks of tropical cumulus building ominously over the land.

At 16.40 the five destroyers were reorganized onto a line of bearing with the *Saumarez* at the centre. This meant that, although in visual contact, they could search a broad swathe of the strait. The afternoon turned to short tropical dusk, the cloud moving off the land and the oncoming humid darkness becoming shot with flickers of lightning.

The face of the waters was increasingly lashed by heavy showers, ideal destroyer weather, particularly with the superior British gunnery radars and, at 22.40, the *Venus* detected a target at nearly 40-mile range.

The flotilla overtook its target, no more than 22.5 km (14 miles) wide to starboard of its track, then hooked to the northward in a curved line abeam, the aim being to pinpoint the target, envelop it and attack from each quarter.

At 00.45 on 16 May the *Haguro*, with the *Kamikaze* on her port quarter, was 10 miles distant from the centre of the British line and closing when her radar detected the destroyers. She manoeuvred as if unsure of their identity (they were approaching from the unlikely direction of Singapore) but then, with sudden resolve, reversed course.

While Power's other destroyers bent on speed to overtake, the *Venus* crossed the *Haguro*'s bows to attack from a forward bearing to starboard, missed her chance and had to make a rapid 300° turn to port to disengage. The Japanese again reversed course but still without opening fire. Power's four destroyers were now closing through the velvet darkness at a relative speed of over 50 kts.

It was just after 01.30 and both sides fired starshell. The *Saumarez* was bathed by the greenish glare at only 3,000 yards from the *Haguro*, which opened a brisk fire. The destroyer was soon hit in a boiler room but skidded around in a tight turn to port and launched a full outfit of torpedoes. Almost simultaneously the *Verulam* was attacking from the adjacent quadrant.

The now violently manoeuvring cruiser was hit forward by three torpedoes. Her forward armament went silent and she began to list, only to be hit by one, possibly two, further torpedoes in the machinery spaces.

For 10 minutes the *Haguro* was teased by destroyer gunfire from various directions until, seizing their chance, the *Venus* and *Virago* ran in from both starboard quadrants, launching 11 torpedoes between them. There were three likely hits but the return fire was now only sporadic and under local control. It fell to the *Venus* with just two torpedoes remaining to sink her. At 02.06 the *Haguro* went down, some 45 miles south west of Penang.

The jubilant destroyers retired almost immediately, but the *Kamikaze* later returned to retrieve 400 survivors from the dark waters. Of the British flotilla only *Saumarez* had been damaged, suffering two dead. In the words of Admiral Lord Mountbatten, the supreme commander in South East Asia, it had been 'an outstanding example of a night attack by destroyers'.

Above: Hit by three torpedoes almost simultaneously,* Haguro *began to list and burn. Further hits made central fire control impossible and cut fighting efficiency considerably. Handicapped in this way, she stood little chance against so many fast moving targets. She went down a little over 30 minutes after the first star shell was fired.

Left: Typical of the heavy cruisers built by Japan in the 1930s,* Haguro *supposedly displaced 10,000 tons but in fact was much heavier. By the end of the war this powerful vessel was approaching 15,000 tons, and her 10 8-in guns and eight 'Long Lance' torpedo tubes should have been able to cope with Manley Powers' 26th Destroyer Flotilla.

Below: HMS* Verulam *makes 27 kts through the tropical squalls in the straits of Malacca in company with one of her flotilla mates. Trained to a fine pitch, the 26th Flotilla were to accomplish a classic night action.

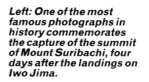

Left: One of the most famous photographs in history commemorates the capture of the summit of Mount Suribachi, four days after the landings on Iwo Jima.

Right: The heavy cruiser USS Salt Lake City bombards Iwo Jima in the months before the landings. She had a distinguished career, seeing action in the Solomons, the Aleutians, the Gilbert Islands, at Kwajalein, Leyte, here at Iwo Jima and later off Okinawa.

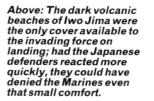

Above: The dark volcanic beaches of Iwo Jima were the only cover available to the invading force on landing; had the Japanese defenders reacted more quickly, they could have denied the Marines even that small comfort.

Right: The mountain of spent brass cartridge cases around this machine-gun position testifies to the amount of suppressive fire required by the troops assaulting deeply dug in Japanese troops on Iwo Jima.

Left: Well dug in artillery fires on Japanese positions at Mount Suribachi, less than a mile away. The bare volcanic soil of Iwo Jima afforded little in the way of cover which made the dominating height of the hill the first Marine Corps target.

Three days into the battle, and the 1st Battalion, 27th Marines are relieved. The 'Thousand Yard Stare' was the trance like state that soldiers could fall into after the sort of intense combat seen on Iwo Jima.

For the defenders this was just as well, because, in order to 'soften up' the island before the landing, both the US Navy and the USAAF carried out massive bombardments. The US Navy began its assault in November 1944 with fire from the guns of six destroyers and four heavy cruisers which lasted a whole morning and was repeated at regular intervals until February, while on 8 December Consolidated B-24s and North American B-25s began an assault which was to last 72 days before climaxing on the morning of 19 February with an attack by 120 carrier-borne planes, dropping napalm along the strip of ground just inland of the proposed landing beaches. From then on the bombardment took the form of a creeping barrage from the massive guns of seven battleships, four heavy cruisers and three light cruisers.

Four hundred and fifty vessels of the US 5th Fleet were offshore at dawn on the morning of 19 February, and around and among them swarmed 482 landing craft of various descriptions, bearing the men of eight US Marine battalions; and at 9.02 the first wave hit the landing beaches, 5th Marine Division platoons on the left, 4th Marine Division platoons on the right.

For the first 20 minutes it seemed as though the US Navy and the USAAF had done the job for the marines, who met only sporadic and scattered resistance, apparently totally unorganized. Then as the marines moved up towards a low sand ridge, concentrated fire from concealed machine-gun and mortar posts opened, and a deadly rain of metal swept the 1-mile strip; the most costly operation in the history of the US Marine Corps had begun.

For a matter of seconds the shock of the sudden deluge of Japanese fire froze the marines where they lay, then training and the realities of the situation galvanized them into action. They could not stay where they were and live; they could not go back, for despite the shot and shell which furrowed the beach behind them LCVs were still swimming in through the surf, and waves of supporting companies were flooding ashore and packing the beach-head.

Sheer pressure drove the leading platoons forward out of the maelstrom behind them into and over the nearest Japanese defensive positions, some of which they destroyed, leaving others to their comrades coming up behind; and in less than an hour they had widened the beach-head to half a mile. Seven whole Marine battalions were ashore with their essential equipment, forward patrols had reached the edge of the main airfield and another was in sight of the western beach.

Undoubtedly Kuribayashi had made a fundamental error in allowing that first wave of Marines to get ashore, for by the end of the day 30,000 Marines and their weapons and stores had been landed, and they were there to stay. Their casualties had been high (that had been expected), but the combination of pressure from behind and desperation had flung the leading elements straight across the neck of the island, isolating Mount Suribachi and its garrison from the main defending force, and placing the southern end of the main airfield firmly in American hands.

Raising the flag

The ensuing four days were spent in capturing Mount Suribachi (the most famous photograph in American history, of the flag being raised by a Marine patrol on the summit, was taken on 23 February), and from then on a savage battle of attrition was fought as the marines assaulted the defence lines to the north. Bayonet, rifle, flamethrower and grenade were the weapons with which the fighting was conducted for the next 21 days, for the Japanese defenders were not only fighting from well dug-in positions, but followed the practice of waiting in deep cover until the marines were closed up to within 50 yards or less before manning their guns and thus betraying their positions, seemingly to vanish again after a violent spasm of vicious and costly close-quarter battle.

Time after time the marines moved in behind an apparently devastating barrage, to be greeted when the guns lifted by fierce resistance from virtually invisible positions. Then after half an hour of bitter and costly fighting, they would rush the post to find only a few dead Japanese and perhaps one wrecked machine-gun; and as they moved forward again the post would spring to life behind them as the defenders reoccupied the post through the tunnels.

By D+10 many marine formations were down to half strength, and although the 3rd Marine Division had now been put ashore, it soon found itself blocked by a positive lattice of defensive positions which constituted the northern half of the island. Complexities of underground bunkers faced them, and mazes of interwoven caves, in one area 1,000 yards wide and 200 yards deep; 800 pillboxes, blockhouses and dugouts each held fanatical defenders every one of whom, it was afterwards revealed, had sworn to kill at least 10 marines.

It was not until D+18 that the first marine patrols reached the north-east shore of the island, and then it became possible to partition the area still in Japanese hands into small pieces and gnaw away at each piece until the defence was crushed. But at last it was done. On the night of 25/26 March the last defenders launched a final Banzai charge against their attackers, and the following morning the bodies of the 300 devoted servants of the Emperor who had carried it out littered the ground around the entrance to their last position.

By this time the first B-29s had landed on the island's main airstrip, and by the end of March squadrons of P-51s were flying in to take up their role of escorting the heavy bombers against the Japanese mainland. It all formed a significant step in the defeat of Japan, but it had cost the marines 6,821 killed and three times that number wounded; and of the 23,000 Japanese who had been on the island when the first landings took place, only 216 were ever taken prisoner, most of them badly wounded.

Iwo Jima was less than 10 sq miles in area. It had taken 72 days of air bombardment, three days of concentrated naval hammering and 36 days of the most bitter infantry fighting to conquer it.

How long, and at what cost, would it take to conquer the Japanese homelands by the same methods?

Japanese infantry weapons

Japanese military equipment was a curious mixture, superlative naval weaponry and manoeuvrable aircraft being balanced by inferior army equipment, which in the case of small arms include a number of contenders for the title 'the worst ever'.

The Type 100 sub-machine gun was a sound but uninspired design, firing the unsatisfactory Japanese 8-mm pistol round. It was not easy to produce, and in spite of some manufacturing short cuts such as spot welding and the use of pressings there were never enough to meet demand.

Influenced by French Hotchkiss and Czech ZB.26 designs, the 6.5-mm Type 96 LMG retained some of the bad features so typical of earlier Japanese machine-guns. With no primary extraction system, rounds had to be oiled to allow easy withdrawal from the chamber, and this oil collected dust to clog the firing mechanism.

Derived from the Arisaka-type rifle introduced in 1905 as the Type 38, the Type 99 was a monopod fitted version of the older weapon employing the 7.7-mm round first introduced during the 1930s. The basic design was a blend of Mauser and Männlicher features.

The 94 Shiki Kenju (or Type 94 pistol) was one of the worst pistol designs ever to go into production, being cumbersome, awkward to use and basically unsafe, as the firing mechanism projected from the side of the gun. If this was pushed while the chamber was loaded, the weapon would fire without the trigger being pulled.

Okinawa

Iwo Jima had given the Marines a taste of what was to come in any invasion of the Japanese home islands. Okinawa, in the Ryuku island group, was to provide an even more sanguinary experience.

In the early hours of 1 April 1945 the US Tenth Army, commanded by General Simon Bolivar Buckner, began landing on the island of Okinawa – the main island of the Ryukyu group, 66 miles long and between three and 10 miles across. The operation was the largest amphibious asault yet undertaken in the Pacific and involved nearly 550,000 personnel, including 180,000 combat troops. Carrier air strikes against the Japanese airfields on Kyushu in mid-March left the facilities in ruins and destroyed some 500 aircraft, thus ensuring little interference to the landing front from that quarter. Only slight opposition faced the US forces for the first few days, the location of the Japanese garrison remaining a mystery until 5 April when it became clear that the southern half of Okinawa had been painstakingly fortified. Ensconsed in a formidable network of bunkers and entrenchments were some 85,000 Japanese troops, commanded by General Mitsuru Ushijima. Part of the force was made up of fresh conscripts, but the backbone of the defence was the veteran 62nd Division, brought back from China.

The infantry battle for Okinawa had barely begun when the Imperial Japanese Navy launched its last major operation of the war, a kamikaze mission on the grand scale involving the magnificent battleship *Yamato*. Rejoicing in the title of the 'Special Sea Attack Force', *Yamato* and a destroyer force was dispatched on a one-way voyage to Okinawa, where they were to inflict the maximum damage possible before meeting their inevitable destruction. *Yamato* was the largest and mightiest battleship of all time, displacing nearly 70,000 tons at full load; crewed by 2,500 officers and ratings, she was armed with nine 18-in guns with a range of 45,000 yards, and over 150 anti-aircraft guns. Flying the flag of Vice Admiral Ito, she sailed from the Inland Sea on 6 April accompanied by the light cruiser *Yahagi* and eight destroyers. US submarines spotted the leviathan as she steamed past Kyushu before steering into the East China Sea. Carrierborne reconnaissance aircraft located her again on the morning of 7 April, and 380 aircraft were launched from Task Force 58. Low clouds and rain squalls proved a slight inconvenience to the aircraft but *Yamato* had no fighter cover, and the bombers were able to make their attacks uninterrupted. The giant battleship greeted its deceptively puny attackers with a hail of anti-aircraft fire and manoeuvred to the best of its ability as it began to fight for its life. The US aircraft swarmed around its monstrous bulk, scoring hit after hit, but *Yamato* absorbed them without any apparent effect. But gradually she began to slow, and the volume of fire coming up at the bombers noticeably diminished; meanwhile her diminutive consorts had lost all trace of formation, four of the destroyers had been sunk and *Yahagi* went down at 14.00. Half-an-hour later the desperate attempts at counter-flooding could postpone the end no longer, and *Yamato* rolled over and sank. Her magazines exploded, and a tall column of smoke some 200 miles short of Okinawa marked the grave of a proud warship and almost all of its crew.

The heroic failure of this last attempt at surface intervention was followed by a savage series of kamikaze air attacks on the US warships off shore, while Ushijima's troops stubbornly contested every yard of their island. On 19 April, Buckner essayed a concentrated attack to punch a hole in the Japanese defences but it failed with nearly 1,000 casualties. For the rest of the month and into May the 10th Army battered against the 'Shuri' line in a remorseless routine of colossal bombardments followed by desperate assaults against blockhouses and bunkers cunningly sited and fanatically defended. Although the Americans knew that the casualty rate was running wildly in their favour as the occupants of each position were killed to a man, US casualties were mounting at an alarming rate. By the end of May it seemed a breakthrough might at last be achieved, but the sudden onset of torrential rains bogged down operations for over a week. Taking full advantage of the weather, Ushijima extracted his surviving units from the battle and began to withdraw to the south. An American attempt to break through his rearguard was repulsed, and the Japanese occupied new positions on the southern tip of Okinawa and prepared to make their last stand.

The Tenth Army pushed forward for the last stage of the battle and set about the grisly task of breaking into the Japanese positions. Finally, on 17 June the Japanese garrison was divided into three encircled pockets, no longer capable of a coherent defence, and some of the more recent conscripts began to surrender. General Buckner broadcast a message to Ushijima urging him to stop the fighting and save the lives of his surviving soldiers, since the end was inevitable. Ironically, Buckner himself was killed the next day when a Japanese shell blew lethal slivers of coral into him while he inspected the 8th Marines. Ushijima survived him by a week, committing ritual suicide with his chief of staff after sending a last report to Tokyo. "Our strategy, tactics and equipment were used to the utmost and we fought valiantly . . . but it was nothing before the material might of the enemy", He was perfectly correct; Japan was doomed.

Left: *The kamikaze was the 'divine wind' that saved Japan from subjugation under the Mongols by wrecking Kublai Khan's invasion fleet. Parallels with the mighty armada approaching Japan's shores led to the same name being applied to the suicide pilots determined to destroy the US Fleet. First seen in the Philippines, off Okinawa, they became a considerable threat. This is the carrier USS* **Bunker Hill***, after being hit twice in 30 minutes.*

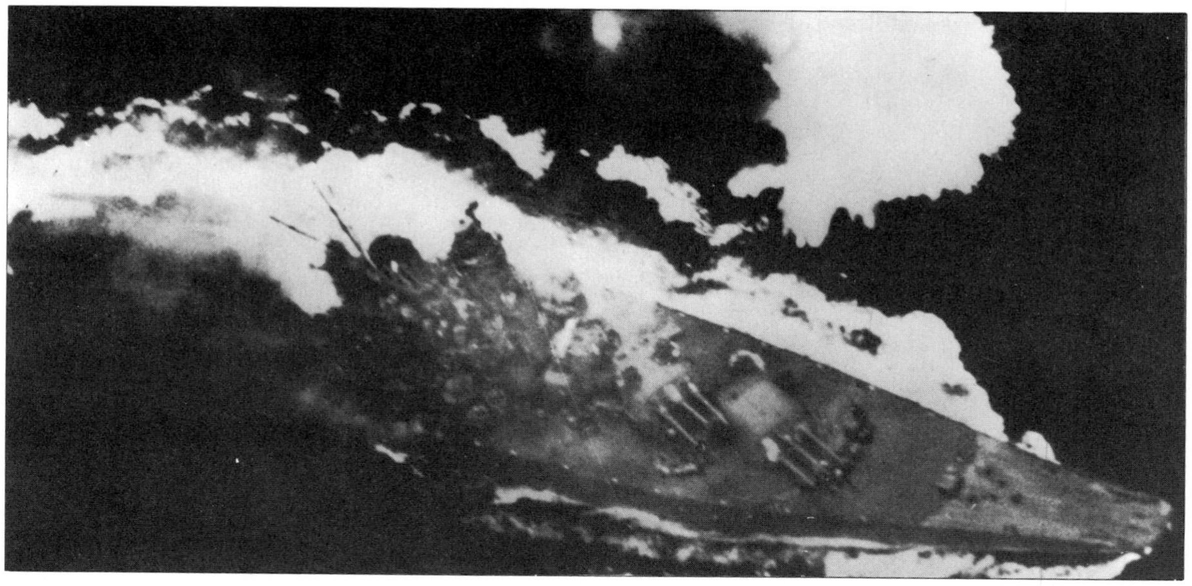

Below: *The mighty* **Yamato** *is attacked on her suicide mission to disrupt the Okinawa landings on 7 April 1945. The last sortie by a unit of the battlefleet, it was overwhelmed by US naval air power.*

Above: *Ground crew cheer and salute as a kamikaze pilot taxis his bomb-laden Mitsubishi A6M towards the runway. Such attacks caused a great amount of problems to the Allied fleets.*

Above: *Dramatic photograph as an A6M tries to slam into the USS* **Missouri***. Many of the kamikazes ended their flight being shot down by flak or fighters. However, a good few made it through.*

One of the two 'California' class battleships present at Okinawa continues to charge the Japanese a heavy price for the damage both ships sustained at Pearl Harbor. In the foreground, Amtracs (Amphibious Tractors) take the first wave of the US Tenth Army ashore.

Left: ***An M4 Sherman medium tank rolls into the outskirts of Naha, in the south of Okinawa, with a company from the 22nd Marines.***

Above: ***Infantrymen of the 27th Infantry Division deal with a bunker in what they have learned by bitter experience is the only safe way.***

Above: ***A Marine dives through Japanese machine-gun fire at 'Death Valley', one regiment. taking 125 casualties in eight hours.***

Right: ***The end of*** Yamato, ***after being attacked and hit by up to 13 torpedoes and six bombs from 380 attacking US Navy aircraft.***

Left: ***The Vought F4U Corsair was widely employed over Okinawa on ground attack duties.***

Below: ***The Fleet Air Arm aided the US attacks on Okinawa, HMS*** Indomitable ***shown here returning from the attack.***

Left: ***Japanese snipers were a considerable problem all over the Pacific. Often camouflaged in trees, one of the primary means of winkling them out was with the Thompson sub-machine gun.***

Below: ***While no large carriers were lost to kamikaze attacks, the wooden-decked US Navy ships were much more vulnerable than the steel-decked vessels of the Royal Navy. USS*** Franklin ***was nearest to being sunk, but she made it back to the USA.***

THE B-29 RAIDS

Once war with Japan became reality in December 1941, it was accepted by the United States that final victory could be achieved by only two means: an appallingly costly land invasion of the Japanese homeland, or the blasting of the enemy into submission from the air. There were no other options. And the Boeing B-29 Superfortress long-range heavy bomber was produced for exactly the latter purpose.

This aircraft had in fact been conceived in 1940 simply as a successor to the B-17, almost two years before the United States entered the war, but after Pearl Harbor great urgency was lent to the process of putting the big bomber into production; its specification was the only one that envisaged delivering a worthwhile bomb load over the vast distances involved in the Pacific war, and in general terms it possessed about twice the performance of the B-17. Once the B-29 entered production it came to be regarded as the single weapon that might bring Japan to her knees, so the application of manpower to bring this weapon into service was nothing short of prodigious.

First flight by the prototype XB-29 took place on 21 September 1942, by which time 1,664 production aircraft had been ordered; the following June the 58th Bombardment Wing (Very Heavy) was activated at Marietta, Georgia, and seven pre-production YB-29s were delivered for crew training the following month.

Meanwhile 700,000 Chinese labourers were set to work to construct nine huge airfields, four in China and five in north-east India, and a new command, the US 20th Air Force, was constituted under General of the Army Henry H. Arnold, on 4 April 1944. On 5 June India-based B-29s of the 58th BW took off to bomb railway yards at Bangkok in Thailand.

Above: Flying from bases in the Marianas, the USAAF stepped up raids on Japan. In order to navigate across the featureless ocean, the fighters (in this case P-51D Mustangs) were shepherded by a B-29.

The first raids

The logistic effort required to support the operations from these bases was enormous, and involved the B-29s themselves ferrying huge quantities of fuel and ordnance over the Himalayas to their staging bases in China, a task which cost many aircraft, as well as accelerated wear on engines and airframes.

The first B-29 raid on the Japanese mainland was flown on 15 June by 50 aircraft against Yawata; seven bombers were lost, but of these only one fell to the enemy. These difficult raids against Japan continued for some months with fairly heavy casualties (at least three B-29s force-landed in the USSR, where they were copied as the Tupolev Tu-4).

When American forces captured the Marianas in 1944 five great bases were constructed, two on Tinian, two on Guam and one on Saipan, each large enough to accommodate a 180-aircraft wing. The first Marianas-based raid on Japan was flown on 24 November by 111 B-29s of the 73rd Wing led by Brigadier-General Emmett O'Donnell against the Musashino engine plant at Tokyo, but as a result of navigating difficulties only 24 aircraft bombed the target.

In the meantime the 58th Wing had moved to the Marianas, to be joined by the 313th, 314th and 315th Wings, representing an initial force of almost 600 aircraft. On 20 January 1944 Major-General Curtis E. LeMay assumed command of the XXI Bomber Command with headquarters on Guam, his task being to initiate a series of devastating fire raids on Japan. The first such raid, on the night of 9/10 March 1945, involved 302 aircraft attacking individually from between 5,000 and 10,000 ft. Crews were reduced and gun armament omitted in the interests of increased bombload, which comprised more than six tons of the new M69 fire bombs, each of which was in effect a cluster of napalm containers. For the loss of 14 B-29s, 16.9 sq miles of Tokyo were reduced to ashes. Five such fire raids were flown in this initial phase against Japan, the cities of Nagoya (two raids), Osaka and Kobe sharing the fate of Tokyo.

As the Japanese fighter defences were increased to meet this tremendous onslaught, the B-29s had their tail guns reinstated, and in May raids by more than 400 aircraft were frequently flown, with losses gradually dropping from 1.3 per cent to 0.02 in August. The greatest raid was mounted on 25/26 May when 464 B-29s out of 498 despatched raided Tokyo, led by 12 Pathfinders. This raid, Mission 183, resulted in over 2,200 tons of incendiaries falling on the predominantly timber-built areas of the Japanese capital, of which 18.9 sq miles were devastated. In the 200-odd fire raids carried out by the B-29s over Japan the USAAF dropped 169,676 tons of bombs, of which 105,486 tons were incendiaries. In Tokyo alone more than 80,000 people were killed and over one million rendered homeless.

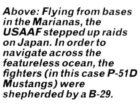

Below: The aerial armadas set out from the Marianas daily to rain death and destruction on to Japan's industry and cities. These B-29s are from Guam. The formation would tighten up as the target was approached.

One hundred and forty five B-29s are in this photograph of Saipan airfield, preparing to take off on a supply drop to PoWs. Such aerial armadas would be seen again in the Marianas some 20 years later as the Boeing B-52s arrived to bomb Vietnam and Laos.

Although the atomic bomb raids caused greater emotional and political fallout, the firestorms on Yokohama caused far greater damage and casualties. Seven square miles of the city were completely razed by these B-29s.

As the Japanese warlords watched the inexorable advances by American forces northwards through the Philippines and began to anticipate the inevitable retribution against the homeland that would follow the seizure of air bases in the Marianas, frantic attempts were being made to create an air-defence system capable of protecting metropolitan Japan from the might of the US air forces. When the blows fell they came with unimagined weight and devastation.

For many months before the opening of the great American bombing raids, the home-based Japanese fighter force had been bottom of the priority list, the 17th, 18th and 19th Hikodans being still largely equipped with 1942-vintage Nakajima Ki-43 Oscar fighters (top speed 329 mph and armed with two 12.7 mm machine-guns). At that time only 13 per cent of Japan's total fighter strength was based at home. Radar equipment ringing the Japanese islands was rudimentary in the extreme, without height definition and capable of 'seeing' no more than 40 miles; considerable reliance was still placed upon sighting reports radioed from picket boats, whose performance would be unreliable to say the least when the huge B-29 formations approached at 30,000 ft.

Nevertheless the early American raids were by no means as effective as planned, the raids being scattered as a result of long-range navigational problems, and the Japanese fighters managed to score a number of successes despite the fact that the B-29 could almost outdistance a Ki-43, even when carrying a full bombload. However, the bomber crews' proficiency quickly improved and devastating daylight attacks were soon made by increasing numbers of B-29s upon Akashi, Kobe, Musashino and Nagoya.

Defending the homeland

Meanwhile the Japanese army air force upgraded the three Hikodans in the 1st Kokugan to divisional status, and new equipment was rushed out from the factories. The Nakajima Ki-44-II Tojo (top speed 375 mph and armed with four 20-mm cannon) equipped several Sentais including the 47th, one of whose Chutais used the aircraft for suicidal ramming attacks against B-29s in defence of Tokyo.

Surprisingly, both the Ki-44 and the much respected Nakajima Ki-84 Frank (top speed 392 mph and armed with four 20-mm cannon) were flown more effectively by the relatively inexperienced Japanese pilots than those who had been flying the earlier generations of much lighter fighters for many months: the older pilots instinctively attempted manoeuvres that caused the new fighters with higher wing loadings to flick, stall and spin. Certainly the introduction of 20-, 37- and 40-mm cannon did much to offset the earlier fighters' inability to carry out normal quarter attacks on the B-29s (owing to inadequate speed margin), but when in 1945 the Americans were able to send powerful formations of long-range North American P-51D escort fighters with the bombers the Japanese interceptors were once more at a tactical disadvantage.

Recognizing that the Japanese army air force by itself would be unable to stem the big American bomber formations, the Japanese navy air force participated in the defence of metropolitan Japan from the outset, contributing some of the best fighters and pilots. Best of all was the Kawanishi N1K2 (369 mph and armed with four 20-mm cannon and two 12.7-mm guns), but deliveries of this aircraft, which was perfectly capable of matching any of the American naval fighters that started operating over Japan in 1945, were badly disrupted by the B-29 attacks against its factories.

When the Americans switched to night attacks by the B-29s on 9/10 March 1945 the Japanese were even more helpless in defence, once more the rudimentary state of their radar technology severely limiting the performance of the defending night fighters, such as they were. Far too late had the Japanese high command recognized the possibility of a threat to the homeland.

With such poor ground radar at their disposal, the Japanese tended to emulate the German *wilde Sau* tactics, using freelancing day fighters against the night raiders, which were frequently silhouetted against the great expanses of fire below, and the defending fighter pilots paid little heed to the flak, whose gunners in turn recognized no restriction of fire against the raiders. Much greater success attended the efforts by Japanese night intruders (usually in such aircraft as the Mitsubishi Ki-46 which, like the German night-fighters, came to be fitted with upward-firing cannon) which prowled over the B-29 bases in the Marianas; when the Americans introduced their big Northrop P-61 Black Widow night fighters, however, the depredations of the Japanese night fighters ended abruptly.

Although in the final weeks of World War II Japan was making some remarkable progress in developing effective interceptors, both as bomber-destroyers and as dogfighters capable of matching the superlative P-51D, the constant attacks on the factories of Japan (particularly those turning out aircraft engines) put paid to stemming the devastating raids. The dropping of the two atomic bombs in any case rendered their efforts superfluous.

That any individual Japanese fighter pilot should have achieved outstanding success was perhaps extraordinary having regard to the absolute American air superiority over Japan in the final nine months of the war. Yet, spurred by the ultimate motivation (defence of one's home) many such men fought with considerable skill and bravery against the great bomber armadas. The legendary Saburo Sakai, who had shot down the first American aircraft to fall in the Philippines on 8 December 1941 and who was appallingly wounded and lost an eye over Guadalcanal, joined in the defence of Japan and destroyed an American aircraft on the last day of the war, thereby completing a personal tally of 62 air victories. Among the most successful of the night-fighter pilots was the naval pilot Sachio Endo who, flying a Nakajima J1N Irving, destroyed a total of seven B-29s, but was killed in a daylight combat with American fighters. An army pilot, Captain Totaro Ito, who flew Kawasaki Ki-45s, destroyed nine of the big bombers and was one of the very small number of pilots to receive the coveted Bukosho award. Another recipient of the Bukosho was Kawasaki Ki-61 pilot Major Teruhiko Kobayishi, the army's youngest *Sentai* commander, who was shot down in his first attack on a B-29; he escaped from this ordeal without injury, and again miraculously survived after ramming another B-29 on 27 January 1945.

Like the Germans the Japanese were forced to embark on desperate expedients in their attempts to stem the great American bomber offensive, and had progressed a considerable distance on the road to developing jet fighters. Several examples of the navy's Mitsubishi J8M1 rocket interceptor (closely resembling the Messerschmitt Me 163 Komet) and the Nakajima Kikka twin-jet fighter (similar to the Me 262) had been completed before the end of the war, but neither reached a service unit before the two final bombs burst above the doomed cities of Hiroshima and Nagasaki.

The US Navy carrier strikes continued against Japan, led by the Curtiss SB2C Helldiver and Vought Corsair. Examples of the former are seen here entering the landing pattern, with some aircraft already deploying their arrester hooks.

Above: Japanese aircraft continued to put up a brave and often suicidal defence against the incessant tide of bombers. Among the more successful aircraft was the Kawasaki Ki-61 Hien, which had the excellent high-altitude performance necessary to reach the bombers.

Numerous last-ditch efforts were mounted against the US bombers, including the use of air-dropped phosphorus bombs, which were fused to explode in the bomber formation. Success was very limited.

Hamamatsu lays wasted after a visit from the B-29 fire-raisers. Most of the Japanese cities were constructed of wood, which proved easy meat to the incendiary bombs raining from above.

JAPAN'S DESPERATE STATE

By the end of June 1945, the reality of their situation could no longer be denied by even the most fanatical or fatalistic of the Japanese people. Their leaders may have been able to inculcate a spirit of unswerving loyalty and obedience into their servicemen, but the Japanese civilians, especially the mothers, wives and daughters, had a more basic belief in their own right to live – even, if necessary, without the approval of their Emperor, who, to be fair, was as appalled by their position as they were themselves.

That position was now disastrous. Tens of square miles of the main Japanese cities had been burned to the ground in March, and the only reason the raids had stopped on 19 March was that the Americans had used up their 10,000 tons of incendiaries. Now more had been manufactured and flown out to Iwo Jima, Saipan and Okinawa, and the B-29s were back almost every night – and for much longer and with heavier bomb loads as they had not so far to fly and there was only the most exiguous Japanese air defence left.

Eight and a half million civilians fled into the countryside from the towns and cities, leaving even those factories which had not been destroyed bereft of labour. Oil refining had practically stopped – not that that mattered much because so had aircraft production and ship-building; and, if home production was at a virtual standstill, so was the arrival of imports. Japan had gone to war to obtain from the 'Greater East Asia Co-prosperity Sphere' the necessary raw materials with which to dominate the East, and now none of them were arriving because the Allied fleets – especially the American submarine packs operating from Luzon or the Marianas – had locked a stranglehold upon all the seas and channels through which they must pass.

Desperate straits

Not only were the people of Japan facing starvation, the strategic position to which the country had been brought should have been obvious to the most basically trained soldier. Yet many of the senior generals and admirals still would not accept that the gamble they had been instrumental in taking when Japan struck at Pearl Harbour had not come off – nor would they accept that, if it had all been a mistake, then the whole Japanese race should not perish rather than their honour, enshrined in the reluctant figure of the Emperor, should be belittled or besmirched.

Fortunately, the Emperor himself was not of so rigid a mind, and since April the Japanese government had been headed by Admiral Suzuki, who like the Emperor was in favour of making peace – at almost any price. But they were puzzled, for as early as February they had made approaches through both the Russian ambassador in Tokyo and their own ambassador in Moscow, begging Russia 'as a neutral' to arrange surrender terms for them with the Western Allies; and no answer had been received.

The reason for this was that the Russians had not passed on the message. It was the end of May before Stalin mentioned the matter to Harry Hopkins, now President Truman's representative, Roosevelt having died suddenly on 12 April, and in the intervening weeks and months, it had been agreed that the Red Army and Navy should soon be deployed against Japan – for which Stalin expected in return to receive the Kurile Islands, the whole of Sakhalin and control throughout Manchuria. Now, at the end of talks with Hopkins, Stalin mentioned that he had 'heard of some peace feelers' put out by 'certain quarters in Japan', and that if Allied demands for 'unconditional surrender' could be modified, Russia's task of arrang-

***Above:* 'Little Boy' was the atomic bomb exploded over Hiroshima at about 9.30 in the morning of 6 August 1945. Made with uranium, it exploded with a force equivalent to 20,000 tonnes of TNT.**

***Right:* The 6,000-m, high mushroom cloud towering over Nagasaki marks the second of the two devastating punches, 'Fat Man' that knocked the Japanese empire out of the war.**

***Below:* Hiroshima is seen devastated by the bomb. It was not the scale of the destruction that was so shocking (after all, more people had been killed or made homeless in firebombing raids on Dresden and Tokyo) but the sheer power of a single weapon, and the insidious deadliness of radioactive fallout and the sickness it caused.**

Chronology of War: 1945

July 18
US carrier aircraft sink battleship Nagato and other ships in Tokyo Bay

July 26
Labour Party wins British elections. Attlee becomes Prime Minister

July 28
Two thousand Allied carrier aircraft attack Kure, Kobe and targets around the Inland Sea

July 31
Field Marshal Alexander appointed Governor-General of Canada

August 2
Potsdam Conference ends. Boeing Superfortresses drop 6,600 tons of incendiaries on five Japanese cities

August 3
Japan completely blockaded by US Navy with the assistance of the British Pacific Fleet

August 6
Atomic bomb dropped on Hiroshima. About 80,000 dead and 80,000 injured

August 8
Russia declares war on Japan. Russian invasion of Manchukuo is along a 1609-km front and involves 76 divisions

August 9
Atomic bomb dropped on Nagasaki. About 40,000 dead and 60,000 injured

August 10
Japanese broadcast qualified willingness to surrender

August 13
Carrier aircraft launch 1,600 plane attack on Tokyo

August 14
Japan agrees to accept unconditional surrender

August 15
VJ-Day. MacArthur appointed Supreme Commander for the Allies

August 16
Emperor Hirohito broadcasts orders to all Japanese troops to surrender

August 19
Japanese surrender in Manila and Java

August 21
Japanese surrender in Manchuria

August 27
US Navy enters Bay of Sagami, Tokyo

August 28
Japanese surrender in Rangoon

September 2
Japanese surrender document signed formally on battleship US Missouri in Tokyo Bay

September 5
British land on Singapore Island

September 7
Japanese surrender in Shanghai

September 9
Japanese surrender in China

September 12
Admiral Mountbatten accepts surrender of all Japanese forces in South East Asia

September 13
Japanese surrender in Burma

September 16
Japanese surrender in Hong Kong

ing Japan's surrender would be easier – a task for which Russia would, of course, expect a place at the peace talks and a share of the occupation of Japan.

By this time, even Truman was beginning to think that perhaps the America–Russia accord which Roosevelt had been so certain would create a new world of trust and reason was not quite so close as had been hoped. Moreover, the Americans then received evidence that Stalin was equivocating to an even greater extent than they had thought, for their signals and codebreaking services – just as efficient as the British at Bletchley Park – had intercepted messages passing between the Japanese Foreign Office and their Moscow ambassador, on both 13 and 27 July, instructing the ambassador that the 'Emperor is desirous of peace.' On 28 July Stalin did inform those attending the Potsdam Conference that 'further approaches' had been made, but at no time did he give an indication that they were being made at a high official level; and Truman was becoming more and more certain that some other factor would be necessary, not only to give the Japanese rulers convincing evidence that the Allies would win the war against them, but also Stalin that his help would not be needed and his conditions for such help not met.

The Manhattan Project had begun in mid-1942, and was the result of scientific collaboration between scientists of practically every Western nationality – many of them, ironically enough, Germans who had been forced to leave their native country because of either Jewish ancestry or suspected anti-Nazi sympathies.

A great deal of the research had been carried out at the Clarendon Laboratory at Oxford – where Rutherford had first 'split the atom' in 1919 - but after Pearl Harbor and Churchill's decisions that everything must be done to increase trust and co-operation with the United States, all information was freely given to American scientists and by early 1942 it was rightly agreed that only in America was there the unthreatened space and the industrial capacity to take the project to its logical end – an atomic bomb.

The first truly significant milestone on the road to atomic power was passed on the afternoon of 2 December 1942 in a squash court at Chicago University, when a team working under Professor Enrico Fermi carefully withdrew cadmium control rods from a huge block of graphite and uranium, thus starting the first man-made self-sustaining chain-reaction.

The atomic bomb

Two-and-a-half years later, at 5.50 a.m. on 16 July 1945, at Los Alamos in New Mexico, the plutonium bomb 'Fat Man' was detonated, and even while the results were being evaluated, the first uranium bomb, 'Little Boy', was being shipped to Tinian, where a B-29 Superfortress was being adapted to carry it. There was not enough Uranium 235 to make two bombs, so a successor to the plutonium 'Fat Man' was put together and sent off in pursuit to the Pacific, both awaiting the political decision.

Churchill was later to write:

> To avert a vast, indefinite butchery, to bring the war to an end, to give peace to the world, to lay healing hands upon its tortured peoples by a manifestation of overwhelming power at the cost of a few explosions, seemed, after all our toils and perils, a miracle of development.
>
> British consent in principle to the use of the weapon had been given on July 4th, before the test had taken place. The final decision now lay in the main with President Truman, who had the weapon: but I never doubted what it would be, nor have I ever doubted since that he was right.

On 6 August 1945 the first atomic bomb was dropped on Hiroshima, destroying most of the city and killing some 80,000 people. Three days later the second bomb was dropped on Nagasaki with similar results.

The explosions made far less impact on the Japanese people than the news of the explosions made in Western circles – principally because the vast majority of the Japanese knew nothing about what had happened until after their government had surrendered. And the Japanese government was split about what to do, for three of its six members were respectively the Army Minister and the Army and Navy Chiefs of Staff, who still believed in fighting on. It was the Emperor who cut the Gordian Knot on 14 August at a meeting of 'elder statesmen', when, the arguments having briefly died down, he announced, 'If nobody else has any opinion to express, we will express our own. We demand that you will agree to it. We see only one way left for Japan to save herself. That is the reason we have made this determination to endure the unendurable and suffer the insufferable.'

That evening the announcement was made by radio that Japan surrendered unconditionally, and Truman agreed that the Emperor's position would be respected. As the Emperor by this time was the single figure in his realm who seemed to possess both authority and common sense, this would appear to have been an eminently reasonable compromise.

On 2 September 1945, the Japanese representatives signed the instrument of surrender in front of General Douglas MacArthur, designated Supreme Commander for the Allied Powers, standing on the quarterdeck of the vast battleship *Missouri*. Officially the war had thus lasted six years and one day from the moment it had been started by Hitler's attack on Poland, though in fact fighting was to continue in some theatres for several more months – and in 1985, an elderly Japanese soldier gave himself up on one of the remote Pacific Islands having in his own mind borne arms during the intervening period; possibly there are others even now.

Fifty-six combatant nations had been engaged in the conflict – some, obviously, much more than others – and if one includes the numbers killed in the course of Hitler's insane attempts at genocide, World War II caused the death of over 50,000,000 people. It was thus the most violent and prolonged self-inflicted injury upon mankind of which history has record, for if the conflicts which have followed have in some cases been of longer duration, they have not been of so wide a scope.

There seems to be good reason for believing that one major factor in the avoidance of a world-wide conflict for such a prolonged period as that which has elapsed since 1945 (longer than any other period in history without great wars between major powers) is the existence of first the atomic and then the nuclear bomb. The 'nuclear balance' – however precarious – has provided an umbrella, and for that practicality, whatever the theoretical or ethical arguments against it, the world should be grateful.

Or at least as grateful as were the soldiers, sailors and airmen of the Allied Powers in 1945, when they learned that, after all, they would not have to take part in an invasion of Japan. They would thus be spared a violent battle across the Japanese homeland, of the type and ferocity which experience of fighting the Japanese soldier had taught them would be necessary. It was a great relief.

Japanese prisoners on Guam bow as they hear the Emperor's voice, broadcast for the first time, as he tells the Japanese people that they have to 'endure the unendurable and suffer the insufferable' i.e. surrender.

General Douglas MacArthur reads the terms of the Japanese surrender aboard the USS Missouri in Tokyo Bay. Behind him stand the representatives of the victorious Allied powers. In the background (flown from the USA by Admiral Halsey) can be seen the Stars and Stripes flown by Commodore Perry's flagship when 92 years before he forced open the doors of Japan to the rest of the world.

Mamoru Shigemitsu, the Japanese Foreign Minister, signs the formal surrender document on behalf of the Emperor and the Japanese Government. There, on the quarterdeck of USS Missouri, on the morning of 2 September 1945, World War II officially came to an end.

INDEX

Page numbers in **bold** denote an illustration. Entries in **bold** denote a special feature.

All military units are grouped under the names of their respective countries.

J

K

L

M

N

Picture acknowledgements

The publishers would like to thank the following individuals and organisations for their help in supplying photographs for this book.

Imperial War Museum: 8, 14, 15, 16, 17, 18, 20, 22, 24, 26, 28, 30, 31, 32, 33, 36, 37, 39, 40, 44, 48, 50, 51, 52, 60, 61, 63, 65, 66, 67, 68, 70, 71, 74, 75, 77, 84, 91, 95, 96, 97, 99, 101, 112, 114, 115, 117, 118, 119, 124, 126, 127, 128, 129, 140, 141, 145, 146, 147, 148, 149, 150, 151, 153, 154, 155, 156, 158, 159, 160, 161, 162, 167, 168, 169, 175, 176, 177, 178, 179, 180, 182, 183, 184, 186, 187, 189, 191, 192, 197, 208, 209, 211, 216, 218, 221, 225, 226, 228, 229, 230, 232, 233, 235, 237, 238, 246, 252, 254, 256, 258, 259, 260, 261, 262, 263, 265, 266, 268, 269, 270, 275, 280, 282, 283, 284, 286, 287, 289, 290, 291, 293, 299, 305, 306
MacClancy Collection: 7, 8, 9, 10, 11, 13, 18, 19, 20, 22, 26, 28, 30, 34, 35, 39, 42, 54, 55, 56, 58, 60, 63, 64, 66, 67, 68, 69, 70, 71, 72, 73, 74, 75, 76, 78, 80, 81, 82, 83, 84, 92, 96, 97, 98, 100, 108, 109, 110, 111, 112, 113, 114, 116, 118, 119, 120, 122, 123, 124, 126, 127, 128, 130, 131, 132, 133, 134, 135, 136, 137, 138, 140, 142, 143, 144, 146, 149, 150, 153, 154, 156, 158, 162, 164, 166, 168, 169, 170, 171, 172, 173, 176, 177, 178, 182, 183, 184, 185, 187, 188, 192, 193, 198, 211, 214, 215, 216, 217, 221, 222, 223, 224, 225, 232, 236, 240, 241, 242, 243, 244, 245, 246, 248, 249, 251, 252, 254, 256, 257, 258, 259, 260, 262, 263, 264, 266, 268, 270, 277, 279, 280, 282, 290, 294, 295, 296, 298, 299, 305, 307, 308, 310
United States National Archives: 6, 9, 10, 11, 18, 21, 24, 26, 29, 38, 63, 85, 86, 87, 88, 92, 97, 102, 104, 105, 113, 119, 144, 148, 152, 153, 154, 155, 165, 166, 168, 174, 180, 185, 196, 200, 222, 227, 228, 236, 250, 251, 257, 272, 273, 277, 280, 298, 300, 302, 304, 309, 311
Royal Air Force Museum, Hendon: 32, 34, 35, 237, 291
Associated Press: 40, 269
Novosti Press Agency: 7, 222, 241, 247, 292, 297
Tass: 247, 310
Robert Hunt Library: 46, 91, 94, 170, 295, 296
United States Navy: 86, 89, 93, 100, 101, 102, 104, 106, 145, 163, 166, 167, 169, 197, 198, 199, 200, 202, 204, 205, 206, 223, 269, 271, 272, 273, 274, 275, 299, 301, 302, 304, 305, 307
United States Army: 6, 98, 100, 102, 150, 175, 176, 180, 188, 190, 192, 193, 225, 230, 234, 236, 238, 239, 253, 259, 276, 278, 279, 284, 288, 289, 290, 300, 305, 309
United States Air Force: 166, 172, 176, 181, 186, 193, 206, 207, 210, 212, 214, 216, 217, 220, 224, 236, 255, 257, 267, 274, 277, 281, 287, 291, 299, 306, 307, 308
Australian War Memorial: 101
Warren Thompson: 186, 229
Sikorsky Museum: 188
Public Archives of Canada: 188, 238
United States Navy via Robert L. Lawson Collection: 195, 200, 205
United States Marine Corps: 197, 200, 204, 206, 302, 305, 311
United States Coast Guard: 225